# THE BOOKFINDER

## Volume 3

# THE BOOKFINDER

## Volume 3

Annotations of Books Published
1979 through 1982
Includes Cumulative Subject Index

## A Guide to Children's Literature About the Needs and Problems of Youth Aged 2 and Up

Sharon Spredemann Dreyer, M.Ed.

**AGS**®

American Guidance Service, Circle Pines, Minnesota 55014-1796

AGS staff participating in the development and production of this publication:

**Program Development**
Dorothy Chapman, Director
Bonnie Goldsmith, Senior Project Editor
Janice Cauley, Copy Editor

**Support Services**
David Youngquist, Director
Lynne Cromwell and Solveig Tyler-Robinson, Production Coordinators
Carol McLean, Production Manager
Maureen Wilson, Art Director

Hardcover design by Gene Roeckers.
Softcover design by Terry Dugan Design.

With love to Bev — My sister, my friend.

# CONTENTS

# INTRODUCTION

A GUIDE TO
CHILDREN'S LITERATURE
ABOUT THE NEEDS AND PROBLEMS
OF YOUTH AGED 2 AND UP

# ACKNOWLEDGMENTS

The *Bookfinder* represents the talents and efforts of many people. The following persons, especially, are acknowledged with gratitude:

Caroljean Wagner, Head of the Central Youth Library, Milwaukee Public Library, was the chief consultant throughout the development of all three volumes of the *Bookfinder.* Her commitment and expertise have been invaluable to this project.

Marianna Markowetz, Curriculum Librarian, University of Wisconsin-Milwaukee, and Ervin S. Yanke, Coordinator of Elementary Education, West Allis-West Milwaukee Public Schools, acted as consultants, contributing valuable suggestions and criticism as the concept of the *Bookfinder* was researched and developed.

Carl Malmquist, M.D., psychiatrist in private practice, Minneapolis, reviewed the *Bookfinder* as it was developed and offered constructive suggestions for expansion and clarification of the Subject Index.

Jane Laswell, Librarian, Bowling Green, Kentucky, carefully researched the great amount of recent material about bibliotherapy and the trends in reading education. She was responsible for the arrangement and cross-referencing of the *Bookfinder* indexes and the Publishers/Producers Directory. The excellence of the *Bookfinder* indexing is to her credit.

Karen Radtke of Milwaukee helped edit annotations when time was short and her assistance especially valued.

Corliss Rice and the staff members at the Wisconsin Regional Library for the Blind and Physically Handicapped, Milwaukee, Wisconsin, helped identify the books available in materials for blind and physically handicapped persons.

Many librarians made extra efforts to locate and lend the books reviewed and indexed in the *Bookfinder.* The staff at the Milwaukee Public Library was extraordinarily helpful, as were the staffs at the New Berlin Public Library, Frank Lloyd Wright Middle School (West Allis), both in Wisconsin, and the Western Kentucky University Library.

Children's book editors and subsidiary-rights departments of over 65 publishing companies graciously worked to identify which of the publications listed in the *Bookfinder* are also available in other printed or audiovisual media. They also supplied hundreds of books for review.

Sixteen people who participated in a field trial during the spring of 1974—teachers, librarians, counselors, and psychologists from the Milwaukee metropolitan area—provided reactions and suggestions in the initial stages of the development of the *Bookfinder.* Participants were Carol Bahr, Shirley Conlon, Delma Erickson, Suzanne Felan, Dorothy Frana, Ruth George, Bernice Harper, Patricia Hoppe, Stanley Ladich, Marilee McMullen, Marianna Markowetz, Marion Pagenkopf, John Peters, John Ricci, Ellen Rubin, and Kathleen Rudes.

Professionals in 16 field-test sites contributed valuable suggestions during the spring of 1976 to help refine the publication. They were:

Georgia Bouda, Children's Librarian, Mill Road Public Library, Milwaukee, Wisconsin.

Jim Bray, Children's Librarian, Rochester Public Library, Rochester, Minnesota.

Betty Charley, Children's Librarian, Minot Public Library, Minot, North Dakota.

Shirley Conlon, Librarian, Irving Elementary School, West Allis, Wisconsin.

Eleanore Donnelly, Coordinator of Branch Services, London Public Library and Art Museum, London, Ontario, Canada.

Suzanne Felan, Assistant Principal, Richfield Elementary School, Richfield, Wisconsin.

Ruth George, Children's Librarian, Atkinson Public Library, Milwaukee, Wisconsin.

Donna Goff, Director of Day Care Services, Child Development Centers of Minnesota, St. Paul, Minnesota.

Joseph Hallein, Chief Librarian/Lecturer, School of Library and Information Science, The University of Western Ontario, London, Ontario, Canada.

Kathleen Israel, Coordinator, Adult and Children's Services, Windsor Public Library, Windsor, Ontario, Canada.

Margaret E. Johnston, Coordinator of Boys and Girls Resources, Boys and Girls House, The Toronto Public Library, Toronto, Ontario, Canada.

Amy Kellman, Reviewer of Books for Children, *Teacher Magazine,* Pittsburgh, Pennsylvania.

Marilee McMullen, Librarian, Frank Lloyd Wright Junior High School, West Allis, Wisconsin.

John Ricci, Coordinator of Pupil Services, West Allis-West Milwaukee Public Schools, Wisconsin.

MaryLett Robertson, School Library Media Specialist, West Hills Elementary School, Knoxville, Tennessee.

Mary Claire Sherman, Coordinator, Library/Media Services, Juneau School District, Douglas, Alaska.

JoAnn Urlocker, Head of Central Children's Branch, London Public Library and Art Museum, London, Ontario, Canada.

Phillis M. Wilson, Director, Rochester Public Library, Rochester, Minnesota.

Everett Chard, Lynda Collins, Mary Graf, Sharon Greeley, Marjorie Lisovskis, Patty Mamula, Judith Melquist, and John Pelnar read and summarized hundreds of children's books. Rosalie Koskenmaki was responsible for an exceptional number of quality annotations.

Judith Grabowski and Verona Ufford worked many hours typing *Bookfinder* correspondence, preliminary indexes, and edited manuscript.

Finally, my appreciation and gratitude to the staff at American Guidance Service. Their talent and dedication to quality result in outstanding educational materials for children and young people.

# AN INTRODUCTION TO THE BOOKFINDER

*Bookfinder 3 begins where Bookfinder 2 leaves off, indexing and reviewing 725 children's books published from 1979 through 1982. It maintains the same easy indexing system and offers new, incisive annotations. Bookfinder 3 expands the Subject Index to include contemporary topics —anorexia nervosa, school mainstreaming, epilepsy, parental custody, school retention—reflected in recent children's literature. Widely reviewed and acclaimed by professionals and lay persons who work with children, Bookfinders 1 and 2 remain vital references for school and public libraries, churches, synagogues, YMCAs, YWCAs, psychologists, psychiatrists, social service agencies, and other groups and individuals who work with children and young people. Bookfinder 3 is their perfect companion.*

Written words have influenced the attitudes, decisions, and behavior of humankind since the beginning of recorded history. An inscription over a library in ancient Thebes proclaimed it "the Healing Place of the Soul." The written word has also been credited with less benign effects: Abraham Lincoln once greeted Harriet Beecher Stowe, author of *Uncle Tom's Cabin,* as "the little lady who wrote the book that made this big war."

Books have an important role in everyday life. Through well-chosen books, readers may increase their self-knowledge and self-esteem, gain relief from unconscious conflicts, clarify their values, and better understand other people. By identifying with characters in books, people may come to realize that they are part of humanity, that they are not alone in their struggles with reality. Reading increases personal knowledge and invites readers to consider themselves objectively.

If children who are experiencing difficulties can read about others who have solved similar problems, they may see alternatives for themselves. By presenting possible solutions, books can help prevent some difficult situations from becoming full-blown problems. Through encountering frustrations and anxieties, hopes and disappointments, successes and failures in fictional situations, youngsters may gain insights applicable to situations they meet in real life. All three volumes of the *Bookfinder: A Guide to Children's Literature About the Needs and Problems of Youth* were developed with these effects in mind.

*Bookfinder 3* is a reference work that describes and categorizes 725 current children's books according to more than 450 psychological, behavioral, and developmental topics of concern to children and adolescents, aged 2 and up. It is written primarily for parents, teachers, librarians, counselors, psychologists, psychiatrists, and other adults who want to identify books that may help children cope with the challenges of life. In short, the *Bookfinder* was created to fill the need for a way to match children and books.

## Bibliotherapy

As people became aware that the written word could influence behavior, they began to develop ways to apply this power. During the first half of the nineteenth century, American doctors Benjamin Rush and John Minson Galt II recommended reading as part of the treatment for patients physically and/or mentally ill. During the early 1900s, French psychiatrist Pierre Janet believed that patients could be helped toward a better life through assigned readings. The term "bibliotherapy" was first used by Samuel McChord Crothers in a 1916 *Atlantic Monthly* article. More recently, in the 1930s, Doctors Karl and William Menninger advocated the use of literature in the treatment of their patients. Publications by the two brothers encouraged others, both professional and lay people, to use literature to help solve problems and promote coping behavior.

Bibliotherapy, the use of reading material to help solve emotional problems and to promote mental health, was used with military personnel during both world wars and with civilians in rehabilitation hospitals, tuberculosis sanatoriums, and general hospitals. Schools have used books and stories as "social helpers" for over a century.

During the last 40 years, many theses and dissertations have been written about various aspects of bibliotherapy. One of the most significant, by Caroline Shrodes in 1949, was especially important in establishing the background for much of the recent research into the theory and practice of bibliotherapy and the psychology of reading. Bibliotherapy continues to grow in popularity, with more research being done, more articles and papers being published. A number of colleges and universities offer class work, conduct seminars, and provide practicum experiences for people interested in learning more about the process and practice, the methods and materials of bibliotherapy.

If youngsters who are experiencing difficulties can read about children who have encountered and solved similar problems, they may see hope for themselves. For example, young children suffering the loss of a loved one may feel comforted after Margaret Stevens's *When Grandpa Died* or Trudy Madler's *Why Did Grandma Die?* is read aloud and discussed with them. Older children may receive comfort after reading and discussing Jill Krementz's *How It Feels When a Parent Dies* or Gloria McLendon's *My Brother Joey Died.* Children who are upset and confused as they face their parents' divorcing may come to terms with their feelings of anger, guilt, and fear after reading Barbara Park's *Don't Make Me Smile* or Jean Okimoto's *My Mother Is Not Married to My Father.* Children may also become better equipped for tomorrow's challenges by meeting similar challenges in today's reading. For example, children who read about Timothy as he enters school in Rosemary Wells's *Timothy Goes to School* may find their own adjustment to school much easier. Young people who have read Elizabeth Richter's *The Teenage Hospital Experience: You Can Handle It!* may adjust better when a hospital stay is necessary.

Three main steps are usually present in the process of bibliotherapy:

1. **Universalization and identification.** From their reading, children come to see that they are not the only persons with particular fears, frustrations, worries, or living conditions. Recognizing similarities between themselves and fictional or biographical characters, they see themselves in those characters and thus may work out their problems vicariously.

Identification is not limited to a reader's identification of self with a story character. A child may also see his or her own mother, father, or other important person in the story. As a result, the child may develop a better understanding and appreciation of the real person.

Children may identify with characters in animal stories as well as with fictional human beings, when the animals have believable human characteristics. Children's reactions to James Marshall's picture books about George and Martha, two hippopotamuses, are examples. Children readily identify with these two animal friends who experience the same feelings, expectations, and companionship typical of childhood friendships.

When the parents, older siblings, and peers in a child's life are inappropriate models of behavior, characters in books may fill that child's need for an ego ideal.

2. **Catharsis.** A child who identifies with a fictional character lives through situations and shares feelings with that character. This vicarious experience may produce a release of tension or an imitation of the character's behavior. (When this happens, it is important that the child have someone with whom to discuss the reading, either individually or in a group.)

An advantage of reading as a therapeutic experience is that it does not force a child to participate. If the fictional situation becomes too intense, too stimulating, too painful, the reader can back off and assume the role of observer. Control rests with the reader, not with someone else. This sort of self-direction is reassuring and can help the child learn to look at problems objectively.

3. **Insight.** Through reading, children may become more aware of human motivations and of rationalizations for their own behavior. They may develop a more realistic view of their abilities and self-worth.

Because the written word tends to carry a special kind of authority, children who feel doubt and suspicion toward adults and peers tend to be less doubtful and suspicious of books. Authors of fiction generally become trusted, because they rarely impose judgment explicitly.

Thus books can become valuable companions to a developing child. Indeed, children often read beyond their tested reading levels in order to read about people faced with situations or problems similar to their own. Adults who want to help children locate the most appropriate and therapeutic books should find the *Bookfinder* a handy guide.

## Using the Bookfinder

Annotations of 725 children's books are the heart of *Bookfinder 3*. There are three ways to locate annotations of particular books:

1. Locate the desired subject in the Subject Index. Under the subject heading, identify the most promising books listed. Then refer to the annotations section to find summaries of those books.

2. Locate the author's name in the Author Index. Identify the desired book and then refer to the annotations for the book summary.

3. Locate the book title in the Title Index. Identify its author and then refer to the annotations for the book summary.

For quick and easy reference, the annotations are arranged alphabetically by author's last name; they are also numbered sequentially.

Each annotation contains the following information:

1. The *bibliographic information* includes the author's complete name. Any pseudonyms are noted. Annotations of books that have been translated into English from another language name the translator and the language of the original publication. Information about illustrations and photographs includes the name of the artist and whether the illustrations or photographs are in black and white or in color. The name of the publisher appears for each book. (All publishers' addresses* are listed in the Publishers/Producers Directory, located after the *Bookfinder 3* indexes.) The book's original copyright date is listed; or, in the case of a translation, the date of the original United States copyright is listed. A book that has already gone out of print is indicated by "o.p." Some out-of-print titles are included because many libraries already have them on their shelves, and it is always possible that an out-of-print title will be reprinted. Also indicated are the number of pages in the book. If the book's pages have not been numbered, the total number of printed pages is indicated by a number followed by the word "counted."

2. The *main subject headings,* or primary themes of the book, are listed alphabetically in upper-case letters near the top of each annotation. Significant secondary themes are listed alphabetically in upper- and lower-case letters under the main subject headings.

3. The first paragraph of each annotation is a *synopsis* of the book. It introduces the main character and describes the plot and the character relationships that provide the main and secondary themes. Whenever possible, the main character's name, sex, and age or grade level are mentioned in the first sentence of the synopsis. Race, culture, religion, and social class of the characters are indicated only when they are pertinent issues in the story. Each summary is carried through to the conclusion of the story.

4. The second paragraph of each annotation is usually a *commentary* that restates the book's main message and indicates strengths or limitations of the way the message is presented. Potential uses of the book may also be suggested. Literary merit, special qualifications of the author, sequels, and the significance of illustrations or photographs may be mentioned here. Points of special concern or interest (such as premeditated violence, explicit sex, controversial language) are also mentioned.

5. A *general reading level* is indicated at or near the end of the annotation. Often, children within the stated age range will be interested in and able to read the book independently or with minimal help. All of the books listed for preschool children, and many of the books listed for primary-age children, are read-aloud volumes.

6. The final element of each annotation is information about *other forms of the publication,* such as films, filmstrips, tapes, cassettes, discs, records, paperbound editions, and materials for blind or other physically handicapped people.

## Application

The person who wants to use books to help children understand the challenges and problems of growing up need not

---

*With cross-referencing to current names in cases where publishing companies have merged or changed their names.

be a professional counselor. Indeed, the main qualifications are an interest in and a concern for children and a willingness to become familiar with children's literature. Reading guidance can be a simple procedure. Of course, professional therapeutic skills are necessary if the child's problem is severe. But in general, the *Bookfinder* can be used to good effect by nearly everyone who works with children.

Parents are in an ideal position to use the *Bookfinder* to help their children cope with new situations. Consider the following examples: Six-year-old Timmy is scheduled to see the doctor for an examination; his symptoms indicate that surgery might be necessary. Timmy's parents tell him of the planned visit to the doctor but never mention the possibility of surgery or going to the hospital. They intend to wait until the doctor has made a definite diagnosis. But when Timmy tells his playmates about his appointment with the doctor, they eagerly embellish their own experiences and what they have heard about doctors, hospitals, and surgery. A very frightened little boy comes home and announces, "I may go to the doctor's office, but I'm not going to any hospital!" Acknowledging his fears, Timmy's parents refer to the *Bookfinder* for stories about hospitals. At Timmy's level of understanding, they find Claire Ciliotta and Carole Livingston's *Why Am I Going to the Hospital?* and Paula and Kirk Hogan's *The Hospital Scares Me.* Timmy's parents read the books to him and candidly discuss the stories and illustrations. Several days later, when Timmy's doctor does confirm the need for surgery, Timmy confidently tells his friends, "I'm going to the hospital to have an operation."

Another family has four young teenagers—two from each of the parents' previous marriages—who are having difficulty living together as a family. Referring to the *Bookfinder*, the family identifies several books about families in circumstances such as theirs. After everyone reads Jean Okimoto's *It's Just Too Much*, Susan Terris's *No Scarlet Ribbons*, and Joan Oppenheimer's *Gardine vs. Hanover*, the family spends time discussing the situations and relationships in each book. Discussing the fictional families offers some insights into this family's relationships. They recognize similarities, explore possible solutions to problems and disagreements, and are even able to laugh at incidents much like those which had led to heated arguments in the past. The reading and discussion do not solve all problems, but the foundations for meaningful communication are laid and everyone feels that the future could be compatible and satisfying and that it's worth working at.

A child can more easily understand and accept other difficult experiences—death of a loved person or pet, parental divorce, transfer to a new school, arrival of a new baby in the family—through reading about similar situations. The child's parents can use the *Bookfinder* to find an appropriate book. In sharing that book and in expressing feelings about the story, family members can increase their understanding of themselves and others. This appreciation can, in turn, lead to stronger and more trusting relationships.

School and public librarians may find the *Bookfinder* useful for helping children find books to meet their individual needs, and for helping parents, teachers, and other professionals find materials appropriate for the special needs of an individual or group. For example, an elementary school is about to include handicapped children in existing classes —mainstreaming. To help the students in the school understand the feelings and needs, the strengths and limitations of handicapped children, the librarian and teachers refer to the *Bookfinder* and identify appropriate books. Several of the books are read aloud and discussed in classes. Others are attractively displayed, encouraging students to do additional reading on their own. The insights the students derive from these books may increase their effectiveness in helping their handicapped classmates feel comfortable in the new surroundings.

Public librarians frequently have specific requests—from children, parents, teachers, and other adults who work with children—for books about particular concerns, attitudes, and developmental tasks. A librarian, sensing that some children have interests or concerns that they prefer not to talk about, puts a copy of the *Bookfinder* on top of the card catalog. A poster, mounted above it, invites students to peruse the index on their own, to find books of personal interest.

Librarians in children's hospitals have a special role as they work with medical professionals to meet the emotional and physical needs of sick children. Hospital librarians usually seek books that promote understanding and acceptance of hospital routines and medical procedures. Lengthy and depressing hospital confinement can be made brighter and more hopeful through carefully prescribed reading.

Teachers are in a good position to match books with children's needs and concerns. A kindergarten teacher who knows that one of her or his students has had a new baby join the family may see that that child is having trouble adjusting. Consulting the *Bookfinder*, the teacher may choose Nicki Weiss's *Chuckie* as a read-aloud story. The teacher can then invite the children to share their experiences with the class. They can compare their feelings with those of Lucy, Chuckie's older sister, and consider some of the happy aspects of having a new baby at home. After such reading and discussion, a child is likely to become more patient and less jealous of the new sibling than before.

Teachers can often promote students' understanding of themselves and others through books, by reading aloud to the class or by encouraging independent reading. This reading can be enjoyable when books are chosen with reader interests and needs in mind. Then readers are likely to want to read more, and reading skills will probably improve in the process.

For example, a teacher has the class agree on one topic of interest—aging, fear, prejudice, sibling relationships— locate the topic in the *Bookfinder*, and select books to read individually. The teacher then chooses one especially pertinent book to read aloud to the class. After all the reading is completed, discussion and other activities are organized to integrate ideas from the children's varied reading experiences.

A teacher divides the class into small groups with each group first selecting a topic of interest, finding the topic in the *Bookfinder*, and then choosing a book (or books) to be read within the group. As the books are read, groups discuss them. When the reading is completed, each group prepares a culminating activity to present to the class.

The following are examples of thought-provoking activities that can follow the reading: role-playing, dramatization, mock interview with the book's main character, bulletin boards, recordings, films, filmstrips, supplemental reading lists, and radio and television programs related to the reading. Teachers can read open-ended stories. Or they can stop reading a story just short of the conclusion and ask the class to end the story. (The teacher should then finish reading the story to the class so students can compare their conclusion with the author's.)

Teachers who read aloud to their classes have many opportunities for discussing how a character felt about something or why the character made particular decisions. Good questions and discussions can broaden students' decision-making abilities and increase their understanding of other people.

A teacher who knows that a child has a problem might introduce the child to a book about "someone who was very much like you" or "someone who also. . . ." Or, to be more subtle, teachers can introduce, to the whole class, that book and other books the class might enjoy. If the teacher sees the troubled child reading one of the suggested books, the teacher might show a willingness to discuss the book with the child.

The school counselor can work with the teacher and the librarian to select books for special study units—for example, on friendship, courage, fear, or other pertinent topics. Counselors working with individual children or small groups of children can choose books to suit personal needs. For example, a new student is transferring into the school. The counselor consults the *Bookfinder*, selects several appropriate titles, and suggests that the new student might like to read about others who have experienced the same kind of change. Reading about someone else in the same situation may provide some hints for making the adjustment easier.

The school counselor can use the *Bookfinder* to help students in individual or group counseling select appropriate reading to be done between counseling sessions. Such reading can extend the counseling experience and serve as a point of reference for beginning the next counseling session.

The foregoing examples are meant to show how children might face everyday problems—as well as more severe problems—more confidently if they have also faced them vicariously, through books. The use of books to help children can be simple or complex, depending on the children's needs and on the confidence and background of the adults who want to help. Parents, teachers, librarians, and counselors and other mental health specialists may find the *Bookfinder* useful. So may nurses, providers of day care, scout leaders, recreation leaders, camp counselors, church and synagogue youth leaders—and anyone else in a position to help youngsters expand their understanding, tolerance, and ability to cope with the challenges of life.

# DEVELOPMENT OF THE BOOKFINDER

The *Bookfinder* was conceived in 1968 as a supplement to the author's thesis for the master's degree. The bibliography then included over 300 books for children aged 9 through 15. The need for easy access to children's literature about developmental problems became more apparent,

and the author decided to update, expand, and reorganize the original bibliography.

Formal development of the *Bookfinder* was initiated in 1973. It began with an extensive new review of current children's literature.

## Book Selection

All available bibliographies and children's book review sources were examined in the search for appropriate books. Children's book publishers submitted hundreds of books for the author to consider. Books familiar to the author, consultants, and field-trial participants were considered, as were books within the collection of the Central Youth Library in Milwaukee. Over 2500 books were considered for each volume of the *Bookfinder*.

All of the books annotated in *Bookfinder 3* were published from 1979 through 1982. (*Bookfinder 1* covers books published through 1974; *Bookfinder 2* covers books published from 1975 through 1978.) Books published after 1982 are not included because they could not be reviewed properly before *Bookfinder 3* was printed. In addition, the selected books were required to be in hardbound form and to be available through ordinary means: libraries, bookstores, book jobbers, and publishers.

Timeliness and appropriateness of content were other important criteria. Timely, "here and now" books are usually more helpful to children with problems than older books are, unless the older books speak to timeless issues. The selected books are, therefore, about the modern child or are so universal in appeal that the difference in time or place is unimportant.

The book plots and themes had to be carried through to resolution or presented completely enough to provoke thoughtful consideration or discussion. The characters had to be realistic. The problems faced by the characters had to be brought out clearly and explored without moralizing.

Artistic quality was also a consideration. Literary quality, although not the prime concern, had to be acceptable to the author of the *Bookfinder*. Where many books on a particular topic were available, only the best were selected for annotation. Illustrations or photographs also had to be of acceptable quality, appropriate to the story, and supportive of its message.

Despite the author's careful concern for proper book selection criteria, the selection of each book was necessarily a subjective process. Some users of the *Bookfinder* will disagree with the inclusion of some titles or will look in vain for some of their favorites.* But every user should find many pertinent and applicable books among the 725 entries, which represent more than 496 authors and 70 publishing companies.

Many picture books are included in the *Bookfinder*. They are not just cute stories; they have plots and characters that encourage reader identification. These books should help prepare young children for new experiences and new stages of development and help solve current problems.

---

*\*Bookfinder users are invited to send their comments and suggestions to the publisher: American Guidance Service, Publishers' Building, Circle Pines, Minnesota 55014-1796.*

About 75 percent of the books annotated in *Bookfinder 3* have main characters of the white middle class. This is a reflection on these authors' own choice of characters. A great effort was made to select books which are honest, realistic representations of people, and which treat characters' ethnic, religious, economic, or other social identity with intelligence and sensitivity.

The nature of existing children's literature is also reflected in the percentages of books included in *Bookfinder 3* for various age levels. About 34 percent of the books in *Bookfinder 3* are classified for ages 12 and up, 33 percent for ages 8 through 11, and 33 percent for ages 2 through 7.

The vast majority of the indexed books—about 90 percent—are fiction. About 10 percent are biography, and there are a few especially significant nonfiction publications.

Clues to meaningful book selection may come from knowledge of the child's home life, family, out-of-school activities, personal ambitions, and other interests. It is important also to consider the reader's vocabulary and comprehension levels, because children should not be forced to read beyond their skills. The reading should be a voluntary and pleasant experience—not another assignment.

## Annotations

The first step in writing annotations was to categorize each book according to its main theme and any relevant subthemes. For example, a subject heading *FRIENDSHIP: Best Friend* means that the plot of the book centers around the thoughts, feelings, and activities of people who regard themselves as best friends. Much care has been taken to ensure that the subject headings accurately indicate the content of the book.

What may appear as an obvious theme to some readers may seem less so to others. A concentrated effort has been made to define themes by asking, "Does this book offer enough information about a particular situation or problem to warrant recommending it to a child who is facing that situation or problem?" Beyond that guideline, only the user can determine whether a book is suitable for a specific child with a specific need. The *Bookfinder* was not developed to prescribe books for particular children; it was developed as a reference that categorizes and describes books as objectively as possible.

As the annotations were prepared, publishing information was carefully checked and rechecked for uniformity and accuracy. Discrepancies were found. Therefore, book titles with idiosyncratic capitalization have been given standard capitalization.

The original book publishers were asked to tell which of their publications listed in the *Bookfinder* are available in Braille, film, filmstrip, tape or cassette, disc, record, paperbound, or large-print editions. If a book's subsidiary rights were retained by the author or the author's agent, there is no way that the book publisher would be aware of rights sold for other formats. Some books, therefore, may be available in other media not known to either the book's publisher or the *Bookfinder*'s author. Although these are very recent materials, it is possible that some items may already be out of stock. Producers (addresses are included in the Publishers/Producers Directory) should be contacted directly for further information. *Paperbound Books*

*in Print* was also used to identify books available in paperbound form. Materials available for blind people—tapes, cassettes, talking books, Braille editions, and large-print volumes—were identified through the indexes and catalogs of the Library of Congress, Wisconsin Regional Library for the Blind and Physically Handicapped. (Most of these materials are available only through regional branches of the Library of Congress [National Library Service for the Blind and Physically Handicapped] and can be obtained only by persons who are legally blind or physically handicapped. Questions regarding materials for blind and physically handicapped people should be directed to local public librarians, who can supply more information about the program and explain how to apply for service.)

Since descriptions of the plots, themes, and characters are meant to be of greatest service to the adult user, the book summaries have been written for adults. No deliberate attempt has been made to whet the reader's appetite. Nevertheless, a child with sixth-grade reading and comprehension skills could probably browse through the annotations and select books without adult assistance.

## Subject Index

The Subject Index lists the primary and secondary themes of all the books in the *Bookfinder*. To compile the working Subject Index, the author, publisher, and project consultants identified over 600 topics they considered important to children and adolescents. Following final book selection for *Bookfinder 1*, the number of topics decreased to about 450. In the development of *Bookfinders 2* and *3*, some headings were deleted because no appropriate books were found to cover those themes in a significant manner. New headings were added, such as anorexia nervosa, epilepsy, school mainstreaming, parental custody, and school retention.

## Cumulative Subject Index

The Cumulative Subject Index, found only in the hardcover edition of *Bookfinder 3*, merges the subject indexes of *Bookfinders 1, 2,* and *3*. Under each topic, books indexed by that topic from all three volumes are listed alphabetically by author's last name. The appropriate volume number is provided.

## Field Test

Field testing of the *Bookfinder* took place during the spring of 1976 in six states—Alaska, Minnesota, North Dakota, Pennsylvania, Tennessee, and Wisconsin—and in the province of Ontario. Sixteen field-test sites provided information from four types of libraries: school, general public, college/consultant, and children's public. Each site was given a field-test version of the annotated bibliography, along with limited subject, author, and title indexes and 453 rough-draft annotations. Parents, counselors, teachers, librarians, and psychologists were asked to review this material, and their comments contributed to the refinement of the *Bookfinder*. Psychiatrists and supervising librarians also suggested ways to make the *Bookfinder* more useful.

# BOOK SELECTION AIDS

For more help in finding appropriate children's books, the reader may want to use the following references, many of which include titles not found in the *Bookfinder*. *Bookfinder* titles that are included in these references are reviewed from various points of view or for purposes that may differ from the *Bookfinder*'s. Titles preceded by an asterisk (*) are more recent, and thus did not appear in *Bookfinders* 1 or 2 Book Selection Aids bibliographies.

Baskin, Barbara H. and Karen H. Harris. *Notes from a Different Drummer: A Guide to Juvenile Fiction Portraying the Handicapped.* New York: R. R. Bowker Company, 1977.

This guide to children's literature about mentally and/or physically handicapped people is divided into five main sections. The first four discuss handicapped people in society and literature, evaluate children's fiction and its application, and investigate patterns and trends in children's fiction, 1940-1975. A fifth section summarizes and evaluates 311 books written between 1940 and 1975. A broad-range reading level (e.g., YC—Young Child; MC—Mature Child) is given for each entry.

*Bernstein, Joanne E. *Books to Help Children Cope with Separation and Loss.* 2d ed. New York: R. R. Bowker Company, 1983.

The introduction to this reference describes how the bibliography was compiled, discusses separation and loss as they relate to children, and defines and explains bibliotherapy. The bibliography itself contains 633 titles (400 new to this edition), most of which are fiction, though some nonfiction is included. Each entry contains bibliographic information, reading interest and reading grade levels, and a comprehensive summary of the plot. The entries are divided into subjects including death, divorce, war, living with new stepparents, and entering a new school. The guide concludes with extensive professional bibliographies on agencies which provide services to children and adults who are facing separation and loss.

*Fassler, Joan. *Helping Children Cope: Mastering Stress Through Books and Stories.* New York: The Free Press, 1978.

This resource provides access to children's books which can lead to "experiences that initiate communication, reduce anxieties, enhance development, and encourage growth." It concentrates on possible stressful situations such as: hospitalization, illness, separation experiences, financial crisis, moving, divorce, and new sibling. Each of five main sections offers professional viewpoints about the topic, followed by a description of selected children's books which might help foster effective coping skills for a given situation. Suggested discussion questions and techniques, proved successful in using literature to help children face stressful situations, are included in each section of the reference, followed by appropriate children's books, listed alphabetically by author.

Feminists on Children's Media. *Little Miss Muffet Fights Back.* New York, 1971. (Available through Feminists on Children's Literature, P.O. Box 4315, Grand Central Station, New York 10017.)

This 48-page pamphlet is a bibliography of children's literature selected for its "positive and nonstereotyped portrayal of girls and women." Each book is briefly annotated, and the collection is divided into 15 categories, including Fiction, From the Past, Science Fiction, and Sex Education.

Gillespie, John T. *More Junior Plots: A Guide for Teachers and Librarians.* New York: R. R. Bowker Company, 1977.

This guide describes 72 books for children aged 11 through 16 years. Books are arranged according to nine developmental goals related to adolescence. These include: Getting Along in the Family, Developing Lasting Values, Understanding Social Problems, Understanding Physical and Emotional Problems, Becoming Self-Reliant, and Developing a Wholesome Self-Image. Each entry includes bibliographic information, plot summary, discussion of themes within the book, techniques for "book talks," suggestions for other uses or activities (additional similar books are listed here), and information about the author.

Lass-Woodfin, Mary Jo, ed. *Books on American Indians and Eskimos: A Selection Guide for Children and Young Adults.* Chicago: American Library Association, 1978.

Reviews of 807 children's books written before 1977 are included in this reference. In addition to bibliographic information and estimated reading grade level, each entry has a summary of content, comments on possible uses, comments on strengths and weaknesses in "writing, accuracy, format, and feel," and a rating of Good, Adequate, or Poor. Two persons reviewed each book; where opinions differed, both points of view are included.

*Lima, Carolyn W. *A to Zoo: Subject Access to Children's Picture Books.* New York: R. R. Bowker Company, 1982.

Over 4400 picture books for preschool children through second grade are indexed under 543 categories in this guide. Picture books relating to more than one subject are listed under each relevant category. An introduction briefly tracing the evolution of the English-language picture book is followed by an alphabetical listing of subject headings and subheadings used in the guide. The subject guide lists books alphabetically, by author and title only, for each subject heading. Complete bibliographic information for each of the books is included in the bibliographic guide. Title and illustrator indexes are also provided.

*McDonough, Irma, ed. *Canadian Books for Young People.* 3d ed. Toronto: University of Toronto Press, 1980.

This revised index includes Canadian children's books (preschool age through age 9) written in English and/or French. All of these books were in print at the time the reference was printed. Each entry includes bibliographic information and an annotative sentence. The reference is divided into two sections: the first lists books in English; the second (written in French) lists books in French. Books are organized in such categories as Picture Books, Sports and Recreation, and Fiction: Stories, Fantasy, and Historical Fiction.

*Mills, Joyce White, ed. *The Black World in Literature: A Bibliography of Print and Non-Print Materials.* Atlanta: School of Library Service of Atlanta University, 1978.

This 56-page booklet indexes and briefly annotates children's books published in 1976 and 1977 about black people in the United States and Africa. Each book is rated Highly Recommended, Recommended, or Not Recommended. Audiovisual titles are interfiled with book titles and briefly described, but not rated. The bibliography is divided into two sections: For Younger Children, ages 3-8; and For Older Children, ages 9-13. Eight subdivisions within these sections include Picture and Easy Materials; Biography; Folklore; Literature; Arts, Crafts, and Recreation; History and Travel; Sociology; and Junior Fiction. A list of adult reference sources is included.

*Rollock, Barbara, ed. *The Black Experience in Children's Books.* New York: The New York Public Library, 1984.

This comprehensive bibliography of black literature includes books for children and books to be shared by children and adults. It covers "a wide range of subjects reflecting the social, political, and economic contributions Blacks are making in this country (USA) and in the developing nations in Africa." Entries are briefly annotated.

Spirit, Diana L. *Introducing More Books: A Guide for the Middle Grades.* New York: R. R. Bowker, 1978.

This reference includes plot summaries of 72 books and lists additional related materials for each entry for reading, viewing, and listening. Altogether, about 500 titles are mentioned. Books are listed according to nine developmental goals for children aged 8 through 14. Among these goals are: Understanding Social Problems, Understanding Physical and Emotional Problems, Developing Values, and Making Friends. Each entry includes bibliographic information and a paragraph of thematic analysis followed by material for discussion and other related materials.

*Sutherland, Zena, ed. *The Best in Children's Books.* Vol. 2. Chicago: The University of Chicago Press, 1980.

This is a collection of 1400 book reviews previously published in the *Bulletin of the Center for Children's Books.* Most of the books were rated as "recommended" reading. The entries are listed alphabetically by the author's name and are categorized in several indexes. The section on developmental values may aid book selection.

*Tway, Eileen, ed. *Reading Ladders for Human Relations.* 6th ed. Washington, DC: American Council on Education, 1981.

This reference was compiled to help teachers, librarians, and other adults select appropriate reading material for children and young people. Books are briefly annotated and divided into age levels—ages 1-5, 5-8, 8-11, 11-14, and 14 and up. They are arranged in five Reading Ladders: Growing into Self,

Relating to Wide Individual Differences, Interacting in Groups, Appreciating Different Cultures, and Coping in a Changing World. Each ladder has several pertinent subheadings. The introduction contains an explanation of the purpose of the reference and practical suggestions for using books with children and young people "to advance the cause of human relations."

Wilkin, Binnie Tate. *Survival Themes in Fiction for Children and Young People.* Metuchen, NJ: The Scarecrow Press, 1978.

This reference, which has comments and suggestions interspersed in the list of titles, divides entries into three main areas—The Individual, Pairings and Groupings, and Views of the World—which are then subdivided. The author believes "that a realistic presentation of human existence will help the children develop their own capabilities in problem solving." The books selected (some nonfiction is included) "are intended as samples that offer certain sensitivity to some of the individual and societal issues of the day." Bibliographic information is followed by a short summary of the book. Most titles included are from the 1970s.

# PROFESSIONAL READINGS

This bibliography includes professional books and articles that describe, analyze, and apply bibliotherapy. Titles preceded by an asterisk (*) are more recent, and thus did not appear in *Bookfinders 1* or *2* Professional Readings bibliographies.

Brown, Eleanor Frances. *Bibliotherapy and Its Widening Applications.* Metuchen, NJ: The Scarecrow Press, 1975.

Carner, Charles. "Reaching Troubled Minds Through Reading." *Today's Health* 44 (1966): 32-33, 75-77.

Cianciolo, Patricia Jean. "Children's Literature Can Effect Coping Behavior." *Personnel and Guidance Journal* 43 (1965): 897-903.

Cianciolo, Patricia Jean. "Interaction Between the Personality of the Reader and Literature." *School Libraries* 17 (1968): 13-17, 19-21.

Darling, R. L. "Mental Hygiene and Books." *Wilson Library Bulletin* 32 (1957): 293-296.

*Davison, Maureen McKinney. "Classroom Bibliotherapy: Why and How." *Reading World* 23 (1983): 103-107.

Edwards, Beverly Sigler. "The Therapeutic Value of Reading." *Elementary English* 49 (1972): 213-218.

*Engelbert, Alan. "In Search of Bibliotherapy." *Show-Me Libraries* 9 (1982): 8-13.

*Frasier, Mary M. and Carolyn McCannon. "Using Bibliotherapy with Gifted Children." *Gifted Child Quarterly* 25 (1981): 81-85.

Gray, Maxine. "Books—Another Use in Our Classroom." *Education* 79 (1959): 487-490.

Hartley, Helene W. "Developing Personality Through Books." *The English Journal* 40 (1951): 198-204.

Heitzmann, Kathleen E. and William Ray Heitzmann. "Science of Bibliotherapy: A Critical Review of Research Findings." *Reading Improvement* 12 (1975): 120-124.

Hoagland, Joan. "Bibliotherapy: Aiding Children in Personality Development." *Elementary English* 49 (1972): 390-394.

*Jalongo, Mary Renck. "Bibliotherapy: Literature to Promote Socioemotional Growth." *Reading Teacher* 36 (1983): 796-803.

*Jalongo, Mary Renck. "Using Crisis-Oriented Books with Young Children." *Young Children* 38 (1983): 29-35.

Lejeune, Archie L. "Bibliocounseling as a Guidance Technique." *Catholic Library World* 41 (1969): 156-164.

Lenkowsky, Barbara E. and Ronald S. Lenkowsky. "Bibliotherapy for the LD Adolescent." *Academic Therapy* 14 (1978): 179-185.

Lindahl, Hannah M. and Katherine Koch. "Bibliotherapy in the Middle Grades." *Elementary English* 29 (1952): 390-396.

Lunsteen, Sara W. "A Thinking Improvement Program Through Literature." *Elementary English* 49 (1972): 505-512.

*McInnis, Kathleen M. "Bibliotherapy: Adjunct to Traditional Counseling with Children of Stepfamilies." *Child Welfare* 61 (1982): 153-160.

Monroe, Margaret E. *Reading Guidance and Bibliotherapy in Public, Hospital, and Institutional Libraries.* Madison: Library School of the University of Wisconsin, 1971.

Monroe, Margaret E., ed. *Seminar on Bibliotherapy.* Madison: Library School of the University of Wisconsin, 1978.

Moses, Harold A. and Joseph S. Zaccaria. "Bibliotherapy in an Educational Context: Rationale and Principles." In *Advances in Librarianship,* vol. 1, edited by Melvin J. Voigt. New York: Academic Press, 1970.

Newell, Ethel. "At the North End of Pooh: A Study of Bibliotherapy." *Elementary English* 34 (1957): 22-25.

Nickerson, Eileen T. "Bibliotherapy: A Therapeutic Medium for Helping Children." *Psychotherapy: Theory, Research and Practice* 12 (1975): 258-261.

Olsen, Henry D. "Bibliotherapy to Help Children Solve Problems." *Elementary School Journal* 75 (1975): 423-429.

*Rakes, Thomas A. and Annabelle Buchanan. "Using Bibliotherapy: A Synthesis of Current Practice." Memphis: Department of Curriculum and Instruction of Tennessee State University, 1980.

Rongione, Louis A. "Bibliotherapy: Its Nature and Uses." *Catholic Library World* 43 (1972): 495-500.

Rubin, Dorothy. "Bibliotherapy: Reading Towards Mental Health." *Children's House* 9 (1976): 6-9.

Rubin, Rhea Joyce. *Bibliotherapy: A Guide to Theory and Practice.* Phoenix: The Oryx Press, 1978.

*Rubin, Rhea Joyce. "Uses of Bibliotherapy in Response to the 1970s." *Library Trends* 28 (1979): 239-252.

Rubin, Rhea Joyce, ed. *Bibliotherapy Sourcebook.* Phoenix: The Oryx Press, 1978.

Russell, Alma E. and William A. Russell. "Using Bibliotherapy with Emotionally Disturbed Children." *Teaching Exceptional Children* 11 (1979): 168-169.

Russell, David H. "Reading and the Healthy Personality." *Elementary English* 29 (1952): 195-200.

Russell, David H. and Caroline Shrodes. "Contributions of Research in Bibliotherapy to the Language Arts Program, I." *School Review* 58 (1950): 335-342.

Russell, David H. and Caroline Shrodes. "Contributions of Research in Bibliotherapy to the Language Arts Program, II." *School Review* 58 (1950): 411-420.

Sanders, Jacquelyn. "Psychological Significance of Children's Literature." *Library Trends* 37 (1967): 15-22.

*Schrank, Frederick A. and Dennis W. Engels. "Bibliotherapy as a Counseling Adjunct: Research Findings." *Personnel and Guidance Journal* 60 (1981): 143-147.

Schwoebel, Barbara. "Bibliotherapy: A Guide to Materials." *Catholic Library World* 44 (1973): 586-592.

Sclabassi, Sharon Henderson. "Literature as a Therapeutic Tool: A Review of the Literature on Bibliotherapy." *American Journal of Psychotherapy* 27 (1973): 70-77.

Shepherd, Terry and Lynn B. Iles. "What is Bibliotherapy?" *Language Arts* 53 (1976): 569-571.

Shrodes, Caroline. "Bibliotherapy." *The Reading Teacher* 9 (1955): 24-29.

Spache, George D. *Good Reading for Poor Readers.* 9th rev. ed. Champaign, IL: Garrard Publishing, 1974. Chapter 3, "Using Books to Help Solve Children's Problems."

Strunk, Orlo, Jr. "Bibliotherapy Revisited." *Journal of Religion and Health* 11 (1972): 218-228.

Tartagni, Donna. "Using Bibliotherapy with Adolescents." *School Counselor* 24 (1976): 28-35.

Tews, Ruth M. "Progress in Bibliotherapy." In *Advances in Librarianship*, vol. 1, edited by Melvin J. Voigt. New York: Academic Press, 1970.

Tews, Ruth M., ed. "Bibliotherapy." *Library Trends* 11, No. 2 (October 1962). Entire issue.

Tiller, Karen. "Bibliotherapy and the Treatment of Emotional Disturbances." *Catholic Library World* 45 (1974): 428-431.

Wass, Hannelore and Judith Shaak. "Helping Children Understand Death Through Literature." *Childhood Education* 53 (1976): 80-85.

Witty, Paul. "Promoting Growth and Development Through Reading." *Elementary English* 27 (1950): 493-500, 556.

Witty, Paul. "Reading to Meet Emotional Needs." *Elementary English* 29 (1952): 75-84.

Zaccaria, Joseph S. and Harold A. Moses. *Facilitating Human Development Through Reading: The Use of Bibliotherapy in Teaching and Counseling.* Champaign, IL: Stipes Publishing, 1968.

# ANNOTATIONS

A GUIDE TO
CHILDREN'S LITERATURE
ABOUT THE NEEDS AND PROBLEMS
OF YOUTH AGED 2 AND UP

**1**

Abercrombie, Barbara Mattes

## Cat-Man's Daughter

Harper & Row, Publishers, Inc., 1981.
(154 pages)

---

*DIVORCE: of Parents*
*Belonging*
*Change: accepting*
*Grandparent: love for*

---

For two years, thirteen-year-old Kate has lived in New York with her divorced mother. Several times during the year she goes to Los Angeles to visit her father, who stars as "Cat-Man" in a popular television show. "I get bounced back and forth between New York and Los Angeles so much, I feel like a Ping-Pong ball," laments Kate. She longs for a return to a settled life with her parents together again. Kate's favorite person is her paternal grandmother, Riley McAllister, who also lives in California. To Kate, Riley is the one person who has always been loving and trustworthy. On one of Kate's visits to her father, Riley arranges to have the girl "kidnapped," spiriting her out of the house in the middle of the night. The grandmother hopes the bogus kidnapping will bring Kate's parents together again in their shared concern for Kate. Sure enough, by the third day of the "kidnapping" Kate's mother is in Los Angeles, the disappearance of Cat-Man's daughter has made the national news, and the police are investigating. Meanwhile, Kate is loving her life at Riley's, a place filled with eccentric people who call Riley's house their home. Finally, suspicious at not hearing more from Riley, Kate's parents converge on Riley's home and discover the hoax. By this time, Kate has begun to realize that a "normal" family is not as important as a family that really loves her—Riley's "family." Kate's mother tells her that she is remarrying and that she and her fiancé plan to put Kate in a boarding school. Now Kate must do a little manipulating to get her mother to agree to her living with Riley. She and her mother decide that Kate will live with Riley and her household for most of the year and take turns visiting her parents on holidays and during the summer. This is not quite the happy ending that Kate wanted. "But," she decides, "with a little work and some luck you might get a good beginning."

Kate is a plucky girl who perceives herself as a pawn in her divorced parents' power struggle. She longs for life to return to "normal," but discovers she'll have to make the best of what she has—and what she has with her grandmother is a very special relationship. As told by Kate, the story is upbeat and humorous. Readers will sympathize with the heroine as she searches for and finds a "real family" to care for her. Although the situation is a bit far-fetched, the characters and their feelings are entirely credible.

Ages 11-13

**Also available in:**
Paperbound—*Cat-Man's Daughter*
Scholastic Book Services

**2**

Addy, Sharon

## We Didn't Mean To

Color illustrations by Jay Blair.
Raintree Publishers, Inc., 1981.
(31 pages)

---

*VANDALISM*
*Practical jokes/pranks*
*Sports/Sportsmanship*

---

Before a track meet between the Hawks, their school's team, and the rival Rockets, Tommy and his friend Brent, both about ten, decide to spray-paint "HAWKS ARE WINNERS" on a bridge wall. While Brent works, his older sister and Tommy's older brother, both members of the Hawks, alert the boys to a Rockets slogan painted on a wall across the street. Brent goes over and changes "Best" to "Losers," and the driver of a passing car threatens to report them for vandalism. They run off but defend their actions to one another as fun, not vandalism. The night of the meet Tommy and Brent watch from the stands, cheering the Hawks and booing the Rockets. When it becomes evident that the Rockets will win, Brent leads Tommy to what he thinks is the Rockets' locker room and suggests they throw everything out of the lockers. The boys are just starting on the second row of lockers when they hear voices and hide in a storage closet. To their chagrin, their own Hawks enter the locker room. Peeking through the door, Tommy watches his angry brother pick up his clothes and hears the coach say he will report this to the opposing team's coach. "Let this be an end to the pranks and the vandalism," he advises the Hawks. Now Brent and Tommy, further distressed when a player discovers his glasses are broken, begin to realize the consequences of their fun. The locker room grows quiet and the boys try to escape, but the coach, working in his office, hears them. He knows right away that they, not the Rockets, are the culprits. "We didn't mean to—," the boys begin, but the coach interrupts and asks if they were also responsible for the bridge painting. They confess, saying it was only a joke. "That kind of joke is called vandalism," he says. "It hurts people." He tells them to report to him in the morning with ideas on how to make up for their actions. Walking home in the rain, the boys pass their fading slogan on the bridge and speed its disappearance by rubbing out the letters themselves.

Two boys show their excessive team loyalty by acts of vandalism. When the "fun" backfires, Tommy and Brent learn the seriousness of their behavior and are eager to make amends. Very simply written with full-page illustrations, the format might deter some prospective older readers, although it enhances the book's suitability for reading with a group. The two culprits are pictured as older than the intended audience, another potential source of confusion. Still, the story encourages children "to define, analyze, and develop constructive alternatives to vandalism," and so is valuable.

Ages 8-10

**Also available in:**
No other form known

**3**

Adler, Carole Schwerdtfeger

## The Cat That Was Left Behind

Houghton Mifflin Company, 1981.
(146 pages)

---

*BELONGING*
*FOSTER HOME*
*REJECTION: Parental*
   *Adoption: feelings about*
   *Animals: love for*
   *Dependence/Independence*

---

For thirteen-year-old Chad a summer at Cape Cod with the Sorenics, his new foster family, is just another temporary situation to be endured until the time when he can live with his mother again. Although Chad has been in foster homes since he was four and his mother got sick, she has always promised that one day she would take him back. Thus, he refuses to believe she would really give him up for adoption, as she suggested in a recent letter. The first days at the Sorenics' cottage are awkward for Chad. He is afraid of the ocean, disdainful of the athletic skills of Bob, the twelve-year-old son, and wary of his foster father's gruff, commanding manner. He often withdraws to a quiet spot behind the cottage to feed and watch a stray cat he has discovered. His foster mother seems to understand his need for a retreat, as does Polly, the quiet, fourteen-year-old daughter. In time, the cat trusts Chad, approaching when he calls and sitting contentedly in the boy's lap. So too does Chad become more comfortable with his new family and he enters willingly into their activities—swimming, jogging, household chores, repair work. The cat, his cat as he has come to think of it, leads Chad to new interests. He goes fishing with Chester, a crusty old-timer, and he works for Mrs. Saugerty, a sour old woman who chases off his cat whenever it comes around. Even so, Chad eagerly does her yard work and sends his earnings to his mother, suggesting that now is the time for them to reunite. Then concern for his cat, which Mrs. Saugerty has threatened to poison, takes his mind off his mother. The Sorenics share his concern and offer to help, but there seems no clear solution. Even locking the cat in the cottage does not work since the animal, desperate for freedom, escapes the first chance it gets. However, it remains unharmed and often returns to be with Chad. As the summer draws to a close, Chad receives the much-awaited reply from his mother: "My new husband don't want me to have nothing to do with you now and maybe it is all for the best for both of us." Chad's hurt increases as he realizes that when he leaves the Sorenics he'll have to leave the cat. He thinks, "It was a rotten thing to teach someone to love you and then to leave him." The Sorenics feel the same way. They love Chad and want to adopt him, if he is willing. It takes Chad a few days to decide to join their family, days in which they are all drawn together as they search for the cat, who has again disappeared. The cat suddenly returns when they are ready to leave and just as suddenly escapes from the car as they prepare to drive away. It is Chad who decides to leave the cat, knowing it can survive on its own and prefers to do so.

A boy adopts a stray cat that is much like him. Abandoned, it is wary of strangers and has learned to fend for itself. The main difference between the two is that the cat takes what it can get and Chad wants what he cannot have—his mother. The animal becomes a catalyst, bringing out Chad's sense of responsibility and drawing his foster family to him by their willingness to protect what is important to him. The relative ease with which Chad relinquishes his long-held dream of living with his mother and adjusts to his prospective adoption demonstrates his realization that he, unlike the cat, wants and needs someone to care for him. The story is told with sensitivity but is not sentimental.

Ages 9-12

**Also available in:**
Paperbound—*The Cat That Was Left Behind*
Doubleday & Company, Inc.

---

**4**

Adler, Carole Schwerdtfeger

## Down by the River

Coward, McCann & Geoghegan, Inc., 1981.
(206 pages)

---

*LOVE, MEANING OF*
   *Boy-girl relationships: dating*
   *Cerebral palsy*
   *Child abuse*
   *Parent/Parents: single*
   *Sex: attitude toward*
   *Sex: premarital*
   *Sibling: love for*

---

While her husband sleeps beside her, Marybeth looks out her window at the dark river and tries to find "the answer to the question of how she had come to be here." She and Peter had been a twosome since sixth grade. He lived with his wealthy grandparents, she with her sister, Lily, who has cerebral palsy, and her mother. When she told her mother she would be happy spending her whole life on the river bluff, her mother called her a fool. Don't follow my example, she constantly preached: a young marriage, two babies, a husband who deserted them. She desperately wanted Marybeth to have a career, to be a success. But Marybeth simply wanted to love someone who loved her back. As she and Peter got older, he asked her more and more frequently for sex. But Marybeth wanted to wait. She baby-sat for the Fraziers, a young couple across the street with two small children. Marybeth was afraid the mother neglected and abused her children, but before she could pursue her suspicions the woman left her family. Marybeth took over for a few days while Garth Frazier looked for permanent help. When their junior year started, Peter began paying court to a new girl, Hillary, who lived in the best part of town and went to party after party. Meanwhile, Garth Frazier's Aunt Florence was caring for the children, but Marybeth and Lily thought the children seemed unhappy and listless. They subsequently learned that the aunt sedated them. Marybeth's relationship with Peter worsened, until finally she considered yielding to his constant demands for sex. Peter continued to see Hillary and lie about it to Marybeth, all the time assuring Marybeth that he really loved her. One night, feeling like "a robot under his control," Marybeth let Peter make love to her. Later, he gave her a gold chain and heart, which she took as proof of his love. But that evening Hillary called to inform her that she and Peter had made love the previous night, that the two of them must "share" Peter. Devastated both by Peter's telling Hillary about their making love and by Peter's sleeping with them both, Marybeth confronted Peter and learned that his definition of love was far different from hers. From then on, Marybeth played a waiting game, convinced that in time Peter would return to her. But the waiting was hard. After their junior year, Peter went to Alaska with a buddy, and Marybeth took a waitressing job at the diner where her mother worked. When Garth Frazier asked her why a beautiful girl like her was always available to baby-sit for his children on Saturday nights, she began to notice him in a new way. When Peter returned from Alaska, he hadn't changed at all. His grandmother had died, but he abandoned his grieving grandfather to go to Phoenix with the mother who had abandoned him years earlier. He promised Marybeth that he would come back in time to take her to the senior prom. But after he left, she began dating Garth. Though nine years older than she, it was Garth, steady, kind, and gentle, who took her to the prom. She saw Peter there, but as she looked from Peter to Garth she realized which was the man she loved, which the boy. Now as Marybeth stands at the window, her husband wakes up and speaks to her. It is Garth. She has found someone to love who loves her back, and she lives happily with him and his children on the river bluff.

After being part of a couple for five years, a girl tests out her own ideas about love and her future. This absorbing story is enhanced by strong characterizations. Garth and Peter present interesting contrasts. Lily is a well-drawn, appealing girl whose cerebral palsy doesn't limit or label her. Marybeth's long-suffering mother loves her girls even when they don't follow her constantly offered advice. Marybeth herself is a thoughtful, loving girl who matures enough to appreciate and finally love Garth over the charming but irresponsible Peter. Several descriptions of lovemaking and the importance of the theme of premarital sex make this a book for mature readers.

Ages 12 and up

**Also available in:**
Cassette—*Down by the River*
Library of Congress (NLSBPH)

Paperbound—*Down by the River*
Pocket Books, Inc.

---

**5**

Adler, Carole Schwerdtfeger

## In Our House Scott Is My Brother

Macmillan Publishing Company, Inc., 1980.
(139 pages)

---

*ALCOHOLISM: of Mother*
*STEPBROTHER/STEPSISTER*
*STEPPARENT: Mother*
  *Change: resisting*
  *Stealing*
  *Values/Valuing: moral/ethical*

---

A

For three years now, since her mother's death, thirteen-year-old Jodi and her father have been a team. Suddenly her father announces his remarriage and just as suddenly, it seems, Jodi's new stepmother, Donna, moves in with her thirteen-year-old son, Scott. Glamorous, volatile Donna, so different from Jodi's understanding, motherly mother, seems intent on redoing everything in her new home—Jodi, the house, even herself. Jodi responds with what Donna feels is cool politeness, frustrating Donna's attempts at friendship. Donna is further frustrated by the suburban housewife role she tries to play, finding it a stifling contrast to her previous life in Los Angeles. She turns to her son for support and Scott, dropping his mask of indifference, surprises Jodi by gently bolstering his mother, becoming as protective and loving as a parent, smoothing over her irritability and dissatisfaction. When, in preparation for a dinner party, Donna orders Jodi to bathe her aging dog and keep her away from the guests, Scott both excuses his mother's abruptness and helps Jodi with the required task. Then, just when Jodi begins to like him, she learns that the street-wise Scott has stolen an African necklace from a school exhibit. Feeling that her knowledge of the theft makes her responsible for undoing it, she returns the necklace, risking being called the thief herself. She resolves to tell her father about the incident when he returns from a business trip. But before he comes home, Jodi notices Donna retreat to her room one evening with a bucket of ice. Scott tells Jodi that his mother has started drinking again and confides that he expects to watch helplessly while she destroys this marriage as she has several others. The boy asks Jodi not to tell her father, the first decent man he and his mother have known, about his theft, and Jodi agrees. Family life continues to deteriorate. Jodi's dog dies and she wrongly accuses Donna of having had her destroyed. Scott helps save Jodi's favorite retreat, a glen behind their house, from being sold to a developer. As Christmas approaches, Scott is spending more and more time shoring Donna up. Jodi wants to ask for her father's help, but Scott knows his mother will refuse it. Finally, as the boy expects, Donna abruptly gives up, buys plane tickets, and decides to exit this marriage also. Scott gives Jodi an early Christmas present—he has told her teacher the truth about the necklace, thereby removing any lingering suspicions of Jodi's complicity in the theft. Then he stuns Jodi by announcing that he and his mother are leaving the next day. Next morning, Jodi begs her father to make them stay. To her surprise, she discovers that he has tried hard to do that, even suggesting Alcoholics Anonymous, but Donna has refused all help. When Jodi returns from school that day, Scott and his mother are gone. In her room, Scott has left a framed picture resembling the glen. On it he's written, "I liked having you for a sister, even if it was only for a little while. With love, Your brother, Scott."

Because she is shown to be honest, fair, and realistic, Jodi is a dependable narrator for this story of family change. She naturally resents the intrusion of a stepmother she considers pushy and intolerant, but gradually learns that the woman is a complex person, insecure and unhappy; not a "mean stepmother," but an alcoholic who cannot be helped until she admits her problem. From her very temporary stepbrother, in some ways more mature and sensitive—certainly more worldly—than she, Jodi comes to understand a bit more about family love and survival.

Ages 10-13

**Also available in:**
Paperbound—*In Our House Scott Is My Brother*
Bantam Books, Inc.


## 6

Adler, Carole Schwerdtfeger

**The Magic of the Glits**
Black/white illustrations by Ati Forberg.
Macmillan Publishing Company, Inc., 1979.
(112 pages)

---

FRIENDSHIP: Meaning of
RESPONSIBILITY: Accepting
  Fear: of water
  Imagination

---

A broken leg and a seven-year-old girl named Lynette whom his mother expects him to entertain threaten to spoil the summer at Cape Cod for twelve-year-old Jeremy. Jeremy's parents have volunteered to care for Lynette while her stepfather, Dave, an old family friend, recuperates from the recent death by drowning of his wife, Lynette's mother. At first Jeremy pays little attention to Lynette, but he soon grows to like the shy, withdrawn little girl who, since the drowning, is terrified of water. He teaches her to make sand castles, skip stones, and run, rediscovering the pleasures of the beach through her. To entertain her, he invents the magical Glits; if she sees one, he tells her, the small, bright creature will grant her a wish. Lynette blossoms under Jeremy's attention. But as their friendship grows, so does Jeremy's concern about the girl's future. He believes her stepfather has little interest in her and that she has no relatives who want her. Thinking to make her invaluable to Dave, he tries to teach her to cook, but Lynette burns her knee. When Jeremy's mother takes them out to eat on Lynette's birthday, the boy is so outraged by Dave's thoughtlessness—he didn't even send a card—that he ruins the evening. Later, he goes to Lynette's room to apologize and finds her gone. Worried and frightened, he searches through the misty darkness for her and finds her huddled by a fire on the beach, dazed from a dream she had about her mother. Jeremy comforts her in her grief and loneliness. Once Jeremy is free of his cast, he meets his friends for a baseball game. Accompanied by Lynette, he is driven by their teasing to

say he is baby-sitting. Afterwards, Lynette will not speak to him and he apologizes, promising never to deny their friendship again. As the time draws near for Dave to return, Jeremy is near panic. Afraid that Lynette might be sent to a boarding school or, even worse, to an orphanage, he tries to coach her on how to behave around her stepfather. But Lynette is more interested in making sand castles for the Glits. When a worried Jeremy goes in for a swim, Lynette, remembering his story about the boy who swam until he drowned, goes in after him. She is knocked under by the current, Jeremy rescues her, and when she recovers he congratulates her on overcoming her fear of the water. Lynette believes she sees a Glit and, excited, nearly forgets to make her wish until Jeremy reminds her. Soon after this, Dave arrives. Jeremy tries to get Lynette to show off all her new accomplishments, but the girl retreats to her quiet manner and his efforts are in vain. Two days later, Lynette answers a phone call from her uncle and happily announces that he wants her to come and live with his family. She explains that she wrote to him weeks ago. Later, at the beach with Jeremy, who feels a little foolish and let down, she reveals her wish—that they will always remain friends. He doesn't think that possible since she will be so far away. She replies, "You can be friends with someone even if you never see them again so long as you don't ever forget them."

The sincere friendship between a young boy and a little girl is plausibly described in this involving story. Although Jeremy sees himself as a teacher and Lynette as his little project, he realizes, through her, the deep, abiding meaning of friendship and the importance of mutual respect. Readers will sympathize with his frustration as he thinks himself the only person concerned with the girl's fate, only to discover that she herself has been arranging a happy future. The two are unusually imaginative and sensitive, lending added interest to the realistic details of the plot. The illustrations capture the essence of the story, the sequel to which is *Some Other Summer*.

Ages 9-12

**Also available in:**
No other form known


## 7

Adler, Carole Schwerdtfeger

**The Once in a While Hero**
Coward, McCann & Geoghegan, Inc., 1982.
(111 pages)

---

BULLY: Being Bothered by
GENDER ROLE IDENTITY: Male
  Courage, meaning of
  Family: relationships
  School: classmate relationships

---

Patrick Simpson offers to be buddy-for-the-day to the new boy in the seventh grade, Maurice (Mud) Muldowny. But he quickly regrets his offer. During the course of the day, Mud asks Pat if he's sure he's not a girl, accuses him of being gay, a teacher's pet, and—when Pat backs down from bully Chuck McGrew's threats—a chicken. That evening, Pat asks his older sister, Julie, what she thinks of him as a boy. Julie points out that their mother is a human dynamo and a college physics professor, their father a quiet man who makes fine furniture. Neither of them fits the sexual stereotypes. Pat isn't completely reassured, though. He wonders if being the only boy in a family of five girls has made him too comfortable around girls. When he makes a list of male attributes he finds only one that fits him: "Don't do homework usually." He decides to begin lifting weights to develop some muscles. The next day Pat volunteers to be Mud's bodyguard when he hears that McGrew has vowed to get Mud. The bully does manage to "get" Mud, sending a friend to tell the principal it was Mud who urinated on the heat ducts in the boys' restroom. Mud's parents are to be called in. Then Pat's father proposes a father-son fishing trip for that weekend, an unusual event in this family. Meanwhile, Mud is avoiding his parents by hiding out in an old storeroom in the school basement. He tells Pat that his parents are always saying he's rotten, that sometimes they put a sign on him saying he's a pig or a thief. As Pat waits outside the school building he is accosted by McGrew, who twists his arm painfully and demands to know where Mud is hiding out. Pat yields; his resulting shame and worry take the edge off the weekend fishing trip. He and his father talk some, but Pat senses his father's unease with him. Seeing that the fishing trip hasn't brought father and son closer together, Julie asks Pat what's been bothering him. He blurts out that since he's a chicken he should have been a girl. Julie tries to convince him that both boys and girls need courage, but that it's not necessary for either to be physically tough. Pat's still worried about Mud, so he bikes down to the school with some food. While they're eating they hear McGrew and his pals come in. Mud and Pat hide in a crawl space, coming out to find a badly vandalized storeroom. Soon two policemen arrive and accuse Pat and Mud of being the vandals; McGrew has evidently phoned in a report. At the police station, Mud's parents readily believe the charges. But Pat's father defends the boys, and they are let off with a warning. Meanwhile, McGrew continues to terrorize the seventh grade. A classmate defends him, saying he's under a lot of pressure from a father who teaches his boys to be tougher than everyone else. At the seventh-grade party that evening, McGrew tries to appropriate Pat's date. She resists, McGrew twists her arm, and an enraged Pat punches McGrew in the nose. McGrew gets off a return punch, but runs to the restroom when he sees what blood is doing to his new cream-colored suit bought for his brother's wedding. He ends up getting hauled off by the ear by his mother, to everyone's amusement. Pat is a hero but, as he tells his sympathetic father, he simply got in a lucky punch. "There wasn't all that much difference between boys and girls, at least in how they were supposed to act. . . . If he lost some, well, he'd win some too, learn how to talk his way out of trouble maybe. That'd be more his style. No need to be a hero all the time anyway."

A boy discovers for himself what it means to be male, what true courage consists of, and how to read between the lines in a friendship. Many boys will find their own doubts expressed here; girls may be better able to appreciate the conflicts some boys experience. All readers should have a clearer idea of what strength of character can accomplish. Characters are well drawn, their motivations clear. The reader is left with a set of new friends.

Ages 10-13

**Also available in:**
No other form known

# 8

### Adler, Carole Schwerdtfeger

## The Silver Coach

Coward, McCann & Geoghegan, Inc., 1979.
(122 pages)

---

COMMUNICATION: Parent-Child
DIVORCE: of Parents
SELF, ATTITUDE TOWARD: Accepting
   Grandparent: living in home of
   Imagination
   Maturation
   Rejection: parental
   Separation from loved ones

---

A

Twelve-year-old Chris, who lives with her mother and sister Jackie, seven, misses her father terribly since he moved out last year. She blames her mother for the upcoming divorce. Now, while her mother attends summer school to complete her nursing studies, Chris and Jackie will spend the summer with their father's mother. Chris feels angry and afraid at the prospect. After all, she has only met Grandmother Wallace once and that was years ago. The first night at her grandmother's remote Vermont mountain home, Chris resolves to write to her father and ask him to come get her. But the days pass quickly. Chris learns to bake bread and make preserves. Soothed by their grandmother's warm acceptance and the peaceful outdoor life, both girls thrive. Still, her father is never far from Chris's thoughts. One day Grandmother Wallace shows the girls her magic silver coach, a miniature her husband had given her when they lived in Morocco and had to make the difficult decision to send Chris's father, then seven, to boarding school in England. She had used the coach to visit her son in her imagination whenever she missed him. She tells Chris that even now, whenever she feels lonely, she uses the coach to visit friends, but that Chris must discover its secret herself. Chris soon does and imagines several perfect days with her adoring father. Then her father actually does come for a visit, an event both girls have planned for and awaited. But he arrives with a woman and her children. They are all going on vacation together and are anxious to get started. Stunned, Chris desperately asks her father for a few minutes alone with him, but he does not have time. Once she recovers a bit from the blow of discovering that her father does not love her or her family best, she begins to understand what her grandmother had told her earlier, that her father "takes care of himself first, before anybody else gets taken care of—always has, most likely always will. Your mother, on the other hand, strikes me as a lady nobody's cared about enough." One afternoon, after helping Jackie retrieve the silver coach from the pond where the younger girl accidentally dropped it, Chris invites her sister to take an imaginary ride. She imagines them visiting not their father, but their home and their mother. A few days later, their mother actually arrives to take them home. She notices approvingly how both girls have changed; they seem less self-centered, more considerate. As they leave, Grandmother Wallace offers Chris the silver coach but she refuses, realizing that her grandmother, saddened by their departure, needs it more than she.

A summer away from her mother coupled with an eye-opening visit from her father allows Chris the time and space she needs to gain a new perspective on her parents' divorce and a deeper understanding of and appreciation for her mother. Although Chris receives welcome support and advice from her grandmother, she cannot give up her romantic vision of her father until he himself callously dispels it. Both Chris and Jackie become more loving and less self-centered under the influence of the serene, realistic grandmother, who shows them how to use fantasy to heal, rather than to delude themselves. This is their father's mother but, perhaps because she knows her son's faults, she aligns herself with the mother and daughters. The changes in the two girls are made believable by strong, well-developed characterizations.

Ages 9-12

**Also available in:**
Paperbound—*The Silver Coach*
Scholastic Book Services

## 9

Adler, Carole Schwerdtfeger

## Some Other Summer

Macmillan Publishing Company, Inc., 1982.
(126 pages)

---

*BELONGING*
*MATURATION*
   *Boy-girl relationships*
   *Expectations*
   *Identity, search for*
   *Jealousy*
   *Relatives: living in home of*

---

After her mother died and her stepfather left her temporarily with family friends, Lynette, then seven, had called her Uncle Josh herself to ask if she could come and stay. But in the five years that she has lived with her uncle and his family on their upstate New York ranch, she has never really felt at home. Summer is approaching and Lynette, now twelve, looks forward to her friend Jeremy's coming to help with the horses. Jeremy, now seventeen, had helped her adjust to her mother's death and her move to Uncle Josh's ranch, promising to be her friend forever. But the Jeremy who arrives seems somehow different. He befriends her cousin Eddie, whom Lynette considers a spoiled brat, and pays a great deal of attention to her other cousin, Debbie, fifteen and boy-crazy. Lynette even overhears Jeremy say that coming to the ranch was his second choice for the summer. Perhaps nobody wants or loves her, Lynette fears. Maybe Uncle Josh will get rid of her as he gets rid of his old horses. She devotes herself more and more to the horses, especially Penny, her favorite, but still longs for Jeremy's attention. Expecting the family to forget her

birthday as they did last year, Lynette is pleasantly surprised when they remember. But at a rodeo the family attends, she is jealous of Jeremy's preoccupation with Debbie. She also resents the time Jeremy spends building a fort with Eddie. Both Debbie and Marie, Josh's wife, warn Lynette not to crowd Jeremy so much. One day while Lynette is riding Penny, Eddie drops a glass jar of water on them and a piece of glass gets embedded in the horse's foot. Everyone insists it was an accident, but a furious Lynette seeks revenge. Several days later she takes an ax and destroys Eddie's fort. Afterwards, she feels no satisfaction: only immense guilt. Word comes of a spreading brush fire, and Uncle Josh and the neighbors battle it. Lynette finds Eddie crying over the loss of his fort, and when she admits what she has done, the two apologize to each other. After the fire is contained, Uncle Josh accuses Jeremy of starting it through his carelessness with a campfire. Lynette confesses that when she chopped down the fort, the broken pieces of wood probably stirred up the buried campfire. She then tells Uncle Josh he can send her away. To her surprise and relief, Uncle Josh tells her she is a loved part of the family and will stay. "For the first time, she had no doubt of her welcome. She was one of them. She belonged." At summer's end Lynette says goodbye to Jeremy, knowing now that her relationship with him may someday be different—maybe some other summer.

Feeling unloved and unwanted in her uncle's family, Lynette counts on her friend Jeremy's arrival to change things. But he is seventeen now and has no interest in a twelve-year-old girl. A nearly disastrous fire provides the occasion for Lynette to discover that her place in the family is secure. Characterizations are strong and dialogue realistic in this perceptive sequel to *The Magic of the Glits*. Readers of the earlier book will probably be disappointed that Jeremy ignores Lynette, but the story shows clearly that Lynette's possessiveness does much to drive her former friend away.

Ages 10-13

**Also available in:**
No other form known

## 10

Alda, Arlene

## Sonya's Mommy Works

Black/white photographs by the author.
Simon & Schuster, Inc., 1982.
(46 pages counted)

---

*PARENT/PARENTS: Mother Working Outside Home*
   *Change: accepting*
   *Communication: parent-child*

---

Sonya loves weekends because then she and her parents can be home together. Since her mother started to work in an office, Sonya doesn't get to see her as often as before. On Saturdays the two of them try to do some special thing together. Sonya also has time alone with her father. During the week she must be quite independent. Sometimes she wishes her mother would help her more, as she used to. One day Sonya announces that she is going to be in a class play. Her mother promises to get time off from work to come. The day of the event, however, her parents get tied up in traffic and Sonya worries they won't be able to make it. But they arrive just in time and watch the performance proudly. After the play Sonya's father goes with her class to the playground and is there to comfort Sonya when she falls off the monkey bars. She sheds some tears when she realizes her mother has gone back to work. Then one day Sonya's mother tells her she is going away on a five-day business trip. Sonya doesn't like the idea very much, but is glad that Mommy will be home before her birthday. "Would you go if it weren't for business?" asks Sonya. "No," her mother answers. "I wouldn't leave you for even one day, unless I had to." Sonya marks off the days on her calendar and looks forward to her mother's calls every night. Finally, bubbling with excitement, she goes with her father to meet her mother's plane. The next day life is back to normal, but at night the family bakes cookies together for Sonya's birthday party. All Sonya's favorite people come to help celebrate. After she has opened all her presents, she says, "It sure is a happy birthday. I like my party and, most of all, I like being six!"

Life is complicated for little Sonya when her mother begins to work away from home. However, with the loving support of both parents, she manages to accept the things she cannot change and live a normal, happy life. Realistic photographs add interest to this honest look at family feelings and adjustments.

Ages 4-7

**Also available in:**
No other form known

## 11

Alexander, Martha G.

## Move Over, Twerp

Color illustrations by the author.
The Dial Press, Inc., 1981.
(32 pages counted)

---

*PROBLEM SOLVING*
 *Bully: being bothered by*
 *Resourcefulness*

---

An excited Jeffrey, about six, is told by his mother that she soon will stop driving him to school—he is old enough now to ride the school bus. The big day arrives, and Jeffrey finds a perfect seat in the back of the bus. The bus begins to fill up and an older boy, about eight, tells Jeffrey to move, calling him a "twerp." When Jeffrey reports the incident at home that evening, his father and older sister, Katie, give him advice about being tough. The next day on the bus, Jeffrey refuses to move. The older boy again calls him "Twerp" and then picks Jeffrey up and deposits him in a different seat. Once again, Jeffrey is defeated. But that night, while reading a book about super creatures, he comes upon a solution. The next morning on the school bus when the bully calls him "Twerp" and orders him to move, Jeffrey says, "My name isn't Twerp. It's SUPERTWERP." With this, he opens his jacket to reveal a T-shirt on which he's

colored a monster and the word "Supertwerp." The older boys laugh, but show a certain respect for Jeffrey's ingenuity. Jeffrey keeps his seat.

A small boy defuses a bully by using both resourcefulness and humor. Although the solution to Jeffrey's problem may seem oversimplified, it does demonstrate that children can counter superior force with ingenuity. Young readers can also discuss the power of humor to overcome obstacles. Apt illustrations are used in place of narrative occasionally to move the story along.

Ages 5-8

**Also available in:**
Paperbound—*Move Over, Twerp*
The Dial Press, Inc.

## 12

Alexander, Martha G.

## When the New Baby Comes, I'm Moving Out

Color illustrations by the author.
The Dial Press, Inc., 1979.
(32 pages counted)

A

---

*SIBLING: New Baby*
 *Communication: parent-child*

---

When young Oliver discovers his mother painting his old high chair in preparation for the new baby, he is angry. She is giving all his old things to the baby, and he insists he still needs them: the high chair for a launching pad, the crib for his wild animals. His mother apologizes and he tearfully goes to her for comfort, but the unborn baby has taken up all the room on her lap. Now he is really angry at his mother and threatens to throw her in a garbage can, take her to the dump, and leave her. On second thought, he decides his mother can stay and he will leave and live in his tree house or his tent. He is surprised when his mother says she would miss him. She needs him to cut out the cookies and play games with her. "I guess that baby won't be much fun for you either. I better stay with you," says Oliver. When she suggests that he will get to do many special things in his new role of big brother, Oliver feels better. With hands on his mother's swollen abdomen he says, "Hurry up, baby, I have lots of plans. I can't wait to be a big brother."

Told in dialogue, this story succinctly captures the hurt and fear an only child feels at the thought of being displaced by a sibling. Oliver's mother, realizing what a threat the baby poses to her son, reacts calmly to his angry, hateful words. Simple illustrations match a concise, sympathetic text. The contrast between Oliver's idea of being a big brother (watching late-night television and eating treats) and his mother's (Oliver minding the baby while she relaxes) is perceptive and funny. This is a companion to *Nobody Asked Me If I Wanted a Baby Sister*, which continues Oliver's story after the new baby is born.

Ages 2-5

**Also available in:**
Paperbound—*When the New Baby Comes, I'm Moving Out*
The Dial Press, Inc.

**13**

Allen, Marjorie N.

## One, Two, Three—Ah-Choo!

Color illustrations by Dick Gackenbach.
Coward, McCann & Geoghegan, Inc., 1980.
(63 pages)

---

*ALLERGIES*
*PETS*

---

Young Wally Springer is allergic to feathers, dust, and—worst of all—his new puppy. Shots and medicine control his allergies but do not completely stop the sneezing, so Wally's puppy has to be exchanged for a pet that will not make him sneeze. Frogs are too noisy and jump out of their bowl. The water snake comes out of hibernation when Wally's aunt discovers it in the refrigerator. Since Wally cannot bear to feed it live mice, he exchanges the snake for a hermit crab. Wally and his father read about hermit crabs and discover that they make their homes in the cast-off shells of sea creatures, moving into bigger ones as they grow. Wally names his crab Harold and carries him around in his pocket to show his friends. They suggest he enter Harold in the pet show. The morning of the show Wally rushes to the terrarium for Harold, but the crab is still trying on new shells. Once he decides on one, Wally puts him in his pocket and sets off for the park. While Wally watches a friend's chameleon, Harold gets out of his pocket and walks away, and Wally must rescue him from a curious cat. The judges, impressed by Wally's information about hermit crabs, award him a prize for the most unusual pet. As Wally walks past the other animals to receive his trophy, he begins to sneeze.

Sympathetic parents help a young boy with allergies find a pet they can all tolerate. In the process, Wally learns a lot about some unusual animals. His matter-of-fact attitude toward his medicine and allergies might help young readers with similar conditions adjust to their frustrations and deprivations. Delightful, humorous illustrations keep the text from lagging and give the book appeal as a read-aloud and as a beginning reader.

Ages 4-7

**Also available in:**
No other form known

**14**

Ames, Mildred

## Nicky and the Joyous Noise

Charles Scribner's Sons, 1980.
(130 pages)

---

*GRANDPARENT: Living in Home of*
*SELF, ATTITUDE TOWARD: Respect*
*VALUES/VALUING: Aesthetic*
  *Autonomy*
  *Change: accepting*
  *Parental: absence*
  *Security/Insecurity*
  *Talents: artistic*
  *Talents: musical*

---

One summer while his unmarried mother is off pursuing another get-rich-quick scheme, Nicky, eleven, is foisted upon his maternal grandmother, Ruby, a woman he has never met. Neither Ruby nor Nicky likes the arrangement but, when the next day Nicky is returned by the police after attempting to run away, they each agree to give the other a chance. While Ruby is at work, Nicky explores the neighborhood. He is stunned to discover in the midst of this California city an elaborate structure of ornately decorated spires surrounded by a high wall. The owner and creator, Eduardo Estrada, calls his beautiful oasis El Cielito Mio and has devoted over thirty years to the spires, despite the ridicule and hostility of many of his neighbors. Nicky begins visiting Eduardo nearly every day, often accompanied by Velveteen Smith, a neighbor girl his age who comes from a large and overcrowded family. Together they help locate discarded materials to decorate the spires: pop bottles, broken pottery, anything that glitters. After Señor Estrada tells Nicky that he is building the towers because it makes God happy when a man pursues what he does best, Nicky decides to concentrate on what he feels is his special talent—playing the piano by ear. Ruby agrees to have her old piano tuned; unlike Nicky's mother, Ruby is impressed by his playing. When Nicky becomes discouraged by his inability to reproduce the intricate Bach chorale he hears at church, Ruby makes arrangements for him to have lessons. The choirmaster recognizes Nicky's natural talent, but feels it will undermine the self-discipline he needs to develop as a pianist. Nicky argues that he will faithfully do the necessary exercise and practice routines, and the choirmaster finally agrees to accept him as a pupil. Taking a cue from Nicky, Velveteen begins to write poetry. Nicky soon finds the practice exercises tedious and difficult, but Señor Estrada and Ruby encourage him to make the most of his talent. Meanwhile, a magazine article about El Cielito Mio that Velveteen and Nicky had persuaded Señor Estrada to allow has brought the spires to the attention of the city building department: Señor Estrada is ordered to demolish and remove them because they are unsafe. The author of the article rallies to the defense of what he considers the most important piece of folk art in the country, as do many people in the neighborhood, including Ruby. Eventually, it is agreed to call in a stress engineer to put the towers to a test. The day of the test Ruby stands with Nicky, Velveteen, and hundreds of other onlookers, cheering when the spires are proved safe. Ruby then invites Velveteen over for a celebration, and Nicky notices that she calls the house "our house." Thinking about that, he decides that he wants to stay at Ruby's and continue taking piano lessons, "because those stupid old exercises were like building the foundation for a tower like Señor Estrada's, a tower that no one could pull down."

In this story of self-discovery, a dedicated folk artist encourages a boy to make the most of his musical talent. In the process, Nicky comes to replace in his affections his irresponsible, often absent mother with his loving grandmother. While Nicky concentrates on the piano, his friend discovers a talent for poetry that offers her a mental refuge from her chaotic home life. Velveteen's discovery demonstrates an important secondary theme of this book: pursuit of a vision, dedication to a craft, can sustain one through many of life's hardships. In the end, Nicky is able to provide encouragement and inspiration to Señor Estrada, bringing the story full circle. This warm, perceptive account is filled with well-drawn characters, each full of life.

Ages 9-12

**Also available in:**
No other form known

## 15

Andersen, Karen Born

**What's the Matter, Sylvie, Can't You Ride?**
Color illustrations by the author.
The Dial Press, Inc., 1981.
(30 pages counted)

---

*FEAR: of Physical Harm*
*PERSEVERANCE*
  *Success*

---

One morning little Sylvie sits on her new two-wheeled bike and wonders if she will ever be able to ride down the big hill by George's house. She makes several attempts but the bike always wobbles and her feet keep coming off the pedals, back to the safety of the sidewalk. That afternoon Sylvie sits on her bike while her mother and a neighbor girl ride past. "Can't you ride?" yells the girl. She passes Sylvie again, repeating the question, and this time her mother answers that Sylvie is just practicing and really can ride. "Now she knows my mother's a liar," Sylvie thinks. The following morning Sylvie's father watches her pushing the bike along with her feet and praises her efforts, but Sylvie only walks away disgusted. She tries practicing at the basketball court where no one will see her, but fails again. This time she gets angry. "She hated the way she got so scared. . . . Nobody else thought they would splat all bloody on the cement." She kicks the bike and leaves it lying on the ground. That night, though, she worries about her birthday bike and in the morning is delighted to find it right where she left it. The next day she tries to ride, and again her feet keep slipping off the pedals. Angry, she sits on the bike, pushing with her feet faster and faster, thinking of how she will demolish the bike

when she gets home. Too late to stop and too angry to care, she heads down the hill she has always avoided. To her surprise, everything goes right. She has a smooth ride. At the bottom of the hill she starts pedaling and passes George sitting on his bike watching her enviously. "Can't you ride?" Sylvie yells.

Fear prevents Sylvie from learning to ride her new bicycle. Only when she gets reckless, so frustrated and angry that the possibility of physical harm is momentarily unimportant, does she conquer the bike. "It was terrific to be speeding along, surely, swiftly, with no fear at all." Though aimed at young readers, this story captures that familiar struggle between the drive to succeed and the fear of failure. Delightfully humorous illustrations, particularly the ones of Sylvie's uncooperative feet and her assorted costumes (athletic garb and playclothes), emphasize the child's frustration and determination. Sylvie's closing taunt after her own recent struggle could prompt discussion.

Ages 4-7

**Also available in:**
No other form known

## 16

Anderson, Leone Castell

**It's O.K. to Cry**
Color illustrations by Richard Wahl.
The Child's World, Inc., 1979.
(32 pages)

---

*DEATH: Attitude Toward*
  *Death: of relative*

---

Nine-year-old Ben learns that his Uncle Jeff has died in a motorcycle accident. Full of grief and anger, Ben feels he should be the one to explain the event to his five-year-old brother, Jeremy. As the two boys talk about Uncle Jeff and all the wonderful things the three have done together, Ben gently leads Jeremy to realize that Uncle Jeff has died. Jeremy too reacts with anger. As both boys cry, Ben reminds Jeremy of what Uncle Jeff had once told them—"It's O.K. to cry." Ben then promises to teach Jeremy all he's learned from Uncle Jeff. Jeremy is happy then, and Ben feels his Uncle Jeff would approve.

Two brothers come to grips with the death of their favorite uncle. At first angry, then very sad, they talk and reminisce about their uncle as they work through their initial grief. Colorful illustrations enhance the story. This book is one in a series—Handling Difficult Times. Following the story is a guide suggesting discussion questions and offering additional information about death, including an explanation of burial and pictures of a closed casket at a grave and at a mausoleum.

Ages 5-8

**Also available in:**
No other form known

A

**17**

Anderson, Penny S.

## The Operation

Color illustrations by Paul Karch.
The Child's World, Inc., 1979.
(32 pages)

---

*HOSPITAL, GOING TO*
*Surgery: tonsillectomy*

---

When little Tangie is told by her doctor that she has to have her tonsils and adenoids removed, she is frightened and thinks of the terrible things that could happen to her. Tangie's mother reassures her, reminding her that Darlene, her cousin, has had her tonsils out. Several days later, Tangie goes to the hospital. The gaily decorated children's section pleases her. In her room she meets Alicia, who has already had her tonsils and adenoids taken out. Alicia tells Tangie that the worst part is the sore throat and being thirsty after the surgery. But she also tells her that the nurse will give her ice chips, jello, and ice cream. Tangie is then given a blood test. Later, a nurse gives her crayons and a coloring book. Soon she gets a shot to make her sleepy. While her mother waits in the room, Tangie is placed on a cart-bed and taken to surgery, so sleepy she really does not care what is happening. The next thing Tangie is aware of is the operation being over and a nurse talking to her. Back in her room, her mother is waiting. Tangie's throat hurts, but she is glad Alicia had warned her. Tangie decides the surgery was not so bad. She plans to tell that to her new roommate when she feels better.

Although the shots, tests, and surgery are treated lightly, this simple story may help to reassure a young child about a hospital stay, without going into any details. Colorful illustrations show Tangie at home and in the hospital. This book is one in a series—Handling Difficult Times. Following the story is a guide suggesting discussion questions and offering additional information about hospitals.

Ages 3-8

**Also available in:**
No other form known

**18**

Anderson, Penny S.

## A Pretty Good Team

Color illustrations by Richard Wahl.
The Child's World, Inc., 1979.
(32 pages)

---

*DIVORCE: of Parents*

---

Young Jeff is upset by all the fighting between his parents and feels alone and lost. One night the arguing is so loud Jeff puts his pillow over his head. He remembers how happy they all used to be and wonders why everything has changed. He also worries that the fighting may be his fault. Later that night Jeff hears a door slam. The next day at school, he is so upset he throws up. He tells his mother about this, but feels she doesn't care. So he

screams at her and runs and hides under his bed. His mother angrily tells him that she and his father are divorcing. An anguished Jeff remembers that two of his friends are from divorced homes. His mother comes back to his room and they comfort each other, crying and hugging. She assures him that the divorce is not his fault, that both parents love him very much. Jeff is then told his father is moving to another city and he will live with his mother. But he will see his father and visit with him during vacations. When Jeff's mother begins to cry again, the boy provides the reassurance: they will get along just fine, he tells her, because they make a good team.

A little boy whose parents are divorcing fears he may be causing the family's troubles. Once Jeff and his mother talk, however, he realizes that both parents love him very much. Colorful illustrations show Jeff trying to cope with the distressing events. This reassuring book is one in a series—Handling Difficult Times. Following the story is a guide suggesting discussion questions and offering additional information about divorce.

Ages 5-8

**Also available in:**
No other form known

**19**

Angell, Judie

## Dear Lola or How to Build Your Own Family

Bradbury Press, Inc., 1980.
(166 pages)

---

*ORPHAN*
*RUNNING AWAY*
*Belonging*
*Family: extended*
*Love, meaning of*

---

Six residents of St. Theresa's Orphanage—Lola, eighteen; James, thirteen; ten-year-old twins Annie and Al-Willie; nine-year-old Edmund; and Ben, five—consider themselves a family. Rather than chance being separated, they leave the orphanage to find a home of their own. Lola, whose real name is Arthur Beniker, is the organizer and provider for the group. He got his name from his pseudonym as a writer of a syndicated newspaper advice column called "Dear Lola." His advice is based on all he learned as an orphaned child, and his assumed name gives him credibility. As they search for a home, the friends camp in parks and vacant garages. They spend many days in libraries where Lola, a great believer in the value of reading, introduces them to books by numerous authors and has them read practical handbooks on home maintenance. After a few months on the road, the family settles in the small town of Sweet River, where Lola buys a run-down house and they all help fix it up. They agree on the fabricated story that they live with their retired grandfather and decide to take Lola's last name of Beniker as their own. Things go fairly smoothly until the children start school. Ben, who has the terrible habit of eating all small things, is suspected of stealing from the kindergarten room. Annie is called to the principal's office about this because "sometimes a sibling can be helpful in dealing with certain kinds of problems, where a parent might be emotionally involved. . . ." Edmund and a friend have a messy birthday party for cats. At the school Halloween party two of the children win prizes for their costumes, but they run away to avoid the newspaper photographers who are about to take their pictures. The children's notoriety, coupled with the postmaster's curiosity about the large packages that Lola gets each week (the letters for "Dear Lola"), prompt the formation of a town committee to investigate the situation at the Beniker house. Before the visit all the children, including James, the "anchorite" who never leaves his room, help Lola dress up as a grandfather. They hope that with this ruse they can continue living together. But Lola is not a very convincing grandfather, especially when his false moustache slips during the visit. The townspeople insist that the case go to court. Lola decides he will try to become the children's legal guardian, rather than run away with them again. The court, however, decides that certain needs are not being met, and the children are to be turned over to the social services agency. During the session, Lola's identity is made public and he loses his credibility: "people don't want to take advice from an eighteen-year-old boy." Suddenly, as the children's fate is being decided, the Benikers dash out of the courtroom and leave town. Picking up another orphan along the way, they move to California. A year later, they have managed to keep a low profile and are continuing to live as a happy family.

This first-person narrative, perceptively told by Annie, provides good discussion material about familial ties outside the conventional family unit and should have considerable appeal for older, less-skilled readers. The book is enjoyable and often humorous, despite implausible situations and a lack of attention to everyday details, such as the necessity for furniture in a house. Some younger readers might infer from the Benikers' adventures that running away is the perfect solution to problems.

Ages 10-13

**Also available in:**
Braille—*Dear Lola or How to Build Your Own Family*
Library of Congress (NLSBPH)

Cassette—*Dear Lola or How to Build Your Own Family*
Library of Congress (NLSBPH)

Film—*Dear Lola or How to Build Your Own Family*
Scholastic Book Services

Paperbound—*Dear Lola or How to Build Your Own Family*
Dell Publishing Company, Inc.

**20**

Angell, Judie

## Secret Selves

Bradbury Press, Inc., 1979.
(177 pages)

---

*IDENTITY, SEARCH FOR*
  *Boy-girl relationships*
  *Grandparent: living in child's home*
  *Prejudice: sexual*

---

On a dare from her best friend, thirteen-year-old Julie Ann Novick phones her crush, Rusty Parmette, introduces herself as "Barbara Birdsong," and asks to speak to "Wendell Farnham." When Rusty, who has envied his older brother his calls from girls, answers coolly, "Do you want Wendell Farnham Junior or Senior?" a new relationship begins—between "Wendell Farnham" and "Barbara Birdsong." These made-up selves are able to talk freely to each other, but in reality Rusty considers Julie a pest and Julie fears that Rusty is an MCP (male chauvinist pig). She fervently hopes that Wendell, who confesses to liking classical music and needing help in math, who isn't afraid to talk seriously and honestly, is the "real" Rusty. Rusty must decide whether his views on women are truly his own or whether they come from his three "macho" older brothers and his father, who owns a sporting-goods store and coaches a soccer team. Julie gets some help from her grandmother, an eccentric who lives with Julie's family and eavesdrops on all Julie's telephone conversations with "Wendell." Together they discuss how people use words to cover up their true feelings and identities. Rusty and Julie go from their private selves to public ones when they are chosen by their respective classes to debate each other on the topic of a woman in the White House. During the debate—a draw, although Rusty really agrees with Julie's position—the girl and boy show both sides of themselves to each other, not just Julie and Rusty, but also "Barbara" and "Wendell." Rusty senses a bond between them, but it isn't until later that day when Julie's grandmother introduces "Barbara" to "Wendell" that Rusty learns who his mysterious caller has been. The next evening it is Rusty who calls Julie, instead of "Barbara" calling "Wendell."

Two introspective young people grope with the confusing and conflicting elements in themselves, playing one role at school and another on the telephone. They and their classmates and friends discuss sexual prejudice in theory and in practice, making this book a good stimulus for discussion. Although the basic premise is a bit far-fetched, the challenges of a young teenager's world are perceptively described here: establishing identity, developing relationships with family and friends, exploring and testing society's values. The natural dialogue contributes realism; the humor adds appeal. The character of the grandmother is especially well drawn.

Ages 11-13

**Also available in:**
Braille—*Secret Selves*
Library of Congress (NLSBPH)

Cassette—*Secret Selves*
Library of Congress (NLSBPH)

Paperbound—*Secret Selves*
Dell Publishing Company, Inc.

A

**21**

Angell, Judie

**What's Best for You**

Bradbury Press, Inc., 1981.
(187 pages)

DIVORCE: of Parents
FAMILY: Relationships
    Boy-girl relationships: dating
    Change: accepting
    Communication: parent-child
    Friendship: best friend
    Parental: custody

Their parents' recent divorce has Lee, Allison, and Joel in a flurry of packing, moving, and mixed emotions. Lee, fifteen, will stay with her father on Long Island for the summer; Allison, twelve, and Joel, seven, will move into New York City with their mother. Lee, who doesn't get along with her mother, is thrilled. Secretly she hopes she and her father can live together permanently. Her summer begins perfectly. She and her three best friends work part of the day for the Parks Department and spend the lazy afternoons at the beach. They call themselves the "Shuffleboard Generation," as each is shuffled between divorced parents. When Lee's mother invites her to spend the Fourth of July with her, Lee reluctantly accepts, vowing to avoid all arguments. But she quickly decides—unjustly—that her mother doesn't want any of her new friends to know Lee is her daughter. After the inevitable fight, Lee runs away, returning later to apologize. Later in July, Lee and her friends decide to have a party. They invite four boys, and Lee finds herself paired with Warren, who is new to the neighborhood. The two soon begin dating and are constantly together. Their relationship helps Lee accept her father's dating more easily. As the summer progresses, both Lee and her father realize how much they enjoy and need each other. Then Warren breaks up with Lee, and both parents try to console her. Meanwhile, Joel keeps hoping that everything will magically revert to the way it was, and, toward the end of the summer, Allison's behavior begins to worry her mother. The girl has become "mother" to Joel and spends all her time caring for him and their new apartment. The parents agree Allison will spend that weekend with her father while Lee stays with her mother. Soon after her father, Allison, and Joel leave, Lee and her mother argue. During the evening, Lee slips out of the apartment. She takes a train back to Long Beach and spends the night with a girlfriend, forgetting to call her father. When she does phone he calls her mother, calling Lee back to say her mother will come to meet with them. When Lee returns home the next morning, the entire family discusses the divorce and their living arrangements. Angrily, Lee insists, "You keep saying you want the best for us, only you're the ones who decide what's best, not us!" She declares she wants to stay with her father. Several days later her parents agree on professional counseling for Allison. They also decide that Lee can stay permanently with her father. Finally Lee has what she thinks is best, although her father helps her to keep an open mind. She and her mother may develop a less volatile relationship as time goes on.

This well-done story focuses on Lee and her family relationships, but the reader is also given candid insights into the convictions and misgivings of each family member as each struggles to adapt to the divorce. Characters emerge as many-sided human beings, and the complexities of feeling created by a family breakup are clearly and sensitively conveyed. This slice of life offers considerable insight into family dynamics during difficult times.

Ages 11-14

**Also available in:**
Braille—What's Best for You
Library of Congress (NLSBPH)

Cassette—What's Best for You
Library of Congress (NLSBPH)

Paperbound—What's Best for You
Dell Publishing Company, Inc.

**22**

Armstrong, Louise

**Saving the Big-Deal Baby**

Black/white illustrations by Jack Hearne.
E. P. Dutton & Company, Inc., 1980.
(42 pages)

CHILD ABUSE
    Marriage: teenage

Robbie, nineteen, and his wife, Janine, have a fourteen-month-old baby boy named P.J. At first they were excited about their "big-deal" baby. Recently, however, their lives have begun to unravel. Because P.J. cries all night and Robbie gets little sleep, he has priced grocery items incorrectly and his job is in jeopardy. Janine has begun to resent the baby and finds no one to talk to about her feelings. One day at the park she gets so angry at P.J. that she grabs his arm and squeezes hard, so hard that the arm turns bright red. Marla Holt, sitting nearby, notices P.J.'s badly bruised arm and walks over to Janine. Marla tells Janine she also used to get very angry at her children and hit them. Then she received help. Marla gives Janine her name and address and tells her to call if she ever wants to talk. When Robbie comes home that evening and discovers P.J.'s swollen and bruised arm, Janine lies about how it happened. Robbie insists Janine take the baby to a doctor, but she says they can't afford it. In anger Robbie strikes Janine and then, after they both calm down, says they need to get help. The next day Janine, in a rage, feels she wants to hurt P.J. Suddenly she remembers Marla. She calls her and finds herself confiding "how she felt. Things that she didn't even know she knew." As a result of the conversation, Robbie and Janine are invited to a parents help group. At the first meeting Janine confesses that she hurt P.J. and then lied about it. She and Robbie are relieved by the group's reassuring response and, in subsequent meetings, learn ways of controlling and redirecting their anger. After six months of meetings, however, Janine decides she doesn't want to continue with the group. She calls Marla and tells her she can't attend because she has no baby-sitter. That same day P.J. knocks over his toy shelf. Janine discovers the mess and in a rage starts pounding on the baby's drum. But she calms herself by realizing that no damage has been done and she needn't pick up the toys that minute. She calls Marla again and asks for a list of baby-sitters. Realizing that she and Robbie need to go out occasionally, Janine also sees that she is indeed benefiting from the group meetings. She will continue to attend them.

A teenage mother falls into a pattern of taking out her frustrations on her baby son, and her harassed young husband reacts with violence towards her. A parents help group provides Robbie and Janine with insight into their problems and support for their frustrations and resentments. This brief, believable story, illustrated for added interest, provides a glimpse into the stresses that can exist in a teenage marriage, stresses that sometimes result in child abuse and domestic violence. The message about the benefits of support groups is a timely one. This is a Skinny Book, part of a series designed for older readers with limited reading skills. These well-written books focus on the interests and concerns of today's young people and should have great appeal.

Ages 10 and up

**Also available in:**
No other form known

## 23

Arrick, Fran

**Chernowitz!**

Bradbury Press, Inc., 1981.
(165 pages)

---

*HARASSMENT*
*PREJUDICE: Religious*
   *Guilt, feelings of*
   *Hatred*
   *Hostility*
   *Jewish*
   *Ostracism*
   *Revenge*

---

Bob Cherno's troubles with Emmett Sundback started when he was fifteen and in the ninth grade. At first it was just a few remarks and some name-calling. Then Emmett began encouraging others to jeer at Bob for being Jewish. On Halloween Bob's house was defaced with eggs and a burning cross thrown on the lawn. Though filled with fear and anger, Bob threw the cross into the lake and kept his feelings to himself. Soon Bob's best friend, Brian Denny, and other boys began ignoring him and even joining in Sundback's taunts. Martha (Matty) Greeley seemed friendly and Bob asked her out. But after the movie they ran into Sundback and his crew. After that he wouldn't even look at Matty, even though she seemed ready to encourage him. Sundback's methods of terrorizing and torturing Bob were varied and numerous; Bob began to understand what mental anguish was. He couldn't understand hatred based solely on his being Jewish—his family isn't even religious. Now it's summer. Brian makes friendly overtures to him, but Bob knows it's only because Brian has nobody else to sail with. How can Brian expect him to dismiss the ugliness of the past year? Then, while substituting on a paper route, Bob has to deliver the Sundbacks' newspaper. One day when Emmett pays him, he gives Bob a "tip": a piece of paper with a swastika on it. One morning, Bob's mother's car is defaced by

a huge, black swastika. Instead of washing it off immediately, she insists on calling the newspaper. Bob and his father confront the Sundbacks, but Emmett denies painting the swastika and his father defends him. On the last day of summer, Bob's mother finds their cat with a broken leg. The next day, the first day of school, Emmett sidles up to Bob and asks him how his kitty is— Bob remembers that Emmett had threatened to harm the cat in the past. Filled with rage, Bob plans his revenge. From September until December he plots and spies on Emmett and then sets in motion an elaborate scenario in which Emmett is framed as the thief of Bob's new radio. Because of Emmett's reputation, everyone supports Bob, and Emmett is suspended from school. Bob later learns that Emmett's father beat him so badly for getting in trouble that the boy spent Christmas vacation in a hospital. However, Bob can't seem to feel good about the success of his plan. Matty Greeley all but asks him out, and even that doesn't lift his spirits. Bob decides the problem is that Emmett didn't get punished for his anti-Semitism; instead, he was punished for something he didn't even do. He resolves to talk to Emmett, to confess what he's done and explain why. But the confrontation isn't at all what he expects. Emmett appears totally oblivious to the damage his bigotry is causing and has absolutely no intention of changing. Finally, Bob tells his parents the whole story. They are shocked at what he went through alone, but they agree his solution was not a good one. His mother points out that revenge never changes anyone's attitudes. Bob knows he must tell the principal too, because she was "used" in his revenge. He and his father tell her together and, though sympathetic, she says categorically that Bob was wrong to wreak revenge the way he did. They call in Emmett, but he will not respond to questions. In the end, all he wants to know is if his father will be told about him being called to the principal's office. When the principal says she won't tell him, Emmett is relieved and goes back to class. The principal promises to think of a way to handle the situation. Her solution is a special all-school assembly presenting several films showing the closing days of World War II and the Jews who were liberated from concentration camps. Everyone is appalled by the shocking images: some cry, some are sick. Afterwards, Bob's father talks to them about the dangers of allowing hatred and bigotry to exist. Bob later sees Emmett in the hall and finds him completely unaffected and unchanged by what he has seen. Shocked, Bob realizes that nothing in the world will change an Emmett Sundback. But he remembers the students who cried and were sick; he knows that people like them far outnumber the Emmetts of this world.

A teenage boy is exposed to a particularly brutal and unrelenting form of anti-Semitism, and he takes revenge upon the ringleader only to learn that revenge solves nothing. Not much attention is paid to the many followers of the chief tormentor, but thoughtful readers will recognize these students' terrible responsibility; without a crew of attendants, Sundback would not have had as much power. Bob's mother believes that people like Emmett are usually fearful, insecure, and deprived, people who can't think rationally, historically, or reasonably. Emmett's brutalization by his father seems one clue to his own brutality. Bob wants to know how such hatefulness can be stopped. This complex question has

A

no easy answer; people like Emmett, the book concludes, cannot be changed. But there are appropriate and inappropriate ways of responding to bigotry. This is a powerful, wrenching first-person narrative. Readers will feel Bob's pain and plot his revenge with him, even though they know—as the principal clearly points out—that framing Emmett was not an acceptable action. A tense, memorable book, this should prompt considerable discussion.

Ages 12 and up

**Also available in:**
Braille—*Chernowitz!*
Library of Congress (NLSBPH)

Cassette—*Chernowitz!*
Library of Congress (NLSBPH)

Paperbound—*Chernowitz!*
New American Library

## 24

**Arrick, Fran**

**Tunnel Vision**

Bradbury Press, Inc., 1980.
(167 pages)

---

*MOURNING, STAGES OF*
*SUICIDE*
  *Communication: lack of*
  *Depression*
  *Expectations*
  *Guilt, feelings of*
  *Reality, escaping*
  *Sibling: relationships*

---

Anthony Hamil, fifteen, has committed suicide, hanging himself in his room with his father's neckties. He left no note, only a theme for English class in which he equated death with peace, peace both for the dead and for the family and friends from whom a troublesome personality has been removed. One by one, those closest to Anthony learn the news and, in their shock and grief, think about him. His mother, while being questioned by the police she called when she found her son, breaks down and cannot function. Her sister, Ruth, must take over, making the funeral arrangements and calling Anthony's father, away on a business trip. In order for Anthony's younger sister, Denise, to be told, the police must pick her up; overweight, unkempt, she has skipped school as she often does and is stoned on drugs. Bitterly, she blames their perfectionist father for Anthony's death. Her brother had been popular, a top student, a superior athlete; she had envied him his success, resented the attention their parents paid him, avoided or ignored him when she could. But Anthony's success had come at a terrible price. Pushed relentlessly by his father, the boy had descended further and further into depression in recent months, staying in his room, not bathing or changing clothes, skipping school, quitting the swim team. At various times Anthony had mentioned death or suicide to his friends Carl and Ditto and to his girlfriend, Jana, but they never believed he was really contemplating such an act. Friends, family, and teachers were all concerned about him; his mother had wanted to get psychiatric help for him. But Anthony's

father, denying to himself that anything was wrong with his son, refused to consider it. Jana would never let Anthony touch her but never told him the reason: she had once been raped. As the people who'd shared Anthony's life now share their guilt and sense of loss, they come to realize that no one person was responsible for this tragedy. As the police officer describes adolescents who attempt or commit suicide, "It's like each of them was caught inside a tunnel, and they couldn't see any end to it or anything at all outside."

This moving, understated exploration of teenage suicide offers no pat answers or solutions. As each character learns of Anthony's death, the reader learns of Anthony's life through their italicized flashbacks. The diversity allows a many-faceted view of the troubled boy. By confiding their grief and guilt to each other, Anthony's family and friends demonstrate how healing it can be to express painful feelings. It becomes clear that no one person was responsible for this death. The dialogue is natural, with occasional profanity.

Ages 12 and up

**Also available in:**
Braille—*Tunnel Vision*
Library of Congress (NLSBPH)

Cassette—*Tunnel Vision*
Library of Congress (NLSBPH)

Paperbound—*Tunnel Vision*
Dell Publishing Company, Inc.

## 25

**Arthur, Catherine**

**My Sister's Silent World**

Color photographs by Nathan Talbot.
Children's Press, Inc., 1979.
(31 pages)

---

*DEAFNESS*
  *Sibling: love for*

---

Today is Heather's eighth birthday. As a special treat, she is allowed to choose what she, her parents, and her older sister will do to celebrate. She chooses a trip to her favorite place, the zoo. The fact that Heather is deaf doesn't prevent her from having a wonderful birthday. Heather has a hearing aid that helps her hear sounds. But she can't distinguish words or hear conversation, and she has trouble determining the direction from which a sound is coming. She is learning to talk by reading lips, by feeling the speaking person's throat and face and then imitating the sound and throat movement, and by sign language. Heather even has a private code in sign language that only she and her sister understand. At her special school she is learning to communicate more easily. Although some children are afraid of Heather or laugh at her, she is a healthy, active girl who loves to ride her bike, go to the zoo, and play. And, notes her sister, Heather especially loves her birthday!

Heather's older sister perceptively describes the vibrant world of her deaf sister. Although written about an eight-year-old and easily read independently by primary readers, the book could also be read to younger

16

children as an introduction to deafness. The photographs of Heather and her sister at the zoo and at home are lively and unposed, giving an added dimension to Heather's story.

Ages 5-9

**Also available in:**
Paperbound—*My Sister's Silent World*
Children's Press, Inc.

## 26

**Asher, Sandra Fenichel**

## Daughters of the Law

Beaufort Books, Inc., 1980.
(157 pages)

---

*JEWISH*
   *Change: resisting*
   *Communication: parent-child*
   *Courage, meaning of*
   *Friendship: best friend*
   *Guilt, feelings of*
   *Identity, search for*
   *Internment*
   *Prejudice: religious*

---

At twelve, Denise Riley is interested in "saving the world" and caring for the "homeless, suffering thousands." She'll begin with Ruthie Morgenstern, her age and new to the neighborhood. Ruthie's father died two months ago and her mother, now as in the past, is subject to nightmares and to "odd changes of mood . . . mysterious nods, silences, and screams." Ruthie's Aunt Sarah helps them move in and speaks enthusiastically about Ruthie's upcoming bat mitzvah when, according to Jewish tradition, she will be acknowledged as an adult, a "daughter of the law." On Ruthie's first day at school, Denise takes her under her wing; eventually they become close friends and "sisters." One day Denise sees Ruthie slip some library books into her bag without checking them out. She is puzzled, but says nothing. Despite Aunt Sarah, Ruthie still has not decided what to do about her bat mitzvah. Her father was very opposed to organized religion, and she feels she will be betraying him. But Aunt Sarah says Ruthie must live her own life. Ruthie finally agrees to the bat mitzvah when her mother hesitatingly approves. But the woman is increasingly remote, and Ruthie's tension builds. One night when her mother goes to her aunt's house, Ruthie invites Denise to spend the night with her. She shows Denise the locket containing a picture of her sister who died in a German concentration camp. Her parents survived the camps, but Ruthie feels her mother's pain is so great that it shuts her out and suffocates her at the same time. "If only I could make it up to her. If only I could just once see her smiling and happy like your mother is every day." She shows Denise the box of old photographs hidden in her mother's drawer, pictures of skeletons, bodies, suffering eyes; she confesses that the books she took from the library were about the Holocaust. Her parents reacted to the tragedy in very different ways: her father raged outwardly; her mother turned inward. Their house has always been full of "sadness, anger, and silence." Ruthie also explains to Denise her ambivalent feelings about the bat mitzvah. Later, Ruthie wakes, frightened by a nightmare. Denise feels helpless, but Ruthie assures her that their talk has helped her a great deal, that she has never before confided in anyone. Meanwhile, Aunt Sarah, a member of the city council, opposes the sale of some land to a local builder and explains her feelings on television. The next day, she is hit in the head with a rock thrown by someone who calls her a "Jew bastard." When Ruthie and her mother go to the emergency room to be with Sarah, Ruthie's mother faints and is admitted to the hospital. Ruthie realizes later that wounded Aunt Sarah, with shaved head and haggard look, reminded her mother of a concentration-camp victim. Ruthie stays home alone in spite of invitations from the Rileys, sunk in grief, emptiness, and despair. Denise can't seem to reach her so she calls Rabbi Davis, with whom Ruthie has been studying, and he goes to visit Ruthie. They talk about the girl's fears and confusion and about her mother's fear of ever letting herself care for anything again. The rabbi also talks to Ruthie's mother and her Aunt Sarah, telling them that her mother's silence about the tragic past has hurt Ruthie. So her mother tells Ruthie everything—how she was married very young and lost her first husband, their small daughter, and her will to live in the camp; how she was sustained and strengthened by Ruthie's father and later married him. She describes how Ruthie's father's strength and determination gradually turned to rage. Rabbi Davis helps the family see that the children of concentration-camp survivors carry a tremendous burden in trying to make up to their parents for all they suffered. He asks Ruthie's mother and aunt to let Ruthie find her own way of surviving. At Ruthie's bat mitzvah some months later, she shares with the large assembly of friends and neighbors, including Denise, the thoughts and feelings that went into her decision to proceed with the celebration. Most important was the fact that she has a lot to celebrate.

A number of crises converge on a young Jewish girl in her thirteenth year, forcing her to make some choices. Her father has just died; she and her emotionally fragile mother have moved to a new town where Ruthie faces a new school and new friends; her Aunt Sarah wants Ruthie to prepare for her bat mitzvah, although her father had been hostile to religion; her mother's remoteness and despair increase. A rabbi's advice to tell Ruthie about her family's horrific past helps Ruthie face the future. As the child of concentration-camp survivors, Ruthie struggles with a nameless guilt she must be helped to understand and overcome. The book's viewpoint alternates: it is told from Denise's perspective in the first chapter, from Ruthie's in the second, and so on. Denise's theme throughout is a cry for involvement, for shouldering responsibility. She wants to know what people should do, "just let people suffer and die? Just go on as if nothing bad ever happened?" The subject of world apathy to the plight of Europe's Jews is not mentioned in the book and many readers will not make the association, but Denise's attitude provides a backdrop for considering the crimes of World War II. This is a strong, affecting story.

Ages 11-13

**Also available in:**
Paperbound—*Daughters of the Law*
Dell Publishing Company, Inc.

**A**

**27**

Asher, Sandra Fenichel

## Just Like Jenny

Delacorte Press, 1982.
(148 pages)

---

*IDENTITY, SEARCH FOR*
*TALENTS*
  *Anxiety*
  *Boy-girl relationships*
  *Family: relationships*
  *Friendship: best friend*
  *Jealousy: peer*

---

To thirteen-year-old Stephie Nordland, pleasing Mr. Oldham and being like Jenny are two of the most important things in life. Mr. Oldham is Stephie's ballet teacher, who believes only "the gifted, gutsy few" will break into professional dancing. Jenny, fifteen, is Stephie's best friend, to Stephie one of the "gutsy few." But Stephie isn't at all sure about herself. At school Mrs. Deveraux, the music teacher, announces a talent show and asks Stephie to dance in it. Thrilled, she asks Jenny to help her choreograph a routine. That night, the two create Stephie's routine and also write application letters to producers of summer stock. Jenny tells Mr. Oldham about Stephie's talent show, but after he watches her routine he merely tells Stephie she had better do well and not embarrass him. Disappointed by his lack of enthusiasm, Stephie is further upset when her mother says she could have created her routine by herself, without Jenny's help. At the school auditions, Matt Greenspan sits by Stephie and encourages her, making her feel both flattered and nervous. Then, at her ballet lesson, Mr. Oldham asks both Stephie and Jenny to audition for his special Workshop. After thinking it over Stephie declines, convinced she isn't good enough, that he only asked her because of her friendship with Jenny. When Jenny makes the Workshop, Stephie feels jealous and begins seeing less of her friend. She is edgy, tired of her constant efforts to prove herself, wondering if she should quit dancing. Even Matt is ignoring her. Her part in the talent show goes very well, but Stephie's jealousy of Jenny's success in the Workshop increases anyway. Finally, her parents take her to see Mr. Oldham, wondering if Stephie should continue dancing. When Stephie says she doesn't feel she's good enough to make it as a dancer, her teacher informs her that she is in fact very talented. But it takes more than talent to be a dancer. It takes a gutsiness that Stephie appears to have lost. Shaken, Stephie talks with Jenny and apologizes for her jealousy. Things start coming together for Stephie; even Matt renews his interest in her. Several weeks later, the two girls audition for summer stock. Stephie makes the final audition, but Jenny does not. The two decide together that, make it or not, they will always be lucky people because they'll always be dancers.

Afraid she is not one of the "gutsy few," living only to please her ballet teacher and emulate her best friend, Stephie begins to give up on herself and her talent. A successful performance, a frank discussion with her teacher, and Jenny's constant support help her regain her confidence. The book clearly conveys the dedication and hard work necessary to become a dancer, has much to say about friendship, and should have great appeal.

Ages 10-12

**Also available in:**
Paperbound—*Just Like Jenny*
Dell Publishing Company, Inc.

**28**

Asher, Sandra Fenichel

## Summer Begins

Elsevier/Nelson Books, 1980.
(173 pages) o.p.

---

*COMMUNICATION: Parent-Child*
*IDENTITY, SEARCH FOR*
*VALUES/VALUING: Moral/Ethical*
  *Friendship: meaning of*
  *School: classmate relationships*

---

Thirteen-year-old Summer Smith makes a point of never expressing a strong opinion. So she's shocked to find herself the instigator of the greatest controversy in her school life. It begins with her eighth-grade class's decision to print a newspaper. Summer's best friends, Terry and Reggie, are serving as editor and gossip columnist respectively, but Summer can't decide how she should participate. Then she overhears the mother of a Jewish student complain about the traditional school Christmas program. Certain everyone will agree with her editorial calling for a new holiday program that encompasses all beliefs, Summer is dismayed when Dr. Kyle, the principal, insists she print an apology. He is furious because he believes the school's conservative benefactor will now cease all funding. In vehement disagreement with Dr. Kyle's attitude, Mrs. Morton, Summer's Jewish homeroom teacher, resigns. Though Summer's father supports her in her refusal to apologize, her mother is devastated when the ensuing publicity revives interest in her as a middle-aged, former Olympic swimming champion, attention she has tried hard to avoid. On the day of the Christmas program, Terry and Reggie stage a protest, and a reluctant Summer finds herself joining them. They march through the auditorium and out the door chanting, "We want Mrs. Morton" while the audience roars and flashbulbs explode. To Summer's relief, the school's benefactor turns out to favor a change in the program and Mrs. Morton is asked to stay. But Summer's problems aren't over. Her mother is still being harassed by the press. Furthermore, many of Summer's classmates avoid or taunt her for her stand. To complicate matters, Reggie has a crush on Rod Whitman, a senior, and when by chance Summer meets Rod during Christmas vacation while Reggie is away, a friendship develops between them. Summer doesn't know whether to feel ecstatic or guilty. She and Rod have a conversation during which he admires her for the strength of her convictions and confesses to an ongoing, if unsatisfying, sexual relationship with his vacationing girlfriend, Cindy. Summer sadly admits to herself that her relationship with Rod must continue to be strictly platonic, but that doesn't displease her because Rod makes her feel important—

unlike her mother, with whom she has never been able to communicate. Summer is convinced her mother would have aborted her if such things were legal when she was conceived. When Reggie and Cindy return from their vacations, they shun Summer for her friendship with Rod. Then Rod decides that having Cindy and being a basketball star are what he really wants, and he too turns away from Summer. She is crushed until she realizes Rod is right about her: she does have strength and she will survive. Summer's friction with her mother gets worse when, during an argument, Summer asserts herself for the first time. But the girl begins to understand her mother better after her father tells her that her mother had suffered two miscarriages before Summer was born and now fears aging. Summer was no mistake or accident, he convinces her. Not long after, Reggie makes a friendly overture to Summer and their relationship is soon restored.

Out of the tumultuous events of her eighth-grade year, a girl finds her own strength and learns to assert herself instead of meekly fading into the background. As Summer's self-esteem improves, so does her capacity to get along with others—including her troubled, preoccupied mother. A warm affinity between father and daughter helps unite the family. Summer's entertaining first-person account rings true.

Ages 10-13

**Also available in:**
No other form known

## 29

Ashley, Bernard

**Break in the Sun**

Black/white illustrations by Charles Keeping.
S. G. Phillips, Inc., 1980.
(185 pages)

---

CHILD ABUSE
RUNNING AWAY
  Enuresis
  Stepparent: father

---

Patsy Bligh, eleven, has lived all her life alone with her mother in the upstairs apartment of Mrs. Broadley's house in Margate, England. When her mother marries Eddie Green, the three move to another suburb farther north. Patsy hates Eddie, who relentlessly insults and beats her. When her mother has a baby and can't give much attention to Patsy, the girl starts wetting the bed at night and her stepfather beats her even more. Patsy dreams of running away, back to Mrs. Broadley who she believes would take care of her and make everything all right again. She shares her hope with her only friend, Kenny Granger, a fat, lonely boy. One day while walking home from school to beg a permission slip for a field trip, Patsy notices a riverboat docked by a wharf on the

Thames. She chats briefly with a pretty girl on the boat, Jenny, who tells Patsy she is a member of a theater group touring downriver, stopping at small towns to perform. Jenny offhandedly remarks that the group could use someone like Patsy to play in a short scene, also mentioning that the boat will stop in Margate. Excitedly, Patsy returns home, where Eddie shouts at her and hits her. But he does write the note she dictates, stating that she has her parents' permission to travel. Patsy takes the note to Jenny, who interprets it as parental consent for Patsy to join the theater group. Patsy convinces the other players that her note is authentic, and the boat is launched. Vastly relieved, Patsy waves goodbye to Kenny on the bank. Meanwhile, the police notify Patsy's parents of her absence from school. Patsy's mother accuses Eddie of driving Patsy away and demands that he find her. Eddie questions Kenny, whose enjoyment of all the attention leads him to agree, reluctantly, that Patsy might have run away on a riverboat. So Eddie, enlisting Kenny's assistance, starts downriver by train. That night when they camp together on the riverbank, Eddie confesses that he always hated his own father, who mistreated him as a child. His reflections give him the first faint glimmer of insight into his relationship with Patsy. Meanwhile, Patsy is enjoying her new companions and her first performance goes well. One morning she sees a London paper carrying a description of her. She panics and is unable to say one word of her lines during that evening's performance. That night she wets the bed. She awakens filled with anxiety and runs away from the boat. Unknown to her, however, Eddie is closing in. He has found the boat and has wheedled the whole story out of Kenny. Patsy manages to hitchhike to Margate and makes her way to Mrs. Broadley's house. There a stranger answers the door and tells her Mrs. Broadley is dead. Meanwhile, Eddie has talked with the theater people and deduces that Patsy must have gone to Margate. He follows her to Mrs. Broadley's house, finding her standing dazed in the yard. In terror, she runs to a nearby amusement park, climbs to the top of a scaffolding, and tries to jump off. Eddie follows. He pleads with her to come down and Patsy, sensing a change in him and realizing she cannot jump, does what he asks. He takes her for tea and talks with her.

A young girl runs away to escape an abusive stepfather. By the time he finds her, both have gained some insight into themselves and each other. Suspense builds gradually here, as scenes of Patsy's adventures alternate with scenes of her pursuers. Character growth is credible and the believable, if not happy, resolution makes for satisfying reading. Scattered illustrations of English life help establish atmosphere and setting.

Ages 11 and up

**Also available in:**
No other form known

A

**30**

Ashley, Bernard

## A Kind of Wild Justice

Black/white illustrations by Charles Keeping.
S. G. Phillips, Inc., 1979.
(182 pages)

---

FEAR: of Physical Harm
REVENGE
  Belonging
  Inferiority, feelings of
  Parental: negligence
  School: achievement/underachievement
  School: pupil-teacher relationships
  Security/Insecurity
  Trust/Distrust
  Violence

---

Ronnie Webster, an English teenager, lives in fear. Four years earlier, he overheard the Bradshaw brothers, gang leaders for whom Ronnie's father, Steve, does odd jobs, threaten to break Ronnie's back if Steve ever disclosed any of their illegal activities. Since then, Ronnie's fear has become all-consuming. Any day, he feels sure, his drunkard father will betray the Bradshaws and then they will come after him. The boy makes no friends, cannot concentrate in school, is a nonreader in a special class. He goes directly home from school each day, always watching over his shoulder for the thugs he expects to be following him. His mother, Val, cares little for anyone but herself; she offers no protection. Now the Bradshaws want Steve, a former race car driver, to drive their loot away after a robbery at the football stadium. The plan: Steve, with Ronnie in tow, will drive to the stadium in a stolen car provided by the Bradshaws. They will park under a specified window from which the money bags containing stolen entry fees will be dropped through the open top of the car. All goes well. Speeding out of the parking lot Steve follows the predetermined path, parks the car with the loot inside, and then makes a run for it with Ronnie. But as they flee Ronnie spots Manjit Mirzar, the Indian girl from his special reading class, looking right at him from a window across the way. The next day, Officer Kingsland arrests Steve: one of Ronnie's reading flash cards was found in the abandoned car. Ronnie suspects Manjit of planting the card and threatens her the next day about keeping her mouth shut, emphasizing those threats with kicks. The girl does not understand, but she is frequently mistreated by whites and has come to expect abuse. Later, Ronnie finds out from Charlie Whitelaw, the school bus driver, that his mother, who abandoned him after Steve was arrested, is now living with Bernie Bradshaw. Ronnie realizes then that his mother planted the reading card in the car to get rid of Steve. The kindly Charlie offers to help Ronnie, and the boy finally turns to the older man and his wife, finding with them a sense of security and belonging he has never had. But the security soon ends. Charlie too is being intimidated by the Bradshaws, forced to use his bus in a plan to smuggle Indians from France into England. He is to drive a group of senior citizens on a weekend tour of Paris; at a designated time during their return trip, he is to pick up the Indians and bring them along to England. Ronnie overhears the plan discussed and becomes convinced, wrongly, that Charlie is a willing participant. Having nowhere to turn, he goes to the police. Officer Kingsland urges Ronnie to return to the Whitelaws so he doesn't arouse anyone's suspicion. Upon returning, Ronnie realizes that the Whitelaws are being victimized just as he is. He also discovers that the smuggling has something to do with Manjit's family. Now Ronnie is determined to get his revenge by beating the Bradshaws at their own game. Forced to go along on Charlie's bus when the Bradshaws discover he knows of the smuggling operation (Roy Bradshaw is also along as "tour guide"), Ronnie runs from the bus during the return trip, just before they are to pick up the Indians. The passengers refuse to continue until the boy is found, the bus is delayed, and the plot is foiled. When he knows time is up, Ronnie gets the assistance of the French police, who see that the Bradshaws are turned over to the British authorities. Since the Indians were not picked up, Charlie escapes arrest, but Ronnie provides Kingsland with the evidence needed to arrest the Bradshaws: the inspector has told Ronnie that during the robbery, one of the stadium officials had managed to spray a gang member with a permanent purple dye. Ronnie noticed on the bus trip that Roy Bradshaw had purple dye on the skin under his watchband. Ronnie gets his revenge and still manages to protect his friend Charlie. His brave action wins him the respect of the neighborhood; more important, it gives him a sense of self-respect. Manjit's sadness is one discordant note: her father was to have been smuggled into the country that night. Still, as one of the officers says, "They call revenge a kind of wild justice."

A young man overcomes the paralyzing power of fear and learns to act, saving himself and other victims of terror in the process. Ronnie goes from trusting no one, least of all himself, to learning where trust can safely be placed. Suspenseful, action-packed, filled with well-drawn characters, containing some street language, this is a powerful book for the better reader. Premeditated violence runs through the plot, but it is never condoned.

Ages 12 and up

**Also available in:**
No other form known

**31**

Atkinson, Linda

## Hit and Run

Black/white photographs by Susan Kuklin.
Franklin Watts, Inc., 1981.
(89 pages)

---

ACCIDENTS: Hit and Run
GUILT, FEELINGS OF
  Honesty/Dishonesty
  Responsibility: avoiding

---

Susan Silver, about sixteen, never saw the boy until she hit him. That particular Saturday evening, on a deserted country road full of twists and turns, it was dark and the rain was pouring down. Once out of the car, she saw a boy about her age, semi-conscious and bleeding. Terrified, Susan covered him with her raincoat, drove to the nearest phone, and told the operator to send an ambulance. Then she went back, but before she got to the boy a police car and an ambulance arrived. Unwilling to return to the scene, Susan drove home. Once there, alone because her parents are gone for the weekend, she tries to rationalize away her fear and guilt. The next morning she discovers her broken headlight and the blood, mud, and scratches all over her car. Panic-stricken, she washes the car and tries to figure out how she can get it fixed Monday without her parents' knowledge. Sunday evening Susan's parents return. Her father mentions the hit-and-run accident that happened Saturday evening; her mother has learned the victim's name from a neighbor. To her horror, Susan realizes she met the boy briefly last summer. She longs to tell her parents the truth, but believes she would rather die than face them. Monday morning, Susan's mother asks where she was Saturday evening; a neighbor has mentioned that she had gone away. Susan says she drove into the city to see her brother, Willie, angering her mother because she wasn't supposed to drive where she's never driven before. When her mother wants to borrow Susan's raincoat, she must lie again. At school that day Susan tries to call Willie to have him back up her story, but he isn't home. Desperate, she drives to his apartment, but it's still empty. Sitting in a nearby park, Susan agonizes about all her lies and her awful predicament. Suddenly she overhears a radio announcement that a woman has been arrested for the accident. Momentarily relieved, Susan races for her car, thinking it is safe to go home again. Just as quickly her feelings change. She cannot keep silent anymore. She cannot allow someone else to be blamed for what she did. Knowing that she will now face the truth and its consequences, she is strangely relieved. "Whatever happened, whatever lay ahead, she knew that the worst part was behind her."

A teenage girl is finally able to admit her part in a hit-and-run accident. This is a taut, realistic story of the effects of fear and guilt, illustrated with believable photographs. Suitable for the reluctant reader, the book could be a valuable teaching aid for young people beginning to drive.

Ages 11 and up

**Also available in:**
No other form known

## 32

Bach, Alice Hendricks

### Waiting for Johnny Miracle

Harper & Row, Publishers, Inc., 1980.
(240 pages)

CANCER
  Boy-girl relationships
  Courage, meaning of
  Family: relationships
  Hospital, going to
  Illnesses: terminal
  Surgery
  Twins: identical

Ever since they were children, identical twins Theo and Becky Maitland, now seventeen, have been playing competitive sports. As high school seniors they are stars of the girls' basketball team. One afternoon Becky's right leg gives out during a game and she collapses. Hospital X rays reveal no injury, so Becky tries to go ahead with her active life. Her boyfriend, Jay, who will only date a "complete lady in full working order," teases her if she complains about her aching leg. So Becky tells no one, not even Theo, that the pain in her leg has intensified and that she feels exhausted much of the time. One day, almost a month after her collapse on the basketball court, she cries to Theo about a burning sensation that has developed in the leg. Her anxious parents rush her to her doctor and then to a specialist who, after initial tests, discovers a tumor on the bone in her right thigh. Becky is admitted to the children's cancer ward of a hospital for a biopsy. She is shocked by the other young patients—their skin color, their thinness, their baldness. Unable to imagine that she too might be a cancer victim, Becky longs to resume her familiar routines. But soon she and her family learn that her tumor is malignant and she must begin chemotherapy at once. Courageously Becky begins the treatment, alternately accepting and despising her illness. When Jay hears that she has cancer, he runs from her house, leaving her broken-hearted. During treatment at the hospital clinic, however, Becky makes new friends, other young people who are able to empathize because they too have some form of cancer. After several months of chemotherapy as an outpatient, Becky is hospitalized for surgery. The tumor is successfully removed and the cancerous piece of bone replaced by a piece of metal. She is to remain in the hospital for two months, her mother with her. Becky's prognosis is pronounced excellent. But her convalescence is difficult for the whole family. The world of the hospital is permeated with pain and death. Becky's younger brothers miss their mother. Mr. Maitland must drive many miles a day to visit his wife and daughter. Theo bears extra responsibilities at home. Her personal life has been so altered by the absence of her twin that she feels estranged from Becky. But gradually Theo gets to know Becky's friends in the hospital. When she comes to stay with Becky for a few days during her winter break, she joins in a scheme to devise an exciting interlude for Mariela, Becky's roommate. Mariela, who has a rare, incurable leukemia, has grown steadily worse; she has told the girls she does not want to die a virgin. The girls convince Matthew, the good-looking therapist, to visit Mariela late that evening. As Theo and Becky whisper together, they reestablish their old relationship. They look forward to Becky's homecoming and being together.

A teenage cancer victim and her family struggle against the emotional trauma and physical pain of the girl's illness. Also prominent in this powerful story is the special relationship between Becky and her twin sister, an intimacy threatened but undefeated by the family catastrophe. Vivid, detailed descriptions of the treatments for cancer and their aftereffects make this a novel for mature readers, as does the language.

B

Ages 12 and up

Also available in:
Paperbound—*Waiting for Johnny Miracle*
Bantam Books, Inc.

## 33

**Banks, Lynne Reid**

## The Writing on the Wall

Harper & Row, Publishers, Inc., 1981.
(244 pages)

---

*IDENTITY, SEARCH FOR*
*REBELLION*
  *Boy-girl relationships: dating*
  *Crime/Criminals*
  *Drugs*
  *Family: relationships*
  *Peer relationships*
  *Self, attitude toward: accepting*
  *Sex: premarital*

Sixteen-year-old Tracy Just loves Kevin because of his punk look and defiant rebelliousness. Her parents dislike Kevin for the same reasons. Kevin and Tracy start dating regularly, and she becomes his eager pupil. Once, at his prodding, Tracy paints "Kevin is a bastard" on a bridge wall. Kevin tells her that once school is out he wants her to leave London with him and go to Holland on a holiday. Tracy's father forbids it, so Tracy sulks and feels persecuted. Refusing to give up, Kevin comes to Tracy's house with Michael, the nineteen-year-old brother of a friend. Michael assures Tracy's father that he will chaperone the three couples planning to go, that Mr. Just can trust him. Tracy's father finally agrees, and the kids make elaborate plans for their seven-day bike trip. Kevin wants Tracy to go to Amsterdam with him alone, but Tracy hedges. The seven take a boat to Holland and camp for the night. The next day they bike to Rotterdam. Tracy refuses Kevin's advances and his suggestions that they split from the others. In Rotterdam Kevin desecrates a statue of Erasmus, infuriating Michael, who demands that Kevin clean it up. Kevin screams defiantly that he is leaving for Amsterdam; Tracy follows. They take a train to Amsterdam and get a hotel room. The clerk directs them to a nightclub that turns out to be for homosexuals. In a fury, Kevin tries to attack the clerk and Tracy must drag him off. They are thrown out of the hotel and spend the night in a youth hostel. The next day, while sightseeing, Kevin meets two men, Neils and Yohan, who invite them to spend the night at their apartment. Kevin and the two men leave Tracy alone in the apartment while they go to nightclubs, and Tracy finds that the two deal in pornographic materials. Frightened, she calls Michael at the youth hostel in Rotterdam. He tells her to take a train back to the group. She does and spends some time alone with Michael, beginning to enjoy his company. Then the group returns to the boat, where Kevin joins them. He apologizes to Tracy and returns her missing bicycle pump. Before they can disembark, Tracy is detained when a police dog smells something in the pump. Kevin has disappeared, and Tracy is arrested and charged with smuggling drugs. Her father comes for her and Tracy tells him everything. Home on bail, Tracy finds that her father is the only one in the family who believes in her innocence. Feeling totally alone, hating Kevin, Tracy goes to church. On her way out she meets Michael, who reassures her and reports that Kevin has confessed to placing the drugs in the pump. Relieved, Tracy returns home, reflects on what has happened, and concludes that her life will now change for the better.

Defiant and "in love," Tracy searches for an identity apart from her Polish immigrant father and rigidly Irish-Catholic mother, one that will secure her place with her English peers. Yet she is restrained by her love and respect for both parents and by a basic decency that eventually allows her to appreciate the differences between her punk boyfriend, Kevin, and the mature, down-to-earth Michael. Tracy's first-person narrative includes some profanity and sexual talk, and several sexual encounters. English slang and attitudes, though they contribute to the atmosphere and tone, could make the story difficult reading for some.

Ages 12 and up

Also available in:
No other form known

## 34

**Bargar, Gary W.**

## What Happened to Mr. Forster?

Clarion Books, 1981.
(169 pages)

---

*SCHOOL: Pupil-Teacher Relationships*
  *Homosexuality: male*
  *Maturation*
  *Prejudice: sexual*
  *School: classmate relationships*
  *Self, attitude toward: feeling different*

It's the fall of 1958, sixth grade is starting, and Louis Lamb vows things will be different this year. This year he'll no longer be an outsider and no one will call him "Billy Lou." The first day of school, two things happen: Louis has a new teacher, Mr. Forster, whom he quickly admires and respects, and he is befriended by a new boy, Paul Harte. Mr. Forster encourages Louis in his creative writing and even gives him a special book to use as his journal. He also coaches Louis in softball, privately, after school. Throughout the fall, Louis feels better and better about himself. His classmates seem to accept him more, even respect him, and his friendship with Paul grows. Then, at the school Open House, after a man arrives to drive Mr. Forster home, Louis overhears several parents quietly talking about his teacher. When they notice several students listening, one asks if Mr. Forster is married. The last day before Christmas vacation, Louis's class puts on a play. The whole class is invited to that evening's cast party—except for Ellie Siegel, whom no one likes. Mrs. Siegel appears at the party with Ellie in tow, accusing Mr. Forster of persecuting her daughter, blaming him for Ellie's exclusion from the party. The teacher had known nothing of this slight. She also informs Mr. Forster that she knows about him and that he won't be a teacher much longer. Confused, Louis worries all through the vacation. School resumes on a Monday with mothers attending and observing. All treat Mr. Forster coolly, if not rudely. By the following Monday, Mr. Forster is gone. At recess a classmate informs everyone that their teacher was "a queer." Heartbroken, Louis leaves school and runs home. Aunt Zona, with whom he lives, tries to explain that Mr. Forster is not fit to be around young people. Not satisfied and very upset, Louis goes to Mr. Forster's house. Once there they talk—after Mr. Forster insists on calling Aunt Zona to tell her where Louis is. She says she will come to get him immediately. Before she arrives, Mr. Forster explains to the boy that he is homosexual, that there are many ways of loving and this is his way. Louis tells Mr. Forster he needs him to be his teacher. Mr. Forster assures him he will do fine on his own with the new teacher. On Wednesday Louis returns to class and resolves to make something out of all that has happened. With that, he opens his journal, so far untouched, and begins to write.

This sensitive story, told by Louis, revolves around the boy's changing relationships with his classmates and, particularly, with Mr. Forster. Unpopular and sheltered, Louis gains self-confidence through the gentle encouragement of his teacher. He is devastated by Mr. Forster's persecution and removal. The homosexuality issue is handled nonjudgmentally: Mr. Forster says he'll "wait and let God come to his own decision about my eternal destiny." Several other adult characters seem exaggerated, perhaps because they are viewed through a child's eyes. Overall, this is a realistic, sometimes humorous portrayal of classroom situations and classmate relationships. The issues it raises are timeless and could stimulate discussion.

Ages 10-13

**Also available in:**
No other form known

## 35

**Barrett, John M.**

### Daniel Discovers Daniel

Color illustrations by Joe Servello.
Human Sciences Press, 1980.
(32 pages counted)

---

*IDENTITY, SEARCH FOR*
  *Family: relationships*
  *Inferiority, feelings of*
  *Jealousy: sibling*
  *Rejection: parental*
  *Self, attitude toward: feeling different*

---

Nine-year-old Daniel, a reader and stamp collector, is sure that his father prefers his younger brother, Peter, to him. His mother helps him see that Peter and his father have one thing in common: they both love sports. So Daniel decides to take an interest in athletics. When he asks his father to play basketball with him, however, it becomes painfully clear that Daniel can't dribble, aim, or shoot. Later, Daniel sits close to his father during a football game on television; his father asks him to move a little so they can both see and be comfortable. Discouraged, Daniel gets on his bike and soon finds himself in front of his teacher's house. Mr. Johnson is washing his car, and he invites Daniel to help in exchange for a

glass of cider. Mr. Johnson tells Daniel how proud he is of him in class. Overcome, Daniel blurts out through his tears that his father hates him. He tells his teacher how his father favors Peter. Mr. Johnson suggests he ask his father for help sometimes. Daniel replies that when he asks for help his father is always busy. He's sure his father would help him with schoolwork, but he never needs help. To cheer him up, Mr. Johnson tells Daniel that he has won the part of Captain Hook in the class play, *Peter Pan*. He suggests that Daniel ask his father to help him learn his part. Elated, Daniel rides home, beginning to realize that even if he "stinks" at sports he is smart and funny and a lot of people like him. Not only does his father agree to help him learn his part, he also helps plan Daniel's costume—which he'll help to make —and tells Daniel he's proud of him. When he asks Daniel to join Peter and him in a game of football, Daniel declines happily and heads for the library for books about Peter Pan. He feels just fine about himself.

Filled with doubts, his self-esteem low, Daniel longs for his father to love him as he loves Peter, his younger brother, although Daniel will never be sportsminded or athletic. A sympathetic teacher helps Daniel see what a talented, important person he is in his own right, and his new self-confidence is gladly shared by his proud father. The compassionate story is greatly enhanced by illustrations that superimpose what is actually happening in Daniel's life over sketches of what the boy imagines or hopes will happen. Readers will respond warmly to Daniel's happy discovery of his own individual worth.

Ages 7-9

**Also available in:**
No other form known

**B**

## 36

**Barrett, Judith**

### I'm too small. YOU'RE TOO BIG.

Color illustrations by David S. Rose.
Atheneum Publishers, 1981.
(31 pages counted)

---

*HEIGHT: Short*

---

"I'm too small to be a grown-up. But you're too big to be a kid." A five-year-old boy wishes he were big like his father, but he notes that both childhood and adulthood have certain advantages and disadvantages. He's too small to drive a car, but his father's too big to ride a tricycle. He's too small to reach the tabletop, but his father's too big to play under it. He's too small to see over the fence, but his father's too big to sit on his son's shoulders. He's too small to play in Little League, but his father's too big. "But," concludes the little boy, "someday I'll be as big as you are. MAYBE EVEN BIGGER."

Though rather slight in content, this book may be encouraging to those dissatisfied with their size, prompting them to share their feelings. Each page begins either with "I'm too small to" or "But you're too big," making for an amusing read-aloud book. The illustrations complement the text nicely.

Ages 4-6

**Also available in:**
No other form known

## 37

**Bates, Betty**

## It Must've Been the Fish Sticks

Holiday House, Inc., 1982.
(136 pages)

---

*ADOPTION: Feelings About*
  *Adoption: identity questions*

---

Thirteen-year-old Brian is sure things would be much better if he hadn't lost his mother when he was a baby. His mother wouldn't nag or worry him or lay down rules as his adoptive mother, his father's second wife, does. His real mother would understand his problems. Then, during a fight with another boy, Brian learns that his mother is still alive. He refuses to believe that she just walked off and left him, although Nat, their Jamaican servant, tells him she did. Ashamed and deeply resentful, Brian tells his distressed parents that he simply must find his birth mother. His father agrees to let him visit her—in three or four years. When Brian insists and threatens to go on his own, his father promises to find Imogene through the bank and allow Brian to spend two weeks with her if she's willing. After arrangements are made, Nat drives Brian to Mount Carmel, Ohio, where they find Imogene living in a small, run-down house surrounded by tall weeds. She shares the house with a rough, rude stock-car racer named Kelsey. Imogene explains to Brian that she had to leave him and his father to find herself, to express herself; she needed space. She tells him she has experimented, she has lived. After brief immersions in ceramics, astrology, ballet, mind control, poetry, and other things, she is now doing welded sculpture. Nat spends the night, but insists on sleeping outside in the fresh air. He sums Kelsey up as a lazy, drunken, pot-smoking freeloader. Then Brian is on his own in a life very different from what he's used to. Kelsey and Imogene aren't courteous to each other, as his parents are. They kiss a lot in front of him, though, and ignore him most of the time. He has no bed of his own and Kelsey's a thoroughgoing bum, prone to swearing at Imogene and making her sign over her support checks to him. They attend a stock-car race where Brian sees that Kelsey has a reputation for dirty tricks. Brian feels helplessly fond of Imogene. She seems so little and powerless. He calls home, feeling ripped apart by having two mothers, and asks for another week with Imogene. Then Kelsey says he's sick of Imogene's whining and sick of her pipsqueak son. He lunges drunkenly toward Brian, but all Brian has to do is step backwards and Kelsey falls on the floor, out cold. Brian realizes that Imogene isn't safe. He has to protect her, angry as he is that she got herself into this mess. He'll just have to stay with her forever, although he misses his family and friends. Most of all, he misses the good meals at home. Imogene and Kelsey live on frozen convenience foods —they even have fish sticks for breakfast. Meanwhile, Brian's father refuses to allow the boy to stay with Imogene, vowing legal action if Brian doesn't return. Nat comes to pick him up. That night Kelsey falls asleep smoking a joint and sets the couch on fire. Nat and Brian rescue the unconscious Imogene and then tell Kelsey that Imogene doesn't want him around anymore. They tell Imogene that Kelsey just moved on. Imogene seems a little disoriented, but she perks up when she notices the ruined couch. Maybe she could learn upholstery. Later, Brian asks Nat if Imogene will ever change; Nat doesn't think so. When Imogene talks about her future it never includes Brian, and the boy realizes she isn't capable of taking responsibility for him. He decides to go home. When his sister asks him why he came back, he says he isn't sure. But maybe it was the fish sticks.

Interesting characters populate this first-person narrative about a boy who feels caught between conflicting ways of life when he has to choose between his helpless, immature birth mother and a stable life with his father and adoptive mother. Although Brian's choice is perhaps not a real one—his father would never have let him stay with Imogene—he does discover his true feelings about family life as he learns a sad little lesson about charming but irresponsible adults. The book is well written and the contemporary topic will appeal to young people. Good discussion material can be found in Brian's relationship with the hapless Imogene and his eventual decision to return home.

Ages 10-13

**Also available in:**
Paperbound—*It Must've Been the Fish Sticks*
Pocket Books, Inc.

## 38

**Bates, Betty**

## Love Is Like Peanuts

Holiday House, Inc., 1980.
(125 pages)

---

*BOY-GIRL RELATIONSHIPS*
*MENTAL RETARDATION*
  *Baby-sitting*
  *Friendship: meaning of*
  *Maturation*
  *Money: earning*

---

During the summer of her fourteenth year, to pay for ballet lessons, Marianne Mandic takes a job caring for a brain-damaged child, Catsy Kranz, age eight. At first the child makes her uncomfortable. But soon Marianne becomes familiar with Catsy and protective of her, especially when she witnesses the longtime housekeeper, Mrs. Johansen, verbally abuse and sometimes physically shake the child. Mrs. Johansen also tells Catsy scary stories to frighten her into behaving. Still, there are times when even Marianne's patience wears thin at Catsy's slowness and her clinging need for love and attention. Then Marianne, attractive to boys but so far uninterested in them, meets Toby, Catsy's eighteen-year-old brother who lives with his mother in the winter and his father in the summer. When Toby invites Marianne to go sailing, along with Catsy, their friendship blossoms, much to the disapproval of Marianne's parents who feel she is too young for Toby. Marianne is perplexed and hurt when Toby suddenly seems cool. She continues to care for Catsy though, taking her to the park where Benji, Marianne's young brother, befriends her and teaches her not to fear the swings. The day comes when Marianne must tell Mr. Kranz about Mrs. Johansen's treatment of Catsy. Even though Toby supports Marianne, Mr. Kranz seems to side with the housekeeper and Marianne nearly loses her job. Toby intervenes, demanding to know why his father can't see what is going on in his own house. Settling on a compromise, Mr. Kranz, with Mrs. Johansen's approval, retires her with a pension, and Catsy is no longer made to fear that spirits will get her if she misbehaves. Marianne's Aunt Sis, a widowed nurse, is hired as Mrs. Johansen's replacement. Toby remains distant and Marianne at last learns why. Two years earlier he had gotten a girl pregnant and she had had an abortion. When summer nears its end Marianne, unable to control her feelings, offers herself to Toby. He gently refuses, hurting her deeply. Soon, however, she comes to realize that he feels as bad as she that he must leave her. By his rejection, Marianne understands, he showed his love and respect. He kisses her goodbye and promises to call.

This enjoyable story describes the confusion many young people face when their bodies mature before their emotions. Toby's maturity, gained from an earlier lesson, saves the day for Marianne. She, in turn, grows emotionally and develops an appreciation for special children as she cares for young Catsy, who is lavish with affection for those who befriend her. The perceptive characterization of Catsy and the descriptions of people's varied responses to retarded children enhance the story.

Ages 10-14

**Also available in:**
Paperbound—*Love Is Like Peanuts*
Pocket Books, Inc.

## 39

Bates, Betty

**My Mom, the Money Nut**

Holiday House, Inc., 1979.
(158 pages)

---

*FAMILY: Relationships*
*VALUES/VALUING: Materialistic*
  *Communication: parent-child*
  *Grandparent: love for*
  *Maturation*
  *School: classmate relationships*
  *School: pupil-teacher relationships*
  *Talents: musical*

---

Eighth-grader Fritzi Zimmer and her parents have just moved from the city to a suburban apartment. Fritzi hates the apartment with its little rooms, hates her school, is ashamed of her father, a maintenance man, and fights constantly with her mother. Overweight and self-conscious, Fritzi believes her mother's main concerns are money and buying. The only school subject Fritzi enjoys is music. She makes friends with a classmate, Hope, who teaches her to play the guitar and helps her with math. Then Mrs. Torcom, the music teacher, asks Fritzi to join the eighth-grade choir. She is elated, her father is proud, her mother is seemingly uninterested. Shortly after she joins the choir, Mrs.

Torcom asks her to sing a solo at the upcoming May music festival. During spring vacation Fritzi's parents send her by bus to the mountains for a week's stay with Poppy, her maternal grandfather. Because she has seldom seen him, Fritzi is apprehensive. Once there, though, she enjoys the farm life and Poppy. She also comes to understand something of why her mother refuses to return to Poppy's farm: the place brings back memories of her motherless, poverty-stricken childhood. Returning home, Fritzi asks her mother to go see Poppy but her mother puts her off with "maybe" and "someday." Frustrated, Fritzi finally tells her troubles to Mrs. Torcom. The music teacher helps her realize how hard motherhood may be for someone who "never had much of a chance to be a child." At the music festival, Fritzi is nervous and sure her voice will fail her, but she sings her solo beautifully and her friends and teacher are proud of her. So are her parents. As the girl reflects on her love of music and her relationship with her mother, she decides that, although her mother may be caught up in money and what it buys, she herself is glad to have her singing and her friends.

A lonely, discontented girl learns during a stay with her sympathetic grandfather that her mother's deprived childhood helps explain the woman's emphasis on money and material possessions. Accepting her mother as she is allows Fritzi to choose her own way of living, helped by an understanding teacher who encourages the girl's love of music. Fritzi tells her own story perceptively. The descriptions of her home life are nicely balanced with observations about school and friends.

Ages 10-12

**Also available in:**
Paperbound—*My Mom, the Money Nut*
Pocket Books, Inc.

B

## 40

Bates, Betty

**Picking Up the Pieces**

Holiday House, Inc., 1981.
(157 pages)

---

*BOY-GIRL RELATIONSHIPS*
  *Accidents: automobile*
  *Age: respect for*
  *Change: accepting*
  *Friendship: meaning of*
  *Love, meaning of*
  *Peer relationships: peer pressures*
  *School: classmate relationships*

---

Ninth-graders Nell Beaumont and Dexter Mead are old friends with a "tame boy-girl relationship." Now that they're in their final year at Troyer Junior High, things are changing. Dexter, athletic and sports-minded, is being pursued by Lacey Dunn. When Nell sees that Dexter is enjoying Lacey's attention, she gives up her relationship with him. Upset, Nell finds she can confide her feelings only to her best friend, Bonnie, and her Great-Uncle Charlie. Dexter begins associating with Lacey and four other classmates, and Nell hears about their drinking and troublemaking. Several months later, Bonnie and Nell celebrate Bonnie's birthday with a big cookout at the river. To Nell's dismay, she sees Dexter and his drunken friends in another area of the park. At the school dance the night before graduation, Dexter and Lacey are drunk and rowdy, and they and their four friends are asked to leave. Several hours later the six are involved in a serious automobile accident. At graduation, the principal announces that Dexter and one other boy are still hospitalized. Nell also hears that Dexter's leg has been permanently injured; he will limp. As the weeks go by, Nell learns that Dexter's new friends have dropped him and that he is deeply depressed. Several friends and Uncle Charlie persuade her to go see him. She is frightened, but when she notices that Dexter is surprised and happy to see her, she's glad she came. By the end of the summer Uncle Charlie, who has had a heart attack, has decided to move to Florida to live with Nell's grandparents. Dexter, on crutches, is coming home from the hospital. Nell and her friends plan a welcome-home party for Dexter, and Nell gives him Uncle Charlie's golf clubs because she knows golf is something he will be able to do. Dexter disparages his ability to play and then ignores Nell for the remainder of the party. Several days later, he calls her to apologize for his behavior, asking her to walk to school with him. So the next day they walk to high school—together again.

Nell's first-person narrative reflects many relationships in her life but focuses on the development of her love for Dexter. This special relationship survives the boy's wild phase, his accident, and his permanent injury. At the end, the reader feels that the bond between Dexter and Nell has been strengthened. Also important is Nell's love and care for her aging great-uncle. Believable character development and authentic plot details enhance the story.

Ages 10-13

**Also available in:**
Paperbound—*Picking Up the Pieces*
Pocket Books, Inc.

## 41

**Bates, Betty**

## That's What T.J. Says

Holiday House, Inc., 1982.
(133 pages)

---

*INFERIORITY, FEELINGS OF*
*MATURATION*
    *Boy-girl relationships*
    *Grandparent: living in home of*
    *Parent/Parents: single*
    *Parental: absence*
    *School: classmate relationships*
    *Sibling: love for*

---

At twelve, Monica Sue Brinker, nicknamed Mouse from her brother's pronunciation of "Monica" when they were little, is a mass of uncertainties. She and her brother, T.J., thirteen, live with their father and paternal grandparents. Their mother has been dead for eight years, and their father travels a lot on business. Mouse worries that he is seeing a woman, worries that her grandparents do not love her, and worries about school. She is very self-conscious about her dental braces and her complexion. The one person she really trusts and

listens to is T.J. Her other love is Patches, her pet rabbit. When she is expelled from Honor Club for the disruption created when another girl locked her in the janitor's closet, she is miserable but can't bring herself to protest. After school one day she talks to Roland Durovic, another shy, outcast seventh grader, and they begin a tenuous friendship. Mouse even shows Roland her rabbit. Then, during the spring music concert, Roland freezes during his trumpet solo and is so embarrassed he can't face his classmates—although he's very talented and has played perfectly during every rehearsal. He even avoids Mouse. Soon afterward, Mouse's father announces that the family will be moving to Sioux City, Iowa, where he spends most of his business time. He is buying a house and won't be traveling anymore. Excited about the move, Mouse still worries that there is a woman in his life he is not telling them about. Later that week Mouse sees Roland and encourages him about his music and the botched solo. As always, she continually refers to what T.J. says. Finally Roland asks her if she ever thinks for herself. Mouse suddenly realizes she does not. She also realizes something about Roland and herself. "We're two nothings turning each other into something." Mouse tells Roland of the prospective move and gives him Patches; she can't take the rabbit along if she is to have the dog her father has promised her. She talks to her father and asks if he is going to marry. He tells Mouse he has been dating for years, but that she will never be left out of his plans if he finds the right woman. Mouse is greatly relieved. The three pack. As they prepare to leave Mouse realizes, when she sees how sad they are at the family's departure, that her grandparents really do love her. She also realizes she is growing up and that things will be different in Sioux City. There, no one will call her Mouse.

Timid, anxious, and self-conscious, forever deferring to her adored older brother, Mouse befriends a shy, unpopular boy and discovers they are helping each other to mature. Her first-person narrative describes this slow process of growth that finally begins to triumph over doubts and fears. The story is thoroughly believable, if less than exciting.

Ages 9-11

**Also available in:**
No other form known

## 42

**Bauer, Caroline Feller**

## My Mom Travels a Lot

Color illustrations by Nancy Winslow Parker.
Frederick Warne & Company, Inc., 1981.
(38 pages counted)

---

*PARENT/PARENTS: Mother Working Outside Home*
    *Family: unity*
    *Life style*

---

A little girl misses her mother, who travels a lot as part of her job. There are, however, good points and bad points to her mother's travel. Some of the good points are going to the airport, long-distance phone calls, postcards, eating out with her father, presents, and staying up late. The bad points are only one kiss at night, her mother missing out on new puppies and school plays, the droopy plants that the little girl forgets to water, and, especially, missing her mother. But the very best thing about her mother's traveling is, "She always comes back!"

A little girl describes the good and bad aspects of her working mother's frequent traveling, and these are cleverly illustrated by colorful, action-filled pictures. Text and illustrations suggest a strong family unity not broken by a mother who travels. Children in similar situations will benefit by seeing both sides of the experience and by reading about another family's way of dealing with a mother's absence. Children whose parents don't travel will be introduced to a different life style.

Ages 5-8

**Also available in:**
Cassette—*My Mom Travels a Lot*
Live Oak Media

Filmstrip—*My Mom Travels a Lot*
Live Oak Media

Paperbound—*My Mom Travels a Lot*
Frederick Warne & Company, Inc.

## 43

**Bawden, Nina Mary Kark**

## The Robbers

Lothrop, Lee & Shepard Company, 1979.
(155 pages)

---

*CHANGE: Accepting*
*COMMUNICATION: Lack of*
   *Crime/Criminals*
   *Friendship: best friend*
   *Grandparent: love for*
   *Parent/Parents: remarriage of*
   *Rejection: parental*
   *Values/Valuing: moral/ethical*

---

All is well with nine-year-old Philip Holbein, who lives with his widowed paternal grandmother in a castle apartment "by the Grace and Favor" of the Queen of England—his grandfather had been a famous British general. Philip's widowed father, Henry, an international news correspondent, visits infrequently, and this Philip finds acceptable also. But then Henry Holbein marries a young American, Maggie, buys a house in London, and, urged by his wife, decides to reclaim his son. Unaware of these plans, Philip visits his father and Maggie. He is angry when he learns the visit is to be permanent, but then decides to hold his peace. A chance meeting with Darcy Jones, a boy about his age, introduces Philip to city life—with a vengeance. Darcy's father is disabled, his mother dead, and the family must scramble for money. Darcy's brother, Bing, sells his goods at a street market and Bing's wife, Adelaide, works too. Though Philip attends school and Darcy often does not, Philip's real education comes from the street-wise, perceptive city boy. Philip learns about school bullies, illegal street markets, and scheming landlords. Along the way, he also learns that it is Maggie, more than his father, who wants him. Nonetheless, Philip accepts the situation and plans to live permanently in London. Still, he's glad enough to return to his grandmother's for the summer vacation, taking Darcy along. During their stay, his grandmother discovers Darcy's "gift from God," his beautiful singing voice, and makes plans to develop it. Before his training can get very far, however, Adelaide comes to fetch Darcy. Bing has been imprisoned for receiving stolen goods. When Philip returns to London several days later, he finds the Jones family in crisis. They are struggling with the shock of Bing's crime and trying desperately to make ends meet; Adelaide has been fired because of the scandal. The boys attend Bing's trial and hear him plead guilty. Throughout the fall, the family's financial condition worsens. To help, Philip and Darcy decide to sing Christmas carols door-to-door. Their search for handouts takes them to Philip's father's next-door neighbor, an extremely wealthy old woman who gives them a pittance for their songs. Darcy decides to rob her house and loyal Philip, the smaller of the two, agrees to squirm in an open window. But his efforts trip a clanging burglar alarm. The boys scramble across to Philip's father's house, but the police soon find them there. They take Darcy away but Philip, scion of a wealthy, famous family, gets off with a lecture and is outraged at this double standard. His father, after a stern reprimand, announces that Philip will pay for damages and then be packed off to a boarding school. The boy is saved by his grandmother, who sees that Henry is now bored with his son and about to travel again. After scolding Henry, she prepares to take Philip back to the castle apartment. Before they leave London, however, Philip and his grandmother visit Darcy's family. Darcy has been placed on probation, and Philip's grandmother tries to arrange for him to come for a visit to pursue his vocal training. She's sure Darcy could win a music scholarship. But the boy, though grateful for the offer, refuses; his family needs him. Philip returns to the castle, happy to be home again with his grandmother but troubled by all that has passed.

A sheltered boy becomes immersed in the harshness and double standards of London life in this suspenseful story. Although there is a fairy-tale quality about the outward circumstances of Philip's life, his warm, open personality and his courage and loyalty come through clearly and believably. The story skillfully combines human interest, humor, and a fast-moving plot.

Ages 9-12

**Also available in:**
Cassette—*The Robbers*
Library of Congress (NLSBPH)

Paperbound—*The Robbers*
Dell Publishing Company, Inc.

## 44

**Belair, Richard L.**

## Double Take

William Morrow & Company, Inc., 1979.
(190 pages)

---

*SELF, ATTITUDE TOWARD: Feeling Different*
   *Appearance: concern about*
   *Attention seeking*
   *Boy-girl relationships: dating*
   *Job*

---

High school senior Robert Beaudette, called Beau, believes people judge others by appearance, not by who they really are. He is sure people judge him critically and fail to give him a chance just because of the way he looks. To prove his point, the tall, overweight, swarthy boy has a scruffy mustache, wears a leather jacket and boots, and drives a hearse. At the beginning of the school year, Beau decides to have his yearbook picture taken. He is encouraged to do so by Claudia LaRosa, a classmate he has admired and tried for years to impress. He decides to make the picture memorable and goes to Litton's Studio wearing a tight shirt and jacket and a tie with a naked woman painted on it. Mr. Litton is amused. When Beau, returning to pick up the photographs, silently but obviously notices the general disarray of the studio, Mr. Litton offers him a part-time job filing and doing odd jobs. Always surprised by kindness, Beau accepts the job. Knowing that Claudia has entered a beauty contest, he dreams of photographing her and Mr. Litton lends him a camera. Claudia and Beau start dating, and she poses for him in various settings. Soon Mr. Litton asks Beau to assist Tommy Sayles, who is photographing a wedding for him. Sayles previously worked for Litton and still helps when needed. Beau's main job is to keep Sayles sober. But Tommy manages to get drunk anyway, and the inexperienced Beau takes most of the pictures. Beau's failure to watch Sayles closely enough upsets Mr. Litton. On Columbus Day, Beau goes to a nearby city to photograph the parade. While there he also captures on film the drunks in a park and a prostitute named Beebee, whom he befriends. Shortly thereafter, two police officers question him at school about a break-in at Litton's Studio. Beau goes to the studio and finds that equipment has been stolen and files dumped and strewn around. He stays to help clean up, but feels Mr. Litton is accusing him. The photos Beau took on Columbus Day and during a second visit to the city have been developed. As he studies the pictures of the drunks and of Beebee, he sees that he has captured and exposed "something human, something touching and pathetic" in these down-and-out folks. He decides that if he really works at photography he will learn to get beyond the surface and show everyone what he's always believed about himself: "that there can be something very touching beneath first impressions." Inspired, Beau returns to the city that evening with a camera in his pocket, intending to take some candid shots. Beebee tells him she knows of someone selling photographic equipment. After he leaves her he spots Tommy Sayles's car and gets suspicious. The next evening Beau has Beebee lead him to Sayles, and he secretly photographs Tommy's transactions with his friends. Beau then goes to Mr. Litton, who alerts the police. Sayles is arrested. A grateful Mr. Litton gives Beau a new camera to keep and even asks him to help photograph weddings.

In this touching, often humorous, first-person narrative, an outcast young man comes to realize through his own photography that he is like the pictures he takes—more than just an outward appearance. Although the story never fully resolves Beau's feelings about himself, the reader is left with the impression that he is developing a healthy self-respect, helped along by the kindness and trust of a classmate and an employer. The profanity and street language in Beau's narrative seem natural to his character.

Ages 13 and up

**Also available in:**
Paperbound—*Double Take*
Dell Publishing Company, Inc.

## 45

**Bennett, Jack**

## The Voyage of the Lucky Dragon
Prentice-Hall, Inc., 1981.
(149 pages)

---

*COURAGE, MEANING OF*
*REFUGEES*
    *Change: accepting*
    *Family: unity*
    *Fear: of physical harm*
    *Freedom, meaning of*
    *Resourcefulness*
    *Vietnam*
    *War*

---

At fourteen, Quan Thi Chi and his younger sister, Ly, know only war. When the Americans withdraw from Saigon and then from all of Vietnam, Quan hopes he and his family will finally know peace. Unfortunately, North Vietnamese officials soon move into Saigon, now called Ho Chi Minh City, and soon Quan is afraid again. He and Ly are ridiculed at school for having a "capitalist" father; the man ekes out a living in a tiny store. Knowing that families are being split up and forced to move into labor camps, the children's terrified father, Phan, writes to his father in Rach Gia on the Gulf of Siam, asking to take the family there to work on the old man's boat. Then officials tell Phan that his shop is now owned by the government and the whole family will be relocated. They begin planning to leave for Rach Gia, even though Phan's father's response hasn't come. But soon the response arrives: the government has confiscated the old man's boat. Quan suggests the family go to Rach Gia anyway, steal the boat back, and escape to Malaysia. The idea terrifies Phan, but several days later the family sneaks out of Saigon in pairs. Quan leaves with Uncle Tan. The housekeeper, elderly Ah Soong, goes off with Aunt Binh, whose home has been destroyed and her husband and daughter killed. She is depressed, withdrawn, virtually unable to take care of herself. Phan, his wife, Xuyen, and Ly leave later, and all meet in Rach Gia. Phan's father has died. Quan devises a plan to get back the boat, *Lucky Dragon*. That night he and his father climb under the pier, steal the boat, and pick up the rest of the family waiting on a sandbar. The tide floats them out into the Gulf. Early the next morning, to their horror, a figure rises up out of the fish-hold: Captain Cu, who works on the boat and had slept in the hold all night. He agrees to flee with them. Several days later they reach Malaysian shores, only to be refused entry. The naval boat does give the family rice and fuel. They try again, are again refused, and then are towed to the island of Bidong where the United Nations is helping to relocate refugees. But they see that

Bidong is a "seething garbage dump of unwanted people." Bitterly disappointed, they cut the towline and head out to sea. Quan suggests they go on to Australia. As the trip becomes more and more perilous, Aunt Binh reveals an almost uncanny ability to work with the others, at times as their leader. Phan, on the other hand, blaming himself for the family's plight, sinks deeper into depression. They manage to survive Thai pirates and a typhoon, but are then out of food and increasingly weakened. By now the engine pump is broken, and the family takes turns bailing water. When they finally reach Indonesia, they are again turned away. Eventually Phan is reduced to madness, and Xuyen tells Quan he must take over as head of the family. Several days after Phan dies, the exhausted, starving Ah Soong jumps overboard, after giving Quan her life savings. They spot land, and the family frantically bails as fast as possible. The *Lucky Dragon* breaks apart; the survivors cling to a makeshift raft as they swim for shore. Utterly exhausted, they crawl to the beach and sleep. The next morning Quan, his family, and Captain Cu are discovered by men in a Land Rover. Their new life in Australia begins.

Centering on the character of young Quan, who never loses hope, this is a memorable, unsentimental account of a courageous pursuit of freedom. It is also a study of various people's reactions to tremendous stress. Exciting, tense, and filled with action, the story brings to dramatic life the plight of war refugees and the strength to be found in unshakeable family loyalty.

Ages 11 and up

**Also available in:**
No other form known

## 46
**Benson, Ellen**
### Philip's Little Sister
Color photographs by Rachael Davis.
Children's Press, Inc., 1979.
(31 pages)

---

SIBLING: Younger
    Resourcefulness
    Sharing/Not sharing

---

It's not always easy being a little sister. Lynn Tucker, age seven, has to put up with a lot from her brother, Philip, who is two years older. Philip has just taken the skateboard away from Lynn. Her mother comforts her, reminding her of the importance of sharing and how Lynn too sometimes fails to share. Lynn reflects bitterly on the injustices of being a little sister, the comparisons between her and Philip made by teachers and relatives, all the hand-me-downs: bike, toys, books, even clothing. To add insult to injury, Philip makes fun of her, sometimes in front of his friends, calling her "Baby" or telling her, "You're just not much good for anything." One morning, as Philip rides his new bicycle to the grocery store, Lynn follows at a safe distance. When she comes around the corner, she sees her brother's bicycle being ridden by someone else, an older boy. Lynn bravely decides to follow and manages, with the help of some children playing nearby, to find out the boy's name and

where he lives. She hurries home to tell her unhappy brother, and their mother informs the police, who retrieve the stolen bicycle. A very grateful Philip assures Lynn that they will be friends forever. He will never again say anything bad about his little sister.

Some of the drawbacks of being a younger sibling are realistically presented in this easy-to-read story that should stimulate discussion. Readers will appreciate Lynn's successful attempt to win her brother's respect. Several photographs are obviously posed, but this should not be distracting to young children. Neither should the ending, which is overly optimistic as children often are: "I won't ever say anything bad about you again."

Ages 5-8

**Also available in:**
Paperbound—*Philip's Little Sister*
Children's Press, Inc.

## 47
**Benson, Kathleen**
### Joseph on the Subway Trains
Black/white illustrations by Emily Arnold McCully.
Addison-Wesley Publishing Company, Inc., 1981.
(45 pages counted)

B

---

LOST, BEING

---

Joseph's second-grade class is taking a subway trip from Brooklyn to a museum in Manhattan, and Joseph is very excited. As the class stands on the platform with their teacher, Joseph notices a mouse between the tracks. Walking beside a waiting train to follow the mouse, Joseph is suddenly carried along with the rush of people boarding and finds himself on the subway. As the train leaves the station, he sees with dismay that his class is still on the platform and the train is moving away from them. Joseph shouts that he is not supposed to be on this train, but everyone ignores him. When the train stops, Joseph is carried by the crowd onto the platform. He asks how to get back to Brooklyn. Finally, a man tells him to get on the train to his right. Joseph obeys, but soon finds he is on a train going to Manhattan. He gets off at the next stop and wonders what to do. He has no money and no lunch. Two boys, Billy and Fatso, approach him. Joseph confesses he got the trains mixed up and wants to get back to Brooklyn. Billy says he will help, but first Joseph has to play a game. Billy and Fatso stand between two cars of a moving train, one foot on the ledge of one car, one foot on the other car. Fearfully, Joseph does the same, but he jumps off when the train stops. He finally admits to himself that he is lost and needs help. He tells a man in a token booth what has happened. The man calls the Transit Police. Soon a patrolman comes and tells Joseph that people are looking for him. Joseph and the patrolman leave the underground subway system and prepare to go back to Brooklyn.

An excited, curious little boy gets swept onto a New York subway train without the rest of his class. There's just enough suspense in this easy reader to maintain interest, and full-page illustrations help readers and listeners identify with Joseph's plight.

Ages 7-9

**Also available in:**
No other form known

## 48

**Berger, Terry**

## Friends

Black/white photographs by Alice Kandell.
Julian Messner, Inc., 1981.
(61 pages)

---

*FRIENDSHIP: Meaning of*

---

Simon, about eleven, loves horses, movies, listening to music, and, especially, being with his friends. He introduces five friends and tells how each is special. Oliver is very smart and helps Simon with his schoolwork. When they go places together, Oliver reports interesting facts. Occasionally Oliver forgets his lunch, and then Simon shares his. Peter is in a wheelchair. Simon helps him use the elevator at school, and Peter teaches Simon about photography—he has his own darkroom. When Simon needs someone to talk to, he confides in Peter, a good listener. David loves to act, wrestle, and be the best at everything. He lets Simon help him walk dogs after school and shares his pay. George is strong and the biggest kid in the neighborhood. But he cried when his dog died and then was embarrassed. George helps Simon with his paper route. Harry loves adventure. He reads about diving for treasure and promises to let Simon come along. Harry and Simon like to explore the city together. But when Harry gets too adventurous and tries smoking, Simon tells him about his grandfather, who is now very ill with a lung disease caused by smoking. Simon likes all his friends because they share things, trust each other, and have fun together.

This uncomplicated first-person narrative explores a boy's friendships with five other boys. Each has varied interests and a distinct personality, but they all like and trust each other. Believable, realistic photographs on every other page depict the daily activities of these six friends.

Ages 7-11

**Also available in:**
No other form known

## 49

**Berger, Terry**

## Special Friends

Black/white photographs by David Hechtlinger.
Julian Messner, Inc., 1979.
(64 pages)

---

*AGE: Respect for*
  *Friendship: meaning of*

---

A young girl often visits Aunt Rose, who lives next door and is not really related to her. She tells Aunt Rose about her life at home and school, and Aunt Rose shares her own experiences. They read books, eat cookies together, and look at Aunt Rose's photographs. Aunt Rose is teaching her young friend to dance so she'll be prepared for her uncle's wedding. Sometimes Aunt Rose's family visits; the old woman enjoys caring for her great-grandchild. She also gardens and sews, although she has some trouble sewing because of her eyes. The girl tries on Aunt Rose's clothes and tells jokes. They sing old songs. "When I leave, Aunt Rose holds me close to her. I feel her warm hands touching me long after I say goodbye."

In this photo story, a young girl describes simply and poignantly the everyday conversations and activities she shares with the aging widow next door. The photographs avoid looking posed, and they tell many stories themselves. The spare, direct prose also lingers, like the touch of Aunt Rose's hands.

Ages 8-11

**Also available in:**
No other form known

## 50

**Berger, Terry**

## Stepchild

Black/white photographs by David Hechtlinger.
Julian Messner, Inc., 1980.
(63 pages)

---

*PARENT/PARENTS: Remarriage of*
*STEPPARENT: Father*
  *Change: resisting*
  *Stepbrother/Stepsister*

---

Eleven-year-old David Miller is confused and fearful about his mother's decision to marry Peter Green. Even though David's father reassures him of his love, David suspects that if there were no Peter his parents might get together again—although they've been divorced for two years. After the marriage David, his mother, and Peter move to a new apartment. David has trouble adjusting to his new school, making new friends, accepting Peter's two children who visit once a week, and responding to Peter's discipline. David's mother listens to his complaints and defends him occasionally, but he is afraid to tell her everything. He doesn't want her to fight with Peter over him. He wants his mother to be happy. He tells his troubles to his father, but when he asks to live with him his father explains that his long working hours and frequent traveling make that impossible. Gradually David begins to open his eyes and realize his life is not so bad. His friend Richard's father yells a lot and his friend Jennifer's stepmother is mean. David's own father can be moody and silent. David still doesn't like his "steps," Joel and Alice, because he has to share his things with them and they pick on him. But all three share a concern about their place in the family now that David's mother and Peter are going to have a baby. Slowly David begins to feel at home with his new family. Peter helps him draw, and the two help his mother prepare dinner. Best of all, Peter and David begin talking together as friends.

A boy suffering through the early days of his mother's remarriage tells of his big adjustments: to a stepfather, two stepsiblings, a new home. Emotionally torn between his father and Peter, his stepfather, David moves from resentment of Peter to acceptance and then gratitude for his affection, since "he doesn't have to like me." The photographs are somewhat stiff and the narration often stilted, but this book should be helpful to children in similar situations. Many issues of divorce and remarriage are presented here in a high-interest, low-vocabulary format.

Ages 7-11

**Also available in:**
No other form known

## 51

**Berman, Claire**

### What Am I Doing in a Step-Family?

Color illustrations by Dick Wilson.
Lyle Stuart, Inc., 1982.
(47 pages counted)

---

*STEPBROTHER/STEPSISTER*
*STEPPARENT*
   *Change: accepting*
   *Emotions: accepting*
   *Family: relationships*
   *Parent/Parents: remarriage of*
   *Parent/Parents: single*

---

Sometimes families get rearranged. If you suddenly find yourself in a stepfamily, there may be a lot you don't understand. Children become members of stepfamilies in a number of ways. Sometimes parents get divorced. What you have to remember is that your parents divorced each other; they did not divorce you. Sometimes a parent dies and the other parent remarries. Having a stepparent doesn't mean you have to forget about the parent who died. Sometimes memories of your own father or mother interfere with your relationship with your new stepparent. But people aren't all good or all bad. In real life, stepparents are not like Cinderella's wicked stepmother. They have feelings, just as you do, and they worry about whether you'll like them. One of the first problems is what to call your stepparent, and this needs to be discussed with your family. But more important than a name is how you feel about your stepparent. If you have stepbrothers and stepsisters, it may take some time to learn to live together. Stepfamilies do not have to love each other right away—or even ever. But they should try to get along. You could be right when you feel your stepparent is playing favorites with your stepbrothers or stepsisters, but realize that you may play favorites too: you probably don't treat your stepparent exactly as you treat your own mother or father. "People who have lived in stepfamilies for a while say that when everyone gets to know each other, the game of playing favorites comes to an end." Learning the rules of your new family may be difficult at first, but it helps if everyone compromises just a little. If your parents are divorced, you may travel back and forth from one to the other. Traveling can be fun, but it can also be confusing. You may sometimes wonder where you really belong. The answer is that you belong with both parents, both families, because both love you. While you're learning how things are done in each home, ask questions and tell your family how you

feel. You might want to ask for a special space in your other home, even a few drawers. You'll like knowing that some of your things are waiting for you to come back. Remember that you can love your stepparent without affecting your own parent's feelings for you. We love different people in different ways. You don't have to report back to each family about how the other lives; each family is entitled to privacy. Belonging to a stepfamily means you have a lot more people in your life. Getting to know them and like them is one of the best parts of belonging to a stepfamily.

One of a series on issues of importance to children, this oversized book with its delightful, full-page illustrations examines the many fears, thoughts, and questions that children have about being part of a stepfamily. Informative, candid, and reassuring, the book provides simple, sound advice and encourages children to ask questions so they do not feel helplessly manipulated. A serious topic is balanced here with touches of humor.

Ages 5-10

**Also available in:**
No other form known

B

## 52

**Bernstein, Joanne Eckstein**

### Dmitry: A Young Soviet Immigrant

Black/white photographs by Michael J. Bernstein.
Clarion Books, 1981.
(80 pages)

---

*IMMIGRANTS*
   *Change: accepting*
   *Jewish*
   *Life style: change in*
   *Prejudice: ethnic/racial*
   *Russia*

---

Dmitry Gindin and his parents emigrate from Russia to find a better life in either Israel or the United States. Because they do not feel "Jewish enough" to settle in Israel, they choose the United States. From Moscow, they follow the established pattern of going first to Vienna and then to Italy, where they wait for their papers to be processed. Three months after their arrival in Rome they leave for New York. The American city overwhelms them: the language, the incredible number of cars, the difficult-to-decipher street signs, their tiny, dirty hotel room. Still, they enjoy outings to museums and appreciate such minor successes as locating the supermarket. Two months after their arrival they find, with some difficulty, an apartment they can afford in a Brooklyn neighborhood housing project. They try then to begin living a normal life. Dmitry starts school in a fifth-grade class, although he had finished fifth grade in Moscow. Some of his new classmates make fun of him for being Russian, and Dmitry thinks about changing his name to something more American. He notices many differences between Russian and American schools: longer days but much easier work, for example. In Russia children are considered the privileged class; adults may go without things, but children always get the best. Not so in the United States. Dmitry finds that Americans have many false ideas about Russians, although he also had mistaken ideas about the United States. For instance, he didn't know it was so hard to get a job or that certain people faced discrimination. Dmitry's father is a musician. After months of trying to find a job, he wins a one-year contract to play viola with the Syracuse Symphony. At first they decide that he will live by himself in Syracuse. Since the job doesn't start until fall, that summer Dmitry is sent to a camp, his father teaches viola in Massachusetts, and his mother stays by herself in New York. The three suffer so much loneliness that they vow never to be separated again. So they all move to Syracuse in the fall. But Dmitry hates his new school, and his mother, an economic analyst, still cannot find work. Dmitry passes the entrance exam for an excellent private school and then wins a scholarship to go there. They buy a car, but still owe money to the refugee organizations that helped them. Dmitry's mother feels useless, as if her soul is dying. But in spite of their nostalgia, homesickness, and day-to-day difficulties, they know they would never return to Russia. A year later, things are somewhat better for the family. Dmitry's father's contract is renewed and the number of his private students is growing. Dmitry has made several friends. They are able to buy a few things. They are happier and make fewer comparisons. Dmitry's mother is overqualified for every job available in Syracuse and her days remain empty. But her mother has emigrated from Russia and lives in the same building, so the two spend time together. And "people are beginning to think of me as just another kid," Dmitry finds, "not the kid from Russia."

A Soviet Jewish boy and his parents emigrate from Moscow and face a multitude of resettlement problems in the United States. Through the book's documentary approach and realistic photographs, the reader gets an immediate sense of the family's thoughts, feelings, and reactions. This is a story of real people struggling in an imperfect world and there is no happy ending—although the family's circumstances do improve. Readers, especially those who have changed schools or moved, will sympathize with Dmitry's sense of dislocation. They will also be enlightened about life in Russia. The book's emphasis on the ways strangers can become friends, making ill-founded hatreds disappear, gives it particular value.

Ages 11-13

**Also available in:**
No other form known

## 53

**Billington, Elizabeth T.**

### Part-time Boy

Black/white illustrations by Diane de Groat.
Frederick Warne & Company, Inc., 1980.
(89 pages)

---

FRIENDSHIP: Meaning of
  Animals: responsibility for
  Autonomy
  Differences, human
  Privacy, need for
  Self, attitude toward: accepting
  Shyness

---

Ten-year-old Jamie Johnson, quiet and solitary, lives uneasily with two noisy, teasing older brothers and a mother who worries that he is alone too much. Then he meets Mattie Swenson, a spirited young woman who works at the Natural Science Center. Mattie shares her home with her cat, several rabbits and goats, a lamb, and a parakeet—some from the Center, some that she's tending for friends and acquaintances. Mattie befriends the lonely boy and Jamie helps her plant her vegetable garden, take care of the animals, even build a closet. To his delight, he is allowed to spend the summer as Mattie's "part-time boy," helping out at her part-time home in the country. Independent Mattie accepts Jamie just as he is, welcoming him into her peaceful outdoor life. He does chores, learns about their wilderness surroundings, makes friends with an equally solitary farm boy his own age, and learns to play soccer. Jamie returns home at summer's end still quiet, still fond of being alone, but newly self-confident. At peace with himself, he is better able to live peacefully with his family.

This perceptive first-person narrative is a happy story with a reassuring message for quiet, shy children, their friends and families. Mattie's acceptance, her understanding of the human need for privacy, and her peaceful wilderness home help Jamie learn to cherish his own individuality. Young readers will especially enjoy the details about living in the country and caring for animals. Sensitive illustrations enhance the story's tranquil tone.

Ages 8-10

**Also available in:**
Braille—*Part-time Boy*
Library of Congress (NLSBPH)

Cassette—*Part-time Boy*
Library of Congress (NLSBPH)

## 54

**Blue, Rose**

### Wishful Lying

Black/white illustrations by Laura Hartman.
Human Sciences Press, 1980.
(47 pages counted)

---

ATTENTION SEEKING
HONESTY/DISHONESTY
  Boasting
  Communication: parent-child
  Family: relationships
  Illnesses: of parent

---

With his mother frequently ill and his father busy with his job, Jody, about six, often feels unloved and unwanted. When his mother can't take him to his friend's birthday party, she asks another woman to drive him and Jody arrives late, when most of the festivities are over. Needing to cover up the real story, Jody says he and his father were at the zoo and lost track of the time. Then, when his father doesn't pick him up promptly, an embarrassed Jody announces that his father is building him a tree house and must have wanted to finish it before he came. His father finally arrives, apologizing for having been detained at work. When they get home, he gives Jody a present, a ceramic boat picked out by his associate, who "knows what kids like." Angrily, Jody unwraps the boat and deliberately lets it drop to the floor. Jody realizes that his mother's frequent illnesses aren't her fault. Still, he resents being taken care of by housekeepers. "Taking care wasn't the same as caring." At school on Monday, still stewing, he does poorly on a math test. But he tells his mother he received a gold star. When he brags the next day in class that his father is taking him to the carnival, Pete, a classmate, declares him a liar since the carnival has already left town. Furious, Jody pushes Pete down, causing him to skin his knee. That evening his parents and Pete's mother confront him. In his own defense, Jody blurts out that Pete called him a liar. His parents agree that wasn't nice, but they wonder sadly why Jody has not always been truthful lately. He explains he only lies about things he wishes would happen. Swallowing tears, he tells his father, "You're always too busy. You buy me things instead of taking me places. And Mom doesn't act like she cares either. Sometimes I don't feel like I'm your real son." Angry now, his parents call Jody ungrateful and selfish and send him to his room. Later, Jody overhears them talking. When they notice him listening, they share their thoughts with him. All three agree to try harder. His parents will pay more attention to him, and Jody will work at being honest. Then his mother suggests that she and he go to the puppet show the next day. However, when Jody comes home he knows his mother isn't feeling well. She wants to go with him anyway, but Jody insists they stay home. When she asks what his classmates will say about the change in plans, Jody replies, "I'll just tell them the truth."

A little boy battles for his parents' time and attention. The need for communication between parent and child is made clear here, although the text suffers from heavy-handedness. Effective illustrations convey Jody's need for repeated assurances that he is loved. This would be most suitable for prescribed reading with specific follow-up activities.

Ages 6-9

**Also available in:**
No other form known

## 55

Blume, Judy Sussman

### The One in the Middle Is the Green Kangaroo

Color illustrations by Amy Aitken.
Bradbury Press, Inc., 1981.
(39 pages)

SIBLING: Middle
  Identity, search for
  Success

Freddy Dissel, about seven, has two problems—his older brother, Mike, and his younger sister, Ellen. "He felt like the peanut butter part of a sandwich, squeezed between Mike and Ellen," like "a great big middle nothing." One day at school, Freddy hears about a school play and decides this could be his chance to distinguish himself. His teacher tells him the play is for fifth and sixth graders, but she will see if they have a part for a second grader. They do, it seems, have a

special part, and Freddy goes to audition. He is asked to jump all around. Then he's told he will play the part of the Green Kangaroo and must speak in a loud voice. At dinner, a proud Freddy announces to his family that he will be the Green Kangaroo in the school play. For two weeks he practices his part at school and at home. The day of the play Freddy nervously puts on the Green Kangaroo costume. He realizes he "wasn't in the middle. He was all by himself up on the stage." So he resolves to do a great job. The play is funny, and Freddy likes it when the audience laughs. When it's over, the director gives him a special thanks for playing the part of the Green Kangaroo. Everyone applauds. Now, at home, Freddy is not as concerned about being the middle child. "He felt just great being Freddy Dissel."

The middle child in a family finds his individuality when he plays the Green Kangaroo in a school play. Freddy's triumph should have great appeal for other "middle children," and for younger, older, and only children also. A green kangaroo highlights the illustrations in this energetic, easy-to-read, believable tale.

Ages 7-9

**Also available in:**
Braille—The One in the Middle Is the Green Kangaroo
Library of Congress (NLSBPH)

Cassette—The One in the Middle Is the Green Kangaroo
Library of Congress (NLSBPH)

## 56

Blume, Judy Sussman

### Superfudge

E. P. Dutton & Company, Inc., 1980.
(166 pages)

FAMILY: Relationships
  Change: new home
  Friendship: making friends
  Sibling: new baby
  Sibling: relationships

Peter Hatcher, ten, feels he's adjusted very well to life with his pesky little brother, Fudge. Then his parents drop a bomb: his mother is going to have another baby. With that news Peter threatens to run away. Persuaded to stay, he agrees on the condition that he can leave if he doesn't like the baby. Five months later Tamara, called Tootsie, is born. To his surprise, Peter adjusts quite well; it's Fudge who wants to get rid of her. First he tries to sell her, then to give her away, and finally he offers to pay someone to take her. Then, once school is out, Peter must cope with more unsettling news. The family is moving from their apartment in New York City to a rented house in Princeton, New Jersey, where his father will take a year's leave to write a book. Disgusted, Peter wishes his parents would ask his opinion before making big decisions like having a baby or moving. Once in Princeton, Peter finds a friend in Alex Santo, a neighbor boy his age. Peter and Alex make extra money during the summer digging up and selling worms. When school starts, Fudge is allowed into kindergarten after being tested, although he's not yet five. The first day of school Peter is called out of class to help with Fudge, who is refusing to get off a high cabinet until his teacher calls him Fudge instead of his real name, Farley Drexel. This she refuses to do, so Fudge is transferred to the other kindergarten class, whose teacher is willing to call him Fudge. There Fudge does so well that his parents say he can have a pet. At Peter's suggestion he chooses a myna bird that he calls Uncle Feather. Fudge even makes a best friend in Princeton. At the end of the year, the family must make a choice—stay in Princeton or return to New York. They vote to return to New York. This time they've made the decision together.

Peter narrates this story of life in the Hatcher family, and all the adventures and misadventures ring true. The boy and his irrepressible little brother, Fudge, manage to adjust to a new baby and a move, but life is smoother when the whole family shares in a major decision. Written with a wonderful sense of family life and great humor, this would be especially fun to read aloud. It is a continuation of *Tales of a Fourth Grade Nothing*.

Ages 8-10

**Also available in:**
Disc—*Superfudge*
Library of Congress (NLSBPH)

Paperbound—*Superfudge*
Dell Publishing Company, Inc.

## 57

**Blume, Judy Sussman**

**Tiger Eyes**
Bradbury Press, Inc., 1981.
(206 pages)

*MOURNING, STAGES OF*
*Communication: parent-child*
*Death: of father*
*Friendship: meaning of*
*Guilt, feelings of*
*Maturation*
*Relatives: living in home of*

After her father's funeral, fifteen-year-old Davey Wexler feels totally alone. She can't shake the memory of how her young father died after being shot by robbers in his Atlantic City store. Haunted, Davey begins keeping a bread knife under her pillow for protection. She gradually withdraws from other people, wishing she could stay home in bed with the blankets pulled over her head. School starts, and on the first and second days, Davey passes out. Her anxiety is causing her to hyperventilate, and her doctor advises a change for the whole family. Soon Davey, her mother, and her seven-year-old brother, Jason, go to stay with Walter and Elizabeth (Bitsy) Kronick, Davey's father's sister and her husband, in Los Alamos, New Mexico. After a week of sightseeing, Davey needs to be alone for a while. She rides a bike to a nearby canyon and decides to climb down. The beautiful landscape brings thoughts of the father she can never share it with, and she is overcome by grief. Suddenly she hears a voice and is confronted by a young hiker who calls himself Wolf. Davey tells Wolf her name is Tiger and begins to meet him daily at the same spot. Wolf asks no questions, and she appreciates that. Meanwhile, Davey's mother is put on medication for the headaches caused by her tension and depression. The medication leaves her listless and she

begins delegating most of her parental responsibilities to the overprotective Kronicks, who have no children of their own. She also begins seeing a psychologist, Ms. Olnick. It is decided to enroll Davey and Jason in school in Los Alamos. Davey's anger and feelings of isolation increase with her continuing inability to talk with her mother about her father's death. When Davey volunteers as a candy striper at the hospital, she meets Willie Ortiz, who is dying of cancer. She learns that Willie is Wolf's father and that the boy has taken a semester off from college to be with the dying man. After Christmas Davey's mother improves enough to take a part-time job. But Davey's own situation worsens. Her mother begins dating a man Davey dislikes, her uncle won't let her take driver's education and the two have a running battle, Mr. Ortiz dies, and Wolf returns to college. Finally, in desperation, Davey agrees to see Ms. Olnick. Gradually able to confide in the psychologist, she tells of her fears that her mother is becoming as overprotective as her aunt and uncle. Later, she also describes the horrible night when her father died in her arms. As she leaves that memorable session, Davey realizes she had not mentioned the way her clothes had been covered with her father's blood. With sudden resolution, she hurries back to the Kronicks' house, takes a bag from her closet, and rides her bike to the canyon. There, under a pyramid of rocks, she buries the blood-stained clothes she has kept with her, resolving now to remember only the good times with her father. Two days later the mail brings Davey a tiger's-eye stone from Wolf. She and her mother go to a restaurant and finally share their grief, longing, and loss. They decide to return to Atlantic City once school is out. When they do go back home, Davey feels like a new person—not on the outside, but on the inside.

A teenage girl tells how she came to resolve her grief over her father's violent death. Details of the shocking event are revealed little by little until Davey is finally able to describe to a psychologist how she could not help her father and he died in her arms. This is a compelling, well-written story of a young girl's stages of grief and a family's efforts to cope with their sudden loss. Davey's believable narrative will capture the attention and sympathy of readers.

Ages 11 and up

**Also available in:**
Cassette—*Tiger Eyes*
Library of Congress (NLSBPH)

Paperbound—*Tiger Eyes*
Dell Publishing Company, Inc.

## 58

**Bograd, Larry**

**Lost in the Store**
Color illustrations by Victoria Chess.
Macmillan Publishing Company, Inc., 1981.
(32 pages counted)

*LOST, BEING*
*Friendship: making friends*

When Bruno, about five, becomes separated from his parents at a busy department store, he is frightened and begins to cry. The tears quickly stop when he meets Molly, also about five, also lost, but not at all afraid. Being lost is fun, she tells Bruno, and then proceeds to show him why. First the two ride up and down in the elevator. Then they go to the sporting goods department. Putting on demonstration roller skates, they skate to the pet department and visit the animals. Next they try on hats. In the housewares department they pretend to eat at a table set with dinnerware. Then, after they return the skates, Bruno and Molly go to the food department and sample cookies, cheese, and crackers. Soon they find two large mannequins to imitate. From there they visit the make-up department and the television department. Then they try on jewelry and pretend to be rich. In the bed department they take naps, awakening when they hear Molly's name over the store's loudspeaker. Molly hurries to the office to be reunited with her mother, and Bruno returns to the place where he was first lost. There he finds his anxious parents waiting for him. As he leaves the store, Bruno waves goodbye to his new friend, Molly.

Although this tale of two lively children enjoying the freedom of being lost in a department store is a bit farfetched, young readers should be greatly entertained by it. Colorful pictures convey the exhilaration of the characters' escapades. The story could initiate discussion about what children might actually do if they are lost.

Ages 4-7

**Also available in:**
No other form known

## 59

Bond, Felicia

## Poinsettia & Her Family

Color illustrations by the author.
Thomas Y. Crowell Company, Inc., 1981.
(32 pages)

---

*FAMILY: Unity*
*Privacy, need for*
*Sibling: relationships*

---

Poinsettia the pig, along with her parents and her six brothers and sisters, lives in a fine old house that she thinks perfect. One day she returns from the library and hurries excitedly to her favorite reading spot, the soft, red leather window seat. Unfortunately, that spot is occupied by one of her siblings, so Poinsettia hurries to the rock out front to read in peace. But she discovers piglets lying all around the rock. Next she tries the bathtub, but her sister Chick Pea is soaking. Poinsettia decides the house is not perfect after all; it is too crowded. She rebels against having no privacy, pinches and yells, and is sent to bed early for misbehaving. But the next day her father says they will all go look for a new and bigger house. Poinsettia hides and stays behind to read. She reads on the leather chair, on the rock, and in the bathtub. By nighttime it is snowing, and the family still has not returned. A lonely Poinsettia is afraid they will not come back, but just then they arrive. Now Poinsettia realizes her family is more important to her than the inconvenience of a crowded house.

In this colorfully illustrated story of a large family of pigs, Poinsettia's desire for privacy and more room is one many children share and most will sympathize with. After a day spent alone, however, Poinsettia realizes how important her family is to her. Crowded or not, the house is lonely without them.

Ages 4-7

**Also available in:**
No other form known

## 60

Bond, Nancy Barbara

## The Voyage Begun

Atheneum Publishers, 1981.
(319 pages)

---

*COOPERATION: in Work*
*MATURATION*
*NATURE: Living in Harmony with*
  *Age: respect for*
  *Change: accepting*
  *Determination*
  *Friendship: meaning of*
  *Gangs: being bothered by*
  *Helping*

---

It is the not-too-distant future and Paul Vickers, sixteen, wanders along the coast of Cape Cod. The world is in an environmental crisis: food and energy are in very limited supply, due mainly to greed and pollution; the fishing industry has disappeared; most wildlife is gone. The abandoned summer communities on Cape Cod resemble ghost towns. Paul and his family have moved here, to the town of Warren, because his stern, unbending father has been appointed director of the local government research station. His luxury-loving mother complains continually about their hard life and deprivations. In the course of his wanderings along the shore, Paul finds an injured Canada goose in a trap. When he can't free it he goes for help to Maggie Rudd, a local conservationist. He and she slowly develop a friendship. Meanwhile, Mickey Cafferty, an eleven-year-old native of the area, spends her spare time scouting the shoreline for anything salvageable to add to her collection of bits and pieces. She meets Walter Jepson, an old man who also works at salvaging, when both find and want an old canvas raft that has washed ashore. Neither can move the raft alone and an uneasy, almost hostile relationship develops as they move the old raft to a building in the abandoned boatyard where Walter lives in a shack he's fixed up. Daily they work on the raft, and soon Mickey discovers why Walter is so secretive and suspicious. In that same building the old man is making a beautiful sailboat, an activity he has made the center of his life. Fearing people might destroy his creation, he swears Mickey to secrecy. But her brother, Shawn, suspicious about Mickey's daily disappearances, follows her to Walter's shack. Later, he and his gang, the Salvages, break into the shack while Walter is visiting a friend in a nursing home. The gang steals everything of value and sets fire to the place to cover their tracks. Mickey discovers the fire raging out of control and meets Paul as she is wandering disconsolately among the ruins. She is hostile and suspicious towards him but gradually, realizing she needs help restoring Walter's shack, comes to accept his assistance. Though they manage to make the shack livable again, Walter, now living in the nursing home himself, refuses to come back. The violence and the loss of his beloved boat have filled him with despair. Mickey, blaming herself for Walter's troubles, thinks that if she can retrieve the old man's tools and find a boat for him to restore, Walter will want to come back. So she and Paul break into the Salvages's hideout to take back Walter's tools. They are caught. Paul is beaten up and dumped on his parents' front lawn. Once he recovers, he arranges a meeting with Shawn and agrees not to press charges if Shawn will help him. Reluctantly Shawn agrees, returning the tools and soon locating an old, abandoned boat at another deserted boatyard farther along the coast. Paul, Mickey, Shawn, Maggie, and Maggie's friend Gabe, once a fisherman, now an artist, secretly work to make the sailboat seaworthy. Late one night, Gabe and Paul steal the research station's powerboat and the five manage to pull the sailboat into Warren's harbor. There they meet Paul's outraged father and many government officials. When he hears the story, Paul's father drops charges but forbids Paul to see his friends again except to say goodbye: he has requested a transfer. A month later, Paul's family is about to move and Paul returns to the boatyard. He finds Walter happily working on the sailboat, with Gabe, Maggie, and Shawn helping. Mickey, who has said her goodbyes to Paul at school, can't bring herself to speak to him. As he walks away, though, he turns to see her waving to him from Walter's little house. Paul, who at first had hated the town as much as his mother did, leaves now vowing to return someday to his friends.

Living in a bleak, exhausted landscape of the future, a group of highly individual people come together in the never-obsolete task of helping one another. Chapters are presented from either Paul's or Mickey's perspective, and the detailed plot and characterizations develop carefully and believably. This well-written story vividly conveys the isolation of these people in relation to their stricken environment and to each other. The subtle picture of what the world could become, both in human and natural terms, will be appreciated most fully by the mature reader.

Ages 12 and up

**Also available in:**
No other form known

## 61

**Bonham, Frank**

### Gimme an H, Gimme an E, Gimme an L, Gimme a P

Charles Scribner's Sons, 1980.
(210 pages)

---

*BOY-GIRL RELATIONSHIPS: Dating*
*SUICIDE: Attempted*
  *Deprivation, emotional*
  *Mental illness: of adolescent*
  *Parental: absence*
  *School: classmate relationships*
  *Stepparent: mother*

---

Dana Furlong, a bright, serious sixteen-year-old who raises lovebirds for fun and profit, is fascinated by his biology lab partner, Katie Norman. Katie, who recently transferred to Dana's high school, is an attractive, vivacious, popular cheerleader. Although they verbally snipe at each other, the two feel a mutual attraction. But under her social facade, Katie is an emotionally distraught girl struggling to cope with the haunting memory of a mother who deserted her when she was nine; a neurotic stepmother, Marcia, only nine years older than she, who resents and emotionally abuses Katie; frequent moves; and an absentee father. Katie has had several "accidents" in which she almost died. She does book reports on famous people who have committed suicide and suffers from blackouts in which she dreams she is dying, with her mother and Dana Furlong as observers. Sensing Dana's interest in Katie and because Katie distrusts adults, Mrs. Allen, the English teacher and guidance counselor, enlists Dana to help find out what is troubling Katie and if she has suicidal tendencies. Wanting to help, Dana invites Katie to the beach. While she is swimming she nearly drowns, convincing Dana that she is indeed suicidal. For several weeks, Dana has been worried about recent fraudulent ads for lovebirds which are hurting his business. Now he is shocked to find that it is Katie who is placing the ads in a bid for Dana's attention and help. Katie is so distraught by Dana's discovery that she takes an overdose of tranquilizers and alcohol and must be rushed to the hospital, where she is treated and released. Katie is then threatened by Marcia with being placed in an institution or foster home. Her father, currently in Honolulu, has not been informed of Katie's actions and knows little about the relationship between Katie and Marcia; Mrs. Allen contacts him. Katie agrees to a second date with Dana as a way to foil Marcia, who has grounded her. During dinner, Katie begins to open up and confide in Dana, but later, when Dana responds to her teasing with a sexual advance, she withdraws from him. After Dana takes her home, Katie gets in Marcia's car and drives away. She makes several silent phone calls to Dana, who discovers where she is and goes to her. He convinces Katie that her returning father is worried about her and angry with Marcia, not with her. On the advice of Mrs. Allen and at Dana's insistence, Katie calls a psychologist for help, feeling reassured by her father's support and Dana's friendship.

A teenage girl feels driven to commit suicide, but attempts to save herself with behavior that translates into a vivid cry for help. Katie sweeps the admiring, sympathetic Dana into her emotional turmoil, and he is instrumental in getting her the support and help she desperately needs. Although not totally realistic, since it's unlikely a teacher would enlist another student's help in such a potentially dangerous situation, the book does provide an opportunity to consider the distress signals sent out by a troubled human being. No simple solutions are offered, only a hope for Katie's recovery. The characterizations are sound, the dialogue natural, and the story a dramatic one.

Ages 12 and up

**Also available in:**
No other form known

**62**

Bonsall, Crosby Newell

## The Case of the Double Cross

Color illustrations by the author.
Harper & Row, Publishers, Inc., 1980.
(64 pages)

---

*CLUBS*
*PREJUDICE: Sexual*
  *Peer relationships*
  *Problem solving*

---

Marigold, about five, and her friends Gussie and Rosie
want to belong to Wizard's private-detective club. But
Wizard and his friends Snitch, Skinny, and Tubby want
nothing to do with girls—especially Marigold. In fact,
the sign on the door of their clubhouse says "NO
GIRLS." Marigold daydreams of situations that will
make the boys beg her to join their club: she has a horse,
she saves them from a flood, she runs an ice cream
stand. Finally she devises a plan. Snitch receives a
coded letter for the club members from a funny little
man with a long beard. When the four boys cannot
decipher the letter's code, they decide they have to get
the little man back again. They set a trap and, after some
time and confusion, catch not one little man but three.
The boys soon discover they have been double-crossed:
the three little men are really Marigold, Gussie, and
Rosie. Just as Wizard is asking the girls to join the club
so they can explain the code, Skinny figures it out. At
that, the girls declare they do not want to join the boys'
club; they will start their own. After much arguing, it is
decided that Marigold, Gussie, and Rosie will join Wizard's club, the "NO GIRLS" sign will be taken down,
and the new club will be called "Wizmars," for Wizard
and Marigold.

Three little girls eager to join a boys-only club succeed
by a clever trick in this delightful "I Can Read" book.
Colorful illustrations capture the characters' feelings
and add details not included in the text. Young children
will enjoy this one.

Ages 6-8

**Also available in:**
Filmstrip—*The Case of the Double Cross*
BFA Educational Media

Paperbound—*The Case of the Double Cross*
Harper & Row, Publishers, Inc.

**63**

Bonsall, Crosby Newell

## The Goodbye Summer

William Morrow & Company, Inc., 1979.
(148 pages)

---

*CHANGE: Resisting*
  *Friendship: best friend*
  *Friendship: meaning of*
  *Loss: feelings of*
  *Maturation*
  *Parent/Parents: single*

---

Allie Pratt, about nine, hates separations and goodbyes.
Her father died in Vietnam when she was only ten
months old, before he had ever seen her. She recalls
how attached she was not long ago to a baby she used to
push in his carriage whenever his mother brought him
to the park. When the family moved, Allie was devastated. Now it is summer vacation again, and the girl
dreads the goodbyes of school and the endlessness of
summer. Allie is a collector—of unhatched duck eggs,
mail-order catalogues, rocks, postcards, pinecones. One
day her mother demands that she clean her room, get
rid of her junk, and hang up her clothes. Allie reluctantly fills up fourteen garbage bags in the process.
When Mr. Waco, the trash collector, hauls off her possessions, she suddenly fears that he is removing her
entire life. Panic-stricken, Allie hops on top of the garbage truck and is carted off to the dump. By the time Mr.
Waco pulls in, a procession of cars with anxious drivers
is following behind his truck. The procession includes a
police car, and Mr. Waco and Allie are taken to the
station. When an angry Mrs. Pratt comes for Allie, she
agrees that the girl will do chores until she can repay
Mr. Waco the twenty-five dollars he paid for his police
fine. Allie is also grounded and must stay inside her
mother's boardinghouse for two weeks. Sure that her
two-week "probation" will never end, Allie is further
upset when she learns that her best friend, Molly Levinson, is leaving to stay with her grandmother before
going on to camp. Then, a few days later, Ms. Wanda
Lenya rents a room at the boardinghouse. The flamboyant former actress, now elderly, is delightfully eccentric, and she and Allie strike up a friendship. They share
secrets, talk, go on walks, and have special times
together. Allie even holds a celebration in Ms. Lenya's
honor on the Fourth of July, a date the woman associates
fondly with small-town festivities of the past. Then one
afternoon, when Allie returns from a corn bake, her
mother tells her that Ms. Lenya received a telegram and
suddenly moved out of the boardinghouse. She left no
message. Brokenhearted, Allie cries and refuses to eat.
Her mother tells her there have to be goodbyes in life;
Allie retorts that her mother couldn't possibly understand how "rotten" she feels. To the girl's surprise, her
mother begins to cry for the first time in Allie's memory.
She tells Allie angrily that losing a husband, being left
with a tiny baby and no money—"that's what rotten
means, and I know all about it!" After several days of
serious thinking and discussions with Molly, who has
returned from camp, Allie gains some understanding of
her feelings about Ms. Lenya's departure and her fear
of goodbyes. Talking with her mother late one night,
Allie notes sympathetically how alone her mother must
have felt after her father died. She concludes that Ms.
Lenya's leaving was not so bad. They have shared a
"nifty" summer, and Allie has many happy memories.
Allie's mother recalls how thankful she was to have
Allie when she lost her husband.

A young, fatherless girl dreads all separations from
those she loves until she learns that change is part of life
and that happy memories will stay with her forever.
Allie is an imaginative, creative child, and her story is
told with humor and insight.

**B**

Ages 9-11

Also available in:
Braille—*The Goodbye Summer*
Library of Congress (NLSBPH)

Cassette—*The Goodbye Summer*
Library of Congress (NLSBPH)

Paperbound—*The Goodbye Summer*
Pocket Books, Inc.

## 64

**Bonsall, Crosby Newell**

### Who's Afraid of the Dark?

Color illustrations by the author.
Harper & Row, Publishers, Inc., 1980.
(32 pages)

*FEAR: of Darkness*

A little boy tells his friend how concerned he is about his dog, Stella, who is afraid of the dark. Stella trembles and shakes and sees frightening shapes when they go to bed. She also hears scary sounds and is not comforted when the boy assures her they are only the wind. When it rains, Stella hides and thinks the sounds on the roof are footsteps. The boy's friend, a patient listener, suggests that it is up to the boy to teach Stella not to be afraid of the dark. "Hold her and hug her," she advises. "Hang on to her in the dark. Let her know you are there. Take care of her!" The boy decides to take the advice that night. All the holding and hugging works—he and Stella are able to sleep peacefully.

A little boy describes his dog's fear of the dark, and his sympathetic friend, recognizing that it is the boy himself who is afraid, gives helpful advice. Expressive illustrations show not the boy's version of the situation, but the real one: they show him hiding, cowering, hunting for the source of the scary sounds while his dog sleeps peacefully nearby. Beginning readers will enjoy the humor in this skillful book, and read-aloud audiences will too.

Ages 3-7

Also available in:
No other form known

## 65

**Bosse, Malcolm Joseph**

### Ganesh

Thomas Y. Crowell Company, Inc., 1981.
(185 pages)

*CHANGE: Accepting*
*DEATH: of Father*
  *Identity, search for*
  *Life style: change in*
  *Perseverance*
  *Problem solving*
  *Relatives: living in home of*

Jeffrey Moore has lived all his fourteen years in India. His American parents had gone there on business and remained to immerse themselves in the culture. Living one step above poverty, the family was completely accepted in their small Indian village. Jeffrey's mother died when the boy was nine; his father, who worked for the national welfare organization, studied Yoga and became a Hindu. Jeffrey acquired an Indian name: Ganesh, after a Hindu god who is the overcomer of obstacles. Now, when his father dies, Jeffrey goes to live with his Aunt Betty in the midwestern United States. He struggles with the clash of cultures, missing his friends and the familiarity of life in India. In the U.S. he is small for his age; in India he was large. Unlike his aunt or classmates, he is a vegetarian and has the habit, expected in India, of belching unrestrainedly while eating. He is used to boys holding hands with boys and keeping their distance from girls. Here boys and girls hold hands and sit close to one another. Jeffrey gains some attention in swimming class when he holds his breath longer than anyone else by using a Yoga way of breathing. Soon afterwards a classmate, Tom Carrington, invites him to a party. There Jeffrey teaches Lucy Smith a mantra, or sacred chant. Lucy teaches it to others at school, and they tease Jeffrey by chanting it in the halls. But they nullify the chant's power with their mispronunciation, Jeffrey consoles himself. When Tom sees Jeffrey practicing Yoga in the wrestling room, he persuades Jeffrey to demonstrate Yoga for the other athletes. Soon the two are friends, with Tom beginning to use Jeffrey's Indian name, Ganesh. Then Aunt Betty tearfully tells Jeffrey that the state is claiming their land for a new highway. They will soon lose their house, which had been built by Jeffrey's great-grandfather. Tom and Jeffrey, now called Ganesh by all his friends, enlist the help of classmates to save the house by the practice of Satyagraha, meaning "a grip on the truth." When the authorities—the police and State Highway Commissioner Walton—come to encourage and then force Aunt Betty to vacate, the young people vow to remain. They decide to fast until the authorities reconsider; at their last meal together, Ganesh makes a gesture of unity by eating his first meat. Their cause attracts statewide attention and newspaper coverage. When people begin to suffer adverse effects from the fast and Aunt Betty becomes ill and is warned of possible kidney failure, Ganesh doubts the wisdom of continued resistance. But his friends, especially the determined Lucy Smith, refuse to give up. Under the pressure of impending television news coverage, Commissioner Walton comes to tell them that the state is designating the house a Landmark Building, safeguarding it against destruction and permitting Aunt Betty to continue living there. Ganesh and his friends have won.

A boy raised in India and his American classmates develop a mutual understanding and respect for each other's cultural heritage when they unite against injustice in this dramatic story. Although the overall circumstances of the plot, especially the resistance to the law, are somewhat improbable, overdrawn, and occasionally melodramatic, the book does present two cultures learning to live together amicably and so could promote tolerance and understanding. The many insights into Indian culture include a detailed and vivid description of Jeffrey's father's funeral, cremation, and burial in a sacred river, a section that could distress some readers.

Ages 11-14

Also available in:
No other form known

**66**

Bottner, Barbara

**Dumb Old Casey Is a Fat Tree**

Black/white illustrations by the author.
Harper & Row, Publishers, Inc., 1979.
(42 pages)

---

*DETERMINATION*
*PERSEVERANCE*
*Peer relationships*
*Success*
*Weight control: overweight*

---

Casey Stoner, a chubby seven-year-old, dreams of becoming a ballet dancer, but remains the clumsiest member of her dancing class. When her ballet teacher, Mrs. Bellanova, announces the roles for the annual recital, Casey is determined to play the evil prince. "Snotty" Marion, "prissy" Evelyn, and "stuck-up" Betsy compete for the roles of princess, queen, and king. Jealous of the three, Casey practices hard, even turning down all sweets and forgetting to watch television. When a skinny new girl, Elizabeth, joins the class as the new worst dancer, Casey quickly befriends her in sympathy. The cast is finally announced: Marion is princess, Evelyn is queen, Betsy is king, and Marybeth is the evil prince. Casey, along with the rest of the class, will be a tree. Hurt and angry, she lies and tells the girls she may not be able to dance in the recital after all: her family may be on vacation. After she stops feeling sorry for herself, though, Casey decides she will prove herself by practicing harder than ever. As the friendship between Casey and Elizabeth grows, they practice together and encourage each other with compliments. At the first rehearsal, the trees bump into each other. Having noticed Casey's hard work, Mrs. Bellanova asks her to be the Head Tree that all the other trees will follow. Marion, Evelyn, and Betsy make fun of Casey's new role, but their teasing only makes her practice harder. The night of the recital, Casey decides she can either be a "dumb old fat tree, or a lovely tree, the best, most feeling tree in the forest." She performs as a lovely tree and receives many compliments, even from Marion. Casey realizes she can be a dancer—or anything else—if she is determined enough.

The story of Casey's determination and triumph is told with humorous sympathy. Any child who has faced and overcome a seemingly insurmountable obstacle will identify with the heroine, as will overweight children. Casey's parents are understanding and supportive. The illustrations of pert, pixie-faced children with Casey a plump, pear-shaped figure add personality to the characters.

Ages 6-9

**Also available in:**
Cassette—*Dumb Old Casey Is a Fat Tree*
Library of Congress (NLSBPH)

**67**

Bottner, Barbara

**Mean Maxine**

Color illustrations by the author.
Pantheon Books, 1980.
(31 pages counted)

---

*NAME-CALLING*
*Problem solving*
*Teasing*

---

Maxine calls Ralph names like "Dummo" and "Owl Eyes." Ralph's older brother tells him to stand up to Maxine, who is only acting tough. As Ralph practices, posing and growling as he imagines himself scaring Maxine away, the little girl walks up, calling names as usual. Ralph whirls around and confronts her with "You . . . better not mess with me! Boooo!" Maxine is impressed, admitting that Ralph "almost" scared her. She wonders how Ralph has become such a good monster, a skill she's been practicing all week. When he volunteers to teach her, she is delighted: "At last—someone to play with."

A little boy's imagination and some coaching from his big brother help him stand up to and win over his young tormentor. This light, simple, humorous tale may encourage children to defend themselves against those who tease or bully them. Purple highlights in the illustrations represent Ralph's imaginings and help tell the story.

Ages 4-6

**Also available in:**
No other form known

**68**

Bottner, Barbara

**Messy**

Color illustrations by the author.
Delacorte Press, 1979.
(29 pages counted)

---

*MESSINESS*

---

Harriet, who likes to be called Harry, is six and very messy. In fact, her mother thinks Harry is the messiest child in town. Her hair is messy, her clothes are messy, and her room is messy. Harry's favorite place to play is under her bed so she will not have to clean her room. Even when Harry helps her mother in the kitchen, she is messy. At dance class all the girls look like ballerinas; Harry looks messy. But Harry is the best dancer. The teacher announces a recital for which everyone will wear a costume. Harry is chosen to be the princess and is given a beautiful white tutu with ruffles. She does not want to rumple the costume and so informs her mother that she will be neat from now on, "just like a princess." All week Harry keeps her room clean and herself neat. During the recital, she looks very neat and pretty and feels like a princess. Afterwards, her proud parents take

B

her to a restaurant for dessert. When the food arrives, Harry twirls her napkin and spills the desserts. Messy again!

A little girl is very content to be messy until she is chosen to be the princess in a dance recital. After a week of being neat, though, Harry seems happy to be messy again. The numerous illustrations show an engaging—but messy—little girl. Children will like Harry; adults will sympathize with Harry's long-suffering mother.

Ages 4-7

**Also available in:**
No other form known

## 69

**Boutis, Victoria**

## Katy Did It

Black/white illustrations by Gail Owens.
Greenwillow Books, 1982.
(88 pages)

---

DETERMINATION
 Communication: parent-child
 Nature: appreciation of
 Success

---

When Katy Milonas's father announces he wants a companion for a three-day hike to Big Dix in the Adirondacks, no one expects eight-year-old Katy to go. She has camped once, with a friend in the backyard, and they slept in the house most of the night. And Katy hates hiking. But when her mother and brother can't go and her father asks her, Katy feels special. She will not only go; she will sleep alone in her own tent. She breaks in a new pair of hiking boots and looks forward to the trip. They'll take along the dog, Toby, who will carry his own pack. As they drive to the trail, Katy begins to worry about wild animals. Her father reassures her. The first day of hiking is fun until it starts to rain. By the time they stop for the night, Katy's shoulders are sore. She makes stew, and her unfailingly cheerful father sets up the two tents. In the process the tarp falls, dropping rain and leaves into the stew. Katy refuses to eat it. Hungry and tired, she goes to bed, only to lay awake listening to scary noises. But after a breakfast of hot oatmeal, which she has always refused to eat but now finds delicious, Katy feels better. The second day of hiking is uphill and Katy finishes it tired. At suppertime Toby fights with a porcupine and gets quills stuck in his face, upsetting Katy into another sleepless night. The third day's climb is hard, and Katy is deeply distressed when she sees a dead, decaying deer. Her father comforts the sobbing girl, saying that even this awful sight is part of nature. Katy keeps climbing, determined to reach the top of Big Dix. When she does, she surveys a magnificent vista. Katy's father is proud of her—and she is proud of herself.

A girl who hates camping and hiking surprises herself when she not only accompanies her father on a three-day hike up a mountain, but also enjoys and is exhilarated by the experience. Included in this simple, well-written story is much basic information about camping, lending additional interest. Also noteworthy is the warm relationship between the supportive, experienced father and his novice daughter. They enjoy each other and respond to the beauty of the mountains. Numerous pencil sketches complement the text.

Ages 8-10

**Also available in:**
No other form known

## 70

**Brancato, Robin Fidler**

## Sweet Bells Jangled out of Tune

Alfred A. Knopf, Inc., 1982.
(200 pages)

---

AGE: Aging
MENTAL ILLNESS
RESPONSIBILITY: Accepting
 Grandparent: love for
 Illnesses: of grandparent
 Loyalty

---

Fifteen-year-old Ellen Dohrmann hasn't been allowed to see or talk to her dead father's mother, Eva Dohrmann, for seven years, ever since the day Eva picked Ellen up from school without telling anyone. Ellen was found when police went to question Eva about a ring missing from a local jewelry store and discovered the child at the eccentric woman's mansion. Ellen remembers how she slipped the ring out of her grandmother's cape pocket so the police wouldn't find it on her. She also remembers all the delightful times she spent with Grandma Eva, attending the elegant teas, making paper flowers, eating fresh strawberries out of season. She's recently seen her grandmother at a restaurant and now, against her mother's wishes, Ellen goes to visit Eva. She finds her grandmother wrinkled, gaunt, and unwashed. The house is piled high with newspapers, cartons, and old junk. Unopened mail dating back several years sits in stacks. Grandma Eva talks about trying to keep "them" out and refers apprehensively to a mysterious "he." Ellen is further appalled to discover that Eva has no telephone, water, electricity, or gas. The next day Ellen brings her friend Josie to visit Eva, but Eva thinks Josie wants to take her things. She locks her in a clothes closet and leaves with the key. Ben and Buddha, two friends, come by and rescue Josie. Ellen deeply resents her grandmother now—almost hates her. She begins to remember some of the scary aspects of the old days with Eva, the wild way she used to talk about the two of them going away to New York or Philadelphia. One day, after visiting her maternal grandfather in the hospital, Ellen finds Eva blocking the emergency room driveway with her old car. Only Ellen can get her to move. Eva tells Ellen about "them"—the officials of the Health Department who plan to remove debris from her property and who will be holding an inspection to determine the future of her home. Ellen promises to help. To do so, she has to tell her mother that she's been visiting Eva. Her mother eventually agrees that they cannot abandon the old woman. The next day a social worker meets with Ellen, her mother, and Eva's doctor and lawyer. They all conclude that Eva cannot be allowed to continue living as she has been. The head of the hospital's psychiatric unit takes Ellen on a tour of the ward, and she begins to see this as the best option open to them. Then Ben tells Ellen he saw smoke coming from Eva's house. Ellen finds Eva burning papers and apparently attempting to burn the house down. Her father, the old woman tells Ellen, once wrote her a letter saying it was better to burn the house down than to let it go to strangers. Ellen takes Eva to the hospital. There the doctor convinces Ellen to help get Eva to sign herself into the psychiatric ward. So Ellen tricks her grandmother into signing the papers, asking her to write her initials as she used to years earlier. Not knowing what she's signing, Eva commits herself. Ellen hates herself afterwards, yet knows the trickery was necessary and that Eva can sign herself out later if she wishes. Ellen even suspects Eva might enjoy herself in the hospital once she adapts a little. Feeling better about her decision, Ellen goes to the hospital "for her first visit with Eva in their new lives."

A teenager takes responsibility for her aging, confused grandmother, who is not the same person she once loved and idolized. Ellen carries this task to its ultimate and painful conclusion when she oversees Eva's commitment to a psychiatric ward. This is a smoothly written story of loyalty and acceptance of responsibility. It falters somewhat with an incomplete characterization of the grandmother as she was in her early relationship with Ellen.

Ages 11-14

**Also available in:**
Paperbound—*Sweet Bells Jangled out of Tune*
Scholastic Book Services

## 71

Brandenberg, Aliki Liacouras

### The Two of Them

Color illustrations by the author.
Greenwillow Books, 1979.
(29 pages counted)

---

*DEATH: of Grandparent*
*GRANDPARENT: Love for*
  *Love, meaning of*

---

A loving grandfather makes a silver ring for his newborn granddaughter. He also makes her a bed and sings her soft lullabies. When she outgrows her bed, he makes her a bigger one and a shelf for her books. At night he tells her stories—stories that had been told to him, stories just for fun, and stories about his love for her. He takes her swimming in the ocean and walking in the woods. After school the girl helps out in her grandfather's grocery store. Sometimes she gives the wrong change but the grandfather only laughs, realizing she is just learning to count. When the grandfather retires, he and the girl spend much time in his garden where he cultivates fruit trees. In time, the silver ring fits the girl. Suddenly the grandfather becomes ill and seems old. He recovers, but is partially paralyzed and confined to a wheelchair. Now the girl cares for him. She wheels him through the garden, sings to him at night, and tells him stories. He dies in the springtime. "She knew that one day he would die. But when he did, she was not ready, and she hurt inside and out." She cuts blossoms for him from his tree and says goodnight,

but her grandfather is silent. In the fall she sits in the garden and looks at the apple tree, thinking of how it will change with the seasons. "She would be there to watch it grow, to pick the fruit, and to remember."

Illustrations and text are equally important in this sad, gentle story of love between a grandfather and his granddaughter. The soft shadings, kind faces, and warm, domestic scenes in the drawings complement the bittersweet, sometimes lyrical, text. The final picture of the girl looking at an empty chair under an apple tree skillfully captures her sense of loss and longing.

Ages 3-7

**Also available in:**
Cassette—*The Two of Them*
Miller-Brody Productions

Filmstrip—*The Two of Them*
Miller-Brody Productions

Paperbound—*The Two of Them*
Dell Publishing Company, Inc.

## 72

Brandenberg, Aliki Liacouras

### We Are Best Friends

B

Color illustrations by the author.
Greenwillow Books, 1982.
(32 pages counted)

---

*FRIENDSHIP: Best Friend*
*FRIENDSHIP: Making Friends*
  *Change: accepting*
  *Moving*

---

When young Peter announces he is moving, Robert replies that he can't because they are best friends. They play together, fight together, and attend each other's parties. "You will miss me too much," he says. But Peter moves anyway, and Robert is lonely without him. He has nobody to play with, share with, even fight with. One day at school a new boy named Will talks to Robert, who silently looks him over. Robert decides he dislikes the boy's name, glasses, and freckles. Then Robert receives a letter from Peter telling him about the new friend he's made. Even though Robert will always be his best friend, writes Peter, he likes his new home better now that he has somebody to play with. Robert writes back, reminding Peter of all the fun things they used to do together and telling him about Will. Later, he sees Will sitting by a fence looking for a frog to replace the pet one he used to have at his other house. Robert tells Will there are frogs in his garden. "If I had a frog in my garden, I'd share it," says Will. "That's what I'm doing," replies Robert. They ride their bikes to Robert's yard, where Will catches a frog and names it after his first one. Robert tells Will how his friend Peter used to come every year to watch the tadpoles in their garden pond and how he called them "Inkywiggles." Will suggests he write and tell Peter about the new crop of "Inkywiggles." They laugh, each happy to be having fun again. Robert writes the letter and tells Peter about his new friend and their fun with the "Inkywiggles." He mails the letter and then rides his bike over to Will's.

In this story of friendship, a young boy finds that a new friend can relieve the loneliness left by his departed best friend. The new friend does not replace the old, but he makes life full and fun again. This gentle tale, with its believable dialogue and sunny, colorful illustrations, would be an excellent read-aloud story.

Ages 3-6

**Also available in:**
Cassette—*We Are Best Friends*
Miller-Brody Productions

## 73

**Branscum, Robbie**

### For Love of Jody

Black/white illustrations by Allen Davis.
Lothrop, Lee & Shepard Company, 1979.
(111 pages)

---

*JEALOUSY: Sibling*
*MENTAL RETARDATION*
  *Ambivalence, feelings of*
  *Family: relationships*
  *Poverty*
  *Responsibility: accepting*
  *Sibling: older*

---

The Depression presents no new problems for twelve-year-old Frankie and her family. Farming in the Arkansas hills has always meant poverty. Frankie's problem continues to be her sister, Jody, ten but with a mental age of two. Jody can only say a few words, is not toilet trained, eats with her hands, and requires total care. But Jody, jealous Frankie is convinced, has managed to steal their mother's love. Sometimes Frankie and Pa have the task of burying the baby animals that Jody, who loves young, cuddly things, has hugged to death. Now Ma is in "the birthing way" and, to protect her from the shock, Pa urges Frankie to take the blame for Jody's latest hugging mishaps. Ma's anger drives Frankie to the refuge of her garden. There she worries about the child expected later that summer. Will Jody hug the baby too hard? Pa wants Jody sent to the state hospital, but Ma won't hear of it. As the summer wears on, both the Depression and the Arkansas drought worsen. Aunt Bonnie Lee and her son, Tad, arrive from the city and all struggle to save the crops. Tad discovers the animal burying place behind the barn and then is horrified to see Jody hug to death the kitten he's given her. When it becomes obvious to Frankie that Tad knows about Jody's "bad habit," she tells him about her troubles with her sister and Ma. He is sympathetic, but tells her she is wrong to treat Jody like a baby rather than a sister. Accepting the advice, Frankie, with Tad's help, works hard to teach Jody to care for herself more and to say more words. But Jody still manages to evade supervision and get into trouble; during a terrible dust storm she wanders from the house, gets lost, and must be rescued by Frankie and Tad. The baby arrives just as the drought breaks in a welcome rain, and matters seem to be improving. Then Jody, again unnoticed, carries the baby to a nearby creek and wades in. Frankie and her father rescue the infant, Frankie talking to Jody to distract her while Pa moves up behind her to retrieve the baby. Though Pa defends Frankie for having saved the baby, Ma blames her for not watching Jody properly. Frankie explodes at this, unleashing her pent-up anger

and resentment. Threatening to leave home, she asks why Ma hates her, why Ma lavishes all her love on Jody. She tells Ma the truth about all the dead animals. Pa leads Ma away, but a miserable Frankie stays by the creek. Her mother rejoins her there and confesses her own mixed feelings about her retarded child. Sometimes Ma feels shame and even anger toward Jody, "and it makes my insides so sick I love her more." She assures Frankie that she also is loved very much. When Pa joins them and the subject of institutionalizing Jody comes up again, he confesses to a change in his own feelings about the matter: "Pears I been wrong too. . . . Maybe folks do best takin' keer of their own, be they right or not." Frankie finds that she too wants Jody to stay with them. Whatever they decide, Ma replies, "it's all outa love of Jody."

A poor Arkansas farm family living through the Depression must come to terms with their responsibility for a severely retarded child who sometimes hugs to death the things she loves. Although the book makes no judgment on whether a child with such a severe handicap and so dangerous a habit can fit into a family, the story does show Frankie and her cousin training Jody to help herself a bit more. Frankie's first-person narration is filled with a vivid sense of place: the heat, dust, and poverty. Characters and situations are believable, and readers will gain considerable insight into what living with a profoundly retarded sibling involves. Softly shaded illustrations complement the story. Frankie narrates in a pronounced hills dialect, which could make the reading difficult for some.

Ages 9-12

**Also available in:**
No other form known

## 74

**Bridgers, Sue Ellen**

### All Together Now

Alfred A. Knopf, Inc., 1979.
(238 pages)

---

*GRANDPARENT: Living in Home of*
  *Friendship: meaning of*
  *Love, meaning of*
  *Maturation*
  *Mental retardation*

---

Casey Flanagan, twelve years old, comes to spend the summer with her father's parents. The United States is engaged in the Korean War, and Casey's father is a military pilot in Korea. Her mother is working two jobs to maintain the family's income. Casey has visited her grandparents' small-town home before, but the prospect of spending an entire summer with them is not appealing to her. Then she meets their neighbor, Dwayne Pickens, a retarded man who has "the mind of a 12-year-old." Dwayne grew up with Casey's father. The young girl and the childlike man become inseparable. Dwayne does not like girls. But he likes Casey because he assumes she is a boy, and she doesn't pursue the point. Casey is rapidly drawn into family and community life. Her Uncle Taylor, a race car driver, has a new girlfriend, Gwen. Casey watches the family's initial apprehension about this "race-track girl" change into fondness and acceptance. Taylor entertains Casey with stories of his and his brother's childhood; Casey had known very little about her father's early years. Hazard Whitaker returns to the town after many years of wandering and finally asks Pansy, his longtime love and Casey's grandmother's best friend, to marry him. Their honeymoon almost ends their marriage, however, when Hazard forgets to reserve a sleeping car for their wedding night on the train. Pansy worries that her marriage is a mistake, and Casey and Dwayne join the effort to reconcile the couple. Then Dwayne, angry and frustrated when his brother Alva's wife yells at him, takes his brother's car and drives it recklessly. Alva, who says he's concerned for Dwayne's welfare, signs a petition to have Dwayne committed to an institution. Casey and many of the townspeople, led by Uncle Taylor, gather forces to get the petition withdrawn. They are able to convince Alva that Dwayne is much loved by his friends and deserves to be happy. Towards the end of the summer, Casey contracts polio. During her convalescence, the family is drawn even closer together. Her grandparents come to regard her as the daughter they always wanted. When Dwayne finally learns that Casey is a girl he is furious at first, but then decides he loves her anyway. Casey has become an important member of her father's family and community. Now, though, the summer is over. Casey goes home to her mother, knowing that she will probably return for other summers, but none quite as special as this one.

A young girl learns much about the love of family and friends in this well-told story. Readers will easily empathize with Casey and the various people in her world, all of whom are realistically and believably drawn. The strengths and weaknesses of individuals and the complexities of relationships are nicely detailed.

Ages 11 and up

**Also available in:**
Cassette—*All Together Now*
Library of Congress (NLSBPH)

Paperbound—*All Together Now*
Bantam Books, Inc.

## 75

**Bridgers, Sue Ellen**

## Notes for Another Life

Alfred A. Knopf, Inc., 1981.
(252 pages)

---

*CHANGE: Resisting*
*GRANDPARENT: Living in Home of*
*LOSS: Feelings of*
*PARENTAL: Absence*
*SIBLING: Relationships*
  *Boy-girl relationships: dating*
  *Depression*
  *Grandparent: love for*
  *Mental illness: of parent*
  *Suicide: attempted*
  *Talents: musical*

---

For the past six years, since their father was first hospitalized for mental illness and their mother moved to

nearby Atlanta to pursue a fashion career, sixteen-year-old Kevin and his thirteen-year-old sister, Wren, have lived with their grandparents, Bill and Bliss Jackson. One Saturday, after she and Bliss have made their usual hospital visit, Wren stops at her grandfather's drugstore where Kevin works to tell him that their mother is coming to see them. Wren is hopeful that this time she might stay, but Kevin discourages such optimism. Bliss is apprehensive about the visit because of Kevin's increasing moodiness, which disappears only when he is with his girlfriend, Melanie. Bliss knows how his mother's absence has hurt Kevin, understands his feeling "that she didn't need them enough, want them enough, love them enough." Their mother, Karen, arrives with the news that she has taken a new job in Chicago and that though she had always intended for Kevin and Wren to come stay with her, they won't be able to now. Wren resolves to accept her life as it is, to concentrate on her piano studies (she is talented and plans a professional career) and the family she has. Kevin, however, broods, and Wren senses and sympathizes with his disappointment. Meanwhile, Wren has captured the interest of Sam Holland, one year older and a boy she had always thought she disliked. She is warmly accepted by his large, loving family. That spring, Bliss must tell Wren and Kevin that Karen is divorcing their father. Wren simply asks if Karen will still visit. As Bliss feared, Kevin reacts by stalking silently out of the house and taking the car. Devastated, he cries for a long time. For Wren's eighth-grade graduation her grandparents take her, Sam, Kevin, and Melanie out to dinner. While dancing with Sam, Wren giddily asks him about their future. Caught up in his confidence, she believes his picture of college, marriage, and children. Another evening, alone in her house with Sam, she agrees to play the piano for him. But she finds his compliments patronizing and tersely corrects his assumption that she will one day teach piano as Bliss does; she informs him that she intends to play concert piano on stage. For Kevin, the summer begins badly. When he talks to his father about the divorce, he is shocked to learn that the man didn't know of Karen's intentions. Despite Melanie's continual efforts to buoy him up, Kevin remains depressed. Bliss asks Jack Kensley, a new minister in town, to talk with the boy. Then their father, temporarily recovered, returns home. Wren readily draws him into the family circle, but Kevin holds back. Karen comes for another visit, raising Kevin's hopes. But she soon makes clear that she really is moving to Chicago. Later, Kevin takes out his frustration on Melanie, challenging her to prove her love for him, and she calls a halt to their relationship. The following day, Karen hesitates a bit before she agrees that Kevin could come live with her. That night, Kevin takes an overdose of sleeping pills. Bliss discovers him in time and as he recovers, she asks Mr. Kensley to begin counseling him. The minister, kind yet tough, helps Kevin think through his actions and face the truth. When Karen prepares to move and invites Kevin to come with her, he is strong enough to decline, realizing it would never work. The day she is to leave, Karen takes Wren out to celebrate her birthday. As she listens distantly to Karen's attempts to explain her past, Wren realizes her mother is trying to help her make the decisions Karen "didn't know how to make." Then, just as

B

43

Kevin begins to regain confidence and emotional strength, his father's illness returns. As he feeds and cares for the listless man, Kevin realizes he will always love him. After a small family birthday celebration, Sam and Wren talk. Wren confesses that "sometimes I can't see room for anything but music." Sam recognizes the conflict, the ambition Wren shares with her mother, but thinks their relationship can weather it. That day Karen calls, and Kevin requests a real, honest talk with her when they meet again at Thanksgiving. Then it is Saturday again and Bliss prepares to return the children's father to the hospital. This time Kevin decides to accompany her and Wren.

In this complex story of loss and change, a brother and sister come to accept and understand their parents. In so doing, they learn much about themselves and their power to shape their own futures. The strong bond between the two, partially in response to their shared loss, shows up time and again in their concern for and sensitivity to one another. Though they want to help each other, in the end they each must work through their own conflicts—Kevin his depression that so resembles his father's, Wren her ambition, so like her mother's. Only when they accept themselves can they be a real support to one another.

Ages 12 and up

**Also available in:**
Cassette—*Notes for Another Life*
Library of Congress (NLSBPH)

Paperbound—*Notes for Another Life*
Bantam Books, Inc.

## 76

**Brochmann, Elizabeth**

**What's the Matter, Girl?**

Harper & Row, Publishers, Inc., 1980.
(121 pages)

---

*EGOCENTRISM*
*LOSS: Feelings of*
  *Change: resisting*
  *Family: relationships*
  *Mental illness*
  *War*

---

It has been four years since Uncle Arion left Vancouver to fight in World War II. Now he'll be home in a week, and thirteen-year-old Anna is camped on her German-born grandparents' front porch, anxiously awaiting her favorite uncle's return. Even though his last letters to her are more than a year old, dating from just before the war ended, Anna refuses to believe that anything is wrong. She ignores the attempted warnings from Gemma, her young aunt, and blocks out the whispering of other family members as they prepare for Arion's homecoming. During the tense week of waiting Anna remembers the fun she and Arion, her handsome prince, used to have. She remembers how he rode her around on his shoulders, how the three of them—she, Arion, and her brother, Marsh—enjoyed the salmon

run, how she confided in Arion, how he made her feel special and pretty even though she knew she was awkward. Anna remembers his letters: how he answered all her intimate questions and told her more than she wanted to know of war; how she ached for him when his girlfriend stopped writing; how she cried when his best friend at the front was killed. As the homecoming day approaches, tension builds and the traffic in and out of the family home increases. Everyone has some comment for Anna—most are annoyed with her for just sitting—but her beloved Gramps, always her champion, tells them to leave her alone. At one point Anna, enraged by Gemma's self-righteous advice, becomes hysterical and hits her grandmother. Anna is frightened by her own behavior and by the uncharacteristic way those around her are behaving. Finally, the family gathers around the gate as the taxi arrives. Anna waits on the porch steps, ready to leap into Arion's arms. She watches as Arion, dressed in white, is guided to the house by a man who is also dressed in white. Anna is shocked at Arion's dazed, unseeing appearance. Still she runs to him, grabs him, tells him to look at her, his favorite niece; but he seems not to hear. Even Gramps must choke back tears as Arion is guided inside. Anna retreats to her own front porch and will not be comforted by anyone. She feels betrayed, cannot believe what has happened, and will not visit Arion. Time passes. One day Marsh hands her a packet of letters—tortured, irrational letters—that Arion wrote him from the hospital. Nobody told Marsh what had happened to Arion either; he just knew when he read the letters. Tired of his sister's self-pity and lonely for a companion, Marsh teases her and she comes back to life and reacts normally. When Marsh brings Arion over to see her, she is able to greet him cordially. But when she is out walking the next day, Anna stands near the barbed wire fence around her grandparents' field and watches Arion, set out in his wheelchair in the sun. "I won't come, not until you ask for me!" she screams, grabbing the wire. Anna despairs at the thought of Arion becoming a fixture, of family routines developing around him. She realizes that "we will never be the same again—none of us."

In this unsettling first-person narrative, a young girl with a romantic view of her youthful uncle must come to grips with his shell-shocked condition when he returns from World War II. Anna gradually sheds her self-centered anger at the change in Uncle Arion and at the varying responses of family members to Arion's plight. She comes to see that all are suffering and that nothing will be the same again. The book is organized in a "countdown" of chapters leading to Arion's actual homecoming. Each chapter is filled with flashbacks to happy times with Arion and to his letters from the war, providing hints of the man's condition that Anna doesn't understand. This is a study of people and their reactions to family trouble, appealing to the mature reader.

Ages 12 and up

**Also available in:**
No other form known

**Brooks, Jerome**

## The Big Dipper Marathon

E. P. Dutton & Company, Inc., 1979.
(134 pages) o.p.

---

*SELF, ATTITUDE TOWARD: Accepting*
  *Braces on body/limbs*
  *Communication: parent-child*
  *Differences, human*
  *Parental: overprotection*
  *Visiting*

---

Horace Zweig, called Ace, his legs paralyzed and his hands weak and disfigured by polio, has tried for years to cope with his limits and frustrations. Now fifteen, he has been "mainstreamed" at school; both there and at home he is told he can do anything he wants. Still, his parents intercept mail they think will disturb him, friends at school seem uneasy with him, and his limitations make him angry. When summer vacation begins his parents arrange for him to visit relatives in Chicago, his first trip alone. Ace is thrilled by his first plane ride, but bothered when his relatives don't know what to make of his handicap. They've brought a wheelchair to take him through the airport. He never uses a wheelchair and is angered and insulted. When he suggests they go ahead and he'll catch up, his aunt replies, "We treat our guests to what they're entitled to. So either we slow down to keep up with you, or you get on that wheelchair and keep up with us!" He gets on the chair. Soon Ace and the family can speak openly. He and his cousin BC become friends, BC sympathetic, Ace realizing that BC's acne and long nose are handicaps in their own ways. When BC's pretty friend Clarissa Schwartz suggests a trip to an amusement park, Ace is eager to go and ride the Big Dipper roller coaster, although he knows this plan worries BC and his family. Late one night, when Ace tries to stand without braces, he falls noisily. His aunt hears him and comes to help him up. He insists that he can be like anyone else. She replies, "What's the big deal about being like everyone?" At the amusement park, riding bumper cars, Ace is exultant, although he has difficulty getting in and out of the cars. When BC refuses to go on the Big Dipper, Ace and Clarissa ride it together. When the exciting ride is nearly over he kisses her. But he can't move fast enough to get off the car when it slows down. After three nightmarish rides, Ace is finally helped to get off. He admits that he has gone beyond the boundaries set by his handicap. Leaving the park, they pass near the carousel. The music lifts Ace from his depression and the three ride it twice, Ace in the middle. When the visit to Chicago ends, Ace and Clarissa agree to write one another. BC is to return the visit, and BC's parents will attend Ace's graduation in two years. On the plane, Ace is able to accept help graciously. At home a letter from BC arrives, but Ace can tell that the envelope has been steamed open. His parents have again intercepted his mail. He manages to divert an angry scene by acknowledging that they were just looking out for his interests. All three finally admit that Ace is different, that his handicap does in fact keep him from doing what everybody else does. His father admits, "Okay, you've got a . . . you've got . . . you've got a problem that makes you different. Now where do we go from here?"

With the help of sympathetic relatives, a disabled boy and his overprotective parents learn to be realistic about his needs and limitations as well as his strengths and potential. Ace tells his story candidly, seriously, but with touches of humor, and the reader becomes well acquainted with him. The dialogue is a bit contrived and stilted, but this doesn't make the characterizations unbelievable. The story provides a clear, instructive look at the life of a disabled teenage boy.

Ages 11-14

**Also available in:**
Paperbound—*The Big Dipper Marathon*
Pocket Books, Inc.

## 78

**Brooks, Jerome**

## Make Me a Hero

E. P. Dutton & Company, Inc., 1980.
(152 pages) o.p.

---

*INFERIORITY, FEELINGS OF*
  *Bully: being bothered by*
  *Courage, meaning of*
  *Death: of friend*
  *Friendship: meaning of*
  *Jealousy: peer*
  *Jewish*

---

In 1943, twelve-year-old Jacob (Jake) Ackerman's three brothers are drafted, leaving Jake feeling even more useless and helpless than usual. He thinks often of Chris Petropolous, his friend when both were seven, who climbed to the top of a telephone pole on a dare and plunged to his death. Chris has become an immortal hero to Jake, the epitome of all that is brave. As for Jake, he recalls with horror and humiliation the day not long ago when Howie Woscowicz and his buddies forced him inside a trash can and urinated on him. His self-contempt returns as they waylay him after school and beat him up. In spite of his black eye and torn fingernail, he walks into Mr. Gold's desk-pad shop and nervously applies for a job. A job will prove to everyone that he is a man, he believes. To his amazement, Mr. Gold hires him on the spot. Jake works hard at making desk pads, embracing Mr. Gold's philosophy: "Make everything into something." Soon he and his employer develop a special friendship. Jake makes another friend at Gold's, a boy named Harry Katz who swaggers and brags just as Jake longs to. Jake decides that his new image demands a pair of high-topped boots with a knife pocket like his brothers wear. He must also train for his Bar Mitzvah, as Harry is doing. Jake's regard for Harry is tarnished somewhat the day they unexpectedly meet up with Howie and his gang. Harry turns tail and runs with a disgusted Jake following, straight into the nearby Hebrew school. At the top of a narrow stairwell, Harry grabs the fire extinguisher and gets rid of Howie by shooting jets of foam at him. Jake is relieved to be safe, but would have preferred a fair fight. He perseveres with his Bar Mitzvah training, however, tutored by

Harry, even though the rabbi and his fellow students torment him for being a late starter. When his brother Max is wounded, Jake helps calm his hysterical mother; though he is proud of the Purple Heart Max is awarded, a renewed sense of dissatisfaction with himself washes over him. It helps when Mr. Gold chooses him from among all the employees to create a special desk pad ordered for a general, but when Jake sees that Harry is jealous he tries to give the job to him. Mr. Gold won't allow it. In a last effort to retain Harry's friendship, Jake promises to come to his house early on the morning of his Bar Mitzvah to help him practice his speech. After a sleepless night, he gets up before dawn, dons his new boots, and walks eight blocks through a blizzard. He arrives soaked, cold, and exhausted to discover that Harry has forgotten him and is still sleeping. Jake waits outside, trying to get Harry's attention for quite some time before the boy wakes up. After this, Jake renounces Harry. He develops pneumonia from his exposure to the storm and in his fevered delirium apologizes to Howie for the fire-extinguisher attack. Although he has his Bar Mitzvah six months later, Jake now knows that a gold medal, even a Bar Mitzvah medal, does not make a man. Realizing that he only went through the training because of Harry, not because he really believed in it, he buries his medal at the base of the pole where Chris Petropolous died, thinking, "You're more one of the Chosen People than I am." Newly content to be himself and to live life as best he can, Jake is aware that Chris's central place in his thoughts is finally fading.

This is a well-told, absorbing novel of a young boy's sense of worthlessness in the face of a world crisis he can do nothing about, a crisis mirrored by his struggles against bullies and false friends. As Jake strives to find his niche in the strained atmosphere of World War II America, he grows painfully to the realization that a person's value has less to do with actions and words than with subtler qualities of character. There is more than one kind of hero. Readers will sympathize with his realistically presented travails.

Ages 9-12

**Also available in:**
No other form known

## 79

**Brown, Marc Tolan**

### Arthur Goes to Camp

Color illustrations by the author.
The Atlantic Monthly Press, 1982.
(32 pages counted)

---

*CAMP EXPERIENCES*
 *Homesickness*
 *Running away*
 *Success*

---

Arthur's parents tell him of the fun he will have at Camp Meadowcroak, but Arthur the aardvark is determined not to go. Even though his friends get on the bus with him, Arthur is unhappy. When they pass Camp Horsewater, Meadowcroak's rival in the traditional scavenger hunt, and see all the tough-looking campers

there, Arthur's distress increases. He even writes his parents a letter on the bus, telling them he is already homesick. The campers arrive and meet their counselors. Arthur finds the girls' counselor sweet and understanding, but the boys' counselor seems mean and demanding. That night the boys discover frogs in their beds and are sure the girls did it. Arthur writes home complaining about the food. In sports the girls beat the boys at everything, and as campers they are even better. Arthur continues to send home sad postcards. Then strange things begin to happen. The girls discover a smoke bomb in their tent. The boys' clothes are stolen. Everyone begins hearing strange noises at night. Arthur writes home that camp gives him the creeps. One night all the campers decide to stand watch. They soon discover that campers from Camp Horsewater are causing all the trouble. Camp Meadowcroak vows revenge. Arthur writes home vowing to run away. During the scavenger hunt he takes his backpack and a flashlight and leaves. The Meadowcroak campers scare their opponents by dressing up one of their members in a fur coat so he looks like a bear. It gets dark and all Meadowcroak needs to win is a flashlight. But there is no flashlight and no Arthur. In fact, Arthur is lost. But his friends find him—he is using the flashlight to light his way—and he helps them win the scavenger hunt. After this victory, Arthur writes home to announce, "Camp is great. I want to come back next year."

Arthur the aardvark is woefully unhappy at camp until he becomes the hero of the scavenger hunt. Then he decides camp isn't so bad after all. Bold, colorful illustrations, the amusing progression of Arthur's letters home, and the familiar camp experiences will delight the read-aloud audience. This is one of several stories about Arthur the aardvark and his animal friends.

Ages 5-8

**Also available in:**
No other form known

## 80

**Brown, Marc Tolan**

### Arthur's Eyes

Color illustrations by the author.
Little, Brown and Company, 1979.
(32 pages)

---

*GLASSES, WEARING OF*
 *Appearance: concern about*
 *Name-calling*
 *Peer relationships: peer pressures*

---

Arthur the aardvark, a second grader, is having trouble seeing the books he reads and the blackboard at school. Sometimes he has headaches. His friends—a rabbit, a cat, a chimpanzee, a dog, and a moose—are becoming irritated because Arthur is constantly asking for help. He ruins their basketball games because he can't see the basket. Then Arthur gets glasses. Now he can see. He loves wearing his glasses until some of his schoolmates begin calling him "four eyes" and "sissy." So Arthur tries to get along without his glasses. He even tries to lose them. When he walks into the girls' lavatory at school because he can't see the sign on the door, he causes a huge screaming scene. The principal understands what Arthur is going through and reassures him about wearing glasses. Finally, Arthur learns to accept his need for glasses. He even begins to feel proud of them.

Although the text and illustrations are funny, children who are sensitive about wearing glasses will identify with Arthur the aardvark's mixed emotions. Children who don't wear glasses may begin to understand the feelings of those who do. The characters, all animals, are delightfully illustrated. This is one of several stories about Arthur and his friends.

Ages 4-7

**Also available in:**
Paperbound—*Arthur's Eyes*
Avon Books

## 81

**Bruna, Dick**

## When I'm Big

Color illustrations by the author.
Methuen, Inc., 1981.
(25 pages counted)

---

*MATURATION*
 *Careers: planning*
 *Identity, search for*

---

Two very young children consider what they'll do and be when they are older. They plan to be a racing skater, a gardener, a dancer; to learn judo, play the flute, go swimming. "When I'm big," one child concludes, "I'm going to do lots of things."

Two little children list the things they'll be and do in the near future and also in adulthood. Each plan, such as "I'll do gymnastics," is illustrated on the opposite page in vivid colors. The boy and girl, virtually indistinguishable in many pictures, propose positive, active future activities.

Ages 2-4

**Also available in:**
No other form known

## 82

**Buchan, Stuart**

## A Space of His Own

Charles Scribner's Sons, 1979.
(197 pages) o.p.

---

*FAMILY: Relationships*
*IDENTITY, SEARCH FOR*
 *Maturation*
 *Responsibility: accepting*

---

At the age of eighteen, Michael Carver is being released from the state correctional farm where he has served an eighteen-month sentence for holding up a pharmacy. His father, Sam Carver, hard-working owner of a small construction company, meets Michael at the gates and takes his son to the beautiful home he shares with his young second wife, Betsy. Betsy greets Michael cordially, but Michael is aloof. He has resented his father ever since he divorced his mother nine years ago to marry Betsy. Through those years, Michael let his bitterness get him into trouble; he made new friends, they started stealing, and he ended up at the correctional farm. Now his mother wants his father to take some responsibility for Michael. As they discuss the past, Mr. Carver demands an explanation for Michael's conduct all those years. Michael replies that when his father left his family for Betsy, Michael lost respect for him, his mother, even himself. He says he is not sorry for all the trouble he has caused both parents, only sorry he got caught. Angry, his father tells Michael he may stay only until he can find a job and a place of his own. Michael walks out. On the highway he gets picked up by a disheveled drifter named Merriweather, who drives him to an employment agency. Michael is hired by Christine Trask, a seventeen-year-old girl who owns her own landscaping business. His first job will be working with Christine in the gardens of the estate belonging to Granowska, an old woman who lives in seclusion with an elderly manservant. Michael loves the work. After receiving his first paycheck, he goes out to find a place to live. He runs into Merriweather, who tells him he won't be able to afford anything on his own. Reluctantly, Michael agrees to live with Merriweather in his run-down shack in the mountains. The next morning, Merriweather insists on driving Michael to Granowska's. He drives right up to the door, although Michael asks him not to. Granowska comes out, furious at this intrusion. She tells Christine never to come back; Christine in turn fires Michael. Merriweather considers the whole situation a joke. He convinces Michael to help him rob Granowska, and the two go back at night to look the place over. But Michael has second thoughts about the proposed robbery. The next day, Betsy comes to the shack to bring Michael some clean clothes. She invites them to dinner, during which Michael sees that Merriweather is rude, gluttonous, crude. He realizes how similar his own behavior has been over the years. Mr. Carver throws Merriweather out of the house and demands that Michael get his belongings out of Merriweather's shack. He takes Michael there, but Merriweather is gone—and so is his gun. Michael knows immediately where he's gone, and he and his father rush over to Granowska's estate. In the struggle to protect the old people, Mr. Carver gets shot; Merriweather escapes. After his father is rushed to the hospital with a shoulder wound, Michael calls his mother. But she refuses to come, telling him he must call Betsy. Michael finally accepts the fact that the little family unit of nine years ago does not exist anymore. He tries to comfort Betsy and decides to forgive his father, to make up to him all the years he has tried to punish him. Mr. Carver replies that a gunshot wound is a small price to pay if he gets his son back. Later, Christine Trask offers Michael her friendship and Granowska comes by to say she has spoken favorably of him to the police. Relieved, Michael is ready at last to begin a new life. As Granowska says, "Nothing goes on unchanged forever. . . . Life is change."

A young man for whom anger and bitterness have become a way of life regains his self-respect and learns to accept responsibility for himself. When he forgives his father for deserting him, he forgives himself for being deserted. A real sense of family emerges here through the absorbing development of relationships among the people in Michael's life. This is a fast-paced, realistic slice of life.

Ages 12 and up

**Also available in:**
No other form known

## 83

**Buerger, Jane**

## Obedience

Color illustrations by Helen Endres.
Children's Press, Inc., 1981.
(29 pages)

---

*DISCIPLINE, MEANING OF*

---

Obedience is turning off the television when Mom or Dad says to. It's staying off the roller coaster at the amusement park, even though your parents would never know you disobeyed them. When Dad says the dog can't come inside at night, obedience is not sneaking him in anyway. It's obeying even when nobody can see whether you do or not. Making your bed and hanging up your clothes as you've been asked is also obedience. When the teacher asks you to line up, obedience means taking your place instead of running to the front of the line. Obedience means stopping for a red light, even though you're trying to catch up with your friend on the other side of the street. When you have a baby-sitter, obedience means going to bed when you're supposed to instead of begging to stay up longer. It's staying inside as your mother told you to when all your friends are playing outside. Obedience is following classroom rules even when you have a substitute teacher. Waiting for the crossing guard to say you can cross the street is also obedience.

Part of a series for the very young about behavior and feelings, this extremely simple, colorfully illustrated book provides repetition and reinforcement of a basic concept—in this case, obedience. The book ends with the question, "Can you think of other ways to be obedient?" and may stimulate discussion for this age group.

Ages 3-6

**Also available in:**
No other form known

## 84

**Bulla, Clyde Robert**

## Almost a Hero

Black/white illustrations by Ben Stahl.
E. P. Dutton & Company, Inc., 1981.
(40 pages)

---

*CHILDREN'S HOME, LIVING IN*
  *Boy-girl relationships*
  *Child abuse*
  *Orphan*
  *Revenge*

---

At the age of six, Chiefie, so named because once when he was very small he played an Indian with chicken feathers in his hair, is sent to the Oakdale School for orphans. The boy's father deserted the family when Chiefie was an infant, and now his mother is dead. The superintendent at Oakdale, Mr. Hatfield, takes an early dislike to Chiefie after the boy sees him slip and fall on an icy sidewalk, and he proceeds to make life miserable for him. At one point, Hatfield has Chiefie locked up without food in a small space under the stairs. The boy has one ally, a teacher named Mrs. Janis. When Chiefie accidentally burns a hole in one of his two shirts, she lies to protect him. Chiefie's best friend among the children is Maggie, but when she is taken out of the school, he doesn't know and can't find out where she's gone. Mr. Hatfield sends Chiefie to The Farm, a place of detention for incorrigible children. There he lives in fear of the older boys, who at one point use him for a football and cause him to require ten stitches in his head. Chiefie is eventually returned to Oakdale, where he graduates from high school and gets a job in a gas station. He stays with kindly looking Mrs. Deal, who turns out to be a friend of Mr. Hatfield's. She offers to keep part of his pay for him so he'll have a nest egg when he leaves. But when he asks for the money she insists he never gave her any. When he protests she calls Mr. Hatfield, and together they threaten to tell the police that Chiefie is trying to rob Mrs. Deal. He knows the police will believe them so he just leaves, but promises revenge. After serving in the navy, Chiefie returns to Oakdale School, determined to make Mr. Hatfield squirm. But he learns that his enemy was dismissed when he beat a boy and the boy's family sued the school. At Mrs. Deal's he finds his old friend Maggie, now a nurse. She is caring for Mrs. Deal, who's had a stroke. Chiefie believed nothing could stop him from unburdening his mind to Mrs. Deal and Mr. Hatfield. But when he sees the sick old woman lying in bed, he knows he can't vent his anger. If Mr. Hatfield were there, he realizes, he couldn't have said the words to him either. Mrs. Deal mumbles "good boy" to Chiefie. But he is no longer interested in talking to her. He wants to talk to Maggie.

In this tightly written, well-illustrated book, a young man narrates his return to the orphanage where he was abused and to the woman who swindled him out of his earnings. Chiefie finds his planned revenge meaningless; readers will find his story compelling, if almost painful to read. This is a Skinny Book, part of a series designed for older readers with limited reading skills. These well-written books focus on the interests and concerns of today's young people and should have great appeal.

Ages 11 and up

**Also available in:**
No other form known

**85**

Bulla, Clyde Robert

## Daniel's Duck

Color illustrations by Joan Sandin.
Harper & Row, Publishers, Inc., 1979.
(64 pages)

---

*CREATIVITY*
*TALENTS: Artistic*
  *Appalachia*
  *Pride/False pride*

---

It is the early 1900s. In the mountains of Tennessee,
where young Daniel and his family live, wood carving is
an art and Henry Pettigrew is the acclaimed master.
Inspired by Mr. Pettigrew's lifelike animals, Daniel
decides to carve something for the spring fair. But it isn't
until late in the winter, after the rest of the family are
well into their projects, that Daniel starts on his block of
wood. His father makes moccasins, his mother sews a
quilt, his brother carves a box, and Daniel carves a duck.
He makes his duck different from most, however; his
duck is looking back. His brother insists the head is
backward, but his father encourages him to do it his
own way. Daniel is very proud of his duck. Spring and
the fair come, and the family rides the wagon to town.
The father takes their handmade articles to the town
hall. When the hall opens, Daniel heads for the wood
carvings and joins the other onlookers in admiring a
deer made by Henry Pettigrew. He is puzzled when he
hears people laughing, but then realizes they are laughing at his duck. Hurt, then angry, he grabs the duck and
runs down to the river. He starts to throw the duck in,
but a man stops him. The man tells Daniel that the
people really liked his duck; they laughed because the
duck made them feel good. Daniel is not convinced. The
man suggests they sit and rest. He asks Daniel if he
would be willing to sell the duck, and Daniel wonders
who would buy it. Some passing children greet the man
and call him by name—Henry Pettigrew. Daniel looks
again at his duck and now believes it must be good.
Henry wants to buy the duck, but Daniel will not sell it.
Instead, he shyly gives it to the master.

A little boy, proud of his first attempt at wood carving, is
hurt by the reaction of others to his work. An older,
more accomplished carver helps him to appreciate his
work anew and understand the laughter it encourages.
Appalachian life, while secondary to the story itself, is
represented at its authentic best in the softly shaded
illustrations touched with color. This is an "I Can Read"
book, appropriate for young readers.

Ages 5-8

**Also available in:**
Paperbound—*Daniel's Duck*
Harper & Row, Publishers, Inc.

**86**

Bulla, Clyde Robert

## Last Look

Black/white illustrations by Emily Arnold McCully.
Thomas Y. Crowell Company, Inc., 1979.
(81 pages)

---

*PEER RELATIONSHIPS*
  *Aggression*
  *Rejection: peer*
  *Revenge*
  *School: transfer*

---

Monica and her friends Fran and Audrey attend
Madame Vere's summer school for girls. The three are
annoyed to find a new student, Rhoda, attaching herself
to their group. Monica knows that Madame Vere
approves of the way they have apparently made friends
with the new girl, so she rather grudgingly tolerates
Rhoda. Sometimes the girls play a childhood game: last
look. When two of them leave each other, one gets the
other's attention and yells "last look." Then the other
must try to attract the first one's glance. The object for
the person who yelled "last look" is not to look. One
day, Madame Vere asks for volunteers to play the roles
in *Beauty and the Beast,* the school play. Everyone
wants Monica to play Beauty, but Rhoda, daughter of an
actress, insists there should be tryouts. Although Rhoda
gives a better reading than Monica, the girls all insist
that Monica be given the part anyway. As they walk
home together, Rhoda tells the others that she never
really wanted the part. As Monica turns into her yard,
she yells "last look" at Rhoda. Behind her she hears
Rhoda yelling for help, but she is determined not to lose
the game and so doesn't turn around. The next day
Rhoda's grandmother stops by Monica's house looking
for Rhoda, who has not been home since the day before.
She suspects that Rhoda has taken a bus to be with her
mother in New York. That night, as Monica sleeps in her
tent in the yard, she is awakened by a noise. She finds a
note telling her that Rhoda is in danger and that she is to
go alone to the deserted Fenwick house—the haunted
house—at midnight on Tuesday. Monica shows her
mother the note and her mother calls the sheriff. He,
however, is skeptical. The next day, Rhoda is still not at
school. That night at midnight, the sheriff goes by the
haunted house but finds nothing. Then Monica receives
another note saying she has one more chance to save
her friend. Late that night, she steals out of the house
and goes to the Fenwick place. Suddenly a figure tries to
blindfold her, but she manages to unmask it. It's Rhoda.
She explains that her disappearance started out as a
response to the game, but that she really hates Monica.
She tries to push Monica into a nearby well, and they
both fall in. It's not very deep and the muddy bottom is
soft. Rhoda apologizes. Monica tries to get out by standing on Rhoda's back, planning to push herself out and
then help Rhoda escape. But Rhoda wants to stand on
Monica's back instead. Once she's out, however, Rhoda
replaces the well cover over Monica and shouts down,
"Last look!" Much later, the sheriff and Monica's
mother come to rescue her. Having found her bed
empty and the note beside it, her mother had contacted
the sheriff. They caught Rhoda as she was running

**B**

away and made her tell them where Monica was. Later they learn that Rhoda's mother has been sent for and is to take Rhoda home with her. When Monica goes back to school, she finds another new girl. Shaken by her experience, she wonders whether the girl will turn out to be friend or foe. She is sure of one thing: she will keep an open mind until she knows.

A girl extends a reluctant hand of friendship to a new-comer and comes in for the new girl's violent attempt at revenge for the rejection she feels. Monica, unnerved by the dangerous behavior she evoked in Rhoda, resolves to be more genuinely open to new people in the future. Rhoda's extreme reaction, however, is seen to stem from deep-seated problems she brought with her; her lack of acceptance by Monica and her circle merely served as the catalyst. This is a rather suspenseful story that could stimulate discussion of how damaging peer rejection can be. Line drawings amplify the strong feelings of the characters.

Ages 8-10

**Also available in:**
No other form known

## 87

Bulla, Clyde Robert

### Poor Boy, Rich Boy

Color illustrations by Marcia Sewall.
Harper & Row, Publishers, Inc., 1982.
(63 pages)

---

ORPHAN
   Freedom, meaning of
   Life style: change in
   Love, meaning of
   Relatives: living in home of
   Values/Valuing: materialistic

---

During the war, when Coco was a baby, a soldier found him lying next to the road near some bombed buildings. The soldier couldn't keep Coco and so gave him to a woman named Rosa, whose home had been partially destroyed by bombs. Rosa took the gold ring from the baby's finger and sold it to buy food. Now she works at a bakery and Coco, about seven, helps her. They are poor. She knows his parents may still be alive and will some-day come for him. So she believes they must not grow too fond of one another. One day a man comes to the bakery and inquires about Coco, explaining that he is the boy's uncle and had given him the ring. He also reveals that Coco's parents died in the war. The man hugs Coco and says, "I was all alone. Now I have you, and you have me." Before taking Coco to his large home in the country, Uncle Paul offers Rosa money, which she refuses. He tells Coco he can have anything he wants. Coco wants only to walk alone in the woods. Uncle Paul says Coco needs clothes and buys him boxes and boxes of them. Because Coco has never seen the sea, Uncle Paul takes him there, and Coco sees horses running free along the beach. He loves watching them, especially one small white horse running with its mother. Several days later Uncle Paul surprises Coco with the white colt. But Coco is troubled that the horse

has been separated from its mother and denied its free-dom. That night the boy packs the few belongings he brought with him and sneaks out to release the horse. Uncle Paul appears and asks Coco to explain himself. He wants the horse to be free, says Coco, and he wants to return to Rosa if she will have him. Uncle Paul agrees to return the horse to the wild, but the next morning he tells Coco he wants him to stay. Coco realizes that Rosa may not want him, that Uncle Paul has said, "But I want you." Uncle Paul tells Coco he may walk in the woods, something the boy has never gotten around to doing. He asks his uncle to come too. They both feel happy.

A young war orphan raised by a poor woman is adopted by a rich uncle. Coco must learn to adjust to a life of luxury, and Uncle Paul must learn to respect Coco's simple needs. This is an especially well-done and rather offbeat easy reader that emphasizes the impor-tance of people and relationships over material posses-sions. Simple drawings help express the feelings of the man and boy and illustrate the differences in their backgrounds.

Ages 5-8

**Also available in:**
No other form known

## 88

Bunting, Anne Evelyn

### The Big Red Barn

Black/white illustrations by Howard Knotts.
Harcourt Brace Jovanovich, Inc., 1979.
(31 pages)

---

CHANGE: Accepting
   Security/Insecurity
   Stepparent: mother

---

For a young boy, the big red barn on his family's farm is a warm, friendly place filled with pleasant memories and a sense of permanence. It is where his younger sister keeps her pet goat, where the hens and pet rooster live, and where the kangaroo mice have built their nest hidden from a hungry barn owl. Despite the boy's objections, the sister shows this nest to Emma, their new stepmother. In the barn too is the hayloft, the boy's special hiding place. He remembers how he went there to cry when his mother died and how he hid there when his father brought Emma home. He wonders why they always paint the barn red and his grandfather gives him the best answer: "Red's the easiest color to see." Then one night the barn catches fire and is destroyed even before the fire engines arrive. Thinking of what he has lost, the boy begins to cry, realizing "that I had no place to go now when I needed to cry." In a few days a new, prefabricated aluminum barn is put into place. The boy hates it. So do the animals. "Change is hard. They'll take to it in time," Emma says. The boy fiercely disagrees and runs to the river, where he is soon joined by his grandfather. They talk about painting the barn red, but the boy feels it will never be the same. His grandfather agrees. "The new barn has to make its own place. It will if we give it a chance." The boy knows his grandfather is referring as much to Emma as the barn. When he real-izes that he, like his grandfather, will never forget the past, he feels calmer. He shows his acceptance of the new barn when he says, "I expect silver's the next best color for a barn after red."

In this first-person story, the family barn symbolizes the permanence and security a young boy longs for after the death of his mother and the arrival of his stepmother. When the barn is destroyed, the boy feels doubly threatened. Through the help of his understanding grandfather, he comes to accept the new barn and his new stepmother. Softly defined illustrations emphasize the tender tone of this subtle beginning reader. But because of its subtlety, young readers may need help interpreting the story.

Ages 4-7

**Also available in:**
Paperbound—*The Big Red Barn*
Harcourt Brace Jovanovich, Inc.

## 89

Bunting, Anne Evelyn

**The Empty Window**
Black/white illustrations by Judy Clifford.
Frederick Warne & Company, Inc., 1980.
(46 pages counted)

---

*DEATH: of Friend*
  *Fear: of death*
  *Friendship: meaning of*
  *Sibling: relationships*

---

Seventh-grader C.G. and his eight-year-old brother, Sweeney, want to give a special present to their friend Joe Rizzio, who has been terminally ill for a year and is now close to death. The three boys live in the same California apartment building, and C.G. knows that Joe likes to watch the red-headed Amazon parrots that nest in trees outside his window. C.G. has already made four attempts to trap one of the parrots for Joe. Now, after observing them so often that he knows their habits, he and Sweeney are determined to catch the bird they call Tag-Along Charlie, a misfit from which the flock keeps its distance. Taking a net and heavy gloves, C.G. climbs a tree, crawls across to a drainpipe running up the side of a house, and hauls himself up to the roof. When the birds fly by, C.G. throws the net over Tag-Along. Net and bird fall to the ground and C.G. clambers down. Trying to get the bird into a box, he forgets to put on the gloves and the parrot tears at his hands. C.G. does manage to get Tag-Along into the box, his mother bandages his hands while Sweeney eases the bird into the cage C.G. bought at the Salvation Army, and the two boys take their gift over to Joe's apartment. They plan simply to leave the bird with Joe's parents, but Joe's father insists they take it in to Joe themselves. C.G. hasn't been able to bring himself to visit Joe for some time. He's afraid "he'll look the way he does in my nightmares, with a skeleton head and a skeleton smile. . . . What do you say to someone who's dying?" Now the boy is shocked to realize that he has captured the parrot to "keep [Joe] company so I wouldn't have to. The parrot was to get me off the hook." Once with Joe, however, C.G. is no longer afraid. He presents the bird to Joe, but is surprised when his friend asks him to let Tag-Along

go; the birds mean freedom to Joe and he likes to see them fly. Joe dies that night. C.G. cries when he sees the parrots, because Joe's window is now empty.

A boy gains valuable insights into death in this first-person narrative. He has been afraid to confront his dying friend, but when he does he loses his fear. C.G.'s matter-of-fact storytelling keeps the account from melodrama, and the photograph-like illustrations complement it beautifully. The feelings and relationships, especially the friendship between the brothers, are realistically and sensitively portrayed.

Ages 8-12

**Also available in:**
No other form known

## 90

Bunting, Anne Evelyn

**The Happy Funeral**
Black/white illustrations by Vo-Dinh Mai.
Harper & Row, Publishers, Inc., 1982.
(40 pages)

B

---

*CHINESE-AMERICAN*
*DEATH: of Grandparent*
  *Death: funeral issues*

---

Laura's mother tells Laura and her older sister, May-May, that Grandfather is going to have a happy funeral. May-May protests that a happy funeral is a contradiction in terms, but her mother maintains that when someone is very old and has lived a good life, death is a happy event. That night they all go to the funeral home in Chinatown. There are flowers, incense sticks, and many relatives with gifts for the dead man. Grandmother gives him a map of the spirit world, and Laura's mother gives him a little bag of food for his journey. People burn paper money, a cardboard house, and other things they want Grandfather to have in his new life in the spirit world. May-May burns a picture of a red car with a silver stripe that she thinks Grandfather might like. Laura burns a picture of a dog he had when he was a boy. That night Laura thinks about Grandfather and cries herself to sleep. At the funeral the next day, people tell how Grandfather was an honorable man and taught them so much. Laura remembers all the things she herself learned from him. She notices that Grandmother is holding half a comb and has placed the other half in the casket. Her father explains that when Grandmother and Grandfather meet again, the two parts of the comb can be joined. Laura and her sister see Grandfather in his coffin. He is covered with "colored cloth squares, like a patchwork quilt," made by his daughters to keep him warm. Laura discovers that Grandfather isn't at all scary in his coffin; he is still Grandfather with his familiar smile. At the door of the church a woman hands them candy to sweeten their sorrow. They ride to the cemetery accompanied by a band that plays "jazzed-up" hymns. Laura tries to think of how happy Grandfather is going to be in his new life, but she still feels awful. As they stand near the burial spot, many people cry. Suddenly Laura realizes what had struck her about Grandfather's smile when she looked at him in the coffin: it was a happy smile. She remembers what her mother said about someone who has lived a good life being happy to go. But, Laura reflects, "she never said it was happy for us to have him go."

A little Chinese-American girl gives a first-person account of her grandfather's funeral and puzzles through an apparent contradiction: if Grandfather is so happy to go, why is everyone so sad? The last line of the book resolves the dilemma beautifully and should be of comfort to children who have experienced the death of someone close to them. The descriptions of the wake and funeral are as delicately done as are the fine, shaded pencil illustrations. Chinese customs are presented simply and reverently in this candid, lyrical account.

Ages 5-9

**Also available in:**
No other form known

## 91

**Bunting, Anne Evelyn**

## The Waiting Game

J. B. Lippincott Company, 1981.
(56 pages)

---

FRIENDSHIP: Meaning of
GOALS
  Deafness
  Self, attitude toward: respect

---

Seniors Luther, Griff, and Dan were a formidable trio on their California high school football team, so good that the coach of the Ohio Buckeyes had talked with Luther and Griff at the end of the season. Now both boys are set on playing for Ohio State, and they've turned down many other offers. Dan, who is deaf, does not expect any offers. Instead, he will attend the local junior college and play on its team. The news that a player from their conference has just heard from Ohio sets Luther and Griff on edge. Luther jumps every time the phone rings. When Dan's mother calls, wishing him well and thanking him for all his past help, Luther remembers how well he and Dan played together. He would tap Dan before every play and Dan, trusting him completely, would run to whichever side he signaled. Griff calls, his waiting over: Ohio State wants him. Luther hopes desperately that his call will come on Monday. A bundle of nerves, he leaves the house for a while. The Ohio coach calls while he's out and promises to call back the next day. That is all Luther needs to know. He is sure Ohio wants him too and rushes to tell his friends the good news. Luther senses Dan's disappointment; he knows Dan had hoped he would play with him at Queens, the junior college, but Luther is too happy now to consider Dan's feelings. Then Luther finds out that the celebration has been premature. Ohio State turns him down; he is too small this year. Maybe next year, when he has thirty more pounds on him, they will look at him again. Devastated, without telling anyone what's happened, Luther leaves the apartment to walk and think. When he gets back, his mother and sister are eager to hear the good news. His divorced mother has even made up her mind to ask his father for help with tuition if necessary. Luther, feeling trapped, suddenly sees a way out. He tells them he turned Ohio down. "I'll go to Queens," he says. "I'll stick with Dan." His family and friends are surprised, but they respect his decision. Dan, however, who hates getting special consideration because of his disability, threatens not to play at all. When Luther suddenly blurts out the truth, Dan explodes. "Just because I'm deaf doesn't mean I'm a moron." Luther knows how much Dan loves football, how he plays for the sheer joy and not for any reward. He goes to Dan and explains everything. Just when Luther and Dan are set to play together, Luther receives an attractive offer from another school. He considers it for a few minutes and then decides against it—not because of Dan, he tells himself, but "because he needed to stay free."

A boy's fierce desire for a football scholarship and his bitter disappointment when it doesn't come through threaten his relationship with a good friend. Luther only recovers his self-respect when he admits that he's used loyalty to Dan, whose deafness takes him out of the running for scholarships but who loves to play football, to cover up his own failure. Limited vocabulary but mature, complex themes make this an excellent, suspenseful, high-interest book even for older reluctant readers.

Ages 10 and up

**Also available in:**
No other form known

## 92

**Burch, Robert Joseph**

## Ida Early Comes Over the Mountain

The Viking Press, Inc., 1980.
(145 pages)

---

DIFFERENCES, HUMAN
  Family: relationships
  Love, meaning of
  Peer relationships: peer pressures

---

It is the end of the Depression in the Blue Ridge Mountains of Georgia. One day, Ida Early appears on the doorstep of the Sutton house looking for work. Since Mrs. Sutton died several months ago, Mr. Sutton and his four children, Randall, eleven, Ellen, twelve, and the twins Clay and Dewey, five, have been under the domination of Aunt Ernestine, Mr. Sutton's testy sister. Aunt Ernestine feels the very tall, plain, ruddy-faced Ida is too eccentric to hire, with her patchwork shirt, baggy brown sweater, overalls, and clodhoppers. But Mr. Sutton watches the children with Ida and comments, "The children are happy for the first time in months." He hires her. The Sutton children soon make the lively, playful Ida their hero; she has been tiddly-wink champion of the world, she tells them, cook on a pirate ship, tamer of wild lions. Randall doubts that anything could ever get the best of Ida. But it does. Ida goes to the children's school one day and is ridiculed by their friends for her strange appearance. The Sutton children do not come to her aid. After this incident, Ida stops wearing her baggy, patched overalls and buys a skirt.

She tries to curl her stringy hair. She becomes withdrawn. The children come to realize how they have hurt Ida, how important she is to them, and how ashamed they are at not having helped her when she needed them. They pledge "never again to fail to come to the aid of someone we love." They ask Ida to visit the school again and, after some hesitation, she agrees. She makes a tremendous hit with her rope tricks, and this time the Suttons openly express their affection for her. Then one day Ida moves on, just as she once said she would. The family manages, but misses her terribly. About two months later Ida returns, because she "missed her true friends."

Despite the fact that the story evolves from the mother's death, what unfolds is the sometimes hilarious account of the delightfully eccentric Ida Early's unorthodox approach to managing the Sutton household. But the book also emphasizes the responsibility we have to other people and their feelings. The turning point comes when the children resist peer pressure in favor of honest pride and affection. The book's rapid pace, easy dialogue, and many amusing scenes make it suitable for reading aloud.

Ages 8-10

**Also available in:**
Cassette—*Ida Early Comes Over the Mountain*
Library of Congress (NLSBPH)

Paperbound—*Ida Early Comes Over the Mountain*
Avon Books

## 93

**Butterworth, William Edmund**

**LeRoy and the Old Man**

Four Winds Press, 1980.
(154 pages)

---

*DECISION MAKING*
*VALUES/VALUING: Moral/Ethical*
  *Afro-American*
  *Crime/Criminals*
  *Fear: of physical harm*
  *Gangs: being bothered by*
  *Grandparent: living in home of*
  *Grandparent: respect for*
  *Life style: change in*
  *Responsibility: accepting*

---

Eighteen-year-old LeRoy Chambers sees three members of the Wolves gang mug and stab an old woman in his Chicago housing project. When questioned by police he denies having seen anything, fearing reprisals, but the victim has told police LeRoy was a witness. Threatened by the gang, his family's apartment vandalized, LeRoy takes a bus to New Orleans. There his father's father meets him and takes him to his home in Pass Christian, Mississippi, where he'll stay until the trial is over. His grandfather refuses to mention LeRoy's father's name; he deserted LeRoy and his mother six years ago. When LeRoy explains why he needs to stay far away from Chicago, his grandfather says the place for people who knife old women is behind bars, and he suggests that LeRoy ought to help put them there. The old man is a fisherman and LeRoy, though he feels superior toward his grandfather at first, is soon working

six days a week hauling in nets and then delivering the shrimp and crabs to restaurants and stores in New Orleans. To help him make these deliveries, his grandfather teaches him to drive. They also begin to rebuild the old man's house, which was destroyed by a hurricane. (He now lives in a shack.) They decide to go into business for themselves, buying catches each day and then marketing them. When his grandfather comes home with a panel truck that says, "A. Chambers & Grandson," LeRoy's eyes fill with tears. The day the roof on the house is finished they drink champagne together. Then police officers from Chicago come to get LeRoy's statement about the crime. He is reluctant to get involved, insisting that the Wolves will cut him to pieces if he testifies. He does give his statement, but before he signs it the officers admit that the victim has died and they are now dealing with a murder charge. LeRoy's grandfather promises the officers that LeRoy will testify and he tells the boy he'll protect him, which strikes LeRoy as a bit ludicrous. A few weeks later the local sheriff receives orders to place LeRoy in custody as a material witness. This usually involves jail unless bond is paid. Because the sheriff is a good friend of LeRoy's grandfather, he asks LeRoy for just ten dollars bail, but warns him not to go anywhere. Then one night LeRoy finds his long-missing father waiting for him at one of the restaurants where he delivers shrimp. LeRoy meets him later at his hotel. His father wants him to jump bail and hide out in New York with him and his lady friend. He can't ask for a divorce from LeRoy's mother because she'll want six years' child support if she finds out where he is. LeRoy notes with disgust his father's diamond ring and gold watch. He and his mother have had to scrape by for so long. He excuses himself to use the restroom and ducks out. But his father catches up with him another night, claiming to have inside information that the Wolves don't intend to let LeRoy live long enough to reach the witness stand. Again he urges the boy to come to New York with him. He runs his own little numbers racket, and LeRoy could make some easy money. Knowing that LeRoy disapproves of him, he remarks, "I may not be the father you want, but I'm doing the best I know how." When the call comes for LeRoy to testify before the grand jury, his grandfather buys himself and LeRoy new suits. Now LeRoy has a choice: he can use the money his father gave him and go to New York, or he can return to Chicago and testify. But he realizes that he fears one thing even more than he fears the Wolves: the loss of his grandfather's affection and respect. When the old man takes LeRoy to the airport, he mentions that there will probably be a plane for New York at the St. Louis stop. LeRoy realizes that his grandfather has known all along about his father's visit. The two embrace and weep. LeRoy assures the old man that he'll never go the way of his father.

In this outstanding, memorable story, an inner-city teenager learns that the harsh rules and twisted values he picked up in Chicago don't apply in rural Mississippi. LeRoy arrives at his grandfather's shack a cynical, suspicious product of the ghetto, only to hear the old man insist that there are more good people in the world than the other kind. His grandfather's respectful, deep friendships with black and white people surprise and impress LeRoy, giving him a powerful counterweight to his father's seductive promises of easy money in New

B

53

York. Both LeRoy and his grandfather come vividly alive for the reader in language that is delightfully immediate and colorful. The subtle wit and teasing interplay between the two contribute to the lively, realistic tone of this richly rewarding book.

Ages 12 and up

**Also available in:**
No other form known

## 94

**Butterworth, William Edmund**

**Under the Influence**

Four Winds Press, 1979.
(247 pages)

---

ALCOHOLISM: Adolescent
  Accidents: automobile
  Boy-girl relationships: dating
  Friendship: best friend
  Parent/Parents: single

---

High school seniors Allan Corelli, son of the new police chief and brother of two other police officers, and wealthy Keith Stevens—Keith from a private boarding school—have each transferred to Richard Stockton High—and are vying for halfback positions on the football team. During practice one day, the coach harasses Keith unbearably and Keith punches him in the face. When three players gang up on Keith, Allan comes to his defense; both are thrown off the team. In appreciation for his support, Keith offers Allan a ride home in the classy Mercedes he drives. Allan learns that the Mercedes belonged to Keith's father, who died a year ago. He also learns that his own widowed father has recently met Keith's mother, and as Allan's and Keith's friendship develops, the two parents begin dating. Allan soon discovers that Keith drinks too much beer and has a knack for getting into trouble. When Mr. Corelli gives an engagement party for his oldest son, Paul, Keith gets so drunk Allan has to take him home. A few nights later Keith and Allan go to a party given by a friend of Keith's, Marilyn, whom Allan would like to date. While Allan is getting acquainted with Marilyn, Keith drinks too much and gets in a fight. Allan takes him home again, but Keith doesn't stay there. He passes Allan on his way to a bar and urges him to come along. But Allan, disgusted with Keith, refuses and goes home. On Keith's way back home after drinking a few more beers, his car is struck by a drunk driver, Thomas Waldron. The Mercedes is a total loss, and Keith's knee is badly smashed. When he is released from the hospital, he appoints Allan to chauffeur him in his mother's station wagon. Marilyn often comes along with Allan and brings her friend Helen to be with Keith. Meanwhile, Keith must appear as a witness in Waldron's trial for drunk driving. Waldron's attorney accuses Keith of having been drinking too, and in the end Waldron is acquitted. Yet despite Allan's growing concern, Keith refuses to recognize that he can no longer get along without alcohol. Finally, Keith's mother asks Allan's father for help. Mr. Corelli arranges to have Keith see several graphic, often gruesome driver-education movies about the possible consequences of driving while drunk. Convinced he must and will quit drinking, Keith promises Allan to stay "dry" for six months. For several days, he is successful. But at Paul Corelli's wedding reception, Keith is unbearably tempted by the abundance of alcohol. Reluctant to be seen drinking at the Corellis, he has Helen drive him to a bar. There, Helen too gets drunk and cannot drive the car properly. A police officer sees her weaving down the street and turns on his siren. Keith, hoping to avoid any more run-ins with the law, tells Helen to outrun the officer. She crashes the car into the concrete wall of a viaduct and is killed; Keith is seriously injured. Eventually his physical wounds heal, but Keith, filled with guilt over Helen's death, retreats into himself, staring into space and refusing to speak. His mother commits him to a mental institution, where doctors hope for his recovery "in time."

A teenage boy's alcoholism leads to tragedy for himself and others. Keith's friend, steady, reliable Allan, tells this compelling story with authentic dialogue and enough wit and humor to prevent its becoming maudlin. He includes a believable portrayal of family relationships, showing the Corelli police officers to be responsible, humane public servants. This is a realistic, serious story that demonstrates, without preaching, the dangers of alcoholism.

Ages 12 and up

**Also available in:**
No other form known

## 95

**Byars, Betsy Cromer**

**The Animal, the Vegetable, and John D Jones**

Black/white illustrations by Ruth Sanderson.
Delacorte Press, 1982.
(150 pages)

---

MATURATION
  Arguing
  Change: accepting
  Jealousy: sibling
  Parent/Parents: single
  Peer relationships

---

Sisters Clara and Deanie are looking forward to their vacation alone with their divorced father. When he informs the girls that a widowed friend of his, Delores Jones, and her son, John D, will be sharing the beach house, both are very upset. Meanwhile, John D is totally opposed to a vacation with anyone but his mother. She warns him that he'd better be nice. He will go because he has to, replies John D, and he will "do nothing crude. I will cause you no embarrassment. My perfect behavior will quite possibly make Sam's daughters look like the Wicked Stepsisters." The meeting of the two families is extremely uncomfortable. As Delores and John D approach the beach house they overhear Clara and Deanie sniping at each other but uniting in their derogatory remarks about the two of them. But John D, master of the verbal putdown, feels far superior to the girls, labeling Clara "animal" and Deanie "vegetable." For their part, the sisters vow to make weird John D miserable. He silently vows the same thing but, although he normally enjoys being alone and special, can't help feeling lonely here and out of place. Several days of strain and even open hostility pass. One day the two adults go into town, Clara and Deanie go to the beach, and John D stays on the porch. Clara takes a rubber raft and floats around on the waves near the shore. Feeling at peace for the first time since her vacation started, she falls asleep. Several hours later, John D suddenly notices that Clara is not in sight. He recalls the warning he heard about the dangerous ocean currents in the area and runs to tell Deanie, blaming her for the disaster since she should have been watching her younger sister. The two hitchhike into town and find their parents. Soon the four are at the Coast Guard station awaiting word on Clara's rescue. They get discouraging reports at first and are especially frightened when Clara's empty raft is found. Meanwhile, Clara wakes up to realize she has been swept out to sea. Cold and terrified, she drifts for several more hours, steadily losing hope. Finally she is found by a fishing boat with no radio and returned to her father. Everyone is emotionally drained, and the two girls are told they can go home if they want. Deanie wants to leave, but Clara decides to stay. If she left now, it would be like running away and she would always recall "The Terrible Thing That Broke Up the Vacation." "But," she tells Deanie, "it won't be as terrible if I stay." John D seems happy at her announcement, but he's also confused. He knows that for the first time he has allowed himself to care about other people.

In this perceptive, deftly written story, three children from two different families are forced together on a two-week vacation. Two perspectives, the girls' and John D's, help to define the characters. Witty and believable, the story leaves the reader feeling optimistic about the future of all concerned. Several well-placed illustrations capture the mood.

Ages 10-12

**Also available in:**
Braille—*The Animal, the Vegetable, and John D Jones*
Library of Congress (NLSBPH)

Cassette—*The Animal, the Vegetable, and John D Jones*
Library of Congress (NLSBPH)

Paperbound—*The Animal, the Vegetable, and John D Jones*
Dell Publishing Company, Inc.

## 96

**Byars, Betsy Cromer**

**The Cybil War**

Black/white illustrations by Gail Owens.
The Viking Press, Inc., 1981.
(126 pages)

FRIENDSHIP: Best Friend
FRIENDSHIP: Meaning of
PARENTAL: Absence
    Boy-girl relationships

The friendship between ten-year-olds Simon and Tony, formed in second grade by their mutual fatherlessness,

cracks when Simon realizes they are rivals for the same girl, Cybil Ackerman, his secret love since first grade. It begins when Tony calls Cybil and her friends names and, in his customary way, attributes the deed to Simon. Simon goes to Cybil's house to apologize, but finds Tony already there. Hiding in the bushes, he hears himself vilified by his supposed best friend. Cybil is not interested and closes the door. Simon and Tony are soon face to face in the bushes but Tony, recovering his bravado, excuses himself with some story that Simon pretends to believe. Furious, Simon has a hard time remembering what he ever liked about Tony. His memory of his father is also beginning to blur. He is delighted when Tony's costume for a contest backfires and Tony appears a complete fool in front of Cybil. At school, Simon is constantly on guard, watching Tony and Cybil, trying to prevent them from looking at each other. He thinks he has succeeded until Tony tells him he has invited Cybil to a movie. Simon feels utterly lost: "It was like the enemy taking the castle without the moat." Then Tony tricks him into coming along and accompanying Cybil's friend, a girl Simon detests. A letter from his father, who walked out on the family over two years ago, only increases Simon's misery. After the movie, as she walks him home, Simon's date tells him about Tony's deception. Cybil had only agreed to the movie on the condition that she would be with Simon. Explaining the whole miserable mess to his mother, who has always cautioned Simon about letting Tony take advantage of him, Simon is surprised to hear her say, "Tony is his own worst enemy." She is on her way to a date, of sorts, the first since Simon's father left, and is pleased that Simon finally sees Tony clearly. Tired of the lies and plots, Simon confesses the mix-up to Cybil, who promptly invites him for a bike ride. She lends him her sister's bike, and they head for the gas station to put air in the tire. On the way they pass Tony's house and Simon gives a small wave to his rival, feeling triumphant at last.

A boy begins to grow away from his best friend when they become rivals for a girl in this humorous, deceptively simple story. Competition makes Simon assert himself for once, and in doing so, he comes out from Tony's shadow and sees that their friendship was one of mutual fatherlessness, not necessarily mutual admiration. Once he sheds his sense of himself as a loser, Simon sees that he needn't try to emulate his wandering, irresponsible father. The real impact of this story lies in Simon's feelings about his absent father. In the end, "It was the first time he had felt sorry for his father rather than himself." Illustrations are full of vitality.

Ages 9-12

**Also available in:**
Cassette—*The Cybil War*
Library of Congress (NLSBPH)

Paperbound—*The Cybil War*
Scholastic Book Services

B

**97**

Byars, Betsy Cromer

## Goodbye, Chicken Little

Harper & Row, Publishers, Inc., 1979.
(103 pages)

---

*DEATH: of Relative*
*GUILT, FEELINGS OF*
  *Anxiety*
  *Family: relationships*
  *Fear: of death*
  *Friendship: best friend*
  *Mourning, stages of*

---

It is four days before Christmas when Jimmie Little, about ten, is summoned by his best friend, Conrad, to the banks of the Monday River. There Jimmie finds that his Uncle Pete has accepted a dare to walk across the ice. Though Jimmie, once again embarrassed by the foolhardy actions of his family, asks him to give up the idea, Uncle Pete forges ahead, entertaining a small crowd with his antics. Halfway across, he falls through the ice and drowns. When Jimmie returns home to tell his mother, she accuses him of encouraging Pete to attempt the crossing. Jimmie is overcome by guilt. His mother later apologizes, saying Jimmie was in no way responsible for Uncle Pete's death and that she tends to say things she doesn't mean when she is distraught. But Jimmie is not comforted. When his father died in a coal mine accident years earlier, the boy had started to call himself Chicken Little. He had been overwhelmed with nameless fears then, and the feelings have returned now, with Uncle Pete's death. He is unable to put the drowning out of his mind and neglects the loyal Conrad. Conrad is hurt, Jimmie thinks him uncaring, and the two fight. In an attempt to overcome her own grief, Mrs. Little decides to throw a party for the remaining family members in Pete's honor, even fetching ninety-two-year-old Uncle C.C. from the nursing home. Watching his colorful family enjoy themselves recalling Uncle Pete's pranks, what fun he was and how he had enjoyed life, Jimmie sees that people can express and cope with grief in different ways. Comforted, he feels proud to be a Little. When he notices Conrad peeking in a window, watching the festivities enviously, Jimmie invites him in.

In this fast-moving story, a quiet, cautious boy comes to grips with several disturbing events and emotions: grief and guilt over the accidental deaths of close family members; confusion about a friendship; anxiety about his place in an outgoing, often unpredictable family. Jimmie's growth in understanding and insight is realistically developed and the story told with warmth and humor.

Ages 9-11

**Also available in:**
Paperbound—*Goodbye, Chicken Little*
Scholastic Book Services

**98**

Byars, Betsy Cromer

## The Night Swimmers

Black/white illustrations by Troy Howell.
Delacorte Press, 1980.
(131 pages)

---

*PARENT/PARENTS: Single*
*RESPONSIBILITY: Accepting*
  *Baby-sitting*
  *Change: accepting*
  *Loneliness*
  *Sibling: oldest*

---

Eleven-year-old Retta (for Loretta Lynn) and her two younger brothers are night swimmers. Although they're always fearful of being discovered, they sneak into Colonel Roberts's pool at night after he and his wife go to bed. This is one of many diversions Retta has found for nine-year-old Johnny (for Johnny Cash) and little Roy (for Roy Acuff). The children's mother died two years ago and their father, Shorty, works nights as a country-western singer and sleeps during the day. So Retta is in charge of the boys day and night. The neighbors disapprove of the lack of adult supervision, but the girl cooks, cleans, shops, and tries to make a home for her brothers. She picks up homemaking tips from television and from observation, but sometimes feels no one appreciates her. Shorty loves his children but, in his drive to become a star, doesn't have much time for them. However, his girlfriend, Brendelle, is sympathetic to Retta's position and feelings. Johnny has made friends with Arthur, a boy his age, and Retta fears she is losing control over him. She also feels a bit resentful that Johnny has turned to someone other than her. One night Johnny slips out when the children are supposed to be sleeping. Retta hears him leave and follows him, discovering Johnny and Arthur at a park launching a small hot-air balloon. Meanwhile, Roy awakes, discovers both Retta and Johnny gone, and decides they have gone swimming at the Colonel's without him. He sneaks over to surprise them, runs up on the diving board, and dives in—even though he can't swim. Retta and Johnny return home from the park to discover Colonel Roberts, who has saved Roy from drowning. Shorty is called home. Retta feels everything has been her fault, but as the adults and children talk she realizes that she must give the boys more room to grow as individuals. Perhaps she has needed them more than they needed her. This becomes clear to her later, when she and Brendelle discuss the evening's events. Sadder but wiser, Retta is somewhat comforted by the hope that Shorty and Brendelle will marry.

Although their life is lonely and largely unsupervised, three siblings stick together, trying to make the most of each day. This is a touching, understated story of a young girl who takes seriously the adult responsibilities thrust upon her, though her family fails to realize she is too young for such demands. Well-done illustrations give an added dimension to the characters and situations. The lack of a standard happy ending seems appropriate to a story that is believable throughout.

Ages 10-12

**Also available in:**
Cassette—*The Night Swimmers*
Library of Congress (NLSBPH)

Paperbound—*The Night Swimmers*
Dell Publishing Company, Inc.

## 99

**Byars, Betsy Cromer**

### The Two-Thousand-Pound Goldfish

Harper & Row, Publishers, Inc., 1982.
(152 pages)

*DAYDREAMING*
*MATURATION*
  *Abandonment*
  *Death: of grandparent*
  *Grandparent: living in home of*
  *Imagination*
  *Parental: absence*

Warren Otis, eight, loves to watch horror movies. When he isn't watching them, he daydreams about monsters, cows with radioactive milk, man-eating snails, and other scary creatures. Since his sister Weezie's goldfish was flushed down the toilet, Warren's daydream has been about a two-thousand-pound goldfish named Bubbles. The children's mother, Saffron, is a fugitive from the law. She has gone from peaceful protests to pipe bombs and is wanted by the FBI. Warren has not seen her in three years, yet he dreams that someday she will return and make his loneliness go away. He and Weezie live with their grandmother, who considers her daughter dead and refuses to talk about her. Warren asks Aunt Pepper, Saffron's sister, about his mother. She tells him that at seven o'clock the first Monday of every month, she or Weezie waits at a public phone near the library for a call from Saffron. Occasionally a call comes. When Warren excitedly tells Weezie he knows about the phone calls, she replies that he doesn't really want to learn what their mother is like and should stop idolizing her. Disappointed, Warren continues to daydream about his mother and about Bubbles the goldfish trapped in the sewer. One day after school, Warren and a neighbor discover his grandmother unconscious. She is rushed to the hospital where it is learned she has had a stroke. Warren wonders if his mother will come home to care for them if their grandmother dies. Weezie scorns the idea, later accusing him of being "a daydream freak. You're not in the world ninety-five percent of the time." Running away from life is not healthy, she proclaims. Aunt Pepper moves in with Warren and Weezie while their grandmother is in the hospital. From her, Warren learns that his mother had been in town for three months last spring and never came to see him. The boy is devastated. Several days later the grandmother dies. Warren cries at the funeral—not for his grandmother, but because his mother fails to appear. Aunt Pepper moves permanently into their apartment. The following Monday Warren insists on accompanying Weezie to the phone booth. He talks to his mother briefly, she cries at the sound of his voice, and Warren is overcome with conflicting emotions. Afterwards, talking with Weezie, Warren decides that real-life problems need to get his full attention. He finishes his daydream movie about Bubbles the huge goldfish and vows that it will be his last. He will face the reality of his life, including the occasional three-minute phone call from his mother.

A lonely young boy whose mother has abandoned her children except for an infrequent phone call escapes into a world of fantasy and daydreams. Eventually, Warren decides to face the fact that his mother isn't coming home and life must continue without her. Deft writing, believable characters, and humor help the reader understand and sympathize with Warren's feelings.

Ages 9-12

**Also available in:**
Paperbound—*The Two-Thousand-Pound Goldfish*
Scholastic Book Services

## 100

**C**

**Caines, Jeannette Franklin**

### Window Wishing

Black/white illustrations by Kevin Brooks.
Harper & Row, Publishers, Inc., 1980.
(20 pages)

*GRANDPARENT: Love for*
  *Visiting*

Summer vacation for Bootsie, about four, and his sister, about seven, is spent with Grandma Mag. The children think Grandma Mag is special, and they love visiting her. She wears sneakers all the time, raises worms for fishing, and likes picnicking in the cemetery because it is a peaceful place. She makes special lemonade, lets them set the table with different-colored dishes, and always gives them gingersnaps and cheese with sassafras tea for dessert. They especially enjoy their bike trips downtown to "window wish." Every week each child has two special evenings for looking in store windows and wishing for toys and books. One summer day is particularly special for Bootsie—it's his birthday and he can wish all day long.

Bootsie's sister tells of the joys of visiting Grandma Mag, who enjoys sharing herself with her visiting grandchildren. The story has no problem to solve or situation to resolve; it simply describes the special love between a grandmother and her two beautiful grandchildren. The book is enhanced by softly shaded pictures that help convey the mood of the visits.

Ages 4-7

**Also available in:**
No other form known

## 101

**Calhoun, Mary Huiskamp**

### Katie John and Heathcliff

Harper & Row, Publishers, Inc., 1980.
(154 pages)

---

*BOY-GIRL RELATIONSHIPS*
  *Maturation*
  *School: classmate relationships*

---

The summer before seventh grade, Katie John Tucker reads and rereads *Wuthering Heights,* mooning over the book's dark, mysterious hero, Heathcliff. When she starts junior high that fall, she begins looking at all the boys as potential Heathcliffs. This is a radical switch for the girl who, the year before, started a boy-haters' club. Now she thinks of little else—as she says, it's a case of "here a boy, there a boy, everywhere a boy-boy!" Romance colors all her activities; even the elderly, unmarried woman whose room she helps clean becomes an aged Cinderella whose prince has never come. Katie has had a satisfying, long-standing friendship with Edwin, a fellow adventurer who lives in the cemetery where his father is caretaker. But the boy she feels could be Heathcliff is shaggy-haired, pale-eyed Jason, an eighth grader in her cooking class. As she tries to interest Jason in a "relationship," Katie becomes involved in school activities and in new and continuing friendships. She tries out for the cheerleading squad but loses the spot to Trish, a more sophisticated classmate. Instead, Katie ends up in a comic five-girl kazoo band that becomes a real crowd pleaser at football games. Always trying to be more "romantical," she has her ears pierced. Some of her friends pair off with boys, but Katie has mixed feelings when the K. C. (Kissed Club) is formed. She is sorry not to be a member, yet secretly glad she has so far escaped being kissed. Having attended her first boy-girl party, Katie decides at Halloween to have her own and to invite Jason. At the party she sees Jason in his true colors: rather cynical and bored, interested only in his date with Trish afterwards, no romantic hero at all. When Edwin invites her to his house "to see what a cemetery is like on Halloween," Katie realizes that this is the boy she really admires. She gladly accepts the invitation.

Although there is little real conflict in this light, humorous treatment of a girl's awakening to boys, readers enjoy Katie John (this is the fourth novel about her) and will find this book appealing, despite its predictable ending. Certain expressions and phrases have become dated, however, and may strike some readers as corny.

Ages 9-11

**Also available in:**
Cassette—*Katie John and Heathcliff*
Library of Congress (NLSBPH)

Paperbound—*Katie John and Heathcliff*
Harper & Row, Publishers, Inc.

## 102

**Calhoun, Mary Huiskamp**

### The Night the Monster Came

Black/white illustrations by Leslie Morrill.
William Morrow & Company, Inc., 1982.
(62 pages)

---

*COURAGE, MEANING OF*
*FEAR: of the Unknown*
  *Imagination*
  *Resourcefulness*

---

Nine-year-old Andy O'Reilly is afraid of all monsters but especially of Bigfoot, who he fears may live in the woods behind his house. Alone one evening while his father, a sheriff's deputy, works and his mother attends a real-estate class, Andy looks out the window and sees giant footprints in the snow. Frightened, he waits anxiously for his mother. There must be a reasonable explanation, she decides, but by the time she looks for the tracks, they've been erased by dogs nosing around the garbage cans. The next night Andy is again alone. He looks outside and sees a huge beast jumping over the back fence. Terrified, he phones his mother and she comes angrily home. It was Bigfoot, Andy cries, but his father and others search outside in vain. The next evening Andy's parents try to find a sitter for him, but can't. Andy says he'll be fine. Later he hears a noise, looks out the long, narrow window in the front door, and sees fur. Once again terrified, Andy calls the sheriff's department and reports a prowler, asking them to send out his father quickly. When he looks outside again, however, Andy realizes the monster is a wounded bear. He decides he had better trap the bear before his mother or father arrives and the bear attacks them. So he throws out a trail of bacon leading to the garage. The bear smells the bacon, follows the trail, and is soon trapped inside the garage when the automatic door closes. Just then Mr. O'Reilly and his partner arrive. A veterinarian is summoned, and the bear is sedated with a tranquilizer gun. His wounded leg is attended to, and then the animal is hauled away to a deeper part of the woods where he won't be tempted to forage for food in garbage cans. Congratulated for his fast thinking, Andy is delighted, proud, and secretly happy that the legend of Bigfoot remains intact.

Andy "cries wolf" several times before the monster he sees, a wounded bear, impels him to consider the safety of others as he overcomes his fear and traps the animal. Quick thinking and ingenuity make Andy a hero, and readers will applaud his triumph. They may also be moved to discuss fears, real and imaginary, and the meaning of courage. Appropriate illustrations complement the text.

Ages 8-10

**Also available in:**
Paperbound—*The Night the Monster Came*
Xerox Publishing Company

**103**

Callen, Lawrence Willard

## Sorrow's Song

Black/white illustrations by Marvin Friedman.
Little, Brown and Company, 1979.
(150 pages)

---

FREEDOM, MEANING OF
FRIENDSHIP: Meaning of
MUTENESS
    Animals: love for
    Nature: respect for

---

Pinch, about ten, and his best friend, Sorrow Nix, mute since birth, are on their way to school when they meet the Zoo Man, who is looking for unusual animals to buy for his traveling zoo. Sorrow's inability to talk upsets the man. On his next trip to Four Corners, in search of a white whooping crane he had spotted by Blind River, he stops first at Sorrow's house and loudly tells Mrs. Nix to have something done about the girl. Sorrow hears his comments and later talks to Pinch, in writing, about her feelings concerning her father's death last year and her desire, especially when she feels happy, to sing. At the river the next morning Sorrow spots the white crane, which she sketches for a class assignment, and a smaller brown one with an injured wing. She and Pinch decide to help the smaller crane and plan to capture it after school. However, several people visiting the school that day spot Sorrow's drawing and know she didn't copy the white crane from a book, as the teacher assumes. Mr. John Barrow, a friend of both Pinch and Sorrow, wants to catch the white crane to sell to the Zoo Man. So do the Sweet brothers, a mean, unsavory pair, at the school for some arithmetic help and just as likely to eat the crane as sell it. The Zoo Man continues to feel protective towards Sorrow and comes to school to ask the teacher about her. Firmly the teacher tells him, "Sorrow Nix is more normal than the two of us. Don't you do anything that will make her feel otherwise." While the others are out searching for the white crane, Sorrow and Pinch easily capture the young brown one and pen it up in the woods behind Sorrow's house. Sorrow spends all her free time tending to the bird. Gradually, it loses its brown feathers and they find they have a white crane. When the crane is able to fly in and out of its pen, Pinch thinks they should let it go before it is discovered. But Sorrow is not yet ready to part with it. One morning they discover the crane penned up outside Mr. John Barrow's house. He claims it was destroying his sweet-potato patch and is rightfully his to sell to the Zoo Man. That night Sorrow and Pinch steal the crane, row it across Blind River, and set it free. Freezing water pours into the rotted boat on their return trip, and Sorrow is sick for several weeks after the rescue. Among her many visitors is the Zoo Man, who continues his search for the crane, aided by Mr. John Barrow. After school, Sorrow, Pinch, and their teacher hurry to the boat dock and find Mr. John Barrow loading the crane into his wagon. They silently climb in for a ride back to town, but are accosted by the jealous and wildly drunk Sweet brothers who cruelly humiliate Mr. John Barrow, frighten Sorrow, and later steal the crane. When Mr. John Barrow recovers the crane, Pinch angrily reminds

him that the bird belongs to Sorrow. The next morning Mr. John Barrow informs Pinch that he has set the crane loose down by the river. He felt Sorrow was talking to him just by looking at him, and he knew her heart was breaking. Pinch runs to tell Sorrow the good news. "Now I can tell Sorrow what it feels like to sing," he says.

In this third book about life in Four Corners, Pinch tells the story of his best friend, Sorrow, a mute but remarkably expressive girl who develops an attachment to a white crane. The fate of the crane is the central issue through which the various characters reveal themselves. Sorrow and the crane are much alike—at times her muteness is equated with being locked in a cage—which is supposedly why the Zoo Man wants to care for and protect them both. But Sorrow, like the crane, needs to be free. Mr. John Barrow, the funniest character in the book, nearly lets his preoccupation with the money he hopes to earn from the crane take precedence over what is right for Sorrow, his longtime friend. This is a thoughtful book, peopled with marvelously real, if eccentric, characters. It presents some difficult issues that would be excellent for discussion. Most of the inhabitants of this small, Southern town are warm, amusing, and refreshingly honest.

Ages 9-12

**Also available in:**
Disc—Sorrow's Song
Library of Congress (NLSBPH)

**C**

**104**

Cameron, Ann

## The Stories Julian Tells

Black/white illustrations by Ann Strugnell.
Pantheon Books, 1981.
(71 pages)

---

FAMILY: Relationships
IMAGINATION
    Friendship: making friends
    Sibling: relationships
    Tooth, loss of

---

When Julian, about seven, and his younger brother, Huey, disobey orders and eat most of the lemon pudding their father has painstakingly made for their mother, their father threatens a beating and a whipping. The boys' fear turns to surprise when they discover they are to beat and whip another pudding for their mother! Then the family decides to plant a garden, and the father sends for a seed catalog. When Huey asks what a catalog is, Julian tells him that a catalog has cats in it, that "cats help with the garden." When the catalog arrives and the father discovers why Huey is so disappointed (no cats), he saves the day by telling the boys that catalog cats are so fast that most people never see them. They can't be ordered; they just help in gardens whenever they please, making the work go faster. Since Huey expects the garden to grow especially fast with the help of the catalog cats, Julian spends an evening outside once everything is planted, whispering encouragement to the seeds. Julian receives a fig tree for his birthday. His father tells him the tree will grow as fast as he does. So Julian, who notices that the tree is growing more than he is, secretly eats each new leaf to speed up his own growth. When the tree hasn't grown at all in a year, his father threatens to dig it up and replace it. Only then does Julian decide to leave it alone and let it grow. This same tactic makes Julian change his mind about having his tooth pulled. When he asks his father to pull his baby tooth because the permanent tooth has come in, his father suggests using a pliers and other unacceptable methods. His mother mentions that a cave boy would have been grateful for that extra tooth when eating tough mastodon meat, and Julian takes to this idea immediately. But just as he is thoroughly enjoying his "cave-boy tooth," it comes out when he eats an apple. A new girl, Gloria, moves into the neighborhood, and she and Julian get along famously from the start. She shows him how to make a kite and tie little slips of paper to the tail with secret wishes on them. "When the wind takes all your wishes, that's when you know it's going to work," says Gloria. When they draw the kite in, all the wishes are gone. Julian guesses that one of Gloria's wishes is the same as his—that they will be best friends for a long time.

Julian tells the stories in this easy reader, and he is a curious child eager to learn about and master his world. His parents, especially his father, firmly yet kindly guide him toward acceptable outlets for his energy and creativity. Warm family relationships are emphasized in these chapters, each of which can be read independently as a short story. The illustrations are especially lively, with Julian's alert look as constant as his wild-haired father's calm, steady expression.

Ages 7-9

**Also available in:**
No other form known

## 105

Carrick, Carol

## A Rabbit for Easter

Color illustrations by Donald Carrick.
Greenwillow Books, 1979.
(32 pages)

---

*ANIMALS: Responsibility for*

---

Paul is always eager to come to kindergarten and visit Sam, their pet rabbit. He especially enjoys feeding Sam and watching him hop about the classroom during storytime. Every day, before recess, Sam goes back in his cage and the teacher patiently reminds the children to latch the cage door so Sam will not get lost. Paul is delighted when Easter vacation arrives and he is appointed Sam's caretaker. Paul's father takes the cage home and sets it up on the clothes dryer where the whole family can watch Sam. Right away, Paul must chase his cat off the cage. Friends from next door come to see Sam, and Paul shows them how to pet him. The next morning, after feeding the rabbit, Paul lets him out for his daily run. A knock at the door sends Sam scurrying behind the living-room couch and draws Paul outside to ride his friend's new bike. He lingers longer than he intended, and when he returns to the house he cannot find Sam anywhere. Although his mother assures him that Sam is just hiding, Paul worries that he

is outside and in danger. Just after checking on the cat's whereabouts, Paul hears a sound from the dirty-clothes pile. He is vastly relieved to discover Sam chewing on the wicker clothes basket. When vacation is over, Paul returns Sam to school, keeping silent about the mishap. However, after Sam's daily run, Paul is very careful to hook the cage door just right.

Entrusted with his classroom's pet rabbit, an earnest little boy is careless just once and loses track of the animal for several frightening minutes. From this mishap, Paul and readers too may gain a new understanding of responsibility and its demands. This is a quiet story, appropriately illustrated in quiet, cool colors.

Ages 3-7

**Also available in:**
Disc—*A Rabbit for Easter*
Library of Congress (NLSBPH)

## 106

Carrick, Carol

## Some Friend!

Black/white illustrations by Donald Carrick.
Houghton Mifflin Company, 1979.
(111 pages)

---

*FRIENDSHIP: Best Friend*
*FRIENDSHIP: Meaning of*
  *Loyalty*
  *Self, attitude toward: respect*

---

Mike and Rob, each about ten, have been friends since kindergarten but have had their share of quarrels, mostly over Rob's insistence on having everything his way. For Mike, however, there is no one else he would rather be with. That is why he usually gives in to Rob, why he is now selling greeting cards door-to-door with him. After Rob makes a particularly good sale, he spots his mother driving by and abruptly goes off with her, leaving Mike standing there holding the cards. The next morning Rob calls Mike all excited about plans for a club; Mike, remembering how Rob's many other clubs have fizzled, is less enthusiastic. The first meeting at Rob's house includes the usual group and one extra— Kenny, the class oddball, there because Mike felt sorry for him. Through a fluke, Kenny is elected president. Rob promptly disbands the club, using his mother and her supposed disapproval as an excuse. Mike knows he is just being a poor loser and angrily starts to leave. Then Kenny, playing the clown, accidentally bumps Mike into Rob's bicycle, knocking it into the street. Rob orders Mike to pick it up, but he refuses and goes home. That night, after waiting in vain for Rob, Mike hurries alone to the movie at the Boy's Club. He grabs the last empty seat, which turns out to be right in front of Rob and his friend Bubba. At intermission, as Mike stands by himself drinking a can of pop, Rob deliberately bumps him. While Mike is brushing himself off, Bubba steals his treasured baseball cap, given to him by a Red Sox coach. Rob and Bubba and several others toss the hat back and forth, ignoring Mike's pleas to give it back. Finally, Rob heads downstairs with the hat and throws it over the railing when Mike grabs him. For the first time in the history of their friendship Mike attacks Rob in earnest and ends up shoving him down the stairs. He is immediately regretful, but simply retrieves his cap and leaves. At home, Mike decides to call Rob and apologize, only to find that Rob has gone to spend the night at Bubba's. At baseball practice the following morning, Mike tries to ignore Rob. But when he and Rob make a double play on their opponents, Rob smiles at him and Mike is encouraged to approach him after practice. He apologizes for Rob's black eye, anticipating an apology in return, but Rob just shrugs. Mike suggests they take the greeting cards around, but they quarrel again when Rob tells him of his new plan to buy a BB gun with both their profits. At home, Mike tells his mother how angry he is at Rob. "He is the way he is," observes Mike's mother. "You have to decide whether his friendship is worth it." Soon Rob shows up with a bag from a sporting goods store. But instead of a new cap for Mike, he pulls out a new baseball glove for himself. Mike realizes then that to Rob, everything, even friendship, can be replaced. Still, they have a good time together. Mike concludes, "I knew it wasn't going to last—Rob would still make me mad sometimes. But I wasn't going to expect him to be someone he wasn't. It was enough that we were still friends."

In this first-person story of friendship, Mike learns as much about his own personal limits and principles as he does about Rob's weaknesses and lack of loyalty. After a serious quarrel he must face what he has sensed for some time: he cares more about their friendship than Rob does. In the end, though wiser, he renews the friendship anyway. This well-told account describes believable, everyday events and relationships. Interesting illustrations that extend the text give the book special appeal for the reluctant reader.

Ages 9-12

**Also available in:**
Braille—*Some Friend!*
Library of Congress (NLSBPH)

Cassette—*Some Friend!*
Library of Congress (NLSBPH)

Paperbound—*Some Friend!*
Doubleday & Company, Inc.

Paperbound—*Some Friend!*
Scholastic Book Services

## 107

**Carrick, Malcolm**

**I'll Get You**

Black/white illustrations by the author.
Harper & Row, Publishers, Inc., 1979.
(188 pages)

*IDENTITY, SEARCH FOR*
  *Belonging*
  *Family: relationships*
  *Fear: of physical harm*
  *Friendship: making friends*
  *Justice/Injustice*
  *Loneliness*
  *Parent/Parents: respect for/lack of respect for*
  *Prejudice: social class*

Michael "Carrot" Perkins, not quite ten, feels he is losing his struggle to fit into his post-World War II London neighborhood. Classmates and neighborhood boys subject him to teasing, taunts, and physical abuse, because his family is different. His father owns a printing business and a house; his mother, all respectability, dislikes the predominantly working-class neighborhood; Carrot and his fifteen-year-old brother, Dick, take music lessons. Yet Dick, musically gifted, friendly, and confident, fits in anywhere and Carrot, not gifted at anything, nowhere. Carrot hates danger; he cries easily. Still, wanting very much to belong, he is drawn to the people living at the council flats, a housing project. His best friend, Jimmy Webb, lives there, as does his enemy, Tommy Barker. Both boys' fathers work for Mr. Perkins. Tensions rise at the flats because of a strike against Mr. Perkins's business. They heighten when Fred Webb, Jimmy's father, who led the walkout after Tommy Barker's father was fired for alleged thievery, finds out that Barker actually was stealing. Although the other workers return when the truth about Barker is revealed, Webb remains out and Carrot tries to find out why. He suspects his father won't take Webb back. The plight of the Webb family worries Carrot: Jimmy has even had to pawn his bicycle for money. Still, Carrot can't find the courage to plead Webb's case with his father. He wishes he could and dreams of becoming like his now-dead grandfather, certain of what he believes and willing to stand up for it. But what does Carrot believe? He hates his piano classes, but obeys his mother and endures them. His one delight is helping Charlie, a street vendor, sell ice cream. But Mr. Barker plans to drive Charlie out of business by starting his own vending business on Charlie's route. Once Carrot and his friends learn of the plan—Tommy Barker tries to bully Carrot into supporting his father—they devise a scheme to foil it. The scheme works and Carrot takes an active role in stopping Barker. Soon after, Carrot learns from his father why Mr. Webb hasn't returned to work: he needs eye surgery and Carrot's father has helped arrange it. To cap Carrot's returned high spirits, his music teacher moves and his parents finally agree to his giving up the despised piano and switching to vocal music. A happy, newly confident Carrot now returns Jimmy's bike to him; Mr. Perkins had unwittingly bought it for Carrot's birthday. Returning the bike is hard for Carrot—he's longed for a bike. But now he has the courage to do what he feels is right.

A young boy begins to overcome his fears and live life courageously, helped by a newfound respect for and understanding of his ambitious father. This is a colorful, rather complicated story, filled with subplots and set in England with accompanying British terms and phrases. Carrot's vivid, compassionate first-person narration is engaging and believable.

Ages 11-13

**Also available in:**
No other form known

C

**108**

Carris, Joan Davenport

## When the Boys Ran the House

Black/white illustrations by Carol Newsom.
J. B. Lippincott Company, 1982.
(150 pages)

---

*RESPONSIBILITY: Accepting*
 *Illnesses: of parent*
 *Parental: absence*
 *Problem solving*
 *Sibling: relationships*

---

Twelve-year-old Justin (Jut) Howard's mother needs four or five weeks of bed rest to recuperate from encephalitis, and she and her boys don't want to worry Mr. Howard, who is in Europe giving demonstrations essential to his new computer business. Jut and his brothers, ten-year-old Marty and seven-year-old Nick, think they can manage to run the house and care for two-year-old Gus with a little help from neighbors and a visiting nurse. But they quickly must contend with an invasion of bees, the awkwardness of grocery shopping by bike, Gus eating a live goldfish, and a pregnant cat that was supposedly spayed. Nurse "Amazon" Brown turns out to be a former basketball star who coaches Jut for his basketball tryouts. She also takes the four boys to a World Series game in Cincinnati, during which Gus gets lost in the crowd. Jut and Marty go hunting on the opening day of the season. It's Marty's first year and he's delighted, but Jut finds that hunting bothers him for some reason. They bring home squirrels to freeze for a future dinner. They also kill two crows, and Jut is determined to eat them right away since good hunters eat all they kill. Nurse Brown contributes her fresh garden vegetables to the dinner, not realizing until it's too late that the meat pie she is eating is crow. The boys don't like her vegetables any better than she likes the crow. While Mrs. Howard continues to recuperate, Jut sees that the laundry is done and the house kept clean, and Marty takes over meal preparations. When Nick accidentally steps on a lever and discovers a secret compartment in the wood molding, they find the source of the persistent smell in the living room: a pile of dead mice set aside by the pregnant cat for her confinement. The week before their father returns, Jut makes the basketball team, thanks to Amazon Brown's insistence that being good at basketball is simply a matter of planning and determination. The boys are relieved and overjoyed to have their father back again. He, in turn, is impressed by their efforts and proud of them. For his part, Jut is glad he doesn't have to play father anymore. At last he can lay to rest his talents as a housekeeper.

Three resourceful brothers take over housekeeping and child-care responsibilities during their mother's illness and their father's absence. They survive numerous mishaps, solve their problems themselves, and learn some practical skills in the process. Detailed drawings and a funny, clever text make the Howard family hard to leave behind when the book ends.

Ages 8-12

**Also available in:**
Paperbound—*When the Boys Ran the House*
Dell Publishing Company, Inc.

**109**

Carroll, Theodorus C.

## The Lost Christmas Star

Based on a story by Elizabeth Yates.
Color illustrations by William Hutchinson.
Garrard Publishing Company, 1979.
(64 pages)

---

*BLAME*
*TRUST/DISTRUST*
 *Communication: misunderstandings*
 *Judgment, effect of emotions on*
 *Peer relationships*
 *Shyness*

---

Friends Judy and Matthew, both about twelve, meet in River Junction's park with other townspeople to trim the communal Christmas tree. Noticing Tim Stevens, a shy boy new to the town, Judy invites him to help string tinsel. Later, Matt asks Judy why she made such a big fuss over Tim. When she replies that she did no such thing, Matt stalks off and Judy concludes that he's jealous. That afternoon, the town holds a Christmas pageant during which Matt places an old, valued star atop the tree. That night a great wind rises, blowing nearly all the ornaments from the tree, including the irreplaceable star. Next day the townspeople search diligently for it, but without success. When Matt spots several sets of footprints near the tree, he wonders to Judy if the fellow with the star-marked boots took the star—or perhaps the boy with a dog. In fact, Judy saw Tim and his dog, Rex, playing near the tree last night but had refrained from telling Matt, fearing the information would only feed his suspicions. Though she reprimands Matt for suspecting Tim without evidence, he remains suspicious and continues searching for the culprit. His pursuit of the star-marked boots ends when Judy spots them on the town policeman; Matt also clears a classmate. That leaves Tim. Matt almost accuses him outright at a school workshop when he sees Tim edging a birdhouse with tin exactly like that covering the star. Tim hears his muttered suspicions and the teacher's warning to Matt about the lack of evidence. Matt's certainty that Tim is the thief frightens Judy, yet she accompanies him to Tim's house in search of evidence. They find Tim's father, a carpenter, using tin strips identical to those Tim used. Thinking this exonerates Tim, Judy implores Matt to apologize. But Matt objects. Why does Tim act guilty? Why did he miss school today? On Monday Tim comes to school looking pale and thinner. Judy insists she knows he is innocent, but Tim can't believe her. In fact, he worries that Rex, who brings everything home, found the star and buried it somewhere. After school, Matt follows the unsuspecting Tim. When Tim leaves his house carrying a box and begins to bury it, Matt rushes to accost him, demanding that Tim open the box. Tim complies. Inside is a dead bird his dog brought home. Mortified, Matt apologizes, but Tim angrily refuses to accept the apology. Later, he refuses to accept Judy's invitation to a Christmas Eve party. Depressed about losing a potential friend, Judy and Matt go into Matt's barn to gather hay for the manger. They scarcely notice Jingles, Matt's dog, worrying something in the hay—until he drags out the star. As soon as they realize what's happened they rush to Tim's house to explain and again apologize. This time he accepts and, with his father, accompanies them to the party.

Matt allows his jealous dislike of a new boy in town to lead him to the unwarranted and damaging conclusion that Tim is a thief. Once he decides that, everything he sees—Tim working with tin, Tim burying a box—confirms his suspicions. This is a good book for young, independent readers, but could also work well as a read-aloud. The use of shifting viewpoints among the three principal characters helps readers distinguish fact from speculation. Illustrations are simple and satisfactory.

Ages 7-9

**Also available in:**
No other form known

## 110

**Chaffin, Lillie Dorton**

### We Be Warm till Springtime Comes

Black/white illustrations by Lloyd Bloom.
Macmillan Publishing Company, Inc., 1980.
(28 pages counted) o.p.

---

*POVERTY*
*RESPONSIBILITY: Accepting*
   *Appalachia*
   *Courage, meaning of*
   *Determination*
   *Parent/Parents: single*
   *Resourcefulness*

---

One winter morning in the Appalachian mountains, little Jimmy Jack Blackburn awakes shivering and numb from the cold that penetrates his family's poor house. "Think about summer," his mother advises as she cuddles close to the baby. It doesn't help. There is no coal or wood to use in their "giant dragon" of a fireplace, but Jimmy Jack knows of an old coal bank in the hill. "You're not big enough to dig coal," his mama says, but she cannot go in her "old rag shoes." "I'm big enough to freeze to death," he answers, "but I'm not going to." The little boy dons his worn but heavy boots, takes a rusty pick, and drags an old toy wagon up the hill. He climbs into a hole dug long ago in the coal bank. Although he knows the top could fall in and squash him like a bug, he lifts the pick and swings it into the coal, over and over. He pulls the first wagonload of coal back to the house and watches his mother make a fire. Then he returns to the coal bank and works until sundown, making several trips home with more coal. That evening he sits with his mother at the hearth, talking and singing. When they are in bed, the wind begins to howl. Jimmy Jack wonders if the house can withstand the wind and is relieved when, the next morning, it is still standing. But when he goes to the coal bank, he discovers that the rock roof was crushed during the night when a nearby tree was blown down by the wind. "Thank you for waiting to fall at night," he says to the rock and the tree. The wind has calmed and the sun is bright and warm. Jimmy Jack

loads up his wagon with a good bunch of firewood from the fallen tree. "We be toasty warm till springtime comes."

A little boy living in Appalachian poverty tells of his triumph over the elements and his success in keeping his family warm. This is a read-aloud book of unusual depth, its somber mood captured well by beautiful, dark-tinged pictures. The dialect Jimmy Jack uses to tell his story does not obscure this lyrical account of hardship and resourcefulness.

Ages 6-9

**Also available in:**
No other form known

## 111

**Chaikin, Miriam**

### I Should Worry, I Should Care

Black/white illustrations by Richard Egielski.
Harper & Row, Publishers, Inc., 1979.
(103 pages)

C

---

*CHANGE: New Home*
   *Family: relationships*
   *Friendship: making friends*
   *Jewish*

---

Molly, about nine and the oldest of four children, is very bitter and depressed when her family moves, in the summer of 1941, from a small walk-up in Manhattan to a larger, first-floor apartment in Brooklyn. She misses her friends, hates the new apartment—although it's easier to get the baby carriage in and out and easier on her father, who has a heart condition—and refuses to help her mother get them moved in. Despondent, she steps outside to see if there are any girls her age around. The only person she sees is a very fat woman sitting on the stoop across the street. Then she hears two girls yell, "Fat Anna, fat Anna!" Shocked, Molly wonders how those girls could be so mean. When she meets the two, Julie and Celia, she finds Celia very domineering and Julie under her sway. Julie's mother, a hypochondriac, often plays on Julie's sympathy and compels the girl to stay home with her. The bossy Celia does do Molly one favor; she takes her to summer school where Molly meets Norma, a girl from her apartment building with whom she quickly becomes friends. Gradually, through the summer, Molly settles into her new neighborhood. She and her parents anxiously gather around their radio each night, listening to the war news. They try to maintain their customary lives, despite their fears for the fate of Europe's Jews—Molly's mother goes to a matchmaker to arrange for Aunt Bessie's marriage. Molly and Julie, who has freed herself from Celia's domination, become friends. Before the school term begins, Celia moves to another town. As Molly watches the movers, she thinks about her first best friend in Manhattan, Selma. She realizes that she can't really remember what Selma looks like. She remembers how she felt about her and the things they did together, but not her face. When a family with two boys moves into Celia's old apartment, one of the boys mistakes Molly for a sixth grader. Even better, the boys have a girl cousin Molly's age who often comes to visit. Thinking over the summer that has passed, eager to start school, Molly's old happy feelings begin to steal over her as she sings, "I should worry, I should care."

A young girl's loneliness in her new surroundings and slowly returning joy as she makes friends are in sharp contrast to the background scene, just prior to America's involvement in World War II. Molly's family is Jewish and they reflect much anxiety over the fate of Europe's Jews as they listen to news of Hitler on the radio. But particular as the story is in place and time, the heroine's feelings are universal, readily understandable to any child who has worried about moving, losing friends, and adapting to a new environment. Almost anecdotal, enriched by Jewish phrases and customs, the story is filled with the everyday activities of home, family, and school. The illustrations capture the warm tone. This is one of several books about Molly's family and friends.

Ages 8-11

**Also available in:**
No other form known

## 112

### Chalmers, Mary Eileen

## Come to the Doctor, Harry

Color illustrations by the author.
Harper & Row, Publishers, Inc., 1981.
(32 pages)

---

*DOCTOR, GOING TO*

---

When young Harry's tail is accidentally slammed in the door, his mother, Mrs. Cat, tells him she must take him to the doctor. But Harry says he doesn't like doctors. "Why?" wonders his mother. Harry replies, "Because." Telling him that's not a good enough reason, the mother cat hurries her kitten off to the doctor's office. There Harry meets a variety of interesting patients: a large dog with a cast on his leg, a small dog with a bandage on his ear, a rooster with a sore throat. The friendly doctor puts some powder and a bandage on Harry's injured tail and tells Mrs. Cat that Harry will be better tomorrow. As he's leaving, Harry comforts three kittens in the waiting room, telling them not to be afraid because "there's nothing to it!" Mother and son head home, with Harry showing off his bandage and relating to everyone he meets the story of how brave he was at the doctor's office.

Simple illustrations and language, humorously combined, make this little book a charming read-aloud. The story offers a completely reassuring view of what goes on at a medical clinic, and so may not prepare children for what might actually be in store for them on their own visit to the doctor. But the animal characters and the warm, friendly experience depicted will appeal to very young children. This book is one in a series about Harry.

Ages 2-5

**Also available in:**
No other form known

## 113

### Chapman, Carol

## Herbie's Troubles

Color illustrations by Kelly Oechsli.
E. P. Dutton & Company, Inc., 1981.
(32 pages counted)

---

*BULLY: Being Bothered by*
*PROBLEM SOLVING*
  *School: classmate relationships*

---

Herbie, six-and-a-half, likes school until he meets Jimmy John. Jimmy John wrecks the tunnel Herbie makes in the sandbox. He splashes paint on Herbie's picture. He smashes Herbie's granola bar. He ties knots in Herbie's jacket sleeves. The last day of this miserable week, Jimmy John holds the bathroom door shut so Herbie cannot get out. The torment continues until finally, Herbie decides not to go to school anymore. One Monday morning, he resolves to stay home. Sophie, from down the block, suggests that Herbie go to school and be assertive. So Herbie goes to school and tries to stand up to Jimmy John; Jimmy John pulls a button off Herbie's sweater. The next day Herbie decides he really will not go to school. Mary Ellen, from across the street, advises Herbie to share a treat with Jimmy John. So Herbie goes to school and, at lunchtime, tries to share his cake with Jimmy John. Jimmy John smears it all over Herbie's shirt. The next day Herbie vows to stay home. Jake, from around the corner, tells him to punch Jimmy John in the nose. So Herbie goes to school and punches Jimmy John in the nose. Jimmy John punches Herbie in the stomach. They both get sent to the office. The next day Herbie vows he will never go to school again. No one's advice has worked. Then Herbie has an idea of his own and he goes to school. When Jimmy John splashes paint, Herbie ignores him. When he wrecks Herbie's tunnel in the sandbox, Herbie ignores him. Jimmy John swipes his granola bar; Herbie ignores him. Finally Jimmy John declares that Herbie is no fun anymore. And Herbie once again likes school.

After trying the advice of each of his friends on how to deal with a bully, Herbie solves his problem himself— he cuts off the bully's fun by simply ignoring him. No adults ever get involved. The listening and reading audience should derive great satisfaction from this cleverly illustrated tale about a triumph over adversity.

Ages 5-7

**Also available in:**
No other form known

**114**

Cheatham, Karyn Follis

## The Best Way Out

Harcourt Brace Jovanovich, Inc., 1982.
(168 pages)

---

EDUCATION: Special
IDENTITY, SEARCH FOR
  Afro-American
  Change: accepting
  Family: relationships
  Integration: school busing
  Prejudice: ethnic/racial
  School: pupil-teacher relationships

---

Thirteen-year-old Haywood Romby hates being bused to Gill Memorial Junior High, a middle-class school where blacks are considered "inner city" kids, and he hates repeating seventh grade. In grade school Haywood was on the honor roll and intended to finish high school and attend college. But two years ago his neighborhood junior high was closed, and he and his friends began being bused to Gill, sixteen miles away. Resentful and angry, Haywood failed seventh grade. One day in the fall he decides to skip school, but then reconsiders and catches the other bus headed for Gill. Unfortunately his long-time enemy, Phillip Duvall, is on this bus. As Haywood steps off the bus, Phillip pushes him and two of Haywood's fingers are crushed by the bus door, the tips severed. When the bandages are finally removed, Haywood, horrified at the sight of his maimed fingers, begins to skip school more and more. He and Phillip fight again, and both are called into the principal's office. After warning Haywood, the principal suggests that he get a tutor to help him improve his grades. Several days later as they wait for the bus, Haywood and his friends drink some whiskey. Haywood passes out on the bus and is suspended. His father is furious. A counselor from school, Mrs. Bennett, talks to the boy and his father. They agree Haywood will begin attending SHOP, Student High School Orientation Program. Still resentful, Haywood does little to cooperate. His father, who has a sixth-grade education, suggests he quit school and start working, since he is doing so poorly. Still reluctant to quit school entirely, Haywood begins working part-time as a janitor. As a cruel joke, he makes a collage of Mrs. Bennett, but even though she recognizes the insult she also sees the quality and has it hung in the school art show. Soon the principal informs Haywood that a SHOP Outlet has opened downtown and Haywood is to finish seventh grade there. He feels he is being kicked out of Gill, but Mrs. Bennett challenges him to stop letting other people influence his life. Haywood accepts the challenge and becomes excited by the SHOP program and the points he can earn for special privileges. His collage wins an honorable mention in the city-wide contest, and Haywood is surprised to see that his friends are genuinely impressed and his family proud. Beginning to feel loved and accepted at last, Haywood vows to himself and to Mrs. Bennett that he will go to summer school, catch up with his class, and get himself back into the proper grade.

Angry and resentful, dislocated by the closing of his neighborhood school and his forced enrollment in an all-white school, Haywood is ready to give up on himself and his future. Then a special counselor and a special school program help him recover his sense of worth and dignity. Well written and fast moving, the book captures Haywood's conflicting emotions and illustrates the unfair burden busing can place on black children.

Ages 12 and up

**Also available in:**
No other form known

**115**

Childress, Alice

## Rainbow Jordan

Coward, McCann & Geoghegan, Inc., 1981.
(142 pages)

---

AFRO-AMERICAN
FOSTER HOME
PARENTAL: Negligence
PARENTAL: Unreliability
SELF, ATTITUDE TOWARD: Accepting
  Fear
  Honesty/Dishonesty
  Love, meaning of
  Sex: attitude toward

---

At fourteen, Rainbow Jordan is used to being left alone. But this time her young mother, Kathie, is stranded at a resort with her latest boyfriend, waiting for a go-go dancing job, and Rainbow is faced with an eviction notice on their apartment door. So the social worker takes her to an interim foster home again, to Miss Josie. Not wanting anyone to know about her mother's absence, Rainbow tells her boyfriend, Eljay, and her best friend, Beryl, that Miss Josie is her aunt. When Rainbow arrives, Miss Josie says that her husband, Hal, is out of town on business. Aware that the first days for her "repeat" children, particularly Rainbow, are often difficult, Miss Josie tries to ease the tension by keeping the girl busy. She's a seamstress and has Rainbow help with the sewing. She takes Rainbow to a fitting, plans outings to museums, and teaches the girl to prepare meals and set an attractive table. On one of her previous visits Rainbow started her first menstrual period. Miss Josie had gently talked with her about sex, a subject Kathie evades; Kathie also refuses to give Rainbow permission for sex education classes at school. Miss Josie's advice is to use self-control. "Don't let mother nature decide your future too soon. She'll take over and run you ragged." Rainbow appreciates Miss Josie, even if she is "square," but her mother is rarely out of her mind. She worries about her safety and when she'll return. At school Rainbow is studying death. "But how bout the loss of a loved one who still livin?" she wonders, thinking of the times her mother is away, or Eljay stops speaking to her because she won't "go all the way," or Beryl and she start drifting apart. Besides these troubles with her friends, Rainbow is under pressure from her teachers. One needs her mother to come in for a conference by Tuesday at the latest. Rainbow has run out of excuses, and by Monday Kathie has not returned. She

**C**

has telephoned, however, promised to be back for the conference, and had her ex-husband send a check for the rent. The longer she stays with Miss Josie, the more Rainbow notices that the woman, usually patient and polite, seems short-tempered and snappish, particularly when questioned about her husband. Then Miss Josie, realizing she has been overly strict with Rainbow, grants her permission to go to the teen center after school. Instead, Rainbow takes the key to her mother's apartment, which Miss Josie has denied her time and again, and plans a rendezvous there with Eljay. Although she is terrified of getting pregnant, she has decided to give in to him because she fears losing him to another girl. Eljay finally arrives—with his new girlfriend. Rainbow is at first polite, but eventually orders them out. Miss Josie arrives soon after that and, though relieved to learn that nothing happened, lectures Rainbow all the way back to her house. Once there, Miss Josie must leave again on a quick errand and Rainbow waits for her on the front steps. She learns from a nosy neighbor the truth about Miss Josie's husband: he has run off with another woman. At this, Rainbow rushes into Miss Josie's apartment and finds her secret papers strewn all over, including her passport listing her age as fifty-seven, not fifty as she tells everyone. When Miss Josie returns, Rainbow demands to know why she lied about her age, why she's been pretending. This time it is Rainbow giving advice about facing up to things, Rainbow who reads the letter Miss Josie has received from Hal asking for a divorce. The next morning at breakfast, conference day, Miss Josie must tell Rainbow that Kathie called late last night and cannot get back. "Miss Josie," Rainbow says, "my mother doesn't love me as much as I love her." Then she asks if Miss Josie loves her. Miss Josie assures Rainbow that she cares about her deeply and will go to school with her. Furthermore, she suggests that Rainbow stay on with her for six months or so, and Rainbow agrees. On the way to school, Miss Josie volunteers to tell the teachers she is Rainbow's aunt, but Rainbow says no. She recognizes that the lie Miss Josie tells about her age is a little one, not one that hurts anyone. She decides to stop her own big lies about her mother.

This story of emotional growth is written from three viewpoints—Rainbow's, Kathie's and Miss Josie's—but it is focused on Rainbow. It is she who comes to realize that her mother will not change and so she herself must stop pretending and start living. For all her years Rainbow has lived in fear—fear that Kathie will hurt her, fear that she will do something Kathie disapproves of, fear that Kathie will not return, fear that Kathie does not love her. The quiet support she receives from Miss Josie and the way Miss Josie faces her own lie and fear of abandonment encourage and strengthen Rainbow, enabling her to admit her fears. In the end, she reveals a budding inner strength. By presenting the viewpoints of all three characters and thus gaining sympathy or understanding for each, the author demonstrates the complexity of their situations. Use of black dialect strengthens, rather than obscures, this memorable story, which includes several candid discussions about sex and some profanity.

Ages 12 and up

**Also available in:**
Cassette—*Rainbow Jordan*
Library of Congress (NLSBPH)

Paperbound—*Rainbow Jordan*
Avon Books

## 116

**Chorao, Kay**

**Molly's Lies**

Black/white illustrations by the author.
The Seabury Press, Inc., 1979.
(30 pages counted)

*HONESTY/DISHONESTY*
 *School: entering*
 *Thumb sucking*

Molly is starting school today. Since she doesn't want to go, she tells her mother she has lost her clothes. She puts on her cowgirl costume instead and then announces that the school called to say she could have the day off. Her mother understands that Molly is frightened and tries to allay her fears. The children at school, however, are not as understanding about her lies. When she tells Joseph, the boy from Apartment 7A in her building, that her thumbs are wrapped in bandages because her pet crocodile bit them, he says she is lying. Molly's feelings are hurt, but instead of crying she goes to the paint room. She tells a red-haired girl that she is a "good painter." Then she proceeds to dribble paint all over her paper and the floor. The children giggle and call her a liar. Later, when she says that her picture, which looks like a bird, is really just a printing of her name, Joseph tells the others not to believe her. But Molly discovers that Joseph has his problems too. When he refuses to climb a rope hanging from the platform over the doll corner, the other boys call him "Skeerty-cat." Molly sympathizes and asks him why he doesn't want to climb the rope. To Molly's surprise, Joseph confides that he is scared. "Why did you say that?" asks Molly. "Weren't you afraid I would laugh at you?" Joseph replies, "If I lied you would know I was lying. . . . Then you would laugh." This bit of honesty encourages Molly to try truthfulness. "My Mom wraps my thumbs because . . . I suck my thumbs," whispers Molly. Joseph doesn't laugh, and now he is her friend. That afternoon on the way home from school, Molly tells her mother that the children didn't believe her when she told the truth. That, continues Molly, is because "I USED to tell sooo many lies!"

In this companion story to *Molly's Moe*, little Molly learns that lying is not the way to make friends or get along well at school. Readers may note that people usually laugh at what others do, not at who or what they are. Soft pencil drawings add to the book's warmth and humor.

Ages 4-7

**Also available in:**
No other form known

**117**

Ciliotta, Claire and Carole Livingston

**Why Am I Going to the Hospital?**

Color illustrations by Dick Wilson.
Lyle Stuart, Inc., 1981.
(47 pages counted)

---

*HOSPITAL, GOING TO*
  *Surgery*

---

Although nobody likes going to a hospital (except perhaps mothers going there to have their babies), it is sometimes necessary. A hospital is a little like a factory: doctors, nurses, aides, technicians, clerks, pharmacists, and other personnel all have specific jobs to do. Doctors, who have different specialties, are your body's mechanics; they work to fix whatever isn't working properly. Children who come to the hospital because of accidents are generally taken to the Emergency Room first, because there they can receive help quickly. You may be hurting, and doctors and nurses may have to do things that hurt you, but it's all done so that you'll feel better soon. If you know in advance when you're going to the hospital, you can bring your favorite toys and books. At first you'll be very busy, with many people working to find out what's ailing you. They will test your urine and probably your blood. You'll be in the Pediatrics Ward, a part of the hospital that's just for children. You may feel scared, angry, lonely, even bored. But everyone is working as fast as possible to help you go home soon. You may make friends there; sometimes other patients can answer questions you might have. If they can't, ask your doctor or the nurses. If you're in the hospital for an operation, you won't be allowed to eat or drink anything for at least twelve hours before your surgery. You'll be awakened early that day and given medicine to make you sleepy again. ("The medicine may be put into you with a needle. Yucch!") Doctors and nurses you see will be dressed in special clothes, including masks, in order to keep everything as clean as possible. All kinds of machines will be hooked up to you. But soon you'll be asleep—a different kind of sleep from the kind at night—and you won't feel anything or know anything until your operation is over. You'll stay in the Recovery Room for a while and then you'll go back to your own room. You might not feel well at first, but when you do, your doctor will send you home.

Part of a series on issues of importance to children, this oversized book with its delightful, full-page illustrations emphasizes that while hospitals aren't places we'd choose to stay in, they're not that bad, serve a necessary function, and are sometimes unavoidable. Children will be reassured by the simple, practical, accurate descriptions of hospital routines. The book's focus on asking questions and getting information is valuable, and the down-to-earth tone gives its suggestions credibility, especially in answer to the universal question: But does it hurt? (The answers vary from "sometimes" to "not much.") Also notable is the message that people are hospitalized solely because they are ill, not because they've been naughty and are being punished. Here is a great deal of useful information for children facing a hospital experience—expected or unexpected.

Ages 5-10

**Also available in:**
No other form known

**118**

Cleary, Beverly Bunn

**Ramona and Her Mother**

Black/white illustrations by Alan Tiegreen.
William Morrow & Company, Inc., 1979.
(208 pages)

---

*CHANGE: Accepting*
*FAMILY: Relationships*
  *Parent/Parents: mother working outside home*
  *School: pupil-teacher relationships*
  *Sibling: rivalry*
  *Sibling: younger*

---

Howie Kemp is Ramona Quimby's best friend, but Willa Jean is his little sister—and a pest. When Ramona, seven-and-a-half, overhears neighbors say that little Willa Jean reminds them of her when she was younger, the girl is highly insulted. She thinks Willa Jean is spoiled and a show-off, not at all like her. But when she asks her mother about it later, her mother tells her that she was indeed a lively little girl with a lot of imagination. This information upsets Ramona, as do other events in the Quimby household. Ramona's father, after being out of work for quite a while, at last has a job, as cashier at the Shop-Rite Market. But he hates it and sometimes comes home grouchy. Ramona is sure her mother will now quit her full-time job and once again become a full-time mother; she misses their times together. However, to her disappointment, she learns that her mother plans to continue working. This means Ramona has to go to the Kemps' house after school. She worries that she and her mother have grown apart since her mother started working. She also feels that Beezus, her seventh-grade sister, gets more of their mother's attention. When her mother and Beezus quarrel over Beezus's hairdo, Ramona is glad to see they aren't getting along. Yet she worries a little because she wants the family to be happy. Several weeks later, Ramona is given a new pair of flannel pajamas. She loves them so much she decides to wear them to school under her clothes. Her teacher, Mrs. Rucker, notices how hot Ramona looks, and finally Ramona tells her about the pajamas. To the girl's surprise, Mrs. Rucker does not laugh at her, and Ramona feels they share a special secret. That Saturday she overhears her mother talking to Mrs. Rucker on the phone. Sure that her teacher is telling her mother their secret about the pajamas, Ramona screams that she hates Mrs. Rucker. She also screams that nobody likes her, not even her own mother and father, and that Beezus gets all the attention. Beezus, in turn, argues that Ramona gets more attention and has fewer chores than she does. Ramona then declares she is running away. Her mother helps her pack, all the while explaining how to pack a suitcase properly. When Romana finds that the suitcase is so full she can't lift it, she knows her mother didn't mean to let her go. She also learns that Mrs. Rucker's call was about Ramona's nose twitching. She was wondering if Ramona was nervous about something. Ramona explains

C

that she was pretending to be a rabbit. Assured of her family's love and Mrs. Rucker's concern, Ramona goes happily off to roller skate.

This funny and touching story shows the struggles of a little girl to cope with changes in her family's life style resulting from hard economic times. Ramona comes to realize that these changes, while upsetting, do not affect her parents' love for her. This is one in a series of books about Ramona and her family and friends, and it makes appealing, satisfying reading. Each episode is appropriately illustrated and exceptionally true to life.

Ages 7-10

**Also available in:**
Cassette—*Ramona and Her Mother*
Miller-Brody Productions

Filmstrip—*Ramona and Her Mother*
Miller-Brody Productions

Paperbound—*Ramona and Her Mother*
Dell Publishing Company, Inc.

## 119

**Cleary, Beverly Bunn**

## Ramona Quimby, Age 8

Black/white illustrations by Alan Tiegreen.
William Morrow & Company, Inc., 1981.
(190 pages)

---

*FAMILY: Relationships*
    *Money: management*
    *School: classmate relationships*
    *School: pupil-teacher relationships*

---

It's the first day of school and things are a bit different in the Quimby family. Ramona will be riding the bus for the first time and, because of changes in the system, she and the other third graders will be the oldest kids at school. Beatrice (called Beezus) is starting junior high. Their mother has taken a job, and their father is returning to school to become a teacher. Ramona still has to go to Howie Kemp's grandmother's house after school, where Howie's little sister, Willa Jean, still drives her crazy. One week, all the kids bring hard-boiled eggs for lunch. A clowning Ramona becomes an angry and embarrassed Ramona when she cracks her egg open on her head and discovers her mother hasn't boiled it. While the principal helps her wash the egg out, she overhears some teachers talking and is devastated when her teacher, Mrs. Whaley, refers to her as a show-off and a nuisance. From then on, Ramona tries anxiously to avoid being a nuisance. One day she ruins everything by throwing up in the classroom. Sick as she is, she must wait in the office for some time before her mother can leave work and come for her. Then she finds that the car has broken down and they must take a taxi. In other circumstances, Ramona would have loved the excitement of her first taxi ride. But now she's too distressed and ill. She can't bear to tell her mother that she didn't let Mrs. Whaley know she felt sick because she was trying hard not to be a nuisance. But her mother stays home from work to take care of her and doesn't seem to mind. The family continues to have its ups and downs. The car needs a

new transmission, which they can't afford; Beezus is worried about a party she's invited to; and Ramona is worried about a book report she has to give. Searching for inspiration, she decides to give the report as if it were a cat-food commercial. She even wears a cat mask. From behind it, she feels brave enough to tell Mrs. Whaley about her fears of being a nuisance. The teacher explains that Ramona misunderstood; Mrs. Whaley meant that washing egg out of hair was a nuisance, not that Ramona was a nuisance. Restored to good spirits at school, Ramona worries anew about her family. Her parents, she knows, fret about the future. Ramona herself worries about her father getting locked in the frozen-food warehouse where he now works part-time. One rainy Sunday when the Quimby house seems particularly small and its inhabitants especially grouchy, Mr. Quimby suggests they all go to a fast-food restaurant and never mind the cost. A stranger, an older gentleman, pays for their dinner because, he tells the waitress, they look like such a nice family. On the way home, Mrs. Quimby says she thinks the man was right—they are a nice family. Not all the time, maintains Ramona. But her father says nobody is nice all the time unless they're very boring. Ramona decides in the end that "she was a member of a nice sticking-together family."

Well known to most young readers, Ramona Quimby stars in another story of everyday life in the Quimby family home and at school. This time the Quimbys must cope with the changes that attend the father's decision to return to school. Plucky Ramona must also learn to adjust to a new teacher she's sure dislikes her. But all is either resolved or accepted in this realistic, appealing, and funny story with its whimsical illustrations. Old and new fans of Ramona Quimby will be thoroughly pleased.

Ages 8-10

**Also available in:**
Braille—*Ramona Quimby, Age 8*
Library of Congress (NLSBPH)

Cassette—*Ramona Quimby, Age 8*
Library of Congress (NLSBPH)

Cassette—*Ramona Quimby, Age 8*
Miller-Brody Productions

Filmstrip—*Ramona Quimby, Age 8*
Miller-Brody Productions

Paperbound—*Ramona Quimby, Age 8*
Dell Publishing Company, Inc.

## 120

**Clifford, Ethel Rosenberg**

## The Killer Swan

Houghton Mifflin Company, 1980.
(114 pages)

---

*PARENT/PARENTS: Remarriage of*
*SUICIDE: of Parent*
    *Guilt, feelings of*
    *Pets: love for*
    *Stepparent: father*
    *Violence*

---

Fourteen-year-old Lex Mebbin has had an emotionally wrenching year, and the boy has reacted by withdrawing into himself. Several years ago his father, an ironworker and a moody, emotional man who boasted of being "a bird. Free as the breeze," had an accident that cost him one of his arms. Totally unable to live with his handicap, angry and morose, he committed suicide. Lex feels guilty still—there were bad times when he had wished his father dead. Then, a year ago, Lex's mother, Stella, married Steve Mebbin and the three of them moved from the city to the country. Although Steve is a calm, quiet man, Lex has not been able to accept affection from him. Lately, two swans have settled on the pond in front of their home. Stella, who sees their arrival as an omen, has been researching the birds' behavior. The male swan, the cob, is sightless in one eye, which periodically causes him much pain. During these times he is especially aggressive about protecting his territory and his babies, the cygnets. One day as Lex is absent-mindedly throwing pebbles into the pond, two cygnets, attracted by the sound, head toward him. The cob, in his attack position, grabs the first cygnet by the neck and snaps the baby back and forth until its neck breaks. Lex manages to rescue the second cygnet, but is then himself attacked by the cob. Lex falls, injuring his wrist, and his stepfather frantically helps him to safety from the murderous swan. Lex decides to raise the small cygnet whom he names Survivor, and the two become inseparable. He and Steve build an enclosure that allows Survivor to go to the pond, yet protects him from the cob. During the Fourth of July holidays, Caleb, Lex's only friend and fellow archery enthusiast, stays with the Mebbins. One day Caleb's puppy, Shadow, a playmate to Survivor, ventures too close to the pond and is attacked by the killer swan. When he sees Shadow's lifeless body, Lex shoots an arrow into the cob's breast, killing him. Steve puts his arm around Lex to comfort him and Lex, for the first time, doesn't pull away. Later that evening he willingly accepts the companionship of Steve and his mother. The barriers are gone.

Lex struggles with two enemies: a murderous swan and all the unanswered questions surrounding his father's violent death. The parallel between the cob and Lex's strange, morose father is sustained throughout this thought-provoking story, particularly in several arresting chapters written from the swan's viewpoint. As Lex works through his feelings about the swan, flashbacks allow the reader to relive some of his good and bad times with his father. When he kills the swan he seems also to destroy his grief and guilt, allowing him to accept the love of his understanding stepfather. Slow-paced, at times almost brooding in tone, this unusual and well-written book merits discussion.

Ages 10-12

**Also available in:**
Cassette—*The Killer Swan*
Library of Congress (NLSBPH)

**121**

Clifton, Lucille

**The Lucky Stone**
Black/white illustrations by Dale Payson.
Delacorte Press, 1979.
(64 pages)

GRANDPARENT: Love for
  Afro-American

Tee, about seven, enjoys listening to tales told by her beloved great-grandmother, Mrs. Elzie F. Pickens. Long ago Mrs. Pickens, then a young girl, received a small, black stone with an "A" scratched on it. Vashti, the woman who gave it to her in exchange for the child's getting her a glass of water on a hot day, told Elzie a story about her mother, then a slave. Vashti's mother, fearing a beating because she had spilled the cotton she picked, had run away and desperately needed help. She attracted the attention of a passing slave by throwing the stone out of the cave where she was hiding. Vashti's life also was saved by the stone when, scrambling after it, she narrowly escaped being struck by lightning. Mrs. Pickens then tells Tee how a chain of circumstances involving the stone meant luck for her also. At first Tee cannot understand the luck of her great-grandmother's being chased by a dog who was hit by the stone, only to be saved by young Amos, the future Mr. Pickens, but years later she does. Now a teenager, Tee wants to receive a valentine from a boy at school but doubts she will. She fears that her only love in life will be her great-grandmother. But that love is imperiled when pneumonia forces Mrs. Pickens into a hospital. No visitors are allowed, but Tee manages to sneak in. Her great-grandmother tells her about an envelope Tee must find at home. Inside the envelope, Tee discovers the lucky stone, now hers. She falls asleep clutching it and is awakened that evening by her parents and her great-grandmother, well again and back from the hospital. Later that day Tee receives a valentine from the boy she likes. She concludes, "Now that is the story of how I got my lucky stone and it started being lucky for me."

This series of stories, beginning just before the Emancipation Proclamation and spanning many decades, is skillfully tied together by a lucky stone and by the love between a great-grandmother and her young great-granddaughter. This love permeates all the accounts of the workings of luck in people's lives, luck arising not from magic but from circumstances and human effort. Realistic drawings underscore the naturalness of the events depicted. Black English lends interest and character to the text without obscuring the story.

Ages 8-10

**Also available in:**
No other form known

**C**

**122**

Clifton, Lucille

## My Friend Jacob

Black/white illustrations by Thomas Di Grazia.
E. P. Dutton & Company, Inc., 1980.
(31 pages counted)

---

*FRIENDSHIP: Best Friend*
*MENTAL RETARDATION*

---

Sam, black and eight years old, and Jacob, white and seventeen, are best friends and enjoy helping one another. Jacob gives Sam pointers about basketball. Since he is bigger, he often carries groceries home from the store for Sam. And Jacob is teaching Sam to identify the make of any car as it passes. Sometimes, however, Jacob forgets things, such as what color the traffic light should be when they cross the street, and then Sam helps his friend remember. Since the boys' birthdays are only two days apart, they celebrate together. This year Jacob has a special present for Sam, a homemade card with the words, "Happy Birthday Sam—Jacob." The printing has taken Jacob "weeks and weeks," and Sam is very excited about his friend's accomplishment. Jacob has a bad habit: he always walks into Sam's house without knocking first, as he does at the home of everyone he knows. If he doesn't know anyone at a house, he stands outside the door "until somebody notices him and lets him in." So Sam decides to help his friend learn how to knock before entering. Every day Sam reminds Jacob about knocking, but Jacob always forgets. After a while, Sam gets discouraged and begins to think Jacob will never learn. But the following day, while Sam and his parents are eating dinner, they hear a loud knock at the door. Jacob peeks inside, yelling, "I'm knocking, Sam!" An elated Sam jumps up to give Jacob a big best-friend hug, exclaiming, "He is my very very very best friend in the whole wide world!"

Sam and Jacob's friendship is nurtured by their acceptance of each other's limitations and by their willingness to help one another. The fact that the older Jacob is mentally slower than young Sam or that their races are different presents no barriers to their friendship. This uncomplicated first-person narrative, told by Sam and enhanced by pencil drawings, would be an outstanding introduction to mental retardation, offering examples of appreciation, respect, patience, love.

Ages 4-7

**Also available in:**
No other form known

---

**123**

Clifton, Lucille

## Sonora Beautiful

Black/white illustrations by Michael Garland.
E. P. Dutton & Company, Inc., 1981.
(22 pages)

---

*LIFE STYLE*
*SELF, ATTITUDE TOWARD: Feeling Different*
  *Appearance: concern about*
  *Family: relationships*
  *Name, dissatisfaction with*

---

Some mornings when Sonora wakes up, she is sure she's ugly. She's convinced that her face is broken out, her ears are waving, and everything is hanging loose. She goes across the hall, bangs on her mother's door, and tells her that something happened in the night. "I got real ugly." Her mother tells her she's beautiful. Sonora says nobody else in her whole school has a name like Sonora, that only she was named after the desert where her mother first saw her father. When she begs her parents to change her name they just look at her, and her mother tells her it's a beautiful name. Another thing that bothers Sonora is that her father is a poet. She has told her friends at school that her father is a boxer (he works out with weights). She's asked her mother many times to talk to her father about perhaps getting a job at the supermarket or someplace. But her mother says that poetry and poets like her father are beautiful. Sonora also dislikes her house. "Honestly, no other person in my whole school lives in a house like this one. I have spoken to them a million times about moving to a nice house with regular rooms and maybe a fence and a dog." But her mother tells her that their home—with one room for lifting weights, another for writing poetry, another filled with plants—is beautiful. Sonora and her parents go for lots of walks, often at dawn. Sometimes they go to a park. They all smile and hug each other, and then her father reads a beautiful poem. Sonora concludes, "We're a family and it's beautiful. Beautiful."

A teenage girl complains about the peculiarities of her life: her changing body, her unusual name, her father's atypical profession, and the irregular house they live in. Her mother sees the beauty in each of these things, and eventually Sonora is able to see it too. This brief, unusual book is written rather like a song or poem, with the mother's refrain ending each chapter: "It's beautiful, Sonora. Beautiful." Sonora's laments are interspersed with pleas for credibility: "I'm not joking." Expressive drawings take up nearly half of the book's pages. The first-person approach makes Sonora very real and allows readers to sympathize with all the family nonconformity she endures and learns to appreciate. This is a Skinny Book, part of a series designed for older readers with limited reading skills. These well-written books focus on the interests and concerns of today's young people and should have great appeal.

Ages 12-14

**Also available in:**
No other form known

**124**

**Coates, Belle**

**Mak**

Houghton Mifflin Company, 1981.
(214 pages)

---

CHANGE: Accepting
NATIVE AMERICAN
    Change: resisting
    Courage, meaning of
    Decision making
    Fear: of the unknown
    Orphan

---

When Pop Williams picks up Makosica Mike Malloy (Mak), his teenage foster son, from the Indian Boarding School for summer vacation, he tells Mak that the recent drought on the Montana reservation lands has ruined business for Halfway House, his lunch counter and gas station. So Pop will retire and soon head for California. With special permission of the authorities, he plans to take Mak with him. An orphan and ward of the government, Mak is biologically only one-quarter Indian, but he wants to stay in Montana to search for "his wa-sic, symbol of a personal power that would help preserve his Indianness." Wa-sic is only found through struggle and danger. One day an old Indian man asks Mak to find his horse, lost in the badlands on Big Bench, near the fearful Spirit Face that grins from the canyon wall. After a hot, difficult day, Mak finds the horse right in front of the evil Spirit Face. Overcome with fear of the face, Mak drops his rope and begins to back away. Just then he stumbles and his hand touches an odd bone that seems made of stone and has a hole down its center. He puts it in his pocket. Immediately the horse gallops toward him and Mak is able to lasso it. Later he tells Mary Sits, the Indian housekeeper at Halfway House and Mak's mentor, that he has found his wa-sic. One day Mary asks Mak to go with her to the Barrack ranch to deliver some moccasins she made for young Gail Barrack. The Barracks, a white family of wheat farmers, are being driven off their ranch by the drought. Their only hope is Chuck Engle, a paleontologist searching for badland fossils. If he finds fossils, the College Foundation will send out a crew to do further work, boarding them at the ranch and thus providing the Barracks with a little income. But Chuck's search has so far been fruitless. Jim Barrack, a little older than Mak, sees that Mak's wa-sic is a fossil and asks Mak to guide Chuck back to the place where he found it. Mak has no desire to go anywhere near the Spirit Face again but Jim is adamant, determined to help save his family's ranch. Uncertain about getting involved, Mak eventually agrees, but guides Chuck only along the highways. He knows the Barracks are counting on him, but he is letting them down "for a reason so deeply Indian that it couldn't be explained or denied." Then Chuck is invited to the Indian council meeting to discuss his permit to excavate. Mak is torn between supporting Chuck and adhering to Indian beliefs about not interfering with Mother Earth. Sentiment is strong against Chuck. When Mak translates Chuck's scientific terminology, he is accused of disloyalty and branded an outcast. However, Chuck has an ace up his sleeve. He says his studies have shown that there is a great deal of wealth in the Indians' land: gypsum, sand to make cement, tungsten, and other minerals. The council votes to allow Chuck his permit and to reinstate Mak. Mak finally agrees to guide Chuck to Spirit Face. When they get near Big Bench, Chuck offers the boy a way out: he can return to fetch a whiskbroom. Mak protests, but then goes. A violent duststorm springs up. Realizing that Chuck is in the midst of it, Mak returns in the jeep. A sudden rainstorm hits and a flash flood nearly carries Mak off, but Chuck reaches down from the canyon wall to pull him up. From their vantage point they see the outline of a huge mastodon. Spirit Face! Now Mak can relinquish some of his fear. The excavations and the drought's end have saved the Barrack ranch. Pop writes from California, enclosing a round-trip bus ticket for Mak to come visit him. Mary shows Mak her savings book; for years she has saved her money so Mak can go to college. She also gives Mak her great-grandfather's chieftain headdress so Gail can complete her collection of Indian beadwork, sell it, and use the money for college. Gail intends to return to the badlands to teach in an Indian school. Mary tells Mak to remind Gail that Indian children must grow up knowing how to stay Indian inside, yet adapt to external changes.

In this slowly unfolding, well-written story of an orphaned boy torn between two cultures, the reader gains considerable insight into the feelings, beliefs, and way of life of Native Americans, particularly their struggle to retain their culture. A lengthy drought is the catalyst for the choices both Mak and his people have to make. Change is essential, they find, and yet change often pits the old ways against the new. After much soul-searching, Mak manages to make the right choices.

Ages 12 and up

**Also available in:**
No other form known

C

**125**

**Cohen, Barbara Nash**

**Fat Jack**

Atheneum Publishers, 1980.
(182 pages)

---

BOY-GIRL RELATIONSHIPS
SELF, ATTITUDE TOWARD: Feeling Different
    Ostracism
    School: classmate relationships
    School: pupil-teacher relationships
    Teasing
    Weight control: overweight

---

Judy Goldstein, a high school senior, is annoyed with a clique of popular girls who like to tease Jack Muldoon, an extremely overweight transfer student. When the girls go to great lengths to ridicule and humiliate Jack, Judy defends him and becomes his first and only friend. Soon afterwards, Miss DeLorenzo, an English teacher, announces that she has no time to direct the senior class play this year. She suggests that the play committee, of which Judy is a member, ask the new librarian, Mr. Sharf, to direct, since he has theater experience. Mr. Sharf, a cool, aloof man, agrees to take responsibility on two conditions. He will have "absolute control of every aspect of the entire production," and the play will be his selection. Though the committee agrees, they groan when he announces his choice: *Henry IV, Part I.* Mr. Sharf tells Jack that he is expected to try out for the part of the overweight comic hero, Falstaff. Jack refuses, fearing ridicule. He appeals to Judy to change Mr. Sharf's mind, but Mr. Sharf insists. In fact, he admits to Judy that he chose the play because he knows Jack has the intelligence and talent to play the role. Deciding his unpopularity can get no worse, Jack finally agrees to play Falstaff. Judy is given a small part. Mr. Sharf, who has dropped casual references to swords, fighting, and singing parts to attract participants and to create student interest in the play, proceeds to show his expertise in directing. Little by little the cast begins to understand the play, even to like it. One afternoon the rehearsal is particularly exciting. Jack and Craig, as Falstaff and the Prince, have learned their lines perfectly. As they move through their scene the other players, for the first time, catch the spirit of the play and the humor of the scene before them. Everyone applauds. Later, in the hallway, Jack kisses Judy, and to her surprise she likes it. From then on, rehearsals improve. The first performance is a real test of how Shakespeare—and Jack—will be received by the student body. The play is a great success and Jack becomes, at least temporarily, a hero. In two succeeding performances, the play is enthusiastically received by the community. After the final performance, Judy gives a cast party. Through the many weeks of rehearsals she has been paired with Jack, and the two sincerely admire one another. But recently a classmate, Joan, who formerly teased and tormented Jack, has begun to show an interest in him. At the party Joan appropriates Jack, and Judy ends up with Joan's former boyfriend, Al. After the excitement of the play dies down, Jack and Judy see less and less of one another, each thinking the other is interested in someone else. Late in the school year the two learn that Mr. Sharf has been asked to leave his position. The wife of a school board member wants to be the school librarian, so her cronies threaten to reveal that Mr. Sharf was once a patient in a psychiatric hospital. Judy wants to help him fight for his position, but Mr. Sharf prefers to resign and Jack insists they respect his decision. As the school year ends, Mr. Sharf departs quietly.

This bittersweet story of friendship is told by Judy as a flashback. In the first chapter, Jack, now married and an award-winning writer, visits Judy, married and with children. In the final chapter, the two admit that each thought the other responsible for their long-ago breakup. Even so, their mutual admiration and tenderness have endured through the years. The themes of a great play are expertly interwoven with modern high school life in this accomplished book. The friendship between two lonely young people is beautifully developed, and all the characters have an unusual depth and breadth. There is enough here to invite a second reading.

Ages 11 and up

**Also available in:**
No other form known

## 126

**Cohen, Barbara Nash**

## The Innkeeper's Daughter

Lothrop, Lee & Shepard Company, 1979.
(159 pages)

---

*INFERIORITY, FEELINGS OF*
*Boy-girl relationships*
*Family: unity*
*Life style*
*Parent/Parents: single*
*Weight control: overweight*

---

Sixteen, overweight, and self-conscious, Rachel Gold spends her time reading and studying, rather than socializing. She wishes she could live like "ordinary people." Instead, she lives with her mother and younger brother and sister in the Waterbridge Inn in New Jersey. Her attractive, self-assured mother owns the Inn and has successfully run it alone since Rachel's father died seven years earlier, in 1941. Rachel's mother loves antiques and one Saturday morning returns with a huge painting, a portrait of an eighteenth- or early nineteenth-century Scottish laird, which she hangs in the Inn's entry. Rachel hates it. Even when an antique dealer says it may be worth one thousand dollars, Rachel is unimpressed. She hates the Inn and now she hates the painting. She also dislikes Ted Jensen, a divorced businessman who frequently stays at the Inn, because she suspects that he and her mother are having an affair. This is later confirmed when, late one night, she hears them together in her mother's bedroom. Ted introduces the Golds to Jeff Dulac, his special accountant, and Jeff temporarily moves in while working on the Jensen account. Rachel and Jeff, eleven years her senior, find they share an interest in books. At the Inn's Christmas party, the two spend the evening dancing and Jeff even kisses Rachel. But he also tells her he has completed his job with Jensen and is leaving the Inn. Despite herself, Rachel is heartbroken. Her mother, while noting that Jeff is too old for her, comforts the girl by suggesting that his attentions should prove to her that she really is attractive after all. Then disaster strikes. As the Golds prepare for their New Year's Eve party, an electrical fire starting in the attic forces them to vacate the Inn. Before the fire can be contained, the place is destroyed. The firefighters do save one thing—the antique painting. After the Golds settle in a small apartment and Mrs. Gold announces her plans to marry Ted Jensen, Rachel decides to find out more about the painting she hates. Researching at the library, she discovers they are owners of a very valuable painting worth thousands of dollars. She and her brother and sister happily approve of their mother's marriage plans, but they insist that the Inn be rebuilt, wedding or not. Rachel has found a new satisfaction in being an innkeeper's daughter.

A girl's fears about her own unattractiveness are remedied by the attentions of an admirer and by an improved relationship with her attractive mother in this entertaining first-person narrative. The story and characters are interesting and believable, never dated, although the events take place in the 1940s. The reader shares Rachel's trials and triumphs as the girl grows in self-awareness.

Ages 11-14

**Also available in:**
No other form known

## 127

Cohen, Miriam

**First Grade Takes a Test**

Color illustrations by Lillian Aberman Hoban.
Greenwillow Books, 1980.
(32 pages counted)

---

*SCHOOL: Classmate Relationships*
   *Education: special*
   *School: pupil-teacher relationships*

---

A woman from the principal's office gives the first grade a standardized multiple-choice test. All but Anna Maria have some trouble with the test. She is the only one to finish and declares it easy. Sometime later the woman returns and takes Anna Maria to a special class because she did so well on the test. The remaining children begin to call each other "dummy" because they weren't selected for the special class. Their teacher reassures them that a test cannot measure important things like drawing pictures, building things, reading books, or being kind to friends. Then she gives them cookies, and the children feel better. Despite her transfer, Anna Maria stops by her old classroom each morning. She worries that the plants may not get watered and that George isn't getting enough help with his arithmetic. At the end of the week she returns to her old class to stay. When the other children ask why, Anna Maria says, "I told them I had to come back. I told them first grade needs me." The teacher remarks that it's good to be all together again.

A standardized test that results in a bright classmate's temporary placement in a special class causes some unhappiness for a group of first graders. But the teacher discounts the test's ability to measure "important things" about a person, and soon Anna Maria returns happily to her old class. The damage to children's self-esteem that can result from school placement based on test scores is worth considering, and the book provides an amusing look at the ways children react to standardized test items. (Sammy, for example, when asked what firemen do, thinks of his uncle being helped by firemen when he got his head stuck in a pipe.) But an anti-intellectual bias is present here, and the idea that a child could leave a special class after one week because her friends need her is farfetched indeed. This cleverly illustrated story is one in a series.

Ages 5-7

**Also available in:**
Cassette—*First Grade Takes a Test*
Educational Enrichment Corporation

Filmstrip—*First Grade Takes a Test*
Educational Enrichment Corporation

Paperback—*First Grade Takes a Test*
Dell Publishing Company, Inc.

## 128

Cohen, Miriam

**No Good in Art**

Color illustrations by Lillian Aberman Hoban.
Greenwillow Books, 1980.
(32 pages counted)

---

*TALENTS: Artistic*
   *School: classmate relationships*
   *School: negative experiences*
   *School: pupil-teacher relationships*

---

When Jim was in kindergarten, his art teacher criticized his drawing, saying the man in the picture had no neck and the grass should be drawn with thin lines. She even painted over the boy's work. Now Jim is in first grade. His new art teacher asks the children to paint a picture about what they want to be when they grow up. Jim's classmates begin eagerly and the teacher praises everyone's picture, even though some do not meet the assignment. But Jim doesn't even attempt a picture. He's "no good in art," he says, and doesn't know what he wants to be. So the teacher tells him to paint a picture of what he likes to do. Reluctantly Jim begins, and as he continues to paint he thinks of many ways to make his picture beautiful. When the teacher asks the class to put their names on their pictures and turn them in, only Jim hides his picture under his desk. But classmates Willy and Sammy take Jim's picture and hand it in. The teacher hangs up all the pictures and everyone admires Jim's, wondering whose it is. Willy and Sammy identify the artist by pulling Jim to the front of the room. His classmates ask what the picture shows. He tells them, "It's me eating pizza." Then Sara, another classmate, asks Jim what he is going to be when he grows up. Willy and Sammy suggest that Jim might be an artist. The art teacher agrees. Another classmate, Paul, tells Jim, "You're good." Finally Jim is convinced he has actually drawn a beautiful picture.

With encouragement from his new art teacher and his classmates, a talented little boy overcomes the insecurity and fear of drawing planted in him by a former teacher. Young readers will sympathize with Jim's feelings, and adults may be helped to remember how powerful their influence on children can be. This colorfully illustrated book is one in a series about Jim and his classmates.

Ages 5-7

**Also available in:**
Cassette—*No Good in Art*
Educational Enrichment Corporation

Filmstrip—*No Good in Art*
Educational Enrichment Corporation

C

## 129

**Cohen, Miriam**

**So What?**

Color illustrations by Lillian Aberman Hoban.
Greenwillow Books, 1982.
(32 pages counted)

---

*SELF, ATTITUDE TOWARD: Feeling Different*
 *Differences, human*
 *School: classmate relationships*

---

Jim is upset because all his friends can hang upside down by their knees on the jungle gym. Jim can hang upside down, but "Jim's hands would not let go." He overhears Anna Maria talking about the most popular children in first grade. He is not one of them. So, to be more popular, Jim decides to start a club. Everyone wants to join except Elinor, the new girl from Chicago. But when Jim explains the complicated rules of his club, no one wants to belong anymore. Jim is disappointed; Elinor says, "So what?" When the nurse measures the class, Jim discovers he is the shortest. Once again Elinor says, "So what?" Dejected by his failure to keep step during square dancing, Jim is sure he can't do anything right. But Elinor maintains, "Some things are easy for some people and hard for other people. So what?" Every day, Jim practices hanging upside down. One day he notices Elinor is missing and learns she has moved back to Chicago. As he hangs upside down on the jungle gym he thinks through all the things that have made him feel left out. Suddenly he lets go with his hands and yells, "So what?"

A little boy who feels left out and incapable of success is encouraged by a classmate's "so what" attitude. Jim's concerns and interests are typical of this age group and will appeal to young readers. However, the message—that people aren't the same and shouldn't worry about being different—is rather subtle and may need some explanation. Colorful, lively illustrations capture the mood of the story, one in a series about Jim and his classmates.

Ages 4-7

**Also available in:**
No other form known

## 130

**Cole, Brock**

**No More Baths**

Color illustrations by the author.
Doubleday & Company, Inc., 1980.
(40 pages counted)

---

*BATHS, TAKING OF*
 *Running away*

---

An indignant little Jessie McWhistle has decided to run away from home rather than take a bath in the middle of the day. "Don't think I'm ever coming back, because I've got friends and none of them ever has to take a bath in the middle of the day," she proclaims. On her way along the path by the river Jessie meets Mrs. Chicken, who tries to convince the girl to come live with her. Mrs. Chicken mentions and demonstrates how lovely it is to frazzle, finding a dusty spot where you "squoosh down and ruffle up and shake sand all over your feathers." But Jessie can't get the sand off the way Mrs. Chicken can and just feels like scratching all over. Next Jessie greets Mrs. Cat, who explains her technique of licking to keep clean. Jessie tries it, but is left with sticky, tangled hair. "'Well,' sighed Mrs. Cat, 'I'm afraid you aren't meant to be a cat.'" Jessie encounters Mrs. Pig next and follows her into a big mud puddle to cool off. But Jessie doesn't like feeling so cold and wet. Thinking of peanut butter sandwiches and clean sheets, Jessie heads back home. Without speaking to anyone, she goes directly upstairs and fills the tub for her bath. When she is clean her mother wraps her in a big, fluffy towel and gives her a warm hug. But Jessie still does not admit that there are worse things than taking a bath.

A little girl who doesn't like baths finds that her animal friends have nothing better to offer—but despite her experiences and the pleasantness of being clean, Jessie is still not ready to admit that baths have their good points. This is an amusing story enhanced by whimsical illustrations of a scruffy-looking little heroine moving through a colorful rural setting. It would be an appealing story to read aloud.

Ages 3-6

**Also available in:**
No other form known

## 131

**Collins, David R.**

**If I Could, I Would**

Color illustrations by Kelly Oechsli.
Garrard Publishing Company, 1979.
(47 pages)

---

*LOVE, MEANING OF*
 *Giving, meaning of*
 *Imagination*
 *Wishes*

---

A young boy thinks mothers are nice and his own the best of all. If he could, he would give her candy, lollipops, and a trip to the moon in his wagon pulled by flying horses. If he could, he would eat everything she fixed for him, buy her a haunted house, and give her lots of pets. He'd give her a mountain of ice cream and a big ship with him as captain to scare off pirates. He would take her to the movies, especially monster shows and cartoons. He would let her play all her favorite games and even see that she won some. He would buy a castle for her, if he could, and guard her from dragons. If he could, he would stay in her bedroom on stormy nights and shout away the thunder so she could sleep. He would dress up like a clown and make her laugh, fix her breakfast so she could sleep late, and take her to the amusement park where he and she could sit "real close" on the roller coaster. He would give her a glass car so they could drive under the sea, and he would show her how to make mud pies. He and his mother would each have a rocket ship, and they would play hide-and-seek in the sky. But what he would most like to do, if he could, is read her a story every night and wish her happy dreams. Then she would smile, kiss him, and say she loves him.

A little boy brimming over with love for his mother describes all the wonderful things he'd like to give her and do for her. Predictably enough, all the gifts he dreams of presenting her with are things he himself wants, from a trip to the moon to a goodnight kiss. Filled with colorful drawings, this exceptionally appealing beginning reader may inspire discussion of what might really make parents happy.

Ages 6-8

**Also available in:**
No other form known

## 132

Colman, Hila Crayder

**Accident**

William Morrow & Company, Inc., 1980.
(154 pages)

---

*ACCIDENTS*
*ANGER*
 *Boy-girl relationships*
 *Change: accepting*
 *Guilt, feelings of*
 *Wheelchair, dependence on*

---

Fifteen-year-old Jenny Melino is excited when her secret crush, wealthy Adam DeWitt, asks her out. Adam picks her up that Saturday evening on his motorcycle. He has forgotten the extra helmet and goggles, but they decide not to go back and get them. On their way home, a rock flies up and hits Jenny in the head. She lets go of Adam, the motorcycle hits a bump, and she is thrown off. Adam goes for help, and soon Jenny is rushed unconscious to the hospital. Four days later, she comes to and realizes she cannot move her right side. Meanwhile, Adam is tormented by what has happened. Finally allowed to see Jenny, he is devastated by her anger and begins to question his life and his plans for Harvard in the fall. After several weeks in the hospital, Jenny is moved to Hilltop House, a rehabilitation center. Sally Flanner, Jenny's social worker at Hilltop, confronts the girl about her bitter conviction that she'll never walk again. But Jenny can't even feed herself and exists in a state of rage and frustration. Sally reminds her that if she gives up she will indeed remain helpless. Jenny begins to realize that her recovery is up to her. After she has lived for several weeks at the center, Adam visits. He presents Jenny with the picture he has won first prize with at a photography exhibition, a picture of Jenny on her roller skates, taken several days before the accident. Furious, Jenny refuses to accept a picture that is no longer her, but Adam says it shows her spirit and love for life and sets it on her bureau. Jenny looks at it for a while and sees that Adam is right. She begins trying harder in her therapy sessions. After ten weeks at Hilltop, Jenny is put in a walker. Excited, she calls Adam and asks him to come see her. But after she proudly shows him her progress, Jenny realizes that she

doesn't need Adam to make her feel special anymore. She looks forward to returning home. The future seems bright.

The lives of two young people become intertwined when their first date ends in a tragic motorcycle accident. Jenny must work through her anger and hopelessness; Adam must confront his guilt. This is a fairly perceptive look at the changing feelings and slow rehabilitation process of a recently paralyzed teenager. It is marred by superficial characterizations, but could provoke substantial discussion.

Ages 11 and up

**Also available in:**
Paperbound—*Accident*
Pocket Books, Inc.

## 133

Colman, Hila Crayder

**Confession of a Storyteller**

Crown Publishers, Inc., 1981.
(91 pages) o.p.

---

*HONESTY/DISHONESTY*
 *Boy-girl relationships*
 *Emotions: accepting*
 *Guilt, feelings of*
 *Identification with others: adults*
 *Jealousy*
 *Loneliness*
 *School: pupil-teacher relationships*
 *Self, attitude toward: accepting*

---

Annie Kruger remembers the year gone by, when she was twelve and certainly never meant to hurt Miss Jones. From the very beginning, Annie had found the new music teacher "special and different." Miss Jones is a loner, a lover of music, nature, poetry. Annie's father is rarely home, she has no brothers or sisters, and her mother seldom shares her feelings. Annie has decided she is "cool toward marriage," and she finds the solitary Miss Jones a kindred spirit. After her first piano lesson, Miss Jones invites Annie to a chamber music concert that afternoon. The two become companions and Annie is there when Miss Jones orders a wood-burning stove from a handsome salesman, Jason Pascal. Annie sees his interest in her teacher and takes an immediate dislike to him. Annie herself has an admirer, Brian. One day as she and he walk in the woods, they meet Miss Jones and Jason there. For reasons the girl doesn't quite understand, this encounter leaves her shocked and angry. Despite Brian's interest in her, Annie is not at all sure she wants a boyfriend. So when Brian kisses her and she finds she likes it very much, she is mortified. After her next music lesson she asks Miss Jones about "bad" thoughts and feelings. Miss Jones tries to reassure her, urging her not to be afraid of her emotions. Somehow, this response disappoints Annie. At her next lesson, Annie sees unmistakable evidence that Jason is living with Miss Jones. "I was in a state of shock. . . . She was sleeping with a man—she was gross and ordinary like everybody else. I cried over a loss I could not name." Later that depressing winter, on Miss Jones's birthday, Annie is invited to have birthday cake with Jason and Miss Jones. The encounter makes Annie feel awkward and uncomfortable. When Miss Jones and Jason have to leave, Annie waits in the apartment for her mother to pick her up. Before she calls her, however, she finishes the pitcher of martinis that Jason and Miss Jones made for themselves. She and her mother arrange to meet at a nearby store, and there her mother discovers her all but drunk. Annie lets her think Miss Jones served her the alcohol. When Annie wakes up that evening, the living room is full of her parents' friends, all of whom are discussing what has happened. The matter reaches a member of the school board, who is determined to have Miss Jones fired for serving alcohol to a minor. Annie knows she should tell the truth, but she angrily tries to convince herself that it really was Miss Jones's fault anyway. She also expects the adults will forget about it in a day or two. But on Monday Annie is called to the principal's office where the school board member and the principal question her. She sticks to her story. After school, Miss Jones takes her for tea and asks her why she made up the story. Little by little she draws Annie out until the girl confesses her anger, jealousy, and confusion. A big meeting is called at the home of the school board member. When the talk centers on dismissing Miss Jones, Annie yells out the truth and will not be swayed from it. Then she apologizes to Miss Jones and to the principal. As punishment, Annie is removed from the spring music festival she'd been eagerly anticipating. Her parents cancel her very first date—with Brian. When she explains to Brian why she can't go out with him this time, he promptly makes a date with her for the following Saturday.

A solitary young girl who fears her new feelings and longings fixes her affections on her young piano teacher, only to be "betrayed" by Miss Jones's romance with a man. When Annie lets her jealousy and anger lead her into making a false and hurtful accusation against Miss Jones, she begins to see how dangerous it can be to ignore what is real in life in preference for what one would like to be true. Annie's first-person narrative, told as a flashback, lacks depth, and Annie is the only well-developed character. But the story adequately describes the emotional dependence a lonely young adolescent can develop on an adult, particularly an adult of the same sex. At the end, the reader feels that Annie's somewhat improved relationship with her parents and the affection and sympathy she gets from Brian will help her accept the world as it is.

Ages 10-13

**Also available in:**
No other form known

## 134

**Colman, Hila Crayder**

### The Family Trap

William Morrow & Company, Inc., 1982.
(190 pages)

*AUTONOMY*
*EMANCIPATION OF MINOR*
  *Boy-girl relationships: dating*
  *Dependence/Independence*
  *Freedom, meaning of*
  *Sex: attitude toward*
  *Sibling: relationships*

Fifteen-year-old Rebecca (Becky) Jones, whose father recently died in a factory accident and whose mother has since been admitted to a mental institution, resents the way her older sister, Nancy, tries to "mother" and control her and their younger sister, Stacey. The girls have frequent flare-ups. Nancy sees sisterhood primarily in terms of responsibility, but Becky wants an intimate, loving, supportive relationship. Then Becky meets Tim Harmon and they begin to date. When he wants to make love to her, she refuses, saying she's not ready for sex. On the advice of a friend, the sisters are suing the factory where their father was killed. Young lawyer David Cimino is handling the case and also seeing a lot of Nancy. When the possibility is mentioned of Nancy being named guardian of Becky and Stacey, Becky objects strenuously. She gets a job helping at Mr. Kowalski's coffee shop, and it's he who first suggests to her that she could become an emancipated minor when she turns sixteen. One night Becky has a party that goes well until three people she hardly knows barge in and refuse to leave. They drink beer and throw pizza all over the house. Nancy comes home with David and goes into a rage, refusing to listen to Becky's explanation. The evening intensifies Becky's feelings that she must move out of the house. She asks David to look into the statute on emancipated minors. He wants to stay uninvolved in this conflict, but does get a copy of the statute for her. When Becky finally explains to Nancy what she's doing, they argue again. Nancy insists that Becky is not capable of taking care of herself. Before the juvenile court hearing on her emancipation, Becky visits her mother for the first time. The woman doesn't seem to understand anything Becky says, and Becky realizes her mother will probably never come home. At the hearing, Nancy can't conceal her jealousy of Becky and her need to control her. Although Becky cries, she manages to state her case clearly, including the fact that she will share in the accident settlement and that she has a job. The judge says a decision will be announced later. Mr. Kowalski shows Becky an apartment she could rent from him. She loves it and is determined to have it. When Tim mentions the privacy they'll have if she's living alone in an apartment, Becky reiterates that she's not ready for sex and not willing to get involved with him until she straightens out her life. They part good friends and hope their feelings will survive their upcoming separation when Tim leaves for college. Becky is granted her emancipated minor status, and she moves into the apartment after a few rude shocks about the cost of furniture. David has asked Nancy to marry him, and Becky gives a party for them in her new apartment. After David and Nancy leave, Becky confesses to friends that she's a little disappointed in Nancy's lack of interest in her new life. She'd always thought they could be good friends if they were on more equal footing. Now she is really alone. But she has friends, school, and her job. When Tim asks her if she's happy, she says she just might be.

A girl applies for and receives emancipated minor status when she turns sixteen. The novel outlines one set of circumstances that could lead to a granting of this special status; some information on the Connecticut statute (including the statute itself) is given. The only caution to readers might be that Becky's situation makes things seem easier than they would likely be. The story stops at the point where her emotional problems may have lightened, but her practical problems are beginning. Also, few teenagers have fifty thousand dollars (Becky's share of the accident award) to count on, or a nice gentleman offering a perfect, low-priced apartment. This is a very readable book, and it does provide information about the emancipated minor statute. But it tends to understate both Becky's problems beforehand and the difficulties she may encounter afterwards.

Ages 12 and up

**Also available in:**
No other form known

## 135

**Colman, Hila Crayder**

**What's the Matter with the Dobsons?**

Crown Publishers, Inc., 1980.
(113 pages) o.p.

---

*FAMILY: Relationships*
*PARENT/PARENTS: Fighting Between*
  *Jealousy: sibling*
  *Separation, marital*

---

On her thirteenth birthday several weeks ago, Amanda Dobson had vowed she would make an effort to get along better with her father, Mark. Amanda's mother's theory is that the two fight because they are both stubborn and oversensitive to criticism. But Amanda feels her troubles with her father can be laid at the door of her sister, eleven-year-old Lisa, who can wheedle anything out of their father. When Amanda shows Mark, an architect, the miniature log house she has made, he criticizes the work instead of complimenting it. Furious, Amanda breaks her model house and overhears her mother, Kate, telling Mark he is spoiling Lisa and being beastly to Amanda. Meanwhile, Lisa is jealous of the secrets Amanda and her mother share. The fighting continues, and the two girls endure daily battles between their parents. Amanda asks her grandmother for advice and is told she has to compromise more. Then, after a dance, Amanda rides in a car with a boy too young to drive who has a six-pack of beer. She is grounded. Again her parents fight over her, confirming Amanda's belief that her parents would be happy if only she had not been born. Saturday night while her family is away, Amanda sneaks out of the house for a time. She is home when her parents return, but learns

her father had called the house several times, getting no answer. A fight ensues, Mark slaps Amanda, and Kate announces she is on Amanda's side. From then on, the fighting between the parents worsens and soon Mark moves out. Lisa cries; Amanda blames herself; Kate assures them the situation is not their fault. Several days later, Lisa goes to stay with her father. During Lisa's stay, Amanda and her father go to dinner and talk. He claims his criticism of her reflects his high expectations for her. After a month, Lisa gets bored and returns to the house. The sisters talk. Lisa promises not to cozy up to her father as much if Amanda and Kate will share their secrets with her. Amanda's grandmother remarries, and after the wedding Kate and Mark announce that Mark is coming home. He tells the family they will probably still disagree and fight, but now he knows that struggle is part of loving, part of life. Each will have to try and accommodate the others, because "we're a family of four, not two and two."

A family is torn apart when the parents fight over their children, each child becoming aligned with one parent. The viewpoint shifts between Amanda and Lisa, slowing the action a bit but making vivid the girls' feelings and their reactions to the family turmoil. This story illustrates very well the dangers of favoritism or suspected favoritism within a family and provides rich discussion material.

Ages 10-13

**Also available in:**
No other form known

## 136

**Conford, Ellen**

**Anything for a Friend**

Little, Brown and Company, 1979.
(180 pages)

---

*CHANGE: New Home*
*FRIENDSHIP: Lack of*
*FRIENDSHIP: Making Friends*
  *Change: resisting*
  *Moving*
  *Name, dissatisfaction with*

---

Eleven-year-old Wallis Greene is sure that her new home near New York City will be just like her past new homes: she will hate the place and make no friends. Her mother and grandmother urge Wallis to change her attitudes, to be a friend in order to make friends. Unconvinced, Wallis replies that her father's frequent career-related moves are selfish and have forced her into a friendless life. Furthermore, her parents' naming her after the Duchess of Windsor has compelled her to spell and explain her first name constantly. Now she has one more cross to bear: her embarrassment over the fact that the former owner of their new house was murdered by his wife. Still, Wallis does consider changing her attitudes and lets a boy her age, Stuffy (for Stafford W. Sternwood), walk her to school the first day. Once there, Wallis immediately spots "The Girl Nobody Likes," Ruth, and shuns her. She tries to cultivate "The Important Girls," but feels thwarted when Ruth seeks her out. Annoyed by Ruth's attention, Wallis goes along with Stuffy's scheme to write a phony love letter from their teacher, Mr. Ryan, to Ruth, who has a crush on him. After they give Ruth the letter, Stuffy enjoys watching the girl moon over Mr. Ryan, but Wallis wishes she had never gotten involved in the distasteful scheme. Again at Stuffy's urging she writes another letter, but so dislikes watching Ruth make a fool of herself that she tells Stuffy she is through. When Ruth asks her for help in writing a letter to Mr. Ryan that will end their "affair," Wallis writes one for her, promises to mail it, and then secretly tears it up, concluding the deception. Then word gets out that Wallis lives in a house where a murder took place. She fears the news will end her chances for friendship, but of course it makes her the center of interest. Wallis takes advantage of the interest and makes two friends. Meanwhile, the resourceful Stuffy decides to capitalize on the interest in the murder and talks Wallis into holding a séance-party to contact the dead man. Wallis, lured by the prospect of making more friends, agrees. Stuffy insists that he will handle everything. The séance goes well until Wallis learns that Stuffy has charged admission. Outraged, she forces him to repay her guests. In the following months, Wallis makes friends and begins to feel she belongs. Then a position in her father's company opens up on the West Coast. Wallis despairs, but her mother and grandmother reason with her. If she has made friends here, why not in California? With help and encouragement from her friends and family, Wallis soon accepts the argument: she made friends here, and now she expects to make friends in her new home.

A young girl forced to make frequent moves as her father's career advances refuses even to try making friends. But she gradually comes to see that she can have friends, and that she really won't do "anything for a friend" if it means compromising her self-respect and hurting others. Stuffy, the young con man, adds interest and humor to this first-person account.

Ages 9-11

**Also available in:**
Paperbound—*Anything for a Friend*
Pocket Books, Inc.

## 137

Conford, Ellen

## The Revenge of the Incredible Dr. Rancid and His Youthful Assistant, Jeffrey

Little, Brown and Company, 1980.
(119 pages)

---

*SELF, ATTITUDE TOWARD: Feeling Different*
  Bully: being bothered by
  Courage, meaning of
  Friendship: meaning of
  Imagination
  Reality, escaping
  School: classmate relationships

---

Jeffrey Childs hates it when bully Dewey Belasco calls him "chicken," "coward," and "childish." Although he's in sixth grade, Jeffrey considers his best friend to be Bix, a neighbor three years younger. Since Dewey came into his life a year ago, Jeffrey's main form of enjoyment and escape from his problems has been secretly writing a book called "The Revenge of the Incredible Dr. Rancid and His Youthful Assistant, Jeffrey." At school Jeffrey's seat partner is Coco Siegelman, whom he likes very much. One day he sees Coco with a "slam" book. He grabs the book and reads what the girls in his class have written about him. Always sure no one likes him, Jeffrey finds his suspicions confirmed. In the most recent chapter of his book, Jeffrey writes of rescuing Coco from Dewey with his stun gun. His writing is interrupted by a telephone call and he ends up baby-sitting for a neighbor. While he's there, the youngest boy cuts his lip and Jeffrey rushes him to the doctor. He's hailed for his quick thinking and begins to feel a bit heroic for a change. At school the next day, Dewey makes fun of Coco. Jeffrey makes a weak attempt to step in, only to have Coco herself hit Dewey. Humiliated at being unable to defend Coco, let alone himself, Jeffrey pretends to have a virus the next day and is allowed to stay home from school. He longs to tell his parents about Dewey, but is afraid they will also think him a coward. Jeffrey returns to school with a new determination to stand up to Dewey. He's tired of feeling bad about himself and pretending everything is fine. When Dewey taunts him in class, Jeffrey tells Dewey he has incurable stupidity. At lunch Dewey challenges him, Bix steps in, and a fight ensues. Jeffrey holds his own. The fight is stopped by a teacher, and the two are required to shake hands and apologize. When he realizes the class is on his side, Jeffrey feels great. "I'd stood up to the guy who'd been terrorizing me for months, and I'd lived to tell the tale." A proud Jeffrey tells his parents what has happened. That weekend several school friends stop by, and even Coco visits. Jeffrey realizes his classmates do like him, and he writes the final chapter in his book: Dewey is dead from a pulverizer gun and Jeffrey is Coco's hero.

A shy young boy feels himself a coward for not standing up to a bully, relieving his feelings by writing a book about his own imagined heroic deeds. Finally determined not to back down anymore, Jeffrey stands up to the bully and not only wins the self-respect he needs, but also the admiration of his classmates. This first-person narrative describes with humor and insight the feelings and fears of a likeable, imaginative boy.

Ages 10-12

**Also available in:**
Cassette—*The Revenge of the Incredible Dr. Rancid and His Youthful Assistant, Jeffrey*
Library of Congress (NLSBPH)

Paperbound—*The Revenge of the Incredible Dr. Rancid and His Youthful Assistant, Jeffrey*
Scholastic Book Services

**138**

Cooney, Nancy Evans

## The Blanket That Had to Go

Color illustrations by Diane Dawson.
G. P. Putnam's Sons, 1981.
(30 pages counted)

---

*TRANSITIONAL OBJECTS: Security Blanket*
  *Problem solving*
  *School: entering*

---

Little Susi loves her blanket and carries it wherever she goes. She wears it to watch cartoons and to read, she uses it as a vampire cape and a raft, and she makes her brother laugh when she and her blanket become the blue blob slinking along the floor. Susi's blanket is her "great, good friend." Then her mother tells her that children are not allowed to bring blanket friends to kindergarten with them. But Susi can't go anywhere without her blanket. "Certainly she could never start school without it." She tries to devise a plan for getting her blanket to school, including stuffing it under her T-shirt, making a skirt out of it, or using it for a book bag. Nothing works. Susi mopes around and nobody can cheer her up. When the start of kindergarten is just a week away, she cuts her blanket in half. Two days later when she goes with her father to buy school shoes, her blanket is smaller and raggedy at both ends. On Saturday when she goes with her brother to buy school supplies, it's even smaller and ragged all around the edges. By the first day of school her blanket is a postage-stamp-size piece of blue, "just the right size to go to school with Susi."

Susi has to devise a way of taking her beloved blanket to kindergarten without breaking the rules. Delightful illustrations punctuate her search for a solution, as the blanket gradually shrinks to an acceptable size. All children who have ever had a blanket or special toy will love this book; those facing separation from a blanket may be inspired by Susi's solution.

Ages 3-5

**Also available in:**
Paperbound—*The Blanket That Had to Go*
G. P. Putnam's Sons

**139**

Corcoran, Barbara

## Child of the Morning

Atheneum Publishers, 1982.
(112 pages)

---

*EPILEPSY*
*SELF, ATTITUDE TOWARD: Accepting*
  *Fear: of the unknown*
  *Friendship: making friends*
  *Talents*

---

Susan Bishop has had "little spells" for almost a year. They started after she suffered a concussion playing volleyball. The family's doctor, Dr. Blake, is not overly concerned about the injury, so the family tries to ignore Susan's occasional spells and blackouts. When school lets out for the summer between her sophomore and junior years, Susan begins looking for a job. But the people in her small Maine town are afraid to hire her: local gossip about her blackouts has spread. At a church supper, Susan meets several people from New York City who are in Maine to start a summer theater. The next day she rides her bike to this theater and gets a job distributing posters advertising the weekly productions. She is thrilled when Steve, the young man who hired her, tells her she can also watch rehearsals. Soon she is coming to the theater daily, helping Steve. Since she loves to dance, she begins watching the dance class, memorizing the steps and practicing them when she's alone. Mr. Ross, the producer, is so impressed with her skills at helping Steve that he hires her as a full-time summer member of the company. Although elated, Susan fears she will have a spell and be fired. Usually she can feel a spell coming—a headache comes first—and can sit down and breathe deeply until it passes. But the episodes are beginning to occur more frequently. When she suffers a blackout in Steve's presence, he encourages her to see a neurologist. Instead, Susan returns to Dr. Blake, who gives her headache pills. He also mentions he is retiring and a Dr. Magone will take over his practice. Back at the theater Susan is asked to do three short dance numbers for the upcoming show. She reluctantly agrees, terrified she will have a spell. The week of performances goes well. Then, during the last scene of the second-last performance, Susan blacks out. She awakens to find Dr. Magone helping her. He asks how long she has had epilepsy, and Susan is dumbfounded. Dr. Magone takes her to a neurologist in Boston. He explains epilepsy to her and the drugs used to control it. For three months, Susan's doctors try various drugs, many with bad side effects, to control her seizures. Finally a medicine without side effects is found to help her. For the first time in over a year, Susan feels well enough to be truly hopeful about her future.

A teenage girl who has "little spells" that her family doctor discounts is finally diagnosed as having epilepsy and can be treated and helped to live a normal life. Susan manages to break free of the scary state of not knowing what's wrong with her and of denying that anything is wrong. Although shallow in characterization, the book does offer insight into the symptoms, effects, and treatment for epilepsy. Also clear is the need for intelligent, specialized medical care. Susan's experiences with the theater group will add appeal for some readers.

Ages 10 and up

**Also available in:**
No other form known

**140**

Corey, Dorothy

## Everybody Takes Turns

Color illustrations by Lois Axeman.
Albert Whitman & Company, 1980.
(32 pages counted)

---

*SHARING/NOT SHARING*
  *Patience/Impatience*

---

**C**

"I take a turn. You take a turn." Some people get the first turn. Other people get the second turn. When one person's turn is up, it's somebody else's turn. Small children, big children, and adults all take turns sometimes. Even pedestrians and drivers take turns. "It's fun to have your turn!"

By alternating simple, colorfully illustrated examples of "my turn, your turn," this little book presents sharing and taking turns as facts of life. One short sentence accompanies each illustration; young children will enjoy the repetition of "my turn, your turn." This is a useful, if not exciting, single-concept book, which could be elaborated upon in discussion.

Ages 2-6

**Also available in:**
Large Print—*Everybody Takes Turns*
Albert Whitman & Company

## 141

**Corey, Dorothy**

## We All Share

Color illustrations by Rondi Collette.
Albert Whitman & Company, 1980.
(32 pages counted)

---

*SHARING/NOT SHARING*

---

A young boy shares his puppy, and his friend shares his kitten. When a third boy joins with a rabbit, they all share their pets. The boys also share popcorn and a sandwich. Later, the narrator's friend shares some paper, the narrator shares his paints, and they both share their paintings with his mother. A tent, a swimming pool, bubbles, cars, and a fire truck are all shared. So is a baby brother. The narrator and his friends share drums, Halloween candy, mittens, and a sled. "We all share!"

Alternating brightly colored, appealing illustrations with black-and-white ones, this simple, engaging book shows children sharing their pets, toys, and favorite things. The young narrator presents sharing as fun and rewarding.

Ages 2-6

**Also available in:**
Large Print—*We All Share*
Albert Whitman & Company

## 142

**Crofford, Emily**

## A Matter of Pride

Color illustrations by Jim LaMarche.
Carolrhoda Books, Inc., 1981.
(48 pages)

---

*COURAGE, MEANING OF*
  *Family: unity*
  *Fear*
  *Poverty*

---

The year is 1932 and the father of ten-year-old Meg has lost his job in Memphis, necessitating the family's recent move to an Arkansas cotton plantation where the father works as a farmhand. They had to sell most of their belongings to finance the move and now they live in a crude, isolated shack whose walls are patched with newspaper. Meg's only friend is classmate Grace Bowers, who lives on the other side of the canal. But Meg has trouble visiting Grace. Meg's mother is terrified of snakes and bridges and is afraid to permit her children to cross the bridge over the canal. Meg's father tells Meg that all bridges, not just this one, frighten her mother, for unknown reasons. Meg equates this fear with her own panic when she must read aloud in school, but she still is embarrassed over what she considers her mother's cowardice. One morning their newly bought cow, Dolly, breaks loose and wanders off. Her mother must give Meg permission to cross the bridge and search for Dolly. Meg finds the cow tied up at the Bowerses' farm and returns home to tell her mother. The mother knows that she herself must retrieve Dolly; she cannot allow Meg's father to go. Weeks earlier, the father had snatched the rope away from Mr. Bowers as the man was unmercifully whipping a mule, and now the mother worries about a second confrontation between the two men. So, with Meg, she resolutely crosses the feared bridge, her face pale, her jaw tight, and her eyes straight ahead. As she is cutting Dolly loose Mr. Bowers appears, his eyes "hard and mean," challenging Meg's mother to leave the animal where it is. But she stands her ground, cuts Dolly free, and remarks calmly that if the cow ever strays again, Mr. Bowers should send word and they will come immediately. Returning over the bridge with her mother and their cow, Meg recalls her teacher explaining that "you had to be especially brave to do things that frightened you." She swells with pride. Her mother is afraid of snakes and bridges but is no coward.

A young girl learns what courage can entail through her mother's brave overcoming of her fears in the interest of protecting her family and preserving their few possessions. Vivid illustrations combined with easy reading aptly depict impoverished rural life during the Depression. This is a book both for independent reading and for reading aloud.

Ages 8-11

**Also available in:**
No other form known

## 143

**Crofford, Emily**

## Stories from the Blue Road

Black/white illustrations by C. A. Nobens.
Carolrhoda Books, Inc., 1982.
(167 pages)

---

*FAMILY: Relationships*
  *Animals: love for*
  *Death: of pet*
  *Differences, human*
  *Honesty/Dishonesty*
  *Peer relationships*
  *Poverty*

---

Eleven-year-old Meg Weston, her younger brothers, Bill and Correy, and their parents live on an Arkansas cotton plantation right off Blue Road, so named because after a rain its mud turns a bluish color. Daddy warns the three children not to name any animals that will later have to be butchered, but Bill insists that Otis the pig has adopted him. Otis even joins Brownie the dog in chasing the few cars that come along Blue Road. One day, as the doctor drives away from visiting Mother, who has a migraine, Otis chases the car and gets killed. Even though it's the Depression and the family could use the meat or the money from selling the pork, Daddy says Bill can decide what to do with Otis's body. Bill decides to give it to a neighbor's family, and Daddy approves. Meg's sixth-grade class gets a new boy: Talmadge McLinn. His hair is too long, he's poorly dressed, and he has a clubfoot, but he smiles broadly and looks eagerly for friends. His classmates, however, led by mean-natured Stinky, ostracize him. Meg likes him, but is afraid to be seen talking to him or even looking kindly at him. Talmadge hates to fight. Stinky makes it impossible to avoid, however, and Talmadge wins—but he cries at being forced to fight. The other kids yell at him to go back where he came from, and Meg adds her voice when he looks at her. Later that year, Meg makes valentines for everyone in her class, including Talmadge. He apologizes for not getting her one and that Saturday shows up at her home with a store-bought valentine. She is touched that he walked into town with his clubfoot just to buy her a valentine, though she doesn't let on. After Talmadge leaves, Meg's father congratulates her on choosing her friends for their inner qualities instead of going along with the crowd. Meg goes upstairs and bursts into tears. Lady Merida is the plantation owner's English mother-in-law. People say she has cancer and is crazy to boot; the schoolchildren cross the street to avoid the house and especially the strange piano music that pours out the windows. Mother explains to Meg that Lady Merida is simply different, and people always fear what they don't understand. So Meg gets up the courage to ask Lady Merida to give her piano lessons, in spite of her friend Josie Tomkin's antagonism. Josie's father thinks Lady Merida is crazy. However, Meg discovers that Josie's mother secretly studies piano with the old woman. Lady Merida explains that Mrs. Tomkin has the soul of an artist and has been stifled, first by an impoverished childhood and now by a domineering, insensitive husband. Meg objects, as Mr. Tomkin has always been nice to her, but when she has dinner at the Tomkin house, she sees how the man subtly and genially controls and belittles his wife and children. When Lady Merida dies, she leaves her grand piano to Mrs. Tomkin. Her husband tries to sell it, but Mrs. Tomkin says "if he did he'd never get another meal in that house." When Mrs. Tomkin plays the piano, Meg hears its beauty with her soul, as Lady Merida taught her to. Mother and Daddy's anniversary arrives, and Daddy is depressed because he can't even afford a gift for his wife. He remembers what life used to be like in Memphis before he lost his job. Meg suggests he take Mother dancing. While they're gone, the children make an anniversary cake. The cake is inedibly hard, but Mother says it's the loving that counts. On one of the hottest days of summer, Meg and her friends go swimming in the canal with no clothes on. When they see a man coming toward them they dash out, and Meg runs into a water moccasin. She escapes unbitten, but the girls worry whether the snake will bite the next person to come along. They can't warn people, though, because that would mean admitting where they were. Meg is overcome with guilt and worry, nearly making herself sick. Her mother draws the story from her, comforting her by admitting that when she was a girl she too went swimming naked with her friends.

Meg perceptively narrates five stories about life in Depression-era Arkansas. Accompanied by illustrations that capture the flavor of the countryside and its people, the stories believably describe certain everyday events of a loving family. They also touch upon several universal experiences of growing children: lying to parents, peer pressures, the ostracized classmate, the loss of a pet.

Ages 9-12

**Also available in:**
No other form known

## 144

Crowley, Arthur

**Bonzo Beaver**

Color illustrations by Annie Gusman.
Houghton Mifflin Company, 1980.
(32 pages)

---

*RESOURCEFULNESS*
*SIBLING: Younger*
  *Rejection: sibling*

---

Five-year-old Bonzo Beaver hurries out of bed in the morning, excited about his mother's promise to let him play outside all day with his older brother, Boo. Boo doesn't want Bonzo tagging along, spoiling his fun, but their mother insists. "What good is a little brother?" wonders the unhappy Boo as he walks around the block with Bonzo. Boo picks a peach from a tree and makes fun of Bonzo because he can't reach one. Then he takes a shortcut and climbs across a brick wall, taunting Bonzo for having to walk around. They pass Mrs. Grisley's lawn—which Boo warns Bonzo not to walk on—and the elementary school. As Boo taunts Bonzo about having to be with the babies next year in school, he suddenly realizes Bonzo isn't there anymore. He's run onto the forbidden lawn. Mrs. Grisley, hearing a noise, comes out with her stick, but softens when she finds Bonzo sitting under her tree crying. She befriends him and together they come up with a plan to teach Boo a lesson. Bonzo calls Boo into Mrs. Grisley's yard, and she pretends to catch them there. Boo cowers and begs her not to hurt them, but Bonzo speaks right out and tells her what a mess her yard is. He suggests she find a beaver or two to get rid of all the sticks by building a dam and creating a pleasant wading pool. What a good idea, pretends Mrs. Grisley, deciding to let them go if they will return in the morning to build the dam. Boo is impressed with his brother's quick thinking and good ideas and tells him so. At home, he tells his mother what happened and how Bonzo saved the day. She wonders if Bonzo wasn't frightened and he says, "We Beaver brothers do okay."

Trying to keep up with an older sibling can be pretty miserable at times. But little Bonzo Beaver makes a friend who shows him a way to impress his big brother. A clever idea, learns Bonzo, can be far more important than size or strength. Exuberant illustrations enhance the simple, appealing verse narration.

Ages 3-6

**Also available in:**
No other form known

## 145

Culin, Charlotte

### Cages of Glass, Flowers of Time

Bradbury Press, Inc., 1979.
(316 pages)

---

*CHILD ABUSE*
  *Abandonment*
  *Boy-girl relationships*
  *Fear: of physical harm*
  *Friendship: meaning of*
  *Loss: feelings of*
  *School: pupil-teacher relationships*
  *Talents: artistic*
  *Trust/Distrust*

---

Claire Burden, now fourteen, had a lonely but peaceful life with her beloved paternal grandmother and her alcoholic artist father, who encouraged her own artistic talents. Then her grandmother died and, due to the agitation of friends and neighbors, a court found her father an unfit guardian. Her grandmother had willed her house (where they'd lived) and money to Claire, to be held in trust until the girl is twenty-one. When her father was declared unfit, he abandoned Claire and the court awarded her to her mother, also an alcoholic and someone Claire has never known. Now Claire's nightmare has begun. Angry at being saddled with a daughter and hating Claire's artistic talents because they remind her of her ex-husband, Claire's mother verbally abuses her, buys almost no food for her, and burns her arms with cigarettes. One day Claire escapes to her grandmother's house, gets in through a basement window, and retrieves some of her father's sketches and her own art supplies. When her mother finds these she burns them in a blind rage. Soon after Claire moves in with her mother, her maternal grandmother comes to visit. Accusing her daughter of neglecting Claire, she beats Claire's mother and demands that Claire come to live with her. She'd started beating Claire's mother too late for it to do any good, the grandmother snarls, but she'd not make the same mistake with Claire. Terrified, Claire runs to the woods and hides. There she meets Daniel Beasley, a black man with a gift for music who is playing Bach on his guitar, and they begin an initially tentative, then deeply supportive, friendship. At Claire's new school she is teased about her unstylish appearance but is befriended by Clyde, her partner in biology lab, who notices the talent in her lab drawings. The brutalized girl is afraid to trust him. Slowly, though, she begins to believe he really likes her. Claire also

attracts the attention of Miss Joyce, her art teacher. But it was caring, pitying people who took her from her father and destroyed her life, Claire believes, and she's reluctant to trust anyone. Watching her grandmother batter her drunken, terror-stricken mother, Claire sees the roots of her mother's own behavior. She defends her mother against her grandmother, impressing her mother into a sincere but pathetic effort to stop drinking. When Claire's mother bitterly describes her ex-husband's treatment of her as an art object to be shoved aside when no longer needed, Claire is shocked into realizing that her father has treated her the same way: when the neighbors and authorities put pressure on him about Claire, he told his daughter she was ugly and abruptly left. But Claire is still afraid to confess to anyone that her mother beats her, fearing the authorities will award her custody to her grandmother, which would be infinitely worse. As her dead grandmother always asked, Mr. Beasley urges Claire to model herself after her namesake, Great-Aunt Claire, whom he recalls and the girl resembles. Constantly Claire strives to be like that good, kind, gentle person, but inside she seethes with fear, anger, hatred, and a sense of failure. Meanwhile, Clyde gradually wins Claire's trust and persuades her to approach Miss Joyce for help with her art. Miss Joyce, warm and friendly, is so impressed with Claire's talent and dedication that she devotes her free time to teaching her. Yet despite her affection for the teacher, Claire can't bring herself to confide the secret of her mother's abuse. Then one day Claire's mother returns early from work, drunk and furious because she's been told (falsely) that Claire reported her to the authorities as an unfit mother. When she sees that Claire has been drawing she feels further betrayed and beats Claire senseless. Then she is herself battered by her own mother, who comes in during the fray. Claire is hospitalized with a broken arm and terrible bruises, but she continues to tell everyone that her grandmother battered both her and her mother. Later, though, she is able to tell Miss Joyce, her new guardian, what really happened. The girl begs Miss Joyce to sell some of her father's paintings so her mother can start a new life elsewhere. She feels a great need to give her mother a decent life after all the years she was herself mistreated. Miss Joyce does as Claire asks. The court has Claire's grandmother's house reopened so she and Miss Joyce can live there. Then Clyde reads to Claire from her Great-Aunt Claire's diary, proving to her that her relative made mistakes, was often unhappy, and finally resorted to suicide. Claire need not model herself after anyone—her friends love her for herself.

Claire's haunting, poignant first-person narrative vividly conveys the complex emotions of an abused, brutalized young girl struggling to escape her terrifying life but reluctant to trust anyone who tries to help her. With the help of Mr. Beasley, Clyde, and Miss Joyce, Claire at last learns to hope again, to take pride in herself and her artistic talents, to believe she is lovable. Thought-provoking, introspective, serious, featuring Claire's thoughts interspersed throughout the narrative in italics, this book encourages understanding both of the abused person and the abuser; Claire's pathetic mother learned to abuse from her own brutal mother. Although the romantic possibilities of Claire's relationship with Clyde add appeal and suggest a brighter, happier future for Claire, much of the story could depress and even frighten some readers. Mature readers, however, will find this an unusually memorable book.

Ages 12 and up

Also available in:
Paperbound—*Cages of Glass, Flowers of Time*
Dell Publishing Company, Inc.

## 146

**Cunningham, Julia Woolfolk**

**The Silent Voice**

E. P. Dutton & Company, Inc., 1981.
(145 pages)

---

MUTENESS
TALENTS
  Bully: being bothered by
  Orphan
  Success

---

Fourteen-year-old Auguste, a mute orphan, is rescued by Astair and her small band of street urchins as he lies near death on a Paris street. Through Astair he meets Monsieur Bernard, France's greatest living mime, and his housekeeper, Madame Louva. Auguste possesses only one thing of value: a gold medallion given to him by Hercule Hilaire, the late, renowned master mime and the only person who ever loved Auguste. Before his death, Hercule taught Auguste, who seemed to have a natural gift for mime, much of what he knew. Monsieur Bernard also recognizes Auguste's gift and allows him to join his mime school while doing odd jobs to earn his keep. Another student, Philippe, whose mother is one of the principal backers of the school, hates Auguste, sensing the power of the orphan's gift. He and his two side-kicks, Raymond and Jean-Louis, dispose somehow of Auguste's newfound pet cat. One day Philippe and Raymond discover Auguste's gold medallion. Their ensuing fight over it takes them up on the rooftops. Philippe shoves Raymond off a roof. Then he runs back to Auguste's room and replaces the medallion. Auguste, who has just found his cat on the rooftops, witnesses the shoving. But Philippe tells everyone that Auguste shoved Raymond, who is now in the hospital claiming he just fell. Philippe's mother insists that Auguste be expelled from the school. However, Monsieur Bernard knows by now about the medallion and about Auguste's relationship with the great Hilaire. He is determined to keep Auguste and coach him privately. Meanwhile, Auguste finds Astair in her tiny room, very ill. She is moved to Monsieur Bernard's school to be nursed by Madame Louva and Auguste. Then Monsieur Bernard tells Auguste to learn Phillipe's part for the next performance. When Philippe sees Monsieur Bernard training Auguste in his role, he brings in his mother. But Monsieur Bernard manages to reassure her by talking about the need for understudies. Philippe is not reassured, however, and he and Jean-Louis threaten Auguste. The night of the performance, Astair and her friends kidnap Philippe. Auguste is persuaded to take the missing boy's part and does a halfhearted job for the first half of the program. Then Philippe, who has been released, returns and attacks Auguste. Auguste now realizes he must put his whole heart into the production.

He is brilliant during the second half, and Monsieur Bernard is content to know that he has a worthy successor to his art. Because of Auguste's success with the critics and the audience, Monsieur Bernard also knows he is no longer dependent on Philippe's mother for backing. Raymond has regained his courage with his health, and he confesses that Philippe pushed him. With this information revealed, Philippe and his mother are no longer a threat to anyone. Astair and her gang share Auguste's success, as he will share what he has with them.

A mute Parisian urchin with a unique gift for mime uses his art to express all the poetry and feeling in his heart. This beautifully written, emotionally satisfying story has strong elements that will appeal to readers—unlikeable villains, rewards for goodness, loyalty, and hard work, suspense. It is an unusual and compelling story.

Ages 11-14

Also available in:
Paperbound—*The Silent Voice*
Dell Publishing Company, Inc.

## 147

**Cuyler, Margery S.**

**The Trouble with Soap**

E. P. Dutton & Company, Inc., 1982.
(104 pages)

---

FRIENDSHIP: Best Friend
  Friendship: making friends
  Peer relationships: peer pressures
  School: behavior
  Schools, private: girls'

---

Thirteen-year-old Laurie Endersby's best friend and partner in crime is Lucinda Sokoloff, otherwise known as Soap. When the two put Saran Wrap over the toilet bowls in the boys' restroom at school, they are suspended for two weeks. Soap's mother decides to send Soap to Miss Pringle's school, an elite private girls' academy. Soap pressures Laurie into applying there too, and so the girls change schools together. Laurie wants to make new friends at Miss Pringle's, but Soap snubs everyone and sticks to Laurie. A classmate, Hilary, invites Laurie to spend the night with her. Against her better judgment but believing Hilary to be more sophisticated than she, Laurie allows Hilary to cut her hair. Then, feeling guilty, Laurie goes to see Soap—but Soap only wants to make trick phone calls. Laurie thinks the activity very immature, but allows herself to be persuaded. However, when Soap picks up the phone she overhears her father telling some woman that he can hardly wait to see her. Soon after, Soap writes a derogatory limerick on the board. Although everyone knows she did it, she declines to confess and the whole class is punished. Laurie wonders why Soap is so negative, so eager to make enemies. Feeling torn between Hilary and Soap, she decides that Soap will just have to make it on her own; Laurie really wants Hilary's friendship. Then Soap finds out that her father is meeting his woman friend at noon in the park. She talks Laurie into coming with her to spy on them. It turns out that Mr. Sokoloff's friend is none other than Miss Helms, the

C

girls' English teacher. Soap feels betrayed and demoralized. They arrive back at school late and get in trouble with Miss Pringle. Hilary begs Laurie to tell her where they were, but loyal Laurie won't. Next evening Laurie, nervous and excited, goes to Hilary's party. One boy upsets her; another, Oliver, is comfortable to be with. After the party, Laurie and two other girls sleep over. The others pressure Laurie to tell what she and Soap were doing when they skipped school. Enjoying being the center of attention, Laurie tells them all about Soap's father and Miss Helms. The next week, Soap discovers what Laurie's done. She doesn't return to school for two days. Hilary fixes Laurie up with a blind date, Anthony, and the four get stoned on marijuana. Laurie gets up and leaves in the middle of the movie when Anthony persists in his advances. She calls her older brother to pick her up, telling him all her troubles. When she asks him why it's so hard for her to say no, he says all people want to be liked. Laurie apologizes to Soap for what she's done and Soap forgives her, although she notes that she wouldn't have betrayed Laurie. In any case, her father has told her mother about Miss Helms, so it's public knowledge. Laurie feels somehow comforted, realizing that Hilary isn't as perfect as she thought and that Soap is changing and maturing. She suspects she has a lot to look forward to—maybe even Oliver.

A young girl is torn between loyalty to an old friend who often gets her into trouble and new friends who seem more sophisticated and mature. Laurie is easily manipulated; even when she's talked into doing something fairly innocent, she often goes against her own feelings. But she recognizes this tendency and by book's end is beginning to remedy it. She also comes to a more realistic view both of the flighty but endearing Soap and of the attractions of her new friends. A delightful—in some spots, very funny—book, this first-person story is a quick, entertaining read that touches on some very real problems of early adolescence.

Ages 10-13

**Also available in:**
Paperbound—*The Trouble with Soap*
Scholastic Book Services

## 148

Dacquino, Vincent T.

### Kiss the Candy Days Good-Bye

Delacorte Press, 1982.
(129 pages)

---

*DIABETES*
   *Boy-girl relationships: dating*
   *Change: accepting*
   *Communication: importance of*
   *Family: relationships*
   *Hospital, going to*
   *School: classmate relationships*

---

Seventh-grader Jimmy Jones loves wrestling and is excited about being workout partner with Butch Farelli, the team's captain. But Jimmy has a secret worry. Although he's eating more—trying to equal Butch's weight—he is losing weight. He'd like to talk to his girlfriend, Margaret, but she hasn't been to school for the past few days. Afraid to confide in his parents or younger brother, Jimmy worries silently, not only about his weight loss but also his temper flare-ups, continual hunger, frequent urination, and great thirst. He's afraid something serious is happening to him. Determined to talk to Margaret, he goes to her neighborhood one day after school and learns from a neighbor that she has moved. Confused and distressed, Jimmy walks home feeling very weak and dizzy. When he reaches his apartment building, he passes out. An ambulance takes Jimmy and his mother to the hospital. The results of Jimmy's blood and urine tests lead the doctors to suspect diabetes mellitus. Jimmy, feeling like part of a horror movie, spends the next seven days in the hospital. He undergoes more tests and starts a series of insulin shots to control his sugar level. Along the way, Jimmy learns about diabetes and struggles to accept everything that is happening to him, unjust as it seems. He is relieved when his doctor tells him he can still wrestle. When Margaret, now living with relatives, visits Jimmy in the hospital, she brings her cousin Santiago with her. Santiago will be attending their school, and Margaret asks Jimmy to help him adjust. Finally, Jimmy is released from the hospital. He and his parents now know how to give him insulin injections, rotate the site of the shots, check his urine, and watch his diet. The family plans to spend the weekend in their cabin in the mountains, and Jimmy asks Margaret to come too. She accepts, but only if Santiago comes along. Jealous, Jimmy reluctantly agrees. Soon, though, they're all enjoying the hiking, fishing, and swimming. But all this vigorous exercise lowers Jimmy's blood-sugar level, and he has an insulin reaction during one of their outings. He feels sweaty and clammy and his arms and legs tingle. Recovering by eating the candy he carries for emergencies, he laughs off the episode. Later he feels miserable, not about the reaction but "that I wasn't man enough to admit what was happening." He must agree when his brother confronts him about the incident: if he lies about a reaction, no one will ever know when he needs help. Jimmy returns to school with his new friend Santiago and everything returns to normal—except the candy days are over.

A young teenager is found to be diabetic and must learn to accept the new conditions of his life. Although somewhat didactic, the story gives an excellent description of the early struggles and necessary education of a newly diagnosed diabetic boy and, secondarily, his family and friends. It emphasizes that although diabetes can't be cured it can be controlled, that diabetic people are not abnormal but different, with certain special needs. Jimmy's story encourages openness with others to increase understanding of diabetes. Young diabetic readers may find the book useful and comforting; others will increase their awareness and understanding. Although the book is detailed, home blood-testing isn't mentioned.

Ages 10-14

**Also available in:**
Paperbound—*Kiss the Candy Days Good-Bye*
Dell Publishing Company, Inc.

**149**

Danziger, Paula

## Can You Sue Your Parents for Malpractice?

Delacorte Press, 1979.
(152 pages)

---

*AUTONOMY*
  *Boy-girl relationships: dating*
  *Family: relationships*
  *Peer relationships: peer pressures*
  *School: classmate relationships*

---

Lauren Allen finds it disgusting to be fourteen and have no rights. She is looking forward to a special elective class at school called "Law for Children and Young People." Lauren wants eventually to be a lawyer so she can help kids get an even break, something she never gets. Her entire family is a trial to her. Melissa, her older sister, goes to college and never seems to be home, although she still lives there. Lauren has to share a bedroom with her younger sister, Linda, who tells jokes incessantly. Her mother is forever writing to quiz shows asking to be a contestant, and her father, an insurance salesman, complains constantly about the family's finances. To make matters worse, Lauren's boyfriend just broke up with her to date another girl. The Saturday before the special class starts, Lauren and her best friend go to the shopping mall and have their ears pierced, against Lauren's parents' wishes. At the mall she meets Zack Davids, an eighth grader whose family recently moved to the neighborhood. Lauren is attracted to Zack but can't understand why, since he is a year younger than she is. When she returns home, her father is furious about her pierced ears. She yells that she will sue him for malpractice for being a lousy father. On Monday, Lauren discovers Zack is also in the special class. The group is assigned to do a paper on laws affecting children and young people, and Zack asks Lauren to be his partner. Hesitant because of what classmates might say about the age difference, Lauren finally agrees. But if her social life is improving, her home life is exploding. Melissa has moved in with her boyfriend, and her father is not speaking to her. He is also furious at her mother for returning to substitute teaching. Lauren's life has become a soap opera, she feels. At school, her fellow ninth graders begin teasing her about Zack, saying she is robbing the cradle. Confused and hurt, Lauren is soon angry at everyone. She visits Melissa, hoping for help in understanding her mixed-up feelings about Zack, her friends, and her father. Zack and Lauren continue working on their law project together, and Lauren decides she really cares for him despite the kidding. When her former boyfriend comes back, expecting her to go steady with him, Lauren finds she prefers Zack, even if he is younger and can't drive a car. As she contemplates her family, her friends, her class, and her relationship with Zack, Lauren realizes she is beginning to cope better with each upsetting situation in her life. "Maybe suing my parents for malpractice isn't as important as making sure that I don't do malpractice on myself."

A feisty teenage girl struggles for her own individuality against family and peer pressures. Told by Lauren, the story is well paced with believable characters. It is written with a delightful sense of humor and with considerable insight into young adolescents—their special code of living, their pains and joys.

Ages 10-14

**Also available in:**
Braille—*Can You Sue Your Parents for Malpractice?*
Library of Congress (NLSBPH)

Cassette—*Can You Sue Your Parents for Malpractice?*
Library of Congress (NLSBPH)

Paperbound—*Can You Sue Your Parents for Malpractice?*
Dell Publishing Company, Inc.

**150**

Danziger, Paula

## The Divorce Express

Delacorte Press, 1982.
(148 pages)

---

*DIVORCE: of Parents*
  *Boy-girl relationships*
  *Change: accepting*
  *Change: new home*
  *Communication: parent-child*
  *Friendship: best friend*
  *Parent/Parents: remarriage of*
  *School: behavior*

---

Fourteen-year-old Phoebe's divorced parents have joint custody of her, which means she lives half the week with one parent, half with the other. She needs a calendar to avoid becoming hopelessly confused, as she was the weekend each parent thought she was staying with the other and she had no place to go. When she gets in trouble at school, her parents decide she'll live with her father in Woodstock all week and spend the weekends with her mother in New York City, "riding the Divorce Express," a bus filled with kids whose divorced parents have made similar living arrangements for them. Phoebe is sure the transportation industry would go bankrupt without divorce; she wonders if it will ever stop hurting to think about her family's breakup. Her best friend, Katie, and her boyfriend, Andy, live in New York, and Phoebe is lonely in Woodstock until she befriends Rosie, the half-black, half-white daughter of divorced parents. She's doubly glad to have Rosie when she learns that Katie and Andy have started dating each other in her absence. When Rosie stays overnight with Phoebe at Phoebe's mother's New York apartment, the girls overhear a comment that suggests Rosie's mother and Phoebe's father are interested in each other. Phoebe wonders how Rosie can take this news so calmly. Phoebe doesn't take it calmly at all when she learns that her mother is planning to marry Duane, a man Phoebe positively detests. Duane likes hunting, thinks children should be seen and not heard, and doesn't like emotional displays. Phoebe tries to tell her mother how she feels, but they don't really listen to each other. Phoebe rides the Divorce Express back to Woodstock very upset. Waiting for her and Rosie at the bus depot are Rosie's mother and Phoebe's father. They all go home and talk about her mother's remarriage until Phoebe feels somewhat better about the situation. Then Rosie interrogates her mother and Phoebe's father

**D**

about their own relationship, which turns out to be fairly serious. They hadn't wanted to tell the girls, for fear of interfering with their friendship. But both say they don't mind at all. Phoebe even decides to attend her mother's wedding. She's not feeling so trapped anymore: "I'm learning to have my own place in the world."

A teenage girl manages to survive a number of changes in her life and recovers her balance with more self-confidence and self-knowledge than she had before. Readers will feel for Phoebe as she struggles to accept her parents' divorce, their new partners, her own loss of friends, her new school, and, ultimately, her need to find a sense of self independent of either parent. This is a perceptive, humorous first-person narrative that should have great appeal.

Ages 11-14

**Also available in:**
Cassette—*The Divorce Express*
Library of Congress (NLSBPH)

Paperbound—*The Divorce Express*
Dell Publishing Company, Inc.

## 151

Danziger, Paula

**There's a Bat in Bunk Five**

Delacorte Press, 1982.
(150 pages)

---

*CAMP EXPERIENCES*
*MATURATION*
 *Boy-girl relationships*
 *Responsibility: accepting*

---

Marcy, almost fifteen, is excited about her upcoming job as a counselor-in-training at a creative arts camp. She is a last-minute replacement, picked by a favorite former teacher. Marcy decides that at camp she will concentrate on developing her character and growing up. In short order she meets Ted, a counselor and high school senior; Corrine, the head counselor in her bunkhouse; and the ten girls she is to work with. All the girls seem pleasant except ten-year-old Ginger, who was nasty last year and is ornery and unkind still. Marcy soon enjoys camp life and falls hard for Ted. Corrine, regarding Marcy as a little sister, helps her with the girls and encourages her, suggesting she not expect too much from herself or others. Ted and Marcy get a day off together and spend it in nearby Woodstock, shopping and walking around—Marcy is sure she's in love. They return to pandemonium in Marcy's bunk number five, caused by a bat that Ted kills with a broom. The girls conduct a short funeral service for it. When Corrine goes into the infirmary with poison ivy—caused by Ginger who rubbed wet poison ivy over her sheets—Marcy is left in charge of the girls. They trick her into believing there's another bat in the bunk, but this time it's only a baseball bat. Then Ginger runs away and Marcy blames herself for not giving her more attention. When the girl is found in Woodstock, Marcy realizes how troubled Ginger is. She also sees that she herself has been focusing too much on her own feelings and problems, not enough on the lives of others. This insight makes it hard for Marcy to face the end of her

stay at camp, yet intensifies her desire to go home and get on with her life. "It's all kind of funny and sad and joyful and exciting at the same time."

This humorous first-person narrative follows the adventures and maturation of a young camp counselor. All the people Marcy works with, staff members and campers alike, help her lose some of her self-absorption and begin to look around her. This sequel to *The Cat Ate My Gymsuit* is easy to read and should appeal to reluctant readers.

Ages 10-14

**Also available in:**
Disc—*There's a Bat in Bunk Five*
Library of Congress (NLSBPH)

Paperbound—*There's a Bat in Bunk Five*
Dell Publishing Company, Inc.

## 152

DeClements, Barthe

**Nothing's Fair in Fifth Grade**

The Viking Press, Inc., 1981.
(137 pages)

---

*REJECTION: Peer*
 *Differences, human*
 *Friendship: making friends*
 *Friendship: meaning of*
 *Parental: negligence*
 *Rejection: parental*
 *School: transfer*
 *Weight control: overweight*

---

The new girl in Jenifer's fifth-grade class, Elsie Edwards, is grossly overweight and fast becomes the "classroom reject." When money begins disappearing from the classroom, Jenifer suspects Elsie; she's seen her buying licorice and knows Elsie's harsh mother, who demands that the girl lose weight, doesn't give her money for food. Elsie is caught and has to spend recess in the principal's office. Jenifer and her best friends, Diane and Sharon, are as scornful of Elsie as everyone is until the day Elsie's skirt falls off in class; she's been losing weight, but her mother hasn't bought her any new clothes or altered her old ones. The teacher asks Jenifer to help Elsie. Elsie tells Jenifer her father was the only person who ever loved her—before he left home about five years ago and her parents divorced. Jenifer offers to be friends, although Elsie doesn't respond, and she defends Elsie to her classmates. When Jenifer comes home with a low grade in math, her parents suggest a tutor. Since Elsie is excellent at math, Jenifer's parents pay her fifty cents an hour to tutor Jenifer; with the money, Elsie can repay what she took from classmates. Elsie is a natural teacher, and Jenifer does much better on her next math test. One day Jenifer visits Elsie's house and is appalled at Elsie's mother's hostility toward her daughter. At Diane's slumber party, Elsie tells the others that her weight problems began with her parents' marital troubles and got worse after her father left home. She's only seen her father once since the divorce and then, when he talked about seeing her again, the woman with him signaled no. Diane's mother sews Elsie's slacks, which have gotten so big for her that she has them all pinned together. Later, Elsie's mother calls and screams at Diane's mother for touching her daughter's clothes. Diane's mother retorts, "It's about time you paid attention to her!" On Monday, Elsie is wearing a new jumper and shoes. One Saturday the four girls, along with Jenifer's and Elsie's younger siblings, decide to attend a carnival. Diane flags a truck driver and, against Elsie's opposition, they all climb on. The truck driver drives for a long time, and the girls notice they're in the country. They manage to jump off, but the truck drives away with Robyn, Elsie's little sister, still aboard. They call the police. When Elsie's mother arrives at the police station she blames Elsie for the crisis and tells her she'll soon be sent away to a boarding school. After Robyn is found unharmed, apparently only the victim of an innocent mix-up, Jenifer's mother tries to dissuade Mrs. Edwards. But the woman seems determined to get rid of Elsie. Then their teacher tells Mrs. Edwards that Elsie has improved more than any other student in their class. She would never steal money again, she helps others with their schoolwork, and she is successfully losing weight. Elsie's mother and the principal agree to give Elsie another chance. She'll return to school in the fall, to the delight of all the girls—especially Elsie.

Jenifer tells this episodic but compelling story of pathetic, overweight Elsie, class outcast until the other students learn to see beyond her physical appearance to the suffering human being inside. Jenifer is appalled by Elsie's hostile, unloving, neglectful mother, and she and her friends unite to defend and protect Elsie. Readers will see how family turmoil—in this case, a divorce with custody going to a parent with little affection for her child—can cause a person to become an overweight outcast. Friendship redeems Elsie, and the relationships among the girls are well drawn.

Ages 8-11

**Also available in:**
Cassette—*Nothing's Fair in Fifth Grade*
Library of Congress (NLSBPH)

Paperbound—*Nothing's Fair in Fifth Grade*
Scholastic Book Services

## 153

Delaney, Ned

**Bert and Barney**

Color illustrations by the author.
Houghton Mifflin Company, 1979.
(32 pages)

*FRIENDSHIP: Best Friend*
 *Arguing*
 *Cooperation*

Bert the frog and Barney the alligator are inseparable friends who continually praise each other. Even when they wrestle to a deadlock, they are mutual boosters; Barney praises Bert as the better wrestler, and Bert maintains that Barney is. So it goes until Bert tells Barney not to be a jerk—they are both good wrestlers. Barney interrupts to dare Bert to call him a jerk just once more. "Jerk!" Bert yells. Whereupon Barney pushes Bert into the swamp and stalks off. Alone, telling himself he is having a grand time, Barney sits on a seesaw but of course cannot seesaw by himself. He plays hide-and-seek and winds up seeking himself. The next day he looks for Bert and spots him swinging. But Bert ignores him until Barney, chasing a ball he is playing with, disappears over a cliff. Bert plunges into the river to save Barney, only to remember he cannot swim. Barney then saves Bert by pulling him onto a floating log. Both remark on how pleasant it is to sit together on the same log. Suddenly they enter rough waters caused by an approaching waterfall. Bert implores Barney to save them, and Barney asks Bert to do the same. Seeing they must both work at it, Barney boosts Bert onto his shoulders to grab an overhanging tree branch. Both escape just before the log plummets over the falls. They immediately begin arguing about the right path home, but quickly discover they are getting nowhere. Next they decide that each will follow the other, but find they can't each do that. Finally, spotting a new path, both yell, "The real path home!" and go along side by side.

Two friends find it impossible to stop quarreling because of their fondness for continually deferring to each other. Only after a narrow escape from danger do they show signs of recognizing how much they appreciate each other and how much more pleasant it is to cooperate than to argue. Detailed illustrations of these animal characters emphasize the humor of their exploits. Young children will enjoy all the action.

Ages 3-7

**Also available in:**
No other form known

## 154

Delton, Judy

**I Never Win!**

Color illustrations by Cathy Gilchrist.
Carolrhoda Books, Inc., 1981.
(32 pages)

*SELF, ATTITUDE TOWARD: Accepting*
 *Identity, search for*
 *Inferiority, feelings of*
 *Success*
 *Talents: musical*

Charlie, about six, never wins at anything. He comes in second in a sack race at school. In Monopoly he lands on Boardwalk and must pay a lot of money. In Little League he strikes out. At a friend's birthday party, he loses at all the games. Other kids win prizes, but not Charlie. Terribly upset, he goes home and practices the piano, playing very rapidly because he's so angry. When his grandfather comes to visit on Monday, Charlie loses four games of checkers to him. Wednesday at a potluck dinner with his family everyone wins at Bingo except him. Charlie is so upset he screams at his mother when she tries to reassure him. At home again he plays the piano, practicing "The Flight of the Bumblebee" until he can play it perfectly. On Friday Charlie goes to the State Fair with his friend Tim and Tim's father. Tim and his father win at games; Charlie does not. Frustrated beyond endurance, he returns home and works some more on "The Flight of the Bumblebee." The next morning Mrs. Teasley, his piano teacher, calls and invites Charlie to her house that evening. He is to play the piano for "some important people." He plays "The Flight of the Bumblebee" and then three other songs on request. Mrs. Teasley calls Charlie her very best student. At last Charlie feels like a winner! "I guess not every prize is one you can see."

A little boy's frustration at always losing translates into great success at the piano, since whenever Charlie loses at something he practices the piano furiously. Thus his playing becomes more than just a way of releasing his anger. It becomes his means of discovering his own worth. Children will appreciate Charlie's unexpected triumph in this beginning reader, also a good read-aloud selection. Simple illustrations accented with red help convey Charlie's feelings.

Ages 4-7

**Also available in:**
No other form known

## 155

Delton, Judy

**Lee Henry's Best Friend**

Color illustrations by John Faulkner.
Albert Whitman & Company, 1980.
(32 pages counted)

---

*FRIENDSHIP: Best Friend*
*Change: resisting*
*Friendship: making friends*
*Moving*

---

Lee Henry and Blair Andrew, both about eight, are best friends. They take turns at batting practice and never cheat at games. Blair Andrew even claps for Lee Henry's report on spiders, although their classmates find it dull. The boys have promised to be best friends forever, so the news that Blair Andrew's family will soon be moving to Cincinnati is quite a blow to both. They decide to run away together, but Blair Andrew's father talks them out of it. After the move, Lee Henry mopes around, refusing to believe his mother when she says he will make other friends. One day a new boy asks Lee Henry to come see his fort. Reluctantly, Lee Henry does. When they play a game together, Lee Henry discovers that the new boy plays fair and likes the games that he likes. But Lee Henry, loyal to Blair Andrew, warns the new boy that they cannot be best friends. To his surprise, the new boy agrees. He too already has a best friend—in California. With that settled, both boys feel free to be friends. They discover a common interest in dinosaurs and make plans to visit a museum together.

With a mixture of humor and matter-of-factness, a boy describes his loneliness when his best friend moves away and his happiness when he makes a new friend. The light but telling approach to the subject is enhanced by cartoonlike illustrations that convey the main character's emotional highs and lows. This is one of several books about Lee Henry.

Ages 4-8

**Also available in:**
Large Print—*Lee Henry's Best Friend*
Albert Whitman & Company

## 156

Delton, Judy

**My Mother Lost Her Job Today**

Color illustrations by Irene Trivas.
Albert Whitman & Company, 1980.
(32 pages counted)

---

*PARENT/PARENTS: Unemployed*
*Anxiety*
*Communication: parent-child*
*Imagination*
*Security/Insecurity*

---

Barbara Anne, about six, worries that things will never be the same now that her mother has lost her job. Her fears grow as she watches her mother work around the house with tears in her eyes, bang silverware, slam the door, and fail to notice the dandelion bouquet Barbara Anne picks. That evening, Barbara Anne puts herself to bed, dirty knees and all, imagining the worst: no more birthday parties, no more Christmas, no more visits to the zoo. When her mother comes in to say goodnight, Barbara Anne offers to help out by baby-sitting, shoveling snow, cutting grass. Realizing how upset the child is, her mother assures her that she won't need to get a job. As mother and daughter snuggle together, the mother explains that right now she feels "sad and mad and all mixed up," but that things will eventually work out for them. She'll get another job, maybe a better job than she had. Comforted, Barbara Anne goes to sleep.

Small children will readily understand the plight of a little girl frightened by the signs of distress in her newly unemployed mother and needing to be reassured that life will eventually return to normal. Text and illustrations complement each other especially well in this first-person narrative. Pictures of Barbara Anne's fearful imaginings are distinct enough from those of real occurrences to be easily distinguished by young children.

Ages 3-7

**Also available in:**
Large Print—*My Mother Lost Her Job Today*
Albert Whitman & Company

## 157

Delton, Judy

**The New Girl at School**

Color illustrations by Lillian Aberman Hoban.
E. P. Dutton & Company, Inc., 1979.
(30 pages counted)

---

*SCHOOL: Transfer*
*Change: accepting*
*Fear: of school*

---

Marcia, about six, is the new girl at school. The first day, the other children stare at her and do not even notice she has on her new dress with the octopus. Marcia feels out of place, doesn't know where things are, doesn't understand subtraction. That night when she tells her mother she does not like her new school, her mother tells her it will be better tomorrow. But Tuesday Marcia still feels out of place and tells her mother so. Marcia's mother encourages her to "give it time." Wednesday Marcia cries and doesn't want to get on the bus, but her mother insists. At recess that day Marcia plays Captain-May-I with the other girls and even makes it to second base when they all play baseball. That night when her mother asks about school, Marcia says, "Give it time." On Thursday her teacher displays Marcia's paper airplane, and a boy notices the octopus on the dress she has worn again. A new friend even invites Marcia to her birthday party. On Friday, when Marcia's mother suggests that perhaps Marcia can stay with her grandmother and go back to her old school, Marcia replies that she is used to this new school now. Besides, there was a new girl at school today and she doesn't understand subtraction either.

Nervous about going to a new school, a little girl finds the adjustment difficult at first. But before too long she begins to make friends and feel at home—and soon there's a newer student than she. Children will find it easy to sympathize with and discuss Marcia and the feelings of new students. Turquoise-tinted illustrations add a light touch.

Ages 4-7

**Also available in:**
No other form known

## 158

Delton, Judy

**A Walk on a Snowy Night**

Color illustrations by Ruth Rosner.
Harper & Row, Publishers, Inc., 1982.
(28 pages)

COMMUNICATION: Parent-Child
    Nature: appreciation of

After a day-long snowfall, a little girl's father invites her to go with him for a walk in the snow. They dress in warm clothes and step out into the night. She puts her arm through his and sticks her hand in his pocket. They make tracks in the snow, admire the falling snowflakes twinkling under the streetlight, and listen to the scrape of someone's snow shovel. They pass by familiar sights that are distorted by layers of snow and watch people inside their Christmas-card houses. They stop in a cafe to have hot chocolate with marshmallows, and the owner says the little girl is the picture of her old man. They get home just in time, says her father, because it's getting colder. But the little girl says she's as warm as she can be.

A little girl narrates the simple pleasures of a walk in the snow with her father. The loving relationship depicted here, enhanced by soft, expressive illustrations, might stimulate discussion of happy times readers have had with one parent to themselves. Also noteworthy is the quiet appreciation for nature shown by the two wintertime walkers.

Ages 5-8

**Also available in:**
Paperbound—A Walk on a Snowy Night
Xerox Publishing Company

## 159

Delton, Judy and Elaine Knox-Wagner

**The Best Mom in the World**

Color illustrations by John Faulkner.
Albert Whitman & Company, 1979.
(32 pages counted)

DEPENDENCE/INDEPENDENCE
PARENT/PARENTS: Mother Working Outside Home
    Baby-sitter
    Communication: parent-child
    Helping
    Responsibility: avoiding

Lee Henry used to have the best mom in the world. She found his missing shoes, fixed him cocoa for breakfast, and prepared after-school snacks for him and his best friend, George. Then one day he and George arrive home from school to find that his mother is working late and has left a baby-sitter whom Lee Henry considers highly unsatisfactory. Sarah Louise is not willing to provide the services Lee Henry is accustomed to. When she does fix them a snack she cuts Lee Henry's sandwich the wrong way, and when she ties his shoes she remarks, "You sure can't do much alone, can you?" When his mother arrives home, Lee Henry reproaches her with all the things she wasn't there to do for him and finishes with, "You're not the best mom at all!" After Sarah Louise leaves, Lee Henry waits for his mother's apologies, but they are not forthcoming. Instead, she asks him to set the table and shows him how to do it. After dinner she asks him to clear the table. Both times Lee Henry objects that it's she who usually does those jobs. When his mother is too tired to play Monopoly after dinner, Lee Henry begins to cry. His mother does not take care of him as she should and he cannot do everything by himself, he wails. His mother agrees, but points out that there are some things he can do. She needs his help to be the best mother in the world. She convinces Lee Henry that the best moms in the world teach their children how to tie their own shoelaces and how to make themselves snacks—and proceeds to show him how to do both. Lee Henry decides he will try to do more things for himself. He takes a bath, washes his ears, puts his clothes in the hamper, and dresses himself —with no help from his mother. When she comes to tuck him in, she brings him one of his shoes that she found in the garage. Lee Henry decides, "I used to have the best mom in the whole world. And I guess I still do."

This is a lively first-person account of the anger and betrayal a small boy feels when his hardworking mother begins asking him to do things for himself, and of his satisfaction in learning to be more self-reliant. The attractive illustrations reflect the changes in Lee Henry as he turns from a happy, dependent child into a doubtful, bewildered, angry boy, and then into a proud, pleased, more capable person—in his mother's words, "the best kid in the whole world." This is one of several books about Lee Henry.

Ages 4-7

**Also available in:**
Large Print—The Best Mom in the World
Albert Whitman & Company

**D**

## 160

De Paola, Thomas Anthony

**Now One Foot, Now the Other**
Color illustrations by the author.
G. P. Putnam's Sons, 1981.
(45 pages counted)

GRANDPARENT: Love for
ILLNESSES: of Grandparent
    Helping

Bobby was named after his grandfather, Bob. Bob has often told Bobby how he taught him to walk, holding his hands and saying, "Now one foot, now the other." The two like to play with wooden blocks, stacking them into a tall tower. When the last block—the elephant block—is put on top, Bob pretends to sneeze and the tower comes tumbling down. One day, not long after Bobby's fifth birthday, Bob has a stroke and is hospitalized. Bobby misses his grandfather terribly, but it is many months before Bob comes home again. When he does he can't walk or talk, and he doesn't seem to know any of the family. He frightens the little boy now, especially one day when he makes a strange noise. His mother tells Bobby that Bob can't help himself. When the boy returns to his grandfather, he seems to see a tear rolling down Bob's face. Bobby begins to talk to him and is convinced Bob knows him, although his mother thinks it's Bobby's imagination. When Bobby builds a tower of blocks and places the elephant block on top, Bob makes a noise like a sneeze. "Bobby laughed and laughed. Now he knew that Bob would get better." Bob slowly begins to talk a little, to move his fingers and hands, and to attempt feeding himself. Bobby helps him. Bob requests stories, so Bobby tells him some. Then Bob rests his hands on Bobby's shoulders and learns to walk as Bobby tells him, "Now one foot. . . . Now the other foot." On Bobby's sixth birthday, he builds the block tower and Bob sneezes as the last block goes on. Bobby asks Bob to tell him some stories, and Bob does. Then Bobby tells the story of how he helped his grandfather learn to walk again.

A little boy and his grandfather exchange roles when, after a stroke, the grandfather is helped to walk by the child he taught to walk years earlier. Bobby helps the man who once helped him, telling him stories, playing their special game with blocks, helping his grandfather feed himself. It is Bobby who first realizes that Bob does recognize and understand people, even though he cannot speak or move. Beautifully and simply illustrated in soft colors, this warm story is about intergenerational love and respect. Young children will easily understand the text and may learn something of what a stroke is and means. Although all stroke victims do not have the rapid recovery shown here, the book suggests the value to them of a caring, supportive relationship. This is a companion volume to Nana Upstairs and Nana Downstairs.

Ages 4-7

**Also available in:**
Paperbound—Now One Foot, Now the Other
G. P. Putnam's Sons

## 161

De Paola, Thomas Anthony

**Oliver Button Is a Sissy**
Color illustrations by the author.
Harcourt Brace Jovanovich, Inc., 1979.
(46 pages counted)

GENDER ROLE IDENTITY: Male
    Name-calling
    Success
    Teasing

There is one little boy in the neighborhood who doesn't like to play ball. His name is Oliver Button. He doesn't like to do the other things boys are supposed to do either. Instead, he enjoys reading books, drawing pictures, jumping rope, and playing dress-up. Since he also likes to dance, his parents decide to send him to Ms. Leah's Dancing School. His father, who is uncomfortable with his son's interests, rationalizes that the dancing is "especially for the exercise." When Oliver takes his shiny new tap shoes to school, the boys tease him and write on the wall that "Oliver Button is a Sissy." But in spite of the continued teasing, Oliver keeps working on his dancing. When Ms. Leah asks him to be in a talent show, Oliver joyfully accepts the challenge. He gets a new costume and practices his routine tirelessly. On the Friday before his performance, his teacher at school announces the time and place of the show and encourages the other children to go and cheer for their classmate. On Sunday afternoon Oliver performs before a packed theater. The audience claps and claps. But when the prizes are announced, Oliver is left out. He is very disappointed and afraid of what people will think of him now. Ms. Leah and his parents, however, greet him with big hugs. His father rewards his "great dancer" by taking him out for a "great pizza." Nevertheless, the next day Oliver doesn't want to go to school and face the other children. But he does go, and as he walks by the wall where the cruel message about him is written, he is surprised to see that the word "Sissy" has been crossed out. The message now reads, "Oliver Button is a Star."

This is a book about the pain of being different, especially of varying from the accepted activities and interests of one's sex. It illustrates the struggle the nonconforming child may have in winning acceptance. Oliver does not fight back; he just endures and continues to find his happiness in doing his special things. The talent competition gives him his chance to prove to himself and others that what he does is worthwhile. Although things do not turn out as he had hoped, he does win the admiration of his family and classmates— the most important prize of all. Expressive illustrations help to emphasize the uniqueness of the main character and of his way of experiencing life.

Ages 4-7

**Also available in:**
Paperbound—Oliver Button Is a Sissy
Harcourt Brace Jovanovich, Inc.

**162**

De Roo, Anne Louise

**Scrub Fire**

Atheneum Publishers, 1980.
(106 pages)

---

COURAGE, MEANING OF
LOST, BEING
  Determination
  Fear
  Resourcefulness
  Sibling: relationships

---

When fourteen-year-old Michelle Seton is informed
that her aunt and uncle want to take her and her two
younger brothers camping in the wild bush country of
their native New Zealand, she wants nothing to do with
the plan. But her parents insist she go along to help with
Andrew and Jason. The second day out Uncle Don,
rather inept at camping, makes a fire to cook dinner.
Suddenly the fire wall breaks and the dry grass goes up
in flames. Jason runs for something to carry water in,
grabs the petrol container, and fuels the fire. Michelle
flees the roaring, spreading blaze, running until she
collapses. She wakes up at night, alone. Frightened, she
finally sleeps again. Next morning she decides to follow
the creek and soon discovers Andrew and Jason. They
continue to follow the creek, hoping to find a search
party but finding only a swamp. Andrew picks some
fruit for them to eat. Then he climbs some rocks and
spots a river, telling Michelle they should follow it.
Michelle smarts at his assumption of leadership—she's
the oldest, she should decide—but Andrew knows
something of wilderness camping and survival from the
experiences he and a friend had when the friend's
father took them camping in the bush. The next day
they follow the river, find a flat beach with a makeshift
shelter, and decide to stay there awhile. On the third
day there, Andrew falls into the churning water and is
rescued by a frantic Michelle. Jason, who's had a cough,
becomes frighteningly sick with a high fever. One day
they spot a helicopter, but the pilot doesn't see them.
After more than five days at their camp, Michelle and
Andrew decide they must get help for Jason, who is at
times delirious. They walk all day and sleep in a cave
that night. Finally Jason is so weak that the two make a
hammock out of vines and carry him. The fourth day
after leaving the river camp, Andrew spots Mount
Egmont and knows they can now find their way out if
they are strong enough to survive a few more days' trek.
By nightfall the three are exhausted and starved. Feeling defeated, Andrew refuses to go on the next morning.
Michelle bullies him until he gets angry and finally
agrees to continue. He collapses after crossing a muddy
river, and Michelle is the only one strong enough to
struggle on. When she hears voices through the haze she
is living in, she tells the men about Andrew and Jason
and then passes out. Michelle and the boys spend the
next two days in the hospital, sleeping. Then Michelle
tells the story of their twelve harrowing days to the man
in charge of the rescue team. That rescue team had not
saved the three; Michelle had been found by hunters
who knew nothing of the lost children. The rescue team
had never dreamed these town kids could get so far

away from their original campsite. Michelle learns her
aunt and uncle escaped the fire, but were cut off by it
from the three of them. She surprises herself by deciding she would like to return to the wilderness someday
—but only "if the campfire was built in a sensible place
by a sensible person." She knows people have been lost
and never found in the bush where she and her brothers had struggled to survive.

In this exciting story, a teenage girl and her two younger
brothers embark on a desperate attempt to survive in
the New Zealand wilderness. Instead of arguing and
challenging each other as they always have in the past,
the three learn to cooperate and to respect each other's
strengths. Michelle and Andrew discover a capacity for
endurance they didn't know they had. Detailed descriptions of survival techniques and of the New Zealand
wilderness enhance this action-filled, realistic
adventure.

Ages 9-12

**Also available in:**
No other form known

**163**

Dickinson, Mary

**Alex's Bed**

Color illustrations by Charlotte Firmin.
André Deutsch Ltd., 1980.
(31 pages counted)

---

MESSINESS
PROBLEM SOLVING

---

Little Alex's mother tells him that his room is a mess:
why can't he keep it tidy? He replies that his room is too
small. Glancing up at the ceiling, he notices there is
plenty of space up there. Nobody uses that space
"except those flies and that spider. If only I could fly."
His mother suggests they think about the problem over a
"nice cup of tea." As they think, Alex eats half a box of
marshmallows and his mother drinks three cups of tea.
Finally, she suggests they put his bed up in that empty
ceiling space and use the space underneath for more
storage. Alex says, "I don't think I have ever seen a
flying bed in the shops, Mum. Where do we get one
from?" We will make it, she answers, and they go to
purchase the lumber and other supplies. Back at home,
she takes the old legs off the bed and carefully nails the
new, long ones on, making sure the bed is level. The
new bed does not at first suit Alex; he thinks it needs a
ladder. His mother agrees. This time, after they buy
more lumber, Alex helps his mother saw, drill, and glue.
Once the ladder is finished she reorganizes his room,
but Alex still isn't terribly thrilled. The first night in his
new bed he nearly falls out, so his mother builds a
safety rail. Then Alex makes a hanging table for his
toys, suspended out from the side of the bed. His mother
is pleased with their inventions and the added space
Alex now has. Alex, however, merely expands his clutter to fill the new space. She must conclude that "there
was one little problem she could never solve . . . Alex."

When Alex's mother decides to put his bed on stilts in
order to create more space for his clutter, Alex simply
expands his mess. His mother observes that her boy, not

the room, is the problem. The familiar subject, the vivid, detailed illustrations of Alex's clutter, the everyday scenes between mother and child, and the simple explanations of the various construction projects make this a comfortable, nonthreatening story for little children—whether they are messy or not. Published in England, the book contains a few characteristic English phrases.

Ages 3-6

**Also available in:**
No other form known

## 164

Dixon, Jeanne

**Lady Cat Lost**

Atheneum Publishers, 1981.
(193 pages)

---

*CHANGE: New Home*
  *Family: relationships*
  *Friendship: making friends*
  *Loss: feelings of*
  *Parental: absence*
  *Pets: love for*
  *Reality, escaping*
  *Self, attitude toward: feeling different*

---

When Mr. Fergusson leaves his family, his wife is forced to sell most of the household goods and all the furniture to pay the bills. Then she moves her family to Montana, where she plans to live with her mother on the family farm. Her children—Kenneth, twelve; Oona, ten; Marlow, seven; and little Angel—all must leave friends and familiar things behind them. When they arrive at Grandma's house, they find an empty shell and no sign of Grandma. Two contractors come by and tell them to get off the land; they've bought it from Mrs. Fergusson's mother and she has moved to Arizona. The house is to be torn down the next day. Mr. and Mrs. Getz, Grandma's neighbors and dearest friends, invite the family to stay with them until they get their bearings. Mrs. Getz explains that Grandma sold the farm thinking the land would be used to build a medical center named after her husband; instead, developers plan to build small homes and trailer courts. The contractors' dog frightens off Kenneth's Lady Cat, one of two sealpoint Siamese that their father won in a poker game. Mrs. Getz can't understand why it's so important to Kenneth to find his cat. "He could never explain that the cats had held the family together after their father had gone. . . . had helped ease the pain of loss." He searches for Lady Cat everywhere, but avoids the cave he's been warned not to go near: Auntie Blossom, who lives with the Getzes, had a son, William, who disappeared years ago and was thought lost in the cave. Meanwhile Oona, who has always felt different and unloved and is sure that Mrs. Getz dislikes her, writes a long letter to her father. She tells him she often thinks of killing herself, but now plans to do something unselfish—find Kenneth's cat for him—to see if that will make people like her any better. She doesn't send the letter, but she does shave off her eyebrows and cut off all her hair. The Getz children, thirteen-year-old Ross and ten-year-old Miranda, return from a visit with their cousins accompanied by

two of the cousins, Dorin and Izzy. Miranda and Oona like each other at once, and Ross and Kenneth find a mutual interest in moto-cross bikes. But despite all the original good feeling, tension builds in the house as the two families try to live together. One night, as the children are all sleeping outdoors in a field, Oona feels something cold around her and hears a breath of a voice saying that they've come for her, that her struggles and heartbreak are now over. Upset by this visitation and by an argument she's had with Miranda, Oona doesn't return to the house with the others. The next day, Ross and Kenneth find her footprints leading into the cave. The Getzes and all the children form a search party, including Auntie Blossom who thinks they are going to rescue her son. While they are searching the cave, Kenneth's resentment toward Mr. and Mrs. Getz dissolves in his gratitude for their care and concern. Then Dragon, Oona's cat, bolts deeper into the cave and Kenneth follows—only to become thoroughly lost. But he and Dragon eventually find Oona and Lady Cat. Oona is staring vacantly and hardly seems alive. Kenneth looks around and realizes she too has seen the bones, undoubtedly William's, laying nearby. They find a hole, shout for help, and are rescued by the construction crew. The contractor is pleased to discover the system of caves beneath his land—now, instead of in a few years when homes might have caved in. He'll leave the land as a park. Grandma writes that she has set aside half the money from the sale of the farm for the family's use, so they will be able to buy a house after all. Ross tells Kenneth they'll probably always be best friends.

Four children find themselves in a changing world when their father leaves them and they move into another family's house. The two oldest, Kenneth and Oona, face especially difficult adjustments. Kenneth's missing cat epitomizes the family's sense of loss, but does serve to focus the boy's anxiety on something concrete. Oona, however, a solitary and impulsive child, gives way for a time to her nightmares and forebodings. The book's viewpoint ranges from Kenneth's to Oona's to Mrs. Fergusson's, even to Lady Cat's, as each tries to make sense of changed circumstances. The introduction of "spirits" (Oona's unexplained encounter with a ghostly presence, the mysterious cave) injects an unnecessary note of unreality into this otherwise realistic story of a family struggling to find its bearings in a new place.

Ages 10-12

**Also available in:**
No other form known

## 165

Dixon, Paige, pseud.

**Skipper**

Atheneum Publishers, 1979.
(110 pages)

---

*DEATH: of Sibling*
*IDENTITY, SEARCH FOR*
  *Abandonment*
  *Family: extended*
  *Family: relationships*
  *Mourning, stages of*
  *Rejection: parental*

---

Five months after the wrenching loss of his older brother, Jordan, teenager Skipper Phillips continues to talk with him at his gravesite and through a journal he keeps that's like a long letter to Jordie. His mother and remaining older siblings worry over what they consider Skipper's morbid preoccupation. The boy's sudden decision to use his summer vacation to find his father, who left before Skipper was born, at first stuns his family. But they soon offer their support in the hope that this quest will cure Skipper's depression. Skipper's mother doesn't know much about her former husband's family, just that they live in the small town of Llangollen, North Carolina. So Skipper leaves Colorado and goes there, discovering an entire clan of Phillipses, including a spoiled half-brother, Gerald, thirteen, who bears an astonishing resemblance to Jordan. Jealous and suspicious, Gerald believes his absent father sent Skipper to ingratiate himself with their wealthy great-grandfather, thereby usurping Gerald's own position and eventual inheritance. Influenced by his greedy uncle, Gerald intends to sell the family estate after his great-grandfather dies. The boys' charming but irresponsible father, George, who now lives somewhere in the northern part of the state with a black woman (to the family's chagrin), promises to visit Skipper. Meanwhile, Skipper grows close to his cousin, Mary Gwyn, a promising pianist whose musical career was ended when she fell from a horse. As he cheers her and carries her to and from her wheelchair, Skipper is reminded of Jordan's last days. True to his character, George calls to postpone his visit, glibly apologizing to the disappointed Skipper. Then, to prevent his father's cabin from being readied for his eventual visit, Gerald puts a dead skunk outside the place—he's determined not to lose his inheritance. Skipper phones his father and once again George promises to come and set things right. But when Gerald sees that George still plans to come, he burns the cabin to the ground. Now George says there is nothing in Llangollen for him, and Skipper realizes to his sorrow that he'll never actually meet his father. But he wants to help his half-brother see things more clearly and accept his friendship. He asks Gerald if he started the fire, reminding him that such an act is arson, a crime. In response, Gerald pushes Skipper into the water and into the path of a deadly cottonmouth snake. Skipper saves himself and then begins to wrestle Gerald furiously. But he can't bring himself to hit the boy who looks so much like Jordan. Packing his bag, Skipper resigns himself to the fact that some people cannot be helped. Then the family gets the news that the great-grandfather is dead. At the funeral, the terms of the old man's will are revealed: Gerald inherits most of his money, but all the relatives have been left their own homes, so Llangollen can never be developed or sold out of the family. Skipper is relieved, but Gerald runs from the church in tears. At the airport, Skipper writes for the last time in his journal: "I'm glad I came. This is the end of my journey and the end of my journal. To my brother Jordan, good-bye and hello."

Although the reasons for Skipper's release from despondency are never clearly delineated, his journey to his absent father's family seems to help him overcome his confusion and paralyzing sense of loss after the death of a beloved brother. This sequel to *May I Cross Your Golden River?* the account of Jordan's illness and death, lacks the poignancy of its predecessor but does offer a vivid picture of a boy floundering in grief, searching for his own identity. After his journey, Skipper is ready to return to his own home, to resume living.

Ages 12 and up

**Also available in:**
No other form known

## 166

**Dodson, Susan**

### Have You Seen This Girl?

Four Winds Press, 1982.
(182 pages)

---

*RUNNING AWAY*
  Child abuse
  Drugs: abuse of
  Family: relationships
  Maturation
  Rebellion

---

Sixteen-year-old Tom Carpenter feels deserted when Kathy, the only girl he has ever cared about, runs away and leaves him behind. They had often talked about fleeing together, Kathy from a mother who beats her and Tom from parents he feels do not understand him. So when Tom receives Kathy's postcard from New York City, he leaves Ann Arbor to find and join her. He goes first to his Aunt Maggie in New York, letting her think he plans to return home after the Easter break. Maggie, divorced and very busy, reluctantly agrees to take him in and help him search for Kathy, calling his parents first to reassure them. They start by talking to an officer at the Runaway Unit in the bus terminal, learning that Kathy escaped from him soon after she arrived. From there they proceed to the library at Bryant Park, which was pictured on Kathy's postcard, and show her photograph to people in the area. As they walk through the Times Square district, Tom is overwhelmed by the open prostitution, pornography, and dope peddling. He begins to realize that the ten days Kathy has been gone is a long time for a defenseless, vulnerable girl to avoid the obvious snares of New York. He doesn't know that in another part of town, Kathy is being well cared for by a wealthy and benevolent widow named Jane Kent. She was brought to Mrs. Kent's posh Greenwich Village apartment after Dee Dee, another runaway who'd grown jealous of Kathy, pushed her in front of the woman's car. Having barely escaped injury, Kathy is now nestling in the lap of luxury while Tom and his aunt visit runaway centers and Tom sees something of the porn "supermarket" of the "Big Apple's Core." Kathy has convinced Mrs. Kent that she is an actress. She has also decided to get Brian, Mrs. Kent's son, to fall in love with her and keep her "safe forever and ever." One day, as she sits at a sidewalk cafe, a photographer named Teddy approaches her. He snaps several candid pictures and later invites her to his apartment for a real photo session. Flattered, Kathy dreams about becoming a famous New York model and actress. Tom, however, is discouraged by his search and depressed about the sordid lives he has seen. Gradually, his aunt helps him see that many of his own family problems are self-induced. He has just about decided to return to the clean streets

**D**

and fresh air of home when he accepts his aunt's and her boyfriend's invitation to go out on the town. In the middle of dinner at an exclusive restaurant, he looks up and sees Kathy preparing to leave with her elegant escort, Brian Kent. He rushes after them, but Kathy wants nothing to do with him. After a fight with Brian and his chauffeur, Tom is left lying semi-conscious on the curb as the car speeds away. Back at the Kents' apartment, however, Kathy finds a surprise: her mother, whom Mrs. Kent has brought to New York. Kathy knows she'll be beaten if she goes home, so the next morning she sneaks out of the apartment to Teddy's place. They have had their first photo session (most of it nude or semi-nude), and now Teddy enthusiastically tells Kathy she will be starring in a movie. Two days later Tom leaves New York, knowing he can do nothing to help Kathy but determined to save himself.

This is the dual story of Tom's eye-opening search for Kathy and Kathy's gradual immersion in the fast life and easy promises of New York. As Tom pursues his studies at "Street-wise University," he realizes where his pointless rebellion is taking him and starts to grow up. Kathy, on the other hand, lonely and desperate, is vulnerable to the charms of operators like Teddy, who "can give more in fifteen minutes than some parents do in fifteen years." Scenes of the runaway network in New York are vivid, as are the portrayals of the manipulating characters who exploit it—although Kathy's rescue, perhaps temporary, by the wealthy Mrs. Kent is hardly the usual pattern for runaway teenagers. Oddly, the only controversial aspect of the book is the attitude of the respectable adults toward alcohol and drugs. Tom's parents believe in letting him drink at home so he won't be "curious outside," and Aunt Maggie gets drunk with him. She has also smoked marijuana off and on and wants to purchase his so she can make sure it's pure.

Ages 13 and up

**Also available in:**
No other form known

## 167

Dolan, Sheila

### The Wishing Bottle

Black/white illustrations by Leslie Morrill.
Houghton Mifflin Company, 1979.
(81 pages)

---

*MAGICAL THINKING*
*WISHES*
   *Animals: love for*
   *Animals: responsibility for*
   *Determination*
   *Money: earning*

---

Nora, about eight, lives in an old farmhouse with her mother and older brother and sister. Her special wish is

for a pony to put life into their empty barn. When Nora's mother reminds her that ponies are expensive, the girl begins to save her weekly allowance. She picks and sells blackberries and wild flowers, collects nuts, and helps her mother in the garden, but the money accumulates very slowly. One day in the meadow, she discovers a circle of dark green grass and is sure it must be a fairy ring. She is also certain that elves have turned themselves into the goldfinches in the nearby pear tree. Every day she feeds the "elves" milk left from her cereal and then runs to the barn to see if they have brought her pony. Nora's family is concerned about her absorption in fantasy, but not even her discovery that a cat is drinking her milk—not elves—discourages her. It's a sad day when she finds the fairy ring has faded and the goldfinch elves have flown away. Then, in the woods, she finds what she believes must be a magic bottle. She cleans it thoroughly and wishes three times for a pony. In an effort to dissuade her from this new obsession, her mother tells her, "Nora, if wishes were horses, beggars would ride." But one miraculous day, Nora awakes from a nap in the barn to find a beautiful copper-colored pony there with her. Nora's mother insists that she and her brother and sister look for the owner. They find him, a farmer named Mr. Gruber, and he explains that the pony, Sam, often escapes now that the grandchildren are grown and gone. He says Nora may come to visit Sam anytime; when she does, he teaches her how to care for the pony. In her happiness Nora decides the magic bottle almost worked, but as she grips it tightly for one more wish, it flies from her hands and crashes to the floor. Summer ends and school begins, with Nora continuing to care for Sam on weekends. She is distressed to learn that Mr. and Mrs. Gruber will be visiting their son in Florida for the winter and plan to send all the farm animals to Mr. Gruber's brother, who lives farther away from Nora's house. After one of Nora's last visits to Sam before the Grubers leave, she returns home to find Mr. Gruber and her family engaged in a "barn warming." To her delight, her mother has given permission for her to care for Sam during the winter. An overjoyed Nora wonders if all this would have happened without the magic bottle. She thinks not.

A little girl who loves horses believes steadfastly in the magic she feels is all around her, despite her family's concern over her preoccupation with fairies, elves, and magic bottles. But Nora finds that even a granted wish must be rooted in solid ground as she works to earn money and then accepts the responsibility of learning to care for a pony. Delicate illustrations reinforce the charm of this imaginative story.

Ages 7-9

**Also available in:**
No other form known

**168**

**Donnelly, Elfie**

## So Long, Grandpa

Translated from the German by Anthea Bell.
Crown Publishers, Inc., 1981.
(92 pages)

---

DEATH: Attitude Toward
GRANDPARENT: Love for
  Cancer
  Death: of grandparent
  Family: relationships
  Grandparent: living in child's home
  Illnesses: terminal

---

Micky Nidetzky holds strong opinions for a boy of ten. For example, his mother is not to enter his room without knocking. But she does, and this, along with her strictness, her close supervision, and especially her criticism of his beloved grandfather, drives him wild. He's also at his wit's end about his older sister, Linda, who takes after their mother in all things and never fails to tattle on Micky. Dad is all right but it is Grandpa Nidetzky, who lives with the family, that Micky especially loves. Still, the boy doesn't seem particularly concerned when his father tells him that Grandpa has cancer. To Micky, cancer is just another illness, like flu. When Dad announces that he has bought a vacation home in the Canary Islands and that the family will go there next week, Micky becomes engrossed in vacation plans. There is a brief flare-up when Micky, assuming Grandpa will accompany them, talks with him about the trip before his parents have decided if the old man's health will permit him to go. But then his parents decide Grandpa should come along and they fly from their home in Austria to their vacation place adjoining a beach. At first, Micky loves his vacation. But then he sees Grandpa's condition worsen, so dramatically that Micky asks his parents if Grandpa will die. Shocked, his mother replies, "People don't talk about that kind of thing!" After Grandpa suffers a sharp attack of pain, Mrs. Nidetzky asks angrily why they brought along such a "sick old man." Grandpa overhears and the two have a long argument. Next morning, Grandpa is gone. Mrs. Nidetzky blames herself. Later in the day, Micky finds Grandpa calmly working crossword puzzles in an empty fisherman's hut. He wanted some peace and quiet and soon announces his intention to stay on the island until he dies. But the family persuades him to return with them. From then on, Grandpa rapidly loses weight and has increased pain and fatigue. Micky tries to grasp the fact that Grandpa will never recover. When he and Grandpa talk, Grandpa admits he doesn't believe in God. After Micky accompanies Grandpa to the funeral of an old friend, the two talk about people's odd ceremonies of burial, their use of phrases like "passing on" to conceal the fact of death. Although Grandpa's health steadily deteriorates, he remains cheerful and refuses to be morbid. Micky profits from Grandpa's straightforward attitude and is able to ask the doctor how long Grandpa has left, a question his father is unable to complete. About two to four weeks, the doctor replies. And soon Grandpa is dead, dying in his sleep. Seeing the body in bed, Micky suddenly feels cheerful: "Grandpa's alright now!" But when the time comes to throw earth on the coffin, a ritual he and Grandpa had smiled about, Micky faints and is confined to bed. His father comforts him by showing him a letter Grandpa had written asking Micky to take care of all his little "treasures." Micky is not to be sorry about Grandpa's death, the old man wrote. He hopes Micky's life will be as happy as his own has been. Himself again, Micky tells his mother to stop crying. Grandpa lives as long as someone thinks of him, and Micky always will.

A young boy whose beloved grandfather is dying of cancer learns to disentangle death from its social trappings and see it clearly in this thoughtful first-person narrative. Micky's is an honest account of death, dying, and mourning, one that could comfort children in similar situations. Though not at all antireligious, the book does present a humanistic approach to death in its criticism of the various social and religious rituals that surround human mortality, and so calls for a discerning reader or an adult's explanation. Family relationships, strained by terminal illness, are realistically presented.

Ages 9-11

**Also available in:**
No other form known

---

**D**

---

**169**

**Donovan, Pete**

## Carol Johnston: The One-armed Gymnast

Black/white photographs by Mitchell Rose, David Hopley, Lynn Rogers, and Carol Johnston.
Children's Press, Inc., 1982.
(42 pages)

---

LIMBS, ABNORMAL OR MISSING
SPORTS/SPORTSMANSHIP
  Perseverance
  Talents: athletic

---

In May of 1978, twenty-year-old Carol Johnston competed in the national gymnastics championship and was named All-American in both her floor exercises and beam routines. Carol was born with only one arm, but that hasn't kept her from becoming tops in a sport that is demanding even for people with two arms. A small person physically, Carol admits she was probably not meant to be a gymnast, but no one ever told her she couldn't be creative with just one arm. Born in Calgary, Canada, she moved after high school to Fullerton, California, encouraged by the Cal State-Fullerton gymnastics coach. At Fullerton she astonished coach and teammates with her abilities. "But I still wanted to be treated as a gymnast, not as a one-armed gymnast." During her freshman year, Carol almost made it to the national gymnastics finals. As a sophomore she won her college conference championship in two categories and went on to be named All-American in the national championships. A year later, she suffered a knee injury. Following surgery and months of wearing a cast, she returned to gymnastics because her life seemed to be missing something without it. But when she reinjured her knee, she was told that if she ever injured it again she might not be able to walk normally. She decided to retire and live a normal life: "Having one arm was never a limitation, but my knee was." Nobody knows why Carol was born with just one arm, reports her mother, but it never stopped her. As a child she took piano and skating lessons. She has appeared on television to tell her story and has inspired many people. Says Carol, "The most important thing in life is not to put yourself in a box. Don't ever say I can't do it."

This biography of the Canadian gymnast who won All-American honors with a physical handicap emphasizes that limitations are often only what people think they are. Illustrated with photographs, this is primarily the story of a talented athlete, only secondarily the story of a handicap. Readers with limited reading skills might find this especially appealing; many readers will find it inspiring.

Ages 8-12

**Also available in:**
Paperbound—*Carol Johnston: The One-armed Gymnast*
Children's Press, Inc.

## 170

### Douglass, Barbara

### Skateboard Scramble

Black/white illustrations by Alex Stein.
The Westminster Press, 1979.
(90 pages)

---

*COMPETITION*
  *Friendship: best friend*
  *Parental: interference*
  *Prejudice: sexual*
  *Sharing/Not sharing*
  *Sports/Sportsmanship*

---

Jody Flynn, about eleven and new in town, first hears of the Skateboard Scramble from Andrea Masters, the daughter of her father's new boss. Jody's father insists she enter the skateboard contest, and he speaks often of how proud he'll be when she wins it. He encourages Jody to make friends with Andrea, who doesn't appear to want Jody's friendship, and to practice with her skateboard every day. When Jody goes to practice at the new skateboard park, she meets Carmen, a fearless skateboarder with a clumsy old skateboard who shares some of her expertise with Jody. When the girls go to sign up for the contest, however, they discover that girls are not allowed to enter it. Jody agonizes over whether or not to tell her father about the boys-only rule. If she tells him, she knows he'll get the rules changed and she'll have to enter "that schlumpy scramble." After a nearly sleepless night, Jody decides that trying to enter the contest is the lesser of two evils: arguments with her father are worse. Since she realizes she won't have much of a chance of winning against Carmen, she considers trying to enter without telling her friend. In the end, though, Jody takes Carmen with her to the hobby shop, and they complain about the boys-only rule until the man lets them sign up. On the day of the tournament trials, Jody is too tense to eat breakfast. Her father, also tense, says sharply, "Missing one meal never hurt anybody." All the way to the tournament he talks about "the Flynn fighting spirit." To her father's disappointment, Jody and Sean Masters tie for second place—Carmen is

first. At the next set of trials, Sean, Jody, and Carmen all tie for first place. Carmen's skateboard is so old that the wheels wobble, spoiling what might have been a superior performance. Jody's father soon gives her a new skateboard so she can beat Sean the next week, and he advises her to practice by herself at home. On Monday, Jody is kept from telling Carmen she won't be practicing at the park anymore; Jody's mother has invited Andrea Masters for lunch. According to Andrea's mother, Andrea is very shy and needs to make friends, although Jody has trouble believing this of the girl she calls Miss Perfection. At the last minute, Andrea's mother cancels the lunch, but it's Wednesday before Jody realizes Carmen herself isn't practicing at the skateboard park anymore. She goes to Carmen's house and overhears her friend telling her young, wheelchair-bound brother that she is determined to win the Skateboard Scramble and the first prize of a trip to Disneyland for him, in spite of her old, wobbly skateboard. Determined to help Carmen, Jody lends the girl her new skateboard for the third and final competition, and Carmen wins. Jody finishes second and Sean is third. Jody expects her father to be angry, but he only remarks that if she hadn't given her board to Carmen, she would probably have won. Then he adds that she's a trophy of a daughter and invites Carmen and her little brother to join them for hamburgers. Jody sees Andrea hanging back and wonders if perhaps Andrea really is shy. She invites her to come with them. Andrea's smile and the group's high spirits are proof that Jody has made some good decisions.

A young girl must cope with several kinds of pressures: pressure from her father to compete and win; pressure from herself to overcome fears and be loyal to her friend. She responds out of her own sense of loyalty and fairness, helping a talented friend and winning her competitive father's respect at the same time. She also reaches out to a shy girl she's envied, deciding that just as there's more than one way to be a champion, so shyness can take different forms. This is a tightly written and appealing story.

Ages 9-11

**Also available in:**
Cassette—*Skateboard Scramble*
Library of Congress (NLSBPH)

Film—*A Different Kind of Winning*
Learning Corporation of America

## 171

### Drescher, Joan Elizabeth

### I'm In Charge!

Color illustrations by the author.
Little, Brown and Company, 1981.
(32 pages)

---

*RESPONSIBILITY: Accepting*
  *Communication: parent-child*
  *Resourcefulness*

---

A little boy is in charge of the house. Upstairs, his father writes on and on, needing to make a deadline. He tells the boy to call if he needs help, but his eyebrows say "not unless it's an emergency." Mother is at work. The boy feels sure he can handle anything, even an emergency. A woman telephones for his mother, and the boy takes down her phone number and her name, Mrs. Car, drawing a car on the blackboard for good measure. Then he paints. Hungry, he goes to the refrigerator and messily prepares an enormous snack for himself and his dog. Then the boy stuffs his food-sticky clothes in the washer and has just managed to dump soap in when the doorbell rings. The boy opens the door to find a salesman, but quickly shuts it again when he remembers that strangers aren't allowed in. Soon the bell rings once more. This time it's his friend, Marshall, with a jar full of grasshoppers. Marshall comes in, immediately trips, and the grasshoppers escape. While chasing them, the boys bump into the painting easel, spilling green paint on the rug. The boy firmly orders Marshall home and begins to clean the rug. Then he spots soapsuds oozing from the laundry room. "Dad!" he calls out. "It's an emergency." After helping him clean up, his father assures the boy that knowing when to call for help is still being in charge. By the time his mother gets home, the boy has prepared the living room for a party celebrating his being in charge. But as he rushes to welcome his mother he must admit, "I'm really glad to see you."

A little boy temporarily responsible for his house remains "in charge" through several calamities. Readers might question the father's calm acceptance of the soapsuds mishap and find the boy's trials a bit exaggerated, but this is a funny, cleverly illustrated tale of a child's enjoyment of responsibility and of his parents' faith in him.

Ages 5-8

**Also available in:**
No other form known

## 172

**Drescher, Joan Elizabeth**
**The Marvelous Mess**
Color illustrations by the author.
Houghton Mifflin Company, 1980.
(32 pages counted)

*MESSINESS*
*Chores*
*Jealousy: sibling*
*Responsibility: avoiding*

A little boy has a very messy room and his parents order him to clean it. Instead he plays, imagining himself a circus juggler and a pirate. Meanwhile, his mother worries that she has been too harsh and his father assures her they are doing the right thing. The boy's sister makes several sarcastic comments about her messy brother. The next morning the parents announce they are going up to see the boy's room. The boy quickly shoves everything into the closet, and his parents praise him for doing what he was told. His jealous sister slams his door as she leaves, causing everything to fall out of the closet.

But his parents, not realizing what has happened, conclude he has learned his lesson and that this has been a good experience for him. Left alone at last, the boy sits down amongst the mess, continuing to play and daydream.

This is a comical story of a small boy with a very messy room. Instead of cleaning his room as he has been told, he plays and daydreams in his "marvelous mess." But, although he succeeds in hiding the mess from his parents, a slammed door assures that his ruse will sooner or later be discovered. Parents and children alike will enjoy the situation. Cartoonlike, the text appears in balloons within the colorful, zany illustrations.

Ages 4-6

**Also available in:**
No other form known

## 173

**Drescher, Joan Elizabeth**
**Your Family, My Family**
Color illustrations by the author.
Walker and Company, 1980.
(32 pages)

**D**

*FAMILY: Relationships*
*Adoption: explaining*
*Belonging*
*Divorce: of parents*
*Family: extended*
*Life style*

"A family is people, living together, sharing, caring." There are all kinds of families. A child can be born into one, adopted into one, or taken into one as a foster member. Families can be big or small. A child can have one parent, two parents, grandparents, or foster parents. Some families have two working parents and others have one; maybe the mother works and the father takes care of the house. Some children, because of divorce, have two families. Other children may live in a house with an extended family, many single people and families living together. Just as every child needs a family, every child also needs time alone—this is easier in some families than in others. Having a family means sharing and helping. It also means communicating feelings, being yourself, fighting, being angry, and yet loving and knowing you are loved. A family cares for one another.

Young children are shown and described in many kinds of families, each one emphasizing the bond of love and sense of belonging. Although the families pictured are all happy ones, they represent quite a diversity of living arrangements, and so the book could be instructive and reassuring to young readers of various backgrounds. The illustrations are highlighted in gold.

Ages 5-7

**Also available in:**
No other form known

**174**

Due, Linnea A.

## High and Outside

Harper & Row, Publishers, Inc., 1980.
(195 pages)

---

*ALCOHOLISM: Adolescent*
  *Friendship: best friend*
  *Loneliness*
  *Suicide: attempted*

---

Niki Etchen seems to have everything going for her. A junior at Lincoln High, Niki is the champion pitcher on the girls' softball team, an honors student, an editor on the school paper. But Niki is also an alcoholic. Three years ago her parents allowed her to start drinking wine, and she has gradually worked her way to gin-and-tonic cocktails, wine at dinner, and beer after dinner. Her parents don't see the problem. Her best friend, Martha, tries hard to cover up for Niki's erratic behavior and changing moods. When Niki's drinking begins noticeably affecting her pitching game, her coach, Scotty, offers to talk with her about her drinking and then gives her an ultimatum: no more hangovers at practices or games or Niki will be off the team. After she skips practice the following day because of a hangover, Scotty tells Niki that she will either join Alcoholics Anonymous or leave the team. In a rage, Niki quits the team. Another teammate, Teri, who goes to Al Anon because her father is an alcoholic, encourages Niki to go to AA. But Niki keeps denying she is an alcoholic, although she has blackouts almost every time she drinks. Finally, after a dramatic confrontation with Martha, Niki tries AA. But she finds that sobriety leaves her angry and irritable, and she rationalizes that she is probably not an alcoholic. Niki starts drinking again, but feels depressed and resentful toward herself and others. After school ends for the summer, her drinking gets worse. Then Martha, who has been attending Al Anon with Teri, confronts Niki, saying she no longer wants the pressure of Niki's drinking and never wants to see her again. Niki continues drinking heavily and one day attempts to slash her wrists. But even alcohol doesn't allow her to cut deeply enough. In despair, Niki decides on her own to concentrate on the AA slogans, "first things first" and "one day at a time." After six weeks of lonely sobriety, she decides to attend an AA and then an Al Anon meeting. At the Al Anon meeting she sees Martha, and they have an emotional reunion. Niki is finally able to acknowledge that she has to conquer her drinking problem one day at a time.

A teenage alcoholic graphically describes her blackouts, loneliness, and suicidal feelings. Though her parents give her little support when she confronts them with her alcoholism, Niki finds her friends and coach very supportive, even when she is not willing to accept their concern and advice. The characteristics of teenage alcoholism and its effects on the young victim and her friends are handled realistically. Much less convincing is the shallow characterization of Niki's parents, whose obtuseness seems highly unlikely. The dialogue is generally believable and includes some profanity.

Ages 13 and up

**Also available in:**
No other form known

---

**175**

Dunlop, Eileen Rhona

## Fox Farm

Holt, Rinehart and Winston, Inc., 1979.
(149 pages)

---

*ABANDONMENT*
*FOSTER HOME*
*PETS: Love for*
  *Belonging*
  *Friendship: meaning of*

---

Ten-year-old Adam Hewitt and his foster brother, Richard Darke, share everything—a bedroom, a bike, chores on Fox Farm in Scotland where Richard's father works —yet seldom talk about anything. Adam's conviction that he will soon join his father in Australia keeps him distanced from the Darke family, despite their efforts to befriend and show affection for him. Adam was abandoned six years earlier when his widowed father emigrated to Australia with a new wife. At first the boy lived with his aunt, but when his father stopped sending support money, Adam was turned over to the Social Work Department. He blames his stepmother, believing his father wants him and will soon send for him—although it's been three years since he heard from the man. Meanwhile, the boy resists showing any affection to the Darkes. In fact, he resolves to keep the fox cub he finds partly to spite Mr. Darke, who Adam thinks cold-heartedly killed its mother. Knowing Richard's conscientiousness and sense of responsibility, Adam enlists his help with the cub to prevent him from telling his parents. Richard finds a place for Foxy in Fox Tower, an ancient watchtower on the property, and devises a way to feed him by sneaking him food they buy with pocket money. Adam quickly becomes so attached to Foxy that he spends his precious Australia money for the animal's food. Allied in the scheme, the boys come to appreciate each other: Adam values Richard's loyalty and practicality, and Richard values Adam's cleverness and courage. Adam devotes all his extra time, effort, and resources to the little animal he loves dearly. Then Mr. Darke, who has been struggling to maintain the farm, announces that he has found a job in the city and the family must move in the fall. At first, Adam is not concerned—he figures he and Foxy will be in Australia by then, since he has written asking his father for the fare —but as money to feed Foxy runs out, he is driven to steal a valuable microscope from Richard's brother. Unable to sell it, he brings it back to find that Richard has covered for him. Then a letter arrives from Australia. His father's new wife, dominated by her husband, tells him he is not wanted. His dreams shattered, Adam's reality is now threatened. The son of the owner of Fox Farm has been lost on an expedition. A local newspaper publishes an article linking the boy's disappearance to the Weird, an ancient curse put upon the family's ancestors for stealing a chalice. People hunting the chalice come to the Tower, but Adam and Foxy scare them off. The boys' struggle to keep Foxy secret ends when a flood threatens the Tower. As a last resort, Adam fearfully shows Foxy to the Darkes. Mr. Darke laughs: Foxy is not a fox after all but a mongrel dog. The owner's lost son comes back, Mr. Darke is offered a partnership in managing the farm, and Adam joins the family.

In this beautifully written story, foster brothers share time and activities, but not friendship, until they are united in their dedication to an animal. Bit by bit, as his attachment to his pet expands to the family that cares for him rather than to the father who abandoned him, Adam tears down the wall he's built around his feelings. All characters are realistically portrayed. The subplot of the Weird is peripheral to the story, but is developed just enough to create suspense and move things along. Throughout, the book imparts a sense of the Scottish countryside and its people.

Ages 10-12

**Also available in:**
No other form known

**176**

Dunne, Mary Collins

**Hoby & Stub**

Atheneum Publishers, 1981.
(156 pages)

---

*RUNNING AWAY*
  *Animals: love for*
  *Belonging*
  *Delinquency, juvenile*
  *Determination*
  *Hitchhiking*
  *Orphan*

---

Thirteen-year-old John Hobart (Hoby) is surprised when Virgil, the ex-convict who lived with his mother before her death and is now caring for Hoby until he can be placed in a foster home, brings home a puppy with good bloodlines. But Hoby soon discovers that Virgil, a mean man, intends raising the pup to compete in dog fights. Dogs seldom last more than one or two fights in the ring. Hoby becomes fond of the pit bull terrier he calls Stub, short for stubborn, and is determined to save him. Together, Hoby and Stub leave Albion, Texas, on a freight car, headed for Hoby's only living relative, his Aunt Elva in Gentry, Illinois. But they end up near New Mexico, having taken the train in the wrong direction. There two boys steal Hoby's wallet and his only picture of his parents before their divorce. He picks cotton—dirty, hard, low-paying work—and rolls a sleeping drunk for his money. Then he and Stub take the train back through Texas to Arkansas. While trying to hitchhike, Hoby is offered a ride he rejects because the man looks at him strangely, possessively. Soon he meets fifteen-year-old Ariel, who's running away from her stepmother and her boarding school. Ariel describes a man she saw at the bus station asking about a boy and a dog: Virgil. To avoid his pursuer,

Hoby works all day at a chicken factory while Ariel watches Stub. Then Ariel gets a ride to Nashville, her destination, and has the man give Hoby and Stub a ride for the first twenty miles. After they are dropped off, a motorcycle gang harasses and frightens Hoby and tries to steal Stub. Some truckers rescue him and give him a lift. Later, again hitchhiking, he meets two young runaways headed for Chicago, and for several days enjoys their friendship—although he spots Virgil's car. Hoby's two friends shoplift, vandalize an old man's garden, and steal a toolbox from a man who gave them a long ride. Disgusted, Hoby takes off again. A farm girl and her mother take him in for a meal and a shower. He stops at a commune Ariel mentioned, and at first it seems like paradise to him. But then a man steals Stub, probably intending to sell him for drug money. Hoby and the man's friend spend several days tracking Stub down. He's been sold to a farmer, Aaron Kendrew, some distance away. Arriving at the well-tended farm, Hoby finds that Stub was bought for the pretty young daughter, Betty Faye. Her father offers to let Hoby work in his peach orchard to earn Stub back. At first, Hoby decides Stub would be better off left on the farm. But then he realizes that Betty Faye has a mean, selfish streak, and he resolves to leave. Betty Faye blackmails Hoby into promising her his watch, the last memento from his mother. Hoby finally gets his pay from Mr. Kendrew, who has overworked him for the price of the dog. Before he leaves, he hands over the watch to Betty Faye—with its insides destroyed. Finally, after several bus rides, Hoby and Stub reach Gentry, Illinois. Aunt Elva, Uncle Doyne, and cousin Jed welcome them, but Hoby overhears his aunt and uncle discussing whether or not to keep him. His uncle fears Hoby might get in trouble and be a nuisance. Apologizing for overhearing them, Hoby defends himself, telling them he's used to hard work and has rejected many opportunities to commit crimes. Impressed, they invite him to stay. But later that day, while walking through the woods, Hoby is jumped on by Virgil, who needs the boy's testimony about the last night Hoby lived with him. Virgil is being accused of committing a murder that night and only Hoby can clear him. Since Virgil also wants Stub back, Hoby makes a deal with him: his testimony for Stub. When Virgil agrees, Hoby realizes how much he has learned. He can even handle Virgil now.

A young, orphaned runaway and his dog encounter friends and enemies, generosity and suspicion, danger and last-minute rescues on their trek from Texas to Illinois. Finding a home at last with his only relative and her family, Hoby learns to be neither victim nor victimizer. Many of his adventures could provide springboards for discussion, including the overriding issue of running away. Although the character of Virgil and of certain other people Hoby encounters are stereotypical, the boy's odyssey is always believable.

Ages 10-13

**Also available in:**
No other form known

**D**

**177**

Dyer, Thomas A.

## The Whipman Is Watching

Houghton Mifflin Company, 1979.
(177 pages)

---

*GRANDPARENT: Living in Home of
NATIVE AMERICAN*
  *Ambivalence, feelings of*
  *Discipline, meaning of*
  *Identity, search for*
  *Rebellion*
  *School: negative experiences*

---

Thirteen-year-old Angie lives on an Indian reservation in Oregon with her grandmother, called Katla, her younger sister, Carysa, and her older cousins, Cultus and Marta. Katla is very mindful of Indian traditions, clinging tenaciously to the old ways, and Marta follows her example. Angie is somewhat impatient with the discipline of Indian life. But Cultus is more than impatient—he is a troublemaker, the kind that gives Indians a bad name, according to Katla. Angie can't understand Cultus's bull-headedness when it is so much easier "just to get along." The reservation is forty-nine miles from the school, so the children take the bus there and back every day. Although many of them behave badly, Cultus is the worst, fighting and instigating fights whenever he can. One day the bus driver tells Katla that Cultus will not be allowed to ride the bus for a week. The grandmother says it's up to the driver to make the children behave. In the old days, she remembers, Indian children behaved because they got whipped regularly by the Whipman, a tribe member responsible for discipline. Cultus has no other way to get to school, but the bus driver refuses to relent. That night Cultus doesn't come home. He returns the next day accompanied by his Uncle Dan, who agrees with the boy that he shouldn't have to attend the white people's school. Although it is Saturday, Katla insists that Dan drive her to the principal's home so she can talk to him about Cultus. Angie, horribly embarrassed, must accompany her, but to her relief the principal isn't home. On Monday the bus driver refuses to take Cultus, so Katla gets on instead and rides to school to see the principal. Again she makes Angie, deeply mortified at being singled out, come with her. Distressed by the wild, destructive behavior of all the children on the bus, Katla tells the principal that someone must make them behave. But he says discipline is up to the parents. Katla spends the school day with Angie, since she must wait for the bus to get home. Angie's best friend, Lois, with whom she's quarreled, makes fun of Katla and is sent out of the classroom. As they wait for the bus, Katla sees Lois write a dirty word in a white girl's textbook. When Katla slaps her Lois fights back, pushing the old woman down and fracturing her arm. While Katla is in the hospital, things fall apart at home and Angie's desperation mounts. Carysa won't wash in cold water the traditional Indian way, and Cultus won't ride the bus even with permission. Angie's friendship with Lois continues to deteriorate. When Katla comes home, there are only two days left before Powwow, a time of dancing and feasting, and Angie stays home from school to help with the preparations. Despite her gloom, she and Lois make up their quarrel, and after Powwow the family goes home and falls asleep by the fire while Katla tells a story about the old days. When Angie returns to school on Monday, her health teacher refuses to let her make up the test she missed and gives her an F: "we just can't let our students miss school for every little thing." That afternoon, Cultus pushes Lois down while they're waiting for the bus, and when the driver tries to discipline him Cultus runs off. He is brought home later that day by Jobie Sohappy, a sympathetic young reservation policeman who is the current Whipman. Cultus has stolen and wrecked a pickup truck and will have to stay in Group Home until a court hearing decides what should be done about him. When the case comes up, the judge orders the whole family into her chambers for a discussion. There Katla speaks eloquently about the struggles Indian children have at the white school where there is little understanding of their culture. The judge invites Katla to address the school board and puts Cultus on two years' probation under Jobie's supervision. When Cultus returns home after his stay in Group Home, his attitude toward his culture has changed. He has been strengthened by Katla's words and Jobie's support. "I'm going to show them I ain't afraid to be Indian." Angie, who has recognized some of Cultus's doubts within herself, begins to rethink her own attitudes about being Indian. Feeling that their life may now begin to right itself, Angie looks to the future with some hope.

The struggles of young Native Americans to find a place in white society without surrendering their traditional culture are believably described in this tightly written story. Angie and Cultus both find that even the smallest rebellion is, in effect, a denial of part of themselves. Their grandmother, strong in her tradition but confused and frustrated by the turmoil of the young people, finally succeeds by sheer eloquence and determination in strengthening her grandchildren's sense of identity. This is a sympathetic portrayal of characters and situations, enriched by details of traditional Indian culture.

Ages 10-14

**Also available in:**
Braille—*The Whipman Is Watching*
Library of Congress (NLSBPH)

Disc—*The Whipman Is Watching*
Library of Congress (NLSBPH)

**178**

Dygard, Thomas J.

## Point Spread

William Morrow & Company, Inc., 1980.
(192 pages)

---

*VALUES/VALUING: Moral/Ethical*
  *Crime/Criminals*
  *Gambling*
  *Sports/Sportsmanship*

---

Meridian University senior Lou Powers feels on top of the world. His picture has just appeared on the cover of *Sports Illustrated,* he is a candidate for the Heisman Trophy, and he is his school's star defensive lineman.

Then a mysterious man approaches Lou with talk about a fourteen-point victory in the upcoming game. When Meridian does win by fourteen points, the man appears again and thrusts an envelope into Lou's hand, an envelope containing five hundred dollars. Fearful that any suspicions of gambling will stain his record and ruin his future, Lou decides against telling Coach Foster. Wednesday after practice Lou sees the man again and demands a meeting that evening. When they meet, he returns the money. The man threatens him with physical harm if he tells anyone of their encounters. After the following Saturday's game, Lou spots a newspaper headline about three men arrested in a scheme to fix football scores. One of the men pictured in the story, Charles Dryden, is Lou's mystery man. The next day Dryden implicates the Meridian quarterback, who is immediately expelled. No one else on the team is named. By now Lou is terrified and, sure enough, the next day he is summoned to the coach's office. A random picture, taken by a television camera crew during practice, shows Lou and Dryden talking. Lou confesses everything, and he and the coach prepare a written statement of his innocence for the newspapers. The next day the FBI arrives at Meridian, and one by one all the team members are questioned. An air of mistrust hangs over each practice. By Saturday the team is so splintered that Lou realizes they cannot win. Knowing that everyone has doubts about the depth of his involvement in the scandal, he volunteers to stay out of the game. When the coach won't allow it, Lou asks him to call the U.S. district attorney investigating the case. He must know if any other team members have been implicated. The coach insists that Lou make the call. He does, reporting to the team that no one else has been implicated or is under suspicion. Hearing this, the players go out and win the game—a team once more.

In ten days, Lou Powers goes from being the star defensive lineman on a college team headed for the national championship to a suspect in a game-fixing scheme. The focus throughout is on the ethical questions raised and their effects on Lou's conscience as he ponders the consequences of admitting his own (innocent) part in the scandal. The topic is sensitively handled. Football talk and vivid descriptions of games add texture and appeal.

Ages 10 and up

**Also available in:**
No other form known

## 179
**Dygard, Thomas J.**

## Soccer Duel
William Morrow & Company, Inc., 1981.
(221 pages)

---

ATTENTION SEEKING
SPORTS/SPORTSMANSHIP
   Decision making
   Expectations
   School: classmate relationships
   Talents: athletic

---

At the beginning of his junior year at Windsor High School, Terry Masters, last year's football star, also outstanding in baseball and basketball, signs up for soccer. He has come to love the game while playing in the summer park league. No problem there. His problem is explaining his choice to the football coach, to his father, a former All-American halfback, and to the other football players. To his surprise, Coach Brundage takes his decision calmly. Terry's father refrains from trying to change his mind. But a friend tells Terry that Bones Nelson, star of last year's soccer team, has wondered how Terry will take not being a star. Terry quickly dismisses Nelson's gibe as sour grapes and just as quickly recognizes he will, in fact, not be the star of the soccer team, called the Eagles. Krystian Wisniewski, a new student born in Poland and raised in England, immediately proves his mastery on the practice field. Coach Schmidt, formerly a soccer star in Germany, works the team hard in practice and stresses team play. Throughout, Terry steadfastly maintains he feels no rivalry with Krystian and no disappointment at not being the star. But Bones Nelson remains skeptical, and Terry is secretly unsure about his true feelings. The first game, which the Eagles win easily, leaves Terry happy, certain he chose the right sport, yet uneasy about the strange feeling of not being in the spotlight. To his father, he announces that he is tired of being Alvin Masters' son on the football field; he prefers being Terry Masters on the soccer field, without anyone pressuring him. His father insists that Terry is pressuring himself. When the Eagles keep winning, their following builds and so does publicity about Krystian Wisniewski, "Wiz the Whiz." Meanwhile, Terry is the perfect team player: he defers to the star even when he himself is in shooting position; he cheers when the Wiz scores. Secretly, he feels disappointed and left out. Nonetheless, he's sure his act is fooling his teammates until, during a game, Bones accuses him of showboating. When no one on the team rebuts the accusation, Terry resolves to show them what real showboating is. He proceeds to shoot the ball whenever he gets his foot on it, delighting the fans, angering Coach Schmidt, and eventually causing his teammates to refuse to pass to him. So it continues until Coach Schmidt pulls Terry out of the game in favor of a weaker but more cooperative player. At this Terry comes to his senses, but Schmidt reminds him that actions count, not words. Before the next game, the team receives a blow when Henrik, their sweeper (key to the defense), breaks an ankle and the coach must start an inexperienced player. As the game develops, Terry realizes how much Henrik, more than Terry, perhaps more than Wiz, was the pillar of the team. Without him, the Eagles find themselves losing to a far weaker team. At half-time, Terry persuades the coach to let him replace the sweeper. He too lacks experience in the position, but he is a better athlete than the other player. Still, Terry has no instincts about where to position himself as the play ebbs and flows. His teammates support him, advise him on where to play, and congratulate him heartily after their narrow victory. Terry realizes he did not play well but decides to continue playing sweeper, a position without glory but offering great satisfaction. Bones Nelson apologizes for his previous cracks about showboating. Terry replies that no apology is necessary. Bones was right earlier, but not anymore.

When a football star chooses a new sport, soccer, he must call on different emotions and find new sources of satisfaction as a team player, no longer a star. It is a hard lesson, and at the end Terry sees that he needn't sacrifice himself for the team, just be part of it. The soccer sequences add appeal to this interesting, convincing story that avoids a predictable ending.

Ages 11-14

**Also available in:**
No other form known

## 180

**Elfman, Blossom**

## The Butterfly Girl

Houghton Mifflin Company, 1980.
(146 pages)

---

*RUNNING AWAY*
*UNWED MOTHER*
  *Boy-girl relationships*
  *Commune*
  *Communication: parent-child*
  *Dependence/Independence*
  *Determination*
  *Pregnancy*
  *Sex: premarital*

---

Sixteen-year-old Florrie and her father argue constantly. An impulsive girl and a dreamer, prone to cutting classes and flitting from interest to interest, Florrie chafes under what she considers unreasonable demands. Her mother is no help, since she also is dominated by the father. Fed up, Florrie goes to spend the weekend with two friends in Baja. There she meets and is attracted to Del Robertson. Florrie allows Del to take her home when the weekend is over, causing a scene with her father, who calls her a whore. Furious, Florrie flees her house with Del and they head up the coast to Berkeley where Del is house-sitting for a cousin. Florrie lives with Del happily for a month, but then he tells her he must return to college in Los Angeles. Although she knows his wealthy parents are pressuring him to return to school, Florrie storms angrily out of the house—but not before informing Del that she might be pregnant. She returns home to her father's ultimatum: she must either go back to school or get a job. Instead, Florrie leaves home once again, finds a job in Los Angeles at a health-food cafe, and takes a room with a new friend, Catherine. She also goes to a free clinic to see about an abortion and there meets Madge, a social worker and midwife. Del finds Florrie and asks her if she is pregnant. Afraid to tell him and sure he'll soon want her back, Florrie denies her pregnancy but keeps putting off the abortion. By the time she sees Del with another girl, her pregnancy is too far advanced for a safe abortion. Soon, in her apartment, with Madge's help, Florrie gives birth to a boy she names David. Del comes to see the baby, but doesn't make any overtures toward Florrie. Meanwhile, an admiring friend, Charlie, overweight and self-deprecating, begs Florrie to go with him to Phoenix. But Florrie, although she cares for Charlie, cannot give up her dreams of Del. She decides to move into Orion House, a shelter for abused women that Madge operates, to work in the nursery. But soon Del's

mother begins watching Florrie and starts legal proceedings to gain custody of David. Afraid that the woman might win her case and wanting to protect Madge, a lesbian, from ugly publicity, Florrie takes the baby to Eugene, Oregon, where she has learned Del is living. But he lives there, she finds, with another woman. Again Florrie flees, after her father arrives to take her home and Del and his girlfriend attempt to take David from her. She goes to live in the Family Place, a commune near Eugene where she tries unsuccessfully to find peace and happiness. She is visited there by Charlie, who asks her to let him take her home. Hard as she knows it will be to return to her parents, Florrie agrees. She calls home and her mother begs her to come soon; her father is very ill. So Florrie, Charlie, and David start home.

In this skillful first-person narrative, a flighty young girl, at odds with her parents, becomes an unwed mother and struggles to find a place for herself and her child. More a sequence of events than a story, the book features believable characters and situations. Florrie's naiveté is obvious and the lessons she learns are painful. This story about the confusions of growing up makes for compelling reading. The realistic dialogue includes occasional profanity.

Ages 13 and up

**Also available in:**
Paperbound—*The Butterfly Girl*
Bantam Books, Inc.

## 181

**Ellis, Ella Thorp**

## Sleepwalker's Moon

Atheneum Publishers, 1980.
(234 pages)

---

*BELONGING*
*EXPECTATIONS*
  *Boy-girl relationships: dating*
  *Change: accepting*
  *Life style: change in*
  *Maturation*
  *Separation from loved ones*
  *War*

---

It is 1942. Anna's widowed father is going off to war, and Anna, fourteen, will live with the Raymond family until his return. Anna is sure the Raymonds are a perfect family; she has longed to be a Raymond since she began visiting them each summer seven years ago. But she soon discovers that living with them is not quite the same as visiting for a short time. Paula, a year older than Anna, loves and then hates Anna with such frequency that Anna is never sure where she stands. Hans, the father, has a temper she had not remembered and he frets about the girls getting in trouble with boys. Rosamund, the mother, is quiet, but beneath the calm, Anna feels she does not want her there. Roger, the twelve-year-old son, is quiet and withdrawn. Anna and Paula get jobs in the flower fields picking seeds, and Paula dates the farm owner's son. When Anna starts school in the fall, she and a young soldier date and grow fond of one another. Then he is sent overseas, where he is killed in combat. Anna is comforted by the mementos he has left her, including his Bible. Fear of being sent away leads Anna to try being indispensable to the Raymonds. But, though she still longs to be a full-fledged member of the family, she gradually realizes that the quiet life with her father in San Francisco had had its advantages. "Pretty soon I knew what it was I'd had with my father all those years of my life. I'd had my own family." When summer returns, the two girls again work in the flower fields. One night Hans angrily confronts Anna, saying he is worried that her behavior with boys will cause her to be raped. Anna knows he is concerned not about her, but about his own daughter. They argue bitterly, and Anna screams that he has never trusted her and only cares about Paula. She calls her uncle in Washington, D.C., and receives permission to come and live there. While preparing to leave, Anna is amazed at the relief she feels. "How could I know that I was half-dead with trying to be a Raymond, that I had to give it up, to go on becoming myself? I knew only that it was over. All over."

Anna discovers that the "perfect" family she's living with until her father returns from the war is, in fact, far from perfect, that her quiet life with her father had its advantages. This realistic first-person narrative gives insight into the dislocations war can bring as it describes Anna's struggles to fit into the Raymond family. Slowly and believably, she learns that real life can differ dramatically from one's expectations and that she can never be a full member of a family not her own.

Ages 12 and up

**Also available in:**
No other form known

## 182

Ewing, Kathryn

**Things Won't Be the Same**

Harcourt Brace Jovanovich, Inc., 1980.
(92 pages)

---

PARENT/PARENTS: Remarriage of
  Change: resisting
  Jealousy: sibling
  Life style: change in
  Stepbrother/Stepsister
  Stepparent: father
  Stepparent: mother

---

Ten-year-old Marcy knows that things won't be the same after her mother marries Bill Compton. The three of them are moving to a new home in a suburb, she is changing schools, and she must leave her best friend, Wendy. During her mother and Bill's honeymoon, Marcy is to choose between staying with Wendy or staying with her father in California. Marcy's father seems a stranger to her, but when he calls urging her to visit, she accepts. After the wedding, she flies out to San Francisco all by herself. Her father, his wife, and her toddler stepbrother live a relaxed and casual life, so different from her mother's neat and structured home that Marcy feels awkward and out of place at first. She adjusts quickly, though, and soon loves going to her father's store with him. He is a coin and stamp dealer, a family business he inherited from his father. Marcy learns to

help him sort stamps and starts her own collection. The four weeks pass quickly and soon Marcy must return to Pennsylvania. Home seems terribly changed. Bill is kind, but a man with definite ideas and preferences that must be considered. When, during a heated disagreement, Marcy tells her mother that she thinks her father is better than Bill, she is sent to her room for the first time in years. Things get even worse when Bill's ten-year-old daughter from Colorado, Carole Anne, comes for a visit. Marcy is jealous of Carole Anne, thinks her mother spoils her, and is sure that Wendy likes Carole Anne better than she likes her. Desperate, Marcy mails a letter to her father saying she wants to live with him. Once the letter is mailed, however, she knows she has made a mistake. She begins realizing that life with Bill is not really that bad and that Carole Anne is fun to have visit. A few days later, Marcy's father calls to say she may come if she wants to. Marcy and her mother cry together, and Marcy admits she doesn't want to leave. She sees now that things have to change and she has to adjust. But she can also begin to look forward to "new things to do, new places, new friends."

Marcy slowly realizes that life involves changes and that she must learn to accept rather than fight them. This is a sympathetic, perceptive exploration of evolving family relationships. Marcy is an extremely likeable character; children in similar circumstances will easily identify with her and be reassured by her story. Convincing dialogue, relationships, and situations distinguish this sequel to A Private Matter.

Ages 8-10

**Also available in:**
No other form known

## 183

Eyerly, Jeannette Hyde

**The Seeing Summer**

Black/white illustrations by Emily Arnold McCully.
J. B. Lippincott Company, 1981.
(153 pages)

---

BLINDNESS
  Friendship: best friend
  Kidnapping

---

When ten-year-old Carey learns that the house next door has been bought by a family with a girl her age, she's ecstatic. Then her other next-door neighbor tells her the new girl is blind. Appalled, Carey doesn't want to believe her. When she finally sees Jenny with her white cane, she tells Aunt Richard, who keeps house for her and her widowed father, that she doesn't want blind people living next door to her and doesn't want to play with them. But Aunt Richard sends her over with a plate of cookies, and Carey watches Jenny walk easily through her new house, transfer the cookies to another plate, and make chocolate pudding. When she gets home, Aunt Richard remarks that "there's probably not much the child can do." But Carey remembers how well Jenny made the pudding. She still isn't sure she wants to be friends, but she and Jenny play cards one morning using Jenny's Braille cards. Jenny begins teaching Carey how to read and write in Braille. To her surprise, Carey

E

enjoys it. She is intrigued by Jenny's abacus, talking-book machine, and tape recorder. When the girls make cookies together at Carey's house, Aunt Richard won't leave them alone, fussing over Jenny and making remarks about a blind child trying to cook until Jenny leaves in tears. One day when Jenny asks Carey to come with her to the drugstore, Carey imagines herself Jenny's protector: "In her mind she could hear people say, 'Isn't that sweet? That little girl helping that poor blind child.'" But Carey soon realizes that Jenny is independent and self-reliant, and it's Carey who gets upset when clerks direct their questions to her as if Jenny were deaf and mute as well as blind. At the store, Carey sees a picture of Jenny's father, a renowned scientist and the heir to a fortune, on the cover of a national news magazine. A man wearing a shabby gray suit asks if Jenny is really the daughter of the man on the cover. Neither Carey nor Jenny likes him. While the girls are running in the park one day, Jenny literally runs into Adam, the coach of a junior track club. He thinks Jenny would make a great sprinter. On the way home Carey stops at the market to pick up something for Aunt Richard. Jenny waits outside, but when Carey returns, Jenny is gone. The next day Carey sees the man in the shabby gray suit and follows him, accusing him of stealing Jenny. In order to keep her from attracting the attention of a passing policeman, the man says he'll take her to Jenny. He puts her in his van and drives to an abandoned warehouse, where Jenny is being held. The frightened girls eventually discover they've been left alone in the warehouse. After considerable searching and exploring, they make their way to the roof. At the same time, firefighters, police, and newspaper reporters begin pulling up; the kidnappers had phoned the police to say where the girls were, but had not picked up the ransom. A few weeks after the kidnapping, Adam stops by with a device for Jenny to wear while she runs. Carey will broadcast instructions to her so that she doesn't run into the other racers. Carey has learned that "seeing with one's eyes wasn't the only way of seeing. Jenny had taught her that."

In this well-written and fast-paced book, a young girl learns a great deal about what it means to be blind. Her friend Jenny teaches her that blind people don't like to be yelled at, stared at, helped unnecessarily, or pitied. In subtle, unobtrusive ways the reader also learns a great deal about the nonsighted and their ways of coping with everyday life. The lightly illustrated book is also a good story about friendship, with a touch of mystery and suspense. The improbabilities of the kidnapping plot will probably not deter the intended audience.

Ages 8-10

**Also available in:**
Cassette—*The Seeing Summer*
Library of Congress (NLSBPH)

Paperbound—*The Seeing Summer*
Pocket Books

**184**

**Fairless, Caroline**

**Hambone**

Black/white illustrations by Wendy Edelson.
Tundra Books, 1980.
(48 pages)

---

LOSS: Feelings of
    Abandonment
Animals: love for
Death: of pet
Family: unity

---

Jeremy, about ten, lives on a farm with Papa; Ramona, the housekeeper and surrogate mother; Stoner, his teenage sister; and Alec, his older brother. When his pet pig, Hambone, must be butchered, Jeremy suffers feelings that remind him of the day, four years ago, when his mother left them to live in the city. Though Jeremy is proud of his father's reputation for a magic hand with his crops, he knows from personal experience that farming is hard work. The boy gets up early each morning to do his chores. His big dream is to have his own garden, an idea scoffed at by Alec, who considers gardening woman's work. When Papa demands Jeremy's help in butchering Hambone, Jeremy adamantly refuses. With some trepidation, Stoner also stands up to their father, declaring that Jeremy will instead help her in the garden. Their father's shoulders slump in defeat, touching Jeremy's heart but not swaying his decision. At Stoner's suggestion and with her help, Jeremy uses the time to plant a memorial for Hambone. Since Hambone loved tomatoes, it will be a tomato memorial. Jeremy digs a deep hole and fills it with Hambone's favorite things, such as manure and the slops from the kitchen. As he fills the hole, memories of his pet flood his mind. Suddenly, though no sound is heard from the barn, Jeremy knows Hambone is dead. With tears streaming, he carefully chooses the strongest tomato seedling, plants it carefully, then kisses the earth. Stoner does the same. The tomato plant called Hambone soon outgrows any other. People praise Jeremy for his magic fingers. Jeremy knows it isn't magic but Hambone come to life. One day a terrible thunderstorm blows up, and Jeremy races through the rain and lightning to protect Hambone. "Lightning!" Jeremy cries. "Strike me dead. But leave old Hambone alone. He's a memorial now, and he can't die again!" Jeremy talks to the plant soothingly as the storm rages, about the things he and Hambone did together and even about his mother, who writes to him every two weeks even though he never answers. At last the storm subsides. Hambone has survived. Jeremy's father finds the boy lying exhausted in the dirt. Stoner has explained to him that the plant is a memorial, but the father cares only about Jeremy. From his back pocket, Papa pulls out Hambone's comb, which Jeremy sinks deep into the earth. Three weeks after the storm, Jeremy reaps well over one hundred tomatoes from Hambone. The phenomenal plant is written about in the local paper. At his father's suggestion, Jeremy sends a copy of the article to his mother. When the plant is through bearing, Jeremy's father tells him to dig Hambone up and replant him next year. Thinks Jeremy, "Hambone will live forever."

This is a touching, sometimes humorous story of a young boy's painful adjustment to the loss of a beloved pet. In a vibrant first-person narration, Jeremy expresses his feelings of grief, feelings intensified by their similarity to his sorrow and anger over his mother's desertion. His decision to plant a living memorial to Hambone suggests a creative outlet for the pain of loss—and provides him an opening for a reconciliation with his mother. Delicate line drawings help convey mood and character.

Ages 8-11

**Also available in:**
No other form known

## 185

Farber, Norma

### How Does It Feel to be Old?

Color illustrations by Trina Schart Hyman.
E. P. Dutton & Company, Inc., 1979.
(30 pages counted)

---

*AGE: Aging*
*GRANDPARENT: Love for*
*GRANDPARENT: Respect for*

---

A grandmother tells her visiting granddaughter what it is like to be old. She is free of parents' advice and free to eat what and when she wants, but she admits that treats don't taste as good as they used to. As they look in a mirror together, she urges the girl to see past the wrinkled face to the full life behind it: bride, mother of four, traveler, and now grandmother. She notes that her hearing and strength are failing and that she misses being needed. Reflecting calmly on her death, she assures the girl that death is normal and that it should cause no alarm. "Soon you'll be knowing that Grandma has died while you are still growing in inches and pride."

A grandmother's lyrical monologues deal openly with loss, aging, independence, and death. Vivid, detailed illustrations capture the mood and complete the image of an aging woman who sees her life with serenity, her death with courage, and her granddaughter with love. This poignant, unusually honest book may increase young readers' compassion and understanding for the trials and joys of growing old.

Ages 8 and up

**Also available in:**
No other form known

## 186

Farley, Carol J.

### Twilight Waves

Atheneum Publishers, 1981.
(131 pages)

---

*IDENTITY, SEARCH FOR*
*LOVE, MEANING OF*
  *Baby-sitting*
  *Belonging*
  *Determination*
  *Grandparent: living in home of*
  *Orphan*

---

Browning Wilds, thirteen, accompanies Mrs. Hudson and her little son, Gavin, whom Browning will baby-sit for, on a vacation in Michigan. It's Browning, in fact, who has suggested the small town where they'll be staying: Seagulls Point. Before the boy was born, his father's ship went down; the newspaper article about the tragedy listed Seagulls Point as the man's hometown. Browning yearns to know more about his father, but Great Gram, with whom Browning lives, cautions him about breaking his heart looking for something that isn't there. Years ago she and Browning's mother had sent letters to Seagulls Point that were returned unclaimed. Gram believes Browning's mother died of heartbreak because his father ran off just a couple of weeks after their wedding and then drowned. But Browning begins asking people if they remember his father or the sinking of the *Neptune II.* Nobody does. He becomes terribly angry at the father who gave him life, disappeared, and now is inspiring this painful search. At the local museum, Browning studies the "Last-Message file": notes and inscriptions that have washed ashore from sailors on sinking ships. He wonders why this search matters so much to him. After all, he'll still be himself no matter what. But despite his love for Gram, Browning wants a father. "The hollow ache inside him pressed against his throat and chest. He was weary of this foolish, futile search. But he knew he could never stop." Mrs. Hudson persuades him to tell her what's bothering him. After hearing the whole story, she is sympathetic and offers to check the newspaper files of fourteen years ago. While she's doing that, Browning daydreams wonderful scenarios in which his father is either still alive, dies a hero, or is trying to come back from his watery resting place. But the truth, which Mrs. Hudson discovers, is far different. Browning's father's name was James C. Edwards, and he was from Indiana. It was his first wife who was from Seagulls Point. They had a baby girl before Jim Edwards left on his ship, and there had been some talk of divorce. But Browning's father committed bigamy when he married Browning's mother. Mrs. Hudson has visited Edwards' first wife's parents and was shown a picture of him. Browning looks just like him. The boy is devastated; not only was his father a liar and a cheat, he was weak and foolish too. Now he knows what Gram meant when she said not to wish too hard for something because you might get it. He thinks about the feeling of attachment he longs for, the web that binds people together, and realizes attachments are

F

based on love, not on accidents of birth. His mind turns toward Mrs. Hudson, Gavin, and especially Gram—the people who matter, the people he loves.

In this straightforward, believable story, a boy who has dreamed for years of finding information about his long-dead father that will confirm his romantic fantasies about him finds that the sordid truth makes him appreciate the bonds created by love, not by birth. Although he has love, pride, and a sense of belonging from his grandmother, Browning thinks he wants something more, and he pursues the memory of his father with unswerving determination. Only when his dream comes crashing down can he fully recognize the value of his real attachments and roots.

Ages 10-13

**Also available in:**
No other form known

## 187

**First, Julia**

### I, Rebekah, Take You, the Lawrences

Franklin Watts, Inc., 1981.
(123 pages)

---

ADOPTION: Feelings About
  Change: accepting
  Children's home, living in
  Friendship: meaning of
  Love, meaning of
  Orphan

---

Twelve-year-old Rebekah Blount has lived in the Meacham County Home for Little Wanderers for over five years. She likens the orphanage to a "maximum security prison," although she has only the vaguest memories about her early childhood and sees Meacham as her home, the other children as her family. As for the housemother, Mrs. Baker: "No matter how hard you tried, you couldn't have squeezed a drop of love juice out of Baker because she didn't have even an ounce of it in her veins." Baker takes a strong dislike to Rebekah's shy best friend, Mildred. Rebekah responds by comforting and protecting Mildred whenever she can. Though Baker makes life unpleasant by taunting the children—and "with an assortment like us it was easy for someone like Baker to hurt our feelings"— Baker is not the worst of their problems. They are often "borrowed" by foster families who do not then adopt them. Consequently, the children must adjust to life in the foster home and then readjust to life at Meacham. Since these repeated partings are extremely painful, when Rosemary and Tom Lawrence come for Rebekah as prospective foster parents, she decides she is not going to like them or let them like her. "I wasn't going to get borrowed again, and then have grief when I had to leave." But on her second weekend outing with the loving, generous Lawrences she must remind herself, "No matter how much fun I was having . . . I was a summer fill-in for them, and come fall they'd forget they ever met me." Rebekah finally admits to herself that she wants to become this couple's foster child. Instead Tom, a real estate agent, and Rosemary, an architect, tell her they want to adopt her. Dizzy and

numb at the prospect, Rebekah wonders why she isn't wildly happy. She feels guilty leaving Meacham and the other children, like a deserter saying goodbye to Mildred. Out of embarrassment that she's come from the Home, she doesn't tell any of her new classmates that she's come from the Home, although Rosemary encourages her to be honest and open about her background. She helps Rebekah wrestle with the fact that her biological parents didn't want her, but the Lawrences do. Then, seven months after her adoption, the Lawrences ask Rebekah what she thinks about them looking for a boy to adopt. She runs angrily to her bedroom and slams the door, and the subject is dropped until two weeks later when Tom and Rosemary hear of a boy about Rebekah's age, David, who was recently orphaned when a mountain-climbing accident killed his parents. They make plans to adopt David; Rebekah plots to return to Meacham. Feeling betrayed, she decides she's better off at the Home. Mildred needs her. But as she prepares to enter the Meacham gates, Rebekah feels the place's threatening power. "Ohmygod, I thought, how could I have left Mildred in this place? And how can I go back in?" After she talks with Mildred, however, two things become clear to Rebekah. First, the Lawrences love her as their own and she needn't doubt them. Second, Mildred doesn't need her protection anymore. Rebekah returns home and, for the first time, anticipates the arrival of a brother.

A young girl from an orphanage tries to understand her conflicting emotions about her adoption by a generous, loving couple. Because of the revolving door she's used to between foster homes and the Meacham Home, Rebekah has gotten cynical and hesitates to reveal her true emotions to adults. In this first-person account, the reader shares her gradual journey towards love and trust. Throughout the book, Rebekah recalls incidents from the orphanage that typify the life there—the time, for example, when one of the girls in her dorm began menstruating and was terrified because no one had ever explained this phenomenon to her. Easy to read and well-paced, Rebekah's story is compelling and satisfying.

Ages 11-13

**Also available in:**
No other form known

## 188

**First, Julia**

### Look Who's Beautiful!

Franklin Watts, Inc., 1980.
(122 pages) o.p.

---

AGE: Aging
APPEARANCE: Concern About
  Age: respect for
  Communication: parent-child
  Friendship: meaning of
  Money: earning
  Self, attitude toward: body concept

---

Thirteen-year-old Cornelia (Connie) Griswold has braces, allergies, a weight problem, and an inability to communicate with her mother. "My mother and I always seemed to be on opposite sides of everything."

Connie's mother is also very beautiful and judges on appearances. When Connie's class plans a spring-break trip to Washington, D.C., she and three friends decide to ask the residents of Coolidge Housing for the Elderly for small jobs that will earn them the ninety dollars each needs for the trip. Connie has reservations about being around old people, because in her mother's "youth philosophy" old age is unattractive and to be avoided. But when Connie eventually joins her friends, she meets the elderly Mrs. Marston and knows at once that she has found someone very special. She feels so protective of Mrs. Marston, so drawn to her, that she offers to work for less money: "I'd have worked for her for nothing." But Mrs. Marston insists on paying her. The old woman's love of poetry inspires Connie to check out some books of poetry from the library. She looks through Mrs. Marston's photograph albums and enjoys her wonderful fresh-baked bread. Mrs. Marston encourages Connie to look more charitably at Icky Birnbaum, a boy who has teased Connie since fourth grade. He too may have problems, she suggests. Then one day Connie finds Mrs. Marston's apartment empty. A neighbor tells her that the old woman fell and broke her hip. Connie runs to the hospital, telling the receptionist she is Mrs. Marston's granddaughter. But she's not allowed in anyway, because she's under fourteen. Grief-stricken, Connie rejects her mother's casual words of comfort. When her mother says it's painful becoming involved with someone, Connie thinks, "So far as I knew Mom was never involved with anyone except herself." Still, she knows her mother has spoken with Mrs. Marston's daughter, who has come into town. Connie is some eight dollars short of her quota for the spring trip and the deadline is drawing near, but she can't seem to make the effort to find jobs. All she can think about is Mrs. Marston. Finally, Connie decides not to go to Washington with her class. Mrs. Marston will be entering a nursing home at the time the class plans to leave, and Connie will spend the week visiting with her. When she tells her mother of her decision, her mother cries and tells Connie how proud she is of her. To her surprise, Connie realizes her mother "looked at me as if I were beautiful." Her mother even offers to take her place with Mrs. Marston so she can go to Washington. Connie is "conscious of a new feeling between us. Not new that minute, but one that must have been slowly getting there." When she visits Mrs. Marston in the nursing home, she is relieved to see that it is quite a pleasant place after all. Then Connie goes for her allergy shot and finds Icky Birnbaum, of all people, in the waiting room. Icky has teased Connie about her allergies for years, telling her they're all in her mind. She is delighted to be able to tease him back. After they talk for a while, Connie sees the possibility of being friends with Ricky—Icky no longer. She offers to treat him to a very special sundae, something his health-fanatic father has long denied him.

An unbeautiful young girl with a lovely, age-fearing mother forms a close relationship with an old woman and learns what "beautiful" really means. In the process, she wins her mother's admiration and decides to keep an open mind about people—even "Icky" Birnbaum. There is insight to be found in Connie's humorous first-person narrative, although characterizations and the development of relationships remain somewhat superficial.

Ages 10-12

**Also available in:**
No other form known

## 189

**Fisher, Aileen Lucia**
**I Stood upon a Mountain**
Color illustrations by Blair Lent.
Thomas Y. Crowell Company, Inc., 1979.
(40 pages counted)

NATURE: Appreciation of
VALUES/VALUING: Aesthetic
    Curiosity
    Religion: questioning

A young girl stands upon a mountain and wonders how the world came to be. "I stood upon a mountain when the year was spring and dwarf forget-me-nots scented the air with spice. A great blue shell of sky curved above me. Hills of pine and fir swelled green below me, and in the valleys between I saw mirrors for the sun." Meeting an old man on the trail, she greets him, saying, "Wonderful world!" He tells her that the world began from nothing more than an "egg." But what, the girl wonders, "had turned nothing into an egg in the first place?" The man cannot answer. And so it goes. At the seashore, she meets a woman who tells her the world began with a "Word." In the desert, an Indian explains the creation of the earth by "fire." On a snowy hilltop she meets two children who explain that all began from a great "explosion." Each explanation leaves the girl wondering what caused the egg, the Word, the fire, the explosion. Even though there are many answers, the girl decides that when she looks at the world and all its faces she is "filled with a wonder that needs no answer, no answer at all."

Inspired by the natural beauty of the world around her, an inquisitive girl seeks the answer to an age-old question. The discovery of many explanations does nothing to diminish the awe she feels. Exceptional illustrations accompany this rhythmic, simple, yet profound first-person text.

Ages 4-8

**Also available in:**
No other form known

**190**

Fitzhugh, Louise

# Sport

Delacorte Press, 1979.
(218 pages)

KIDNAPPING
PARENTAL: Custody
   Death: of grandparent
   Greed
   Parent/Parents: remarriage of

Eleven-year-old Simon, nicknamed Sport, has lived with his absentminded but loving father since his parents were divorced when he was four years old. Sport's mother is a ruthless woman who does not hesitate to let Sport know that she loves money and hates little boys. When Sport's maternal grandfather dies, he leaves his estate of thirty million dollars to be divided between his daughter and Sport. Sport's mother gets a fourth of the estate unless she agrees to keep Sport with her for six months of the year, in which case she gets half. She decides that having the whole estate beats either of her options and sets about trying to get complete custody of Sport. At any time, Sport would object vigorously to living with his mother, but he especially resists now that he's grown to love his new stepmother, Kate. While Kate and Sport's father are on their honeymoon, however, Sport must stay with his mother. To his disgust, he is forced to attend a large cocktail party given by Aunt Carrie, his mother's sister. When he insults a guest, his mother sends him to his room without dinner. Instead, he goes back to his father's empty apartment. Mr. Wilton, his mother's lawyer, finds him there and returns him to his mother. The day his father and Kate are expected to return, his mother wakes him early. They get into her car, but don't go back to his father's apartment. Instead, the chauffeur drives to the Plaza Hotel, where Sport is locked in a room and guarded around the clock. All his attempts to escape fail until his good friend Chi-Chi, a busboy at the Plaza, sneaks him out on the room-service wagon. Sport has a joyful reunion with Kate and his father. But that afternoon, as he and his friends walk home from school, a big black car pulls alongside them and someone grabs Sport and throws him in the car. At the next stoplight, Sport manages to open a door and call to his friends. They surround the car and are attempting to free Sport when the police arrive and take all the boys into custody. Aunt Carrie convinces the police with her tale of innocence. It takes a lot of explaining and some assertive behavior from Sport's father before the boys are released and the true situation revealed. Sport's father calls his lawyer, who later tells them that Sport's mother has renounced all claims to Sport and is on her way to Europe.

A young boy is the victim of the greedy machinations of a ruthless, unloving parent. Although Sport's mother is painted in very dark colors, the story is still believable and emotionally gripping. Sport shows a sense of values: his inheritance means far less to him than the love and companionship of his father and Kate. Characters are strongly and memorably drawn.

Ages 9-12

Also available in:
Paperbound—Sport
Dell Publishing Company, Inc.

**191**

Flournoy, Valerie

# The Twins Strike Back

Black/white illustrations by Diane de Groat
The Dial Press, Inc., 1980.
(30 pages counted)

TWINS: Identical
   Problem solving
   Teasing

Identical twins Ivy and May are tired of being teased, of being regarded as duplicates or as two halves of a whole, of always being referred to as "the twins." So they devise a plan to get back at their chief tormentors, their older sister, Bernadine, and cousin Nate. Since Bernadine says they think alike, the girls decide to pretend they can read each other's minds. On the morning of their eighth birthday, Bernadine is to give them breakfast and take them and Nate to the movies. After Nate arrives, Ivy comes down to the kitchen and requests Corn Flakes for herself and May. But Bernadine gives May her usual Rice Krispies. Ivy then remembers she forgot her sneakers and holds her hand to her head. When May comes down she brings the sneakers and says, "Hey, Ivy, I told you I wanted Corn Flakes today!" Ivy says she heard the request, but Bernadine did not. A skeptical Bernadine and Nate begin to believe the girls can really read each other's minds when Ivy rushes upstairs and returns fastening her bracelet, just as May predicted. After the movie the group cannot find May, and Bernadine asks Ivy for her telepathic help. Ivy leads them to the park where they discover from Fish, a friend of the twins who is in on the hoax, that May left a few minutes earlier. Next, Ivy leads them to the grocery store; again they are too late. They learn that May had a soda, as Ivy said she had, and left. Now Ivy says they will find May at their grandparents. And so they do. May tells them the truth, and she and Ivy have a good laugh. Their grandmother scolds Nate and Bernadine for treating the girls as beings with special powers instead of as individuals. Nate and Bernadine apologize. Then they call the girls' parents to come over so they can start the birthday party.

Exasperated twin sisters trick their older sister and cousin into believing they really are of one mind. In the process, their need for individuality is demonstrated and recognized. This is a familiar problem for many twins—how to make others realize you are two separate people—and the young twins in this story devise a good-natured solution. Illustrations show two lively girls, rightfully proud of their ingenuity.

Ages 6-8

Also available in:
No other form known

**192**

Foley, June

**It's No Crush, I'm in Love!**

Delacorte Press, 1982.
(215 pages)

---

IDENTITY, SEARCH FOR
SCHOOL: Pupil-Teacher Relationships
   Boy-girl relationships
   Death: of father
   Family: relationships
   Friendship: best friend
   Identification with others: story characters
   Parent/Parents: single
   Roman Catholic

---

At fourteen, Annie Cassidy wants to be exactly like her favorite heroine, Elizabeth Bennet of *Pride and Prejudice*. There are already similarities: Annie too has three sisters, her mother isn't a very "scintillating" person, and she obviously takes after her father. He, however, died in an automobile accident nearly two years ago. Now Annie plans to find a perfect man with whom she can lead a perfect life teaching in a university and writing scholarly books about the novels of Jane Austen. On her first day at Sacred Heart High School, she meets the man she has been looking for: David Angelucci, her dignified and handsome English teacher. Annie's best friend, Susanna Siegelbaum, well acquainted with Annie's idealism but the practical type herself, asks immediately what Annie is "going to do about it." Annie responds that she's going to think about David a lot. She also, of course, studies harder for English than for any other subject and looks for chances to impress her teacher. After a couple of months of this, however, Annie grows impatient. When Mr. Angelucci asks for help with the school newspaper he advises, she quickly volunteers. Instead of being with him, though, she finds herself frequently in the company of the newspaper's editor, Robby Pols. Robby is the exact "opposite of Mr. Angelucci. Not brilliant. Not handsome. Not charming. Not mature. Not very pleasant, even." But because her mother has gotten a job and Annie has to care for her sisters after school, Robby must come to her house to work on the paper and before long is practically one of the family. Annie tolerates him, but dreams about David Angelucci. With Susanna for company, she starts to spend Saturdays secretly observing David in his "natural habitat," the public library. When Robby agrees to let her interview David for the paper, she learns that he is doing research for his doctoral dissertation and needs a research assistant. She volunteers. In the meantime, though, another relationship has started to demand some of her attention: her mother is dating a man in her office and seems "looser" and more carefree than usual. She confides to Annie that, as the oldest of eight children, she never before had time to play. As Annie's attitude toward her mother softens, she also starts to appreciate Robby and accepts when he invites her to Saturday's Winter Dance. Then, unexpectedly, David calls and asks her to work late Saturday night and to share a surprise with him afterwards. Sure he will now admit his love for her, Annie cancels her date for the dance. She is a bit disturbed when Robby invites

Susanna to go in her place. At the library on Saturday she watches David intently for some sign of affection. She notices nothing but a few flaws in his appearance she hadn't seen before. Finally, at ten o'clock that evening, he announces that he has to pick up his date who will help him chaperone the Winter Dance. When Annie reminds him of the surprise, he shows her a rough draft of his dissertation. Devastated, she runs all the way home. Later, as she talks to her mother, Annie is comforted by the rare closeness she and her mother share. She also cheers up when Susanna reports that she spent most of the evening listening to Robby talk about Annie. Annie decides that most people don't care if she never becomes perfect like Elizabeth Bennet—it's all right for her just to be Annie Cassidy.

Though Annie imagines she is nothing like her mother, both seek perfection: Annie models herself after a Jane Austen heroine and her widowed mother has tried hard to be the ideal homemaker, mother, and Catholic layperson. Both become more realistic as they learn more about life and other people, and in so doing they grow closer to each other. The realism of Annie's crush on her English teacher is marred somewhat by the reader's early recognition that Mr. Angelucci is callous, uncaring, and dislikes teaching teenagers, a task he'll soon be free of. However, readers will cheer Annie's realization that "ordinary" people like Robby and her mother are special after all, and they'll like the delicious humor throughout the story. Especially funny are Susanna's loyal attempts to trail Mr. Angelucci for Annie. Each time, her prey turns out to be someone else —a priest, a janitor.

Ages 11-13

**Also available in:**
Paperbound—*It's No Crush, I'm in Love!*
Dell Publishing Company, Inc.

**193**

Fox, Paula

**A Place Apart**

Farrar, Straus & Giroux, Inc., 1980.
(184 pages)

---

FRIENDSHIP: Meaning of
   Change: resisting
   Cruelty
   Death: of father
   Parent/Parents: remarriage of
   School: classmate relationships

---

After the sudden death of her father, thirteen-year-old Victoria Finch finds her life completely changed. Their income reduced, she and her mother must move from Boston to a small, ramshackle house in the town of New Oxford. There Victoria meets and is captivated by wealthy, sixteen-year-old Hugh Todd, who seems impressed by a dramatic scene she has written for English class. Full of self-importance, Hugh urges her to expand the scene into a play so he can direct its performance—as he has other school plays—the next year when he'll be a senior. Victoria isn't interested in writing a play, but has neither the strength nor the desire to oppose Hugh's wishes. Her best friend, Elizabeth, considers Hugh a high-handed egotist whose humor is most

F

often at the expense of others. Victoria realizes Hugh's shortcomings, but for her they enhance his attractiveness. When the school year ends, Hugh, about to leave for Italy with his parents, tells Victoria to spend her vacation getting her play in shape. She tries, but hers is a difficult summer. Still grieving for her father, Victoria is hurt when her mother begins dating Lawrence Grady. When school resumes, Victoria discovers that Hugh is not interested in her, only in enhancing his reputation by directing her play. She refuses to continue with it, and so Hugh finds someone else to manipulate: Tom Kyle. When Elizabeth finds a boyfriend and her mother announces plans to remarry, Victoria's loneliness intensifies. She tries to maintain her relationship with Elizabeth by agreeing to join her and her boyfriend on a dangerous drive up to Mt. Crystal. By chance, Tom Kyle is invited along. The mountain road is slick with ice and they almost crash. In his fear Tom wets his pants and he is humiliated before the entire school when the incident is made known, probably by Hugh. To prove himself, Tom repeats the treacherous trip up the mountain and has a near-fatal accident. Disgusted by the cruelty and callousness of people, Victoria is almost glad her mother is marrying Lawrence Grady and they are moving back to Boston. After her hurt and anger have subsided, however, she comes to appreciate all she has learned during her year in New Oxford.

This moving story, told by Victoria herself, recounts a year's worth of emotional upheavals in the life of a young girl. The death of a beloved parent is wrenching; learning the difference between true and false friends brings both suffering and joy; the spite of her peers fills her with disgust. Sorting out these experiences leads to maturity. The book is realistic and well written, with believable dialogue and relationships.

Ages 12 and up

**Also available in:**
Braille—*A Place Apart*
Library of Congress (NLSBPH)

Cassette—*A Place Apart*
Library of Congress (NLSBPH)

Paperbound—*A Place Apart*
New American Library

## 194

**Franco, Marjorie**

### So Who Hasn't Got Problems?

Houghton Mifflin Company, 1979.
(153 pages)

---

*PEER RELATIONSHIPS*
 *Boy-girl relationships*
 *Friendship: best friend*
 *Moving*
 *Neighbors/Neighborhood*

---

Thirteen-year-old Jennifer and her friends Dorothy and Myra watch a new family move into their neighborhood on Chicago's north side. Later they go visit the newcomer, Angela, who is also thirteen. Angela soon announces that her family is very rich and that Jennifer's stories, on which she prides herself, are boring. Jennifer hates Angela for trying to take her friends away

from her. Meanwhile, Dorothy is desperate. Her stepfather and her mother fight constantly, and her mother often threatens to send Dorothy to New York to live with her father. Convinced that her mother wants to get rid of her, she and Jennifer compose a letter to Dorothy's father asking if she can come live with him. Then Eddie Sebastian, who lives next door to Jennifer, invites her to help him paint a mural on his basement walls. Dorothy offers to help too, and the three begin spending every spare moment working in Eddie's basement. Although she's expected it, Jennifer is very hurt when Myra announces that she has invited Angela, rather than Jennifer, to go with her on a planned trip to San Francisco. Later, Jennifer meets Angela on the street and is shocked to see her wearing a skirt and blouse that Jennifer had given to Catholic Charities. Obviously, Angela isn't rich. This is her chance to get even with the new girl by ruining her credibility with Myra and the others. But Jennifer's older sister suggests that Angela may have her reasons for lying, and Jennifer decides to say nothing for the moment. Then Dorothy, whose father hasn't responded to her letter, announces her plan to run away to New York. Jennifer tries to discourage her and makes Dorothy promise to tell her if she ever actually decides to run away. Meanwhile, Jennifer and Eddie are becoming a twosome as they and Dorothy work on the mural. One afternoon, Myra tells Jennifer she has made the wrong decision about the San Francisco trip. She has learned that Angela lied about being rich, and now she wants to tell everyone what a phony Angela is. Jennifer helps Myra see what she now understands: Angela lies to feel important. She urges Myra to take Angela on the trip as planned. The mural is almost finished. All that's left is to paint in Dorothy and Jennifer sitting in their favorite place—on the steps of the Catholic school across the street from their homes. But early the next morning, Dorothy's mother calls Jennifer to say Dorothy is missing. The mother, feeling responsible, admits she may sometimes say things she doesn't mean. A frightened Jennifer points out that Dorothy believes what her mother says. They call New York to alert Dorothy's father, who has been out of town and only read Dorothy's letter the day before. Then Jennifer gets more bad news: Eddie and his family are moving. Depressed, she goes into the Catholic church to dip her hand in the holy water font—although she is not Catholic, this has been a practice of hers and Dorothy's whenever they were upset. She meets a sympathetic priest, Father Gordon, who listens to her troubles and suggests that if he were running away, he'd head for the airport. Quickly Jennifer calls the airport and has Dorothy paged. When Dorothy comes to the phone, Jennifer tells her how upset her mother is. Dorothy takes a taxi home. Two days later, Myra and Angela leave for San Francisco. Eddie, Dorothy, and Jennifer finish the mural—even adding Father Gordon—and Dorothy's father invites her and Jennifer to spend a week in New York with him. Since Eddie has moved to New York, he is invited to join their sightseeing party. September finds Jennifer, Dorothy, Myra, and Angela waiting for the moving van to arrive at the house where Eddie used to live.

This is a briskly paced first-person narrative about an eventful summer in the life of a young teenage girl and her friends. Jennifer is an appealing storyteller and the changes she describes, in friends and in herself, will be familiar to many readers. Characters are well drawn and the book's similar first and last scenes make for a satisfying reading experience.

Ages 10-12

**Also available in:**
No other form known

## 195

**Freeman, Gaail**

### Out from Under

Bradbury Press, Inc., 1982.
(166 pages)

---

*MATURATION*
  *Change: accepting*
  *Friendship: best friend*
  *Jealousy*
  *Manipulation: peer*
  *Mental illness: of adolescent*
  *Parent/Parents: single*
  *Suicide: attempted*
  *Suicide: consideration of*

---

A year after her father's death, fifteen-year-old Emily Corson is just beginning to feel like living again. Two major problems confront her. Her best friend, Carla, is obsessed with suicide, and she herself has a crush on her school bus driver, Tank, who is at least twenty years older than she is. When Emily and Carla audition for parts in the school play, Emily is called back and Carla is not. During an overnight stay with Carla, Emily must contend with her jealous friend's talk of death and suicide. She is repelled by Carla, yet feels drawn to her too. Then Emily's mother drags a large loom out of the attic and tells Emily that she has signed her up for weaving lessons. Pleased, Emily eagerly goes to class and discovers that her teacher is Tank, real name Mort Hammond. That evening Emily and Carla go to a party. A boy named Ernie tries to befriend Emily, but she holds back shyly. Suddenly Carla, in tears, grabs Emily and demands they leave. Emily almost suspects that Carla has been raped, but Carla refuses to discuss it. "What does it look like happened?" she exclaims. The next day, after a weaving lesson, Tank and Emily go to a diner. She sees Carla's father there and learns Carla has tried to slit her wrists. She has been placed in a hospital for treatment of depression. Still, life goes on for Emily. There is school, her weaving, letters from Carla, her continuing crush on Tank. Finally allowed to visit Carla, Emily spends an emotionally wrenching time with her friend and then tearfully leaves. Tank sees her walking in the pouring rain and takes her home. Soon after that, Tank and Emily's mother begin a close relationship. When her mother confronts her about her jealousy, Emily's anger deepens. Then Ernie asks Emily to help with costumes for the play—she hadn't returned to read again after her successful audition—and she and he become friends. She quits her weaving lessons, hating Tank and her mother and their relationship. Carla comes home for a weekend, and Emily is appalled at how manipulative she is. "Suicide is my destiny," she proclaims. By spring Emily feels less close to Carla and more comfortable with Ernie. When Tank announces

he is moving to California, Emily finds that she hurts for her mother. But she herself feels better, stronger; she even begins weaving again.

A teenage girl must cope with her father's death, the manipulative behavior of a disturbed friend, a crush on her bus driver-turned-weaving teacher, a tenuous relationship with her mother, and her developing friendship with a boy her age. It's a tall order, but Emily emerges from her struggles with a determination to get on with her life. Well written and insightful, the book convinces and involves the reader throughout.

Ages 12 and up

**Also available in:**
No other form known

## 196

**Gaeddert, LouAnn Bigge**

### Just Like Sisters

Black/white illustrations by Gail Owens.
E. P. Dutton & Company, Inc., 1981.
(90 pages)

---

*DIVORCE: of Parents*
*RELATIVES: Living in Child's Home*
  *Family: relationships*
  *Hostility*
  *Only child*
  *Rejection: parental*

---

Carrie Clark, an only child, is very excited about the upcoming visit of her cousin Kate, also an only child, who will spend the summer. Carrie has always wanted a sister, and she writes out three pages of activities she can share with Kate. But nothing works out as planned. Kate, whose mother has recently left the family in New Jersey and moved to New York to be a designer, is unfriendly, rude, and uncooperative. She takes an immediate dislike to Anne Riley, Carrie's best friend, pronouncing her family "disgusting" because they have five children and Anne's mother so enjoys homemaking. Anne is puzzled by Kate's hostility but allows Kate to teach her to swim, something she's failed to learn for many summers. Gradually, Carrie begins to feel sorry for Kate, although she still doesn't like her. One day, Kate writes and mails a letter, appearing noticeably cheerful afterwards. Later, she tells Carrie and her parents that she's written to ask her father to take her home for the weekend. However, after a painful weekend spent waiting in vain for Kate's father, he calls to say he's been out of town and didn't get her letter until he got back. He'll see Kate the next weekend when he takes her to look at a boarding school he and her mother are considering for her. Carrie wants to know, "Doesn't anybody care about Kate?" The next day Kate tells Anne that she now swims well enough to make it out to the raft. Afraid, Anne makes Kate promise to keep a hand on her all the time. But halfway there, Kate leaves Anne's side and swims to the raft, where she taunts Anne. Anne sinks. Carrie tries to help her but can't, so she yells for help and the lifeguard rescues Anne. Furious, Carrie turns on Kate, telling her she's horrible, mean, despicable, and it's no wonder her mother left her. She also accuses her of being jealous of Anne's happy home life. Kate disappears with her bicycle. By evening her parents are on their way, state troopers are looking for her, and Carrie's family is helping with the search. When, hours later, Kate is found forty miles away, headed for her mother in New York, she ignores her parents and tells Carrie she has no home. Carrie and her parents discuss the possibility of inviting Kate to live with them. Her parents emphasize that once they make the invitation there will be no going back. Carrie realizes she actually likes being an only child. Furthermore, Kate has not exactly been the sister she dreamed about. But when her father suggests sharing their happiness, Carrie consents to the plan. Kate and her parents, however, have made their own plans and Kate, now convinced of her parents' love, will attend the boarding school after all. She will divide her vacations between New York and Tulsa, where her father will be living. She will also visit Carrie for shorter vacations and weekends. "We can't be sisters, but we are cousins after all."

In this tightly written and beautifully illustrated story, a young girl adjusts to the often unpleasant and unpredictable realities of her troubled cousin's visit, emerging with an appreciation of her own family life as it is, not as she sometimes wishes it would be. Carrie becomes more understanding as her perspective widens, and readers will enjoy her gradual transition from hostility to empathy.

Ages 8-12

**Also available in:**
No other form known

## 197

Galbraith, Kathryn Osebold

### Come Spring

Atheneum Publishers, 1979.
(198 pages)

---

CHANGE: New Home
  Chores
  Family: relationships
  Friendship: making friends
  Moving
  Pets: love for

---

Redheaded Reenie Broden, about eleven, must reluctantly leave her best friend when the Broden family moves from Grandma Allen's house to a rented house in a town near Detroit. Reenie and her family move often. Her handyman father is a dreamer, drifting from job to job, from town to town. This time Reenie hopes they can put down real roots. She tells herself, "We'll never move again; I'll have lots of friends." She loves their new house, where she finally has her own room. She makes friends with the little boy next door and adopts a stray police dog, Star. When her mother begins working at Kresge's lunch counter so there will be extra money to fix up the house, it means Reenie must do chores after school. She is embarrassed about her mother's job because some of the girls at school consider Kresge's a "twirpy" store. At first Reenie has some problems making friends, telling her older brother that school is full of "snotty snobs." In fact, one girl, Janice, makes fun of

Reenie's freckles. But soon Reenie makes friends. She, along with the rest of the girls in the class, is invited to Janice's Halloween party, where Reenie proudly dresses as the red-haired Queen Elizabeth I. She enjoys herself at the party and feels part of the group at last. But later that night, Reenie hears her parents arguing. Her father wants to move again in the spring. He tells Reenie that the town of Silver Lake would be a good place for them; there would be plenty of work for him there. Distressed, Reenie says she doesn't want to move. She likes her new house and school and worries that there will be no place for her dog in Silver Lake. Her mother talks with her alone, saying Reenie is an Allen, one of the lucky ones, not a dreamer like the Brodens. Her mother doesn't want to move either, but she assures Reenie that if they do move, Star will come with them. Meanwhile, they are going to continue fixing up the house, since they might not move after all. Encouraged, Reenie goes to her room, thinking that spring is a long way off. Maybe she can put down roots before it comes.

A young girl longing for the security of a permanent home manages to remain optimistic about the future despite the discord caused by parents who dream different dreams. No pat solutions are offered in this realistically told story, but the reader feels that Reenie is resilient enough to cope, helped by a loving, if unsettled, family. The story offers believable characters, dialogue, and situations.

Ages 9-13

**Also available in:**
Cassette—Come Spring
Library of Congress (NLSBPH)

## 198

Galbraith, Kathryn Osebold

### Katie Did!

Black/white illustrations by Ted Ramsey.
Atheneum Publishers, 1982.
(30 pages counted)

---

SIBLING: New Baby
  Attention seeking
  Belonging
  Communication: parent-child

---

When little Mary Rose dances to entertain her new baby brother, Mama asks her to stop jumping up and down because she wants Peter to sleep. Then when Mary Rose sings him a lullaby, Mama asks her to stop making "all that noise." So Mary Rose pours a glass of orange juice all by herself and then fills Peter's little bathtub with lilac bubble bath and green alligators because she knows he loves his bath. She starts making presents for Mama and Peter in the sandbox, but gets lonely all by herself. Since Mama is still busy with Peter, Mary Rose takes Tuffy the turtle out to play. Then Mama wants to know who spilled orange juice and got the kitchen floor all sticky. Mary Rose says her doll Katie did that. Katie is also responsible for filling Peter's tub; Mary Rose insists she saw Katie do it. When Mama asks who left all the pots and pans in the sandbox, Katie is again the culprit. Then Mama wonders why Katie took Tuffy the turtle out of his bowl and put him in with the fish. Because Tuffy was lonely, replies Mary Rose. "I think his mama was too busy to play with him." Mama sits in the rocker with Mary Rose on her lap. The little girl says she thinks she'll throw Katie away because she's been so naughty. But Mama objects. She says she'd never throw Mary Rose away. The pots and pans are now all sandy, points out Mary Rose, but Mama says they'll brush off. Mary Rose explains that Katie just wanted to make sand pies for Mama and Peter. She guessed that, Mama says. She suggests they go outside, make sand pies together, and then come in and have tea—just Mama, Mary Rose, and Katie.

In this well-illustrated book, a little girl with a new baby brother lets her mother know she too needs attention by attributing her own behavior to her doll and her own loneliness to her pet turtle. Mama understands. This warmly reassuring book would be a good one for parents and children to share.

Ages 3-7

**Also available in:**
No other form known

## 199

Gambill, Henrietta

### Self-Control

Color illustrations by Kathryn Hutton.
Children's Press, Inc., 1982.
(29 pages)

*SELF-DISCIPLINE*

Self-control, "a good thing to have," is listening to your friend when you'd rather he listen to you. It's letting someone else have the biggest piece of candy and then waiting until after dinner to eat your piece. It's letting your cat down when she doesn't want to be held anymore and not laughing when your sister falls down. It's refraining from punching your brother after he's punched you. When you let your baby sister sleep, even though you want to play with her, that's self-control. It's not feeding the dog at the table, even though he begs you to. It's not throwing your bat down when your strike-out loses the baseball game. Self-control is being quiet in the library, lining up when the teacher asks you to, and not pushing the people in front of you. It's waiting for the scissors when a friend is using them, and it's keeping your eyes on your paper when you don't know the answers. Self-control is listening quietly when the teacher reads a story, waiting patiently for your parents to finish talking to friends, and deciding on the right thing to do when you have a choice.

Part of a series for the very young about behavior and feelings, this extremely simple, colorfully illustrated book provides repetition and reinforcement of a basic concept—in this case, self-control. The book ends with the statement, "Having self-control will help you to be a happy person," and may stimulate discussion for this age group.

Ages 3-6

**Also available in:**
No other form known

## 200

Gantos, Jack

### The Perfect Pal

Color illustrations by Nicole Rubel.
Houghton Mifflin Company, 1979.
(30 pages)

*FRIENDSHIP: Meaning of*
  *Pets*

One day Vanessa, about six, decides she wants a cheerful pet that will make a good pal. She hurries off to the pet store. There Wendell, the sales assistant, suggests a fish. Vanessa, though, decides on a pig because it could eat milk and cookies with her. Unfortunately, the pig has horrible table manners. So Vanessa puts him in her bathroom and returns to the pet store. This time she comes home with a sloth. But the sloth is no fun because all it wants to do is sleep. She tucks the sloth in bed and again returns to the pet store. Vanessa wants lively conversation, so she leaves with a parrot. But at the soda shop the parrot insults people. Wendell next suggests a friendly sheep dog. But on a rowboat ride the frisky dog, busily scratching fleas, nearly upsets the boat, so Vanessa leaves him in her backyard. Rejecting a snake, Vanessa decides to try a quiet hermit crab. But while she is taking a nap, the crab bites her toe. She places it in a bucket of water. Next, Vanessa decides monkeys are almost human. But once home the monkey ignores her and plays with the other animals. Vanessa feels even less cheerful than when she started. She returns for the last time to the pet store with all her pets in tow, telling Wendell she cannot find a pal. Wendell suggests there is one pal, the "perfect pal," she has not yet tried—him. So Vanessa and Wendell become pals.

Through trial and error, Vanessa discovers her perfect pal is actually a human being like herself, not all the pets she tries to befriend. Simple, colorful illustrations bring to life this imaginative story about finding a friend. Written for a beginning reader, the book would also be an enjoyable read-aloud selection. With all its humor, the story might well lead to discussions about the qualities of friendship.

Ages 4-7

**Also available in:**
No other form known

## 201

Garden, Nancy

### Annie on My Mind

Farrar, Straus & Giroux, Inc., 1982.
(234 pages)

*HOMOSEXUALITY: Female*
  *Guilt, feelings of*
  *Harassment*
  *Justice/Injustice*
  *Love, meaning of*
  *School: negative experiences*

G

Liza Winthrop, a freshman at MIT, tries to write a letter to Annie. To organize her thoughts, she thinks back over the past year. It's the previous November and Liza is president of the student council at coed Foster Academy. At a museum she meets Annie Kenyon, who attends a public high school, and they exchange a look like nothing Liza's ever experienced. The meeting leaves her so off-balance that she fails to report her friend Sally for piercing students' ears in the basement, and she and Sally are suspended for a week. Ms. Baxter, assistant to Mrs. Poindexter, the director, points out that Foster Academy is in danger of closing because of lack of funds, and that the current fund-raising drive will be hurt by any adverse publicity. During Liza's week of suspension, she spends every possible moment with Annie. "Just sitting there in the growing darkness with Annie was so special and so unlike anything that had ever happened to me before that magical seemed like a good word for it and for her." That Sunday as they sit on the Coney Island beach watching the sun go down, they suddenly begin hugging and kissing. After the first startling moments, Annie admits that she's always wondered if she were gay. Later, Liza remembers her own feelings of being different, isolated, of preferring to be with girls rather than boys, of imagining her future with another woman instead of a man. That winter the two see each other often, and Liza daydreams constantly about Annie. Her younger brother, Chad, teases her about being in love, but thinks it's with a boy. Liza admits to herself and to Annie that she really is in love. For Christmas they give each other rings. Liza feels that Annie is her other half. They talk about the physical part of their love, but have no place to be alone. Then Liza offers to feed the cats of two teachers during their absence over the two-week spring vacation: Ms. Widmer, who teaches English, and Ms. Stevenson, the art teacher. Liza and Annie meet daily at the teachers' house and gradually become lovers. To their surprise, they discover that Ms. Widmer and Ms. Stevenson share the large double bed and that the bookcases upstairs are full of books about homosexual love. On Sunday, the day the teachers are expected home, Annie and Liza decide to make love in the big double bed. They are discovered by Ms. Baxter and Sally, who have come to find out why Liza skipped the fund-raising meeting that morning. The girls are barely dressed, and Ms. Baxter storms upstairs to find that the bed has been used. She talks about sin and ugliness. Just then the two teachers arrive home. They try talking to Liza and Annie, but all are too upset to make any decisions. The first thing Monday morning, Mrs. Poindexter tells Liza she's suspended pending an expulsion hearing. She must go before the Board of Trustees, and her parents must be notified. Liza's mother is supportive, remembering that when she was young, she and a friend had experimented in a giggly way with hugging and kissing each other. Seeing the fear, pain, and love in her mother's eyes, Liza lies and says she and Annie never went further than that. But when her father comes home, he admits to having recognized the intense nature of Liza's relationship with Annie. He used to think he was open-minded about homosexuality, but now that it involves Liza he's frightened and unhappy. Chad, after being questioned privately by Mrs.

Poindexter, cries himself to sleep. The Board of Trustees hearing is unbearable for Liza, but they decide that her actions don't involve the school or other students and so are not in their province. However, they hold a hearing for Ms. Widmer and Ms. Stevenson during which Sally testifies that their lesbian relationship influenced Liza, who admired them very much. The two teachers are fired. In reality, Liza never even knew they were gay. At school, Chad is teased but sticks up for Liza. Liza too has her tormentors. She and Annie visit Ms. Stevenson and Ms. Widmer, who have each taught for twenty years. They are making the best of their forced retirements and advise the girls not to punish themselves for something that really isn't their fault. Losing a job is a small matter, as long as nobody separates them. After reflecting on all the happiness and sadness of the past year, Liza decides not to write the letter to Annie. Instead, she telephones and tells Annie she loves her. They make plans to meet during the Christmas vacation.

A high school senior discovers her love for another young woman and tries to cope with the effects the relationship has on her family, school, and friends. On one level, this is a simple love story: recognition, attraction, growing love, delight in the other person, physical expression of the love, and a feeling of wholeness when together. Because it is a love not generally approved and encouraged by society, there are other levels to the story. Written largely in the first person (transition passages of Liza at college are third person), the book doesn't answer the many questions it raises. It comes closest to offering a message when Ms. Stevenson says that "what matters is the truth of loving, of two people finding each other." Annie and Liza's lovemaking is not described in detail, and the physical side of their love is not emphasized except insofar as it intensifies all their feelings. Not all young people who may feel homosexual actually are; Liza's mother points out that it is normal for adolescents to be confused about their sexual feelings and even to experiment. But Liza's feelings about Annie are quite well delineated, and Liza herself is sure she loves Annie. This is a strong, convincing, affecting story.

Ages 13 and up

**Also available in:**
Paperbound—*Annie on My Mind*
Farrar, Straus & Giroux, Inc.

## 202

**Gardiner, John Reynolds**

### Stone Fox

Black/white illustrations by Marcia Sewall.
Thomas Y. Crowell Company, Inc., 1980.
(81 pages)

---

*DETERMINATION*
*Grandparent: living in home of*
*Grandparent: love for*
*Illnesses: of grandparent*
*Pets: love for*
*Resourcefulness*

---

Ten-year-old Willy, his grandfather, and Willy's big dog, Searchlight, live together on a potato farm outside

Jackson, Wyoming. When Grandfather becomes ill, Willy goes for Doc Smith. Doc says Grandfather is not really sick; he simply does not want to live anymore. But neither of them knows why. Willy is determined to make Grandfather want to live again and feels the problem will be solved if he harvests the potato crop. By hooking Searchlight to the plow, Willy harvests the potatoes and then sells them. He prepares for winter by stacking wood and stocking up on food, but Grandfather does not improve. Willy goes to school that fall with Searchlight pulling him over the snow on his sled five miles each way. One day when Willy returns home, a state official awaits him. He has come to collect five hundred dollars in back taxes. Without it, the state will take the farm. Willy tries to borrow money, but without success. Then he sees a poster at the general store in Jackson announcing the National Dogsled Race in February—a race ten miles long over snow-covered countryside. The prize is five hundred dollars. Willy withdraws his college savings of fifty dollars to enter the race. Also entered is Stone Fox, a giant of an Indian who has never lost a dogsled race. By the day of the race, the odds are heavily in favor of Stone Fox. At the sound of the gun, Willy and Searchlight jump out to a huge lead. As they race past their farm, Willy is encouraged to go even faster when he sees Grandfather sitting by the window. Close to the finish, Stone Fox and his five Samoyeds are neck and neck with Willy and Searchlight. One hundred feet from the finish line, old Searchlight's heart bursts and she dies instantly. Stone Fox, who knows Willy's story, stops and fires his rifle, signaling the other approaching racers to stop. He motions to Willy, who carries Searchlight across the finish line.

Based on a legend from the Rocky Mountains, this story of a boy's devotion to his grandfather and to his faithful dog is believed to be true. The dog seems almost human, able to understand her master's needs and struggling to help him all she can. The setting is of an earlier era, and the pencil illustrations add to that feeling. Although this is written for an older child, younger children would enjoy having it read aloud.

Ages 8-10

**Also available in:**
Paperbound—*Stone Fox*
Harper & Row, Publishers, Inc.

## 203

**Gates, Doris**

## A Morgan for Melinda

The Viking Press, Inc., 1980.
(189 pages)

---

*FEAR: of Animals*
*FRIENDSHIP: Meaning of*
*GUILT, FEELINGS OF*
   *Animals: responsibility for*
   *Courage, meaning of*
   *Death: of sibling*
   *Family: relationships*
   *Maturation*

Ten-year-old Melinda Ross loves her father, Cal, and more than anything wants him to be proud of her. So when he announces he wants to buy her a horse, Melinda pretends to be enthusiastic. But she is terrified of horses. When she was five, her brother, Martin, who was ten, died of leukemia. Martin had loved horses and wanted one. Now Melinda feels her father, who also loves horses, is buying one for her because it's too late for Martin to have one. Soon after they begin looking for a horse, Melinda sees a film at school about a Morgan horse and "that was just about the darlingest animal I had ever seen." Melinda asks for a Morgan, but her parents are afraid they can't afford one. Then her father finds a seven-year-old Morgan they can afford, Aranaway Ethan. The horse is delivered to their farm and Melinda, thinking the horse beautiful but still afraid of him, decides to call him Ethan. Melinda finds that the more she takes care of Ethan, the less she fears him. At this time, Muriel Zinn, whom Melinda later nicknames Missy, contacts the Ross family. Missy, in her seventies, wants to lease a horse and learn to ride. Although Cal doesn't have a horse for her to lease, one is found and boarded at the Ross barn, and Cal begins giving Missy lessons. Melinda sees how easily Missy rides her horse, Merry Jo, and confides to the old woman that she is afraid to ride Ethan but feels she must. For the first time, she confesses how guilty she feels about continuing to live although Martin died. Missy gives Melinda two pieces of advice: "That which you fear will come to pass. If you fear something, you see, it will happen. So don't fear it"; and "You can't live forever in the shadow of your dead brother, dear. It's not your fault that he died, and nothing you can do will bring him back." With Missy's encouragement, Melinda begins riding Ethan more frequently. She finds that the more she rides, the more confident she feels. In the fall Missy decides to buy and breed Merry Jo. But before Merry Jo gives birth to a foal, Missy dies suddenly of a heart attack. In her will, she leaves Merry Jo to Melinda. Melinda knows that with Missy's help she has conquered her fear of horses and her guilt about Martin's death. "I knew I had grown a lot, not only on the outside, but on the inside, too."

Guided by a wise old woman, a young girl conquers fear and guilt, the legacy of her brother's death. Written as Melinda's first attempted novel, this poignant story features natural dialogue and strong, carefully delineated family relationships. Melinda's release from her burden of guilt comes slowly and believably. Readers, especially those who love horses, will find her a highly sympathetic character.

Ages 10-12

**Also available in:**
No other form known

G

**204**

Gauch, Patricia Lee

**Fridays**

G. P. Putnam's Sons, 1979.
(159 pages)

---

PEER RELATIONSHIPS: Peer Pressures
  Belonging
  Clubs
  Ostracism
  Rebellion
  School: classmate relationships
  Stealing: shoplifting

---

Winter drags on in Corey Martin's dull suburb. Like her eighth-grade classmates, Corey wants a boyfriend, exciting people to be with, and adventures. But she's never really been popular and tends to be quiet and unassertive. When a school dance is announced she feels the "heat" begin to build; pent-up emotions seem to be stirring in everyone. At Deejays, the local hangout, she and seven other restless girls discuss the dance, still six weeks away. Jan, the sophisticated, attractive leader of the group, announces a sleep-over at her house the next Friday. At the sleep-over, the other girls imitate Jan's every action. Boys arrive and a hilarious water fight follows. Soon, unsupervised Friday nights at Jan's luxurious home become near-rituals, each intended to be "something bigger, something crazier, something more fun." At school the girls become known as "the Eight." They dress alike and wear their hair the same way. Corey, just barely part of this group, marvels at her good fortune. One member, a new girl in school named Terry McCue, even turns down a date to be with her friends. One Friday two girls arrive at Jan's sleep-over with beer stolen from their parents. After everyone drinks, they decide to hold running races in the yard, for which Terry and another girl strip to underpants and T-shirts. When the racing ends the girls toast the victors. Corey, exhilarated, realizes they are having fun even without boys. At school she quarrels with her old friend, level-headed Paul Wimbush, regarding him as a throwback to another time; belonging to the Eight is enough for her. Her schoolwork suffers. On the next Friday the girls, led by Jan, start a follow-the-leader prank: shoplifting. Corey, terrified, steals a scarf, but Terry cannot bring herself to steal. When the school is vandalized Corey assumes, as does everyone, that another old friend, Johnny Culbers, is responsible, since Johnny is often in trouble. Only Terry, whom Johnny was the first to befriend when she was new in town, doubts his involvement. At the next sleep-over Jan provides champagne. After three quick glasses Terry begins to dance and remove her clothes. When the music stops all the girls except Corey, quietly uncomfortable, egg her on. To new music she removes her bra. The boys, hiding outside, tap on the windows and applaud. Suddenly Jan's parents appear and the party abruptly ends. At school Monday Terry is called a stripper. The girls ostracize her; boys cluster around. Corey, deeply upset, does not know what to do. At the long-awaited dance, the girls hear a commotion outside and find that Terry has been in an accident while in a stolen car. Corey assumes Johnny is involved, since Terry is dating him,

but learns that the boy with Terry was clean-cut, well-dressed Woody Anson. She tries to go to Terry, but the police hold her back. After Terry is taken away, Corey tries to sort out her feelings. Paul, whom she has continued to avoid, sits and talks with her. When she expresses shock at Woody's involvement with the stolen car and dismay at Johnny's vandalizing the school, Paul tells her that Woody, not Johnny, was the vandal. Wondering how she could have "figured everything and everybody so wrong," Corey senses that something new is beginning for her, some new insight into herself and what she really wants. What she really wants is a fresh start.

The need to make and keep friends and the strength of peer pressure persuade a young teenager to drink, shoplift, and ostracize a good friend who attempts to warn her about her new friends. Corey's first-person account captures a contemporary situation with realism and appeal. Her conclusions are uncertain and open-ended, allowing readers to discuss what she learns and how it changes her.

Ages 11-13

**Also available in:**
Paperbound—Fridays
Pocket Books, Inc.

---

**205**

Geibel, James

**The Blond Brother**

G. P. Putnam's Sons, 1979.
(201 pages) o.p.

---

DETERMINATION
PREJUDICE: Ethnic/Racial
SPORTS/SPORTSMANSHIP
  Boy-girl relationships: dating
  School: classmate relationships
  Talents: athletic
  Violence

---

For Rich Gaskins, to live is to play basketball. A star in his former school, Rich's reputation has preceded his family's recent move, and he looks forward to his senior year playing for Marchmont High School. Unfortunately, tensions are high between black and white students in the recently integrated school system. All five members of last year's starting basketball team are black, all have returned this year, and Rich finds the atmosphere charged when he turns out for the team. He has other strikes against him in the minds of the black players. His father is an executive in the town's most prominent company and the family lives in an expensive part of town. Rich is attractive, a good student, drives a Corvette. The first time Rich scrimmages with the other players, they freeze him out. Rich eventually makes first string, but the others ignore him on the court and are openly antagonistic off the court. The absence of teamwork shows during the first few games; the team wins largely because Rich pulls them through. As the outstanding player, Rich is dubbed the "Blond Panther" by the local sports newswriter. Then another player harasses Rich after a game, shoving him and severely bruising his wrist. Rich plays that week despite considerable pain and tells no one the circumstances of his

---

116

injury. His determination to play at all costs impresses the other players. Gradually they begin to play as a team. Rich asks Rosie Turner, a teammate, why he has finally been accepted. Because, Rosie explains, he's proven he wants to play with them, not to be better than they are. Rosie and his friends invite Rich to the Belles Ball, an annual dance for black students. Rich accepts and asks a girl from the social set he could be in if he wanted. But when she finds out which dance it is she weasels out of the date by lying about a previous engagement. So Rich goes alone and discovers that Rosie has set him up with Glen Jackson, a beautiful black student whom Rich begins dating steadily. His parents are surprised when they learn Glen is black, but they seem to accept her totally. By March the team is undefeated and wins the District Championship. Rich wins the Most Valuable Player trophy. After the championship game, Rich walks to his car and finds three white teammates and the football captain. They taunt Rich, calling him "The Blond Brother" and goading him to fight. Rich is knocked unconscious, terribly battered. Bruised and still weak, he insists on playing in the state tournament despite the cast on his arm and his aching body. His decision is applauded by the senior coach, who sees this as perhaps his last chance to win the championship. The coach's young assistant deplores the whole situation, but is not allowed to interfere. The team wins the first two games, with Rich playing as much as he can. He is thoroughly exhausted and in a lot of pain as the final game begins, but is determined to play. He's knocked down, reinjuring the hand in the cast and having to be carried off with two minutes left to play. The team loses. Then, painfully and reluctantly, Glen breaks off their relationship. She cares for him, yet knows she'll never be able to endure the prejudice that will always surround them. Hurt, stunned, and miserable, Rich begins to hate basketball, school, and the social upheavals he never wanted to be part of. In May Rich is awarded Marchmont's Male Athlete of the Year award, but he feigns illness to avoid the presentation assembly. When Rosie and the other starting players bring the trophy to his house later that day, he and Rosie talk. Rich realizes the year was not all bad. When the four scrimmage in his driveway, "for the first time in a long time, he was starting to feel like the Blond Brother again."

An action-filled basketball season is the backdrop for a compelling look at the racial prejudice that surrounds an athlete who wants only to play his game. Through sheer determination and single-mindedness, Rich wins the respect of his teammates and his coach. This well-written, nicely paced book deals honestly and candidly with prejudice, interracial dating, and the struggles of young people to find a place in the world they inherit. Exciting sports sequences add interest for basketball fans.

Ages 12 and up

**Also available in:**
No other form known

**206**

**Gerber, Merrill Joan**

**Please Don't Kiss Me Now**
The Dial Press, Inc., 1981.
(218 pages)

---

*PARENT/PARENTS: Single*
  *Boy-girl relationships*
  *Communication: parent-child*
  *Death: of friend*
  *Parent/Parents: remarriage of*
  *School: classmate relationships*
  *Sex: attitude toward*

---

Since her parents' divorce, fifteen-year-old Leslie's life has grown increasingly complicated. Her mother, "like some desperate teenager," has been preoccupied with dates, boyfriends, her appearance—everything but her daughter. Leslie's father has remarried, and Leslie dislikes his new family. Most distressing at the moment is her mother's interest in Mr. Kesey, a favorite former teacher of Leslie's and supposedly a devoted family man. When her mother asks Leslie to accompany her and Eric, the boyfriend of the moment, to the desert for the weekend, Leslie begs off since, as a violinist in the school orchestra, she can't miss opening night of the musical. After the performance the good-looking lead, Brian Sweeney, takes her out for ice cream and then home in his van, complete with waterbed. He tries to persuade her to loosen up with a bit of marijuana and some hugging, but she sends him away. When she gets inside, she finds a note from her mother. Leslie is to spend the weekend with her father, since if he discovers she is unsupervised he may begin a custody suit. Unhappily, Leslie goes to bed. Towards morning she is awakened by Mr. Kesey, who knocks on the window of her mother's bedroom (where Leslie has slept). She questions him about his relationship with her mother. Kesey replies that they have a lot in common and that he thinks he can help her. Asking Leslie to trust him, he takes her to her father's apartment. The weekend is ghastly. Back home, Leslie finds Eric—her mother is shopping—and he makes a pass at her. She flees to her friend Ron Bernstein's house, and he implores her to tell her father. But Leslie doesn't want to live with her father. She begins to see Brian with some regularity, although she knows that Ron cares for her more. She likes necking with Brian; with him, she doesn't have to think. Then Leslie finally gets a real girlfriend: Lois, a senior she's admired, who offers to be her roommate when the musical's cast travels to San Diego for a performance. Meanwhile, Leslie's mother and Mr. Kesey become more involved, especially after Leslie tells her mother about Eric. Before too long, her mother announces plans to marry Mr. Kesey. His marriage has been over for a long time, she tells Leslie. The two plan to build a geodesic home in the Sacramento Valley for themselves and Leslie. Determined to keep Kesey from ruining his life, Leslie tries to persuade him of her mother's flightiness and her own unwillingness to move to Sacramento. On the bus trip to San Diego, the cast members witness a fiery car accident. Leslie's horror intensifies when she learns that the death car held Lois and her parents. Returning to her hotel room, Leslie

**G**

discovers her mother and Kesey, who have impulsively decided to come see the show. She tells them about Lois and asks them to leave her alone. Ron slips into her room to comfort her, offering to have her live with him and his mother. Then Brian visits her and suggests they make love—they may as well take advantage of the room now that Lois won't be back. Disgusted, Leslie sends him away, goes to her mother's and Kesey's room, and announces her decision to live with them. She will move away, away from Ron's and his mother's affectionate concern, away from Brian's attentions, away from everything. But she'll return for visits. And now she'd rather ride home with her mother and Kesey than with the kids on the bus.

A teenage girl struggles for equilibrium in a year filled with conflicts: her mother's post-divorce antics and her prospective remarriage, her father's new and unlovable family, a steady boyfriend and a male friend who wants to be more, the death of her only girlfriend, the prospect of moving. Through it all runs the thread of Leslie's central conflict, with her mother; both are bewildered and searching for themselves, each resents the other. After Lois's shocking death, Leslie realizes that at least "she was alive and had choices!" The convincing, fast-paced story remains uncluttered despite numerous characters and events. Dialogue is realistic, with occasional profanity. This is competent writing about contemporary issues.

Ages 13 and up

**Also available in:**
Paperbound—*Please Don't Kiss Me Now*
New American Library

## 207

**Gerson, Corinne**

**How I Put My Mother Through College**
Atheneum Publishers, 1981.
(136 pages)

---

COMMUNICATION: Parent-Child
PARENTAL: Unreliability
  Divorce: of parents
  Parent/Parents: remarriage of

---

Thirteen-year-old Jessica greets her mother's news that she has registered for college with, "Anything was worth trying if it made Mom act so happy." Since her parents split up that spring, her mother has spent a lot of time in her room crying. She explains to Jessica and to nine-year-old Ben that she had her children first and is now, at thirty-two, going to college. "I guess you could say I'm just doing my life a little backwards." But from that point on, life for all three of them goes backwards. Jessica soon discovers that she must "mother" both her mother and Ben, just when she herself is having trouble adjusting to junior high. None of her old friends are in her classes, she doesn't like any of her teachers, and she keeps getting lost in the big, new school. Then she comes home to a mother who rapidly looks, sounds, and acts like a young college student. The two have nightly talks during which Jessica says little and just tries to provide the encouragement her mother needs. As Jessica becomes more and more isolated at school, she takes on more chores at home. If she can't make it at school, she decides, she can succeed at what she "seemed to be best at: being a mother." Jessica and Ben get used to several of their mother's boyfriends, but not Randy. Ben hates Randy and the man makes Jessica uncomfortable too. When their parents finally get divorced, their father introduces them to Margie, who seems very nice and very young. The day after their mother makes cheerleader, their father announces his plans to marry Margie. Meanwhile, Randy continues to be their mother's favorite, although Jessica tries to tell her he's a freeloader. At the big Thanksgiving Day football game, Jessica's mother breaks her arm while cheerleading and is escorted home by one of the players, Augie, who then begins to take her out. On the Saturday after Thanksgiving, their father and Margie are married. Then their mother becomes a political activist. When she takes part in a protest rally, she faints and is taken to the police station along with other demonstrators. Soon after, Jessica and Ben see a TV movie about a girl who runs away because her parents are getting a divorce. In the end, the girl is found and the parents decide they don't want a divorce after all. Several days later, Ben runs away. While he's being searched for, Randy makes some uncomplimentary remarks about the boy to his mother—who finally asks Randy to leave and not come back. Ben has unwittingly gotten rid of Randy after all. After Ben is found, the parents decide that family therapy might be helpful. When the children hear that Margie and their father are expecting a baby, both Jessica and Ben finally accept the way things really are. Jessica's mother is seeing a lot of her psychology professor and she appears to be changing. She isn't asking Jessica's opinion about everything, and she's beginning to wear skirts and blouses instead of jeans and plaid shirts. Jessica is glad because she needs a little advice about her own love life. She thinks it's time the tables were turned and her mother helped her.

A young girl must switch roles for a time with her newly divorced mother as the woman enters college life with a vengeance. This amusing first-person account lets the reader see some of Jessica's feelings, but the book's central premise—a teenager taking over the role and duties of her mother while the mother becomes "one of the kids"—will be difficult for most young people to accept. While some children no doubt do take over certain parental functions, the situation here is so exaggerated as to keep readers from entering wholeheartedly into the story. Still, they will enjoy the brief glimpses of Jessica's own life, and the story of her and her brother's gradual acceptance of their parents' divorce is handled well. At the end, the reader can only hope that Jessica's mother really has changed enough to resume the role her children need her to play.

Ages 11 and up

**Also available in:**
No other form known

**208**

**Gerson, Corinne**

## Son for a Day

Black/white illustrations by Velma Ilsley.
Atheneum Publishers, 1980.
(140 pages)

---

FRIENDSHIP: Making Friends
PARENT/PARENTS: Substitute
RESOURCEFULNESS
    Parent/Parents: single
    Parental: absence

---

Danny is eleven and lives with his aunt in an apartment in The Bronx. He has never known his father; his mother has moved to California to try to make it in show business. Aunt Dorothy works, even on weekends. So when Danny discovers a way to have a substitute father each weekend, he designs a plan of action. He frequents the local zoo, where he often sees various fathers and sons together. He calls these fathers "zoodaddies" and develops a technique for getting in on their conversations, usually by giving information about a particular animal. Before long, he is invited to join them for lunch. After a pleasant day, he's often invited to dinner at a restaurant. Soon Danny has an address book, phone numbers, and a schedule of weekend outings. He figures he is even luckier than kids who have regular fathers, because he gets only the benefits. Danny has never sought a "zoomommy," but one day he unintentionally joins Mike Anderson and his mother. Ms. Anderson, a television news commentator, proves so much fun that Danny soon adds her to his list of regulars. One day when Mike is out of town with his father, Ms. Anderson and Danny have lunch together. Danny shares his entire plan with her, happy to have made a friend to whom he can entrust all the details. The next week, as he watches her evening show, "Everyday People," Danny is horrified to hear Ms. Anderson tell his whole story, even showing scenes from the zoo and other favorite spots. She doesn't give his name, but Danny is afraid to go to school the next day. His friends, however, have not yet identified him. Then the evening paper continues the story, reporting that several of Danny's zoodaddies have called the television station telling of their admiration for the boy. The morning paper carries a composite picture drawn from the descriptions given by the various zoodaddies. That day the principal calls Danny into his office. Thinking he is in big trouble, Danny quickly confesses that he is "son for a day." Suddenly he is surrounded by newspeople and cameras. Ms. Anderson arrives, and even Aunt Dorothy. When Danny realizes that Ms. Anderson told his story because she found it so endearing and that no one is angry with him, he decides to enjoy all the publicity. That night he is a special guest on "Everyday People," and all the zoodaddies and their sons meet at a restaurant for a big party. Even his mother returns home and attends. For several days, Danny is a celebrity. Then his mother is offered a job in Chicago. At first Danny finds it hard to think of leaving The Bronx and his friends. But when he realizes he will have new opportunities for meeting fathers with sons, he buys a new date calendar.

A lonely, resourceful boy applies his charm and ingenuity to just the right opportunities and ends up with new friendships and a whole collection of substitute parents in this clever, believable story. Danny's first-person narrative is spiced with humorous observations about people and events. Amusing illustrations add to the appeal.

Ages 10-12

**Also available in:**
Paperbound—Son for a Day
Scholastic Book Services

**209**

**Gerson, Corinne**

## Tread Softly

The Dial Press, Inc., 1979.
(133 pages)

---

GRANDPARENT: Living in Home of
HONESTY/DISHONESTY
    Baby-sitting
    Friendship: meaning of
    Imagination
    Orphan

---

G

Twelve-year-old Carol Ann Tate, called Kitten by family and friends, has two families, the one she lives with and the one she dreams of, and she much prefers the second. Her actual family consists of Peter, her pesky ten-year-old brother, and her proverb-quoting grandparents. Her dream family consists of her dead parents, whom she dimly remembers, a teenage brother, Buck, and a little sister, Gabrielle. At a store, Kitten meets and strikes up a conversation with an attractive young mother, Mrs. Fulsom, who is shopping with her three-year-old son, Tommy. Kitten tells the woman about her dream family and how she cares for young Gaby, but neglects to mention that this family is imaginary. Mrs. Fulsom, believing Kitten is experienced in handling youngsters, offers the girl a daily baby-sitting job as her helper. Ignoring her friends' warning that Mrs. Fulsom isn't as nice as she seems, Kitten appears at the Fulsom home the next morning. She rapidly falls in love with the job, the house, Tommy, and the lovely Mrs. Fulsom. Though Kitten wants to tell the truth about her family and home life and makes several attempts, Mrs. Fulsom never finds time to listen to her and Kitten finally stops trying. Meanwhile, Kitten's real family pales more and more when compared with the Fulsoms and their luxurious surroundings. When Mr. and Mrs. Fulsom invite Kitten along on a vacation to care for Tommy, Kitten must be devious to conceal her real family and keep her secret. Lulu, the baby-sitter for the family accompanying the Fulsoms, helps her and quickly becomes her best friend. Lulu's large, busy family captivates Kitten, who finds them a welcome contrast to her own quiet relatives. All goes well on the vacation until the last day, when Kitten and Lulu have a falling-out over a boy. Soon after their return home, Mrs. Fulsom learns about Kitten's real family, concludes that having a dream family is "sick," and fires her. Still angry, Mrs. Fulsom visits Kitten's grandparents to tell them of the situation, urging them to get psychiatric help for Kitten. Kitten realizes how much her grandparents love her when she overhears them defending her. The newly recognized virtues of her family are underscored when Lulu, who has made up with Kitten, reveals that her family only puts on a smiling face for visitors; at other times they often quarrel and fight. Kitten now realizes just how lucky she is: "I knew then that [Grandma] and Grandpa and Peter were all the family I had. And all I really needed."

A young, orphaned girl who lives with her grandparents expresses her longing for a conventional family life by creating an imaginary family and by seeing other people's home lives through idealistic eyes. As she discovers that no families are perfect, she also comes to see the virtues of her own loving home environment. Kitten tells her own story and it will appeal to the intended audience, at an age when all nonconformity is shunned. The story unfolds logically, with the tension of Kitten's secret building to a believable conclusion.

Ages 9-12

**Also available in:**
Paperbound—*Tread Softly*
Scholastic Book Services

## 210

**Giff, Patricia Reilly**

**Fourth Grade Celebrity**

Black/white illustrations by Leslie Morrill.
Delacorte Press, 1979.
(117 pages)

---

*RESOURCEFULNESS*
*SELF, ATTITUDE TOWARD: Accepting*
  *Attention seeking*
  *Friendship: best friend*
  *Imagination*
  *Inferiority, feelings of*
  *Jealousy: sibling*
  *School: classmate relationships*

---

Casey Valentine, nine, wants to be popular like her pretty older sister, Van. "I have no zip. No style. I'm a lump of vanilla pudding." Determined to become a celebrity, Casey decides to be president of the fourth-grade class. Walter Mole, her best friend, agrees to nominate her on one condition: Casey must take Walter's place as pen pal to Tracy Matson. The Moles and Matsons met on vacation, and Walter's mother has been forcing this correspondence. Casey does become class president, although not by a popularity vote. Her name is drawn out of a box in which every fourth grader's name has been placed after all the other contenders drop out of the race. Undaunted by how she was "elected," a thrilled Casey promptly starts a school newspaper, with the approval of her teacher, Mrs. Petty. Casey picks a committee of three others, names herself editor, and the work begins. To help promote the paper, the four decide to sell raffle tickets for a mystery prize. Casey is determined to sell the most tickets. She and Walter sneak into school on a Saturday to steal Van's class list of the sixth grade so Casey can get a head start over the weekend. While in the building, Casey also uses the school ditto machine to run off a newsletter to Tracy in which she tells an imaginary story of how she has received a medal for saving her school from a fire.

The following Monday, Casey and her news reporters try to run off copies of the newspaper, only to have the school secretary, Mrs. Crump, scoot them out of the ditto room. But Mrs. Crump promises to run off and staple the papers for them. At lunchtime, as they're selling the newspapers, Casey notices there is one more page than she expected. To her horror, she realizes she left the ditto master for Tracy's letter at school on Saturday and Mrs. Crump has mistakenly run it off too. A mortified Casey runs home after school to hide. There Van tells her the letter was terrific and reports that Mrs. Petty called Casey creative. Casey is a celebrity after all.

A young girl living in the shadow of an older sister tries to get out in various elaborate, sometimes underhanded ways. She finally becomes a "celebrity"—but legitimately, because of her writing ability. This funny story captures the whirlwind life of a messy, active, imaginative fourth grader. Portions of Casey's story are told in letters to her pen pal, Tracy. Pencil drawings enhance the story, a companion volume to *The Girl Who Knew It All.*

Ages 8-10

**Also available in:**
Paperbound—*Fourth Grade Celebrity*
Dell Publishing Company, Inc.

## 211

**Giff, Patricia Reilly**

**The Gift of the Pirate Queen**

Black/white illustrations by Jenny Rutherford.
Delacorte Press, 1982.
(164 pages)

---

*COURAGE, MEANING OF*
  *Death: of mother*
  *Diabetes*
  *Family: relationships*
  *Relatives: living in child's home*
  *School: classmate relationships*

---

Since her mother's death the year before, eleven-year-old Grace O'Malley has tried to take care of her father and her younger sister, Amy, who has diabetes and worries Grace by ignoring her special diet. Grace is apprehensive when her father says his cousin, Fiona, is coming from Ireland to visit them. Just before Fiona's arrival, Grace accidentally breaks her teacher's prized glass Christmas bell. All the sixth graders fear and dislike Mrs. Raphael, and Grace knows she can never confess what she's done. Fiona arrives bearing little gifts and immediately tells Grace that she reminds her of the other Grace O'Malley, the brave and bold pirate queen. Fiona's love for Katie, Grace's mother, inspires her father to explain the circumstances of Katie's accidental death for the first time. Meanwhile, Grace worries about Mrs. Raphael's broken bell. Lisa, a new girl in school, always unkempt and the butt of her classmates' jokes, mentions that she saw a bell just like it in a shopping mall thirty miles away. Grace's father is too busy to take her there, so Fiona does. After buying the bell, Grace feels less relieved than she'd expected to; something is still nagging at her. Fiona tells Grace that this is her happiest Christmas: after years of living alone, working in the parish rectory in Ireland, she finally has a family to love. When Grace slips the new bell under the classroom Christmas tree, she decides to improve Lisa's standing with Mrs. Raphael by writing that the bell is from Lisa. But her plan backfires when Mrs. Raphael suspects Lisa of replacing the bell because she broke it. That afternoon Amy gets sick and must go to the hospital. Grace handles the emergency with Fiona's help. Later, Amy jokes about Grace bringing her a box of candy, and Grace bursts out that she hates Amy for frightening her all the time and for not doing what she ought to do. The next day Grace's father brings her a message from Amy: she loves Grace and wants Grace to know that it's very hard to stay on her diet, that sometimes she just wants to pretend she doesn't have diabetes at all. Grace's father admits he's guilty of the same thing. If he just didn't talk about Katie's death, he'd thought, he could pretend she was around somewhere. Now he and Grace need to help Amy stop running away from her diabetes and become "everyday brave." Remembering her own words to Amy about doing what she ought to do, Grace tells Mrs. Raphael the truth about the bell. The teacher is surprised to learn the children fear her, saying she must think about that and how she has changed over the years. She and Grace both apologize to Lisa. After school, Grace can't find Fiona at first and realizes how much she needs and loves her. When Fiona comes in, Grace begs her to stay with them permanently. Fiona had told Grace's father she would only stay if she were asked, and only until they didn't need her anymore. She talks about courage. When Grace tells her about the bell, adding that she is not bold and brave like the pirate queen, Fiona says courage is a gift that we don't always have with us. For Christmas, Fiona gives Grace an old photograph of her mother and Fiona herself, taken long ago in Ireland. For Grace, who has no pictures of her mother and has begun to forget what she looked like, it is a gift almost as precious as the gift of courage.

A young girl discovers there are many kinds of courage and that all the important people in her life struggle with fears just as she does. In this beautifully illustrated, well-written, and touching story, various examples of courage are presented in terms easy to understand and apply to readers' own lives. The stages of mourning and the trials of diabetes are skillfully woven through the plot, as are details of Irish customs and folklore.

Ages 9-12

**Also available in:**
Paperbound—*The Gift of the Pirate Queen*
Dell Publishing Company, Inc.

**212**

Giff, Patricia Reilly

**The Girl Who Knew It All**
Black/white illustrations by Leslie Morrill.
Delacorte Press, 1979.
(118 pages)

---

FRIENDSHIP: Meaning of
SCHOOL: Achievement/Underachievement
  Inferiority, feelings of
  Responsibility: avoiding
  Self-discipline
  Teasing

---

Tracy Matson, about nine, has just started summer vacation, and she wants Leroy Wilson to be her summertime best friend. Unfortunately, Leroy wants to play with his friend Richard, and both boys love to tease Tracy for being a slow reader. Tracy likes to ignore her reading problems by showing off and acting like a know-it-all. Her father has asked her to read fifteen minutes every day during the summer. Instead of the daily readings, she keeps track of the minutes she owes and always writes an IOU. Tracy does try to be helpful, but something always seems to go wrong. As a surprise, she decides to touch up a newly painted shutter on the house of Mrs. Bemus, the new school principal. Reaching for a can of turpentine, she misreads the label and uses Turkey Red paint. To cover up her mistake, Tracy paints a red rose on the shutter. When she hears voices, she hides and then sneaks away. Vacation begins to improve when Casey Valentine, Tracy's pen pal, comes to town with her parents for the summer. Tracy and Casey quickly become the best of friends. They decide they need to earn money for the County Fair, so they get a joint baby-sitting job. When this doesn't bring in the revenue they need, they enlist Leroy, Richard, and two other children from town to plan a play they can present and charge admission for. As usual, Leroy and Richard tease Tracy about her poor reading ability, surprising Casey, whom Tracy has told that she loves to read. Casey offers to help Tracy with her reading. Embarrassed, Tracy screams for everyone to leave. She then runs into her house, discovering that her dog, Rebel, is sick. Both parents are working and no one else is available, so when Tracy spots Mrs. Bemus outside her house, she asks the principal to drive her to the veterinarian's. On the way home, overcome with guilt, Tracy blurts out that it was she who painted the shutter because she misread the label on the can. Mrs. Bemus invites Tracy into her house to talk. She encourages the girl to let Casey help her with her reading. She also offers to help the group earn money for the fair by having them paint her garage. A grateful Tracy apologizes to Leroy and Richard for her outburst and tells them about the garage. She then offers to teach Casey to paint a garage if Casey will help teach her to read.

A girl covers up her reading deficiencies by showing off and playing tricks. When a friend discovers her secret and a sympathetic principal takes an interest in her, Tracy can finally admit to herself that she needs help. Though her problem is not solved, Tracy becomes

**G**

determined to improve her reading. This is an enjoy-able story, filled with humor and true-to-life characters. Lively pencil drawings enhance this companion volume to *Fourth Grade Celebrity*.

Ages 8-10

Also available in:
Paperbound—*The Girl Who Knew It All*
Dell Publishing Company, Inc.

## 213

Giff, Patricia Reilly

### Today Was a Terrible Day

Color illustrations by Susanna Natti.
The Viking Press, Inc., 1980.
(26 pages)

---

SCHOOL: Achievement/Underachievement
   Inferiority, feelings of
   Success

---

Ronald Morgan, in second grade, is having a terrible day at school. When he crawls under his desk to retrieve his pencil, his classmates call him Snakey. Then, because his mother forgot to sign his homework, he signs her name. Not only does Miss Tyler, his teacher, tell him that forgery is a crime; she informs him that he spelled his mother's name incorrectly. The children all laugh. During reading time Ronald, hungry, sneaks to the closet and eats a sandwich—from Jimmy's lunch bag. Then Ronald, who knows he is in the "dumb group" in reading, has to ask how to do a workbook page. He feels even dumber when Rosemary, also in his group, asks, "Don't you even know how to do that?" In line to get a drink of water, Ronald holds his finger on the water and splashes a girl's dress. A third-grade teacher marches him back to his class, warning him that if he doesn't learn to behave he will never get into third grade. A classmate says Ronald may not get to third grade anyway because he can't read. At recess, Ronald misses a fly ball and loses his ice cream money. That afternoon he makes mistakes while reading aloud for his teacher. Just before it is finally time to go home, Ronald is reminded that it is his turn to water the plants. While watering, he knocks a pot off the windowsill. As he leaves for the day, Miss Tyler hands him a note and tells him to read it himself, with help from his mother if necessary. Ronald surprises himself by reading the whole note without help. It says that Miss Tyler is sorry for his bad day and hopes tomorrow will be better. Ronald can read after all! Elated, he runs home to tell his best friend. He also decides to take Miss Tyler a new plant tomorrow for her birthday.

A day of assorted mishaps and failures ends trium-phantly for a little boy when he is able to read his teacher's encouraging note all by himself. Ronald, in the "dumb" reading group, tells his own story, and his feel-ings of inferiority and incompetence, changing to hap-piness and pride, come through clearly. Colorfully illustrated, this beginning reader tells a lighthearted but sympathetic story.

Ages 6-7

Also available in:
Paperbound—*Today Was a Terrible Day*
The Viking Press, Inc.

## 214

Giff, Patricia Reilly

### The Winter Worm Business

Black/white illustrations by Leslie Morrill.
Delacorte Press, 1981.
(132 pages)

---

FRIENDSHIP: Making Friends
REJECTION: Peer
   Change: new home
   Family: relationships

---

LeRoy Wilson is less than thrilled when his cousin Mitchell, also ten, moves to town with his mother and younger sister after his father leaves the family. Winter is just beginning, and LeRoy and his friend Tracy expect their worm business to pick up smartly when the ice-fishing season gets underway. Mitchell wants painfully to be part of LeRoy's life, but he does one thing after another that LeRoy considers intrusive, obnoxious, or embarrassing. Furthermore, LeRoy's mother signs LeRoy up as Aunt Louise's first piano student, over his strenuous objections. Mitchell tags along when LeRoy goes to visit his bachelor friend, Gideon Cole, who lives in a mountain cabin by himself during the winter and goes deep-sea fishing in the Atlantic during the sum-mer. To keep Mitchell away from Gideon's mountain, LeRoy tells him about the fearsome mountain monkeys, which resemble Abominable Snowmen. Gideon, how-ever, praises LeRoy for helping Mitchell; it must be hard to move to a new place, he remarks, and he's sure LeRoy is introducing Mitchell around and helping him get set-tled. LeRoy thinks to himself that Mitchell has no trou-ble at all—he just moves in and takes over. On the first snowy morning, Mitchell gets up early and contracts with just about everyone in town to shovel their walks. LeRoy, beaten to this job opportunity, is incensed to the point of tears. As it turns out, though, Mitchell intends for both of them to do the walks and split the money. Then, at his first piano recital, LeRoy can't remember how his piece ends so he just keeps repeating it—whereupon Mitchell pretends to faint, releasing LeRoy from his endless loop. The next day the ice fishermen arrive. Tracy, LeRoy, and Mitchell take the worms out onto the ice to sell. But Mitchell's sister bumps into him as he's holding the worms and almost all of them fall in an ice hole. Even Tracy gets mad at Mitchell then. When Mitchell leaves, his sister reports his intention of saving LeRoy; LeRoy realizes that his cousin has gone to protect him from the mountain monkeys (they eat any-one who warns another person against them). Tracy says Mitchell really needs a friend. He tries so hard to help other people. LeRoy reluctantly agrees and decides to go after him. When he finds Mitchell, he tells him that the mountain monkey story is a hoax told to all new kids. Mitchell is glad to know he's not a new kid anymore.

LeRoy realizes that nobody is perfect and that his cousin's good points far outweigh his bad ones. This is not a profound tale, but readers may see past Mitchell's apparently abundant self-confidence to the trials of the new kid on the block trying to fit in. Attractive, lively illustrations perk up this story of cousins' rivalry.

Ages 8-10

**Also available in:**
Paperbound—*The Winter Worm Business*
Dell Publishing Company, Inc.

## 215
Gilbert, Harriett

### Running Away
Harper & Row, Publishers, Inc., 1979.
(266 pages)

---

*AUTONOMY*
*MATURATION*
*Friendship: best friend*
*Peer relationships: avoiding others*
*Schools, private: girls'*
*Separation from loved ones*

---

Sixteen-year-old Jane Rackham, a student in an English boarding school, receives a letter from her father saying that her mother has prematurely given birth to a seventh child. Her mother and the new baby are having problems, but Jane is told not to worry. Upset and frightened, Jane welcomes an invitation from her best friend, Audrey Croft, to spend the weekend in London with Audrey and her mother. But her expectations of a carefree time soon evaporate. Audrey, her mother, and her sister, Henrietta, bicker and fight at every opportunity. Audrey's brother-in-law, Gary, tries to explain the family discord to Jane, saying that Audrey's divorced mother "sees her baby growing up, growing away from her, so she does what she can to make her a baby again." Henrietta, on the other hand, was "her dad's little girl," and her mother actually dislikes her. Sensing Jane's need for someone to talk to, Gary tells her she can call him any time. But once again, Jane feels afraid and lonely. She also has a terrible fight with Audrey, and by Sunday neither girl is speaking to the other. Back at school, Jane withdraws into herself. After another fight with Audrey, she sneaks away from school and telephones Gary in London, hysterical. He drives down to the village, and Jane tries to explain her feelings. She believes her parents have forgotten about her and do not need her. Then, persuading Gary to let her drive his car, Jane speeds back toward the school and hits Aziz, the favorite kitten of the headmistress, Miss Anthony. When she gets back, Jane tries to tell Miss Anthony what has happened, but the woman is preoccupied and refuses to listen. Jane continues to exist in a daze, feeling friendless, unloved, and guilty. One night later that week, she sneaks out of the dorm to find the kitten's body. Audrey follows and they renew their friendship. Jane tells Audrey that she has killed Aziz, but Audrey insists she has seen the cat since the accident. Sure enough, the girls finally find Aziz, hurt but alive. They return the cat to Miss Anthony in the morning. Jane is run down from not eating much the past week, and the cold night spent outdoors makes her ill. As she recovers in the infirmary, she begins to realize that she cannot cling to her parents forever. She is a separate person.

A lonely girl who lives apart from her large family at an English boarding school longs for her parents' love and attention but comes to realize that she must make a life for herself. The family troubles of a friend help Jane see that discord and conflict exist in many people's lives. This is an introspective story about a slow, painful maturation process. Some profanity is included in the dialogue.

Ages 11-14

**Also available in:**
No other form known

## 216
Gilson, Jamie

### Do Bananas Chew Gum?
Lothrop, Lee & Shepard Company, 1980.
(158 pages)

---

*LEARNING DISABILITIES*
*Baby-sitting*
*Education: special*
*Inferiority, feelings of*
*School: achievement/underachievement*
*School: classmate relationships*
*Self, attitude toward: feeling different*

---

Sam Mott is twelve and in the sixth grade, but he reads on a second-grade level. His parents believe his reading difficulties stem from the family's frequent moves. Sam believes he can't read because he's dumb. When they lived in California, Sam was tested and said to have "learning disabilities." But now, in Illinois, Sam has been placed in a regular sixth-grade class and doesn't want to take any more tests. He overhears his parents discussing him, his mother worrying that he might be retarded. Sam knows he is just dumb. Then Sam is hired to baby-sit for two little boys after school. The first afternoon, he can't read the note from their mother and so does not let the dog out or give one of the boys his medicine. The mother, Mrs. Glass, is angry, and Sam promises to do better. She then asks Sam to write down his orthodontist's name; Sam is sure he'll now be fired for stupidity because he can't spell and his writing is illegible. The next day Mrs. Glass asks Sam to read to her boys, but he cannot. At school Alicia, the smartest student in class but highly disliked because of her boasting and superior attitude, asks Sam if he can read; she has seen through his bluffing and joking. He ignores her. The next day, while he's baby-sitting, Alicia comes by and offers to help him with his spelling. Angry that now Alicia, Mrs. Glass, and his teacher know he can't read, Sam refuses when his parents tell him he is to be tested again. Then Mrs. Glass confronts Sam about not being able to read. She tells him he is not stupid—he has proved that by being such a good baby-sitter—but he needs help. So Sam agrees to be tested by Ms. Huggins, the special education teacher whom Sam, unaware of her position, has seen and admired before. When Sam tells her he is dumb she replies, "You're not allowed in my door unless you're smart." (Another teacher works with children who have lower ability.) Ms. Huggins finds that Sam is excellent in math, but that he learns better by hearing than by reading. She shows him some easier ways to read and encourages him to use a tape recorder, reading into it so he can hear himself and taking notes with it. These are just the first of the things she'll work through with him, she promises. After the testing, Sam talks with Alicia. He tells her he feels better about himself and is determined not to feel dumb anymore. They agree that, just as Sam has told Alicia not to keep telling people she's smart, Sam will stop telling people he is dumb.

Feeling dumb and different, a young boy with a learning disability stumbles through school until he agrees to be retested and is given the special help he needs. This isn't an in-depth account, but it does offer a sympathetic and hopeful look at someone living with a learning disability. Humor lightens the mood, but the painful feelings that can result from repeated school failures are clearly drawn. Also effectively done is Sam's friendship with Alicia, who lacks friends because she thinks too much of herself, rather than too little. Oddly, the story is written in the first person (quite a feat for someone who can't read or write), but most readers will not notice this discrepancy.

Ages 9-11

**Also available in:**
Cassette—*Do Bananas Chew Gum?*
Library of Congress (NLSBPH)

Paperbound—*Do Bananas Chew Gum?*
Pocket Books, Inc.

## 217

**Girion, Barbara**

**A Handful of Stars**

Charles Scribner's Sons, 1981.
(179 pages)

---

*EPILEPSY*
*Boy-girl relationships: dating*
*Family: relationships*
*Maturation*
*School: classmate relationships*
*School: pupil-teacher relationships*

---

Julie Meyers, in cap and gown waiting for high school graduation ceremonies to begin, reminisces about a time early in her sophomore year. It is during a party at Elyssa Winston's house that Julie suddenly begins walking in circles, talking about algebra and then pounding on the door. Afterwards, she has no recollection of anything. One day she finds herself in the gym holding a notebook she doesn't recognize. After several more episodes, Julie begins to wonder if she's going crazy. But how could she be, she, Julie Meyers, member of the "in" crowd, one of the stars of the first school play, the object of Steve Marks's attentions! At the tryouts for *Guys and Dolls,* the spring play for which parts usually go to juniors and seniors, Julie gets an enthusiastic response to her audition. The next day, increasingly worried about her health, she sees Dr. Carlson, a neurologist, who administers a number of tests. Dr. Carlson explains to Julie and her parents that Julie has epilepsy. "The word epilepsy dropped into that room like a punch in the stomach." Dr. Carlson gives her medication and the family is relieved to think the pills will stop her spells. Several days later, Julie is delighted to learn she got a part in *Guys and Dolls.* But that evening she has another

seizure, this time right in front of a horrified Steve. When she recovers he is polite but distant. Julie remembers her extreme sense of isolation: "As if I was struggling alone in some deep dark tunnel." Every time she has a seizure Dr. Carlson readjusts her medication. After a basketball game, the kids try to coax her into having some beer. Knowing that alcohol could be very dangerous combined with her medications, Julie pretends to drink some and spills the rest. Her parents and grandmother watch her constantly and the household revolves around Julie and her spells, to her older sister Nancy's growing resentment. Then Julie has a particularly public seizure, in the school cafeteria. She hears the kids talking about her, calling her names. Ms. Barish, the drama teacher and Julie's idol, finds her crying behind the stage. When Julie confides in her, the woman "relieves" her of her part in the play—she will not risk a seizure in the middle of a production. Her cowardice is hard for the girl to accept. Little by little, Julie's life begins to shred "the way a tissue will when it's held under a water faucet." Classmates are nice enough in school, but Julie is no longer included in parties and extracurricular activities. The night *Guys and Dolls* opens, Julie feels her heart is truly breaking. Several weeks later Elyssa invites Julie to a slumber party. But that Friday Julie has a seizure in school, and Elyssa's mother calls Julie's mother to say it would probably be better if Julie didn't sleep overnight. Julie locks herself in her bedroom all weekend and meticulously cuts up her new pajamas. She also dumps all her pills in the wastebasket, though later she retrieves a few. She withdraws even more from those around her. During her junior year, Julie's parents send her to visit Nancy, now a freshman at Duke University. With Nancy and her friends, who don't seem to care about her epilepsy or her pills, Julie feels more like her old self. At a fraternity party, she meets freshman David Seegar, who takes her announcement about her epilepsy very calmly. They dance and talk and plan to keep in touch, possibly to see each other during Christmas vacation. That visit doesn't materialize, but David does manage to come at the end of Julie's junior year and Julie falls in love with him. During her senior year, Julie is accepted at three universities, including Duke. Duke seems such a safe choice: Nancy and David are there to smooth her way. But Julie decides that a safe choice isn't necessarily a good one; she will attend Colgate instead. Her parents are upset but her grandmother, who has so often come to her rescue, insists that Julie must be allowed to make her own decisions. David attends her graduation ceremony, and Julie looks forward with confidence to whatever the future brings.

When a teenage girl learns she has epilepsy, she must cope not only with unexpected seizures and continual medication, but with the ignorance and small cruelties of classmates and adults. Julie tells her own story in flashbacks and, although in her case it's epilepsy that sets her apart, it is the story of any teenager ostracized by peers. Well-written and perceptive, the book presents an accurate picture of epilepsy, its symptoms, treatment, and social implications, without obscuring a compelling story about growing up. It is dedicated to the author's son Eric, "who faced it all with courage and grace."

Ages 12 and up

Also available in:
Paperbound—*A Handful of Stars*
Dell Publishing Company, Inc.

## 218

Girion, Barbara

**Like Everybody Else**

Charles Scribner's Sons, 1980.
(169 pages)

---

FAMILY: Relationships
LIFE STYLE
    Friendship: best friend
    Jewish
    Maturation
    Parent/Parents: mother working outside home
    School: classmate relationships

---

Samantha Gold, Sam to her friends, is twelve-and-a-half and wants to be like everybody else. Her best friend, Sue Ellen, has a mother who stays home all day, cooks and bakes for the family, and even has matching towels in the bathroom. Sam's mother, Eileen, is a well-known writer of children's books. That is fine with Sam. What bothers her is that the house is only clean when the housekeeper comes, the family eats TV dinners and fast foods, and the towels in the bathroom never match. Sam feels responsible for Eileen's health and nutrition, mothering her mother with snacks and encouraging her to eat. But Sam's life is hectic too. She has just started junior high and also goes to Hebrew school to prepare for her Bat Mitzvah the following April. What's more, she has decided to run for student council, her mother has just written an adult love story, and *People* magazine is coming to interview the whole family. During the magazine interview, Sam discovers that her mother's new book is more than just an adult love story; it is about marital infidelity and includes explicit sex. Hugely embarrassed, Sam is sure she will have "to go to another planet to get away from being Eileen Gold's daughter." Once the news about Eileen's book gets around, Sam quits the student council race and tries to endure the teasing at school and the weird phone calls. She desperately wants to confide her troubles to her mother, but decides not to add to Eileen's burdens. Eileen is miserable over her bad reviews and the adverse reactions to her book in the community. Finally, after a fight with Sam's father, Eileen announces that she is hereby quitting and will write no more. Ignoring the typewriter in the back room, Sam's mother begins cooking and cleaning for all she's worth. Because everything is so crazy at home and at school, Sam concentrates on her Bat Mitzvah speech. One day her mother discovers the speech and, when the family discusses some of Sam's thoughts, is overwhelmed by the simple truths her daughter has expressed. Sam has written, "The important thing is to find out what kind of woman you are and not let anyone stop you." Eileen realizes that writing is what she loves, not housework. The family's old routine resumes with Sam's mother typing and Sam worrying about her—but happy to be doing just that.

A young girl who hates being different from her peers teaches her busy mother something about being true to oneself, learning at the same time that her unconventional family life is just fine with her. This is a warm, funny first-person narrative. The characters and situations are believable and should appeal to the intended audience.

Ages 10-13

Also available in:
Paperbound—*Like Everybody Else*
Dell Publishing Company, Inc.

## 219

Girion, Barbara

**Misty and Me**

Charles Scribner's Sons, 1979.
(139 pages)

---

BABY-SITTING: Involuntary
PETS: Responsibility for
SECRET, KEEPING
    Age: aging
    Friendship: meaning of
    Honesty/Dishonesty
    Parent/Parents: mother working outside home
    Sibling: older

---

Eleven-year-old Kim Bowman initiates a secret plan to make her dream of owning a dog come true. Kim's mother has decided to return to work, and both parents feel Kim will have her hands full before and after school baby-sitting for Willie, her six-year-old brother, and helping with other chores. They think Kim should postpone getting a dog. Kim is determined to change their minds, despite "Willie the Whiner." One day after school, Kim and Willie visit the animal shelter, just to have a look. Unable to resist the idea of adopting a puppy, Kim tells Norman, the man in charge, that she wants to be placed on the waiting list. Not long after, she learns a puppy is available. To raise the money she'll need for the dog's registration fee, shots, veterinarian, and food, Kim takes Willie's milk money and the PTA dues her mother had given her. She plans to pay this back from the money she's earning baby-sitting for Willie. Knowing she can't yet bring a puppy home, Kim enlists an elderly neighbor, Mrs. Macvey, who does odd jobs to supplement her Social Security income, to take care of the dog for six dollars a week. When they arrive to pick up the puppy, Kim tells Norman, who won't give them the dog without their parents' consent, that Mrs. Mac, waiting outside the shelter, is their grandmother. Willie and Kim are delighted with the "mostly beagle" puppy they name Misty. Every day after school they rush to Mrs. Mac's house to feed Misty, take her for walks, and help Mrs. Mac. Kim can't resist letting her two friends, Lisa and Eddie, in on the secret. Lately Lisa, always Kim's best friend, has only been interested in things like shopping, makeup, and boys, and the two had been drifting apart. Sharing the excitement of Misty renews their friendship. Keeping a secret puppy costs more than Kim had anticipated, and she has to use half of her disco class money to cover the additional expenses. Several weeks later, the puppy is secret no longer. Late one night, two policemen arrive at the Bowmans' home with Misty, and Kim is awakened to explain the situation to her parents. Mrs. Mac has

G

suffered a heart attack and asked the policemen in the first-aid squad to take Misty to Kim. The Bowmans, very disappointed in their daughter's behavior, finally agree to keep Misty, and Kim promises to repay all the money she has taken. Kim and Willie have become very attached to Mrs. Mac and are concerned about her health. It is decided that the woman will go to live with her daughter in Ohio. On the day she is to leave, the Bowman family comes to say goodbye. Aching for Mrs. Macvey, who is leaving all she loves, Kim impulsively gives her the dog they both love, to make the move easier.

This uncomplicated first-person narrative captures a young girl's love for her puppy. Although she gets immersed in the complexities of deceit as she struggles to care for her secret pet, Kim fulfills her responsibilities faithfully. Along the way, she and her little brother draw closer together, and she learns enough about love and loss to be able to give Misty away to the ailing Mrs. Mac. Anecdotes about Kim and her classmates add interest.

Ages 10-12

Also available in:
Paperbound—*Misty and Me*
Scholastic Book Services

## 220

Girion, Barbara

**A Tangle of Roots**

Charles Scribner's Sons, 1979.
(154 pages)

---

*DEATH: of Mother*
*MOURNING, STAGES OF*
  *Boy-girl relationships: dating*
  *Family: unity*
  *Friendship: best friend*
  *Jewish*
  *Maturation*

---

When sixteen-year-old Beth Frankle is called out of class by the principal and told her mother is dead, she is sure there must be some mistake. But there is no mistake; Beth's young mother has died instantly from a cerebral hemorrhage. Beth and her father, grandmother, and Aunt Nina somehow manage to stumble through the funeral and the week of Shiva, the traditional Jewish period of mourning. When Beth returns to school, Joyce, her best friend, and Kenny, her boyfriend, try to help her adjust to her mother's death. But Beth cannot. She misses her mother terribly, she hates seeing her father so sad and lonely, and she resents her grandmother's attempts to take over their household. Then Beth's father, trying to recover, invites her to go with him into New York City from their home in New Jersey for an evening of fun. Beth would rather go out with Kenny, but feels she must accompany her father. Although she has a good time, she realizes again how lonely her father is. Her emotions receive another jolt when she hears from Joyce that Kenny was with someone else that night. At Thanksgiving her father invites her to go with him on a business-vacation trip to Miami. This time too Beth would rather stay home with Kenny but, although she feels torn, she chooses to go with her

father. In Miami she is disturbed when Stacy Arnold, a business associate, seems to be interested in her father. Beth accepts a date with a tennis pro, but ends it early and abruptly when he tries to seduce her. She begins to see that she is angry at her mother for dying and causing her this emotional upheaval. Back home, Beth learns that Kenny has begun dating another girl. As the weeks pass, Beth sees her father looking happier and going out more. She is glad, yet fears that he is already forgetting her mother. Beth is also afraid that her father's increasingly independent life will leave her all alone. Over Christmas vacation, her father goes on a ski trip to Vermont with Stacy and some other couples. On New Year's Eve day, Beth is filled with loneliness as she remembers how her father always gave her mother a dozen yellow roses on this day. Terribly sad, she asks Aunt Nina to drive her to the cemetery. Alone at her mother's grave, she discovers a dozen yellow roses under the newly fallen snow. She sees that, although his life has to go on, her father still loves and misses her mother. Relieved and somehow comforted, Beth leaves the cemetery.

A girl shares her feelings of grief, anger, guilt, and loneliness following the sudden death of her mother. Stricken anew by the breakup with her boyfriend, Beth at first resists her father's efforts to recover from his grief and go on living. But time and a moving visit to her mother's grave help her come to some acceptance of what has happened. Beth is a compassionate, believable narrator, and her story is enriched by details of Jewish family life.

Ages 12-16

Also available in:
Paperbound—*A Tangle of Roots*
Dell Publishing Company, Inc.

## 221

Goldman, Susan

**Grandpa and Me Together**

Color illustrations by the author.
Albert Whitman & Company, 1980.
(32 pages counted)

---

*GRANDPARENT: Love for*

---

Katherine, about six, is visiting her grandparents. Today, while Grandma attends an art show, Katherine will have Grandpa all to herself. As always, Grandpa has planned special things for them to do together. This time they will stop at the store where Grandpa used to work and then go to a baseball game. At the store, while Grandpa helps solve a problem in the shipping department, Katherine types him a letter that says, "I love you, Grandpa." At the baseball game, Grandpa gives Katherine money to pay for the tickets and to buy their hot dogs and peanuts. On the way home, the two sing Grandpa's old college song. Grandpa does special things for Katherine throughout the day. That night, as he and Grandma give the little girl her bath, Grandpa even powders Katherine's toes.

A little girl tells about the special friendship she has with her grandfather. This charming story might prompt a read-aloud audience to tell of similar experiences with grandparents. Soft, uncluttered illustrations will hold the attention of young children.

Ages 2-6

**Also available in:**
Large Print—*Grandpa and Me Together*
Albert Whitman & Company

## 222

**Gordon, Shirley**

### The Boy Who Wanted a Family

Black/white illustrations by Charles Robinson.
Harper & Row, Publishers, Inc., 1980.
(90 pages)

---

*ADOPTION: Feelings About*
  *Anxiety*
  *Change: accepting*
  *Change: new home*
  *Foster home*
  *Parent/Parents: single*

---

Michael wants a real family with real parents. Instead he lives in various foster homes and never knows when he will be moving again. At a birthday party for several foster children at the social service office, Michael's wish when he blows out the candles on his cake—he is seven—is to be adopted. One day shortly after the party, Miss Finch, his social worker, takes him to meet Miss Graham, who wants to adopt him. When Michael learns she is single and a writer, he fears she won't be the ordinary mother he craves. But then he remembers he is not an ordinary boy. Michael and Miss Graham are introduced and then left alone to get acquainted. They talk, see the room that would be his, wash her car, and drive to a hot-dog stand for lunch. Miss Finch returns and tells Michael that it will take a year for the adoption to become legal. Twice before, the boy was almost adopted. The first family couldn't get along with him. The second simply changed their minds, hurting him deeply and making him wary. But Michael moves in with his new "mom" and makes friends in the neighborhood and at school. By Christmas Michael's fear of rejection has eased. But one day he asks Miss Graham why his real mother didn't want him. Miss Graham explains, "No one knows about your real mother, Michael. . . . But sometimes a mother can't keep her baby because she doesn't have a place for him. . . . I'm sure she would have kept you if she could." She herself is very glad to have Michael, she tells him. At the end of the year Miss Graham signs the adoption papers. She and Michael then go to court, where a judge makes the adoption legal. After a big hug, Michael and his mother start planning for the future.

Weary of a succession of foster homes, Michael longs to be adopted. His trial year with Miss Graham eases his anxieties about change and rejection. The story presents no real adjustment problems for Michael or his new mother, but it is a touching account and could help explain adoption to children. Notable is the fact that a single woman adopts Michael, suggesting the various possibilities on the adoption scene today. Pencil sketches add interest.

Ages 7-9

**Also available in:**
Paperbound—*The Boy Who Wanted a Family*
Dell Publishing Company, Inc.

## 223

**Gould, Marilyn**

### Golden Daffodils

Addison-Wesley Publishing Company, Inc., 1982.
(172 pages)

---

*CEREBRAL PALSY*
*SCHOOL: Mainstreaming*
  *Epilepsy*
  *Friendship: meaning of*
  *School: classmate relationships*
  *Teasing*

---

Janis Ward, who has cerebral palsy, is attending a regular school for the first time and wants badly to be perfect—no limp, no funny wrist, no epileptic seizures, no facial twitches. When she needs bright, happy thoughts she imagines golden daffodils. But she's discouraged on her very first day in the fifth grade at Wilson School. Her teacher asks Rhoda, Janis's overly helpful cousin and now her classmate, to do things for her that Janis could do and prefers to do herself. From the beginning, two classmates, Cheryl and Garth, make life difficult for Janis, tripping her, calling her names, pinching her. But Barney Fuchs befriends her. Barney has a special interest in Janis because his brother, David, has returned from Vietnam a paraplegic and now won't leave his room or be helped in any way. In a hasty reaction to one of Cheryl's put-downs, Janis challenges Cheryl and Garth to a handball match against her and Barney during the school's upcoming Junior Olympics Day. Though Janis was a good handball player at her old school, she isn't very optimistic about beating Cheryl and Garth. Then Barney talks Janis into visiting his brother. At first she resents his request, accusing him of befriending her only as a way of influencing his brother. But Barney replies firmly that he is her friend because he likes her. Janis agrees to ask David, a former coach, for some tips on how to win the handball match. David proves less than cordial, but he does provide some pointers. When Janis returns to her old school for her swimming therapy she's surprised at how changed everything seems. She doesn't feel she belongs anymore. Later, in talking with her mother, she realizes that the school hasn't changed: she has. Her world is expanding. Janis and Barney begin practicing for the handball match, coached at times by Janis's athletic older sister, Stell. Several days before the match, Janis and Barney practice before school as usual. They have always stopped before anyone else arrived on the playground, but this morning they forget the time. Cheryl, Garth, Rhoda, and several others arrive. Cheryl and Garth begin their taunts, Barney and Garth fight, Garth trips Janis, and Rhoda pulls Garth off. That weekend, Janis and Barney take the train to visit their grandparents, who live in the same town. On a visit to the beach, Janis tries to follow Barney into the deep water and has to be rescued by her grandfather. He cautions her that what's safe for other people

**G**

may not be safe for her. The morning of Junior Olympics Day is so hectic at home that Janis forgets to take her anti-seizure medicine. Cheryl and Garth begin the long-awaited handball match with a quick nine points. But then Janis and Barney start concentrating and play a great game, winning 21 to 17. As their victory is being announced, Janis has a seizure. Recovering at home the next day, mortified at having made a spectacle of herself, she rails against life's unfairness. Her father agrees that life isn't fair and that there are some things she may never be able to do. But he reassures Janis of her family's love. Stell adds her love and support as Janis reads get-well notes from her classmates. Barney comes by bearing a beautiful daffodil with a champion's blue ribbon on it. He challenges Janis to a game of handball and she accepts—but warns him that she intends to win.

A young girl with cerebral palsy is mainstreamed for the first time and overcomes the natural obstacles imposed by her condition, as well as some very unnatural obstacles presented by a couple of cruel, spoiled classmates. Some of the dialogue and situations here may seem a bit contrived, but Janis's first-person story allows readers to enter the life of a disabled person. Primarily the story of a young girl with grit, only secondarily about a child with cerebral palsy, this is a worthy addition to readable stories with handicapped protagonists.

Ages 8-12

**Also available in:**
No other form known

## 224

Graber, Richard Fredrick

**Black Cow Summer**

Harper & Row, Publishers, Inc., 1980.
(212 pages)

---

BOY-GIRL RELATIONSHIPS: Dating
  Harassment
  Loss: feelings of
  Love, meaning of
  Prejudice: social class

---

It is the Depression year of 1938 and Ray Decker is beginning his sixteenth summer in Rock River, a small town in Minnesota. Ray's prime interest this summer is Mary Ellen Brandt, who has recently moved with her remarried mother from Missouri to a farm in Rock River. Ray adores the independent Mary Ellen, but the girl's three rough, boisterous stepbrothers, especially Claude, the oldest, vigorously oppose this relationship with a "town boy." They harass Ray on several painful occasions, roughing him up, forcing liquor down him, taking him for a wild ride perched on their car's running board. Further opposition comes from Ray's nagging, at times meddlesome, mother who considers Mary Ellen an Ozark hillbilly. Despite all this interference, the two young people continue to see each other, often over black cow sodas at Dawson's Drugstore. Then Mary Ellen's stepfather, Rudi Brandt, dies of pneumonia. Ray is reconciled with the Brandt family—even Claude drops his hostility—as he shares their feelings of sorrow and loss. The farm is sold, and Mary Ellen and her mother prepare to return to Missouri where they have

relatives and friends. Claude will leave the farm, but the other two brothers will work as tenant farmers for the new owners. Just before they must part, Ray and Mary Ellen become lovers and Ray asks the girl to marry him. She is amazed at his proposal. "Just look at what has happened in the past few months!" she exclaims. Although they hope to continue their relationship, they must accept an uncertain future. The summer ends with Ray possessing a deeper understanding of friendship, love, and loss.

With humor, candor, and vivid characterizations, a romantic and awkward teenage boy relates his thoughts and feelings about an important summer in his life. This is the third novel about Ray Decker, and it is a first-person account of relationships rather than a heavily plotted story. The frequent use of dialogue, occasionally including profanity, may be cumbersome to some readers, especially since thoughts are not always distinguished from speech. Readers may also find Claude's transformation somewhat contrived. The sexual incident is presented tastefully.

Ages 12 and up

**Also available in:**
No other form known

## 225

Grace, Fran

**Branigan's Dog**

Bradbury Press, Inc., 1981.
(189 pages)

---

COMMUNICATION: Lack of
PETS: Love for
REALITY, ESCAPING
  Anger
  Death: of pet
  Detention home, living in
  Identity, search for
  Parent/Parents: remarriage of
  School: classmate relationships

---

Casey Branigan, fifteen, considers his dog, called D-Dog, his partner and best friend. Instead of talking directly to people, Casey either looks somewhere else or talks through D-Dog. He imagines that he and D-Dog live in the Old West and ride the range together. Being with D-Dog is infinitely preferable to being at home. Casey loathes his stepfather, Rush, and Rush's young daughter, Melanie. Although Casey continues to be an honors student who peppers his speech with ready quotes from famous writers, he spends more and more time fantasizing about his English teacher, seeing the two of them as lovers in the Old West. In real life, however, Candy Sweetwater traps Casey into taking her to the Senior Court Dance. Since he doesn't want to go, Casey is relieved when he's grounded for setting fire to some of Melanie's clothes. Unfortunately, as part of his punishment he must take Candy to the dance. There Candy mortifies Casey by sneaking off with Thad Duvall, a black athlete from school. A few nights later a cross is burned on the Duvall lawn. Thad's best friend says he knows who did it. The following day the school paper prints a large article suggesting that Casey is the culprit. A police officer questions Casey, but no charges are filed. Still, the article has raised questions in everyone's mind. Feeling humiliated, Casey decides to take D-Dog and go north to Berkeley where his father lives, although he hasn't seen the man in seven years. He discovers his father living with a woman and drinking heavily; the discovery upsets him into "accidentally" setting the curtains on fire. Since his father is cool and remote with him, Casey is thrilled when he suggests the two go camping. But the experience ends badly when his drunken father screams at him and then disappears. Casey flies home the next day. On the way home from the airport, he and his mother stop at a roadside stand. D-Dog runs after a rabbit and eats it. When Casey finds the dog, she is lying quietly in a field. On the way to the vet she dies in his arms of strychnine poisoning. Two weeks later, still distraught, Casey lights a fire in his wastebasket in an attempt to recreate an Old West campfire—he can no longer daydream about the West unless he lights a fire first. He falls asleep and is rescued, unconscious, by Rush. Both are treated at the hospital; the house is heavily damaged. The neighbors, whose garage and fence were also damaged, charge Casey with arson. He is sent to a reform school, Camp Kenyon, for four months. There he begins regular sessions with a counselor, Mr. Wells. The boy remains uncommunicative, staring off into space, until Mr. Wells goads him by mentioning his love for D-Dog and his setting the house on fire. Enraged, Casey screams back at him. From then on, Mr. Wells helps him begin to evaluate his actions and find alternative ways to express his anger. When his four months are up, Casey can look directly at people, no longer needs his fantasies, and sets no more fires. Delighted to learn he's been exonerated from starting the burning cross at the Duvalls' house, Casey begins to help Rush repair their home. "We're better than a family now," he reports. "It looks as though we're on the way to being friends."

An angry, frustrated boy sets fires and lives in a fantasy world as a way of escaping from an intolerable reality. A skillful therapist helps Casey become reconciled to his parents' divorce, his dog's death, and his need to find constructive outlets for his anger. Careful research into Casey's brand of pyromania is evident in this well-written, realistic narrative. Casey's story lets readers sympathize with him and recognize his need for help. This is a serious book about a profoundly troubled boy; the text includes some profanity and several brief sexual encounters.

Ages 10 and up

**Also available in:**
Braille—*Branigan's Dog*
Library of Congress (NLSBPH)

Cassette—*Branigan's Dog*
Library of Congress (NLSBPH)

**226**
**Graeber, Charlotte Towner**

**Grey Cloud**
Black/white illustrations by Lloyd Bloom.
Four Winds Press, 1979.
(124 pages)

---

*CHANGE: New Home*
*LIFE STYLE: Change in*
*Animals: responsibility for*
*Friendship: meaning of*
*Responsibility: accepting*

---

In all his twelve years, Tom has never met anyone like tall, thin, solitary, bespectacled Orville Breen. To Tom, Orville is as strange as the rural countryside Tom now unwillingly calls home. Tom's family has recently moved from the city after his father had a heart attack and required a quieter life style. Tom has found an injured pigeon—banded, so he is obligated to find its owner. When he is told by his sister that Orville raises racing pigeons, Tom reluctantly comes to him with the bird. Orville takes the injured pigeon, names it Grey Cloud, and says little else. The boy lives with his mother and works the Breen farm alone, although he is scarcely older than Tom. Despite his distaste for country living, Tom is drawn to the Breen farm and slowly enters Orville's world. Fascinated at Orville's being able to drive, Tom accompanies him on long truck rides to release pigeons on training flights and gradually begins to help out with the farm chores. Tom's growing attachment to the routine is briefly interrupted when he falls in with classmates more like those he associated with in the city. But he soon parts company with them when they call Orville names and say Mr. Breen is in an insane asylum. Tom learns that in fact Orville's father is in a VA hospital, a piece of shrapnel in his brain, unable even to recognize his own family. Tom's fascination with driving is put to a test when Orville has an attack of appendicitis while driving the truck and Tom must drive him home. While Orville recuperates in the hospital from his emergency surgery, Tom does the farm chores, caring for Orville's birds and continuing their training. Disaster strikes, however, when the boys from school come over and dare Tom to prove he can drive. Leaving the pigeon loft open and unprotected, Tom drives off. He returns to find that the cat has killed the prize racer and mauled Grey Cloud. Tom's fury at the cat wears off quickly enough, but his personal anger and guilt do not: he knows he let Orville down. He is immensely relieved when Orville, after hearing the news, forgives him. With their best racer dead, the boys don't expect much from the first race of the season. But to their surprise, one of Orville's pigeons places second. With the prize money, Orville buys back his father's breeding pigeons, which he had been forced to sell for feed, something Tom never knew. Then Orville gives Grey Cloud to Tom.

Tom's unhappiness with his unfamiliar rural environment turns to satisfaction when he befriends the solitary

G

Orville Breen and begins to share his interests and values in this convincing, quietly told story. The emphasis on plot over introspection and the relatively plain writing style should appeal to many readers.

Ages 9-11

**Also available in:**
No other form known

## 227

### Graeber, Charlotte Towner

## Mustard

Black/white illustrations by Donna Diamond.
Macmillan Publishing Company, Inc., 1982.
(42 pages)

---

DEATH: of Pet
  Communication: parent-child
  Loss: feelings of

---

Eight-year-old Alex insists that his family's cat, Mustard, is not really getting old. He accuses his younger sister, Annie, of bothering the cat. But when Mustard is taken for a check-up, the veterinarian says his heart is not as strong as it used to be; Mustard must take medicine and shouldn't be subjected to any stress. Unfortunately, a few days later, the big dog belonging to the newspaper boy corners Mustard and frightens him so badly he suffers a heart attack. That night Alex has Mustard sleep next to him. The boy is awakened in the middle of the night by strange noises. He finds Mustard walking back and forth in the closet, making awful crying noises and bumping into the walls. He can't seem to see or to walk straight. For the rest of that night, Alex's parents keep Mustard in their room. The next morning Mustard looks worse, but Alex must go to school while his father takes Mustard to the vet. His parents warn Alex that Mustard will probably not get better and that the best the vet can do is make his death painless. Alex comes home from school to see his father standing in the backyard with a small box and a shovel. Alex looks at Mustard one last time, and then they bury him. Alex keeps Mustard's collar and Annie his catnip mouse, but Alex and his father take the rest of Mustard's things to the animal shelter. When the woman there hears about the loss of their pet, she asks if they'd like a kitten. Alex and his father agree they aren't yet ready for another cat. Maybe next year.

Fine pencil drawings distinguish this story of how a boy and his family cope with the illness and death of a much-loved pet. Alex is supported by parents who share his grief, show their own, and are honest about what is happening to Mustard. The book could be helpful to children whose pet has died or is old and ill.

Ages 4-10

**Also available in:**
Paperbound—Mustard
Bantam Books, Inc.

## 228

### Graham, Ada and Frank Graham

## Jacob and Owl

Black/white photographs by Frank and Dorothea Stoke.
Coward, McCann & Geoghegan, Inc., 1981.
(63 pages)

---

ANIMALS: Love for
  Divorce: of parents
  Friendship: lack of
  Maturation
  Pets: substitute for human relationship

---

Eleven-year-old Jacob and his mother have lived in their northern New England town for three months and Jacob still has not made any friends at school, just as he had not made any friends the previous summer at camp. Reaching out for friendship is difficult for the independent, solitude-loving Jacob. One day he overhears two boys on the bus talking about an owl they've seen in Clark's woods. Jacob takes the first opportunity to go looking for it. The owl appears to be wounded, and Jacob carries it home in his jacket. His mother points out that wild creatures aren't like pets and that he can't keep the owl in the house. Jacob is hurt; he and his mother have been particularly close since his father left them and moved to California. Finally she agrees to let Jacob keep Owl in the shed. At first Owl won't eat, but Jacob is very patient and wins him over. The boy reads a lot about owls over the next three months, and Owl becomes a very important part of his life. One day his mother takes him to a nearby bird sanctuary where the proprietor, Mr. Redmond, tells him that injured wild birds must eventually be turned over either to a government agency or to a licensed sanctuary. Jacob, angry at his mother's bringing him there, insists he won't give up Owl. During a severe winter storm, Owl escapes through a broken window. Weeks pass and the bird doesn't return. Jacob is inconsolable. Then, a month after he left, Owl returns, hungry and bedraggled, but alive. Jacob's mother asks him to go with her once again to the sanctuary. Jacob is still determined not to give up Owl, but he goes. Mr. Redmond assures Jacob that he could come and help out at the sanctuary any time he liked. Then Jacob's father writes and invites him to come to California for a visit after school is out. Jacob worries about leaving Owl, but his mother observes that he soon must make a decision about Owl anyway. Owl needs more freedom and care than they can give him, she explains; he needs to be with other owls. Jacob begins helping Mr. Redmond on Saturdays. One day he tells the man that he won't be able to help out for a while because he'll be going to California. Soon after, he brings Owl to the sanctuary. Before he leaves on his trip, Jacob stops by to visit Owl, telling Mr. Redmond that Owl looks good. "It was his way of saying 'thank you' to the older man." Jacob mentions that his new friend, Nelson, has lent him a book to read on the plane. When Mr. Redmond notes that Owl was lucky to have found Jacob for a friend, Jacob replies that he was lucky too.

A boy who has trouble making friends takes in an injured owl and then must make a decision about the animal's future. Gradually, helped by the patience and kindness of his mother, Jacob learns the meaning of friendship: doing what's best for the other. At the same time, Jacob begins to adapt to his own life in a new community without his father. He makes a friend at school, agrees to a visit with his father, and is able to let Owl go—all clear steps in his maturation. Posed but natural-looking photographs illustrate an undidactic text that contains accurate and informative material on owls and other wild "pets."

Ages 8-11

**Also available in:**
No other form known

## 229

**Grant, Cynthia D.**

### Joshua Fortune

Atheneum Publishers, 1980.
(152 pages)

CHANGE: Resisting
LIFE STYLE: Change in
  Divorce: of parents
  Family: relationships
  Name, dissatisfaction with
  Parent/Parents: remarriage of

"I'd skate through life like mayonnaise on wheels if it weren't for my drippy name," says Joshua Fortune George, fourteen. His parents were Haight-Ashbury hippies when he was born and the family still lives there. Josh knows kids his age named Peace and Love; his younger sister is named Sarah Sunshine. Besides his name, Josh does not like the neighborhood, his family's casual apartment and life style, or his father's eagerness to travel. Eventually his father, Timothy, leaves for good and his mother, Suzanne, moves Josh and Sarah from apartment to apartment, each smaller and more run-down than the last. Finally Suzanne returns to school and gets a teaching degree. By then she has divorced Timothy, and Josh's "Phantom Father" only rarely sends them postcards. When Suzanne meets Harley Frazier, a toy salesman, she moves the children to Santa Rosa to live near him. Josh calls Harley "Frog Man" because when Harley gets mad he blows up like a bull-frog. And Harley gets mad at Josh a lot. Not only does Josh not like Harley, he is not crazy about the kids at his new high school. Still, although he thinks Alexa Wells is crazy and Richard Johnson weird, they soon become a threesome. To Josh's horror, Harley and Suzanne decide to marry. He protests until Suzanne finally tells him that she and Harley will marry and become a fam-ily whether Josh likes it or not. The boy dreams about his father returning to stop the marriage, but he buys Harley and Suzanne a frog cookie jar for a wedding gift. Josh's father shows up the day of the wedding with his new wife. Harley and Suzanne marry. As for Josh, he realizes life has to change and he has to get used to it.

Joshua has had many burdens to bear in his fourteen years, and his lively first-person narrative describes his painful adjustment. Interesting characters, vivid descriptions (occasionally laced with profanity), and a warm, funny tone distinguish this story, which the unat-tractive jacket cover does nothing to recommend. Read-ers will be glad they looked inside.

Ages 10-13

**Also available in:**
No other form known

## 230

**Grant, Eva**

### I Hate My Name

Color illustrations by Gretchen Mayo.
Raintree Publishers, Inc., 1980.
(31 pages)

NAME, DISSATISFACTION WITH
  Teasing

When Demelza Smith starts school she begins hating her name. Her classmates laugh when her name is called. Demelza's parents explain that she was named after her great-grandmother, a beauty and an accom-plished pianist. Demelza admires her great-grand-mother's pictures in the old photo album, but she still hates her name. The teasing at school continues and is more and more hurtful. Finally, Demelza's parents explain that when they named her, they gave her the middle initial "J." They tell Demelza to pick out any "J" name she likes and they will call her by it. Excitedly, Demelza tries on various names but finds something wrong with each of them. "They all sounded so . . . boring." Demelza decides that her own name is the most interesting. From then on, when she's teased, she stands up for herself. One day she overhears two girls talking. One insists she sees nothing wrong with the name Demelza. Demelza breaks in emphatically. "It may not be the most beautiful name in the world, but I think it's the most interesting!" She is surprised when some of her classmates cheer.

This spirited first-person narrative considers the prob-lems an unusual name can cause a child. Helped by her supportive parents, Demelza learns to take pride in her name. Although the resolution is oversimplified, the book would be appropriate for discussions about how teasing hurts. Colorful illustrations help sustain interest.

Ages 5-8

**Also available in:**
No other form known

## 231

**Grant, Eva**

### Will I Ever Be Older?

Color illustrations by Susan Lexa.
Raintree Publishers, Inc., 1981.
(31 pages)

SIBLING: Rivalry
  Sibling: love for
  Sibling: younger

David is seven and fears he will "never catch up" with his ten-year-old brother, Steven. David gets Steven's

G

hand-me-downs, and the jeans often have patches. He gets Steven's old soccer shoes, his old roller skates, even his former teachers, who compare the younger boy unfavorably with his brother. Sometimes his grandmother forgets and calls him Steven. David wishes that Steven didn't exist. One day, when David and his mother go to pick Steven up after soccer practice, Steven isn't there. His mother is worried but David is delighted: maybe they'll never find Steven and then he, David, will get to be the oldest. He asks his mother if it's possible for him ever to be older than Steven. She tells him it's not, but that perhaps being the oldest isn't always best. She explains that she and the boys' father had practiced child rearing on Steven because he was first. When Steven was David's age, he had to go to bed much earlier than David does now. As David starts to look for Steven, the older boy runs out, eager to tell his mother that he's been selected to attend a soccer clinic that weekend. On Saturday, David finds there's nobody to kick the soccer ball around with. Steven's not there to fix his roller skates or to watch a favorite show with him. When his brother finally comes home, David admits, "I was surprised at how nice it felt to have Steven back." After they're in bed for the night, David tells Steven how he feels about the hand-me-downs and about Grandma forgetting his name. Half asleep, Steven confesses that sometimes Grandma forgets and calls him David!

This gentle, low-key account of sibling rivalry is narrated by the younger brother and provides a simple example of what can become a more serious problem. David begins by detailing his complaints about being number two in the family, but ends by showing that he does love and appreciate his brother. An introductory page for parents and teachers suggests that the story "will stimulate many discussions, as it provides a useful reminder to both parent and child of the universal nature of the sibling experience." The illustrations are outstanding: charming, detailed, appealing.

Ages 5-8

**Also available in:**
No other form known

## 232

**Grant, Jan**

### Our New Baby

Color illustrations by Phillip Lanier.
Children's Press, Inc., 1980.
(31 pages)

*SIBLING: New Baby*

A little girl knows her mother looks the way she does because she is going to have a baby. Lately, both her parents have been so busy getting ready for this new baby that they have no time for her. Last week they told her she would have to share her room with the baby. She doesn't want to. Her parents think it will be fun to have a new child. The little girl doesn't think it's going to be fun at all. Why does her mother want a new baby when she has her? One day, the girl goes with her mother to the doctor. "The new baby in your family will

be lucky to have a big sister like you," Dr. Foley says, giving her a book about babies. Then he lets her listen to the baby's heartbeat through a stethoscope and has her put her hand on her mother's stomach to feel the baby move. She is much happier when she leaves Dr. Foley's office. Her brother, Steven, is born on Sunday, and on Monday the girl goes to the hospital to see him and visit her mother. She had expected Steven to be bigger so she could play with him. After her mother comes home, many people come by with presents for Steven. Angrily, the little girl wonders why everyone is making such a fuss over "a dumb old baby" who "can't even do anything." After everyone leaves, her mother sits and talks with her, recalling how everyone brought presents to the girl when she was a baby. She and her mother talk and laugh. Then Steven starts to cry and won't stop. His sister has an idea—she rocks the cradle and sings her favorite song. The baby stops crying. Happy now, the little girl decides, "Mom and Dad are really going to need my help with our new baby."

A young child tells how neglected she feels as her parents prepare for their new baby. With a lot of understanding and support, including help from a perceptive obstetrician, she comes to join in the enthusiasm and begins to enjoy her role as big sister. Color photographs expand this short account, which could be helpful in preparing a child for the advent of a sibling.

Ages 4-7

**Also available in:**
No other form known

## 233

**Gray, Nigel**

### It'll All Come Out in the Wash

Color illustrations by Edward Frascino.
Harper & Row, Publishers, Inc., 1979.
(32 pages)

*HELPING*
*RESOURCEFULNESS*
*Family: unity*

Disaster results when a little girl tries to be helpful and grown-up. She gets paint in her hair when she "helps" her father paint a room and floods the kitchen when she "helps" wash dishes. When she pours juice, she pours juice everywhere. Breakfast in bed for her parents produces a jumble of cereal, milk, and bedsheets. "Look what you've done," her mother chides. But her father's refrain, "Don't worry, Love, that's how you learn. And it'll all come out in the wash," is comforting to the child as she learns it isn't the failure that counts, but the trying. Then she helps with the washing.

This warm, whimsical story will amuse and reassure children who have tried to be grown-up and found themselves wanting. Delightful, cartoonlike illustrations enhance the story. This is appealing read-aloud material.

Ages 4-6

**Also available in:**
No other form known

132

**234**

Green, Phyllis

**Gloomy Louie**

Black/white illustrations by John Wallner.
Albert Whitman & Company, 1980.
(63 pages)

CHANGE: Accepting
INFERIORITY, FEELINGS OF
SELF, ATTITUDE TOWARD: Accepting
  Family: relationships
  Helping
  Moving

Louie Bix, about ten, arrives home from his baseball game glum and disgusted with himself. Though his team won, all he can think about are his own two strike-outs. He is greeted with the news that his family is moving from Detroit to Phoenix. His mother has been promoted to vice-president of her company and is being transferred. His father, a teacher, has found another teaching job. Louie is immediately plunged into deeper gloom. He pictures deserts, cactuses, and snakes. His father talks with him about the sadness of moving from Detroit, but emphasizes the excitement of moving to Phoenix. Louie is not convinced. He worries about telling his best friend, Chubby, but Chubby seems unconcerned. Even Louie's mother, happy about the move and her promotion, cannot cheer him up. The next Saturday at the baseball game, gloomy Louie keeps striking out. He complains so much that finally his older brother, Base, names him the Doom King. "You're the gloomiest kid I ever saw." Base asks if Louie realizes how the rest of the family feels about the move. His father will have to teach first grade in Phoenix, although he teaches fifth grade in Detroit. He's not complaining. Both their parents are a bit apprehensive about the move but they're trying to be optimistic. That night, Louie overhears his parents talking about a person who is a loser and no fun. Since that's how he sees himself, he is sure they're talking about him. But when they realize he has overheard them they quickly explain they were discussing Mrs. Calaban, a crabby, gloomy neighbor for whom Louie mows grass. Louie thinks maybe he should figure out how to be happy. Several days later, while walking home from a baseball game, Louie discovers smoke coming from Mrs. Calaban's house. He rings the bell, pounds on the door, and finally stops a car, telling the driver to call the fire department. Then he breaks a window, crawls in, and rescues Mrs. Calaban by helping her out the bedroom window. Mrs. Calaban thanks Louie profusely for saving her life, vowing to turn over a new leaf and "live my life appreciating how lucky I am." Perhaps Louie should turn over the same new leaf. Filled with self-confidence after his heroic rescue, he decides he might even be happy in Phoenix.

A boy without much self-confidence resolves to overcome his characteristic gloominess and seek life's brighter side in this believable, lightly humorous story. A talk with his brother helps Louie realize that others in his family will make sacrifices when they move to Phoenix; a brave rescue allows him to feel better about himself. Simply drawn illustrations help convey Louie's moods.

Ages 8-9

**Also available in:**
No other form known

**235**

Greenberg, Jan

**The Iceberg and Its Shadow**

Farrar, Straus & Giroux, Inc., 1980.
(119 pages)

FRIENDSHIP: Best Friend
FRIENDSHIP: Meaning of
  Family: relationships
  Ostracism
  Peer relationships: peer pressures
  School: classmate relationships

Anabeth, a sixth grader at Skokie Elementary School, is one of the most popular girls at school. She is student council president, loves her teacher, Mrs. Thilling, and is best friends with Rachel. Although Anabeth is outgoing and Rachel quiet and withdrawn, they have been best friends since kindergarten. Then one day everything changes. Mindy—loud, aggressive, and bossy—moves to Skokie and joins their class. Anabeth finds her exciting. Before long Mindy is the unofficial class leader, disturbing others and demanding her own way. Soon Anabeth, Mindy, Carolyn, and Tracy dub themselves the "Fabulous Foursome," excluding Rachel because she has told Mrs. Thilling that Mindy copied her work. Anabeth feels guilty about ignoring Rachel and not defending her, but seems compelled to follow Mindy; she is half-afraid not to. "I felt like a rubber ball bouncing back and forth between them, but I didn't want to land on either side." Finally, Anabeth confronts Mindy about her bossiness and accuses her of being mean. At a class party later that day, Mindy, Carolyn, and Tracy ignore Anabeth and later harass her. They rename themselves the "Three Musketeers" and soon get others to shun Anabeth. Anabeth now realizes what Rachel must be feeling, but she is too embarrassed to apologize. Finally she breaks down and tells her parents the whole story. They've suspected that something was amiss and react with concern and support, helping Anabeth realize that as a leader in the class, she could have and should have stuck up for Rachel. By the end of the school year, Anabeth has managed to regain the respect of her classmates. Feeling confident at last, she calls Rachel to apologize and they agree to meet. Anabeth hopes to show Rachel she really cares.

Anabeth finds that the excitement of being notorious is less satisfying than a real friendship. When she herself is ostracized, she understands how unfair she has been toward her best friend. Told by Anabeth, this well-paced story is filled with humor, interesting characters, and satisfying family relationships. It describes problems of peer pressure common to this age group.

G

Ages 10-12

**Also available in:**
Paperbound—*The Iceberg and Its Shadow*
Dell Publishing Company, Inc.

## 236

### Greenberg, Jan

### The Pig-Out Blues

Farrar, Straus & Giroux, Inc., 1982.
(121 pages)

---

*WEIGHT CONTROL: Overweight*
  *Autonomy*
  *Boy-girl relationships*
  *Communication: parent-child*
  *Expectations*
  *Parent/Parents: power struggle with*
  *Parental: control*
  *Self-esteem*

---

At fifteen, Jodie Firestone is overweight, broke, and
bored. She lives in Connecticut with a beautiful mother,
Vanessa, who despises anything fat. Until Jodie was
thirteen she was a stringbean, but then as she stopped
growing taller she began to grow wider. Her mother
nags her constantly about being a walrus, which makes
Jodie run for the refrigerator. The girl's favorite activity
is the school drama group, and when they decide to
present *Romeo and Juliet,* Jodie decides to lose weight
so she can be Juliet. Her mother puts her on a strict diet;
the only restaurant in town she's allowed to patronize is
Mr. Wheatley's Health Food Store. She jogs with her
mother and takes a laxative every night before bed. She
loses twenty pounds. But the tryouts for the play are a
disaster. The role of Juliet goes to Maude St. James, a
newcomer from England—partly because while Jodie is
reading the part of Juliet she faints, and the director says
she needs to build herself back up before she can handle a heavy role. David Simms, older brother of Jodie's
best friend, Heather, gets the part of Romeo. Though
Jodie would love to play Juliet to his Romeo, on or off
stage, she is given the role of the old nurse. When she
gets home, her mother screams at her as if she lost the
role deliberately. The girl goes into hiding after that.
She skips school, forging a note of excuse, and spends
her days eating great quantities of food. The sympathetic Mr. Wheatley offers her a part-time job, and she
accepts it gratefully. But Vanessa doesn't want Jodie
working anywhere near food and considers waitressing
a low-status job. The two scream at each other and end
up physically fighting. After that, Vanessa leaves Jodie
alone. The girl returns to school and works at her job,
but the silent battle with her mother goes on. "With
every bite of food I took, I knew I was the loser, but I
couldn't stop. Why should I starve myself for her?"
Rehearsals are going very badly; Maude St. James is a
poor actress, unable to learn her lines or respond to
direction. When Jodie tries to help, Maude has a tantrum. Then life gets a little easier for Jodie. Wanda Sue,
a likeable and popular classmate who is even heavier
than Jodie, helps Jodie see that she can be loved despite
her size. Vanessa and Jodie hug each other for the first
time in years. When Vanessa and her friend decide to
spend two weeks in the Caribbean, Jodie stays with the
Simms, who give her a hearty welcome and seem to love

her for herself. After ten days of the family's normal,
healthy meals, Mr. Wheatley's sprout sandwiches, and
no Vanessa to nag her, Jodie is considerably thinner.
"There were moments when I was tempted to take a
second helping or sneak into the icebox, but no one
cared whether I did or not, so I didn't.'' One night when
she goes to the refrigerator for comfort after a stressful
dream, she says no to herself and wakes up the next
morning feeling strong and renewed. Vanessa writes a
letter admitting she's made mistakes and offering a
truce. The troubled production of *Romeo and Juliet* is
cancelled, and David, dogged by a sense of failure,
disappears. Jodie has heard him speak of spending days
in the Metropolitan Museum of Art in New York, two
hours away, and after he's been gone two days she goes
there and finds him. They talk and then take the train
home. Vanessa has returned. Jodie hates the thought of
going back home to their dingy apartment where everything will be the same. But then she realizes that if she
can change, situations can too. Maybe even Vanessa can
change. Her mother has brought her a yellow bed-
spread, the first time she's ever given Jodie anything that
wasn't a reward for losing weight or getting good grades.
She suggests that if she were Jodie, she'd redo her bedroom in bright colors. Jodie says quietly that she loves
the spread and will use it. However, she will consider
the color scheme more carefully before deciding. She is
not, after all, her mother.

An overweight teenager learns that she, not her fierce
mother, is in control of her body. Along the way she
learns that it's also up to her to choose her own values
and friends. Jodie's is a compelling first-person narrative with well-drawn characters, especially that of
Vanessa, who, though she's rather likeable, is actually a
verbally and psychologically abusive parent from whom
Jodie must free herself. Jodie's success with her weight
is entirely realistic as presented, although readers with
more serious weight problems may find her victory
superficial and unlikely. However, Jodie's weight problem is secondary to her struggle for autonomy, and her
efforts to define herself in the face of parental controls
will speak to many readers.

Ages 12 and up

**Also available in:**
Paperbound—*The Pig-Out Blues*
Dell Publishing Company, Inc.

## 237

### Greenberg, Jan

### A Season In-Between

Farrar, Straus & Giroux, Inc., 1979.
(150 pages)

---

*ILLNESSES: Terminal*
*MATURATION*
  *Anxiety*
  *Death: of father*
  *Family: unity*
  *School: classmate relationships*
  *Self, attitude toward: accepting*
  *Self, attitude toward: feeling different*

---

For as long as she can remember, thirteen-year-old Carrie Singer has been awkward, too tall, and teased by

other kids. In fourth grade Carrie decided to protect herself by adopting an indifferent attitude. By now she and Fran Steiner, the other Jewish student at Miss Elliot's Academy, stand leagued against the school and the middle-class values it epitomizes. Yet Carrie's moods continually shift. One moment she is withering in her criticism of Courtney Allen, a "golden girl"; the next, she considers Courtney to be perfection. Never before interested in boys, Carrie still convinces herself to avoid them. Secretly, though, she hopes Dewy Daumatt, an athletic neighbor, will ask her out. Easily hurt, Carrie just as quickly conceals the hurt with a wisecrack or an indifferent shrug. Her isolation deepens when her father, a warm and friendly man, must go away for cancer surgery, and Carrie's mother accompanies him. Carrie becomes increasingly troubled. She feuds constantly with Sonny, her eight-year-old brother; their live-in maid, Dorothy, is sorely tried to keep the peace. Carrie also does badly at school, and her parents' return does not lift her anxiety. The already strained relationship with her mother, to Carrie a cool perfectionist, deteriorates. Though her father steadily weakens, Carrie cannot break through her shell to tell him of her love and anxiety. One night she hears him coughing and buries her head under her pillow. Gradually, though, Carrie lets her feelings show. She tearfully tells Dewy her worries; she takes a night walk with her father and talks to him. He tells her that he too is frightened, but is grateful for his family's support. It is only after her father dies, however, that Carrie's anxiety dissolves under the pressure of her grief. She comes to see that behind her mother's cool exterior is a great need for her daughter. Carrie also understands Sonny's bewilderment at their father's death and comforts him. She helps as her mother takes over the father's business, and she and Dewy begin dating. More and more, Carrie learns to accept people for what they are—including herself.

A lonely, troubled young girl endures the illness and death of her father, pulling out of her grief and self-absorption as she gains insight into herself and the people around her. Carrie tells her own story with a serious, but not morbid, tone. Her maturation and the closer relationship developing with her mother provide an encouraging conclusion.

Ages 11-13

**Also available in:**
Paperbound—*A Season In-Between*
Dell Publishing Company, Inc.

## 238

Greene, Bette

### Get On Out of Here, Philip Hall

The Dial Press, Inc., 1981.
(150 pages)

---

BOASTING
LEADER/LEADERSHIP
  Boy-girl relationships
  Clubs
  Peer relationships
  Self, attitude toward: confidence
  Success

---

As teenager Beth Lambert practices her acceptance speech for the Brady leadership award to be given that evening at the Old Rugged Cross Church in Pocahontas, Arkansas, her mother comes in and advises her not to count her Bradys before they hatch. Later, at the awards ceremony, when Rev. Ross begins to describe the winner—someone who uses leadership ability quietly and humbly—Beth stands up and waits for her name. Instead, the award goes to Philip Hall, and Beth is ridiculed and laughed at for her presumption. She runs out of the tent and hides in the woods all night. When she finally goes home, she tells her mother that she's planning something so important people will remember it for years. She calls an emergency meeting of the Pretty Pennies Girls Club and, as its president, announces that they will challenge the boys' club, the Tiger Hunters, to a relay race on the town's Dollar Day. She herself will coach the team. A big, excited crowd assembles on the great day, and the mayor publicly praises Beth for her involvement, inspiration, and hard work. The relay begins with Philip Hall and Beth. She runs as fast as she's ever run in her life, but Philip is faster. In desperation, she throws the red handkerchief to the second runner, Bonnie, instead of handing it over as she's supposed to. As a penalty, the sheriff makes Beth do the hand-off again, losing them valuable time. Bonnie takes off and runs as hard as she can, but the race is already lost—"a race that I had lost singlehandedly, without a bit of help from anybody." Afterwards, Beth tries to disappear but is confronted by angry members of the Pretty Pennies. She knows that "even a hundred years won't be nearly time enough for me to forgive myself for what I had done here today." A week later, Philip Hall, who's still her friend, tells her the Pennies are having a meeting without her and that Bonnie hopes to take over the presidency. Beth, outside the window, listens to their meeting, and when she hears that they plan to boot her out, she rushes in to protest and apologize. But when the vote is in, Bonnie is elected the new president. Overwhelmed by her failures, Beth tells her mother she wants to move to a different town, a different county, where nobody will know her. Her sympathetic parents agree to her moving to Walnut Ridge to live with her grandmother. Once there, she promptly organizes a girls' club, but declines the presidency when they offer it to her; she's come to Walnut Ridge to be a follower, not a leader. But she can't help whispering suggestions to B.J., the new president, although she berates herself later. The club is sponsoring the town's New Year's Day party, and B.J. admits she has no idea how to plan a party for two thousand people. So Beth offers to do it. On Christmas Day her family all comes to Grandma's house. Her parents ask Beth when she's coming home. She tells them she can't until she gets through the New Year's Day party. To Beth's relief, the party is a great success, not only for Walnut Ridge but for the many Pocahontas people who attend. Philip Hall is one of them, and he urges Beth to come home again. She sees what a true friend Philip has been and tells him he deserved the Brady leadership award. Three of the Pretty Pennies ask Beth to return and be their president again, since Bonnie hasn't done anything. As long as there aren't any more secret meetings, Beth replies, because they hurt people. For the first time, Beth can laugh about her mistake in the relay race. She tells her parents she's ready to go home.

Beth Lambert is an energetic, idea-filled girl who's gotten a bit big for her britches since readers last met her in *Philip Hall Likes Me. I Reckon Maybe.* Through several humbling experiences and a few successes, she learns not to be so full of her own importance and to appreciate the true nature of her leadership abilities. This fast-moving, entertaining book asks, "How can others toot your horn when you're so busy doing it yourself?" Beth changes believably from cocky to quietly competent. The black dialect in her first-person narrative adds authenticity and doesn't obstruct the story line.

Ages 9-12

**Also available in:**
Paperbound—*Get On Out of Here, Philip Hall*
Dell Publishing Company, Inc.

## 239

Greene, Constance Clarke

**Al(exandra) the Great**

The Viking Press, Inc., 1982.
(133 pages)

FRIENDSHIP: Best Friend
Decision making
Illnesses: of parent
Maturation
Parent/Parents: single

At twelve, the narrator is a year younger than her best friend, Al, short for Alexandra. Now that school is out for the summer, Al is looking forward to leaving New York City and visiting her father and his new family on their farm in Ohio. However, Al, who "suffers a lot from role reversal," worries that her mother works too hard and coughs too much. She insists that her mother go to the doctor, who discovers she has pneumonia and immediately puts her in a hospital. The narrator's father has Al stay with them in her mother's absence. That evening he even takes his daughter and Al to a fancy restaurant—secretly upsetting the narrator, who would prefer to be alone with her father. Al visits her mother daily and envies her best friend's stable family. For her part, the friend envies Al going to Ohio and the farm. But Al finally decides she cannot leave her mother. Reluctantly she telephones her father and explains the situation. Al's mother is proud of her daughter's decision, and she cheers Al up by promising her a vacation in a beach cottage on the Jersey shore. Several days later Al receives a package from Ohio, a T-shirt saying "AL(exandra) THE GREAT." An enclosed note from her father praises her for her devotion. Al hugs her best friend and her new shirt.

Excited about spending three weeks with her father and his new family, Al's dream is dashed when her mother becomes ill. But as the narrator—Al's best friend—notes, Al's decision to stay with her mother was the right one. This warm, humorous book shows two best friends learning a lot about responsibility. The story is a sequel to three previous books about Al, her best friend, their families, and their other friends.

Ages 10-12

**Also available in:**
Cassette—*Al(exandra) the Great*
Library of Congress (NLSBPH)

Paperbound—*Al(exandra) the Great*
Dell Publishing Company, Inc.

## 240

Greene, Constance Clarke

**Double-Dare O'Toole**

The Viking Press, Inc., 1981.
(158 pages)

RISK, TAKING OF
Death: of friend
Friendship: meaning of
School: classmate relationships
Sibling: relationships

When Francis Xavier O'Toole, known as Fex, was five, his older brother, Pete, dared him to walk on his hands up the center aisle of a store. The applause of Fex's first audience hooked him into taking all dares offered him. Now Fex is almost twelve and, though he knows that accepting dares always gets him into trouble, he continues to succumb to every challenge. He is frequently victimized by a classmate, Barney Barnes, who exploits Fex's weakness by daring him into escapades that Barney himself would never attempt. Barney's latest dare, to put "Palinkas is a pig," complete with illustration, on the desk of Mr. Palinkas, the principal, has cost Fex a week of mandatory after-school chores. Mr. Palinkas, however, is sympathetic to Fex and encourages him to resist his compulsion to take dares. As Fex knows, "There's nothing worse than knowing you've been a fool and have no one to blame but yourself." Pete is now a good-looking, athletic, fifteen-year-old sophisticate who offers Fex instructions about "making out" with girls. The inexperienced Fex, taking the instructions for a dare, attempts to try them out on his childhood friend, Audrey. But Audrey calls him "cuckoo" and runs into the kitchen. Barney gives a boy-girl party at which he dares Fex to "make a move" on an older girl when the lights are turned off. The lights come back on to reveal Fex being dumped on the floor by the indignant girl. Everyone but Audrey laughs at him. Several days later, Fex takes his young baby-sitting charge, Charlie, to the fishing pond. Barney and his gang appear and dare Fex to jump in the water. Fex is determined to avoid dares and does not oblige. But when the gang dares Charlie, the little boy plunges into the water and is swept away by the current. Fex manages to save the child, with the aid of two men, and becomes a local hero, complete with picture and story in the newspaper. Slowly, with his parents' and younger brother Jerry's support and sympathy, the new "hero" begins to gain the self-confidence he needs to withstand Pete's teasing and Barney's bullying. He has been helped all along by the good advice of his main confidante, Angie, a sixtyish storekeeper. Shortly after the rescue of Charlie, Angie dies suddenly. Audrey and Fex go together to the wake, where Fex faints from the pressure of his emotions. When he revives, he and Audrey walk home hand in hand.

A boy begins to overcome his weakness for accepting dares in this sympathetic, entertaining account. Supported by understanding family members and friends, Fex gains the self-confidence he needs. The relationships between Fex and the other characters, especially Audrey and Angie, are well drawn and the dialogue is natural, although the plot itself is a bit thin.

Ages 9-11

**Also available in:**
Braille—*Double-Dare O'Toole*
Library of Congress (NLSBPH)

Paperbound—*Double-Dare O'Toole*
Dell Publishing Company, Inc.

## 241

Greene, Constance Clarke

**Your Old Pal, Al**

The Viking Press, Inc., 1979.
(149 pages)

---

FRIENDSHIP: Best Friend
  Anger
  Expectations
  Jealousy: peer

---

Thirteen-year-old Al's best friend tries to encourage her as she waits expectantly for promised letters from her father and his new wife and from a boy named Brian whom she met at her father's wedding. But despite her friend's efforts, Al's moods swing uncontrollably from eager anticipation to crushing disappointment. After meticulously composing a letter to Brian, Al reads it to her friend. The friend advises Al never to mail such a self-deprecating letter; it's "bad," she tells her, "it stinks," "it's a bummer." As Al vacillates between sending and not sending it, her friend accepts an invitation for a two-week stay with Polly, whose parents are going on safari in Africa. This latest desertion is the last straw, and Al's emotional turmoil erupts in anger. She insults her friend and impulsively mails the letter. Meanwhile, Al's friend, angry also, picks a fight with Polly, and a temperamental triangle results. Tension grows until at last, ashamed of themselves, the girls apologize to each other and become friends again. Al has received her long-awaited invitation for a month's stay with her father and new stepfamily. Then, soon after the friends' reconciliation, an excited Al gets a postcard from Brian. In the same mail, her ill-considered letter is returned because of insufficient postage. On friendly terms once more with her friends and the world, Al decides, "If only I could figure some way to get mad and not say anything mean until I got over being mad. It's the things people say to each other when they're mad that cause the trouble."

As three volatile young teenagers work through their jealousy and anger, they learn the hurting power of thoughtless words. They also make some discoveries about apologizing and forgiving. As told by Al's unnamed best friend, this perceptive and funny story will strike responsive chords in anyone who has ever been estranged from a best friend. This is the third book about Al and her best friend.

Ages 9-13

**Also available in:**
Braille—*Your Old Pal, Al*
Library of Congress (NLSBPH)

Cassette—*Your Old Pal, Al*
Library of Congress (NLSBPH)

Paperbound—*Your Old Pal, Al*
Dell Publishing Company, Inc.

## 242

Greene, Sheppard M.

**The Boy Who Drank Too Much**

The Viking Press, Inc., 1979.
(149 pages)

---

ALCOHOLISM: Adolescent
ALCOHOLISM: of Father
  Boy-girl relationships
  Child abuse
  Deprivation, emotional
  Friendship: best friend
  Parent/Parents: single
  Sports/Sportsmanship

---

The fifteen-year-old narrator (whose name is never given) is intrigued by Buff Saunders, a fellow player on the school hockey team. But the narrator's best friend, Art, warns that Buff is nothing but a troublemaker, a liar, a wise guy. In spite of the warning, the narrator accompanies Buff to the hospital the day he is hit in the face by a hockey puck during a game and loses four teeth. Afterwards, he takes Buff home to a "dump" of an apartment in an old house and shares a can of stew with him and his father. Buff's father, who begins drinking as soon as he walks in the door, is a former hockey player who takes great pride in Buff's game. He is delighted by the missing teeth, gleefully predicting that Buff, like him, won't have a tooth left by the age of eighteen. Buff says he'd like to quit hockey, but his father won't hear of it. The argument ends when the drunken father slaps his son in the face, right on the twelve stitches he's just had. The narrator later describes the evening to Ruth Benedict, a recovered alcoholic for whom he does odd jobs. They talk about why people drink. Ruth tells him it's a way, a bad way, of coping with problems. The narrator is first exposed to Buff's own drinking at a party given by Tina, Art's girlfriend. There the narrator meets a girl named Julie. When Buff arrives with a case of beer, three cans missing, he says he needed to "limber up" before the party. Tension grows during the evening because of Buff's attentions to Tina, and he and Art end up fighting. Art nearly severs a tendon when he steps on a broken bottle during the fight, and he must give up hockey for the rest of the year. He demands that the narrator end his friendship with Buff, but the narrator feels grateful to Buff for his help with hockey and sorry for his troubles. One day he learns that Buff keeps miniature bottles of liquor in his pocket "for emergency use only"—whenever he gets tensed up at practice. The narrator gives up his first date with Julie to keep Buff from drinking after a disappointing performance in a hockey game. But Buff doesn't show up that night and is missing for the next several days. Then Julie calls the narrator out of class to say that she's found Buff, dead drunk, behind the school. They call Ruth, who comes at

**G**

once and takes Buff home with her. Julie and the narrator then go to Buff's father in an attempt to enlist his help and support for Buff. But the drunken Mr. Saunders roughs up the narrator trying to find out where Buff is. When they get back to Ruth's, Buff tells them how he tried to run away, but began drinking instead. Then his father, having discovered where Buff is, arrives at Ruth's, violently drunk. When they won't let him in, the man throws a barbecue grill through Ruth's window. Buff calls the police and finally strikes his father after Saunders taunts and ridicules him. Then Buff runs off and the narrator follows him to a garage, hoping to comfort him. He finds Buff sitting in a 1960 T-bird that his father completely rebuilt. It is the car his mother was killed in, his drunken father at the wheel. Buff believes his father loves the car far more than he loves him. He then announces his plans to take the car and head for Canada, where he was born. He challenges the narrator to go with him. His friend pledges his loyalty, promising to stick with Buff. Finally convinced that this friendship is real, Buff tells the narrator that if he will help him get through a rehabilitation program Ruth has mentioned, he will postpone going to Canada. In a playoff game at the end of the season, the narrator and Buff, now living at Ruth's house, both play well. Afterwards, Buff tells his friend that he now realizes he doesn't have to be exactly like his father. He is his own person. Buff receives the Most Improved Player trophy, but still hasn't made up his mind whether or not he will play hockey next season.

As he wrestles with his own drinking problem as well as his father's, a boy finds support in the friendship of several peers and of an older, recovered alcoholic. Buff desperately wants his father's love and approval, but comes to realize he probably won't ever have it and can live without it if he must. The sympathetic narrator must cope with troubles of his own, as he is torn between his old and new friend and enters his first boy-girl relationship. He also has to come to terms with the violence and abuse he sees between Buff and his father. The story is believable, and readers are left feeling that Buff has his drinking problem under control.

Ages 12 and up

**Also available in:**
Paperbound—*The Boy Who Drank Too Much*
Dell Publishing Company, Inc. [Laurel Leaf Library]

## 243

**Greenfield, Eloise**

### Darlene

Black/white illustrations by George Ford.
Methuen, Inc., 1980.
(29 pages counted)

---

*CHANGE: Accepting*
  *Visiting*
  *Wheelchair, dependence on*

---

Darlene, about six and confined to a wheelchair, is left by her mother at her Uncle Eddie's for the day. She resents being left there. When her cousin Joanne asks her to play, Darlene says she wants to go home. She finally agrees reluctantly to play board games with

Joanne, but soon asks if it is two o'clock, the time her mother is to come for her. It isn't, so Joanne tosses Darlene a ball and the two girls play catch. Then Darlene asks Uncle Eddie if it's two o'clock yet. It's still early and so Darlene and Joanne play jump rope, Darlene turning a rope tied to a chest and Joanne jumping. Again Darlene asks if it is two o'clock. It still is not, so Uncle Eddie plays his guitar and the three sing songs. Finally, Darlene's mother returns to pick her up. But now Darlene is having so much fun that she wants to stay.

Unhappy about being left with her uncle and cousin, a little girl is determined not to enjoy herself. Before long, though, Darlene discovers she is having so much fun that she hates to leave. The child's confinement to a wheelchair is never mentioned in the text. It is depicted in the large, unusually attractive, softly shaded illustrations that bring the characters to life. The story, although slight, could stimulate discussion both of Darlene's gradual change in attitude and of the physical activities she enjoys.

Ages 5-7

**Also available in:**
No other form known

## 244

**Greenfield, Eloise**

### Grandmama's Joy

Color illustrations by Carole Byard.
William Collins Publishers, Inc., 1980.
(32 pages counted)

---

*GRANDPARENT: Love for*
  *Change: accepting*
  *Empathy*
  *Grandparent: living in home of*
  *Moving*

---

Grandmama is sad and little Rhondy doesn't know why. To cheer her, Rhondy has Grandmama stop taking old clothes out of the closet and stuffing them in a box; she must watch Rhondy put on one of her singing shows. But the show doesn't make Grandmama smile as it usually does. So Rhondy goes to visit Mrs. Bennett and suggests that Mrs. Bennett give Grandmama a call to make her feel better. But Grandmama doesn't answer the phone. Then Rhondy finds a pretty, speckled rock in the yard and gives it to Grandmama, explaining that there are lots of pretty things in their yard. Grandmama starts crying. She says they have to move because the rent is too high. Rhondy thinks about missing her friends, her school, and her neighbors, but she doesn't dwell on that now. Instead, she asks Grandmama to tell her the story once again of how the two of them came to live together. Grandmama recalls that after an accident that took Rhondy's parents' lives, she picked up the infant Rhondy from the hospital and declared that Rhondy would always be her joy. As long as she had her joy, she always thought, she'd be all right. Rhondy wants to know if she is still Grandmama's joy. And will she be Grandmama's joy when they move? Grandmama, "smiling a real smile," says yes and hugs

Rhondy. The little girl "felt so happy in her grand-mama's arms because as much as she was Grand-mama's joy, Grandmama was her joy, too."

When her grandmother is unhappy and discouraged about being forced to move from her house, little Rhondy reminds her of the really important things in life: the love and concern the two have for each other. This beautiful portrayal of the affection between a child and an aging adult features outstanding illustrations and a simple, tender text. The younger audience might need adult guidance in fully appreciating the love, concern, and care that remain for Rhondy and Grandmama despite difficult times.

Ages 4-8

**Also available in:**
No other form known

## 245

### Greenfield, Eloise and Alesia Revis

### Alesia

Black/white illustrations by George Ford.
Black/white photographs by Sandra Turner Bond.
Philomel Books, 1981.
(61 pages)

*HANDICAPS: Multiple*
 *Determination*
 *Wheelchair, dependence on*

Alesia was nine years old when she was hit by a car and almost completely disabled. Now she is seventeen and a junior in high school. Although usually confined to a wheelchair she has, after many years of hard work, regained some movement in her body. One of her best friends is Lisa Hall, a girl she met at a summer camp for disabled children. One Saturday in March Alesia attends a party at Lisa's house and enjoys dancing. She loves parties, even though she has to lean against the wall or put her weight on the boy in order to dance. Some boys just say "never mind" when she has to lean on them, but she doesn't waste her time with people like that. Besides parties and dancing, Alesia enjoys most things other teenage girls do: going to movies, attending basketball games, shopping for clothes. When Alesia goes out in public she doesn't like adults to stare at her, although she doesn't mind answering children's questions. Some people move away when they see her wheelchair, as if she has some kind of disease. When this happens, she thinks to herself, "They have disabilities, too—faults and things like that, everybody has them. Mine is just more noticeable." Some people try too hard to help her, and she doesn't like that either. She wants to do as many things as she can by herself. If anyone were to ask her what she wants "most in the whole world," she'd say, "To be able to walk again." She recalls her accident. After coming out of a five-week coma, she had first to learn to crawl. Years of physical therapy followed. Gradually she tried to take steps, first with help and then by herself, wearing leg braces. Now she can go for walks outdoors, always holding onto and supported by friends. At the Interstate

Commerce Commission, where she works for the sum-mer, she often gets around by holding onto her wheel-chair and pushing it in front of her. When school starts in September, Alesia has just about decided to go to college. She wants to live on campus and be on her own. Alesia feels she would be letting down all the people who are pulling for her if she doesn't keep trying to do more things. When she worries about her future, she remembers how the doctors told her parents at the time of the accident that she would probably be a "vegeta-ble" the rest of her life. Knowing that didn't come true gives her faith and courage. One goal dominates her thoughts about graduation. She wants to walk across the stage all by herself to get her diploma. She practices faithfully and dreams of the day when this will be possible.

This book consists of the entries in Alesia Revis's diary between March 19 and October 24, 1980. The reader gets a very personal look at the daily life of a disabled teenage girl determined to overcome her physical limi-tations. As we follow her thoughts and observe the accompanying photographs and illustrations, it is impossible not to admire Alesia's courage and buoyant spirit. The diary format does make for somewhat dis-jointed reading, but the story is an inspiring one.

Ages 10-14

**Also available in:**
Cassette—*Alesia*
Library of Congress (NLSBPH)

G

## 246

### Greenwald, Sheila

### Give Us a Great Big Smile, Rosy Cole

Black/white illustrations by the author.
Little, Brown and Company, 1981.
(76 pages)

*EXPECTATIONS*
*RESOURCEFULNESS*
 *Family: relationships*
 *Friendship: meaning of*
 *Problem solving*
 *Talents: musical*

Six weeks ago Rosy Cole turned ten, and ever since her birthday she's been worried. Rosy's Uncle Ralph is a successful photographer. When Rosy's two older sisters turned ten her uncle made each famous by publishing a book of photographs of them, along with a short story about each girl. Anitra excels at ballet and Pippa is a good horseback rider, but Rosy is convinced she excels at nothing. One evening Rosy's mother announces that Uncle Ralph is going to accompany her to her violin lesson. Now Rosy, who hates her lessons and tries hard to miss them, is really worried. As she feared, Uncle Ralph takes lots of pictures during the lesson and announces that the title of his new book will be *A Very Little Fiddler*. When news about Rosy's book gets around, everyone wants to be her best friend—espe-cially Hermione Wong, who plays in a quartet with her. Even Ms. Radzinoff, her music teacher, begins to be nicer to her, announcing that Rosy will play a solo at the

May music recital. Until then, she will have daily lessons. Despite herself, Rosy begins to enjoy all the attention. Maybe she really is a "rising star." Then one day, just before her lesson, Rosy overhears a tape of a perfectly awful violinist. Chagrined, she realizes the miserable tape is her own. A mortified Rosy informs her parents she will not play at the recital and then decides to run away. But while walking through Central Park, Rosy hatches a plan. She runs home, returning to the park with her violin and a sign—"Help me  I have no talent  Should not get lessons  recitals  publicity or encouragement  If you agree  sign petition" Someone calls Rosy's mother, who comes to the park and, hearing Rosy play the violin, soon joins the others in signing the petition. Rosy wins. Uncle Ralph decides to do a story about a racehorse instead and also announces his engagement to Ms. Radzinoff. Rosy loses some of her "best friends," but her friendship with Hermione, a genuine one, continues.

In this amusing first-person narrative, a clever young girl sees how right she was to be realistic about herself and her talents. She's no violinist, but Rosy Cole is an exceptional problem solver. With all the humor, her feelings about her predicament come through clearly. Numerous drawings enhance this well-paced story.

Ages 8-10

**Also available in:**
Braille—*Give Us a Great Big Smile, Rosy Cole*
Library of Congress (NLSBPH)

Cassette—*Give Us a Great Big Smile, Rosy Cole*
Library of Congress (NLSBPH)

Paperbound—*Give Us a Great Big Smile, Rosy Cole*
Dell Publishing Company, Inc.

## 247

**Gregory, Diana**

## There's a Caterpillar in My Lemonade

Addison-Wesley Publishing Company, Inc., 1980.
(123 pages)

---

*CHANGE: Resisting*
*PARENT/PARENTS: Remarriage of*
  *Friendship: best friend*
  *Maturation*
  *Sports/Sportsmanship*
  *Stepparent: father*

---

For all of her fourteen years Samantha, called Sam, has been perfectly happy with only her widowed mother for a parent. So she is very upset by her mother's decision to remarry. Sam has nothing in particular against Mr. Hooten; she simply does not want a stranger intruding in their life. She finds little sympathy, however. Her best friend, Cathy, comes from a large family and does not seem to appreciate Sam's despair. Furthermore Cathy, motivated by what is to Sam an incomprehensible interest in boys, has decided to join the school swim team. Sam cannot understand why her friend would want to clutter up her summer with such a structured activity. Soon, however, to avoid a dinner date with Mr.

Hooten, Sam tells her mother she's promised to meet with Cathy and discuss joining the swim team. Her mother is delighted, especially since Mr. Hooten was on the swim team in college. What started out as an excuse turns into a reality as Sam, tired of being cut off from her friends, tries out for the team and makes it. In the meantime, her favorite aunt arrives to help with the wedding preparations and then to stay on with Sam while her mother and her new husband go on their honeymoon. Out shopping one day for Sam's dress, her aunt can't help but notice the girl's gloominess. She tells Sam the story about the caterpillar that drops into a glass of lemonade, advising her to look at the situation from both sides—the caterpillar's and the person with the lemonade—before making a final judgment. Although Sam understands what her aunt means, she avoids thinking about her mother's marriage. The day of the wedding is a bad blur for Sam, a day she tries to forget while her mother and Mr. Hooten are away on their honeymoon. On the day they are to return, her aunt talks to Sam about how her mother's dreams had been thwarted when Sam's father was killed in the war. Listening to her and drinking her lemonade, Sam reflects on the tale of the caterpillar. However, when the couple returns Sam avoids Mr. Hooten. Then comes Sam's first big swim meet. She has been chosen to swim the relay, an honor for one so new to the team. She begins well by placing in her first two events and then prepares for the relay, aware that their team needs to place to win the meet. Preoccupied by this thought and by her teammates' urging her to be the first in the pool, she jumps in before she realizes there is still a swimmer in the pool completing the previous event. Her mistake means their relay team is disqualified. Mortified, Sam leaves the meet, still wearing her swimsuit, and hides behind some folding chairs in a hallway. It is Mr. Hooten who finds her, gently puts a towel around her, and tells her how he made a similar mistake when he was on his college swim team. When Sam decides she wants to walk home, Mr. Hooten quietly hands her the bag containing her clothes so she does not have to return to the locker room. One of the boys from the team walks her home, assuring Sam that he does not blame her. She appreciates his concern, even though nothing can change what she did or how bad she feels about it.

A teenage girl whose mother remarries refuses to believe that any good can come out of changes in her life. But her involvement with the swim team, begun as a way to avoid contact with her mother's new husband, serves to bring the two together and opens up communication and understanding between them. Sam's first-person account moves quickly and is told with insight and humor. The girl at the end of the book, horrified by her own foolish mistake but confident she will survive, has changed a great deal. She has matured, made new friends, found new interests, and begun a warm relationship with her "new father."

Ages 10-12

**Also available in:**
No other form known

**248**

Griffith, Helen V.

**Mine Will, Said John**

Color illustrations by Muriel Batherman.
Greenwillow Books, 1980.
(32 pages counted)

---

*IMAGINATION*
*PETS*

---

Young John and his parents go to the pet shop. He wants a puppy, but his mother wants a nice, quiet gerbil. John insists that his gerbil will cry at night. Sure enough, it does, whimpering and yelping until John's parents come into his room to see what is happening. All they see is a sleeping gerbil, but John says it has been crying and keeping him awake. The next day they return to the pet shop and exchange the gerbil for a chameleon. John insists that chameleons, though quiet, glow in the dark and turn bright colors. When his father says they do no such thing, John says, "Mine will." That night the chameleon begins to glow, and even under John's blanket its bright colors shine through. John's parents come into his room, wondering about the light. John reports that the glowing chameleon, now asleep, is keeping him awake. They return to the pet shop in the morning. This time John's parents suggest a frog, but they change their minds when John tells them his frog will chew on furniture all night long. They tell John to go ahead and pick out a puppy. He chooses one that will not cry, glow in the dark, or chew on furniture. "He will always mind me, and he will love me better than anything," says John. His mother is not convinced a puppy can be that perfect. "Mine will," says John. "And it was."

When a young boy's parents select pets for him other than the puppy he really wants, he concocts a disturbing habit for each that keeps him, and thus his parents, awake at night. He gets his puppy. Young readers will delight in John's imaginative determination to win a small contest of wills. The matter-of-fact tone and pleasing illustrations accent the humor.

Ages 4-6

**Also available in:**
No other form known

**249**

Gross, Alan

**The I Don't Want to Go to School Book**

Color illustrations by Mike Venezia.
Children's Press, Inc., 1982.
(31 pages)

---

*FEAR: of School*
*Decision making*
*Imagination*

---

A young boy isn't sure he's well enough to go to school. He's certainly not well enough to face such things as forgetting his bus money, getting all sweated up in gym, or perhaps having to wrestle with Big Bruce Novak again. He could catch a bad cold from the chilly shower after gym and an older boy might snap him with a towel. What if he forgets his locker combination again or can't tell which boots are his? What if his zipper breaks! Somebody might throw up in school, or he could be reported by the crossing guards for something he didn't do. He might get caught passing a note and have to read it aloud, or the kids could make fun of his lunch, or he might have to raise his hand to go to the bathroom and everybody would know why his hand was up. Of course, on the other hand, if he stays home he won't get to see his friends or play with them after school. There's nothing on daytime television and nobody will feed the homeroom fish if he's not there to do it. Sometimes his teacher is funny and shows them interesting things; sometimes they work with clay. He'll fall behind in his work if he misses a day. So maybe he'd better go to school. "But if school doesn't work out today, I'm going to stay home tomorrow."

This humorous look at a boy trying to evaluate the pros and cons of going to school will appeal to any reader who's ever had a bad day at school. The realistic ending keeps the door open for the boy to reconsider his decision tomorrow. Some of the school incidents seem more appropriate for older readers, although the reading level and format of the book seem geared for younger students. Still, this will be great fun for the read-aloud audience. Large, bold illustrations enhance the text.

Ages 5-9

**Also available in:**
No other form known

**250**

Gross, Alan

**What If the Teacher Calls On Me?**

Color illustrations by Mike Venezia.
Children's Press, Inc., 1980.
(31 pages)

---

*SCHOOL: Pupil-Teacher Relationships*
*Self, attitude toward: confidence*

---

A little boy worries about being called on in class. Even when he knows the answer, he gets "mixed up" with everyone looking at him and the teacher waiting. She tries to help by rephrasing the question and asking if he understands, but still he sits tongue-tied. Certain that his classmates think him stupid, he tells himself that he knows the answers but just cannot say them. He's noticed that he's usually called on when he's not paying attention—when he's daydreaming or making paper airplanes. So he decides his teacher will not call on him if he pretends to know the answer and is eager to volunteer it. But he has outfoxed himself: "Oh, no. Me? Um . . . ah, repeat the question, please?"

This first-person story presents a familiar classroom dilemma and should be a good discussion starter. Cartoonlike illustrations add humor, but the situation remains real. Readers will notice that the narrator ponders his dilemma instead of paying attention in class and so is caught answerless once again.

G

Ages 5-7

**Also available in:**
No other form known

## 251

**Guest, Elissa Haden**

### The Handsome Man

Four Winds Press, 1980.
(184 pages)

---

*AMBIVALENCE, FEELINGS OF*
*LOVE, MEANING OF*
  *Boy-girl relationships*
  *Family: relationships*
  *Friendship: best friend*
  *Friendship: meaning of*
  *Separation, marital*

---

Fourteen-year-old Alexandra Barnes lives in Greenwich Village, attends a private, progressive school, worries a lot, and wears a black-and-white-checked newsboy cap everywhere she goes. When she notices a handsome man in the neighborhood, she and her best friend, Angela Sinclair, decide to follow and find out about him. They record everything they discover in their notebooks. Alex daydreams about meeting H.M., their code name for Handsome Man. One day Alex and Angie spot H.M. sitting at a cafe by himself. They take the next table. He notices Alex's cap, tells her he's a photographer, and invites her to his apartment some Saturday so he can take her picture. Alex can't go the next weekend because the headmaster from her brother Nigel's school calls with the news that Nigel and a girl have been found together in bed smoking pot. Alex's parents leave for Nigel's school, putting her in charge of her little sister, Eloise. When her parents return they report that Nigel is on probation, but Alex senses that something even more serious is wrong although her parents deny it. Upset about the missed meeting with H.M., Alex sees him later and he says she can come by on Friday. Friday arrives and Alex, who has invented a school activity to explain her absence, goes to H.M.'s apartment—although she's filled with last-minute fears about the wisdom of what she's doing. H.M., actually Terry Gray, takes many pictures of Alex in her newsboy cap, telling her she reminds him of turn-of-the-century New York. Afterwards, he takes one last picture: Alex holding Tallahassee, the neighborhood cat. As she runs home she thinks, "I love him so much it feels like I'm dying." A week later, Terry tells Alex that the picture of her and Tallahassee made a big hit at an ad agency he contacted. They want to use it for a cat-food advertisement. Her parents need to sign a release, and then Alex will earn three hundred fifty dollars for modeling. But Alex is afraid to tell her parents because she's sure they'll disapprove of how she met Terry. Angie accuses Alex of neglecting her, of being totally wrapped up in H.M. Alex reassures her, but she herself is anything but reassured when she overhears her mother crying to her father that she knows all about "her." A few days later, she and her mother have a celebration dinner for her mother's good grades—she is working for a master's degree. But Alex senses undercurrents. "Something is happening at home and I think maybe if I stay away long enough it will disappear." She does tell her father, who tells her mother, about the cat-food advertisement, and her father signs the release. Terry calls and invites her over, and Alex is cheered at the thought of seeing him again. But that evening her mother announces that she, Alex, and Eloise will be spending the summer at the Cape. Her father will stay in New York. Alex objects and pleads and argues, but her mother is adamant. It is "best" this way. When her father comes home, Alex fearfully asks him if he and her mother are getting a divorce, but he says it's just a "breather." Alex storms out of the house and runs to Terry Gray's apartment. The visit ends with Alex crying on his shoulder, telling him about her family's troubles. He comforts and kisses her, saying she's a lovely girl and he'll miss her. She leaves and goes down by the dock, knowing she'll never see Handsome Man again, that all her daydreams of him are over. But the kiss is real and hers forever. She tosses her cap into the river where it sinks out of sight.

This first-person novel is a warm and humorous portrayal of the crush of a teenage girl on an older man. Terry, unaware of Alex's feelings, is merely kind, interested only in photographing her. Many readers will identify with Alex's conflicts, her ambivalent feelings toward her parents, the Handsome Man, even her best friend. Her parents' impending separation is not dealt with in depth; it provides part of the uneasy background against which Alex tries to make sense of her changing emotions and attitudes.

Ages 12 and up

**Also available in:**
No other form known

## 252

**Guy, Rosa Cuthbert**

### The Disappearance

Delacorte Press, 1979.
(246 pages)

---

*PREJUDICE: Ethnic/Racial*
  *Alcoholism: of mother*
  *Appearance: concern about*
  *Crime/Criminals*
  *Death: murder*
  *Foster home*
  *Friendship: meaning of*
  *Justice/Injustice*
  *Reputation*
  *Trust/Distrust*

---

When sixteen-year-old Imamu is falsely accused of murder, his mother is noticeably absent from the court hearing. But Ann Aimsley sits in on all the proceedings and her calm, cool presence helps the boy through. Ann has escaped the ghetto's poverty and when, after Imamu's case is dismissed, she offers him her help and her home, he gladly, if apprehensively, accepts. Packing his meager belongings, Imamu moves from his filthy, cockroach-ridden apartment in Harlem to Ann's middle-class home in Brooklyn. As he leaves he remembers that before his father was killed in Vietnam he had a mother who loved and cared for him. Toward the woman she was, rather than the helpless alcoholic she has become, he feels a deep sense of responsibility.

Originally named John Jones, Imamu became a Muslim to keep himself from alcohol and drugs, which are forbidden by Islam. Besides Ann, whom he adores, his new family includes her husband, Peter, strong-willed with set ideas; Gail, seventeen and a bright college freshman who feels a secret affinity for Imamu; and little Perk, full of laughter and mischief. Close to the family is Perk's godmother and Ann's best friend, Dora Belle, whose whole life revolves around her appearance—especially her long, black hair—her home, and her two rental properties. Imamu is surprised when the beautiful, sultry West Indian woman seems interested in him, a Harlem street kid. On Imamu's second day in Brooklyn, Perk disappears. Blood from a cut on his hand and a yellow ribbon belonging to Perk that is found in his room seem to incriminate Imamu. He is terribly hurt when Ann looks accusingly at him, and his tenuous relationship with Peter is destroyed. Hauled down to police headquarters, Imamu is wrapped in cold towels and beaten with rubber hoses. Gail is furious at her mother for her hasty judgment. She finds evidence to prove Imamu had cut himself on a broken glass and, despite her parents' protests, she goes to the police in his defense. The next day Imamu is released for lack of evidence, and although Gail pleads with him to return to her home, he picks up his drunken mother from the police bench and takes her back to Harlem. Determined to solve the mystery and to clear himself, he does return to Brooklyn that night, but intends to stay only until he and Gail have found Perk. Responding to Dora Belle's flirtations, Imamu goes to her house one evening and surprises her getting out of the shower. Shocked by the sight of her bald head dotted with tufts of gray hair, Imamu is unprepared for her violent, furious attack. He escapes, but suddenly remembers several other odd incidents that now convince him of what has happened to Perk. Stealthily, by flashlight, he climbs in the cellar window of one of Dora Belle's rental properties and in a patch of new cement begins hacking with a pick. Someone tells Dora Belle of an intruder on her property, and she and the Aimsleys find him there. When he explains his purpose Dora Belle goes berserk and reveals her terrible crime. The day Perk disappeared, the girl had gone to her godmother's house to have her hair combed specially for a school party. She also had intruded upon Dora Belle without her wig. In a murderous rage Dora Belle had shaken her goddaughter and then let her go suddenly, causing Perk to fall and fatally hit her head. Some years earlier, the Aimsleys learn from a mutual friend, Dora Belle had suffered a tropical fever that destroyed her hair and affected her mind. The grief-stricken Aimsleys again offer their home to Imamu, this time with sincerity, but his conscience forces him back to Harlem to care for his mother. He does accept a job from Peter Aimsley, however, for he has begun to see his way out of Harlem, perhaps with Gail.

A Harlem teenager struggles to rise above the violence all around him in this harsh, powerful novel. Tied to his nightmare existence by his sense of responsibility for his alcoholic mother, Imamu strives to be neither victim nor criminal. Finding violence and murder even in the comfortable surroundings of his foster family, he resolves to find his way out of poverty without abandoning his mother. Vivid characterizations make this suspense-filled story memorable; West Indian dialect lends it authenticity.

Ages 12 and up

**Also available in:**
Paperbound—*The Disappearance*
Dell Publishing Company, Inc.

**253**

**Haas, Dorothy**

**Poppy and the Outdoors Cat**
Black/white illustrations by Margot Apple.
Albert Whitman & Company, 1981.
(128 pages)

*PETS: Love for*
 *Family: relationships*
 *Friendship: best friend*
 *Problem solving*

Poppy Flower, about nine, longs for a pet. But with seven children and two parents living in a small, third-floor apartment, there just isn't room. One day, on the way to school with her best friend, Tink, Poppy rescues a kitten from a trash can. Several days later Poppy helps rescue the same kitten from the school fire escape. Now the kitten must be hers, Poppy believes, because she has saved it twice. She takes the kitten home, but her mother won't allow her to keep it. Her father tells her she cannot have an indoors cat. So Poppy decides to have an outdoors cat. With Tink's help, she discovers a perfect spot under the back steps. There she fixes a bed for the kitten out of a box and an old sweater she buys at a resale shop. She names the cat Rosebud and spends her spring days playing with Tink and teaching Rosebud about bugs, birds, cars, and crossing the street. Just before school is out, the Flower family gets a windfall. Through a sweepstakes that Poppy's mother had entered, they have won a four-bedroom home to be built in the suburbs. But despite the family's need for more room, the children, especially the older ones, worry about leaving their friends and school. After much thought, Poppy's parents decide they too would rather stay in the city. They take cash instead of the new, suburban home and use it to buy an older house one block from their apartment. Though Poppy can now have a pet, she must accept the fact that Rosebud, her outdoors cat, would rather continue to live outside. One summer day while Poppy and Tink are playing, Rosebud brings over her two kittens. She seems to want Poppy to take them, and Poppy realizes the kittens are not safe under the steps. So Poppy takes one kitten and Tink takes the other one. Now Poppy's happiness is complete.

A little girl who longs for a pet manages to get both an outdoors and an indoors cat in this warm story of family life. Poppy is an appealing and resourceful heroine, and the tales of her large family are funny and believable. Nondescript illustrations neither add to nor detract from the amusing story.

H

Ages 7-10

**Also available in:**
Cassette—*Poppy and the Outdoors Cat*
Library of Congress (NLSBPH)

## 254

**Hall, Lynn**

### Danza!

Charles Scribner's Sons, 1981.
(186 pages)

---

*ANIMALS: Love for*
  *Family: relationships*
  *Grandparent: respect for*
  *Identification with others: adults*
  *Responsibility: accepting*

---

Eleven-year-old Paulo is with the Paso Fino mare named Twenty the day she gives birth to a stud colt they call Danza. Paulo thinks Twenty is the best of all his grandfather's horses even if she is only a mare. His grandfather has nothing but contempt for the mares and for a boy who prefers riding a mare to riding a stallion. Paulo feels himself an outcast in the family. He is uncomfortable with his father, dislikes his older brother, and sees the younger children get love and hugs aplenty while he gets none. One day when Paulo is home alone, an American, Major Kessler, comes to inquire about buying some Paso Fino horses to take back to the States with him. The boy meets Kessler several months later at a horse show in which Danza places second in the weanling class. Paulo's grandfather refuses to discuss selling any of his horses to an American. Major Kessler confides his frustration to Paulo, who is flattered by the man's attention. Major Kessler doesn't treat him like a "no-account little kid." Three years later, when Danza has developed into a magnificent stallion and Paulo is fourteen, Major Kessler returns to Puerto Rico, still trying to buy a Paso Fino stallion. After a horse show, while the Major and his grandfather are discussing business, Paulo puts Danza in his stall but fails to shut the gate properly. Thirsty, Danza gets out of his stall, drinks the water left in the trough, and then knocks over an ice chest and finishes off the ice and ice cream he finds there. The next morning the horse is seriously ill; for many days he lies near death. Guilt-ridden, Paulo believes he's killed "the only thing in the world that loves me"; his grandfather has been right to distrust him. Just after his grandfather decides Danza will have to be shot, Major Kessler proposes taking the horse to the States where he's sure the university veterinarians can save him. There's one condition: Danza will then be his. The grandfather consents to send Danza to the States, but insists the Major must return him. He does agree that the Major can breed Danza. Paulo volunteers to go along to do round-the-clock nursing, and they soon leave for Louisiana. From the start Danza makes progress, and Paulo enjoys being useful and independent. He basks in the Major's praise and approval, which "came down on him like winter sunshine." When spring comes and Danza is well enough to be ridden and to breed, the Major tells Paulo about his plan to show Danza in a couple of months. The boy is a little confused. Will the Major be pocketing stud fees and prize money that ought to go to his grandfather? And shouldn't he and Danza return home? At Danza's first show, the pressure is on. If Danza doesn't win under Paulo, he is to be turned over to a professional trainer. Paulo knows that Danza's legs aren't back to normal yet. Danza places third; another horse fancier remarks that the judges won't take seriously a horse that can be managed by a youngster. So the Major brings in Jordan Welch to train and ride Danza. Danza promptly takes two firsts, including a championship. The Major is elated, but Paulo has noticed that Danza moves as if in pain. He overhears some talk about how Welch was once blacklisted because of his illegal methods, particularly his use of "soring," putting something painful on the horses' feet to make them lift their feet snappily. Welch will not allow Paulo near Danza to verify his suspicions, but the next morning Paulo forces a confrontation before witnesses with the Major and Welch. A show official says Welch has acted illegally and that Paulo may take Danza home with him. Paulo writes to his grandfather for the money to return home. Instead, his grandfather comes to Louisiana. Since the National is only a few days away, they decide to stay for it. In a superb performance Danza wins the stallion class, but immediately afterwards he begins limping and can't go on to compete in the Championship class. Paulo and his grandfather talk, and the old man confesses his fear of losing Paulo as he lost all his sons except Paulo's father—all went to the States. They return to Puerto Rico with a new sympathy for each other.

A boy's love for a horse takes him far from his home in Puerto Rico and helps him mature and grow closer to his family. In some ways a typical horse story, this has added interest because of its Puerto Rican hero and his difficult family relationships, the details about an unusual breed of horse, and a secondary plot about admiring the wrong sort of person. Readers will find the book involving.

Ages 9-12

**Also available in:**
Cassette—*Danza!*
Library of Congress (NLSBPH)

Paperbound—*Danza!*
Grosset & Dunlap, Inc.

## 255

**Hall, Lynn**

### Half the Battle

Charles Scribner's Sons, 1982.
(151 pages)

---

*BLINDNESS*
*SIBLING: Rivalry*
  *Competition*
  *Courage, meaning of*
  *Security/Insecurity*

---

Blair Liskey, whose visual impairment leaves him all but blind, and his younger brother, Loren, are preparing for the Sangre Trek, a grueling, hundred-mile, two-day endurance ride on horseback over rugged mountain country. The ride is dangerous even for sighted people, but Blair needs to prove to himself that he has courage enough to attend college next year and begin living life on his own. He is also enjoying the publicity he is getting for attempting the Trek. Loren, who will act as Blair's companion and guide, resents his brother's getting all the credit. Just once Loren would like to come in first, instead of always taking second place to Blair. Loren has a good chance of winning the Trek in his age group with his high-spirited, fast Arabian horse, El Kadir—but only if he's not held back by Blair's slower pace. During the eight weeks' training period, Loren pushes Blair to the limit, hoping he'll back out. When Blair's horse strains a tendon halfway through his training, Loren again hopes Blair will withdraw. Instead, Blair begins training another horse, Raven. But he's become aware of Loren's hostility. Then a girl expresses interest in Blair, and he asks Loren if they can double with him and his date. Loren, tired of being his brother's keeper, tells Blair the girl only felt sorry for him and is actually dating someone else, which isn't true. Loren doesn't enjoy his date that night, because he keeps seeing Blair's disappointed face. Tension builds in Loren as the Trek date approaches. His brother is "so damned sweet and helpless and brave. There was no way, ever, to strike at a brother like that without being a terrible person yourself. The frustration was overwhelming sometimes." Loren begins to think he will have to sabotage Blair during the Trek, leave him behind and go ahead to win on his own. Meanwhile, Blair continues training with Raven, working very hard to condition the horse and get himself ready. One of the other riders is Sandy Fields, whom Loren likes but who seems interested in Blair. When Loren sees Blair kissing Sandy, his anger and frustration increase. Blair and Raven pass the vet check (Loren was hoping the horse would be disqualified). The first day of the Trek is exhausting but they complete it, although Loren and El Kadir have to hold themselves back to stay with Blair. The next day, Loren leads Blair off the trail and then abandons him to complete the Trek alone. Blair's horse bolts, and he tries to find his way back to the trail by feeling for hoofprints. He falls and tumbles down an incline. Loren hears the scream and then suddenly comes upon Blair, who has quickly climbed back onto the trail. Loren's startled horse kicks Blair in the head (a glancing blow) and Loren himself is thrown, suffering a broken leg, a concussion, and other injuries. Blair, not seriously hurt, elects to stay in the hospital overnight with his brother. When Loren regains consciousness, Blair begins talking about next year's Trek. Loren wonders how Blair could trust him again after what he's done. But Blair, although he's well aware that Loren "did a rotten thing," is willing to forgive. "Being me isn't easy sometimes," he tells Loren, "but being my brother probably isn't always beer and skittles, either."

Two brothers, one blind and striving to rise above his physical limitations, the other resentful of the limelight his brother's blindness always attracts, learn to put themselves in each other's shoes for the first time. The narrative viewpoint in this exceptionally well-told story switches from brother to brother, allowing the reader to empathize with both and to see the complexity of their conflict and their affection. Although there is much here for the lover of horse stories, the book offers more:

an unusually well-defined sibling relationship and a tension and suspense that are sustained from beginning to end.

Ages 11 and up

**Also available in:**
Paperbound—*Half the Battle*
Grosset & Dunlap, Inc.

## 256
**Hall, Lynn**

**The Leaving**
Charles Scribner's Sons, 1980.
(116 pages)

---

*IDENTITY, SEARCH FOR*
  *Communication: lack of*
  *Communication: parent-child*
  *Decision making*
  *Family: relationships*

---

Roxanne Armstrong, eighteen, is moving to Des Moines to find a job, leaving behind her parents and the family's small farm in northern Iowa. She'll miss the security of the farm but feels she must prove her worth—not only to herself, but to her parents. Roxanne's mother, Thora, is quiet, withdrawn, seemingly without affection for her daughter or her husband, Clete. Clete takes no obvious interest in either wife or daughter, apparently preferring the company of his drinking buddies. Roxanne's leaving is painful and awkward for all three. Clete hopes Roxanne will hug him, but she does not, and he feels a stranger to his only child. In his mind he reviews his plan for escape from the farm and Thora: he has sold Roxanne's horse and will use the money to return to the city of Waterloo, to his former job and his friends. Thora longs to tell Roxanne how much she loves her, but she can't find the words. As the two drive to Des Moines that Thanksgiving weekend, Thora tells her daughter not to compromise, not to settle for anything less than the best for her life. Slowly Roxanne realizes that her mother's life has been nothing but compromises. "She felt suddenly as though she were a repeat of her mother, starting over again with a new life, and it was crucial that she know what mistakes to avoid." During the car ride, Thora also manages to convey her love to Roxanne, something Roxanne has never felt. Between Thanksgiving and Christmas, Roxanne finds a room and a job in Des Moines, Clete leaves Thora and the farm (he is gone when Thora returns from Des Moines), and Thora finds the first real peace she's known in thirty years. Roxanne comes home for Christmas, and she and her mother celebrate the best Christmas she can remember. That spring two friends invite Roxanne to share an apartment with them. Now the girl must decide: should she stay in Des Moines or should she return home? Roxanne decides to go home—to the farm, to the life she loves, to the mother she has come to understand only by leaving.

A girl's bid for independence provides the occasion for a shake-up of her unhappy family that leaves each member changed. Moving from the present to the past, the narrative brings the reader close to all three characters, detailing the nature of each person's dissatisfaction

H

and search for release. Roxanne, the main character, discovers her mother's love for her and her own love for their farm life, bringing her search full circle. This is a thoughtful story of the unexpressed pain some families endure and of the inner resources people discover to lessen that pain.

Ages 12 and up

**Also available in:**
Paperbound—*The Leaving*
Grosset & Dunlap, Inc.

## 257

**Hallman, Ruth**

**Breakaway**

The Westminster Press, 1981.
(92 pages)

---

*DEAFNESS*
*RUNNING AWAY*
  *Boy-girl relationships*
  *Love, meaning of*
  *Maturation*
  *Parental: overprotection*
  *Self, attitude toward: accepting*
  *Success*
  *Talents: athletic*

---

A diving accident has left seventeen-year-old Rob Cory, a talented athlete, almost totally deaf. His return to normal life is hampered by his mother, who seems unable to cope with her son's impairment and won't let him out of her sight. Rob's girlfriend, Kate, cannot bear seeing him shut out of life and insists on visiting him every day. When an angry Mrs. Cory forbids Kate to come back, Kate persuades Rob to run away with her. After she tells her parents that she's off to spend the rest of the summer with a friend, as in other years, she and Rob take a bus to a large city in another state. There they rent a room in a seedy boardinghouse in a rough neighborhood. The owner, a feisty old woman named Hattie Gogan who also runs the grocery store next door, doesn't really believe the two are brother and sister, as they claim, but she takes them in anyway after insisting there be no "hanky-panky." That first night, Hattie has a stroke and must be hospitalized. She asks Rob and Kate to look after the house during her absence, in exchange for their room and board. Besides taking on the cleaning and cooking, the two devise a course of study for Rob; he learns lipreading and some sign language. When Hattie returns, she demands to know their real story and Kate confesses all, sure now that the woman enjoys helping people in trouble. Sure enough, Hattie encourages Rob in his efforts to accept and adjust to his deafness. She even manages to get him a dog trained to assist the deaf. One day Rob comes home covered with mud. He's been plastered by some neighborhood kids after he failed to answer their calls. Spurred on by Kate, Rob goes back out and finds the boys, angrily explaining that he is deaf. In time, he begins coaching them in football and basketball, and they become special to each other. Their mutual admiration proves unexpectedly valuable when Rob and the boys subdue two robbers who hold up Hattie's grocery store and are about to take Kate hostage. As a grateful

Hattie and Kate prepare a surprise dinner for the boys, Kate hears a familiar voice at the door. Rob's mother has arrived with a policeman and a judge—unknown to her, both friends of Hattie's. Rob is not yet home, and after the two law officers persuade Hattie to let Mrs. Cory in, his mother is told all about his rehabilitation. When Rob and the boys enter the yard, Mrs. Cory watches through the window as her son communicates successfully with his friends. Convinced and grateful, Mrs. Cory begins to thank Hattie, but Hattie insists she is not the one to be thanked. So Mrs. Cory thanks Kate.

An overprotective mother, both domineering and dependent, keeps a teenage boy from accepting his hearing loss and getting on with his life. The boy's determined girlfriend, a sympathetic landlady, and Rob's own will to recover help him learn the skills he needs to cope successfully with his disability. No judgment is made on Rob and Kate's decision to run away, but the successful outcome could be read as an endorsement. This story is very simply written, perhaps a bit contrived, but should be appealing to young people with limited reading skills. Especially worth notice are the descriptions of Rob as he learns to live with his deafness.

Ages 12 and up

**Also available in:**
Paperbound—*Breakaway*
Dell Publishing Company, Inc.

## 258

**Hamilton, Morse**

**Big Sisters Are Bad Witches**

Color illustrations by Marylin Hafner.
Greenwillow Books, 1981.
(32 pages counted)

---

*SIBLING: Younger*
  *Sibling: new baby*

---

Little Kate would like to have a baby brother. She thinks she would make a good big sister. Her brother would say, "You know what, Kate? Big sisters are bad witches," and she would agree. Kate is unhappy with her own big sister, Emily, who she believes has been bad to her tonight. She is also feeling guilty about her own behavior because when she climbed on the desk to watch Emily type on their father's typewriter, the giraffe figurine got knocked off and broken. Then Emily, angered by her sister's interference, pulled on Kate's sweater, tearing off one of the buttons. So Kate hit Emily on the arm. Now Kate is waiting for her father to get home. She has apologized to Emily, but her big sister still won't let her sit by her to watch TV. Alone with her thoughts, Kate thinks about how she will hug and kiss her father when he arrives. At the same time, she anticipates the spanking she will probably get for fighting with Emily. She remembers, however, that she is not the only one who has misbehaved; if her father spanks her and not Emily too, he will also be bad. Perhaps, she thinks, everyone in the house is bad except her mother and her spider, Jennifer, named after Emily's best friend. But the human Jennifer doesn't like to play with Kate because Kate is too small. After visiting her spider, Kate goes to greet her father who has just come home. Emily immediately tells him he should spank Kate, but instead he hugs both his girls and informs them of their new baby brother. Now, he says, "Kate will know what it's like to be a little sister and a big sister." Since this news puts everyone in a good mood, Emily plays dolls with Kate, teaches her a new song, and reads her a story. Kate reconsiders and decides that "Emily's not really a bad witch."

This book follows the somewhat erratic thought processes of an imaginative child who is trying to establish her own identity as well as her place in the family. Kate knows the trials of being a younger sibling and vows not to be "bad" to the coming new baby. When her older sister is kind to her, however, Kate quickly forgets her grievances. Colorful pictures of scruffy children reflect the lively personalities of Kate and Emily.

Ages 3-6

**Also available in:**
No other form known

## 259

Hamilton, Morse and Emily Hamilton

**My Name Is Emily**
Color illustrations by Jenni Oliver.
Greenwillow Books, 1979.
(30 pages counted)

---

*SIBLING: New Baby*
  *Communication: parent-child*
  *Running away*

---

Returning home about suppertime after having run away, five-year-old Emily comes upon a man raking leaves in his front yard. With grave politeness the man asks her if she lives nearby and what her name is. When she replies the man expresses amazement, for his daughter also is named Emily. Further coincidences are revealed as they continue the conversation. Both Emilys have brown hair and gray eyes, were born June 12, and can count to twenty in Spanish. Emily covers her mouth with her hand to suppress a giggle and then confesses that she is his little girl. Disbelieving, the man explains that his daughter has run away. Then he looks deeply into Emily's eyes and seriously asks her one more question. "Do you have a little sister who wets her bed and cries and takes up your parents' time, but who needs their love just the same?" Emily admits this is true. Just then a woman comes to the door with a baby in her arms and calls out, "Supper's ready, you two." Emily's father grabs her up, hugs her tightly, and carries her into the house.

A delightfully different way of dealing with sibling rivalry is depicted here. The verbal play between father and daughter cleverly returns to the child the feelings of love and security she'd missed since the arrival of a new baby. Although the father acknowledges Emily and her feelings about her sister, he also carefully emphasizes the needs of the new baby as part of the family. Delicately colored illustrations capture the warm, quiet tone of the story.

Ages 3-6

**Also available in:**
No other form known

## 260

Hamilton-Merritt, Jane

**My First Day of School**
Black/white photographs by the author.
Julian Messner, Inc., 1982.
(30 pages counted)

---

*SCHOOL: Entering*
  *Friendship: making friends*
  *Transitional objects: toys*

---

Kate and her best friend, Bear, are starting kindergarten today. Kate feels prepared because she and her mother have shopped for a new dress and visited the school. Kate has also written her name on her lunchbox. Kate gets up early on this first day of school because she has so much to do before the bus comes: get dressed, eat a good breakfast, fix her snack for school. Her older sister, Sarah, helps her get on the bus. At school Kate is glad to have Bear with her and wonders if she'll make any new friends. She learns where to keep her things, where the bathroom is, and the various school rules. Her teacher and class talk about families and pets, the children draw pictures of their families, and they meet the principal. At the school library, Kate and Bear find a book about bears and the librarian reads another book to the class. After their busy day, Kate and Bear have lots of things to tell Mommy and Daddy. When Mommy asks, Kate says she hasn't made a new friend yet but plans to tomorrow. On the second day of school, the teacher tells Kate that Bear must stay in the cubbyhole where Kate keeps her other things. Kate has art, music, gym, and work periods. After snack time she sweeps the floor— her responsibility—and goes to the playground for play time. There she meets a possible new friend. She asks another possible new friend to play on the slide with her. "It's easier than I thought to make friends," says Kate. That night Kate tells Bear that he doesn't have to come to school with her anymore. Her teacher is so nice, and she knows now that she has friends at school too.

Kate narrates her experiences during the first and second days of kindergarten as she learns that she is capable of making friends and that school is a good place to be. Kate's tone is matter-of-fact, but listeners and readers will suspect that Bear is a great comfort to her those first two days. When Kate decides to leave him at home it's plain that she has overcome some doubts and fears about school. The photographs of typical kindergarten activities and facilities sometimes appear posed, but that doesn't detract from the value of this reassuring book.

Ages 3-6

**Also available in:**
No other form known

**261**

Hanlon, Emily

**The Swing**

Bradbury Press, Inc., 1979.
(209 pages)

---

FRIENDSHIP: Meaning of
  Communication: parent-child
  Deafness
  Honesty/Dishonesty
  Stepparent: father

---

Though they have different problems, both eleven-year-old Beth Hampton and Danny Grady, thirteen, find solace in the same place: at the swing hanging from the gnarled oak that stands on the lot between their houses in the town of Chester Falls. Danny misses his father; his stepfather, earthy and practical Clyde, is no substitute. Owner of a smokehouse, he forces Danny, who has no stomach for slaughtering animals, to participate in the butchering of a cow. A terrible nausea wells within the boy and he vomits. Later, he is dismayed to learn that although his mother sympathizes with him she also understands Clyde's viewpoint, since Danny will one day inherit the business. Beth, deaf from birth, has come to Chester Falls with her parents for the summer, as she does every year. She has high-spirited plans to climb the mountain that towers above the field near their summer home. When her mother withholds permission, a furious Beth rebelliously scales not only the mountain, but also the unstable old tower perched at its peak. Danny and two other boys, Willy and Brian, find her there. While Danny stands by, the other two torment Beth, calling her "Dummy" and shaking the rickety steps of the tower. Ashamed of his silent acquiescence, Danny wishes he still had his father to confide in. Meanwhile, Beth's parents, who don't know about her escapade on the mountain, relent and give her permission to go there. She returns and sees a mother bear and its cub. Thrilled, she secretly claims them for herself. One day while Beth is visiting her bears, Danny goes rabbit hunting on the mountain with a rifle Clyde gave him as part payment for mending pigsties—Clyde has been giving Danny work that doesn't offend the boy's sensibilities. This is Danny's first solo hunting expedition and he trips and drops the gun, which fires, frightening the mother bear into menacing the two children. Danny panics and Beth saves their lives by getting him to climb a tree. The two make a pact of secrecy about the incident, but when Danny arrives home dirty and scratched, Clyde is suspicious and questions him. Ashamed to admit the truth, Danny blurts out that Beth was attacked by a bear and he rescued her. His falsehood balloons as Clyde rounds up a hunting party. Learning of this, Beth heads up the mountain intent on saving her bears. She confronts the hunters and her father, who is searching for her, and tells them the truth. The hunt is not cancelled, but Danny is tormented by Willy and Brian, who are part of the group. Clyde defends Danny, persuading him to fight Willy. Danny goes berserk, beats Willy to the ground, and then turns on Clyde. Danny and Beth are in town the following day when the triumphant hunters march by with the dead mother bear and her cub. The next morning Beth slips away to the swing for consolation, only to discover that someone has tied the dead bear cub to it. When Danny approaches her, she attacks him with flying fists, certain that he has committed this atrocity. Danny covers his head and waits for Beth to exhaust herself. Then he tells her he didn't tie the bear to the swing. As she lipreads his words, her eyes are cold and disbelieving. He continues, forming his words carefully: "I'm sorry the bears are dead, Beth. I know it's my fault. But I didn't mean to break our pact. . . . This is my place here as much as it's yours. I couldn't lie here." Beth understands for the first time that Danny too has experienced pain and fear. Together they bury the bear cub beneath the oak and vow to share the swing forever.

Written from the alternating viewpoints of Beth and Danny, this is a poignant story about two young people struggling to adjust to a world of conflicting values where human differences are poorly tolerated. Feisty Beth learns not only the perils of surviving with a hearing impairment, but also how to listen with her heart as she is awakened to Danny's suffering. Gentle Danny, still mourning for his father, comes to understand a stepfather whose values are different from his own. The two children develop a bond out of their love of animals and their need for the consolation of the swing.

Ages 10-12

**Also available in:**
Braille—The Swing
Library of Congress (NLSBPH)

Cassette—The Swing
Library of Congress (NLSBPH)

**262**

Hanlon, Emily

**The Wing and the Flame**

Bradbury Press, Inc., 1980.
(147 pages)

---

FRIENDSHIP: Meaning of
  Differences, human
  Homosexuality: male
  Love, meaning of
  Maturation

---

During his Christmas vacation from college, on a cold, snowy New Year's Eve day, Eric Nicholson, nineteen, sets out on a bicycle trek to visit his friend Owen Cassell, a sculptor in his seventies who lives alone on Stoneface Mountain. While searching for the reclusive Owen, Eric recalls the events of his fourteenth year, the year he met Owen. At first afraid of the "seedy-looking" old man who seemed to be watching him, Eric came to love and respect Owen and happily served as model for Owen's sculpture of his dead son, whom Eric resembled. The son had died in his burning house along with his mother, and from then on, Owen had lived apart from society. Owen had been watching Eric, the boy found, because of this resemblance to his son; ever since the fire, Owen had been unable to complete the sculpture. The fire had destroyed all his photographs of his son, and grief had wiped out Owen's memory of the boy's face. Eric, at odds with his own family and touched by Owen's story, became devoted to the old man. That summer Eric had divided his time between this new friendship and an old one, with his best friend, Chris Praeger. During one trip to the mountain, Owen had shown Eric an eerie hidden cave, used as a burial place by the Indians of the area. Eric later brought Chris there to experience the special, almost magical feelings the cave generated. The boys' closeness resulted in a sexual encounter, which at first frightened and confused both of them, but which they gradually learned to understand and accept. Now, five years later, Eric returns to the cave in his search for Owen and discovers the sculptor's body, frozen to death. For Eric, Owen has left burial instructions and his will, with Eric named as beneficiary. Chris has followed Eric to the cave. Equally moved by the life and death of Owen Cassell, the two friends leave together.

This unusual story centers on a time in a boy's life when his feelings—about himself, his family, his friends—threaten to overwhelm him. He finds comfort and matures emotionally by learning from an old man and a young boy the many ways one can accept and express love. Eric's relationship with Owen is sensitively described, although Owen's otherworldliness and mystical observations make him at times an unsatisfactory character. Especially well done is the depiction of the stages in Eric's relationship with Chris. Their physical attraction is handled with great delicacy and is seen as only one component of a many-faceted friendship. A perceptive exploration of relationships, the story shows how a true friendship can span years and endure changes.

Ages 13 and up

**Also available in:**
No other form known

## 263

Hansen, Joyce

### The Gift-Giver

Houghton Mifflin Company, 1980.
(118 pages)

---

*AUTONOMY*
*FRIENDSHIP: Meaning of*
  *Afro-American*
  *Boy-girl relationships*
  *Change: accepting*
  *Foster home*
  *Maturation*
  *Parent/Parents: unemployed*
  *Responsibility: accepting*

---

Doris and her friends Sherman, Russell, Yellow Bird, Dotty, and Mickey are in the same fifth-grade class. They also all live on 163rd Street in The Bronx. But Doris feels less fortunate than her friends because her parents want her to avoid the playground. They're afraid of the gangs and the drug dealing. Since Doris wants to play with her friends, she occasionally gets grounded for defying her parents and going to the playground. One day in April, Amir joins their class. He is quiet and solitary, more content to observe than to take part in games. Doris is drawn to the boy and his quiet spirit, and soon a friendship develops. When Sherman runs away from the foster home he has just been placed

in, Amir persuades him to return and make the best of it. Doris then discovers that not only is Amir himself now in a foster home, but that he has been in many such homes. He's also run away repeatedly, for which he spent time in reform school. After school is out for the summer, Doris, more and more curious about Amir, finally asks him how he managed to adjust to all the homes and changes he has known. Amir tells her of an old man he befriended in one home. "He said kindness always comes back to you. He told me I'd been a blessing to him. He called me the little gift-giver." Shortly thereafter, Doris's father is laid off. Her parents discuss sending Doris and her baby brother to live with separate relatives so both parents can work. Terrified at the prospect of the family breaking up, Doris begs them to give her a chance to watch Gerald and take care of the apartment. Reluctantly, her parents agree. To everyone's surprise, Doris proves to be a capable baby-sitter and a responsible housekeeper. Although in two weeks Doris's father returns to his old job and the house returns to normal, the girl feels she has proven her worth. Just before school starts in the fall, Doris learns that Amir's foster family is moving to California, and so he must go upstate to a group home. Doris will lose a good friend, but he has been a gift-giver. He has helped her understand herself and others a bit better.

A young girl growing up in a tough urban ghetto tells a poignant story of survival and friendship. The author understands her characters and their milieu and makes events come alive for the reader. The dialect adds to the story's authenticity and should present no difficulties in comprehension.

Ages 9-12

**Also available in:**
No other form known

## 264

Hargreaves, Roger

### Mr. Noisy

Color illustrations by the author.
Creative Education, Inc., 1980.
(32 pages counted)

---

*CHANGE*
*SELF-DISCIPLINE*
  *Consideration, meaning of*

---

When Mr. Noisy reads a book, he does so at the top of his lungs and can be heard a hundred miles away. He snores loudly. His alarm clock is so loud it wakes up the people who live at the bottom of the hill in Wobbleville. When he leaves his house, he slams the door so hard that the door, house, hill, and all of Wobbleville wobble. At the bakery, he gives his order in such a loud voice that Mrs. Crumb trembles. He does the same thing to Mr. Bacon, the butcher. When Mr. Bacon and Mrs. Crumb meet in the street, Mrs. Crumb tells Mr. Bacon her idea about a way to change Mr. Noisy. The next time he orders his loaf of bread in Mrs. Crumb's bakery, she pretends she cannot hear him. He ends up yelling more and more loudly, but to no avail. The same thing happens at the butcher's, and Mr. Noisy goes to bed hungry that night. But the next day at the bakery, after

H

beginning to shout, Mr. Noisy speaks very quietly . . . and gets his bread. Again, at the butcher's, he tries his usual shouting, but only receives his meat when he speaks quietly. After that Mr. Noisy learns to tiptoe, to open and shut doors quietly, and even to whisper.

With the help of Mrs. Crumb and Mr. Bacon, Mr. Noisy learns to lower his voice and generally to go more gently through life. The extensive Mr. Book Series (originally published in Great Britain) features colorful, cartoon-like illustrations and presents characters with various flaws or personality defects who are changed or reformed, temporarily or permanently, usually by some outside agency—magic, tricks, happenstance, or, as in this case, friends. These amusing little books have a special appeal for children and, since each focuses on a single personality trait, can be useful in introducing a topic.

Ages 3-7

**Also available in:**
No other form known

## 265

Harlan, Elizabeth

**Footfalls**

Atheneum Publishers, 1982.
(128 pages)

---

*DEATH: of Father*
  *Boy-girl relationships*
  *Family: relationships*
  *Illnesses: terminal*
  *Sex: attitude toward*
  *Sports/Sportsmanship*

---

Stephanie (Stevie) Farr is the only freshman on the girls' varsity track team, a long-distance runner with a good chance of winning the regional cross-country race. But her mother is more interested in Stevie's grades than in her running, too busy to help Stevie clock distances on weekends. Her father is usually too tired to help. For a while, her father stays home from work with "the flu," although Stevie hears her mother talking to the surgeon who removed the growth on her father's back the previous year. One night, after a disastrous dinner of quarrels about inconsequential things, her father decides to get dressed and take Stevie out to clock distances. But he returns to the kitchen, still in his pajamas and robe, saying he's just too beat to do it. Stevie screams that he's always "too beat" to do anything with her. The night of her fourteenth birthday party, with six of her friends staying overnight, her father is taken to the hospital with severe bleeding. In the middle of the night, Stevie finds her younger brother, Robby, huddled on the couch. She'd asked that he not be in the house for her party, but since he has few friends and had no place to go, he hid in a crawl space near his parents' bedroom. There he saw his father bleeding copiously. On their way to a track meet, Mr. Desnick, the boys' track coach, sits next to Stevie on the bus and rubs his thigh against hers. Although Stevie has often fantasized about Mr. Desnick, she finds his behavior disgusting. Then she wonders if she's going to be frigid. During the race, she falls and sprains her ankle. Jeb Gray, a junior, helps her; she

decides from her reactions to him that she's probably not going to grow up frigid after all. That afternoon her mother returns from the hospital looking haggard. Stevie's father has had surgery. Stevie asks her mother if her father will be all right. When her mother hesitates, Stevie remembers all the checkups and doctor's appointments over the last year. Suddenly she realizes her father has cancer and is dying. She screams at her mother for keeping the truth from her. During the next several weeks, Stevie's grandparents stay with her and Robby while their mother spends all her time at the hospital. Stevie and Robby visit their father once and find him pale, weak, drifting in and out of sleep. Stevie trains furiously for the cross-country meet, telling herself that if she completes a certain distance or achieves a certain time her father will live. Then, on her way to winning the long-awaited race, she suddenly realizes that her father is going to die anyway. She gives up and loses the race; her father dies two days later. Although she knows he's dead, Stevie keeps waiting to hear his distinctive footfalls in the house. Numb and apathetic, she stops running and her grades fall. At a party Jeb kisses her, but it's anything but memorable. She talks to Robby about things in life that are outside their control. In the spring she begins running again, but wishes she could have slowed down enough to share some of her father's dying time with him. Her sessions with a school counselor help her understand and accept some of her feelings, even about the disappointing kiss from Jeb. Then Jeb invites her to run with him on Saturday morning. He tells her Mr. Desnick has been fired for kissing one of the students. After they run, Jeb kisses Stevie again and unfastens her bra. She stops him but that night, remembering, she begins to masturbate. Then she thinks of her father. She gets out of bed and studies his picture. She realizes she is angry at him for dying, but then understands that he didn't choose to die. "I guess . . . I'm beginning to accept the fact that Daddy isn't ever coming back, because he can't come back, because he's dead. And death lasts forever." She places his picture face down, returns to bed, and masturbates to orgasm. She wonders "if this was what Daddy meant when he said I would do lots of things for myself when I got older."

A teenage girl recounts a traumatic year in her life: the year she trains so hard for the regional track meet, the year she finds her first boyfriend, the year her father dies. Stevie doesn't realize the seriousness of her father's condition (which her parents have kept from her) until near the end. Even then she is unable to cope with it, and no one helps or encourages her to take stock of her relationship with him before he dies. Further complicating her emotions is her emerging sexuality, stimulated by an overly friendly teacher and then a boyfriend. Relationships and situations are perceptively and sensitively described, although the masturbation sequences seem both superfluous and contrived. Stevie's conflicting feelings about her father's death have the ring of truth, perhaps because the author has translated into fictional terms her own feelings as a young girl when her father died of cancer.

Ages 12-14

**Also available in:**
Paperbound—*Footfalls*
Ballantine Books, Inc.

**266**

**Harrah, Michael**

## First Offender

William Collins Publishers, Inc., 1980.
(186 pages) o.p.

---

*DELINQUENCY, JUVENILE*
*DETENTION HOME, LIVING IN*
   *Alcoholism: of mother*
   *Family: extended*
   *Justice/Injustice*
   *Violence*

---

Thirteen-year-old Freddy Godwin is approached by Ron Cummings about helping him steal money from an old woman. Freddy thinks it's a joke and laughs, angering Ron into starting a fight. Freddy returns home with bruises and scrapes. Home is an abandoned hotel where he lives with Ma, who drinks too much; Birdie, her cousin and friend; and the kind, homosexual Jerome. When Freddy tells Ma who his adversary was, Jerome recognizes the name. He reports that Ron's father runs a pornographic bookstore, his mother runs a whorehouse in the back, and Ron's been jailed twice already. That night, Ma is fired from her waitressing job for getting drunk and insulting a customer, and she disappears. When Freddy finds her, she reminisces about her past happiness. Ever since the fire that took her husband's and daughter's life, she's been in pieces. When they get back to the hotel, a police car is waiting in front. Freddy, bewildered and frightened, is taken to the station and interrogated by Detective Moran. He is accused of robbing an elderly woman; Ron Cummings has confessed and named Freddy as his partner. Freddy thinks that if he just keeps telling the truth, everything will be all right. But he is taken to the Juvenile Detention Center where he spends hours waiting with his arms strapped painfully to his sides. He is given nothing to eat the entire day and is not allowed to go to the bathroom. Two policemen bully and threaten him until he tries to fight them—for which he's put in the first-offenders section. There he finds a complicated set of rules and a rigid point system requiring him to earn anything beyond his basic food, shelter, and clothing. Moran questions Freddy again, telling him he could go home right away if he would just confess. Otherwise he'll return to the main detention center where, says Moran, the record for a little guy like Freddy avoiding homosexual rape is about two days. Terrified, Freddy continues to insist he's innocent. But in a lineup, he is identified by the victim as the thief. As days pass, Freddy's moods alternate wildly. Sometimes he is sure his innocence will be proved. Other times he knows that Ron's testimony and the victim's identification could carry the day. One of the wardens is Mr. Willie, a black policeman working a second job, who feels that Freddy just doesn't fit the usual delinquent profile. He calls Moran and asks if he remembers Ron Cumming's old sidekick, Tom Silvers. Tom bears a distinct resemblance to Freddy. Moran doesn't think much of the question and says the case is all wrapped up. But Mr. Willie remembers a cabdriver who was murdered the previous week by two boys resembling Ron and either Tom or Freddy. He checks and finds that Tom was released from his last

sentence three weeks ago. Mr. Willie gets Tom to testify about the breaking-and-entering cases in exchange for silence on the greater charge of murder. Later that day, Mr. Willie tells Freddy he's been released. Moran apologizes for the error. When Freddy discovers that Mr. Willie was responsible for his release, he runs back to thank him. On Christmas Eve, Freddy, Ma, Birdie, and Jerome all contribute something to the celebration. Freddy's heart sinks when Birdie sets out a bottle of scotch she bought with some money left over from what Freddy had given her to buy a Christmas tree. He hopes Ma won't have any, but she insists she's in control and starts drinking. Freddy angrily breaks the bottle and runs out of the hotel. They run after him and he sees Ma slip on the steps. He goes back to make sure his Ma isn't really hurt.

An innocent boy is held in a juvenile detention center, unable to prove he doesn't belong there. This nightmarish, wrenching book introduces a likeable, memorable character in Freddy as it exposes inequities in the juvenile justice system. Freddy's helplessness in the face of circumstantial evidence and his financial and social powerlessness are deeply affecting. Rough street language, the pervasive tone of suppressed violence, and some overt violence may render the book inappropriate for certain readers. The negative aspects of juvenile detention may seem overplayed here, but—unfortunately—they are entirely credible.

Ages 11-13

**Also available in:**
Paperbound—*First Offender*
Grosset & Dunlap, Inc.

**267**

**Harris, Mark Jonathan**

## With a Wave of the Wand

Lothrop, Lee & Shepard Company, 1980.
(191 pages)

---

*CHANGE: New Home*
*CHANGE: Resisting*
*MAGICAL THINKING*
*SEPARATION, MARITAL*
   *Friendship: meaning of*
   *Sibling: relationships*

---

Marlee has had such a streak of rotten Mondays during her fifth-grade year that when her father moves out on a Monday in May—the crowning disaster—she is sure he will be back the next morning. He is not. In August her mother decides to move with Marlee and her younger brother, Jeremy, to nearby Venice, California, where she has taken a job. This is a lonely time for Marlee; she hates their quaint old house, hates the free-spirited ocean town, and most of all, she hates the separation. She even finds something to dislike about the kindly old magician next door, Mr. Tomaro, who by way of introduction pulls two roses from his sleeve. Marlee simply dismisses his magic as trickery. One particularly bad day, she thinks about how much she would prefer living with her father. During the following weekend visit with him, Marlee proposes this move. Her father gently maintains that their current arrangement is the best. That night Marlee and Jeremy talk about the separation

**H**

and wonder if they could have caused it. Back home on Sunday, Marlee tells her mother that the barrenness of her father's apartment seems a sign that he is planning to move back. Her mother replies that the separation "has nothing to do with our feelings about you. Whatever we decide, we'll both still love you." Marlee is not convinced. Soon after this, when Mr. Tomaro pulls a live rabbit out of a hat without first removing one from the rabbit cage, she finally believes his magic is real. Once school starts Marlee asks him to help her put a spell on Dee, a classmate, to make her be her friend. Mr. Tomaro teaches her a spell she is to repeat every night as she imagines herself and Dee together. The next day Marlee approaches Dee, and they soon do become friends. Impressed, Marlee then decides to cast a spell on her parents to get them back together. She asks Jeremy to help, but their plan seems to have backfired when their mother invites a male friend over. Each weekend, Marlee finds her father more and more distracted. She also realizes, after a visit to her old neighborhood, that she likes her new home and no longer wants to move back. Even though she is unsure about the effects of her spell, she notices that her mother seems changed, happier, that things are going more smoothly at home. Her father has promised to attend her upcoming twelfth birthday party. Marlee becomes convinced that during her party, her father will announce he is returning home; she secretly imagines the scene every night, as Mr. Tomaro advised her to do with Dee. Thus, when her father arrives the day before the party and announces that he will be moving to New York to take a new job and that her mother and he have decided to get a divorce, Marlee feels utterly betrayed. She throws the inscribed locket he brought her into the canal and locks herself in her bedroom. The next morning, on her birthday, she runs away. Mr. Tomaro finds her that night and takes her home after explaining the rabbit trick and telling her the secret behind her friendship with Dee: her own self-confidence won her a friend. Marlee avoids her father in the coming weeks, but when it appears she may not see him before he leaves, she begins to regret her behavior. One night Marlee and Jeremy are sent to the store. They return to a gathering of everyone who'd been invited to Marlee's birthday party, including their father. Mr. Tomaro performs and suggests that he might share his secrets with Marlee if she were interested in becoming a magician. Eventually, Marlee is alone with her father. "I just couldn't hate him anymore. Dad wasn't the same person I'd thought he was, but then, I decided, neither was I." The next day she uses her birthday money to buy a cape and top hat, presenting herself to Mr. Tomaro for instruction.

In this story of painful changes, a young girl feels trapped in situations she cannot control or avoid. After a bad year at school, her parents' separation, and a move to a strange town, Marlee feels cheated and rather cynical. Through her friendship with Mr. Tomaro, she decides magic is the only way to win back her adored father and reunite the family. But eventually Marlee understands that everyone, including her magician friend and her father, is human and therefore imperfect. This recognition allows her to stop grieving for the past and begin to accept the present. With interesting characters and a complicated yet believable plot, this

excellent novel features a heroine with that mixture of toughness and vulnerability so appealing to many young readers.

Ages 9-12

**Also available in:**
Paperbound—*With a Wave of the Wand*
Scholastic Book Services

## 268

**Harris, Robie H.**

## I Hate Kisses

Color illustrations by Diane Paterson.
Alfred A. Knopf, Inc., 1981.
(31 pages counted)

*MATURATION*
  *Transitional objects: toys*

Some sudden changes have taken place in little Peter. He decides he is now too grown up for some of the things he liked a short time ago. For one thing, he now hates kisses. He doesn't want his stuffed dinosaur, Nellie, anymore and gives her to his father, along with her baseball cap, quilt, and sweater. He'd rather play with his new robot. At dinner Peter wants to eat string beans, something he's never liked before, so his muscles will grow big. After dinner, however, Peter falls on top of his robot and hurts his knee. "Where's my Nellie?" Peter sobs. That night the dinosaur stays on Peter's pillow, and there is a goodnight hug for both his parents. Still no kisses, but Peter decides, "Maybe I'll have some . . . in the morning."

This is a charming, reassuring book for children who are trying to grow up but still need kisses and a favorite toy now and then. When Peter falls and hurts himself, he forgets for a time how big and strong he's become. Bright illustrations add to the warmth and humor of the story.

Ages 2-5

**Also available in:**
No other form known

## 269

**Harris, Robin**

## Hello Kitty Sleeps Over

Color illustrations by J.M.L. Gray.
Random House, Inc., 1982.
(24 pages counted)

*SEPARATION ANXIETY*
*VISITING*
  *Grandparent: love for*

Kitty gets ready early to sleep over at Grandma's house. She packs socks, overalls, her favorite T-shirt, and slippers. Her mother reminds her to take her pajamas and toothbrush. Kitty will bring Grandma some flowers she and Mama gathered from their yard, and Grandpa some home-baked cookies. When it's time to go, Mama carries the flowers and cookies, and Kitty carries Lucy, her favorite bear, and two storybooks. When she arrives,

Kitty gets big kisses from her happy grandparents. Then Mama kisses her too and drives away. Kitty is momentarily sad to see her mother go, but she's comforted by a hug from Grandma and the familiar feel of Lucy. For a while Kitty plays games with Grandma and then she plays with the toys that are kept at this house especially for her. Later, Grandma makes a special dinner and a dessert of ice cream with chocolate sauce and cherries. Just before bedtime, Grandpa helps Kitty bathe and brush her teeth. Then Grandma reads her two stories and kisses her goodnight. Once again Kitty isn't sure she wants to sleep here, but Grandma holds her hand until she drifts off. In the morning Kitty helps make the pancakes and then packs her things to go home. She is ready when Mama comes, but decides she really would like to sleep at Grandma's house again.

Many small children are already familiar with "Hello Kitty," and they will enjoy this story of the character's sleepover with her grandparents. Clearly communicated is the warm, loving relationship that helps Kitty overcome her anxiety about being away from home. Simple, bold illustrations add appeal.

Ages 2-5

**Also available in:**
No other form known

## 270

**Hassler, Jon Francis**

**Jemmy**

Atheneum Publishers, 1980.
(175 pages)

---

*IDENTITY, SEARCH FOR*
  *Alcoholism: of father*
  *Deformities*
  *Dropout, school*
  *Friendship: meaning of*
  *Native American*
  *Prejudice: ethnic/racial*
  *Sibling: relationships*
  *Talents: artistic*

---

In October of Jemmy Stott's senior year, her father tells her to quit school. A house painter turned alcoholic, he wants Jemmy to keep up the house and take care of her eleven-year-old brother, Marty, and her six-year-old sister, Candy. Jemmy accepts the news calmly; most Indians in northern Minnesota don't finish high school anyway. Actually, Jemmy is a "half-breed." Her mother, dead for almost six years, was a Chippewa, and her father is white. The girl has never felt herself a full member of either race. The next day Jemmy drives to school and withdraws herself. For a change, she decides to go home by way of the forest road. A blizzard begins to rage and Jemmy's car runs out of gas. She stumbles along the road on foot until she finds a barn. Once inside she collapses from exhaustion and cold. There she is discovered by Otis Chapman. He and his wife, Ann, feed Jemmy and give her warm clothes and shelter for the night. Jemmy learns that Otis is a famous artist commissioned to paint a large mural for a building in Minneapolis. The painting is to commemorate Minnesota's Indian heritage, and Otis is in the area researching the lore about the Maiden of Eagle Rock. Studying

Jemmy's features, Otis asks if he can use her as his model. Jemmy readily agrees, happy for the first time in years to be an Indian. Otis and Ann discover Jemmy's interest in sketching and buy her a sketchbook. Soon the Chapmans get to know Jemmy's family. Marty and Candy quickly adore them, but Mr. Stott avoids them, obscurely resentful of their generosity to his children. Otis and Ann give Jemmy a paint box and easel, and Otis begins teaching her to paint. When Christmas comes Mr. Stott refuses the Chapmans' invitation, preferring to take Marty into town to celebrate. When his father gets drunk, the mortified boy runs to hide in the schoolhouse. He is accidentally trapped in the unheated building and is found unconscious with frostbitten hands. Two fingers must be amputated and Marty, fearing ridicule, refuses to return to school. With the Chapmans' help, Jemmy persuades him to go back. Meanwhile, Jemmy learns from Ann that Otis himself used to be an alcoholic. Before one of his frequent trips to Minneapolis to work on his mural, Otis suggests that Jemmy's father paint his dilapidated barn. When he returns and finds that Mr. Stott has barely touched the barn, he shocks the man by calling him a no-good drunken bum. Otis finally finishes his mural and Jemmy, knowing the couple will now move from the area, can't bring herself to attend the dedication. But to her surprise she realizes that her father has become kinder towards his children, that he isn't drinking as much. He even begins scraping their house in preparation for painting. Otis Chapman's rebuke has changed him. Several days after the Minneapolis dedication, Jemmy drives in to see the mural. She is astonished at the painting's beauty and at the likeness of herself. When she recognizes the Indian brave in the mural's background as Otis, both loss and joy wash over her. She realizes that in the six months she has known the Chapmans, they have made a painter out of her and a new man out of her father. She is grateful.

Half Indian and half white, a demoralized girl is helped by generous, loving friends to discover her artistic talents, her identity as a Native American, and her individual worth. In the process she witnesses the start of a recovery for her alcoholic father and a drawing together of her family. This low-key, well-written story is distinguished by vivid descriptions of the natural and human scene and by strong characterizations.

Ages 11 and up

**Also available in:**
No other form known

## 271

**Hautzig, Deborah**

**The Handsomest Father**

Color illustrations by Muriel Batherman.
Greenwillow Books, 1979.
(47 pages)

---

*DIFFERENCES, HUMAN*
  *School: classmate relationships*

---

As Father's Visiting Day at school approaches, Marsha, about seven, becomes more and more worried. What if her father doesn't look like other fathers? Suppose he does something awful and everyone laughs? She asks her friend Kathryn if her father is handsome, and Kathryn replies that he is the handsomest man in the world. Marsha grows more nervous, for she is certain her father is not. The evening before the big day, Marsha glances at her father's old hat and decides it looks hopelessly stupid. With sudden decision she puts her forehead against the hot radiator and then runs to inform her mother she has a fever. When her mother declares her the picture of health, she suggests to her father that he may be too busy to come to school with her. But the next morning father and daughter attend on schedule. Marsha looks around for Kathryn's handsome father. She sees several fathers, including one standing by the blackboard who is fat and not handsome at all. Kathryn joins Marsha and leads her excitedly to her father, the fat man standing by the blackboard! As Marsha introduces her father to Kathryn's, Marsha's father sneezes and blows his nose with a loud honk. Ready to climb under the desk with humiliation, Marsha waits for the laughter, but there is none. Instead, Kathryn and her father say, "Bless you!" and the day continues. Soon Marsha relaxes. In the afternoon, when the class has science, Marsha is proud that her father knows so much about dinosaurs. At the day's end, she whispers to him, "You are the handsomest father here."

As Marsha discovers it is all right for her father to be himself, she also gains insight into what individuality means. She learns too that beauty is truly in the eye of the beholder. Simple, appealing illustrations add a lighthearted touch to this beginning reader, also an entertaining read-aloud story.

Ages 4-7

**Also available in:**
No other form known

## 272

**Hautzig, Deborah**

**Second Star to the Right**
Greenwillow Books, 1981.
(151 pages)

---

*ANOREXIA NERVOSA*
*GUILT, FEELINGS OF*
*SELF, ATTITUDE TOWARD: Body Concept*
  *Family: relationships*
  *Friendship: best friend*
  *Hospital, going to*

---

At fourteen, Leslie Hiller tries to feel happy about her family, her good friend Cavett French, and the girls' school she and Cavett attend. Yet deep inside she is dissatisfied, unable to resolve her guilt over her stormy relationship with her mother. She decides that if she lost ten pounds she would like herself more: "If I were thin, my life would be perfect." During Christmas vacation Leslie gets the flu and loses a few pounds. She decides that now is the time to diet and begins counting calories

and doing sit-ups. Soon she is losing weight rapidly. She begins to enjoy feeling hungry. She also feels the presence inside her of a "dictator" who forbids her to eat. Her parents, afraid she is losing too much weight, insist that she eat. So Leslie does—and then induces herself to vomit. She reaches her goal of one hundred and five pounds, a loss of twenty pounds. But Leslie can't understand why she still doesn't feel thin. She decides her goal will be ninety-nine pounds. By early spring Leslie is no longer menstruating, her fingernails are blue, and she is always tired. She insists on eating dinner in her room, but instead of eating she throws the food out the window. Her parents, Cavett, and her teachers are distraught over Leslie's appearance. Existing on three curds of cottage cheese a day, she is constantly nauseated, cold, and weak. Her lips are cracked and will not heal, and her hair is falling out. Yet Leslie feels fat and unhappy. In desperation her mother takes her to a doctor who weighs her at eighty-six pounds. He tells her to eat and come back in two weeks. After a week Leslie is too weak to go to school. She returns to the doctor weighing seventy-six pounds and is placed in the hospital. There a psychologist tells Leslie she has anorexia nervosa, Latin for "nervous loss of appetite," but does little to help her. Her parents find two specialists at a different hospital, and there Leslie is befriended by two other girls with the same condition. Discovering she is not the only person in the world with the problem relieves her somewhat. She's not forced to eat, but must drink five glasses of caloric liquids a day. She also begins sessions with Dr. Wilcox, a psychiatrist, who tells her that starving will not make her unhappiness go away. With his help and the encouragement of other anorexia nervosa patients at the hospital, Leslie begins to maintain her weight and feel a little better about herself. Although her problems are not solved, she gains some insight into herself and her relationship with her mother and slowly starts coming around.

Confused about her feelings toward herself and her mother, Leslie decides her happiness will begin when she is thin. Her first-person narrative leads the reader through her long and torturous journey of near-starvation. Though her problems are left unresolved, it appears that Leslie will eventually recover from anorexia nervosa with psychiatric help. It may seem a bit unlikely that Leslie's first doctor and psychologist fail to diagnose or treat her true condition, but there is value here for siblings and peers of those with anorexia and for those curious about the illness. Written with compassion, this book deals honestly with the emotional upheaval suffered by a girl who wants to please and be good and in striving to improve almost kills herself.

Ages 12 and up

**Also available in:**
Braille—*Second Star to the Right*
Library of Congress (NLSBPH)

Cassette—*Second Star to the Right*
Library of Congress (NLSBPH)

Paperbound—*Second Star to the Right*
Avon Books

**273**

Hautzig, Esther Rudomin

**A Gift for Mama**

Black/white illustrations by Donna Diamond.
The Viking Press, Inc., 1981.
(56 pages)

---

*GIVING, MEANING OF*
 *Family: relationships*
 *Love, meaning of*
 *Resourcefulness*

---

Sara Domin, about ten, has always followed the "family tradition" of making gifts for birthdays, Hanukkah, and other special occasions. Her artistic mother believes that the best presents are handmade. Sara, however, does not agree. With Mother's Day coming soon, she is determined to give Mama a pair of black satin slippers to wear with her new black satin robe. Since Sara does not get an allowance, she must find a way of raising the nine zlotys she needs. She decides to discuss the matter with her Aunt Margola, her mother's younger sister, a student at the university near their home in Vilna, Poland. Margola always comes to Sara's house the day after Sara's parents have given a party. She brings her friends to help eat the delicious leftovers. Since there was a party on Sunday, Margola and her friends come as expected, after classes on Monday. As Sara watches the students eat, she notices that much of their clothing needs repair. She asks Margola to find out if her friends would be willing to pay her for mending their clothes. Margola comes back a few days later with the good news that the students agree to let Sara be their "clothes doctor." For the next two weeks Sara goes straight from school to Grandmother Hanna's house to work on her secret project. As she mends, darns, and turns worn collars, she and Grandmother talk together. She learns about her mother as a child. Although Sara is not overly fond of making things, Mama always loved to paint and draw and make objects out of clay. Sara earns her money just in time to buy the slippers for Mother's Day. She is very pleased with herself as she presents the shoe box to her mother on Sunday morning. But, much to her sorrow, Mama is not very enthusiastic about her "store-bought" gift. Later in the day, however, Margola brings her friends by in their newly mended clothing. Each one shows Mama the bit of work that Sara did for them to earn money for the gift. Mama is deeply touched. She leaves the room and returns in her black satin robe and matching slippers. Sara watches happily as her mother, looking "just like a movie star," serves her guests around their dining room table.

In this gentle story of family love and understanding, a young girl comes to recognize that her mother's insistence on handmade presents stems mainly from her own artistic yearnings. Only when Mama learns that Sara earned the money for her "store-bought" slippers by mending clothing does she accept and appreciate her daughter's gift. Expressive illustrations contribute greatly to the old-country atmosphere of the book, which takes place in pre-World War II Poland.

Ages 8-12

**Also available in:**
No other form known

**274**

Hayes, Sheila

**Me and My Mona Lisa Smile**

E. P. Dutton & Company, Inc., 1981.
(116 pages)

---

*BOY-GIRL RELATIONSHIPS: Dating*
*FRIENDSHIP: Meaning of*
*MATURATION*
 *Communication: rumor*
 *Daydreaming*
 *Shyness*

---

In her first year of high school, Rowena Swift is sure she's the only girl with no boy in her life. She feels too tall, too drab, too flat-chested. And she has to smile with her mouth shut because of the dental braces she still must wear. On a quiz about experience in "Modern Woman" magazine, she scores seven out of a possible 40: "You haven't left the garage yet." Rowena's once-close friend, Kate, has become part of a small clique of popular girls. Another, newer friend, Beth, is being pursued by Jim Dennison, a boy Rowena dislikes. But when Alan Phillips, the new English teacher, appears in class for the first time, Rowena herself is finally smitten. He encourages her fledgling interest in poetry, suggesting that she attend an out-of-town poetry reading with him and various students from the Writing Club. But there Rowena feels out of place, suspicious of the girls who've come, girls she has never liked much. Her dislike is confirmed when she discovers they smoke pot and treat her condescendingly. But Mr. Phillips sits next to her on the bus ride home, unwittingly feeding her infatuation. Once back, she writes another letter to advice columnist Trudy Potts, saying that she and "Alan" have had their "first chance to be . . . really together, if you know what I mean!" Rowena never mails her letters to Trudy; she always tears them up and flushes them down the toilet. She intends to do the same with this letter, but when her mother comes in she shoves it into her history book and then forgets about it. The next day at school, Kate borrows the history book. A day later, Rowena overhears some gossip about a student-teacher romance, recalls the note in the borrowed book, and feels certain that Kate has read it and talked. At first she's upset, but then decides the gossip will provide the limelight she's craved. At a meeting at Beth's house to plan the school's holiday dance, Gary Finch flirts with Rowena; he must have heard the rumor about her, she decides. Flustered, but pleased to be noticed, Rowena realizes she has never felt so good about herself. But when Jim Dennison begins to show an interest in her too and she inadvertently encourages his meaningful glances, Beth gets angry and stops speaking to her. Meanwhile, Rowena continues her attempts to impress Alan Phillips, turning in feverishly emotional poems. Then Kate shows a new interest in her old friend, which Rowena attributes to the rumors about her love life. Kate invites her to join her group and go to one of the football players' homes after the game. There Brad McKenna, a junior, latches on to Rowena and gives her a long, sloppy kiss. Gary invites Rowena to the holiday dance, mainly, she feels sure, because of her secret reputation. Then Alan Phillips shows up at a school variety show with a date. Word spreads quickly that the woman is his fiancée. Rowena burns with embarrassment, sure she will be found out. At the holiday dance, Mr. Phillips and his fiancée are chaperones. Rowena tries hard to stay far away from them, but because she and Gary are part of the dance committee, they are asked to take a turn entertaining the chaperones. Mortified, Rowena tries to run from the room. Gary follows, thinking she's upset, as he is, by the intergalactic theme of the dance. Finally Beth makes up with Rowena and innocently mentions that the gossip about a student-teacher affair involved a girl named Ginger. At last Rowena realizes that there never was any talk about her and Mr. Phillips. She need not hide from him or anyone else. Gary truly likes her for herself.

Rowena narrates this light, amusing story of a girl's discovery that she is indeed likeable and attractive— without benefit of provocative rumors she nourishes about herself and her glamorous English teacher. Rowena also gains some understanding of her friends Kate and Beth, both of whom she has misjudged. There is considerable insight here into the trying world of young teenagers.

Ages 11-13

**Also available in:**
Paperbound—*Me and My Mona Lisa Smile*
Lodestar Books

## 275

Hazen, Barbara Shook

**Even If I Did Something Awful**
Color illustrations by Nancy Kincade.
Atheneum Publishers, 1981.
(30 pages counted)

---

*GUILT, FEELINGS OF*
*LOVE, MEANING OF*
*Discipline, meaning of*

---

A little girl breaks the special vase that Daddy gave to Mommy for her birthday. What will Mommy do? The child asks, "Would you love me no matter what I did?" When the mother assures her that she would, the little girl persists. "Even if I did something awful?" "Like what kind of awful?" asks Mommy. The little girl imagines many things she might have done. What if she had gotten orange crayon on the carpet? Her mother answers, "I'd love you even if you crayoned the whole house. But I'd make you clean it up." "Would you love me if Mouser and I were playing rough and we pulled down the dining room curtains?" asks the girl. Says Mommy, "I'd love you even if you played so rough you pulled down the Empire State Building. But I'd make you pick it up." The game goes on with the same kind of questions and the same kind of answers until the little girl finds the courage to mention the real incident. If she broke the vase while playing ball in the living room after being told not to, would her mother still love her? Mommy, realizing that the pretending is over, still answers yes. She goes on to say that she "might be mad

and yell things like 'I told you a thousand times!' and 'This is the last straw!' and 'I've had it with your disobeying!'" She might also send the little girl to her room without dessert. But then, after tears on both sides, Mommy says, "I'd still love you no matter what, no matter how mad, no matter how awful. And I always will."

A little girl who needs to confess that she has disobeyed her mother and broken a vase bolsters her courage by proposing imaginary misdeeds and asking, "Would you still love me?" Her mother counters with imaginative responses that emphasize both love and discipline. The little girl learns that even though she may make her mother unhappy or angry, and even though she may be punished, she cannot destroy the love that Mommy has for her. This message will be reassuring to young children. The illustrations enhance the fanciful quality of the dialogue.

Ages 3-6

**Also available in:**
No other form known

## 276

Hazen, Barbara Shook

**If It Weren't for Benjamin (I'd Always Get to Lick the Icing Spoon)**
Color illustrations by Laura Hartman.
Human Sciences Press, 1979.
(30 pages counted)

---

*SIBLING: Rivalry*
*Sibling: relationships*

---

A little boy maintains that if it weren't for Benjamin, his older brother, he'd get to lick the icing spoon, receive all the Christmas gifts, and never have to share. He wants to be bigger than Benjamin, but he never is, and Benjamin gets to do things he can't do. He does realize that Benjamin sometimes wishes he were the younger brother so he could be babied. And although the younger brother never quite catches up with Benjamin, he can do a few things Benjamin can't, such as whistle, wiggle his ears, and make up songs. Still, after thinking about what life would be like "if it weren't for Benjamin," he tells his mother it's not fair. She says it's not possible to be absolutely fair. The little boy feels slighted when his grandmother makes a fuss over Benjamin's drawing, but she explains that both boys are special to her and each is good at different things. She then asks him to make up a song for her. When his father takes Benjamin to a double-header, the smaller boy decides his father must love Benjamin more. But his father points out that he gets to go to shows and to the zoo. He asks his mother whom she loves better. She says she loves them both very much, each one for what he is. He tells his mother that he wishes sometimes for Benjamin to disappear. His mother explains that parents' love for their children is different from siblings' love for each other and that it's okay to feel the way he does, as long as there's no hitting or hurting. That night, he begins to think of all that he'd be missing "if it weren't for Benjamin": the jokes, the helping hand, the encouragement. "Funny," he muses, "how you can hate someone sometimes and other times be glad he's your brother."

A younger brother gives a first-person account of life with an older sibling: the advantages and disadvantages as well as the vain search for absolute equality and justice. The book touches on many of the feelings children have about their siblings, but it does not convey (perhaps intentionally) the clenched-teeth, urge-to-kill emotions often found in real life. The low-key, slightly pedantic tone does reassure children that their feelings of doubt, resentment, even hate, are normal. The book could be used to initiate a helpful discussion on sibling rivalry. The illustrations clearly depict the emotions and activities described.

Ages 3-7

**Also available in:**
Paperbound—*If It Weren't for Benjamin (I'd Always Get to Lick the Icing Spoon)*
Human Sciences Press

## 277

### Hazen, Barbara Shook

### Tight Times

Black/white illustrations by Trina Schart Hyman.
The Viking Press, Inc., 1979.
(32 pages counted)

*PARENT/PARENTS: Mother Working Outside Home*
*PARENT/PARENTS: Unemployed*

A little boy wants a dog. His working mother brushes aside the request. His father says no also because of "tight times," claiming the child is too little to understand. But after his mother goes to work, his father explains over breakfast that tight times are "the times when everything keeps going up." Tight times are the reason the family eats Mr. Bulk instead of cereal in little boxes, and why they went not to the lake but "to the sprinkler" last summer. Tight times are also why they eat soupy things with lima beans instead of roast beef on Sundays, and why a baby-sitter, rather than his mother, picks the boy up from school. One afternoon the father comes home looking angry and dismisses the sitter. He makes "special drinks" and explains to the boy that he has lost his job—it seems to the child as if something were lost behind a radiator. When his mother returns from work, she gives the child a candy bar and says she wants to talk to Daddy alone. Outside, the boy hears crying coming from a trash can. A passerby rescues a bedraggled kitten from the can. The kitten seems hungry but refuses a part of the child's candy bar, and the passerby says it wants milk. The boy takes the kitten into the kitchen and tries to give it a dish of milk, but instead spills the container. As the kitten rushes to the milk, the parents run into the kitchen. The child explains that a nice lady said he could keep the kitten. Suddenly both parents begin to cry. They make "a sandwich hug with me in the middle." Then the boy starts to cry and his father says the kitten can stay, so long as there is no more talk about wanting a dog. After dinner, while the father reads the want ads and the

child rests on his thigh, kitten on chest, the father asks the kitten's name. "Dog," the child replies. He plays with the "great cat," gets tickled by chin whiskers, and hopes Dog likes lima beans.

The everyday meaning of economic hard times, parental love, and the company of pets is made clear in this compact work. The little boy who tells the story sees his parents harried and depressed, and his father explains "tight times" in comprehensible terms. The parents affirm their enduring love in a tearful hug, and the kitten—even if it isn't a dog—quickly wins the child's heart. Detailed illustrations supplement the slender but effective text.

Ages 5-7

**Also available in:**
Paperbound—*Tight Times*
The Viking Press, Inc.

## 278

### Heck, Bessie Holland

### Cave-in at Mason's Mine

Black/white illustrations by Charles Robinson.
Charles Scribner's Sons, 1980.
(64 pages)

H

*COURAGE, MEANING OF*
*FAMILY: Relationships*
*Fear*

Joey Johnson, nine, is traveling with his parents to spend their vacation in a cabin in the Rocky Mountains. Joey is especially interested in exploring an abandoned gold mine that his father had discovered when he was a boy. But he's nervous about hiking, because the previous summer he got lost in the woods. The first morning, he and his father set out to find Mason's Mine. Joey enjoys the chipmunks and even sees a bear rambling a short distance away. He and his father slide down a steep bank and cross the cold mountain stream below, stopping to drink. His father continually points out landmarks, trying to teach him what signs to watch for in case he must retrace his trail back to the cabin. At last they arrive at Mason's Mine. His father checks the entrance for safety, and then he and Joey take their flashlights and begin to explore. They have only been inside the cave for a few minutes when they hear a loud rumbling. His father yells at him to run for the entrance. Joey makes it outside, but his father is trapped in the fallen logs that had been at the mine's entrance. Unable to move, he tells Joey to return to the cabin and have his mother call the forest ranger. Joey is desperately afraid of getting lost, but knows he must get help for his father. He runs, crosses the stream, climbs the slippery slope, able to find his way by the landmarks his father had shown him earlier. He reaches the cabin exhausted, only to find a note that says his mother has gone to buy groceries. Joey races out to the main highway and tries flagging down two passing trucks. They ignore him, so when he sees a car coming down the mountain, he stands in the middle of the highway to make it stop. The two men in the car are furious, but when they hear his story they take him right to the ranger's station. The ranger sends out a rescue helicopter, and the two men take Joey back to the cabin to wait for his mother. When she returns, Joey directs her to the hospital where the ranger has told them to go. His father has been rescued and is being cared for in the emergency room. He has a broken bone in his foot and a couple of broken ribs, but he is well enough to return to the cabin. Joey is a hero. His father thinks he will be able to sleep out in the pup tent in a couple of nights and knows he will feel good enough to go fishing. Joey, who only that morning was afraid of the mountains, now decides they are beautiful, wonderful.

A young boy must overcome his fears and practice the new skills his father has taught him in order to save his father's life in this suspenseful adventure. Simply written, with numerous illustrations that add appeal, this is a story both of courage and of a warm father-son relationship.

Ages 8-10

**Also available in:**
No other form known

## 279

**Helmering, Doris Wild**

## I Have Two Families

Color illustrations by Heidi Palmer.
Abingdon Press, 1981.
(46 pages counted)

---

*DIVORCE: of Parents*
*Anxiety*

---

Eight-year-old Patty and her younger brother, Michael, have two homes. One is with their mother and a cat named Harry at 22C Park Street. The other is with their father and a dog, Pancake, at 1622A Skinker Avenue. When Patty first learned that her parents were getting a divorce, she worried about what would happen to her. Maybe she would be separated from Michael. Or maybe, if her mother and father could fall out of love with each other, they could also stop loving her. Perhaps neither one would want her anymore. Then one day the uncertainty ended. Mom and Dad called a conference to discuss the family's future. They announced that since Dad had a job with regular hours, both children would live mainly with him. Since Mom worked for an airline and had irregular hours, they would stay with her when she was home. Now Patty and Michael have a happy life again. At their Skinker Avenue apartment they share the chores and follow a now-familiar routine. Michael goes to day care, and Patty goes to her friend Jane's house after school. As they ride home in their father's car, they play a game Patty loves called "catch-up." Each person has to tell at least two things that happened during the day. When they get home, Patty feeds the dog and sets the table while Dad makes dinner. Sometimes Michael helps by getting out the napkins. In the evening the children watch television, read books, or play Chinese Checkers. They go to bed at 8:30. Wednesdays, however, are different. Mom picks Michael up from day care and Patty from school. She takes them to their home at 22C Park. There, life is not quite the same because "every family is different, you know." At this home Patty empties the dishwasher and

helps get dinner, while Michael feeds the cat and sets the table. After dinner they play cards or watch television. Sometimes Mom reads to them. As always, they go to bed at 8:30. On Thursday morning Patty gets her hair braided. If Mom doesn't have to work, she keeps Michael with her all day, making Patty a little jealous. Thursday night, the children go back to Skinker Avenue. Saturday morning, Dad takes them grocery shopping. In the afternoon they go roller skating or to a movie. On Saturday night Dad usually goes out on a date. Michael and Patty don't like this very much, but they understand that they must be "pleasant" to the person Dad is dating. Sundays are always spent with Mom. After Sunday school, they go to a movie, go bowling, or visit relatives. If Mom's schedule permits, they get to stay overnight. Life is quite agreeable for Patty and Michael. The only difference between them and most of their friends is that they are part of two families —one on Park Street and one on Skinker Avenue.

This timely first-person narrative, told by Patty, shows that children can live a normal, stable life after their parents' divorce. Patty and Michael experience all the fears and uncertainties that most children of divorce feel. Yet, because their parents are supportive and cooperative, they are able to adjust and make a new life much like the old one. The book may be reassuring for children in a similar situation, enlightening for those who need to understand what divorce means. The illustrations complement the text, which is optimistic without being sugar-coated.

Ages 6-8

**Also available in:**
No other form known

## 280

**Henkes, Kevin**

## All Alone

Color illustrations by the author.
Greenwillow Books, 1981.
(30 pages counted)

---

*AUTONOMY*
*PRIVACY, NEED FOR*

---

A young boy sometimes likes to spend time all by himself. When he is alone, he hears and sees and feels much more than when he's with other people. He hears the trees breathing in the wind. He sees roots tangling their way down into the ground. He feels the warmth of the sun on his body. When he's alone, he can pretend he's tall enough to lick the sky or small enough to hide behind a little stone. He asks himself questions he can't answer, thinks about things he's enjoyed doing, and looks at himself "inside and out." By and by, though, he wonders what his friends are doing. Being alone can be fun sometimes, but just for a while.

The young, introspective narrator is beginning to develop a separate sense of himself, starting to enjoy experiencing the world in his own way. He concludes that "no one looks just like me or thinks just like I do." Young readers or listeners will agree and may see some relevance to their own sense of themselves. Pastel illustrations—showing a child who appears to be a boy, but could also be a girl—support the quiet, reflective tone of the book.

Ages 3-6

**Also available in:**
No other form known

## 281

Henriod, Lorraine

**Grandma's Wheelchair**

Color illustrations by Christa Chevalier.
Albert Whitman & Company, 1982.
(32 pages counted)

*GRANDPARENT: Love for*
*WHEELCHAIR, DEPENDENCE ON*
   *Helping*

Four-year-old Thomas gets dressed in the morning just as his older brother does, but when Nate goes off to kindergarten, Thomas runs down the street to Grandma's house. As soon as Thomas arrives, he and Grandma telephone to let his mother know he arrived safely. Thomas thinks his mother probably lies down for a while after she hangs up the phone; she's been getting a lot of rest lately while waiting for the new baby. His mother doesn't have much of a lap anymore for Thomas to sit in, but Grandma always has a lap because she is always sitting in a chair—a wheelchair. After Grandma reads Thomas some stories, they do her work together. He helps her make applesauce, fold the clothes, and dust. When his stuffed hippopotamus falls and spills a lot of sawdust out of a hole in its head, he gets the vacuum. It's heavy, but he and Grandma pull it into the living room. "We are strong, Grandma and me, together." Then, when they go outside to wait for Nate to come home at lunchtime, Grandma's wheelchair tire has a blowout. Thomas tries to push her, but the chair is too heavy. Grandma remembers an old wheelchair in the garage. Thomas digs it out and watches as Grandma uses her "slippery board" to change from one wheelchair to the other. When Nate comes to Grandma's house after school and tells Thomas that he has his own special seat in kindergarten and that you need to be five years old to attend, Thomas replies that he doesn't care. At Grandma's house, there's always a special seat for a four-year-old whenever he needs it.

A preschooler spends his mornings helping his wheelchair-bound grandmother in this realistic, sometimes amusing first-person account. Chores that might be too much for either one are easily done when they work together. Having a special function in Grandma's life gives Thomas a sense of pride and accomplishment that young children will find especially satisfying. Even his older brother's glowing descriptions of kindergarten do not lessen Thomas's pleasure. The warm, domestic tone is accented by drawings of homely, but appealing, characters.

Ages 3-7

**Also available in:**
Large Print—*Grandma's Wheelchair*
Albert Whitman & Company

## 282

Hentoff, Nat

**Does This School Have Capital Punishment?**

Delacorte Press, 1981.
(170 pages)

*SCHOOL: Classmate Relationships*
*VALUES/VALUING: Moral/Ethical*
   *Age: aging*
   *Communication: parent-child*
   *Justice/Injustice*
   *Marijuana*
   *Schools, private: boys'*

Sam Davidson is beginning the ninth grade as a new student at Burr Academy, one of New York's most prestigious private schools. On his first day he meets Rob Holmes, with whom he has much in common. Both boys have "inflammable" tempers and reputations for being quick with their fists. When they meet, Sam is waiting to see Mr. Monk, the headmaster. Rob rushes into the office. He has promised Mr. Monk that whenever he is "seized with an overwhelming urge to strike someone," he will come to see him first. The person he wants to hit is Jeremiah Saddlefield, a very unpopular student who has destroyed a rare book of American Indian history given to Rob by his father. But Jeremiah has his defenders on the faculty. Mrs. Wolf, who has a "thing about misfits," spends a lot of time with Jeremiah and other "castoffs" who need help. As a teacher, Mrs. Wolf has a reputation for being tough. She gives her students difficult assignments, like the one in Oral History to interview and write a report about the life and times of some person over sixty—not a relative. At his father's suggestion, Sam decides to study Major Kelley, a renowned jazz trumpeter. Sam, who plays the trumpet himself, begins to attend Kelley's performances and is able to "open himself to the music." Appreciating this, Major Kelley allows Sam an inside look at his world. He teaches him about jazz and shares his personal philosophy of life. Meanwhile, Rob's troubles with Jeremiah intensify when Jeremiah frames both Sam and Rob for possessing marijuana. He throws one of his own butts on the floor, the two boys pick it up to throw it away, and they are intercepted by Mr. Levine-Griffin, director of the high school, who won't believe their explanation. When Sam tells Major Kelley of the frame-up and the possibility of their expulsion, Kelley goes to a friend who works for Jeremiah's father and finds out that Jeremiah has had emotional problems requiring psychiatric counseling. With this information Major Kelley decides that the best way to help Sam and Rob is to help Jeremiah. So when he comes to Mrs. Wolf's class with Sam, he pays special attention to Jeremiah, inviting him to his performances. Sam feels betrayed and angry, but Kelley wants to help Jeremiah take that "terrible weight off his soul" and confess. Jeremiah does come and hear the jazz musicians play, and their music seems to awaken something in him "from a long, long sleep." But when they stop, he feels alone again. He manages to tell Major Kelley about the frame-up, but explains that if his father finds out he will cut him out of his life. Mr.

H

Saddlefield, a powerful newspaperman with a reputation for ruthlessness, has many enemies and would never allow Jeremiah's pranks to fuel their fires. Major Kelley suggests that if his father is really that bad, Jeremiah needn't care what he thinks. So Jeremiah does tell his father—who respects his son for having the backbone to confess. When he tells the truth to Mr. Monk, the headmaster decides to be lenient. He suspends Jeremiah for the rest of the year, but will allow him to make a "new beginning" in the fall. Jeremiah also volunteers and is required to apologize publicly to Rob and Sam. A grateful Sam realizes that somehow his "fairy godfather" has set him, as well as Jeremiah, free.

Boys at a private school are changed for the better by a famous jazz trumpeter, a man as "sharp and clean" as his music. A delightful sequel to an earlier story about Sam Davidson, *This School Is Driving Me Crazy*, the story beautifully captures both life in the world of professional jazz and life in a boys' private academy. The development of the relationship between Sam and the elderly Major Kelley adds humor and poignancy. Readers will revel in the story and emerge with food for thought.

Ages 11 and up

**Also available in:**
Paperbound—*Does This School Have Capital Punishment?*
Dell Publishing Company, Inc.

## 283

**Herman, Charlotte**

### What Happened to Heather Hopkowitz?

E. P. Dutton & Company, Inc., 1981.
(186 pages) o.p.

---

*JEWISH*
*Family: relationships*
*Identity, search for*
*Perseverance*
*Religion: faith*
*Responsibility: accepting*
*Secret, keeping*

---

Heather Hopkowitz, fourteen, makes a fundamental change in her life. It all starts when her parents decide to take a month-long Caribbean cruise. Heather's little brother, Shawn, is sent to stay with Aunt Gloria, but her house is too far from Heather's school. After some deliberation, Heather's parents arrange for her to stay with Barbara and Nate Greenwald, old friends of Heather's father. The Greenwalds have a daughter, Shani, who is Heather's age. Heather's mother objects to this idea at first because the Greenwalds are Orthodox Jews and she's afraid Heather will be uncomfortable trying to adapt to their life style. Heather's parents are also Jewish, but nonobservant. The only truly "Jewish Jewish" person in the family is Grandpa Morris Hopkowitz, currently living in a convalescent home while he recovers from a stroke. Aunt Gloria plans to take Heather and Shawn to visit him every weekend. During their first visit, Grandpa is delighted to hear that Heather is staying with the religious Greenwalds and that she went to shul—synagogue—with them on the Sabbath. The only other time Heather can remember being in an Orthodox synagogue was when she was very small and went with her grandparents. Memories of Grandma Hannah had also come into her mind as she shared the traditional Sabbath meal with her hosts. During the following week, Chanukah is celebrated in the Greenwald home. Heather also spends time with the youth group at the synagogue. On Sunday afternoon she accompanies Shani and her parents into New York City for a special photo exhibit at The Jewish Museum. As Heather studies the old photographs of Jewish life, she is filled with a sense of belonging. By the end of her second week with the Greenwalds, she believes she is "undergoing some sort of metamorphosis." When Aunt Gloria comes to get her for Christmas vacation she feels herself a "complete stranger" to her family. She has secretly decided to become Orthodox. Since her aunt is on a low-meat, natural food diet, she has no problem keeping kosher while she is with her. When her parents return, however, it becomes much harder. She pretends she has become a vegetarian and sneaks kosher food into her room. She uses candleholders from the Greenwalds for a private Sabbath celebration. She lies to get out of the house on Saturday morning to attend shul. Her only support comes from Shani, her other friends, and Grandpa Morris, who tells her that if she is "acting out of true belief," any other way would be cheating herself. Finally, after weeks, Heather cannot stand the deception any longer and lets a boy from the synagogue youth group pick her up for a concert wearing his kipa (skullcap). That night the story comes out. Her mother, feeling betrayed, refuses to help her with her food or cooperate with her observance in any way. Her father asks her to postpone her religious transformation until she has grown up and is on her own. Heather, however, is steadfast. After her grandfather dies, she decides to assume her grandmother's Hebrew name, Chana. As Passover approaches, she asks if her family can have an authentic Seder, the ceremonial meal, this year. Her parents consent and agree to help. It is a beginning. Heather is overjoyed.

A teenage girl decides to become an Orthodox Jew and withstands the opposition of her unreligious parents until they realize and begin to accept the depth of her belief. Heather's first-person narrative allows the reader to follow her transformation closely and to empathize with her determination to follow her faith despite the guilt she feels from her parents' resistance. Heather comes across as a serious, responsible girl who is quite capable of choosing her own way and accepting the responsibilities inherent in her decision. Readers will gain considerable insight into the forms and customs of Orthodox Judaism.

Ages 10-13

**Also available in:**
No other form known

**284**

**Hermes, Patricia**

**Nobody's Fault**

Harcourt Brace Jovanovich, Inc., 1981.
(107 pages)

---

*DEATH: of Sibling*
*GUILT, FEELINGS OF*
  *Reality, escaping*

---

Emily Taylor doesn't like her older brother's teasing, especially when he makes fun of her ability to play baseball. Emily dreams about being the first woman in the major leagues, but Matthew (Emily calls him Monse, short for Monster) knows she is afraid of the ball and insists she will never make it. He also deliberately causes trouble between her and her best friend, Mary Elizabeth, and Emily decides she must get even. Knowing he is afraid of snakes, she decides to find a dead one and put it in his bed. While she is busily carrying out her plan Monse is cutting the grass in the backyard with the riding mower—despite Emily's reminding him of their father's rule that neither child may use the mower unless an adult is around. On this morning both parents have gone to work and Millie, the housekeeper, has not yet arrived. But Monse is anxious to finish his job so he can go to baseball practice. When Emily returns to the kitchen, she notices that the mower sounds a bit strange. Then she sees it, riderless, pushing against the stone wall in the back field. She runs outside and finds her brother lying in the grass with blood all over him. Frantically she tries to get him up, but can't. She runs inside and calls the emergency number, bringing the police and ambulance. Monse is rushed away and it is only later that her parents tell Emily what they think happened. Monse apparently had hit a wasps' nest and had fallen or jumped off the mower to escape the attacking insects. The mower ran over him, and he has bled to death. Emily's responsibility for this tragedy comes over her in a flash; if she hadn't been hiding the snake in Monse's bed, she would have heard his cries and been able to save him. The enormity of her guilt overwhelms the girl and her mind begins to shut out reality. She writes in her diary that Monse is hurt and will be in the hospital for a while. She becomes physically ill and can't even leave her bed to attend the funeral. She stops eating and spends most of her time sleeping. When the family doctor comes to see Emily, she suggests that the girl is "coping with something she hasn't told anyone about" and should get psychiatric help. Emily then begins to see Dr. Weintraub, an older man with a small, friendly voice and penetrating eyes. One day Emily hears the sound of air drills on the street below his office and is reminded of the noise the mower made. Frightened, she begins to confide in the doctor but then stops. He gently explains that she can't run away from her thoughts indefinitely. Even sleeping can't keep the pain away forever. Realizing he is right, Emily tells the doctor what has been tormenting her. Dr. Weintraub asks her to consider what might have happened if her father had not told Monse to cut the grass before going to practice that day, or if her mother had

stayed home until the housekeeper came. Perhaps Millie could have skipped her hair appointment that morning and not been late. Emily finds herself responding automatically, "It's nobody's fault! . . . Accidents happen." Surprised by her own words, she quickly realizes that they apply to her as well. Finally able to acknowledge Monse's death and to face her grief, she visits the cemetery to say goodbye. Then, wearing her brother's baseball hat, she is ready to play baseball again, to talk to Mary Elizabeth again, to get on with her life.

Like most siblings, Emily and Monse have a complicated relationship—part love, part rivalry. After Monse's death, Emily poignantly describes her emotional journey from guilt and denial to acceptance and honest grief. Neither gory nor maudlin, the story has a realism that will attract readers who have had to struggle with their own feelings of guilt or who have observed others in mourning.

Ages 10-12

**Also available in:**
Paperbound—*Nobody's Fault*
Dell Publishing Company, Inc.

**285**

**Hermes, Patricia**

**What If They Knew?**

Harcourt Brace Jovanovich, Inc., 1980.
(121 pages)

---

*EPILEPSY*
*FRIENDSHIP: Meaning of*
  *Grandparent: living in home of*
  *School: transfer*
  *Secret, keeping*
  *Self, attitude toward: feeling different*

---

Jeremy Marin, age ten, is enjoying her summer in Brooklyn with her grandparents until she learns she will be attending school there while her parents remain in England on business. She is very much afraid that everyone will discover her well-kept secret: Jeremy has epilepsy. Before getting the news about school, she had been having a better summer than she ever anticipated and has also made some good friends—notably, twins Mimi and Libby. Then there is Carrie, another classmate, small in size but an awfully big pain to Jeremy. The girls' summer adventures have included exploring a sewer filled with rats and playing tricks on Carrie. Before school starts, Mimi shows Jeremy a notebook in which she has written characteristics or peculiarities of all the kids in the class. Jeremy does not want her friends and classmates to think her odd because of her epilepsy. Her grandparents find it difficult to discuss her condition, but Jeremy decides to talk over her fears with Grandpa and feels much better afterwards. He reassures her; she hasn't had a seizure all summer, which shows that her daily medication is effective. And, if she should have a seizure, "you'll cope just fine." School begins well for Jeremy. After several weeks, the girls in the class get together to plan their revenge on Carrie for all the nasty things she's done recently. One of Carrie's misdeeds involved Jeremy. After finding one of Jeremy's anti-seizure pills, Carrie has started the rumor that Jeremy is on drugs. In revenge, the girls decide to put dead mice in Carrie's desk and in the folder containing her speech for Parents' Night. Two days before Parents' Night, Jeremy has several spells of not feeling well, and later that day she has a seizure at school. She has been careless about taking her medicine. Mimi and Libby are concerned and very supportive, but Carrie decides everyone should know about Jeremy's "fit" and proceeds to spread the word. The day of Parents' Night, Carrie finds the mice and runs screaming from the building, yelling that she will not give her speech to the parents that evening as planned. Miss Tuller, the principal, asks Jeremy to give the address about friendship instead. Overcoming her nervousness, Jeremy speaks very personally: "A friend doesn't really care if you're—different in some ways." Seeing Carrie in the audience, Jeremy finds herself including something she had not planned: "And a friend can be—a friend can even be—somebody who's mean to you sometimes."

A young girl with epilepsy hates to be different from her classmates and so tries to keep her condition a secret. But in the process, as Jeremy's first-person narrative describes humorously and believably, she learns quite a bit about the highs and lows of friendship. Finding friends who are supportive and accepting of her epilepsy leads Jeremy to be more tolerant and forgiving herself. The author has epilepsy, and the book provides insight into this often-misunderstood condition.

Ages 9-11

**Also available in:**
Paperbound—*What If They Knew?*
Dell Publishing Company, Inc.

## 286

**Hermes, Patricia**

## You Shouldn't Have to Say Good-bye

Harcourt Brace Jovanovich, Inc., 1982.
(117 pages)

---

*DEATH: of Mother*
*ILLNESSES: Terminal*
  *Cancer*
  *Death: attitude toward*
  *Family: unity*
  *Fear: of open or public places*
  *Loss: feelings of*

---

When thirteen-year-old Sarah Morrow learns early in the school year that her mother is dying of melanoma, a particularly virulent form of cancer, Sarah's first reaction is anger; her mother had postponed seeing a doctor, although she hadn't felt well. When her mother gets home from the hospital, she teaches Sarah how to do the laundry, explaining that she'd been thinking of all the things Sarah needs to know how to do for herself from now on. Sarah tries to ignore what her mother is saying, although her mother pleads with her to face the truth. When she talks about all the good books she wanted to give Sarah and now won't be able to, Sarah finds herself hating her mother for dying. She finally cries, with her mother holding her. They go to a bookstore where her mother buys several books for Sarah to read in the future. Sarah tells herself she'll never read these "getting-ready-to-die books" and hides them in the back of her bookcase. The Saturday before Christmas, Sarah and her parents have a Christmas party for all their friends. Sarah's mother is very happy. But the next day her arms and legs hurt, and her skin has a yellowish tinge. When Sarah comes home from school Monday, nobody is there. She calls her father's office and suspects from his colleague's evasive answers that her mother has been rushed to the hospital. Trying to avoid thinking, she returns to school. But the building is locked, so Sarah goes over to her friend Robin's house, although nobody ever visits Robin at home. Sarah always knew Robin's mother was somehow different, but Robin never talked about it. Today, however, when Sarah asks why her mother looks frightened, Robin explains that her mother has agoraphobia. She appears to be getting a little better, and Robin hopes she will attend their big gymnastics show that evening. Robin, who often does daredevil stunts, is toying with the idea of adding a forbidden, dangerous move to her routine. Before the show, Sarah thinks that since her parents probably won't be there, she could jump off the high bar onto the trampoline, something she's never done and her coach certainly wouldn't allow. But once the girls start their performance, they see their parents in the audience and abandon the dangerous stunts. Sarah's mother is weak, she needs help to get in the house, but she is home. The next day, Christmas Eve morning, she asks Sarah what she was planning to do during her gymnastics act; she had noticed her hesitation at the end. After Sarah tells her, her mother says people often do dangerous things to avoid facing threats from inside. She asks Sarah not to take that way out. Christmas at the Morrow house has its old and loved rituals. So Sarah is very upset when her parents want to open gifts on Christmas Eve afternoon instead of on Christmas morning as they've always done. Her mother is sitting rigidly, seeming to hold tightly onto something. Sarah shouts that they never do things this way and she doesn't like it. But with encouragement she agrees and goes to get her presents for her parents. Before they can be opened, Sarah's mother holds out her hands to Sarah, her eyes pleading, and dies. Sarah screams and screams; then she runs to her room where she is still crying when her father comes to find her. She asks him what her mother wanted from her at the end. He says she just wanted to live, to see Sarah grow up, but of course no one could give her that. Sarah goes to say goodbye to her mother before her body is taken away. Her mother has left Sarah a book. She wrote in it constantly after she learned she was dying, all the things she wanted to tell Sarah. Sarah reads this frequently in the months following her mother's death. Part of it makes her happy; some of it makes her sad. The most comforting lines are the very last ones her mother wrote to her: "Don't let anybody tell you differently. What we're going through stinks. It just plain stinks."

In this moving, first-person story of death and loss, a young girl experiences anger, denial, avoidance, and other wrenching emotions as she does her best to come to terms with her mother's dying. Although few people will be able to read the book with dry eyes, the story is not maudlin or melodramatic. The characters and their emotions seem authentic, and there is a strong emphasis on people's strength and ability to survive even the cruelest of blows. Sarah's father is willing to assume a larger role in her life and is able to share her grief. Also distinctive is the close relationship between mother and daughter and the ways the parents themselves deal with terminal illness and impending death. Readers will remember this sad but basically hopeful book for a long time.

Ages 10-13

**Also available in:**
Paperbound—*You Shouldn't Have to Say Good-bye*
Scholastic Book Services

## 287

**Herzig, Alison Cragin and Jane Lawrence Mali**

### A Season of Secrets

Little, Brown and Company, 1982.
(193 pages)

---

*EPILEPSY*
*ILLNESSES: of Sibling*
*SECRET, KEEPING*
  *Animals: love for*
  *Communication: lack of*
  *Sibling: love for*

---

Brooke Forbes, fourteen, has always had a particularly close relationship with her six-year-old brother, Benji, and is concerned about his fainting episodes. But her parents insist there is nothing wrong with Benji. Brooke is not to speak of his fainting to anyone, not even to her best friend, Izzy. When Benji faints on the last day of school, Brooke overhears her father urging her mother to call the teacher and pass the episode off as flu. The Forbes family has a new next-door neighbor, Dr. Noah Blazer, who Izzy thinks is strange and dangerous. He's very interested in the bat-infested barn on his property. One night when Brooke wakes up and sees that Benji's bed is empty, she finds him next door talking to Noah. An extremely bright child, Benji is fascinated by the experiments Noah plans to carry out with the bats. But Benji continues to spend most of his time in his room, avoiding his friends and looking pale. To Brooke's worried questions her mother snaps that Benji is just fine. One day Benji shares his great secret with Brooke: he has found a tiny young bat that he's keeping in his room. Together they feed "Lucifur," and Benji teaches it to fly to him for water. Because Brooke abruptly leaves Izzy every day to get home in time for Lucifur's feedings, Izzy becomes suspicious and hurt. Knowing that keeping Benji's secret is ruining her friendship, Brooke finally persuades her brother to let Izzy see Lucifur. All goes well until Izzy asks Benji about school in the fall. He becomes very upset, says he won't go, and locks himself in his room. That afternoon, while a group of neighbors and friends, including an employee of Brooke's father named Sam Renwick, talk together in the Forbes's kitchen, Lucifur flies in. Sam, who hates bats, tries to kill it with a broom. In the commotion, Benji faints. Their parents aren't home, and Benji is pale, sluggish, and can't remember anything. When their parents return, Brooke is furious with them. Her mother tries to calm her down but Brooke forces a confrontation, determined to understand the mystery at last. Her parents admit Benji has epilepsy. They hasten to explain that epilepsy is mostly controllable, that there

is a good chance Benji will outgrow it, and that the attacks do not hurt him permanently. But they are absolutely determined to keep Benji's condition a secret so he won't be labeled or stigmatized. That night Noah's barn burns to the ground and arson is suspected. In fact, Brooke remembers hearing the distinctive sound of Sam Renwick's pickup just before the blaze was discovered. In the aftermath of the fire, Sam tells a group of neighbors and townspeople that it's a good thing the barn burned down. Relating what had happened to Benji that afternoon, Sam concludes that bats had infected the boy with rabies or worse and that he doesn't want his children endangered. With that, Brooke explains to everyone that Benji has epilepsy, that his condition has nothing to do with the bats, and that it's in no way contagious. In response, a neighbor tells about her sister who has epilepsy and is an active, competent, "normal" person. Questions are answered, fears allayed. Later, Brooke discovers that Benji hasn't been taking his hated pills all summer; he is soon given more palatable medication to control his seizures. Before school starts Benji frees Lucifur, a wonderful pet but basically a creature of the wild.

Brooke must contend with her parents' determination to keep her brother's epilepsy secret. Memorable characterizations in this well-written book allow the reader to enter Benji's world and to appreciate that people with epilepsy are defined by far more than their disease. The actual information on epilepsy is brief but valuable, and the details about bats add suspense and appeal.

Ages 11-13

**Also available in:**
Paperbound—*A Season of Secrets*
Scholastic Book Services

## 288

**Hest, Amy**

### Maybe Next Year . . .

Clarion Books, 1982.
(153 pages)

---

*MATURATION*
  *Boy-girl relationships*
  *Careers: dancer*
  *Change: accepting*
  *Decision making*
  *Family: extended*
  *Grandparent: living in home of*
  *Talents*

---

Kate Newman loves to dance, loves the long, hard workouts at ballet school and the feeling of accomplishment when she dances well. The one person with whom Kate can really share her feelings about ballet is Peter Robinson. Although Peter is several years older than Kate, who is twelve, they take ballet lessons together and are the best of friends. Kate even suspects she is a little bit in love with Peter. Lately, Peter has encouraged Kate to try out for the National Ballet Summer School. She knows he is good enough to audition, but fears she is not. At home, Kate asks her grandmother, Nana, if she can take supplemental ballet classes to prepare for the upcoming auditions. Nana (Kate and her sister's guardian—their parents are dead) agrees to one extra class a

**H**

week. She also announces that an old family friend, Max Schumacher, will be moving into their apartment and paying rent. Mr. Schumacher, seventy-one and recently forced to retire from his law practice, will take the den as his bedroom, although Kate has wanted it. She resents his intrusion and does little to make him feel welcome. Slowly, though, he wins her over with his kindness and his luscious, homemade chocolate chip cookies. Several weeks later, Peter walks Kate home from ballet class. On the way, he kisses her. He is invited to stay for dinner and, after tasting Mr. Schumacher's cookies, declares the man should sell them. This upsets Mr. Schumacher—"The world doesn't think I'm fit to work anymore"—and Nana accuses him of self-pity. The next day Mr. Schumacher announces he will start a cookie business. In three weeks, Nana and Mr. Schumacher have successfully turned the apartment into Max's Makeshift Cookie House and have a large volume of business. Kate is excited about their success, but a little concerned that the two are becoming romantically involved. Meanwhile, Peter continues to pressure Kate about the audition. She talks to Nana and is relieved when she is encouraged to wait another year. Her decision upsets Peter. She waits for him after his audition, though, and is glad he has been chosen. Despite Kate's dance instructor's disappointment, Kate feels sure she's made the best decision about her own career. Several months later, Nana and Mr. Schumacher marry. Peter is best man.

A young dancer decides she's not yet ready to audition for a national ballet school, and she stands firm against her friend's and teacher's disappointment with the help of her supportive grandmother. Believable relationships and realistic, appealing characters fill Kate's first-person narrative. Descriptions of traditional Jewish celebrations in the Newman home add warmth and richness to the interesting plot.

Ages 9-12

**Also available in:**
No other form known

## 289

Hickman, Janet

### The Thunder-Pup

Macmillan Publishing Company, Inc., 1981.
(114 pages)

---

CHANGE: New Home
PETS: Love for
  Fear: of animals
  Fear: of storms
  Friendship: meaning of
  Moving
  Visiting

---

What Linnie McKay wants more than anything else in the world is a puppy. With her tenth birthday coming up and the whole family whispering about a big surprise, she's sure her dream is about to come true. Besides her birthday, Linnie has something else to look forward to this summer. Darla Champion and her family are stopping for a visit on their way from their house in the city to the country home they've bought. The girls' fathers were Army buddies; they plan to leave Darla with the McKays and have her follow them later on the bus. Although Linnie has never met Darla, she's happy about this visit since there are no other girls her age in town. But when the Champions arrive, Linnie is less sure. For one thing, Darla looks "like an advertisement in American Girl magazine." For another, she hates the country and prefers to spend most of her time dancing and twirling her baton. To make matters even worse, Darla hates dogs. In fact, unknown to Linnie, Darla fears dogs. Linnie, on the other hand, loves living in the country and, of course, loves dogs. She also has a fear, though: thunderstorms. When a storm comes up just as she is performing at the end-of-the-year school program, she runs off the stage in tears. Darla saves the show by performing one of her dance routines, humiliating Linnie and confirming her belief that her guest is the "most stuck-up, disgusting, insensitive, boring, rotten person she has ever known." Then Linnie and her friend Arnold manage to hide a motherless puppy from the dogcatcher. They name the pup Harry and when Linnie discovers that Harry is afraid of storms too, she loves him even more and longs to take him home. But the day before her birthday, her parents take her to Springfield for a "day-before-birthday present, too good to keep." Linnie thinks they are going to pick up her dog, but is chagrined to find that the surprise is a new house. Her family has always lived with her grandfather, and though they've been crowded Linnie has been happy with the arrangement. Shattered by the thought of moving and terribly disappointed to find that the big surprise has nothing to do with a dog, she sneaks Harry into the house and hides him. But the puppy comes out and is chased outside, where he disappears. The next morning Darla finds him nosing around in some weeds across the street. She leads Linnie to him because she's afraid to pick him up. The puppy is shivering with fear at the sound of an approaching thunderstorm. As Linnie and Darla hurry to the house to escape the storm, lightning strikes a tree in the McKays' front yard, causing it to fall and trap Darla underneath. By concentrating on the trembling puppy in her arms, Linnie manages to overcome her own fear enough to run for help. Darla is rescued, safe except for cuts and bruises, and later that day—Linnie's birthday—Linnie is told she may keep the pup. The next morning Darla has to leave to rejoin her parents. By the time she boards the bus, Linnie feels somewhat sympathetic towards her; after all, they both know how hard it is to move and they both have fears. Later, Arnold tells Linnie that Darla had considered her lucky to have a dog and a new house so near her old one. Darla was also impressed by Linnie's ability to overcome her fear of storms enough to get help for her. Linnie decides that maybe Darla isn't such a bad person after all; she may even write to her. And maybe Darla is right—maybe Linnie is lucky.

Set in a small midwestern town in 1950, this is a well-written story about two girls who discover they have more in common than they'd thought. The treatment of the children's fears—of moving, of dogs, of storms—is convincing and the development of their relationship nicely paced. Dog lovers especially will find the book enjoyable.

Ages 9-11

Also available in:
No other form known

## 290

Hickman, Martha Whitmore

**My Friend William Moved Away**

Color illustrations by Bill Myers.
Abingdon Press, 1979.
(28 pages counted)

---

*FRIENDSHIP: Best Friend*
  *Friendship: making friends*
  *Moving*

---

It leaves quite a hole in Jimmy's life when his best friend, William, moves away. The boys, about seven, used to play together every day, either at Jimmy's house or William's. They shared everything, from Jimmy's two hamsters and William's turtle, to Jimmy's Fort Apache and William's Rocket Zoom. The morning after William leaves, a sad Jimmy dresses and eats breakfast. He feeds his hamsters, watches TV, and looks over his Fort Apache—alone. Walking to William's house later, he notes that although the house is still there, along with the tree, the hydrant, and the cracked sidewalk, William is gone. As Jimmy turns slowly toward home, a sudden thought strikes him. He turns back and walks farther down the street to the house of a classmate, Mary Ellen. When she comes out and sees Jimmy eyeing her bicycle with its rocket and blue streamers, she offers him a ride. He agrees, provided she ride his. Back at his house, Jimmy shows Mary Ellen his hamsters while she tells him about her gerbils. He explains to Mary Ellen how strange it feels not to have William around. "I know," she says. "I saw you and William walking to school together. . . . Sometimes I was walking way behind you, by myself." Jimmy grows thoughtful upon hearing that. When Mary Ellen's mother calls her home, the two make arrangements to play together the next day.

A little boy's lonely first day without his best friend becomes a day filled by another friendship in this first-person story. Jimmy expresses with few words but real depth of feeling how it feels to lose a best friend and gain a new friend. Warm, realistic illustrations convey the sentiment as completely as the text. The picture-book format makes this a logical read-aloud selection, but short sentences and simple vocabulary make it suitable for young readers as well.

Ages 4-7

Also available in:
No other form known

## 291

Hill, Margaret

**Turn the Page, Wendy**

Abingdon Press, 1981.
(176 pages)

---

*ABANDONMENT*
*RUNNING AWAY*
  *Belonging*
  *Child abuse*
  *Children's home, living in*
  *Emotions: accepting*
  *Foster home*
  *Guilt, feelings of*
  *School: truancy*

---

At sixteen, after a year in a mental health center and six years at a children's home, Wendy Carmichael has been living in Virginia Hall for two years. Dr. Elizabeth Blair, Virginia Hall's superintendent, tells Wendy a foster family wants her and she will spend the weekend with them. The Abbenoth family is kind to her, but Wendy doesn't just want a family: she wants her family. In fact, she hates all families because they're not hers. She also hates the father who never claimed her and the mother who gave her away "to the nightmare couple" who called themselves her foster parents. She thinks about baby Joel who died. Son of her foster parents, he was always hungry and feeble. She used to scavenge food for him. One day, during a school trip to a writing workshop at the high school in Tyler, a nearby college town, Wendy sees a woman who greatly resembles her. Telling her bus driver that she'll return home on the other bus, Wendy slips away to find the woman she thinks may be her mother. She eventually loses sight of her and spends the night in an unlocked car. The next day she finds an old, abandoned boarding school and moves in. Afraid that Virginia Hall will set the police on her trail, Wendy goes to the local high school to lose herself among other teenagers. She remembers that when she was sent to the office to get some papers for the workshop, she overheard discussion about a file on Kim Coverly, a girl who was to attend the school but never showed up. On an impulse, Wendy presents herself as Kim Coverly. She's given the file and told to go to the guidance counselor's office. On the way, Wendy reads the file and learns that Kim is an excellent student who wants to be a clinical psychologist. The counselor, Mr. Platner, looks at her suspiciously, but does not challenge her. He invites her to be part of a special group of students who are working with children having difficulty adjusting to school. He thinks that "Kim," with her interest in psychology, will enjoy the group. When she meets with this special group, Mr. Platner tells Wendy that "her" child is an eight-year-old named Jane who won't speak to anyone. The next day, he lends her a copy of *Throwaway Children*, a book about abused children, and the last period of that day she meets Jane. That night she reads the book and realizes she and Joel were not the only children in the world subject to abuse and neglect. She barely gets through the next school day; both her math and physics teachers are surprised when she fails fairly simple tests. So Wendy decides to leave the school the next day, telling the office that her family is moving. Then she calls Virginia Hall to tell them she's coming back and is surprised when they don't seem either worried about her or particularly glad that she's returning. It seems the Tyler police called them at the beginning of the week. Wendy was "allowed" to stay there while the police and some school staff kept an eye on her. When she gets back to Virginia Hall, she has a rude awakening. She's told they may not be able to keep her because of her truancy, lying (to the bus driver), and lack of any respect or concern for those who care about her. Although she protests she didn't really run away, Dr. Blair condemns her for her years of self-pity, excuses, and impulsive behavior. Wendy tries to explain her actions, but Dr. Blair points out that good intentions are not sufficient. When Wendy mentions Joel, as she so often does, Dr. Blair insists that she finally bring that whole story into the daylight where it can't continue to haunt her. Wendy confesses that she had found a carton of milk the day Joel died. On her way to take it to him, she had drunk it all herself. Ever since, she has been obsessed by guilt, sure Joel would have lived had he gotten that milk. Dr. Blair has Wendy read a poem that the girl herself wrote about Joel; she realizes from her own words that Joel would have died anyway. As they talk, Wendy notes how seldom she has recognized or shared her emotions. The Abbenoth family wants to talk to Wendy again, even though they are disappointed in her. After she explains some of her feelings and actions, they decide having Wendy in their family would be good for all of them.

Abandoned by her parents, left with abusive foster parents, Wendy is a girl of impulsive actions and repressed emotions. A fruitless search for her birth mother leads to her discovery that she has herself abandoned people who care about her. Wendy learns that she need not always be rootless; she can make her own roots. This is a poignant, realistic story about the universal need to belong to someone. The session with the perceptive Dr. Blair is especially well done.

Ages 10-14

**Also available in:**
No other form known

## 292

**Hinton, Susan Eloise**

**Tex**

Delacorte Press, 1979.
(194 pages)

---

*MATURATION*
*SIBLING: Love for*
*Abandonment*
*Boy-girl relationships*
*Friendship: best friend*

---

Fourteen-year-old Texas (Tex) McCormick is never happier than when he is in the saddle of his horse, Negrito. He is devastated when his brother, Mason (Mace), two years his senior, sells the horse to pay the gas bill. In a rage, Tex attacks Mace, who fights back out of his own anger and frustration at the father who has caused their problems. After their mother died of pneumonia when Tex was three, their father became a rodeo circuit rider, leaving the boys alone for weeks and months at a time. Now that they're older, they often must fend for themselves. Easygoing Tex takes it one day at a time, but Mace's sense of responsibility gives him ulcers as he tries to pay the bills, watch over Tex, keep up his own grades, and remain the star high school basketball player in hopes of attending college on a basketball scholarship. Although Tex never questions his father's absences, he does feel his father has always favored Mace and wonders why. After all, it's Tex who tries to be like his father. Mace believes Tex needs more attention and discipline from their father because Tex is always getting into scrapes. When the brothers pick up a hitchhiker who turns out to be a wanted murderer and later dies in a police shoot-out, their involvement is mentioned on national TV, causing their father to take notice of them once again. At first both boys are delighted at Pop's return, but Mace is wary of his father and his promise to stay. Pop promises to buy Negrito back, but then forgets his promise. When Mace and Tex try to buy back the horse, they are told it is not for sale. Losing Negrito for the second time is a heavy blow to Tex but he soon transfers his affections to Jamie, his best friend Johnny's younger sister, and their friendship deepens into love. Wise beyond her years, Jamie says she can picture them married at eighteen and divorced a year later. Crushed, Tex begins to feel that everyone and everything he loves is just out of reach. When Tex and Johnny put explosive caps on the typewriter keys in typing class, Pop is the only one who laughs. Disgusted by Pop's refusal to take Tex's problems seriously, Mace inadvertently reveals to his brother that Tex is not Pop's son, that he was conceived while Pop was serving time in jail for bootlegging. Now Tex knows why Pop withholds his love, why Mace is always his favorite. Desperate, he runs into Lem, an ex-friend of Mace's who has gotten involved in buying, selling, and taking drugs. With Lem he visits a drug dealer, but the spaced-out conversation repels him. As he turns to leave, the drug dealer pulls a gun and Tex is critically wounded. In his fear and pain, Tex's main concern is that Mace should know he forgives him for revealing the truth of his parentage. "I don't hate you, Mace," he intones over and over in his semi-conscious state. When Tex recovers, Mace decides not to go on to college because his brother needs him. But Tex explodes, "You don't go to college because of me, and in two years you'd hate my guts." A fortune-teller once told Tex, "There are people who go, people who stay. You will stay." He knows Mace must go, and he urges him onward. Tex gets a job helping with horses after school and begins to see some hope for his future.

As told by Tex, this powerful and realistic story depicts some of the soaring elation and depths of pain possible in adolescence. Largely abandoned by their father, their mother long-dead, Mace and Tex, their relationship almost that of father and son, struggle to survive in a world whose harshness is tempered by their love and need for each other. Tex, likeable and often witty, grows from a naive, fun-loving prankster to a young man capable of understanding and accepting responsibility for his actions. The problems he resolves and the pain he endures assure him of the reader's sympathy.

Ages 11-15

Also available in:
Braille—*Tex*
Library of Congress (NLSBPH)

Cassette—*Tex*
Library of Congress (NLSBPH)

Paperbound—*Tex*
Dell Publishing Company, Inc.

## 293

### Hlibok, Bruce

### Silent Dancer

Black/white photographs by Liz Glasgow.
Julian Messner, Inc., 1981.
(64 pages)

---

*DEAFNESS*
  *Education: special*
  *Talents*

---

Nancy, ten years old and deaf, likes Fridays best of all because that's when she has her ballet class. After breakfast, during which she communicates with her parents and her deaf brother in sign language, she takes the bus to the Lexington School for the Deaf in New York City. There Nancy checks her two special hearing aids before starting work with her speech teacher, who uses a biofeedback machine to help Nancy form words correctly. After lunch, science class, and a spelling bee, Nancy packs her homework in her knapsack and takes another bus to the Joffrey Ballet School. As she prepares for her ballet class and puts on her slippers, she remembers the benefit at Lincoln Center the year before. Nancy and her deaf classmates danced a special number. Now Ms. Baylis, Nancy's teacher and a former leading ballerina, comes in to check the girls before class. With her is an interpreter who conveys Ms. Baylis's instructions in sign language and speaks for those students whose speech is difficult to understand. The students "hear" the music with the help of a piano connected to a special sound system that causes the floor to vibrate. After their stretching exercises, they practice ballet positions. A television videotape crew comes to film the group, interviewing Nancy afterwards. When she's asked about her dreams for the future, Nancy says she'd like to appear at Lincoln Center again someday.

A deaf youngster achieves confidence, pleasure, and a sense of physical well-being from her Joffrey Ballet School classes, which have been modified somewhat to accommodate deaf students. Striking photographs, starkly simple and unposed, bring the reader into Nancy's story. Ballet vocabulary and information about ballet training are skillfully woven into the text. Readers interested in ballet as well as deaf readers will enjoy this book. The latter may be especially encouraged to note that a field not traditionally open to deaf students has become an option for them.

Ages 8-11

Also available in:
No other form known

## 294

### Hoban, Lillian Aberman

### Arthur's Funny Money

Color illustrations by the author.
Harper & Row, Publishers, Inc., 1981.
(64 pages)

---

*MONEY: Earning*
*PERSEVERANCE*
  *Cooperation: in work*
  *Goals*
  *Resourcefulness*
  *Sibling: relationships*

---

Arthur, a young chimp, needs five dollars so he can buy a special cap and a T-shirt with the name of his team, "Far Out Frisbees," printed on it. He and his younger sister, Violet, decide to have a bike wash so that Arthur can earn the money. They buy soap and scouring pads and set up shop, with Violet, who needs to practice her arithmetic, keeping track of all expenditures and earnings. Things do not go as planned, however. Arthur is charging twenty-five cents per bike, but Norman and his brother want him to wash both a bike and a trike for forty-two cents. Wilma, Peter, and John need a wagon, a scooter, and a skateboard washed, and Arthur is willing to do the jobs until it becomes clear that they expect to receive his services free of charge. Disgusted, Arthur announces that he'll wash bikes only and for exactly twenty-five cents apiece. Then he and Violet run out of soap. They return to the store, only to find that the price has gone up since they were there in the morning. So they decide to look elsewhere for soap. Passing the general store, Violet notices a sign advertising the window-sample "Far Out Frisbees" shirt and cap at a special price. The saleswoman adds the figures on Violet's piece of paper and tells Arthur that he has more than enough to buy the items at the reduced price of $4.25. With the eighteen cents change, sister and brother buy licorice, dividing the five pieces of candy evenly.

This story shows the value of cooperation and the ins and outs of earning and saving money—humorously and not didactically. Arthur, who "knows numbers," discovers the many complicated and frustrating aspects of running a business. His sister proves an alert and able assistant, and she gets some needed practice with her arithmetic. This "I Can Read" book with its colorful illustrations will challenge young readers to solve some of Arthur's and Violet's arithmetic problems on their own.

Ages 6-8

Also available in:
Paperbound—*Arthur's Funny Money*
Harper & Row, Publishers, Inc.

H

**295**

Hobby, Janice Hale with Gabrielle Rubin and Daniel Rubin

## Staying Back

Black/white illustrations by Carol Richardson.
Triad Publishing Company, Inc., 1982.
(93 pages)

SCHOOL: Achievement/Underachievement
SCHOOL: Retention
  School: negative experiences
  Self, attitude toward: accepting
  Success

When Billy hears he has to repeat first grade, he feels terrible at first. He's hated school, never did his work, and was one of the smallest children in class. But now he finds he likes being one of the older and bigger kids in his class. Lyndon has sickle-cell anemia and is usually too tired to keep up with his class. After he misses fifty-three days of second grade, his teacher and parents decide he'll be better off if he repeats the year. Now everything is a little easier and Lyndon knows his subjects better. Lilly, who is deaf, transfers in third grade from a special school to a regular school. Everything goes well at first, but then Lilly's classmates and teacher (who wears a mustache that hinders Lilly's lipreading) grow careless about facing Lilly when they talk. If the teacher asks her if she understands the assignments, she says yes because she's too embarrassed to say no. As a result her schoolwork suffers, even though she's a bright girl. When her parents tell her she must repeat third grade, Lilly gets very upset. Her parents insist she is not a failure, that she is doing very well. After thinking about it, Lilly looks forward to the next school year and is delighted to find that her teacher, who shaved off his mustache, is also looking forward to a good year with her. Fourth grade is the worst year of Jennifer's life. After much arguing and unhappiness her father moves out, her parents get divorced, and she "flunks" fourth grade. The next year, things are better at home and Jennifer's teacher helps her with her schoolwork and tells her she is smart. Jennifer is thrilled, since she is used to thinking of herself as stupid. Chip's teacher thinks he is lazy and fooling around when he can't read simple sentences, so Chip finally stops trying altogether. He begins to feel like the dumbest kid who ever lived. When the school psychologist diagnoses a learning disability, Chip is relieved that someone finally understands. She says he's as smart as anyone else, and he is enrolled in a special school instead of having to repeat fifth grade. There he is happy and successful. When Ryan's family moves to Florida, he finds his new school unfriendly and strict and the schoolwork more advanced than what he is used to. After a difficult year, Ryan is asked to repeat fifth grade. He is comforted when he learns that one of the most popular boys in his class was in his second year of fifth grade. Ryan's own father admits he had to repeat a grade. Ronnie's parents appear to have his whole life planned out for him. They want him to be the best, and by sixth grade he's tired of the pressure. The more they push, the more he resists. When he fails sixth grade his parents enroll him in summer school, but he does no better there. In his second year of sixth grade, his parents leave him strictly alone—Ronnie doesn't know if they were told to or if they just gave up. But he finds he likes discovering his own talents and working for himself. Matthew is one of the smallest and youngest members of the third grade, and he never gets his seatwork done. At first he feels sad when he is told he must repeat third grade. Later he's glad because he feels more competent now academically, socially, and physically.

Seven children relate their experiences of repeating a grade. The reasons for the retentions are familiar but vary widely, from illness to learning disability to parental pressure; none is completely remedied by the repeated year, but each is shown to be improving. Illustrations showing students of various races and ethnic backgrounds accompany the children's reflections on their feelings, fears, and reactions. At the back, a "Message to Parents" and "Let's Talk about Staying Back" provide step-by-step suggestions for parents: how to help the child accept and discuss his or her feelings, how to help other family members express their feelings about the matter, how to help the child view this experience as an opportunity to be successful, how to establish future guidelines and limits, and how to emphasize those things the child does well. Also included are discussion questions based on each child's story.

Ages 6-12

**Also available in:**
Paperbound—Staying Back
Triad Publishing Company, Inc.

**296**

Hogan, Paula Z.

## I Hate Boys  I Hate Girls

Color illustrations by Dennis Hockerman.
Raintree Publishers, Inc., 1980.
(31 pages)

BOY-GIRL RELATIONSHIPS
FRIENDSHIP: Meaning of
  Clubs
  Peer relationships: peer pressures
  Teasing

Peter's long, lonely summer improves rapidly when a girl his own age, about eight, moves next door. He and Dawn spend nearly every day together until school starts. Then Peter, to avoid being teased by his male friends for having a girlfriend, joins the "I Hate Girls Club." In retaliation, Dawn forms her own "I Hate Boys Club." At the boys' first meeting, the leader proposes a mean trick on the girls. Peter silently disapproves but feels pressured to participate. They sneak to the girls' playhouse, and Peter overhears Dawn's comment on boys: "First they're your friends. The next day they're not." He knows she means him. Then the attack begins. The boys throw a pail of dusty dirt inside the playhouse windows while Peter holds the door shut so the girls can't escape. Later, at home, he talks with his father about the club and how the other boys made fun of him for his friendship with Dawn. His father asks, "You mean you just lost a good friend because of what other people were saying about you?" Peter does not answer. The next morning he grabs his squirt gun and goes to visit Dawn. He apologizes for the dirt, but she wants to know why he has the squirt gun. He suggests a squirt gun fight, and she grabs his gun and tries to squirt him with it. Then they laugh and forget about their clubs, friends once again.

A young boy denies his friendship with a girl in order to avoid harassment and teasing from his male friends. His father helps him realize that a true friendship is something to be cherished, not to be subjected to approval by others. Readers of this age group will sympathize with Peter's and Dawn's feelings and may gain a stronger appreciation of their own friendships with the opposite sex. Illustrations show a lively group of ethnically varied boys and girls.

Ages 5-8

**Also available in:**
No other form known

## 297

**Hogan, Paula Z.**

### Sometimes I Don't Like School

Color illustrations by Pam Ford.
Raintree Publishers, Inc., 1980.
(31 pages)

---

*FEAR: of School*
*Perseverance*
*Problem solving*
*School: achievement/underachievement*
*Success*

---

George, about eight, has come to dread school. On this Monday morning he pretends to be ill, but his mother mentions calling the doctor and George suddenly recovers. "He was too miserable to tell his parents the real reason he didn't want to go to school." Every morning his class plays an arithmetic game. George is always the first one out, the first to sit down, because he never knows the answer to the addition problem on the card his teacher holds up. This morning is no exception, even though George has tried to stop the game by letting the classroom hamsters loose. Not only does his teacher wrongly blame another student for the incident, but once the hamsters are retrieved she proceeds with the game. George hears the now-familiar giggles of his classmates when he gives the wrong answer. "I don't like this game!" he thinks. "And sometimes I don't like school, either!" On the way to school the following morning, George passes the muddy baseball field and jumps into the mud, slipping again and again. When thoroughly dirty, he returns home to change and misses the arithmetic game. The next day his mother sees that George is at school early. When his turn comes to solve the addition problem, George stalls. His teacher asks if he's having trouble seeing the card. Seizing this new excuse, George claims he can't see it. But while talking with his teacher after school, he confesses that he really can see, that it was he who let the hamsters out, and that his unhappiness with school is due to the game. "It's hard to do it while everyone's watching," he says. His teacher understands and gives George an extra set of

cards to practice with at home, promising not to tell his classmates. The next morning, after one night's practice with his patient, supportive father, George answers his first problem correctly and then is downed, smiling, on his second problem. Some days later, after much practice and with a newfound enjoyment of arithmetic, George is one of two players left in the game. Although he does not win, he receives a cheer from his classmates for his great improvement. His teacher tells him, "You've worked hard. We're glad you're in this class." "So am I!" thinks George.

Embarrassment about his poor performance in arithmetic clouds a young boy's feelings about school. Rather than confide in his parents or seek help, he desperately tries to avoid the situation entirely. However, his understanding teacher recognizes his need for help and extra practice. Once George admits his problem, he can and does take the necessary steps to solve it. The text is complemented and extended by colorful illustrations.

Ages 6-9

**Also available in:**
No other form known

## 298

**Hogan, Paula Z.**

### Sometimes I Get So Mad

Color illustrations by Karen Shapiro.
Raintree Publishers, Inc., 1980.
(31 pages)

---

*ANGER*
*Emotions: accepting*
*Friendship: meaning of*
*Problem solving*
*Self-discipline*
*Sibling: older*

---

Karen, about eight, has been invited to go swimming with Janet, an older neighborhood girl, and is searching for her beach bag when her mother reminds her that she is responsible for her younger sister, Rosie, that afternoon. Karen grudgingly takes Rosie along, leaving her to trail behind as soon as Janet joins them. At the beach, Rosie plays on shore while Karen and Janet swim. Karen doesn't want to swim past the marker as Janet does and suggests instead that they go back to shore for some cookies. But Janet spots a friend and the two leave Karen and go back in, swimming out past the marker. Karen helps Rosie with her sand castle, now glad for the little girl's company and secretly proud of her efforts. Janet returns from her swim only to tell Karen that she is going home with her friend. Fighting tears, Karen takes out her hurt and anger on Rosie and kicks over her sand castle. A few days later, Karen is surprised and delighted when Janet invites her to go to a movie. She promptly leaves a note for her mother and meets Janet at the theater. When Janet seems to be taking an awfully long time to get popcorn, Karen goes to find her. Janet is not at the refreshment stand so Karen walks back down the aisle with the drinks she has bought. Then she spots Janet sitting with her classmates. When Karen starts to sit next to her, a boy blocks her way, saying those seats are only for fourth graders. Janet joins in the laughter. Speechless with anger, Karen pours her grape drink on Janet's head. That night, after her mother gets a call from Janet's mother, Karen tearfully tells her story and Rosie joins in, mentioning the day at the beach and the sand castle Karen ruined. "Sometimes I get so mad that I just have to do something!" Karen explains. Her mother suggests that the best thing to do is to let people know when and why they make her angry. So next morning, after apologizing to Janet for pouring the drink on her, Karen explains why she was so angry. Janet agrees that she behaved badly and she invites Karen to play. But Karen turns her down—she has promised to help Rosie build a playhouse. "Even though she's just a little kid, she likes me a lot and we have fun together." The two agree to get together another day, and Karen feels so happy she begins to skip.

Angered by the rejection of an older girl she admires, Karen reacts by striking back, first at her sister, then at the older girl. Guided by her mother's advice, she learns to accept her anger and to express it verbally and forthrightly. Then she's ready to express other emotions honestly, such as her affection for her sister. Expressive illustrations extend the text, which, if a bit simplistic, may be useful in discussions of ways to express feelings constructively.

Ages 5-8

**Also available in:**
No other form known

## 299

Hogan, Paula Z.

### Will Dad Ever Move Back Home?

Color illustrations by Dora Leder.
Raintree Publishers, Inc., 1980.
(31 pages)

COMMUNICATION: Parent-Child
DIVORCE: of Parents
    Change: resisting
    Running away

Laura, about nine, is unhappy because her parents don't live together anymore. She hates the too-quiet house when she comes home from school and her mother's irritability when she gets home from work. While Laura sets the table she thinks about her parents but says nothing, aware that her mother dislikes discussions about her father. After dinner she wanders into her brother John's bedroom. Every Saturday they take turns visiting their father. "Do you think Dad will ever move back home?" she wonders. No, says John, not even if they are good, because the problem does not have to do with them. Saturday comes and Laura waits for her father, but her mother disappoints her by leaving before he arrives. She had hoped her parents would talk together, but her mother says there is no point. Things will get better, she tells Laura. But the girl lashes out. "I just wanted us to be a real family again, and you won't even try!" Then Laura has such a good time with her father that she forgets all about the fight with her mother. When they stop for lunch, Laura asks if she can move in with him. He is so much more fun than her

mother. But her father says they need to give this arrangement a fair trial. Besides, he tells her, if she lived with him she would see how busy and tired he is most of the time. Laura accuses him of not wanting her. The next morning she gets up early and sneaks out of the house. She will run away, since her parents hate her. On the way she passes two of her friends, and they suggest she go to the deserted house on Elm Street. She stands hesitating in front of the rundown house with the Keep Out sign, now frightened, but finally finds an open basement window and jumps in, a very long jump. Once inside, she can't get back out. Then she hears noises on the other side of the locked basement door, coming closer and closer. Panicked, she runs, trips, and screams when the door opens. But it's her parents, and she rushes to them. As the three walk back home together, her father tells her that they have decided he will spend more time with her and her brother, time just to be together. When they reach the house, he leaves and Laura goes inside with her mother. They sit and talk, her mother assuring her that both parents still love her even though other things have changed. Laura volunteers to help with some housework, but her mother just wants to sit and talk. Laura hugs her.

The effects of divorce on children are clearly described in this story of Laura's struggle to understand and adapt to the changes in her life. She tries to talk about her feelings with her parents, but they are not always ready to listen; some feelings she keeps to herself. When she runs away, her parents realize the depth of her unhappiness and resolve to be more available to her, reassuring her of their love. The resolution demonstrates how divorced parents can and do unite in caring for their children. This expressively illustrated book may be helpful to some families as they work to establish or maintain communication.

Ages 7-10

**Also available in:**
No other form known

## 300

Hogan, Paula Z. and Kirk Hogan

### The Hospital Scares Me

Color illustrations by Mary Thelen.
Raintree Publishers, Inc., 1980.
(31 pages)

HOSPITAL, GOING TO
    Fear: of the unknown
    Surgery

Young Dan Martin's fall from the monkey bars results in a dreaded trip to the hospital to have his injured ankle mended. His mother's presence and reassurance are not enough to calm the little boy's fears. At the hospital Dan is helped onto a cart and is greeted by people in "funny clothes" under bright lights. A sympathetic nurse explains that she is putting a temporary bandage on his ankle. Then, after examining Dan's ankle, Dr. Waters tells him about the X rays that need to be taken to determine the extent of the injury. While the Martins wait for Dr. Chun, the bone specialist, to arrive, the nurse gives Dan an injection for his pain. Dan hates shots, but this one is not bad enough to make him cry. Dr. Chun explains to the Martins that Dan's ankle is indeed broken and it cannot heal unless he operates on it right away. He gets a room for Dan on the children's floor and reassures him by admitting that "this is all very strange to you, Dan, but there is nothing to be afraid of." But Dan is still afraid. Once upstairs, he is told why he must wear a hospital gown and he meets Dr. Hood, his anesthesiologist, who tells Dan what she'll do during his operation. "I will help you fall into a special sleep . . . so it won't hurt while Dr. Chun is fixing your ankle." Dan continues to learn more about hospital procedures even in the operating room—about the uniforms, lights, and machines—before he falls into a deep sleep. When Dan opens his eyes, he is back in his room with his family. The operation is over. Dan's parents explain to him why his leg is in a cast and how the strange bottle of medicine and the tube attached to his arm will help prevent infection. The next day, Dan worries about missing so much school. His mother tells him about a special worker at the hospital who will help him with his schoolwork. As the days pass, Dan feels better and better. Dr. Chun puts a walking cast on his leg and helps him walk with crutches. Finally, Dan is able to go home and back to school. His teacher encourages him to tell the class about his hospital visit. Then everyone takes a turn signing Dan's cast.

This reassuring, simple, but informative account of a little boy's surgery and hospital stay could help prepare children for a hospital visit. It might also be useful for describing the hospital experience to a patient's siblings and peers. Dan is very clear about his feelings and observations, making him an engaging character. Large, colorful illustrations add to the appeal.

Ages 3-8

**Also available in:**
No other form known

## 301

**Holland, Isabelle**

### Now Is Not Too Late

Lothrop, Lee & Shepard Company, 1980.
(159 pages)

---

*MATURATION*
*Alcoholism: of mother*
*Change: accepting*
*Grandparent: living in home of*
*Love, meaning of*
*Nightmares*
*Stepbrother/Stepsister*

---

Eleven-year-old Cathy Barrett loves spending the summer with her paternal grandmother on an island off the coast of Maine, although she wishes her stepbrother, Andy, could come too. She regards Andy more as a brother than a stepbrother. In his absence, Cathy spends time with Marianne, her summer best friend. Marianne warns Cathy about the Wicked Witch, an odd woman who lives alone in a cottage up a steep hill and has lots of animals. Her curiosity piqued, Cathy asks her grandmother about the woman. Her name is Elizabeth, the grandmother replies; she's known her for thirteen

years. She then changes the subject. Still curious, Cathy decides to go see Elizabeth, this Wicked Witch. She is surprised to meet a woman of about forty, beautiful but sad. Elizabeth paints and does illustrations for children's books, and she asks Cathy to model for her. They dicker about payment, and Cathy agrees to sit two hours a day for twenty-five days. She plans to use the money for the bicycle she wants. As she leaves Elizabeth's cottage, she decides to tell neither Marianne nor her grandmother about the arrangement. That night Cathy has a terrifying nightmare, like the ones she often had as a child. The modeling begins, and Cathy tells Elizabeth that her mother died when she was five. Elizabeth tells Cathy that she had a daughter once, but scared her badly when she was little. Then Andy arrives at Cathy's grandmother's house, coming early from camp. With him is his friend Don, whom Cathy soon resents because of the attention Andy gives him. One day Cathy asks her grandmother about her mother. She was sick in mind as well as body, her grandmother replies, but she encourages Cathy not to judge her mother. While she's with Elizabeth, Cathy begins to draw, and their two hours each day become very important to her. When Andy, Don, Marianne, and Cathy go to the mainland for a movie, they see Elizabeth and follow her into a church. There they overhear her testimony to an Alcoholics Anonymous meeting. She confesses to screaming at and verbally abusing her little daughter. Old memories flood Cathy's mind and her nightmare becomes a reality. She runs away, back to the island, and hides on a cliff over the ocean. Terribly confused, terrified, she nearly falls over but is rescued by an old man and his dog and taken to her grandmother's house. Cathy asks if Elizabeth is her mother. Yes, her grandmother admits; Cathy has been lied to. When she's able to face Elizabeth again, Cathy goes and talks with her. Elizabeth gives the girl a check for her bike. Maybe they can see each other in New York someday. Back at her grandmother's, Cathy has a sense of how much this summer has meant to her.

Cathy's island summer turns dramatic when she learns that Elizabeth, the "Wicked Witch," is the source of her nightmares—the alcoholic mother she'd thought dead. Although the reader realizes this considerably earlier, Cathy's first-person narrative is so compelling that interest never flags. The relationship between the girl and her grandmother is especially well drawn.

Ages 10-13

**Also available in:**
Paperbound—*Now Is Not Too Late*
Bantam Books, Inc.

## 302

**Hoopes, Lyn Littlefield**

### Nana

Color illustrations by Arieh Zeldich.
Harper & Row, Publishers, Inc., 1981.
(29 pages counted)

---

*DEATH: of Grandparent*
*Nature: appreciation of*

---

H

A young girl is at Nana's house, but Nana isn't there. "Our Nana died in the night." She sits on the stool by Nana's window and looks at Nana's slippers and glasses and book. She hopes she and Nana will read a story together, but then realizes they can't do that anymore. In the garden she sees the bird feeder and the baby ferns that Nana said you can hear unfurl if you're very quiet. She wonders what it's like for Nana now. Is being dead like sleeping? The girl lies down in a field and thinks, "I am the me that was me before I was born." She remembers Nana calling to the chickadees and, when she and Nana were quiet, the chickadees' answer. She feels the breeze. Nana can't hear the wind, but she is surely there beside her granddaughter just the same. In the woods the girl is very quiet and hears a fern unfurling. She calls to a chickadee. "I am very still, for I know he is near. And Nana too is here."

This story-poem follows a little girl through the day after her grandmother's death. She has learned from Nana to hear things many people don't listen for and to expect responses from the things around her so subtle that only she is aware of them. She seems comforted and accepting at the end, knowing Nana is near. Soft, gentle drawings reinforce the thoughtful descriptions and observations. The text requires a certain receptivity on the part of the reader; although the book is very short and simple, the meaning may elude younger children without adult-guided discussion.

Ages 5-8

**Also available in:**
No other form known

## 303

Hopkins, Lee Bennett

## Mama & Her Boys

Harper & Row, Publishers, Inc., 1981.
(149 pages)

---

PARENT/PARENTS: Remarriage of
PARENT/PARENTS: Single
  Communication: parent-child
  Decision making
  Love, meaning of
  Sibling: relationships

---

The Kipness family includes Mama and her much-loved sons, Christopher Hugh, four, and Mark Charles, ten. Mama tells her boys that she would like to replace their father, whose love for them died and who walked out on his responsibility to them when Chris was just a baby. But choosing is not easy since Mama will only settle for a very special man, one who will be right for the three of them. The first proposal has come from Mr. Jeremiah Jacobs, owner of the laundry where Mama works, but when she asks her boys' approval, Chris avows he does not "want any more fathers" and Mark begs time to think about it. Neither wants Mr. Jacobs as a father, and so Mama refuses his proposal. Life changes for all of them when, for an article in his class newspaper, Mark interviews Mr. Michael Carlisle, the school maintenance man. Mike offers to help the family with a plumbing problem and is invited to dinner. Gradually he becomes part of the family, spending

many happy hours with Mama and the boys. As Mike's relationship with them develops, Chris must work out strong feelings of jealousy as more and more of Mama's time and attention are given to her suitor. Mark remains more introspective, waiting patiently for events to take their course. Together, the four of them decide that Mama and Mike should marry. As Chris says, "I like the idea, I like it very much."

Mama won't remarry until her sons agree she should. A sequel to *Mama,* this tender, believable story aptly portrays the rewards that come from a sincere effort to consider the best interests of every family member in a decision that affects them all. It is a quiet account of loving family members looking out for each other.

Ages 8-11

**Also available in:**
No other form known

## 304

Hopper, Nancy J.

## Secrets

Elsevier/Nelson Books, 1979.
(138 pages) o.p.

---

MENTAL ILLNESS: of Adolescent
REALITY, ESCAPING
  Death: of father
  Friendship: meaning of
  Kidnapping
  Parent/Parents: remarriage of
  Problem solving

---

Other people's secrets are an obsession with fourteen-year-old Lenore James. Since witnessing the death of her father, who was hit by a car several years earlier, Lenore feels "like a locked box from which nothing can escape . . . nothing can get in either." Her inability to communicate and her blank looks fool people into thinking she's unbalanced and not too intelligent, which is the effect she strives for. Lenore overhears Miss Lisinsky, a new teacher, talking about a coming field trip in conspiratorial tones to a gray-haired stranger. Several days later Lenore follows the stranger, whom she calls Gray Head, and observes him tailing Sammy Loudon, a wealthy classmate. Lenore is certain Miss Lisinsky and Gray Head are conspiring to kidnap Sammy. Knowing no one will believe her, she tries to restore her credibility by bringing up her grades. Her favorite teacher, Mrs. Norris, gives her an A for an essay describing the coming crime using the actual names of those involved, but warns her not to use real names in her stories. In a rare moment of confession, Lenore tells her psychiatrist, Dr. Matthews, of the kidnapping plot. Though pleased at this voluntary communication, he thinks her active imagination has simply returned to life. Frustrated, Lenore tries to warn Sammy himself, but he only laughs and explains that Gray Head is his bodyguard. Lenore is unconvinced and feels powerless to prevent a tragedy. Her emotional turmoil is compounded by her mother's plans to remarry, although she's surprised to discover she actually likes her future stepfather. During the fateful field trip, Miss Lisinsky, as Lenore expects, sends Sammy on an errand alone. Lenore follows nervously, and together they fall into the kidnappers' trap. She and Sammy are bound, gagged, and sedated by two men who take them to a condemned building complex. For two days they are fed carry-out chicken and water. The kidnappers force them to tape-record messages to their parents and finally, when no ransom money is forthcoming, attempt to poison them with tranquilizers and whiskey. Holding the pills in their mouths, they spit out what they can and force themselves to vomit the alcohol. When Sammy falls unconscious, Lenore, groggy herself, kicks and punches her kidnappers and screams at them. A drunken brawl results and then rescue comes at last: Dr. Matthews had gone to the police after reconsidering Lenore's story. Lenore and Sammy are taken, bruised and battered, to a hospital, and Miss Lisinsky and Gray Head (the other man remains at large) are caught at the airport trying to escape to Spain. When her mother and Dr. Matthews visit Lenore in the hospital, they are delighted with how open and communicative the girl is. Lenore is happy too: "I didn't much like the secrets anyway." The future looks even brighter when, after her mother's remarriage, Lenore overhears her stepfather say, "No one is ever going to replace her father. I'd like to be her friend, a good stepfather, if she'll let me."

Lenore tells the story of how her depression ends and her lost grip on reality is regained through her harrowing kidnapping and the purposeful action it evokes from her. Faced with real danger to herself and a friend, Lenore breaks through her illness and finds courage. This unusual, fast-paced story is told with humor as well as suspense. Lenore's matter-of-fact attitude toward her illness and the believable description of her recovery keep the book from melodrama.

Ages 11-14

**Also available in:**
Cassette—*Secrets*
Library of Congress (NLSBPH)

## 305

**Houston, James Archibald**

## Long Claws: An Arctic Adventure

Black/white illustrations by the author.
Atheneum Publishers, 1981.
(32 pages)

---

*COURAGE, MEANING OF*
*ESKIMO*
   *Nature: respect for*
   *Risk, taking of*
   *Sibling: relationships*

---

Pitohok and Upik are the oldest children of an Eskimo family that is near starvation since the death of their father left them unprepared to survive the winter. Newly fortified after eating some frozen trout they found, Pitohok and Upik decide to attempt the three-day walk to retrieve the caribou their grandfather killed last fall but was too weak to carry home. Their grandfather makes them a small sled using frozen caribou skins as runners and the three remaining frozen trout as crossbars. Wearing new fur boots their mother has sewn

for the journey they set out, armed with an old rifle, two hand-carved stone bullets, a snow knife, and an ax to dig out the precious meat. Although their trek across the tundra is slowed by a blizzard, they arrive at their destination unharmed. Just when they discover the caribou's antlers rising above the snow on a ridge near a river, as their grandfather had described, they also see Kugvik, a wolverine, digging near the spot. Pitohok shoots, frightening the intruder away. Heading home the next morning with the caribou lashed onto their small sled, they spot a grizzly bear, known to them as Akla, Long Claws. They walk faster, but cannot outdistance the fearful beast. As night approaches, Pitohok cuts the sled apart, throwing the runners to the hungry bear. Now the boy must carry the heavy caribou on his back, and still the bear follows. Pitohok tells Upik to throw the animal one of their two remaining fish. While Long Claws eats, they shallowly bury the caribou, build an igloo on top of it, and sleep. The next day they trudge on in a heavy ice fog, a sign of spring, unable to see the trail of their old footprints. They are weary, but confident they have lost Akla. That afternoon Upik hears the bear's breath and turns to see it right behind them. Afraid to shoot for fear the bullet will only shatter, she begs her brother to leave the caribou. The bear claws at the meat, knocking Pitohok off balance, but he grimly rises and staggers on. Now they sight their family's igloo and Pitohok, knowing they cannot live without the meat, desperately hangs on to the caribou. He is unable to walk any farther, though, and begs Upik to run. She stays, screaming at the bear to leave her brother alone, aware that the animal is not good or evil but merely a hunter as they are. Their mother and grandfather, hearing Upik's screams, come out and see Pitohok collapse with his arms locked around the caribou. Long Claws drags it slowly away, taking Pitohok also. The grandfather draws his bow but Upik interferes and stands in his way, afraid he will miss and hit Pitohok. Suddenly she runs straight between her brother and the bear, screaming angrily, "You let go of him! Let go!" The surprised bear looks at her, drops the caribou, ambles after the last piece of fish she throws, and disappears. Pitohok asks his grandfather if he would have believed Upik could do what she did. No, the old man replies. "Nobody knows the strength or courage that humans possess until real danger comes to test them."

An authentic and vivid tale of the Innuit people, written by a man who has lived for many years in the Arctic, this story portrays the Eskimo's often-desperate struggle to survive. Also detailed are the people's customs, beliefs, and way of life. The harrowing and courageous journey of the brother and sister is sure to grip young readers and provide abundant material for discussion. Upik's triumph at the end is motivated by a desire to protect and preserve all that is dear to her, and readers will cheer her success. Also notable here is the attitude of partnership with the natural world, enhanced by illustrations that convey, in their simplicity, the starkness and vastness of the landscape.

Ages 9-11

**Also available in:**
No other form known

H

## 306

Houston, James Archibald

### River Runners: A Tale of Hardship and Bravery

Black/white illustrations by the author.
Atheneum Publishers, 1979.
(142 pages)

---

FRIENDSHIP: Meaning of
  Courage, meaning of
  Native American
  Nature: living in harmony with

---

Fifteen-year-old Andrew Stewart arrives in northern Canada to work as a clerk at Fort Chimo, a trading company. There he meets Pashak, a Naskapi Indian boy his own age who helps him learn the ways of the Indians and Eskimos who come to trade their furs for rifles and other goods. The company decides to send Andrew and Pashak to Ghost Lake to set up an outpost. The company's competitor, a French trading post across the river, plans to follow the boys to the new outpost and set up one of their own. So one party of packmen goes noisily off in the other direction as a diversion. Andrew, Pashak, and their packmen quietly slip out at night and head toward Ghost Lake. On the long trek to the new site, Andrew gets separated from the group because he's much slower on snowshoes. He follows their trail until snow obliterates it. Then he finds a marker Pashak left for him and is able to rejoin the others. They stop at Mium-scum's camp where one of Pashak's sisters lives with her husband, Mium-scum's son. Andrew watches a shaman (a priest who uses magic) attempt to find the whereabouts of the much-needed caribou. When he produces no results, he flees. Andrew, Pashak, and their packmen continue on to the outpost site, where they begin laying the foundation. Just before the packmen return to the main trading post, they predict that no one will come to this remote outpost. They are right, and eventually Andrew and Pashak run out of food. They decide to approach the mysterious mountain people, who offer to share their bountiful game. The boys' group witnesses a bear feast, rituals, feasting, drumming, storytelling, and singing. While camping near these mountain people, the group traps furs. Spring arrives. One day the old shaman staggers into camp, nearly dead of starvation. He says that Mium-scum's group is camped only two days away and can't move because they're all starving. Pashak and Andrew pack food and go to the camp, where they find Pashak's sister and her child nearly dead. Her husband and father-in-law have left to search for food. Andrew and Pashak go after them and bring them back safely, although all the rest of their group has died of starvation. The boys then set out to canoe back to Fort Chimo with their six bundles of furs. Andrew's map shows that one branch of the river is very short and straight, the other—the one the Indians have always used—longer and curvy. The boys soon find out why the Indians never use the short, straight branch when their canoe is dashed up on Bad Rock. Five of the bales of furs are lost in the accident and the boys can find no way off the rock island, which is surrounded by treacherous river currents. The others,

traveling on the long branch of the river, decide to check the other branch for the boys. They sight the two on the rock and get them off by hurling a line to them. Pashak goes first. When Andrew crosses over, he manages to bring the bale of furs. Pashak says Andrew definitely has all the makings of a good Scottish trader. However, when they get back to Fort Chimo, Andrew feels a failure; he did not get the outpost built and he lost five of the six bales of furs. But they are warmly welcomed and discover that the price of the otter skins Andrew did bring back has risen quite a bit. The Indians contribute even more furs because of Andrew's help during the long winter. Pashak's family adopts Andrew, giving him the new name "fine man." After the adoption ceremony, Andrew realizes how close he feels to these people and to the natural world all around them. He feels the unity of land, animals, and people. "He felt as though he, too, had become a part of everything upon this earth."

Two boys survive in the harsh but beautiful country of northern Canada during the fur-trading days of the nineteenth century. Andrew learns a great deal from his Indian friend, Pashak, and the book is rich in authentic details of Indian and Eskimo life in the Far North. An appreciation for nature shines through the pages, as do the wisdom, knowledge, and skills of the natives of this difficult land. Andrew learns about steadfastness, courage, and service to others in this exciting account based on true events.

Ages 11 and up

**Also available in:**
No other form known

## 307

Hughes, Dean

### Honestly, Myron

Black/white illustrations by Martha Weston.
Atheneum Publishers, 1982.
(149 pages)

---

HONESTY/DISHONESTY
  Communication: importance of
  Communication: misunderstandings
  Communication: parent-child
  School: classmate relationships

---

Fifth-grader Myron Singleton can't understand why his classmate Lustre Bright would rather lie than tell the truth. She weaves the most fantastic stories in the most convincing manner. When their teacher, Mr. McEnelly, decides to use Lincoln's birthday as an occasion to discuss honesty, he asks Myron's help. Myron suggests that it is always better to tell the truth. But when he tries to discuss the issue with his parents that night he precipitates a near-riot when both discover (thanks to Myron) that the other keeps certain things secret. The next day in school Myron publicly accuses Lustre Bright of lying. Mr. McEnelly tries to soften Myron's statement, but Myron is adamant. In a heated discussion, Mr. McEnelly tries to tell Myron the difference between rudeness and honesty. Myron asks if this means he shouldn't tell Benny that he stinks and Franny that she ought to brush her teeth once in a while. After school,

Benny beats Myron up. That night as he listens to a phone-in radio show, Myron hears the principal, Mrs. Kendall, and the school superintendent, Dr. Monroe, discussing the merits of a bond proposal for a new school. Even though Myron agrees with them, he feels obliged to call in and report that some of their information is false. His father has told him, for example, that a rivet company rumored to be moving into town and thus adding more schoolchildren to the already crowded building will not, in fact, be coming. An angry uproar follows, and Myron is invited to speak on a local television show the next evening. After school the next day, he and his parents are summoned to a conference with Mrs. Kendall and Dr. Monroe. Myron is not to go on television, Mrs. Kendall insists, but Dr. Monroe arrives late to report that the media is accusing them of trying to muzzle Myron, and so they must allow him to go on. They explain very carefully to Myron how badly they need to pass this bond issue. Dr. Monroe mentions the relative lack of intelligence of the electorate. During the television interview Myron defends the need for a new school, but adds that the issue should be decided on its real merits. When questioned, he repeats some of the things Dr. Monroe and Mrs. Kendall said, including Mrs. Kendall's remark that even Abraham Lincoln probably lied through his teeth on occasion. The latter remark receives nationwide publicity in a situation increasingly referred to as Lincolngate. After the story is picked up by national wire services, a press conference is held. The school administrators do not come off well when they attempt to explain what's happened. The reporters keep pressing Myron, trying to discover his motivation since he insists he does believe in the school bond issue. Replies Myron, "Everyone seems to think you have to tell the truth for some reason. I thought you just told it because it was the truth." The town is divided, half thinking Myron a busybody who's done them harm, the other half proud of this native son. The next day, children from Myron's school are interviewed. Lustre Bright, an appealing tear running down her cheek, tells several convincing and utterly false stories about their crowded school. Myron, upset by the lies, visits the local newspaper editor and tells him he can prove Lustre is wrong. He emphasizes again that the bond issue should be judged purely on its merits. The bond issue is defeated. As Myron had predicted, voters felt insulted and manipulated by the whole affair. Even Lustre admits that she too thinks it's always best to be honest. Then she tells how Myron once saved her life by rescuing her from two armed thugs.

A boy ventures into the murky realm of absolute truth and is dismayed by the results. He must endure the anger of nearly everyone close to him, although they all admit the virtues of his beliefs. There is a certain ambivalence in the book; the reader isn't always sure whether to admire Myron or to find him tiresome. His principles seem sound, but his poor, beleaguered parents come across more sympathetically—and the school bond issue is defeated. If nothing else, this entertaining book suggests the complexities of insisting on absolute honesty. There is much here to prompt discussion. Illustrations accent the humor.

Ages 9-11

**Also available in:**
No other form known

## 308
**Hughes, Dean**

### Switching Tracks
Atheneum Publishers, 1982.
(166 pages)

---

*GUILT, FEELINGS OF*
  *Age: aging*
  *Ambivalence, feelings of*
  *Depression*
  *Friendship: making friends*
  *School: classmate relationships*
  *Suicide: of parent*

---

Mark Austin's father has died, he and his mother and younger brother have moved to another house, and Mark is attending a new junior high. An elderly neighbor, Willard, offers to pay Mark to help him put together the model railroad set he has in his basement. Mark refuses at first, but later accepts when he needs money to play the video games at the arcade. Since his father's death, Mark doesn't do schoolwork, he won't make friends, he screams at his brother—all he seems to want to do is play video games. To his concerned mother, Mark says he hated his father and doesn't care that he's dead. But secretly he must spend most of his energy trying to suppress the unidentifiable voices that return to haunt him. The tension builds in the boy: he's failing in school, his mother begins dating a man named Don, some boys on the bus tease him about Willard. The voices in his head try harder to break through, especially when his mother asks how he would feel if she and Don married. Mark continues saying anything he can to hurt his mother, denying that he used to love his father, admitting no good in him. His mother tries to present his father as a man riddled with problems that could explain, if not excuse, his physical abuse and drinking. Only Mark and his mother know that Mark's father's death was not an accident, but she insists they had no choice that last day when he begged his family to take him back—they had to send him away. Willard tries to get through to Mark, accusing him of having chosen hatred as a way of life. But Mark cannot forget the last words he said to his father. Then Willard tells Mark he's dying of cancer and wants to leave Mark his house and his train set. Furious that Willard has kept his illness a secret, feeling cheated and somehow betrayed, Mark spends the following day in such a daze that one teacher asks him if he's on drugs. He can't remember any of the afternoon and, after a hazy incident on the bus, wakes up in a hospital a day later. Mark realizes he has to tell someone all that's burdening him. He asks for Willard, who has also been hospitalized for some tests. He tells Willard the whole story: how his father threatened to kill himself if his family didn't take him back, how he described the exact suicide he planned (which he later carried out). Mark had gone out to talk to him and found him crying by his car. When his father again repeated his intention of killing himself, Mark had told him he didn't have the guts to do it. Those were the last words he ever spoke to his father. Mark believes his father must have hated him to leave him with this legacy of guilt. Gently, Willard points out that Mark both hated and loved his father. The weeping boy

H

admits he misses his father terribly. Willard helps Mark see that while the family gave his father many second chances, Mark was given no second chance to apologize or undo his hasty words. He persuades the boy to talk further with some of the hospital staff. Earlier, when Willard offered him the train set, Mark angrily turned it down. Now he tells Willard he'd like to accept the gift.

In this painful and gripping novel, a boy is driven by guilt to the brink of mental illness when he suppresses his memories of the day his father killed himself. When he finally sees the necessity of unburdening himself, he chooses the elderly man who has befriended him and is himself dying. Mark and Willard take courage from each other: one learns to live and the other to die. Tense and fast-moving, not depressing, the book focuses on the close relationship that develops between the boy and the old man.

Ages 10-14

**Also available in:**
No other form known

## 309

**Hughes, Shirley**

**Alfie Gets In First**
Color illustrations by the author.
Lothrop, Lee & Shepard Company, 1981.
(32 pages counted)

---

*RESOURCEFULNESS*
  *Problem solving*
  *Success*

---

Alfie, his mother, and his little sister, Annie Rose, return from a shopping trip. Mom unlocks the door, sets the basket of groceries and her keys inside, and then walks back down the apartment steps to get Annie Rose out of her stroller. Alfie, pretending to be racing with his mother, runs inside ahead of her shouting, "I've won, I've won!" and slams the door, leaving himself and the keys on the inside, Mom and Annie Rose on the outside. Even with his mother's encouragement he can't reach the door catch, and he's too short to shove the keys through the mail slot. Mrs. MacNally from across the street comes to see what the commotion is about and is soon joined by her daughter, Maureen. Mom suggests Alfie get his little chair from the living room to stand on so he can push the keys through the mail slot. But he is busy crying, Annie Rose is crying, and Mrs. MacNally, Maureen, and Alfie's mother try to think of a way to get inside. The milkman and a window cleaner contribute a ladder and the suggestion that they climb in the bathroom window. But when the window cleaner is halfway up the ladder, the front door suddenly opens. Alfie has used his little chair to climb up and has managed to release the door catch. "He was very pleased with himself." Everyone comes in and they all have tea together.

A little boy who accidentally locks his mother and baby sister outside their apartment overcomes his feelings of helplessness and gets the door open. The delightful illustrations play an integral part in the story. While the text concentrates on the activities of the adults, the reader sees Alfie going for his chair, standing on it, and unlatching the door. The sudden opening of the door

surprises Alfie's mother and the neighbors, but the reader has seen it coming. Children will love this satisfying tale.

Ages 3-5

**Also available in:**
Disc—*Alfie Gets In First*
Library of Congress (NLSBPH)

## 310

**Hughes, Shirley**

**Moving Molly**
Color illustrations by the author.
Prentice-Hall, Inc., 1979.
(32 pages counted)

---

*CHANGE: New Home*
*MOVING*
  *Loneliness*

---

Little Molly and her family move from their basement apartment in an English city to a house in the country. Her mother and father are soon busy fixing up the house and yard. Molly's brother and sister go to school every day, and when they're home Patrick rides his bike and Joanie cares for her guinea pigs. Everybody has something to do but Molly. In the city she'd never been at a loss for friends. She finds a hole in their fence and begins spending her days in the neglected yard next door. It's become a jungle for cats, so she plays with them. She tends some abandoned plants and keeps herself amused. Then one day she sees a moving van pull up next door. Twins Kevin and Kathy, her new neighbors, peek at her through the hole in the fence. They like to do the same things she does, so now Molly is as busy as the rest of her family.

A child adjusts to the move her family makes, once she finds some friends next door. Accompanying the simple, appealing text are lively, old-fashioned illustrations that realistically depict the English setting. Readers will want to linger over some of them.

Ages 3-5

**Also available in:**
Disc—*Moving Molly*
Library of Congress (NLSBPH)

Paperbound—*Moving Molly*
Prentice-Hall, Inc.

## 311

**Hull, Eleanor Means**

**Alice with Golden Hair**
Atheneum Publishers, 1981.
(186 pages)

---

*MENTAL RETARDATION*
  *Age: aging*
  *Friendship: meaning of*
  *Identity, search for*
  *Maturation*
  *Nursing home, living in*
  *Rejection: parental*

---

Alice McMartin is nearly eighteen and has been in institutions for the retarded since she was a small child. She can remember the time when she lived with her family and had a "wonderful," kind mother. But then one day, Alice recalls, her mother sent her away, went to a hospital, and died. In truth, Alice's mother placed her in an institution when she discovered she was dying. Her father left her there because he felt he couldn't manage her care. Despite visits from her father and sister, Alice has grown up believing that her parents gave her up because they didn't love her. Now she is old enough to go out into the world. Mrs. Hones, the social worker, has found her a job at a nursing home, where she can live as well as work. Alice is at first apprehensive about caring for "horrible old things" who drool and shake and probably smell. But she soon learns to like the people on her floor, the second, and is warmed by their acceptance of her. She forms one very special attachment to a patient named Allegra Daniels, an intelligent woman who draws Alice into a "world of knowledge and love." Mrs. Daniels (Leg) helps the girl get acquainted with some of the other people who work at the home. She encourages Alice to get to know Appolonia, whom Alice at first does not like because she is black and has called Alice a "looney." One day, while Alice is talking with Mrs. Daniels instead of watching her patients, a resident named Miss Johnson slips away from the home. Alice knows that Miss Johnson has wanted to visit her niece in a nearby hospital. She goes after her and brings her back, but is still in danger of losing her job. It is Appolonia who defends her to Mr. Bell, the hospital administrator. Alice is allowed to continue her work on the second floor, and when Mrs. Daniels has a stroke and is moved to this section, Alice cares for her too. The staff, however, decides that Alice is too emotionally involved with the patients and she is transferred to another floor. Before she leaves, she promises Leg to come back. But after many attempts to return, Alice finally gives up in despair. She runs away to her father's house, where she is later found by Mrs. Hones and returned to the nursing home. Angry with Mr. Bell for his treatment of Alice, Mrs. Hones reports him to his employer, the state department. In the meantime, theft has become a problem at the home. When it looks like Appolonia is going to be blamed, Alice reveals a crucial bit of information. She tells Mr. Bell that Browny, an orderly, has a key to the laundry-stair door. A patient reports seeing a truck outside the laundry at night. The mystery is solved, and Alice and Appolonia become friends and roommates. Soon after, Mr. Bell is dismissed from his job amid rumors that he was taking rake-offs for allowing certain inefficiencies to persist at the home. Cap Whitby, honest but cold and legalistic, is brought in to replace him. He decides that although Alice is "almost more than adequate" for her job, it doesn't look good to have a retarded girl working with the patients. Mrs. Hones, however, offers him some information that helps him reconsider. She has learned that Alice's mother was also retarded, but that she was "good and respected" and had a "rare gift for love." She had cared very much for her family and had only given Alice up because she knew she was dying. Alice, insists Mrs. Hones, is going to be just like her. When Mrs. Hones tells this to Alice

herself, the girl feels strong enough to face anything. She knows at last that her mother loved her and that, like her mother, she herself is "good and respected."

Here is a rare, poignant look into the mind of a retarded girl. The reader sees clearly both Alice's limitations and her special gift of seeing "more than other people." We empathize with Alice's sense of rejection and isolation and admire her heroic effort to cope with a complicated world. The book would be excellent reading for anyone who wants to look behind the seemingly impassable barrier that surrounds mentally retarded people.

Ages 11 and up

**Also available in:**
Paperbound—*Alice with Golden Hair*
New American Library

## 312

**Hunter, Kristin Eggleston**

## Lou in the Limelight
Charles Scribner's Sons, 1981.
(296 pages)

*IDENTITY, SEARCH FOR*
*TALENTS: Musical*
    *Afro-American*
    *Boy-girl relationships*
    *Crime/Criminals*
    *Drugs: abuse of*
    *Family: relationships*
    *Sex: attitude toward*

Sixteen-year-old Louretta Hawkins knows she has talent and is determined that someday she will make enough money as a singer and songwriter to take herself and her family out of the ghetto. Her mother is convinced that Lou is "running with the Devil and singing his music," but Lou persists with her career. She and the three "Soul Brothers" have acquired a manager named Marty Ross who helps them cut a record album and then gets them bookings in New York and Las Vegas. But gradually Lou and the boys realize that they are sinking more and more into debt to Marty for the luxurious life style he insists they maintain. Worse, Marty expects Lou to sleep with a fat stranger named Bill Bland, who is supposed to be the group's "most valuable contact." The man backs off when Lou tells him she's a minor, but in order to get over her shock and disgust she allows Frank, one of the Soul Brothers, to make love to her. This relationship further complicates Lou's life, since Frank is a playboy who takes her availability for granted even as he flirts with other women. He also manages to run up a huge gambling debt during their first week in Las Vegas. They already owe Marty five thousand dollars. Then Lou finds Frank and the others high on drugs that have been sent to them by the hotel manager, Carl Sipp. Lou herself has been approached by Sipp, who offers to reduce their growing debt if she will sleep with him. Convinced they desperately need help, Lou wires her older brother and is pleased the next morning to receive word that Mrs. Jerutha Jackson is on her way. "Aunt Jerutha" is a friend of her mother's and a "good member of the Cheerful Baptist Church." Practical without being stuffy, Aunt Jerutha assesses the situation and begins to take action. She talks to a United

H

177

States Attorney, Ben Carroll, who has been looking for a way to crack down on some of the illegal activities in Las Vegas. Since Lou and the boys are minors who were brought across state lines to be "corrupted," he is particularly anxious to have their statements. After Carroll threatens Marty with a lawsuit, Lou and the boys are released from their contract. The four young people testify before a grand jury, and Carl Sipp and two other people, all "tentacles" of a "giant octopus of crime," are indicted. Lou and the boys return home to rest and rethink their plans for the future. They decide that since they have missed most of the school year anyway, they will take their music on the road for a while. Their new manager, Sam Banks, sets up a whirlwind schedule of engagements that drains Lou's remaining energy. She begins to take more and more pills to keep going, a trick she learned from Marty. Finally, she collapses and is taken to a hospital in Brunswick, Georgia, suffering from dehydration, malnutrition, and exhaustion. During her stay in the town she learns that her mother's relatives, whom she has never met, are local people. One in particular, Julia Church, takes an interest in Lou. Julia, a concert pianist and music teacher, decides to claim her talented young cousin. She wants to give her a home and an education, to share her life with her. Lou, hungry for knowledge and culture, accepts the offer. Finally, she thinks, she has found where she belongs.

In this sequel to *The Soul Brothers and Sister Lou,* Lou learns that her ambition to become a star is not worth the exploitation that seems to accompany the "limelight." Her chance encounter with a cultured, educated cousin restores her yearning for a solid grounding in real values. Although the book is rich in its depiction of black culture and language, the characterizations of almost all the minor characters are flat and stereotypical. Similarly, the depiction of the casual use of drugs by entertainers is too staged to be completely realistic. There is some explicit sex.

Ages 14 and up

**Also available in:**
No other form known

### 313

**Hurd, Edith Thacher**

### The Black Dog Who Went into the Woods

Color illustrations by Emily Arnold McCully.
Harper & Row, Publishers, Inc., 1980.
(32 pages)

---

*DEATH: of Pet*
  *Family: relationships*
  *Loss: feelings of*

---

Benjamin, about seven, sadly announces to his family, "Black Dog has gone into the woods and died." Rose and Sammy, Benj's older sister and brother, say it cannot be true. Even Benj's mother and father assure him that Black Dog will return. But Benj is adamant. After dinner, the entire family walks through the pasture and meadow to the woods, but finds no trace of Black Dog. Benj is sure she does not want to be found. During the next few days the family, minus Benj, continues to look for Black Dog. Finally they agree that Benj is probably

right: Black Dog is old and has quite likely gone to the woods to die. That night each family member dreams about a past experience with Black Dog. In each dream, Black Dog returns to say goodbye. At breakfast they discuss their dreams and agree that Black Dog came back one last time to each of them. But they're all sure she came closest to Benj.

A young boy and his family adjust to the death of their dog. Although it's not quite believable that each family member dreams about Black Dog on the same night, the story sensitively conveys the feelings of loss a family experiences when a pet dies. Softly shaded pencil sketches enhance the quiet mood.

Ages 5-7

**Also available in:**
No other form known

### 314

**Hurd, Edith Thacher**

### I Dance in My Red Pajamas

Color illustrations by Emily Arnold McCully.
Harper & Row, Publishers, Inc., 1982.
(30 pages counted)

---

*GRANDPARENT: Love for*
*VISITING*
  *Age: aging*

---

Young Jenny's parents warn her not to be loud or boisterous at her grandparents' house when she goes for an overnight visit. Jenny promises but smiles secretly, remembering the lively times she has shared with her grandparents. When she arrives with her red pajamas, toothbrush, and Lion, she is loudly greeted by Grandpa and hugged by Granny. Right away, Grandpa grabs Jenny and she sings as he twirls her around in their familiar whirling game. When she stops, she wobbles and falls into Granny's lap. Then Jenny helps her grandfather build an outside house for Catarina, Granny's big cat. Later, Jenny helps fix supper and set the table. She and her grandfather chuckle at their messy faces after eating the blueberry pie. When the dishes are done, Granny runs Jenny's bath in the big claw-footed tub. Jenny has a grand time splashing and swimming. Then, dressed in her red pajamas, she helps her grandfather bring in firewood. Jenny sits on the floor with Lion and Catarina and watches the fire. Then Granny begins to play the piano softly and Jenny dances. Soon she and her grandfather are clapping, stomping, and dancing as her grandmother plays louder and yells out square-dancing calls. Humming their tunes, her grandparents dance together. Grandpa gives Jenny a piggyback ride upstairs and, after Granny tucks her and Lion in, he says, "Oh, what a beautiful, lovely, noisy day."

This warm story about a little girl's special relationship with her grandparents reminds readers that age is a relative thing. To Jenny, the grandparents who dance and sing and play with her are not old. To her grandparents, Jenny's noise and activity are not bothersome but wonderful. They have much to give each other, and their enriching friendship could encourage readers, young and old, to make and sustain contact with grandparents or grandchildren. Lively illustrations emphasize the loving relationship.

Ages 3-6

Also available in:
Filmstrip—*I Dance in My Red Pajamas*
Random House, Inc.

## 315

Hurmence, Belinda

## Tough Tiffany

Doubleday & Company, Inc., 1980.
(166 pages)

---

FAMILY: Unity
    Afro-American
    Grandparent: respect for
    Money: management
    Poverty
    Privacy, need for
    Unwed mother

---

Tiffany Cox, eleven and the youngest of six children, lives with her family in rural North Carolina. Tiff shares a bedroom with her four sisters. When her mother, a spendthrift, buys two bunk bed sets for the girls, all four are stacked one on top of the other. Tiff is delighted to have the topmost bunk close to the ceiling: privacy at last. Recently the family's happiness has been disturbed and Tiff finally discovers the reason: her fifteen-year-old sister, Dawn, is pregnant. Tiff has the perfect solution: give the baby to Aunt Sister, who baby-sits daily and loves children. Aunt Sister readily agrees to keep the baby, but Dawn is not sure she wants to give it up. She quits school and begins spending time with Aunt Sister, learning how to care for babies. Tiff hates Dawn's boyfriend, Joe, even though he helps pay the doctor's bills and visits Dawn often. Once school is out Tiff must spend time with her arthritic Granny Turner, helping her clean house and weed her yard. This Tiff does grudgingly, since to her Granny is old and mean and stingy. Tiff's pleasant summer hours are spent reading the books she gets from the library. One day while her parents are out, a man comes by to repossess the bunk beds. Tiff is frightened and tearful and finally the man relents, but he promises to return if the payments are not made. In August the family has a large reunion with relatives from all over the country. The affair is a huge success, although Tiff has to spend much of the time with Granny as she prepares food for the gathering. After the relatives are gone, Granny discovers her life's savings missing and frantically searches for her money. Later in the day, Tiff finds the misplaced cash and talks Granny into putting the money in a bank. Then Tiff teaches her to write checks. Granny rewards the girl by writing a check to cover the remaining cost of the bunk beds. Returning home, Tiff finds the family arguing over where Dawn and her baby will live. Several weeks later the whole family goes to a parade, leaving Dawn at home. Tiff returns to get some money and discovers Dawn in labor. She stops a police car and demands that the officer take them to the hospital. Later that day Tiff's parents tell her Dawn has named her girl Tiffany, because of Tiff's help. When Tiff is allowed to

choose a middle name she picks Turner, Granny's family name, assumed in slavery but now worn in freedom. Dawn and the baby have come home to be part of the family.

A young girl living with her large family in a poor, rural area of the South copes with the problems of little money, less privacy, an unwed, pregnant sister, and a difficult grandmother. Tiff is an appealing heroine and the book features warm, believable family relationships. Noteworthy is the compassionate account of the plight of a young unwed mother. This is a thoughtful story of a contemporary family.

Ages 10-13

Also available in:
Cassette—*Tough Tiffany*
Library of Congress (NLSBPH)

Paperbound—*Tough Tiffany*
Library of Congress (NLSBPH)

## 316

Hurwitz, Johanna

## Aldo Applesauce

Black/white illustrations by John Wallner.
William Morrow & Company, Inc., 1979.
(127 pages)

---

CHANGE: New Home
NAME, DISSATISFACTION WITH
    Friendship: making friends
    Moving
    School: classmate relationships
    School: transfer
    Teasing

---

It is January and fourth-grader Aldo Sossi wakes up in his new house, filled with apprehension about entering his new school. For a time, all his fears seem justified. He is assigned a seat next to DeDe, a girl who wears a false mustache. He says the teacher's name wrong. At lunch, when he smells DeDe's tuna sandwich, Aldo explains that he is a vegetarian and wants to become a vet. He likes birds too much to eat them, he tells her, and cannot eat tuna since he read that dolphins are often killed in tuna nets. Then DeDe slips, knocking his applesauce to the floor, and Aldo acquires the embarrassing nickname "Applesauce." Some boys steal his hard-boiled egg and play catch with it. DeDe tells him to bring another the next day, but it too is stolen and tossed around. The third day DeDe herself brings an egg, this one raw. Snatched and tossed, it breaks messily, and a smiling aide tells Aldo and DeDe that she thinks the tricks are over. At home, Aldo pursues his usual animal-loving routine. He saves his toast crusts for the birds and scatters leftover spaghetti and wheat germ. After two months at his new school, Aldo still has only one friend, DeDe, and still suffers the burden of his nickname, Applesauce. He constantly wonders why DeDe wears the mustache, but doesn't ask. Curious about why he has been invited to a classmate's birthday party when the boy has never said a word to him, Aldo learns that all the boys from class were invited. "The more kids, the more presents," says the birthday boy. Since hot dogs and hamburgers are on the birthday menu, Aldo eats only potato chips, a pickle, and orange soda. By the time the cake is served, his stomach is so jumpy he can only eat a little bit. He is despondent on the way home and his father, aware of Aldo's painful nickname, explains his own brother's monicker—Tomato Sauce for Thomas Sossi. At school DeDe is glum, so Aldo invites her to his house. While they wait for Aldo's sister's applesauce cake to bake, DeDe tells him not to be offended by his nickname: "Everybody in the school knows you better if you have a nickname." After lunch at DeDe's the next Saturday, Aldo is finally emboldened enough to ask his friend why she wears a fake mustache. She tells him that she wants to look like her father, divorced from her mother and painfully missed. She has always been told she resembles her father, so now that he's grown a mustache she is wearing one too to maintain the similarity. If her father goes bald, Aldo asks her, will she shave her head? He assures her that her father will remain her father no matter where he is or how much they differ in appearance. Both friends are comforted.

This second of several books about Aldo shows the boy quietly struggling to fit in at his new school without violating his strongly held principles or being something he's not. He befriends another lonely, nonconforming child, and the two comfort and sustain each other. Aldo is gentle and likeable and his story is told with a light, humorous touch that remains true to the concerns and feelings of sensitive, individual children. Amusing illustrations capture the tone.

Ages 7-9

**Also available in:**
Cassette—*Aldo Applesauce*
Library of Congress (NLSBPH)

Paperbound—*Aldo Applesauce*
Scholastic Book Services

## 317

**Hurwitz, Johanna**

### Once I Was a Plum Tree

Black/white illustrations by Ingrid Fetz.
William Morrow & Company, Inc., 1980.
(160 pages)

---

*IDENTITY, SEARCH FOR*
  *Jewish*
  *Prejudice: religious*
  *Religion: questioning*

---

Ten-year-old Gerry Flam (changed from Pflaumenbaum, meaning plum tree) feels different, and she doesn't like it. Her two best friends are Catholic; she is Jewish. Just being Jewish is confusing to her because her parents do not believe in God and are not practicing Jews. Even so, Gerry stays out of school for Jewish holidays—on her parents' orders, although they don't participate in the celebrations. In October Gerry and one of her best friends, Ann, start piano lessons with a new neighbor, Mrs. Wulf. In early December Gerry meets Mrs. Wulf's son, Edgar, who is twelve. She learns the Wulfs are Jewish and that they fled Germany just before World War II. Edgar talks of the war, just ended two years earlier, and of all the Jews killed. He also tells Gerry about the newly formed Jewish state of Palestine. Gerry, confused about all this new information, admits she has never been to a synagogue. She isn't really a Jew, she believes; she is an American. Edgar maintains that the Jewish people have a responsibility to history. For the first time, Gerry begins to consider what her being Jewish means. During the next few weeks she asks each of her parents about their faith. Both say they do not believe in God. Gerry tells both that she does. One day, as she and Edgar walk home from school, they are taunted about being Jewish by a group of classmates. The attack baffles Gerry, who tries to explain she is an American. In April the Wulfs invite Gerry's family to their Passover seder. Gerry's parents decline, but suggest that Gerry and her younger sister attend. As Gerry dresses for the dinner, her mother gives her a tiny six-pointed star on a chain, her necklace when she was a young girl. Feeling very special and very Jewish, Gerry enjoys the seder. She decides to read about Jewish holidays and customs and to study the stories from the Old Testament. As she walks home, Gerry feels genuinely glad about who and what she is.

A young girl whose parents are nonobservant Jews meets a family of Jewish refugees from Hitler's Germany and begins searching for her own ethnic and religious identity. Gerry's first-person narrative, while dealing with a serious theme, is witty and warm. Characters, especially that of Gerry herself, are well developed. Numerous pencil sketches add humor and enhance the story.

Ages 9-11

**Also available in:**
No other form known

## 318

**Hurwitz, Johanna**

### Superduper Teddy

Black/white illustrations by Susan Jeschke.
William Morrow & Company, Inc., 1980.
(80 pages)

---

*SELF, ATTITUDE TOWARD: Confidence*
  *Money: earning*
  *Pets*
  *Separation anxiety*
  *Shyness*
  *Sibling: relationships*

---

In "An Invitation for Teddy," the five-year-old boy, who is much shyer than his older sister, Nora, and who wears a superman cape when he needs to feel brave, is invited to a birthday party but doesn't want to go. His mother leads him there step by step, but when he is confronted with the big, noisy crowd, Teddy insists he doesn't know a soul and won't go in. The gathering turns out to be the wrong party; he is later very happy to spend the afternoon at the real party, which consists only of him and his best friend. In "Grandpa Tells a Story," Teddy and Nora, uneasy and bored when their parents go out of town and leave them with their grandparents, listen to Grandpa's modern version of the Cinderella story. In "Teddy Gets a Job," the little boy cares for a neighbor's cat and earns his first salary, something even Nora has never done. "Squabbling" is what Teddy and Nora do a great deal of, but they end up playing Little Red Riding

Hood together and all ends well. Teddy finds "A Super-duper Pet," solving a longtime family problem. He and Nora have always wanted a pet, but their mother is allergic to anything with fur and objects to anything that's too big, too noisy, or too expensive. Mr. Hush is a tortoise who meets all the requirements. Then in "Teddy Entertains," the shy little boy surprises his mother by bringing his entire kindergarten class to his apartment for cookies and milk on their way home from a class walk through the neighborhood. While they are there, he even donates his superman cape to the kindergarten costume box because he is now too big for it. "Teddy was feeling super."

Six anecdotal chapters show little Teddy growing in self-confidence as he fights shyness, assumes some independence, solves problems, and proudly relinquishes his superman cape. Children will find much that is familiar here, and they will enjoy the lively illustrations of gnomelike characters. Several other books about Nora and Teddy feature Nora as the main character.

Ages 4-7

**Also available in:**
Paperbound—*Superduper Teddy*
Dell Publishing Company, Inc.

## 319

**Hurwitz, Johanna**

### Tough-Luck Karen

Black/white illustrations by Diane de Groat.
William Morrow & Company, Inc., 1982.
(157 pages)

---

SCHOOL: Achievement/Underachievement
  Change: new home
  Family: relationships
  Friendship: making friends
  Self-improvement
  Success

---

Thirteen-year-old Karen Sossi hasn't made any friends since her family moved from New York City to New Jersey, and she blames her "rotten luck" for the trouble she's been having with schoolwork. Schoolwork just isn't important to her, especially compared with her two great loves, cooking and her new baby-sitting job. Her mother, concerned about her lack of friends, gets Karen to attend a Halloween party given by the math teacher. There Karen becomes friendly with Annette and even talks to Roy, a boy she's admired from a distance. But when Annette comes over to spend Saturday afternoon, Karen blames her "bad luck" when Annette is allergic to Karen's two cats and has to leave. Karen continues to do poorly in all her school subjects, and her mother goes with her to talk to the English teacher. Her mother shows the teacher a letter that Karen has written to one of her many pen pals, and the teacher is impressed with Karen's writing. She suggests that Karen write future assignments on stationery, since she seems to have no trouble writing that way. Then Karen must complete a science project and is forbidden to baby-sit and later to use the kitchen for her baking and cooking until the assignment is done. Everyone in the family offers suggestions, but the deadline approaches and Karen still

has no ideas for the project. Her mother allows her to bake bread one day and Karen gets a brainstorm: she'll demonstrate how yeast works to make bread rise. The project is a success, especially since Karen brings along some freshly made bread to share with classmates. Usually silent in class, she now finds she's actually enjoying leading a discussion. Later she realizes that her classmates accept her and that her bad luck this fall has been entirely the result of her own laziness and carelessness. "Good luck was like making bread. It took time and effort."

A young teenager in a new school makes friends and learns to take responsibility for the "bad luck" that dogs her schoolwork. Readers equally disenchanted with school will empathize with Karen and may get some ideas from her use of a favorite activity—baking bread—for a school project. Luck has little to do with Karen's problems and even the encouragement of her family cannot really help her; she must help herself. Expressive illustrations and humorous touches enhance the book. The Sossi family will be known to readers of the books that feature Karen's brother, Aldo.

Ages 10-13

**Also available in:**
Paperbound—*Tough-Luck Karen*
Scholastic Book Services

## 320

**Hutchins, Patricia**

### The Tale of Thomas Meade

Color illustrations by the author.
Greenwillow Books, 1980.
(31 pages counted)

---

EDUCATION: Value of

---

Young Thomas Meade sees no reason to learn to read. While he is walking, a bucket of paint falls on his head. When the painters ask if he can read the "danger" sign, he answers, "Why should I?" A passerby calls him a disgrace and directs him to a store where he can clean up. Thomas pushes a door marked "Pull" and knocks several shoppers down. When they ask if he can read, again he replies, "Why should I?" Then he pushes the wrong button on the elevator and when he finally reaches the washrooms goes into the ladies' room. He is chased out and, unable to read another sign that says "Storeroom: Keep Clear," upsets a loaded wagon. Things get dangerous when he cannot read the "Don't Walk" sign and tries to cross the street. He causes several accidents and barely escapes injury. Since Thomas cannot pay the fine for jaywalking, he is taken to jail. His parents will not pay his bail until he learns to read, so his cellmates teach him and he learns quickly. After he is released from jail, he reads all day and long into the night. Now when his parents ask him to stop reading, he replies, "Why should I?"

Told in rhyme with repeated refrain, Thomas's story points out the drawbacks and dangers of not knowing how to read and hints at the pleasures of reading. Illustrations present many of the important signs nonreaders miss and elaborate on the text by showing all of

Thomas's difficulties. Reluctant readers will find convincing, often humorous, arguments here for learning how to read. This beginning reader, with its skillful blend of text and illustrations, should have great appeal.

Ages 5-7

**Also available in:**
Cassette—*The Tale of Thomas Meade*
Educational Enrichment Corporation

Filmstrip—*The Tale of Thomas Meade*
Educational Enrichment Corporation

## 321

Inkiow, Dimiter

## Me and Clara and Casimer the Cat

Translated from the German by Paula McGuire.
Black/white illustrations by Traudl and Walter Reiner.
Pantheon Books, 1979.
(78 pages) o.p.

---

*RESOURCEFULNESS*
  *Problem solving*
  *Sibling: relationships*

---

Clara, about six, finds a tiny kitten under the currant bush and names it Casimer. She and her younger brother are determined to teach the kitten to be friends with their dog, Snuffy. However, the cat and dog have other ideas and the house is nearly destroyed as they chase each other from room to room. Certain that Casimer is bored, the children take her one day to visit their Aunt Emma. Aunt Emma must leave them alone for an hour. Casimer is fascinated by Aunt Emma's four goldfish, and soon the children find one, two, and then all four missing. Panic-stricken, they call their mother, who comes quickly with four more goldfish. Aunt Emma is none the wiser. Deciding to have a flea circus, Clara has quite a job locating a dog with enough fleas to serve her purpose. Before the fleas can be trained, however, they attack the children, and their mother must spray them with smelly bug spray. The determined Clara secretly gathers the fleas in a matchbox and keeps them in the basement. She reads and rereads a book called *Taming Wild Animals,* talking to the fleas every day in an effort to teach them commands. Finally she considers they must be trained and brings them upstairs to the dining room. When she opens the matchbox they all jump out, but refuse to obey her orders to jump up on the table where she can capture them. That day her mother has guests for coffee, but they do not stay long and when they leave, they do so scratching madly.

These and four other adventures of the resourceful Clara are narrated by Clara's younger brother, who fluctuates between admiration and concern for his sister. Done in chapter form with cartoon illustrations, this lighthearted book is designed to capture the imagination and tickle the funny bone of any young reader.

Ages 7-9

**Also available in:**
No other form known

## 322

Ipswitch, Elaine

## Scott Was Here

Black/white photographs by the author.
Delacorte Press, 1979.
(210 pages)

---

*COURAGE, MEANING OF*
*HODGKIN'S DISEASE*
  *Death: attitude toward*
  *Family: unity*
  *Friendship: meaning of*
  *Hospital, going to*
  *Illnesses: terminal*
  *Love, meaning of*
  *Religion: faith*
  *Twins: identical*

---

In the fall of 1971, when identical twins Scott and Steven Ipswitch are ten years old, Scott begins to lose his appetite and complain of a sore throat. He is taken to the family doctor, who sends him to a throat specialist. Scott is then referred to a pediatrician, who puts him in the hospital for tests. After five days of tests, Scott undergoes a bronchoscopy and a lymph node biopsy. The results confirm that he has Hodgkin's disease, a cancer of the lymph system. More tests and surgery are required to determine the seriousness of the disease, so Scott is transferred to Children's Hospital in Los Angeles. Clinging to their Christian faith, the family waits for the results of more tests, many of them very painful. Then surgery is performed to determine the stage of the disease. It is discovered that Scott has Stage Four B Hodgkin's disease, the worst form. The doctors say he has about two years to live. Fearful that Scott cannot handle all this information, his parents tell him he has Hodgkin's disease but don't mention that it is cancer and, in his case, terminal. Scott, a bright, optimistic, determined boy, remains hopeful and writes and illustrates stories about his hospital experiences. He begins chemotherapy and after three weeks in the hospital goes home and becomes an outpatient. The drugs leave him nauseated, he loses his hair, and he must be monitored by frequent blood tests and regular bone-marrow checks. The family treats Scott as normally as possible. He and Steven fight and play and engage in school and after-school activities. The emotional toll on the family has its effects, though. Scott's mother is finally put on tranquilizers after constant early-morning vomiting and sleepless nights. Steven has his own fears about Scott's illness and is often lonely when Scott is hospitalized and their parents spend time with him. Everyone realizes that nothing will ever be the same again, but believe the outcome is up to God. By summer Scott is gaining weight and looking healthier. He continues to pursue his interest in World War II memorabilia, begun during his first hospitalization, and starts collecting medals and ribbons. In January both boys turn twelve and Scott's disease is in remission. But as sixth grade ends in June, Scott is again bothered by neck and back pain and returns to the hospital. After more painful tests and treatments he returns home and begins seventh grade in the fall. The following summer, Scott has low blood counts and frequent infections. Dr. Williams, his hematologist, is impressed with Scott's writings and illustrations. He asks Scott if he can use them in lectures he gives. In the spring when Scott is fourteen, his parents, after some hesitation, take him to a religious healing service. Although Scott is not healed, they still believe God will eventually cure him. Meanwhile, the hospital begins using Scott's writings in their orientation program for interns. The summer after eighth grade Scott takes a trip to Idaho with a friend and a trip to Yellowstone with his family. In the fall he begins ninth grade and his fifth year with Hodgkin's disease. By the end of September Scott is back in the hospital. From then on, Scott goes back and forth to the hospital with sore throats and excruciating backaches. He is weak and the chemotherapy has stunted his growth. By April the doctors discover that Scott has leukemia. He is now in critical condition and a week later is admitted to intensive care. On Good Friday, April 16, 1976, Scott dies, ending his five-and-a-half-year ordeal.

Scott's mother writes this tribute to her son. It is a candid account of a loving family with believable human frailties struggling to lead as normal a life as possible in the face of catastrophic illness. Although it details the boy's harrowing ordeal, the book is not without humor in its scenes of family life under stress. Woven throughout are examples of Scott's insightful, moving writings and illustrations—some of which his family found only after his death—and the middle of the book contains photographs of Scott and his family. This touching but unsentimental story of a courageous boy would be especially useful to the families and friends of young people suffering from terminal illness. The book concludes with a paper, "Terminal Illness and the Adolescent," written by a doctoral candidate in educational psychology who spent time with terminally ill children and was profoundly moved by her contact with Scott.

Ages 12 and up

**Also available in:**
No other form known

## 323

**Irwin, Hadley, pseud.**

### Bring to a Boil and Separate

Atheneum Publishers, 1980.
(123 pages)

DIVORCE: of Parents
  Change: accepting
  Friendship: best friend

Katie Warner, thirteen, is just finishing four weeks at summer camp and is not sure she wants to return home. Once there she will have to face an unspoken fact: her parents are divorcing. Her older brother, David, nicknamed Dinty, meets her bus, explaining that their parents, both veterinarians, are working. He tries to cheer her up but once she's home and alone, Katie begins to reflect on the divorce, feeling her parents are divorcing her. Although her mother tries to help the girl understand the reasons for the divorce and assures her of both parents' love, Katie finds her only consolation in talking to her horse, Denver. She dreads the next four weeks because her best friend, Marti, will be away at

camp. She fills her days sleeping late, practicing barrel races on Denver, playing tennis, and watching late TV movies. She does manage to start a friendship with her tennis instructor and place third in barrel racing at the County Horse Show. After the race she and her father talk, and he too tries to help her understand the divorce. But he's moved to another town and Katie feels like a yo-yo, balancing herself between her mother and her father. Dinty refuses to discuss the divorce, except to advise Katie not to take it so hard: "Let go! It's over. . . . It's not the end of the world. Quite." Finally the four weeks pass and Marti returns from camp. At last Katie has a friend to talk with, to relax with. The two sign up for a local tennis tournament and end up opponents for the final match. They decide in advance that Marti will win, but Katie becomes so involved in the game she forgets the plan and beats Marti. Although Marti doesn't mind, Katie feels like a traitor. That evening the girls stay alone at Marti's. They experiment with cigarettes and tequila, Marti's parents discover them drunk, and Katie's mother grounds her for the week before school starts. Smarting over the punishment, Katie still is able to see that she has to be responsible for herself. Further, "I wasn't responsible for Mom or for Dad or for the divorce—just for me." The following week, Marti and Katie register for high school and look forward with great excitement to the next four years.

Fearing her parents' divorce and the changes it will bring, a young teenage girl dreads the month-long absence of her best friend. But the friend finally returns, and Katie emerges from her busy summer with some understanding and acceptance of herself and her family situation. Touching, humorous, believable, with realistic characterizations and dialogue, this first-person narrative explores the emotional upheavals a divorce can bring and charts the active life of a perceptive young girl.

Ages 10-12

**Also available in:**
No other form known

## 324

**Irwin, Hadley, pseud.**

### The Lilith Summer

The Feminist Press, 1979.
(109 pages)

AGE: Respect for
  Love, meaning of

Ellen's mother has persuaded her that being a summer companion to elderly Lilith Adams will earn her the money for the bike she wants. At twelve, Ellen considers herself too old to require a baby-sitter, but she needs something to do this summer since her mother is going back to school. Lilith had been her Grandma Pearl's best friend. Ellen's mother and Lilith's daughter have made the arrangements for Ellen's job. Unfortunately, however, Ellen quickly decides that both Lilith and her house are depressingly old. Furthermore, Lilith gives a lot of orders and acts more like a baby-sitter than a helpless old woman who needs a companion. Then one day Ellen sees a check written to Lilith by her mother.

She suddenly realizes that Lilith is her baby-sitter! They are being paid to look after each other. When she tells Lilith about the deception, the old woman, although upset, tries to convince Ellen that daughter and mother are acting out of love and concern. Still, they both feel humiliated and angry—but they need the money. They agree, therefore, to call a "truce" and make the best of the situation. As the mark of their agreement, they set aside one hour of the day, between four and five, to do quiet things together. During this time they read aloud, write poems, draw, and make up a private language called Lilellenish. A sympathy begins to grow between the two. Ellen notes Lilith's kindness toward her aging friends, her tolerance as she explains their oddities. During the course of the summer, Ellen herself has many chances to experience Lilith's love and understanding. When she impulsively steals a pearl ring from a store, Lilith helps her return it with an apology. But then she gives Ellen the money to buy it back. When the girl is frightened by a bad storm, Lilith consoles her by talking about her own fears. Even now, confides Lilith, she has lots of fears. Her daughter and niece want her to give up her house and move to a nursing home. But she is afraid of "not being needed. Only needing. . . . Of being outdated. Of not being old enough to be a genuine antique. Just old enough to be junk." By the end of the summer, Ellen is able to tell Lilith, "I think when I grow old . . . I want to be just like you, Lilith. I think you're very brave and I don't think you're so old . . . or useless . . . or junky." Then she learns, to her sadness, that her family will soon be moving to Minneapolis. Eight years later, Ellen stands at her college dormitory window remembering a song that Lilith used to sing. In her hand she holds a newspaper clipping: "LILITH E. ADAMS, 85, PASSED AWAY YESTERDAY AT HER HOME AT 212 LAKE STREET." Ellen fondly remembers "that summer. The Lilith Summer."

Despite their initial resentment, a young girl and an old woman left to care for each other one summer develop an abiding affection and respect. Ellen and the reader discover the truth of Lilith's conviction that "all of us are many people: the people we once were, the people who have loved us, even the people who have hurt us." Well-drawn characters distinguish this insightful story about the treasures that the old can offer the young.

Ages 9-13

**Also available in:**
No other form known

## 325

Irwin, Hadley, pseud.

## Moon and Me

Atheneum Publishers, 1981.
(150 pages)

---

BOY-GIRL RELATIONSHIPS
FRIENDSHIP: Meaning of
MATURATION
    Grandparent: living in home of
    Parental: absence
    Perseverance
    Resourcefulness

---

E.J. is fourteen and has recently moved to Bluff Farm, Iowa, to live with her grandparents for six months while her mother accompanies her father on a business trip out of the country. E.J. herself has traveled all over the world; prior to coming to Iowa, she lived in France for two years. Now she chafes at the rural, unsophisticated, dull life in Bluff Farm. At the close of the school year, E.J. meets Harmon Wells, known as Moon. He is brilliant and a very mature twelve, but E.J. finds him too young and too short to be interesting. In fact, he irritates her. The only farm activity E.J. likes is riding her horse, Lady Gray. One day during her ride, she meets Moon. He suggests that E.J. enter a one-hundred-mile endurance ride to be held in midsummer—with him as her trainer. Appalled by the boy's persistence, E.J. rides away from him. But the next morning when she gets up, she finds Moon already in the kitchen talking with her grandparents. The three are engrossed in plans for the endurance ride, an event her grandparents used to participate in. Miffed that no one has even consulted her, E.J. reluctantly agrees to enter. The last day of school Moon reminds her that they have exactly fifty-seven days to train for the ride. He has their entire regimen plotted: obstacle courses for the horse, a special diet for E.J., a daily schedule including physical exercises, even a reading program about horses. In spite of her objections, E.J. finds she cannot argue with Moon, so well researched and logical. Besides, both her grandparents support him enthusiastically. So E.J. complies with Moon's rigorous training program. The last few days before the ride, Moon gives E.J. a rest while he rides his bike over the trail so he can make a precise map for her. Then the ride begins. Moon has plotted the course with his usual accuracy; he meets E.J. at every rest point with information and encouragement. All the training pays off: E.J. completes the rugged trip in the allotted three days' time. When she checks in at the finish, Moon is nowhere around. Despite herself, E.J. misses him. When the awards are given out, Moon appears with a big camera to take E.J.'s picture. He is truly proud of her; in fact, a mutual friend, Angie, tells E.J. that Moon loves her. But E.J. wants a romance and not with Moon. Now that the endurance ride is over, Moon decides to enter a bike marathon across Iowa, and E.J. goes with Angie and her mother to their lake cabin. Moon rides eighty-three miles in one day, joining the girls for supper at the lake. The three talk together; E.J. mentions her desire for a real relationship with a boy. Moon is quiet, but after that night E.J. doesn't see him for the rest of the summer. When school starts, she seeks him out. He tells her he is researching meaningful relationships and has planned the strategy for E.J. to get a date with Rick Adams, the tall, handsome senior she has dreamed of dating. Pleased, E.J. follows Moon's directions and, according to schedule, Rick asks her to the homecoming dance. The date, however, is less than exciting. Rick, a true Iowa pig farmer, can only think of his favorite boar who had unexpectedly died that day. His dancing is terrible, he's shy and speaks in monosyllables, and when he suggests she go with him to see a new hog he wants to buy, E.J. excuses herself and says she'll catch a ride home. She starts to walk and along comes Moon. E.J. is happy to see him. Somehow it seems appropriate that he walk her home from her first date. She notices that Moon is now almost as tall as she. When she tells him she will be leaving Bluff Farm the following week, E.J. knows she will truly miss him. Quietly they tell one another how much their friendship means. Both seem to realize that someday it may develop into something more.

An offbeat friendship develops between a sophisticated teenage girl and a younger but unusually bright and mature boy in this enjoyable, often humorous study of relationships and maturation. E.J. ponders the distinction between friendship and romance, discovering that the boundary can change in surprising ways. The riding competition adds interest to this well-written story.

Ages 11-14

**Also available in:**
No other form known

## 326

Irwin, Hadley, pseud.

**What About Grandma?**

Atheneum Publishers, 1982.
(165 pages)

COMMUNICATION: Parent-Child
GRANDPARENT: Love for
  Age: Aging
  Boy-girl relationships: dating
  Death: of grandparent
  Grandparent: living in home of
  Illnesses: terminal

Sixteen-year-old Rhys and her divorced mother, Eve, plan to spend a month with Wyn, Rhys's grandmother, while they list her house for sale, arrange for an auction of her things, and get her settled in a nursing home. But when they arrive, Wyn checks herself out of the hospital where she's been recuperating from a broken hip, insisting that she will return to her own home and stay there. Rhys finds herself watching "a contest between two stubborn, strong-willed women and I wasn't sure whose side I was on." Wyn's best friend, Virene, has a grandson, Lew, who attends medical school and works in the pro shop on the golf course during the summer. An avid golfer, Rhys gets to know and like Lew. But when he comes with Virene to visit, Rhys fears he is really interested in her youthful, attractive mother. Her mother has asked Rhys to gently break the news to Wyn that a room has been reserved for her in Sunset Haven after Eve and Rhys go back home. Her grandmother, in turn, confides to Rhys that she is dying, and she asks Rhys to gently break the news to her mother. Angry at being caught in the middle and upset with their lack of communication, Rhys blurts out both pieces of news. Eve and her mother talk together far into the night. Rhys and Lew continue to see each other. Both sense something strong and important between them, but Lew is concerned about the ten-year age difference. Rhys talks to her mother and discovers that Eve is not interested in Lew but is concerned about Rhys's relationship with him. Rhys helps her grandmother burn what are apparently old love letters, and they talk about dying. Eve decides to remain with Wyn as long as she and Rhys are

needed, keeping her mother in the home she's lived in all her life, even though the doctor warns them that caring for a terminally ill person is difficult, demanding work. The three grow closer, knowing and appreciating each other more. Rhys realizes "that part of me would die with Grandma, but part of her would live in me." Wyn grows weaker and is soon confined to the hospital bed set up on her sun porch. Lew, Virene, and Wid, Wyn's dear friend of many years, are frequent visitors. Then Lew has to return to school. He and Rhys may never see each other again, but they both admit they will always look for a little Lew or Rhys in people they care for. When Wyn dies, Rhys and Wid are with her.

In this poignant and skillfully written first-person account, a teenage girl deepens her understanding of mothers and daughters. Her own mother wonders if she hasn't spent her whole life reacting to her mother instead of acting for herself. She tells Rhys, "It's not always easy to be a daughter." Wyn's rich Welsh heritage is one of several threads in the story; another is the strong relationship between Wyn and Virene, friends for forty years. Reflections on aging (when "the inside and the outside don't match anymore") and Wyn's attitude about dying add depth to this book about beginnings and endings.

Ages 11 and up

**Also available in:**
No other form known

## 327

Iverson, Genie

**I Want to be Big**

Black/white illustrations by David McPhail.
E. P. Dutton & Company, Inc., 1979.
(32 pages counted)

AUTONOMY
MATURATION
  Ambivalence, feelings of

A little girl talks about how big she wants to be: big enough, but not too big. Big enough to go to first grade, eat at a friend's, fix her own breakfast; but not too big for piggyback rides, her vampire costume, or having her mother read her a story. She would like to be big enough to dress herself, but not big enough to hang up her pajamas. Big enough to watch a scary movie, but not too big for a night-light. Big enough to receive a letter in the mail, but not too big for her special blanket. The little girl wants to be big enough for many things—"but not quite big enough to take care of myself all the time."

This is an amusing but serious book about wanting to grow up without losing what's best about being little. Young children will easily identify with the heroine's ambivalent feelings. Charming sketches enhance the first-person text. This would be a good book for sharing in a group.

Ages 3-6

**Also available in:**
No other form known

185

**328**

Jacobs, Dee

## Laura's Gift

Black/white illustrations by Kris Karlsson.
Oriel Press, 1980.
(58 pages)

---

*MATURATION*
*MUSCULAR DYSTROPHY*
  *Death: attitude toward*
  *Family: relationships*
  *Fear: of death*
  *School: behavior*
  *Twins: identical*
  *Wheelchair, dependence on*

---

They are twins, best friends, and eighth graders at St. Hilda's School for Girls, but that's about all Catherine and Laura Devon have in common. Catherine is opinionated, outspoken, and impatient; Laura is quiet, patient, and confined to a wheelchair by muscular dystrophy. Catherine hates Miss Vertue, school principal and English teacher, and is forever receiving demerits. Laura likes her and is always trying to smooth things out between the two. One Saturday afternoon the twins make their weekly trip to the library. Catherine is silly and makes Laura laugh. Eventually Catherine wanders off, intending to look up a word she saw on her mother's desk: "pseudo-hypertrophic." Her good humor turns to fear for her sister when she discovers the term has to do with respiratory weakness and paralysis ending in death. At home Laura promises Catherine candy if she'll practice her piano scales, and Catherine is warmed by her sister's ability to make life's drudgeries a bit more pleasant. Then both girls have fevers and are taken to the hospital. Laura is hospitalized as a precaution; Catherine goes home. After a week Catherine is fine, but Laura has pneumonia, and Catherine convinces herself that her sister is dying. She becomes obsessed with getting Laura back home and stops practicing the piano and doing her homework. Their mother asks Catherine to help her redecorate the twins' room as a surprise for Laura, but Catherine adamantly opposes the change and refuses to help. She is sure her parents are redecorating because Laura is dying. That Saturday Catherine sits on the front steps alone. Miss Vertue joins her and encourages her to be optimistic. Both girls have given gifts to each other, she says: Laura has given Catherine the gift of discipline, and Catherine has given Laura the gift of laughter. Catherine mustn't throw away these gifts, Miss Vertue urges. Catherine's terror resumes when her parents are called to the hospital. But late that evening she learns that Laura's fever has broken and she will be fine. The next morning, Catherine talks with her father, confessing how afraid she was that Laura would die. Her father encourages her to talk to Laura about death, since Laura herself has accepted her condition and her uncertain future. Feeling somehow comforted, Catherine looks forward to Laura's return.

When Catherine believes her beloved sister is dying, she gives up on everything—including herself. Her understanding school principal helps her see that she and Laura have each given the other a special gift. Her father urges her to let Laura's acceptance of her uncertain future guide Catherine's own feelings, and Catherine's deepened understanding is the only resolution to this memorable character study. Not explained is the parents' failure to discuss muscular dystrophy and its dangers with both girls more thoroughly. With its dark, haunting illustrations and probing text, this is a book for mature readers.

Ages 10-13

**Also available in:**
Paperbound—*Laura's Gift*
Oriel Press

**329**

Jenkins, Jordan

## Learning About Love

Color photographs by Gene Ruggles.
Children's Press, Inc., 1979.
(31 pages)

---

*LOVE, MEANING OF*
  *Emotions: accepting*

---

Coming home unhappy after losing several neighborhood games, eight-year-old Alan enters the kitchen to find his parents crying, their arms around each other. Instantly forgetting his disappointments of the day, Alan learns that his mother must go to the hospital for a serious operation. At the news, Alan realizes how much he loves his mother. He has told her this many times without ever thinking what the words really mean. Now, as Alan considers for the first time what his world would be like without his mother, he is able to say the words with feeling. Although his father cannot promise that his mother will be "all right," Alan's mother, touched by her family's loving concern, conveys to the boy her own sense of optimism about the surgery: "No one ever went into an operation feeling as good as I do."

His mother's impending surgery helps a young boy realize how important she is to him. Some stagy photographs and stiff dialogue make this book less than profound in its consideration of family love. Still, the more natural photos emphasize the recognition and expression of feelings; this aspect of the book gives it value for young readers, especially children whose parents have been ill or hospitalized.

Ages 4-8

**Also available in:**
Paperbound—*Learning About Love*
Children's Press, Inc.

**330**

Johnston, Norma

**Myself and I**

Atheneum Publishers, 1981.
(210 pages)

---

AUTONOMY
IDENTITY, SEARCH FOR
   Blame
   Boy-girl relationships: dating
   Love, meaning of
   Responsibility: accepting
   Unwed mother: child of

---

Sarah Anne (Saranne) Albright, almost sixteen, had been "the champion, sweetheart, supporter and mother-hen of the wild Hodge boy." But Paul Hodge has gone to California with his older sister, Mary, a Hollywood actress. Now Tim Molloy asks her to go steady. She's fond of Tim, life seems increasingly unsettled now that the United States is entering World War I, and so Saranne accepts Tim's pin. Then word comes that Paul is returning. Saranne's family and a few others have recently learned that Mary is not Paul's sister after all; she is his mother. She has taken the boy with her to Hollywood to remove him from all the trouble he's been having—trouble with his grandparents, with school, with the police. But Mary and Paul don't get along. Paul desperately wants to find out who his father is, and he resents Mary for withholding that information. He seems almost to resent her for giving birth to him. Anticipating Paul's return, Saranne returns Tim's pin. When she sees Paul again, their intense feelings for each other resume and she determines to help him find his father. Paul's mother returns to California but Saranne's Uncle Ben, very fond of Mary, invites her back for Christmas. Paul is hired by Ken Latham, a friend of Saranne's Aunt Tish, to work in his darkroom. Paul loves the work but is an erratic and undependable employee, often disappearing without explanation. Saranne has heard Paul's grandfather, a drunken bully, refer sneeringly to "Latham" and she tells Paul about it. So when Ken asks Paul about his missed work and insolent attitude, Paul demands to know if Ken is his father. When Ken denies it, Paul is rude and accusing, prompting Aunt Tish to lash out at him for his ingratitude, the chip on his shoulder, his self-pity. Paul runs from the room and the next day has disappeared. Saranne and two friends find him and bring him home for Christmas, but he remains restless and bitter. His mother does return for the holidays and at a New Year's party, Saranne overhears Doug Latham, Ken's ne'er-do-well brother, threatening her. Several days later Doug confronts Paul, demanding to know if the boy is his and Mary's son. Horrified, Paul punches Doug in the jaw. But facts are facts. Doug, as Uncle Ben explains later, "was a spoiled kid who couldn't stand not getting his own way, and he had a kind of demon in him that he wasn't able or willing to control." Saranne sees that the description fits Paul too. Knowing who his father is seems only to increase Paul's unpredictable moods. Saranne, exhausted and fed up, finally tells him that he's simply bound and determined to be life's victim. They break off their relationship. When Saranne's Aunt Sadie, a meddling woman who

had lived with the family, dies during an influenza epidemic, Saranne finds among her effects a letter from Paul that the woman had evidently hidden from her. Paul writes that he has joined the Army and is beginning to understand himself a bit. Expecting to be sent to the Front, he intends to do something to make everyone proud of him. Saranne writes back with the news of his mother's and Uncle Ben's upcoming wedding, suggesting he return for the ceremony. Paul does come back, and he and Saranne renew their love. He wants her to marry him secretly before he leaves, but Saranne refuses. She knows she needs to find her own independence first, so she can be sure she belongs "to myself and I."

Saranne tells this story of an angry young man, and it is more Paul's story than hers. He gradually realizes that the identity of his father has little to do with who he is and what he should do. Saranne in turn learns that just being Paul's girl is an insufficient identity. A sequel to *A Nice Girl Like You* and four other books about Saranne's family, this tautly written, detailed story develops slowly but dramatically. It illustrates by means of two well-drawn characters the difference between healthy and unhealthy dependence on others. Self-definition, Saranne and Paul find, is largely a private matter.

Ages 11 and up

**Also available in:**
Paperbound—*Myself and I*
Grosset & Dunlap, Inc.

---

**331**

Jones, Penelope

**Holding Together**

Bradbury Press, Inc., 1981.
(173 pages)

---

DEATH: of Mother
   Family: unity
   Illnesses: terminal
   Sibling: relationships

---

Vickie Stevenson loves February because of Valentine's Day and her birthday three days later. This February bodes especially well because the fourth-grade play comes right at the beginning of the month. Even though Vickie's mother has been sick a lot lately, she has managed to make Vickie a beautiful costume. Vickie enjoys the fact that Anne, her older sister and a "big deal" fifth grader, has never been in a play. On the day before the performance, Mrs. Stevenson comes to school to help with the dress rehearsal. Vickie is pleased when her friends notice how pretty her mother is. The next morning, however, Mrs. Stevenson is too ill to get out of bed. "Why does she always have to be sick?" Vickie asks her father. "It's not fair." Soon her mother is too weak to get out of bed at all, and she finally decides to go into the hospital. On the morning before their mother leaves, Anne confides to Vickie that she is "scared" about this sickness that seems to be getting worse. It has never occurred to Vickie to be frightened by her mother's illness, but now she wonders if Anne senses something she doesn't. After school, Vickie and Anne find Aunt

Claire, their mother's best friend, at home waiting for them. She tells them Mrs. Poudry will look after them beginning the next day. The girls remember Mrs. Poudry as the elderly baby-sitter who stayed with them two years ago and treated them like babies. Aunt Claire cheers Vickie up, however, by announcing that she herself will be acting as "party mother" next Saturday for Vickie's birthday party. The next day, her actual birthday, is filled with good things for Vickie: her mother calls to wish her a happy day, she receives presents, and the class sings to her. She is especially pleased when her father decides to take them to see their mother. The visit turns out badly, though, when Vickie accidentally falls against her mother's leg, causing her great pain. That night, Vickie hears Anne sobbing and goes to her. "I'm scared that Mom is never going to get better. I'm scared that she's going . . . to die," says Anne. "Don't cry," Vickie whispers. "She can't die." The party on Saturday is wonderful, almost perfect, except for her mother's absence. Then the days seem "to melt into a sameness." Thinking about a topic for a report, Vickie half wishes she could write about cancer, which she suspects her mother has. But she's afraid to research the disease. When Mrs. Stevenson finally comes home from the hospital, she is accompanied by a nurse. It's still February and Vickie happily tells a friend, "The best things always happen to me in February." But after school, when she goes into the bedroom to see her mother, she can hardly believe her eyes. Mrs. Stevenson is very thin and has lost a lot of her hair. Vickie realizes at last that her mother is dying. Her father explains that "there is nothing anyone can do . . . except to see that she is free from pain." The girls sit with their father and cry until the tears stop coming. Their mother goes back to the hospital on Sunday night and Tuesday night she dies. Now the Stevenson house fills with visitors and weeping. By the time Grammy and Aunt Irene leave, however, Vickie is looking forward to going back to school and "having regular things happen." Mrs. Poudry, who isn't so bad after all, moves in permanently, and life starts to settle down. There are moments of intense pain for all of them, times when only crying can help. Their father works hard to help his daughters get through their grief and proceed with their lives. "You both mean more to me now than ever," he tells them. For their part, Vickie and Anne have learned just what it means to be a family.

At first her mother's illness is just an inconvenience that intrudes on the happy pattern of young Vickie's life. Gradually, however, she begins to realize that the problem goes deeper than her small disappointments, and at that point her relationship with her family starts to change. She has to depend more and more on her father and starts to see her sister in a completely new light. This is a believable, tightly woven story of family tragedy, sad but not depressing. Funeral issues aren't dealt with; the focus is on the strengthening effects of family communication and unity.

Ages 9-11

**Also available in:**
No other form known

## 332

**Jones, Penelope**

### I'm Not Moving!

Color illustrations by Amy Aitken.
Bradbury Press, Inc., 1980.
(32 pages counted)

---

*MOVING*
*Change: resisting*

---

Little Emmy's family is moving to a house far away. But she is determined to stay where she is. She doesn't want to leave the digging hole her father helped her dig in the yard, where she enjoys hiding and playing. She visits several neighbors and friends to see if she can stay with them, but each is unsatisfactory in some way. At the Morrises' she doesn't like the looks of the brown rice being prepared for dinner. At her friend Bobby's she doesn't like the smell of the pillow she lies on when they play house in Bobby's room. At Mr. Feldberg's house, she grows weary of helping him weed the garden. Mrs. Robinson, who has no children, keeps a neat, tidy house and tells Emmy not to touch the cat. The cat then stretches, showing teeth and claws. Emmy decides there is no good place to stay except in the digging hole. She begins to dig an even bigger hole. Emmy's father comes to the digging hole and tells her that dinner is ready. Then her mother makes her laugh by asking, "Well, Miss M, what should we wash for dinner? You or the mud?" Finally, her father tells Emmy to save her digging arm for their new backyard; together they can dig an even better hole. Emmy tells her parents she knows where she wants to stay—with them.

This appealing story allows young children both to sympathize with Emmy's determination to stay where she is and to explore some of her alternatives with her. Simple, pastel pictures are appropriate to the uncomplicated first-person narrative.

Ages 3-6

**Also available in:**
No other form known

## 333

**Jones, Rebecca Castaldi**

### Angie and Me

Macmillan Publishing Company, Inc., 1981.
(113 pages)

---

*ARTHRITIS, JUVENILE RHEUMATOID*
*DEATH: of Friend*
*Change: accepting*
*Dependence/Independence*
*Hospital, going to*
*Illnesses: terminal*
*Maturation*

---

When eleven-year-old Jenna sees a doctor about her hot, swollen, painful knees, she is told she has juvenile rheumatoid arthritis and must spend several weeks in a children's hospital in Columbus—a place too far from her home for her parents to visit except on weekends.

She doesn't understand how a child can have arthritis, why she can't just take aspirin, why she must go into the hospital. She's upset when her younger sister refers to her "crippled" legs. Her father helps her see that she has a choice: to stay as she is (she has pain and can barely walk) or get some help. Jenna's hospital roommate is twelve-year-old Angie Salvador, who has some sort of blood ailment. Jenna also meets Bill, whose leg problems eventually lead to an amputation; Sam, who undergoes brain surgery; and Wendy, an accident victim who protects herself from pity by her haughty manner. Wendy announces that the whole hospital is full of losers. Angie replies that Wendy only feels sorry for herself. She, on the other hand, hasn't time for self-pity. One day Angie, who faints frequently, takes a long time to recover from one of her spells. After that she seems weaker and more listless. Her mother takes a room across from the hospital. Angie complains that everyone is too nice to her. As for Jenna, after several weeks of whirlpool baths, physical and occupational therapy, cortisone injections that make her puffy, and a lot of enforced rest, she is told she's making progress and can soon go home. Her parents have kept from her the possibility of surgery if she had not responded to treatment. Now that it's been ruled out, they tell her, and Jenna is angry about being denied information. She pushes them for facts about her future, and they agree she has a right to know. Her future is somewhat uncertain, they tell her. Meanwhile, Angie explains to Jenna that blood is leaking from the capillaries in her brain into her spinal fluid, but her doctor is unable to find which capillaries are involved. The head nurse says Angie must move to a private room. Jenna, Bill, Sam, and Wendy make up a Sunshine Box for Angie, but they aren't allowed to see her for several days. Jenna's legs are getting better, and when she thinks about returning to school she realizes she's changed. She understands Angie's insistence on being independent: "She wanted me to be Jenna Matthews. Not the crippled kid." She wants Angie to tell her how she can keep from being a crippled kid when her legs don't work right. But when she gets to Angie's room, it's empty and the bed is neatly made up. Angie has died. Jenna screams and screams. She feels that Angie abandoned her just when she needed her most. Angie's mother has left Jenna the kite she had given Angie, sure that Angie would want her to have it back. As Jenna goes home with her family, she refuses her sister's offer to fly the kite for her. She knows that Angie would approve of her decision to fly the kite herself, in whatever way she can manage it.

A girl comes to terms with her rheumatoid arthritis and, with the help of a terminally ill roommate, rejects seeing herself as a person defined solely by her illness. This affecting, often humorous first-person account realistically shows Jenna's growth as she learns about and copes with an illness that can create permanent disability. The story line and the medical information are smoothly integrated, although character development, aside from Jenna and Angie, is minimal.

Ages 9-11

**Also available in:**
No other form known

## 334

**Jones, Toeckey**

### Go Well, Stay Well

Harper & Row, Publishers, Inc., 1979.
(202 pages)

*APARTHEID*
*FRIENDSHIP: Meaning of*
  *Dependence/Independence*
  *Education: value of*
  *Maturation*
  *Prejudice: ethnic/racial*
  *Values/Valuing: moral/ethical*

When Candy, a white girl born and raised in South Africa, sprains her ankle, she is helped by Becky, a Zulu girl. A friendship develops between the two fifteen-year-olds. Becky tells an amazed Candy of the prejudice and poverty that her people have endured. South African whites attend school free, but Zulus must pay for their education. An embittered Becky explains that Zulus "mustn't be encouraged to become too educated . . . . Too much education would make us too clever and 'cheeky.'" The girls want to remain friends, but social mores forbid friendships between blacks and whites. To justify their meeting, they decide that Becky will give Candy weekly lessons in the Zulu language. Candy must then persuade her initially resistant parents to allow these lessons. Her bigoted older brother is especially insulting and hostile. But Candy prevails, and Sunday after Sunday the girls sit and talk in her room. They can't go swimming or play tennis together, but their desire to overcome their own prejudices—Becky's bitterness, Candy's unexamined assumptions about the races—bonds their friendship. One Sunday, Becky doesn't come for their usual meeting. There is rioting in Soweto, the black township where she lives. Candy tries desperately to find out what has happened to her friend. Finally Becky comes to Candy's house in urgent need of money. Her family must bribe the officials for a permit to stay in their house. Tension is high between the girls, Candy sensing how deeply Becky's pride must be suffering. She attempts to comfort her, but Becky backs away. She trusts no one; her only goals are survival and education. As the violence in Soweto settles down, Becky resumes her visits. Meanwhile, Candy meets and begins dating Dirk, an Afrikaner. She worries about Dirk's reaction to her friendship with Becky, since the Afrikaner government is largely responsible for the history of black suppression in South Africa. She is surprised and gratified to discover that Dirk has no prejudices against blacks. Determined to widen her awareness and overcome her remaining inner prejudices, Candy proposes to go with Becky to Swaziland to visit Becky's relatives. Candy's parents are shocked at the prospect and deeply opposed, but Candy resolves to defy them and go anyway. Her Uncle Jack comes to the rescue; he and his wife will take the girls to Becky's relatives' home and then vacation nearby. Although this appeases Candy's mother, her father doesn't give his blessing until the girls are about to leave. When he does, Candy can embark on this adventure with happiness.

J

This thought-provoking, well-written book provides a revealing, candid look at South Africa and apartheid. Varied perspectives of South African life are given through the eyes of Candy, her parents and brother, an old, black family employee, her Afrikaner boyfriend, and Becky. Characterizations and relationships have depth and complexity, and the story treats apartheid, a subject rarely found in children's literature, with exceptional clarity.

Ages 12 and up

**Also available in:**
No other form known

## 335

Josephs, Rebecca

**Early Disorder**

Farrar, Straus & Giroux, Inc., 1980.
(186 pages)

---

*ANOREXIA NERVOSA*
  *Ambivalence, feelings of*
  *Change: resisting*
  *Family: relationships*
  *Mental illness: of adolescent*
  *Puberty*
  *Suicide*

---

At fifteen, Willa Rahv is pretty, highly intelligent, and part of a dynamic, happy family. At least, that's what everyone thinks. But inside, Willa is floundering in a sea of insecurity and fear. Her father is a theater critic, her mother a translator; Willa longs for their individual attention, but they seem absorbed in their careers and each other. Willa believes her problems started when she turned thirteen, the year she started menstruating. That was the year she started being afraid of everything. Her only friend is Ellen, although Ellen has parent problems too and Willa can't always feel close to her. The one person she really admires is her French teacher, Mademoiselle Girard, a gentle, unworldly woman. One day, a man peeks into Willa's dressing room at a department store and then follows her partway home, taunting her. Filled with self-loathing, she tells her mother the story. But her mother, reluctant to be drawn away from her work, doesn't seem to consider the incident all that serious. She is kind, but distant. Willa, frantic to find a new identity for herself, makes long lists of self-improvement projects. But the only project she manages to stick with is a diet, to her mother's approval. Soon after she begins dieting, the family goes to stay at their country home. Willa feels increasingly troubled: "Things aren't right, and I don't know why." That month she skips her period and is glad; now she doesn't have to grow up. She accepts a date with Walt Polanski, a boy who lives nearby, and the evening ends with their petting until Walt ejaculates. He apologizes, but Willa has remained completely detached from the whole situation, her mind wandering to random, barely related thoughts. "This is not me," she thinks. When Walt calls her the next morning, Willa remembers an obscene phone call she once received and hears those words as Walt talks. Desperate to be alone, despite her fears, she lies to her mother about a party at Ellen's and takes the train back to the city. On the way, she reads in a magazine about the Ten Day Protein Diet and decides to follow it. On New Year's Eve, she and Ellen drink a whole bottle of champagne, Ellen tries to cut her wrists, and both girls end up in the hospital with alcohol poisoning. Willa finds only one encouraging note emerging from the chaos of the holidays: she's doing well on her diet. Eventually she gets tired and apathetic, her nails turn blue, she gets chills and becomes dizzy. She weighs eighty-three pounds, and her pediatrician tells her mother that Willa has anorexia nervosa. He negotiates an eating plan with her, but Willa knows she won't follow it. No one will be permitted to spoil her diet. One night she collapses, and the pediatrician recommends a psychiatrist, Dr. Jordan. He confirms the diagnosis, but since Willa is adamantly refusing help he suggests she be hospitalized. Her parents prefer to believe they can coax her to eat. Willa will not give in, though; she doesn't need to eat. "This is my single task. I have nothing else to accomplish, other than to abstain. To get skinny." At the same time she thinks, "Somebody, please stop me from doing to myself what I'm doing." She continues to see Dr. Jordan, but her relationship with her parents deteriorates further. Although Willa now weighs seventy-two pounds, Dr. Jordan refuses to force her to eat, maintaining that she must make that choice. Ellen commits suicide, deepening Willa's despair and alienation. Finally, Mademoiselle Girard invites Willa to spend the summer with her in France. Dr. Jordan says the choice is hers. If she'll agree to gain weight before the summer, she can go. Willa isn't sure she wants to do that. But the story ends with her making one very small decision on her own, suggesting that perhaps Willa may find the strength to save herself.

In this well-written, if disturbing, first-person narrative, a deeply troubled teenage girl succumbs to anorexia nervosa. Willa's recorded ordeal—complicated, sometimes almost surreal—powerfully reflects the skewed world of the anorexic. Described are the physical symptoms, the self-hatred, the fear of sexuality, the rage to control some part of one's life regardless of the cost. A book for the mature reader, Willa's story may create awareness and broaden understanding of anorexia nervosa.

Ages 13 and up

**Also available in:**
Paperbound—*Early Disorder*
Fawcett World Library

**336**

Kamien, Janet

## What If You Couldn't . . . ? A Book About Special Needs

Black/white illustrations by Signe Hanson.
Charles Scribner's Sons, 1979.
(83 pages)

---

*DIFFERENCES, HUMAN*
*HANDICAPS*
   *Blindness*
   *Deafness*
   *Emotions: accepting*
   *Learning disabilities*
   *Limbs, abnormal or missing*
   *Mental retardation*

---

Because people with handicaps are in some ways different from other people, they can find themselves the object of unwanted pity, fear, ridicule, or embarrassment. However, most do not mind honest questions, and they hope people will not be hurt if their offers of help are sometimes refused. A person who is blind, for example, can work, learn, read, enjoy life, and do most things sighted people can do. Special training, Braille books and newer, more sophisticated reading equipment, canes, guide dogs, and other aids are available to them. "Being blind would certainly make your life different, but it wouldn't necessarily make your life hopeless, boring, or lonely, unless you let it." The same is true of mental retardation. Some people's mental development, for a variety of reasons, is simply slower than average. People who are mentally retarded can still learn, but they need extra help and encouragement. People with missing or nonfunctioning limbs can move around with the help of wheelchairs, braces, walkers, or crutches. Their biggest problems are functioning in a world unsuited to wheelchairs and coping with other people's reactions to them. Recently, physically handicapped people have been lobbying for new laws promising them equal education and employment opportunities, as well as accessibility to housing and public buildings. Impaired hearing has a number of causes and degrees of severity. Children with mild hearing losses may be wrongly thought lazy or unintelligent. Lipreading, sign language, hearing aids, visual clues, and vibrations all help hearing-impaired people understand others. Some people have trouble controlling their feelings. They may feel angry, depressed, afraid, or out of control most of the time, instead of just occasionally. Some may have behavior problems; others may withdraw and have personality problems. Many people believe that both a person's experiences and a physical predisposition (inborn or resulting from dietary deficiency) can result in serious emotional problems. Therapists have many methods to help people deal with their emotions. Sometimes, in severe cases, hospitalization or simply removal from the family is necessary. Most people are eventually able to overcome their emotional problems. Learning disabilities are problems in visual or auditory perception. People sometimes think students with learning disabilities aren't trying hard enough or are deliberately turning in poor work. With more attention being given to this problem, teachers are much more sensitive to the possibility that students who perform inconsistently may need special help.

In this excellent, detailed overview of handicaps, the author (who often directly addresses the reader) presents information using diagrams, anecdotes, parenthetical remarks, and illustrations. She provides some of what's known about causes, daily living difficulties, physical aids, and recent advancements. Equally important is the view of the handicapped person as a human being who, like everyone else, has unique differences, needs, and talents.

Ages 8-12

**Also available in:**
No other form known

---

**337**

Keller, Holly

## Cromwell's Glasses

Color illustrations by the author.
Greenwillow Books, 1982.
(32 pages counted)

---

*GLASSES, WEARING OF*
   *Sibling: relationships*
   *Teasing*

---

Cromwell looks like all the other little rabbits, but in one way he's very different. As the doctor explains to Mama, "He's terribly nearsighted." Before long, Cromwell knows what the doctor means. He gets lost so many times when he's out playing with his sisters and brother that Mama finally has to tell him he can't go along anymore. He stumbles over things and his sister Lydia calls him "a pain." He tries to be helpful, but something always goes wrong. When Martin gets his kite stuck in a tree and Cromwell thinks it's a bird, Cynthia laughs at him, and a frustrated Cromwell kicks her foot as hard as he can. That night, as Mama tucks him in, she tells him to be patient because soon he'll be old enough to wear eyeglasses. When the day of his appointment with the eye doctor finally arrives, his mother gives him a new doll to help him feel brave. The examination takes a long time, but in a few days Cromwell's glasses are ready. Now he sees so much better that he can help Mama in the supermarket. His sisters and brother, however, make fun of the way he looks, and for a while Cromwell hates his new glasses even more than he hates not being able to see. But when Mama sends the children to the park and someone else makes fun of Cromwell's glasses, Cynthia becomes angry and shouts, "You can't talk about my brother like that!" She then plays with Cromwell on the jungle gym and applauds when he misses only one rung. Martin lets him play marbles, and he hits a shiny red one on the second try. He doesn't miss the ball when he plays catch and gets all the way to four on hopscotch. Cynthia tells him when it's time to leave that she thinks his "glasses are going to be okay," and he agrees. Exhausted, Cromwell sleeps all the way home.

Cromwell is teased when he can't see and teased when he wears glasses. This no-win situation ends when his siblings finally stick up for him. The book will be helpful both to children wearing glasses and to those who should be supportive of them. Softly colored illustrations of the rabbit family add appeal.

Ages 3-6

**Also available in:**
No other form known

## 338
**Kenny, Kevin and Helen Krull**

**Sometimes My Mom Drinks Too Much**
Color illustrations by Helen Cogancherry.
Raintree Publishers, Inc., 1980.
(31 pages)

*ALCOHOLISM: of Mother*
*  Communication: parent-child*

Maureen, about eight, is unhappy because her mother drinks too much. When she does she behaves strangely, upsetting their once-stable family. Sometimes Maureen is afraid of her mother. One day when her mother yells at her about not doing her homework and says she won't get any dinner until the homework is done, Maureen is too frightened to tell her she doesn't have any homework. Later, her mother apologizes and takes her out to eat, confusing Maureen even more. On the day of Maureen's school orchestra concert, which her father is conducting, her mother arrives late and must be helped to her seat. Maureen is embarrassed, especially when her mother claps too long afterwards and Maureen's friend Yoshi asks if her mother is drunk. The mornings when her mother is too sick from drinking to go to work and her father calls her company to say she has the flu, Maureen feels sorry for both of them. The mother is often unpredictable: she arrives late for a special dinner Maureen and her father have prepared and then is not interested in eating. At Maureen's birthday party her mother again disappoints and frightens her when she falls, drops the cake, and then lies on the floor laughing. Neither Maureen nor Yoshi think anything is funny. In fact, Maureen gets angry and wonders why her mother is so mean to her. "Why does Mom hate me?" she asks her father. He explains that her mother has a sickness called alcoholism that makes her drink too much and behave strangely. Her mother's illness, he assures the girl, has nothing to do with Maureen. Still, the mother's behavior affects them all. Sometimes when her father is especially upset with her mother, he yells at Maureen. Maureen is happiest when she is with her friends, and she gets support from her sympathetic teacher. One day, after her mother has been staying home from work more than usual, Maureen comes home from school and finds no one there. A note from her father says he will be home for dinner and not to worry, but Maureen worries anyway. When her father gets home, he tells Maureen her mother will be in a special hospital for a few weeks; she and her boss felt it could help her. Maureen wonders if her mother will be well when she returns; her father tells her that "no one knows for sure." The mother will still need help from them and from other people. "But you and I always have to remember that she has a sickness that's not our fault. We

can help her get well, but she has to help herself too." Maureen wants to help right away by setting the table, but her father suggests she call Yoshi instead and invite her to go out with them for hamburgers.

A young girl struggles to understand and cope with her mother's alcoholism. Her father tries to help by providing information, explaining that her mother's behavior is caused by a sickness called alcoholism, not by anything Maureen has done. Readers experiencing similar emotional turmoil may be helped to understand alcoholism as a disease. The prospects for the woman's recovery are simply and honestly discussed. Of special note is the employer's supportive role in securing treatment for her. Expressive illustrations show an attractive woman trying and failing to maintain even the appearance of normality due to alcohol abuse.

Ages 5-8

**Also available in:**
No other form known

## 339
**Kerr, M. E., pseud.**

**Little Little**
Harper & Row, Publishers, Inc., 1981.
(183 pages)

*BOY-GIRL RELATIONSHIPS*
*DWARFISM*
*  Autonomy*
*  Orphan*
*  Parental: overprotection*

Sydney Cinnamon, a seventeen-year-old dwarf with a humped back, was abandoned by his mother at birth to an orphanage for malformed children. When he was fifteen he designed a "roach costume" for himself and became the mascot for his school's football team. Mr. Palmer, owner of a local pest control company, hired "The Roach," as Sydney came to be called, and the boy became a local hero through public appearances and television advertisements. Bella La Belle, known as Little Little, is the daughter of a prominent businessman in the town of La Belle. She too is a dwarf, though perfectly formed, pretty, and overprotected by her parents. The weekend of her eighteenth birthday an organization called "Tadpoles," a club for dwarfs, is holding a convention in La Belle. Included in the weekend festivities is a huge birthday party for Little Little. By coincidence, as a favor for a business associate, Mr. Palmer has arranged to have "The Roach" make a guest appearance at the party. Sydney comes to town early and, by chance, meets Little Little at an amusement park. The two are attracted to one another. Sydney performs as "The Roach" at an afternoon football game attended by Little Little and her snobbish parents, who tell Little Little that they hope she would never associate with that particular dwarf. They dislike the "offensive, vulgar, show-biz aspects of this fellow." In defiance, Little Little goes to a movie with Sydney that night. Her angry father comes to the theater and carries his daughter out. Meanwhile, another well-known dwarf is coming to La Belle for the weekend: Knox Lionel, a sharply dressed, smooth-talking evangelist and con man, known to all as

Little Lion. Little Lion has been writing love notes to Little Little since last year's Tadpole convention, and this year, convinced she would be an added attraction at his evangelical meetings, he proposes to her. He preaches a Sunday morning church service and gives an altar call especially directed to Little Little. But by now she has decided she is quite uninterested in him, his preaching, and his proposal, and she ignores him. So when another girl, just as pretty, answers his altar call, Lion starts a new romance. The finale of the weekend, Little Little's birthday party, ends in chaos when Lion and his new girlfriend dump Little Little's birthday cake onto her lap. Soon after the party, Sydney moves to La Belle and he and Little Little, to the annoyance of her parents, become close friends. However, when their English teacher prefers Sydney's composition to Little Little's, the competitive girl's interest in Sydney seems to cool.

Growing up as a dwarf can be complicated and frustrating, but it need not be defeating. Despite his size, appearance, and bizarre upbringing, Sydney has become highly motivated and self-educated. Similarly, Little Little's difficulty is not her size but her domineering parents. This unusual and well-written story is told in alternating chapters, first from Sydney's perspective, then from Little Little's. Strong characterizations and believable, often humorous, dialogue overcome the strange details and settings.

Ages 11 and up

**Also available in:**
Paperbound—*Little Little*
Bantam Books, Inc.

## 340

### Kherdian, David

### The Road from Home: The Story of an Armenian Girl

Greenwillow Books, 1979.
(238 pages)

*COURAGE, MEANING OF*
*WAR*
  *Family: relationships*
  *Refugees*

Veron Dumehjian's earliest memories, from 1907, are of her family's white stucco house in the Armenian quarter of Azizya in Turkey. This home was surrounded by beautiful poppy fields belonging to her father, who was a wealthy merchant of the poppy gum used in making opium. Her father's family was large and wealthy, and Veron was surrounded by many relatives. She had an especially loving relationship with her grandmother, her Aunt Lousapere, and her cousin Hrpsime, who was her own age. When she was eight, Veron's idyllic childhood came to an abrupt end. World War I was raging and the Turkish government, allied with Germany, decided to eliminate the Armenians living in their country. Since two uncles were serving in the Turkish army, their wives, children, and mother, Veron's grandmother, were allowed to stay in Azizya. Aunt Lousapere and Hrpsime were also among those permitted to stay. The rest of the family, including Veron, were given

three days to pack their wagon and prepare themselves for deportation. Veron, a happy and optimistic child, was determined that someday she would return to Azizya and the loved ones left behind. On the journey across Turkey, the people suffered from exhaustion and lack of food. Old people who fell along the way were killed by the gendarmes who controlled the procession. The Dumehjians were able to keep going because of their wealth: Papa could bribe the soldiers. After entering Syria, however, many of the deportees contracted cholera. The three younger Dumehjian children died. Veron, however, survived, and in spite of all the sadness still had a strong will to live. But her gentle mother could not bear the loss of her children and soon died also. Knowing now that they were nearing the end of their journey and that death was imminent for all of them, Papa bribed one of the gendarmes to let them escape back into Turkey, which was free again. After arriving in Biriji, Papa was called away with his wagon to serve the Turkish government. He died while on this assignment and Veron was left in the care of her "aunties," solitary Armenian women who had survived the march. Eventually she came to live in an orphanage for Armenian refugee children in Syria. Then, when she was nearly twelve, she was reunited with her grandmother. She found, however, that everything had changed in Azizya. Aunt Lousapere, having lost her husband, had taken Hrpsime to live in Smyrna. The other members of the family did not "know how to be of comfort to one another." Then more fighting broke out. The Greeks, Christians like the Armenians, began to fight the Turks for the control of Smyrna. Azizya was bombed and Veron, severely wounded in the leg, was sent to a hospital in nearby Afyon. A Greek general who came regularly to the hospital met her and, several weeks later, asked to adopt her. He wished to protect her, to take her to his sister's home in Smyrna and later to Athens. Afraid that the Turks might defeat the Greeks in Afyon at any time and then turn against the Armenians again, fearing that she would then be killed, Veron consented. The home in Smyrna was very beautiful, but the girl could not be happy. She started to think about her parents, sister, and brothers: "I felt that if I went to Athens with the general and became Greek, I would not only lose my church and my nation and my grandmother, but in a sense I would lose all of those who had died, as well. I had to remain an Armenian, a Dumehjian, the girl my parents and grandmother had reared." She ran away and, after another hospitalization for her injured leg, was found by her Aunt Lousapere and reunited with Hrpsime. After much more travail, at the age of sixteen, Veron left for America to become the bride of an Armenian refugee who had asked for an Armenian wife. His parents and Veron's aunt had arranged the marriage, and Veron was satisfied with the prospect.

In this wartime biography of his mother, writing in his mother's voice, David Kherdian has described an amazingly resilient young girl's struggle to survive terrible persecution without giving up her "hope and belief in life" or her "faith in God." Veron always knew that she was not made for sadness and it was this natural optimism, along with a desire to bring joy to others, that helped her go on when others could not. The view of the persecution itself, as seen through the eyes of this loving

K

child, is extremely penetrating but not gory, explicit, or melodramatic. The book gives insight into a period of history not commonly known and is eloquent testimony to the grief and futility of war.

Ages 12 and up

**Also available in:**
Cassette—*The Road from Home: The Story of an Armenian Girl*
Library of Congress (NLSBPH)

## 341

**Kingman, Lee**

### The Refiner's Fire

Houghton Mifflin Company, 1981.
(218 pages)

---

CHANGE: Accepting
LIFE STYLE: Change in
  *Belonging*
  *Child abuse*
  *Commune*
  *Family: relationships*
  *Fear: of failure*
  *Identity, search for*
  *Parent/Parents: single*

---

Thirteen-year-old Sara Bradford arrives in Martin's Corners, New Hampshire, to live with her father, Richard, a ceramic historian turned potter, whom she hasn't seen in over four years and scarcely knows. Since the death of her mother, she has been living with Gran, her mother's mother. But now Gran is ill and had to sell her house. Sara's father lives in a huge old barn with a group of craftspeople: Zeke gardens, cooks, and carves wood; Ben is a carpenter; Blanche Wicketts crochets and Harvey Wicketts makes miniature furniture; Gabe Courbeau, a neighbor boy taken in by Richard when he ran away from his drunken, abusive father, cares for the goats and helps out; and Kyra is an artist with a little boy, Demetri. Richard carefully explains to Sara that he and Kyra are involved with each other, but that she is very independent and doesn't want to marry again. Sara has always felt awkward and accident-prone around her artistic father, and her new life with him begins disastrously when her cat streaks into the pottery room and breaks a punch bowl and many cups. Her father explodes in anger, frightening and discouraging her. But gradually Sara settles in, filling the role of messenger when she discovers that each member of the group has a specific responsibility. Her father—she's always called him Richard at his request—wants to teach her to throw a pot. Fearing failure, Sara doesn't want to try, but he insists and she's eager to please him. She can't do it, gets blisters, and seems confirmed as Richard's "inept daughter." Sara badly wants Kyra to marry Richard so that they, she, and Demetri can all be a family. To further their relationship she offers to care for Demetri so the two can have a brief vacation. While they're gone, however, she and Demetri get into various scrapes. When the parents return, Sara asks Kyra why she won't marry Richard. Kyra explains her need to find an individual identity and her fear of a second failure at marriage. At school, Sara is named chairperson of a group of students assigned to write and perform a medieval play. The project is a disaster from start to finish, the

group uncooperative and lazy, the production ill-rehearsed. Mortified at one more failure, Sara flees the school, gets lost in the woods on the way home, and accepts a ride with Gabe's father, who will not allow her to leave the car when she realizes he is drunk. At the barn, he threatens Richard and the others because they are keeping Gabe from him. After he leaves, everyone, including her father, praises Sara for keeping her head in a dangerous situation. They also help her see that the failure of the play wasn't her fault. The companionable atmosphere is spoiled when Kyra announces that she and Demetri are returning to her home in Crete so Demetri's father can visit him. The night Richard returns from taking them to the airport, he discovers a fire in the barn. He gets everyone out, but as they watch firefighters vainly battle the flames, he talks about what has been lost: Harvey and Blanche's life savings, which they refused to bank; all Ben's tools and equipment; Harvey's miniature furniture; the painting Kyra did of Sara; the home he's provided for Gabe. When her father puts his head down and cries, "Sara was appalled. Everything was falling to pieces around her. All the bulwarks built up during the summer were crumbling." They find Gabe's father's body in the debris and suspect that he set the fire. Blanche dies of the shock. Sara and her father (she is calling him Daddy now) go to her friend Margaret's house for the night. There her father confesses the doubts he had about her coming to live with him, especially just as he was trying to develop his relationship with Kyra. But he loves her, he says. Will she stay with him from now on? Deeply relieved, Sara assures him she will. With Ben's enthusiastic help, they discuss ways of building a solar house on the foundations of the old barn.

A young teenager learns to trust the unconventional father she barely knows. Along the way she finds that a family isn't so much a particular group of people or one special place, but a feeling. Likeable characters, an offbeat setting, and vividly descriptive writing distinguish this story. Its leisurely pace allows readers time to get acquainted with Sara, to sympathize with her awkwardness and her yearning for a stable, conventional family.

Ages 12-14

**Also available in:**
Paperbound—*The Refiner's Fire*
Dell Publishing Company, Inc.

## 342

**Kinter, Judith**

### Cross-Country Caper

Black/white illustrations by Furan Illustrators.
Crestwood House, Inc., 1981.
(47 pages)

---

DECISION MAKING
  *Courage, meaning of*
  *Drugs*
  *Sports/Sportsmanship*

---

Scott Stone is a member of the high school track team who hopes to get a trophy for a five-minute-mile cross-country race. While training one day, he takes a horse trail and sees a rider toss something by a tree. Investigating, Scott finds a bottle of pills with a twenty-dollar bill wrapped around it. A teammate, Tim Matson, claims the bottle, giving Scott a mumbled excuse about his medication. The next Saturday Scott hides near the same tree. He sees the same rider, who this time threatens Tim with a knife. Scott knows something is very wrong. Still, he and the team are running well and he has great hopes for the cross-country meet. Then Tim offers him a "job." All he has to do is make one simple delivery and he'll earn fifty dollars, more than enough to buy the new track shoes he needs. Scott's task during the upcoming meet is to pass off a bottle of pills to a runner from another school. He's to wait until no other runner is in sight and then make his delivery. Scott is torn between wanting the money and wanting to win the meet; if he stops for any reason, his team will lose. He is noncommittal when Tim gives him his final instructions because he has decided on a plan. Scott waits until the other runner thinks they're alone, but then doesn't deliver the bottle until Shawn, one of his teammates, is in view. He shouts to Shawn to look at what's going on. Then he grabs the bottle back and races for the finish line. There he collapses, but is later able to tell the police the whole story. When the horse rider tries to claim the bottle, guards grab him. At the awards banquet, Scott is given the trophy he's been coveting. In order to make up his lost time and then some, the coach explains, Scott surely ran a five-minute mile. He tells the gathering that Scott chose to lose for the team in order to win for the school when he exposed a drug ring.

One of a series of high-interest, easy reading books that deal with teenagers' contemporary concerns, this story hinges on a painful decision that Scott must make. In order to expose a drug ring, he has to let his team lose a cross-country race that they have an excellent chance of winning. Scott makes the courageous choice. Although a little less than convincing, the book will appeal to readers who like a short, illustrated book that highlights issues of interest.

Ages 11-14

**Also available in:**
Paperbound—*Cross-Country Caper*
Crestwood House, Inc.

## 343
**Kipnis, Lynne and Susan Adler**

## You Can't Catch Diabetes from a Friend
Black/white photographs by Richard Benkof.
Triad Publishing Company, Inc., 1979.
(64 pages)

---

*DIABETES*

---

Karen, Danny, Colleen, and Robert have diabetes. Ten-year-old Karen knows that her body doesn't make enough insulin and that she must supply herself with insulin injections. She's also aware that many people don't know much about diabetes and that even doctors aren't sure what causes it. In the morning when she and her brother, Michael, get up, Michael wants to play. But both children understand that first Karen must give herself an insulin injection and then she must eat a good breakfast. Though diabetes isn't curable, Karen's twice-daily injections help keep her healthy. A pill or spoonful of insulin won't work. Each shot she gives herself is in a different place on her body so she avoids getting too sore in one place. Sometimes Karen's sister and brother are jealous of the attention she gets because of her diabetes; family members of diabetics are affected even though they don't have diabetes themselves. Eleven-year-old Danny also must give himself insulin injections. At lunchtime his school friends want to trade lunches but Danny refuses, explaining that because of his diabetes he must stick to the meal plan he and his parents prepare each day. Everyone in the family must make adjustments when one member has diabetes. On Halloween Danny couldn't eat the candy he collected so his father traded him a penny for each piece. Seven-year-old Colleen sees her doctor regularly and uses a special kit to check her urine every day for glucose (sugar) and ketones. Glucose appears "when the body is having trouble using sugars and starches," ketones when the body doesn't use proteins and fats properly. Colleen was worried when her urine tests showed the presence of glucose. She is relieved to learn from her doctor that the glucose isn't her fault. But it's important to know about it so that she and her doctor can work together for better control of her diabetes. In order to clear up the glucose problem, Colleen increases her morning insulin injection. Fourteen-year-old Robert's hobby is building models. "To build models all Robert has to know are the basics. And the basics are all Robert's friends need to know about his diabetes." One day, after sweeping the cut grass from a lawn, Robert becomes very dizzy. A friend knows that he needs to swallow some sugar immediately because he is having an insulin reaction. This happens when the amount of food and insulin in his body get out of balance and there is more insulin than sugar. A candy bar or glass of soda pop will restore his sugar level. Robert wears a medallion to alert people to his diabetes in case of emergency. He explains to his friends that diabetes is not something you can catch from someone. Karen, Danny, Colleen, and Robert are four of the almost one million young people in the United States with diabetes. With insulin, well-planned meals, regular urine tests, and regular checkups, they can all lead normal, active lives.

This informative presentation of juvenile diabetes accurately explains the basics of the disease in simple, easy-to-understand terms. Emphasized is the involvement of the diabetic child's family, the changes and adjustments that all must make. Text and photographs provide details of urine testing and insulin injections. One photograph, a close-up of an insulin injection, shows an inaccurate needle position; diabetics will notice the error. Otherwise, the book should help dispel fear and misunderstanding, presenting diabetes as a part of some people's daily lives.

Ages 7-12

**Also available in:**
No other form known

K

**344**

Klass, Sheila Solomon

## To See My Mother Dance

Charles Scribner's Sons, 1981.
(154 pages)

CHANGE: Resisting
FANTASY FORMATION
  Abandonment
  Parent/Parents: remarriage of
  Peer relationships
  Reality, escaping
  Stepparent: mother

When thirteen-year-old Jessica Van Norden's father announces he is marrying Martha, he warns Jessica that he is not changing his mind—not even if Jessica's asthma kicks up as it has every time he's brought a woman home. Jessica's mother, Karen, ran away on the girl's first birthday. Her father later had Karen found by a detective; she was living in California with hippies. Jessica's grandmother hates Karen and has for years filled Jessica's head with stories of her mother's selfishness and irresponsibility. After Karen left, Grandma threw away all her things. But Jessica thinks about her mother constantly, consults with her in imaginary conversations, and fantasizes about meeting her again. In her dreams her mother is the beautiful, successful dancer she wanted to be. Jessica considers asking her grandmother if she can come live with her so she won't have to live with her father and Martha. But Grandma advises Jessica to make things so uncomfortable for Martha that she'll move out. Two of Jessica's friends also have mother problems. Sylvia has a new stepmother too, and hers is gradually making her over, from her clothes to her hair. She even wants Sylvia to have her nose fixed. Brookie's mother drinks. One night Jason Georgiades walks Jessica home and gives her her first kiss. In response, she asks him if he'd like to sleep with her. But Jason declines, knowing Jessica is simply trying to hurt her father and Martha. At home, Jessica is polite but distant. Her grandmother comes to dinner and subjects Martha to a rude and insulting interrogation. When she asks why they married so fast, Jessica's father replies that he knew she and Jessica would try to stop them if they didn't. Later, Jessica overhears her father and Martha talking. Martha is distressed by Jessica's misery and wants to try something to help her. Then Brookie calls, but seems to collapse in the middle of a sentence. Jessica and Jason run to her house and find her very drunk. They start to help her but Jason thinks Brookie may have done this deliberately in an attempt to teach her mother a lesson, so they leave her. Then Martha startles Jessica with the news that she has located Karen. Jessica needs to see her mother as a real person, Martha says. At school the next day, Sylvia won't speak to Jessica. When confronted, she says she's agreed to have the nose surgery and that her parents now feel Jessica and Brookie aren't fit friends for her. Brookie reports that her experiment was a success; her mother is going to Alcoholics Anonymous. Finally, Martha takes Jessica to San Francisco where her mother lives in a run-down house called "Children of the Lotus." Karen's roughly cut hair is dyed an ugly red, and

she wears a pale blue gown. She answers Jessica's questions remotely: she left because she was young and needed peace; no, she didn't worry about leaving Jessica; no, she never thinks of Jessica. Now the big mystery in Jessica's life is over, and she wonders why she doesn't feel any different. Martha attributes Karen's change to her heavy drug use, and Jessica knows how Brookie felt when she had to admit her mother was an alcoholic: "Reality hurts like hell." Glad to have seen her mother, Jessica still has no trouble saying goodbye to her. She suggests to Martha that she be allowed to attend a boarding school, explaining that she needs to straighten things out for herself.

A girl obsessed by the mother who abandoned her years ago finally substitutes reality for fantasy and grows up a little in the process. In this first-person story, Jessica's present life is totally taken up with her fascination with the past and her imaginary visions of the future. Well-defined characters populate this thoughtful book, answering a few questions about life but leaving many more open for the reader to ponder.

Ages 10-13

**Also available in:**
Paperbound—*To See My Mother Dance*
Fawcett World Library

**345**

Klein, Monica

## Backyard Basketball Superstar

Black/white illustrations by Nola Langner.
Pantheon Books, 1981.
(45 pages)

PREJUDICE: Sexual
SIBLING: Rivalry
  Peer relationships
  Talents: athletic

Jeremy, about ten, is the captain of the Flyers, a basketball team in need of someone who can get the ball in the basket. His younger sister, Melanie, can jump high, run fast, and make baskets; she wants to try out for the team. Jeremy tries to bribe her out of doing so, offering to do her chores and give her his allowance, his giant ant farm, and his rock collection. But Melanie will not be deterred. Grimly Jeremy contemplates how all his friends will laugh at him when they learn that Melanie is a better athlete than he. After all the aspirants but Melanie have tried out, Jeremy's teammates call on him as captain to decide whether they can consider a girl. Knowing the team needs his sister's skill, Jeremy gives his consent. Melanie far outshines the others, and the Flyers vote unanimously to make her a member of their team.

Jeremy and his teammates decide that his sister Melanie's talent at basketball, much needed by the Flyers, makes her eligible to join their ranks. The message about sexual equality is decidedly mixed here, its intent almost defeated: "She's really good," say Jeremy's friends, "even if she is a girl." Despite the muddle, this is a likeable easy reader with appealing illustrations. The book may well prompt discussion about gender roles.

Ages 6-8

## 346

Knox-Wagner, Elaine

**My Grandpa Retired Today**

Color illustrations by Charles Robinson.
Albert Whitman & Company, 1982.
(30 pages counted)

---

GRANDPARENT: Love for
RETIREMENT
    Empathy
    Life style: change in
    Loss: feelings of

---

The day her grandfather retires from his barbershop, young Margey is the only child at his party. She eats large quantities of chocolate cake and tidies up the shop, asking her grandfather if she should wash the combs. He tells her to throw out the old newspapers instead and they salute one another in a familiar little ritual. Then comes the big surprise. Grandpa is presented with his own barber chair, now decorated with ribbon and unbolted from the floor. "Since no one can take your place, Al, we decided you should take it with you," Grandpa's partner says. The friends clap, the guest of honor stares, and Margey runs to the bathroom to be sick. When she returns she tells her concerned grandfather that she just had too much cake, and together they clean the shop for the last time. When it is time to leave, she refuses his offer to lock the door, telling him he should do it this time. They walk home slowly. Grandpa suggests activities they could do together during the summer, but Margey only says, "I like barbershops." He tells her he will miss the shop too. That night Margey finds her grandfather sitting in his barber chair, looking lonesome and sad. She jumps on his lap and tells him, "There is more to life than working in a barbershop." He laughs and sends her to bed with a promise of things they will do in the morning. In bed, Margey thinks about those things—the sticky drawers they will fix and the dresser they will paint, the backgammon game her grandfather and his friend will teach her and her friend, and the barbershop they may visit. "But not to stay," she says. "Because, today, my grandpa retired."

This warm story about the feelings of loss that retirement can bring, as seen through the eyes of a little girl, is simple but expressive. Margey shares her grandfather's elation at the party, his emptiness at its end, and his sadness upon leaving his barbershop for the last time. When she begins to see the positive aspects of the change—more time to be together—she cheers her grandfather by telling him what she's discovered. This story, with its detailed illustrations, may help children understand what retirement means.

Ages 4-7

## 347

Knox-Wagner, Elaine

**The Oldest Kid**

Color illustrations by Gail Owens.
Albert Whitman & Company, 1981.
(31 pages counted)

---

SIBLING: Older
    Justice/Injustice
    Sharing/Not sharing

---

"Ever since I was born, I've been the oldest kid. It's not fair," says the big sister. At first being oldest was okay, because she had her parents to herself. But since her brother arrived, she has had to share everything—room, toys, parents. She has to set a good example, but watches her brother do things she would never get away with. At the family picnic, she's the oldest cousin. So, since there's not enough room at the table with the younger kids, she has to wait. She tells her grandfather she hates being the oldest kid. He listens to her as he works on his shiny, old, much-loved car and asks her to hold the flashlight for him. When he needs more than two hands, she holds the wrench while he uses the screwdriver. Then he takes her for a drive alone, in spite of all the younger cousins begging to come with them. One of the cousins yells after her, "You think you're so smart. Just because you're oldest, you get to do EVERYTHING." As she and her grandfather head back home after the drive, she thinks, "Ever since I was born, I've been the oldest kid. It's hardly ever fair. But sometimes it feels fair."

An "oldest kid" tells what it feels like to be one. Accompanied by especially appealing and original illustrations, this is a delightful, sympathetic book that will elicit a response from all readers, no matter where they fall in the family constellation. The girl in the story is older than the picture-book audience, but this might serve to extend the perspective of children who lament being the youngest.

Ages 4-8

## 348

Knudson, R. Rozanne

**Rinehart Lifts**

Farrar, Straus & Giroux, Inc., 1980.
(88 pages)

---

DETERMINATION
FRIENDSHIP: Best Friend
    Friendship: meaning of
    School: classmate relationships
    Sports/Sportsmanship

---

Arthur Rinehart is the fifth grade's Mr. Nice Guy. He is smart, gets A's on tests, and reads aloud to the class. He also loves plants and has all kinds growing in his room at home. But Rinehart, as his best friend, Suzanne "Zan" Hagen, calls him, is not athletic. "Rinehart couldn't roll or toss or pitch or fling or bowl. He was uncoordinated as maple syrup. He was the slowest runner in the fifth grade. Face it. Rinehart was a sports slouch." Zan wants Rinehart to excel in at least one sport. She is tired of Randy, Fritz, Eugene, and Dum-Dum, the "Mighty Four," paying him a quarter not to play with them. Rinehart is satisfied being a sports slouch, but Zan threatens to end their friendship if he can't perform in the next sport she sees on TV. That Saturday, Zan watches weight lifting on TV and decides this is one sport in which Rinehart can be successful. He wants her friendship and agrees to try. The two buy a book about weight lifting and a one-hundred-pound starter set with two dumbbells and one barbell. Zan sets up a gym in Rinehart's garage. He works out each day while Zan encourages him. Zan even decorates the garage with a rug and Rinehart's plants. By December Rinehart has begun to love lifting and has advanced from beginner to intermediate. In January Zan challenges the Mighty Four to a lifting match with Rinehart. They laugh and ignore her, not knowing what she means by "lifting." In February Zan tries them again. Instead, the four boys sneak into Rinehart's garage and destroy the plants and pots. Zan wants revenge; Rinehart wants a contest. In April he is in the advanced weight-lifting program and Zan once again challenges the Mighty Four to a "Lifting Spectacular." Having no idea what they are getting into, they accept. Each wants to win the "Mr. Arlington" contest that Zan has set up. The day of the contest, the four boys arrive confident of victory, only to discover none can lift the one-hundred-pound barbell over his head. Confidently Rinehart poses, flexing his muscles, and then lifts the weights—to the amazement of the Mighty Four and his own and Zan's satisfaction.

Two friends with opposite personalities defeat a band of local "jocks" in this easy-to-read story. Rinehart is indifferent to sports; Zan is athletic, knowledgeable, and competitive. Together they succeed in making Rinehart excel at something besides his schoolwork and his horticulture. In three companion books featuring Zan, *Zanballer*, *Zanboomer*, and *Zanbanger*, Rinehart is Zan's coach. In this book they exchange roles. The ending shows Rinehart a victor at last, but leaves hanging his future relationship with the Mighty Four.

Ages 10-12

**Also available in:**
Paperbound—*Rinehart Lifts*
Avon Books

## 349

**Konigsburg, Elaine Lobl**

**Throwing Shadows**

Atheneum Publishers, 1979.
(151 pages)

*MATURATION*
 *Age: respect for*
 *Responsibility: accepting*

In the first story of this collection, "On Shark's Teeth," Ned tells about meeting a retired college president at his father's Florida fishing camp. President Bob, as he tells Ned to call him, is a braggart who pesters the boy into coming with him to hunt fossilized sharks' teeth. What Bob doesn't know is that Ned and his mother have collected fossils for years and are self-taught authorities on the fossils in the area. Soon the two are locked in competition to find outstanding specimens. When Ned finds several teeth still in a jawbone, an unusually exciting find, Bob becomes a picture of what Ned sees as "Jealousy and Greed." But Ned suddenly becomes aware of his own smugness, and he decides to give Bob the jawbone. In "The Catchee," Avery describes his young life: though shy and unassuming, he is always, and always will be, an innocent victim. For example, there was the time he was accused of burglary while looking for a hose to water the azaleas he'd been hired to care for while their owner was on vacation. His experiences have shown Avery that the world is divided into catchers and catchees, and he will always belong to the second group. "In the Village of the Weavers" is narrated by Ampara, a novice guide in the mountains of Ecuador. She tells about a poor, proud boy named Antonio who sells weavings while his grandfather lays ill. Once the grandfather recovers, Antonio, feeling the need to continue to prove himself, begins singing on Ampara's tourist bus. Soon he brings on more children to sing and help him sell his weavings. Full of his success, Antonio becomes quite bossy. Then his changing voice cracks, and his singing and selling careers are through. He decides to ask Ampara to teach him English so he can be a guide. Philip is laid up with a broken arm in "At the Home." Needing new batteries for his tape recorder, he stops at the nursing home where his mother works. An old man, noticing the tape recorder, sings Ukrainian folk songs into it. Philip begins going to the home often, staying as long as he can. He is persuaded to record a Hungarian man's life story as it rambles from crisis to crisis on the theme "how being ugly saved my life." Fascinated almost in spite of himself, Philip wants to continue the recording. But because he now can't spend so much time at the home, he encourages the residents to listen to and record each other. In "With Bert and Ray," William explains how two antique dealers ask his mother to manage estate sales for them. They tutor her in the business and, loyal to his mentors, his mother gets them into house sales first so they can buy the choice items. Gradually, William's mother begins to surpass Bert and Ray in her knowledge and skill. After she makes a real find, buying a Chinese screen for about one hundred dollars and selling it for over twenty thousand, William resolves to convince his insecure mother—who feels that people won't love her if she is smarter than they are—that she has gone beyond her teachers.

These five stories, each narrated in the first person, all show the male main character coming to a sense of the world and his place in it. Sometimes this insight results from a sudden revelation, as when Ned discovers that his smugness is just as lamentable as Bob's greed and jealousy. Sometimes the realization comes as a summing up of the boy's whole life, as in Avery's tale. Readers will enjoy not only each boy's comprehension and appreciation of life, but the events leading up to the insight. The stories have an appeal and depth that should make them ideal for discussion.

Ages 10-12

**Also available in:**
Braille—*Throwing Shadows*
Library of Congress (NLSBPH)

Cassette—*Throwing Shadows*
Library of Congress (NLSBPH)

## 350

**Korschunow, Irina**

### Who Killed Christopher?

Translated from the German by Eva L. Mayer.
William Collins Publishers, Inc., 1980.
(125 pages) o.p.

---

*AUTONOMY*
*DEATH: of Friend*
*VALUES/VALUING: Moral/Ethical*
  *Friendship: best friend*
  *Identification with others: peers*
  *Identity, search for*
  *Suicide*

---

When seventeen-year-old Martin attends his best friend Christopher's funeral in the small, white church on the hill overlooking their German village, he is bitter about the presence there of the teachers who ridiculed and tormented Christopher and the classmates whom Christopher referred to as a "pack of hounds." He runs away from the funeral and thinks about Christopher, "the only person I could really talk with." As soon as Christopher began attending Martin's school the previous January, Martin knew he was special. It was a troubled time then between Martin and his parents, and he'd begun to question adult values. His parents blamed Christopher for their son's alienation, but it had begun even before he and Christopher talked about "the pressure and the stress on performance." Christopher's father, bewildered by his son's life and death, asks Martin to come talk about Christopher. Martin tells him about his and Christopher's trip to Vienna for spring break. He doesn't mention, however, that they stayed with Akim Lemmert, a friend of Martin's father, rather than at youth hostels. Akim had seen that Christopher was emotionally very fragile and had tried to help him. But Christopher believed that it doesn't pay to get too close to anyone. Nothing really matters, not even sex. Christopher had slept with Ursula, a classmate and good friend of both boys. She'd wanted to help Christopher out of his depression, and it angered Martin that his friend could dismiss so lightly what Ursula had given him. When Martin returns to school several days after the funeral, he wonders if Christopher was right to think their classmates were totally despicable and mediocre. He was certainly right about some of the teachers. One of them invites Martin to his apartment to discuss Christopher, wondering if he is to blame for failing to respond to the boy's troubles or for being abrupt and hostile to Christopher on occasion. They discuss whether or not Christopher's death was an accident or suicide. Martin tells the teacher the whole story of Christopher's last days. He had disappeared one Friday. Everyone searched for him. The Penner brothers, newcomers in the village and with criminal records, had been picked up for questioning. After they were released, local farmers beat one of them severely.

Angry, Martin was determined to find Christopher and tell him that if he'd left a note, they wouldn't have worried so much and the Penner brother would not have been beaten. He thinks back to his conviction that if Christopher were not dead, he must be in Vienna at Akim's apartment. Martin had taken the train to Vienna, finding Christopher as expected. He had talked him into coming back. When they returned to school on Monday, a teacher heckled Christopher and, when Christopher responded, threw him out of school. Martin relives that last bike ride on the hilly, curving road home. As Christopher pedaled faster and faster, he veered and hit a rock in the middle of the road, swerved, and was hit by an oncoming truck. Martin is sure that Christopher "didn't want to live anymore. . . . He was riding that bike like someone who didn't care what happened to him." After telling this story, Martin leaves the teacher's apartment and returns home late. He talks with his father, and the two reach a new understanding. Then Martin goes to meet Ursula. She says Christopher is probably better off dead: "he could never have made it." She thinks he ran away the week before he died because she had told him she thought she was pregnant, although she found out later she wasn't. She asks Martin if he would have acted the way Christopher did. He doesn't know, but is convinced that he and Ursula belong together. The next day, Martin visits Christopher's grave. He wants badly to be able to talk to his friend once more, to tell him all the things he has discovered in the past few days. "But," he concludes, "perhaps he would not have liked to hear about it."

In this memorable first-person narrative, a young man attempts to deal with the death of his best friend, perhaps a suicide, while struggling to understand how he himself feels about life. Martin tries to see the world as Christopher saw it: a meaningless, sterile place. While Christopher was alive, Martin had accepted his values. After Christopher's death, however, he judges things for himself and finally understands the differences between them; he acknowledges at Christopher's grave that his cynical friend would probably not have wanted to hear about the new perceptions Martin has gained in trying to figure out who "killed" Christopher. In an excellent translation of a well-written and engrossing book, the characters ask questions raised by young people all over the world. This insightful story has much to offer the mature reader.

Ages 12 and up

**Also available in:**
No other form known

## 351

**Krementz, Jill**

### How It Feels to Be Adopted

Black/white photographs by the author.
Alfred A. Knopf, Inc., 1982.
(107 pages)

---

*ADOPTION: Feelings About*
  *Adoption: explaining*
  *Adoption: identity questions*
  *Adoption: interracial*

---

**K**

Adopted children consider their special circumstances. Jake doesn't think he'll ever search out his birth mother. Carla agrees that the family who adopted her is her real family, although she is black and they are white. Melinda wasn't adopted until she was seven. Now, at ten, she needs to have one of her parents around all the time because she feels so insecure. Timmy understands how impossible it would have been for his very young, unmarried parents to keep him. Sometimes, though, he's jealous of his younger sister, the child of his adoptive parents, because she's not adopted and doesn't have to answer questions about it. Sue's adoptive family encouraged her in her search for her birth mother, but she considers them her real family. Barbara feels jealous when her friends discuss their ethnic origins and she doesn't know what hers are. When Alfred was eight he was adopted by a single man who had already adopted another son, Wayne. The family has since grown to include three more adopted brothers, one black (as are Alfred and Wayne), one Hispanic, and one Korean. Last year, Holly's birth mother phoned her. Although she now sees her occasionally, Holly still thinks birth mothers should approach children indirectly, through their adoptive parents. Quintana says she probably won't look for her birth mother, for fear of intruding on the woman's life. Jack says his friends think that because he's adopted, his parents treat him better. Gayle loves and admires the seventy-one-year-old woman who has raised her and her adopted siblings: one deaf and mute, one paralyzed, one only four months older than Gayle, who is fourteen. Jane has become much more self-assured since meeting her birth mother, and she and her adoptive family agree that the meeting has added a new dimension to their own relationship. Lulie was adopted along with her twin brother; having someone in the family who's actually related to her has made things easier. Soo-Mee feels her life began at the age of three when she came from Korea to live with Mommy. Joey's mother awarded him to the state because she couldn't handle him. He lived in an orphanage for a year until he came to the attention of Father Clement, a Catholic priest who was urging his parishioners to adopt kids who needed homes. Getting little response, Father Clement decided to set an example by adopting Joey himself. They've gotten a lot of publicity, but Joey knows that "as long as there's love and caring, that's all that matters."

Nineteen adopted children talk candidly about their feelings, including their differing outlooks toward their birth parents. The diversity and wisdom expressed in this beautifully written and photographed book should reassure readers who are adopted and inform others of the broad range of feelings that adoption can inspire. This outstanding book should be an excellent resource for discussion.

Ages 9 and up

**Also available in:**
Cassette—*How It Feels To Be Adopted*
Library of Congress (NLSBPH)

**352**

**Krementz, Jill**

## How It Feels When a Parent Dies

Black/white photographs by the author.
Alfred A. Knopf, Inc., 1981.
(111 pages)

---

*DEATH: of Father*
*DEATH: of Mother*
   *Death: attitude toward*
   *Mourning, stages of*
   *Suicide: of parent*

---

Twelve-year-old Laurie Marshall's father died in a plane crash. She handles her grief by talking to Ingrid, who lost her father two years ago, and by sharing feelings with her mother. One day Jack Hopkins's father, depressed because of an illness, paid all the bills; the next day he fatally shot himself. Although Jack, at eight, will never understand everything that went into his father's decision, he's not angry anymore. For the first three months, though, he didn't talk to anyone about his father's death—especially not his mother. Susan Radin's mother died when Susan was only six. Every now and then, just for a second, Susan can feel her mother's presence. Peggy Laird lost her father two years ago, when she was nine. Her mother has remarried, which was difficult for Peggy. She finds it helpful to write in her diary. Nine-year-old Alletta Laird believes the garage light that shines only in her window is her father's spirit. When Stephen Jayne, then eight, heard his father had died, the first thing he asked was if they could keep their dog and cat and house. He also worried about money and was afraid to ask for anything special the first Christmas. When he went to camp, he pretended to his new friends that his father was still alive. Helen Colón, now sixteen, whose mother died after years of illness, says, "You blame them for a very long time. You think that it's their fault that they died and left you." John Durning was nine when his mother died, and he drew her a picture and wrote a note to put in her coffin. Tora Garone still doesn't know the details of her father's hunting accident or even where he's buried. She thinks she could get over her grief more quickly if her mother wouldn't "spare" her. Meredith Meryman's mother was sick for two years, but Meredith never knew how sick until she died. She hasn't said the word "Mom" in five years. Gardner Harris was twelve when his mother contracted cancer. He still feels guilty about the things he didn't do for her. Father-child night at school is hard for Carla Lehmann, but memories of her father are very important to her. At the very moment Valerie Crowley's father, a firefighter, died, she and her friends were walking home from school talking about another firefighter who'd been killed. "They say that time makes it better, but it hasn't really. It's just made me think about it more. . . ." Nine-year-old Amira Thoron was only three when her father died. Sometimes she thinks it was better that way, because she doesn't miss him so much. David Harris's mother had cancer. Although he didn't want her to die, he did want her to be free of the pain. In some ways her illness made things easier; he spent more time with her that last year and had time to prepare for and to some extent accept her death. Seven-year-old Gail Gugle's father died just nine months ago. She believes she misses him more than her brother does. "A neighbor said Daddy would come to live in our hearts so he would keep living with us but in a different way."

Eighteen youngsters, aged seven to sixteen, tell what it's like to lose a parent. Supplemented by wonderfully vibrant and moving photographs, the text provides readers with an excellent opportunity to reflect on, discuss, or evaluate their own feelings about this sensitive subject. The author found that the children interviewed welcomed the opportunity to talk about their experiences. The book aims to solace and strengthen other children who may share the grief, anger, anxiety, and embarrassment of having lost a parent, to let them know they are not alone and that everyone reacts differently to such an event. The children frequently mention behavior of their peers that either helps or antagonizes them, making the book informative and useful for all children.

Ages 8 and up

**Also available in:**
Cassette—*How It Feels When a Parent Dies*
Library of Congress (NLSBPH)

### 353

**Kroll, Steven**

**Friday the 13th**

Color illustrations by Dick Gackenbach.
Holiday House, Inc., 1981.
(32 pages counted)

---

*INFERIORITY, FEELINGS OF*
*SIBLING: Relationships*
  *Rejection: sibling*
  *Success*

---

With young Harold's bad luck, every day seems like Friday the 13th. Every morning at breakfast, he spills egg on his shirt. Every time he plays soccer, it rains. Every night when he washes dishes, he breaks one. He knows that when Friday the 13th really comes, his luck will be even worse. Harold's misfortunes are not lessened any by his sister, Hilda, who takes every opportunity to point out his ineptness, clumsiness, and overall bad luck. On the morning of Friday the 13th none of Harold's clothes match, he spills his pencils and crayons on the school bus, he skins his knee at recess, and he finds he has an egg-salad sandwich, which he hates, for lunch. "Harold can't do anything right!" taunts Hilda, who happens to have a peanut-butter-and-jelly sandwich, Harold's favorite. That afternoon at his softball game, Harold misses the ball numerous times and is booed, with Hilda leading the assault. In the last inning, with two outs and the opposing team winning, it is Harold's turn at bat. No one is more surprised than he when he hits a home run and gives his team the victory. Harold is a hero, and for once he feels good about himself. It begins to rain on his way home and a car splashes him with mud, but still Harold feels fine. When Hilda slips and knocks a cake off the table and onto herself, Harold triumphantly tells the soggy girl, "Happy Friday the 13th, Hilda!"

One stroke of good luck restores the self-esteem of an unlucky boy plagued by a nasty sister in this humorous tale of sibling strife. Readers will empathize with Harold throughout and will share his satisfaction over Hilda's comeuppance in the end. Amusing illustrations add to the lighthearted tone.

Ages 4-7

**Also available in:**
No other form known

### 354

**Kropp, Paul Stephan**

**Wilted**

Coward, McCann & Geoghegan, Inc., 1980.
(111 pages)

---

*FRIENDSHIP: Making Friends*
*SELF, ATTITUDE TOWARD: Accepting*
  *Boy-girl relationships*
  *Bully: being bothered by*
  *Glasses, wearing of*
  *Parent/Parents: fighting between*

---

Fourteen-year-old Danny Morrison lives in a shabby house with a drunken, abusive father, an angry, defensive mother, a drug-taking older sister, and a frightened, dependent little brother. In a new blow to his self-confidence, Danny has recently gotten glasses and the pair his parents could afford make him look owlish, or "wilted," in the current terminology of his peers. Everyone at school seems to notice his new glasses and he is often teased about them, but classmate Samantha Morgan takes notice of Danny himself and seems to like what she sees. Gradually, with some help and encouragement from friends, a relationship develops between the two. Although Sam is from an affluent family and lives in a big house furnished with antiques, she seems comfortable in Danny's shabby little home. The lonely boy is more and more drawn to the girl, and the two have several tentative sexual experiences together. But despite his relationship with Sam, Danny continues to be buffeted by life. His math teacher, a retired army major who seems to understand the turmoil Danny lives with and who on occasion offers advice and counsel, suddenly dies of a heart attack. Soon after, the discord and fighting in the Morrison household comes to a head when the drunken father finally leaves for good. For some time, Danny has been harassed by another admirer of Samantha, a bully who threatens to pulverize him if he continues to see her. When this bully taunts Danny about the Major's death and his father's departure, Danny strikes out and the two fight viciously until a friend separates them. Danny is shocked by the intensity of his feelings and by his own brutality. He goes to Sam's house where she patches him up and gives him his Christmas presents. Her present, perfume, got broken in the fight. Being with Sam gives Danny confidence and hope, but she will soon be leaving for a Christmas vacation. Her family is already preparing for a summer trip to Europe. Meanwhile, Danny's sister has stopped going to school and stays home to smoke marijuana. Danny worries that he might be somewhat responsible for his parents' separation; he is sure his sister's behavior has contributed to the split. But he

K

knows he is needed at home to provide some comfort and reassurance, some stability, for his confused brother.

Danny fights to keep his head above water as his family life disintegrates. More a description of situations, relationships, and feelings experienced over several months' time than a fully plotted story, this compelling first-person narrative provides insight into the conflicts of a troubled boy's life. Although the reader is left to ponder how Danny will fare after Sam leaves, the tone of his narration is generally optimistic and resilient— and not without humor. Some profanity is sprinkled through the dialogue and several brief, mild sexual encounters are described. Danny is an appealing character and readers will feel for him.

Ages 11-14

Also available in:
Paperbound—*Wilted*
Dell Publishing Company, Inc.

## 355

Landis, James David

**The Sisters Impossible**

Alfred A. Knopf, Inc., 1979.
(172 pages)

---

SIBLING: Younger
  Appearance: concern about
  Careers: dancer
  Competition
  Jealousy: sibling
  Problem solving
  Talents

---

Thinking herself clumsy and graceless, nine-year-old Lily is jealous of her older sister, Saundra, a promising ballet dancer. Their parents want curly-headed Lily to take ballet lessons with tall, long-haired, graceful Saundra. Reluctantly Lily agrees to take the lessons, and with equal reluctance "haughty" Saundra agrees to act as her coach. In private the girls agree that a single lesson should satisfy their parents and leave Lily free to quit. At first Lily is miserable, embarrassed by the casual nudity of the locker room and by the "toilet jokes" she hears, shocked by the dancers' bloody feet. Dance class is cruel: the teacher is abrasive, the work demanding. Yet somehow Lily loves it. After class she is taunted by Meredith, Saundra's only serious rival for a place in the school's professional company. Lily wins their verbal battle, but Saundra is furious with her for even talking to Meredith and won't let Lily explain. As audition time nears Saundra withdraws into herself, losing weight along with her confidence. Meredith again confronts Lily, and this time Saundra sees Lily slap her. The sisters leave class holding hands. At home Lily dances for Saundra, trying to draw her from her isolation. The truth comes out: Saundra is afraid that Meredith will beat her in the audition. Since she believes her parents' love depends on her success as a ballet student, she fears that if she loses the competition she'll lose their love. She also fears her future as a professional dancer. Saundra is afraid to win and afraid to lose. Now Lily understands that her sister's cool, aloof exterior is only a

mask to hide her fears. Together they explain the situation to their concerned parents. Lily proposes to intimidate the intimidating Meredith, but her lawyer father helps her see that this tactic won't work. So Lily takes her father's advice and decides to give Meredith a false sense of security. She will allow the unkind, conceited rival to think that she and Saundra have given up the battle, that they believe Meredith to be the better dancer. Lavishly and openly, Lily praises Meredith, assuring her of easy victory in the audition. In private she bolsters Saundra's sagging will and watches her sister's confidence return. The audition is not yet won, but Lily knows she and Saundra, though different, are both very strong, especially as a team.

A young girl with a talented sister overcomes her jealousy, learns to accept herself as she is, and helps her sister cope with an aggressive rival and a temporary loss of will and self-confidence. Lily's mind is very subtle for her age, but her story remains believable. The keen, bitter battle for the coveted ballet position is well drawn, as is the relationship between the two sisters. The parents—the father a lawyer and the mother a lawyer and judge—are concerned and supportive. However, the father's aid in manipulating the other dancer, although realistically presented, could be construed as negative and undesirable by some readers and adults. The open ending should prompt discussion.

Ages 9-11

Also available in:
Paperbound—*The Sisters Impossible*
Bantam Books, Inc.

## 356

Langner, Nola

**Freddy My Grandfather**

Color illustrations by the author.
Four Winds Press, 1979.
(29 pages counted) o.p.

---

GRANDPARENT: Love for
  Grandparent: living in child's home

---

A little girl's grandfather lives at her house. She calls him by his first name, Freddy. Freddy grew up in Hungary. Sometimes, when the little girl's mother gets angry with her, Freddy says something to her mother in Hungarian. The girl suspects he's telling her mother to leave her alone. Even when Freddy speaks English it sounds funny, but the little girl has no trouble understanding what he means. Sometimes Freddy gets angry, but never at her. He fights with Uncle Jerome and even calls him "buta," which means "stupid." Freddy likes to sew and once had a tailor shop. Now he makes coats just for his granddaughter. Freddy does make the little girl angry sometimes. For example, he teases her at supper by stealing food from her plate, and he takes her to visit his friend Mrs. Flint, whom she doesn't like. Also, Freddy is sometimes too friendly for a grandfather. He greets her friends with a bow and a click of his heels, as he learned to do in Hungary, and stays in her room with them until her friends run out of things to say. Freddy's own room is a very interesting place. He uses his white lamp and red table when he reads his Spanish newspaper and listens to his Spanish radio station—this year he is learning to speak Spanish. There's a special stone in his room that is rough on one side and smooth on the other. The girl's favorite thing is a bowl of glass fruit that lights up and turns red when it is plugged in. The smell in Freddy's room is a mixture of cigars and lemons; Freddy rubs his fingers with lemon to take off the cigar stains. Freddy loves to eat and takes twice as much as anyone else. He makes "shlurping" noises when he eats his soup. The little girl likes that, but her parents don't. Sometimes Freddy gets all dressed up and goes out late at night. He tells the girl's mother he'll be home when he gets home, and this makes her angry. It seems as though he likes to make her angry. Sometimes Freddy takes his granddaughter with him to a Hungarian restaurant. One time, the girl was frightened by a thunderstorm and tried to hide from it. Her grandfather called her to the window and said, "See the sky light up and you'll feel better." She did. There are many wonderful things about Freddy, but for the little girl the best thing is, "I love him."

A little girl vividly describes her old-world grandfather, an engaging eccentric. She is candid about his imperfections as well as his strengths, but always sees Freddy through the eyes of love. In a very few pages, she creates a memorable character. The soft illustrations are bathed in yellow light, adding to the pervasive warmth that fills this book.

Ages 5-8

**Also available in:**
No other form known

## 357

Lasker, Joe

### The Do-Something Day

Color illustrations by the author.
The Viking Press, Inc., 1982.
(32 pages counted)

---

*BELONGING*
  *Helping*
  *Rejection*
  *Running away*

---

On a sparkling, do-something day, little Bernie wants to help his father. But his father says he's too busy just now making plans for tomorrow's big fair. His mother has no time for him either, nor does his brother. Nobody needs him, Bernie thinks angrily, and he decides to run away. When he passes Carl's Garage, Bernie explains that he's running away because no one wants his help. But Carl does. Bernie helps Carl check some headlights, and then Carl gives Bernie a big map to help him on his travels. At Dimple's Delicatessen, Bernie helps Mr. Dimple hang up salamis in his window. Mr. Dimple gives Bernie a salami and a sour pickle to eat on his way. When Bernie goes to say goodbye to Bertha at Bertha's Bakery, she asks him to help date-stamp some paper bags and then gives him a warm rye bread and some cookies to go with his salami and pickle. Mr. Pfeffer of Pfeffer's Fresh Produce asks Bernie to water his horse, giving him some grapes and plums. Bernie then runs an

errand for Tom, of Tom's Shoe Repair, and is given a pair of old high-button shoes to keep his feet warm on the road. When he tells Mrs. Byrd of Byrd's Pet Shop that he's running away, she asks him to help her feed the fish and birds. Then she gives him another runaway, a little dog. After walking until he's tired and the sun begins setting, Bernie sits down to rest. He looks at all the things he's collected and has an idea. He returns home and gives the map to his father, who says it's just what he needs to finish the plans for the big fair tomorrow. His brother needs the high-button shoes to complete his costume. His mother adds the food Bernie has to their picnic lunch. And Bernie's father says the dog is just what Bernie needs, especially when everyone gets too busy for him. Bernie's mother says they need him to love. She gives him a big hug.

In this warm story, a little boy who feels unwanted and unneeded finds he can help others and that people do need him. Children will empathize with Bernie and feel satisfied at the story's end. The illustrations are a delight; listeners and readers will want to linger over the colorful portrayals of inner-city streets, pictures that manage to look both antique and realistic.

Ages 3-7

**Also available in:**
Paperbound—*The Do-Something Day*
Scholastic Book Services

## 358

Lasker, Joe

### Nick Joins In

Color illustrations by the author.
Albert Whitman & Company, 1980.
(32 pages counted)

---

*WHEELCHAIR, DEPENDENCE ON*
  *Differences, human*
  *Fear: of school*
  *School: mainstreaming*

---

Nick, about seven, is frightened at the prospect of going to school for the first time. Nick wears leg braces and gets around in a wheelchair; his teachers have always come to his home. Now he will attend a regular school and many questions plague him. How will he go up and down stairs? Will anyone want to play with him? Will there be others who cannot walk? Meanwhile, at school, a ramp is built and a special desk made to accommodate Nick's wheelchair. The big day arrives. A teacher's aide wheels Nick into the school. He is frightened by the noise and clamor, but as he enters the classroom his teacher, Mrs. Becker, welcomes him with a smile. After checking with Nick, she invites the other children to ask him questions. "Why do you use a wheelchair?" they ask. "Why can't you walk?" Shy at first, Nick gradually relaxes and answers the questions with growing confidence. Days pass, and Nick and the other children grow used to each other. People help Nick and he helps them. One day he even helps the gym teacher open windows with a long pole. Nick especially loves watching the other children run and jump during recess. To him, they seem to be flying. Then, during a basketball game, the ball accidentally lands on the roof.

No one, not even the teachers, can get it down. But Nick can! He wheels off to get the window pole, returning to cries of "Nick to the rescue!" He pokes at the ball with the long pole, and as the ball drops to the ground everybody cheers. Now Nick feels *he* is flying.

A disabled child's initial fear of school dissolves with barely a ripple, thanks to understanding parents, sympathetic teachers, and his own outgoing attitude. The approach to the topic is matter-of-fact, the emphasis positive. Children, disabled or not, who face mainstreaming with some anxiety will find the story reassuring. The illustrations are delightful.

Ages 5-8

**Also available in:**
Large Print—*Nick Joins In*
Albert Whitman & Company

## 359

Lasky, Kathryn

**My Island Grandma**

Color illustrations by Emily Arnold McCully.
Frederick Warne & Company, Inc., 1979.
(30 pages counted)

---

*GRANDPARENT: Love for*
  *Nature: appreciation of*

---

After Abbey's father closes his classroom for the year and her mother changes her winter paints for a box full of summer colors, they all leave together for their special island hideaway. Waiting on the dock with a wheelbarrow to carry their luggage is Abbey's grandmother. Grandma's cabin is over on the sea side of the island, connected to their side by a mossy path that cuts through a pine forest. Every day Abbey runs barefoot over the soft path to join her grandmother for some new adventure. Sometimes, early in the morning, the two of them go swimming in "dark sea pools." Grandma has "strong hands" that hold Abbey "tight and safe" while she is learning to swim. Afterwards, they wrap themselves in towels and sit on a "million-year-old rock" to talk. On their way home Grandma often picks sea herbs to put in salads or gathers periwinkles to make soup. Abbey hates both these foods, but she loves to eat the blueberries they pick in the afternoon. One day as Abbey and Grandma walk home from picking berries, they come across a nest of eggs that are beginning to hatch. Abbey wants very much to stay and watch, but Grandma points to the mother duck circling overhead and insists they leave. "When you're getting born," she says, "you need to be left with your own kind. People with people, ducks with ducks." Sometimes Abbey and Grandma go sailing. If there are lots of big, fluffy clouds in the sky, they tell cloud stories. On rainy days Abbey and her grandmother stay inside and make moss gardens and cookies. Sometimes when Abbey is asleep in the special sleeping bag Grandma made her, Grandma uses her soft night voice to wake her up and direct her outside to look at the starry sky. At the end of the summer they all return to the city. All winter long, however, as Abbey sees her grandmother wearing "shoes that make her taller" and riding the subway, she knows that inside she is still her "Island Grandma."

This is a lyrical, loving account of a special friendship and a perfect summer. Abbey's grandmother gives her a priceless gift, a deep respect and love for the natural world. The pen-and-ink drawings are washed with clear colors that reinforce the happy mood of the book.

Ages 4-7

**Also available in:**
No other form known

## 360

Leach, Michael

**Don't Call Me Orphan!**

The Westminster Press, 1979.
(94 pages)

---

*DEPENDENCE/INDEPENDENCE*
*SELF-ESTEEM*
  *Abandonment*
  *Belonging*
  *Children's home, living in*

---

Thirteen-year-old Kenny runs away from the Bethlehem Home for Boys to visit his father, whom he hasn't seen since the court sent him to the Home four years earlier. He finds his father living in a dirty room, and they have little to say to each other. Upset, Kenny leaves and defiantly buys an adults-only magazine that he reads in an alley. Later he cries and tears it up. He returns to the Home but wonders, "Where do you belong, Kenny? Where do you belong?" He remembers all that led up to the Bethlehem Home: the early companionship with his father, the fights between his parents over his father's increasing drinking, the day his father left them, the "uncles" that came to stay with his mother and him, his truancy and eventual appearance in court. Father McCabe finds Kenny and brings him to his office, offering the boy hot chocolate to drink and a bucket of warm water for his cold feet. When Kenny refers bitterly to himself as an orphan, Father McCabe tells him there are no orphans at Bethlehem; orphans have nobody to care for them and everyone at Bethlehem has someone. There may be no room for Kenny with either of his parents, but there is a place for him at the Bethlehem Home for Boys. Father McCabe asks Kenny if he has any friends. The boy can only think of seven-year-old Joey Sands. When he's asked about Leon Jones, his own age and captain of the swim team, Kenny says he doesn't know him very well and doubts he'd make the swim team anyway. But the next day Leon gets Kenny to try out for the team, and Kenny does well. Afterwards, Father McCabe tells Kenny that his mother is too sick to have him come home for the Christmas holidays. Kenny and Father McCabe both know this is a lie, and Kenny concludes that he doesn't belong anywhere. He decides to run away for good, but remembers that he has promised to take Joey along. Joey tells Kenny about his own home situation, which is very similar to Kenny's. Warmed by their friendship, both boys decide to go back and never run away again. The next day is the swim meet. The boys from Bethlehem try hard, but they are behind four points as they begin the final relay race. Kenny is the key swimmer in this race; he puts his heart and soul into it and wins. Jubilant, Kenny is even happier when he and Joey, the only boys with no place to go for Christmas, are invited to spend the holiday with Father McCabe's family. Father McCabe lets the two boys use the pool after everyone else leaves, normally against the rules. When he comes to get them for lunch, he teases them by asking what they're doing in the pool. Kenny laughingly replies, "We belong here!"

Abandoned by his parents, a lonely boy living in a Catholic Home finds a sense of belonging with the help of a priest and a younger friend, self-confidence as a winning member of the swim team. Kenny is finally able to acknowledge that his parents can love him, yet be unable to care for him—further, that he can survive even if they don't love him. Father McCabe makes much of the fact that the boys are not orphans but "dependent": they need and are worthy of the help and love of others. This moving first-person narrative is rooted in reality; the world constructed within its pages is believable and three-dimensional. Kenny's feelings can probably be shared by many children who are also "dependent," although not "orphans."

Ages 10-12

**Also available in:**
No other form known

### 361

**Leech, Jay and Zane Spencer**

**Bright Fawn and Me**

Color illustrations by Glo Cealson.
Thomas Y. Crowell Company, Inc., 1979.
(32 pages counted)

---

*JEALOUSY: Sibling*
  *Native American*
  *Sibling: love for*

---

A young Cheyenne girl has a little sister named Bright Fawn who shares her sleeping robe but never helps fold it up. Her mother says that Bright Fawn is still young and will learn. Bright Fawn doesn't help with any of the preparations for the trading fair. While her older sister walks, Bright Fawn is allowed to play with her doll as she rides on the travois, a kind of dogsled. When they arrive at the trading camp, the older sister must take Bright Fawn for a walk while their mother prepares food for the great feast. When their grandmother gives each girl a spoonful of honey, a dog takes Bright Fawn's share and the older sister gives up hers so Bright Fawn will stop crying. Lost Star, a friend of the older sister, says she wishes she had a sister. A man from another tribe tells her she has a fine little sister. A young woman going to the river for water stops and also tells her she has a fine little sister. But the girl pretends not to hear. Bright Fawn wants to ride a brave's horse and she begins to cry. The brave allows Bright Fawn to sit on his horse, telling the older sister how lucky she is to have such a fine little sister. A man from a northern tribe and a woman with a papoose also congratulate her on her little sister. But when another girl makes fun of Bright Fawn and calls her a pest, the sister defends Bright Fawn and explains that she is little and will learn. The

other girl says, "I am glad I do not have a sister." Bright Fawn's sister sticks out her tongue at the girl, takes Bright Fawn's hand in hers, and squeezes it tightly.

The narrator tells of her little sister, who seems a pampered nuisance until someone calls her a pest and impels the older sister to jump to the little girl's defense. This simple tale of sibling jealousy, while universal in its appeal, is set in Native American life of long ago. The realistic illustrations, in vibrant shades of brown, sienna, and orange, reflect the authenticity and richness of the text.

Ages 4-8

**Also available in:**
No other form known

### 362

**Leggett, Linda Rodgers and Linda Gambee Andrews**

**The Rose-Colored Glasses: Melanie Adjusts to Poor Vision**

Color illustrations by Laura Hartman.
Human Sciences Press, 1979.
(31 pages)

L

---

*GLASSES, WEARING OF*
*VISUAL IMPAIRMENT*
  *Empathy*
  *School: classmate relationships*
  *Self, attitude toward: accepting*

---

Melanie, about ten, has impaired vision from a car accident. Her family has moved, and she is embarrassed about the round, thick, pink-tinted glasses she needs now. So she struggles along without them. Unaware of her predicament, her new classmates consider her awkward and peculiar. Mrs. Davis, her teacher, asks Melanie and another student, Deborah, to work with her on a project that will help everyone understand and accept Melanie's vision problem. Afterwards, as the girls walk home together, Melanie begins to cry. She admits that she feels hideous in her glasses, that she wishes desperately her eyes were all right again. But Deborah, kind and concerned, assures her that people will like her regardless of her glasses. The next day Deborah and some other girls walk to school with Melanie. Mrs. Davis begins the morning by showing an out-of-focus film. Everyone has to strain to see and no one can follow it; only Melanie and Deborah know what the teacher's purpose is. After the film, students describe the uncertainty and nervousness they felt about watching the blurry screen. Then Melanie tells the class that fuzziness is what she always sees without her glasses. Deborah continues the presentation by having students read the blackboard through squinted eyes, and Mrs. Davis instructs a pupil to walk across the room while squinting. Participants all agree that they feel angry and unsure of themselves when they cannot see well. All—including Melanie—agree that she should wear her glasses rather than suffer unnecessarily the frustration of impaired vision.

A perceptive teacher recognizes that both Melanie and her classmates need to understand and accept her poor vision and the glasses she must wear because of it. Not only does Mrs. Davis encourage Melanie's self-acceptance and self-confidence, but she also helps the other students empathize with the girl's situation by having them actually experience the effects of damaged eyesight. Narrated by Deborah, this aptly illustrated account would be excellent both for visually impaired and visually normal children.

Ages 8-11

**Also available in:**
No other form known

## 363

L'Engle, Madeleine Franklin

**A Ring of Endless Light**

Farrar, Straus & Giroux, Inc., 1980.
(324 pages)

---

ANIMALS: Love for
BOY-GIRL RELATIONSHIPS
DEATH: Attitude Toward
  Family: unity
  Friendship: meaning of
  Grandparent: love for
  Illnesses: of grandparent
  Illnesses: terminal
  Leukemia
  Maturation
  Religion: faith
  Suicide: attempted

---

The family of fifteen-year-old Vicky Austin has come to spend the summer with her maternal grandfather, a retired minister who is dying of leukemia. The old man lives on an island off the New England coast and, despite the reasons for their coming there, Vicky looks forward to the stay. But she soon is caught in what seems an inescapable web of pain and death. First her wealthy, confused friend Zachary tries to drown himself, and a neighbor and close family friend, Commander Rodney of the Coast Guard, dies rescuing him. The Commander's son, Leo, Vicky's age but never her favorite person, now turns to her in his grief, and Vicky finds him more understanding and considerate than she'd ever thought. He becomes especially important to her as her grandfather's death approaches; Leo loves the old man also. The troubled Zachary, on the other hand, continues his erratic behavior, wooing Vicky and then shocking her with his irresponsible stunts and unorthodox way of looking at things. The overwhelming fact for Vicky, though, is the coming death of her beloved grandfather. She is helped to bear up by her close-knit family and by the dying man himself, who discusses death with her, citing the Bible, literature, and philosophy while facing his own death serenely. Vicky has always found satisfaction in writing poetry and she continues to do so now. Best of all, she meets her brother's friend Adam Eddington, a student of marine biology who is studying dolphin communication. Adam, on a summer research grant, introduces Vicky to the dolphins he is studying, and the girl discovers that she and the undersea mammals can communicate with each other telepathically. She is drawn into Adam's life and work, but continues to see Zachary. While on a date with him, Vicky learns that her grandfather has been

rushed to the hospital. Zachary takes her there but then disappears, unable to stand the sights and smells that remind him of his own recent efforts to die. Seeking news of her grandfather, Vicky meets a distraught young mother she's seen at the hospital before. The woman frantically cries that her daughter is dying because the father, for religious reasons, refuses to allow treatment. After thrusting the unconscious little girl, who is having a seizure, into Vicky's arms, she runs for help. No one comes and, needing immediate aid because of a weak heart, the child dies as Vicky holds her. Overwhelmed, Vicky collapses, reviving to find that Adam has come, sensing her need for him. She learns that her grandfather is still alive, but, numbed by grief and depression, she herself is unable to recover. She drifts in and out of consciousness, waking briefly to wonder, "Why be conscious in a world like this?" No one can rouse her, so Adam suggests that he take her to the sea and the dolphins, an environment she's come to love. Vicky awakens some when they get there, and she and Adam swim out. The dolphins come to Vicky, sensing her plight. They lift her between them as they leap and sparkle in the sun. When she fails to respond, they form a circle around her and one dolphin slaps her playfully. Adam laughs, Vicky joins in, and her depression gives way to happiness. The dolphins swim back out to sea, and Vicky returns with Adam to shore and to life.

This fourth book about the Austin family is a dramatic, involved, at times subtle philosophical novel that will appeal to mature readers. Vicky undergoes a massive emotional shock brought on by the death and pain all around her and by her own maturation struggles. She is helped to recover by the support of her family and friends, her grandfather's intelligence and sensitivity, the consolations of poetry and philosophy, and her love for Adam and the dolphins. This last angle, Vicky's communication with the dolphins, lends the book an almost fantasy-like quality that never detracts from the story's realism and believability. A rich brew, the book should reward readers with ample material for thought and discussion.

Ages 11-14

**Also available in:**
Braille—A Ring of Endless Light
Library of Congress (NLSBPH)

Cassette—A Ring of Endless Light
Library of Congress (NLSBPH)

Paperbound—A Ring of Endless Light
Avon Books

## 364

LeRoy, Gen

**Billy's Shoes**

Black/white illustrations by J. Winslow Higginbottom.
McGraw-Hill Book Company, 1981.
(39 pages counted)

---

INFERIORITY, FEELINGS OF
SIBLING: Younger
  Parental: interference
  Sibling: love for

---

Billy wants to be like his older brother, Ben, and doesn't at all mind wearing Ben's hand-me-downs. Most of all, Billy loves wearing Ben's outgrown shoes. When he's wearing them, he can "outrace an angry bee, leap higher than his cat, and kick a ball farther than anyone." He wants Ben's shoes to last forever. One day his mother takes Billy to buy new shoes because his—Ben's old ones—are getting so worn out. But Billy puts the new ones under his bed and wears the old ones to school the next day. His parents want him to wear the new shoes: "They didn't understand how important Ben's shoes were." The next day when he looks for Ben's shoes, they're gone, and he must wear his new shoes to school. He feels like crying, but won't in front of Ben. At school that day, Billy doesn't play with anyone. He's sure there's no use trying to run or jump in the new shoes. "What was the use of anything? No one understood him. He didn't throw his mother's things away. He didn't tell her what she could wear." Billy watches Ben playing and wonders how long he'll have to wait until he gets the shoes Ben is now wearing. Then Billy sees a bike speeding towards a dog that's busy burying a bone. Billy dashes across the schoolyard and grabs the dog out of harm's way. His friends admire his fast running. That night Billy shines his new shoes, which have become dusty and scuffed. He begins to wonder if it isn't his own feet, rather than Ben's shoes, that make him run so fast, leap so high, and kick a ball so far.

An admiring younger brother attaches almost magical importance to his brother's cast-off shoes until his own quick action in an emergency convinces him that all he really needs are his own two feet. Billy's parents are impatient with him and throw away the old shoes while he's asleep, an injustice that comes through clearly. But Billy's story still reaches a satisfying conclusion, and children will like the clever, appealing text and illustrations.

Ages 5-8

**Also available in:**
No other form known

### 365

LeRoy, Gen

**Lucky Stiff!**

Black/white illustrations by J. Winslow Higginbottom.
McGraw-Hill Book Company, 1981.
(39 pages counted)

---

*SIBLING: New Baby*
  *Jealousy: sibling*

---

Little Anabel hates going off to school each morning because she's sure her parents and her new baby brother, Vaughan, are having a great time together while she's away. She thinks Vaughan's name is silly, his crying drives her crazy, and whenever he squeaks her parents get all excited. When Anabel squeaks her parents tell her to calm down. She thinks her little brother is a lucky stiff. On Saturday Anabel suggests to her friends Nina and Spike that they play house with her as the baby. Lying in a lined wagon, Anabel gets fed crushed crackers and water—awful! Nina and Spike go off to play hopscotch, leaving her alone. When Anabel

"cries," Nina and Spike come back, pretend to burp her, and then leave her again to play with three other friends. She coos loudly to attract their attention, but when Amy offers her a cookie Spike takes it away, saying that babies haven't any teeth. So they mash it up and feed it to her. Again they leave her lying in the wagon while they go back to their game. Anabel finally gets up and goes home. She tiptoes into the nursery. "Poor fellow," she says to Vaughan. "Poor little fellow." She tells him that as soon as he learns to talk and walk, she'll help him get out of his crib. Vaughan grabs her finger and holds on. Anabel decides Vaughan isn't such a silly name. She kisses him, promises to talk to him later, and decides she's glad she's grown up.

A little girl resents the intrusion of a new baby brother and is jealous of the attention lavished on him. After playing at being a baby with her friends, however, she realizes that it's more fun to be able to talk, walk, and eat independently—more fun to be "grown up." Busy, whimsical illustrations accompany a simple, straightforward text. Anabel's parents remain in the background; her change in attitude is entirely self-invoked. The book allows children with new siblings to appreciate the advantages of greater independence.

Ages 4-7

**Also available in:**
No other form known

L

### 366

Letchworth, Beverly J.

**Pax and the Mutt**

Black/white illustrations by Tracye Hanson.
Crestwood House, Inc., 1981.
(47 pages)

---

*POVERTY*
  *Pets: love for*
  *Resourcefulness*

---

It's Jamie's eleventh birthday, but there will be no presents. His father is dead; his mother works at a factory to support him and his little sister, Julie; there is no money for anything but the bare essentials. Jamie doesn't understand why they have to be so poor. He feels let down to have no birthday gifts. When he's in Pax's grocery store he starts to steal a candy bar, thinking Pax, an old woman, will never know he took it. But then he remembers his mother telling him that sometimes he will be the only person to know if he does right or wrong. He puts the candy back. Then he finds an adorable puppy that he calls Happy and considers a wonderful birthday gift. But his mother says there is no way she can feed another living thing. Jamie talks her into letting him keep the dog overnight. Tomorrow is Saturday, and he'll spend it figuring out a way to earn money for the dog's food. The next day he and Julie comb the neighborhood looking for bottles to redeem. He finds a half-dollar, but loses that and his other money through a hole in his pocket. When his mother finds out the dog hasn't eaten all day and Jamie has not come up with any means of providing for it, she says it must go. So Jamie asks Pax if he can work in her grocery store to earn a little money. She says she can barely keep herself. Realizing that he simply can't care for Happy, Jamie shoos him away and even throws a rock to scare him. Pax sees this and reconsiders; she'll offer Jamie work in exchange for dog food. But now Jamie can't find Happy. The next morning Pax shows up at Jamie's door with a bag of dog food—and Happy. Jamie agrees to start work for her right away.

One of a series of short, high-interest books for younger children, this story shares with the reader Jamie's anguish when he can't keep a dog he loves because his family is too poor to feed it. Jamie's resourcefulness and willingness to work, along with the generosity of Pax, the store owner, produce a solution that turns the boy's life around. Before, Jamie says, his life had all the excitement of a bowl of oatmeal. Now he has something to look forward to. This simply written story will appeal to the intended audience.

Ages 8-11

**Also available in:**
Paperbound—*Pax and the Mutt*
Crestwood House, Inc.

## 367

Levinson, Nancy Smiler

### Silent Fear

Black/white illustrations by Paul Furan.
Crestwood House, Inc., 1981.
(63 pages)

---

*CHILD ABUSE*
  *Foster home*

---

At thirteen, Sara Michaels is taken to a new foster home. Her mother is dead and her father, whose mental illness was growing worse, has disappeared. Dixie Mack, her new foster mother, also cares for Donald and Alex, eight and ten. Dixie, who has alcohol on her breath, shows Sara to a rough bed on an unheated porch. As soon as the social worker leaves, she announces that Sara will be responsible for the kitchen, bathroom, laundry, and baby-sitting. The social worker has told Dixie that she is to buy Sara a winter coat with her first support check. Instead, she gives Sara a dreadful old coat of hers and buys herself a fur-trimmed jacket. Sara decides her only hope is to find her father. She goes to the newspaper office to place an ad, and there meets Dave Lancaster, a schoolmate and the son of the newspaper owner. When Sara is later than usual getting home, Dixie beats her, threatening the boys with spending Christmas in a closet if they mention Sara's "punishment." Sara would like to tell somebody about her situation, but she remembers a similar one in which authorities believed the adult, not the child. Then Sara wins a prestigious poetry award sponsored by the newspaper and is to receive a plaque the next day. She tries to talk to Ms. Light, her English teacher, about Dixie, but they are interrupted. The next day Donald is sick, and Dixie makes Sara stay home to care for him. Dave comes by the house with her award, saying Ms. Light suspects that all is not well with Sara. He suggests she talk to his father. Then Dixie comes in and rages at him for being there. Both Dave and Ms. Light later

encourage Sara to take some action. She tells her story to Dave's father, but the family is about to go on a ski weekend. They hate to leave her, but she insists she'll be all right. As Dave walks her part way home, Dixie spots them. She beats Sara and then locks her in the closet. Smelling smoke, Sara realizes the house is on fire. Donald lets her out, and she and the boys escape. Dixie, who set the fire to collect insurance, is hospitalized for psychiatric treatment. It's been discovered that she herself was a battered child and has a great deal of unresolved hostility. Sara stays with Ms. Light, where she's welcome to remain until other arrangements are made. Sara knows she has choices to make. Meanwhile, Dave is taking her to the glee club party.

One of a series of high-interest, easy reading books that deal with teenagers' contemporary concerns, Sara's story focuses on the alternatives she has for taking charge of her life. Sara is luckier than many abused children; she does break out of the cycle. Although rather superficial, the book does suggest that no situation is completely hopeless and no abused child totally helpless.

Ages 10-13

**Also available in:**
Paperbound—*Silent Fear*
Crestwood House, Inc.

## 368

Levinson, Nancy Smiler

### World of Her Own

Black/white illustrations by Gene Feller.
Harvey House, Inc., 1981.
(122 pages) o.p.

---

*DEAFNESS*
*SCHOOL: Mainstreaming*
  *Boy-girl relationships*
  *Change: resisting*
  *School: negative experiences*

---

Sixteen-year-old Annie is frightened and angry when her father and older brother tell her she will be leaving the Center, a private school they can no longer afford, to attend Larchmont High School. Annie has gone to the Center for the past nine years, ever since her hearing was impaired after a case of the mumps. She is convinced that at Larchmont she'll be alone, left out, a freak. Reluctantly, Annie goes to the school to meet with Ms. Shoreham, the special education teacher. The girl is especially dismayed by her biology and driver's education teacher, Mr. Tillis. His face remains expressionless when he speaks and his voice, buried in his huge mustache and beard, comes through Annie's hearing aids as a low drone. But Annie says nothing, hoping to fail at Larchmont so she can go back to the Center. When school starts, Annie rejects all friendly overtures. In biology, Mr. Tillis often turns his back to the class and talks while writing on the board. Realizing that Annie needs help but not conscious of his own part in her difficulties, he appoints Rita as her tutor. Rita and her male cronies make fun of Annie. Annie sits with two other girls at lunch, but since she hasn't told them she's deaf, they speak to her while looking at the ground or while eating. Finally, when they ask why she doesn't answer their questions, Annie gets up and runs home. A few days later, Michael Hale, the assistant editor of the school paper and Rita's boyfriend, tries to interview Annie for an article on new students. She is upset and uneasy but he reacts kindly, saying they can do the interview some other time. Mr. Tillis continues to expect Rita to pass on notes and assignments to Annie, but Rita treats her commission as a joke. In driver's ed., Mr. Tillis turns on several old films with poor sound and leaves the room. In homeroom, Ms. Shoreham announces that some equipment has disappeared from the school office. Annie finally decides to confide in Ms. Shoreham when she gets only one question right on a driver's ed. test. But when she gets to the office, she sees a commotion and lipreads Rita's mother complaining that Rita doesn't have time to help someone who's "deaf as a stone." Terribly upset, Annie goes to the Center for comfort. Later, she walks to the park and sees Michael helping some children learn to play tennis. Suddenly a boy takes a spill on a skateboard and breaks his arm. Annie quickly splints it and has Michael call the paramedics. Impressed, he talks with her. She tells him she's deaf, he asks her what it's like, and gradually Annie realizes she really likes him. But the troubles in school persist, and Annie finally confides in Ms. Shoreham. She makes a few suggestions, but reminds Annie that all students confront problems in school and must learn how to solve them. Pondering that idea, Annie returns to the biology room to pick up some papers she's forgotten, running into Rita and two of her friends. They tease her and then continue their talk, assuming she can hear nothing. They are discussing their plans to break into the school. After several days of torment, Annie realizes that she cares very much for the school and would not like to see it vandalized. Believing that the group will act on a Friday night when the school is empty, she goes first to the police department, but they suggest she come back with her parents. Then she tells Michael, but he thinks she has misunderstood. So Annie runs to the school, where she sees a light and some figures moving about. She goes to a nearby house and asks the resident to call the police. They arrive quickly and arrest three boys. The next Monday at school, Rita's involvement in the escapade is established. Michael, apologetic for not believing Annie, invites her to the Disco-Thon and she accepts. There, things are easier than she'd expected. "Step by step, she began to catch on to the beat."

A deaf girl is mainstreamed into a public high school after years of happy attendance at a special center. Slowly and with considerable frustration and pain, Annie makes friends and learns to adapt to a wider world. Helpful illustrations accompany this simply written story, which includes much information about the lives of hearing-impaired people. For example, words are left out of conversations, just as Annie might miss them, and the reader quickly appreciates her frustration. The story, with its high school setting and touches of mystery and romance, should claim the attention of reluctant readers.

Ages 12 and up

**Also available in:**
No other form known

**369**

Levoy, Myron

**A Shadow like a Leopard**

Harper & Row, Publishers, Inc., 1981.
(184 pages)

---

*AUTONOMY*
*FRIENDSHIP: Meaning of*
*MATURATION*
  *Delinquency, juvenile*
  *Gangs: membership in*
  *Gender role identity: male*
  *Parental: absence*
  *Puerto Rican-American*
  *Violence*

---

At fourteen Ramon Santiago wants to be macho almost as much as he wants to be a writer. A gang member, Ramon lives a dangerous, complicated life. He and his friend Harpo steal a woman's Social Security money in a darkened hallway, but Ramon can't forget her eyes bulging with terror. Ramon's mother is in the hospital, and he believes nobody helps her because she's on welfare. "You're no person if you're on welfare. You're just a piece of junk." When he takes a plant to his mother, who has suffered a nervous breakdown, she confuses him with his father, Carlos, in prison for the past year for assaulting a policeman at a "Free Puerto Rico" riot. Carlos's anger and frustration have sometimes been directed at his son, the "sissy" who writes his feelings in a notebook the boy now keeps well hidden. Dopey Luis, a fellow gang member always looking for possible victims, tells Ramon that the artist Arnold Glasser, an old man in a wheelchair, is an easy mark. Ramon talks his way into Glasser's apartment and then pulls a knife. Wildly frightened, Glasser begs the boy to take all his money—twelve dollars. The gang refuses to believe Glasser doesn't have several hundred dollars, as Dopey Luis claims. Determined to get the money if it exists, Ramon puts the twelve dollars and an apology under Glasser's door. When Glasser invites him in, Ramon tears up the apartment looking for money. Only when he sees the pitiful bits of food in the refrigerator does he realize that Glasser truly is poor. But Ramon likes Glasser's paintings and offers to sell them and split the proceeds with the old man. He eventually does sell some of them and returns to Glasser's apartment to fix a celebration dinner. Glasser shows Ramon a book about artists of the 1930s that includes color reproductions of several of the large murals he did for important buildings around the country. Glasser and Ramon spend the next day at the Metropolitan Museum of Art. When Ramon sees Dopey Luis spying on them, he knows the gang is out to get him but refuses to be frightened. He is splitting his half of the painting proceeds with them, but they don't like him hanging around with one of "them." Ramon goes to the art galleries on Madison Avenue to sell more of Glasser's paintings but gets a poor reception everywhere. Then he spots a painting in the window of the Nielsen gallery that he thinks looks like one of Glasser's. Nielsen, citing a revival of 1930s paintings, agrees to hang some of Glasser's work. Ramon plans to surprise Arnold on Wednesday by bringing him in to Nielsen's to sign a contract. Delighted with himself, Ramon decides

L

he has style and brains, which is a lot more than the other members of the gang have. But that night the gang ambushes Ramon and knifes him; a cut in his neck just misses his jugular. They also give him a bad cut in the shoulder, requiring stitches. Now Ramon wants revenge. First, though, he takes Glasser to the Nielsen gallery as arranged. To his amazement Glasser goes wild, ripping down his paintings and refusing to be part of the exhibition. Ramon accuses him of being afraid to be alive, afraid to keep painting, afraid to exhibit his work. Glasser countercharges that Ramon is afraid to go anywhere without his knife. The boy immediately drops his knife in Glasser's lap. "I'll trade you," he says. "My scared for your scared." Glasser agrees. On the street later Ramon sees Harpo, who slinks away, having evidently been part of the ambush. Ramon realizes there is no honor, no macho, in attacking someone four against one. When he arrives home his father is there, out on parole and determined to banish his anger. He's a new person, he says. He thinks Ramon's mother will be better in a few weeks, and the two of them can begin cleaning up the apartment for her. Then his father makes scornful remarks about a studious friend of Ramon's and about the "old bum" Arnold Glasser. He also wants to know if Ramon got his knife cuts with honor. Finally Ramon bursts out, "You want me always to win! To be macho! I'm gonna be macho my way, not your way!" Locking himself in the bathroom to write in his notebook, Ramon thinks, "Nobody's gonna tell me what to be. Not him. Not Harpo. Not Glasser. Nobody. I'm gonna be me, from inside."

A young Puerto Rican-American boy in New York City finds his own definition of macho with the help of an elderly artist and the discipline of keeping a journal. Ramon is a likeable, memorable protagonist who grows and defines himself in believable stages as the story progresses. The friendship between Ramon and the irascible but talented Glasser is based on respect and a growing understanding and sympathy. Although violence, poverty, and prejudice form a backdrop for the story, Ramon's choices are the central issue. He is ultimately true to his own instincts, and therein lies his strength. The colorful milieu includes street language with considerable profanity.

Ages 12 and up

**Also available in:**
Paperbound—*A Shadow like a Leopard*
New American Library

## 370

Levy, Elizabeth

## Come Out Smiling

Delacorte Press, 1981.
(186 pages)

---

*HOMOSEXUALITY: Female*
*PEER RELATIONSHIPS*
    *Camp experiences*
    *Communication: parent-child*
    *Competition*

---

Fourteen-year-old Jenny will be a senior at Camp Sacajawea this summer. As she says goodbye to her parents in Cincinnati and boards the train for New York, she anticipates all the special privileges that senior campers enjoy. Shortly after joining the other girls in the compartment they will share for the trip, she spots her favorite counselor, Peggy, the riding instructor. She has with her a tall, pretty girl named Ann whom she introduces as her assistant for the summer. Since Jenny will be training for the Midsummer Horse Show, she expects to see a lot of Peggy and Ann during the next eight weeks. The camp director believes that competition is a good and natural part of life. To emphasize this, she always divides the camp into two teams, the blues and the greens. They compete in weekend sports matches and earn points during the week for things like flagpole attendance and bed making. Jenny longs to be both color captain and the best rider at camp. She feels on the social borderline—not really popular at school or at camp, but not unpopular either. She has plenty of friends, but no best friend. Ever since her first year at Sacajawea she has wanted Marcie as her special friend, and she is immediately drawn to her again. Marcie is unaffected, noncompetitive, and easy to talk with. Among the things they discuss as they get reacquainted is how far each has gone with a boy during the past school year. When the color war competition begins, Jenny is delighted to come in second on the green team and get to serve as lieutenant. Marcie is placed on the blue team and, as the summer progresses, her dislike for the color war increases. She agrees with Ann, who says "it's insane to have color war all summer long." In fact, Marcie agrees with Ann about a lot of things. Jenny likes Ann too, finding that Ann understands her insecurities and her problems with a sarcastic father who embarrasses her and makes her feel inadequate. Early one morning, Jenny goes to the stable and sees Peggy and Ann holding hands and kissing. Terribly upset, she reasons that since these are two of her favorite people, maybe she is gay too. After all, she has never had a real boyfriend. During the next week as she practices for the Midsummer Show, Jenny can think of nothing but what she has seen. She's not even happy after she wins the blue ribbon. When she finally tells Marcie her secret, Marcie also begins to feel insecure about her sexual identity. Maybe they both will turn out to be lesbians. At the final campfire, each girl is given a candle float to wish on, light, and push out onto the lake. At first Jenny intends to wish that she won't be gay. Instead, however, she thinks about the many times her parents have sent her to her room with instructions not to come out until she is smiling. She places her candle on the water and asks the spirit of Sacajawea to "please give me courage. Give me courage to come out smiling."

A young girl worries about her ambivalent attitude toward boys. She wants to keep up with her friends in their experiments with the opposite sex, but sometimes doubts that she likes boys or thinks about sex as much as a normal girl should. Furthermore, the one man in her life whom Jenny does love, her father, is so sarcastic and insensitive that she's usually angry when she's with him. When she discovers that two of her favorite people are gay, Jenny's questions about her own sexuality intensify. Believable dialogue and skillful characterizations mark this thoughtful story of a girl's unresolved struggle to define herself.

Ages 12 and up

**Also available in:**
No other form known

## 371

Lexau, Joan M.

**I Hate Red Rover**

Color illustrations by Gail Owens.
E. P. Dutton & Company, Inc., 1979.
(56 pages)

---

SCHOOL: Classmate Relationships
TEASING
Determination
Empathy
Grandparent: love for
Play
Sports/Sportsmanship
Success

---

Most of her class likes to play Red Rover, but Jill, about seven, hates it. It hurts when the others try to run through her clasped hands and so she lets go, breaking the rules and letting the other team win. She especially dislikes being laughed at when she can't break through the line on her turn. It's not her fault she's so small. After school she goes straight to her grandfather, who always understands. But this time the tears in his eyes stop her in mid-sentence. He explains he must have all his teeth pulled the next day and he's afraid, not only of the pain, but even more of being laughed at for the way he will look without teeth. Jill assures him she would never laugh. The next day she makes a special effort not to break the rules in Red Rover. She is pleased when, with new determination and tightly closed eyes, she is able to withstand the battering body of a member of the opposite team. Running to her grandfather after school, she laughs with glee and Grandpa gets tears in his eyes thinking Jill is laughing at his toothless mouth. But she isn't, she assures him. They agree that it "feels good to do something hard." The next day, however, Jill is again unable to break through the line. Fortunately, the next several days are rainy and Jill can enjoy the indoor games she plays well. Inevitably, though, a clear day dawns and it is time once more for Red Rover. "Now they will laugh at me again. I hate it! I hate it!" A classmate advises her to look beyond the other team, not at their clasped hands. Jill resolves to try this. Keeping her eyes on the fence behind the players' heads, she runs toward the clasped hands. Angry and determined, she plows straight through the line. Later, she can't wait to tell her grandfather of her feat, but first he has a surprise. He is wearing brand-new dentures, which he proudly removes and displays on his palm. Biting her lip in an effort not to smile, Jill glances into her grandfather's eyes and they both burst out laughing.

A little girl and her grandfather share a fear of being laughed at and later a recognition that some necessary actions entail a certain amount of pain. This is a warm, easy-to-read story with softly colored, detailed illustrations. It describes experiences most children will recognize and suggests that many feelings and fears are not restricted to the very young.

Ages 6-8

**Also available in:**
No other form known

## 372

Lifton, Betty Jean

**I'm Still Me**

Alfred A. Knopf, Inc., 1981.
(243 pages)

---

ADOPTION: Identity Questions
IDENTITY, SEARCH FOR
Family: relationships
Sex: premarital

---

Sixteen-year-old Lori Elkins gets an impossible assignment from her history teacher. As one of his "living" projects designed to help young people "feel" history, Mr. Innskeep asks his students to trace their family trees. Since Lori is adopted, the task raises feelings she has always tried to suppress. Her parents have never been forthcoming about either Lori's or her adopted brother Mike's backgrounds, and Lori has refrained from asking too many questions. But even as a small child she fantasized about her birth parents and their reasons for giving her away. Lori's friend Maggie has a similar problem. Her father died when she was a baby, and her mother has refused to tell her anything about him. Maggie thinks she can use her stepfather for the family tree assignment. But Lori decides she would feel like a "fraud" if she handed in her adoptive parents' tree. She confides her dilemma to Sue O'Brien, her former baby-sitter who lives next door. Sue's boyfriend, Tony Daley, is a law student who thinks Lori has the "human right to know how she got on this earth." He explains, however, that birth records aren't easy to get. Encouraged by Maggie, Lori searches her house and finds an Order of Adoption that gives her mother's name, Barbara Goldman, and the agency in New York City that handled her case. Lori is reluctant to continue the investigation for fear of hurting her parents, but Maggie insists she make an appointment with Ms. Barnes, the director of the adoption agency. What Lori learns from this meeting does not make her happy. Her nineteen-year-old birth mother was not married and did not divulge the father's name. Lori has never considered the possibility that she could be illegitimate. Her first reaction is to give in to her "bad blood" by getting drunk and letting her boyfriend, Chris, make love to her. After all, many of her friends are sleeping with boys. She is humiliated when Chris decides he doesn't want to have sex with her while she's intoxicated. Lori doesn't think she can talk to her mother about any of this, especially during her parents' latest troubles with Mike, always hard to handle both at school and at home. Lori wonders if he too could be troubled by the fact that he is adopted. She has learned by attending a Search and Find group meeting in New York that many adoptees are, like her, disturbed by their mysterious origins. Even Maggie discovers a need to visit her paternal grandparents, who she knows live nearby. Lori goes with her and is impressed by their kindness and delight in being "found." Lori begins to forgive her birth mother when she and Chris start to

L

have sex regularly and she realizes how easy it would be to become an unwed mother herself. Meanwhile, Tony has managed to locate Barbara Goldman's wedding certificate, along with her current address and phone number. Lori phones and arranges a meeting. She finds Barbara to be a warm and sensitive woman who has suffered a great deal from giving up her baby. She tells Lori about her father and the circumstances surrounding her adoption. At last Lori feels she has "been born" and belongs "on this planet." When she returns home she tells her adoptive parents about her discoveries and is surprised by their understanding. They talk frankly about the possibility that some of Mike's problems might be caused by his uncertainty about his origins. Relieved and closer to her adoptive parents than ever, Lori finds that instead of changing her identity, her discoveries have strengthened it.

An adopted teenage girl seeks out her birth mother and learns about her past in this first-person narrative about the turmoil adopted children can face. Lori's search is successful on all fronts—her birth mother is warm and communicative, her adoptive parents completely supportive—not at all the norm, one feels, for such investigations. But the story is insightfully told and should be good reading for adopted young people, their adoptive parents, and other readers. Although the "modern," permissive view of teenage sex goes unquestioned, there is good discussion material for the opposite position.

Ages 12 and up

**Also available in:**
Paperbound—*I'm Still Me*
Bantam Books, Inc.

### 373

Lindgren, Astrid

## I Want a Brother or Sister

Translated from the Swedish by Barbara Lucas.
Color illustrations by Ilon Wikland.
Harcourt Brace Jovanovich, Inc., 1978. (Released 1981)
(29 pages counted)

*SIBLING: New Baby*
 *Attention seeking*

Peter, now three, knows he once was a baby. He knows too that despite his almost constant crying back then, Mama and Papa loved him very much. One day in a park, Peter meets a friend pushing a carriage. "My baby brother," the friend exults, but Peter answers he would rather play with toys than with a baby. Once home, though, Peter promptly asks Mama for a brother or sister. To his surprise, Mama tells him he will soon have one. Peter likes the idea and for a time he even likes Lena, his baby sister. He watches Mama caring for her, and he approves. But soon Peter decides it is "not any fun to have a sister." How can Mama and Papa love Lena—even more than they love him—when all she does is cry? Peter grows furious at them and at Lena too. He throws a tantrum and when Mama comes, Peter is glad. "After all, she was Peter's mama first, and not Lena's." One day Peter confides his feelings to Mama and she replies, "First I loved my little Peter and now I

love my big Peter." She confirms that he too was troublesome and required a lot of attention as a baby, and she asks him to help her tend Lena. Peter decides that maybe it is Lena's turn to be little and troublesome. He pushes her in a carriage, he plays with her, and he enjoys it. When he becomes older still and Lena is three, they both receive a little brother named Mats. The two are able to accept and love Mats right away.

Here is an excellent story for introducing a young child to the idea of a baby brother or sister, not as a rival for affection but as a future playmate. Parents will also discover tips for handling sibling rivalry by enlisting the older child's aid in caring for the baby. Colorful illustrations will charm young readers and listeners.

Ages 3-7

**Also available in:**
No other form known

### 374

Lindgren, Barbro

## Sam's Car

Translated from the Swedish.
Color illustrations by Eva Eriksson.
William Morrow & Company, Inc., 1982.
(29 pages counted)

*PLAY*
*SHARING/NOT SHARING*

Sam is playing with his car when Lisa comes along and wants to play with it. Sam won't let her so "Lisa smacks Sam." "Sam smacks Lisa" in return, and now both Sam and Lisa hurt. They cry. Then their mother brings another car. Happiness is restored as each child plays with a car.

Two very young children fight over a toy until their mother provides a solution. This simple, whimsically illustrated book could be a useful discussion starter about sharing and playing together. Also worthy of discussion is the hitting portrayed. This is one of several books about Sam.

Ages 2-5

**Also available in:**
No other form known

### 375

Lindgren, Barbro

## Sam's Cookie

Translated from the Swedish.
Color illustrations by Eva Eriksson.
William Morrow & Company, Inc., 1982.
(29 pages counted)

*PETS*
 *Sharing/Not sharing*

Sam has a cookie and is just beginning to enjoy it when along comes his dog. The dog wants the cookie and ends up taking it away from Sam. "Sam is angry. Dumb doggie." When he pulls the dog's ear, the dog gets angry too and growls. When the dog begins to chase him, Sam becomes frightened and cries. This brings Mommy, who scolds the dog and tells him not to take Sam's cookie. Then she gives Sam another cookie.

A young child and his dog disagree about the ownership of a cookie. When the dog wins by greater might, Sam's mother has to step in and Sam gets another cookie. This extremely simple book could be used with very young children to stimulate discussion about sharing, pets, and when not to argue with an animal. The brief text and whimsical illustrations are encouraging and inviting. This is one of several books about Sam.

Ages 2-5

**Also available in:**
No other form known

## 376

Lindsay, Jeanne Warren

**Do I Have a Daddy? A Story about a Single-Parent Child**

Black/white illustrations by DeeDee Upton Warr.
Morning Glory Press, 1982.
(44 pages)

PARENT/PARENTS: Single
UNWED MOTHER: Child of
    Communication: parent-child
    Parental: absence

After a run-in with his friend Jennifer who says she's going to tell her father on him, Erik asks his mother where his own father is. Does he have one? His mother explains that it takes both a mommy and a daddy to make a baby and so, yes, he had a daddy in the beginning. She says that some parents love each other so much they get married and live together. But she and Erik's daddy were very young and not ready to get married. She wanted Erik very much, his mother tells him, but, although his father was proud of him, taking care of a baby was too big a job for him then and he left. She suggests that, when he needs to, Erik tell friends that he had a daddy, but he's gone now. A few days later Erik wants to know if his father will ever come back. He wants a daddy like Jennifer's. No, his mother replies, his father will probably never come back. But if she ever gets married Erik will have a father. In the meantime, Erik can spend more time with Uncle Bob. And how about a walk with Grandpa right now?

An unmarried mother explains to her little boy why his father doesn't live with them. Although text and illustrations are not particularly outstanding, the book may be very useful to begin discussions with certain children. In the back, a section for adults explains that one out of six children in the U.S. is born to an unmarried woman and offers suggestions to parents about the need for honesty in speaking to their children about absent parents. Also suggested is that parents examine their own feelings about the absent person to avoid confusing or frightening their children.

Ages 4-8

**Also available in:**
No other form known

## 377

Lipp, Frederick J.

**Some Lose Their Way**

Atheneum Publishers, 1980.
(118 pages)

FRIENDSHIP: Making Friends
    Fear: of physical harm
    Loneliness
    Nature: appreciation of
    Nature: respect for
    Reality, escaping

Vanessa Dunlin is in the eighth grade, but has skipped several grades and is only eleven. Younger and smaller than her classmates, she is often picked on, especially by David Pinkham. When, under pressure from a teacher to name her tormentor, Vanessa names David, the boy promises revenge as soon as school is out. Summer comes, and Gram has to go to West Virginia to help her married daughter. So Vanessa goes to live in the other half of their duplex with Char, the black woman who is like family to them. Because Vanessa fears David, she spends the summer days at the library and the evenings reading, retreating into a fictional world of Camelot and knighthood. But she has recurring nightmares about encountering David in The Bottoms, an overgrown jungle of trees surrounding a pit that holds the sludge dredged from the nearby river, the only place in the neighborhood that Vanessa fears. Resolving to confront her fears, she goes to The Bottoms where she does indeed encounter David. She runs; he chases and tackles her to keep her from walking onto the dangerously unstable mud flats. David feels he is two people, the cool, self-reliant master of his environment and the cowardly, fearful person he knows he often is. He recognizes his fears in Vanessa and regrets having terrorized her. After apologizing, he invites her to help him with his project: studying the effects of pollution on the birds that inhabit the area around The Bottoms. Together they try to rescue a mallard caught in an oil spill and share the wonder of the returning sandpipers on migration. One day a man and his son want to fish near the dangerous mud. David warns them against it. Later Vanessa thinks she hears a cry, but David insists it's nothing. Then they see the man and his son, minus their fishing gear, leave the area all covered with mud. David seems to grow distant after that. He finally confesses to Vanessa that he is afraid of the mud, that he actually saw the man and his son struggling but turned his back on them. His cowardice, he believes, could have cost them their lives. Vanessa asks Char about the best way to help David, but Char says David has to forgive himself first. Soon after, David and Vanessa see a gull with a broken wing fall into the muddy pit. David goes after the bird in spite of the danger, and Vanessa has to bring in the fire department to rescue him. She runs home to tell Char, but there she finds her Uncle Mart waiting to take her to Gram in West Virginia. Vanessa begs to be allowed to visit David in the hospital, but Mart's car is all packed and waiting. She stays in West Virginia with Gram and her aunt's family until November. As soon as they get back home Vanessa runs to The Bottoms, but finds David's tent abandoned and

L

213

ruined. When she goes to his apartment building, the landlady says David and his father have gone, perhaps to Indiana or Illinois. Believing she will never see David again, Vanessa becomes numb, unable to do her schoolwork or to concentrate on anything. A worried Gram meets with the school counselor, who says Vanessa will have to repeat ninth grade unless something changes. Then in March, David's father comes to town and takes Vanessa out to dinner. He thanks her for giving his son back to him. Instead of a mixed-up kid, David is now a real human being, thanks to Vanessa—the first friend he ever had. David has sent Vanessa his binoculars and his bird guide. She returns to The Bottoms, awakens to her surroundings, and starts recording bird information. This will be her project now. The next summer David and his father send Vanessa tickets to visit them in their new home in Provincetown. Without a trace of strain, she and David revert to their easy friendship and make plans for bird watching.

Two lonely young people find their way past the misconceptions they have about each other to form an enduring, nourishing friendship. This engrossing story is generally told from Vanessa's viewpoint, but the reader is several times invited to share David's perspective. The natural history which becomes an integral part of the book will entice budding naturalists, but the inclusion of it does tend to slow the story's pace.

Ages 10-13

**Also available in:**
No other form known

## 378

**Litchfield, Ada Bassett**

### Words in Our Hands

Color illustrations by Helen Cogancherry.
Albert Whitman & Company, 1980.
(32 pages counted)

---

*DEAFNESS*
*Change: new home*
*Self, attitude toward: feeling different*

---

Michael Turner, age nine, and his two sisters, Gina and Diane, have learned several ways to communicate with their deaf parents. Mr. and Mrs. Turner attended schools for the deaf as youngsters, so they did learn to speak. Their speech, however, is often difficult for people outside the family to understand. Lipreading is another way for Mr. and Mrs. Turner to perceive the world around them. Most of the time, though, the Turner family communicates by talking with their hands. They use both finger spelling, in which every letter of the alphabet has a sign, and sign language, in which every sign has a more complete meaning. Sign language is faster and easier than finger spelling. The children began learning sign language as babies and are still learning new signs all the time. The Turner home also has a TTY, a teletypewriter that records messages on tape when attached to the telephone. Lights flash on and off when the telephone or doorbell rings. And Polly, the family dog, is especially helpful in alerting the parents to events like an alarm going off or a knock at the door. The Turners are a very happy family until the

father's company relocates in a new town and they must move. The move is very difficult for everyone. Mrs. Turner feels strange and uncomfortable in the stores, where no one knows her. And when the Turners talk with their hands, people stare at them. For the first time, the children are embarrassed by their parents' deafness. One day Michael sees three boys imitating his parents. Humiliated, he realizes that "just for a minute, I wanted to pretend my mother and father were not my parents." That evening Gina comes home with a note from her teacher inviting her family to attend a performance of the National Theatre of the Deaf. The Turners decide to go and are pleasantly surprised to find many people in the audience using sign language. Some of the actors are deaf, and the entire performance of *The Wooden Boy* is presented in sign. After the play, the Turners go backstage to meet and talk with some of the actors. Gina's teacher is there, and Gina is delighted to learn that she can sign. Michael is very proud of his parents, and the whole family becomes optimistic about their life in the new town. As Michael says, "Being deaf doesn't mean you can't hear or talk. If you have to, you can hear with your eyes and talk with your hands."

In this first-person narrative, Michael describes in both informative and emotional terms his life with his deaf parents. The illustrations include the finger spelling symbols for each letter of the alphabet and several examples of sign language. Deaf children will identify with the parents' problems and feelings, as well as their satisfying experiences. Hearing children will gain insight into the feelings, challenges, and abilities of deaf people.

Ages 7-9

**Also available in:**
No other form known

## 379

**Little, Mary E.**

### Old Cat and the Kitten

Black/white illustrations by the author.
Atheneum Publishers, 1979.
(119 pages)

---

*DECISION MAKING*
*PETS: Responsibility for*
  *Death: of pet*
  *Loyalty*
  *Pets: love for*

---

Twelve-year-old Joel finds a big, ugly, scarred, starving old tomcat and spends weeks patiently and lovingly gentling it, naming it Old Cat. Old Cat had been abandoned to fend for himself for the past five years. Joel's mother initially feels the family can't support a cat. Joel's stepfather has been gone for a year looking for work in the city. She spends long hours working in a beauty shop, and Joel has to spend much of his free time baby-sitting with "the Fiends"—Bitsy and Seth, his stepsister and stepbrother. But Joel promises to feed Old Cat out of the money he's been saving for a second-hand microscope. His mother wonders what he sees in the mangy tom. Replies Joel, "He was a pretty, clean little kitten once, Mom. Ain't his fault nobody gave him a home." Joel makes a home for Old Cat in the garage, but the cat prefers his own haunts, in particular a trash pile where one day he finds a weak little kitten. After several days of cleaning the kitten and trying to bring it food, Old Cat finally gets his charge to walk the two blocks to Joel's house. Joel's mother feeds the kitten and tells Joel how much she always wanted a kitten when she was young. Meanwhile, Joel worries about Old Cat's eye where a film seems to be forming. He has a library book on cats that's now two years overdue. He knows that to get a book on cat care, he'll have to return the other book and pay a big fine. But the librarian only charges him fifty cents and helps him select the book he wants. Joel reads that a veterinarian must examine eye problems in an animal, so he takes Old Cat to the vet. His mother is appalled at all the money he's spent, especially when she learns that the vet can do nothing about Old Cat's impending blindness in one eye. Soon after, Joel's friend Wayne describes what happens in animal shelters when they have too many animals: unwanted animals are put in a decompression chamber, outlawed in many states for being inhumane. Joel's stepfather calls to say he has found a job and wants his family to join him in the city very soon. The problem for Joel is that his stepfather is allergic to cats. Joel puts an ad in the paper but gets no response. He calls the animal shelter to find out if what Wayne told him was true. When he hears that they do indeed use a decompression chamber, he throws up. His mother calls from the beauty shop to tell Joel that a Mrs. Grant might be interested in the kitten, but feels that her third-floor apartment is no place for Old Cat. Mrs. Grant is very sympathetic and shows Joel photographs of her beloved cat, Barney. She explains that when he got old and sick he was in a great deal of pain, so Mrs. Grant had him put to sleep. Joel is horrified, but she explains that she held Barney in her arms while the vet gave him a shot and Barney died painlessly. Just before they're ready to pack up the last of their things, Joel's mother notices that Joel looks odd. She asks where Old Cat is. Joel says he spent the last of his microscope money to have Old Cat put to sleep with an injection, since he could not abandon him. Joel hugs the kitten as she licks the tears from his face.

When Joel must decide between abandoning Old Cat or having him humanely put to death, he chooses the latter. A strong sense of responsibility and loyalty pervades all Joel's actions, and the story clearly conveys the importance of those qualities in our relationships both with animals and people. The spareness and delicacy of the illustrations underscore the same characteristics in the text. However, the description of how animals are destroyed in decompression chambers could disturb some children.

Ages 8-12

Also available in:
Paperbound—*Old Cat and the Kitten*
Xerox Publishing Company

**380**

Liu, Aimee

## Solitaire

Harper & Row, Publishers, Inc., 1979.
(215 pages)

*ANOREXIA NERVOSA*
*GUILT, FEELINGS OF*
*SELF, ATTITUDE TOWARD: Body Concept*
  *Boy-girl relationships: dating*
  *Family: relationships*
  *Friendship: making friends*
  *Maturation*

L

Aimee describes her early childhood as a "cupcake existence," "frosted with affluence, filled with adventure, and sprinkled generously with loving care." But her joy ended brutally at seven when she was raped by two twelve-year-old boys. When Aimee was nine, her grandmother called her "chubby," making the girl wonder for the first time if she was overweight. By twelve, Aimee is filled with doubts about herself, concern that her parents' bickering will end in divorce, worries about her stormy relationship with her mother. That Christmas, weighing one hundred thirty pounds, Aimee decides to diet. She becomes obsessed with calorie counting, calisthenics, dancing, and schoolwork. In three weeks she loses fifteen pounds and feels great satisfaction at having total control over this one part of her life. With the weight loss comes the stopping of her periods and the constant feeling of being cold. But her friends admire her self-discipline and, despite her parents' concern, Aimee loves her sense of control. At fourteen she decides she wants to be a model, and her parents reluctantly agree to let her apply to various agencies in New York City. The Wilhelmina Agency signs her, pleased with her slender, tall figure and good looks, and she begins periodic modeling jobs on weekends and during the summers. But Aimee is still obsessed with her weight. She begins going on eating binges, after which she makes herself throw up and uses laxatives. At fifteen, Aimee weighs ninety-two pounds. She moves to the basement bedroom, seeking refuge from the parental battles. At sixteen her picture begins appearing in magazines. Classmates admire her, especially the girls, and Aimee loves the attention. Dieting becomes gratification. It also serves as an escape from her problems—her parents, pressure to date, school, the future. In her senior year Aimee begins dating for the first time. She goes steady with Ken Webster, who is also obsessed with pushing himself to the limit: doing without sleep, driving fast cars. They take strength in each other, and when both enter Yale they begin living together. Aimee becomes a vegetarian and starts eating a little more regularly. After several months devoted solely to school and Ken, she begins to reevaluate her life. She realizes she and Ken are suffocating each other. She breaks up with him, moves into a dorm, cultivates a more varied social life, and even tries to eat better. In the process, Aimee realizes she had been leading a sick, unnatural life; she had been afraid to grow up. Home for the summer, she even comes to discover that her parents really do love and care for her and each other. They are her support and "I was downright lucky to be their daughter."

In this deeply affecting first-person narrative, Aimee describes the true story of her struggle against anorexia nervosa and other eating disorders. Raped at seven, profoundly disturbed by her parents' constant arguing, Aimee's obsession with losing weight becomes her way to assume control. Overcoming her self-destructive behavior requires her to understand that what she fears most is growing up. In the end, Aimee triumphs over both anorexia and her feelings of worthlessness. The rape scene, though sensitively handled, is detailed and could upset some readers.

Ages 13 and up

**Also available in:**
No other form known

## 381

**Lobel, Arnold**

## Uncle Elephant

Color illustrations by the author.
Harper & Row, Publishers, Inc., 1981.
(64 pages)

---

*PARENTAL: Absence*
  *Mourning, stages of*
  *Relatives: living in home of*
  *Sharing/Not sharing*

---

When his mother and father are reported missing at sea, a young elephant sits sadly in his room with the curtain closed until Uncle Elephant, wrinkled and old, comes to invite him for a visit. They take a long train ride during which Uncle Elephant distracts his young nephew by counting houses, fields, telephone poles, and the shells of the peanuts they are eating. When they arrive, Uncle turns on a lamp, only to have a small voice yell at him. The elephants decide this must be a magic lamp and make many wishes on it before a small spider crawls out and complains about the heat inside. Uncle Elephant welcomes each new day with loud trumpeting. He introduces his nephew to all the flowers in his garden. They wear flowers and welcome the dawn together. When they take a walk Uncle Elephant creaks in all his joints because of his great age, and so he tells his nephew a story to take his mind off his creaks. When the young elephant thinks about his parents he gets very sad, but when Uncle Elephant dresses up in all the clothes he owns they end up laughing so hard they forget to mourn. Uncle Elephant makes up a wonderful elephant song for them to sing. Then comes a telegram announcing that the young elephant's parents have been rescued. Happy Uncle Elephant and his nephew once again ride the train, but this time Uncle is counting the days they have spent together. The elephant family has a happy reunion that evening. Uncle Elephant and his nephew promise to see each other often.

A young elephant grieving for his parents is loved and distracted by his Uncle Elephant. In this first-person story for beginning readers, the young elephant learns that he is not alone, that there are songs, flowers, new dawns, and laughter even in the midst of sorrow. The elephant characters, gentle humor, and happy ending keep the story light, as do the many softly colored illustrations. Still, the book may be helpful for young children whose parents are for any reason absent.

Ages 4-7

**Also available in:**
Braille—*Uncle Elephant*
Library of Congress (NLSBPH)

Disc—*Uncle Elephant*
Library of Congress (NLSBPH)

Paperbound—*Uncle Elephant*
Scholastic Book Services

## 382

**Lorimar, Lawrence T.**

## Secrets

Holt, Rinehart and Winston, Inc., 1981.
(192 pages)

---

*HONESTY/DISHONESTY*
  *Ambivalence, feelings of*
  *Mental illness: of parent*
  *Parental: weakness*
  *Sex: extramarital*
  *Sex: premarital*
  *Suicide: of parent*

---

Sixteen-year-old Maggie Thompson has for some time been puzzled by her father's lies and secrets. She knows that Pastor Thompson, minister of St. John's Church in the affluent community of Mountain View, California, is attractive to women. Even her friend Nell, on first meeting him, blushed and got flustered. Later, Nell tells Maggie that she felt as if Maggie's father were "trying to look at me through my clothes," insisting "that ministers are the world's biggest lechers." Maggie is aware that her father does counsel many "troubled women." Then Maggie begins dating a motorcyclist, Bob, and the two become sexually involved. Maggie finds their first encounter disappointing, but she is thrilled by Bob's slick way of handling his motorcycle and feels relaxed with him and his friends, happy to drop her "minister's daughter" role. Maggie's mother warns her that she is using Bob to run away from something. One day, Maggie goes with Bob to a beach party, where Bob gets very drunk and eventually falls asleep in the sand. Stranded, Maggie calls her father. Pastor Thompson suggests they keep the incident a secret and tell Mrs. Thompson that Bob's motorcycle broke down, since her mother already dislikes Bob. Maggie remarks that what they have is not a secret but a lie. "A secret isn't usually a lie," her father replies. "It's the part of the truth you don't choose to tell." Early in the fall, Pastor Thompson appoints Hedda Fisher, young and pretty, to be the new director of the youth group—instead of Mrs. Horner, who had wanted the job badly and had the support of the group's members. An uproar ensues. The youth group is disappointed and angry; Hedda appears determined to have the job at any cost; Mrs. Horner feels the other woman has weaseled in. Pastor Thompson calls the situation "delicate," explaining to Maggie that he chose Hedda to relieve the depression she has been in since her miscarriage the year before. Maggie's mother tells her they must support her father, because if he "does lose the upper hand, it will be terrible for all of us." She persuades Maggie to go talk to Hedda, who has gotten wind of the complaints and wants to know what the specific objections are. When Maggie goes to Hedda's apartment, the woman is at once nervous and defensive, making vicious remarks about Mrs. Horner while claiming a Christian love for all. Maggie, distressed and confused, decides Hedda is a "little crazy." Later, at home, her father insists she report to the group that Hedda was receptive to her visit and wants very badly to get along with all of them. Maggie complies. Now she suspects her father has a sexual relationship with Hedda. One night Pastor Thompson arrives home late to find Maggie up studying. When he bends down to kiss her, Maggie catches the scent of sandalwood. She has only smelled sandalwood once before: on Hedda Fisher the day she visited her. Nell starts the rumor about the affair, and soon gossip is circulating. Both Maggie and her mother know the story is true, but Mrs. Thompson asks Maggie to try and squelch the talk. Pastor Thompson goes so far as to plead his innocence to the youth group himself. But late one night, Maggie's suspicions are confirmed when she and Bob see her father walk to Hedda's apartment. Hedda's husband calls Pastor Thompson to say he plans to see the bishop about the affair. Maggie's mother tells her that there have been affairs before and that she used to consider her husband a liar. Now she believes he does not really know he is lying. "The biggest secret he has," she tells Maggie, "is not from us but from himself." Called to speak with the bishop, Pastor Thompson reports that his superior now understands the situation better, that things are going to be all right. But the bishop calls Maggie's mother to say that everyone except Pastor Thompson concurs about what has been happening—including Hedda Fisher. He asks Mrs. Thompson to try once more to get her husband to admit his guilt. The next day Maggie is called out of class for an emergency message: her father has committed suicide by driving his car over the guardrail on the canyon road. After this, Maggie finds life simpler, but she has a great sense of sorrow and loss. Her mother tells her that although the family tried to help and understand, the rest was always up to God. Maggie wonders if her father "believed in God's mercy even as he was driving over the side of the mountain."

Maggie tells her own story, and it is a moving and powerful one. The reader comes to see not only Pastor Thompson's deep problems, but also the web of denial and self-deception woven by Maggie's mother and eventually Maggie herself. Both women have a strong impulse to protect the man, the family, and themselves. Maggie must face the tangle of other people's lies as well, realizing that life is often not as simple and harmonious as it appears. Less thoroughly explored are the emotional issues of Maggie's relationship with Bob. Though she feels sad and alone after their first sexual encounter, her reasons for continuing to have relations with him are not pursued. Interestingly, her mother tells Maggie that she "wouldn't be struck dead for it. It's a simple little physical act . . . and the first time it's about as much fun as riding a bicycle for the first time—most people fall off." This is a gripping, incisive story.

Ages 12 and up

**Also available in:**
Paperbound—*Secrets*
Grosset & Dunlap, Inc.

## 383
**Love, Sandra Weller**

**Crossing Over**

Lothrop, Lee & Shepard Company, 1981.
(155 pages)

---

COMMUNICATION: Parent-Child
DISCIPLINE, MEANING OF
DIVORCE: of Parents
    Decision making
    Life style: change in
    Maturation
    Schools, private
    Talents: artistic

---

L

Although Megan Dorenberg's parents were divorced over three years ago, she and her younger brother, Kevin, have had a secure and happy childhood with their mother in Red Lion, Pennsylvania. Now their mother is moving to Boston to attend graduate school for a year, and Megan and Kevin, thirteen and ten, will be living with their father at Kentucky Military Academy (KMA), where he is a beginning teacher. As students at the highly structured school, the two will have to adjust to an entirely new way of life, quite different from the progressive school in Red Lion and the flexible, easygoing life with their mother. Even though she missed half of the third grade because of illness and has been behind in some subjects ever since, Megan's special ability in art has gained her recognition at school and kept her feeling good about herself. Now, however, she will need to catch up academically. Trying to be mature, she is at first determined to think of the year as an "adventure." But soon after she arrives on campus, her good resolution begins to break down. She receives a handbook with an "endless" number of rules and finds that her schedule of classes, tutoring sessions, and study periods will eat up her entire day. Furthermore, eighth graders at KMA are not allowed to take art, and her only time for sketching will be on weekends. To make matters worse, their father is busy and often irritable, convincing Megan that he really doesn't want them around. At the end of the first week, lonely and very unhappy, Megan decides to take a walk. She follows a path that leads away from campus and down to the river. There she discovers a cabin and meets Elise Aberdeen, the school's part-time art teacher, who uses the building for a studio. Elise invites Megan to return the next day, with her father's permission, to sketch with her. But even this prospect does not keep Megan from writing to her mother that night, asking to join her in Boston. When she returns to Elise's cabin the next day it is still without permission. She doesn't want to share this haven with anyone. In the weeks that follow, Elise proves a wise and understanding friend, empathizing with Megan's feelings but trying to persuade her to discuss them with her father. Since Megan has quickly collected three demerits at school, however, she doesn't expect much understanding at home. Instead, she continues to hope that her mother will rescue her. Then their father takes the children for a weekend with his mother. On the way they visit the historic John Rankin house, a stop on the Underground Railway where slaves were helped to "cross over" the Ohio River to freedom. Later, at Grandma's, Megan overhears her father confiding his frustration about his busy schedule and Megan's unhappiness. He says that the children's mother is now asking him to give them up after Christmas, and he doesn't think this would be good for them. Though she is touched by her father's concern for them, Megan dreams that night that she is a slave making her way over the river to freedom. The next day at school, she remembers how her parents used to argue about that very subject of freedom. Their mother believed in plenty of breathing room and independence; their father believed rules would help them develop self-discipline. "If they have rules about small things," he'd say, "they'll have more energy to use thinking about big ones." In the time remaining before the holidays, Megan and her father draw closer. She tells him about her friendship with Elise, and he arranges for Elise to give Megan private art lessons. Now Megan's days take on a new, happier "rhythm." When Elise announces she is leaving to attend art school, Megan can overcome her own disappointment enough to show concern for her father's feelings, since he has begun to fall in love with her friend. When her time to choose finally arrives, Megan confidently decides to complete her year with her father as planned.

A young girl who has never had to make serious decisions for herself learns that tough choices accompany maturity and that a well-organized life, even at a military academy, gives her the freedom to think about these important things. When she further learns that feelings are as important as facts and starts to share hers with her father, she takes another step toward adulthood. This book, filled with believable characters and relationships, manages to be gently persuasive about the merits of a structured life style without being didactic. The idea that parent-child problems can sometimes be solved through communication is also compellingly presented.

Ages 10-12

**Also available in:**
No other form known

## 384

Lowry, Lois

### Anastasia Again!

Black/white illustrations by Diane de Groat.
Houghton Mifflin Company, 1981.
(145 pages)

---

CHANGE: New Home
  Age: aging
  Friendship: making friends
  Moving

---

Twelve-year-old Anastasia Krupnik is alarmed and outraged at the prospect of her family's move from Cambridge, Massachusetts, to the suburbs. She dreads leaving her best friend and thinks suburban lives are played out much like those of the characters in soap operas. She envisions people with no integrity in houses decorated with matching furniture, bowls of fake fruit, and paint-by-number pictures. Her father, a university professor and published poet, cautions her against "premature assumptions." However, both he and her mother, a successful artist, along with her precocious little brother, Sam, suffer and share their own pre- and post-moving blues. But they find and buy an old house that is just right for the family, and having her own room makes Anastasia less resistant to the move. Her spirits rise further when she makes friends with a neighborhood boy who is actually taller than her five feet, seven inches. She determinedly befriends an eccentric old neighbor and, in the end, engineers a party during which she introduces this lonely woman to a group of older people. Helping her friend overcome her fear and shyness shows Anastasia the truth of her father's warning about "premature assumptions." The move to the suburbs hasn't been so bad after all.

In this sequel to *Anastasia Krupnik*, the precocious Anastasia weathers her anxiety about moving, learning, through her friendship with a lonely neighbor, how misconceptions and fear can close off happiness. Anastasia is a resilient, enthusiastic, affecting heroine with a delightful sense of humor. Witty, accurate descriptions and remarkably authentic dialogue give this story great appeal. A hasty summation of the whimsical mystery novel Anastasia is writing provides an amusing ending to the book.

Ages 9-12

**Also available in:**
Braille—*Anastasia Again!*
Library of Congress (NLSBPH)

Cassette—*Anastasia Again!*
Library of Congress (NLSBPH)

Large Print—*Anastasia Again!*
Wisconsin Department of Public Instruction

## 385

Lowry, Lois

### Anastasia at Your Service

Black/white illustrations by Diane de Groat.
Houghton Mifflin Company, 1982.
(149 pages)

---

MONEY: Earning
  Friendship: making friends
  Job
  Practical jokes/pranks
  Prejudice: social class
  Responsibility: accepting
  Revenge

---

Anastasia Krupnik, twelve, recently moved, her only friend gone to camp, suffering from poverty, boredom, and depression, places advertisements around town offering her services as a Companion to a rich older woman. When she reports to her first employer, Mrs. Ferris Bellingham, she is a little surprised to be put to work polishing silver, but she assumes a Companion has to pitch in during emergencies. Then she accidentally drops a silver spoon into the garbage disposal. Mrs. Bellingham tells Anastasia she is to work as a maid at a birthday luncheon for her granddaughter, Daphne, the next day. As if being a maid weren't bad enough, Anastasia learns that the girl she'll be serving will probably be in her class this fall. Mrs. Bellingham also points out that the silver spoon cost thirty-five dollars and Anastasia will have to work another twelve hours to pay for it. The next day Anastasia disguises herself by wearing her mother's bra stuffed with panty hose, powdering her hair, and wearing makeup. But Daphne unmasks her when Anastasia's bosom falls into the platter of deviled eggs she's carrying, and the girls become friends. Daphne's father is a minister, she tells Anastasia, so she has had to become almost a juvenile delinquent in order to rebel. She's angry at her grandmother for insulting her with a doll on her birthday, and Anastasia is angry at being forced to do maid's work when she applied to be a Companion in the best tradition of Gothic mysteries and romances. Daphne proposes that they revenge themselves on Mrs. Bellingham by inviting a neighborhood drunk, a bag lady, two potheads, a couple of recently released psychotics, and people from the low-income housing units to Mrs. Bellingham's upcoming fund-raising party. Meanwhile, Anastasia's little brother, Sam, falls out of a window and is hospitalized with a head injury. While in the hospital, he makes friends with a Mrs. Flypaper, apparently imaginary. Anastasia is horrified when she hears that the money from Mrs. Bellingham's fund raiser is to go to the pediatric wing of Sam's hospital. She and Daphne resolve to head off trouble at the affair by spotting the people Daphne invited and asking them to leave. Unfortunately, Daphne doesn't remember what most of them look like. She asks one disreputable-looking guest to leave and he turns out to be the mayor of Boston. Finally, the girls confess their scheme to Mrs. Bellingham, also confiding their fear of her. She sends them home and soothes her guests. When Anastasia goes to collect her paycheck, she takes Sam along. To her surprise, he embraces Mrs. Bellingham and calls her Mrs. Flypaper. It turns out that Mrs. Bellingham works as a volunteer in the hospital. She is upset that both Anastasia and Daphne were angry with her but were too afraid to confront her with their feelings. Daphne, dealt with severely by her parents for the first time in her life, asks Anastasia's help in keeping out of trouble in the future; school detentions aren't much fun. Anastasia gladly agrees to help her new friend.

In this entertaining sequel to *Anastasia Krupnik* and *Anastasia Again!* the feisty young heroine learns not to prejudge people just because they are very rich. She also accepts the consequences of her actions and realizes, when he is badly hurt, how much she actually loves her precocious little brother. This is easy, appealing reading with several ideas worth thinking about—such as the tendency of revenge to backfire.

Ages 9-12

**Also available in:**
Braille—*Anastasia at Your Service*
Library of Congress (NLSBPH)

Cassette—*Anastasia at Your Service*
Library of Congress (NLSBPH)

Paperbound—*Anastasia at Your Service*
Dell Publishing Company, Inc.

**386**
Lowry, Lois

**Anastasia Krupnik**
Houghton Mifflin Company, 1979.
(113 pages)

*MATURATION*
*SIBLING: New Baby*
　*Age: aging*
　*Loss: feelings of*

At age ten, Anastasia suddenly finds herself possessed of an unpredictable temperament. In a little green book, she keeps two lists headed "Things I Love" and "Things I Hate." One day she loves Washburn Cummings, with his huge Afro; the next day, after he makes insulting remarks about her hairdo, she hates him. She decides to turn Catholic but changes her mind quickly at the idea of confession. She hates pumpkin pie at Thanksgiving, but by Christmas she loves it. Shortly after her tenth birthday, a small, pink wart had appeared on her left thumb. Anastasia loves her wart because her father has told her warts have a kind of magic about them. Angry when she learns that her mother is expecting a child, she immediately adds the baby to her "hate" list. To reconcile her to the loss of her only-child status, her father tells her she can name the baby. In anger, she secretly decides on a terrible name: One-Ball-Reilly, after a classmate she hates. She hates her grandmother for being old and confused and in a nursing home. At Thanksgiving she tries to talk to her, but the old woman lives only in the past and doesn't know Anastasia. The girl is saddened and frightened by the idea of old age. Then one day she learns from a poem by Wordsworth about "the inward eye," the solace of happy memories. Realizing that her grandmother has the inward eye, Anastasia is more sympathetic at Christmas when the old woman talks in the present tense of her deceased husband, Sam. One day, just as suddenly as it came, the wart disappears. Anastasia goes to tell her parents and finds them grieving for her grandmother, who has died. Anastasia is amazed to find herself crying with real feeling. That same day, her mother goes to the hospital to have the baby. Anastasia is convinced these upsetting events are related to the sudden disappearance of her wart. On the way to the hospital to see her baby brother, she crosses out the name she had planned for him and writes down a new one. The name she has chosen is Sam.

One of a series of books about Anastasia Krupnik, this is a sensitive and lively account of a bright young girl beginning the painful process of growing up. Anastasia learns to balance her brimming emotions by becoming attuned to others' needs, and so comes to understand herself a bit better. Told realistically and with humor, the story is consistently involving.

## 387

**Luger, Harriett Mandelay**

## Lauren

The Viking Press, Inc., 1979.
(157 pages)

*DECISION MAKING*
*UNWED MOTHER*
  *Boy-girl relationships: dating*
  *Communication: parent-child*
  *Friendship: meaning of*
  *Parent/Parents: fighting between*

Terribly afraid she's pregnant, seventeen-year-old Lauren Murray changes quickly from a carefree member of the Gruesome Threesome, with friends Judy and Stephanie, into an adult with burdens nearly too great to bear. After telling her boyfriend, Donny, she confides her apprehension to Judy and Stephanie. They accompany her to the Free Clinic where she learns she is twelve to fourteen weeks pregnant, too far along for a simple abortion. Desperately needing support and guidance, Lauren is soon disappointed by friends and family. Judy scoffs at her stupidity for not taking precautions; in response, Stephanie attempts to support Lauren by declaring that love cannot be so cold and calculating. Donny, though supportive, is frightened about his own future and wants Lauren to get an abortion. Lauren's parents, usually at odds, band together in support of their daughter, placing full blame on Donny, while his parents consider Lauren the culprit. Upset by the attitudes of both sets of parents, hurt by her friends' lack of understanding, feeling betrayed by Donny, Lauren packs a bag and, with fifty dollars to her name, leaves home intending to solve her own problems. She goes to the beach, her favorite refuge, and cries out her fear, hurt, and anger. There she is befriended by Liz and Dawn, unwed mothers who offer her shelter in exchange for food and money. Lauren soon learns the difficulties of a life without parental support: Dawn, negligent and immature, eventually loses her child to the courts, and Liz finds herself unable to pay the rent. Through the two, Lauren meets Tom and Andrea, a married couple who have been trying for seven years to have a baby. She and Andrea become friends, but Andrea accuses Lauren of not taking seriously her responsibilities to her unborn child. For the first time, Lauren begins to contemplate what keeping her baby might mean. One day, the tense situation with her roommates explodes as Lauren (now penniless after losing her job in a hamburger joint) is accused by Dawn's boyfriend of leading him on. Depressed, despairing, and alone once more, Lauren packs her bag and again

heads for the beach. Tempted by the soothing rhythm of the waves, she walks into the surf, half intending never to return. She comes to her senses in time and strikes out struggling for the shore. Once safe, she finds herself at a pay phone calling her mother to come for her. Her frightened, concerned family welcomes her home. Donny tells her he still loves her, and at first Lauren believes he will marry her. She tells her parents she will keep the baby, although she doesn't say that she and Donny will marry. When she talks to him of marriage, he reluctantly agrees. But Lauren realizes that he feels trapped and resentful, that their marriage would be much like her parents' unhappy one, and she lets Donny go. Then Carla, Lauren's fourteen-year-old sister, shyly but proudly confides that she and her boyfriend have had sex for the first time. Appalled, Lauren sees history repeating itself. Her thoughts turn to the childless Andrea and Tom and to the need of her unborn child for a family. Her decision is made.

This emotion-packed novel clearly depicts the agonizing decisions young people must face when burdened with premature parenthood. The various options available to Lauren—abortion, single parenthood, marriage, adoption—are sensibly, thoroughly, and impartially examined through the girl's own thoughts and actions. This is a strong, affecting story, filled with possibilities for discussion.

Ages 12 and up

## 388

**Lyle, Katie Letcher**

## Dark But Full of Diamonds

Coward, McCann & Geoghegan, Inc., 1981.
(174 pages)

*COMMUNICATION: Parent-Child*
*DEATH: of Mother*
*LOVE, MEANING OF*
  *Fantasy formation*
  *Loss: feelings of*
  *Parent/Parents: single*

Since Scott Dabney's mother died four years ago, his relationship with his father has grown worse and worse. Not only has Dr. Dabney become emotionally distant, but he spends most of his evenings alone in his office trying to drown his loneliness in bourbon. Scott, about to begin his junior year in high school, believes the "great Dr. Dabney . . . should have been able to save Mama." Furthermore, Scott resents his father's making light of his mother's accomplishments as an actress and playwright. Scott has glowing memories of his mother, not only about her many theatrical ventures but about her childhood in DeLane County. Although he has never been there, he's sure DeLane must have been as perfect as she was. After she died, Scott comforted himself with the thought that she had returned to her childhood home and would always remain there happily "in a past perfect time that was changeless and dependable." Now, in the middle of a long, dismal summer, Scott is unexpectedly cheered by the news that Hilah

Brown has completed her master's degree in drama and is returning to teach English at the high school. Hilah was his swimming teacher the summer his mother died, and although she is nine years older than he, he was "crazy" about her. He has not seen her since, but remembers her teasing promise to wait for him to grow up. When she finally arrives in town, Scott is tense with excitement and determined to "dazzle" her into forgetting the difference in their ages. As a member of her Thespian group, he does his "acting just for her." Yet, in spite of his best efforts to please and impress, Hilah remains just a friend. Everyone but Scott seems to realize that the more likely candidate for her affections is his father. But when Hilah invites Dr. Dabney to escort her to the harvest dance, Scott is forced to face up to reality. He and a friend leave the dance frequently to drink the liquor his friend has in the car. Ultimately, his father and Hilah must take the drunken Scott home. Confused and hurt by his father's interest in Hilah, Scott's resentment increases. His mother's "ghost seems near again," and he is terrified that he will once more lose a woman he loves. He drops out of drama club and tries to deaden his mind by spending hours running under the gray winter sky. Then in January, on Scott's seventeenth birthday, Hilah and his father announce their marriage plans. The following weeks pass away in numbness. Scott talks to people and then cannot recall what they've said. He takes dangerous chances while driving his new car (a birthday present from his father) and then trembles at his narrow escapes. He tries to give credence to a rumor that Hilah is sleeping with him as well as with his father, making himself sick with self-loathing. Finally, Scott gets in trouble with the police by firing a rifle into the concrete swimming pool he sees as a symbol of his unrequited love. Then, as the first signs of spring appear, Scott's "frozen state" starts to melt away. He begins to get used to the idea of the upcoming marriage and even decides privately to try out for the next play. But this change of attitude does not come in time to divert his worried father's announcement that the marriage is off and that Hilah will be leaving at the end of the school year. Scott, now frightened, goes to Hilah's apartment in an attempt to erase all the ugliness of the last year. He coerces her into riding with him to fabled DeLane County. The four-hour trip is miserable and when he finds a resident old enough to remember his mother's family, he is devastated by what the man tells him. His mother's family's house and yard were filthy, and people said chickens roosted in the family's beds. Her father was an unkind man who "wouldn't give away squash in August." Exhausted and almost too ill to walk, Scott allows Hilah to take him to a motel and call his father. Dr. Dabney comes and diagnoses a serious infection. In a trance of high fever, Scott watches his father kiss Hilah's forehead and Hilah kiss his hand. At that moment he feels something inside him let go. Two days later, as they drive home, Scott can acknowledge to himself that his mother did not come from a perfect world and that life itself cannot always be just. Later, since he can't bear to lose her entirely, he asks Hilah to come back to them, even if it means she loves his father more than she does him. In May the two are married. Scott knows he will always be jealous of his father for winning Hilah. But now at least he can accept their love and get on with his own life.

Estranged from his father and nursing an idealized vision of his dead mother, Scott transfers his affections to a theatrical young woman, a "glimmering girl" much like his mother. His despair at losing Hilah to his father is vividly conveyed, as is his horror at discovering that his feelings about his "perfect" mother have been rooted in myth. All the characters and actions are believable, but the book is primarily a study of Scott. His sexual fantasies are described, but not explicitly; however, the relationships and antics of his friends may offend some readers.

Ages 12-14

**Also available in:**
Paperbound—*Dark But Full of Diamonds*
Bantam Books, Inc.

### 389

**McCaffrey, Mary**

**My Brother Ange**

Black/white illustrations by Denise Saldutti.
Thomas Y. Crowell Company, Inc., 1982.
(86 pages)

M

REJECTION: Sibling
   Accidents: automobile
   Baby-sitting: involuntary
   Family: relationships
   Guilt, feelings of
   Sibling: older

Eleven-year-old Michael (Mick) Tooley often feels irritated with his younger brother, Angelo (Ange). He's tired of looking after Ange, tired of helping out at home, tired of his dull, gray life. He still misses Granny Mia dreadfully; things haven't been the same since she died. He tries not to think of his father either—it's been a year since he walked out and didn't come back. One day Mick's friend Leon gives him a souvenir pencil filled with sand from the Isle of Wight. In a scuffle over the pencil, Ange inadvertently knocks it out of Mick's hand and all the special sand spills out. Wild with rage and distress, Mick screams at Ange, calls him names, and tells him to get lost. When Leon tries to calm him down, Mick says the pencil incident has clinched months of frustration at Ange's following him everywhere, talking unceasingly, asking so many questions. The little boy runs off, and Mick lingers behind in spite of strict orders not to let Ange walk home alone from school in the dangerous London traffic. When he finally does head home, he hears a siren and a girl from school runs up to tell him his brother's been killed. Mick races to the scene and has to be restrained from going to Ange, who is underneath a van. A policeman tells him his brother is seriously injured, but not dead. Mick and his mother visit Ange in the hospital. He is bandaged all over except for his eyes and mouth. Mick cries and cries, telling Ange how sorry he is, what a creep he is. Ange accepts Mick's apology, saying they're both creeps. Mick promises to come back and read to Ange, vowing never to tell him to shut up again. A previously bad-tempered neighbor is the soul of comfort and hospitality during the crisis. Mick decides that if adults can change, so can kids. In the apartment that seems so empty without Ange, Mick begins to understand what his mother's lonely life must be like. He realizes that he doesn't need to fantasize anymore about Mr. Rivers, his teacher, becoming his father. When Leon gives Mick his own sand pencil, Mick decides to give it to Ange, even though he loves it himself. He goes to a church and lights candles for his brother's recovery. Walking out, he feels he is a different person.

When his clinging younger brother is seriously injured, Mick's hostility to Ange changes radically as he reconsiders his attitude toward his sibling. This simple, touching story, sparsely illustrated, does not examine the roots of Mick's antipathy toward his brother, but it may inspire some readers to reflect on their own sibling relationships. The dialogue is a bit British at times, but meaning is never obscured.

Ages 8-11

**Also available in:**
No other form known

## 390

McCord, Jean

**Turkeylegs Thompson**

Atheneum Publishers, 1979.
(242 pages)

---

BABY-SITTING: Involuntary
DEATH: of Sibling
MATURATION
REALITY, ESCAPING
   Bully
   Enuresis
   Friendship: making friends
   Guilt, feelings of
   Hostility
   Rejection: sibling
   Sibling: love for
   Stealing

---

At twelve, Betty Ann Thompson wants to hit back at the world. She is called "Turkeylegs" by her schoolmates because of her long, skinny, scabby, knock-kneed legs. Her parents have been divorced for three years and while her mother works, she must care for her two younger siblings, Brother and Laura. Turkey loves Laura but she hates seven-year-old Brother because he wets himself day and night and she must clean up after him. She had to demand that he and his bed be moved from her room because she couldn't stand the smell. Brother constantly smells and is ridiculed and ostracized by his peers. Turkey has no money, can't get anything she wants, and hungers for peace, although she has fought and beaten every boy in school. Running in the hills outside town is her chief happiness. There she meets Charlie, a little older, who also seeks solitude in the hills. Turkey and Charlie become friends, but the girl's frustrations continue. Convinced she'll never get the bike she dreams of, she steals one so she can go anywhere she wants. She takes Brother for a ride to silence him about the theft. But when she takes Laura, the little girl's foot catches in the rear wheel, tearing ligaments and tendons. A frightened, guilt-stricken Turkey heads for home, only to find the police waiting for her. She is instructed to appear in court on Monday but runs away to the hills the day before. There Charlie

convinces her to go back and face the consequences of her theft. The police give her a stern lecture but let her go. Shocked at her own behavior, Turkey tries to improve: she attends school regularly, stops fighting, and plants a garden. But disturbing events keep happening. When she takes Brother and Laura to a museum, a man exposes himself to them. One day when she goes to the hills looking for Charlie, she falls asleep and returns home very late. Her mother and the father she barely remembers are there, the father upset, her mother weeping: Laura, who has been sick for days, is gravely ill. When Laura dies, Turkey withdraws from the world. Her reunited parents try to help by getting her a dog but it runs away, terrified of her. They buy her a bike, but she runs it into a car. One day she walks out and away from school, heading for the hills to "muse backwards into the time when things had been whole in her life and had made some sense in her life." She stays too late and spends the night in a cave. Next morning Charlie finds her and convinces her that, like it or not, she must live in the world. Reluctantly, Turkey leaves the hills and crosses the bridge to find her way back.

A young girl receives a vivid, premature, and painful initiation into adult life. A truant and underachiever at school, an unhappy baby-sitter at home, a child of divorce, a rebel and a fighter, Turkey manages to bounce back from theft, guilt, and the loss of a beloved sister. Although she has been hurt, she will resume the struggle of living. Tough, kind, and brave, Turkey excites sympathy, and her experiences shed light on maturation. The book's length and the complexities of the plot require a mature reader. Some slang and profanity color the dialogue.

Ages 11-14

**Also available in:**
Cassette—Turkeylegs Thompson
Library of Congress (NLSBPH)

## 391

McDonnell, Christine

**Don't Be Mad, Ivy**

Black/white illustrations by Diane de Groat.
The Dial Press, Inc., 1981.
(77 pages)

---

PEER RELATIONSHIPS
   Play
   Problem solving
   Sharing/Not Sharing

---

Ivy Adams, about five, is invited to her friend Bill's birthday party, and she buys him a toy bulldozer. At the party, she wins a game and receives a prize of three little trucks. Later, Bill confesses to her that he really wanted the three trucks. Ivy confesses she really wanted the bulldozer. They laugh and agree to share their toys the next day. At school, when she finishes her work, Ivy plays quietly with Noah's ark. Soon Leo joins her and they put the ark in water, having so much fun that they become noisy and splash water. Their teacher reprimands them and they must miss recess to clean up. Ivy is angry at Leo, but soon forgives him and asks him to play with her again. One hot day, Ivy notices the new neighbor children playing in their pool. She wants to join them, but is too shy to ask. Instead she tries to get their attention by pretending to swim and dive, pouring water on her head, and putting on a sea monster beach toy. The children do not notice her. Finally Ivy holds the hose on her head and then the children do notice. They ask Ivy to join them and she happily agrees. While playing at Phyllis's house one day, Ivy spots a small, fuzzy bear she wants so badly that she sneaks it home. Soon she begins feeling guilty and calls Phyllis, confessing what she did. Phyllis tells Ivy she can borrow the bear for a while, to Ivy's great relief. One day after school Ivy, Bill, and Phyllis decide to go to the park and slide on the icy hill. They have a wonderful time. Then Leo and his older friend Bulldog persuade them to go to dangerous Snake Hill to slide. The children go reluctantly and when Bulldog crashes, they return to the park and continue to enjoy themselves. Christmas Eve finds Ivy's family decorating the tree. The little girl is so excited she can hardly sleep that night. The next morning a delighted Ivy finds the beautiful tree all lit up and a new blue bicycle just for her.

Six humorous episodes explore the world of an adventurous little girl. Young readers will like the lively heroine. Expressive pencil sketches make Ivy's world vivid.

Ages 7-8

**Also available in:**
Paperbound—*Don't Be Mad, Ivy*
Bantam Books, Inc.

## 392

McKay, Robert W.

## The Running Back

Harcourt Brace Jovanovich, Inc., 1979.
(146 pages)

*BELONGING*
*SELF, ATTITUDE TOWARD: Feeling Different*
  *Blame*
  *Boy-girl relationships: dating*
  *Delinquency, juvenile*
  *Reputation*
  *School: classmate relationships*
  *Sports/Sportsmanship*

Jack Delaney is about to start his senior year at a new school in a new home with his aunt and uncle, but he can't forget his troubled past. Jack's mother abandoned him when he was an infant and his alcoholic father is dead. The boy has been a gang member and a reform-school inmate. Now, although he loves football and is a natural athlete, he hesitates to go out for the team. When he finally does he immediately clashes with Peanuts Gilliam, the running back he replaces in the first game. Since he always expects animosity, Jack is surprised when Benny, the quarterback, invites him to a party after the game. There he meets Cindy Farr, a student at a girls' school in another city, whom he immediately likes. Before the next game, one of Jack's teammates warns him that Peanuts's buddies will probably miss

some blocks for him when he's carrying the ball. It seems that Peanuts, son of the wealthiest man in town, views Jack as a threat, particularly since Jack has been befriended by Lori, Peanuts's former girlfriend. The first half of the game goes as predicted; Jack cannot make any yardage. In the locker room at halftime the coach angrily gives the players an ultimatum: either they play as a team or they get out. Nearly half the team, Peanuts included, leaves. The coach quickly patches together a new team, with barely enough players for substitutions. Despite the loss of manpower, they play their hearts out and win. Afterwards, Jack feels he's a real team member at last. From then on, he concentrates so completely on adjusting to life with his aunt and uncle, playing the best football he can, and thinking about Cindy, who has let him know she likes him, that he pays little attention to anything else until Lori tells him the school has been broken into and he's being framed. Money was taken from the office, and Jack's cap, lost several days before, was found there. Although the police chief decides the hat is not proof enough and lets him go, Jack feels accused, a perpetual suspect. He dreads facing his aunt and uncle and is surprised when they defend him. At school he pretends not to care what others think, but when he learns Cindy may not be able to get to town for the coming weekend, he fears she's embarrassed to be seen with him. So when Lori asks him to a drive-in movie that Saturday, he accepts. Before the Saturday game, he learns that Cindy will be coming to town after all. Soon after his date with Lori, to whom he confides his tensions about the break-in, Jack decides to find out the truth. He confronts Peanuts and together they discover what happened: one of Peanuts's buddies framed Jack. Peanuts and Jack, driving around together and talking, find they have much in common and they part friends. Jack then goes to see Cindy, but she has heard of his date with Lori and will not talk to him. In the days before the final football game, days in which Peanuts and Jack cement their friendship and the team struggles to perfect a new game plan, Jack tries unsuccessfully to talk with Cindy. At halftime, Cindy tells him that his friends Peanuts and Lori have explained everything to her. She apologizes for the way she has acted.

In this story of self-acceptance, a young man cannot forgive and forget his own past mistakes and willingly assumes the role of outcast. Only when he decides to stand up for himself, to face his rival honestly and defend his innocence, is Jack able to think well of himself. A secondary theme concerns the necessity of making one's own judgments of people, based on real knowledge. The heavy emphasis on football, coupled with a fast-paced plot, make this a good choice for reluctant readers. Though less than outstanding, its contemporary themes will appeal to readers of both sexes and may encourage them to contemplate some of the issues presented.

Ages 12-14

**Also available in:**
No other form known

M

**393**

MacLachlan, Patricia

## Arthur, for the Very First Time

Black/white illustrations by Lloyd Bloom.
Harper & Row, Publishers, Inc., 1980.
(117 pages)

---

SIBLING: New Baby
  Differences, human
  Identity, search for
  Reality, escaping
  Relatives: living in home of

---

The summer that Arthur Rasby is ten years old, he's sure his mother is going to have a baby, but isn't sure he likes the idea. Because his mother isn't feeling well and he has no friends nearby, Arthur is sent to spend the summer with Great-Aunt Elda and Great-Uncle Wrisby. They live in a huge, rambling old house with a pet chicken, Pauline, who responds only to French. Great-Uncle Wrisby sings to the pig, Bernadette, and Arthur feels that his relatives are "scatty." But he does come to love Pauline and believes she is much nicer than a baby would be. Moira MacAvin, the veterinarian's granddaughter, insists on calling Arthur Mouse. She tells him that her parents have abandoned her. Arthur feels abandoned too and hasn't opened any of his parents' letters. Moira accuses Arthur of writing about things in his journal instead of experiencing them. She says he's like their social worker who comes to ask "meaningful" questions, writes in her notebook, and then does nothing about any of it. Since Bernadette will be giving birth in a few weeks, Moira lends Arthur a book about birthing sows. But when Arthur tries to tell Wrisby about the precautions they must take, Wrisby doesn't want his advice. Elda explains Wrisby's belief that if he doesn't think about bad things, they won't happen. Then Arthur and Moira decide Pauline looks sickly, so they dose her with Great-Uncle Wrisby's "tonic" while he and Elda are in town. In the course of tasting this brew, Moira, Arthur, and Pauline get drunk and reach Moira's house just as the social worker does. Moira's grandfather spanks her, proving to her that he really does love her. The social worker decides that Moira can stay with her grandfather instead of being put in a foster home. Following this, Arthur reads all twelve of his parents' letters. In one of them, his mother mentions that everything takes time. When Arthur tells Moira about the letters, she says his parents sound nice. He agrees. Bernadette starts to have her babies during a storm while Wrisby and Elda are in town. Moira and Arthur find her in the new pen Arthur built for the birthing, and they help until Wrisby comes home. Moira congratulates Arthur on really doing something at last, calling him Arthur instead of Mouse for the very first time.

Spending the summer with his whimsically unconventional great-aunt and great-uncle, a young boy slowly comes to terms with the fact that he will soon have a sibling. From being an observer of life, Arthur becomes a participant. In the process, he begins to know and accept himself and others. In the future he'll be more confident, better able to cope with life's uncertainties. Softly shaded illustrations capture the story's mood.

Ages 8-10

**Also available in:**
Cassette—*Arthur, for the Very First Time*
Library of Congress (NLSBPH)

Filmstrip—*Arthur, for the Very First Time*
Pied Piper Productions

Paperbound—*Arthur, for the Very First Time*
Scholastic Book Services

**394**

MacLachlan, Patricia

## Cassie Binegar

Harper & Row, Publishers, Inc., 1982.
(120 pages)

---

CHANGE: Accepting
PRIVACY, NEED FOR
  Belonging
  Change: new home
  Differences, human
  Family: extended
  Family: relationships
  Guilt, feelings of

---

Cassie Binegar, about eleven, and her family have moved to an old house near the shore. Now her father and brothers can be closer to their fishing boat, and their mother can rent out the little cottages surrounding the house. But Cassie misses her old tree house and feels she now has no private space. She tries making a place for herself in the attic, but is moved out when more storage space is needed. For a while a closet under the stairs seems like a good place, but her father and brothers need it for their gear. Cassie feels so different from her casual, rough family that she's sure she must have been adopted. She likes her new friend's family because they are more formal and unchanging, but Margaret Mary is intrigued by Cassie's relatives and wishes she had some unusual family members. Cassie's Uncle Hat, who even wears a hat to bed, speaks in rhymes; Cousin Coralinda wears a feathered cape and other miscellaneous feathered items. One day Gran comes to visit, followed by Uncle Hat, Cousin Coralinda, and Baby Binnie. Guilty Cassie isn't sure she wants to see Gran; just before her grandfather died Cassie had yelled at him, and she's sure that if she had just apologized, he would be alive today. Gran brings a beautiful tablecloth for the dining room table; it extends to the floor and makes a wonderful hiding place for Cassie. Underneath the table she overhears talk about Cousin Coralinda's husband, who has left her and Baby Binnie. She also hears "the writer" when he comes in to rent a cottage. Cassie falls in love with him and talks to him about her space problem. He says we all carry around our own private space. Gran tells Cassie that the hermit crab changes its space many times, that different kinds of spaces can shelter a person. Cassie begins to feel that perhaps she does have a space of her own after all. She talks to Gran about the time she yelled at her grandfather. Gran explains that Papa died because he was sick, and that he used to yell too. In fact, just before he died he sat up in bed and yelled, "Where in hell are my green socks!" Gran tells Cassie she has to let her guilt go. "The writer" and Cousin Coralinda begin spending a lot of time together. When they marry, Cassie is maid of honor and wears a dress worn by her mother and grandmother at their weddings.

In this rather low-key but delightful book, Cassie, "who wishes that things never changed," learns that things can change and still remain the same. When she wonders if Gran has changed after her husband's death, Cassie's mother explains that Gran is still the same person even though her life has taken on new patterns. Margaret Mary helps Cassie see that what may look static and secure on the outside can actually be very different on the inside. She provides counterpoint for Cassie's feelings; when Margaret Mary delights in the changing images in a kaleidoscope, Cassie wants to pick one picture and keep it the same always. Cassie is ashamed of her family, whom she considers odd, but begins to change her mind when Margaret Mary insists they are all "splendid."

Ages 9-12

**Also available in:**
No other form known

## 395

MacLachlan, Patricia

### Mama One, Mama Two

Color illustrations by Ruth Lercher Bornstein.
Harper & Row, Publishers, Inc., 1982.
(30 pages counted)

---

*FOSTER HOME*
*PARENT/PARENTS: Substitute*
  *Mental illness: of parent*

---

Young Maudie is awakened in the middle of the night by the baby's cries and goes to his room. Soon Katherine appears with the baby's bottle and lets Maudie feed him. Then Katherine comes to sit on Maudie's bed and together they tell the story of "Mama One, Mama Two," which Maudie has again requested. Maudie begins and tells about a girl and her mother, Mama One, and how happy they were together. Mama One painted bright pictures of trees and sunsets. But then, continues Katherine, Mama One became unhappy and did not know why. She painted dark pictures and did not cook or clean. The girl did all the chores, says Maudie. Mama One stayed in her room and the girl was lonely without her. Mama One asked a social worker for help—"Tom, who listens." He took Mama One to a place where she could talk about being sad and find out what it was that made her sad. Tom told the girl it was not her fault that Mama One was unhappy. Then he described a special place where she could live for a while with someone who had helped other children and knew all about Mama One. The girl was afraid but she packed her things, including her blue quilt, and got in the car with Tom, wondering if she'd have a night-light in her new home. Maudie tells about how Tom spotted a bluebird and stopped his car. He told the girl the bird was going south but would be back in the spring, and maybe

Mama One would also. At her new home the girl helped Mama Two with the baby, learned to make pancakes, and made new friends. When Maudie and Katherine finish the story, Katherine puts the sleeping baby in his crib and comes back to sleep with Maudie awhile. Then Maudie—the girl—and Katherine—Mama Two—talk about when spring will come. "Whenever Mama One comes home will be spring," says Katherine. Then they sleep under Maudie's blue quilt.

This gentle story-within-a-story reassures a little girl in a foster home about the eventual return of her mentally ill mother. Even more, it demonstrates the depth of love and understanding of the foster mother who willingly accepts the role of second mother so urgently required by the child. Significantly, little Maudie indicates by her part of the "Mama One, Mama Two" story that she realizes her need for help and recognizes how her life has improved since coming to her foster home. Pastel illustrations emphasize the caring, soothing tone of the book, which could be very helpful in preparing a child for a foster home.

Ages 4-7

**Also available in:**
No other form known

M

## 396

MacLachlan, Patricia

### The Sick Day

Color illustrations by William Pène Du Bois.
Pantheon Books, 1979.
(29 pages counted)

---

*ILLNESSES: Being Ill*
  *Love, meaning of*

---

Dragging Frederick, her blanket, into her father's writing room, little Emily says her head, stomach, and toe hurt. Put to bed, she asks for Moosie, a lost stuffed animal. While looking for Moosie and a thermometer, her father finds her rubber bands and he puts her hair into three ponytails, the one on top making her look like a fountain. When Emily says she may have to "swallow up," he bends down and talks her stomach out of it. Emily says she feels like a sandwich, and her father makes her laugh by saying she doesn't look like a sandwich. When she asks if she is going to die, he says she is going to read instead. She complains that she has read all her books, so he invents a story for her. Then he makes her some broth and draws a picture of a "gentle monster" to chase her sickness away. Emily smiles and says it is fun being sick with him. The next day Emily is better, but her father is sick. Her mother stays home from work and Emily sings to her father, draws him a picture, and finds beneath his bed the missing thermometer and Moosie.

The care and attention of a loving father inject happiness into Emily's day of sickness. Young readers and listeners will be cheered by the father's reassurance and charmed by the clever dialogue and illustrations. Emily's care for her father the next day is a satisfying turn of events.

**Also available in:**
No other form known

## 397

**MacLachlan, Patricia**

**Through Grandpa's Eyes**

Color illustrations by Deborah Ray.
Harper & Row, Publishers, Inc., 1979.
(40 pages counted)

---

*BLINDNESS*
*GRANDPARENT: Love for*

---

Young John loves his grandpa's house. It isn't big or shiny-new like some houses he's seen. But John likes to go there because he can see the house through his grandpa's eyes. His grandpa is blind, but he still has a very special way of seeing and he helps John see this way too. Grandpa gets up when the touch of the sun warms him awake. He can smell the fried eggs and buttered toast Nana has fixed for breakfast and can even sense the fresh bouquet of marigolds in the kitchen. For John the smells are all mixed together until he closes his eyes and concentrates on distinguishing them. Grandpa and John play their cellos together. John uses written music, but Grandpa can play because the notes "are in his fingers." When Nana makes a clay sculpture of Grandpa's head, Grandpa can tell it's a good likeness just by running his fingers over it. When John pretends his fingers are water flowing down the clay head and filling all the spaces, he discovers the head does look like Grandpa. Grandpa sees some things through his memory. When he and his grandson walk across the field, he sees in his mind how the sun shines on the river and how the Queen Anne's lace looks in the meadow. Grandpa tells which direction the wind is coming from by "the feel of the meadow grasses and by the way his hair blows against his face." He can identify birds by their sounds. Grandpa smells lunch when it's ready and feels if John has washed the dishes clean enough to dry and put away. He reads Braille and listens to television. Of course, sometimes Grandpa makes mistakes and needs a little help. But it still seems to John a very special thing to use ears, hands, and nose as Grandpa does. When Nana says goodnight, John can hear the "smile" in her voice. Grandpa always says her voice smiles to him, and John can see it too—if he looks through Grandpa's eyes.

The quiet, gentle tone of this book reflects the loving relationship between John and his grandparents. Young readers may become more aware of their senses and of the extra dimension of experience that can come from using each sense more carefully. They may also gain an appreciation for and understanding of the ways blind people can "see" their world. Delicate, subdued pictures add to the feeling that the reader too has had a chance to look through Grandpa's eyes.

Ages 5-8

**Also available in:**
Paperbound—*Through Grandpa's Eyes*
Harper & Row, Publishers, Inc.

## 398

**McLendon, Gloria Houston**

**My Brother Joey Died**

Black/white photographs by Harvey Kelman.
Julian Messner, Inc., 1982.
(64 pages)

---

*DEATH: of Sibling*
*Family: relationships*
*Loss: feelings of*
*Mourning, stages of*

---

When her older brother, Joey, teases her as she leaves for school, his sister decides he's not so sick after all and yells to him that she hopes she never sees him again. When she comes home from school her grandparents tell her Joey's been hospitalized with Reye's Syndrome, a complication of a virus he probably caught from his sister. She wants to call Joey and tell him she didn't mean what she said when she left that morning, but he's too sick to come to the telephone. He dies during the night. The girl is at first numb and then runs out of the house. Grandpa finds her in a nearby park and holds her close. In the next few days she must endure bewildering remarks by visitors ("the good die young," "God needed Joey"), her parents' grief, and her own feelings of guilt, loneliness, anger, and confusion. Grandma assures her that wishes and angry feelings cannot make a person die. The girl sees her father sitting on Joey's bed and crying, but she doesn't go to him because he has told her men shouldn't cry and she hates to embarrass him. At the funeral home, she looks for a long time at Joey in his coffin. She doesn't want to leave him alone in the cemetery, but Grandpa gently takes her away. Afterwards, she watches Joey's favorite TV program and, although it doesn't seem funny, she laughs. Her father scolds her, saying she's upsetting her mother. But she keeps laughing all the way to her room, where she starts to cry. That night, when she wakes up from a dream about Joey, Grandma comforts her. The girl used to like school, but now she hates it. Her friends seem to be avoiding her. She carries around a picture of her family—all four of them—and pretends that Joey will soon come home from camp. She thinks about running away. One day the school counselor invites her to join a support group of students who have lost someone they loved. After some hesitation, she goes to the meeting and listens to the others share their experiences. The counselor explains the importance of getting feelings out in the open. The girl learns that "crying is a natural reaction to pain" and that adults sometimes don't tell children the truth about death; they may want to protect children or they may have difficulty dealing with their own emotions. One day the girl tells the group that her parents don't love her anymore. Another child says she used to feel that way too, but things change. The girl tells her grandmother what she told the group: her grandmother explains that her parents do love her but their own pain is so great they sometimes forget hers. Eventually, the girl and her parents join a support group together, and their relationship improves. It's now a year since Joey died and his sister still feels sad and lonely sometimes. But she doesn't feel guilty anymore and is able to share things with her parents. She knows that she has survived the very worst thing that could happen, losing someone she loved. She feels brave and strong. Joey would be proud of her.

A young girl gives a first-person account of her adjustment to her older brother's death. Most of the feelings experienced by a grieving child are included in this moving, well-written story. The photographs are realistic, affecting, and appropriate. The book should offer enormous comfort and help to bereaved children as well as inspire insight and compassion in their friends. The value of support groups and professional counseling is clearly stated; the address of a national support group for bereaved parents and children is provided.

Ages 9-11

**Also available in:**
No other form known

## 399

McPhail, David Michael

**A Wolf Story**

Color illustrations by the author.
Charles Scribner's Sons, 1981.
(30 pages counted)

---

ANIMALS: Love for
NATURE: Respect for
    Freedom, meaning of

---

A timber wolf lives in the North Woods. He is a good hunter and knows how to take care of himself. Then one day some men come looking for a wolf to use in a movie. They capture him, take him to their movie set, and chain him to a post. But since the moviemakers want to show the wolf dressed in a man's clothing, they must unchain him in order to get his costume on. As they are trying to button a coat around him, he breaks loose and jumps over the high iron fence to freedom. The police and "soldiers" are called in, and soon many people are chasing the wolf. He runs all day and his feet become sore. At one point he passes a school bus, and the children open the windows and lean out to cheer him on. In the late afternoon the wolf sees a brook and goes to get a drink of water. Instantly he is surrounded by men with guns. Then a good sound reaches the wolf's ears, the sound of the children's voices that had cheered him earlier in the day. The children stream through the circle of guns "holding hands and daring the men to shoot." "Let the wolf go home!" they shout. They stand guard over the wolf, giving him water from their hats, until several government officials arrive. The officials talk to the police and to the children, deciding that the children are right and the wolf should be returned to his home in the woods. In their happiness, the children dance around the wolf and sing:

The Timber Wolf is going home
    Going home
    Going home.
The Timber Wolf is going home
    The Timber Wolf
    Is free!

This unusual story is based on an actual event in London that was observed and memorialized in a song by the author's friend. The wolf's life is endangered by people who don't respect his right to live freely. He is championed by a group of children who persuade the officials to return him to his home in the woods. The story, despite its grounding in truth, has the poetic feel of a legend, giving it added richness. The fact that the animal is a timber wolf, a feared creature threatened with extinction, gives it power. Expressive illustrations capture the plight of the animal and the kindness of the children.

Ages 5-7

**Also available in:**
No other form known

## 400

Madler, Trudy

**Why Did Grandma Die?**

Color illustrations by Gwen Connelly.
Raintree Publishers, Inc., 1980.
(31 pages)

---

DEATH: of Grandparent
    Death: funeral issues
    Family: unity
    Grandparent: love for

---

Young Heidi arrives home from school eager to go with her grandmother to the park for a pony ride. But her grandmother is lying down and promises to take her the next day. Instead, Heidi and her grandmother make horses out of clay. The next day when she comes home from school, Heidi sees her grandmother on a stretcher that is being placed in an ambulance. Heidi's mother explains that her grandmother is sick and is going to the hospital. Mrs. Kane, a neighbor, watches Heidi and her younger brother while her parents are at the hospital. The next morning Heidi's mother comes home and sadly tells her that her grandmother has died. "Death is a natural part of life," she explains. "Your grandma had a long and good life." That day the family stays home and everyone is sad. Heidi decides that if she wishes hard enough, maybe her grandmother will come back. But it doesn't work. She notices her father has also been crying, and the two of them talk about her grandmother. Heidi tells him of her distress over not getting to say goodbye. Her father reassures her: her grandmother knew Heidi loved her. At the funeral Heidi stares at her grandmother's body and says goodbye. Back at the apartment, Mrs. Kane tells Heidi she will now be her baby-sitter after school, but Heidi only wants her grandmother. The little girl and her father go for a walk in the park. There they talk about the grandmother's death and their fond memories of her. Heidi realizes that part of her grandmother will always be with her. She goes back to the apartment to apologize to Mrs. Kane and to water her grandmother's flowers.

A little girl struggles to accept her grandmother's death, coming to realize the value of her loving memories. Bright, detailed illustrations help convey the story, and the picture of the grandmother in her open casket could help prepare children for a funeral. The book handles a difficult subject tastefully.

Ages 4-9

**Also available in:**
No other form known

## 401

**Magorian, Michelle**

**Good Night, Mr. Tom**

Harper & Row, Publishers, Inc., 1981.
(318 pages)

---

*CHILD ABUSE*
*DEPRIVATION, EMOTIONAL*
*LOVE, MEANING OF*
*WAR*
  Death: of friend
  *Friendship: making friends*
  *Friendship: meaning of*
  Orphan
  *Talents: artistic*

---

Just prior to the Second World War, eight-year-old William Beech, pale, weak, and scared, is evacuated from London and sent to live in the town of Little Weirwold with irritable, crusty Thomas Oakley, a widower in his sixties who has decided to do his part for the war effort. Will knows he's a bad boy because Mum often tells him so. A religious fanatic for whom virtually everything is "evil," she even sends along a belt with instructions to whoever gets Will to watch him all the time. When the boy arrives, Tom discovers bruises and sores all over his arms and legs. Will can't read, he sleeps under the bed, and, when persuaded to sleep in it, wets the bed nightly. He suffers from malnutrition, can't keep more than a small amount of food in his stomach, and looks like a waif. Tom buys Will some clothes and boots; even, when Will displays some uncharacteristic interest in them, some paints and brushes. Tom hasn't been near the art supply store since his young wife, Rachel, died over forty years before. Nine-year-old Zacharias Wrench, as energetic and effervescent as Will is quiet, also an evacuee, befriends Will. Will is embarrassed to be placed in a class with younger children because he can't read, but he works industriously at his schoolwork and makes progress. On his ninth birthday he receives many gifts and cards, and Tom has a surprise party for him. He hardly knows how to react: he's never had a present or friends or praise. Meanwhile, his mother writes to repeat over and over that he is bad and that Tom must watch him all the time. After two months with Tom, Will keeps the sheets dry at night, his last sore is healing, and he's making progress in school. Tom himself is changing, coming out of himself into life again. With Will Tom is patient, caring, reassuring. He changes the bed daily without reprimand, takes the boy to the library, reads aloud to him every night. The villagers are delighted and amazed, even more so when Tom joins them more actively in the war effort. In March, Will's mother writes that she is ill and wants her son back for a while. For Will, being back with his mother is like drifting into a nightmare. He finds a baby in their apartment with her little mouth taped shut. When Will questions his mother, she beats him senseless. A month later, when Tom still hasn't heard from Will, he goes to London to investigate. He and a warden find the boy chained to a pipe in a closed alcove, clutching his dead sister's tiny body and nearly dead himself. Will is taken to a hospital, and Tom discovers that the authorities plan to put him in a children's home. Desperate, he kidnaps the sedated boy, wraps him warmly, and takes him back to Little Weirwold. He and Zach nurse Will through weeks of nightmares and fever. When he's better, Will, Tom, and Zach have a happy seaside holiday together. Back home, Will meets Geoffrey Sanderton, an established artist, who begins giving the boy lessons when he sees how talented he is. Authorities from London bring news that Will's mother has committed suicide. They still want to take Will to a children's home, but Tom finds a way to start adoption proceedings instead. The day before Will's tenth birthday, Zach's father is badly wounded in a London air raid and Zach goes to London to see him in spite of his mother's warnings. He is killed in the London bombings. For four months Will is inconsolable. Then Geoffrey tells him about a dead friend of his and how he feels better when he smokes his friend's pipe. Will repairs and learns to ride Zach's old bike, and he begins to heal. He sees that even without Zach it's good to be alive, especially living in Little Weirwold with his "dad."

A young victim of an unbalanced, murderously abusive mother finds a loving home with a reclusive widower in a small English town. In discovering a world he never knew existed, Will also discovers his own artistic talents and begins to emerge as a complete human being. The mutual love and need of the boy and the man are movingly described. Richly detailed, engrossing, and appealing, this story of rural England during World War II illuminates daily life in a small, generous community. The country dialect is easily understood and adds authenticity.

Ages 11 and up

**Also available in:**
Cassette—*Good Night, Mr. Tom*
Library of Congress (NLSBPH)

## 402

**Marangell, Virginia J.**

**Gianna Mia**

Dodd, Mead & Company, Inc., 1979.
(224 pages) o.p.

---

*FAMILY: Unity*
*MATURATION*
  *Change: accepting*
  *Change: resisting*
  *Death: of sibling*
  *Family: extended*
  *Immigrants*
  *Italian-American*
  *Love, meaning of*
  *Religion: faith*
  *Roman Catholic*

---

Life in 1937 for twelve-year-old Gianna Dellesanto is filled with love and a strong sense of family ties. Her Italian immigrant parents work long hours and struggle to make ends meet. But Gianna believes her mother when she tells her, "As long as you have your family to love you, and your religion to believe in, then you will always be all right." Gianna is the youngest of six children. She dreams of becoming an archaeologist and is encouraged in that dream by her adored oldest brother, Eddy. Then World War II intervenes. Eddy quits college to enlist in the Air Force. Gianna, now seventeen, and her sister Annamarie work after school in a bookstore. One afternoon while at home, Gianna answers the door to a Western Union man who gives her a telegram stating that Eddy has been killed in action. Gianna's parents are grief-stricken; the girl herself is devastated. She begins questioning God and is tormented by religious doubt. Several weeks later, after she herself has narrowly escaped death in a freak accident, she comes to grips with her sorrow and confusion, accepting Eddy's death as part of God's plan. She then tries to help her father, who still cannot accept the loss. Over the next few years the family slowly grows apart. An older brother marries and moves away. Another enters the priesthood. A sister marries and soon has a baby. Annamarie causes a family crisis and heartbreak by breaking her engagement to a local boy stationed overseas and instead marrying a Protestant missionary. Because Annamarie's husband is not Catholic, her father refuses to acknowledge his daughter or the marriage. Gianna watches sadly as family ties continue to unravel. Ten years after Annamarie's marriage, the family reunites for the first time. Gianna is now twenty-eight, an archaeologist engaged to another archaeologist. All the Dellesanto children are succeeding in their chosen careers, many have their own children, and Gianna's parents relish their roles as grandparents. Gianna reflects on the happiness surrounding her and prays that this new generation of children will grow up with the same family closeness she once cherished.

The reader shares three stages of Gianna's life—as a young schoolgirl, a high school student during World War II, and a woman returning home for a family reunion—in this warm story of family relationships. Gianna's love for her parents and their traditions conflicts at times with the changes going on around her, both outside the family and within. But Gianna is shown holding onto her dreams and pursuing her goals. The story is enriched by descriptions of Italian customs and by the color of Gianna's Italian community.

Ages 12-15

**Also available in:**
No other form known

## 403

**Marino, Barbara Pavis**

### Eric Needs Stitches

Black/white photographs by Richard Rudinski.
Addison-Wesley Publishing Company, Inc., 1979.
(32 pages)

*HOSPITAL, GOING TO*
*SUTURES*
 *Accidents*

When young Eric has an accident on his bicycle, his father says he needs stitches in his knee. On the way to the hospital, a frightened Eric wants to know what will

happen and if his father will stay with him. His father reassures him, saying he'll stay with Eric if it's all right with the doctor. He explains the procedure for anesthetizing the area and then stitching it, telling Eric why it's important to have some wounds stitched. When Eric tells the emergency-room nurse he's scared and might cry, she says it's okay to cry if it hurts, as long as he holds his leg still. When the doctor joins them he too is reassuring, explaining what he is doing as he proceeds to treat Eric's cut. After the knee is numb, the doctor stitches it up. He congratulates Eric for being such a good patient. The nurse wraps Eric's knee and gives him instructions for keeping it clean and dry so it won't become infected. On the way home, Eric's father takes him for a double-scoop ice-cream cone.

A young boy visits a hospital emergency room to have his knee stitched. Realistic, informative photographs and a simple, candid text give readers a good idea of exactly what's involved in this kind of injury. A note from the author, herself an emergency-room nurse, reports that children who are prepared psychologically for emergency-room care are usually less traumatized and more cooperative than other children. This book is written to help provide good preparation.

Ages 4-10

**Also available in:**
No other form known

**M**

## 404

**Marney, Dean**

### Just Good Friends

Addison-Wesley Publishing Company, Inc., 1982.
(90 pages)

*FRIENDSHIP: Best Friend*
 *Boy-girl relationships*
 *Gender role identity: female*
 *Gender role identity: male*
 *Puberty*
 *School: classmate relationships*
 *Sports/Sportsmanship*

Boyd, about to enter junior high, has two major problems: he has no body hair yet and his two best friends are girls. He wonders what the locker-room crowd will think of him. His friend Marcia is pretty, thin, and long-haired. Lou (for Louella) is overweight with very short hair. She lifts weights, wrestles, and is skilled in self-defense. The three of them tell each other all their "deep dark secrets." Boyd never finds it as easy to talk to boys. Lou talks Boyd into going out for the soccer team with her. Before school starts that fall, he and she practice soccer basics together. Marcia joins them for jogging every morning. The first day of school, when Boyd stops by for Lou, she's wearing a dress. They both agree she's better off in her usual jeans and T-shirt, despite her mother's fervent desire for her to look and act like a lady. Then Jack the Jerk asks Marcia to the dance Saturday night. She refuses, saying she's going with Boyd and Lou. But Boyd's feelings of jealousy make him realize he's beginning to think of Marcia as more than just a friend. He wonders what such a development would do to their threesome. But now, for his first date, he's going to the dance with two girls. Jack the Jerk, Lou, and Boyd are all to be starters in the soccer game. At practice, Jack trips Lou and so Boyd punches Jack, leading Jack to say later that he didn't think Boyd had it in him. Boyd finds it difficult to think of himself as a man who depends on violence. At the first practice, Lou scores the only goal for either side and the coach makes her the captain for the first game. Marcia kisses Boyd, and he likes it. Lou reports that Jack has asked her to the dance and so Marcia and Boyd can go by themselves, but she warns that after this one separation they'll revert to being a threesome. At the dance Marcia and Boyd see Jack but not Lou, and she's not at home when they call. Much later Lou arrives, all disheveled. It seems Jack and an older buddy of his drove her eight miles into the country and then made her get out. Her mother had been thrilled about her first date and Lou, thinking someone actually liked her, had gotten all dressed up. Now she's humiliated and bewildered. Marcia and Boyd comfort her, but Boyd is depressed. Why is it so difficult being male or female? He looks in the mirror and decides he needs a shave.

A young boy's concern about what manliness means is explored in this sensitive, easy-to-read story. Boyd finds no real answers, and he hurts for his "boyish" friend Lou when she is cruelly humiliated; his engaging first-person narrative affirms his loyalty to himself and his friends. Readers may feel comforted to know they are not alone in having doubts about their masculinity or femininity, nor in being concerned about the relative speed or slowness of their physical development. They will also thoroughly like these characters.

Ages 11-13

**Also available in:**
No other form known

## 405

**Marshall, Lydia**

### Nobody Likes to Lose

Color photographs by Eric Oxendorf.
Children's Press, Inc., 1980.
(31 pages)

---

*SPORTS/SPORTSMANSHIP*
*Competition*

---

Even though seven-year-old Sandy is convinced she will lose her swimming match, she swims hard in the race. She does finish last, but her time is her fastest ever. Emily, her nine-year-old friend and teammate, congratulates Sandy on bettering her time. Sandy shouldn't expect to beat girls who are almost nine years old, says Emily. Then Emily's event is announced, but a very disappointed Sandy doesn't even wish her luck. Instead she reflects on all the trophies and medals Emily has won. This time Sandy thinks Emily may lose because she too is racing against older girls. As it turns out, Emily does come in last. But she is happy because she bettered her time and did her best. There are two kinds of winning, Emily believes, "winning against yourself and winning against others." You can't usually win both ways, but "you don't ever really lose if you win against yourself." Sandy feels better and smiles when she hears

her next event announced. She tells Emily, "Maybe I won't win in one way, but if I don't, I think I'll win in another."

With the help of a friend, a girl learns the meaning of winning and being a good sport. An easy reader, this book uses action-filled photographs to help tell the story. The simple concept and ease of resolution may seem contrived, but are in keeping with the intended audience and could be used to promote discussion.

Ages 7-9

**Also available in:**
Paperbound—*Nobody Likes to Lose*
Children's Press, Inc.

## 406

**Maruki, Toshi**

### Hiroshima No Pika

Translated from the Japanese by Komine Shoten.
Color illustrations by the author.
Lothrop, Lee & Shepard Company, 1980.
(47 pages counted)

---

*WAR*
*Death*
*Japan*
*Violence*

---

On August 6, 1945, at 8:15 in the morning, seven-year-old Mii is eating breakfast with her parents in their Hiroshima home. Suddenly a terrible light, ever after known as the Flash, surrounds them. It is followed by shock waves, collapsing buildings, and violent flames. The United States has dropped its top-secret explosive, known as "Little Boy" by the crew of the plane that dropped it, on the city. Mii's father is caught in the flames but his wife rescues him somehow, lifts him onto her back, and sets off with him and Mii to reach the safety of the river. They join crowds of people with clothes burned away, swollen faces, weak voices. Many just drop where they are. Mii sees terrible, horrifying sights: a dead man floating down the river followed by a dead cat; a woman whose baby won't nurse because it's dead, whereupon she wades out into the river and out of sight; hundreds of dead and wounded people. They run through the burning, collapsing city and cross the river. On the beach outside Hiroshima they lie sleeping or dazed, shocked to learn that four days have passed. An old woman sits up, gives Mii a rice ball, and lies down, never to move again. Mii's father is left in a hospital that is little more than shelter—no doctors, medicine, or bandages—while Mii and her mother return to the wasteland that was their city. Since the day the bomb was dropped, Mii stopped growing. Her mother still must remove bits of glass embedded in Mii's skull that eventually work their way out. Her father recovered from the injuries suffered that day, but several months later his hair fell out, he began coughing blood, purple spots appeared on his body, and he died. Many other people later fell ill with this incurable radiation sickness. Some are still in hospitals. Every year on August 6, people from Hiroshima commemorate their dead. They set lighted lanterns afloat on Hiroshima's seven rivers, each with the name of a loved one. Mii's mother says the horror cannot happen again, as long as "no one drops the bomb."

The bombing of Hiroshima is seen through the eyes of a Japanese girl and her family. The vivid, nightmarish, rather surrealistic illustrations tell a story that is often stronger than the text, of death, destruction, horror. Although the material may seem too powerful for young readers, the treatment is factual without being offensive or overly frightening. Readers will understand that Hiroshima must never happen again. One paragraph that describes the bomb contains words children may need to have explained: *explosive, impact, conventional, contaminated, radiation.* This account can serve equally well as a read-aloud or as an independent reading selection for which younger children will need adult guidance. Older readers too will profit from guided discussion.

Ages 7 and up

Also available in:
No other form known

## 407

Marzollo, Jean

**Amy Goes Fishing**

Color illustrations by Ann Schweninger.
The Dial Press, Inc., 1980.
(56 pages)

---

*FAMILY: Relationships*
  *Success*

---

It is Saturday morning and everyone has some place to go except Amy and her father. But her father has an idea. "Let's go catch Old Chinny Whiskers. . . . The biggest, oldest catfish in Morgan Lake." Amy's brother and sister have told her that fishing is boring. But after packing their lunch and taking out the garbage, Amy and her father start out. Near the lake they stop to rent a boat and buy some worms. Amy doesn't really like to touch the worms, but she puts one in the can just to prove she's not afraid of them. Then, after they have rowed out to the middle of the lake and baited their hooks, they drop their lines overboard and begin to wait. In order to help the time pass, Amy's father tells a story about the brown bump they see sticking out of the water. He says it is a muskrat house. Amy enjoys the story, but begins to get tired of sitting. After a while, though, she feels a tug on her line. She is so excited she jumps up, leans over, and falls into the lake. Her father scolds her for being so careless and then asks if she wants to go home. She doesn't; in fact, she picks up a worm and puts it on the hook all by herself. Her father finally gets a bite, but it is only an old black boot. Soon they row to a little island and get out their lunch bag. It smells funny, however, and when they look inside they see orange peels and bits of pancake. They have thrown out their lunch and brought the garbage instead. As they laugh at their mistake, Sam from the gas station walks up and offers to share his catch with them. They cook the fish over a campfire, and Amy thinks it the best meal she has ever eaten. Sam says he caught Old Chinny Whiskers, but threw him back. That fish "is old and has

whiskers, just like me." Then Sam whispers to Amy his secret for catching fish. Back out on the lake she puts two worms on her hook as he advised and sits quietly. Soon she catches a fish—not Old Chinny Whiskers but a "real beauty." On the way home she tells her father how much she enjoyed "worms and muskrats and Old Chinny Whiskers and Sam and my first fish." She has not had a boring day at all.

A little girl and her father go fishing and, despite several minor mishaps, enjoy themselves thoroughly. Readers will too: the father-daughter relationship is warm and believable, and clever pastel pictures enhance the humorous text.

Ages 4-7

Also available in:
Paperbound—*Amy Goes Fishing*
The Dial Press, Inc.

## 408

Matthews, Ellen

**Putting Up with Sherwood**

Black/white illustrations by Unada Gliewe.
The Westminster Press, 1980.
(137 pages)

M

---

*PEER RELATIONSHIPS*
  *Egocentrism*
  *Friendship: lack of*
  *Learning disabilities*

---

Diane Foley begins the fifth grade feeling very sorry for herself. Her best friend has changed schools, and Diane doesn't really get along with anyone else her own age. Even Alice, who tries to be nice to her, is "too eager and too friendly" to suit Diane. When classmates Kerry and Neil start a neighborhood newspaper, Diane wants to be a reporter or nothing at all, so she does nothing. The congenial Alice, however, settles for a job as a delivery girl and is soon writing her own column. When the first issue of the *Snappy Snooper* is distributed, Diane contents herself with making sarcastic comments about the other children's success. Another big source of unhappiness is the fact that Sherwood Willis, the school clown, has just moved next door to her and is in her class. Life gets even worse when their teacher, Mrs. Carver, asks her to help Sherwood with his homework two or three times a week. A very impatient tutor, Diane has no sympathy at all when she learns that Sherwood has a learning disability. To her he is still just a dumb troublemaker, and she is chagrined when some of his original cartoons are printed in the paper. At this point, Diane has accepted Alice's job as delivery girl, but feels infinitely superior to the rest of the workers. When the *Snappy Snooper* staff decides to give a talent show to benefit a needy family in the neighborhood, they only reluctantly include Diane's piano piece. She is not a talented pianist and tries to play overly difficult songs. Kerry and Neil want Sherwood to do a clown routine, but to Diane's amazement he refuses. Although he knows he has a talent for being funny, he is tired of being laughed at. He confides to Diane that he would rather be taken seriously and have friends, but that his disability keeps this from happening. Gradually, Sherwood makes Diane realize that she doesn't have any friends either, because she's selfish and bossy. Besides their loneliness, Diane learns, she and Sherwood have something else in common. When they are asked to give an impromptu skit at school, they find they make a good comedy team. Diane agrees to forget her piano piece and do the skit with Sherwood for the talent show. She is finally part of two real teams—a comedy team and a team of children who raise a lot of money for a good cause.

Young Diane has trouble fitting in and making friends, and for a while she's convinced that other people are at fault. But a lonely, learning-disabled boy shows her the error of her condescending ways. Learning to accept others and to cooperate puts her well on her way to a happier life. The story has considerable humor, emphasized by the illustrations.

Ages 9-11

**Also available in:**
No other form known

## 409

**Matthews, Ellen**

### The Trouble with Leslie

Black/white illustrations by Unada Gliewe.
The Westminster Press, 1979.
(109 pages)

---

RESPONSIBILITY: Accepting
  Baby-sitting: involuntary
  Cooperation: in work
  Friendship: meaning of
  Parental: absence
  Self, attitude toward: confidence
  Sibling: older

---

Eric's mother will only come home on weekends now that she's enrolled in the university's summer school, and ten-year-old Eric is not happy about that. While his father is at work, Eric has to watch his three-year-old sister, Leslie, whom he considers a pest. On Friday, he tells his father he will clean the house and fix dinner in time for his mother's first weekend homecoming. Then he and his friend Tully decide to give the dog, Fred, a bath. Leslie tries to help and gets so dirty that she too needs a bath. But the little girl refuses to take one until Eric suggests that she bathe in the tub with the hose, just like Fred. Eric's housecleaning job is haphazard, his lasagna dinner flops, and Leslie develops a rash from the dog's bath soap. But their mother, happy to be home, laughs and enjoys everything. During the next week, Eric and Tully lose Leslie at the Union Day celebration. After a panicky hour they find her riding a horse in the parade. Eric begins to feel resentful, unappreciated, "like a mother—watching Leslie, cleaning house, and cooking all the time." When his mother comes home for the Fourth of July weekend she is preoccupied with her studies, asking Eric to continue helping out for a few more weeks. But when his father is called out of town, crotchety Mrs. Campbell comes to stay with them. Under her iron rule Leslie and Eric must eat eggplant, take baths in the middle of the day, and miss their favorite TV programs. In retaliation, Eric enlists Tully to

help play a trick on Mrs. Campbell. Later, Eric confesses the prank to his father, who tells him that Mrs. Campbell simply doesn't understand "a family trying something together." On another day, Leslie eats a bottle of pills. Remembering what he learned in first-aid class, Eric has his sister drink several glasses of milk. He fears his father will hold him responsible for Leslie's poisoning, but is relieved to be told his quick action saved his sister's life. Eric's summer continues to have its ups and downs: a pleasurable trip to a Wisconsin lake cabin, a birthday party for Leslie during which Leslie gets her hair full of bubble gum. Then a neighbor offers to pay Eric and Tully to take charge of her son's birthday party. Cheered at the prospect, Eric realizes he must be capable if people are willing to pay him for his help.

In this lively first-person account, a young boy recognizes that mistakes often go hand in hand with new responsibilities. Throughout, Eric shows himself to be resourceful and resilient, even when his loving but busy family leaves him to sort out many of his feelings on his own. Young readers will find it easy to empathize with Eric's trials and triumphs. Clever illustrations add to the fun.

Ages 8-11

**Also available in:**
No other form known

## 410

**Mauser, Pat Rhoads**

### A Bundle of Sticks

Black/white illustrations by Gail Owens.
Atheneum Publishers, 1982.
(169 pages)

---

BULLY: Being Bothered by
  Aggression
  Courage, meaning of
  School: classmate relationships
  Self, attitude toward: accepting
  Violence

---

When eleven-year-old Benjamin Tyler comes home from school with a badly beaten face and torn shirt again, courtesy of Boyd Bradshaw, Ben's angry father says the next time Ben comes home like that he's going to lock him out of the house. He accuses his wife of mollycoddling the boy and says Ben needs lessons in courage. But Ben hates fighting—it makes him sick to his stomach—and only wants to be left alone. He can't understand why Boyd hates him and picks on him. When Boyd calls Ben a faggot in school the next day, the substitute teacher, Miss Fletcher, makes Boyd read the dictionary definition of "faggot": a bundle of sticks. She gives Ben a ride home so he can avoid being attacked again. Then his mother drives him to his first kajukenbo lesson, a self-defense method that includes karate, judo, kenpo, and boxing. Ben is sure he will hate the lessons. But his Sifu (instructor) is patient and understanding, gently instructing Ben in the beginning movements. As the boy's skill grows, his father warns him not to tell anyone about it; then he'll be forced to demonstrate what he knows, like it or not. But Ben can't resist, and then is embarrassed when he falsely claims he has his yellow belt. He continues his kajukenbo lessons and befriends Roger Wilmer, the only other young boy in the class. Then Boyd has an emergency appendectomy, making Ben feel alternately delighted and guilty. With any luck, Boyd will be out until summer vacation. When Ben finally does earn his yellow belt, he is disappointed at his own reaction. He knows that inside he is still not a fighter; the yellow belt has really changed nothing. But his Sifu claims that if Ben ever needs to defend himself, the moves will come automatically. Boyd returns to school and teases Ben. Ben starts to fight back, using one of the kicks he's learned, but stops when he realizes he could seriously damage Boyd's new appendectomy scar. During the summer months, Ben earns his orange belt. His sixth-grade teacher is none other than Miss Fletcher, now married and teaching full-time. But when Boyd turns up in his classroom, still itching for a fight, Ben sees nothing has changed. One afternoon Boyd kicks Ben's dog, Daisy. When Ben sees Daisy lying there, he turns on Boyd and attacks him, winning the fight hands down. But he feels sick afterwards and worries about whether he's knocked out any of Boyd's teeth. He is not happy being the hero his classmates now think him. Ben earns his purple belt in a day-long test and awards ceremony. When he and another student, a brown-belt adult, encounter two characters who want to fight about a dented car door, Ben watches his fellow student use diplomacy to settle the dispute, even though he could also have "settled" it physically. Ben begins to understand what his Sifu means about the freedom never to have to fight. He feels different, yet still the same. He'll always hate fighting, but now knows it is absolutely right to be the Ben Tyler he is.

The young victim of a school bully learns both to defend himself and to accept himself as he is when he takes kajukenbo training. This attractively illustrated book subtly emphasizes the connection between self-image and how a person is perceived by others; as long as Ben felt like a helpless victim, he remained one. Self-defense, as his instructor points out, is partly in the fists and partly in the mind. But the Sifu also maintains that one might never have to use one's fists if one's attitude is right, a philosophy worthy of discussion.

Ages 10-12

**Also available in:**
Cassette—*A Bundle of Sticks*
Library of Congress (NLSBPH)

### 411

Mauser, Pat Rhoads

## How I Found Myself at the Fair

Black/white illustrations by Emily Arnold McCully.
Atheneum Publishers, 1980.
(58 pages)

---

*LOST, BEING*
  *Dependence/Independence*
  *Problem solving*

---

Since her mother is ill, nine-year-old Laura is going to the state fair with her best friend, Mary Denton, and the Denton family. On the way Laura, who sees most things as she thinks her mother would, reflects on "poor Mary, being stuck in a crazy family like this!" Laura is an only child, but the Dentons have six children, all of whom seem to Laura noisy, grubby, carelessly dressed (jeans and T-shirts), and reckless—they don't use seat belts. Furthermore, they don't look out for one another. Once they arrive at the fair they all scatter, leaving Mary and Laura on their own. First the girls get something to eat, and then they go to the 4-H barn where Laura's blue-ribbon painting and Mary's wild flower collection are displayed. From there, Mary runs off to use a restroom and doesn't come back. After wandering around the fairgrounds looking for her, Laura gets on the Ferris wheel, hoping to see at least one Denton face from the top. Instead she finds herself high in the air with a defective bar on her chair. It unhooks and she clings to it and screams all the way to the bottom. But just before the bar came unhooked she had seen Mr. and Mrs. Denton, so she hurries after them filled with misgivings: the Dentons haven't even missed her, she might throw up, she might have to spend the night sleeping on a bench without a blanket or pillow. When she can't find them, she tries to call her mother on a pay phone. After getting a recording about her call being long-distance and finally losing all her money in the phone, Laura gives up. She'll probably have to steal food eventually, she thinks, since her money is gone. She walks aimlessly through barns and exhibits and is allowed into the Mansion of Mirrors free when she tells the woman she's looking for her friend. But once inside, she becomes lost and disoriented: "I was lost inside of being lost." When she finally gets out, she goes back to the 4-H barn, takes down her painting, and hugs it. Then she has an idea. If she stays by Mary's wild flower collection, sooner or later Mary will have to come by to pick it up. Sure enough, Mary finally appears, demanding to know where Laura has been. She's heard that someone was nearly killed on the Ferris wheel! Laura tells Mary about that and everything else. When Mary discovers that Laura has never heard of calling collect and that she didn't get her money back for the uncompleted call, the two run back to the pay phone and collect Laura's money. Impressed by her friend's knowledge and quick action, Laura asks Mary is she's ever been lost and scared. Mary says she gets lost all the time. She usually just tells someone and gets taken to the information booth to wait for her parents. But Mary compliments Laura on the number of different solutions she tried. On the way home, various Dentons tell how they saw Laura at different times during the day, but didn't realize she was lost. Their concern gives Laura "a warm feeling." "What a great family," she thinks.

An only child, used to her mother's close supervision, goes to a state fair with the large, unruly family of a friend and gets lost. After a succession of frightening experiences, Laura uses her head and finds her friend again. Laura tells this story herself, and the panic of a child unaccustomed to being on her own comes through in her exaggerations and convictions of doom. But the style is light and the illustrations emphasize the humor of the situation. Laura gains some self-confidence when her good idea succeeds in reuniting her with her friend; perhaps she won't feel quite so helpless in the future.

Ages 7-9

**Also available in:**
No other form known

**412**

Mazer, Harry

**The Island Keeper**

Delacorte Press, 1981.
(165 pages)

---

*AUTONOMY*
*IDENTITY, SEARCH FOR*
  *Death: of sibling*
  *Family: relationships*
  *Nature: living in harmony with*

---

At sixteen, wealthy Cleo Murphy is overweight and very unhappy. Her mother died nine years ago in a car accident and now her sister, Jam, "the only person she loved in the world," is dead too, having drowned in a boating accident. Her father is emotionally distant, forever occupied with his business affairs. Her grandmother is no comfort, always sending her off to distant places where she's to learn how to conduct herself appropriately. With Jam gone there seems no reason for Cleo to go on enduring the "stiff and artificial" life at home or the endless procession of private schools and camps. Her only desire now is to "disappear completely." Cleo has written out an escape plan that allows her to shed her old identity and steal away to Duck Island, her father's uninhabited property in Canada where she and Jam spent one wonderful summer together. The plan succeeds, and from the first moment she steps onto the beach she feels her sister's presence all around her. Then, however, Cleo senses something else. Smelling ashes, she climbs up the slope and sees that their cabin has burned to the ground. She goes in search of other shelter and finds a small cave where she can sleep and keep her things. But a few days later a raccoon breaks into her knapsack and destroys most of her food supply. She knows she should give up, but she feels such a strong sense of Jam's presence in the "extraordinary emptiness and silence" of the island that she cannot leave. She starts to live on fish and vegetation, amusing herself by imagining her grandmother's reaction to her new way of life: "Pure savagery." She gets to know the animals—a doe with two fawns, a chipmunk, and an injured owl. One day when she is very hungry she knows she is ready to eat a frog as Owl does. She catches several and finds that with each one she kills, something inside of her hardens. She keeps a pot of soup at her camp, each day throwing in whatever she is able to forage. And each day that she survives, she feels happier. Her body becomes thin and strong. When the caretaker of the estate comes to look for her, she eludes him. Life on the island is "simple and real," and she is not ready to leave. One day, however, a bad storm seems to mark the beginning of winter, and Cleo goes to prepare her canoe for departure. She finds it crushed under a fallen tree. Since it will be at least three months until the lake freezes enough to cross on foot, she feels sure she will die on the island. Still, she builds a stone shelter around the opening of the cave and stores up as much food as she can find. She kills a porcupine, a

raccoon, even a small, lame deer. Finally the lake freezes. Cleo straps on her hand-made snowshoes and struggles through the wind and snow to the mainland and her angry father and grandmother. She finds that even though she has changed, home is the same. After a time she decides to return to school, perhaps to become a naturalist. On her trip back to school she considers her previous unhappiness and decides that things don't have to be that way again. "Things had happened—the island had happened."

An unhappy young girl, mourning the death of her sister, embarks on a true voyage of discovery in this engrossing book. By becoming "part of the island," Cleo learns that she, like the animals she befriends, is a survivor. She finds enough inner strength to keep going against formidable odds, accepting and adapting to natural rhythms. The reader is drawn into Cleo's struggle and must applaud the serene, strong young woman who returns to her world not as a passive observer, but as a participant.

Ages 10-14

**Also available in:**
Paperbound—*The Island Keeper*
Dell Publishing Company, Inc.

**413**

Mazer, Harry

**The Last Mission**

Delacorte Press, 1979.
(182 pages)

---

*FEAR: of Physical Harm*
*WAR*
  *Courage, meaning of*
  *Death: of friend*
  *Jewish*
  *Violence*

---

Determined to stop Hitler from killing the Jews, fifteen-year-old Jack Raab steals his older brother Irving's birth certificate and enlists in the Army Air Force. He leaves his family a note saying he is heading out west to travel as his father had before him. He goes through basic training eagerly and impatiently, hoping to be sent overseas as soon as possible. After the training, Jack is made waist gunner on a B-17 bomber based in England. Now he learns what fear is and what it does to people. On his twenty-fifth mission his plane is badly damaged and Chuckie O'Brien, his best friend, is killed. Jack bails out over Czechoslovakia and tries to make his way to Allied territory. After two days he is captured by the Germans. When they read the "H" for Hebrew on his dog tags, Jack is sure he will be killed. Instead, after some weeks, the war ends and he is freed. Later, back in England, he learns that he is the sole survivor of his bomber crew. Desolate at the loss of his crew and at the destruction he has participated in, Jack is sent back to the United States. He wants to be discharged, but at first it seems he will be sent to the Pacific with another bomber crew. Then he confesses to lying about his age and is confined to the guardhouse. He is discharged after a formal hearing reveals his true age and service record. He hadn't contacted his family during the war, but when they received a "Missing in Action" telegram in Irving's name they figured out what had happened to Jack. Jack had sent them a telegram after the war saying he would be home soon, and his family greets him with joy when he returns. Jack then makes a painful visit to the family of his dead friend Chuckie. He admits to Dorothy Landon, the girl he met while he was in basic training and wrote to while overseas, that he is only sixteen, and their romance cools to an enduring friendship. Lost in civilian life, Jack returns to high school, full of doubts about the future and disturbing memories of combat. He tells his classmates, in a speech at a recognition assembly: "War isn't like the movies. It's not fun and songs. It's not about heroes. It's about awful, sad things, like my friend Chuckie that I'm never going to see again."

The experiences of wartime and the difficulties of readjustment to civilian life leave an underage veteran saddened by his role in war and cut off from his family and generation. Separation, fear, death, imprisonment, return—even the casual profanity of Army life—all are included in this portrayal of the bewildering and frightening world of war. Strong on action, without moralizing, the book raises serious questions about war, heroism, duty, and courage.

Ages 12-14

**Also available in:**
Paperbound—*The Last Mission*
Dell Publishing Company, Inc.

## 414

Mazer, Norma Fox

**Mrs. Fish, Ape, and Me, the Dump Queen**
E. P. Dutton & Company, Inc., 1980.
(138 pages)

*DIFFERENCES, HUMAN*
*LIFE STYLE*
*OSTRACISM*
    *Love, meaning of*
    *Name-calling*
    *Parent/Parents: substitute*
    *Relatives: living in home of*
    *School: classmate relationships*

Joyce Adams lives with her mother's brother, whom she calls Old Dad, in a comfortable little house next to the town dump. An orphan, she has lived with her uncle since she was four. Old Dad is the keeper of the Queenship Town Dump and takes great care with his work. Every day he puts biodegradable garbage into the ravine and buries it under fresh earth. After a time, the enriched soil produces huge fruits, vegetables, and sunflowers. Old Dad also has special places for metal, paper, rags, and anything else that comes to the dump. He fixes repairable appliances and furniture and gives them to anyone who asks for them. Joyce is very happy with her uncle, but she sometimes fantasizes about her mother surviving the car accident and returning to live with her daughter and brother. That would make Joyce's home life perfect. But nothing, it seems, could make her life at school anything but miserable. Although she is a good student, Joyce has not had a friend since first grade, when the children found out that her uncle

tended the dump. From then on, she has been ostracized and teased. This year the kids call her the "Dump Queen" and Old Dad, with his long arms, short legs, and sloping shoulders, the "Ape Man." Joyce hopes for a while that the new girl, Lacey Laurence, will be her friend, but then Lacey discovers Joyce's secret and begins to spend her time with more "high-class" people. One day Joyce's classmates put garbage in her desk, and the teacher sends her to get the janitor. Mrs. Fish, the tall, fat custodian with the bright clothes and black whiskers, called "Crazy Fish" by the kids, becomes Joyce's best friend. When Old Dad suffers what appears to be a stroke and cannot tend the dump as usual, Mrs. Fish spends her weekends helping out. She becomes part of their lives, sharing meals and staying over on Saturday nights. Although Old Dad enjoys her cheerful company, he believes that depending on people can only lead to misery. So, as soon as he is able to resume his normal routine, he sends Mrs. Fish away. But Joyce is very unhappy without her. Finally Old Dad, unaccustomed to soft words and sentimentality, takes Mrs. Fish a very special courting present: a pole on which he has, over the years, carved intricate faces and animals, a work of art that Mrs. Fish has greatly admired. With this gift, he asks her to join them at the dump. Now Joyce has a complete family. Nothing changes for her at school, yet in her happiness everything seems different. Joyce feels ready to attempt anything, even trying again to make Lacey her friend.

A girl who is ostracized for her highly unconventional home life learns to take strength from her warm and loving, if unusual, family in this touching first-person account. Readers will readily sympathize with Joyce, Old Dad, and Mrs. Fish, three outcasts who shine beside the cruelty of their tormentors. The attention to detail here, particularly about Old Dad's care for the environment and knowledge of appropriate waste-disposal methods, imparts a quiet dignity to life at the Queenship Town Dump.

Ages 10-12

**Also available in:**
Paperbound—*Mrs. Fish, Ape, and Me, the Dump Queen*
Avon Books

## 415

Mazer, Norma Fox

**Up in Seth's Room**
Delacorte Press, 1979.
(199 pages)

*BOY-GIRL RELATIONSHIPS: Dating*
*SEX: Attitude Toward*
    *Autonomy*
    *Communication: parent-child*
    *Family: relationships*
    *Maturation*
    *Parental: control*
    *Values/Valuing: moral/ethical*

At fifteen, Finn Rousseau looks forward to sexual experiences but for now wants to remain a virgin. At the apartment her sister Maggie shares with a boyfriend, Jim, she meets and is attracted to Jim's brother,

**M**

nineteen-year-old Seth, a handsome high school drop-out. Finn's mother, like her husband furious with Maggie and Jim for living together, forbids Finn to date Seth when she learns that he is Jim's brother. Finn tells Seth of her mother's anger, revealing at the same time that she is only fifteen. Seth is shocked at how young she is, and they part. At a friend's suggestion, Finn considers seeing Seth and lying to her parents about it. Then the two meet by accident at a concert. Seth apologizes for their last encounter and kisses Finn, in sight of her mother, who has come to pick Finn up. At home there is an angry scene, Finn's parents claiming she is too young to know what she is getting into with Seth. When Seth calls, Finn's father tells him not to call again and hangs up on him. A few days later, defiantly, Finn goes to him and returns home late, triggering another scene. During the next weeks they meet secretly at the restaurant where Seth works. Maggie learns of the relationship and takes her parents' side, leaving Finn increasingly cut off from her family. Seth takes her to Maggie and Jim's apartment, where he has been staying, but Jim will not let them remain. So Seth moves out, rents a cheap attic apartment, and takes Finn there. She is nearly as ardent as he, but insists they stop short of intercourse. Late getting home, Finn quarrels with her parents again. Her father slaps her and grounds her for a month. After some time and several calmer discussions, the parents relent and say Finn can see Seth—within limits they propose and she accepts. But when she goes to Seth, he tries to force himself on her. When she refuses he becomes physically aggressive and verbally abusive. Later, their quarrel mended, she learns that he had never taken her refusal to have intercourse seriously. He tells her that she has led him on and explains himself thus: "If at first you don't succeed . . . that's the male creed." This "insight" into the male mind is a major discovery for Finn. After a drive in the country, Seth tells her he is leaving home to work on a distant farm. Finn is heartsick. In a sunny meadow they make love, but again stop short of intercourse. Since Finn has heard that love without intercourse isn't really love, she asks, "Did we just make love?" Seth takes her home and they part tenderly.

Finn's struggle for love, sexual experience, and independence is described clearly and nonjudgmentally. The language is frank, the narrative candid. Strong characterizations enable readers to see the developing relationship between Seth and Finn from varied perspectives. There is much good discussion material here: Finn's emotions, her parents' attempts to control her, the pressures of her friends, and the sometimes aggressive behavior of the boys. Especially provocative is Seth's "male creed." Finn is a heroine with whom many readers will strongly identify.

Ages 13 and up

**Also available in:**

Cassette—*Up in Seth's Room*
Library of Congress (NLSBPH)

Paperbound—*Up in Seth's Room*
Dell Publishing Company, Inc.

**416**

Mazer, Norma Fox

**When We First Met**

Four Winds Press, 1982.
(199 pages)

---

*BLAME*
*BOY-GIRL RELATIONSHIPS: Dating*
*LOVE, MEANING OF*
  *Accidents: automobile*
  *Death: of sibling*
  *Guilt, feelings of*
  *Mourning, stages of*

---

March is a month when seventeen-year-old Jenny Pennoyer's spirits usually sink. It was in March, two years ago, that her sister, Gail, was killed by a drunk driver. Jenny is still tormented by having argued with Gail that dark, stormy night about who would ride her bike to the store; her mother, Amelia, still hates Nell Montana, the woman who hit Gail. Mrs. Montana had been charged with second-degree manslaughter. Amelia tells Jenny that she is sending a blood-red rose to Mrs. Montana, along with a note reminding her of her atrocity. Jenny is surprised when something good happens to her in the midst of all this sorrow; it is early in March when she first sees the handsome, blond boy with the rainbow suspenders and starts to fall in love. One Saturday morning, as Jenny and her best friend, Rhoda, are leaving a shopping mall, they see the boy and one of Rhoda's admirers approaching them. They meet, talk, and agree to have a pizza together. At the end of their lunch, Jenny's happiness disappears; she learns the boy's name is Rob Montana. When Rob learns her last name is Pennoyer, he asks, "Would you know anything about a red rose?" Jenny tries to persuade herself that they can't see each other again, but Rob is persistent and soon they are secretly dating. Then one day they stop in at Rob's house and forget about the time. When Mrs. Montana comes home from work, Jenny suddenly finds herself face-to-face with the woman her mother calls "Mrs. Killer." As they talk it becomes obvious that Nell has suffered a great deal because of the accident. She explains that she wasn't drunk, just a little relaxed by the "drink or two" she had at a party, and that the visibility was so bad she couldn't see Gail until the last moment. Though sympathetic, Jenny knows that out of loyalty to her parents she cannot allow herself to befriend Mrs. Montana. She stays away from their home and resists Rob's arguments for bringing their relationship into the open. Eventually she agrees to let him meet her family, but the resulting scene is as bad as she has feared. Her mother rushes from the room and her father orders Rob out of the house, telling Jenny to break off the relationship. At first she refuses, but can't ignore the pain she is causing everyone and finally gives in. During the weeks that follow, Jenny suffers a great deal. Then, by accident, she and her mother go into the shoe shop where Nell Montana works. Nell takes the opportunity to beg for forgiveness and, although she can't oblige, Amelia begins to see her daughter's "killer" as a human being, one who has the "tense, lined face of a woman in pain." Soon after, a newspaper article reports Nell Montana's near-fatal overdose of sleeping pills. Amelia wonders if she is to blame. She is finally able to dismantle Gail's room—until now, it had been left intact as a shrine. Meanwhile, Jenny sees that no one's life has been changed for the better because she has given up Rob. She goes to him and, after expressing some of his hurt and anger, he acknowledges that he wants her back. Jenny's parents are not overjoyed, but can see that Mrs. Montana is not a monster and that Jenny is still their daughter no matter whom she loves.

The love between a teenage girl and the son of the woman whose car struck and killed the girl's sister helps both families toward recovery from grief and guilt. Rob and Jenny's love begins with physical attraction and develops into a true appreciation of each other's character. This is an affecting story of the healing powers of love and the gradual reawakening to life of several people who have mourned for a long time. Readers will remember Jenny and her family from an earlier book, *A Figure of Speech,* and will be just as caught up in this second story about them.

Ages 12 and up

**Also available in:**
Film—*When We First Met*
Learning Corporation of America

Paperbound—*When We First Met*
Scholastic Book Services

## 417

**Mearian, Judy Frank**

**Someone Slightly Different**

The Dial Press, Inc., 1980.
(197 pages)

---

PARENT/PARENTS: Single
  Alcoholism
  Death: of grandparent
  Grandparent: living in child's home
  Grandparent: love for
  Parental: absence
  School: classmate relationships

---

Twelve-year-old Martha (Marty) Trevor fantasizes about the return of her father, who went out to get gasoline one day when Marty was little and never came back. When her paternal grandmother, Flossie Trevor, and her two cats unexpectedly turn a visit into a permanent arrangement, Marty looks forward to finding out more about her father, since her divorced mother will never speak of him. Flossie bakes bread, fixes french toast for breakfast, sews clothes for Marty and her mother, and generally turns their barren house into a home. Until her arrival, Marty had been bitterly teased by classmates, especially Donna Kett, for being a latchkey kid and for having no father. Attending a Halloween party, Marty wears a superb witch costume made by Flossie and is accompanied by Friend, one of Flossie's cats. But when Donna arrives she tells Marty she's just untied a cat that was leashed to a chair on the front porch. Horrified, thinking Friend will wander away and be killed, Marty dashes out of the party, only to find Friend still tied up. Hurt, she takes Friend and walks home. There she and Flossie talk about Marty's father, Johnny, a charming, good-looking man with a

bad case of wanderlust. On Saturdays Flossie usually attends the horse races; that Saturday Marty talks her grandmother into taking her along, even though she knows the activity offends her mother's religious beliefs. They bet on a long shot that Marty chooses and each wins $75.80 on a one-dollar bet. Marty's mother isn't angry, but she's glad to hear that Marty chose not to bet anymore, even after her win. Both Flossie and Marty turn over their winnings to Marty's mother, who struggles to make ends meet. In Sunday school, the students are asked to sign pledges that they will never take an alcoholic drink. Marty knows her mother, a Sunday school teacher, will expect her to sign the temperance card. But Marty can't bring herself to participate in what she considers a sneaky way of obligating children who don't know their own minds yet. So Marty's mother explains her opposition to drinking: her own father was an alcoholic and her parents died when her drunken father ran the car into a tree. They also lost her mother's family farm because of her father's drinking. Feeling very close to her mother, Marty explains why she doesn't like the temperance card and her mother agrees with her. When Marty and Charlie, her best friend, participate in a spelling contest, Flossie attends and cheers them both on. When Donna tries to mock Flossie and Marty, Marty stares her down and knows she'll never be intimidated by Donna again. Flossie shows Marty a letter she's received from her son; he's recently married a woman who loves to roam as he does. Shocked but also relieved, Marty begins to look toward the future more realistically. Then she becomes very ill with scarlet fever and so does Flossie. As Marty is recovering, she notices that their young doctor and her mother are now on first-name terms. When Flossie seems a little better, Marty visits her in her bedroom and helps her drink water, just as Flossie nursed her. That night Flossie dies. Marty feels horribly guilty about giving the disease to her grandmother; her mother explains that Flossie had serious angina and it's not Marty's fault she died. The next morning when Marty wakes up she smells bread baking and wonders if it's all been a bad dream. But it's her mother baking bread, trying to remember Flossie the best way she can. Marty asks her mother about her relationship with the doctor. She's a long way from making any sort of commitment, her mother replies, and Marty is content. In memory of Flossie, Marty begins beating up the batter for french toast.

A young girl gradually gives up her dream of her missing father reappearing to give her the kind of family life she craves. Her grandmother shows her that a loving family need not be the traditional one. Marty, whose full name is Mary Martha, reflects on the Martha side of her character—the serious, dutiful side—and the Mary side—sociable and eager to please. At the end of the book she seems to have integrated the two and has gained self-confidence and understanding. Along the way is a believable progression of events in the life of a sensible, compassionate young girl. Especially notable are Marty's warm relationships with her mother and grandmother.

Ages 10-12

**Also available in:**
No other form known

M

**418**

Mearian, Judy Frank

## Two Ways about It

The Dial Press, Inc., 1979.
(166 pages)

---

RELATIVES: Living in Child's Home
  Belonging
  Cancer
  Family: unity
  Illnesses: of parent
  Jealousy: peer
  Security/Insecurity

---

Eleven-year-old Annie Reynolds enjoys being an only child and resents her teasing, domineering cousin, Lou, fourteen, invading her life each summer. Annie tries to keep in mind that Lou comes from an unhappy home with parents who fight constantly. Annie's father promises her a restaurant dinner just for the two of them when she can laugh at Lou's teasing. This summer, Lou, an excellent cook, decides she and Annie will sell box lunches to a summer construction crew working nearby. The lunches are a huge success, even more so for Lou when she meets Mike, a young summer worker with the crew. Then Annie has a shock. She learns her mother has a lump in her left breast and must undergo surgery. Mechanically she helps Lou with the cooking and cleaning while her mother is hospitalized, trying to hide her fear. Hospital rules won't let her visit her mother because she's too young. Her anxiety surfaces when a neighbor, in a clumsy attempt to console her, further frightens her with visions of the cancer spreading. Anxiety is compounded by hurt and jealousy when Lou is allowed to visit Annie's mother although Annie can't. Annie is somewhat mollified when her father remembers their dinner for two and praises her for her help, courage, and smiles during these difficult times. Special plans are made for her mother to be brought down to the hospital lobby to see her. Annie is both excited and frightened, and it is with great relief that she observes her mother looking and acting the same as before. But her mother's homecoming is deflating for Annie because, despite her wishes, everything isn't the same. Mrs. Reynolds is tired and in need of rest and exercise to strengthen her left arm. Her father must assist her mother and the two seem wrapped up in each other, excluding Annie. After a scolding from Lou for not appreciating her parents' loving relationship, Annie tries to understand how it would feel to live as Lou must, in abusive turmoil. Lou becomes withdrawn when Mike leaves for college, although he promises to write and send her his class ring. When a manila envelope with a lump the size of a ring box arrives in the mail, Annie's resentment flares anew and she hides the envelope, intending to cause Lou a few more days of suffering. That evening Lou's mother calls, irrationally demanding that her daughter come home. Feeling guilty now as she observes Lou's misery, Annie doesn't know how to return the letter without admitting her deceit. At the train station the next morning, Annie follows Lou to the restroom, hands her the letter with sincere apologies, and awaits the explosion. When Lou smiles and shakes her hand, Annie is so overcome that she grabs Lou in a hug. Another wonderful moment follows. Annie's mother, for the first time since the surgery, raises her left arm high above her head to wave goodbye to Lou.

The loving relationship between Annie's parents and the warm family life they share with their troubled niece enhance this believable first-person narrative. Trying to cope with her unhappy, jealous cousin and her mother's surgery proves more than Annie can handle at first, but as she begins to come to grips with her feelings she is able to see Lou with compassion and even affection. The handling of Annie's mother's recovery from her mastectomy may reassure children that cancer is not necessarily synonomous with death.

Ages 9-12

**Also available in:**
No other form known

**419**

Mendonca, Susan R.

## Tough Choices

The Dial Press, Inc., 1980.
(136 pages)

---

BELONGING
DECISION MAKING
PARENTAL: Custody
  Boy-girl relationships
  Family: relationships
  Guilt, feelings of
  Parental: unreliability
  Running away
  Self, attitude toward: accepting
  Stepbrother/Stepsister
  Stepparent: mother

---

Last year, when Crystal Borne was thirteen, a judge gave her the choice of continuing to live with her flighty mother, Vicki, or of going to live with her concerned father, Adam. After eight years of divorce, Adam had brought this custody suit in an attempt to remove Crystal from her mother's irresponsible care. But Crystal, afraid to be disloyal to her mother, told the judge she couldn't decide. So the judge had her remain with her mother, to Crystal's immediate regret. Now, at fourteen, Crystal is weary of the constant moves, of being left alone or with her grandparents, of her mother's steady stream of boyfriends. One day she overhears Vicki's plans to move away with her current boyfriend and leave Crystal behind with her grandparents. Crystal runs to her grandparents' house and calls her father. He tells her to return home and then threatens her mother with another lawsuit. Vicki agrees to let Crystal go, and the girl happily moves to Monterey County to live with her father, her stepmother, Terry, and her five-year-old stepsister, Casey. Crystal wants to be part of this family, but fears she is "more trouble than she is worth." Several mishaps involving Crystal—Casey almost drowns when Crystal forgets to watch her, Crystal takes an inaccurate phone message for her father with costly consequences—convince the girl that all she does is disappoint people. Crystal does make two friends, Rosey Mendez and her sixteen-year-old brother, Mario. One day at school, Crystal's mother shows up and takes her to lunch and out shopping. She begs Crystal to return to San Francisco with her. Infuriated at her mother for all the emotional upheaval she has caused, Crystal screams she never wants to live with her again. But Crystal is equally sure she is creating tension between Adam and Terry. So when Mario asks her to run away with him she sneaks out of the house and meets him at the bus station. Several hours later, though, Crystal realizes she cannot stay away. She really does love her father and his new family. While waiting for a bus back home, she is found at the station by her father. Happily reunited with the family and assured of their love, Crystal writes a letter to the judge requesting that she be allowed to live with her father permanently. Several months later the judge officially grants her father custody. At last Crystal has a real family.

A young teenager caught in a custody battle struggles to make the right choices in a world of conflicting loyalties. Though marred by shallowness and predictability, the story is believable and could be thought-provoking for young people in similar situations. Since parental custody is rarely treated in children's literature, this book, despite its weaknesses, has value and can promote understanding.

Ages 11 and up

**Also available in:**
Cassette—*Tough Choices*
Library of Congress (NLSBPH)

## 420

Meyer, Carolyn

### The Center: From a Troubled Past to a New Life

Atheneum Publishers, 1979.
(193 pages)

---

*DETENTION HOME, LIVING IN*
*SELF-IMPROVEMENT*
    *Communication: importance of*
    *Delinquency, juvenile*
    *Drugs: abuse of*
    *Guilt, feelings of*
    *Homosexuality: male*
    *Honesty/Dishonesty*
    *Self-discipline*
    *Values/Valuing: moral/ethical*

---

Fifteen-year-old David Peterson is in trouble at school and at home, regularly gets high on drugs, and has now been picked up for stealing mail. His parents enroll him in the Center, a place where troubled teenagers are helped to change themselves. The first thing David sees there is a plaque with the word HONESTY on it. But David has vowed not to stay at the Center, hates everyone there, and has no compunction about lying to the staff and counselors. Meanwhile, David's father, Richard, thinks about his son, reflecting on his doubts about David's paternity and his unsatisfying marriage. Richard is very proud of his successful older son, Richie, and of his bright and pretty daughter, Susie. David's mother, Ellen, remembers all the conflicts between Richard and David, especially the one that led to her husband striking her. She has felt cold towards him ever since. In the privacy of his room, the "good" son, Richie, smokes pot,

listens to acid rock, and thinks about how he wants to be a carpenter instead of the CPA his father expects him to be. Ellen begins attending the Center's Parents Club and learns that a delinquent child is often reflecting the troubles of the whole family. During his first months, David spends time with his counselor, Kevin Murphy, and gradually gives up the idea of escaping the Center. He lies a number of times, but is then subjected to brutal verbal confrontations in encounter groups and eventually confesses his dishonesty. He tells Kevin about his homosexual relationship with his friend on the outside, Billy. David says he doesn't feel homosexual and is ashamed of the relationship. After three months, David is determined to make it at the Center. He is raised to Intermediate status; his new counselor is Betsy Coleman. The first visit home is tense. Billy talks him into sneaking out at night, and they smoke a few joints. When he returns to the Center he lies to Betsy about having seen Billy. From that moment the pressure of his guilt builds until he finally tells a friend the truth about his home visit. As part of the consequences of his dishonesty, he must face the entire group and endure a loud, angry, verbal trimming. David cries and admits that he just wants his father to love him. When a newcomer teases him about his masculinity, David slams him against the wall. But a session with the Center's sexuality expert reassures him somewhat on that point. During his next visit home, David realizes that the real conflict in his home is between his parents. Ellen, who still attends the Parents Club, finally breaks down and tells the group that her marriage is disintegrating. On a family vacation in Maine, David celebrates his sixteenth birthday and learns that his parents are divorcing. Richie has decided to bum around rather than go to college. Susie has constant tantrums, and David worries about her choice of friends. When Doug, a good friend, drops out of the Center, David feels the bottom fall out of his world. Against regulations he goes after Doug. After they share a joint, David calls the Center and says he's coming back. As part of the stringent rules governing readmittance, David has to beg his Center "family" to take him back. His father has moved out, and David visits him in his small, depressing apartment. For the first time, the two express some of their feelings for each other. Moved up to a supervisory position at the Center, David gets a job at a restaurant. One day he finds the courage to ask Heather, one of the waitresses, if he can take her home. She invites him to attend a party with her—a party featuring marijuana, as it turns out. Heather sees nothing wrong with getting high once in a while, but David is now opposed to all drugs and from then on sees Heather only at work. After two years at the Center, David is favorably evaluated. When he graduates, his mother feels that what's happened to him is a miracle. The counselors know it's more a product of energy and hard work. Heather attends the graduation ceremony, telling David she's given up pot after thinking it over what he told her. He asks her out again.

A badly troubled teenager enters a therapeutic community where patients are involved in their own treatment. David emerges two years later having internalized a set of values that will allow him to pursue his own goals and enter into nurturing relationships. Although the book offers a great deal of information and many psychological insights, it is primarily the story of the uneven, painful maturation of a likeable, well-delineated character. Based on reality therapy, treatment at the Center is a combination of psychotherapy and encounter groups. Some of it may seem incomprehensible or even brutal to the reader; in context, however, all the methods make sense and are shown to be effective for many young people. This earnest, involving account would be an excellent choice for discussion because of the broad range of adolescent thoughts and feelings it covers. Because of crude and scatological language and the subtlety of certain ideas and issues, however, the book should generally be recommended for older readers. David Peterson is a composite of the kind of boy found at Vitam Center in Norwalk, Connecticut. The author's own son's residence there led to the writing of this book.

Ages 13 and up

**Also available in:**
No other form known

## 421

Miklowitz, Gloria D.

### Did You Hear What Happened to Andrea?

Delacorte Press, 1979.
(168 pages)

---

*GUILT, FEELINGS OF*
*RAPE*
   *Boy-girl relationships: dating*
   *Family: relationships*
   *Fear: of physical harm*
   *Hitchhiking*

---

Andrea Cranston, fifteen, and her boyfriend, David Hoffman, eighteen, have spent a hot August afternoon at the beach. When they miss their bus home, Andrea convinces David to hitchhike, even though her mother has told her many times not to. An ordinary-looking man in a green Dodge picks them up. He lets David off near his home, saying he will take Andrea on to hers; she agrees. But he passes her street, and when she protests he threatens to kill her if she does not cooperate. He drives to a wooded area in the hills and rapes her at gunpoint. Then he takes her back to the highway and pushes her out, warning her to tell no one or he will come back for her. Numbly she walks down the highway until some classmates pick her up and take her to the police. Andrea's shock and horror are intensified by the reactions of her family. Her mother is ashamed and wants to pretend nothing has happened; she will not permit Andrea to talk about the rape. Her father is angry and wants revenge. Her older sister, Sue, is quite matter-of-fact, encouraging Andrea to act tough. Her little brother is confused because no one will explain what has happened. Her mother questions her decision to go back to her part-time job, but Andrea feels she must take her mind off herself. Still, she fears going out, fears sleeping with her windows open, terrified that the rapist will find her and kill her as he said he would. She avoids David for several days, fearful of his reaction, but when she sees him and tells him she was raped he is grief-stricken and blames himself. He also becomes determined to find the rapist, spending much of his remaining vacation searching for the car. Gradually,

Andrea learns to relax with David again. However, when he goes away to college and school starts for her, she fears the boys and isolates herself from everyone but Kim, one of the girls that found her on the highway. She receives some help by phone through a "Rape Hotline," but her mother doesn't encourage further counseling, nor does she want Andrea to press charges even if the rapist is caught. At Thanksgiving time, while shopping with Kim and Sue, Andrea is sure she sees the green Dodge go past her in the street. Later she recognizes the man—walking right toward her. She faints and when she regains consciousness, all she can do is scream. The rapist has vanished. Sue and Kim take her home and insist to her parents that not only Andrea but they too must have professional help. They begin seeing a counselor, who helps all of them deal with their anger and fear. Just before Christmas, Andrea is summoned to the police station for a line-up. She recognizes the rapist immediately and decides to press charges. Another young victim is also able to identify him; she too will testify. By the time of the trial, five months later, Andrea is feeling more confident and her family has better learned to cope. The rapist is convicted on several counts and gets a sentence of five years to life in prison. Though Andrea knows she will never be the same, she does feel relief and a new sense of freedom knowing the man will be behind bars.

This suspenseful first-person narrative gives a sensitive, perceptive look at the traumas of a young rape victim and her family. It makes clear that others to whom Andrea is important are also victims; they too have been hurt and must be helped to recover. The rape account is straightforward, and the police interrogation uses descriptive language and terms. The book requires a mature reader.

Ages 13 and up

**Also available in:**
Cassette—*Did You Hear What Happened to Andrea?*
Library of Congress (NLSBPH)

Paperbound—*Did You Hear What Happened to Andrea?*
Dell Publishing Company, Inc.

## 422

Miklowitz, Gloria D.

### The Love Bombers

Delacorte Press, 1980.
(199 pages)

---

*CULTS*
*SIBLING: Relationships*
   *Communication: lack of*
   *Self, attitude toward: accepting*

---

First the strange phone call about an Eastern-Western philosophy and now a letter from her brother, Jeremy, saying he is quitting college and joining the "Help Our World Projects"—Jenna Gordon, eighteen, is uneasy and scared. She feels sure that Jeremy is not being truthful with her or their parents. Although he is ten months older, Jenna has always felt they were twins, sharing the same interests and desires. She has never realized that, although Jeremy loves her, he has often resented this "twin" feeling, especially since Jenna has had their parents' constant approval and Jeremy their incessant criticism. Jenna confides her concern about Jeremy to Rick Palmer, Jeremy's best friend. He agrees to drive Jenna to San Francisco, where they will try to see Jeremy. Arriving at the address Jeremy has sent, Rick and Jenna find he is not there. The next morning they decide to go to the Berkeley campus and find out about the group he has joined. They learn the leader is Ibram ben Adam, considered by his followers to be the Messiah, and that members are called "Adamites." The Adamites "bomb" their listeners with love. Jenna and Rick accept an invitation to dinner at the group's Berkeley house, and Jenna feels the strong pull of the members' closeness and apparent love. Rick warns her to be careful. Told Jeremy is at their retreat north of San Francisco, they accept a weekend invitation, Jenna more enthusiastically than Rick. Meanwhile, Jeremy feels "that for him, time started, his life began, on the day he met the Family." At first he was confused about the people in the movement, but now sees the group as a way out of the domination of his parents and sister, a way towards himself. At a weekend retreat, the Family had urged him to stay on for a week-long seminar. Jeremy was concerned that his parents and Jenna would worry about him. He was also uncomfortable about never being left alone, fed enough, or allowed enough sleep, uneasy about having to pray both to the Creator and to the Master, ben Adam. But he was also overwhelmed by the group's love for him. After several intensive weeks of lectures, Jeremy returned to the Berkeley house, starting to "witness" and to sell flowers at the airport. He had requested his bankbook from his parents shortly after joining the group, before his parents had doubts about what he was doing. He has turned it and his credit card (in his parents' name) over to the Family. One night, Jeremy is suddenly sent back to the retreat. Several days later he is reunited with Jenna and Rick—but the three are never allowed to be alone together. After one day of this, Rick devises a plan and tricks Jeremy into an unaccompanied meeting. He and Jenna try to make Jeremy see he is being manipulated and brainwashed. But as Jenna pleads with her brother to remember their good family times, she suddenly realizes that Jeremy only remembers the bad times. She also sees that Jeremy and she are not alike at all, that she has been blind to his desperate search for approval and support. Acknowledging their defeat, Jenna and Rick watch Jeremy walk back to his Family where he feels safe, secure, and loved.

Both sides of a contemporary issue are effectively presented here as a frightened and confused young man joins a religious cult, making his sister and friend realize they've never really known Jeremy at all. Jenna herself is conscious of the group's power, their spellbinding attraction, the lure of being totally controlled in the name of love. At the end, the reader has learned much about the cult phenomenon and is left to ponder if Jeremy will eventually give in to his secret doubts about the Family. In many ways, this interesting story resembles an unsensationalized exposé.

Ages 12 and up

**Also available in:**
Paperbound—*The Love Bombers*
Dell Publishing Company, Inc.

**423**

Miles, Betty

**Maudie and Me and the Dirty Book**
Alfred A. Knopf, Inc., 1980.
(144 pages)

*CENSORSHIP, LITERARY*
*Friendship: making friends*
*School: classmate relationships*

Kate Harris quickly volunteers when her teacher, Ms. Plotkin, asks for sixth graders to read to first graders at an elementary school. But her excitement vanishes just as quickly when the only other volunteer is Maudie Schmidt. Kate and her friends think Maudie is "sort of a dope—one of those kids that everyone wants to avoid." The girls visit the school together and observe Ms. Dwyer's first-grade class. Reluctantly Kate agrees to go with Maudie to the library to pick out a book to read. She is surprised to discover that she and Maudie share a love of reading. After they make their selections, Kate goes to Maudie's house. As she comes to know her, Kate begins to feel more comfortable with Maudie. The following Friday the two girls return to Ms. Dwyer's class, both excited and nervous. Maudie reads *Little Bear* and then Kate reads *The Birthday Dog*, about the birth of a puppy. The children begin to ask questions about how the puppy was born, and soon Kate is stammering through an explanation of mating. Ms. Dwyer nods her approval and later tells Kate she handled the situation well. The following Monday, Kate, Maudie, and Ms. Plotkin are summoned to the principal's office. Over the weekend, it seems, certain parents called to complain about Kate's book and her explanation. Scared and confused, Kate is comforted by her teacher's calm support and acceptance of responsibility. The principal listens to Kate and agrees the incident was innocent, but she decides to suspend the reading project for the time being. Kate's parents are understanding and supportive. Her older brother is upset, however, because the incident almost causes a breakup with his girlfriend, whose parents are angered by what happened. Soon a public controversy begins, to Kate's extreme distress. Letters appear in the newspaper, both for and against the reading project, and an organization is formed called "Parents United for Decency." They want "smut" removed from the school and library bookshelves. Finally the school board calls a meeting, Kate included, to discuss what has happened and whether or not the project should continue. Upset by the discussion, Kate stands and defends the book, the discussion that followed, and the reading project. Her speech receives favorable applause, and the board votes to continue the project. The library begins to hold weekly adult discussions about children's books, more children volunteer for the reading project, and, best of all, Maudie is accepted into Kate's group.

Kate's first-person narrative looks humorously at a serious subject, censorship in school and library. Kate defends the book she read and the discussion that followed, and her courage leads to a defeat for the forces

**M**

of censorship. Along the way, the friendship between Kate and Maudie blossoms. Some thought-provoking discussions may follow the reading here.

Ages 10-12

**Also available in:**
Braille—*Maudie and Me and the Dirty Book*
Library of Congress (NLSBPH)

Cassette—*Maudie and Me and the Dirty Book*
Library of Congress (NLSBPH)

Paperbound—*Maudie and Me and the Dirty Book*
Avon Books

## 424

Miles, Betty

### The Trouble with Thirteen

Alfred A. Knopf, Inc., 1979.
(108 pages)

---

CHANGE: Accepting
 Death: of pet
 Divorce: of parents
 Friendship: best friend
 Loss: feelings of
 Maturation
 Menstruation
 Moving

---

Annie Morrison and Rachel Weiss have been best friends since nursery school. On a perfect spring day, they both wish they could stay twelve forever. Annie doesn't like the way "things are always changing." But she is helpless when Rachel announces that her parents are getting a divorce and she will soon move to the city with her mother. Annie dreads the changes that Rachel's absence will bring. She also dreads the possibility of Rachel becoming a sophisticated New Yorker and leaving her, Annie, far behind. When Kate, one of their friends, announces she's getting her ears pierced, Annie again feels that everything is changing too fast for her. One day Rachel goes into the city with her mother to look at schools and misses the slumber party Kate has for her thirteenth birthday. When she returns, Rachel is excited about her new school, the city, and the friends she is making there; Annie wants to talk about the birthday party and learning how to dance. Rachel and Annie do resume most of their former closeness the next day, however, when Annie's old dog, Nora, dies. Annie grieves for a long time and wonders if the sadness will ever fade. When she gets her first period she wants to tell Rachel about it, but the right moment doesn't seem to come. One Saturday they decide to walk all around town, with Rachel taking pictures of Annie in the old familiar places. While acting silly in the dime store photo booth, Annie tells Rachel she got her period. Rachel says she did too, and their friendship seems stronger than ever. But when they go into New York for a day, their tensions and sadness erupt in a shouting match in front of a dress shop. They are reconciled when each begins yelling that the other is her best friend. They go into the shop and buy two look-alike dresses; now they feel like real New Yorkers. Rachel's young aunt further encourages them when she says that her best friend lives in Bloomington, Indiana, that people can remain best friends even if they don't live in the same city. But the day Rachel moves is a sad one for Annie. She reflects that although she'll probably have fun that summer, life will definitely be different—no Nora and no Rachel. Rachel gives Annie her prized dollhouse that they both have added to and tended over the years. They use the last precious hour left to them to start a quilt for one of the beds. Annie gives Rachel, who dreams of becoming a photographer, a photography book she's admired. On the flyleaf, Annie has written a poem. At the last minute, when Rachel's mother arrives to pick her up, Rachel gives Annie a picture of Nora that she'd taken shortly before the dog's death. Annie muses on how long ago that seems. "We were like children. I remembered how I wished we would never grow up and that things would never change. In the back of my mind I must have known they would."

In this first-person narrative, Annie, who hates changes, details the feelings of young teenage girls facing traumatic alterations in their lives—menstruation, divorce, changes in friends, the death of a beloved pet, separation from a best friend. Her candor adds depth to the characterizations as she and Rachel, about to live apart, manage to preserve the closeness they have always enjoyed.

Ages 9-13

**Also available in:**
Paperbound—*The Trouble with Thirteen*
Avon Books

## 425

Miles, Miska, pseud.

### Jenny's Cat

Black/white illustrations by Wendy Watson.
E. P. Dutton & Company, Inc., 1979.
(40 pages)

---

CHANGE: New Home
 Pets: love for
 Running away

---

Already feeling lonely and friendless in her new house in a new town, young Jenny is especially unhappy when her father, a train conductor, must travel, and she has to share a bed with her mother, who is afraid to sleep alone. One night the two hear sounds outside, and Jenny assures her mother that it is only branches moving in the wind. But in the morning she finds a small cat on the porch. Jenny wants to keep it but her mother is cool to the idea, disliking cats and worrying about unwanted kittens. Though she doesn't really know, Jenny claims the cat is a male. Patches grows dear to Jenny, but when her father returns they discover that Patches is indeed a female and will soon have kittens. Jenny's mother insists the cat must go, and so Jenny takes Patches and runs away. She goes across the street to her new friend Doris's house, and Doris hides the two in the basement. Soon Jenny's parents arrive looking for her. Doris tells them that Jenny ran away to save the cat. When Jenny, still hiding, hears her father say they are not going to take Patches to a farm, she comes upstairs to her angry but relieved parents. Her father says he knows a man who will spay Patches. In spring, three kittens are born. Jenny keeps one and places the other two with neighbors, one of them Doris.

A little girl succeeds in keeping her beloved cat and makes a good friend along the way. Jenny's loneliness in her new neighborhood, her mother's fears, her own love for Patches, and her decision to run away are all realistically described, as is the decision to have the cat spayed. Though the illustrations suggest a time early in the century, the problem of unwanted stray animals remains current.

Ages 6-8

**Also available in:**
Paperbound—*Jenny's Cat*
Bantam Books, Inc.

## 426

**Mills, Claudia**

**At the Back of the Woods**
Four Winds Press, 1982.
(86 pages)

COURAGE, MEANING OF
  Communication: parent-child
  Friendship: meaning of
  Identification with others: peers
  Mental illness: of parent
  Superstition

Ten-year-old Clarisse still remembers the day Emily moved into the neighborhood. She joined the group of friends—Suellen, Mandy, Patsy, Inga, and Clarisse—who play by the brook at the edge of the woods. On the other side of the brook, in an ancient, run-down house, lives Mrs. Spinelli, who keeps chickens and is thought to be a witch. Emily, Clarisse finds, is very brave. She's not afraid to jump off a high branch by the brook and teaches Clarisse to jump too by holding her hand and jumping with her. At Patsy's birthday party, Emily notices that Inga, poorly dressed as usual, is ashamed of the birthday gift she's brought—a can opener, the only thing she could find around the house to give. So Emily trades gifts with her and isn't bothered at all by the others' scorn. Later, Mandy brings in her father's girlie magazines, embarrassing Clarisse because nothing remotely related to sex or even bathrooms is ever mentioned in her house. Emily isn't at all interested in the magazines since she's used to nudity. But she admits she'd like to jump out of the tree naked and soon does so. Emily's shows of bravery continue. To prove that Mrs. Spinelli is not a witch, she crosses the brook, touches the chicken coop, and does not shrivel up and die. Emily also thinks Clarisse's retarded little brother, Davey, is cute and is happy to hold him. When Inga's mother is due home from a mental hospital, Mandy and Suellen tease Inga about the electric shock treatment they've heard rumors about. Emily slaps them both to make them quit. In revenge, Mandy tells her mother that Emily instigated looking at the girlie magazines, adding the story about Emily jumping naked from the tree. All the mothers then shun Emily, except Clarisse's mother, to her daughter's surprise. Just before a hurricane, Emily crosses the brook again and comes back with Mrs. Spinelli's cat to show the others that it's not a witch's familiar. She then lets it go. But the next morning, after the hurricane, the cat is found drowned in the drainpipe and Mrs. Spinelli has a big sign in her yard: "To whoever killed my cat BEWARE I HAVE PUT A CURSE ON YOU." Clarisse stays with her aunt while her parents fly Davey to Tulsa, Oklahoma, to seek some new treatment. They return without Davey and are vague about when he'll come home. Then Emily gets the measles and is delirious, talking about Mrs. Spinelli's cat and the curse. One day after she's well again, when she is about to jump from their tree, Emily looks across the brook and sees Mrs. Spinelli. Clarisse watches as Emily's face turns green with fear. When she jumps, she breaks her leg. Clarisse soon realizes that the accident has changed something inside her friend. Perhaps she'd been so brave and free because nothing had ever before hurt her. "It occurred to me then that I had been braver than Emily when we jumped together from the big tree—because I was jumping in spite of my fear, and Emily had never been afraid. Suddenly the image of Inga waiting for her mother to come home seemed the bravest sight I had ever seen." Emily's cast comes off in December, but the girls don't play in the woods together the way they used to. The next summer, Clarisse and her parents go to visit Davey. When she returns home, she finds that Emily's family has moved away suddenly. She had no chance to say goodbye, but Clarisse knows she will never forget her friend.

A young girl learns the difference between unthinking bravery and real courage in this perceptive first-person narrative. Many issues are well handled here, despite the book's brevity: friendship, family communication, courage, mental illness. Clarisse's brother's mental retardation is smoothly integrated into the plot, but the lack of communication on the subject between Clarisse and her parents strikes a false note. Each of the friends is perceptively characterized, and their sometimes frightening childhood world is vividly conveyed.

Ages 9-11

**Also available in:**
No other form known

## 427

**Milton, Hilary Herbert**

**Mayday! Mayday!**
Franklin Watts, Inc., 1979.
(152 pages)

COURAGE, MEANING OF
  Accidents: airplane
  Fear: of physical harm

The light plane carrying eleven-year-old Allison Parker, her mother, and four family friends crashes on a mountainside in bad weather. Four passengers are injured or unconscious. The bruised Allison and her injured friend Mark Brasfield leave to get help. To keep the site clearly in mind they try to walk in straight lines, but they are thwarted by an impassable thicket, an abandoned mine, and a menacing pack of wild dogs. Meanwhile, rescue efforts begin as airport personnel determine that the plane is missing and contact the Civil Air Patrol. As the cold night drags on, Mark slips and nearly strangles on his makeshift splint. Allison saves him and they continue, weakened by hunger, thirst, and despair. At last they find a small stream and a dirt road, glimpsing a light in the distance. Allison is too weak to continue, but she convinces the reluctant Mark to leave her and press forward alone. Counting his steps in order to return to Allison, Mark reaches the house. Rescue follows: Mark's sister is dead, but the rest survive. As Allison falls asleep nestled against her grandfather, she remembers one of the wild dogs that threatened them. Safe at last, she drifts off thinking she might turn the dog into a pet.

With few survival skills and only a flashlight, two young people endure their own fears and a danger-filled night to bring rescue to air-crash victims. The main characters are believable and their actions intelligent and mature. Experienced flyers might wonder why the plane was allowed to remain aloft in such severe weather.

Ages 9-11

**Also available in:**
No other form known

## 428

Miner, Jane Claypool

### A Day at a Time: Dealing with an Alcoholic
Color illustrations by Vista III Design.
Crestwood House, Inc., 1982.
(63 pages)

*ALCOHOLISM: of Father*
*Family: relationships*

Ellen Russell has grown up with the sounds of her parents fighting about her father's drinking. She wishes she could tell him how awful it is to have a drunk for a father. Lately, he seems to be getting worse again. One day her mother leaves a message at his office asking him to come straight home because of an emergency. When he arrives and asks about the emergency, she explains that since he is usually drunk when he comes home, she needs to talk to him about his drinking while he is sober. But that night there is another fight, and when her father goes after her mother with a broken bottle, Ellen calls the police. Her father is booked and sent to the detoxification center for twenty-one days. Both Ellen and her mother feel torn by guilt. Then Ellen's mother begins attending Alanon meetings and starts to change. She had been obsessed by her husband's drinking, but now she seems almost indifferent. When Ellen asks her what she's going to do when her father comes home from the hospital, her mother says she can't worry about that yet; she takes one day at a time. As expected, after he comes home her father resumes drinking. Ellen is determined to "help" him, despite her mother's opinion that he must help himself. When her mother refuses to bribe or manipulate her father into staying home at night, Ellen blames the Alanon meetings for making everything worse. She has consistently refused to attend any Alateen meetings. Her mother explains what Alanon has taught her: neither she nor Ellen is the cause of the father's drinking and neither can be the cure for it. One night when her father tries to take the car keys after he's been drinking, Ellen tries to stop him. She realizes

she sounds just the way her mother did before she joined Alanon. Her father strikes her. Suddenly Ellen sees very clearly that there is no way she can prevent him from drinking if he wants to. She must live her own life. If she hurries, she can make that night's Alateen meeting.

This book presents a family trapped in the familiar behavior patterns caused by the alcoholism of one member. Two very helpful points are emphasized: no one can prevent the alcoholic from drinking but himself or herself; feeling guilty is both inappropriate and ineffective. Ellen's story ends hopefully when she decides to join Alateen. She has made the choices that affect her, and her father must make his choices. This title is one of the Crisis Series of books, each of which focuses on a significant contemporary topic, making them especially appropriate for initiating discussion. Although characterizations lack depth and resolutions are simplistic, these abundantly illustrated books will appeal to reluctant readers.

Ages 11 and up

**Also available in:**
No other form known

## 429

Miner, Jane Claypool

### A Man's Pride: Losing a Father
Color illustrations by Vista III Design.
Crestwood House, Inc., 1982.
(63 pages)

*PRIDE/FALSE PRIDE*
*Death: of father*
*Job*
*Responsibility: accepting*

Tim Simmons's father died two months ago, and at sixteen Tim is now the man of the family. Remembering how proud his father was, Tim refuses to consider letting his family go on welfare and he rips up the welfare worker's papers when she comes to visit. His mother remarks that his father was a good man and a good worker, but that he had too much pride sometimes. Tim decides not to finish his last year of high school; instead, he will work full-time at a store to support his mother and younger sister. Then a shopper runs her cart into the ladder Tim is standing on and blames Tim for the mess. Tim yells back that it's her fault. When the store manager reprimands Tim but offers to give him a second chance, he quits. "A man has to keep his pride." At his next job, the owner of the store drinks and cheats Tim out of a week's wages. The boy resolves to be more careful about jobs in the future. His mother fears they can't afford to keep the house, but Tim knows his father would not have wanted them to move into a housing project. So he takes a hard, dirty, dangerous job as a furnace cleaner and lies about his age to get it. He feels diminished having to lie, knowing his father would never have done so. But he'll never be the man his father was, Tim decides sadly. He feels guilty knowing his boss could lose his business if it were discovered he had hired someone under eighteen. Then a man, Frank, approaches him about becoming partners. If Tim will put up two hundred dollars, all he has, along with his father's old truck, Frank will supply him with roofing and painting jobs. Tim distrusts the proposition, but he meets Frank in a parking lot anyway to turn over the money as arranged. Before Tim can insist on coming along to purchase the roofing supplies, he's hit over the head. He wakes up in a hospital and is told that Frank is a small-time crook. The truck is recovered, but the money is not. Wiser now, Tim decides he needs a little more school before he's ready to tackle the full-time job world, and he approves of his mother's decision to move into the housing project. Maybe after another year of school, Tim considers, he'll be better prepared to follow in his father's footsteps.

Tim's story conveys with painful clarity the realities of finding and keeping a job that pays a living wage. After several mishaps, he concludes that finishing high school is a good way to prepare for the world of work. He also learns that a man's pride can sometimes be unrealistic and counterproductive. This title is one of the Crisis Series of books, each of which focuses on a significant contemporary topic, making them especially appropriate for initiating discussion. Although characterizations lack depth and resolutions are simplistic, these abundantly illustrated books will appeal to reluctant readers.

Ages 11 and up

**Also available in:**
No other form known

## 430

Miner, Jane Claypool

### Miracle of Time: Adopting a Sister

Color illustrations by Vista III Design.
Crestwood House, Inc., 1982.
(63 pages)

---

ADOPTION: Feelings About
    Orphan
    Sibling: relationships

---

As Shirley helps the younger children with their dance class and prepares for her own lesson, she thinks about Kim, the five-year-old Vietnamese orphan her family is adopting. Kim will be arriving today, and Shirley is so excited about getting the sister she's always wanted that she has given up the space in her bedroom she uses for dancing so she and Kim can share the room. When Shirley gets home that evening, however, Kim is already sleeping. Their first contact is at three in the morning when Kim wakes her with screams. The next day the child looks blank and far away, does not speak, and won't respond to Shirley or her parents. They take her to a doctor who recommends lots of love, rest, and time. To Shirley, sad and a little angry, Kim seems a stranger, not the dream sister she's longed for. When Kim eats she gobbles, snuffles, uses her hands, and makes a mess. She seems to live in a world of her own and continues to resist all attempts to reach her. Shirley retrieves a rag doll that her mother made for her when she was little and spends an evening refurbishing it for Kim. The next morning she finds it on Kim's floor, ripped and destroyed. The doctor now thinks Kim might have to go to a home for disturbed children. That day at

school is disastrous for Shirley: she fails a history exam because she worked on the rag doll instead of studying, her dance teacher reprimands her for slacking off, and she feels like a failure for not being able to reach Kim. She also hates herself for being angry with a helpless orphan. Her parents plan to call the agency on Monday to make arrangements to take Kim to the home. They are deeply distressed, but feel they've made no progress in the months Kim has been with them. Then, as she works with the children at the dance studio, Shirley wonders if dance and music could reach Kim. Saturday morning she puts on a record, dresses in her tutu, and sits Kim on a chair in front of her. For a long time, Shirley dances—beautiful dances, fast dances, comical dances. Nothing seems to reach Kim. Finally, to show her frustration and despair, she mimes banging her head against the wall. She hears a laugh—Kim's. Shirley repeats the mime and then calls her mother. They hug Kim, and Shirley and her mother laugh together. Kim smiles. "It was a small smile, but it was a beginning."

A teenage girl reaches her emotionally scarred adoptive sister through her dancing. Shirley moves from unrealistic expectations for Kim, through anger and sadness, to hope, encouraging readers in similar circumstances to accept their changing, often contradictory feelings. This title is one of the Crisis Series of books, each of which focuses on a significant contemporary topic, making them especially appropriate for initiating discussion. Although characterizations lack depth and resolutions are simplistic, these abundantly illustrated books will appeal to reluctant readers.

Ages 11 and up

**Also available in:**
No other form known

## 431

Miner, Jane Claypool

### Mountain Fear: When a Brother Dies

Color illustrations by Vista III Design.
Crestwood House, Inc., 1982.
(63 pages)

---

DEATH: of Sibling
FEAR
    Loss: feelings of

---

The Murphy twins are hiking in the mountains when Don slips over the edge of a cliff and falls. John hears his scream and tries to reach him, but eventually has to go for help. A fire department crew brings Don's body up on a stretcher. John is devastated by his brother's death. After the funeral, when a doctor advises John to resume his normal life as soon as possible, he can't understand how anything can ever be normal again. "For him, it was normal to be one of the Murphy twins. He couldn't imagine being alone." On his first day back at school his friend Raymond and then a teacher try to talk to him, but John can't respond. In gym class he runs up on the bleachers to recover a ball and then freezes when he looks down to the floor below. It takes both Raymond and the gym teacher to pry him off the bleachers; John discovers he is terrified of heights. He decides to skip school for the next three days. On his way home, he goes to the zoo and meets a ten-year-old boy who's trying to steal his wallet. The boy won't give his name, so John calls him Bozo. He discovers that Bozo is one of six children and is left on his own a lot. The child asks John if he'd like a little brother. John doesn't mention Don, but says he'd be glad to have a brother who will quit stealing and skipping school. When Bozo points out that John is also skipping school, John says he's going back. For the next three weeks, John meets Bozo at the zoo every day. The boy is full of questions and imitates everything John does. Once when John sees Bozo climbing a tall jungle gym, he urges him to get down—and then realizes he has communicated his fear of heights to the impressionable child. Raymond wants John to proceed with plans they made before Don's death to go camping in Canada, but John rudely refuses. He feels sorry as he watches Raymond walk away, but decides it's better to be alone and not care about people; then you're not hurt if you lose them. Bozo asks John to be his big brother at a Boy's Club camping trip. But when John learns they'll be camping on Mt. Washington, where Don died, he refuses, even though he sees how hurt Bozo is. To make amends he invites the boy to the beach and amusement park. While riding a Ferris wheel, Bozo is stuck at the top and becomes hysterically frightened. He starts climbing out, and the young man in charge of the ride doesn't know what to do. John climbs up the spokes of the wheel and sits with Bozo until another park worker frees the lever that works the wheel. Later, John invites Bozo to go for a long bike ride with him and Raymond.

A teenage boy whose twin brother dies in a fall off a cliff overcomes his resulting fear of heights by fearing for someone else's safety more than for his own. Young "Bozo" acts as a catalyst to bring John out of his depression and back to life. The book touches only lightly on Don's death and John's stages of mourning; instead, it concentrates on John's fear and on the healing powers of human relationships. This title is one of the Crisis Series of books, each of which focuses on a significant contemporary topic, making them especially appropriate for initiating discussion. Although characterizations lack depth and resolutions are simplistic, these abundantly illustrated books will appeal to reluctant readers.

Ages 10 and up

**Also available in:**
No other form known

## 432

**Miner, Jane Claypool**

### Navajo Victory: Being a Native American
Color illustrations by Vista III Design.
Crestwood House, Inc., 1982.
(63 pages)

---

*NATIVE AMERICAN*
  *Bully: being bothered by*
  *Expectations*
  *Prejudice: ethnic/racial*
  *School: classmate relationships*
  *School: transfer*

---

Every year the Navajo Tribal Council sends one boy to Los Angeles for schooling, hoping to benefit from new skills and ideas by giving some of their people advanced educations. This year they have sent Manuel to Central Vocational High School, and he's worried. He wonders what his family will say if he fails; his grandfather has told him not to shame them. He worries about being able to learn fast enough and about what the other students think of him. He already knows what Sonny thinks of him. Sonny calls him Injun Boy and harasses him every chance he gets. One day Sonny pulls a knife on Manuel, but Manuel manages to trip him and grab the knife away just as the history teacher comes into view. Both are sent to the principal, who expels Sonny and must also reprimand Manuel since he was involved, however innocently. Manuel's Uncle Luis, with whom he's living, comes to school and defends the boy. Manuel's history class is studying the Indians of the Southwest and one day Manuel describes some of their sand paintings. After class, a girl warns him that Sonny's friends are out to get him. When school is out, as Manuel is erasing the sand painting design he drew on the board, three of Sonny's friends come in and vandalize the room, spray-painting Manuel's name on the wall. Certain he will never prove his innocence, Manuel leaves a note for his uncle and takes a bus back to the reservation. He arrives to find that his grandfather is dying. The old man gives the boy a pouch containing two thousand dollars. Manuel protests that he doesn't deserve the money and tries to tell his grandfather about his problems. But his grandfather maintains that the way he uses the money will show if he deserves it or not. After the old man's funeral, Manuel goes camping in the desert, a traditional Navajo way of working out troubled feelings. He thinks over his life on the reservation and in Los Angeles. He notices the prairie dogs scurrying about, acting largely on unfounded fears of nonexistent wolves. Manuel wonders if he too has been running scared for no reason. He determines to make a go of it at Central or, if that doesn't work out, at some other high school. "No matter what, he would finish his work."

A Native American teenager confronts prejudice and injustice as he tries to succeed at a public school. Manuel's story gives readers a glimpse of the difficulties posed by having to live with two sometimes-contradictory value systems. In the end, Manuel appears to have learned how to respond to the best in both. This title is one of the Crisis Series of books, each of which focuses on a significant contemporary topic, making them especially appropriate for initiating discussion. Although characterizations lack depth and resolutions are simplistic, these abundantly illustrated books will appeal to reluctant readers.

Ages 11 and up

**Also available in:**
No other form known

**433**

Miner, Jane Claypool

## New Beginning: An Athlete Is Paralyzed

Color illustrations by Vista III Design.
Crestwood House, Inc., 1982.
(63 pages)

---

*PARAPLEGIA*
*Change: accepting*
*Sports/Sportsmanship*
*Wheelchair, dependence on*

---

At seventeen, Steve's whole life revolves around football. All his future plans depend on the game, since he wants either to play pro ball or to be a coach. Then, in the first play of the season's first game, he's tackled and suffers a back injury that leaves him paralyzed from the waist down. He can't accept the possibility of spending the rest of his life in a wheelchair. "He would never get used to it! Never." When the paralysis proves permanent, Steve believes his life is ruined, that now he is utterly useless. Back at home, he soon gives up doing things for himself and eventually spends the entire day in bed watching television. A teacher for homebound students visits with schoolwork, but Steve doesn't do it and the teacher doesn't appear to care. Four months after the accident, Steve's mother insists he go back to school. But he can't see the point and doesn't want people feeling sorry for him. Then Coach Stein, whom Steve has refused to see since the accident, comes to replace the homebound teacher. He tells Steve he has four weeks to make up his homework or he'll fail. Steve begins doing his work and looks forward to Coach Stein's visits. When Steve mentions how useless he feels, the coach tells him about a job at a nearby grocery store ringing up sales and bagging groceries. Very doubtful about his ability to do the job, Steve tries to back out of the interview. But the coach insists, and Steve decides to try his best to get the job. He is hired and enjoys the work. One day he notices a little boy named Buddy stealing some candy. Steve gives him the opportunity to put it back quietly. Later he discovers that Buddy wants to learn to play basketball, so Steve gives him a few tips and then takes him to the Y and coaches him. Buddy mentions a team in a nearby town that plays wheelchair basketball. Steve decides that maybe he won't have to give up sports for the rest of his life. "He was feeling alive and hopeful for the first time since the accident."

A young athlete learns to accept his paralysis and find new ways of looking toward his future. Although Steve will have to cope with a great many other changes in his life, the emphasis here is on his self-image. He has to give up a lifelong image of himself as one kind of person in exchange for another view: different, but perhaps equally life-enhancing and satisfying. This title is one of the Crisis Series of books, each of which focuses on a significant contemporary topic, making them especially appropriate for initiating discussion. Although characterizations lack depth and resolutions are simplistic, these abundantly illustrated books will appeal to reluctant readers.

Ages 11 and up

**Also available in:**
No other form known

**434**

Miner, Jane Claypool

## She's My Sister: Having a Retarded Sister

Color illustrations by Vista III Design.
Crestwood House, Inc., 1982.
(63 pages)

---

*MENTAL RETARDATION*
*Egocentrism*
*Peer relationships*
*Rejection: sibling*

---

Sixteen-year-old Mary Lou worries when she learns her retarded older sister, Judy, is coming home from her special school to attend Mary Lou's school. Her mother reassures her that Judy will be in a different part of the school, but since her friends' favorite put-down is "retard," Mary Lou knows it would be a social disaster for her if her friends find out she has a retarded sister. She pleads with her parents to let her transfer to West High, and they eventually give their permission. Then she mentions that it would save her a two-hour bus ride if she could live with her Aunt Helen. She spends a week with Helen before school starts and enjoys it. But living with her aunt proves less pleasant. Aunt Helen accuses Mary Lou of being selfish and spoiled, makes her do everything her way, and insists on absolute neatness. Miserable, Mary Lou moves back home. Judy is glad to see her, but their mother tries to keep Judy out of Mary Lou's way so Mary Lou can live as normal a life as possible. One night when Mary Lou is talking on the phone to a boy she likes, Judy comes along and wants to talk too. Mary Lou quickly ends the call and then complains bitterly to her mother. The mother apologizes, but when Mary Lou remembers some of the things Aunt Helen accused her of, she apologizes herself for overreacting. She still refuses to have a party at her house, absolutely determined that no one ever know about Judy. She turns down invitations and keeps more and more to herself, realizing she's losing friends but terrified that Judy will wander into her part of the school and claim her as her sister. Then one day, while she's on an errand in Judy's part of the school, Mary Lou sees two boys talking to Judy. They call her sweetheart and pretend to fight over her favors. Believing the teasing is harmless, Mary Lou badly wants to walk away before the boys see her. One of them dates her friend, and if he finds out Judy is her sister the story will soon be all over the school. In the end, however, Mary Lou is unable to leave Judy in this uncertain situation. She greets Judy and asks what she's doing. The boys are surprised, but Mary Lou explains in a clear voice that Judy is her sister.

A self-centered teenage girl fears her social life will be ruined if anyone finds out she has a retarded sister. Although Mary Lou, aided and abetted by her mother, goes to great lengths to avoid claiming Judy, she eventually does so when Judy needs her. The reader suspects that Mary Lou's tendency to see people and events only from her own perspective will now begin to change.

M

This title is one of the Crisis Series of books, each of which focuses on a significant contemporary topic, making them especially appropriate for initiating discussion. Although characterizations lack depth and resolutions are simplistic, these abundantly illustrated books will appeal to reluctant readers.

Ages 11 and up

**Also available in:**
No other form known

**435**

Miner, Jane Claypool

**Split Decision: Facing Divorce**
Color illustrations by Vista III Design.
Crestwood House, Inc., 1982.
(63 pages)

---

DIVORCE: of Parents
  Change: accepting
  Decision making
  Family: relationships

---

When sixteen-year-old Ann's parents announce they are getting a divorce, they tell her she can choose whom she will live with. Angry with both for divorcing without what she considers sufficient cause, Ann spends the next weeks trying to bring about a reconciliation. She takes her father a homemade meal and tells him her mother sent the food. But he mentions the messy house when he picked Ann up that morning and says sending food wasn't part of their arrangement. Ann's mother would do better to clean up the house so it will look more attractive to potential buyers. Unable to accept defeat, Ann quickly buys her mother a box of candy and says it's from her father. Her mother knows Ann bought it and thanks her; her husband never once brought her a gift in seventeen years. Now Ann tries to decide which parent to live with. She appreciates her father's dependability and orderliness, but she also enjoys her mother's sociability and sense of fun. She needs them both. She tries another tack, reporting to each the compliments supposedly given by the other, but this backfires and makes them angrier at each other. She makes up a love interest for each, hoping to stir up jealousy, but neither seems to care. When she realizes that her parents actually seem happier since their separation, Ann begins to doubt the wisdom of her efforts. But she insists that all three of them talk, although her parents have decided never to see each other again. They've made some decisions and they have their rights, Ann concedes, but she has rights too. She wants to live with both of them. She wants two bedrooms, two sets of clothes, two sets of furniture. She needs both her parents and will split her time equally between them.

Ann's story reveals the painful and powerful drive some children feel to mend their parents' troubled marriage. Only reluctantly does Ann accept the fact that the marriage is over. The focus of the book is on Ann's determination to affect her parents' decision, a goal usually doomed but shared by many children of divorce. This title is one of the Crisis Series of books, each of which focuses on a significant contemporary topic, making them especially appropriate for initiating discussion.

Although characterizations lack depth and resolutions are simplistic, these abundantly illustrated books will appeal to reluctant readers.

Ages 11 and up

**Also available in:**
No other form known

**436**

Miner, Jane Claypool

**This Day Is Mine: Living with Leukemia**
Color illustrations by Vista III Design.
Crestwood House, Inc., 1982.
(63 pages)

---

LEUKEMIA
  Communication: importance of
  Courage, meaning of
  Hospital, going to
  Illnesses: being ill
  Illnesses: terminal

---

After three weeks of tests, sixteen-year-old Cheryl is finally leaving the hospital. She should be relieved, but she's very worried. No one explains anything to her, people tend to whisper around her, and she doesn't like the way her parents are acting. Seeing her mother with a nurse, Cheryl demands to know what they're talking about. The nurse wants to tell Cheryl the truth, but her mother maintains that Cheryl was just a little tired and now she's better. Cheryl insists on seeing the doctor and is finally told she has leukemia. At first appalled, Cheryl then feels terribly angry at being kept in the dark for three weeks. When her parents want her to return to school, Cheryl asks why she should study. She "had quickly learned that all she had to do was talk about dying and they would give in. They were afraid to face the facts, and they wanted her to stop talking about it, too." Sick of their whispered conversations and evasions, Cheryl runs away in the middle of the night to her Aunt Marsha. None of the family knows about her leukemia, and Cheryl hopes Marsha will treat her normally. But on the way, when she's frightened by a man who approaches her, Cheryl falls and cuts her knee. She remembers that one of the symptoms of leukemia is bleeding that won't stop, so when Marsha takes her to the hospital she doesn't object. Four days later she's still there, but feeling better. She tells her mother, "That trip in the night taught me something I needed to know. Life is important as long as you have it." Her mother apologizes for her own and Cheryl's father's behavior, and Cheryl resolves to be hopeful. But the bad feelings come back anyway. She is sad, frightened, angry, worried. Then a nurse asks Cheryl if she'll spend some time with a younger girl in the next room. Cindy Lou looks very sick, but doesn't seem to feel sorry for herself. After the two play cards and talk, Cheryl leaves, promising to see Cindy Lou tomorrow. The younger girl replies, "I never talk about tomorrow. But this day has been good. This day is mine." In response to Cheryl's questions, the nurse admits that Cindy Lou hasn't much longer to live, but that her leukemia is different from Cheryl's. Cheryl thinks about Cindy Lou, who can't have her parents with her because they live out of town, who will probably never go home again, who has learned to live each day fully. That evening, Cheryl tells her parents that she's going to lead as normal a life as she can for as much time as she has.

A teenage girl learns to accept her leukemia and live for the present instead of worrying about an unpredictable future. Some information about leukemia—life expectancy, symptoms, treatment—is given, but the focus is on appreciating the gift of today. Cheryl deals with a number of different feelings as she confronts her illness, including anger at her parents' reluctance to face the truth. This title is one of the Crisis Series of books, each of which focuses on a significant contemporary topic, making them especially appropriate for initiating discussion. Although characterizations lack depth and resolutions are simplistic, these abundantly illustrated books will appeal to reluctant readers.

Ages 10 and up

**Also available in:**
No other form known

## 437

Miner, Jane Claypool

**The Tough Guy: Black in a White World**
Color illustrations by Vista III Design.
Crestwood House, Inc., 1982.
(63 pages)

*AFRO-AMERICAN*
*INTEGRATION*
  *Courage, meaning of*
  *Prejudice: ethnic/racial*
  *School: classmate relationships*
  *School: transfer*

Fifteen-year-old Larry's family has moved and he is attending a new school, one with exactly six black students. Larry is sure the white kids won't give him a chance. But he's determined to hide his fears and act tough. Accordingly, in his first class on his first day he tangles with a boy named Bob and ends up in the principal's office, refusing to explain what happened. When the teacher suggests that Larry might be a troublemaker, the principal replies that he'll give Larry a chance—he has a good record from his previous school. That afternoon, Larry is attacked from behind by three white boys and beaten unconscious. When the police question him Larry can't identify the boys, although he remembers a bracelet one was wearing. On their way home from the hospital, his parents discuss the possibility that their move was a mistake. But Larry's father points out that only three students were involved, and he asks Larry to give the rest of the school a chance. Mike Jamison, a classmate, tells Larry he's sorry about what happened, but Larry ignores him. When Larry gets the highest grade on a tough science test, the teacher announces it out loud. Larry wonders if the kids looking at him are surprised because they think blacks aren't very smart. Two shy girls approach him about joining the science club, but he refuses. Then Larry seeks out Kevin, a senior with whom he doesn't really have much in common. But at least they're both black. At lunch Bob deliberately pushes Larry and then loudly accuses Larry of pushing him. When Mike defends Larry, Larry is rude

to him. One Saturday afternoon with Kevin convinces Larry that just because they're both black doesn't mean they will automatically be friends. On his way home, he runs into Mike and some other boys playing baseball. He joins them and enjoys himself until he notices that one of the boys, Charlie, is wearing the bracelet Larry remembers from his beating. He decides that if Charlie is Mike's friend, then Mike isn't worth his time. Larry tries to convince his parents to move back to their old town, but they can't and his father asks him not to be a quitter. So Larry plans to run away after school the next day. But the day is an eventful one. He manages to get Bob off his back, has fun in gym, and saves Charlie's life with his resuscitation techniques when Charlie collapses on the track. As Charlie is carried off on a stretcher, he thanks Larry and says he has something to tell him. But Larry shrugs off what's in the past. Mike asks Larry to play ball with him that evening. Larry realizes that going back to his old school isn't the answer. His aunt really doesn't have room for him, and he does hate to be a quitter. Mike and Kevin are already his friends, and Larry knows he'll have more.

A black teenager in an overwhelmingly white school believes everyone's response to him, good or bad, is really just to his skin color. There is real prejudice in Larry's new school, but he brings most of his troubles on himself, and this is the major focus of the book. Readers may be able to identify times when they expected others to react negatively to them because of their looks, grades, athletic ability, and so forth. They will sympathize, however, with Larry's special loneliness. This title is one of the Crisis Series of books, each of which focuses on a significant contemporary topic, making them especially appropriate for initiating discussion. Although characterizations lack depth and resolutions are simplistic, these abundantly illustrated books will appeal to reluctant readers.

Ages 11 and up

**Also available in:**
No other form known

## 438

Moeri, Louise

**First the Egg**
E. P. Dutton & Company, Inc., 1982.
(99 pages)

*RESPONSIBILITY: Accepting*
  *Boy-girl relationships*
  *Egocentrism*
  *Family: relationships*
  *Maturation*
  *Rejection: parental*
  *Values/Valuing: moral/ethical*

High school senior Sarah Webster is as astonished as her classmates when the instructor in her Marriage and Family class pairs the students off, gives each couple a raw egg, and tells them they are to become the egg's parents for the next five days, applying all they've learned about caring for a newborn baby. They are never to leave the egg unattended, unless it is "sleeping" in an adjoining room. They are to keep a baby book,

M

listing everything they do for the egg. Sarah is paired with David Hanna, a handsome but hostile transfer student with an icy personality and a caustic tongue. When Sarah explains her assignment at the dinner table, her father becomes inexplicably and deeply angry about it. Sarah begins to become involved with her egg, waking at two in the morning for its "feeding" and worrying when it's David's turn to watch over it. She's puzzled when her father makes remarks about there being too many babies in the world already. Then she finds her mother crying in the middle of the night and discovers that her father never wanted their last child, nine-year-old Julie. He'd been planning to start his own business when his wife became pregnant and has since blamed her for his failure to make a lot of money. He frequently threatens to leave her. Suddenly Sarah understands the distance she has always sensed between her father and Julie, and she realizes that Julie is a little too quiet, too unassuming. When David, a prospective doctor, turns the egg and the baby book over to Sarah the next day, she reads his entries. He refers to the egg as "the patient" and says it appears to be so severely retarded that several pediatricians have recommended it be institutionalized. Sarah ponders the dilemma of one parent wanting a child institutionalized and the other not. David stops over to say she'll have to finish the egg project alone; he's taking off for Baja with several friends. He's not going to graduate or go on to college. When her friend Becca tells Sarah to alert David's father, Sarah refuses. She suspects that David wants her to do just that, so he will be absolved of all responsibility for his decision. He's not in school the next morning but shows up later in the afternoon, telling Sarah that he left his friends and hitchhiked home. She's glad he's not going to ruin the egg project because she really needs the good grade she's working for. She has not worked up to her potential in high school, she realizes. Then her mother announces she has taken a job. Sarah will have to fix dinner every night and help out while her mother works an evening shift. When she complains that her older brother, Rob, should help, her mother points out that Rob is a full-time student working four hours a day. He's exhausted, and Sarah is shocked to realize that she hadn't even noticed Rob's fatigue. She hadn't really looked at her mother as a person either, until now. Becca calls Sarah in the middle of the night to report on a date she had with Bobby. He wanted to sleep with her and at one time she might have been tempted. But caring for the egg has helped her realize that she and Bobby could create a child between them, an act that would be totally irresponsible. The day the students are to return the eggs, Sarah confesses to David that this week of having to face reality has been terribly hard. David admits he has been shaken up too. They both feel a certain amount of grief at giving up their egg. The last entry in their baby book says, "We will be back to get you."

A school project serves as a catalyst for the maturation of two teenagers, one afraid of responsibility, the other too wrapped up in her own concerns to notice the problems and needs of her family. This is a book that can be read on two levels: as a story and as a study of human behavior and relationships, punctuated by reflections on the meaning and importance of life. Skillfully written in journal form, the story provides sensitive characterizations and believable situations, although some readers may wonder at the speed with which feelings emerge and attitudes change. The premise is based on an assignment that has been given in a number of U.S. schools.

Ages 12 and up

**Also available in:**
Cassette—*First the Egg*
Library of Congress (NLSBPH)

Paperbound—*First the Egg*
Pocket Books, Inc.

## 439

**Moeri, Louise**

### The Girl Who Lived on the Ferris Wheel

E. P. Dutton & Company, Inc., 1979.
(117 pages)

---

*CHILD ABUSE*
*FEAR: of Death*
*FEAR: of Physical Harm*
*MENTAL ILLNESS: of Parent*

---

To eleven-year-old Clotilde Foerester, called Til, living in San Francisco in 1943, even riding the hated Ferris wheel with her mild-mannered father is better than staying home with the mother whose violence she fears more and more. Til's mother, Gertrude, was an unloved daughter and is now a compulsive nag and house cleaner, one for whom nothing in life is good enough. She has driven Til's father to divorce, and now she slaps and punches Til and knocks her down the stairs. Til's father, who avoids the details of his daughter's home life, takes Til to an amusement park every Saturday, his only free time. Til likes the bumper cars, feeling heroic and in control as she drives them, but secretly hates the Ferris wheel, something bigger and stronger that throws her around. Til's father plays his fiddle for her as they walk along the beach in Golden Gate Park, and Til feels cheated of a happy family life. At school a worried Til asks a friend if her mother ever hits her. The friend replies, "Of course not. What do you think my mother is —some kind of nut?" Til tries to attract attention at school by drawing on a math paper a face that calls "Help." Talking with the school nurse, she cannot bring herself to reveal her fears of her mother. Instead, she talks about hating the Ferris wheel because it throws her around. The nurse, concerned about Til's many bruises, constant headaches, and trouble with schoolwork, thinks the girl is complaining about her father. Til cannot correct her and unhappily leaves for home. There she finds a chilling sight: her own place at the dinner table is set as usual, but her mother's is set with butcher knives. Til takes some money and flees, but then tries to sneak back home, confused. She hears her mother calling her softly, knife in hand, and realizes her danger in time to get out of the house. On her way to her father's apartment she stops to eat, and a drunken sailor molests her. The Navy's shore patrol stops him and offers help, but Til runs away again. At her father's apartment she finds not him, but his friend Helga. Again Til flees, and a worried Helga calls Til's father and alerts the police. Bewildered and weary, Til goes home. Her mother is waiting in the shadows with a knife. The police arrive and Gertrude hides the knife, saying she can handle this bad girl who ran away. Til realizes at last that she must act to save her life. She goads her mother, calling Gertrude a slave, herself a princess. Gertrude loses the last shred of control and goes for Til with the knife. The police stop her. Then Til's teacher and the school nurse arrive. The nurse had alerted the teacher to Til's need for help, but they were delayed in coming to the house because of the wartime gas rationing. Til's father comforts the shaken girl, assuring her that the two of them had little to do with Gertrude's madness. Til begins to understand that she had been trying not to believe what she knew to be true about her mother, that her life has been saved by her independent action.

A young girl whose mentally ill mother abuses her and finally threatens her life must break out of her paralyzing fear and guilt and take action to save herself. Described clearly are the sources and signs of Til's mother's illness and the dangerous condition of Til's home life, a setting for disaster both before and after her parents' divorce. Til's difficulty in admitting to herself that her mother means to kill her is both painful and compelling. This book has unusual power and suspense —too much, perhaps, for some readers. Adult support and guidance may help keep the story in perspective. Mature readers will find much to discuss here.

Ages 13 and up

**Also available in:**
Paperbound—*The Girl Who Lived on the Ferris Wheel*
Avon Books

### 440

**Mohr, Nicholasa**

**Felita**

Black/white illustrations by Ray Cruz.
The Dial Press, Inc., 1979.
(112 pages)

---

*MOVING*
*PREJUDICE: Ethnic/Racial*
  *Death: of grandparent*
  *Family: unity*
  *Friendship: best friend*
  *Grandparent: love for*
  *Harassment*
  *Puerto Rican-American*

---

To get the children into better schools, the family of eight-year-old Felita Maldonado moves from an apartment in a Puerto Rican neighborhood to "a way better neighborhood" nearby. Felita is unhappy about the move. But the new apartment is larger and nicer, the area cleaner and quieter, and at first the neighbor girls are friendly. Adults are not so hospitable, however, and soon Felita is asked, "Why don't you stay with your own kind?" The girls, influenced by their parents' attitude, strike her and tear her dress. Johnny, her brother, is beaten and called a "spick." Her younger brother wants to fight back, but is restrained by his father. The family's mailbox is damaged, the mail scattered. Bags of water are dropped on Felita's mother from windows as she

comes home with groceries. The Maldonados decide to move again for safety's sake. Their new apartment in the old neighborhood, across the street from the first, is small; Felita sleeps in a fixed-up storage area. She loves to stay overnight with her grandmother, Abuelita, who lives nearby. Abuelita tells her, "We Puerto Ricans are a rainbow of earth colors . . . like the many flowers of one garden." The two dream of visiting Puerto Rico together. When Felita's fourth-grade class prepares to do "The Courtship of Miles Standish," Felita and her best friend, Gigi, both want to play Priscilla. Felita talks about the play tryouts and her intentions, but Gigi does not. So Felita is amazed and hurt when Gigi tries out and does so well that she gets the part. Felita's teacher reminds her that she is already set designer and assistant stage manager, but the girl is not consoled. The play is a great success, as is Gigi. At the cast party she is friendly towards Felita, who remains resentful. After Thanksgiving dinner Felita again stays with her grandmother. She tells Abuelita that Gigi was sneaky about getting the part, but admits that she herself would not have played it so well. Abuelita's advice, to talk to Gigi, results in a reconciliation between the girls. In spring, Felita's grandmother lies near death. She summons the children for private talks. Always happy to be Felita's confidante and ever involved in family life, she encourages the girl to tell her how things have gone with Gigi. Then she dies. As a grieving Felita walks with her uncle through a park, listening to his proposal of a trip to Puerto Rico, Felita silently promises that if she ever gets there, she will make a big bouquet of the colorful Puerto Rican flowers for her grandmother.

Blind, inherited prejudice and the violence it spawns threaten a trusting young girl but show her the value of her close-knit family and neighborhood life. The large and small concerns of Felita's life will be easily understood and sympathized with by young readers. The story, appropriately illustrated, is enriched by details of Puerto Rican-American life and by the warmth of Felita's relationship with her old-world grandmother.

Ages 8-10

**Also available in:**
Paperbound—*Felita*
Dell Publishing Company, Inc.

### 441

**Moncure, Jane Belk**

**Caring**

Color illustrations by Helen Endres.
Children's Press, Inc., 1981.
(28 pages)

---

*LOVE, MEANING OF*
*RESPONSIBILITY: Accepting*
  *Consideration, meaning of*

---

Caring is lifting a little brother so he can pick apples too, helping a turtle safely cross a path, feeding birds all winter long. Caring is picking up litter and putting it where it belongs. It's pushing a friend on a swing, even if it is the tenth push. It's leaving wild flowers on a mountain trail so others can enjoy them, putting your bike away so it won't get wet or stolen, teaching a friend how to turn cartwheels, and sharing your coat on a chilly day. Caring is making your bed, putting away clothes, and keeping toys picked up. It's replacing a dead tree, bandaging a friend's knee, and caring for your puppy. Cleaning up after yourself, being kind to a new person in the neighborhood, obeying your parents—these too are ways of caring.

Part of a series for the very young about behavior and feelings, this extremely simple, colorfully illustrated book provides repetition and reinforcement of a basic concept—in this case, caring. The book ends with the question, "Can you think of other ways to show caring?" and may stimulate discussion for this age group.

Ages 3-6

**Also available in:**
No other form known

## 442

**Moncure, Jane Belk**

# Courage

Color illustrations by Helen Endres.
Children's Press, Inc., 1981.
(29 pages)

---

*COURAGE, MEANING OF*

---

Courage is getting back on a bicycle after you've fallen off. It's letting a doctor give you a shot, telling a big boy not to tease your little brother, and practicing something until you get it right. Courage is talking to your father when you've done something wrong and telling your best friend you're sorry after a fight. It's also admitting when you've done wrong and not blaming the umpire when you strike out. Courage is refusing to let a friend copy your paper. It's opening your mouth for the dentist, making friends with the dog next door (after your mother says it's okay), and going off cheerfully for the first day at a new school. Courage is staying with friends while your parents go away for the weekend. It's climbing the slide ladder, saying hello to new people, and trying to be the best person you can be.

Part of a series for the very young about behavior and feelings, this extremely simple, colorfully illustrated book provides repetition and reinforcement of a basic concept—in this case, courage. The book ends with the question, "Can you think of other ways to show courage?" and may stimulate discussion for this age group.

Ages 3-6

**Also available in:**
No other form known

## 443

**Moncure, Jane Belk**

# Honesty

Color illustrations by Paul Karch.
Children's Press, Inc., 1981.
(29 pages)

---

*HONESTY/DISHONESTY*
  *Trust/Distrust*

---

Honesty means playing fair. It means taking your place at the end of the line instead of trying to sneak in front of others. It's telling the truth, even when that's very hard to do. Honesty means putting dirty clothes in the hamper instead of hiding them under your bed. Honesty is taking the blame for things you've done instead of blaming others, being willing to admit that you started the fight. "People trust you when you are honest and apologize." Honesty is not taking anything from a store, even when no one is looking. It's turning in the set of baseball cards you found on the playground. It's asking your teacher for help instead of looking at a classmate's paper. It's leaving money on the kitchen table when your mother forgets it there. Honesty is telling the truth, admitting you've forgotten to do a chore, returning the money when a clerk gives you too much change. Honesty is giving credit where it belongs instead of taking it for yourself. "Honesty builds trust, and trust is the most important thing about friendship and love."

Part of a series for the very young about behavior and feelings, this extremely simple, colorfully illustrated book provides repetition and reinforcement of a basic concept—in this case, honesty. The book ends with the question, "Can you think of other ways to show honesty?" and may stimulate discussion for this age group.

Ages 3-6

**Also available in:**
No other form known

## 444

**Moncure, Jane Belk**

# Joy

Color illustrations by Pat Karch.
Children's Press, Inc., 1982.
(29 pages)

---

*EMOTIONS: Identifying*

---

"Joy is a happy feeling inside that bubbles out in a smile when your best friend comes to play." It's making the first snowman of the year, drinking hot cocoa after being out in the snow, and playing the drum in a rhythm band. It's Thanksgiving dinner at Grandma's house, seeing someone you know at your new school, having a part in the Christmas program. Joy is seeing the rainbow after a storm, running barefoot on the beach, finding your kitten after she's been lost. Joy is making a kite that flies, finding a water fountain when you're thirsty, being chosen by your brother for his team even though you're the smallest kid. Joy is holding your baby sister for the first time and having her fall asleep in your arms. It's going for a swim after the hot work of putting up a tent. It's getting hugged by Mom and Dad after they've been away on a long trip.

Part of a series for the very young about behavior and feelings, this extremely simple, colorfully illustrated book provides repetition and reinforcement of a basic concept—in this case, joy. The book ends with the question, "Can you think of other joyful things?" and may stimulate discussion for this age group.

Ages 3-6

**Also available in:**
No other form known

## 445

**Moncure, Jane Belk**

**Kindness**

Color illustrations by Linda Sommers Hohag.
Children's Press, Inc., 1981.
(29 pages)

---

*CONSIDERATION, MEANING OF*
  *Cooperation*
  *Love, meaning of*
  *Sharing/Not sharing*

---

"Kindness is making a card for a friend who has the chicken pox." It's giving your sister a towel when she's wet and shivering after swimming. It's holding your umbrella mostly over your friend when you're walking in the rain. Kindness is helping Grandfather rake the leaves without his asking you. It's buttoning up a younger child's sweater, tying your sister's shoelaces, and being gentle with your puppy. Kindness is surprising Mom with a birthday cake, bringing Dad a cold drink when he's hot, sharing lunch with a friend who forgot his, and graciously accepting a friend's apology. It's sharing ice cream with a friend, giving someone a turn in your swing, slide, or wagon, and giving your friend a piece of your bubble gum even after he's wrecked your model airplane. Thanking your teacher, being friendly to a new classmate, and holding the door for someone with her arms full is kindness too. "Kindness brings happiness to others."

Part of a series for the very young about behavior and feelings, this extremely simple, colorfully illustrated book provides repetition and reinforcement of a basic concept—in this case, kindness. The book ends with the question, "Can you think of other ways to show kindness?" and may stimulate discussion for this age group.

Ages 3-6

**Also available in:**
No other form known

## 446

**Moncure, Jane Belk**

**Love**

Color illustrations by Linda Sommers Hohag.
Children's Press, Inc., 1981.
(29 pages)

---

*CONSIDERATION, MEANING OF*
*LOVE, MEANING OF*
  *Helping*

---

Love is bringing a pan of snow to a sick little brother so he can make his own snowman. Love is telling him you're sorry when he slips off the bed during a pillow fight. Love is bringing Nana a sweater when she's cold and helping Mom bring in the groceries. Love is helping your sister, obeying your parents even when you don't want to, and taking a cake to the new family next door. Love is inviting the new neighbor over to play, showing her your secret hiding place, and walking with her to school on Monday. Love is sharing, love is kindness, and sometimes love is courage—like saying no to a friend who wants to copy your paper. Love is admitting that you, not Tommy, broke the window. It's picking up your toys when Dad says to; love is obeying. Love is caring. It's treating others as we want to be treated. "The feeling of love is the best of all feelings. It comes from caring for others and knowing others care for us."

Part of a series for the very young about behavior and feelings, this extremely simple, colorfully illustrated book provides repetition and reinforcement of a basic concept—in this case, love. The book ends with the question, "Can you think of other ways to show love?" and may stimulate discussion for this age group.

Ages 3-6

**Also available in:**
No other form known

**M**

## 447

**Moncure, Jane Belk**

**My Baby Brother Needs a Friend**

Color illustrations by Frances Hook.
Children's Press, Inc., 1979.
(32 pages)

---

*SIBLING: New Baby*

---

A little girl knows her new baby brother needs someone to look after him, so that's what she does. She sings and rocks him to sleep, plays with him and tickles his toes, and helps bathe him. When she takes him for a walk, she tells him about everything she sees. She holds his hand and helps him stand. When he's older and it rains, she will play with him in her room, and when it snows she'll catch snowflakes for him. When they go to the zoo, she'll lift him up to see the animals; when they go to the park, she'll share her merry-go-round horse with him. When her birthday comes next spring she'll invite him to her party and let him blow out the candles. She'll share her birthday cake with him because he's never had a birthday party of his own. Her brother doesn't have many friends. "That's why he needs a friend like me."

A child with a new baby in the family focuses on all the things she can and will do for her little brother. Part of a series that deals with children's feelings, this book presents only the positive, loving feelings associated with a new sibling. Accompanied by attractive, realistic, pastel illustrations, the text can help children expecting a new sibling to imagine a happy future. It can also reassure those having trouble adjusting to a new baby.

Ages 3-7

**Also available in:**
No other form known

## 448

Montgomery, Elizabeth Rider

### "Seeing" in the Dark

Color illustrations by Troy Howell.
Garrard Publishing Company, 1979.
(48 pages)

---

BLINDNESS
SCHOOL: Mainstreaming
   Courage, meaning of
   Friendship: making friends
   Self, attitude toward: accepting

---

Kay, about eight, is blind. Her family has recently moved and, though she gets around well in their new apartment, the prospect of attending a different school frightens her. On her first day Miss Stone, her special teacher, arrives to walk her to school, as they have practiced. Kay finds her way so well that Miss Stone decides she can come alone the next day. When Kay enters her classroom she is greeted by Mr. Green, her homeroom teacher, who smells clean like soap. Kay walks easily to her desk, on which rests a Braille writer, and then moves to the coatroom to hang up her coat and put her lunchbox away. A bell rings loudly, filling Kay with dread as she listens to the clatter of many feet and the din of children's voices. Mr. Green introduces her to her classmates, answering their many questions. Later in the morning he suggests that the children play a game in which half the class takes turns pretending to be blind. He tells them, "Kay will learn a lot from us, and we will learn a lot from her." Then Mr. Green chooses Jimmy as Kay's sighted guide for the day. Jimmy leads her out to recess, and all the children crowd around. Several tease Kay, saying that because her eyes look normal and she knows her way around, she can't possibly be blind. Ted shoves something hard into her hand, declaring it's candy, but Kay knows a stone when she feels one. Milly hands her a penny, telling her it is a dime, but Kay can feel the smooth edge. The children turn Kay in circles until she is dizzy and then free her to find her classroom. Totally disoriented, she nearly walks into a wall. Her classmates now believe she is blind and they pity her. "Don't feel sorry for me!" Kay begs. "It's no fun being blind, but I'm used to it." Soon Kay is playing partner tag and other games with her classmates. One day she brings her violin to school and plays for the class. The children are impressed and beg for more. Mr. Green suggests she take up drums so she can join the school band. The weeks pass pleasantly. Then one day Kay smells smoke. The hall is so thick with it that not even Mr. Green can see where he is going. "Give me your hand. I know the way," Kay tells Jimmy. Everyone joins hands and Kay leads the way out. Miss Stone hugs her, telling her how proud she is. Kay hugs her back and whispers, "I'm glad I'm in this school."

A young blind girl, mainstreamed in a regular classroom, has some trouble making friends at first. But soon her plucky acceptance of her disability wins over her classmates, and she is already a successful class member when she leads the others out of their burning school to safety. The emphasis is on Kay's compensations for her blindness—the keenness of her other senses, her musical ability, her refusal to pity herself or accept pity from others. This is an easy reader with attractive, realistic illustrations.

Ages 5-7

**Also available in:**
No other form known

## 449

Moore, Emily

### Something to Count On

E. P. Dutton & Company, Inc., 1980.
(103 pages)

---

REJECTION: Parental
SEPARATION, MARITAL
   School: classmate relationships
   School: pupil-teacher relationships
   Self-esteem

---

Lorraine Maybe is just about to start fifth grade when she learns that her parents have decided to separate. Since her mother is always telling her that she's "enough to drive anybody away," Lorraine blames herself for her father's departure. It is true that Lorraine is not a very congenial child. She has had a consistent behavior problem at school, and it looks as though fifth grade will be no different. She immediately decides she doesn't like her new teacher, Mr. Hamilton, and decides to call him Wolfman. A tall, black man with a red beard and red, bushy hair, he has a laugh that sounds like "a pig snorting." To make matters worse, a new girl named Rhonda Elaine Archer is in Lorraine's class. Rhonda is very proud of her IQ. Mr. Hamilton, however, is not impressed by IQ scores. He believes that "everybody is good at something." When he has to punish Lorraine for undone homework by making her miss the class trip to The Metropolitan Museum of Art, he brings her a magazine about the exhibit the class has seen. Lorraine, who has a special interest in art, wonders how a man not even related to her can be so thoughtful when her own father cannot find the time to visit her and her little brother. Her mother tries to explain that it's just their father's way to work hard and neglect everything else. Lorraine, however, holds to the belief that her father's indifference must be caused by her and Jason's behavior. So the two children write him a letter listing the ways they will improve their conduct so he can love them. They wait anxiously for a reply. Their father's only response, however, is to say that since he's their father they shouldn't doubt that he loves them. A disillusioned Lorraine begins to realize—if not to accept—that she will never be able to depend on her father. Her mother, however, will always be there for her: after she and Rhonda are given three-day suspensions for fighting at school, her mother comforts her and goes to see her teacher. As Lorraine walks to school, she finds herself eager to be back in Mr. Hamilton's class. And maybe she and Rhonda can be friends after all.

Lorraine narrates this poignant story, and readers will find it easy to sympathize with this bright child who does not submit easily to events or to the limitations of other people. Her difficulty accepting herself and others causes problems both at school and at home and makes her feel responsible for her parents' separation. An understanding teacher and various proofs of her mother's love help Lorraine accept her father's emotional distance and preoccupation with work. Although her life is changing, Lorraine finds some good things she can count on.

Ages 8-10

**Also available in:**
No other form known

## 450
**Morgan, Alison Mary**

## All Kinds of Prickles
Elsevier/Nelson Books, 1980.
(175 pages) o.p.

---

*BELONGING*
*CHANGE: Resisting*
  *Abandonment*
  *Death: of grandparent*
  *Death: of pet*
  *Loss: feelings of*
  *Reality, escaping*
  *Relatives: living in home of*

---

When Paul's grandfather dies, the boy, in his last year of British primary school, goes to live with his Aunt Jean Dawkes and her family. Abandoned by his parents when he was a baby, Paul must now get used to another home. At first his cousin Joanna isn't too happy about having the unknown Paul come live with them. But she learns to accept him and both children look after Davy, Paul's goat, the only thing left in the world that's really his. But Davy poses problems because he eats every flower he sees. One day, Paul and Joanna see Davy eating his way through the flowers in the traffic circle. They bring him home but say nothing. As Joanna goes into the house, she overhears a telephone conversation between her mother and, she suspects, her mother's sister, Paul's long-missing mother. At tea that day, Joanna mentions to Paul that his mother was Mrs. Dawkes's sister. For the first time, Paul realizes that Mrs. Dawkes is family, and he feels a new fondness for her and a sense of belonging. Jealous about this sudden rapport between her cousin and her mother, Joanna blurts out that Paul's mother may come along and take him away. Mrs. Dawkes promises Paul that if his mother does return, he needn't go with her if he doesn't want to. Then Mr. Dawkes announces that he knows about the damage Davy has done and that Davy must go. An ad is placed in the paper, but none of the people who come to look at Davy find him suitable. That Saturday, Paul, Joanna, and Mrs. Dawkes visit Paul's maternal grandfather, whom he has never met. The boy and the old man take to each other at once, and later they all go down by the sea—another first for Paul. But when they return home, Davy is gone. Mr. Dawkes says that some friends of the farmer next door came and took Davy to a lovely home in the country. Paul's anxious requests to go visit the goat are met with evasions. Finally, suspecting that he has "come out to meet the thing he was more afraid of than anything else in the world," Paul sneaks onto the farm next door. There he finds Davy's body. As he holds it, he knows that the world holds "nothing for him ever again." He does not discuss his discovery, but slowly his grief changes to rage. That night, when the family is asleep, he destroys their flower borders, vegetable garden, bushes, lawn, greenhouse, and rock garden. Toward morning, he views the damage that the old Paul would never have caused. But that Paul is now as dead as Davy and his grandfather. He sets off on his bike for the home he once shared with his grandfather. He gets a ride with a truck driver, inadvertently gets off at the wrong place, and leaves his bike behind in the truck. Meanwhile, the family has discovered Paul's absence and the destruction he caused and are looking for him. They piece together what must have happened, and Joanna is so appalled when she hears that Davy has been killed that she says she would have helped Paul ruin the garden had she known. Paul finally gets near the house where he used to live. He is afraid to go any further, for he knows he will have to face reality once he sees other people living there. He realizes he has been running away, that his "great adventure had been as pointless as the destruction of the garden. There was no way to escape, except to sit here, quite still, until he died." But he goes on and finds a little, white-haired old man hanging from the roof by one hand. Paul quickly replaces the ladder that had fallen and gets invited inside for tea. The old man is using Paul's grandfather's teapot and other things, and Paul feels quite at home. He tells the old man all that's happened and agrees to notify his aunt. They talk about what makes a person want to go on living and decide that it's a certain curiosity about what might come next. That evening Paul finds an injured hedgehog. He cares for it and takes it back with him when his aunt comes. Back with his aunt's family, he is treated with coldness and a certain resigned tolerance. His aunt tells him he will spend some time visiting his mother in London. Frightened, Paul asks how long he'll be gone and why he must go when his aunt promised he wouldn't have to. His aunt makes it clear that he can return if he wants to after his visit. While repairing his rock garden, Mr. Dawkes builds an attractive, flower-bordered home for Prickles, the recovered hedgehog. This Paul welcomes as a breakthrough in his relationship with his new family.

The destruction of a pet means the loss of the only source of continuity in a young boy's life, and he reacts with grief and rage. Eventually Paul realizes that the past is gone, that he must find happiness in the present and look with curiosity, if not hope, toward his future. This is a realistic, involving story with well-developed characters and relationships. The ending, while suggesting future happiness for Paul, is left open, encouraging discussion. Paul's story continues in the sequel, *Paul's Kite*.

Ages 11-13

**Also available in:**
No other form known

**M**

**451**

Morgan, Alison Mary

## Paul's Kite

Atheneum Publishers, 1982.
(113 pages)

---

*BELONGING*
*LONELINESS*
  *Parental: negligence*
  *Rejection: parental*
  *Relatives: living in home of*

---

After Paul's grandfather dies and the Welsh aunt, uncle, and cousin with whom he has lived for a few months have family problems, Paul goes to London to live with his mother—who at various times introduces him as her nephew, little brother, or son. She models and doesn't like her employers or men friends to know she has an eleven-year-old son. Paul is to run errands, keep the apartment clean, and care for himself. Ignored, the boy entertains himself by exploring London. In Hyde Park he watches people flying kites and yearns "to share in their freedom and vitality." Alone nearly every evening, Paul wonders if he'll be lonely all his life. Then his cousin Joanna, who has been kind to him, comes to visit London for a few days while her parents attend to some business. The two try to find all the locations in London that are listed on the British Monopoly board. While running for a bus, Joanna is hit by a van. She is hospitalized with a concussion and a broken leg. Paul stays with her in the hospital until her parents can get there from Wales. He's minus a friend again. Soon after, however, Mr. Abraham, a former judge who befriended Paul when he lived in Wales, arrives to bring the boy news of his father, who Paul had always assumed was dead. The man had been traced after Paul's grandfather's death so he could assume ownership of the small farm. Paul learns that his father has been rescued by a religious cult from alcoholism and drug dependency. He is now living in the cult's commune in America. There will be no reunion with Paul in the near future, but Mr. Abraham suggests that maybe someday Paul will want to know his father. After Paul's aunt and uncle verify that Joanna will be able to leave the hospital soon, Uncle William confesses that he must soon go to prison for embezzling from his firm. Paul will return to Wales to live with his aunt and Joanna while his uncle serves his sentence. To allow his aunt to accompany her husband back to Wales for the sentencing, Paul offers to visit Joanna in the hospital. Joanna asks Paul to fly a kite in the park she can see from her hospital room. So, with the help of an old woman, Paul gets a kite up. He imagines it looking in at Joanna and flying past all the people he knows. He thinks his mother and the man she is to marry soon will be too busy to look up at a kite. But his aunt and Mr. Abraham will see it. Even Uncle William may see it from his prison window.

In this sequel to *All Kinds of Prickles*, Paul is still searching for a place where he can feel he belongs. Left nearly alone in London, the boy gains some self-confidence and isn't unhappy at the prospect of returning to Wales with his aunt and cousin. The characters in this well-paced book are so sharply delineated that the reader will become absorbed in their lives. The ending leaves room for a future book about Paul.

Ages 10-13

**Also available in:**
No other form known

---

**452**

Morgenroth, Barbara

## Tramps Like Us

Atheneum Publishers, 1979.
(145 pages)

---

*EGOCENTRISM*
*REBELLION*
*SELF, ATTITUDE TOWARD: Feeling Different*
*VALUES/VALUING: Moral/Ethical*
  *Discipline, meaning of*
  *Parental: control*
  *Running away*
  *Self, attitude toward: accepting*

---

Sixteen-year-old Vanessa is exceptionally bright and exceptionally bored with her eastern small-town existence under the watchful eyes of her parents. She is ready for excitement and finds it at the forbidden Elks dance in a neighboring town. There she meets Daryl, a brother of one of the band members, and eagerly accepts his invitation for a motorcycle ride. They begin to meet regularly on the sly. Usually they just drive to some woods and talk, but for Vanessa that is enough. She feels so comfortable with Daryl; for the first time in her life she knows someone as bright as she is, as stifled by school and parents. Daryl awakens Vanessa's pride in her own individuality, but she continues to feel misunderstood and unchallenged at school. Daryl gets most of his criticism at home, as Vanessa learns from his brother, Booth. One night their father gets so angry at Daryl's insolence that he smashes Daryl's beloved guitar. Encouraged by Daryl and Booth, like brothers to her now, Vanessa begins to assert herself more at home and at school. First she fights with her math teacher, then with her father over her D in geometry. In gym class, which she detests, she refuses to do an assigned stunt on the trampoline. Her rebellion sends her to the principal's office, where she is belligerent: "This school is trying to rape my mind." By mid-year Vanessa's friendship with Daryl is still undiscovered, but her parents know that something has caused the change in her. One Friday night, Booth tells Vanessa and Daryl about his father's ultimatum to straighten up or get out. In his anger at the recollected scene, Booth smashes his hand through the van window and they must rush him to the emergency room. At the hospital, a nurse who is also a neighbor sees Vanessa and Daryl embracing and reports the incident to Vanessa's parents. After quizzing Vanessa about whom she was with and immediately jumping to conclusions about how low-class this boy must be, even though Vanessa tells them Daryl's father is vice-president of a company, her father telephones Daryl's parents for a showdown. They arrive with Daryl and accusations fly. In the end, the parents agree that their children are both tramps and forbid them to see one another. Vanessa and Daryl decide they have no

256

other option but to run away. Daryl feels sad about it, but Vanessa "had already accepted the disappointment of having my parents fail me." They head for Los Angeles where Daryl hopes to find work as a musician, spending the first night in a deserted shack. The next night they stop at a restaurant for dinner and are seen by a passing policeman and taken to the station. Placed in adjoining cells, they sing—folk songs, songs Daryl and Booth had written, songs of protest. When the parents arrive, explosively angry, they have made plans to keep the two apart. Vanessa is sent away to boarding school, but she is now confident she can survive. She realizes that as an individual she is merely one among many: "I have allowed myself space to be me, and I'm willing and able to allow space to everyone else to be them." Even so, she does not give up hope of seeing Daryl again some day, just one more time.

In this first-person story of rebellion and self-discovery, many readers will recognize the familiar confrontations between teenagers and authority figures. But Vanessa, Daryl, and Booth—while involving as characters—are also intolerant, egocentric, and given to broad generalizations about people and society. Vanessa's highly partisan narration could be viewed as an endorsement of anti-social behavior, an encouragement to rebel. Still, this is strong, thought-provoking material that begs for discussion.

Ages 12 and up

**Also available in:**
No other form known

### 453

**Morgenroth, Barbara**

**Will the Real Renie Lake Please Stand Up?**
Atheneum Publishers, 1981.
(164 pages)

*IDENTITY, SEARCH FOR*
*Deafness*
*Delinquency, juvenile*
*Friendship: meaning of*
*Life style: change in*
*Parent/Parents: remarriage of*
*School: classmate relationships*
*Stepbrother/Stepsister*

Since her parents' divorce, sixteen-year-old Irene (Renie) Lake has lived with her mother in a small apartment in Queens, New York. She attends a tough city high school and tries her best to fit in. "I had blended in like a chameleon. That was my chief talent. Blending in." So Renie joins a gang, carries a switchblade, smokes pot, has a boyfriend, and acts tough. Sometimes, though, she wonders where the other Renie is—the kind, considerate girl whose family is still intact. On Christmas Day Renie and her mother's live-in boyfriend have a big fight, and Renie storms out of the apartment. Her boyfriend, Gary, finds her walking aimlessly and takes her

for a ride in his "new" car. Soon the police stop them. The car, which Gary had stolen, holds a stash of marijuana and barbiturates. The two are arrested, Renie booked as an accessory. She is placed in her mother's custody and given a court date. Renie's father, a lawyer in Connecticut, comes to defend her and asks the judge for temporary custody. The judge agrees, telling Renie he hopes the change of environment helps her; if it doesn't, she could be sent to reform school. Renie packs and leaves with her father that night. His wife, Marlene, has three children, and she and Renie's father have a baby of their own. Renie shares a room with Gretchen, her age, who from the start lets Renie know she is unwelcome. But Renie vows to be a chameleon once more. She becomes a good student and is quiet and obedient at home. Still, one night Gretchen accuses her of stealing away her boyfriend. Resentful and unhappy, Renie leaves the house to walk and think. An old, beat-up car passes her. Then Renie hears a rustling in the woods and discovers a deer has been hit. Not sure where she is, she runs to the nearest house, where she meets a deaf young man. He reads her lips and takes her in his jeep to find the deer and bring it back to his barn. By now the man's mother has returned and explains that Jan is studying to be a veterinarian. Fascinated, Renie watches as mother and son talk through sign language. At the school library the next day, Renie checks out a book on sign language and learns the alphabet. After school she returns to Jan's to check on the deer. To Jan's delight, she signs to him. Meanwhile, Renie's father decides he wants permanent custody and insists she begin seeing a psychiatrist. Gradually, Renie opens up to her stepmother and discovers that Marlene loves and respects her. One day, Renie goes with Jan on a veterinary farm call. He discovers her switchblade and is furious. Afraid to explain why she carries it, Renie runs away from him. After a session with her psychiatrist, though, she decides to be honest with Jan about her past. But before she can go to him and explain, the school principal demands a locker search and marijuana is found in Renie's locker. She is suspended from school, knowing Gretchen planted the pot but unable to prove it. Furious, Renie decides to run away and calls Gary. But as she waits for him, she realizes she is letting Gretchen win. She decides to stay and fight; the real Renie Lake will finally stand up. She and Jan resolve to do battle together.

Changing her identity to fit her changing circumstances leaves Renie confused and disoriented about who she really is. With the help of her psychiatrist and a friend, she finds the courage to be herself and to hold fast to her convictions. This first-person narrative realistically portrays the struggles of a teenager trying to be her own person in the emotional turmoil of her parents' recent divorce.

Ages 12 and up

**Also available in:**
Paperbound—*Will the Real Renie Lake Please Stand Up?*
Fawcett World Library

M

## 454

Morton, Jane

### I Am Rubber, You Are Glue

Beaufort Books, Inc., 1981.
(96 pages)

---

*FAMILY: Relationships*
  *Change: accepting*
  *Helping*
  *Little League*

---

Fourth-grader Bart Barton wants desperately to pitch on the Little League team. But Mr. Simms, the coach, lets his son Randy pitch, making Bart play in right field. Although Bart realizes that Randy is a good pitcher, the two boys don't like each other much. When they argue, as they often do, Bart usually has the last word: "I am rubber, you are glue. Whatever you say bounces back and sticks to you." But getting the last word isn't as good as pitching. One day when Bart comes home from baseball practice, his lawyer father announces his plan to run for mayor. The family is very excited, and Bart and his parents even have their picture in the paper. Unfortunately, the picture shows silly Bart with his eyes crossed and his tongue hanging out. It seems to Bart that no matter how much he wants to help or be good, something always goes wrong. Even when he tells his class about his father, he doesn't feel any increased respect from his friends. Then, during his father's fund-raising dinner, Bart gets his finger stuck in a pop bottle and the fire department must be called. His parents decide he should stay home from such events in the future. Soon both his parents are so busy with the campaign that he sees little of them. After school, he's usually left with his baby-sitter. He worries about burglars because of recent robberies in the neighborhood. He also begins to resent all his work for the campaign. When school begins again in the fall, Bart has a hard time with all the homework and his other worries. Meanwhile, the political race is going badly because his father's opponent is conducting a smear campaign. On his way home from school one day, Bart cuts through an alley and spots two suspicious-looking men apparently breaking into a house. He runs home, calls the police, and hurries back to the men's van, scooping the keys out of the ignition and throwing them into the bushes. Just then the police arrive and arrest the men. Bart is a hero and his picture appears in the paper beside his father's letter denying his opponent's allegations. The next day is the election. As the Barton family awaits the results at headquarters, Mr. Simms and Randy appear. The coach tells Bart that with such a good throwing arm—as demonstrated when he threw the burglars' keys into the bushes—he should be able to pitch occasionally in Little League. Bart's father wins the election. To cap Bart's happiness, it appears that he and Randy will be friends.

A young boy who wants to be liked, to pitch for Little League, and to be useful tells the story of how he achieved all three. Bart's narrative is lively and funny, giving a readable glimpse into the life of a plucky, appealing ten-year-old boy. The Little League angle and the details of a political campaign add interest.

Ages 9-11

**Also available in:**
No other form known

## 455

Morton, Jane

### Running Scared

Elsevier/Nelson Books, 1979.
(118 pages) o.p.

---

*INFERIORITY, FEELINGS OF*
*LEARNING DISABILITIES*
  *Communication: parent-child*
  *Delinquency, juvenile*
  *School: achievement/underachievement*
  *School: behavior*
  *Talents: athletic*

---

Dave Miller is fifteen and has a favorite game—looking at cars as he walks along and deciding which he likes best. One day while he's skipping school, Dave plays the game, only to discover an old car with keys in the ignition. He steals the car for a joyride. After a chase by the police, during which he smashes up the car, Dave is arrested and taken to Juvenile Hall. "As a lesson" Dave's parents refuse to bail him out, so Dave spends two nights at the Hall. Before he is released to his parents he is introduced to Bill Patrick, called Pat, who is to be his counselor. At home that evening, Dave's mother is quietly supportive but his father fumes. Depressed, feeling unloved, a failure, Dave fleetingly considers suicide. After dinner he decides to go running, the one thing he really enjoys. He meets Pat, who invites Dave to run with him each morning at six. They begin the next morning and Pat, impressed with Dave's running, urges him to try out for the junior high track team; Dave is still in junior high because his reading difficulties, which have continued, led to his repeating the first grade. Reluctantly, Dave joins the team. After several weeks of practice he is chosen to run the upcoming two-mile race. But in order to race, he has to have his teachers sign an eligibility card. His English teacher, Miss Finney, refuses because of his poor performance in her class. Dave storms out of her room but then realizes that without track he again has no purpose or goal. Later, after a discussion with Pat, Dave apologizes to Miss Finney. She agrees to sign the card if Dave will agree to special reading classes. The day of the race comes and not only does Dave win, but Pat and Dave's parents are there to cheer him on and congratulate him.

This is a frank story of a learning-disabled boy's frustration and inability to communicate. An understanding counselor discovers and encourages Dave's running ability, engendering new feelings of pride and purpose in the underachieving teenager. Although it lacks depth of character and is predictable in plot, the book adequately portrays a likeable boy who manages to overcome his feelings of inferiority.

Ages 10-14

**Also available in:**
Braille—*Running Scared*
Library of Congress (NLSBPH)

Cassette—*Running Scared*
Library of Congress (NLSBPH)

**456**

Moskin, Marietta Dunston

**Rosie's Birthday Present**

Color illustrations by David S. Rose.
Atheneum Publishers, 1981.
(31 pages)

*PROBLEM SOLVING*
  *Giving, meaning of*

Today is little Rosie's mother's birthday, and she has
nothing to give her. As she sits sadly on the steps of her
baby-sitter's apartment building, Rosie sees a gold button on the sidewalk and decides to give it to her mother.
But Mr. Muldoon, the mailman, says the button is from
his uniform. He trades Rosie a silver ballpoint pen for
the button. At the end of the block Rosie sees Mr. Syl-
vester, the policeman. His pen has run out of ink, so
Rosie trades him her new pen for a key chain with a
penlight. Down the street she meets a cabdriver trying
to fix his cab. He needs a small light to see into the
engine, so he trades Rosie a shopping bag full of party
favors for the penlight. Next Rosie sees Joe, the Good
Humor Man. The bell on Joe's truck is cracked so no
one knows he's around. Rosie trades a horn blower from
her bag of favors for five ice-cream sandwiches, one for
each member of her family. Hurrying back with the ice
cream, Rosie stops to watch the garbage truck. Suddenly
she realizes that the ice-cream sandwiches are rapidly
melting. So she shares them with the four garbagemen.
One of them gives Rosie a cracked mirror with a carved
gold frame. She is delighted with this gift for her mother
until Mrs. Dickey from the second-hand shop comes
running up. She has accidentally thrown away her
antique mirror! When she discovers Rosie has it, Mrs.
Dickey invites her to the shop to find something to trade.
She gives a thrilled Rosie a small, heart-shaped pin
made of silver with tiny red stones. That night at her
mother's birthday party, Rosie proudly presents the
favors and her gift. Her surprised family wants to hear
her story, so Rosie begins to tell them.

A little girl without a birthday present for her mother
ends up after a series of trades with a very beautiful gift.
Simply told, plentifully illustrated, and unpretentious,
this tale of generous little Rosie is easy to read and listen
to.

Ages 4-7

**Also available in:**
No other form known

**457**

Murphy, Jim

**Death Run**

Clarion Books, 1982.
(174 pages)

*DELINQUENCY, JUVENILE*
*GUILT, FEELINGS OF*
  *Peer relationships: peer pressures*
  *Values/Valuing: moral/ethical*
  *Violence*

Sophomore Brian Halihan steals a six-pack of beer to
take to the park where he's meeting his friends Roger,
Al, and Sticks, all older boys. While they're killing time
waiting for a dance to start, they begin hassling a basketball player who's been practicing in the park, taking his
basketball and playing keep-away. Roger pretends to
throw the ball over the boy's head, but when the boy
reaches up for it, Roger slams it into his face instead.
When the boy falls, convulsing and bleeding, the others
run away. The next day Brian learns that William
Janowski, a basketball star, has been found dead in the
park. Detective Sergeant Robert Wheeler, a former
New York City detective who now works in Brian's suburb, senses something peculiar about Janowski's death
—especially when he finds three full beer cans near the
body and marks on Janowski's face that match the pattern on a basketball. Janowski had epilepsy and an
autopsy shows a burst aneurism at the base of his brain,
previously undetected. It ruptured as the result of a
seizure, according to the medical examiner. The police
consider the case solved, but Wheeler doesn't. The four
boys decide to avoid being seen together until the whole
thing blows over. But Brian finds himself walking past
the Janowski house. Wheeler sees Brian and becomes
suspicious. He files his report, but adds a supplemen-
tary page detailing his concerns. The police chief closes
the case anyway. Then Wheeler's daughter, Susan, who
attends the same high school as the boys, decides to do
some detecting on her own. She and several of her
friends discover that Sticks had a locker-room fight with
Janowski several weeks earlier. Without asking her
father, Susan copies his reports and shares them with
R.R., editor of the school newspaper, who is writing an
article on Janowski's death. R.R. decides the next step is
to find out who Sticks's friends are. Meanwhile, Brian
has seen Wheeler's name in the newspapers and calls
the police station, giving a false name, to get his address.
He doesn't want to meet Wheeler, just to observe him.
When he does, Brian knows that Wheeler has not given
up the case. After Susan spends a day trying to track
down Sticks's friends, she is attacked and threatened at
knifepoint but does not see her assailants. However, she
hears one of them call another Sticks. The Janowski
case is reopened, a file is begun on Susan's attack, and
Wheeler is removed from both cases because of his
daughter's involvement. Al and Roger tell Brian that
they staged the attack on Susan in order to incriminate
Sticks; when Brian gets angry they beat him up and
warn him to keep quiet. Brian realizes he's trapped
between Roger and Al on one side, Wheeler on the
other. Disobeying his orders, Wheeler interrogates
Sticks, hoping to make him nervous enough to implicate
his accomplices. Seeing Sticks and Brian together,
Wheeler decides to wait at Brian's home, but Brian sees
his car and flees. Then Brian borrows money from his
girlfriend so that Sticks can run away; because of a
previous juvenile record in Michigan, Sticks is sure to
bear the brunt of Janowski's death. Brian is tempted to
run away too. But "as easy as it sounded, he knew he
could never completely outrun Janowski's ghost or his
own guilt." In studying her notes, R.R. discovers that
one of Sticks's friends is Roger, whose former girlfriend
threw him over to date Janowski. In addition, if someone did hit Janowski with the basketball it had to be a
left-handed person because of the side of his face that

was bruised. Roger is left-handed. She calls the detective on the case with her information. When Roger and Al are found together and questioned, they admit their guilt. After seeing Sticks off on the train, Brian, unaware of Roger's and Al's confession, goes to Wheeler's house and knocks at the door. "I think we should talk," Brian says.

A teenager involved in a fatal incident is unable to live with his guilt. Brian tries to tell himself that he was only an innocent bystander, but knows that once he chose to flee and leave Janowski dying, he became part of the act. He eventually chooses to reveal himself to the detective, Wheeler, not only because he realizes Wheeler will get him anyway, but also because he needs to take responsibility for what he's done. The book presents three viewpoints: Brian's, Wheeler's, and a neutral narrator's. Wheeler's story gives glimpses into the man's job conflicts, self-doubts, even procedural matters. Brian's story, fast-paced and filled with action, is definitely written for adolescents. His parents remain in the background, concerned about the obvious changes in their son. This is a gripping story and a good book for discussion.

Ages 11 and up

**Also available in:**
No other form known

## 458

**Myers, Bernice**

### Not at Home?

Color illustrations by the author.
Lothrop, Lee & Shepard Company, 1981.
(48 pages)

---

COMMUNICATION: Misunderstandings
  Friendship: best friend

---

Sally, about eight, hurries down the apartment stairs with her overnight bag, ready to spend the weekend with her best friend, Lorraine. But when she rings the bell, a woman she doesn't know tells her Lorraine is not home. Bewildered and hurt, Sally runs home crying. Mrs. Allen, who lives in Sally's building, invites the tearful girl in for ice cream. She lends a sympathetic ear to Sally's tale of woe, and Sally goes home feeling a little better. But she stays in her room, ignoring the telephone when she thinks she hears it ring over the sound of her mother's vacuum. All the next week at school, Sally avoids Lorraine. After school Friday, Sally stops at the bakery. There she sees Lorraine, and the two ignore each other. But Sally finally blurts out, "Where were you last weekend?" She was at home, Lorraine answers, wondering why Sally did not come. As they shout at each other, the girls begin to realize their big misunderstanding. Lorraine had gone to borrow a math book, and the baby-sitter never mentioned that Sally had arrived while she was gone. She had waited for Sally all weekend. Soon the girls are giggling friends again. Lorraine invites Sally to her house for the weekend. Sally readily agrees, saying her bag is still packed. She tells Mrs. Allen she is going to Lorraine's house because Lorraine is her best friend.

A misunderstanding separates two friends for a whole week. When they finally confront each other, the girls see what a silly mistake they have made. Colorful, cartoonlike illustrations highlight this warm, funny, and believable beginning reader that may encourage children to suggest alternative ways of handling a familiar experience.

Ages 6-8

**Also available in:**
No other form known

## 459

**Myers, Walter Dean**

### Hoops

Delacorte Press, 1981.
(183 pages)

---

DETERMINATION
MATURATION
  Afro-American
  Boy-girl relationships
  Crime/Criminals
  Friendship: meaning of
  Peer relationships
  Sports/Sportsmanship
  Talents: athletic
  Violence

---

Springtime in Harlem finds Lonnie Jackson, seventeen, living part-time at home and part-time at the Grant Hotel where he works. Fulltime, he thinks about basketball. When all else in his confusing life fails, he has his basketball. "My game was my fame, and I knew it was together." At the gym one day, Lonnie and others are told about an upcoming city-wide basketball tournament. College scouts will be watching the games, especially the finals. This tournament is a chance for kids who did not play high school ball to be recognized. Lonnie is excited about the possibilities until he meets their coach, Cal Jones. Lonnie has seen Cal on the streets, considers him a wino, and refuses to be coached by him. So Cal challenges him to a six-point one-on-one game. If he loses, he will quit. When Cal beats Lonnie, he demands he come to practice the next day. From then on, Cal rides Lonnie constantly, demanding more of him than of the others. Lonnie resents it, yet he knows Cal thinks he has the potential to succeed. When they lose their first game, Cal says they're playing as individuals, not as a team. By now Cal and Lonnie are friends, and Cal invites the boy to his apartment. He shows Lonnie his scrapbook and for the first time Lonnie realizes that Cal is actually Spider Jones, a former professional basketball player. Cal explains that he threw away his one gift, basketball, by getting involved in a point-spread gambling scheme. Meanwhile, Lonnie's girlfriend, Mary-Ann, discovers that her boss, Tyrone Giddins, has her brother Paul's name on an envelope. This worries her: Paul has had lots of money recently and she knows Tyrone can't be trusted. Paul confesses to Lonnie that he is stealing and selling welfare checks. At the same time, Mr. O'Donnel, the head of the basketball tournament, tells Cal he doesn't want any bad publicity and urges him to quit coaching. Lonnie learns that it was Tyrone's bodyguard who told Mr. O'Donnel about Cal's past. Cal fails to show up for the next two games, and Lonnie discovers he's in jail. When he's out on bail, Lonnie learns that he beat up a man who wanted him to shave points again. Then Cal is called back to Mr. O'Donnel's office and told that Lonnie, who was kicked out of one game for arguing with the referee, cannot play in the championship game. Lonnie is furious; Cal tells him he can suit up and watch. Then, in front of Lonnie, Cal calls in a bet against his own team. If he is going down, he tells Lonnie, he intends to take some people with him. The team loses badly in the first half. In the second half, when Cal knows all bets are placed, he sends Lonnie in to play. The team wins the championship by one point. Lonnie sees Cal leave for the locker room and runs after him. Too late, he sees Cal being beaten by Tyrone and his bodyguard. Lonnie tries to help, but Cal is shot and dies. A grieving Lonnie realizes that Cal has made his restitution and his comeback. And Cal has taught him that if he keeps himself and his game together, he might have a chance in this world.

A Harlem teenager determined to have something better than the bleak environment of his childhood finds in basketball and in the courage of his coach the strength and self-confidence he needs. Surrounded by crime and coercion, Lonnie tries not to yield; he even avoids having sex with his girlfriend so their relationship can be special in their world. His first-person narrative is vivid and involving; the basketball sequences add excitement and are woven smoothly into the plot.

Ages 12 and up

**Also available in:**
Paperbound—*Hoops*
Dell Publishing Company, Inc.

## 460

Myers, Walter Dean

### Won't Know Till I Get There

The Viking Press, Inc., 1982.
(176 pages)

---

*AGE: Aging*
*FOSTER HOME*
*MATURATION*
   *Adoption: feelings about*
   *Age: respect for*
   *Delinquency, juvenile*
   *Sibling: rivalry*

---

Fourteen-year-old Steve Perry's parents ask him if he has any objections to their adopting a child. He doesn't and so Earl Goins—thirteen, with a record of disturbing the peace, vandalism, and armed robbery—comes to live with them for a trial period. In an impulsive attempt to look as tough as he thinks Earl is, Steve writes on the side of a train with spray paint. Transit police take him, Earl, and two other boys to the station. When they appear in court, the judge offers them an alternative to the detention center: working six days a week all summer at Micheaux House for Senior Citizens. There Steve and his friends meet the janitor, London Brown, and the five residents left in the home, which is to be shut down at summer's end—Pietro Santini, Esther Cruz, Eileen Lardner, Jack Lasher, and Mabel Jackson.

Steve doesn't know what to think about Earl, who tends to be sarcastic, cool, and remote, but also has nightmares and occasionally wets the bed. When this happens, Steve helps him change the bedding and wash it without his parents' knowledge. Still, Steve resents his loss of privacy. Meanwhile, the residents want to keep their home open and remain independent. Eileen decides they need a source of income. She has a three-thousand-dollar inheritance they can use for seed money. Pietro and Steve decide to set up a sandwich and coffee shop in the deli area of a local supermarket. London is advanced one thousand dollars to start a waxing business, and two others clean sidewalks for local businesses. Then Steve and Earl fight, and the family discusses sending Earl back to the agency. A camping trip suggested by a counselor seems to please Earl; later, Steve's father says the experience made him lean toward keeping Earl. But when they finally decide to adopt the boy, who cries with happiness and apprehension when he learns their intentions, Earl's mother arrives to make sure her son's adoptive home is all it should be. As she has twice before, she refuses permission for him to be adopted. However, the family is granted legal custody of Earl until he is eighteen. The city shuts down the House after all, declining to take responsibility for the residents' business activities. The group is split up, although Steve and Earl visit Mabel and the now-married Pietro and Esther. Steve decides that in trying to understand Earl during the summer, he has come closer to understanding himself. He has also learned a great deal from his association with the old people. At first they all seemed alike to him; now, they are individuals. He wonders what old age will hold for him: "I guess I won't know till I get there."

Written in the form of a diary, Steve's story shows him learning to see beyond preconceived notions about people to the real individuals beneath. The old people at the home and his troubled foster brother all touch Steve's life. Set in Harlem, the book moves as quickly as does its fresh, lively dialogue. The characterizations of the House's residents and their exchanges with Steve and his friends give readers superb insight into some of the problems, feelings, and concerns of older people.

Ages 11-14

**Also available in:**
No other form known

## 461

Myers, Walter Dean

### The Young Landlords

The Viking Press, Inc., 1979.
(197 pages)

---

*NEIGHBORS/NEIGHBORHOOD*
*RESPONSIBILITY: Accepting*
   *Afro-American*
   *Boy-girl relationships*
   *Cooperation: in work*
   *Crime/Criminals*
   *Friendship: meaning of*
   *Ghetto*
   *Problem solving*

---

M

Paul Williams, in his mid-teens, lives in a run-down neighborhood of New York City. It is summer vacation and his friend Gloria wants to spend the time doing neighborhood projects. With Paul and three other friends she starts the "Action Group," whose main target will be to clean up "The Joint," a crumbling apartment building on the block. When they complain about the building's condition to its owner, the man turns to Paul and asks him to invest a dollar towards improving the place. Paul pays. About a week later, an amazed Paul receives the title to "The Joint," made out in his name. He is reluctant to accept the responsibility, but at Gloria's insistence and with his parents' approval he decides the group will try to make some improvements. First they meet the tenants, an odd and demanding bunch. The young people quickly learn that operating an apartment brings much more trouble than profit. They hire an eccentric little man, Mr. Pender, to do the bookkeeping. He shows them that after they make minor repairs and pay the insurance, taxes, and bills, they will have no money left to make any improvements. They will have to raise money, they decide, by doing extra projects. Meanwhile, a neighborhood boy, Chris, has been accused of stealing stereo equipment from the store where he works. The Action Group decides to help clear him, hoping to collect the thousand-dollar reward offered by the owner of the store for the recovery of the equipment. Paul, Gloria, and another group member, Bubba, check out a vacant warehouse for stolen merchandise, but are told by the police to stay out of the case. Mr. Pender suggests they spread the word through the neighborhood that they want to buy stereo equipment; maybe someone will approach them with the stolen goods. In the meantime, they decide to have a street fair to raise money. They set up booths and people donate food to sell. The fair is a great success, netting the group over four hundred dollars. During cleanup, a man who has been lingering in the area tells Paul that the kids should set up a little disco joint in the basement of the building; he can get them some stereo equipment, he says, at half price. Paul's ears perk up. He and Bubba, without asking Gloria or Mr. Pender, take the profit money and meet the man at a warehouse. They spend most of the money on the stereo equipment he shows them, but when they get home and compare the serial numbers of the stolen equipment with the numbers on the boxes of the equipment they've bought, they begin to think they've made a mistake—that this is not, after all, the equipment Chris was accused of stealing. Depressed, Paul tells his father what he's done. His father suggests they recheck the numbers and, sure enough, those on the actual equipment do match the list of stolen numbers. Chris is cleared, but the Action Group refuses the reward money. Chris, they have learned, knew about the theft and was paid to keep quiet. "We didn't feel right taking the reward money. . . . We would just try to do more of the work ourselves and to get by the best we could." But their finances deteriorate even more during the winter, and they realize they can't afford to keep the building. Then the man who heads the local numbers racket, a benevolent soul, buys the building and hires the group to run it. The kids are sure that with a little luck they'll be making a profit in two years.

Five friends attempt to improve living conditions in their depressed neighborhood. Paul tells this warm, realistic story with wit, authentic dialogue, and lively characterizations. The conclusion, in which they must surrender ownership of the building, is credible, but out of their determination to improve "The Joint" comes much good. The group members learn to appreciate each other, the tenants begin to help one another, a crime is solved, and a tentative romance is born between the two leaders, Paul and Gloria.

Ages 11-14

**Also available in:**
Paperbound—*The Young Landlords*
Avon Books

## 462

**Naylor, Phyllis Reynolds**

## All Because I'm Older

Black/white illustrations by Leslie Morrill.
Atheneum Publishers, 1981.
(36 pages)

---

*SIBLING: Older*
  *Justice/Injustice*
  *Resourcefulness*

---

Life is not fair, John believes. Because he is eight and the oldest, he gets blamed for everything. When his younger brother, Peter, starts trouble, John gets punished. Peter even tries to make their little sister, Stephanie, like him best by entertaining her and making her laugh. Peter always manages to undo all John's good resolutions. One Saturday their mother sends their father and the three children to the grocery store. John privately vows to hold his temper and be good. But by the time they get to the store, he and Peter have argued, fought, and caused Stephanie to get a lollipop stuck in her hair. John is now eager to redeem himself by helping their father. But in the fruit section, the boys squabble. In the dairy department, John talks Peter into putting his head in the ice cream case and the manager scolds them. In the seafood lane, Stephanie throws a package of baloney in with the lobsters. Their father, his distress growing, tells John to push Stephanie around in the cart. But when Stephanie eats a banana and gets messy, Peter and John are ordered to take her outside and be good. John sits Stephanie on top of a bag of mulch. When she gets restless, he puts an empty paper grocery sack over her head and makes a hole for her to see through. Stephanie likes the sack so much she wears it home. When she fusses, John and Peter scratch the sack and make noises to amuse her and quiet her down. When they get home, Peter tells his mother how the sack was John's idea. Both parents are proud of John. Delighted, he lets Peter play with his parachute.

A much-tried oldest child figures out a way to keep his baby sister amused, winning praise from his parents, admiration from his pesky younger brother, and a bit of self-respect too. John narrates this light, funny account that "oldest" children will appreciate—and younger siblings may find enlightening. Lively drawings keep the story moving.

**463**

Naylor, Phyllis Reynolds

**Eddie, Incorporated**

Black/white illustrations by Blanche Sims.
Atheneum Publishers, 1980.
(101 pages)

---

*JOB*
*RESOURCEFULNESS*
    *Cooperation: in work*
    *Money: earning*
    *Success*
    *Work, attitude toward*

---

The Anselminos are a business family: the father owns a produce store, the mother sells homemade goods, oldest son Roger works in a shoe store, and middle son Joseph is determined to be a banker. "Everybody, it seemed, was going places and doing things except Eddie." Twelve-year-old Eddie decides that if he's ever to amount to anything, he has to go into business for himself. Mr. Clemmons, the inventor next door, advises Eddie that when he finds a problem, he'll have found a business. The first problem Eddie finds is littered aluminum cans. He and his best friends, Dirk and Elizabeth, go into the aluminum-recycling business, but make only thirteen cents apiece the first day. After several weeks, they close down the business. Next they try lawn mowing, but after two ruined lawnmowers, that business folds too. Eddie feels like a loser. In the hardware store to buy a replacement part for a lawnmower, he sees a new gadget being sold: a lint trap for washing machines. He remembers that Mr. Clemmons has been working on a similar lint trap, so he buys him one. Mr. Clemmons is very discouraged to see that someone got ahead of him on his invention. Eddie feels the same way when he attempts to market a foot deodorant, only to be hooted out of his own living room and later find that foot powder has been available for a long time. The *South End Weekly* newspaper is the next venture; it ceases publication after three weeks. In the meantime, Mr. Clemmons has come up with the idea of disposable lint-trap liners. In September, Eddie and his friends sell protection to the sixth graders for "sing day," during which any seventh or eighth grader can demand that a sixth grader stop and sing the school song. For twenty-five cents, Eddie and his friends will sing along with and support any sixth grader. The day is financially successful, but it is, after all, "a one-time show. What Eddie wanted was a job that lasted all year. He wanted a desk with a telephone on it, a rubber stamp with his name on it, a book for expenses, and a box for cash receipts." Then Eddie hits on a steady business: a baby-sitting agency. He, Dirk, and Elizabeth draw up contracts for sitters and for parents, each of whom pays a small fee to "Eddie, Incorporated" (Elizabeth's idea because no matter what ideas Eddie might subsequently come up with, the company name will be appropriate). Eddie is so busy with his new job that he forgets about his birthday and is pleasantly surprised with a cake—and a desk calendar from his mother, a ledger from his father, a rubber stamp from Joseph, and his own telephone from Roger. That evening a parent needs a sitter, all the agency sitters are busy, and so Eddie himself goes. The baby is none other than Herman the Terrible, and Eddie has a busy, messy, tiring evening. But he decides that "work wasn't always excitement and fun and money. Sometimes it was just plain work."

Young Eddie learns a great deal about the practical aspects of running a business as he attempts several profit-making ventures. Underlying this colorful and funny account of his short-lived projects are business concepts and attitudes that will be easily understood by readers—who may be inspired to pursue a similar endeavor of their own. Droll illustrations and well-drawn characters further enliven this enjoyable book.

**464**

Naylor, Phyllis Reynolds

**A String of Chances**

Atheneum Publishers, 1982.
(244 pages)

---

*DEATH*
*RELIGION: Questioning*
    *Boy-girl relationships*
    *Family: relationships*
    *Maturation*
    *Relatives: living in home of*
    *Values/Valuing: moral/ethical*

---

Sixteen-year-old Evelyn (Evvie) Hutchins will spend the summer with her cousin Donna Jean, who is expecting a baby shortly, and Donna Jean's husband, Tom Rawley. Evvie's father, a Faith Gospel preacher, and her mother, a practical nurse, have always opened their home to elderly and disabled people. Evvie's older sister, Rose, complains about the current crop: an aphasic man, a retarded man, and a senile old woman. Evvie's mother worries because Donna Jean and Tom no longer go to church, but her father thinks Evvie can be a good influence on them. While Evvie is living with the Rawleys, her bedroom will be occupied by Matt Jewel, hired help, her age, and generally in some kind of trouble. Evvie and Donna Jean share a love of making beautiful things, and they plan to start a crafts shop called The Cousins. Evvie enjoys the space, quiet, and affection she finds with the Rawleys. She learns from her cousin that Rose dated Tom in high school and has never forgiven Donna Jean for taking him away. Now Rose won't date, afraid to take any more chances on love. After a long labor with some frightening moments, Donna Jean has her baby at home. Evvie vows she'll never go through the pain and humiliation of childbirth. But she is delighted by little Joshua. Meanwhile, Matt begins to play a larger role in Evvie's life. Evvie's best friend, Sue, likes Chris Lundgren, a friend of Matt's. But Chris likes Evvie and so does Matt. Matt shocks and angers

N

Evvie by challenging her beliefs about the "right religion." He says he could have his prayers answered by a great golden grasshopper in the sky and no one could prove him wrong. Though she rebuffs him, he demands that she examine her beliefs for a change. Donna Jean also admits she has a lot of questions about religion, but no answers. Evvie begins to see Joshua's newness as a sign that she can start over and find God in her own way. But she continues to be irritable and mean-spirited around Matt. With Chris, however, her relationship deepens. One day the two visit Chris's bedroom to see his drums and end up on the bed kissing and hugging. The experience is lovely to Evvie, but a neighbor tells her parents that she was alone with Chris in his house, and Evvie's mother forbids her to do that again. One Sunday Tom and Donna Jean decide to take Joshua to church to show him off. Afterwards, they all go to the Hutchins's for dinner, during which Matt raises some questions about religion. Evvie's father won't allow anyone to condemn Matt: brains are to be used, he maintains, and everyone has to make his or her own journey. Evvie finds herself terribly angry at Matt for saying things she never would dare to say to her parents. Then a particularly happy day, when Joshua laughs his first laugh, turns into the most tragic: Joshua dies during his nap, a victim of crib death. Donna Jean and Tom are inconsolable and separate in their grief. That night they bring Joshua's body home from the coroner's and all night long they walk him, talk to him, and sing to him. The next morning Tom carries his son's body around the yard to show him all the things he meant to show him someday. On their way back to return the baby's body, they stop the car, hold Joshua up, and beg God to return him to life. Afterwards, Donna Jean explains that they simply had to try it. Evvie asks her father why God did not respond. He says he doesn't feel God "took" Joshua in the first place; God doesn't go around making people miserable. Evvie watches helplessly as the warmth and tenderness between Tom and Donna Jean turns to pain, shock, anger, and sadness. Then, when Chris can't promise to return the next summer, Evvie decides you can't really count on anything. During Joshua's funeral people share their thoughts and feelings, and Evvie is astonished to hear Matt quote from one of her favorite poems that expresses her exact feelings about Joshua. Distraught, Evvie wants her father to prove to her that there is a God. He is gentle with her, accepting her doubts and anger about Joshua's death, but he cannot hand her his own beliefs. Donna Jean and Tom beg Evvie to stay with them. She is uncertain. Matt alone seems to understand her, but she can't make herself call out to him. Gradually, Evvie and her family and friends help her devastated cousin take up her life again. Even her parents' three disabled guests manage to aid in the process. The Cousins shop project revives. Evvie and Matt spend time together, and she admits she hated him because he seemed to threaten her with his questions and doubts. They agree that if they're both unmarried by the time they're thirty, they'll consider marrying each other. For now, although she can't prove the existence of God, Evvie begins to sense where and what he must be.

A girl's dormant doubts about her religious beliefs are forced into the open by the crib death of her cousin's cherished son and by the challenging questions posed by a boy her age. Questioning religion means questioning her parents' values, and Evvie wonders how you grow up without growing away. Her loving, open-minded father suggests ways both can happen without undue damage. Although religion is a major theme here, it is not obtrusive or didactic. Evvie's doubts and questions are skillfully woven into the larger picture of a maturing teenager and her relationships with others.

Ages 12 and up

**Also available in:**
Paperbound—*A String of Chances*
Ballantine Books, Inc.

## 465

Neigoff, Mike

### It Will Never Be the Same Again

Black/white illustrations by Gwen Brodkin.
Holt, Rinehart and Winston, Inc., 1979.
(191 pages)

---

*MATURATION*
*PARENT/PARENTS: Unemployed*
 *Family: relationships*
 *Money: earning*
 *Peer relationships: peer pressures*
 *Responsibility: accepting*
 *Work, attitude toward*

---

A week before school lets out for the summer, fifteen-year-old Sid Kaplan's life is turned upside down. His father arrives home with the upsetting news that his job as a respected, established reporter for a downtown Chicago newspaper has been terminated due to cutbacks. At first Sid expects that his father's unemployment will quickly end. But time passes with no change and, after some serious discussions with his mother, the boy becomes more concerned and angry. He had counted on his father's financial help for a school ski trip that winter, but his mother tells him not to plan on it and not to mention the trip to his father. Tutti Bernstein and Angelo Betalucci, Sid's two best friends, have been planning this trip with him; the three intend to get in on the fun, even though only the rich kids usually go. Sid's mother advises him to get a job. Resentfully, Sid applies for a position at the local suburban newspaper office. He is hired by the editor and publisher, Joe Larsen, and starts the next week working four hours each morning developing film and doing odd jobs. Mr. Larsen is always barking orders at him, never praises him, and the job is boring. At home his father is grouchy and hard to live with, but his mother feels Sid expects too much from the family, that he doesn't understand how defeated and incapable his father feels. By the end of July Sid is so bored with his job and distressed by the summer fun he is missing that he tells his boss he's "thinking of quitting." Mr. Larsen asks him to finish out the week. He also assigns Sid several simple photographic stories to cover, telling him in a fatherly way that all jobs are sometimes slow or boring. Mr. Larsen also asks Sid's father to do a special report on the unemployment in their suburb. This assignment leads to a position as managing editor of the paper. It means a cut in pay for Sid's father, but he'll have the opportunity to buy into the business in the future. By the time school starts in the fall, Sid has decided the ski trip is not worth spending his money on. He busies himself with the school newspaper, deciding to major in journalism in college. Two afternoons a week he works for Mr. Larsen, alongside his father. Reflecting on the events of the summer, Sid concludes, "All I know is that I feel surer of myself, confident that I'll be able to muddle through the years ahead, the way we muddled through That Summer. . . . And I know that things will never be the same again."

A teenage boy tells of the summer of his father's unemployment, a time of considerable change for the whole family. At first Sid is bored with his job, resentful of his father's depression, angry about the financial hard times. But as his interest in the newspaper business grows, Sid's perspectives on the world of work and on his own life change. By summer's end, he can reflect on how valuable the whole experience has been. Sid laces his story with considerable humor. Characters, dialogue, and situations all ring true.

Ages 12-14

**Also available in:**
No other form known

## 466

Newton, Suzanne

### M.V. Sexton Speaking

The Viking Press, Inc., 1981.
(196 pages)

---

*IDENTITY, SEARCH FOR*
*MATURATION*
  *Boy-girl relationships*
  *Communication: lack of*
  *Friendship: making friends*
  *Job*
  *Orphan*
  *Relatives: living in home of*
  *Responsibility: accepting*

---

Martha Venable Sexton, sixteen, looks forward to a long, lazy summer. But Great-Aunt Gert informs her she must find a job. Having lived with Aunt Gert for ten years since her parents died, Martha Venable knows it is useless to argue. Even Uncle Milton does not do that. So Martha Venable gets a job at Bradley's Bake Shop, where experience is not required. The owner, Brad Bradley, a playful, fun-loving man, tells her he finds her name intimidating and so will call her M.V. The first day of work is hectic and tiring, but M.V. meets and quickly likes Brad's wife, Rachel, who also helps in the shop. The next day, M.V. learns the Bradleys are considerably in debt. She worries that they can't really afford her, but she's agreed to take the job and knows they need help—although the work is terribly confusing and frustrating. One day M.V. goes to a crowded restaurant for lunch, and a young man offers to share his table with her. Gene Kestler is twenty-five and a jewelry repairman; M.V. enjoys their lunch together. That evening, the girl again asks her aunt and uncle about her parents. She knows so little about them—only that they died in a mountain-climbing accident—and has always felt a mysterious reserve in her aunt and uncle when she mentioned them. As usual, Aunt Gert tries to avoid

the subject and M.V. learns only that her mother was Aunt Gert's sister's child. M.V. resolves to keep asking questions until she knows everything about her parents. Rachel encourages her to assert herself, so once again M.V. asks Aunt Gert about her mother. This time her aunt cries, and the girl is totally baffled. On Saturday, after getting paid, M.V. buys some makeup, which she's never worn before. She wears it to church, infuriating Aunt Gert. "Aunt Gert's everlasting do's and don'ts encircled me like a fence. How could I be my natural self when I didn't even know what my natural self was?" That afternoon M.V. talks to a neighbor, Mrs. Pepper, who went to school with her mother. The woman gives M.V. her high school yearbook. The next day Mrs. Pepper's son Arnold drives M.V. to work and asks her out, and she has another lunch with Gene. But as M.V.'s social life improves, Aunt Gert gets grouchier, distrusting the girl's new friends. Meanwhile, Uncle Milton seems friendlier and one day comes to the bakery to take her to lunch. As they eat, he explains that Aunt Gert is worried that M.V. will follow in her mother's footsteps and eventually leave them. The story finally comes out: M.V.'s mother had lived with Aunt Gert after her own mother died. While away at college, she had secretly married one of her professors. The marriage became known when M.V.'s mother got pregnant and her father subsequently lost his job for marrying a student. Aunt Gert has never gotten over her sense of betrayal. That night, M.V. takes Aunt Gert and Uncle Milton to dinner and is able to claim them as her family. The atmosphere at home improves greatly and M.V. looks forward to finishing her summer job, dating, and enjoying life. She thanks Aunt Gert for making her get a job: "It has changed my life."

A girl living with a staid and reserved great-aunt and an unassertive great-uncle feels stifled, frustrated, and baffled by the mystery surrounding her dead parents. Her friendship with her summer employers encourages her to press for answers and, in the process, she matures and grows closer to the couple who raised her. M.V.'s first-person narrative is laced with humor and filled with fascinating, believable characters and crisp dialogue. This is an outstanding story of personal growth.

Ages 11 and up

**Also available in:**
Paperbound—*M.V. Sexton Speaking*
Fawcett World Library

## 467

O'Connor, Jane

### Yours Till Niagara Falls, Abby

Black/white illustrations by Margot Apple.
Hastings House Publishers, Inc., 1979.
(128 pages)

---

*CAMP EXPERIENCES*
*MATURATION*
  *Friendship: making friends*
  *Friendship: meaning of*
  *Separation anxiety*

---

Having convinced her parents to send her to summer camp with Merle, her best friend, ten-year-old Abby must go alone when Merle breaks an ankle. Abby's

O

misadventures begin almost immediately. Her bunkmates, veteran campers Bonnie and Phyllis, collapse her bed, soak her hand in water as she sleeps, and tease and taunt her at the slightest provocation. Abby forgets to lock the food chest, and seagulls eat the girls' picnic lunch. Abby gets poison ivy. When mice nest in her pajamas her sympathy is awakened and she adopts them as pets, but she still wants to go home. "You must learn to make the best of situations even when they don't turn out like you want," her mother maintains. With the arrival of a new camper, Roberta, Abby finds someone clumsier and more of an outsider than she is. Abby's sympathy for Roberta is strengthened by the overt hostility of Bonnie and Phyllis. The dauntless Roberta leads Abby on a spy mission to the counselor's cabin, and the two girls turn the tables on Bonnie by running off with her robe and towel while she showers. Slowly, Abby's confidence returns, but certain fears persist. Though a good swimmer, she is afraid of diving and pleads with her parents to get her excused from diving lessons. She enjoys her assignment of teaching younger girls to swim, but feels ashamed of her refusal to dive. Then, in an accidental fall from the diving board, she discovers she can indeed dive. She even stars as Dracula in a skit. As camp ends, Abby learns that Merle is spending an extra week away from home with a new friend. At first Abby is hurt, but soon she realizes that change is part of friendship. Her own new friendship, with Roberta, will also be tried by separation. She realizes too that in spite of everything she has enjoyed camp and is sorry to see it end.

On her own for the first time at summer camp, a young girl must cope with separation from her home and best friend, harassment by difficult bunkmates, and her own lack of confidence. She sides with several shy girls and holds back from testing or trusting herself until sympathy for another outsider and success in teaching younger girls enhance her self-esteem. Abby comes to realize that her worth is independent of the people and places she had thought its source. Although Abby's financial security will seem alien to some readers, most will identify with her easily. Her story is told with humor and illustrated invitingly.

Ages 8-10

**Also available in:**
Paperbound—*Yours Till Niagara Falls, Abby*
Scholastic Book Services

## 468

Ofek, Uriel

### Smoke over Golan

Translated from the Hebrew by Israel I. Taslitt.
Black/white illustrations by Lloyd Bloom.
Harper & Row, Publishers, Inc., 1979.
(184 pages)

---

*ISRAEL*
*WAR*
  *Friendship: meaning of*
  *Patriotism*
  *Resourcefulness*

---

When he is five, Eitan Avivi and his family move to Neot-Golan, a farm in the Golan Heights. Eitan and Albert, his father's friend and farmhand, with Nicky, Albert's big dog, become immediate friends. Some months later, Ricky, a young woman soldier and teacher, arrives to open the tiniest school in Israel—she teaches only Eitan, living with his family during the week and at her parents' home on weekends. At this time a friendship begins between Eitan and Saleem, a Syrian boy who crosses the border into Israel one day to find his donkey that wandered off. The boys meet frequently and play together. Eitan and his parents also become acquainted with the soldiers at the nearby military post and soon open their home to them. One soldier, Asher'ke, becomes a special friend of Eitan's. In the fall of 1973, after noticing several Syrian tanks traveling south, Asher'ke sets up a signaling device between Eitan's farm and the post. Eitan's pregnant mother leaves the farm and goes to her parents' home in Hadera to be closer to the hospital. One day Saleem doesn't come to play. Concerned, Eitan looks over the border through his new field glasses. He spies Syrian tanks under camouflage nets. The following morning the Israelis are put on alert, and Albert and Eitan's father join their military units. Eitan waits at the farm for the bus that is coming to take him to safety. But about noon, a sudden, deafening blast signals the beginning of battle, and Eitan realizes that he has inadvertently been left alone on the farm. He and Nicky race for the shelter, where he notices water seeping in. The water line has been hit, Eitan finds, and he turns off the main valve. In the house, he switches on the radio in time to hear Prime Minister Golda Meir announce, "Today, at about two o'clock in the afternoon, the forces of Egypt and Syria launched an attack on Israel." A buzzing from Asher'ke's signal reminds Eitan of the military post and he goes there. He finds it nearly destroyed, deserted except for one dead soldier and Asher'ke, who is wounded. Before returning to the farm with Eitan, Asher'ke raises the Israeli flag over the post. The next day a jeep pulls into the farmyard and Asher'ke holds and questions the driver, a Syrian intelligence officer. In the jeep Eitan finds a satchel with important documents about a secret assignment. They lock the Syrian in Eitan's room. The next day Asher'ke is brought down with pain and fever from his wound, and Eitan wonders fearfully what to do. To his relief, a friend, Tziyon Harari, arrives in his jeep. As Asher'ke's condition worsens, Eitan and Tziyon drive to the post to radio for help. They are promised assistance but when Eitan raises the Israeli flag, which is down, he draws a blast of enemy fire that destroys Tziyon's jeep. They must walk back to Neot-Golan and on the way are trapped in a skirmish during which Eitan receives a superficial arm wound. Soon after they return to the farm a rescue helicopter arrives and takes Asher'ke and the Syrian on board. Just then Eitan sees Israeli tanks moving toward them, and he decides to stay on the farm with Tziyon. Before long his father returns, they call and learn his mother is safe, and Neot-Golan becomes a Tagad, a battalion station for the wounded. One day Eitan gets a ride over the border in an army car and finds Saleem alone in his village. He brings the Syrian boy back to the farm, deciding "if the grown-ups fought one another, maybe we, the youngsters, could live in peace." At last the war ends and Albert comes home, wounded. Eitan has a baby sister and Ricky returns. But she no longer teaches in the tiniest school in Israel. Eitan now goes to school with Ami, the young brother of Asher'ke. Asher'ke and Ami have joined the family on Neot-Golan.

The effects of the 1973 Yom Kippur War on a young Israeli boy are grippingly described in this exciting story. Eitan finds his resourcefulness and maturity challenged as his peaceful country life is abruptly transformed by the terror and destruction of war. He learns much about survival and pride, and his friendship with a Syrian boy reminds the reader that children don't make wars. The earthy realism of the illustrations enhances the vivid narration.

Ages 9-13

**Also available in:**
No other form known

## 469

**Okimoto, Jean Davies**

### It's Just Too Much

G. P. Putnam's Sons, 1980.
(126 pages)

---

PARENT/PARENTS: Remarriage of
  Appearance: concern about
  Change: resisting
  Family: relationships
  Maturation
  Puberty
  Stepbrother/Stepsister
  Stepparent: father

---

Life is not easy for Cynthia. She is one of only five no-bra girls in her sixth-grade class, and her best friend, Trae, is "turning beautiful" right before her eyes. Worst of all, she and her little sister, Sara, are about to acquire two stepbrothers. Cynthia loves her future stepfather, Sam, and is glad about the marriage. But she's not at all sure she will like having David, eight, and Larry, her age, as part of the family. Although the boys only spend weekends with their father, they still manage to add to the misery of Cynthia's life. For one thing, they eat all the snack food. When they all go to the Schwartzes' summer place on Whidbey Island, Helene Schwartz ignores Cynthia and spends all her time trying to impress Larry. Adding insult to injury, Helene is obviously beginning to mature physically and has started wearing a bra. She also happily announces that her period is due any day now. Cynthia sadly reflects that her only signs of growing up are pimples on her nose and forehead. As the wedding day approaches, Cynthia gets less and less excited about it. She is disappointed when she discovers it will not be a grand wedding but a small one in their house. Worse, she learns her father is not happy about the occasion and has planned a long business trip so he won't have to be in town. This means that during the honeymoon she and Sara will be left in the care of a great-aunt who is "a completely terrible person." Eventually, to their great relief, their mother and Sam return. Things further improve when Cynthia goes to Happy Hollow Camp for the summer. She makes new friends and her mother sends her a size 30AAA bra to wear. But when the summer ends, she returns home to the same old problems. Trae is still

beautiful; Larry and David are still eating all the food and getting away with murder. When school starts, however, Cynthia has new things to think about. She is a seventh grader in a large junior high. She must wear braces. She has to take a bus. There are new people to get acquainted with, including Seth Rosen, "the most wonderful boy." When Seth begins to notice her, she's sure she's in love. One weekend Cynthia, Sara, Larry, and David have a pillow fight in the living room. Her mother is furious and punishes them all equally, to Cynthia's satisfaction. When Harry Z, who lives down the street, pushes David off his bike, Cynthia flattens him "with one punch." Then when Harry starts teasing Cynthia about having a boyfriend, Larry punches him too. That night as she goes to bed to dream about Seth, she also thinks about her new stepbrothers. She decides that, like her relationship with Sara, life with Larry and David will have its ups and downs. They are "like my real brothers."

A young girl must cope with momentous changes in her life: the onset of adolescence, her mother's remarriage, two stepbrothers whom her mother, afraid of becoming the "wicked stepmother," at first treats with partiality. However, Cynthia gradually finds her place among her peers and sees her family life return to normal. She emerges as a fairly happy teenager, with a boy to dream about and two new brothers who are really "not so bad" after all. Cynthia's first-person narration is lively and funny. This story is a sequel to *My Mother Is Not Married to My Father*, in which Cynthia describes her feelings and experiences when her parents divorce.

Ages 10-12

**Also available in:**
No other form known

## 470

**Okimoto, Jean Davies**

### My Mother Is Not Married to My Father

G. P. Putnam's Sons, 1979.
(109 pages)

---

DIVORCE: of Parents
  Change: resisting
  Parent/Parents: remarriage of
  Stepparent: father

---

When their mother takes eleven-year-old Cynthia and six-year-old Sara out to dinner, Cynthia knows something is amiss. But the last thing she expects to hear is that her parents are getting a divorce. Over dinner, their mother tells them that their father is moving into an apartment and they will see him every weekend. Sara does not seem to understand the importance of the news, but Cynthia, extremely upset, throws up soon after they return home. When her father calls, she asks him to confirm the news, hoping there has been a mistake. But there hasn't. When the girls and their mother return from a weekend spent with friends, the apartment looks ransacked; their father has been by to pick up his things. That night, Cynthia, Sara, and their mother all sleep together in Mom's king-sized bed. The next night Cynthia moves her favorite things into her closet and sleeps there with her cat. She tells Martha the cat how terribly frightened she is. She admits that she's also very angry, but is afraid to tell her mother so for fear her mother will leave her too. Later, she is able to confide her feelings to her mother during one of their frequent crying sessions. Family life continues to change in disturbing ways. Sara starts carrying around a baby bottle. Their mother buys herself purple clothes and says she might as well drink all the wine they have so she can save the bottles for a terrarium collection. Sara and Cynthia discuss the possibility that it was actually their misbehavior that drove their father away. If they promise to reform, will he come back? He does come back—for the weekend—but the girls notice he is wearing beads around his neck, longer hair, and "teenager pants." The rules at their father's apartment are different from the rules at home, they find, and this confuses them for a while. They soon realize that their parents are anxious to make up to them for the divorce; they are treated to numerous zoo visits, park outings, and movies. Before they are quite used to all the changes, there is another one: their father's friend, Ellen. Cynthia continues trying to make sense of the divorce and eventually drops her efforts to reconcile her parents. When her mother accepts her first date, Cynthia tells Martha the cat how much she hates sharing people. As her mother continues to date, she and Sara get used to it. However, when Cynthia decides that Bill would make an ideal husband and father (he has a horse), she cannot understand why her mother isn't willing to go along with her plan. Later, she has better luck with Sam. To Martha she confesses that she loves Sam herself and almost wishes that Sam wanted to marry her instead of her mother. She worries that her love for Sam is taking something away from her father, but her mother maintains that there's always enough love to go around. For Cynthia, one of the hardest things to understand is why, now that her father has Ellen and her mother has Sam, the two of them continue to fight and argue over the smallest things whenever they see each other. When Cynthia is to appear in a class play, she becomes terribly upset that there are "no married people in my family." Her father is coming with Ellen and her mother with Sam. For just that one night, Cynthia wishes her family were like the Waltons on TV. Later, she tells her mother how she feels. Her mother asks her what she'd think about bringing Sam into the family—along with his two sons, who live with their mother but visit Sam on weekends. Both Cynthia and Sara are delighted. The girls, their mother, and Sam discuss stepfamilies and how they'll need to look for a new house and get to know each other better. Feeling somewhat reassured, Cynthia decides, "Maybe we weren't like the Waltons on TV, but it was okay the way we were."

A rather classic case of divorce is seen through the eyes of Cynthia, who narrates the book. Most of the responses that children have to divorce are included: denial, guilt, anger, confusion, misplaced hope, regression, bargaining, and finally acceptance and adjustment. With the help of a sensitive mother, both Cynthia and her younger sister are able to talk out their feelings and adapt to events beyond their control. Most children involved in divorces will find themselves somewhere in these pages. Others will gain insight. The story continues in the sequel, *It's Just Too Much.*

Ages 9-11

**Also available in:**
Braille—*My Mother Is Not Married to My Father*
Library of Congress (NLSBPH)

Disc—*My Mother Is Not Married to My Father*
Library of Congress (NLSBPH)

**471**

**Okimoto, Jean Davies**

**Norman Schnurman, Average Person**
G. P. Putnam's Sons, 1982.
(125 pages)

*EXPECTATIONS*
*PARENTAL: Interference*
  *Communication: parent-child*
  *Courage, meaning of*
  *Gender role identity: male*
  *Sex: attitude toward*

Sixth-grader Norman Schnurman, who has absolutely no interest in or aptitude for sports, is the son of Mad Dog Dave Schnurman, a former college football star. When Norman's father begins coaching the junior league Bears team, he promises to turn Norman into a first-rate running back. Sure Norman will soon love the game as much as he does, he buys his protesting son a complete football outfit with his old number, 33. Meanwhile Norman, whose main interests are garage sales and video games, has accidentally broken three hula-lady lamps at Reasonably Honest Al's. To repay Al the twelve dollars for the broken lamps, Norman and his friend P.W. repair one of the lamps and then hold a tent show after school. They charge admission to watch the hula-lady lamp light up, look at a poster of a woman in a wet T-shirt, and other raucous goings-on. A mother finds out and tells Norman's parents. For his punishment he has to show the mother the lamp and apologize. Then, at a garage sale, Norman meets Carrie Koski and her grandfather. She's new in school and attractive, and Norman offers to show her around. Since Norman has never seen a naked woman, he decides to hide in his older sister Sally's closet and watch her undress. Instead, he leaps out and scares her. He and his mother talk, Norman blaming his current antics on the pressure to play football. His mother sympathizes, explaining that his father simply wants to relive his happiest times through Norman. Norman helps Carrie find her way around on the first day of school, braving his friends' teasing to sit with her at lunchtime. He goes to his first football practice with much anxiety, and during it he throws up. On his way home in disgrace he meets Mr. Koski, who invites him for tea and tells him that being a man does not depend on size or aggressiveness. During the first football game, Norman makes a touchdown—for the other side. Then P.W. reports that his neighbors have installed a hot tub and use it nude. The two plan to peek from a tree in P.W.'s yard. One day Mr. Koski takes Carrie and Norman to the zoo. When they see a monkey "fooling around with himself in front of all the people and all the other monkeys and everything," Mr. Koski points out that the monkey is not ashamed or unhappy with himself. Norman's father tries with growing desperation to turn his son into a football player.

268

Finally, Norman tells his father he is not cut out for football and is quitting the team. He recommends, though, that his father continue coaching, since it gives him so much pleasure. When Norman tells Mr. Koski he's quit the team, Mr. Koski rewards him with a medal. Whenever he finds an outstanding example of everyday human courage, he bestows a medal; this is the second one he's ever given. Norman takes Carrie out and enjoys their time together: "It sure had been a good day for me, Norman Schnurman, son of Mad Dog."

With the help of his sympathetic mother and understanding friend, Norman arrives at a better understanding of who he is and is not when he's pressured to play football against his own inclinations. Torn between wanting to please his father and needing to be himself, Norman finally finds the courage to make the right choice. Along the way, this funny first-person narrative includes the language and preoccupations of sixth-grade boys, giving it great appeal for the intended audience. But it is also a warm, perceptive story of family relationships and growing up.

Ages 10-12

**Also available in:**
Paperbound—*Norman Schnurman, Average Person*
Dell Publishing Company, Inc.

## 472

**Oneal, Zibby**

## A Formal Feeling

The Viking Press, Inc., 1982.
(162 pages)

---

*DEATH: of Mother*
*MOURNING, STAGES OF*
 *Emotions: accepting*
 *Emotions: identifying*
 *Family: relationships*
 *Guilt, feelings of*
 *Parent/Parents: remarriage of*

---

When sixteen-year-old Anne Cameron returns home from boarding school for Christmas vacation, she has to face an upsetting reality: her mother has been dead for a year and now her father has remarried. She can't understand how her father could have remarried so soon. When her older brother, Spencer, tells her she'll like having Dory around, Anne considers him disloyal. To forget her grief, Anne has taken up running; sometimes even hours later she still feels pleasantly isolated in a crystal shell. As she talks to her father, Dory, and Spencer, she feels detached, as though they are all characters in a play. Even when Eric calls she feels remote, although they'd dated the previous summer. She remembers how she listened to her father read Dante all that summer, how she and Eric dated and kissed, how the heaviness that had been with her since her mother's death began to lift. But since August, since Dory's arrival on the scene, the bleakness has set in again. Spencer believes that getting on with their lives doesn't mean they are forgetting their mother, but to Anne it seems they're all doing just that. She feels obligated to remember her, although Spencer questions, but doesn't correct, Anne's "memory of perfection." Anne envies her best friend Laura's spontaneous warmth and

understanding. When a puppy dies and Laura's mother feels bad, Laura hugs and comforts her, something Anne would have hung back from doing. Seeing the blue sweater her mother knit for her the summer before she died reminds Anne that her mother always provided her with blue clothes because blue was her mother's favorite color. Anne suddenly realizes she hates blue. She begins to remember something about a train trip. When she questions Spencer and he adds to her recollections, she remembers the time when Mother went away to live by herself because she needed time to think. Anne had screamed at her shortly before she left. While living with her grandmother during her mother's absence, Anne had decided that if you lose control, people won't love you anymore. So when her mother did return home, Anne ignored the whole incident and immediately buried the memory. Then Anne sprains her ankle ice skating. When she asks the doctor's permission to go caroling on Christmas Eve, he doesn't think it's a good idea. Anne protests, but he tells her, "Some things you have no control over." His words strike a chord in Anne. She refuses pain medication because, she tells Dory, she wants to feel the pain and be sensitive to her own healing. Now Anne begins to realize that she's always felt responsible for her mother's death. Painful as it is, she must ask herself: Did she actually love her mother? She remembers anger, repressed feelings, and constant efforts to please, but she also recalls their good times. In sum, "they had loved each other in their imperfect ways." Anne finally knows her mother is dead and can say goodbye to her at last.

A teenage girl who has for years denied her feelings about her mother must confront them in order to live and feel again after her mother's death. In the beginning Anne takes a protective, belligerent attitude toward her mother's memory; she was perfect. Anne finally realizes that this willful blindness hides guilt and resentment that must be acknowledged if she is to recover from her grief. This beautifully written, gently suspenseful novel offers little action, but its complex examination of a difficult emotional problem invites and should gain the reader's empathy.

Ages 12 and up

**Also available in:**
Paperbound—*A Formal Feeling*
Fawcett World Library

## 473

**Oneal, Zibby**

## The Language of Goldfish

The Viking Press, Inc., 1980.
(179 pages)

---

*CHANGE: Resisting*
*MATURATION*
*MENTAL ILLNESS: of Adolescent*
 *Depression*
 *Family: relationships*
 *Suicide: attempted*

---

Ever since her family moved to Northpoint, Carrie Stokes, thirteen, has been lonely and unhappy. The only thing Carrie has ever liked about their new house is the fish pond in the backyard with its miniature, moss-covered rock island in the center and the large goldfish that come to the surface whenever Carrie or her older sister, Moira, calls to them in a special way. But now even that pleasure is disappearing. Moira is interested in boys and tells Carrie she is a baby to think about talking to goldfish. Things are no better at school. Except for math and art, her best subjects, Carrie finds school frightening. She has no friends except Mrs. Ramsay, the art teacher, who gives her a private drawing lesson each Saturday morning. In the fall of her eighth-grade year, Carrie begins to notice a strange dizziness come over her whenever she feels afraid or upset. At first she tries to ignore the feeling, telling herself it is the flu. But, though she tries to remain in control of herself, the dizziness persists, sometimes so intensely that she loses consciousness. One day she becomes so frightened that she races to the clinic where her physician father works. He minimizes the problem, telling her she is probably anemic. Her mother, absorbed in her busy social schedule, refuses to listen to Carrie's pleas for help. For several days the world seems blurry to Carrie, until one evening she finds herself far from home. She doesn't know where she's been or how she's gotten where she is. She finds her way home but decides she must be going insane. While her parents are entertaining friends, Carrie goes upstairs and swallows the contents of a bottle of capsules in the medicine chest. She is hospitalized and drifts in and out of consciousness for several days. Her mother still refuses to admit anything is wrong, but her father hires a psychiatrist for her. Gradually, Carrie begins to like and trust the doctor, and the two try to interpret the meaning of the hazy island that sits in the middle of Carrie's escape world and haunts her. Time passes, and though Carrie fears she will try suicide again, she slowly learns to control herself when the dizziness comes over her. When she returns to school, a new boy named Daniel befriends her. He invites her to join a special group for advanced math students, but Carrie declines, unable to admit to him that the club meets at the same time she sees her psychiatrist. She resumes her art lessons though, frequently painting the hazy island of her imagination. Slowly, Carrie's world begins to right itself. She attends a school dance and Daniel walks her home. She even explains to him why she was unable to join the math club and is delighted when he accepts her explanation matter-of-factly. During the summer she learns that her beloved Mrs. Ramsay is divorcing her husband and moving away to be with "another man." Carrie feels betrayed, but by the time she goes to say goodbye she is able to forgive Mrs. Ramsay and be grateful for her loyalty and friendship. As she continues to paint, Carrie begins to understand that the island represents the childhood she is reluctant to leave behind. Given that insight, she decides she will grow up after all. One warm afternoon she takes a little neighbor girl out to the fish pond and shows her how to talk to the goldfish. Suddenly she recognizes the pile of rocks in the middle of the pond as the elusive island of her fantasies. Knowing now that she is truly recovering, Carrie feels renewed courage.

A young girl's recovery from a severe depression is described realistically in this thought-provoking book about the pain of maturation. Carrie's developing emotional problems and her progression toward attempted suicide are believably detailed, as is her gaining of insight into what her symptoms might mean. Readers will feel her relief and sense of freedom as she realizes that she can and will leave childhood behind.

Ages 11-14

**Also available in:**
Cassette—*The Language of Goldfish*
Library of Congress (NLSBPH)

Paperbound—*The Language of Goldfish*
Fawcett World Library

### 474

**Oppenheimer, Joan Letson**

## Gardine vs. Hanover

Thomas Y. Crowell Company, Inc., 1982.
(152 pages)

---

*PARENT/PARENTS: Remarriage of*
*STEPBROTHER/STEPSISTER*
  *Arguing*
  *Differences, human*
  *Family: relationships*
  *Rejection: parental*

---

When Frances Gardine marries Berkley Hanover, their children have varied reactions. Young Abby Gardine and Drew Hanover are pleased, but Jill Gardine, fifteen, hates the whole idea and especially dislikes her new stepsister, Caroline Hanover, sixteen. Jill hadn't been overly happy about her mother remarrying, but she was particularly distressed to learn Berk's two children would live with them. For her part, Caroline has new reason to resent her mother, a famous cancer specialist who claims not to have a maternal bone in her body. It was her mother's idea that she and her brother be sent from New York City to California to live with their father. Then Caroline meets Jason Emery and falls in love for the first time. When she overhears sharp-tongued Jill making fun of her first encounter with Jason, Caroline responds in kind. By the time their parents return from their honeymoon, the battle lines are drawn. Jill's boyfriend, Gary, feels Jill is needlessly hard on Caroline, just as she is on him. Frances and Berk call a family conference to discuss the incessant arguing between Jill and Caroline. Jill becomes very emotional and says she can't live with Caroline. In response, Caroline leaves the room, accusing Jill of being melodramatic. The tension spreads. When Jill and Abby return from a visit with their father, they find strained relations between Frances and Berk and between Frances and Caroline. Even Abby and Drew have their first falling-out. That night, Frances and Berk announce their separation. Drew blames Caroline for the breakup and spends every free minute with Abby at the Gardine house. Meanwhile, Caroline makes her first real friend, Michelle, and learns from her that she intimidates people with her beauty, intelligence, and sophistication. Michelle herself had simply decided to act on her suspicion that Caroline was basically shy and insecure. Then Caroline has a talk with her biology teacher, a career woman like Caroline's mother. The girl begins to see that her mother is simply a limited person, that she doesn't really dislike her daughter. Caroline, who had considered and rejected the idea of becoming a doctor because of her mother's attitude, now realizes she could become one without turning into her mother. Human relationships are important to her; they are not to her mother. Jill's mother is suffering a great deal from the breakup, losing weight and sleep. Jill wants to help mend fences but when Gary says that will mean talking to Caroline, she balks. Then Frances falls seriously ill with the flu and Jill nurses her. When Jill also becomes very sick, Abby, in desperation, calls Caroline. For several days Caroline takes care of them both, and she and Jill have several talks. They agree that they want the families to reunite. When Jill becomes insulting Caroline quietly leaves the room, proud that she hasn't indulged in her usual knee-jerk reaction to Jill's sharp tongue. They talk again, though, and each admits to a secret admiration of the other. Caroline confesses that her mother's rejection has always made her feel like a loser. They decide to call another family conference, confident that this time they can all live together in harmony.

The antagonism between two teenage stepsisters breaks up their new family, but it is the girls' decision to work at resolving the conflict that eventually reunites it. In the process, both Caroline and Jill learn quite a bit about themselves, allowing them greater understanding of the roots of their difficulty. This well-written book, with strong, believable characters and a suspenseful story line, alternates viewpoints between Caroline and Jill so that readers can appreciate both sides of the conflict. There is insight here into the little, everyday habits and routines that can cause friction and must be considered in such a family merger.

Ages 11-14

**Also available in:**
Paperbound—*Stepsisters*
Pocket Books, Inc.

## 475

Oppenheimer, Joan Letson

**Working On It**

Harcourt Brace Jovanovich, Inc., 1980.
(136 pages)

---

*INFERIORITY, FEELINGS OF*
*SHYNESS*
  *Boy-girl relationships*
  *Friendship: best friend*
  *School: classmate relationships*
  *School: pupil-teacher relationships*
  *Self, attitude toward: accepting*

---

Tracy Ayres is convinced "fifteen is the pits" as she joins teacher Eden Lindsay's drama class. She has been talked into taking the class by family members and by Carla, her best friend—they've heard wonderful things about the class and think it will help improve Tracy's sense of herself. But the painfully shy Tracy dreads it. Suffering from a "rotten self-image," a "superwoman" mother, and a bright, popular older brother, Tracy is dismayed when her appointed class partner for improvisations is the popular, good-looking Wylie Babcock.

Each student must keep a personal "Character Notebook" about an emotion frequently felt: Tracy writes about shyness and Wylie writes about "like" because he really has no one to love. At the end of six weeks, each improvisation team is to do a presentation illustrating the feelings in their notebooks. Tracy is at first resentful at being chided for her shyness, goaded to express her real feelings, and analyzed mercilessly by Wylie as they work together. But slowly the girl's "work in progress" becomes a process of building her confidence and self-acceptance. She is almost paralyzed with fright before each class presentation but gradually comes to relax and act freely, the class forgotten. She begins to see how adept both Wylie and her mother are at manipulating responses from her; she works out her frustrations by describing her feelings in the class log, able to recognize changes in herself as the class progresses. As Tracy blossoms, she and Wylie are drawn together. There is one casualty of Tracy's maturation, however: Carla is resentful and hurt when Tracy stops sharing every thought with her and their friendship ends. By the end of "miracle worker" Miss Lindsay's class, many students have grown in self-acceptance and tolerance for others. Tracy especially benefits from her teacher's advice: "Stop and think when you put yourself down. Become aware of what you are doing to yourself."

A painfully shy teenage girl blossoms under the guidance of a wise teacher and the discipline of improvisational acting. In the process, Tracy learns how much people can help one another to gain self-knowledge. Plot development is logical and although the ending is rather tidy, it does not appear contrived. Characterizations lack some depth, but relationships are realistic and the dialogue natural. Readers will easily identify with Tracy and her classmates and will be left hopeful that their growth will continue beyond the class.

Ages 11-13

**Also available in:**
No other form known

## 476

Osborn, Lois

**My Brother Is Afraid of Just About Everything**

Color illustrations by Jennie Williams.
Albert Whitman & Company, 1982.
(31 pages)

---

*FEAR*
*SIBLING: Relationships*

---

A boy of about eight tells of his younger brother's many fears. The little boy hides under his bed during storms and in the bushes when the mailman comes. He screams if the drain is opened while he's in the tub. One day, when their mother starts to vacuum, the older boy takes his frightened little brother out for a walk. They go past the older boy's school, but the little boy only looks frightened when told he will go there one day. When they meet some of the older boy's friends, his little brother clings to him, afraid to talk. On the way home they wait for a passing train and the younger boy, unlike his brother and "most kids" who "think trains are pretty exciting," is again frightened. Back at home the brothers sit under a tree in their backyard. The older boy decides it's time for a talk. He tells his brother that his fears are unreasonable. Though the younger boy looks hurt and in need of comforting, his brother says, "Look, you've got to get tough. It's stupid to keep on being afraid of things that won't hurt you." Just then the younger boy smiles at something he sees approaching. Without turning around, the older brother knows it must be a dog. The younger one happily grabs the large dog while his brother runs behind a tree, hoping the dog will leave. When the dog jumps up and licks him, the older boy runs into the house and latches the screen door behind him. Safe inside, he watches his younger brother play with the dog and wishes he could join him. But he will not go out while the dog is there.

With a touch of scorn and superiority, the narrator describes his younger brother's varied and unfounded fears. However, his lecture to the younger boy is cut short by his own fear of a dog. When the brothers reverse roles, the older boy realizes "everybody's afraid of something." This book, nicely illustrated with line drawings, may help young readers accept their own fears more readily and be more tolerant of others. However, the story lacks any advice or examples about how to overcome fears or calm the fears of someone else.

Ages 4-7

**Also available in:**
Large Print—*My Brother Is Afraid of Just About Everything*
Albert Whitman & Company

## 477

**Osborne, Mary Pope**

**Run, Run, As Fast As You Can**
The Dial Press, Inc., 1982.
(149 pages)

---

*DEATH: of Sibling*
  *Communication: lack of*
  *Peer relationships*
  *School: transfer*

---

When eleven-year-old Hallie Pine moves to Virginia, she expects to be as popular as she's always been. In their frequent moves as an army family, Hallie has always been class president or vice-president, head of the safety patrol, lead in the school play. But this time she finds the popular group in her new school to be smooth, sophisticated, shallow—out of her league. However, Hallie isn't about to be seen with her unpopular next-door neighbor, Laney Bankley, although Laney's been kind to her. When Hallie manages to make the popular girls laugh with a remark about an overweight teacher, she comes up with a few more quick remarks, one of them at Laney's expense. Still, although the three class "stars" seem to be Hallie's friends in school, they never include her in their out-of-school activities. One day in the shopping mall, they actually make a game of running away from her, though she is "desperate to be with that group." Hallie spends the rest of the weekend playing with her eight-year-old brother, Mickey. On Monday Mickey complains of a

stomachache and Hallie stays home with him, unwilling to face the kids at school. She recovers her pluck, but Mickey doesn't get better. After several doctor's appointments, he's taken away in an ambulance. Hallie's parents are evasive about Mickey's condition, although Hallie knows they tell everything to her sister, Anne, a college sophomore. Hallie is only allowed to visit Mickey once. When she sees him crying, she wants to hug him, but is pulled away. She screams hysterically, wanting to stay, wanting assurance that she may return. Her parents spend most of their time in the hospital in Norfolk, telling Hallie very little about Mickey. Her distress increasing, she can't even bear to sit with the popular girls. It's Laney who finds her throwing up in the restroom and suggests she just go home and cry. Then her father tells Hallie she'll spend Christmas in Florida with an aunt and uncle. She pleads to be allowed to visit Mickey, but he makes her flight reservation anyway. Her mother takes her out to dinner, offering to buy her anything she wants. As she watches her mother, noting her unusual behavior, Hallie suddenly realizes that Mickey is dying. Her mother buys her a bathing suit and an ice-cream cone, fends off her questions, and tries to act as if nothing is wrong. The next morning she hurriedly leaves to join her husband at the hospital. Later that day Hallie tries to call Anne, but is told by her sister's roommate that Anne flew suddenly to Norfolk. Then Mrs. Bankley comes to bring Hallie over to their house for the evening. With Laney's encouragement, a determined Hallie takes off on her bike for the bus station, only to find that she's missed the five o'clock bus. She sets off in the rain for Norfolk, biking the twenty-five miles in a daze. Arriving on Mickey's hospital floor, she sees her parents and Anne sitting at the end of the hall. She slips into Mickey's room, but soon realizes that the body on the bed is no longer Mickey. After his funeral, Hallie is able to talk to her mother about everyday things—her hair, the books Laney reads. She begins to feel peaceful. She knows Mickey can get along without her. Now she must learn to get along without him.

In the space of a few months, a young girl moves to a new town, learns that popularity has limited value, and loses her younger brother. The first half of the book concerns Hallie's intense need to be part of the school's popular group, although this theme is not extensively developed. The popular girls are stereotypically portrayed, as is the unpopular friend who comes through in a pinch. The death of Hallie's brother is the significant part of the book and makes heart-wrenching reading because of the parents' unwavering insistence on keeping Hallie in the dark about a family matter that obviously touches her profoundly. Their behavior is costly to their dying son also, since it deprives him of his sister's comfort and company. There is no justification in the book for the parents' attitude, and Hallie seems to bear no resentment. However, readers and parents might want to discuss this aspect of a well-written and believable story.

Ages 9-12

**Also available in:**
Paperbound—*Run, Run, As Fast As You Can*
Scholastic Book Services

## 478

Panek, Dennis

### Matilda Hippo Has a Big Mouth

Color illustrations by the author.
Bradbury Press, Inc., 1980.
(32 pages counted)

---

FRIENDSHIP: Keeping Friends
NAME-CALLING
   Revenge

---

One day as Matilda Hippo skates along the street singing to herself, she greets five of her friends with personal taunts. She calls attention to Elmer the Elephant's big nose: "Isn't it hard to see around that nose?" She notes Alex the Alligator's long teeth: "Gee, Alex, you have the world's biggest teeth." She mentions Mollie the Spoonbill's skinny legs ("Mollie, you have the skinniest legs!"), the leopard's many spots ("Spots! Spots! Lots of spots!"), and Leo the Lion's messy hair ("Such messy hair, Leo, how can you comb it?"). Since Matilda makes these remarks quickly as she skates past, her friends have no chance to defend themselves. Soon after, when Matilda falls into a puddle of water, she wonders why her friends didn't warn her. But her friends feel insulted and hurt. They have posted a sign saying, "Matilda Hippo has a big mouth." Matilda cries when she sees the sign and then both sides apologize. Matilda changes the sign to, "Matilda Hippo had a big mouth." A lesson is learned and friendship restored.

Matilda learns the effects of name-calling in this colorful book about friendship. Then she and her friends decide that friends forgive each other's mistakes and thoughtlessness. The bright, bold illustrations will help young readers understand the changing emotions of the animal characters. Children will see themselves and their friends in these characters, and the story should prompt discussion.

Ages 4-7

**Also available in:**
No other form known

## 479

Parenteau, Shirley

### I'll Bet You Thought I Was Lost

Color illustrations by Lorna Tomei.
Lothrop, Lee & Shepard Company, 1981.
(30 pages counted)

---

LOST, BEING

---

Sandy and his father go to the supermarket to buy the ingredients for a salad. Sandy stops to read cereal boxes and then discovers he cannot find his father. "Now the aisle looked longer and the stacks looked higher. Without my dad, the store seemed bigger than before." Remembering the purpose of this shopping trip, Sandy hurries toward the vegetables. He sees a man weighing mushrooms, but it is not his father. Frightened, he runs right into a cart with a baby inside. He envies the baby, who is not lost. Next Sandy runs to the front of the store and looks out at the parking lot. But he can't spot their car among so many. His panic increasing, Sandy runs up the soup aisle and sees "the whole wall of soup cans leaning toward me from the top. They never looked so scary when I was with my dad!" Finally Sandy sits on a pile of pet-food bags and hopes he will survive to see his dog again. After sitting for a while, he resumes the search for his father, so afraid he almost cries. Passing the bakery, he wishes the huge birthday cake were for him. Then, turning a corner, Sandy bumps into a man who is trying on sunglasses. He starts to ask the man for help when he realizes he's found his father. "Hello, Dad," says a very relieved Sandy. "I'll bet you thought I was lost."

A trip to the supermarket with his father becomes a scary adventure when little Sandy gets lost. He tries hard to find something familiar in the people and products he sees, but his panic steadily increases until he finds his father; then the boy is delightfully plucky and brave. Young readers will feel for Sandy, whose dilemma is vividly conveyed by numerous illustrations and a witty text.

Ages 5-8

**Also available in:**
No other form known

## 480

Paris, Lena

### Mom Is Single

Color illustrations by Mark Christianson.
Children's Press, Inc., 1980.
(31 pages)

---

DIVORCE: of Parents
   Change: accepting

---

When his teacher announces that the class is going to make name tags for parents' night, a little boy is sure everyone else has two names to put down instead of just one. Writing his mother's name makes the boy think about the way things were when Dad was still part of the family. Everything has changed since the divorce, however. Now the boy and his sister, Julie, go to Mrs. Mayer's house after school until their mother comes home from work. Before his mother got her job she went back to school so she would be able to make more money. Even so, the family has to stay on a strict budget. At first the boy didn't know what being on a budget meant. Now he knows that, for one thing, it means getting clothes for your birthday instead of a football. Another change is that now everyone has chores to do. Sometimes the boy gets angry because he doesn't want to help and doesn't understand why things had to change. He'd worried that all their new chores might mean their mother would leave or something might happen to her. After he told his mother how he felt, she talked with Grandma and Grandpa about taking the children if anything ever happened to her. This made the boy feel much better. He still does some things with his father, but it's not like it was. For one thing, his father now lives in another part of town. His father insists that he misses them too, but the boy wonders if Dad's as lonely as he is when they wave goodbye. Last

P

week when Dad said he couldn't go on a camp-out, the boy asked his grandfather. Grandpa said he was too old to sleep in a tent. But then Uncle Kenny agreed to take him, and they had a lot of fun. The boy used to pretend that his parents would get back together again, but now he knows they won't. He has come to realize, however, that their being apart doesn't mean they don't care about their children. It just means that things are different for all of them.

A boy describes the painful changes that his parents' divorce has brought to their family. Simply told and vividly illustrated with photographs, this story may promote understanding of family upheavals as the boy comes to realize that, despite all the changes, his parents continue to love him.

Ages 6-8

**Also available in:**
Paperbound—*Mom Is Single*
Children's Press, Inc.

## 481

Park, Barbara

### Don't Make Me Smile

Alfred A. Knopf, Inc., 1981.
(114 pages)

---

*DIVORCE: of Parents*
  *Anger*
  *Change: resisting*
  *Communication: parent-child*
  *Life style: change in*

---

Charlie Hickle, almost eleven, has had his life turned upside down by the breakup of his parents' marriage. He is angry with both of them and deeply frustrated about his own helplessness: "Divorce is like watching your mother back the car over your brand new bicycle. You know what's about to happen, but there's nothing you can do about it." He's sure he'll never smile again and suspects he might even lose his mind. Life becomes more and more chaotic as Charlie refuses to go to school, tries running away from home to live in a tree, and rejects all his father's overtures during their Saturday visits. Worried about his son, Charlie's father takes the boy to a child psychologist, Dr. Girard, whom Charlie at first resents. But when he learns that Dr. Girard's parents divorced when he was a boy and he didn't let it ruin his life, Charlie decides the doctor might just understand how he, Charlie, feels. Dr. Girard suggests that Charlie share his feelings with his parents. His first attempts are clumsy: during an Easter visit from his mother's cousin, he manages to hurt both her feelings and his mother's. For his eleventh birthday, Charlie wants to have things normal again and convinces his parents to go on a family picnic. But the afternoon ends with the mother and father quarreling bitterly and Charlie, in desperation, calls Dr. Girard and asks what he should do. Advised again to make his feelings known, Charlie returns to his parents and politely asks his father to leave. This his father does, without anger. Over the next two months, Charlie continues to meet with Dr. Girard. The psychologist helps the boy grapple with sinking grades, disruptive school behavior, and the conviction that he will never be truly happy again. At the story's end, Charlie has begun to believe he will survive the divorce. He even catches himself smiling now and then.

A boy troubled and alienated by his parents' divorce is helped to cope by a skillful, sympathetic psychologist. Charlie's sometimes-humorous narration lends his story credibility and saves it from sentimentality. His painful struggle to adjust to the breakup of his family moves believably to his realization that, while the sadness is not completely gone, he is learning to live with his new situation.

Ages 8-11

**Also available in:**
Paperbound—*Don't Make Me Smile*
Avon Books

## 482

Parsons, Elizabeth

### The Upside-Down Cat

Black/white illustrations by Ronald Himler.
Atheneum Publishers, 1981.
(43 pages)

---

*PETS: Love for*
*SHARING/NOT SHARING*
  *Loss: feelings of*

---

Lily Black, a black cat with a white fur bib and four white paws, comes to live with Joe and his parents the year Joe is seven. The family calls her the "Upside-Down Cat" because in the winter she lies on her back on a heat register with her paws in the air. Each summer the family, with Lily, leaves their tiny New York City house to live in their summer home on the Maine coast. There Lily is free to roam the woodlands along the bay, coming and going as she pleases. The summer Joe is ten, Lily's adventures take her farther than usual. One day toward the end of the summer, she wanders into a new territory and cannot find her way back. The family is accustomed to her frequent absences, but when she is gone several days they become worried. Labor Day is fast approaching, time for the family to return to the city. Every day Joe hunts and calls for Lily Black, but she cannot be found and the family has to leave. Now the weather gets colder. Lily Black grows a warm coat. Snow falls. One day Lily finds a little fishing shack perched on a rocky point of land. She judges from the smoke curling out the chimney that someone has been there recently. Investigating further, she discovers a comfortable cushion stuffed under the floorboards. She settles in, feeling secure for the first time in weeks. Several days later Henry, an old fisherman, walks up the wharf and enters the shack. Lily smells a fire being built and then chowder cooking. She observes the man unseen, but when he returns several days later and Lily again smells chowder, she cautiously approaches the shack and sits in the doorway. Henry, who loves cats, feeds Lily, chats with her, and invites her to stay. When he must go back to his home in town, he leaves food for her. He would like to take her along, but his wife is terribly afraid of cats. All winter Lily stays at the fishing shack. Henry comes out every few days, bringing food.

He cooks, checks his traps, fixes his tools. In the spring he brings out his lobster boat and soon Lily begins to ride with him, sitting proudly in the stern. Spring passes, bringing long summer days and the arrival of Joe and his parents. They clean the house, plant the garden, and Joe paints his little boat. One day while rowing in the bay, he notices a fisherman checking his lobster traps. He rows closer and is surprised to see a black and white cat sitting on the stern deck. Lily Black! Rudely he tells Henry that the cat belongs to him. Henry, though surprised, can see that the cat recognizes Joe. Abruptly he hands her to the boy, briefly explaining that she had come to his shack and he had taken care of her through the winter. Joe takes Lily home and the family has a happy reunion. But Joe is troubled. He wonders if Lily Black belongs to Henry now. Joe and Henry become friends, and late in the summer Joe asks Henry if he would like to keep Lily again through the winter. The fisherman is touched by the boy's understanding, but says that Lily must go where she will be cared for best. He says goodbye to Joe and Lily until next summer.

A cat loved by a boy and an old man creates a friendship between the two built of respect and understanding. Parts of this well-written story are told from the cat's perspective, and the total effect is thought-provoking. Illustrations capture both the relationships and the rugged beauty of the Maine coast.

Ages 8-11

Also available in:
No other form known

## 483

Pascal, Francine

**The Hand-Me-Down Kid**

The Viking Press, Inc., 1980.
(172 pages)

SIBLING: Youngest
  Delinquency, juvenile
  Friendship: making friends
  Guilt, feelings of
  Honesty/Dishonesty
  Problem solving
  Sibling: relationships
  Teasing

Arianne (Ari) Jacobs is eleven, the youngest of three children, and gets all the family hand-me-downs: "Everything's all used up just when I'm big enough to get in on it." Besides Ari and her parents, the family's Greenwich Village apartment includes fourteen-year-old Neddy, who teases Ari, and sixteen-year-old Elizabeth (Liz), who gets everything she wants. Ari's new best friend, Rhona Finkelstein, wants to borrow Liz's brand-new bike to use in the marathon qualifying races. Since Ari badly wants Rhona's continuing friendship, she manages to sneak Liz's treasured bike out of the storeroom and walk it carefully to the park where she's to meet Rhona. There she sees several teenage boys harassing an old man, tossing his hat back and forth. Jumping into the fray, Ari rescues the hat. But afterwards, to her horror, she finds that Liz's bike is gone.

When Rhona and her friends arrive, they are unsympathetic. Miserable, Ari goes back to the storeroom to pretend the bike had been stolen from there. Liz is hysterical and Neddy calls the police. After a few questions, the police focus on Eddie, Liz's Puerto Rican boyfriend, but in the end must admit they doubt they'll ever find the bike. So Ari decides to look for it herself. Returning to the park, she meets Jane Richardson, a new girl in school. Jane, easygoing and friendly, also has older siblings but doesn't let them push her around. She advises Ari to quit acting "little" and points out some of the advantages of being the youngest. The two go to Ari's house. When Neddy begins to tease Ari, Jane cleverly turns his taunts back on him. The police return and start to lean on Eddie again. As they are taking him away, Ari bursts out that she took the bike for a ride and left it unlocked. Believing she lied to save Eddie, all are grateful to her, and Jane is very impressed with what she considers Ari's quick thinking. When Ari tells her the truth, Jane promptly offers to help her find the bike. They spend some time searching for Bag Mary, who was in the park when the bike disappeared; when Jane has to go home, Ari finds Bag Mary herself. She learns that a boy named Bucky who hangs out at Delmonte's luncheonette was one of the boys teasing the old man. At Delmonte's Ari discovers that Bucky is often in trouble and that he frequents Reinhardt's bike shop. The bike shop seems a significant clue, but the owner is so mean Ari leaves without any information. At school on Monday, Rhona is still angry about the bike. As Ari is again apologizing, Jane steps in and shows Ari that she need not allow Rhona to treat her badly. Then Ari gets a shock. At Jane's birthday party after school, her big present from her parents turns out to be Liz's bike! Jane's parents bought the bike at Reinhardt's, and so Jane's and Ari's families and the police all meet there. The police say Otto Reinhardt used to own a used-car lot where a lot of stolen cars turned up. Bucky arrives while the group is in the shop, but then realizes something is up and runs away. Ari, Rhona, and Jane catch him. He claims Reinhardt made him and some other boys steal bikes. When confronted, Reinhardt gives Jane a new bike and returns Liz's bike. Ari is then relieved to tell the true story. Later, Rhona admits that she's been a bully, and Jane loans Rhona her new bike for the race. Neddy still picks on Ari now and then, but she has learned not to let the teasing get to her. Now she feels "sort of excited" about herself.

The youngest of three children has trouble asserting herself both at home and at school. Ari cries and whines and pouts ineffectually until she meets confident, self-possessed Jane. Readers will see clearly that nobody needs to allow bullying or teasing. In this first-person story, Ari also demonstrates that lying to evade anger creates so much guilt that the truth is preferable. Prejudice is dealt with briefly in the police's treatment of Eddie. Mainly, though, this is a story for young people unable or unwilling to assert themselves. It provides practical, if not universally laudable, techniques for dealing with teases and bullies; matching insult to insult is sometimes the only effective method.

Ages 10-13

Also available in:
Paperbound—The Hand-Me-Down Kid
Dell Publishing Company, Inc.

P

**484**

Pascal, Francine

## My First Love & Other Disasters

The Viking Press, Inc., 1979.
(186 pages)

---

*BABY-SITTING*
*BOY-GIRL RELATIONSHIPS*
  *Decision making*
  *Dependence/Independence*
  *Maturation*
  *Responsibility: accepting*
  *Values/Valuing: moral/ethical*

---

Victoria, nearly fifteen, has spent her whole freshman year madly in love with seventeen-year-old Jim, who doesn't even know she's alive. Worse yet, he has a clingy girlfriend named Gloria. Determined to win him over, Victoria convinces her parents to let her work as a mother's helper on Fire Island, where Jim will be spending the summer without Gloria. After much pleading and arguing, her parents consent. Their main stipulation is that Victoria must tell Cynthia, the divorced woman she will be working for, that she cannot stay alone overnight with Cynthia's two children. During her first day on the island, Victoria is kept busy helping unload and unpack. When she finally gets down to the pier with the children, she runs into another boy from school, Barry, who she has heard likes her. He is waiting for Jim, soon to arrive on the ferry, so Victoria waits with him, anxious to see her true love. The first meeting goes badly. Jim thinks she is Barry's girl, which Victoria flatly denies. Then later, Barry surprises her by confessing his love for her. Nervous, she laughs, and her later apologies cannot undo the hurt he suffers. Back at the house, Victoria must tend to the children until their bedtime. Coming downstairs from her small, hot, third-floor bedroom, hoping to slip away for a while, she is intercepted by Cynthia, who tells her not to let the children talk to their paternal grandfather if he should call—at least not until his son, her ex-husband, starts paying some of their bills. Uneasy about this situation, Victoria hopes the grandfather will not call. The next day, Victoria stops at the restaurant where Jim works. She surprises herself by telling him she'll be at the local disco on her night off, a place Cynthia has asked her to avoid. He responds rather noncommittally. The next day, Victoria meets several other mother's helpers and soon realizes that she is doing much more and being paid less than any of the others. Still, she feels Cynthia needs and appreciates her. Besides, she leaves Victoria such cute, clever instructions. Later, Jim actually invites Victoria to meet him at the disco that night, but Cynthia has plans for the evening and tells Victoria to stay home with the children. Around midnight, Victoria discovers Cynthia home asleep and, hoping to salvage her long-awaited date, sneaks out. After a few dances, Jim takes her out to the pier where she agrees to the heaviest petting she has ever allowed. She returns home to find that she's locked out and must wake up a furious Cynthia. Soon after, the children's grandfather does call and Victoria allows them to talk to him, swearing them to secrecy. Several days later, at the disco, she refuses Jim's invitation to go

outside and he walks off, ignoring her pleading apology. The next morning, after Cynthia leaves for a day in the city, the grandfather arrives and wants to take the children out fishing. Victoria agrees, certain they'll be back before Cynthia returns. Then Cynthia calls and says she'll be gone for the night also, if that will be all right with Victoria. Again she agrees, certain her parents will never find out. Everything catches up with her when Cynthia unexpectedly returns after learning from Victoria's mother, whom she happened to see and talk to, that Victoria is forbidden to stay alone. Searching for the grandfather and children, Cynthia and Victoria discover that their boat is the only one still out on the bay, now filled with whitecaps. Barry takes Victoria and Jim out in his boat to search for them. It is difficult going and Jim wants to turn back, but Victoria begs Barry to keep looking despite the danger and he willingly obliges. They finally spot the lost boat, and it is Victoria and Barry who risk their lives to rescue the children and the old man. Back on shore, all is soon forgiven as Cynthia learns of their bravery and reconciles with the grandfather. The next morning, when Jim delivers one of his customary take-it-or-leave-it ultimatums, Victoria realizes how spoiled he is. She leaves it. The next time she finds one of Cynthia's clever notes listing extra work for her, she writes a clever note of her own, playfully asking for many outrageous favors in return. And then she calls the person she wants to see—Barry.

In this entertaining first-person story, an engaging, realistic girl finds being in love and on her own more complicated than she had ever imagined. Victoria compromises herself time and again, making ill-considered decisions she soon regrets. In the end, when everything catches up with her, she is relieved, mature enough now to recognize the shallowness of her "love," to assert herself with her employer, to seek out the boy she genuinely likes, and to realize she still values the security of parental supervision. Victoria is an appealing heroine, her story enriched by authentic-sounding dialogue.

Ages 12 and up

**Also available in:**
Cassette—*My First Love & Other Disasters*
Library of Congress (NLSBPH)

Paperbound—*My First Love & Other Disasters*
Dell Publishing Company, Inc.

**485**

**Paterson, Katherine Womeldorf**

## Jacob Have I Loved

Thomas Y. Crowell Company, Inc., 1980.
(216 pages)

---

*TWINS: Fraternal*
  *Age: aging*
  *Grandparent: living in child's home*
  *Jealousy: sibling*
  *Maturation*
  *Self, attitude toward: feeling different*

---

Louise Bradshaw, thirteen, strong and healthy, resents the attention given her frail, musically talented twin, Caroline, by their parents and other inhabitants of Rass Island in Chesapeake Bay. The tiny island, at this time

276

(the late 1930s) populated almost entirely by fishermen, offers Louise few escapes from Caroline and their acid-tongued, Bible-quoting grandmother who lives with the family. Pointedly, the grandmother recites the verse ending "Jacob have I loved, but Esau have I hated." Louise is certain she is Esau. "Progging for crab" with Call Purnell, her only friend, provides Louise with an outlet and a way to contribute to the family's income. When Louise is about fifteen, Captain Wallace returns to the island after a fifty-year absence. The legendary captain had left as a young man, after his behavior during a severe storm resulted in the islanders calling him a coward. Louise and Call quickly befriend the man, but Louise is bitterly jealous when Caroline does so also. Following a hurricane, the Captain briefly moves in with the Bradshaws, causing Louise to feel keenly her need for affection and her embarrassed attraction to the old man. Noticing Louise's emotional turmoil, the insensitive grandmother increases her verbal attacks. Then the Captain uses his inheritance to send Caroline to a Baltimore boarding school to study music. Betrayed, tormented by her grandmother, Louise quits school and joins her father on his fishing boat. Her mother, a former teacher, tutors her at home. Call is drafted early in World War II; when he is discharged, Louise learns to her sorrow that he and Caroline plan to marry. After passing her high school exams, Louise decides to build a life for herself away from Rass Island. Her mother accepts her decision, but tells Louise that they will miss her even more than they miss Caroline. Convinced now of her parents' love, Louise is able to leave the island "and begin to build myself as a soul, separate from the long, long shadow of my twin." The years pass. Louise becomes a nurse-midwife in rural Appalachia, marries, and has a child. Her story comes full circle when she delivers the twins of one of her mountain patients. The first twin is vigorous, the second frail. Secure now about herself and her own family, Louise can advise the mother and grandmother about the special needs of both infants.

Set in the late 1930s and early 1940s, this beautifully written first-person account, told by Louise in retrospect, presents some of the timeless dilemmas of growing up. With its realistic, fully developed characters and its depiction of the slow, painful ways human relationships mature, the story is touching without being sentimental.

Ages 12 and up

**Also available in:**
Cassette—*Jacob Have I Loved*
Library of Congress (NLSBPH)

Paperbound—*Jacob Have I Loved*
Avon Books

**486**

Payne, Sherry Neuwirth

## A Contest
Color illustrations by Jeff Kyle.
Carolrhoda Books, Inc., 1982.
(37 pages counted)

---

*DIFFERENCES, HUMAN*
*SELF, ATTITUDE TOWARD: Feeling Different*
*WHEELCHAIR, DEPENDENCE ON*
   *Cerebral palsy*
   *School: classmate relationships*
   *School: mainstreaming*

---

In fifth grade Mike, confined to a wheelchair because of hemiplegic cerebral palsy, which "means his legs don't work," changes from a special school to a public one. He finds his new school very difficult. He needs help in the cafeteria and in entering the bathroom but is afraid to ask for it. After the first day he tells his father about a kid who took his hat and called him a "spaz." His father says, "It's not easy. . . . But you have to live with all kinds of people. And a good place to start learning about them is in school." The youth center next door to the school is accessible to wheelchairs, and when Mike goes there he finds many of the kids in his class playing pool. He often plays pool at home with his father by leaning against their pool table and would like to play with the kids, but they seem afraid of him. So he just watches. Mike can easily keep up with his classwork, but the loneliness is harder. Then his teacher, noticing his sadness, decides they need to show his classmates the ways he is not so different. The next day she announces an arm wrestling contest. Randy, the strongest boy in the class, beats everyone until Mike is the only one left. Afraid to hurt him, Randy lets Mike win. Then they play again and Mike wins for real. To avoid alienating Randy, he tells him that he has an advantage because pushing his wheelchair has strengthened his arms. Later, Randy is surprised to learn that Mike swam nearly every day at his old school. At lunch the next day, one of the girls from Mike's class sits by him. After lunch there is another classroom contest, this time checkers, and Mike beats Randy again. Randy, friendly and interested, wants to know what else Mike can do. Mike tells him about pool. Randy wonders why he never said anything before. "Because I was afraid no one would want to play with me. Besides, who would stand next to me?" asks Mike, who needs someone there in case he loses his balance. "I will," Randy replies. When they enter the game room that afternoon, some kids make fun of Mike and say he cannot play. Randy only grins and says, "Try him." Mike's second year at his new school is much easier. He has people he can ask for help, and even though some still stare, many have discovered he is not so different from them.

A wheelchair can isolate a person emotionally as well as physically. In this smoothly written story, a sensitive teacher recognizes that the key to understanding and acceptance of her new disabled student is to make his wheelchair "disappear" by structuring contests in which Mike can demonstrate his strengths. Stereotypes are forgotten as Mike and his classmates discover their common interests and forget about the wheelchair. The difficult transition of the main character, portrayed as an average boy who likes sports and competition, from a special to a mainstreamed school and the positive change in his self-concept will be helpful reading for similarly afflicted children, their teachers, parents, and new classmates. Expressive illustrations aptly capture Mike's feelings.

Ages 8-10

Also available in:
No other form known

## 487

Pearson, Susan

### Molly Moves Out

Color illustrations by Steven Kellogg.
The Dial Press, Inc., 1979.
(64 pages)

SIBLING: Relationships
  Change: new home
  Friendship: making friends
  Loneliness

A young rabbit named Molly has six younger brothers and sisters who are constantly taking and often destroying her things. With a tired mother and an angry father, it's up to Molly to do something. She takes her brother Gregory fishing, hoping it will cure him of taking her books. They have such a good day that they decide to repeat it. However, the other siblings have heard about Gregory's wonderful day, and they tag along. There's too much noise and nobody catches any fish. Worse, Gregory still takes Molly's books. Molly tries the same strategy with Mary and John and gets the same results. So she tells her parents there are just too many rabbits in the house, and she moves across the meadow to a little house of her own. For the first two weeks Molly loves living alone, doing all her favorite things with nobody to bother her. By the third week, however, she realizes something is wrong. She tries gardening and swimming and a cookout to lift her spirits, but she finally recognizes the problem: she has nobody to share things with. So she makes friends with her neighbor, Martha, and they go fishing together. One day when she has an I-Am-Glad-You-Are-My-Friend cake in the oven for Martha, the doorbell rings. It's her family, with presents and a cake for a housewarming party. Then Martha arrives with an I-Am-Glad-You-Moved-In cake. When Molly's cake comes out of the oven, they all have milk and cake together. Molly notes that two cakes were never enough for the rabbit family but that "three cakes are just right."

This charmingly illustrated beginning reader describes the daily trials of the oldest sibling in a large family. Molly's solution, moving out, could initiate discussion about what life might be like away from one's family. Molly does eventually recognize her need for companionship, but the reader doesn't know if she will move home again or not. Molly's story will satisfy children who wish they could just move out when siblings

become too troublesome. However, those grappling with sibling conflict will not find any realistic suggestions here.

Ages 5-8

Also available in:
Paperbound—Molly Moves Out
The Dial Press, Inc.

## 488

Pearson, Susan

### Saturday I Ran Away

Black/white illustrations by Susan Jeschke.
J. B. Lippincott Company, 1981.
(39 pages)

RUNNING AWAY
  Family: relationships
  Resourcefulness
  Sibling: youngest

Little Emily hates being the youngest and smallest. Her sister, Katy, blames everything on her. Her older brother, Tom, won't let her play with him. So Emily decides to run away. While she's making a list of what to take, her mother talks to her. She tells Emily that sometimes she wishes she could run away too. The next morning as Emily fixes a snack, Tom says he wishes he could join her. As she fills her thermos, her father says he would like to disappear for a day. As Emily packs, Katy tells her she would like to run away from Tom. Since the whole family would like to run away, Emily posts a note on the refrigerator door inviting anyone who wants to run away to meet her at the bend in the creek. Before long Tom shows up with his fishing pole. Soon Katy arrives and begins sketching. Next, Emily's father comes with his fishing pole and joins Tom. Then Emily's mother arrives. Soon the whole family is laughing together, enjoying their outing and admiring Emily's good idea. They spend a pleasant day by the creek and conclude that if they were nicer to each other, no one would ever want to run away.

When Emily discovers that every person in her family wants to run away, she revises her own plans to include them all in a lazy, relaxing day together. All members of families, young and old, will recognize themselves in this charming, expressively illustrated tale.

Ages 5-7

Also available in:
No other form known

## 489

Peavy, Linda S.

### Allison's Grandfather

Black/white illustrations by Ronald Himler.
Charles Scribner's Sons, 1981.
(32 pages)

DEATH: of Grandparent
  Death: attitude toward
  Illnesses: terminal

Erica wonders if her friend Allison knows that her grandfather is dying. She wants to ask her mother, but doesn't feel like talking or even thinking about this subject "just yet." She can't help wondering, however, if it's very hard to die. Erica remembers when Allison spent the summer with her grandparents and Erica visited the ranch several weekends to keep her company. Late in the evenings the two friends often sat by the fire and listened to Allison's grandfather telling stories about his days as a cowboy. Sometimes he would show the girls his shiny, silver spurs, spinning the wheel of a spur with his finger as he described one of his many adventures. One story was about nearly freezing to death one winter while leading his horses to food. Erica remembers him saying, "Yes, sir, little girls, Old Man Death got surprised that day. Thought he had me for sure, figured I'd be froze stiff. But I wasn't ready to die that day, little girls, I wasn't ready to die." Erica wonders if Allison's grandfather is ready to die now. She knows that grandfathers die because one of hers died before she was born and she only knows about him from his pictures. That evening, Erica's mother goes to the hospital to sit with Allison's grandfather so Allison's grandmother can get some rest. Mama says that even though he's usually sleeping, Allison's grandfather likes to have someone hold his hand. Erica remembers last summer when he carried buckets of gooseberries in his big, strong hands and let the girls spin the wheel of his silver spur. Allison's grandfather's hands are very busy in Erica's dreams that night. When her mother comes home the next morning, she sits in the rocking chair near the window and takes Erica on her lap. When she stops rocking, she tells Erica that Allison's grandfather has died. Erica wonders how it felt to be holding his hand when he died. Mama replies softly, "It was all right, Erica. . . . It was even beautiful. He opened his eyes and looked straight at me and smiled. Then he died." Perhaps he was smiling because "the part of him that's light and life" was "somehow riding over the mountains again instead of lying in that hospital knowing he couldn't get well." Erica likes this idea and wants to think of him that way. "Just now" she doesn't want to think of him being dead. She wants "to think about Allison's grandfather riding over the mountains with the sunlight dancing and sparkling off his bright silver spurs."

A little girl finds that her first encounter with death raises many questions in her mind. But until she feels ready to cope with the answers, she postpones asking the questions. The philosophy that the "light and life" of a person goes on after death will be comforting to many young children, as will the love, kindness, and caring reflected in the quiet text and soft, appealing illustrations. Erica confronts death, but it is the death of her friend's grandfather; the distance softens the blow. Suitable for reading aloud to younger children, the book can also be read by independent readers. It should prove a good book for sharing.

Ages 6-9

**Also available in:**
No other form known

490

**Peck, Richard**

## Close Enough to Touch

Delacorte Press, 1981.
(133 pages)

---

*DEATH: of Friend*
*MOURNING, STAGES OF*
  *Boy-girl relationships: dating*
  *Loss: feelings of*
  *Love, meaning of*

---

During the Fourth of July fireworks, sixteen-year-old Matt Moran gets up his courage and tells Dory Gunderson he loves her. She wants to know what took him so long; she loves him too. The following March, Dory dies suddenly and unexpectedly of a ruptured aneurysm. Matt is one of six pallbearers. After the funeral, he stops by the Gundersons' home at Mrs. Gunderson's invitation. Wealthy and snobbish, she tells Matt things would never have worked out between him and Dory anyway, and that he'll soon forget her. His father and stepmother attempt to comfort him, but Matt refuses to eat that day. The next day he goes to school, but "by lunch I'm only about 10 percent there." A locker-room acquaintance, Joe Hoenig, tries to comfort him and tells him he should cry. Matt decides that a "simple solution" to his pain would be to get roaring drunk. He does so. Police pick him up and call his father, who continues to be sympathetic. "Something had to happen. You wouldn't grieve." Matt says he was grieving but his father insists, "You didn't grieve. You just got quiet. That's the way I was when your mom died." Matt's next solution is to drop out of school. Over spring break, he announces that he's going up to the family's lake cottage for a few days. He doesn't intend to return. When he's jogging the first day, however, he finds an injured girl lying in a ditch. A horse with a sidesaddle stands nearby. Matt takes the girl to the local emergency room, where her dislocated shoulder is bandaged, and then drives her home. He learns her name is Margaret and she's a senior at his school. Matt returns to school and seeks out the Hopkins poem that Margaret says she was named after. When he suggests they get together to talk about it she refuses, saying they would just be talking about Dory, since the poem concerns death. Matt doesn't see Margaret again for several days, but he's not looking too hard. "I'm making a pretty good adjustment to being miserable. I may be able to make a lifetime career out of it." He does drive past Margaret's house and around the block several times until her father comes outside and signals him into the driveway. Margaret explains why she doesn't want to talk about Dory: "She meant too much to you. She can't mean enough to me." Some friends of Dory's tell Matt that instead of going to the junior dance, they plan to spend the evening together in memory of Dory. Matt has just asked Margaret to the junior dance, but she's refused because it's the same night as the senior prom, which she's attending with Joe Hoenig. So Matt decides to join the memorial. He now suspects he loves Margaret, but feels guilty since he once told Dory he would love her forever. The memorial evening is uncomfortable and Matt leaves early. He goes to the country club where the senior prom is being held and finds Margaret and Joe. He explains to Joe that he's crazy about a senior girl and plans to abduct her. Joe thinks it's a great idea until he finds out the girl is Margaret. However, Joe is interested in another girl anyway and agrees to leave the prom with Margaret and go with Matt to the lake cottage. Once there, Joe goes straight to sleep. Matt and Margaret walk down to the beach to watch the sunrise.

A teenage boy whose girlfriend has died tries to cope with his grief and make a new beginning. Written in the first person, this beautifully crafted story is moving, witty, and grounded in reality. Matt has trouble identifying his own feelings and conveying what he feels to others. Defending himself from the pain of losing Dory, he shuts off his emotions for periods of time. But he makes progress in self-knowledge and in reaching out to others, leaving readers hopeful for him at the end. Several stereotypical and undeveloped characters take little from the impact of the story.

Ages 12 and up

**Also available in:**
Cassette—*Close Enough to Touch*
Library of Congress (NLSBPH)

Paperbound—*Close Enough to Touch*
Dell Publishing Company, Inc.

## 491

**Peck, Robert Newton**

## Clunie

Alfred A. Knopf, Inc., 1979.
(124 pages)

---

*MENTAL RETARDATION*
*TEASING*
  *Bully: being bothered by*
  *Friendship: meaning of*
  *Sexual assault*
  *Suicide*

---

Sixteen-year-old Clunie Finn, overweight, awkward, and retarded, hates the teasing and name-calling that follow her wherever she goes. She is furious when the kids chant, "Clunie Finn, Clunie Finn . . . Lock her up in a loony bin." Sometimes the kids are so mean Clunie tries to hide from them. She especially hates Leo Bannon, the bully who taunts and teases her the most. But Clunie loves school, her teacher, the ducks in the pond on her farm, the daisies she picks, and her father. He has been raising her alone since her mother committed suicide. She is also beginning to love fifteen-year-old Braddy Macon, who defends her when the kids, especially Leo, tease her. Braddy even walks Clunie home and talks nicely to her about ducks and daisies. Her father warns her to ignore her tormentors and not to hit them, because Clunie is extremely strong. One afternoon Leo follows Clunie as she walks home from school. In a deserted area he tries to rape her. Clunie hits him repeatedly with a piece of wood and then runs and hides. Soon the whole town has heard that Leo was found murdered. Braddy races to the scene and overhears Clunie's father say Clunie is missing. Guessing what has happened, Braddy runs through the woods searching for Clunie. He spots her in the pond above the dam. She cannot swim and struggles as the current

pushes her. Braddy tries to rescue her and in the process almost drowns. But Clunie screams she does not want to be locked up in a hospital and begs Braddy to let go of her. Too strong for him, Clunie breaks loose from his grip and drowns. Braddy realizes that Clunie is free at last.

A retarded girl arouses opposite reactions in two teenage boys: one taunts and assaults her, the other cares for her. Clunie, loving and emotionally vulnerable, but physically powerful, is overcome by a cycle of violence she can't escape. This is a compelling, tragic story with much to say about the feelings of retarded people and the varied responses they can evoke in others.

Ages 12 and up

**Also available in:**
No other form known

## 492

**Perl, Lila**

## Don't Ask Miranda

The Seabury Press, Inc., 1979.
(164 pages)

---

*HONESTY/DISHONESTY*
*PEER RELATIONSHIPS: Peer Pressures*
  *Family: relationships*
  *Friendship: making friends*
  *Moving*
  *School: classmate relationships*

---

Thirteen-year-old Miranda Sargent hates moving, but her father is a salesman who goes from one "opportunity" to another. Now it is November and they have just moved to Long Island. As usual, Miranda finds it hard changing schools and trying to make new friends. Because of her loneliness at school, she accepts a job working at her Aunt Friedl's Little Vienna Bakery—Friedl isn't really her aunt, just a distant relative. Just before Christmas, classmate Hal Olin comes into the bakery, asking Miranda to help with his campaign for election to the eighth-grade activities committee. Miranda is so thrilled at being asked to join Hal's "team" that she even slips him a cookie, definitely against Aunt Friedl's policy. At a Christmas party, Cassie Wallace, Rosellen Leeds, and Hal ask Miranda to spy on Angela Corcoran, who is running against Hal. Miranda, afraid of losing their friendship, agrees. During Christmas vacation, Rosellen and Cassie visit Miranda at the bakery, and Miranda is caught giving them pastry. Aunt Friedl angrily deducts the cost from her paycheck, and Miranda suspects her job will end when the shop reopens after an upcoming January holiday. To make matters worse, Miranda's parents are fighting again, and Miranda suspects her father is having another affair. After vacation, Miranda finds herself caught up in plans to steal Angela's campaign speech. She accomplishes the theft, but is terrified she will be found out. "There seemed nowhere left to turn. School, home, the Little Vienna—they had all become uneasy, even forbidden territory." A few days later, Miranda stops in front of the bakery and soon finds herself inside confiding her troubles to a sympathetic Aunt Friedl. When she gets home, she is greeted with the news that the family is moving to Atlanta. Miranda feels her parents have made their decision the same way her supposed friends make all of theirs: "Don't ask Miranda." Nobody wants her opinion—but her opinion is that she wants to stay where she is. An agreement is finally reached. Miranda will stay with Aunt Friedl for the remainder of the school year. The election is held at school and a seemingly repentant Hal withdraws his name. One day he even seeks out Miranda after school and apologizes for hurting her and for all the shady dealings. Miranda realizes she too was wrong. In trying to please others she forgot that the only person she needs to please, to answer to, is herself.

Desperately lonely for friendship and feeling powerless to control her troubled home life, a young girl finds herself trapped in a dishonest school campaign. As her story unfolds, Miranda slowly begins to see that a person cannot buy friendship; it has to be earned honestly. Furthermore, she can assert some control over her life by holding to her own values and preferences. Dealing with relationships and situations familiar to the intended audience, this is a candid and convincing story.

Ages 10-13

**Also available in:**
No other form known

## 493

Perl, Lila

### Hey, Remember Fat Glenda?

Clarion Books, 1981.
(168 pages)

---

*SELF, ATTITUDE TOWARD: Body Concept*
*WEIGHT CONTROL: Overweight*
  *Friendship: best friend*
  *School: classmate relationships*
  *School: pupil-teacher relationships*

---

By the time school starts in the fall, eighth-grader Glenda Waite has lost sixteen pounds by dieting all summer. Her best friend, Sara, who just recently moved away, writes Glenda encouraging notes about losing weight and thinking thin. Glenda is really trying, especially now that she has a crush on Mr. Hartley, her English teacher. She is determined to eat less and jog more. Glenda's mother, also overweight, encourages her to join a "dancercise" group. Glenda refuses, preferring to jog. Besides, her mother isn't a great recommendation for dancercise, since she eats the moment she returns from class. One Sunday, two school friends, Mary Lou and Patty, come to Glenda's house to study. They notice some of Sara's encouraging notes about losing weight and laugh. Hurt, Glenda begins to eat more and more. But when Mr. Hartley announces he will be directing the school's musical review, Glenda decides to try to lose weight again. She joins dancercise and discovers that Patty is in her class. Soon people begin to notice a thinner, more attractive Glenda. By the time of the class's Halloween costume party, Glenda feels thin enough to go as a dance-hall queen. No one recognizes her, and she notices the admiring glances and whispered appreciation. When a classmate grabs her mask

and reveals who she is, everyone is surprised. Mr. Hartley arrives to judge the costumes, and Glenda ties for first. Then she and Patty decide to try out for the musical review. They ask their dancercise teacher, Miss Esme, to help them with a routine. Miss Esme, who knows Mr. Hartley, warns the infatuated girls that he is a selfish "user." But when Mr. Hartley asks Glenda to help him with auditions, she works very hard. When the players are announced, however, Glenda and Patty are not on the list. Disappointed, Glenda still agrees to be Mr. Hartley's assistant director. She works hard, continually misses dancercise, and begins eating more. After Christmas she realizes he is simply using her, and she quits. Angry at herself and at Mr. Hartley, Glenda decides she will always be fat. Then fat Robert Fry tells Glenda that with her as his inspiration, he is beginning to lose weight. Glenda begins to put her life in perspective. She may never be skinny, she tells Sara. But maybe she can be somewhere between fat and thin.

A young teenage girl struggles to lose weight, hampered by a mother who can't control her own eating. Glenda must also cope with changing relationships among her classmates and a crush on her glamorous but exploitative English teacher. Slightly exaggerated characterizations add humor to this first-person narrative, a sequel to *Me and Fat Glenda*.

Ages 9-12

**Also available in:**
Paperbound—*Hey, Remember Fat Glenda?*
Pocket Books, Inc.

## 494

Perl, Lila

### Pieface and Daphne

Clarion Books, 1980.
(184 pages)

---

*ONLY CHILD*
  *Age: aging*
  *Egocentrism*
  *Friendship: meaning of*
  *Jealousy: peer*
  *Relatives: living in child's home*
  *Sharing/Not sharing*

---

Pamela Tietelbaum, nine and an only child, is accustomed to being the center of her family's attention. Summer school begins with a project that involves her not watching television for three weeks and finding something constructive to do in its place. At the library she meets Shirley Brummage, a crusty old woman who relies for her income on junk, trash, and coupons (clipping them from library magazines). Pam decides that helping Shirley will be her project, despite the woman's initial resistance. Soon Pam is keeping a diary of her efforts for school. Shirley insists on calling her Pieface, a name she gave her at their first meeting because the girl's face reminded her of a pie. Then Pam is told that Daphne, the eleven-year-old daughter of her mother's cousin, will live with them for the summer. Pam is not at all sure she approves. At school, Pam is crushed when her log book for the Turn-Off-the-Tube project is deemed only second-best in the class. Her distress continues at home as preparations are made for Daphne's

P

arrival. "You'd think the queen was coming." Pam intends to hate Daphne and finds that easy to do: Daphne is pretty, dreamy, and watches TV constantly— "Because the real world, you know . . . it stinks." Pam is hurt when Shirley takes a liking to Daphne. She accuses Daphne of always trying to get attention, of being "a phony." Even hearing that Daphne's adoptive parents are divorcing and neither wants custody of the girl doesn't soften Pam's heart. She throws a tantrum when her mother hints that Daphne may stay indefinitely. That means Daphne will be there for cousin Lainie's wedding, for which Pam will be a flower girl. She does not want to share any part of the wedding with Daphne. The next morning when Pam goes to see Shirley at her apartment, Daphne follows. They find Shirley slumped over. Daphne, insisting the woman is ill, goes for help. It turns out that Shirley has had a stroke and Daphne gets credit for saving her life, much to Pam's dismay. Her mother admonishes her: "Pamela, you're shameless. Why shouldn't it be Daphne's turn to shine?" But Daphne steps into the spotlight again when she tries on —and looks beautiful in—Pam's flower-girl dress. Plans are made to include Daphne as another flower girl. Though her mother compliments her for being mature and sensible about this new development, Pam knows that "inside, I was really hurting." Then Pam finds Daphne crying as she tries to pack. She has decided to go away until the wedding is over because "I've spoiled the wedding for you." The girls have a heart-to-heart talk. Pam admits to being spoiled and bossy, but says she now doesn't mind having Daphne around. Daphne then explains how bad things are between her parents: her mother is in a sanitarium and her father is living with another woman. To make amends, Pam, pretending to be her mother, calls and cancels her own flower-girl dress. At the wedding, as she and her parents watch Daphne come down the aisle, Pam feels only a little regret. She tells her mother that she and Daphne have agreed Pam will be the flower girl if and when Pam's grandmother gets remarried. The trade-off explains Pam's new attitude: "You didn't think I'd changed that much, did you? And, anyhow, this sharing stuff is supposed to work both ways, isn't it?"

A self-centered only child manages to form true friendships with an old woman and a young cousin whose parents are going through a bitter divorce. This first-person narrative lacks a distinctive plot and writing style, and minor characters remain indistinct and stereotypical. But Shirley, the proud, crusty old woman, and Pam herself, jealous and selfish, are very well depicted, both in their own relationship and in their dealings with other people. The story provides enough action to keep the reader involved.

Ages 9-11

Also available in:
Paperbound—*Pieface and Daphne*
Pocket Books, Inc.

## 495

Petersen, P. J.

### Would You Settle for Improbable?

Delacorte Press, 1981.
(185 pages)

---

FRIENDSHIP: Meaning of
  Delinquency, juvenile
  Maturation
  School: classmate relationships
  School: pupil-teacher relationships

---

Ms. Karnisian, the ninth-grade English student-teacher, asks Mike, Warren, and Harry a favor they consider impossible. She replies that it is not impossible, just improbable. She wants the three to befriend Arnold Norberry, a boy from the county juvenile hall where she works nights. Arnold will soon be getting out of juvenile hall and into Marshall Martin Junior High. The boys reluctantly agree to meet Arnold and Ms. Karnisian at the bowling alley that Saturday afternoon. The two are an hour late and after Ms. Karnisian leaves, things don't go well. Trying to befriend Arnold, Mike invites him to his house. Arnold promptly steals Mike's calculator and makes a joke of it when he's caught. At school, most of the ninth graders avoid Arnold with his swaggering walk and cocky attitude. Then one day Warren cuts the wires to the class intercom and Arnold takes the blame, to Mike's puzzlement. Why would Arnold want to protect Warren? Deciding to give friendship another try, Mike rides his bike to Arnold's home in the run-down section of town. There he meets Arnold's drunken mother and sees the kind of life Arnold must contend with every day. As ninth-grade graduation nears, Ms. Karnisian says Arnold can graduate if he passes the eighth-grade constitution test. His friends help him cram, but Arnold doesn't show up to take the test when he is scheduled. So Warren tricks him into taking it another day, and Arnold passes. Elated, he asks Jennifer to the graduation dance. She accepts, making Arnold happy and excited. But then Jennifer's parents plan a family party that Jennifer must attend instead of the dance. Arnold is convinced her father simply didn't want the girl to date him, and he tells Mike he will seek revenge. When Arnold's mother is arrested, he stays with Mike's family for several days, talking to Mike about stealing a car and going to Canada. As the school year ends, the class plans a party and gift for Ms. Karnisian. Mike is treasurer of the fund. When the books they'd intended to buy are sold, Arnold volunteers to get something else and Mike gives him the money. Arnold promptly disappears. Then Mike hears that Jennifer's father's sports car has been vandalized. He's sure Arnold has had his revenge. When Ms. Karnisian reports that Arnold was arrested in a stolen car and will return to juvenile hall, the class, especially Mike, feels hugely let down. Arnold writes a letter to the class explaining his troubles, but Mike doesn't believe the explanation. He still suspects that Arnold took the money and the car to go to Canada. After talking with Ms. Karnisian, however, Mike feels better. He can't stay angry; Arnold needs his support, no matter what really happened.

Despite Arnold's tough-guy attitude, Mike and his friends like and try to help him. When Arnold gets into trouble again anyway, the sympathetic Ms. Karnisian convinces Mike to stand by the incorrigible boy. Mike tells the story with wit and warmth. It is punctuated with excerpts from individual class notebooks that provide in-depth portraits of the main characters. A serious novel about a serious problem, this story's realistic ending leaves open the possibility of Arnold's changing and maturing some day.

Ages 11-13

**Also available in:**
Paperbound—*Would You Settle for Improbable?*
Dell Publishing Company, Inc.


## 496

Peterson, Esther Allen

**Frederick's Alligator**
Color illustrations by Susanna Natti.
Crown Publishers, Inc., 1979.
(30 pages counted)

---

*HONESTY/DISHONESTY*
*IMAGINATION*

---

When Frederick tells his mother about the pet lion in his closet, she replies that he'd better finish breakfast or he'll be late for school. When he warns the mailman about the timber wolf in the basement who likes to eat mailmen, the mailman suggests Frederick put the wolf's name on the mailbox. And when he tells his class about the grizzly bear in his attic, the teacher asks him to sit down. After school that day, Frederick finds an egg down by the river. He packs it in leaves and mud, puts it in a shoebox, and hides it under his bed. When the egg hatches into a baby alligator, Frederick tells his mother about it. She says she hopes his lion doesn't eat it. The mailman, when informed, says that now the wolf has a playmate. Frederick asks his teacher if he can bring his baby alligator to show-and-tell. She gives permission and adds that he can bring his grizzly bear too. The next day, Frederick's mother, the mailman, and his class are all surprised to see that Frederick really does have an alligator. After show-and-tell, the alligator is put on the science projects table, from which it disappears along with the tadpoles and silkworms. Although everyone searches, the alligator is still missing that afternoon. Then, as Frederick's best friend puts on his rain boots, the alligator is found in one of them. Frederick decides he can't keep the alligator. It might grow up to eat his hamster or even his baby brother. First he tries to sell it, but nobody wants it. He finally carries it back to the riverbank where he sets it free. He tells himself that now he'll stick to more familiar pets. Meanwhile, Frederick's mother, although she is convinced there's no lion in his closet, looks anyway. The mailman finds himself wondering about the timber wolf in the basement. "And to this day, his classmates still wonder if there is a grizzly bear in his attic, but Frederick won't tell."

A young boy's switch from tall tales to the truth confounds his family and friends in this amusing book. Frederick makes no distinction between fantasy and fact; the world of his imagination seems as real as the alligator egg under his bed. The illustrations are charming and lighthearted, and the wry ending to Frederick's story will delight young readers.

Ages 4-7

**Also available in:**
Braille—*Frederick's Alligator*
Ginn and Company


## 497

Peterson, Jeanne Whitehouse

**That Is That**
Color illustrations by Deborah Ray.
Harper & Row, Publishers, Inc., 1979.
(32 pages counted)

---

*ABANDONMENT*
*SEPARATION, MARITAL*
  *Change: accepting*
  *Loss: feelings of*
  *Sibling: relationships*

---

P

Young Emma Rose watches her father leave his family, hearing him say, "I am tired of all our shouting and fighting, I need to find my own happiness." Refusing to say goodbye to him, she observes her mother crying as she stirs the soup. Then she tells her little brother, Meko, that their father is gone. Meko cries, hugging his teddy bear. For a while, first with her brother and then alone, Emma Rose plays games that she hopes will magically bring her father back. Then she wonders why he left and why he hasn't returned. She regrets not saying goodbye and decides to make a "Remembering Place" on her desk, placing on it her father's picture and other mementos of him, along with a note she writes saying, "Goodbye Father. So Long." At first she thinks about her father every day, but refuses to talk about him to anyone. Time passes. Emma Rose dumps the Remembering Place in her drawer when she needs space for her microscope. When winter comes, Emma Rose and Meko build a snowman. Looking at the snowman, Emma Rose sings a song she has just made up: "If you are sad and lonely, I wonder why you wander in the night? But if you are happy I understand, and wish you well." Then Meko puts one of their father's old hats on the snowman. Emma Rose is humming; Meko is smiling as he says, "That is that!" They are happy again.

This simple, quiet story captures the complicated emotions, separation process, and eventual acceptance a child experiences when a parent leaves. Soft, poignant, shaded drawings enhance the story's melancholy mood.

Ages 5-8

**Also available in:**
No other form known

**498**

Pevsner, Stella

## Cute Is a Four-Letter Word

Clarion Books, 1980.
(190 pages)

---

VALUES/VALUING: Moral/Ethical
 Boy-girl relationships: dating
 Friendship: meaning of
 Identity, search for

---

Clara Conrad begins eighth grade determined to make herself memorable in her own right. She will no longer be Laurel-the-pianist's younger sister, Mother-the-principal's daughter, or neighbor Jay Frank's baby-sitter. But one of the first big changes in Clara's life is not of her own making. Her mother decides to ease finances by having Laurel, a student at the Juilliard School of Music, live with a couple in New York. The couple's daughter, Halcyon, who refuses to attend a New York public school after years of private boarding schools, will come to the Midwest to live with them. Meanwhile, Clara's best friend, Angel, and Fergy McNutt ask to use Clara's basement to house their laboratory rats and to conduct experiments as they prepare for the science fair. In return, Angel promises to help Clara win a long-coveted position on the Pom Pon cheerleading squad. Then Halcyon arrives—peevish, obnoxious, and condescending—and makes it known that her profession (not her hobby) is photography. She sets up a darkroom in the basement and she, Angel, Fergy, and Jay Frank spend a lot of time down there. Clara feels left out, but she keeps very busy practicing for Pom Pon tryouts. Without much of Angel's promised help, Clara wins a place on the squad. Then Skip Svoboda, captain of the football team and the most popular boy in school, calls Clara, tells her she's cute, and asks when elections for Pom Pon captain will be held. To her amazement, Clara, the newcomer, wins the position. Before long, Clara and Skip are a recognized twosome. Clara can't understand how Angel, who went with Skip last year, can give him up, but Angel suggests that Skip is more of a personality than a person. Clara, her mother, and Halcyon visit Laurel and Halcyon's parents in New York. Clara notes that Halcyon's parents do not appear to appreciate their daughter's photographs of the laboratory rats, that Halcyon wants approval, but that her parents don't give her any. Clara's plans for her big year seem to be bearing fruit: "I felt (without trying to be conceited about it) that I was now one of the cutest girls in the school." She's in with the Pom Pon crowd, dates the most popular boy, and is on everyone's party list. Then Clara discovers that Skip engineered her election as Pom Pon captain because he thought she was cute and he only dates winners. Had she lost the election, he would have switched to the girl who won. When Skip next tells Clara she's cute, she rebuffs him. He warns her not to push her luck with him. Angel and Fergy, with the help of Jay Frank, are almost ready for the science fair. They hold semifinals to choose the five fastest rats. Little Blue (they each have a spot of dye on their head to distinguish them from one another) is Jay Frank's favorite. But since Little Blue is disinclined to run mazes or push levers, he drops out of the running early. Then, just before one of the biggest games of the season, as the Pom Pon squad is waiting to run onto the field, Clara gets an urgent call in the school office. It's Jay Frank and he seems desperate. Clara leaves the squad and dashes home, only to find that the emergency is not life-threatening. Jay Frank had put Little Blue in a cage with one of the semifinalists. Their dye has worn off, and he doesn't know which is which. The rats are due to be picked up any moment to be taken to the science fair. Clara finds minute traces of blue dye on one of them and returns to the game. It's now half-time, and she decides to sit the rest out. Afterwards, Skip goes by and ignores her. When a friend expresses surprise, Clara says that maybe the blue dye on her forehead has faded. The friend doesn't understand the remark, but Angel does. She tells Clara how much she admires Little Blue. "He decided one day that he wasn't going to race pell-mell down the runway just because of the pellet. It wasn't the most important thing in his life, not at that moment." Angel assures Clara that she'll never need blue dye to distinguish her from everyone else. Clara intercepts Skip and tells him what she thinks of him. Then she goes out on the floor and does her Pom Pon routine with extra flair—not for Skip, not for fame, but just for herself.

In this lively and realistic first-person novel, a young teenage girl sorts out superficial values from more authentic ones. Being cute isn't everything, Clara finds. She also comes gradually to understand the abrasive Halcyon. Minor characters here remain one-dimensional, and the heroine herself is concerned with very little besides her popularity. But many young people go through such a phase, and readers will easily identify with Clara. There is good discussion material in her satisfying discovery of the importance of old loyalties and the hollowness of popularity for its own sake.

Ages 10-12

**Also available in:**
Cassette—*Cute Is a Four-Letter Word*
Library of Congress (NLSBPH)

Paperbound—*Cute Is a Four-Letter Word*
Pocket Books, Inc.

**499**

Peyton, K. M., pseud.

## Marion's Angels

Black/white illustrations by Robert Micklewright.
Oxford University Press, 1979.
(152 pages) o.p.

---

IMAGINATION
SELF-DISCIPLINE
 Emotions: accepting
 Parent/Parents: single
 Self, attitude toward: feeling different
 Talents: musical

---

Marion is probably the only twelve-year-old girl in the world with her own medieval church. She keeps the keys to St. Michael's, an abandoned fifteenth-century church overlooking a marsh in her small English town. Marion takes care of the flowers, does the cleaning and some of the maintenance chores, and occasionally gives guided tours. She is particularly attached to the twelve angels carved on the ceiling. Marion's now-dead mother was a medieval scholar who taught the girl the church's history. Marion's preoccupation with the church is not the only reason the villagers think her strange. At times, Marion seems to have perceptions well beyond the usual. Her youthful father, Geoff, says the girl merely has an over-active imagination; those who don't know her well, and no one other than her father really does, prefer to think her mad. St. Michael's is in dire need of restoration work, so a benefit concert has been arranged to raise money for roof repairs. The night before, Marion watches unseen as a young man enters the church and plays the piano that has been brought in for the benefit. Marion feels an affinity with the pianist, who is, it turns out, Patrick Pennington, engaged to play at the concert. Pat's playing so moves Marion that she's afraid the roof will come off the church and the angels will all fly away. She interrupts the benefit by crying out to stop the angels, and the villagers are again convinced that Marion is quite mad. Her father understands, however, and Pat tells her that her intense reaction to his music is a compliment. Pat's wife, Ruth, reminds Marion very much of her own mother, and she notices that her father also sees the resemblance. The young couple lives in a cottage nearby, and they, Geoff, and Marion begin spending a lot of time together. One day when Marion is in the church reflecting on the recent repair estimate, a huge sum, Pat joins her, advising her to pray for a rich American to solve all the church's problems. Marion does just that and has hardly finished her prayer when she hears a loud American voice. The world-renowned American violinist Ephraim Voight, currently performing in England, offers to earn the necessary sum by giving concerts and using his own professional fund raisers to promote the cause. He invites Pat to play with him. For Marion it is, of course, a miracle, but her father, Pat, and Ruth caution her not to speak of miracles to the villagers. From then on, Marion's miracle seems to run away with itself. Her father and Ruth seem to be attracted to each other. The new fund-raising venture has delayed a time together that Pat and Ruth had planned, away from the demands of his music. In fact, he will soon go on a concert tour of the United States without Ruth. Uneasy as Marion feels about losing control over her miracle, she does begin to get a grip on her runaway emotions. She sits through a private concert of Pat's without crying out or running from the room. The night before Pat is to leave, he plays a public concert and takes Marion with him. She listens without causing a scene. They are both in a restless mood during the drive home. The weather is wild and stormy. After Pat drops her off, Marion decides to go to the church and pray for another miracle that will set everything right. As she is praying, the church tower collapses. Pat and Geoff work for hours to rescue her. Marion is unharmed, saved because one of the angels, fallen from the ceiling, made a bridge over her body, protecting her from falling debris. And the miracle she prayed for has happened: Pat has missed his plane. Marion sees Ruth tiptoe into the room where her exhausted husband is sleeping and embrace him, convincing Marion that the two will be reconciled. Seeing this, she is able to let go of her long-held dream of a

substitute mother. "She saw quite plainly that she felt the need no longer. The realization filled her with confidence and a feeling of freedom."

A highly imaginative and impressionable young girl learns to exert some control over her emotions, helped by a supportive father and sympathetic friends. When she relinquishes her dream of a replacement for her mother, she gains self-confidence and a feeling of liberation. Beautifully written, with well-drawn characters, a sense of place, and believable relationships, this is a realistic if unusual story—the reader is never compelled to accept supernatural explanations for Marion's miracles. The sequence of events can easily be explained by coincidence, although the timing is a bit uncanny. The illustrations seem to depict a younger girl and could deter some teenagers from beginning the book. Pat Pennington is the main character in several other books by Peyton.

Ages 11-14

Also available in:
No other form known

## 500
### Pfeffer, Susan Beth
### About David
Delacorte Press, 1980.
(167 pages)

P

---

*SUICIDE*
  *Adoption: feelings about*
  *Boy-girl relationships*
  *Communication: lack of*
  *Death: of friend*
  *Death: murder*
  *Friendship: best friend*
  *Guilt, feelings of*
  *Mourning, stages of*
  *School: classmate relationships*

---

Even as her father tells her the tragic story, seventeen-year-old Lynn Epstein cannot believe it. Her friend for thirteen years is dead. More than that, David Morris has murdered his parents and then committed suicide. Lynn loved David like a brother and felt she knew him well. Why would he do this? David knew he was adopted, and he hated the birth parents who gave him up. He also didn't get along with his adoptive parents, who had great expectations for him but expressed little love, praise, or encouragement. Lynn tries to reconstruct the last conversation she had with David in the school cafeteria, but she draws a blank. After several days she returns to school, but all David's other friends are as confused and grief-stricken as she. Lynn becomes obsessed with that last, forgotten conversation, wondering if it holds the key, wondering if she could have stopped David. Her parents become so concerned about her guilt, nightmares, insomnia, shaking fits, loss of appetite, and shifting moods that a month after the tragedy they suggest she see a psychologist. She readily agrees, knowing she needs to talk to someone. Then Lynn finds and reads David's four notebooks, left to her in his own personal will which was found by Lynn's father, acting as solicitor for the family. The closer she comes to the end of the last notebook, the more she dreads finding out why David murdered his parents and took his own life. When she finally confesses this to her psychologist, he tells her she must finish the notebook and start living her life without David. Back home Lynn finishes the notebook. David wrote that his mother, who had longed for a child of her own, was pregnant. Yet Lynn learns this was not true. An autopsy proved his mother was not pregnant; this was a figment of David's imagination. Her questions unanswered, Lynn remains haunted by that final lunchtime conversation. Back at school, she walks fearfully into the cafeteria she has been avoiding and finally remembers what David said. The conversation was mundane, except that David told her he had a surprise planned for his mother's birthday. The murder/suicide occurred two days before her birthday. Lynn realizes there was no way she could have prevented the tragedy, that David "lived in a world of such misery that the only way he could be happy was by destroying it all, and himself with it." Six months later Lynn stops seeing the psychologist and believes she has successfully adjusted to David's death. She is looking forward to college, knowing she will never forget David but feeling stronger and more mature because of what happened.

Shocked and baffled by her friend's murders and suicide, Lynn struggles to understand the events and to overcome her crushing guilt at failing to predict and avert them. With the help of her parents, friends, and psychologist, she comes through her grief a stronger person as she finds some answers. Told by Lynn in diary form and including some profanity, this is a tense, memorable, emotion-charged story that is neither melodramatic nor morbid. There is much to discuss here, particularly the varied reactions and interactions of classmates and friends, all perceptively presented.

Ages 13 and up

**Also available in:**
Paperbound—*About David*
Dell Publishing Company, Inc.

## 501

**Pfeffer, Susan Beth**

**Awful Evelina**

Color illustrations by Diane Dawson.
Albert Whitman & Company, 1979.
(32 pages counted)

---

*COOPERATION: in Play*
  *Imagination*
  *Visiting*

---

Meredith doesn't mind visiting her aunt and uncle but she hates playing with Cousin Evelina. Evelina always hits her and steps on her toes, and the grown-ups never seem to see what's happening. On the day her family is to go see these relatives, Meredith wakes up unhappy. She thinks of circumstances that would keep them from making the dreaded visit. Having noticed clouds in the sky, she imagines it might rain so hard there would be a flood. If a giant wave swept their house away, her father would cancel the visit. But it doesn't rain and they soon depart. After they have traveled a while Meredith sees cows eating grass. She imagines that the world's largest

bull might charge their car. Her mother, using her red coat, would "whirl . . . and twirl . . . and drive that old bull back to its barn." But then Mommy would be so tired that Daddy would have to take her back home. However, the car drives on by the cows, and soon they are parking in front of Evelina's house. Meredith sees a robin taking a worm to its nest and thinks that perhaps an eagle will swoop down and steal her away to its nest in the top of the tallest tree. A helicopter would have to rescue her. Then, after the newspaper and television cameras had taken her picture, her father would have to take her home. But no eagle comes and Meredith has to go into the house. Much to her surprise, however, Cousin Evelina has changed. She tells Meredith that only babies hit and step on toes. When they both want the same color in the Panda Poohbah game, Evelina decides they will take turns and Meredith can be first. When it is time to go home, Meredith does not want to leave. She tells her father that it might snow and then they would have to stay in Evelina's house forever.

Many children will identify with the plight of a child forced to play with someone who is mean to her. They will be relieved along with Meredith that Cousin Evelina has matured enough to be a nicer person. Detailed illustrations emphasize the richness of the heroine's imagination as she weaves daydreams about escape from this dreaded visit. The humor in the unfolding of the plot and in Meredith's fantasies prevents the tale from becoming didactic.

Ages 6-8

**Also available in:**
Large Print—*Awful Evelina*
Albert Whitman & Company

## 502

**Pfeffer, Susan Beth**

**Just Between Us**

Color illustrations by Lorna Tomei.
Delacorte Press, 1980.
(116 pages)

---

*FRIENDSHIP: Meaning of*
*SECRET, KEEPING*
  *Adoption: feelings about*
  *Divorce: of parents*
  *Trust/Distrust*

---

Cass Miller, eleven, cannot keep a secret. When her best friend, Jenny, confides that she has bought her first bra, Cass's weakness threatens their friendship. Cass's mother, a psychology student, devises a way to teach Cass to be silent: she will be paid for the secrets she keeps. Cass agrees to the arrangement, but then reveals a secret almost immediately. Determined to keep the next secret told to her, she tries not talking at all. Then her second-best friend, Robin, tells Cass that her parents were divorced and that she was adopted by her mother's second husband. Cass keeps this secret, then five others, and feels very good for a little while. Soon, though, she tells three of the secrets. Robin invites Cass and Jenny to dinner and Jenny, resentful since her parents' recent divorce and looking for a way to hurt Robin, whom she dislikes, notices that Robin does not resemble her parents. She becomes convinced Robin is

286

adopted and tries to think of a way to reveal this news. Meanwhile, Cass manages to reveal no secrets during a visit to relatives by keeping quiet, eating, and coughing a lot. Jenny confesses that her mother is short of money since the divorce. Robin advises her to call her father for help. But when Jenny calls, she repeats her mother's angry remarks about her father's new girlfriend, infuriating her father into hanging up on her. Since the call was Robin's idea, Jenny vows revenge. Cass is sure that if Robin just apologizes to Jenny, all will be well, but Robin refuses. Knowing none of this because Cass, though increasingly distressed, hasn't revealed the secret, Cass's mother takes the girl to her psychology class to show her off; her classmates know about their agreement. When Jenny announces her intention to spread the word that Robin is adopted, Cass threatens to lie and say Jenny is a bed-wetter. The blackmail works. Jenny confesses that she'd really like to stop being mean and losing friends. Cass realizes that the secret to keeping secrets is to consider, "Would she want other people to know about this?" The tension breaks, the three girls become friends again, and Cass treats Robin and Jenny to lunch with the money she has earned keeping secrets.

Three young girls learn how important it is to keep secrets in this warm, funny first-person narrative. Cass sets out her problem clearly—she simply talks without considering the consequences—and her realistic attempts to change could be useful to readers. The reasons why some secrets shouldn't be told warrant discussion. Clever illustrations complement the text.

Ages 10-12

**Also available in:**
No other form known

## 503

**Pfeffer, Susan Beth**

**Starring Peter and Leigh**

Delacorte Press, 1979.
(200 pages)

---

*DECISION MAKING*
*IDENTIFICATION WITH OTHERS: Peers*
*IDENTITY, SEARCH FOR*
  *Divorce: of parents*
  *Hemophilia*
  *Parent/Parents: remarriage of*
  *Stepbrother/Stepsister*

---

Leigh Thorpe, sixteen, has chosen to leave Los Angeles and her career as a television actress to move to Long Island with her divorced mother, who has recently remarried. After spending four years playing the part of Chris Kampbell on "The Kampbell Kids," a family program, Leigh feels she has missed out on normal teenage life. Her new stepbrother, Peter, one year older than she, has hemophilia. Like Leigh, Peter has missed out on much of the usual teenage social scene. Because of his illness he is frequently confined to home, sometimes to bed, and has not been in school for months. He now plans to enjoy a social life vicariously, through his stepsister. The two discuss how Leigh should dress and behave in order to be accepted by the right crowd and to

overcome her "star" status. Leigh is soon befriended by Anna, an eccentric loner who is not intimidated by Leigh's television career. Gradually the two girls are accepted by a popular group of students. But when a movie Leigh made before leaving California is televised, some of her new friends have difficulty separating the real Leigh from the runaway alcoholic prostitute she portrayed. The school drama teacher, impressed with her performance, pressures Leigh to star in the class play, *Antigone*. But she decides not to audition, and Anna gets the lead. Coaching Anna and several other actors and then seeing *Antigone* performed make Leigh miss acting. A visit to her actor father and his live-in girlfriend in New York City, where she spends a day on the set of his soap opera and has her picture taken for a fan magazine, stirs more restlessness in Leigh. Back at home, she decides she still prefers a "normal" life. But she finds it increasingly difficult to juggle ex-stardom and her new friendships: she has yet to be asked on a date and her friends, with the exception of Anna, are still somewhat uncomfortable in her presence. Peter, whose intermittent bouts with internal bleeding are often brought on by routine colds and infections, comes down with the flu, and his father, Ben, argues with Leigh's mother about his care. Seeing that the argument bothers Peter, Leigh reminds him that all married people fight. But Peter believes his parents divorced because of his illness, and he fears he may destroy this marriage too. Leigh begins dating the class president, but finds that Peter is not interested in hearing about her newfound romance. Realizing she is now living the life she has always dreamed of, Leigh decides to let the future take care of itself for a while. Then she is offered the role of Anne Frank in a four-month tour. Her father, now out of work, is offered a job with the touring company if Leigh will play Anne. The girl, conscious of her responsibility to her father, decides to take the job. Her mother and stepfather support her decision, but Peter is upset. Ill again, the boy confesses his love to Leigh, who finally perceives that his affection for her has for some time been more than brotherly. He compels her to consider her own feelings, which she finds she doesn't fully understand. She tells him time will help them both sort things out. Peter decides to go to California for some specialized and intensive physical therapy. When he is better he plans to visit his mother to try to reconcile some of the anger and guilt that has alienated them since the divorce.

Although few readers will be able to identify with Leigh's specific plight—that of choosing between a regulated home life and a career as a successful actress—many will sympathize with her wish to be accepted by her peers, her search for stability, and her undefined love for her stepbrother. Although the story line at times seems shallow and the heroine's first-person narration is less than sparkling, themes are clearly developed and the hemophiliac Peter is an interesting character. His guilt and alienation resulting from his parents' divorce are not explored in great depth. But Leigh's philosophical, almost jaunty, attitude toward her parents' breakup certainly presents the case that divorce is something to which teenagers can adjust. The dialogue includes some profanity.

**P**

Ages 12-14

**Also available in:**
Cassette—*Starring Peter and Leigh*
Library of Congress (NLSPBH)

Paperbound—*Starring Peter and Leigh*
Dell Publishing Company, Inc.

## 504

**Pfeffer, Susan Beth**

### Starting with Melodie

Four Winds Press, 1982.
(122 pages)

---

*DIVORCE: of Parents*
  *Boy-girl relationships: dating*
  *Friendship: best friend*
  *Jealousy: peer*
  *Parental: custody*

---

Fifteen-year-old Elaine Zuckerman has always been a bit jealous of her best friend, Melodie St. Clare Ashford. Melodie's parents are Constance King, Broadway star, and Trevor Ashford, successful movie producer, and they live in an elegant mansion. Elaine's mother is a dentist, her father works with computer chips, and her life seems terribly dull compared with Melodie's. But now Melodie's parents are embroiled in a messy, publicized divorce. Melodie's grades have plummeted and she seems depressed all the time, helpless to stop her parents' wrangling over her and her little sister, Lissa. Elaine, eager to help her friend, is pulled two ways when her boyfriend, Steve, asks her out for Friday night. Melodie and Lissa have eaten Sabbath dinner at Elaine's house every Friday night for years. So Elaine invites Steve to join them. After dinner, Trevor Ashford arrives for his daughters. Elaine's parents aren't sure he has his wife's permission to take them, but the girls are willing to go with him and so he gets his way. On Monday Melodie and Elaine overhear Melodie's parents having a loud, bitter argument, during which Trevor says he's going to sue for custody of his daughters. When Steve invites Elaine to have dinner with his family on Tuesday, she accepts, even though Tuesday dinners at Melodie's house are an institution. She leaves a message with Melodie's governess that she won't be coming. When Melodie calls to accuse Elaine of preferring Steve to her, Elaine tells Melodie that she's been a little tiresome lately. Melodie hangs up. The next day in school Melodie looks terrible, but Elaine ignores her. When friends report that Melodie is crying in the girls' room and suggest that Elaine help her, Elaine replies that Melodie is capable of blowing her own nose. She herself is entitled to live her life with sane, normal people, Elaine decides. But after considering how painful a custody fight must be and talking with her older brothers, Elaine repairs her friendship with Melodie. Then Lissa disappears, unhappy about being shuffled off to Boston to stay with her grandparents. After an entire day's search, the Zuckermans find her asleep in their car. Both Trevor and Constance come to Elaine's house that evening and begin, theatrically and noisily, to accuse each other of negligence. Elaine's mother points out that they risk losing their daughters' love and respect, that they must find a solution ensuring the girls'

happiness and security. Melodie proposes an acceptable idea: a move to New York where both parents work, so the girls needn't stay in the suburbs with only household servants for much of the week. Elaine and Melodie will miss each other but they make plans for visits, and Elaine knows this solution is best for Melodie. She also feels a renewed appreciation for her own stable family.

A teenage girl becomes involved with her best friend's deteriorating family situation, helping her survive it and coming to appreciate her own stable family life—it may be conventional, but it's also safe and loving. This first-person story brings likeable characters into strong relationships and builds considerable sympathy for children who are victims of divorce. Although Elaine and Melodie are sometimes characterized as younger than they are supposed to be, the story resolves itself realistically.

Ages 11-13

**Also available in:**
No other form known

## 505

**Pfeffer, Susan Beth**

### What Do You Do When Your Mouth Won't Open?

Black/white illustrations by Lorna Tomei.
Delacorte Press, 1981.
(114 pages)

---

*FEAR*
  *Family: relationships*
  *Friendship: best friend*
  *Jealousy: sibling*
  *Perseverance*
  *Problem solving*
  *Success*

---

It started in kindergarten when she forgot her lines in a play. Since then Reesa Nathan, now twelve, has had a fear of talking in public. Her teachers respect her phobia and do not call on her to speak in class. One day Reesa's language arts teacher tells her she has won the school's writing contest on "What I Like Best About America." Delighted, Reesa happily tells her family at dinner. But her older sister, Robby, informs her that she will have to read her essay at the county-wide contest. If that is true, Reesa declares, she will drop out of the contest. The principal confirms Reesa's fears: in two weeks she will read her essay in front of five hundred people. Her presentation will constitute fifty percent of the final judging. Terrified, Reesa turns to her best friend, Heather, for advice. Heather tells Reesa to see a psychiatrist who will cure her of the phobia. Reesa sees a psychologist, Dr. Marks, and asks her, "What do you do when your mouth won't open?" Dr. Marks is sympathetic, but can't promise to cure the girl's phobia in two weeks. Several days later Dr. Marks calls Reesa and tells her to pick up some library books about public speaking. She also asks the girl to return to her office that Friday to learn some relaxation techniques. Reesa learns from the books that fear of public speaking is normal and that it helps to become very familiar with one's speech. She begins practicing diligently, even summoning the courage to read her essay to Heather. Robby, though, tells Reesa she will freeze up and embarrass the family and urges her to quit. That Friday at Dr. Marks's office, Reesa learns breathing exercises and other ways to relax. That weekend Robby persuades Reesa to practice by reading to her language arts class. So that Monday Reesa volunteers to read part of a play aloud. Unfortunately, she freezes and is unable to speak. Furious at her sister, Reesa messes up Robby's file cabinets, Robby slaps her, and soon both girls are crying. Each confesses she is jealous of the other: Reesa of Robby's extra privileges, Robby of Reesa's prettiness and their mother's view of her as a talented writer. They make up and Reesa reads her essay to Robby, who encourages her. The night of the contest arrives, and a frightened Reesa practices her relaxation techniques. But when it is her turn, she begins to panic. Seeing her family and Dr. Marks helps her regain control, and she concentrates on looking at Robby. Reesa begins reading her essay, but ends up speaking extemporaneously; she has changed since she wrote the essay, and the attitudes expressed have changed too. She decides to put forth her new ideas and feels good about herself when she's done. Although she doesn't win, "I'd won what I wanted to win." Tremendously encouraged, Reesa begins to consider the upcoming auditions for the school play.

A young girl with a deep fear of public speaking is helped to overcome her phobia in this lively first-person narrative. Although it seems odd that Reesa has never gotten help from parents or teachers and must seek it out herself, her encounters with the psychologist are convincing and the book's other relationships and situations ring true. Despite unattractive illustrations, this is a most appealing story.

Ages 10-13

**Also available in:**
No other form known

## 506

**Phelan, Terry Wolfe**

### The Week Mom Unplugged the TVs

Black/white illustrations by Joel Schick.
Four Winds Press, 1979.
(37 pages)

---

*CREATIVITY*
*PARENTAL: Control*
  *Nature: appreciation of*
  *Resourcefulness*

---

No matter how poorly ten-year-old Steve may do on a math test, when he gets home from school he can turn on a good TV cartoon chase and instantly feel better. Since Steve's family has three TVs, his viewing does not interfere with his sisters' preferences, Beth's soap operas or Stacey's game shows. But one day their mother declares, "You're all zombies—not people. You spend all your waking hours glued to the TV screen. I can't stand it anymore. I'm going to pull out all the plugs." She decrees that the sets will stay unplugged for one whole school week, from Monday morning until sundown Friday night. On the first day without TV,

Steve invites every friend he has to his house after school. When they leave at five, however, he is so overcome by the silence that he starts to scream. Eventually he quiets down and begins to listen to the crickets. He has never heard crickets in the afternoon before and walks around the house trying to find "those clickers" and wondering if the cats are "still bopping the mice on the five-thirty TV show." He feels like "bopping" his mother on the head but decides instead to try even harder to accept the situation, as his sisters are. That evening he notices that a "nosey star" is following him. The second day without TV is almost a rerun of the first. That night, going to bed nearly two hours before his usual time, Steve looks out the window for the "nosey star" and decides to spend Day Three building a telescope. He does, out of two cardboard tubes, two magnifying glasses, and chewing gum for glue. On Day Four he is able to view insects, birds, and then a sparkling night sky. He dreams that night that he discovers a new comet. Day Five dawns—only five hours until the end of the TV ban! Since he can't look for comets during the day, Steve focuses on leaves, blades of grass, and other small outdoor things. When Stacey and Beth join him, they too enjoy the "lightweight, portable TV screen" that doesn't need any plugs. Then a sudden downpour washes away the "live shows." When the time comes to plug in the TVs again, the power is out. Stacey suggests they use the time without electricity to make more equipment to go with the telescope. They are working busily when their mother flicks on the overhead light. The three children stare at each other—now they can watch any program they want. Steve looks at his watch: six-thirty and time for reruns. Then he notices that the sky is clearing. He decides he would rather see a "first run." Maybe he'll even discover a UFO circling that comet.

This first-person account of a child's withdrawal from television addiction is bound to interest most young readers. They will know exactly how Steve feels as he lives through the initial days of boredom and will share his rediscovery both of the world around him and of his own imagination. Clever illustrations add to the humor of this timely book.

Ages 8-10

**Also available in:**
No other form known

## 507

**Philips, Barbara**

### Don't Call Me Fatso

Color illustrations by Helen Cogancherry.
Raintree Publishers, Inc., 1980.
(31 pages)

---

*NAME-CALLING*
*WEIGHT CONTROL: Overweight*
  *Responsibility: accepting*
  *Self, attitude toward: feeling different*

---

Rita, about seven, is the heaviest child in her class. At school she quickly eats a big lunch and then tries to trade her carrots for cookies. When the children line up to be weighed, someone whispers, "Let's see if Fatso

P

breaks the scale!" Rita weighs seventy-five pounds, and the nurse quietly says they may have to come up with a diet for her. Embarrassed, Rita thinks she will feel better in art class. But when they are assigned to draw someone in the class, two boys draw "Fatso" and snicker. The teacher scolds them, saying, "People come in all shapes and sizes, and that's no reason to make fun of them." At home Rita's stepfather asks what's bothering her, and she tells him that everyone at school calls her names. He suggests they both diet by not eating sweet things or drinking soda pop. She hesitates, but then runs to ask her mother to leave the cookies out of tomorrow's lunch. "I don't want to be fat anymore." Her mother also likes the idea of losing weight and suggests they go jogging together. Rita hates even thinking about exercise, much preferring to watch TV, but she agrees to take swimming lessons with a friend. When she jumps off the board for the first time she hears a whisper: "She's so fat that she sinks when she dives!" In frustration, she eats three candy bars on the way home. Her stepfather reassures her, saying that losing weight takes time and she will feel better about herself if she keeps trying. So Rita decides to continue her diet. Her parents thank her for changing the eating habits of the whole family. Some weeks later, when she is again weighed at school, she has lost only five pounds. But the nurse is enthusiastic. Rita has also grown an inch and "a growing girl shouldn't lose too much weight." Rita runs off to join her friends, too happy to notice that no one is calling her names.

An overweight young girl, teased at school, finds the determination to lose weight. Although Rita's family's attitude may seem idealized and her success a bit too easy, readers will sympathize with her hurt feelings as the victim of name-calling. Overweight children will be cheered by Rita's story; others may gain understanding. The text is enriched by colorful illustrations that reflect the characters' emotions.

Ages 5-9

**Also available in:**
No other form known

## 508

**Phipson, Joan Nash, pseud.**

**Fly Free**

Atheneum Publishers, 1979.
(134 pages)

---

FRIENDSHIP: Best Friend
VALUES/VALUING: Moral/Ethical
   Australia
   Fear: of enclosed spaces
   Freedom, meaning of
   Nature: appreciation of

---

Australian Johnny Johnson, seventeen, is a slow, easygoing, good-natured fellow. His classmate Wilfred Manning is a serious-minded, studious boy who suffers from claustrophobia. When Johnny discovers Wilfred accidentally locked in a storage closet at school, he releases the terrified boy. During subsequent conversations, the two discover a mutual love of the out-of-doors and they become friends. Wilfred's love of nature stems from the

sense of freedom he finds in wide-open spaces; Johnny's is largely practical. He traps the foxes and rabbits of the Australian countryside for the money he can make selling furs. Since Johnny lives with his parents and three sisters in a small farm cottage, he also uses trapping as an excuse to be by himself. Wilfred, who can easily imagine the panic of a trapped animal, hates Johnny's trapping. At school a special excursion for seniors is announced, a trip to a remote island off the Australian coast. Wilfred longs to go. Johnny is at first not interested, thinking the trip too expensive. But when he quarrels with his family, he decides that a trip away from home is just what he needs. He convinces Wilfred to help him with the trapping so both can earn money for the excursion. With Wilfred along, Johnny can venture into rougher country for a previously untapped source of skins. One day while checking the traps alone, Johnny observes strange wheel tracks. He follows the tracks to a beautiful, but cold and menacing, clearing. Realizing that the place would be great for trapping, he takes Wilfred there with him after school and they set their traps. When they return the next day, they find a colorful, rare species of parrot caught alive in one of the rabbit traps. As they release the bird and prepare to let it fly away, two men drive up. They offer to buy the bird, first for ten dollars, then for fifty, promising even more money for more birds. Johnny grabs at the offer, but Wilfred is suspicious. The next time the four meet, Wilfred accuses the men of poaching protected birds. The men will admit to nothing; Wilfred makes no comment but has had enough of trapping. During the following week, the boys avoid one another at school. On Friday, Johnny goes to Wilfred's house to plead for his continued help just until they have enough money for the trip. But Wilfred refuses. The next day Wilfred again stands his ground, and the boys begin to fight. Johnny shoves Wilfred into an open shed and bangs the door shut. Unknown to him, the door latches tight, trapping Wilfred inside. Johnny then rides off on his motorbike. The claustrophobic Wilfred panics and is only half-conscious when his father finds him five hours later. Meanwhile, Johnny has headed for the clearing. There he sees that he has caught another of the beautiful parrots and has trapped a rabbit. As he works to transfer the live rabbit into a bag, he slips. His foot is caught in one trap, his hand in another, and no matter how he struggles he cannot free himself. He remains trapped all afternoon and through the night. As he tries again and again to free himself, he sees the bird and the rabbit go through the same motions and finally understands what Wilfred was protesting all along. Sunday morning, Johnny's family finally notices his absence. His father goes to Wilfred, who is not yet completely recovered from his ordeal in the shed. The two rush to the clearing, where they find Johnny unconscious. As they revive him, the poachers arrive. Both boys gather all their strength and courage and manage to release the parrot before the men can seize it. Johnny cries when he sees that the rabbit has died in the night. As soon as he is able, he sells his traps and gives all the money they've saved to Wilfred for the trip. Wilfred doesn't want to accept the money but Johnny assures him, "I'd feel better if you took it and went. Honest."

This is a compassionate portrayal of two boys, their friendship, and their feelings for nature. The story is enhanced by the development between the boys of a serious conflict of values, leading to an angry confrontation that results in complete disregard for each other's feelings and welfare. Wilfred's claustrophobia has taught him the horrors of confinement; Johnny's frightening experience of being trapped leads him to appreciate the right of every creature to live freely. The Australian setting adds interest.

Ages 11 and up

**Also available in:**
Cassette—*Fly Free*
Library of Congress (NLSBPH)

Paperbound—*Fly Into Danger*
Scholastic Book Services

## 509

Phipson, Joan Nash, pseud.

### A Tide Flowing

Atheneum Publishers, 1981.
(156 pages)

---

*FRIENDSHIP: Meaning of*
  *Death: of friend*
  *Death: of mother*
  *Grandparent: living in home of*
  *Loneliness*
  *Loss: feelings of*
  *Paraplegia*
  *Rejection: parental*

---

Fourteen-year-old Mark Taylor vividly remembers the disastrous boat trip he took four years ago with his mother. They were sailing to Sydney on a friend's boat, intending to go on to England. Mark saw his mother either slip or jump overboard—he's not sure which, although he later testified she fell. Her body was never recovered, and the boy is haunted by his last sight of her. He also can't forget the white albatross he saw flying up out of the water the next morning as the crew searched for her. Mark goes to live with his paternal grandparents but keeps wondering when his father, who lives in a remote part of Australia, will come for him. He looks forward to telling him exactly what happened to his mother so he can get it out of his system. But his father eventually shows up with his new wife, telling Mark he's sold their family home and that Mark will continue to live with his grandparents. One day Mark asks his grandparents, avid sailors, to take him out on their big boat. On the water, Mark finds himself looking for his mother's body. When an albatross follows the boat for a while, he thinks of his mother and feels more at peace than he has in a long time. But at school he has few friends; he becomes even more solitary and remains obsessed by the albatross. His cousins, uncle, and grandparents are angry at his inability to recover from the tragedy. One day Mark runs away to a headland near the sea, and a passerby must grab him back when he steps dangerously close to the edge, caught up in the wonder of an albatross wheeling overhead. After that his grandparents treat him gently, and Mark tries to avoid friction with them. One day he sees Connie Peterson, in her wheelchair, careening down

the hill out of control, her mother running desperately behind her. Determined to stop her before she reaches the road, Mark pushes the chair to one side, but is himself hit by a car and badly injured. Connie's mother visits him in the hospital every day. He learns that Connie became paraplegic two years ago in a car accident that killed her father. She'll take longer to mend from this second accident since her resistance is lower. Mark finds it very easy to talk to Mrs. Peterson and then to Connie. He tells the girl about his mother's death, how he can never be sure if she meant to go over or not. Connie reveals that she believes her accident was her father's fault, something she's never told anyone. They talk about their loneliness and their past lives. Mark is impressed by Connie's ability to face her life and her future with such serenity. He invites her to go sailing with his grandparents once they've both recovered. When they do go sailing, Mark sees a great joy in Connie's face. But as they're docking, Mark's grandfather, who is holding Connie, loses his balance and they go overboard. Although it appears that Connie has only gotten wet, her eyes look haunted. Mark begins taking her out frequently to show her things. When Connie hears of the rift between Mark and his cousins, she helps mend it and soon becomes like one of the family. Mark himself "expanded and flowered in the warmth of undemanding friendship." His affection for his grandparents grows, and his grades at school improve. One day Mrs. Peterson calls and says Connie needs Mark. The girl seems filled with some great inner turmoil and wants to get out, at once. Mark knows the perfect place, a deserted beach on the bay. There Connie professes to see the albatross, although Mark sees nothing. Afterwards, she seems calm and satisfied. That night, Connie becomes ill and is hospitalized. When Mark goes to see her, he realizes she is dying. After she dies, Mark stays with her mother for a while. He plans to earn money to visit his English relatives, particularly his maternal grandparents, who write to him but who Mark feels have failed him. His "loneliness was something he had put by, like childhood."

In this strong and affecting story of friendship and recovery from pain, a boy grieving for his mother and a paraplegic girl learn the difference between being solitary and being lonely. For Connie, their easy friendship "was a door into the living world that she had thought shut forever. For Mark it meant the cracking of his carapace and the end of loneliness." Mark has to deal with three instances of overwhelming rejection by those whom he expects to nurture him: his mother, who apparently commits suicide; his father, who retreats from him and remarries; and his maternal grandparents, who he feels have failed him too. The symbolism of the albatross and what it comes to mean for both Mark and Connie is clear and vivid. A powerful story for any adolescent, this would be particularly appropriate for those who have suffered the loss of a loved one or the end of a relationship.

Ages 12 and up

**Also available in:**
No other form known

P

## 510

Pieper, Elizabeth

**A School for Tommy**

Color illustrations by Mina Gow McLean.
The Child's World, Inc., 1979.
(32 pages)

---

*HANDICAPS*
 *School: mainstreaming*
 *Wheelchair, dependence on*

---

Tommy Williams, a bright and happy seven-year-old, is confined to a wheelchair. When he is ready for second grade, his mother decides he should go to a regular school. He is admitted on a "trial basis." The first day of school his classmates are curious about his wheelchair and his legs. Very matter-of-factly, Tommy explains that his legs do not work. He also lets the children try his crutches and take turns riding in his wheelchair. Tommy notices, though, that Mrs. Jones, his teacher, appears worried or sad. One day Tommy asks to play baseball at recess. He hits the ball from his wheelchair and his best friend, Joel, runs for him. Even though in the excitement of hitting the ball Tommy falls out of his wheelchair and hurts his side, he is happy to be part of the class. Several days later, Tommy watches while his class has gym. After observing for a while, he asks the gym teacher, Mr. Miller, if the class can have a wheelbarrow race. Mr. Miller agrees. Joel holds Tommy's legs and the two boys win the race. Another classmate, Billy, hurts his nose when he falls, and the whole class laughs when Tommy says he is glad he is not the only one who gets hurt at school. Even Mrs. Jones laughs at that.

Although confined to a wheelchair, Tommy is a bright, charming boy who wants to be accepted as he is. With perseverance and humor he easily wins over his classmates, and finally even his teacher is able to relax. Although this colorfully illustrated story is very simply presented and doesn't dwell on the difficulties a handicapped child could encounter in a regular classroom, it may help children understand that someone confined to a wheelchair can still participate in many activities. This book is one in a series—Handling Difficult Times. Following the story is a guide suggesting discussion questions and offering additional information about handicapped children.

Ages 5-8

**Also available in:**
No other form known

## 511

Piepgras, Ruth

**My Name Is Mike Trumsky**

Color illustrations by Peg Roth Haag.
The Child's World, Inc., 1979.
(32 pages)

---

*FOSTER HOME*

---

Little Mike Trumsky lives in a foster home with the Weston family, and so enjoys it that he occasionally calls

himself Mike Weston. This is the second time the boy has lived in a foster home. The first time he was very young. He and his mother had been living with his grandmother, and when she died Mike stayed in a foster home while his mother got resituated. Now he's been with the Westons three months and, despite his happiness with them, Mike is beginning to worry. The first time they lived apart, his mother wrote and called; this time she has not. He knows she has gone to a hospital for surgery and fears she has forgotten him. One day, as he's coming home from school, Mike is greeted by Miss Hunt, his caseworker. She has come to take him to see his mother. Will she remember me? Mike worries. But his fears are put to rest when he and his mother are happily and tearfully reunited. She assures him that as soon as she starts her job and can get a place for them to live, the two will be together. Mike is happy again to be Mike Trumsky.

A child in a foster home is confused and worried about his sick mother, but his fears dissolve when he is reunited with her. Mike's feelings of displacement are too easily resolved, and his lack of information about his mother is puzzling. Still, the book could lead to helpful discussions about the various reasons a child may need foster care. Colorful illustrations show Mike with his friends, foster family, and mother. This book is one in a series—Handling Difficult Times. Following the story is a guide suggesting discussion questions and offering additional information about foster home care.

Ages 5-8

**Also available in:**
No other form known

## 512

Pierik, Robert

**Rookfleas in the Cellar**

Black/white illustrations by Beth and Joe Krush.
The Westminster Press, 1979.
(102 pages)

---

*LOSS: Feelings of*
*RESPONSIBILITY: Accepting*
 *Death: of father*
 *Family: unity*
 *Mourning, stages of*
 *Sibling: relationships*

---

After Danny Van Doren's father dies of emphysema, the twelve-year-old is plagued by nightmares of himself coughing and gasping for breath. Danny's younger brother, Stevie, and little sister, Carrie, also have difficult adjustments to make. Stevie holds imaginary conversations with his father; Carrie believes their father has been kidnapped by the Skeleton Man and will return. Then their mother decides they can't afford to keep the house their father built. Crushed, Danny decides to prove he can be the man of the house, but his efforts to apply for a job, paint the family room, and repair the plumbing don't work out as he plans. The children discourage a family of potential buyers with made-up stories of crime in the streets, the murder of a neighbor, leaks in the house, and "rookfleas" in the cellar. An important memory for Danny is his winning the Pinewood Derby with a model car he and his father built. Now it is Stevie's turn to enter, and Danny is determined to help him. Their mother surprises them with gifts from their father purchased just before he died, including a model car kit for Stevie. The boys work hard on the car, dubbed the Silver Streak, but it is slow, and Stevie runs off in frustration. Danny recalls their father lubing his car with graphite and that does improve the new car's speed. When he goes to tell Stevie he finds him perched precariously on the roof, frightened, yelling that everything is his fault and he's sorry. Danny doesn't understand any of this, but he cautiously and as calmly as possible talks Stevie down. Then he spanks him soundly for risking his life. But Stevie continues to believe his father's death was his fault; when he climbed the roof once before and his father spanked him, he had wished his father dead. He's sure his father wouldn't want him to win the Pinewood Derby. But he does win, in a close race. Before the race, Stevie had built a live trap for a scout project, and now he catches a young possum that Carrie names Pretend because he plays dead. In the meantime, Danny's mother sells the house and signs a lease on an apartment. At this time Carrie begins to worry that their mother may also die. Elmo, a neighborhood boy, jealous that Stevie won the derby race, comes over one day and teases Pretend unmercifully. Stevie fights Elmo to make him stop and Elmo vows revenge. Now Danny feels it is time to release poor Pretend. But as the possum lumbers from the cage, Elmo appears and throws a rock that kills him. At this Carrie cries, not only for Pretend, but for her father. She can now be helped to understand that her father lives only in her heart. Then the family learns that their dear friends the Weilers, an older childless couple, must move from their duplex because the owner is selling. Danny's mother, a newly licensed real-estate agent, decides to buy the house. The Van Dorens will live upstairs and continue to rent the downstairs to the Weilers. In the new house, Danny celebrates his thirteenth birthday with two cakes, one from his mother and one from Mrs. Weiler. When his mother plays the piano while everyone sings, life seems more like the old days than it has in a long time.

Three children struggle to accept their father's death, and the oldest, Danny, tries to assume responsibility for his younger brother and sister. Characterizations lack depth here, but the situations and relationships are believable, and the story encourages understanding of a family's trauma when a parent dies. The vocabulary level is low, the interest level high, and the book well suited to the reluctant reader. Illustrations enhance the text.

Ages 8-13

**Also available in:**
No other form known

**513**

**Platt, Kin**

## The Ape Inside Me

J. B. Lippincott Company, 1979.
(117 pages)

*ANGER*
*Aggression*
*Peer relationships*
*Self-discipline*

Ed Hill is a fifteen-year-old boy with a problem. He has a terrible temper that rises up inside him and explodes "like a volcano." Since he feels incapable of controlling it, he thinks of this temper as a separate being, an ape he calls "Kong." No amount of reasoning by Eddie's rational side can bring Kong into line. On several occasions his temper almost gets him killed because it will not let him back down when the odds are against him. But in spite of the trouble Kong causes, Ed is not sure he really wants to control him. After all, Ed likes to fight and Kong is good at finding opportunities—in fact, the boy dreams of becoming a professional boxer. But he is small and doesn't really think he has a chance. Besides, Ed without Kong is a very nice person. He loves his divorced mother and wants to earn a lot of money so he can give her nice things. He tries to put up with Les, who lives with them, although Les dislikes Eddie and deliberately irritates and berates him. Eddie works hard at Sal's Body Shop and tries to justify Sal's faith in him. He chooses friends like Debbie Donaldson, the shyest girl in school, and Bobby Penna, gentle and studious. When Debbie wins a national poetry contest and learns she must give a speech to the student body, she's sure she will die of fright. She wishes she could be more like Eddie; Sal and Bobby, however, do not admire Eddie's irascible ways. They both try to convince him that anger starts in the mind and his mind must control Kong. Sal, however, realizes that part of Ed's problem is that he likes to fight. So he sends the boy to see Phil Sierra, a friend who runs a gym and can tell Eddie if he has what it takes to become a professional fighter. Phil watches Eddie in the ring and concludes that he is "a fighter already," that fighting is obviously part of his nature. But he warns the boy that he must learn to control his temper. "Otherwise, when your temper is up, you're like a runaway car with no brakes. You got no steering power either, because the control is gone." He explains that when a person is angry he isn't thinking clearly, "and it's easy to pick him apart and then put him away." Phil tells Eddie to come back when he has Kong under control. Eddie resolves to subdue his temper and soon has a chance. During Debbie's speech in the school auditorium, Mike Boyd, sitting behind Eddie, starts to disrupt the assembly by making fun of the girl. Kong roars, "You letting him get away with this? . . . Kill the bum, hit him!" But even after Boyd jams the heel of his hand into Eddie's face, Eddie remains calm. He is in charge now. Determined to control himself, he thinks, "No more, Kong. I'm boss. Get back in your tree."

A teenage boy gives his uncontrollable temper a separate identity but realizes he'll never get anywhere until

P

he takes charge of "Kong." Eddie's first-person narrative is peppered with his conversations with other characters and his dialogues with Kong. Thought-provoking and full of discussion possibilities, the story makes a valuable distinction between the discipline required for prizefighting and untempered anger. Ed's story may help readers with similar temperaments and should have special appeal for the reluctant reader.

Ages 12 and up

**Also available in:**
Paperbound—*The Ape Inside Me*
Bantam Books, Inc.

## 514

Platt, Kin

### Brogg's Brain

J. B. Lippincott Company, 1981.
(123 pages)

---

*AMBIVALENCE, FEELINGS OF*
*EXPECTATIONS*
  *Boy-girl relationships: dating*
  *Communication: parent-child*
  *Competition*
  *Maturation*
  *Sports/Sportsmanship*
  *Talents: athletic*

---

Fifteen-year-old Monty Davis runs the mile for the school track team because he enjoys running, not because he wishes to compete or loves to win. The adults around him, however, don't accept what they consider his lack of drive. His coach thinks he should demand more of himself. His father, who had also been a runner in high school, wants him to work harder. Even his English teacher urges him to be more ambitious, suggesting that most people need to win. Monty disagrees. In fact, he is irritated by all these demands to excel, telling himself that all he has ever wanted to do is run for fun. Then, in contradiction of his own philosophy, he starts training harder. He begins running a course around a park near his home and there sees a blonde girl with a ponytail who can outrun him every time. He begins dating a school friend, Cindy, a marathon runner and Japanese-American, although his father would much prefer him to date an "American" girl. He takes her to a movie called "Brogg's Brain," in which a talking brain dominates the other characters. Afterwards, the two discuss the possibilities of Monty's controlling his running by sending positive messages to himself. One night Monty's father again prods him about doing better. Angrily Monty leaves the house and heads for the park. There he speaks with the ponytail girl, Julie Mars, a champion marathon runner. She suggests they run together and gives him some pointers. The day of the big meet with arch-rival Culver arrives. Monty will compete with his own teammates, Cott and Rose, and with a runner from Culver named Bunny Ellison. Now the coach, after all his lectures about winning, tells Monty that today he is to be a "rabbit"—he is to run hard in order to wear out Ellison, letting Cott and Rose take first and second place so their school can win the meet. But a voice inside Monty tells him that today he can run better than he ever has before. He runs for

all he is worth, yet is unable to "wear out" Ellison. Monty beats him by less than ten yards, with Cott and Rose left behind.

A boy who runs for the pleasure of it resists adult demands that he run to win and then discovers that he has a competitive spirit after all. Furthermore, once he begins competing he decides he wants to win. Monty's first-person narrative will compel the attention of readers, especially budding athletes. His discovery of the joys of competition merits discussion.

Ages 12 and up

**Also available in:**
Paperbound—*Brogg's Brain*
Scholastic Book Services

## 515

Pollock, Penny

### Keeping It Secret

Black/white illustrations by Donna Diamond.
G. P. Putnam's Sons, 1982.
(110 pages)

---

*CHANGE: Resisting*
*DEAFNESS*
*SCHOOL: Transfer*
  *Dependence/Independence*
  *Friendship: making friends*
  *Moving*
  *School: mainstreaming*
  *Self, attitude toward: accepting*
  *Self, attitude toward: feeling different*

---

When Mary Lou Spangler, nicknamed Wisconsin for the state she loves and has lived in until now, enters her new sixth-grade class in New Jersey, she decides no one will ever know about the hearing aids hidden by her hair. Her former classmates knew all about her hearing problem, but that was different because they were her friends. She meets Jason Wainwright, a class leader, and Maria Maracosa, beautiful and seemingly without problems. One day Wisconsin sees Jason writing her name on a wall, except that he starts it with a *P*. She stays home "sick" for three days and concentrates on ways to revenge herself on Jason. The rest of her time is spent trying to figure out how to get out of a class spelling bee (she hates them), how to avoid a class picnic to be held at Jason's house (the swimming would ruin her hearing aids if she wore them, and if she took them out, everyone would see), and how to become sick enough to escape Field Day (her hearing aids could fall out during the games). She wants to learn to play softball, but her father doesn't want her to; he's been overly protective since her ear surgery. Wisconsin gets her revenge on Jason during the spelling bee by asking him to spell Wisconsin. Everyone but the teacher knows how Jason previously spelled it, so they all laugh at his embarrassment. Then Wisconsin overhears her mother talking to her older brother, Will, about a conference she had with Wisconsin's teacher. Her classmates won't accept Wisconsin, her mother says, because Wisconsin won't accept herself. Will tells Wisconsin that Jason asked him if she had a boyfriend. He wondered if she is so unfriendly because of her bum ear. Wisconsin is shocked: how does he know about her hearing? It seems their teacher had told the entire class about Wisconsin's hearing aids when she was playing sick, advising the students not to mention it, that Wisconsin would show them her hearing aids when she was ready to. Wisconsin is angry and embarrassed. Then, when Jason calls to ask her to bring brownies to the picnic, he confesses that the reason he wrote "Pisconsin" was that the boys had been teasing him ever since he said she was cute. When the picnic has to be cancelled because of rain, Wisconsin is actually disappointed. She starts practicing softball by herself. When Will sees her trying so hard he begins to help her, and soon her father joins in. On Field Day, Wisconsin is paired with Maria for the three-legged race. When Maria trips six inches short of the finish line, she is deeply dismayed. Her mother, it turns out, is very athletic and competitive, and Maria's life is far from trouble-free. The two girls move toward friendship. In the big softball game, Wisconsin finds herself at bat with the score tied. At the worst possible moment one of her hearing aids falls out, right on Jason's toe. But he returns it to her with a wink, and when Wisconsin faces the batter she's determined to hit the ball into the middle of Wisconsin!

A young girl adjusts poorly to her new school because her determination to hide her hearing aids leads her to hide her feelings about many things. Anticipating rejection, she in fact triggers it, and she refuses several overtures of friendship. With help from her family, Wisconsin finally sees that the only barrier to making new friends has been her own attitude. Soft illustrations accompany this well-told story of life in the mainstream for a hearing-impaired child.

Ages 9-12

**Also available in:**
No other form known

## 516

Posner, Grace

### In My Sister's Eyes

Beaufort Books, Inc., 1980.
(144 pages)

---

MENTAL RETARDATION
    Abortion
    Boy-girl relationships: dating
    Family: relationships
    Pregnancy
    Sex: premarital
    Sibling: love for

---

When Christine Ockham, co-captain of the cheerleading squad, congratulates Billy Roster on his tennis game and asks for help with hers, it's the start of a caring, mutually supportive relationship. Billy does wonder, though, what Chrissie will think of his retarded sister, Jen, "the skeleton in his closet." Meanwhile, Chrissie is trying to decide whether or not to give up cheerleading to get on the tennis team. Her best friend and fellow co-captain, Beth, seems oddly desperate for Chrissie to stay with cheerleading. Finally, Beth breaks down and admits she needs Chrissie: she's afraid she's pregnant. She is "pre-engaged" to Pete Sloan, a football star, but she hasn't told Pete or her parents and doesn't know

what to do. At this time, Jen's residential school asks her family to keep her at home for a while because there's been an outbreak of virus. With both his parents working, Billy knows some of the responsibility for Jen's care will be his. And "he did love his sister. She was good and innocent and vulnerable. She touched something very deep inside him." Billy takes Chrissie home to meet Jen, and they get on well together. Meanwhile, Beth is very bitter: "The next guy who wants me will have to damn well wait till I'm a woman and know exactly what I'm doing." She still doesn't want to tell Pete; she doesn't love him and never did. But she finally decides it's unfair not to tell him. When Billy asks Chrissie to the prom she refuses abruptly, with no explanations. Later she comes to Billy's house and invites him and Jen to go with her to the beach. There she explains that she'd just heard that Beth is pregnant after all. She'd felt momentarily that she was Beth and that Billy was another Pete Sloan. While they talk, Jen wanders off. It is nearly dawn when they find her, sleeping under a dock. Chrissie goes to visit Beth, who is brittle and flip about what has just happened to her. She had pains, went to the doctor, and had "polyps" removed from her uterine wall. No more pregnancy. But now she needs to talk to someone about her feelings of loss and the fact that her mother insists on acting as though nothing has happened. The big crime in her house, according to Beth, is not having sex, but being found out. Billy's parents and Jen come to his tennis tournament. He worries at first about Jen having a seizure there or acting inappropriately, but she does neither and he wins the tournament. Later, while playing cards with his sister, he reflects on her "beautiful but vacant" eyes. Sometimes, as they were growing up, he'd felt, "There's someone locked up in there, a real, living, thinking, feeling person is locked up in the body of my sister. And she wants to get out." When the school calls to say Jen can come back, Billy asks if the family could keep her. But Jen's own delight at the thought of going back shows them that she is actually happier at the school. The family is asked to decide if Jen can participate in an experimental surgical program to stop her seizures. They decide against it. Jen's present quality of life is "simple but good" and makes her happy; she has too much to lose. Beth's father has had a heart attack, and she is sure that if it weren't for her "trouble," her father would not be sick. Chrissie and Beth's father himself reassure and comfort her. At the prom, Beth is touched by Pete's concern for her. Billy and Chrissie look to the future as they talk about Jen.

Two young people attempt to integrate into their own lives the problems of those close to them and to respond in helpful, appropriate ways. Most of the book is told from Billy's or Chrissie's viewpoints, but exceptions are made twice: once when Jen's mother thinks about her retarded daughter, and once when Jen herself thinks about her environment. Readers may find it a bit disconcerting to be suddenly in the mind of an adult, but this section does give additional insight into an important theme. Jen's reflections are what one would like to believe she feels, but of course the reader can't be sure how authentic they are. Beth's pregnancy and its aftermath point up her changing attitudes about sex; it may be that "all the kids were doing it," but Beth concludes

P

she's not ready for the responsibility of physical intimacy and won't be for quite a while. Both Billy and Chrissie are just a little too good to be true, but they are appealing characters and provide continuity in a book that is more a string of interrelated situations than a strongly plotted story.

Ages 12 and up

**Also available in:**
Paperbound—*In My Sister's Eyes*
Fawcett World Library

## 517

Potter, Marian

### The Shared Room

William Morrow & Company, Inc., 1979.
(192 pages)

---

*MENTAL ILLNESS: of Parent*
*Family: relationships*
*Grandparent: living in home of*
*Maturation*
*Parental: absence*
*Perseverance*
*School: classmate relationships*

---

At the beginning of fifth grade, Catherine Doyle is required to write her autobiography. Living with her grandparents, she does not remember her mother or father and wants to know more about them both. Catherine sleeps in her mother's old room and has cherished a few possessions of hers that the grandmother had missed when she cleared things out. Catherine likes to think she is "sharing" her mother's room. But her grandmother, Nana, refuses to tell her anything except that her mother is in a hospital. When Catherine tells her grandfather, Pop, that she wants to see her mother, Pop says such a visit will confuse Catherine and make her sad. Several days later, at school, Catherine tells her teacher that her mother is sick. But when a classmate announces that Catherine's mother is "crazy," the girl begins to realize what is actually wrong with her mother. After school, when she is teased and taunted, Catherine fights back with her fists and earns the nickname Muhammad Ali. The name sticks; she is soon called Ali by almost everyone. Ali has discovered that her mother is in a mental hospital in a nearby town. She tells Pop she wants to visit her at Christmas and buys a blouse to give her. But Nana adamantly refuses permission, and so Ali finally mails the gift. Soon she receives a short letter of thanks from her mother. Despite Nana's distress, Ali writes back asking her mother to come home for a visit. Sometime later she overhears Nana on the telephone refusing to have Kathleen, Ali's mother, home for Easter. Ali is angry and puzzled, but Nana insists she will understand when she is older. The school year ends and summer passes quickly. Soon after school starts again, Nana has major surgery. Ali helps out at home and comes to appreciate Nana more than she ever has. But soon after Nana returns home, Ali renews her plea for permission to visit her mother. Nana finally gives in. She and Pop take the excited but frightened Ali to her mother's hospital. There they find that Kathleen is responding beautifully to new drug therapy and has shown signs of a renewed interest in

life. Several weeks later Ali furtively opens a letter from the hospital addressed to her grandparents. The hospital wants permission for Kathleen to come home for a short visit. Ali types a letter of permission and forges her grandmother's signature. Then, because their car isn't running, she writes to her uncle, asking him to get Kathleen and bring her home. That Saturday her mother arrives. Nana is furious; Pop and Ali are elated. Later, while Nana and Kathleen nap, Pop finally explains to Ali about her mother's breakdown, her father's desertion, and Nana's struggle to accept what had happened. At the end of the week's stay, a weary Kathleen tells Ali that she wants to return to the hospital. She feels unable to cope with the demands of living in the world again. Ali begs her to reconsider, and Kathleen decides to make an effort for her daughter's sake. She will stay in town at a halfway house where she can gradually adjust to living outside the hospital. Ali is thrilled.

A determined young girl, discovering that her mother is in a mental hospital, battles to have her come home. Though levels of characterization vary here from thoughtful to superficial, and though some of Ali's efforts seem a bit farfetched, this is a believable story offering insight into the fears and misunderstandings that still surround mental illness. Ali's grandmother has forbidden herself to hope for her daughter's recovery and must be wrenched back to a cautious optimism when Ali forces the issue by establishing contact with her mother. Kathleen's illness, described as manic-depressive psychosis newly controlled by lithium, is realistically portrayed in this warm, sometimes humorous story of family relationships.

Ages 10-12

**Also available in:**
No other form known

## 518

Power, Barbara

### I Wish Laura's Mommy Was My Mommy

Black/white illustrations by Marylin Hafner.
J. B. Lippincott Company, 1979.
(47 pages)

---

*FAMILY: Relationships*
*Love, meaning of*
*Parent/Parents: mother working outside home*

---

Jennifer thinks her friend Laura's mother is just about perfect. As a matter of fact, she wishes she could have Laura's mommy for her own. After-school snacks at Laura's house consist of things like punch and donuts. Her own mother thinks that "snacks should be real food, not just sugar." Laura's family eats in the dining room, sometimes by candlelight. But Jennifer's little brothers are messy eaters, so her family has to eat in the kitchen. When Jennifer eats at Laura's the girls are served seconds of dessert, and then they are allowed to leave the table and play. At her house Jennifer has to help clear the table and get her own seconds of dessert —if there are any. When Jennifer sleeps over at Laura's house, Laura's mother lets the girls stay up late and gives them a breakfast of pancakes shaped like little people. Jennifer's mother makes them go to bed early and be quiet so they won't disturb the boys. In the morning they have to make the beds and fix their own breakfast. One day everything changes. Jennifer's mother goes back to work, and Laura's mother begins babysitting for Jennifer and her brothers. Jennifer is sure life will be wonderful now. But instead of donuts after school, the children are given apples. "Donuts are fine for a treat once in a while, but fruit is much better for you," says the new baby-sitter. Then, since Laura's mother is busier now, Jennifer is asked to teach Laura how to make her own bed. When Jennifer and her brothers have to stay late one evening, the family eats in the kitchen, "the way they had when Laura was little." The girls are asked to help clear the table; Laura has to learn how to scrape and stack the plates. By the end of the first week of this new arrangement, Jennifer is delighted to go out for pizza with her own family. On Saturday she and her mother bake a chocolate cake together. Mommy even calls her "Pumpkin Princess," as she did when Jennifer was little. A happy Jennifer decides that even though Laura's mother is nice, she's glad her mommy is still her mommy.

Jennifer comes to appreciate her own home and mother when the "perfect" mother of a friend becomes Jennifer's baby-sitter, rather than her hostess. This amusing story allows children to compare two life styles and to evaluate the old adage, "The grass is always greener." Expressive illustrations add to the humor of this easy reader.

Ages 4-7

**Also available in:**
No other form known

## 519

**Powers, Bill**

### A Test of Love

Black/white photographs by Bill Aron.
Franklin Watts, Inc., 1979.
(90 pages) o.p.

---

*PREGNANCY*
  *Boy-girl relationships*
  *Communication: importance of*

---

When sixteen-year-old Patricia Calder learns from a local birth control clinic that she is six weeks pregnant, she confides her shock and confusion to her best friend and fellow cheerleader, Linda. But to her mother she denies that anything is wrong. However, she unknowingly drops a scrap of paper with the clinic's name and address written on it. The next day, when Pat announces her intention to visit her eighteen-year-old boyfriend, Tommy, who attends college in a nearby town, her mother confronts the girl with the scrap of paper, demanding to know if she and Tommy are sleeping together. Pat longs to tell her mother everything but can only answer the specific question. She adds that she doesn't want to hurt anyone. To her anger and disappointment, when Pat tells Tommy she is pregnant, he refuses to make marriage plans and recommends that she have an abortion. At Monday's cheerleading practice, Pat tells Linda what Tommy said and expresses her fear that everyone who loves her will be hurt by her

dilemma. Her mother, she predicts, will hate her. The next day she is incensed by the casualness with which Sally, the head cheerleader, takes her birth control pill. That night Tommy calls, pressing Pat to have an abortion, and she realizes that he is concerned only with himself. On Wednesday, the day before Thanksgiving, Pat goes home early from the pep rally because she feels sick. She finds Tommy waiting to talk to her but refuses to see him, saying they can talk before the Thanksgiving game. On the day of the game, Pat's mother insists that after dinner the two of them talk about whatever is bothering Pat. Frightened at the prospect, the girl leaves for the football field. There, Tommy confronts her with more insistence on secrecy and an abortion. Sick, confused, and crying, Pat runs into the parking lot, where a backing school bus strikes her. She wakes up in the hospital with a broken leg and learns that the accident caused a miscarriage and that Tommy has told her parents everything. When her parents come into the room, Pat admits that withholding truth was worse than being pregnant. She had planned to tell her mother everything that night, no matter what.

This is a thought-provoking book with a rather contrived ending. It does demonstrate that teenagers in trouble must know whom they can and cannot depend on and so provides good discussion material, especially since the main character is shown to grow emotionally from her experience. Although an accident ends Pat's pregnancy and cancels her immediate dilemma, she does learn how valuable and comforting honest communication with family and friends can be. Photographs, some looking posed, help tell this high-interest, low-vocabulary story.

Ages 12 and up

**Also available in:**
Braille—*A Test of Love*
Library of Congress (NLSBPH)

Cassette—*A Test of Love*
Library of Congress (NLSBPH)

## 520

**Prince, Alison**

### The Turkey's Nest

William Morrow & Company, Inc., 1980.
(223 pages)

---

*BELONGING*
  *Abortion*
  *Life style: change in*
  *Love, meaning of*
  *Pregnancy*
  *Relatives: living in home of*
  *Unwed mother*

---

Kate Carling, seventeen, is pregnant by Laurie Coppersmith, whose wife, Barbara, had left him but now has come back because she has leukemia. Kate's divorced "Mum" is planning to marry a man named Nigel, so, despite her mother's reservations, Kate plans to stay with her widowed Aunt Beth on her farm in Suffolk. Co-workers in the London snack bar where she works, her mother, and later the doctors in Suffolk bring up the question of abortion. Laurie especially thinks this is the answer, and he gives her money for one when she leaves London. But Kate isn't sure. Although she considers herself a London girl, Kate gradually familiarizes herself with the farm routine, beginning to enjoy being there and to love Aunt Beth, a brusque but kind woman. But Kate doesn't really feel at home because Beth refuses to let the pregnant girl help with the work. One day, feeling homesick, depressed, and bored, Kate breaks down and cries. Realizing that she needs something to do, Beth puts her in charge of the chickens. About the same time, Kate's London girlfriends send her a package of art materials and Kate begins to draw. She helps with the lambing and begins sewing maternity clothes. Then Beth falls and has to be hospitalized. Peter, a neighbor, helps out, soon confessing to Kate that he's always loved Beth. Alec Fairchild, the son of another neighbor, drives Kate in to visit her aunt. Later, after Beth is home but her leg is too stiff to drive, Alec begins driving Kate to her prenatal clinic. Life in Suffolk continues to be sweet for Kate. Then, sometime after Laurie's wife dies, he comes to the country to visit Kate. During his stay he asks her to marry him and tries to make love to her, but she realizes he has no feeling at all for the coming baby and she refuses him. After Kate has her baby, a boy, her mother and Nigel come to visit. Kate asks Beth if she can stay on at the farm instead of returning to London. Beth is glad to have her, but warns Kate that Peter has asked her to marry him and eventually she'll be leaving the farm. Now Kate's newfound home seems to be slipping away. Then her father, whom she hasn't seen for many years, flies in from Australia and invites her to bring the baby and return with him to meet his wife and three young sons. Kate has nowhere else to go, so she accepts his offer. Shortly before she is to leave, Alec declares his love for her and the baby and asks Kate to marry him. Kate realizes that this, the perfect answer for her, has been there all the time. They will live in Aunt Beth's house; Alec's father had always intended to buy it from Beth someday for his son.

A young, unmarried London girl, pregnant and without many options, learns to love farm living and embarks on a country life with her baby and a young farmer husband. This book gives an excellent view of farm life, of the relationship between city-bred Kate and her country Aunt Beth, and of the problems created by a pregnancy outside of marriage. Its virtues are marred, however, by shallow and stereotyped characters and by a glossing over of the decisions such a pregnancy requires. There is interest here, but little depth.

Ages 12 and up

**Also available in:**
Paperbound—*The Turkey's Nest*
Grosset & Dunlap, Inc.

## 521

**Quackenbush, Robert M.**

### First Grade Jitters

Color illustrations by the author.
J. B. Lippincott Company, 1982.
(32 pages)

---

*FEAR: of School*
  *Identification with others: peers*

---

Told by his mother that he has "first grade jitters" and by his father that he is cranky and out-of-sorts, a young rabbit denies that he is behaving any differently. He is the same as always and still likes the same things—except for food, of course. He's not very hungry lately. According to the young rabbit, the reason he yelled and kicked at the shoe store was that he preferred his old, pinching shoes to new ones. He certainly is not worried about school, he says, and remembers the fun he had in kindergarten last year with his friends Tammy, Kevin, and Jason. Sometimes he does wonder about first grade and whether his friends, not seen all summer, will be there. He wonders too about his teacher and whether she will expect him to know how to read and spell and do arithmetic. Imagining that the teacher might speak strangely in a language he doesn't understand scares the rabbit so much he goes to bed. He tells his mother that his leg is bothering him and he can't walk. He doesn't expect to improve before school starts, but when Tammy calls he manages to hobble to the telephone. Newly returned from a summer with her grandparents, Tammy comes over to play blocks and is soon joined by Jason and Kevin. Tammy tells them she has already met their teacher, Miss Welsh, and likes her. Miss Welsh does not expect them to know how to read and write, and she talks just like them, reports Tammy. Greatly reassured, the young rabbit says, "My jitters are gone! Let's play big yellow school bus, and I'll be the driver."

In this short, simple tale of apprehension about school, the young rabbit narrator feels defensive when his parents try to define his "jitters." Only when he learns from his friends that his fears about first grade are unfounded does he feel better and regain his self-confidence. Though fear of school may not always be so quickly and easily resolved, this book could help comfort young children for whom the reassurance of peers is beginning to be important. Crisp illustrations deftly catch the essence of the text.

Ages 5-7

**Also available in:**
No other form known

## 522

**Rabe, Berniece Louise**

### The Balancing Girl

Color illustrations by Lillian Aberman Hoban.
E. P. Dutton & Company, Inc., 1981.
(32 pages counted)

---

*SCHOOL: Classmate Relationships*
  *Braces on body/limbs*
  *School: mainstreaming*
  *Wheelchair, dependence on*

---

Margaret, a first grader, gets around either in a wheelchair or with leg braces and crutches. Even so, she is an expert at balancing. She can balance her books on her head, can balance a high tower of blocks, can balance her body on her crutches. Her classmate Tommy ridicules Margaret's balancing skills and frequently destroys the towers and castles she builds. Now Margaret's school is planning a carnival to raise money for gym equipment. The first grade will have a "fish pond" operated by Tommy and his father. William, another classmate, will dress up as a clown and sell balloons. Margaret decides that for her booth she will make an entire village of dominoes, each standing on end and properly spaced so that when the first domino is tipped, the next will fall and the next until the whole village topples. People will pay to have their names placed in a hat; the person whose name is drawn the night of the carnival will get to push the first domino. Margaret works on her village for days, using all the dominoes in the school. Her teacher watches Tommy carefully so he doesn't succeed in tipping the dominoes. The night of the carnival, Margaret buys three balloons from William and catches a big spider in Tommy's fish pond. Soon it is time to draw the name of the person who will push the first domino. Tommy's name is drawn, and he is thrilled at the opportunity to destroy something of Margaret's with permission. The domino village falls, according to Margaret's design, and her booth earns the most money for the carnival.

Margaret's disability is illustrated, but not mentioned in the text. She is shown to be a happy child functioning normally in a typical classroom. Even Tommy's continual provocation does not upset Margaret, and his characterization adds reality to a simply told story.

Ages 5-7

**Also available in:**
Disc—*The Balancing Girl*
Library of Congress (NLSBPH)

## 523

**Rabinowich, Ellen**

## Rock Fever

Black/white photographs by Mauro Marinelli.
Franklin Watts, Inc., 1979.
(85 pages)

---

*ALCOHOLISM: of Mother*
*DRUGS: Abuse of*
  *Boy-girl relationships*
  *Divorce: of parents*
  *Reality, escaping*

---

Sixteen-year-old Doug is the lead singer of a rock group that performs in a local nightclub. Agents hear the group and want the boys to "cut a demo" record, but Doug is worried. Each boy will need to contribute one hundred dollars for studio rental and Doug has only one source for that kind of money: his father, a physician. But ever since his parents' divorce a year ago, Doug's father never seems to have time or money for his younger son, although he's very proud of Doug's older brother, an honors student in college. Doug's mother drinks and lately has become violent with Doug when she's drunk. Determined to get the money, Doug goes to his father's office. His father informs him that he will never invest money in a music venture and suggests Doug concentrate on his studies and pursue a career in medicine. As Doug walks away, he passes the office dispensary and gets an idea. He'll steal drugs from his father and sell them to get the money he needs. He grabs some bottles and many sample packages. Later, nervous and depressed, he tries a Quaalude to calm himself. He sells most of the pills to a dealer at school

and gets the money for the demo. One night at rehearsal, he meets a girl named Valerie and later walks home with her. The next week he takes her out to dinner. He likes her and is leery when his mother invites Valerie to the house to celebrate her birthday. The three have a pleasant time until Doug's mother gets drunk and starts screaming and clawing at Doug. Embarrassed, he tells Valerie to leave and puts his mother to bed. To calm himself, he takes another Quaalude. He stays high all the next day. That night at rehearsal he gets into a fight with Alex, the drummer. Tony, the leader of the group, postpones the demo. Another twenty-four hours pass and Doug is still stoned. He decides to run away. His mother, drunk as usual, grabs at Doug to stop him. When he pulls away from her, she falls down the stairs and lies at the bottom, unconscious. Doug gets her to the hospital, where his father meets them. His mother will be all right, but her excessive drinking must end. Doug's father apologizes to the boy for not recognizing what was happening and promises to help Doug get his mother to join Alcoholics Anonymous. Doug returns to his group and apologizes. Next, he flushes the rest of his Quaaludes down the toilet. Finally, he calls Valerie and the two happily agree to meet.

The younger son of divorced parents, his mother an alcoholic and his father cold and remote, has only his rock group to sustain him. Lonely, depressed, and needing money, Doug's easy access to drugs gives him the funds he needs, as well as a way to escape the pain of reality. But drugs, he finds, erect barriers between himself and the only friends he has: his fellow musicians and his girlfriend. To preserve himself and the friendships he values, he gets rid of the drugs. Simply written with a relatively uncomplicated resolution, this story will appeal to reluctant readers. Photographs are an added attraction.

Ages 12 and up

**Also available in:**
Braille—*Rock Fever*
Library of Congress (NLSBPH)

Cassette—*Rock Fever*
Library of Congress (NLSBPH)

## 524

**Radley, Gail**

## Nothing Stays the Same Forever

Crown Publishers, Inc., 1981.
(148 pages)

---

*PARENT/PARENTS: Remarriage of*
  *Age: aging*
  *Change: resisting*
  *Death: of mother*
  *Friendship: meaning of*
  *Loss: feelings of*
  *Maturation*

---

Everything seems to be changing for twelve-year-old Carolyn (Carrie) Moyer. Her father seems very serious about Sharon, the first time he's been serious about a woman since Carrie's mother died of cancer four years ago. Carrie is unhappy about the developing relationship and feels her older sister, Phyllis, is disloyal to their mother's memory because she likes Sharon. Carrie's

R

299

friend Bridget tells her about an art workshop in New York. Carrie's father isn't encouraging about the possibility of her attending, but since he says that money is one of the obstacles, she begins looking for jobs. She works in the garden of Grace Stebbins, an elderly neighbor, and gets a few other odd jobs. She also enrolls in an art class at the recreation center, even though she feels it's beneath her. Her teacher appreciates her caricatures and cartoons. When Sharon comes for dinner, Carrie is antagonistic; when her father tries to talk to her about including Sharon in their lives, she refuses to listen. Only with Grace can Carrie talk about her feelings. When her father takes her, Sharon, Phyllis, and her boyfriend, Al, out for dinner, Carrie feels lonelier and lonelier as everyone else seems happier. Then her father announces that he and Sharon will be married in September. Carrie dashes into the restroom. Sharon follows her, but Carrie rudely rebuffs her overtures. Then Grace has a heart attack. Carrie visits her often in the hospital, becoming so absorbed in her friend's illness that the New York workshop seems unimportant and Carrie sees Bridget off on the train without a qualm. When Carrie next goes to visit Grace in the hospital, she's told the woman has been moved to a nursing home. Carrie is very upset, but Grace reassures her. As Carrie watches Grace's belongings being carried out of her house, she feels that familiar sense of loss. Sharon understands and is kind and supportive. Carrie makes a small gesture of goodwill toward Sharon when she brings her some of Grace's flowers. Al and Phyllis also announce their engagement. When Bridget returns from her workshop, Carrie can tell her that all is well.

Carrie stops fighting the changes in her life with the help of an elderly woman who knows how to listen and how to accept whatever life deals her. Carrie tells her own story and it is well written, with perceptive characterizations. Children whose parents are remarrying or whose classmates are going through family realignments will empathize with Carrie's resistance, anger, fear, and loneliness.

Ages 9-12

**Also available in:**
No other form known

**525**

**Reader, Dennis J.**

## Coming Back Alive

Random House, Inc., 1981.
(233 pages)

---

*MOURNING, STAGES OF*
*NATURE: Living in Harmony with*
*REALITY, ESCAPING*
  *Boy-girl relationships*
  *Death: of father*
  *Death: of mother*
  *Divorce: of parents*
  *Dropout, school*
  *Resourcefulness*

---

Bridget and Dylan are both the only children of affluent parents and live in a "sweet expensive" suburb of San Francisco. Now in high school, they have been best friends and "fellow confessors" since second grade.

Besides being bright, both are attractive and accomplished. About a year ago, however, the "cold winds" started blowing through Dylan's life. His father moved away, taking another woman with him, and his mother acquired a live-in boyfriend. Now Dylan believes "that only two kinds of people populated the earth, the beat-up ones and their beaters." Since he doesn't want to be a beater but can't let himself be beaten anymore, the only alternative is to form a "special shell" around himself. Then the winds blow over Bridget. She is home alone when the news comes that her parents have been killed in an automobile accident caused by a drunk driver. She spends the first days wandering from room to room, listening to the voices that seem to have been soaked up by the walls and furniture. Then Aunt Charlene arrives on the scene, followed by Mrs. Pace, a school counselor; both try to persuade her to forget the past. Bridget resents these people's attempts to put her life in order. When Charlene announces that she will be selling the house and taking Bridget back to Santa Barbara, Bridget is desperate. She turns to Dylan, agreeing to accompany him on the escape he has already planned to the Primitive Area of Trinity National Forest in northern California. Leaving their homes secretly one night, the two travel by bus, hitchhike, walk, and run from the police until they reach the mountain wilderness. There they find a secluded side canyon and build their shelter. They live there, foraging and killing wild animals for food, until they are spotted by campers. Soon after, they find a discarded newspaper with an article captioned WILD YOUTHS REPORTED IN MOUNTAINS. They are shot at and pursued until they find another canyon that can only be reached by a hole in the face of a steep, slippery rock wall. They name this new home Secret Creek and come to think of it as their own "private paradise." In the days that follow, their brother-sister existence gives way to acknowledged physical attraction. But Dylan insists their relationship return to platonic, since a pregnancy would mean returning to civilization. Bridget cooperates, but knows from this time on that Dylan is afraid of her, afraid to love anyone. As summer moves into autumn, they perfect their deer-snaring method and are able to store away a good supply of food for the colder days ahead. Now they have the spare time to sit and debate what to do with themselves. Bridget has begun to question their staying forever in the mountains, but Dylan insists he will never leave. Then a gentle, sensitive stranger comes briefly to Secret Creek, bidding them to "forgive the people you love for not being what you want them to be. . . . Because, you know, the whole business of living is never what you want it to be or what it should be." A short time later, while hunting outside the canyon, Bridget is captured by six campers who intend to take her back to the civilized world. Dylan rescues her, but not before she has realized that "not all people are fanged monsters." She returns to the canyon knowing she cannot spend the rest of her life in the mountains. She must return to the world. Dylan, however, with living parents who continue to betray him, will not return with her. They part, each accepting the other's decision.

The flowing, lyrical style of Bridget's first-person narrative sustains this romantic adventure and keeps it believable. The characters of Bridget and Dylan are well developed and compelling; readers will share their pain and understand their differing reactions to it. The book's emotional intensity could be therapeutic for readers who have experienced similar misfortunes. Although Dylan's conflict is not resolved, there is hope that someday he will be able to "bring the mountains down to the town." The ending provides good discussion material about an idealistic versus a practical approach to life.

Ages 12 and up

**Also available in:**
Paperbound—*Coming Back Alive*
New American Library

## 526

**Redpath, Ann**

### Jim Boen: A Man of Opposites

Black/white photographs courtesy of James Boen family.
Creative Education, Inc., 1980.
(48 pages)

---

*PARAPLEGIA*
  *Courage, meaning of*
  *Wheelchair, dependence on*

---

Jim Boen lives a full life as a coach, statistician, teacher, hunter, husband, and father—in a wheelchair. On October 15, 1951, Jim, a dedicated and skilled Dartmouth University athlete of nineteen, broke his neck in a gymnastics accident. He had to stay in the hospital for months, two holes drilled in the outer layer of his skull so that tongs could be inserted and thirty-pound weights hung from them to stretch his neck and relieve pressure on his spinal cord. He was placed in a "foster frame," a canvas tray stretched over metal pipes, spending two hours facing the floor and then two hours facing the ceiling. Friends visited him often and helped him write letters cautioning his parents back in Wisconsin not to expect too much too fast. Although doctors did not hold out much hope that Jim would ever walk again, he kept his parents informed of each bit of progress: using his hands, regaining feeling in his toes, being able to sleep in a real bed again, brushing his own teeth. Although Jim professed to realize he might never recover, he didn't really believe his own words. He dreamed of someday playing volleyball and swinging on the high bar again. After five months in the hospital, he entered a rehabilitation center, but his condition didn't improve much. He returned home to Wisconsin where, with his parents' help, he established a daily routine. He spent eight years trying unsuccessfully to walk. After he earned his B.A. in mathematics by transferring credits from a nearby college to Dartmouth, he moved from his parents' home to the University of Illinois where he met and married Dorothy Frey. Jim went on for his M.A. and Ph.D. while Dorothy finished her degree in education and began teaching. They moved around the country several times, eventually settling in Minnesota where today Jim teaches biometry, the study of statistics as applied to health research. They've adopted a son and daughter and Dorothy, originally a musician, has returned to her violin and plays professionally. In addition to his teaching schedule, Jim also hunts and travels by himself. He organized wheelchair

basketball in Minnesota and coached it for five years. He also likes speaking to groups about the lives of disabled people. "He thinks it's important for people to know that disabled people have feelings and desires just like everyone else."

This undramatic, realistic biography of a courageous athlete who became paraplegic tells how one person came to terms with his disability. Photographs flesh out a story that will appeal to and inform both disabled and nondisabled readers. The author introduces the book by asking, "Who is this man who, after his injury, refused to be treated like a victim?" The question is satisfyingly answered.

Ages 9 and up

**Also available in:**
No other form known

## 527

**Reece, Colleen L.**

### The Outsider

Black/white illustrations by Furan Illustrators.
Crestwood House, Inc., 1981.
(47 pages)

---

*BELONGING*
*SIBLING: Relationships*
  *Honesty/Dishonesty*
  *Rejection: parental*
  *Self-esteem*
  *Twins: fraternal*

---

At seventeen, Susan Ackley has heard a million times that she and her twin, Sally, don't look at all alike. Susan thinks of herself as the ugly twin, the overweight one, the outsider. Her mother thinks everything Sally does is wonderful; her father, to whom Susan was close, died recently, just before their high school graduation. There's little money and their mother has no work experience, so it's up to the twins to find jobs. Susan's dream is to be a nurse, partly because nursing would never interest Sally and so there would be no competition from her. Susan begs her mother to borrow the money for her to start a two-year LPN program, but her mother says they can't afford it—even when Susan points out bitterly that the graduation clothes bought for Sally would have paid for her first year. Jeff Kincaid, a good-looking college sophomore, comes to take Sally out, but meets Susan in front of the house. Since Sally's not ready yet, he drives Susan to the library and they sit in the car and talk. He's impressed with her desire to be a nurse, and they so enjoy talking that he is late picking up Sally. One of Sally's friends has seen Jeff and Susan together and calls Sally immediately; she's furious. The next day Jeff sends Susan roses with a note wishing her well in her dream of nursing school. Sally gets Susan a job where she works, at a clothing store, with the understanding that she doesn't want anyone to know that Susan is her sister. One day Susan overhears two of the girls talking about a little racket they have going. When a new outfit comes in that one of the girls likes, they see that it gets soiled. It's then put on a special sale rack where the clerk who likes it can snap it up at a reduced price. Susan is horrified to hear that Sally is the ringleader of the operation. She has no one to talk to but Jeff, so she calls him and he suggests they go out. She tells him what she's discovered and cries on his shoulder. He says the only solution is to confront Sally and ask her to stop. Susan does this and, although Sally is furious at first, Susan notices that the rack of sale clothes diminishes. One day, just before closing time, Susan and Sally see two people stealing jewelry. Susan boldly dashes after them, but is knocked aside and hits her head. Sally tackles one of the robbers and another clerk gets the other. The store's owner, who happens to be Jeff Kincaid's uncle, gives each of the girls a thousand-dollar reward. Susan promptly decides to use the money for her first year of nursing school. Sally says she's going too. She felt so useless when she saw Susan hurt and wants to learn how to help people. To her surprise, Susan finds that the idea of her sister going into her field no longer bothers her. She looks forward to the two of them being real twins, neither one an outsider.

One of a series of high-interest, easy reading books that deal with teenagers' contemporary concerns, this story describes a young woman's struggle to build her self-esteem and achieve her goals. She is handicapped by the death of her beloved father, her mother's bias toward her twin, and feelings of inadequacy encouraged by her more popular, outgoing sister. Although the writing is awkward and the dialogue somewhat dated, the book will find readers to appreciate its brevity and easy reading level. The story could prompt discussion.

Ages 12 and up

**Also available in:**
Paperbound—*The Outsider*
Crestwood House, Inc.

## 528

Relf, Patricia

**That New Baby!**

Color illustrations by DyAnne DiSalvo.
Golden Press, 1980.
(21 pages counted)

---

*SIBLING: New Baby*

---

When Elizabeth's parents bring her new baby brother home from the hospital, she is waiting on the porch with Grandma. Elizabeth doesn't understand why everyone is making such a fuss when "all Mikey ever does is eat and sleep and cry." But when Mikey is old enough for her to take him places, Elizabeth begins to enjoy being his big sister. She likes teaching him things. Still, most of the time Elizabeth thinks her baby brother is just a lot of trouble. He makes messes when he eats and always seems to need his diaper changed. Furthermore, Elizabeth has to walk around on tiptoe whenever Mikey takes a nap. One day while Mommy is resting, Elizabeth tries to entertain Mikey by setting up her racing car track inside his playpen. But when she turns on the power, he gets frightened and begins to cry. Mommy, very upset, says Mikey could have hurt himself! She sends Elizabeth to her room. Elizabeth slams the door, shouting that she hates being a big sister and hates that

"dumb baby." She tells herself she will stay in her room "for always!" Later, when her parents knock on the door, she refuses to let them in. For the rest of the day Elizabeth stays in her room. After a while she begins to feel lonely. Then, suddenly, she hears Mikey crying and her mother calling her to look in on him. Forgetting about her anger, she runs to the baby's room. "Poor Mikey," she thinks. He is probably lonely too. But his big sister knows exactly what to do. She makes a funny face and he promptly stops crying. At bedtime that night Elizabeth and her parents apologize to each other. Elizabeth even admits that she really does like being Mikey's big sister. "Mikey thinks you're the best big sister in the world," says Dad. Then he adds, "And so do we!"

A little girl endures the emotional ups and downs of adjusting to a new baby brother. Because Elizabeth is no longer the center of attention, she has to struggle with her jealousy and hurt feelings. In the end, however, she feels secure and happy, her importance in the family reinforced by her parents' apology and praise. This story should motivate discussion about a familiar situation. Bright illustrations accent the humor.

Ages 4-7

**Also available in:**
No other form known

## 529

Reuter, Margaret

**My Mother Is Blind**

Color photographs by Philip Lanier.
Children's Press, Inc., 1979.
(31 pages)

---

*BLINDNESS*
  *Family: unity*

---

A mother and father and their son, about eight, have prepared a picnic lunch to take to the park. The mother has recently gone blind. She must hold her husband's arm as she walks. When she first became blind, the boy and his father had to do all the housework because the mother was sad and fearful. Then a special teacher began coming to the house. He taught Mother new ways to perform household tasks. Now she listens to recipes on a tape recorder and is able to cook and bake. She cleans and even does the grocery shopping again. She reads Braille and labels foods with Braille labels. She uses a special cane to walk outside, and at the park she distinguishes each plant by its smell and the shape of its leaves. Various sounds help her know where she is and what and who might be around her. The boy is glad his mother has learned to do so much, but "I wish she could see."

A boy describes his mother's and the family's adjustment to her blindness. The emphasis is on the woman's strengths and growing independence. Photographs illustrate the steps of her progress; illustrations of a Braille book and of writing in Braille with a stylus are of special interest. The text can be easily understood by young children.

## 530

### Reuter, Margaret

### You Can Depend on Me

Color photographs by Joe Weinshel and Seri Swenson.
Children's Press, Inc., 1980.
(31 pages)

---

*RESPONSIBILITY: Accepting*
  *Chores*
  *Helping*
  *Sibling: younger*

---

Dan's older brother, David, gets to help their mother paint the lawn furniture and their father fix his workbench drawer. Dad never tells David he's in the way. But although Dan helps in small ways—picking up little branches in the yard, stirring paint for Mom, or holding the flashlight for Dad—he never gets to do anything he considers very important. And he's always making mistakes and getting yelled at. When he helps his mother weed the garden, he pulls up some flowers by mistake. His father finds his rusted dump truck in the grass. When Dan borrows David's truck, he returns it with sand stuck in the wheels. One day Dan offers to go to the store to buy nuts so his mother, who's just started mixing up his favorite cookies, can put nuts into them. On the way home, he stops to talk to Mrs. Beck, who offers to let Dan walk her dog, Honey. By the time he gets home, the cookies are already baked—without nuts. Although his mother praises him for successfully buying the nuts and getting the correct change, Dan decides that the next time he's running an errand, he won't stop to take Honey for a walk. Then Dan learns that the Becks are going on a weekend trip and will be leaving Honey at a kennel. He offers to take care of the dog while they're gone. The Becks ask Dan's parents if they can depend on the boy, and Dan wonders if his parents will tell them about the times he has been careless. But his parents assure the Becks that Dan will do his very best. Relieved and proud, Dan resolves not to disappoint them or the Becks. "They can depend on me."

When faced with a welcome responsibility, young Dan, with the warm support of his parents, is determined to be dependable and trustworthy. This first-person account of a boy with good intentions and little follow-through is a bit stilted, but could lead to useful discussion about what responsibility means. The boy in the photographs appears older than is implied in the text.

Ages 6-9

## 531

### Richter, Alice and Laura Joffe Numeroff

### You Can't Put Braces on Spaces

Color illustrations by Laura Joffe Numeroff.
Greenwillow Books, 1979.
(56 pages)

---

*ORTHODONTIA*
  *Family: relationships*

---

A little boy wants three things for his birthday: ice skates, a Hank Aaron baseball, and braces. His older brother, Neil, needs braces and soon will get them, numerous friends have them—they make kids look older. He and Neil are both examined by the orthodontist, Dr. Sherman, but the smaller boy has no front teeth. "You can't put braces on spaces," Dr. Sherman says. He does think, however, that someday the boy will need braces. On Neil's next visit, a nurse X-rays his teeth and then traces drawings from some of them. A small tray of white, gluey alginate is prepared, and a plaster-of-paris mold from the alginate imprint creates a perfect impression of Neil's teeth. Back home the younger brother wistfully wraps a strip of aluminum foil around his teeth. The next week, Neil and his brother learn there are many different kinds of braces and that people wear them for varying lengths of time. Neil's must be worn for two-and-a-half years. Some people need rubber bands and others have night braces, but not Neil. Neil feels nervous the day Dr. Sherman is to apply his braces, but the dentist is reassuring and explains procedures while he works. First he cements brackets to Neil's front teeth and thin silver rings with little tubes to the back teeth. He puts silver wires through the tubes and attaches these to the brackets. When the wires are tightened every few weeks, they will slowly, a little at a time, move the teeth into their proper position. It takes nearly two hours to attach the braces. Neil's mouth is a bit sore and he feels self-conscious at first. His mother reminds him of the time the barber cut his hair too short; Neil expected his friends to tease him, but nobody did. Neil's little brother puts on his aluminum-foil braces and they all laugh. Neil learns that he mustn't chew bubble gum or sticky stuff, he must be cautious eating apples, and he has to brush his teeth carefully. Shortly thereafter, the boys' mother decides she will get braces to straighten her two front teeth. When their father complains that he will soon be the only one in the family without them, his younger son says, "Don't worry, Dad. There's always plenty of aluminum foil."

This delightful first-person account informs young readers in simple terms about the application of braces, the reasons for them, and the restrictions they entail. Children are reminded that, although braces may seem desirable, they can be uncomfortable and cause some self-consciousness at first. The self-consciousness soon passes, however, and the end result is worth the discomfort. Cartoonlike illustrations add humor and warmth.

**R**

Ages 5-9

**Also available in:**
Cassette—*You Can't Put Braces on Spaces*
Westport Communications

Filmstrip—*You Can't Put Braces on Spaces*
Westport Communications

## 532

Richter, Elizabeth

### The Teenage Hospital Experience: You Can Handle It!

Black/white photographs by the author.
Coward, McCann & Geoghegan, Inc., 1982.
(128 pages)

---

HOSPITAL, GOING TO
  Accidents
  Anorexia nervosa
  Birth defects
  Cancer
  Cardiac conditions
  Cleft lip/palate
  Diabetes
  Fractures
  Illnesses: being ill
  Limbs, abnormal or missing
  Scoliosis
  Surgery

---

Hospitalization is often a special ordeal for teenagers, for whom strength, beauty, and independence tend to be extremely important. In these interviews with hospitalized teenagers, Michael talks about his injured pancreas, the IV in his arm, and the difficulties of talking to his female doctor. Debbie is discovering that having diabetes isn't as scary as she thought it was, although she misses her family and worries a little about how she'll manage once she leaves the hospital. Frank has been in and out of hospitals all his life because of his osteomyelitis. Chris is adjusting to the fact that since his cliff-climbing accident he will always wear a brace on his paralyzed leg; he is gradually becoming less hostile and demanding. Karen has a rare form of cancer, currently in remission. She still manages to be cheerful and says it helps to know what to expect in a hospital. Edith has a lot of questions for the orthopedic surgeon who will be doing corrective surgery on her leg. James is afraid of waking up to great pain after his upcoming surgery. After her corrective surgery for scoliosis, Lourdes must wear a body cast for eight or nine months. She worries about having a scar and about her ability to have babies later on. John urges patients to ask questions of their doctors and to be aware of treatment procedures. "If two nurses come into your room within ten minutes of each other to give you what seems to be the same medication, ask about it." Peter is about to leave the hospital after radiation treatment for cancer. He and his mother share their feelings and talk about dying. Emmett, whose blood clots excessively, warns patients to question doctors, who like to use big words. He is in a teaching hospital, so he's seen daily by medical students as well as doctors. For him, the worst part of hospitalization is boredom. Lynn has been hospitalized for anorexia nervosa. She feared the hospital because she knew the staff would make her eat and she doesn't want

to get "fat." Unbearable pelvic pain brought Gina to the hospital, where she was diagnosed as having pelvic inflammatory disease (PID), the result of gonorrhea untreated in the early stages. The worst aspects of hospitalization for Gina are the IV and the loneliness. "I feel so old. . . . I was pregnant too. I want these girls coming up now to know. . . . a saline abortion is very painful. You'll never forget it, never." In interviews with hospital professionals, Dr. Jaffe discusses admission procedures, Linda Larson talks about getting to know your nurses, and Dr. Ellis discusses teenagers' relationships with their surgeons. Dr. Raphaely reassures and informs patients about anesthesia. Dr. Showalter says hospital patients often have reduced sexual desire, fewer interests, fewer fantasies, but things usually return to normal when the person recovers. It's important to realize that it's common to feel depressed while hospitalized or ill.

Interviews with hospitalized teenagers and hospital professionals offer readers a wealth of information and advice. A position statement on hospital care for adolescents and a list of potential questions that a hospitalized teenager might ask are included in the back of the book, as are a glossary of medical terms and an index. The interviews and photographs are graphic, well presented, and interesting. Both patients and professionals are represented by an excellent cross-section of ages, sexes, and races. A fine book for any teenager, this will be particularly valuable for those facing hospitalization.

Ages 12 and up

**Also available in:**
No other form known

## 533

Riley, Jocelyn

### Only My Mouth Is Smiling

William Morrow & Company, Inc., 1982.
(222 pages)

---

FAMILY: Relationships
MENTAL ILLNESS: of Parent
  Boy-girl relationships: dating
  School: classmate relationships
  Violence

---

Thirteen-year-old Merle Carlson has learned how to paste on a smile that has nothing to do with how she's feeling inside, a handy device when you have a frequent mental patient for a mother. Elaine Carlson has stayed well for so long this time, however, that Merle and her younger brother and sister are beginning to believe she's cured. She has kept the same job for nearly two years and has been paying rent all this time to Grandma. Her face is even fairly clear; it is always covered with "red zits" just before she has a nervous breakdown. The children are not, therefore, prepared for what happens one Saturday morning in July when Grandma gets home from having her hair done. She and their mother get into a fight over the rent money that culminates in Grandma pushing Mrs. Carlson onto the floor and kicking her. Even though the scene has been violent, the children leave the house with their mother thinking they are just accompanying her on her usual Saturday escape to the movie theater. They end up at the Chicago bus depot buying one-way tickets to northern Wisconsin. After riding all afternoon and night, they finally arrive at Lake Lune, where last spring their mother made the down payment on a lakefront lot. Mrs. Carlson buys a tent, a few clothes, and other necessities. With the exception of a once-a-week hike into town for supplies, the family stays in this secluded spot for the rest of the summer. Their lives are uninterrupted except for one visit from Grandma, who has traced their whereabouts. The women have a loud argument during which the children feel torn in their loyalties to both adults. Merle later wonders why, "if Grandma is so sane," she can't see that "she always sets Mother off with the things she says." As autumn approaches, Mrs. Carlson rents a small house in town. At least now they have running water. The children sleep on a mattress and box-spring set left on the floor of one of the bedrooms. Their mother finds a part-time job as bookkeeper for a feed-and-grain company and brings home bags of free oatmeal for them to eat. On the first day of school, Merle walks to the junior-senior high feeling happy about the few hours she will have each day to live her own private life. She makes friends and meets Ricky Ellesen, to whom she's very attracted. Eventually she discovers that Ricky's apparent interest in her is only his way of making a former girlfriend jealous. One day Mr. Hall, the school counselor, calls Merle in for a conference. He explains that he has had a letter from her grandmother detailing her mother's mental problems and expressing concern for the children's welfare. Reluctant to confide anything that might get back to her mother, Merle does her best to make him think everything is fine. Then Merle returns home after the Homecoming Dance to find her mother sitting alone in the dark, smoking two cigarettes at one time, and talking about the evil forces that wish her ill. Her skin lately has become "pasty white" with "big red zits popping out," so Merle knows something bad is about to happen. Elaine behaves strangely all weekend and on Sunday afternoon Merle calls her grandmother; returning to Chicago seems "the least worst of all the possible terrible solutions." Grandma promises that she and the children will go to family counseling sessions while Elaine is in the hospital. By Monday morning, Mrs. Carlson is completely irrational. Early in the morning, a social worker comes to the door with two policemen. They take Mrs. Carlson away in a straitjacket. Shortly afterward, Grandma arrives to take the children home. She explains that part of the reason for their mother's relapses is her reluctance to take anti-psychotic drugs. When she stops taking them she can't sleep, her skin breaks out, and she eventually has a breakdown. Even with this explanation, there are many questions left in Merle's mind. She can only hope the family therapy sessions will help them all understand mental illness a little better.

Three children live at the mercy of their mother's eccentric whims and occasionally psychotic behavior in this serious, believable first-person narrative. They can't argue with her because she becomes irrational, and they can't always turn to their grandmother because her brutality with her daughter only makes things worse. They know that confiding in anyone or acknowledging that anything is wrong will ultimately reinforce their mother's paranoia. The only alternative is to pretend that everything is fine. The story offers considerable insight into the trauma of being part of a family touched by mental illness. Merle's tone is rather matter-of-fact, never maudlin, but the terror of her life comes through clearly.

Ages 12-14

**Also available in:**
No other form known

## 534

**Rinaldi, Ann**

**Promises Are for Keeping**
Walker and Company, 1982.
(187 pages)

---

*LOVE, MEANING OF*
*RELATIVES: Living in Home of*
*Abortion*
*Ambivalence, feelings of*
*Boy-girl relationships*
*Communication: rumor*
*Rebellion*
*Sibling: relationships*

R

---

Fourteen-year-old Nicole (Nicki) DeBonis lives with her older brother Tony, a popular high school football coach, and his wife, Carol. She often spends weekends with her other brother, Larry, a doctor who shares Nicki's guardianship with Tony; their mother died at Nicki's birth and their father died of a heart attack several years ago. Nicki is dating Eric, one of Tony's star football players. Both young people have heard rumors about Tony and Eric's divorced mother. They dated in high school, and the gossips say that Tony is really Eric's father. Nicki's best friend, Meredith, wants to sleep with her boyfriend and manages to wring a promise from Nicki to get her some birth control pills from Larry's office. Then Tony forbids Eric and Nicki to go out the night before a big football game. They defy him and go to a local pizza place where Eric fights with boys from the other team when they taunt him about being Tony's son. Soon after, to Nicki's shocked surprise, Eric is picked up for selling drugs. When she disobeys Tony's orders not to see Eric while his drug case is pending, Tony grounds her. About that time, Larry's nurse catches Nicki taking the birth control pills for Meredith. Now Nicki is in trouble with both brothers. Larry demands the name of the friend she got the pills for, and when Nicki won't tell he forbids her to enter his home or office again. An angry Tony tells her, "You trample on everybody who loves you. You always did. Ever since you were a little kid." He adds that he's not Eric's father and warns her not to break the bonds that tie their family together. Nicki, who had at times thought she hated her brothers, now is filled with confusion. At her new job as a candy striper at the hospital, she meets some of Larry's patients and discovers how highly respected and loved he is. Largely due to Tony's taking custody of him, Eric is placed on probation. Tony tells the boy he isn't his father, although he wishes he were. For Nicki's fifteenth birthday Larry, Tony, and Carol take her out to dinner. Larry gives her a silver bracelet, telling Nicki he loves her and wishes she'd let him back

305

in her life. Then Meredith asks Larry to give her an abortion. He refuses and asks Nicki to talk to her friend. Before she can, Meredith has her abortion at a clinic with a poor reputation. She almost dies and has probably become sterile. Larry blames himself for handling the situation badly. Then Tony asks Nicki for her help. He wants her to reconcile with Larry. He also wants her to encourage Eric to choose the out-of-state college that has accepted him but that he is thinking of turning down so he can stay near Nicki. Nicki accuses Eric of caring for her just because she's Tony's sister. Hurt, he replies, "You don't even recognize it when somebody thinks a lot of you. When they do, you're rotten to them." They declare their love for each other. For the first time in months, Nicki goes to spend a weekend with Larry. She urges him to stop blaming himself for what happened to Meredith, to accept life's imperfections instead of railing against them. He has recently broken up with his girlfriend, Molly, partly because he couldn't shake his feelings of guilt. Larry serves as "parallel parent" to a young, institutionalized boy named Jeremy, who is to return to his own home in two weeks. Nicki asks Jeremy to go with her by train to Philadelphia to visit Molly. Her motives: if Jeremy travels out of state and misses his curfew, he will have to remain in the state training school another six to eight months, more time for him to see Larry. Nicki believes Jeremy needs more of Larry. She also hopes that Molly, who will have to bring them both home, will reconcile with Larry. When the three return to town, Nicki calls Larry to hint about his inviting Molly over to thank her for helping them out. But an angry Larry tells Nicki to go straight to Tony's house that evening. He doesn't want to see her again. Puzzled, Nicki replays their conversation in her mind. Convinced that something odd is happening, she runs to Larry's house, overhears people inside demanding drugs and money, and calls the police. As she waits anxiously for Larry's rescue, Nicki realizes that "you have to be nice to people you love because you don't know when you walk out of the house in the morning, if you'll ever see them again!" Larry is saved and Nicki now knows that love is stronger than anything, that her love for her brothers cannot be explained or argued away.

In this rich, powerful sequel to *Term Paper,* Nicki tests the limits of her relationship with her guardian brothers. She is both drawn to and repelled by their authority and strength, and her confusion leads her to acts of rebellion she often hadn't planned and knows are foolhardy. Nicki's first-person descriptions of her ambivalent feelings reach to the heart of much adolescent agony. At various times she perceives her brothers as siblings, parents, friends, teachers, role models, heroes, even lovers, changing views that buffet her complex emotions until all three characters deepen their understanding of family relationships. Readers of the earlier novel will be eager to meet these old friends again.

Ages 12 and up

**Also available in:**
Paperbound—*Promises Are for Keeping*
Bantam Books, Inc.

## 535

**Rinaldi, Ann**

**Term Paper**

Walker and Company, 1980.
(202 pages)

---

*DEATH: of Father*
*SIBLING: Relationships*
  *Alcoholism: adult*
  *Family: relationships*
  *Guilt, feelings of*
  *Love, meaning of*
  *Rebellion*

---

When Nicki DeBonis's brother Tony, a substitute teacher, takes over her freshman English literature class, he allows students to choose their own topics for term papers—except for Nicki, who is required to write about the death of her father. Tony wants Nicki to rid herself of some of the grief she's been carrying since their father died six months ago. She won't talk about it to him or to her other brother, Larry, a doctor, and she's just received three warning notices about her poor schoolwork. Tony is eighteen years older than Nicki, and Larry is fifteen years older. Their father disappeared for three years when the boys were eleven and fourteen. After his return their mother became pregnant, and she died when Nicki was born. Although Nicki had always lived with her father, Tony actually raised her. As Nicki tries to write her paper, she thinks back to the events that led to her father's death. She remembers when Tony returned from Vietnam, insisting that Nicki treat her father with respect, although he has never been a real father to her. He had a heart attack the year before, and Tony warns her never to upset him. When Aunt Ro, Nicki's mother's sister, returns to her old mansion after two years in Europe, she tells Nicki that her father saw other women even while her mother was pregnant with her. Then Carol, Tony's wife, who began drinking a little wine when Tony was in Vietnam, begins to drink more heavily. She's just discovered she's pregnant. Worried that Tony will discover Carol's drinking, Nicki disposes of her empty bottles. When Tony finds out that Aunt Ro has been feeding Nicki's resentment toward her father, he forbids her to visit anymore. He explains that his own resentment of his father led him to turn down a career in pro football because he knew it would hurt his father; he doesn't want Nicki to ruin her life with resentment too. Then Nicki overhears her father asking Tony to offer Larry's girlfriend, Ruth, five thousand dollars to leave Larry and move to Florida. Their father doesn't like Ruth because she's divorced and has a small son. Tony refuses to meddle. One day, Nicki finds Carol drunk. After a fight during which Carol slaps her hard, Nicki puts Carol to bed and then goes to tell Aunt Ro she can't come over anymore. But while she's gone Carol wakes up, tries to find Nicki to apologize to her, and falls down the stairs. She loses the baby. Meanwhile, Aunt Ro leaves suddenly for Europe, unwilling to worsen family tensions for Nicki. Nicki's father, a realtor, attempts to sell her house as she's authorized and so remove her permanently from their lives. He's also succeeded in convincing Ruth, who really loved Larry, that she'd ruin his life if she married him; in response, Larry is deeply depressed and taking pills. Nicki and her father talk. He wants to know how she feels about him; she can only say she loves him sometimes. When he makes disparaging remarks about Larry, Nicki defends her brother. Her father maintains that he loved her mother and that his leaving the family actually made Tony the strong person he is today. Nicki responds that he has hurt all three of them. He starts to leave the room, collapses, and dies of a heart attack. Nicki decides never to tell anyone she was arguing with her father just before he died. Tony allows Virginia, their father's companion, to complete the real estate work, even giving her a key to the house. Distressed, Nicki runs off to Aunt Ro's empty house where she finds a box that her aunt left for her. In it are love letters to Nicki's father from Virginia—the woman he was seeing regularly while her mother was pregnant with her. Her brothers find Nicki hysterical, throwing things and screaming abuse, calling Larry a junkie and berating Tony for tolerating Virginia. The next morning Larry is gone, but to clarify his intentions he has left a half-bottle of his pills for Nicki to destroy. She does, with relief. Six months later, Nicki, Tony, and Carol are living in Nicki's father's house. For three weeks after she hands in her term paper, Tony ignores her. They finally talk. Tony asks Nicki if she still hates her father. She doesn't. He helps her see that her father's death was not her fault; his health was precarious. He gives her an A on the paper.

As she writes a term paper about the events leading up to her father's death, Nicki relives the story in an attempt to deal with feelings she has repressed. This first-person narrative is powerfully written, with strongly delineated characters and great intensity of feeling. Nicki, living with her father and yet tied to brothers so much older than she that they function almost as parents, is the focus or recipient of some thoroughly adult emotions. Tony expects her to grow up, to act mature; yet he, Carol, and Larry hover over her, unsure of how far to take their authority. Tony is almost a caricature of integrity, yet he demands a sort of dishonesty from Nicki with respect to her father. She is never to tell her father what she really thinks, and so she remains a resented stranger whose sudden death fills her with guilt. Few readers will forget this book quickly. The story continues in the sequel, *Promises Are for Keeping*.

Ages 12 and up

**Also available in:**
Paperbound—*Term Paper*
Bantam Books, Inc.

**536**

Riskind, Mary L.

## Apple Is My Sign

Houghton Mifflin Company, 1981.
(146 pages)

---

*DEAFNESS*
*FRIENDSHIP: Making Friends*
  *Change: accepting*
  *Communication: importance of*
  *Education: special*
  *Family: relationships*
  *Schools, private*

---

In Philadelphia in 1899, ten-year-old Harry Apple is beginning his second week at The Bertie School for the Deaf. Harry's parents own a farm in rural Pennsylvania. They are also deaf, as are his brother and sisters. His father, proud and independent, is unschooled. Because he mistrusts most hearing people, he wants Harry to have an education in a school with other deaf children. At first Harry is frightened and homesick, but when he makes friends he begins to enjoy himself. He learns to play football and, because of his artistic talents, is given training in drawing and tailoring. After the Thanksgiving football game he travels by train to his hometown to spend the Christmas holidays with his family. At first it seems odd to Harry to be back home. His parents treat him more as a grown-up, his little sisters are shy with him, and his brother has taken over his chores. The end of harvest has come, a time for the family to take apples to town to be pressed into cider. Harry is pleased to meet his hearing friend Freckles in town, especially when Freckles shows interest in learning the sign-language alphabet. Several days later the town hosts a "harvest fair," a day for displaying sewing and produce and for judging preserves and canned goods. Special events for the children include a magic show and a spell-down. This time when Harry sees Freckles, Freckles ignores him. Puzzled, Harry goes to see the magic show. He sees Freckles again at the spell-down, sitting in the audience, finger spelling the contest words to a participant friend. Angrily, Harry realizes that the boys are cheating. The commotion he makes catches the attention both of the judges and of his own father, who thinks Harry is in on the cheating and lashes out furiously at him. When he ignores Harry's attempts to explain, Harry flees. He starts following the railroad tracks and then notices that Freckles is trailing him. Freckles tries to apologize, but Harry slugs him. Freckles continues to follow, suddenly tackling Harry and rolling him away from the tracks just as a freight train he couldn't hear thunders past. Harry's father appears, expressing his gratitude to Freckles and explaining to his son that he has learned of his innocence in the spell-down episode. After the Christmas holidays, Harry must return to school. Freckles comes to the train depot to see him off. He offers Harry a cat's-eye marble, but Harry is still confused and embarrassed over the cheating incident and refuses the gift. Freckles explains that the finger spelling was to be a joke on the judges, not an insult to Harry. He offers the marble again and Harry accepts, feeling that he has made his

R

first true friend among the hearing. He is eager to return to school to tell his friends there of his vacation adventures.

In this well-developed story, a deaf boy in turn-of-the-century Philadelphia adapts to a private school and makes a good friend. Harry Apple, a member of an all-deaf family, is an appealing, courageous boy, and the story, while not minimizing the problems of deafness, emphasizes the essential normality of deaf people. In a twelve-page foreword the author, the hearing child of deaf parents, explains various sign languages—signing, finger spelling, pantomime. She describes some of the complexities of each system and the constant evolution of sign language. In the story, she features the system taught her by her parents.

Ages 10-14

Also available in:
Braille—*Apple Is My Sign*
Library of Congress (NLSBPH)

Disc—*Apple Is My Sign*
Library of Congress (NLSBPH)

## 537

**Robinet, Harriette Gillem**

## Ride the Red Cycle

Black/white illustrations by David Brown.
Houghton Mifflin Company, 1980.
(34 pages)

---

*HANDICAPS: Multiple*
*PERSEVERANCE*
 *Brain injury*
 *Courage, meaning of*
 *Sibling: relationships*
 *Success*
 *Wheelchair, dependence on*

---

Eleven-year-old Jerome Johnson wears thick eyeglasses, special shoes, and leg braces. He speaks slowly and his speech is slurred. Because his legs have been paralyzed since a viral infection left him with brain damage at the age of two, Jerome has spent most of his life in a wheelchair. Now he has convinced himself that he can make his legs work again. He has shared his secret dream of owning a three-wheel cycle with his older sister, Tilly, who helps him ask Mama and Papa about buying one. Mama, who Jerome knows fusses and fumes to hide her fears for him, is angered by his request, but Papa is sympathetic. He asks Mama what the physical therapists say, and she answers softly that they think a cycle would strengthen Jerome's legs. So Papa takes Jerome and Tilly to buy a large, red, three-wheel cycle. He puts a special seat on it and alters the pedals. The first time Jerome sits on the cycle, the whole neighborhood comes to watch him. His legs tremble, he's nervous, and he drools, but Jerome cannot make the pedals go. His audience slowly drifts away. Every day Jerome sits on the cycle for hours, but nothing happens. One day he has an idea. He asks Tilly to take him up by the alley where the pavement slopes to the street. Here the cycle can build some momentum, and his legs can learn the motions of pedaling. All summer long Tilly takes Jerome to this secret place, and little by little his legs begin to work as the muscles grow stronger. Jerome has another secret

too, something that not even Tilly knows about, something that he practices nightly in his room. Summer ends, and the neighborhood plans a Labor Day block party. One of the events is a talent show, and Tilly enters Jerome. At the time of his performance, she brings Jerome out to the sidewalk on his cycle. Slowly he pedals to the middle of the block. There he stops, bows, and climbs off the cycle. Standing alone, he haltingly stammers a thank-you to Tilly, Papa, and Mama. Then he takes the few cautious steps toward his wheelchair, showing family and friends what he has practiced late at night. His family is ecstatic, his neighbors overjoyed. For Jerome, it is the greatest victory of his life—so far!

A brain-damaged boy makes great progress because of his courage and determination. Jerome's handicaps, limitations, and perseverance are all realistically portrayed, and readers will empathize with him and cheer him on. Especially well described are Jerome's relationships with his loving family. Pencil drawings further illustrate the rare qualities of this special boy, whose dreams and frustrations match those of the author's son.

Ages 7-11

Also available in:
No other form known

## 538

**Robinson, Barbara Webb**

## Temporary Times, Temporary Places

Harper & Row, Publishers, Inc., 1982.
(113 pages)

---

*BOY-GIRL RELATIONSHIPS: Dating*
 *Empathy*
 *Family: relationships*
 *Relatives: living in child's home*

---

Fifteen-year-old Janet has had a crush on Eddie Walsh for so long that she is stunned into silence when he suddenly walks her home one Sunday evening after the Methodist youth-group meeting. They sit on the porch swing and kiss, and he says he'll see her Wednesday evening. Janet's impressive, flamboyant Aunt May has come to stay for a while as she recuperates from a broken heart; she was in love with a married man and her life is now a shambles. When Janet has a slumber party, Aunt May objects to the noise and slaps Janet. Janet's mother asks Aunt May not to begrudge the girls their happiness just because she is unhappy. Wednesday evening, as promised, Eddie comes for Janet, and they visit all the local hangouts. Janet has a perfect evening; Eddie asks her out again for Friday and Saturday nights. After that they are always together. As they watch the sun rise after a special midsummer swim night, Janet thinks life has never been so wonderful. But she must have forgotten to wish on the last star and knock on wood, because she comes down with poison ivy. Not wanting Eddie to see her all broken out, she stays at home for the next three weeks. He only calls twice, but Janet looks forward to seeing him at the Methodist retreat camp. Once there, however, she spots him with a blonde girl, and he appears to be avoiding her. At the square dance she starts to speak to him, but changes her mind when she realizes there will be no happy ending to this particular story. She puts a good face on it and is complimented by a counselor for being so cheerful. She doesn't even admit her complete misery to her best friend. When she returns home, she finds herself feeling more sympathetic toward Aunt May. One day she asks her mother why Aunt May doesn't go somewhere else instead of returning to Detroit, the scene of her heartbreak. "Most people just take up where they are and go on from there," her mother replies. Janet realizes she lost Eddie "as I would no doubt lose, and gain, much over the years —simply because things change." But she is convinced that a person can't just quit living for fear of being hurt.

A teenager falls in love for the first time and discovers how much it hurts to lose love, an insight that makes her more sympathetic toward her eccentric, unlucky-in-love Aunt May. This delightfully written first-person account conveys the flavors and scents of a small-town summer and a gentle first love that mysteriously comes and then mysteriously goes. Several details suggest an earlier time period, but the story itself is timeless.

Ages 11-13

**Also available in:**
Braille—*Temporary Times, Temporary Places*
Library of Congress (NLSBPH)

Cassette—*Temporary Times, Temporary Places*
Library of Congress (NLSBPH)

Paperbound—*Temporary Times, Temporary Places*
Avon Books

## 539

Robinson, Nancy Konheim

**Wendy and the Bullies**

Black/white illustrations by Ingrid Fetz.
Hastings House Publishers, Inc., 1980.
(128 pages)

BULLY: Being Bothered by
BULLY: Fear of
   *Communication: parent-child*
   *Friendship: making friends*
   *Peer relationships: avoiding others*

Wendy, about eight, lives in mortal fear of bullies. She is especially afraid of Pat, a neighborhood girl who once hit her in the head with a rock, sending her to the doctor and so incensing her mother that she called Pat's mother. Now, because Wendy does not want to be called a tattletale, she will not tell her mother about another bully, Stanley Kane, who's been tormenting her at school. She won't even tell her teacher when Stanley spoils her painting, trips her in the aisle, and pushes her against a tree, stunning her and again sending her to the doctor. Still the terrorized Wendy remains silent, although she's too upset to eat supper and refuses to return to school the next day, feigning illness. That evening her father, thinking an early birthday present might cheer her up, brings home a cocker spaniel puppy. Wendy is thrilled with the little dog she calls Shep, though she was secretly hoping for a larger dog to protect her from the bullies. On Friday, her mother insists she return to school. Wendy obediently leaves the house, but then sneaks back in and hides in her secret closet, a dark place that frightens her. When her mother walks past the closet she notices the door open a crack,

pushes it shut, and fixes the padlock. Wendy screams, startling and angering her mother. The girl still will not explain why she's afraid to go to school, so her mother takes her. During art class, Wendy draws a picture of Shep. Stanley scribbles a beard on the puppy and then scribbles on Roger's painting too. It's the last straw for Wendy, who knocks over Stanley and his easel. Roger joins in and punches Stanley in the nose. Stanley wails, and Wendy and Roger feel proud of themselves for a change. Then, when Wendy gets home from school, she cannot find Shep. Thinking her mother has taken the dog back, she begins to cry and then blurts out the truth about Stanley's bullying. Shep is outside, her mother tells her, and the two sit down to talk, soon joined by Wendy's father. Her parents comfort her by telling about bullies they themselves overcame as children. Feeling better, Wendy goes outside to take Shep for a ride in her doll buggy. Pat appears and gives the buggy a shove, sending it racing down a hill. Wendy screams and Pat, seeing the terrified puppy dangling from its leash at the bottom of the hill, seems genuinely upset over what she has done. She apologizes and the two talk civilly for the first time. Then Wendy's class decides to sell raffle tickets but can't agree on an orderly way to canvas the neighborhood. Wendy has the best idea: students will go in pairs, each pair being assigned to a specific area. When she volunteers the use of her own map—carefully drawn with every street marked and places indicated where bullies might be found—even Stanley is impressed.

A young girl is tormented by several children in her neighborhood and school and is too terrorized to ask for help. A talk with her parents strengthens her and an assertive confrontation with each of her two chief enemies restores some of Wendy's self-esteem. Although the story moves much too quickly to its satisfying conclusion, this is a realistic depiction of a common childhood dilemma. Wendy's terror comes through vividly. Dialogue rings true, and the relationship of parents and child is nicely drawn.

Ages 7-10

**Also available in:**
Paperbound—*Wendy and the Bullies*
Scholastic Book Services

## 540

Robison, Deborah

**No Elephants Allowed**

Color illustrations by the author.
Clarion Books, 1981.
(29 pages counted)

BEDTIME
FEAR: of Darkness
   *Imagination*

Every night after little Justin gets in bed, an elephant comes into his room. Sometimes it's two elephants and sometimes even lions and alligators. Everyone disputes his story, but Justin knows what goes on in his room. His father gives him a toy rabbit to help with his elephant problem. It's nice and cuddly, but it doesn't help. His mother makes him a strong, new bed, but that doesn't

R

keep the elephants away either. His sister gives him a night-light so he can see there are no elephants or lions in his room. But they're still there. Then one night Justin finds a picture in a magazine that he cuts out and hangs up in his room. When his family comes in to see what it is, Justin shows them his picture of a huge, scary gorilla and says, "Now I have a gorilla to protect me!" He climbs into bed and goes right to sleep. The elephants never come back.

After receiving well-meant but ineffective help from his family, a little boy deals successfully and in his own way with his nighttime fears. Colorful, bold illustrations enhance this whimsical story that will comfort young children and promote discussion.

Ages 3-6

**Also available in:**
No other form known

## 541

Robison, Nancy Louise

**Ballet Magic**

Black/white illustrations by Karen Loccisano.
Albert Whitman & Company, 1981.
(95 pages)

---

APPEARANCE: Concern About
HEIGHT: Tall
SELF, ATTITUDE TOWARD: Body Concept
  Encouragement
  Success
  Talents

---

Although she has taken ballet lessons for seven years, Stacey feels newly awkward and self-conscious this fall. About fourteen, she's grown three inches in the last three months. Now she's taller than her classmates and thinks her friends Pam and Lynn are ignoring her because of her height. Then Ida May, their ballet teacher, announces that for this year's Christmas recital, all her classes will combine to perform "The Nutcracker." Stacey wants to play the Sugar Plum Fairy, but fears she will be cast as the Nutcracker because of her height. No one wants that role because of the heavy, unglamorous costume and because the Nutcracker does so little dancing. Stacey leaves class feeling grumpy. On her way home she meets a short, chubby woman named Mrs. Fremple, who cheerily strikes up a conversation with her. When Stacey tells Mrs. Fremple her troubles, the good-natured woman assures the girl that tall people can be good dancers. That weekend Stacey attends Lynn's end-of-summer party and attracts the attention of Lynn's older brother, Mark, who is also a dancer— and taller than Stacey. The time for "Nutcracker" try-outs arrives, and a disappointed Stacey is cast as the understudy for the Sugar Plum Fairy. Then she meets Maria, the tall girl who has won the coveted part. Under Maria's kind guidance, Stacey rehearses until she can dance the part perfectly. She is proud to learn that Ida May is grooming her for next year's Sugar Plum Fairy. Stacey becomes a sort of rehearsal assistant, helping where she's needed and learning other parts, including that of the Nutcracker. Then, the morning of the opening performance, Ida May calls and asks Stacey to come to the auditorium right away. Mark, the Nutcracker, has sprained his ankle, and Stacey must dance the part. Though she fears being teased, Stacey agrees for the sake of the show. Mrs. Fremple has sewn the costumes and she alters the Nutcracker's costume to fit Stacey, telling her she must play the part with spirit even if her heart isn't in it. Then Stacey gets an idea. She will tell no one that it is she, not Mark, inside the Nutcracker head. She dresses alone before the performance and lets everyone call her "Mark." She performs joyfully, doing her best and enjoying every minute of the applause. At the end of the performance, Ida May insists Stacey remove the head so everyone can see her. Before she can protest, Pam and Lynn help lift the heavy head. Everyone gasps and then applauds wildly. Stacey stands tall and proud.

Although extremely self-conscious about her height, Stacey develops a new poise and self-confidence through the reassurance of several important people in her life: her mother, Mrs. Fremple, Ida May, and Mark. Illustrations lend interest to this simple story for young, independent readers. Although the resolution may seem pat, Stacey's feelings about her height are real enough, and readers will share in her triumph as the Nutcracker.

Ages 9-11

**Also available in:**
No other form known

## 542

Roche, Patricia K.

**Good-bye, Arnold**

Color illustrations by the author.
The Dial Press, Inc., 1979.
(32 pages counted)

---

SIBLING: Younger
  Sibling: rivalry

---

Little Webster Mouse resents his older brother, Arnold, resents his selfishness, his bossiness, his snoring. Webster dreams of Arnold's leaving home and his being the only Mouse child. He is elated when Arnold does leave for a whole week to visit Grandma. As soon as his brother is out the front door, Webster plays with all Arnold's toys. He's usually forbidden to go near Arnold's side of the room, but now he sits in Arnold's chair at the table, gets the biggest piece of pie, and sleeps in the top bunk bed. He also helps his mother paint and bake. By the middle of the week, however, the house seems too quiet. Webster has no one with whom to share a picnic lunch or act out bedtime stories. On the day of Arnold's return, Webster makes a cave of blankets between the two bunk beds. When Arnold arrives, he compliments Webster on his cave and the two brothers, happy to be reunited, have a rollicking game of caveman. When Webster wakes up in the middle of the night it is no longer too quiet, and he smiles as he listens to Arnold's soft snoring.

The younger of two mice brothers enjoys a few days of being an only child. But sooner than he expects, Webster begins to miss his playmate. Detailed, colorful illustrations of the mice characters elaborate on the familiar situations in the text and add humor to this appealing tale of sibling rivalry.

Ages 3-7

**Also available in:**
Paperbound—*Good-bye Arnold*
The Dial Press, Inc.

## 543

**Rockwell, Anne F. and Harlow Rockwell**

## Can I Help?

Color illustrations by the authors.
Macmillan Publishing Company, Inc., 1982.
(24 pages counted)

*HELPING*

A little girl often asks, "Can I help?" She likes, for example, to "squish the suds in the sponge" and "squirt the hose all over the car," polishing it "until it shines in the sun." Sometimes she helps set the table or wash clothes. Sometimes she helps with the grocery shopping, picking out cereal and the kind of peanut butter she likes best, even pushing the big, heavy shopping cart. The next-door neighbors like the way the little girl helps them by entertaining their baby when they're busy. In the fall she rakes leaves, in the winter she shovels snow, and she's always ready to make cookies. There are some jobs, however, that her parents won't let her help with until she's bigger. One is mowing the lawn; another is painting the walls; another is slicing onions. The little girl's parents help her too. As a matter of fact, when they ask if they can help her tie her shoes, make her bed, or pick up her toys, she likes to say, "Yes!"

This first-person account, engagingly illustrated, captures the joy young children feel when adults have the patience to let them help. One of the Rockwells' My World series, the book could inspire the read-aloud audience with some new ideas for "helping."

Ages 3-6

**Also available in:**
Disc—*Can I Help?*
Library of Congress (NLSBPH)

## 544

**Rockwell, Anne F. and Harlow Rockwell**

## I Love My Pets

Color illustrations by the authors.
Macmillan Publishing Company, Inc., 1982.
(24 pages counted)

*PETS: Responsibility for*
  *Pets: love for*

A little boy has two pets, a dog and a goldfish. He feeds the dog three times a day and never bothers him while he's eating. When they play in the backyard, the boy throws a stick and the dog brings it back. He plays with his goldfish in a very different way, by making funny faces and watching the fish make them in return. The boy has to be careful when he feeds the goldfish because too much food would make him sick. The goldfish has a plant, a castle, and a mermaid in his bowl. "He likes to hide in his castle and swim around his mermaid." The boy brushes his dog and tucks him into bed at night with a blanket that used to be his. When it is time to clean the fishbowl, the boy and his father fill a pitcher with cold water and let it stand overnight. Then, in the morning, they put the goldfish in a paper cup with some of the old water while they wash the bowl and fill it with water from the pitcher. When they're finished, the boy empties the cup into the clean bowl. Whenever the dog drinks water, he gets his whiskers wet and drips onto the floor. The boy wipes up after him. On the dog's red collar are a license, a rabies tag, and a silver name tag that says Mac. These tags jingle when he walks. The goldfish's name is Goldie and he "wiggles and waves his tail when he swims." Mac wags his tail whenever he sees the boy. The boy loves his pets and agrees with his friend next door who thinks he's very lucky to have two.

A little boy tells how he cares for and loves his pets. Listeners and readers will learn some basics of pet care in this cheerful, vibrantly illustrated book, another in the Rockwells' My World series.

Ages 3-5

**Also available in:**
No other form known

## 545

**Rockwell, Anne F. and Harlow Rockwell**

## My Barber

Color illustrations by the authors.
Macmillan Publishing Company, Inc., 1981.
(24 pages counted)

*APPEARANCE: Concern About*
*BARBER, GOING TO*

A young boy's hair is too long, so he and his father go to the barbershop. The boy sits in the fire-engine chair and his father in a regular barber chair. Once the boy's clothes are covered with a plastic cloth, his hair is wetted, combed, and cut with scissors, thinning shears, and electric clippers. After the haircut, the barber uses a suction tube to draw the loose hair off the boy's neck. Next the barber puts pleasant-smelling talcum powder on the boy's neck and uses a towel to dust the powder off. While the boy is having his hair cut, his father's barber cuts his father's hair and trims his beard. Then another barber sweeps the hair off the floor and prepares to cut someone else's hair. The boy and his father return home, and the mother compliments them both on their haircuts.

A young boy describes his adventure of going to the barbershop. Each thing the barber does is carefully explained. Colorful, bold illustrations bring the barbershop to life and provide detailed pictures of the barber's equipment. The book could be reassuring to a young child going to the barber for the first time.

**R**

Ages 3-6

Also available in:
No other form known

## 546

**Rockwell, Anne F. and Harlow Rockwell**

## Sick in Bed

Color illustrations by the authors.
Macmillan Publishing Company, Inc., 1982.
(24 pages counted)

---

*ILLNESSES: Being Ill*
  *Doctor, going to*

---

A little boy comes home from school cranky and unable to eat his supper. He goes to bed early but wakes in the middle of the night shivering and feeling sick all over. His parents take his temperature, rub him down with warm water and alcohol, and stay with him until he goes back to sleep. In the morning he sucks on ice to soothe his sore throat until it is time to go to the doctor, who examines him thoroughly. Later, at home, his mother explains that the throat culture the doctor took is a way of finding out what kinds of germs are causing the sore throat. Then the doctor will know what medicine to prescribe. The rest of the day the boy drinks ginger ale and sucks cracked ice while his mother reads to him or he watches television in his room. The next morning his mother calls the doctor's office and learns that he has to go back and get a "big shot." It hurts, but he is very brave and doesn't cry. By that evening the boy feels well enough to eat, and the next day he plays in his room. On the weekend he goes outside with his dog and on Monday morning is ready to return to school. His teacher and friends all tell him how much they missed him.

This charmingly illustrated book moves step-by-step through a typical bout of childhood illness and a trip to the doctor. The examination is described and pictured and could help prepare a child for something other than a routine physical. The young narrator includes reassuringly familiar objects and experiences that enhance this addition to the Rockwells' My World series.

Ages 3-6

Also available in:
No other form known

## 547

**Rodowsky, Colby F.**

## H. My Name Is Henley

Farrar, Straus & Giroux, Inc., 1982.
(184 pages)

---

*PARENTAL: Unreliability*
  *Belonging*
  *Change: new home*
  *Decision making*
  *Parent/Parents: single*
  *Security/Insecurity*

---

Twelve-year-old Henley and her mother, Patti, are always on the move. Patti is eternally restless, believing that each of her jobs stifles her creativity. The next move, she's always sure, will make them both completely happy. On a casually extended, unthinking invitation from acquaintances, Patti uproots them once again to move to New York City, though Henley begs her not to, reminding Patti that this time she promised to stay put for a while. But Patti uses the thousand dollars sent to Henley by her paternal grandparents when her father died, although on Henley's insistence she leaves fifty dollars for "emergencies." When they arrive in New York, they find that Roger, a hard-working law student, and his wife, Margery, a nurse, are hardly the free-living, "creative," relaxed people Patti was expecting. Patti promises she'll look for an apartment and a job, but she insists on showing Henley around New York first. Henley is extremely uncomfortable about imposing on their unwilling hosts, but Patti begs Henley to trust her; this time things are going to be different. After all, Patti reminds her daughter, she gave up her job and everything just to bring Henley to New York where she could have "advantages." Despairing, Henley feels she is wearing away like a snake shedding skin after skin. Then Roger asks them to leave. Patti decides to return to Baltimore, although she changes her mind again at the bus depot and Henley must urge her on. In Baltimore they stay with a friend, Angel, who lectures Patti about being immature and unfair to Henley. Patti resents the lectures and soon leaves. Henley is torn between wanting to defend Patti and needing to agree with Angel. They drive south of Baltimore, wildly, and Henley's "head throbbed with Patti's refrain: round and round and round she goes—where she stops, nobody knows." They drive endlessly, aimlessly, stopping at hotels and eating in restaurants. When they have less than one hundred dollars left and their car breaks down, they head for Aunt Mercy, a woman Henley's heard many stories about. Aunt Mercy is a doctor in a small town and lives with Booshie, an old, slightly demented woman. Aunt Mercy accepts their arrival calmly. As the summer days go by, Henley comes to love the stability of the small town. But Patti begins complaining about feeling trapped. After two weeks in a job Aunt Mercy got for her, she is already bored. She admits what Henley has suspected all along: she's not a real niece of Aunt Mercy's, just an old friend of one of her nieces. Patti teases Booshie, and Henley doesn't like the meanness she feels coming from her mother. One day Henley is enjoying herself at the Fourth of July carnival when Patti pulls her away and tells her to grab a few things so they can catch a train out of town. She makes all her usual promises, but this time Henley refuses to go along. She spends the time until Patti's train leaves with Slug, a girl her own age. The rest of the summer is solid contentment for Henley. When school starts that fall, she feels close to Aunt Mercy, Booshie, and the others. But she always remembers that it was Patti who brought her here.

In this tense and memorable first-person narrative, a young girl plays mother to her own restless, immature parent, following her unwillingly from town to town until the girl finally makes the break to achieve the security she needs. Henley's situation is an agonizing one, and readers will get deeply involved in her plight. Her sense of coming home after she realizes she can't survive with Patti any longer provides a satisfying conclusion to a very affecting book.

Ages 10-13

**Also available in:**
No other form known

## 548

Rodowsky, Colby F.

## A Summer's Worth of Shame

Franklin Watts, Inc., 1980.
(150 pages)

---

*SHAME*
*Ambivalence, feelings of*
*Crime/Criminals*
*Family: relationships*
*Friendship: meaning of*
*Imprisonment*
*Life style: change in*
*Parental: absence*

---

Fourteen-year-old Thadeus St. Clair waits for his friend Peter Hunter, with whom he's spent every August at this particular ocean beach for as long as he can remember. This summer, though, he almost doesn't want Peter to arrive. Everything's changed, and he doesn't relish telling Peter what's happened. His mother now works as a cashier; his older sister, Bridget, is a waitress; he is taking care of his younger sister, Muppy; and his father, who used to be a prominent banker, is in prison for embezzlement. Peter and his family have experienced many emotions the past months, including embarrassment, guilt, unease, tension—and anger. "He was angry with his father for being where he was, for doing what he had done." When he overhears women in the public library gossiping about his family, he is torn between wanting to hear and wanting not to hear. They remark on how well his mother has stood by his father, and Thad thinks that's more than he has done. He is unable even to answer his father's letters. Although their mother claims the children understand their father has made a mistake, Thad does not understand and he wants nothing to do with his father. Fortunately, when he finally tells the story to Peter, he finds that Peter already knows what happened and it makes no difference to their friendship. Thad gets a job working nights in the House of Terror on the boardwalk, as a monster in a cage. He gives his boss a false name, because his own is so well known he'd rather not use it. Every night it's the same, "the snarling and roaring and the clanging of bars, the crowds and the heat and the suffocating dark." People who lost money through Mr. St. Clair's embezzling begin filing suit against him, and the story hits the newspapers. There is no way the family can pay back all the money, but Thad wishes he could help. "Part of him wanted to do something for all of them, to take charge, to solve all their problems. Another part of him wanted to run and hide. . . . He wanted his father to come home and not to come home; he wanted to be able to talk to him and never to see him again. The wanting and the not wanting made him hurt inside." When Thad's boss tells him one night to get in his cell where he belongs, something snaps. Thad runs home, gets some camping gear, and flees to a campground on Watch Island. There he realizes that what he can't tolerate in his father is the man's weakness. Thad could have

forgiven his father if he had taken charge. Instead, it was his mother who broke the news and held things together, while for months on end his father stared out the window and waited for dinner. Early the next morning his mother arrives on the island. She tells him people cope with calamity in different ways. They discuss Muppy and her recent irrational, obsessive concern with the weather. His mother starts to say once again that his father has made a mistake, but then she faces the thing squarely and says unequivocally that his father has done wrong, has stolen money. Thad accompanies her home, finding that something in their talk has relieved his restlessness and bitterness. He is still not ready to visit his father in prison, but the next time his mother and Bridget go, Thad sends a loving letter. It isn't quite sincere, but Thad hopes that by the time his father comes home he can really feel love for him again.

A boy whose father is imprisoned for embezzlement gropes for ways of dealing with his anger, bitterness, and confusion. When he roars and growls in the House of Terror, Thad imagines that the patrons who pass by him include his grandmother (who has disowned his father), the state auditors, his father's boss, the judge, even his father himself. His father's actual crime is less hurtful to his relationship with his son than his incapacity for strength, leadership, or decision making after he's found out. Accepting his parent's weakness is Thad's triumph. Never moralistic, this is a compelling, believable, suspenseful story.

Ages 12-14

**Also available in:**
No other form known

## 549

Rosen, Lillian D.

## Just Like Everybody Else

Harcourt Brace Jovanovich, Inc., 1981.
(155 pages)

---

*COMMUNICATION: Importance of*
*DEAFNESS*
*Family: unity*
*Friendship: meaning of*

---

After a bus accident, fifteen-year-old Jenny is left totally deaf. Angry and resentful, she is not convinced she even wants to live. She does begin taking lessons in lip-reading, practicing with family and friends. Still, the first time after the accident that Jenny goes to a party, she leaves in despair after realizing how impossible it is to read lips in a group and still keep up with what's going on. Wondering if anyone will ever want her, she briefly thinks about killing herself. In the summer her world shrinks even more when a good friend moves away and other friends take summer jobs. She can't use the phone, no one asks her to baby-sit anymore, and when a new girl her age moves into the neighborhood she rejects Jenny when she discovers she's deaf. One day Joe Benton comes to visit her; they have mutual friends. Joe has been deaf since birth and his "deaf" speech is sometimes difficult for hearing people to understand. But Jenny can read his lips. He begins to teach her to sign and takes her to her first captioned

R

movie. She enjoys meeting other hearing-impaired people, so encouraging and accepting, and she's relieved to be able to communicate again. She and Joe spend a lot of time together, sharing ideas and practicing signing. He takes her to his house where a number of special electronic devices make life easier for him and his deaf parents. One night when she's there, the police call and ask his father to come see if a child found by the highway is deaf. Jenny goes with them and watches the relief on little Mary's face when Mr. Benton begins signing to her. She has run away from an abusive foster home and a school where no allowances are made for her deafness. Mr. Benton comforts her, suggesting the police call the state deaf association's hotline. Joe has told Jenny how difficult school is for him. He understands very little and faces continual frustration, yet he's learning more in a regular school than he did in the too-easy school for the deaf. He intends to go on to college. When Jenny's parents tell her she must return to school in a month, she is distressed at having to go through the motions of attending school when she will understand so little. Then Joe comes over and says he's been accepted at several colleges, including two that are just for the deaf. He tells Jenny to continue her education, suggesting that she can help change the current unworkable system. Jenny's parents discover that under the law she has a right to a proper education, and they are prepared to stand behind her and work for a solution. With the support and encouragement of her parents and Joe, Jenny feels ready to return to school.

This first-person narrative of a teenager who loses her hearing is an appealing story in itself, but it also contains a great deal of information about living with this disability. At times the need to convey information overpowers the story line, but this doesn't happen often enough to alienate the reader. Jenny's insistence on her need for human contact, which her deafness has radically affected, will be illuminating for hearing readers, as will her hatred of pity and her desire to show she can function in a hearing world, given half a chance. She reproaches hearing people for not even trying to meet her special needs—small things such as facing her when they talk and speaking more slowly. This readable and informative book offers the special insight of an author who is deaf.

Ages 11 and up

**Also available in:**
No other form known

### 550

Ross, Pat

## M and M and the Big Bag

Black/white illustrations by Marylin Hafner.
Pantheon Books, 1981.
(43 pages)

---

*RESPONSIBILITY: Accepting*
*SUCCESS*
  *Education: value of*

---

Little Mandy and Mimi are best friends who pretend to be twins. Today Mimi's mother is sending them alone to the supermarket for the very first time. Their shopping list includes five items: butter, bread, two apples, a box of trash bags, milk. Mandy carries the list, Mimi the money. As they prepare to leave, Mimi's dog, Maxi, begs to go along. The girls put Maxi on his leash and walk to the store. But because dogs are not allowed in, they tie him outside. Then Mandy, without realizing it, drops the shopping list. When the two begin to shop, they have no list and have forgotten what to buy. Mimi thinks she remembers. They begin filling their cart with possibilities: popcorn, soda, chocolate ice cream, grape bubble gum. As they stand in line at the checkout, they look woefully at their five-dollar bill. They have too little money and all the wrong items. Abandoning their cart, they go outside and find Maxi with the list in his mouth—slimy, filled with tooth holes, but still decipherable. Happy again, the girls go back inside and make their purchases. Then, returning the list to Maxi, they take turns carrying the bag of groceries home.

Two little girls are eager to take on the responsibility of their first solo shopping trip. But having lost their list, surrounded by many tasty temptations, they briefly lose track of their assignment. Their ability to read the list, dog-eared as it is, allows them to complete their errand successfully. Beginning readers will appreciate this familiar situation, and they'll like Maxi the dog's role in resolving the girls' problem. The amusingly illustrated story is one of several about M and M.

Ages 6-8

**Also available in:**
No other form known

### 551

Ross, Pat

## Meet M and M

Black/white illustrations by Marylin Hafner.
Pantheon Books, 1980.
(41 pages)

---

*FRIENDSHIP: Best Friend*
  *Arguing*

---

Little Mandy and Mimi are best friends. Mandy is taller and Mimi wears one size bigger, but even so they pretend to be twins. Each girl is missing the same front tooth and both wear matching shirts with an M on the front. They live in the same apartment building, Mimi right above Mandy. Sometimes they take bubble baths together, sharing the yellow pail that belongs to both of them. They share each other's pets too, Mandy's guinea pig named Baby and Mimi's dog named Maxi. One day at Mandy's apartment, she and Mimi quarrel—over everything. They cannot agree what to play or where to play and soon are calling each other names. Angrily Mimi goes home, vowing not to return, and they do not speak to each other for three days. Each attempts to have fun alone in the other's line of vision, but their efforts fall flat. On the third day each girl sits by herself in her room, bored. Suddenly Mandy hears a noise at her window. Mimi has lowered a message to her in their yellow pail. All afternoon the girls send messages and small gifts to one another: crackers, a comic book, racing cars. The last note from Mandy says, "Meet me on the stairs." Mimi replies, "Just what I was thinking!" She races down the back stairs, and Mandy races up. When they meet on the landing, they make plans for the next day.

A quarrel temporarily disrupts the lives of two best friends. Mimi's ingenuity and the fun of playing a new game restore the girls' friendship. Amusing illustrations enhance this easy reader, one of several about M and M.

Ages 6-8

**Also available in:**
Cassette—*Meet M and M*
Miller-Brody Productions

## 552

**Ross, Pat**

**Molly and the Slow Teeth**

Color illustrations by Jerry E. Milord.
Lothrop, Lee & Shepard Company, 1980.
(47 pages)

---

*TOOTH, LOSS OF*
    *School: classmate relationships*

---

Each of Molly Davis's second-grade classmates has lost at least one baby tooth, but Molly hasn't lost any. She doesn't even have a loose tooth. Her parents try to reassure her, but when Molly sees her friends with empty spaces in their mouths, she is distressed about her slow teeth. She hates to read the "Tooth Chart," a special poster on which each child records the loss of teeth. Molly tries several schemes to keep up with her classmates. She blackens one tooth, but no one is fooled. She puts a tiny white stone under her pillow for the tooth fairy; the tooth fairy leaves a dime for a good try. She ties a string between her tooth and a doorknob, but her father warns that she will hurt her mouth. So Molly ignores her teeth for a week. When she checks, she actually has a loose front tooth. Day after day she wiggles it. Then one day at lunch, while pretending to be a hungry dinosaur, Molly takes a big bite out of an apple and her tooth sticks in it. That night the tooth fairy brings her a quarter and lets her keep the tooth besides. The next day at school Molly proudly writes her name on the "Tooth Chart."

A little girl is anxious to lose her baby teeth so she can be like the other children in her class. Zany illustrations enhance this beginning reader, which could be comforting to others with "slow teeth." Helpful also is the message that losing teeth is usually simple and painless.

Ages 6-8

**Also available in:**
Paperbound—*Molly and the Slow Teeth*
Scholastic Book Services

## 553

**Roth, David**

**The Hermit of Fog Hollow Station**

Beaufort Books, Inc., 1980.
(96 pages)

---

*FRIENDSHIP: Meaning of*
*VALUES/VALUING: Moral/Ethical*
    *Age: respect for*
    *Change: new home*
    *Rejection: peer*

---

Soon after his family moves from Boston to a semi-rural suburb, twelve-year-old Alex meets two local boys, Fritz and Benny, who invite him to come fishing. On the way to the lake they tell Alex to be on the lookout for Old Man Turner, who "thinks he owns the whole woods." They tell him, "If Old Man Turner catches you there he'll fry your heart for supper." While they are fishing, Turner appears, "a large, hulking figure . . . his face hidden by the tangle of his white beard." Fritz throws rocks at him and as Fritz and Benny run away, Alex sees the man fall into the stream. Hesitating for just a moment, Alex struggles to pull Turner partway out of the water and then goes for help. After the ambulance takes Turner away, Police Chief Bicks tells Alex about the man he saved. "He's hid himself away in that old station by the tracks, but whatever demon plagues him, it's living right there with him." Later, Alex learns that Turner has had a heart attack. Frightened, he says nothing about Fritz and Benny, but the chief guesses independently that the two were involved. The next day, the boys beat Alex up, accusing him of being "the new fink in town." Alex refuses to let his mother call Bicks about the assault; he must live in this town and won't compound his reputation as a snitch. Anxious to apologize to Mr. Turner, Alex sneaks into his hospital room, but is caught by a doctor and sent away before he can say anything. Still, he thinks he noticed Mr. Turner giving him a small wave. It isn't until the end of the summer that Alex encounters Mr. Turner again in the woods. The boy apologizes, Turner takes him to a choice fishing spot, and the two become friends. Fritz and Benny have remained Alex's enemies, however, and soon after school starts they make sure Alex becomes a social outcast. But the friendship with Turner continues. The two talk, argue, and have spirited discussions of *Walden*, which Turner has given Alex to read. Alex's parents worry that his time is not being spent on schoolwork and with friends his own age. On one visit to Turner, Alex goes with him to another town and helps him dig up an old steel cashbox. He returns home very late and is grounded for a week, but Chief Bicks, pleased about the friendship with Turner, offers some solace. When Alex next visits Turner, he sees the old man return letters and old, faded photographs to his cashbox. Although Turner is ailing, they go out together to pick winter apples. When they return, the cashbox is gone. Alex knows who the culprits are. He finds Fritz and Benny in a hut about to open the box. He shakes the flimsy hut until it collapses and then pounds on the rubble with a board until the frightened boys run off, leaving the box. Alex returns Turner's property to him but the old man's privacy has been violated and Alex sees him change, his

R

health failing rapidly. One November morning, Alex finds Turner dead. He also finds a note: "Take the box, Alex." He takes the box home and hides it in his closet unopened, calling Chief Bicks and returning to Turner's place to wait until his body is taken away. While he waits he thinks of his friend "and wished him well, wished him peace."

A lonely boy offers his friendship to an eccentric recluse, enriching both their lives. The closeness of the relationship between Turner and Alex is believable and touching, and the lyrically written text powerfully conveys their enduring affection. True friendship, Alex finds, has nothing to do with age or circumstance, everything to do with loyalty and concern.

Ages 9-12

**Also available in:**
No other form known

## 554

**Rounds, Glen Harold**

**Blind Outlaw**

Black/white illustrations by the author.
Holiday House, Inc., 1980.
(94 pages)

---

*BLINDNESS*
*MUTENESS*
   *Animals: love for*
   *Patience/Impatience*
   *Trust/Distrust*

---

In the course of drifting across the range, the Blind Horse gets mixed up with a herd of range horses and is driven into a corral on a Montana ranch. The Boy, a young teenager who had himself drifted onto the ranch earlier that year, can hear and understand but can't speak: he can only make wordless sounds. He has a special rapport with animals, and as he goes about his chores he is followed by a magpie, a family of rabbits, and a coyote pup. The other ranch hands and the Ranch Owner accept the Boy because he "was a good worker. . . . And after a while, nobody paid attention to the fact he could not speak." The Horsebreaker in charge of taming the herd of range horses discovers that the Blind Horse is "pure outlaw" and blind to boot. When he fails to gentle the Blind Horse, the Boy communicates his wish to try. The Ranch Owner tells the Boy, "If you think you can gentle that Blind Outlaw in your spare time, he's yours." The Blind Horse is put in a corral by himself, and every day the Boy sits on the fence and talks to the animal in his own strange fashion. As he does his chores, the Boy goes back and forth near the Horse, accustoming the animal to his comings and goings. The Boy also brings in his old saddle horse so the Horse can get used to the other animal. At night the Boy sleeps next to the corral. He works patiently for days and weeks, teaching the Horse to tolerate his presence and that of the old saddle horse, to eat from his hand, to allow a saddle on his back. The Boy makes chirping, crooning sounds that the Horse seems to understand. The animal begins to trust and accept the Boy. Then one day, when all the ranch hands are out fighting a range fire, a Stranger inadvertently lets the Blind Horse out of

his corral. The Boy spends several days looking for him. When he finds him, the Boy is again patient and woos the Horse with his voice and a brown-sugar sandwich. He succeeds in bringing the Horse back and trains the Horse so well that the two participate in the fall roundup, to the amazement of the men from other ranches. They can't believe that a blind horse and a mute boy can do the same work they do. When some Horse Buyers visit the ranch and talk about other places they've seen and the land in Oklahoma where they're headed, the Boy decides he wants to go with them. The Ranch Owner gives him a bill of sale for the Blind Horse, along with some money, a saddle, a sheepskin coat, and a shirt. The Boy and the Blind Horse set out for Oklahoma, the magpie perched on the Boy's shoulder.

Companion volume to *The Blind Colt* and *Stolen Pony,* this book details the gentling of a badly spooked, probably mistreated, blind horse by a patient, loving, mute boy. Horse and boy, both handicapped, respond deeply to each other and form a lasting bond. Readers will enjoy this well-done, rather unusual horse story, to which small line drawings add texture and even whimsy. The characters are all nameless throughout, a touch that contributes a certain remote, legendary, at times distracting quality.

Ages 9-11

**Also available in:**
Braille—*Blind Outlaw*
Library of Congress (NLSBPH)

Cassette—*Blind Outlaw*
Library of Congress (NLSBPH)

Paperbound—*Blind Outlaw*
Scholastic Book Services

## 555

**Roy, Ronald**

**Avalanche!**

Black/white illustrations by Robert MacLean.
E. P. Dutton & Company, Inc., 1981.
(58 pages)

---

*RESOURCEFULNESS*
*SIBLING: Love for*
   *Change: accepting*
   *Courage, meaning of*

---

Right after Scott Turner's parents announce that they are sending him to Aspen to visit his brother, Tony, they tell him they will be going to St. Thomas to work out the details of a divorce. Scott is fourteen and has not seen his brother for six years, ever since Tony abruptly left Connecticut. Scott was hurt by his brother's sudden departure, and his sense of rejection was compounded when his parents sent him to boarding school. Now the upcoming divorce further uproots him emotionally. Tony welcomes Scott warmly. It is snowing heavily, but by noon the next day the weather is much warmer, so warm that the ski patrol is shutting down most of the trails because of the danger of avalanches. But Tony has promised to take Scott skiing on Smuggler, a mountain not used by many tourists. They ascend the steep trail in Tony's pickup. When they reach the desired spot, a meadow, Tony turns the truck around in case it snows and driving becomes even more difficult. While the two stand gazing at the beautiful scene they begin to hear the sound of dynamite. The ski patrol is bringing down some of the snow on the regular "avalanche chutes" while the people are off the slopes; these controlled avalanches are to prevent uncontrolled ones. Tony assures Scott that there's never been an avalanche on Smuggler. They ignore other blasts that follow, and a happy Scott feels "as though he's never lost Tony." Suddenly a "breeze from nowhere" is followed by rumbling, a white wave comes plunging down the mountainside above them, and they are both buried by snow. At first filled with panic, Scott's determination and sense of reason gradually take over. He begins to inch his way upward with a broken ski and finally sees light. He doesn't see Tony, however, and knows he must go for help. Maneuvering the truck down the treacherous road, he stumbles into a local store and the people there notify the ski patrol. Soon Scott is back in the meadow showing the patrol where he dug out. They probe the snow with bamboo rods until one member strikes something that seems soft. She moves her probe around to make the hole larger and then calls the dogs to sniff. They react excitedly and everyone begins digging. Tony is found alive and is quickly sent to a Denver hospital by helicopter, accompanied by Scott. A few days later, Tony is recuperating and Scott reluctantly prepares to go back to Connecticut. Troubled, he realizes that Tony's little apartment has become more of a home to him than his parents' large house. As Scott rides to the hospital to visit his brother one last time, Tony's friend Dave insists that the trouble in Scott's life is not his fault. Scott should try not "to think about how the world is messing around with your life; think about what you can do to the world." Scott tells his brother that he'd like to come back and is delighted when Tony insists that he stay for the whole summer next time.

A boy from a troubled family is reunited with his rebellious older brother. Tony's example of making a life for himself gives Scott the determination to do the same, to rise above his circumstances. Characters are superficially developed here, but the action-filled plot, complementary illustrations, and limited vocabulary should attract the reluctant reader. The book is successful in portraying the rekindling of a warm relationship between brothers.

Ages 10 and up

**Also available in:**
No other form known

**556**

Roy, Ronald

**Frankie Is Staying Back**
Black/white illustrations by Walter Kessell.
Clarion Books, 1981.
(82 pages)

*FRIENDSHIP: Best Friend*
*SCHOOL: Retention*
  *Empathy*
  *School: Achievement/Underachievement*

R

Jonas and Frankie have been inseparable best friends for years. Then, near the end of third grade, Frankie must tell Jonas that he will not be going on to fourth grade. He'll have to repeat third grade. Frankie is very upset, Jonas depressed. Each boy secretly wonders how this turn of events will affect their friendship. Jonas wants very much to help Frankie feel better. At dinner that day he tells his family the news: Frankie will be staying back because of his troubles with math and reading. Can Frankie sleep over that night? Concerned for Frankie, especially since his father has recently left the family, Jonas's parents say yes. Frankie comes but he's still upset, and the evening goes badly. He accidentally breaks Jonas's model airplane. Then he tries to read aloud from Jonas's jokebook and has trouble. When Jonas tries to help, Frankie begins to cry and Jonas gets mad at him. After a fight at the breakfast table, Frankie leaves and Jonas goes off to play baseball. But during the game, he resolves again to help Frankie. Monday morning Jonas tells his teacher that he didn't do his homework. During reading he stumbles and pretends he can't read. His angry teacher calls his mother, and Jonas explains that he was trying to be like Frankie so he could be held back too. To his chagrin, he learns that his teacher and Frankie had misunderstood: they thought he was making fun of Frankie. His mother suggests he was thinking more of himself than of Frankie. Then she tells him about a plan that the school and Frankie's parents have worked out to help Frankie. Jonas runs to Frankie's house, apologizes for the misunderstanding, and explains the plan. Frankie will attend summer school, working five hours every day on his math and reading. Then he'll take a test. If he passes, he can go on to fourth grade. Now Frankie and Jonas, still best friends, can be happy about the future again.

Best friends find their relationship at risk when one boy is told he'll have to repeat third grade. Simply and warmly written, this story offers insight into the importance of a supportive friendship during difficult times. Illustrations show two engaging little boys who will claim the sympathy of readers. The ending, however, could raise false hopes in a child who faces retention; the book should be recommended with this reservation in mind.

Ages 8-10

**Also available in:**
No other form known

**557**

Ruby, Lois

**Two Truths in My Pocket**

The Viking Press, Inc., 1982.
(137 pages)

---

FAMILY: Relationships
JEWISH
  Age: aging
  Belonging
  Boy-girl relationships: dating
  Death: of grandparent
  Determination
  Differences, human
  Love, meaning of
  Mental retardation
  Prejudice: ethnic/racial

---

The first story in this collection, "Inscriptions on Stone," has sixteen-year-old Micah Wexroth newly moved to Middlebury, Vermont, where he's the only Jewish boy. Trying hard to fit in, Micah calls himself Mike, eats his first non-kosher hamburger, and goes along with new friends to a nearby ski resort where they tamper with the wiring of the ski lift. As a result, a worker is nearly electrocuted. Micah doesn't tell his father. He also can't bring himself to announce his plans to break a long family tradition and not become a rabbi. His younger sister, Chava, decides she will be the rabbi in their generation. In "Forgetting Me, Remember Me," fifteen-year-old Tracy, minimally brain damaged and "Little Miss Super Jew," as her father calls her, is angry at being the only one in the family who seems truly to care about the meaning of her brother Alan's Bar Mitzvah. She insists on being part of the ceremony and vows to learn all the prayers for her own Bat Mitzvah. In "Lighter Than Air," fifteen-year-old Bobby Kornfeld fears other people will notice his severe case of unrequited love for his American Lit teacher. He goes for counsel to old Rabbi Shuman, who sends him to see a young priest. The priest suggests trying to focus on something ridiculous about Mrs. Blimton so that he won't be so distracted by her. Bobby decides to picture his teacher as a blimp. In "Hasty Vows," Lauren Zebroski ponders her on-again, off-again relationship with Stuart, who isn't Jewish. She recalls the time he came to dinner during one of her mother's periods of intense Jewishness and about how uncomfortable he was at her cousin Estelle's wedding. Now Lauren realizes what the real difference between them is: "Stuart knew just who he was. But she and her people were forever unraveling the mystery of their own heritage. She felt suddenly that she rather liked living with the mystery of untold, untolled generations." Lauren decides to break off the relationship. "Strangers in the Land of Egypt" features fifteen-year-old Barry Wyman who, during Sabbath services, sees a black family participating in all the prayers and responses: "These people thought they were Jews!" The family's daughter, Esther, shocks Barry's youth group when she announces that her family is Hebrew and chides them for their ignorance and elitism. Barry goes to Esther's apartment to apologize. Her father explains that his family,

although very well assimilated into the white community, is still ostracized by the Jewish community. Barry asks Esther out. When he explains to his mother that Esther is simply his good friend, she accepts the relationship. But when he gets to Esther's house, her parents inform him that she is not going anywhere with a white boy. Later that night Esther calls, explaining that her father isn't as liberal as he sounds about certain things. In "Frail Bridge," sixteen-year-old Rochela cannot mourn the death of her great-grandmother until she hears the relatives talking about her. "And the more I listened to my relatives, the more I realized that what I knew of her, had always known, was wrong." Rochela only remembers all the grim Sunday afternoons spent visiting the nursing home, all the summer camps she couldn't attend because of the costs of Bubbie Yetta's care. But Bubbie has left Rochela her wedding ring and pearls because, she said, she recognized early on that Rochela had compassion. When at last the girl senses the connections between her great-grandmother and herself, she is able to cry.

Six strongly written stories about Jewish teenagers present a variety of characters and settings, all ineffably and sometimes irreverently Jewish. The stories, three of them first-person narratives, concern important issues of growing up and of growing up Jewish: family relationships and expectations, encounters with prejudice, dating and friendships. All are realistic and believable, vividly conveying the influence of the characters' Jewish heritage on their daily lives.

Ages 12 and up

**Also available in:**
Paperbound—*Two Truths in My Pocket*
Fawcett World Library

---

**558**

**Ruby, Lois**

**What Do You Do in Quicksand?**

The Viking Press, Inc., 1979.
(199 pages)

---

MENTAL ILLNESS: of Adolescent
UNWED FATHER
  Baby-sitting
  Love, meaning of
  Reality, escaping

---

The lives of Leah Aaronson, fifteen, and Matt Russell, sixteen, cross unexpectedly and constantly when Matt, whose family recently moved next door to Leah's, brings home his newborn baby daughter, Barbara. Matt's first, brief sexual encounter with his girlfriend resulted in her pregnancy; the girl, uninterested in their baby, has moved to another state. Since Matt cannot bear to give the baby up for adoption, he has decided to raise her himself. His father applauds his decision; his mother tolerates it after trying to dissuade him. Leah lives with her mother's third husband, Moe, who loves her like a daughter, and her earthy, honest grandmother, Glen. She has a chaotic past: deserted by her father, sexually abused at six by her mother's second husband, her mother dying when Leah was eight. Now the girl becomes totally absorbed in Matt's baby, whom she considers her own soul daughter. Leah spends every minute she has and that Matt and his family will allow caring for Barbara, even urging Matt to give the baby to her. At first Matt welcomes Leah's help, which has relieved some of his exhaustion and resentment at trying simultaneously to be a father and a high school senior. But when he realizes that Leah's interest in Barbara is excessive, he shuns her help. As Leah becomes more and more afraid of losing Barbara, she tries to find out about her past. She questions Moe and Glen about her parents but, for what they consider her own good, the two refuse to answer her questions. When Moe contemplates remarriage, Leah feels threatened by yet another painful loss. Unable to express her mounting desperation, Leah finally explodes. She kidnaps Barbara and locks herself and the baby in her bedroom. When at last the emotional turmoil overwhelms her and she faints, Matt breaks down the door. Leah is briefly hospitalized and then continues to see a psychologist, who helps her come to grips with her painful past. As for Matt, the day comes when Barbara calls him Daddy and he realizes with awe that what he feels for her is not merely duty any longer, but love. Leah's breakdown gives him the impetus to do something for all of them. Impressed with the idea of the cool cleanliness of Oregon, he decides to move there. He gives Leah his new address so she can communicate with him when she's ready. Leaving Barbara in a day-care center while he works and with a baby-sitter two nights a week while he attends college, he sees that both their needs are met.

This study of human relationships is written from the first-person viewpoints of both Leah and Matt, in alternating chapters. Logically and believably developed, with realistic characters and dialogue, this is a story with considerable interest and insight. It is also refreshingly laced with humor.

Ages 12-14

**Also available in:**
Paperbound—*What Do You Do in Quicksand?*
Fawcett World Library

## 559

**Ruffins, Reynold**

**My Brother Never Feeds the Cat**
Color illustrations by the author.
Charles Scribner's Sons, 1979.
(29 pages counted)

*SIBLING: New Baby*
 *Helping*

Little Anna describes all the household chores that need to be done, chores that she does or helps with. She takes out the garbage, helps her father rake leaves, walks the dog, shops for groceries. As she performs each task, she remarks to any available listener that, while she works hard, her brother does nothing but play. By bedtime, as she feeds the cat, she figures she's done ten jobs that day. After a bath, she snuggles on the bed with her unhelpful but lovable brother. He is a tiny baby!

A little girl complains about all the work she has to do, in contrast to her brother who plays all day. But the detailed illustrations—complete with a delightfully sly

family cat—reveal Anna's pride and pleasure in the tasks she often takes on voluntarily. Young children will appreciate the humor of the surprise ending and may be moved to discuss their own feelings about new siblings.

Ages 3-7

**Also available in:**
No other form known

## 560

**Ruthstrom, Dorotha**

**The Big Kite Contest**
Black/white illustrations by Lillian Aberman Hoban.
Pantheon Books, 1980.
(47 pages)

R

*PROBLEM SOLVING*
 *Money: earning*
 *Resourcefulness*
 *Sibling: relationships*

Stephen's younger sister asks him if she can have the blue ribbon he hopes to win in the big kite contest. He tells her the prize wouldn't mean anything if she didn't win it herself. Then Stephen's batwing kite crashes into a tree. Stephen tries to trade for a new kite, but nobody wants to trade—not even for a pregnant hamster. New kites cost two dollars, but he only has ten cents. So he uses the dime to buy lemonade mix and sets up a stand. He earns fifty cents, buys a box of soap, and offers to "wash anything" for ten cents. His sister helps out by riding up and down on her tricycle with a sign on the back advertising Stephen's various enterprises. After washing five bikes, two trikes, two wagons, and his little sister, Stephen has one dollar. With it, he buys a dog brush and offers to groom dogs for ten cents. He grooms one dollar's worth of dogs, sells his dog brush to a friend for fifty cents, and buys a large bottle of glue with the $1.50. Now he will try repairing toys. His first attempt is a disaster, however, and nobody will give him another chance. He is left with a large bottle of glue and no money. His sister approaches him with an idea, but he won't listen. On the morning of the kite contest, Stephen gets a note saying that if he wants to win the blue ribbon, he should come to the park. It is signed, "ME." At the park, where everyone but Stephen seems to have a kite, he sees his sister with his batwing kite! She tells him she fixed it with his glue. The contest begins, and Stephen watches as his sister tries to get the kite into the air. He calls out directions and coaches her to a win. Stephen takes the shiny blue ribbon that he wanted so much and hands it to his sister. She couldn't have won without him, she insists, but Stephen says she deserves the ribbon. She had the good idea.

A little girl trying to help her brother win a blue ribbon in a kite contest learns it's more fun to win one on her own. Stephen shows ingenuity and perseverance in his attempts to earn enough money to buy a new kite, and his sister is an eager helper. This amusing story for the beginning reader, accompanied by whimsical illustrations that extend the text, shows two independent children looking for the solution to a problem in two very different, but equally creative, ways.

Ages 6-8

**Also available in:**
Cassette—*The Big Kite Contest*
Miller-Brody Productions

## 561

**Sachs, Elizabeth-Ann**

### Just Like Always

Atheneum Publishers, 1981.
(160 pages)

HOSPITAL, GOING TO
SCOLIOSIS
 Fear
 Friendship: meaning of
 Imagination

Janie Tannenbaum, about ten, is admitted to the children's ward of a hospital for treatment of scoliosis (curvature of the spine). Janie, whose parents can visit only on weekends because of their work and the distance, is rambunctious and prone to mischief. Her roommate is Courtney-Ann Schaeffer, about the same age though opposite in personality. Soft-spoken and cooperative, Courtney loves to imagine herself in a make-believe world called "Greno." Janie would rather play baseball or read a mystery. In spite of their differences the two quickly become friends, although Janie cannot fathom Courtney's preoccupation with an imaginary kingdom. One night when they sneak out of their room and sit on a fire escape stairway overlooking the city, Courtney shows Janie a bridge that shines like a jeweled necklace. But Janie angers Courtney by showing the "necklace" to one of the nurses. Then, when Courtney discovers that Janie has read a page in her secret diary, she refuses to speak to Janie until Janie shares a "deep secret" with her. Janie confesses that she hates her real name, which is Janice, and Courtney is satisfied. The time comes when both girls must endure body casts. Courtney is shocked to learn she must first have her beautiful long hair cut off. Janie is scared too, but her young, handsome doctor convinces her to be brave. Until now, both girls have been throwing their hospital food out the window for the pigeons, eating only the snack foods their parents bring them. Now Janie wonders how they will get rid of the hospital fare while wearing the restrictive body casts. Before she can devise a new plan, however, the old one abruptly stops when breakfast eggs land on a policeman's head. The girls are scolded and moved to a room nearer the nurses' station. There Janie contrives a new scheme to keep herself busy. She enlists Courtney to help her with a questionnaire about love and begins interviewing each member of the hospital staff. Next she must decide what to do with the information she has collected. She decides to create a romance between their favorite nurse, Ms. Rogers, and their favorite doctor, Dr. Michaels. She and Courtney arrange a meeting of the two at a certain time, so the girls can watch from their window. Later Ms. Rogers explains to Janie that love can't be tricked into happening. Janie is more puzzled than ever about the subject. Then Janie has her surgery and is moved to a different floor to recover. Courtney too has surgery and she too is moved, but to another part of the hospital where she

must await a second operation. Janie is released in a body cast to recuperate at home. She does not even get to say goodbye to Courtney and is heartbroken. Ms. Rogers tells her that if the friendship is real the two will find a way to see each other again, and it will be "just like always" between them.

A spunky young girl hospitalized for treatment of scoliosis learns the meaning and importance of love and friendship. This is an interesting, often funny look at a long-term hospital stay and the resilience of two young roommates. Although some of the scoliosis treatment is described, the pain and discomfort are glossed over in the interest of the story's real focus: the developing friendship between Janie and Courtney. Furthermore, it seems highly unlikely that the girls' parents would play so small a part at such a serious time for their daughters. Still, the book may be a good introduction to life in a hospital for someone facing an extended stay.

Ages 10-13

**Also available in:**
Paperbound—*Just Like Always*
Xerox Publishing Company

## 562

**Sachs, Marilyn**

### Beach Towels

Black/white illustrations by Jim Spence.
E. P. Dutton & Company, Inc., 1982.
(76 pages)

BOY-GIRL RELATIONSHIPS
 Communication: importance of
 Death: of mother
 Friendship: making friends

Sixteen-year-old Lori Fisher meets seventeen-year-old Phil Rivers on the beach and, after a rocky start, they begin to talk to each other. He decides to overlook her blaring radio; she overlooks his self-centeredness. Phil tells Lori that he waits at the beach every day for his girlfriend, Ronda, who seems to have a different excuse each day for not showing up. Sick of school and sick of home, Phil wants only to drop out, move away, and marry Ronda. When Ronda finally does come to the beach, Phil plays up to Lori, using her to make Ronda jealous. At the same time, he's quick to do everything Ronda asks. Lori finds his attitude disgusting and is angry at being used. When Phil goes to get something to drink, Lori leaves before he gets back. The next day at the beach he asks why she left so suddenly. She explains. He insists that Ronda loves him, that it was she who started chasing him. Lori asks him how Ronda makes him feel, insisting he's confusing love with sex. After telling Phil just how she feels about his using her to make Ronda jealous, she accuses him of being like all boys—selfish and interested only in his own affairs. Lori spends the next week at another beach. When she returns Phil is upset, saying he's been trying to find her. He apologizes for being selfish and asks her about herself. Why is she always at the beach alone? Why does she have scars on her legs? Reluctant at first to talk, Lori finally tells Phil about the accident that killed her mother. Lori was driving. She was hospitalized for several months with serious injuries. They've healed, but "inside—inside I'm still limping." Although she wasn't at fault, she still has nightmares. Her doctor has recommended a summer of relaxation, a time without serious thinking. Affected by her story, Phil says he's through with Ronda. He wants to get to know Lori better and asks her out to dinner.

Two troubled young people come to share each other's problems and feelings in this sensitive story whose plot develops almost completely in dialogue. Sparely but skillfully written, the short book manages to be both appealing and thought-provoking. Illustrations add interest and expand meaning. This is a Skinny Book, part of a series designed for older readers with limited reading skills. These well-written books focus on the interests and concerns of today's young people and should have great appeal.

Ages 12 and up

Also available in:
Paperbound—*Beach Towels*
Avon Books

## 563

Sachs, Marilyn

**Bus Ride**

Black/white illustrations by Amy Rowen.
E. P. Dutton & Company, Inc., 1980.
(107 pages)

---

*BOY-GIRL RELATIONSHIPS*
*SELF, ATTITUDE TOWARD: Accepting*
*Appearance: concern about*

---

Judy and Ernie are high school juniors who meet one morning on the school bus. Ernie has small eyes, a large mouth, and crooked front teeth. Judy thinks he is a "funny-looking boy—but funny-looking in a nice way." She assumes at first that their meeting is just an accident, perhaps a fortunate one. But then she realizes that all Ernie really wants is to meet Karen Shepherd, Judy's friend. Karen is pretty, bright, and very popular. Judy, on the other hand, doesn't think of herself as "anything special." She is very conscious of her acne and wears her hair unattractively down over her face to cover her broken-out skin. She is an average student and has not been at all successful with the opposite sex. Yet she and Karen have been friends for a long time, although they aren't as close now as they were when younger. When Ernie first suggests that he and Judy help each other get dates, she is angry at the insinuation that she needs help. But then she admits that she really is a "loser" and can use assistance. As Judy and Ernie develop their plans during the next few rides to school, they become good friends. Judy discusses her dreams for the future and confesses how hard it is for her to get along with her father. Ernie talks about the difficulty of being the only male in a house with a mother and two sisters. He confesses his fear that he will "go through life sitting on the bench" and never find the one thing he can be good at. They arrange a double date to a ball game on Thursday evening—Ernie with Karen, Judy with Ernie's friend Alex. Everything goes well, except that Alex is too quiet

to please Judy. Ernie and Karen, however, arrange for another date on Saturday night. On the bus the following Monday, Ernie tells Judy that he's not sure he can handle Karen's bubbly personality. It might be hard for him "to stand around watching her be friendly with the whole world." Judy reveals that Karen told her how Ernie spent most of their date talking about Judy. They decide the friendship they've built on the bus is very special and that perhaps "two losers can make one winning combination."

Two rather average young people who lack self-confidence build a friendship almost in spite of themselves. This outstanding, unusual book consists entirely of dialogue between the two, dialogue that naturally and smoothly moves the story along. The surprise ending is delightful and believable; soft-toned illustrations complement the text. This is a Skinny Book, part of a series designed for older readers with limited reading skills. These well-written books focus on the interests and concerns of today's young people and should have great appeal.

Ages 11-14

Also available in:
Braille—*Bus Ride*
Library of Congress (NLSBPH)

Cassette—*Bus Ride*
Library of Congress (NLSBPH)

## 564

Sachs, Marilyn

**Class Pictures**

E. P. Dutton & Company, Inc., 1980.
(138 pages)

---

*FRIENDSHIP: Best Friend*
*MATURATION*
*Grandparent: living in child's home*
*Loyalty*

---

Patricia Maddox (Pat) and Lorraine Scheiner (Lolly) become best friends in kindergarten. In first grade, they attend each other's birthday parties, which are as different as the girls themselves—Lolly with all the advantages an affluent family can provide, Pat living in a small apartment above a store with her widowed mother, her grandmother, and two brothers. In second grade, it is popular, outgoing Pat who protects funny, artistic, unpopular Lolly. That year, Pat learns that the man she always thought of as her daddy was not really her father, that her mother was married once before. By fourth grade the girls are in separate classrooms, since Pat has been placed in the gifted class. She talks to Mr. Evans, her third-grade teacher, about her dislike of the class. When the girls are in sixth grade, Pat's grandmother has a romantic interest, Mr. Nagel. Although Pat and her mother do not get along, they both dislike Mr. Nagel. He and Grandma eventually marry; Pat's mother does not attend the wedding. Pat becomes extremely interested in rocketry and begins spending time at Mr. Evans's house using his tools to build a reflecting telescope. She baby-sits for his young son, Luke, and becomes friendly with his wife, Meg. When seventh-grade class pictures come out, Pat realizes that "Lolly had become a beauty." As an eighth grader, Lolly blossoms socially and is very popular. But she refuses to go to a party unless Pat is invited. Pat thinks of herself more and more as a scientist, but it is Lolly who manipulates a teacher into allowing Pat to enroll in a metal shop class. "There was a reshuffling in our friendship too. After all those years of looking after Lolly and protecting her, suddenly she didn't need my protection anymore. Suddenly, it looked as if I might need hers. And I hated it." In ninth grade, Lolly and Pat admit they have each been jealous of the other over the years: Lolly envying Pat's firmness of purpose, Pat envying Lolly's beauty. In tenth grade, Pat confides more in Mr. Evans than in Lolly, becoming almost a part of the Evans family. When Pat and Lolly double-date, Pat's date has eyes only for Lolly. Lolly's picture is all over the yearbook, but Pat is considered "a brain." Sometimes their friendship seems finished, but they still retain ties to each other. As a junior, Pat has "shameful daydreams" about Meg dying and herself ending up in Mr. Evans's arms. That year Lolly is president of the Ecology Club. It starts with five members but swells to many more under her leadership; most are boys. As seniors, both girls want to demonstrate against a nuclear power plant, but Lolly's mother won't permit her to take part. Pat does, and Mr. Evans picks her up at the detention center after she is arrested. Pat is accepted by both Stanford and MIT. She and Mr. Evans have an emotional scene when he tells her Meg is pregnant and she cries and says she can't bear to leave him. The summer after graduation, Lolly prepares to move away from home and Pat to leave for MIT. They are still best friends, but both admit they are glad to be going away from each other for a while. They share their fears about the future and the changes it might bring. Lolly suggests that, instead of the dire things Pat thinks might happen to their friendship, "maybe it will be even better than it's ever been."

Pat narrates these fourteen chapters that chronicle her fourteen-year and continuing friendship with Lolly. The complementary nature of friendship, the give-and-take, the enduring loyalty are all part of Pat and Lolly's relationship. Each becomes an individual in her own right, their friendship having to change and adapt as they grow; sometimes keeping pace, sometimes not. Giving strength to Pat's lyrical reflections on a childhood friendship is the well-drawn story of two girls and how they grew.

Ages 10-13

**Also available in:**
Paperbound—*Class Pictures*
Avon Books

## 565

**Sachs, Marilyn**

### Hello. . . . Wrong Number

Black/white illustrations by Pamela Johnson.
E. P. Dutton & Company, Inc., 1981.
(106 pages)

---

*BOY-GIRL RELATIONSHIPS*
  *Appearance: concern about*
  *Self, attitude toward: accepting*

---

When Angie calls Jim McCone to apologize for telling him to get lost at the dance Saturday night, she misdials and gets another Jim, beginning her apology before she realizes her mistake. She quickly hangs up, but then calls the boy back for his promise not to tell Jim McCone of her intention to apologize. She has reconsidered: Jim McCone had his hands all over her while they were dancing. The next night Angie calls Jim again to make him promise not to say a word to Jim McCone. He promises, after supplying his own evidence that McCone is not worth her attention. The next night, Angie asks Jim to tell her all the bad things he knows about McCone so she won't be tempted to call him. Jim does—and also tells Angie a little about himself. The next night they talk again, but not about anything that would allow them to identify each other. Angie says she'd just be a pest, bringing all her problems to him. And she likes being able to tell him things she can't tell anyone else. She muses about why people treat her as a helpless, silly blonde, deciding it's partly because she plays that game. Jim plays and sings some sad songs he's written. He tells Angie about breaking up with his last girlfriend, who crowded him and tried to change herself to be more what he wanted. When Angie asks if he only writes sad songs, he sings her a bouncy tune that he recently composed. But he won't tell her the occasion for it. The next time she calls him, Jim sings her "Angie's Song." Now she wants them to meet, but Jim refuses. Maybe there are things about him that Angie wouldn't like. Nobody is perfect, she replies, mentioning a funny-looking boy who followed her around in school that day and even asked someone who Angie was. Jim points out that even such a funny-looking boy might be beautiful on the inside. But Angie insists that this boy with the big nose couldn't be anything like Jim. When Angie calls again, she says she saw the short, funny-looking boy with the big nose again. She's discovered that he is Lisa Franklin's former boyfriend named Jim, that he is musically talented but was too shy to sing any of his songs for Lisa, that he and Lisa broke up because he was crowding her and trying to change himself to be more what she wanted. Angie and Jim both admit that the time they spent talking to each other on the phone was the happiest of their lives, but Angie says she can't continue now that she knows he has lied to her. In their last phone call, they review the nine hours they have just spent together, decide to go dancing soon, and make plans to meet the next day. They finish by telling each other the love they feel.

Two teenagers begin their relationship entirely over the phone and get to know a great deal about each other. Both learn not to judge on externals. Written entirely in dialogue, the book focuses on the things that are really important in a relationship: kindness, sharing, support, encouragement. Considering that they only picture nightly phone calls, the illustrations are well done, although the characters appear younger than their ages. Cleverly, Jim is seen only from the back until the end. This is a Skinny Book, part of a series designed for older readers with limited reading skills. These well-written books focus on the interests and concerns of today's young people and should have great appeal.

Ages 12-16

**Also available in:**
Braille—*Hello. . . . Wrong Number*
Library of Congress (NLSBPH)

Paperbound—*Hello. . . . Wrong Number*
Scholastic Book Services

**566**

Sachs, Marilyn

## A Summer's Lease

E. P. Dutton & Company, Inc., 1979.
(124 pages)

---

*EGOCENTRISM*
*JEALOUSY: Peer*
*SCHOOL: Pupil-Teacher Relationships*
  *Cooperation: in work*
  *Determination*
  *Friendship: lack of*
  *Maturation*
  *School: classmate relationships*
  *Talents*

---

It is June, 1943, the end of the school year, and fifteen-year-old Gloria Rein wants one thing only: to be appointed next year's assistant editor of *Wings,* the school literary magazine. As one of the most talented writers in her class, she would appear to be a likely candidate. But her adviser, Mrs. Horne, feels Gloria is not qualified to do the job alone, for the girl does not get along well with others. When Gloria learns that Mrs. Horne plans for her to share the coveted editorial job with Jerry Lieberman, she becomes physically ill. Burningly jealous of other writers, Gloria is filled with hatred at the very sight of other students' writing and tells herself that she is more "versatile," more "extraordinarily talented" than anyone else. She gets little understanding from her widowed mother, who works in a factory and aims to save Gloria from that fate by convincing her to take a "commercial" course so she can get a job in an office. Gloria, however, considers herself a "genius" and is determined to go to college. Mrs. Horne invites both Jerry and Gloria to spend their vacation helping take care of a group of children at her family's summer home in the Catskills. Never having spent time out of the city, Gloria is enchanted with the mountain retreat. She basks in nighttime conversations with Mrs. Horne, who treats Gloria as a friend and equal and is one of the few people the girl admires and respects. But when Mrs. Horne speaks to Jerry with similar intimacy, Gloria storms out of the room. She glories in being the leader of a group of young boys who admire her skills in punchball and wrestling. For Jerry, who is clumsy and has no stomach for rough play, Gloria has only taunts and disdain. She takes Jerry's kindness and his patience in the face of her own rudeness as signs of his weakness. After witnessing an incident in which Gloria leads the others in ridiculing Jerry, Mrs. Horne cuts off her confidential nightly chats with the girl. Aching for her teacher's approval, Gloria apologizes to her for treating Jerry unkindly. But Mrs. Horne tells her it's too late for being sorry. She reminds her that Jerry should no more have to be "locked inside of being a boy" than Gloria should into being a girl. After this, Gloria begins at last

to warm up to Jerry, and one night the two openly discuss their feelings. Gloria admits that she hates feeling jealous all the time, that she knows she has no friends. Jerry tells her that many people like her and would befriend her if she would only show an interest. Then Dorothy, a little girl who has shared a special relationship with Jerry during the summer, falls into a coma. While Mrs. Horne calls frantically for a doctor, Jerry sits paralyzed and Gloria tends to the child. But later, in the hospital, Dorothy dies, and Jerry and Gloria each confess a regret: Jerry that he was unable to help Dorothy while she was dying, and Gloria that she was never kind to the girl while she was living. During the next school year, Gloria and Jerry work together as co-editors, though not without "disputes and differences." Gloria is even able to respond without jealousy to a poem of Jerry's. Shortly before the end of the term, the two quarrel over a submission to *Wings.* Jerry, busy with other projects and perhaps weary of quarreling, resigns. They reestablish a relationship after this, but it's never what it was. Gloria knows their real friendship is over, but she looks forward to being sole editor-in-chief of *Wings* in the fall. "I gloated. . . . It was all mine now, . . . all mine!" She understands herself a bit better, though: "It was still there, to my shame—my need to contend against him."

Wrapped up in her talent, eager for recognition, a teenage girl has immersed herself in lonely, bitter isolation. A perceptive teacher recognizes Gloria's need for love and friendship, and a gentle friend helps her begin to find them. Although Gloria matures and mellows through her experiences with Jerry and Mrs. Horne, her basic personality doesn't change. But she is able to consider the feelings of others upon occasion, discovering "it's a better world . . . if you let your compassion grow bigger than your jealousy." The plot proceeds logically, and character development is strong. Much of this first-person account is in the form of a diary.

Ages 11-14

**Also available in:**
Paperbound—*A Summer's Lease*
Dell Publishing Company, Inc.

**567**

St. George, Judith

## Call Me Margo

G. P. Putnam's Sons, 1981.
(173 pages)

---

*INFERIORITY, FEELINGS OF*
*SCHOOLS, PRIVATE: Girls'*
*SHYNESS*
  *Friendship: meaning of*
  *Homosexuality: female*

---

In all her fifteen years, Margo Allinger has never lived anywhere long enough to feel at home. Her father's job as a government adviser has meant that the family lived outside the U.S. more than inside. Now her parents are on assignment and have decided to let Margo stay in one place for high school: at Haywood, a boarding school near Philadelphia. Though very shy, Margo looks forward to making some lasting friendships. Two sophomore girls, "Stretch" and "Cricket," are kind to her, but they attract so much attention by their uninhibited behavior that Margo feels uncomfortable being with them. It is not until she meets Miss Frye, the tennis coach, that things start to look up. Tennis is the one thing in Margo's life she feels confident about, and Miss Frye seems genuinely to like her. Her brief happiness, however, lasts only until her roommates, both juniors, arrive. She sees right away that these are best friends who don't really need her companionship. Furthermore, B.J. McIver is "outrageously beautiful" and Eva Gordon looks like a model. On the first day of classes, Margo has another setback. When Miss Durrett, the feared English teacher who is "a horror and gives terrible grades," calls on her, she freezes. She's always been shy about talking in class, but never this bad. She tries to forget her humiliation by playing hard at afternoon tennis practice, but the other team members are very unfriendly. That evening, however, B.J. and Eva talk with her, promising to help her with her problems and "stick up" for her. Against her better judgment but out of gratitude, Margo agrees in return to sign their initials on the breakfast register so they can skip the meal and to cover up for them when they come in after curfew "smelling of beer and acting silly." One Friday, Miss Durrett calls on her again. When her throat closes up as it had that first day, she knows the teacher is taking pleasure in her embarrassment. For some reason, an undeclared battle between the two has begun. As Margo's fear of speaking in English class starts to affect her other courses, Miss Frye and their Saturday tennis matches are all that keep her going. It is here that Margo meets Pete Montgomery, who also enjoys tennis. But Miss Frye, Margo notices, doesn't like her to pay much attention to Pete. The coach also sours Margo's relationship with the team by publicly praising her and by displacing a senior and moving her up to third singles. One Saturday when Miss Frye is out of town, Pete cautions Margo about spending so much time with her. Later, Eva bluntly tells her that the tennis coach is gay and that her and B.J.'s reputations are suffering because of Margo's interest in her. Not wanting to believe this about Miss Frye, Margo tries to carry on their relationship as usual. Then, while visiting the coach's apartment, she sees a pair of orthopedic shoes in the closet, considers other observations she's made, and suddenly understands why Miss Durrett hates her so much: she used to live with Miss Frye and is now jealous of Margo. Furthermore, it becomes apparent that many people, her roommates as well as the entire tennis team, believe she is having an affair with Miss Frye. One day Margo is set up by the tennis team to read announcements during the school's public assembly. She is scared speechless until she sees Cricket and Stretch pulling for her in the audience and knows they are her friends. Later, when Eva and B.J. make fun of her nervousness, she realizes they enjoy her failures. "If she were weak and a failure, if she were gay even, they could control her." Feeling comfortable at last, Margo decides to accept Cricket and Stretch's offer to room with them. With Pete and her new roommates believing in her, maybe everything will work out.

A shy and insecure girl must painfully separate friends from enemies at her new boarding school. When she learns her admired tennis coach is gay, she doubts her

own sexuality as she doubts everything else about herself. But new roommates and a sympathetic boy help Margo relax and find her own strengths. The story is believable and satisfying, providing a good view of life in a boarding school.

Ages 12-14

**Also available in:**
Paperbound—*Call Me Margo*
New American Library

## 568

**Sallis, Susan Diana**

**Only Love**

Harper & Row, Publishers, Inc., 1980.
(250 pages)

*BOY-GIRL RELATIONSHIPS*
*LOVE, MEANING OF*
*WHEELCHAIR, DEPENDENCE ON*
Amputee
Death: attitude toward
Nursing home, living in
Paraplegia
Reality, escaping

Frances (Fran) Adamson is sixteen, high-spirited, mischievous, strong-willed, and paraplegic. Newly at Thornton Hall, the last in a series of institutions she has lived in since being abandoned as an infant, Fran meets "Aunt" Nell and "Uncle" Roger, a childless couple who befriend youngsters at Thornton. They enlist her help with another resident, Luke Hawkins, who recently lost both legs in a motorcycle accident. The eighteen-year-old son of wealthy parents, he has withdrawn from all human contact. Fran invites Luke to attend a planning meeting for the upcoming Fete Day at Thornton, but he doesn't appear; instead, Fran learns, he listens to the proceedings from next door. In time, she and Luke begin talking frequently on the telephone, but Luke doesn't want her or anyone to see him. Meanwhile, Fran helps keep things lively at Thornton Hall. She plays matchmaker. She befriends Granny Gorman, full of life despite being crippled by arthritis. Then Fran has a long bout with pneumonia that saps her vitality and drains her spirits. When she is somewhat recovered, Luke finally agrees to meet her—outdoors, after everyone is asleep. When he demands to know why he should respond to her urgings and begin thinking about crutches and artificial legs and walking again, Fran informs him jauntily that he has to have legs to carry her over the threshhold. Fran doesn't hear from Luke again for the next two weeks. On the day of the Fete, he appears triumphantly on crutches with one artificial leg in place. After that, their relationship deepens, impelling Dr. Beamish, the head of Thornton, to advise Fran to tell Luke about her serious heart and lung condition, about the fact that she hasn't long to live. She is not being fair to Luke, the doctor warns. All Fran wants is a year or two of happiness, but she decides to stay away from Luke. That night, however, she can't resist meeting him and returning his embraces. He talks about marriage, but all Fran can see is a future in which everyone but she can walk. Luke invites his parents to visit Thornton for the first time so they can meet Fran. They are shocked at the idea of marriage between a paraplegic girl and a boy with no legs. Fran's disclosure that she can't have children doesn't dissuade Luke, but she is still unable to tell him she is dying. To Granny Gorman, though, she expresses her "calm certainty that it was a privilege to die young. . . . Something to do with a journey; a journey toward something pretty good. And I would get there early." That night, in the garden, Fran tells Luke her secret. He wheels away, devastated. Then Nell and Roger fail to appear as usual on Sunday, and Fran discovers that Roger has left Nell. Fran spends three days with Nell, and the two make plans to swim in the Channel the next weekend. When their scheduled day for the swim arrives, Fran waits for Nell but instead sees Roger and Luke drive up. Gently they break the news: Nell has drowned. Roger seems to think she has killed herself because he left her, but a sorrowful Fran convinces him that Nell was probably just testing the Channel waters in preparation for their swim. When she returns to her room, Luke is waiting outside her door. He lifts the blanket over his legs and she sees jeans and shoes. Awkwardly and with difficulty, he carries Fran over the threshhold of her room. Nobody disturbs them, and they talk together until they fall asleep. In the middle of the night, Luke goes back to his room and telephones Fran, saying that he will always hold her hand on this side and Nell will surely hold her hand on the other. Luke narrates the last chapter of the book. Two years have passed since the six months he knew Fran. She is buried next to Nell. Luke now works in the family business and goes back to Thornton once a week to help out.

Fran's poignant and unforgettable first-person narrative, set in England, is both a love story and a perceptive, useful, and sometimes lyrical view of life from a wheelchair. Her candid storytelling gives vivid life to all the characters. Although the book deals with heavy and sometimes depressing subjects and ends sadly, it has such authenticity and Fran such an irrepressible spirit that it can't be put down. One of the helpers in the institution asks, "What has she got to laugh about? What have any of us here got to laugh about?" But Fran knows what there is to laugh about and shares her laughter with others.

Ages 12 and up

**Also available in:**
Disc—*Only Love*
Library of Congress (NLSBPH)

Paperbound—*Only Love*
Dell Publishing Company, Inc.

**569**

**Sallis, Susan Diana**

## A Time for Everything

Harper & Row, Publishers, Inc., 1979.
(218 pages)

---

*LOVE, MEANING OF*
*MATURATION*
   *Communication: parent-child*
   *Death*
   *Guilt, feelings of*
   *Loneliness*
   *Mental retardation*
   *Prejudice: social class*
   *Sex: extramarital*
   *War*

---

Eleven-year-old Lily Freeman, living with her parents and grandfather in the Cotswold hills of England during World War II, is reasonably contented with her life. But her mother, a "foreigner" rather than a lifelong hill-dweller like her husband, is unhappy, and the parents quarrel often. Then, because London is being bombed, Lily's aunt and her frail, disabled cousin, Philippa, come to live with them. When Lily's father enlists in the infantry, Lily asks old Nanny Dexter to read her tea leaves. She is relieved when Nanny tells her the leaves show loneliness in her future, but not death. She wins a scholarship to high school in Gloucester, but the new school is difficult for Lily and the villagers' snobbish disapproval of her mother and aunt is hard for her to bear. She confides in Philippa who, though clumsy and unable to give words to things, understands. During a summer trip to Cornwall their beach is bombed, bringing the war terrifyingly close. Back at home in the fall, Lily's beloved Grandad dies unexpectedly and Lily goes accusingly to Nanny Dexter, screaming that the tea leaves lied. Nanny confirms the girl's suspicions that her parents had to marry because her mother was pregnant with her. When Mavis, the evacuee Lily's family has taken in, shows Lily a note that says "you are a hoar," Lily immediately assumes that local gossip about her mother and Mr. Edwards, the schoolteacher, is true. When the angry villagers storm to Mr. Edwards's home, Philippa averts any possible violence by seating herself at his front door and playing ball. Then an American Air Force officer, Bob Critchley, begins coming regularly to their house on weekends; Lily, now more and more alienated from her mother, basks in the love she feels for him. When the girl senses a relationship growing between her mother and Bob, she tells him that her mother was pregnant with her before she married, thinking this information will disgust him. But Bob replies that Mum has always put Lily first. Lily is devastated when Mum reveals she is pregnant with Bob's child, and then disgusted when she decides they must not see any more of Bob; she doesn't want him to feel pressured. A day later, word is sent that he has been killed in action. Lily, deeply depressed, cannot forgive her mother, not even for her own begetting. When she learns that the villagers are coming with a petition asking her mother to leave town, Lily decides Mum must face her "punishment" alone and arranges to take Philippa and leave the house. But Philippa, sensing danger,

S

hides in the woods, forcing the townspeople to search for her instead of confronting Mum. The exposure further weakens Philippa, who dies soon after, leaving a terrible void in Lily's life. When Mum enters the hospital to give birth, Lily can tell her honestly that she does not hate her. But she still feels lonely and torn. Then Lily discovers that Mavis herself had made the notes calling her mother a "hoar." Unexpectedly, her father walks in the door, having gotten a "compassionate leave," and says he plans to stay. Lily asks if he'll mind about Mum's new baby, and he says he will. But he knows he'll feel worse if he goes away and never sees Lily and Mum again.

Regional English dialect adds authenticity to this first-person account of a young girl's maturation during the difficult years of World War II. At first Lily's growing awareness of life's complexity and people's fallibility—notably her mother's—causes her to retreat in angry confusion. But partly through the example of her remarkable cousin, ill and disabled but a constant source of love, Lily finds strength, courage, and a new bond with her parents. Her father's timely return seems contrived, but the reader senses that Lily could have found her way even without it. The book's realistic dialogue includes occasional profanity.

Ages 13 and up

**Also available in:**
No other form known

## 570

**Sargent, Sarah**

## Secret Lies

Crown Publishers, Inc., 1981.
(118 pages)

---

*IDENTITY, SEARCH FOR*
*MATURATION*
   *Abandonment*
   *Change: accepting*
   *Fantasy formation*
   *Loneliness*
   *Parental: absence*
   *Relatives: living in home of*

---

One day Elvira Judson, thirteen, comes home from school in Chicago and discovers a note from her mother that makes her furious. Elvira's mother has run off to marry her boyfriend and has left Elvira money to go to her Aunt Carrie's in Charlottesville, Virginia. Elvira has no intention of leaving Chicago, but when school officials discover her situation they turn her over to a social worker who makes the arrangements for her. Elvira must resign herself to the fact that while her mother is gone, she will have to stay with relatives. "She was a deserted daughter going to stay with an old aunt back in the bushes, and she might as well start facing up to it." Elvira's passion has always been to fantasize about the father she never knew and knows nothing about. Now, traveling by train to her aunt's, she dreams of him. Aunt Carrie, a semi-retired nurse, meets Elvira and drives her to her home thirty miles outside of Charlottesville. Living with her also is Cousin Henry, past eighty and an invalid. The next day Elvira goes for a hike in the woods and comes upon a deserted, dilapidated old plantation.

There she discovers Michael, about sixteen, who has run away from his nearby home. Elvira falls in love with the old house that fits so well the life she imagines with her handsome, rich father. She begins asking her aunt about her parents. Aunt Carrie is vague, saying only that they were too young to face up to family life. She does mention that Elvira's father's sister lives in Charlottesville. Elvira begs to see her and a meeting day is set. But Aunt Joyce is a bitter disappointment. The visit is made even worse when Elvira is shown a recent picture of her father. He is fat and bald. Her dreams of him fade, and she realizes how alone she really is. She begs Michael to let her go with him when he leaves the plantation. He tells her the tragedy of Aunt Carrie's childhood and why Cousin Henry is an invalid. Aunt Carrie's "deranged" father, discovering that his young wife and Cousin Henry loved each other, had shot and killed his wife and himself. Henry too was shot and crippled. Suddenly Elvira feels great sympathy toward these two who have suffered as she has and who also keep secrets. Back at the house, Aunt Carrie warns Elvira to stay out of the woods; the sheriff thinks someone is staying at the old plantation. That night Elvira sneaks away and warns Michael. He asks her to join him in his escape, but she refuses: Aunt Carrie and Cousin Henry are her family now.

Abandoned by both parents, a young teenage girl must leave her home in Chicago to live with an aging aunt and cousin. When her fantasy life with her glamorized father is shattered by the truth of his appearance and nature, Elvira comes to see that the security and love she longs for can be found with her relatives in her new home. Enhancing the story are the sympathetic tone, strong characterizations, and vividly described setting; detracting a bit is the superficially handled relationship with the runaway, Michael.

Ages 11 and up

**Also available in:**
No other form known

## 571

**Sarnoff, Jane and Reynold Ruffins**

## That's Not Fair

Color illustrations by Reynold Ruffins.
Charles Scribner's Sons, 1980.
(30 pages counted)

---

*JUSTICE/INJUSTICE*
   *Sibling: relationships*

---

Becky, about five, is bored. Her older brother, Bert, is too busy reading to play. When her mother suggests she dust the furniture or peel potatoes, Becky insists that "sissy silly girls' work" is not fair. Father suggests she clean her room. Becky thinks that's not fair either. Bert informs Becky that she must not say "that's not fair" every time she does not get her way. Elephants, he explains, have four knees, whereas other animals have only two. Elephants do not say "that's not fair." Instead, they accept the way things are. But if he, Bert, cut pieces of cake for the two of them, a large one for himself and a very small one for Becky, that would be unfair. Becky tries the new philosophy, applying Bert's examples of fair and unfair to various situations. She understands when her friend Ben cannot play, when everyone gets mail except her, and when her best friend goes away and can't be with her. But when Father says he will take Bert downtown, Becky complains, "That's not fair." Then she discovers that Father is taking Bert to have a haircut that Bert does not want. Now it is Bert's turn to say, "That's not fair." But, as Becky hastens to explain, it's "as fair as an elephant's knees."

An older brother uses logic to teach his sister the difference between fair and unfair. But when the tables are turned and Bert meets injustice, Becky is quick to apply his logic to his own situation. Softly colored illustrations extend the story with details not included in the text, adding humor to this lighthearted account.

Ages 4-7

**Also available in:**
No other form known

## 572

**Savitz, Harriet May**

### Run, Don't Walk

Franklin Watts, Inc., 1979.
(122 pages)

---

*PARAPLEGIA*
*SCHOOL: Mainstreaming*
*WHEELCHAIR, DEPENDENCE ON*
  *Boy-girl relationships: dating*
  *Perseverance*
  *Pets: love for*
  *Prejudice: toward handicapped persons*
  *School: pupil-teacher relationships*
  *Self, attitude toward: accepting*

---

Since a diving accident a year ago that left her paralyzed from the waist down, Samantha Lee Anderson (called Sam) has lived in her own world. Her only friend and constant companion is her dog, Mandy, whom she rescued from an animal shelter. After missing a year of school, Sam returns for her senior year. She longs to be inconspicuous, left alone with her dreams and her writing. Unfortunately for Sam, classmate Johnny Jay feels differently. Johnny too is in a wheelchair, but he is a fighter and an attention seeker for his cause, the rights of the disabled. With the support of NOD, Now Organized Disabled, Johnny has been picketing the school's restrooms because they are inaccessible to wheelchairs. Sam avoids Johnny, snubbing him when he asks her to join the protests. Coming gradually out of her shell, she joins the school paper in November and for her first interview chooses Ms. Jenkins, her English teacher, who is a runner. Sam is taken by the similarities between running and writing—both are exhilarating and solitary. A few days after the interview, Sam asks Ms. Jenkins if she can work out with her. They do so three mornings a week before school and an hour on Saturdays, Ms. Jenkins running, Sam in her chair. Sam begins to confide in her teacher and gets so caught up in training that she asks Ms. Jenkins to help her sign up for the city's twenty-six-mile marathon scheduled for April. By early spring Sam and Johnny have become friends, though they avoid the issue of Johnny's militancy. On a date, Johnny takes Sam to a protest demonstration for the blind. They are counted in the masses of people giving support to the cause, and an angry Sam ends the relationship. Johnny organizes another protest at school over the restroom issue, bringing in people from NOD to picket with him. He is expelled for two weeks. Soon after, Ms. Jenkins breaks the news to Sam that she cannot "run" in the marathon. The officials said their decision "was only for her own good." A stunned Sam is finally able to share Johnny's anger and take up his cause. She organizes a student walkout and, after three days, school officials agree to remodel the restrooms. NOD also helps Sam get approval to participate in the marathon. She begins the race fifteen minutes early to avoid injury to herself or the runners. Four hours and twenty-six miles later, Sam triumphantly crosses the finish line to the cheers of the onlookers, including her parents, Ms. Jenkins, and Johnny.

Withdrawn and refusing to consider the implications of her condition, a newly paraplegic girl is at first content to go through high school unnoticed and alone. A militant disabled classmate and an understanding teacher help Sam confront her paralysis and her feelings. She is finally able to admit she is disabled and has special needs that deserve to be met. The author is well qualified to be a spokesperson for the handicapped, having worked for many years with disabled people and with wheelchair sports teams.

Ages 12 and up

**Also available in:**
Cassette—*Run, Don't Walk*
Library of Congress (NLSBPH)

## 573

**Schick, Eleanor Grossman**

### Home Alone

Color illustrations by the author.
The Dial Press, Inc., 1980.
(56 pages)

---

*DEPENDENCE/INDEPENDENCE*
  *Change: accepting*
  *Parent/Parents: mother working outside home*

---

Little Andy's mother began working full-time today, so no one will be home when he returns from school. He has his own keys and has practiced using them. Mrs. Scott, who lives next door, will be available if he needs anything or gets lonely. As soon as Andy steps inside the apartment, he locks the door behind him as instructed. Then he calls his mother at her office to say he's home. She is happy to hear all is well and tells him to look for the note she left for him. He remembers that he's not to open the door to anyone, and he follows the directions in the note: have cookies and milk, do homework, take hamburgers out of the freezer. The rooms seem bigger to Andy today and the noises louder. He builds a big play town in his room for all his toy animals. He turns on the radio to shut out the sounds of creaking stairs in the building's hallway whenever someone comes home. When the phone rings, he takes a message for his mother, knowing he should not tell anyone he is home alone. She arrives a few minutes before she said she would. Andy shows her the town he built, the telephone message, and the defrosting hamburgers. "Mom says I did a good job, and she is very proud of me." Then Andy tells his mother about his day at school and she tells him about her new office. He helps her with dinner and gets to peek at the lemon cake she brought home for dessert.

In this first-person account, a little boy comes home to an empty house for the first time and acts responsibly and self-reliantly. Attractive illustrations dress up this beginning reader, well suited for use by parents and children together as they prepare for a similar new experience.

Ages 5-8

Also available in:
Paperbound—*Home Alone*
The Dial Press, Inc.

## 574

### Schick, Eleanor Grossman

### Joey on His Own

Color illustrations by the author.
The Dial Press, Inc., 1982.
(56 pages)

---

*DEPENDENCE/INDEPENDENCE*
  *Helping*
  *Self-esteem*
  *Success*

---

When little Joey's mother discovers they're out of bread and she can't leave Joey's sick younger sister, she asks Joey to go to the store. She shows him the empty bread bag and tells him to get another loaf like it. She puts money and the empty bread bag in his pocket and hands him his jacket, mittens, and hat. Says Joey, "And she didn't even give me a chance to say no." Joey's never been shopping without his mother before, and on the way to the store he notices that the buildings seem much bigger, the traffic noisier, and the mean kid down the block meaner. The dog behind the fence barks more loudly, and the store seems very far away. When he gets there he asks a man where the bread is, and the man tells Joey he's very grown-up to be shopping by himself. In the bread aisle, a woman helps him find the right kind of bread. In the checkout line Joey keeps a toddler in a cart entertained. The cashier takes his money, gives him change, and says, "Thank you very much, sir." On his way home, Joey feels terrific. The dog isn't barking anymore, and he shows the mean kid he doesn't care how mean he is. The traffic isn't as loud and the buildings are about the right size. When he gets home, Joey brings the mail up to his mother. She says he did a perfect job. Lunch never tasted so good!

In this engaging beginning reader, a little boy goes to the store by himself for the first time, completing his errand with resounding success. Simple, attractive illustrations follow Joey as he describes his progress toward self-assurance. The pithy story will appeal to many children on the verge of this sort of independence. Reading it over and over will help prepare them for stepping out on their own.

Ages 5-8

Also available in:
Paperbound—*Joey on His Own*
The Dial Press, Inc.

## 575

### Schotter, Roni

### A Matter of Time

William Collins Publishers, Inc., 1979.
(128 pages)

---

*DEATH: of Mother*
*IDENTITY, SEARCH FOR*
  *Cancer*
  *Communication: parent-child*
  *Friendship: best friend*
  *Guilt, feelings of*
  *Illnesses: terminal*

---

Lisl Gilbert is sixteen and a senior in high school when she learns that her attractive, artistic, dynamic mother is dying of cancer. Lisl has always admired, even envied, her mother, sometimes trying to outdo her but always feeling eclipsed. There have been times when boyfriends who called for Lisl became so enthralled with her mother that they didn't notice Lisl enter the room. Jean Gilbert, her daughter thinks, is a "special person"; she, on the other hand, is a "nothing." She should be the one to die. But as her mother's body grows weaker, Lisl begins to realize that behind the woman's superstar image is a frail human being, as confused about life and as insecure as her daughter. Lisl is helped through her emotional ordeal by her loyal, understanding best friend, Jo, and by a surprising source of counsel—a social worker, Samantha Canby, called Sam. Lisl's older sister had suggested that Lisl contact a social worker, although both expect a "gray-haired lady with heavy shoes and a high-collared dress." Instead, young Sam makes her first appearance in denim skirt, Mexican shirt, sandals, and shawl. Lisl is initially unimpressed, but gradually comes to value having Sam to talk to as her mother's condition worsens. Lisl's father, out of work, always overshadowed by his wife, is of little help. When her mother entreats her to stay home from school with her, Lisl is torn apart with guilt. But she manages to express both her love for her mother and her need to maintain her own life as normally as possible. Her mother understands, and Sam helps Lisl see that if she is to survive this tragedy, she must begin to establish her own identity, must find out how she herself is special. She learns to choose the things she likes best about her mother's spirit and personality and incorporate these into her own individual style of living. Her mother's life ends on Lisl's graduation day. By then, the girl has begun to discover her own uniqueness. Realizing that her father will now be alone, she resolves to improve their relationship. Although she is sadder than she has ever been before, Lisl knows that life is worth living and that she is a person worth being.

This first-person narrative, told in retrospect by a girl who has survived a terrible ordeal and, as a result, has done a lot of thinking and growing in a short time, is a moving, but not morbid, story. Lisl's struggle to establish her own identity and her recognition that her idolized mother is only human after all will have implications for many readers in similar situations. The story is occasionally a bit didactic in its attempt to present a contemporary philosophy of death and dying.

Ages 12 and up

Also available in:
Paperbound—*A Matter of Time*
Grosset & Dunlap, Inc.

## 576
**Schubert, Ingrid and Dieter Schubert**

## There's a Crocodile Under My Bed!
Translated from the Dutch.
Color illustrations by the authors.
McGraw-Hill Book Company, 1981.
(24 pages counted)

---

*BEDTIME*
*FEAR: of Darkness*
*IMAGINATION*

---

Before Peggy's parents go out for the evening, Peggy reports a crocodile under her bed. Her father reassures her that crocodiles exist only in the zoo and in places like Africa. He checks under the bed where Peggy has seen two glowing eyes, but finds nothing. However, when Peggy turns out the light, she hears giggling. It's coming from a large crocodile on top of the wardrobe. Peggy is frightened at first, but the crocodile immediately reassures her by saying his name is James and showing her that he can shrink until he's quite small. No longer frightened, Peggy says she prefers him his usual size. He returns to it and says he'd like a wash as he's very dusty. Peggy and James take a bath together, dance to the stereo (he teaches her the Crocodile Rock), and make a small crocodile out of an old egg carton, paint, paper, and glue. Peggy is getting sleepy, so James carries her to bed and tells her about the Land of Crocodiles. He was a very mischievous young crocodile, he says. Once he exchanged crocodile eggs with ostrich eggs, confusing and frightening all the crocodile and ostrich parents. He was brought before the Council of the Seven Wise Crocodiles. For his punishment he has been sent to the Land of Man, where he must love and comfort one thousand children who are afraid of the dark. He was given two gifts: the language of people and the ability to shrink so he would not frighten them. When his task is completed, he will once again be welcome in the Land of Crocodiles. After telling his story, James slips quietly out of the sleeping Peggy's room. The next morning her father sees the egg-box crocodile under Peggy's bed and says, "So there was a crocodile under your bed after all!" Peggy just smiles.

A little girl copes with her bedtime fears by turning the frightening crocodile of her imagination into a gentle, entertaining fantasy, spending an evening with a delightful crocodile whose very job is to reassure her. Marvelous, whimsical illustrations take almost as long to "read" as the book and may produce as much discussion. Illustrated directions for making the egg-box crocodile are included. Some readers might notice that there is no mention of a baby-sitter for Peggy.

Ages 3-6

Also available in:
No other form known

## 577
**Schuchman, Joan**

## Two Places to Sleep
Color illustrations by Jim LaMarche.
Carolrhoda Books, Inc., 1979.
(31 pages counted)

---

*DIVORCE: of Parents*
 *Anxiety*
 *Change: accepting*
 *Guilt, feelings of*

---

David's parents are divorced and the seven-year-old spends weekdays with his father, weekends with his mother. During the week, David is in the family home: familiar surroundings. His father's kindly housekeeper assures him that he can and will get over his parents' breakup, but David is uncertain and fearful, continuing to hope his parents will be reunited. Despite the patience and reassurance of both parents, David dreads losing their love and feels that he is somehow the cause of the family's troubles. One Saturday his mother buys him a kite and races him through the park. At dinner after this happy afternoon, David spills his malt. Although his mother does not scold him, the episode lingers in the boy's mind. Finally, he asks his mother if she will "get undivorced from Dad" if he is careful not to spill anything and keeps his room clean. She assures David that he is not the cause of the divorce, that her need not change—he is loved by both parents just as he is. After she tucks him in bed, reads him a story, and kisses him goodnight, David decides he is getting used to having two places to sleep.

Despite patient, supportive, reassuring parents, a young boy needs time and abundant love to accept the breakup of his family. The first-person narrator is convincing, even touching, a figure young readers should find easy to understand and trust. The characters, though lightly developed, are deftly drawn. Handsome illustrations complement the compact text. David's insights—that divorces happen but that parents don't "get divorced from their children," that he can get used to his new life—have wide application and should provoke useful discussion between parents and children.

Ages 5-7

Also available in:
No other form known

## 578
**Schultz, Gwendolyn**

## The Blue Valentine
Black/white illustrations by Elizabeth Coberly.
William Morrow & Company, Inc., 1979.
(64 pages)

---

*SCHOOL: Transfer*
 *Friendship: making friends*

---

Cindy and her parents move to a new house, and Cindy enters first grade in a new school. Although none of the children in her class seem friendly, the teacher, Miss Kelly, tries to make her feel welcome. Cindy discovers that she and Miss Kelly share a favorite color: blue. A week before Valentine's Day, Cindy works hard to make a beautiful blue card for Miss Kelly. She is the first in the class to put her card into the classroom box, and for a week she anticipates the opening. When the valentines have been distributed, Cindy feels sad because she received very few, but she feels especially hurt because Miss Kelly does not hang up the blue valentine with her others. The next morning Miss Kelly explains that after all the children went home, she found Cindy's card stuck to the bottom of the box. She tells the class it is so beautiful that she wants Cindy to show how the card was made. After school one of the girls in her class walks Cindy home.

A young girl seeks to win her teacher's approval and her classmates' acceptance through the use of her artistic talent. An understanding mother and a sensitive teacher give her gentle encouragement. Updated illustrations make the book more timely and give new appeal for young readers. Detailed instructions for making the valentine card are included.

Ages 5-8

**Also available in:**
No other form known

## 579

**Sebestyen, Ouida**

**Far from Home**

Little, Brown and Company, 1980.
(191 pages)

---

CHANGE: Accepting
IDENTITY, SEARCH FOR
UNWED MOTHER: Child of
  Belonging
  Communication: parent-child
  Grandparent: love for
  Love, meaning of
  Maturation
  Rejection: parental

---

After the death of his unmarried mother, thirteen-year-old Salty Yeager must find some way for himself and his great-grandmother, Mam, to live. He promised his mother that he would always care for Mam. His mother has left him a note: "GO TO TOM BUCKLEY HE TAKE YOU IN LOVE HIM." It's 1929 in a small Texas town, and Tom Buckley is the owner of the run-down Buckley Arms, a boardinghouse. At present the only permanent guests are Hardy McCaslin, Tom's wife Babe's unemployed nephew, and his wife, Rose Ann. Salty's mother had worked at the Buckley Arms for fifteen years, and Salty hopes they will hire him to replace her. Tom seems to want nothing to do with Salty, but Babe has Salty and Mam move into the boardinghouse. There Salty helps Babe with the housework and lives in his mother's basement room. Hardy is a practical joker who spends the little money he has on rubber centipedes and other joke items he orders from catalogs. His and Rose Ann's relationship is shaky, and things get worse

when he learns Rose Ann is pregnant. She had thought a baby would save their marriage. While running an errand one morning, Salty meets Jo Miller, a young, pregnant woman, who asks him about the nearest hotel and then faints as he is trying to help her into the boardinghouse. She has just fled Dallas, where her husband perjured himself in a trial. She knows he was guilty; at least seven people lost their eyesight because of the liquor he "cut" with grain alcohol to make more profits. She begins living at the Buckley Arms. When Salty tells Tom that he's determined to find out who his father is, Tom coldly discourages him. Then Salty goes to help Tom at the ice dock where Tom has taken a job, accidentally touches a live wire, and is nearly electrocuted. Afterwards, Tom and Salty cling to each other with unguarded affection. When Hardy leads Salty to realize that Tom is his father, Salty understands that the idea has been unacknowledged in the back of his mind. He is terribly angry at Tom's neglect, "passing him on the street all his life without wanting to love or even know him." Now Salty wants recognition from Tom, but Hardy warns him that Tom isn't about to let Salty "mess up his life." Salty realizes that for the first time he has the power to hurt other people—Babe doesn't know about Tom's involvement with Salty's mother. After much arguing with Hardy, Rose Ann leaves to visit her sister. While she's gone, Hardy broods over her attempt to tie him to her by means of a baby. Tom and Salty are often angry at each other. One day when Salty gets home, his beloved pet goose is gone. He blames Tom and threatens to tell Babe who he really is. During the Fourth of July parade, news comes to Hardy that Rose Ann is suffering from infection because of a self-induced abortion. Salty wonders why Rose Ann thought that killing their baby would make Hardy love her more. Then he realizes that he was doing something similar when he threatened to tell Babe—by hurting Tom and Babe's relationship, he was expecting to bind Tom to him. Before Hardy leaves to go to Rose Ann, he and Tom sit in the front seat of Tom's car drinking, Salty in the back seat. The two men talk as if Salty weren't there. Tom tells Hardy what Salty and his mother meant in his life and why he intends to keep from hurting Babe at all costs, even if it means never telling Salty that he loves him. Salty understands. When they get back to the boardinghouse, they find that Mam is missing. Salty and Tom find her where her house used to be. She has evidently had a stroke. Tom offers to share Salty's responsibility for Mam. Late that night, Salty and Idalee, a neighbor girl, climb on the roof to set off Hardy's Fourth of July firecrackers. Salty objects because Hardy isn't there, but Idalee says, "Well, we are."

A motherless young boy's struggle to force his father to acknowledge and love him on his own terms must be modified as he fits himself into his father's world. Tom's growing acceptance of Salty in his life is almost as painful for him as Salty's fight for recognition and love. Three relationships reflect each other here: Salty and Tom's; Jo and her husband's; Hardy and Rose Ann's. In each case, at least one person must decide whether life is better lived without the other person or with that person along with considerable compromise. As Jo says, "To be bonded so closely to somebody, and then to be opposed. It must be the most terrible thing that can happen to people." In this sober but poignant period piece, the reader watches as Salty takes the first steps toward maturity. He stops being solely self-regarding and begins to look at and care about others in a realistic light.

Ages 12 and up

**Also available in:**
Paperbound—*Far from Home*
Dell Publishing Company, Inc.

## 580

Sebestyen, Ouida

**Words by Heart**

Little, Brown and Company, 1979.
(162 pages)

---

*AFRO-AMERICAN*
*COURAGE, MEANING OF*
*PREJUDICE: Ethnic/Racial*
  *Communication: parent-child*
  *Death: of father*
  *Death: murder*
  *Love, meaning of*
  *Religion: faith*
  *Values/Valuing: moral/ethical*

---

The year is 1910 and twelve-year-old Lena Sills's family is the only black family living in the cotton-growing community of Bethel Springs, Mississippi. For most of her life Lena has lived in the all-black town of Scattercreek. Here in Bethel Springs she begins for the first time to feel vulnerable. When she wins first prize in a scripture-memorizing contest, over a favored white boy, her victory surprises and upsets people. She and her parents return home to find a butcher knife stabbed through a fresh-baked loaf of bread and into the table. Then her father is hired to replace Mr. Haney, an irresponsible white field hand, and Lena realizes that the community's apparent acceptance of her family is both superficial and fragile. Old Bullet, the family dog, is mysteriously killed, but Papa tells Lena she must not hold anyone in Bethel Springs responsible for the deed. Lena is troubled by her father's unwillingness to seek justice, but she shares his empathy for other people. When Mr. Haney's son, Tater, is taunted in school, the girl offers her lunch to him, even though she privately suspects that it was he who killed Old Bullet. The boy's father gets violent when he drinks; at one point he menaces Lena and her younger brother and sister when he comes to make her father "pay" for taking his job. Lena's heart goes out to the Haney family, with their shiftless father and many mouths to feed. She even comes to feel sorry for lonely, crotchety Mrs. Chism, owner of the land where Lena's father and Claudie, her stepmother, work. Lena wins over Mrs. Chism enough to persuade her to lend books that had been her children's. Then Mrs. Chism sends Papa on a fence-mending trip that will take him away from home alone for a few days, to both parents' dismay. Sensing danger when Papa fails to return on schedule, Lena sets off on her own to look for him. She finds him close to death from a bullet wound. His assailant, Tater, is also lying helpless, severely hurt from being thrown and dragged by his horse, drifting in and out of consciousness. Told by her

father that he himself will die shortly, Lena wonders if God has betrayed them. Papa gently acknowledges that she must grapple with the question, but she will surely find an answer. He insists she must help Tater home. In the next agonizing minutes, Lena's father dies and Tater begs Lena for help. The girl struggles with the choice of helping him ("love your enemies and do good to those who hate you") or leaving him to die ("a tooth for a tooth"). Finally she decides she must help him: even though she cannot love Tater, "she loved someone who knew how to love him, and that was a beginning." In silence, Lena returns Tater to his family and then takes her dead father home with the horse and wagon. She resolves never to reveal to anyone who was responsible for the killing. Claudie, despite her grief, announces to the white neighbors who have gathered that the Sills family will remain in Bethel Springs to fulfill Papa's dream of a better life for his children.

A young black girl looks to her father and to her Christian faith to help her cope with injustice and racial violence. This is a poignant, powerfully written story. Characters are carefully and completely drawn, with realistic, occasionally profane, dialogue. Both Lena's moral strength and her shock and confusion at each new injustice are sensitively depicted. Some readers may question her decision not to hold Tater responsible for her father's death, but the story's emphasis is on the triumph of love and forgiveness, even in the face of premeditated murder. Lena's decision is balanced by Claudie's newfound determination to stay in the hostile white community, rather than return to Scattercreek.

Ages 10-13

**Also available in:**
Cassette—*Words by Heart*
Library of Congress (NLSBPH)

Paperbound—*Words by Heart*
Dell Publishing Company, Inc.

## 581

Seuling, Barbara

**The Triplets**

Color illustrations by the author.
Clarion Books, 1980.
(32 pages counted)

---

*AUTONOMY*
*TRIPLETS*
  *Problem solving*

---

Hattie, Patty, and Mattie are identical triplets and nobody can tell them apart. Even worse, nobody seems to try. People point and stare at them. Kids call them Huey, Dewey, and Louie. Their father cheers for Patty when it is Mattie who catches the last baseball in the game. Everyone refers to them as "the triplets" or to one as "the triplet who . . ." They want to play the parts of the shepherd, Herod, and an angel in the school Christmas play. Instead, they become the Three Wise Men. So it goes. Finally, the three retire to their bedroom and refuse to come out until they are recognized as individuals. The police cannot help because the girls are not breaking any laws. The firefighters cannot help because they are not in danger. But when a firefighter recognizes one of his two identical dogs by its love of flowers, everybody sees a way to tell the triplets apart. Lists of each girl's likes, dislikes, talents, and interests are drawn up and memorized. The dog carries three separate notes upstairs, each informing one girl that she is now recognized individually. Soon all three are out of their room and back with their family and friends.

Identical triplets have to insist on being known as individuals in this gently humorous story that twins also will appreciate—as will anyone tired of being identified only as a part of something. Cartoonlike illustrations capture the spirit of the text and help point out differences among the three heroines.

Ages 4-7

**Also available in:**
No other form known

## 582

**Shane, Ruth and Harold Shane**

## The New Baby

Color illustrations by Eloise Wilkin.
Western Publishing Company, Inc., 1980.
(24 pages counted)

---

*SIBLING: New Baby*

---

When a deliveryman brings a large box to little Mike's house, his parents tell him it is a buggy for the new baby. Mike is amazed to learn he will soon have a brother or sister, and he has many questions. On the day Aunt Pat comes to stay for a while, Mike asks his parents, "Who'll bring the baby?" His mother explains that the baby will be born in the hospital. That very night Mike wakes to find the hall light on and Aunt Pat in her robe. His mother kisses him and says she is going to the hospital to have their baby. The next morning Daddy calls from the hospital: "Mike, you have a beautiful baby sister!" Mike hands the phone to Aunt Pat and runs next door to tell Mrs. Blair the exciting news. His father returns home and a green truck delivers another big box, this time for Mike. He wonders if this means they are going to have another baby. But in the box is Mike's big new bed, and the boy happily helps his father assemble it. Now the baby can have his small one. It seems forever before Mommy brings little Pat home. Mike gazes in awe at his sister's tiny hands, blue eyes, and soft, wispy hair. He sits way back on the couch and holds her just right. "How proud Mike is."

This story, to be read to young children, gently expresses a little boy's excitement and awe over the arrival of a new baby. Softly colored illustrations reinforce the positive tone, aimed at helping young children ease into the adjustment of sharing life with a new brother or sister.

Ages 2-6

**Also available in:**
No other form known

## 583

**Sharmat, Marjorie Weinman**

## Lucretia the Unbearable

Black/white illustrations by Janet Stevens.
Holiday House, Inc., 1981.
(38 pages counted)

---

*IMAGINATION*
*Friendship: keeping friends*

---

Lucretia Bear prepares for her bicycle ride by packing drops for her throat, a handkerchief for her nose, a thermometer in case of fever, and bandages in case she gets hurt. Once started, she meets Hunkly Lion, who tells her she has a wart on her nose. This news makes Lucretia feel sick, and she goes to Hunkly's for warm milk. There she smells fresh paint and feels sicker. Then she fears she is losing her memory. Finally, Lucretia agrees to see the doctor. Fatso Tiger is waiting to see the doctor too, but Lucretia refuses to sit by him because she suspects he has a sore throat. She finally sits by Loretta Sue Turtle, who is there to have her shell checked for cracks. The doctor pronounces Lucretia fit so she hurries away. Then, on a bike trip with Hunkly, Lucretia falls and hurts her knee. She declares she is dead; Hunkly says all she needs is a Band-Aid. Lucretia insists she is much worse than he thinks. Finally Hunkly tells her she is unbearable and rides away. Even Loretta Sue and Fatso have no sympathy for her. Lucretia begins to realize that the scrape on her knee is little and her friends are few. Maybe Hunkly is right; she is unbearable. So Lucretia packs a picnic basket and hurries to Hunkly's house, where she finds Loretta Sue and Fatso. Lucretia tells them she feels so good she wants to have a picnic. After convincing them that she is "not on the lookout for germy flies, ants . . . food poisoning . . . or a jaw ache," the four friends have a picnic. And they never call Lucretia unbearable again.

Overly concerned about her health, a young bear quickly discovers that her friends find her complaints unbearable. Once Lucretia resolves to be happy and feel good, she renews her friendships. This simple, charming tale with its simple solution invites discussion. Pencil drawings of the animal characters increase the appeal for young readers.

Ages 4-7

**Also available in:**
No other form known

## 584

**Sharmat, Marjorie Weinman**

## Rollo and Juliet, Forever!

Color illustrations by Marylin Hafner.
Doubleday & Company, Inc., 1981.
(32 pages counted)

---

*FRIENDSHIP: Best Friend*
*Anger*

---

Rollo Cat and Juliet Cat are best friends. "Our friendship is true blue," Juliet says. "Through sad times, good times, rain, sleet, crackling thunder and prickly heat, our friendship will go on." Rollo wholeheartedly agrees. Then one day Rollo does not come to Juliet's house to play tag. Juliet discovers him at his own house with August, a new cat in the neighborhood. An angry Juliet pours a pitcher of tomato juice on Rollo's head. Rollo retaliates by pouring a carton of buttermilk on Juliet. Juliet runs away screaming she hates Rollo; Rollo screams that he hates Juliet. Each pledges never to speak to the other. For a while Juliet and Rollo "enjoyed hating each other." Then, after several weeks, both become calmer. Juliet wants to tell Rollo she's not angry anymore. But she doesn't know how, since they aren't talking. So she calls Rollo on the telephone, says hello, and hangs up. Rollo calls back and says, "Hello back." He knows she wants to make up so he goes to her house and tells her she can apologize. She must miss all his "wonderful qualities." Juliet promptly dumps a pitcher of limeade over Rollo. But both realize they really do want to talk to each other. When they meet on the street, they say a few words. Each time they meet the conversations get longer. Finally they agree that they like being friends. Rollo and Juliet make up and, even though they will still argue occasionally, pledge to be friends forever.

This is a delightful, imaginative account of a friendship, a quarrel that interrupts the friendship, and the renewing of the relationship. Pastel illustrations capture the moods of the two feline friends and the action of the story. Young readers and the read-aloud set will enjoy discussing the friendship of Rollo and Juliet.

Ages 4-8

**Also available in:**
No other form known

## 585

**Sharmat, Marjorie Weinman**

## Say Hello, Vanessa

Black/white illustrations by Lillian Hoban.
Holiday House, Inc., 1979.
(29 pages counted)

---

*FRIENDSHIP: Making Friends*
*SHYNESS*

---

Vanessa the mouse is so bashful she hides under the sofa when company comes. She has no friends at school and is glad to be seated behind Quincy Moose, whose large antlers hide her. "Trying to make friends must be the scariest thing in the world," Vanessa tells her mother. One day Mr. Mitchell, the teacher, asks the students to spell *country*. Vanessa knows how, but is afraid to raise her hand. After class she watches enviously as her classmates gather together. "Bunches and groups, bunches and groups," she thinks. "Everybody has enough friends already. They don't need me." When Vanessa arrives home by herself, her mother suggests she find someone else in her class who is alone and then say hello. Vanessa agrees to try. The next day she walks slowly toward Lisa Goat and, in a tiny whisper, says hello. Lisa doesn't hear her, so Vanessa whispers hello once more before turning away in defeat. The following day, with new purpose, Vanessa

approaches Sigmund Toad. She shouts hello so loudly he covers his ears and hops away. Vanessa vows then to say nothing to anyone. But when Mr. Mitchell asks the children to spell *tooth*, Vanessa, with an eagerness she can't conceal, raises her hand high and spells *tooth* perfectly. Everyone looks at her, but she doesn't mind. In fact, it feels good. After class Quincy Moose tells her he wishes he could spell *tooth* and even *moose*. As they walk out of class together, Vanessa happily teaches Quincy to spell *moose*. On the way home, with Quincy at her side, Vanessa calls out greetings to everyone, her shyness forgotten.

In this perceptive story told through animals, the sensitive problem of a shy child's making friends is addressed in a gently humorous way. Vanessa Mouse, unable to conceal her spelling ability, learns there are simple and natural ways of offering friendship to others. Pencil illustrations showing the characters in old-fashioned dress and surroundings add a charming warmth to the story.

Ages 4-7

**Also available in:**
Paperbound—*Say Hello, Vanessa*
Scholastic Book Services

## S

## 586

**Sharmat, Marjorie Weinman**

## Sometimes Mama and Papa Fight

Color illustrations by Kay Chorao.
Harper & Row, Publishers, Inc., 1980.
(31 pages)

---

*PARENT/PARENTS: Fighting Between*

---

Even though Kevin and Millicent, about six and eight, cover their ears, they can still hear their parents arguing. Kevin is scared. He wishes it were a school day so he could leave, but it's Sunday. He tries to invent ways to tune out the sounds. He thinks about something funny, and then he and Millicent sing a loud song. He wants to say, "Hey, Mama. Hey, Papa. That's a silly fight you're having, so stop that silly fight." He thinks of ways to draw their attention to him and away from the fight, saying he doesn't feel well. He remembers when there was a fight about a new chair that his mother liked but his father thought was ugly. He remembers telling them that he hates fights and they agreed that they do too. "But they happen sometimes, and then they get over with." He thinks about the happy times they have when Mama and Papa are not fighting, when they all sing together or draw pictures. Suddenly Millicent and Kevin hear their parents coming up the stairs. The quarrel is over. Mama and Papa have smiles on their faces and hugs for their children.

As his parents fight, a little boy tries to keep in mind that their arguments are usually resolved. In the meantime, he discovers some useful methods of making those arguments less miserable for himself. The book may reassure young children and is sure to create discussion. Adults may find it helpful to remember how upsetting their quarrels can be to children. Colorful illustrations expand the text.

**Also available in:**
No other form known

## 587

**Sharmat, Marjorie Weinman**

### Taking Care of Melvin

Black/white illustrations by Victoria Chess.
Holiday House, Inc., 1980.
(30 pages counted)

---

FRIENDSHIP: Meaning of
GIVING, MEANING OF
    Helping

---

Melvin Dog is the most generous, helpful animal in his neighborhood. His friends say, "Melvin Dog has always been kind, generous, thoughtful, dear, and altogether wonderful." He washes clothes for his friends, waters their plants, baby-sits with their children. He is so busy doing things for everyone that he needs five bulletin boards to keep track of each day's activities. As a result, Melvin has no time for himself. He does not get enough sleep, never has time to eat wholesome meals, and seldom has clean clothes to wear. One day, when Laverne Cat brings over her entire rock garden for Melvin to polish, he faints from exhaustion. The doctor orders bed rest for a day, with others giving Melvin complete care. At first Melvin is reluctant even to ask for a bowl of cereal. But when he realizes how wonderful it is to be waited on, he becomes more and more demanding. As his friends stop by, his requests get more outrageous, ranging from an exotic lunch to new wallpaper for his room. His friends declare that he has become an ogre. Melvin decides it is fun to be an ogre. But the next day his phone doesn't ring and no one comes with chores for him to do. Lonely, he seeks out his friends and they agree to let him do some things for them—but not everything. When Melvin realizes he will finally have time to take better care of himself, he is happy.

This humorous tale teaches a valuable lesson, without preaching, about the balance between give and take: too much of either can be disastrous. Illustrations of the animal neighborhood add to the fun.

Ages 4-8

**Also available in:**
No other form known

## 588

**Sharmat, Mitchell**

### Come Home, Wilma

Color illustrations by Rosekrans Hoffman.
Albert Whitman & Company, 1980.
(32 pages counted)

---

IMAGINATION
    Anger
    Discipline, meaning of

---

Because little Wilma has hit her brother, her mother orders her to stay in her room. So Wilma decides to run away. She draws a picture of a horse and pretends the horse becomes real and carries her on a journey all over the world. Her mother calls Wilma to come back, but Wilma ignores her. In her imagination, she and the horse travel to a candy store, a drive-in movie, the plains of Africa, a parade through the jungle. At each stop her mother pleads with Wilma to be obedient, but Wilma only scoffs. Finally Wilma imagines that she and the horse go to the top of the highest mountain. There her mother tells Wilma she misses her, and Wilma finally relents. She has the horse stop at Macy's Department Store where she buys gifts for her mother. Then she comes home for a hug.

An exceptionally imaginative little girl works out her anger at her mother by taking a fantasy journey on a fantasy horse, at each stop refusing her mother's entreaties until her mother admits missing her—at which Wilma "comes home." Bright illustrations blend real with imaginary in depicting Wilma's wild journey.

Ages 6-8

**Also available in:**
No other form known

## 589

**Shreve, Susan Richards**

### The Bad Dreams of a Good Girl

Black/white illustrations by Diane de Groat.
Alfred A. Knopf, Inc., 1982.
(92 pages)

---

FAMILY: Relationships
    Daydreaming
    Parent/Parents: mother working outside home
    School: classmate relationships
    Sibling: rivalry

---

Fourth-grader Carlotta McDaniel is, by default, the good girl in her family. With three teenage brothers who steal street signs, lie, and even smoke cigarettes, all Lotty can do is dream about being bad. At Lotty's new school for gifted children, Kathy Sanders—class president, all-around leader, and former friend—has started the I Hate Lotty Club. When Lotty's family finds out, her brothers are unexpectedly supportive and comforting. But Lotty's schoolwork worsens, and she feels an academic failure as well as a social one. Her brother Nicholas suggests that she herself join the hateful club, but after she requests membership it loses members and folds. When Lotty's mother returns to work after twelve years at home, the girl feels like an orphan. She daydreams about running away from home and how her family will beg her to come back. She is somewhat comforted by a note her mother leaves under her pillow, reminiscing about Lotty as a toddler. Growth is always painful, her mother suggests, but eventually welcome. That evening Lotty makes dinner, cleans the house a little, and makes a valentine to put on her mother's bed. Then her father's week of bed rest for a back injury coincides with a day off from school for Lotty, who doesn't feel she knows her father very well. She fixes him a special breakfast, he writes her little notes, they talk. When her brothers come home and monopolize their father, Lotty fantasizes about burning up all his nice little notes; he only seems to like her when nobody else is around. Then the doorbell rings. It's the florist with roses for Lotty and a note from her father thanking her for one of the nicest days he's had in years. Although Lotty spars with all her brothers, most of her fights are with Philip. After one incident in which she dumps a can of tuna on his head and he dumps a pan of lumpy white sauce on hers, Lotty dreams about Philip's upcoming camping trip and how she rescues him when he breaks his leg. When he actually does break his arm, she and he promise not to have any more bad dreams about each other. Sometimes bad dreams come true.

A young girl daydreams to work out feelings she can't express as a real-life good girl. Lotty details several situations that mark her year as a fourth grader: peer rejection, her mother returning to work, getting to know her father, and a fight with one of her brothers. These separate episodes flow together smoothly in this entertaining first-person narrative. Charming drawings illustrate both Lotty's real world and her dreamworld.

Ages 8-10

Also available in:
Cassette—*The Bad Dreams of a Good Girl*
Library of Congress (NLSBPH)

Paperbound—*The Bad Dreams of a Good Girl*
Avon Books

## 590

Shreve, Susan Richards

### Family Secrets: Five Very Important Stories

Black/white illustrations by Richard Cuffari.
Alfred A. Knopf, Inc., 1979.
(56 pages)

---

*FAMILY: Relationships*
  *Death: of pet*
  *Divorce*
  *Friendship: best friend*
  *Grandparent: living in child's home*
  *Guilt, feelings of*
  *Honesty/Dishonesty*
  *Illnesses: terminal*
  *Suicide*

---

Sammy, about ten, wakes up one morning to find that his old dog, Giles, is dead. Though he grieves, he surprises himself with his ability to proceed through the day's normal routines. The family buries the dog in the backyard, and Sammy explains to his younger brother that although they'll never see Giles again, they'll remember him in their hearts. In the months that follow, several other events cause Sammy to look at life from different perspectives. He's shocked when his aunt and uncle get a divorce and worries that his parents too might separate. He anxiously questions them, but they think he's joking and reply accordingly. When they realize he is genuinely troubled, his parents talk about divorce and reassure him that a divorce is not in their plans, that he's not to worry. They also reaffirm their love for him. Sammy's best friend, Willy, has lived next door for several years. One day everyone is shocked and saddened when Willy's popular, athletic older brother, Michael, hangs himself in the basement. Because Sammy had been one of the last people to talk

with Michael, he wonders if somehow he has caused the suicide. He confesses his feelings to his father, who reassures him and is glad Sammy confided in him. Sammy's greatest grief is that Willy and his parents soon move to another part of town. Sammy and Willy will still see each other and do things together, but it will never be the same. Then Sammy's Grandmama comes to live in his home after surgery; she has terminal cancer and the doctors can't help her anymore. Grandmama is absent-minded, looks "terrible," according to Sammy's friend, and coughs all day. Sammy and his family treat her kindly, although sometimes it's difficult for his mother to cope with her ailing mother-in-law, especially when the older woman drinks too much. Sammy's father explains that his mother drinks because she is in so much pain. When Sammy's new friend Amos refuses to come over because Grandmama looks too scary, Sammy abandons Amos to play gin rummy with Grandmama. In math class, Sammy has had difficulty learning the multiplication tables, and the night before the test he doesn't study. Rather than fail his second test in a row, he decides to copy answers from a boy across the aisle. But after he cheats, he's afraid he's turning into an evil person, a criminal, and he can't even eat his supper. When his father comes in at bedtime to talk, Sammy admits he has cheated and says he must run away. His father advises him to call the math teacher and confess. He does, and his teacher, understanding but firm, says Sammy must come to school on Saturday and take another test. Sammy thanks him. Then his father, in a rather rare gesture, kisses his son goodnight.

Though all the issues Sammy faces during an upsetting year are serious, some even tragic, the combined effect of these easy-to-read episodes is not morbid: at times, there are even touches of humor. Sammy brings to each event a blend of youthful innocence and a kind of budding introspection. Because wise, loving parents help him cope and build his self-esteem and his appreciation of others, he is able to feel secure in spite of the troubles around him. Each chapter is written as a complete short story, and each could be used separately to initiate discussion and promote understanding. Sketchy, shaded illustrations complement the text.

Ages 9-11

Also available in:
Cassette—*Family Secrets: Five Very Important Stories*
Library of Congress (NLSBPH)

Paperbound—*Family Secrets: Five Very Important Stories*
Dell Publishing Company, Inc.

## 591

Shreve, Susan Richards

### The Masquerade

Alfred A. Knopf, Inc., 1980.
(184 pages)

---

*FAMILY: Relationships*
*IMPRISONMENT*
  *Ambivalence, feelings of*
  *Life style: change in*
  *Mental illness: of parent*
  *Parental: weakness*
  *Responsibility: accepting*

---

**S**

Eighteen-year-old Rebecca Walker is making fudge in the kitchen when her older brother, Eric, tells her that two policemen are leading their father away from the house; he is being arrested for embezzlement. The anguished days that follow are particularly difficult for Rebecca, who must assume even more responsibility for the family than she already has. Because of her remote, genteel mother's emotional fragility, Rebecca's father, a lawyer and accountant, has always depended on her. Eric has always been the difficult child; Sarah, now sixteen and a talented dancer, the self-centered child; and Eliza, now seven, the favorite. It's been up to Rebecca, the "good" child, to hold the family together. Now the four must read about their father in the newspaper. They are forced to sell their beautiful house on the Sound in Greenwich, Connecticut, and move to a two-bedroom apartment over a drugstore. Their mother takes a job in the drugstore as a cashier, the first job she has ever had. Eric returns abruptly to medical school and to Gayatri, the Pakistani woman he lives with. Through the turmoil of their lives their mother moves like someone untouched, but her behavior becomes increasingly bizarre. Then Sarah does not come home from a gymnastics tournament, and the family hears nothing of her for many days. One night during Sarah's absence, their mother dresses up in her high school prom dress and tells the children her date will be picking her up at eight. The owner of the drugstore has spoken to Eric about his mother, afraid that something is wrong with her. Sarah finally returns home. She has been in New York, pursuing her dream of becoming a professional dancer, but makes Rebecca promise not to ask her anything about her stay there. Soon after, Sarah quits dancing. Their father seems to have lost all interest in his children. Their mother is put in the state mental hospital after she is found wandering around one night in her prom dress. Their father has her transferred to a private institution, but will not explain to Rebecca how they can afford it. Then a representative from a local church group organized to "support the Walker children" approaches Rebecca about putting Sarah and Eliza in two local homes. She refuses. The frustrated representative promises to come up with another solution. She returns and asks Rebecca and Sarah to attend a benefit dance at the country club. There they discover halfway through the evening that the "benefit" is for their mother's stay in the private hospital and that their father has okayed it. Still, Rebecca clings to the belief that her father will be found innocent. She tells herself she can tolerate anything, now and in the future, if he is exonerated. When her father pleads guilty at his trial, Rebecca turns "mean," as Eliza puts it. She talks about sleeping with everyone she meets. She begins running with a wild crowd, staying out until nearly dawn night after night. Although she doesn't actually sleep with any of the boys, she thinks often of her father's reaction should he see her with them. When summer comes, Eric and Gayatri move into the small family apartment while both work at the local hospital. Eric is sick a great deal, primarily psychosomatic illnesses culled from his medical textbooks. Sarah receives a ballet scholarship, but refuses it. Rebecca herself is getting a "bad reputation." Their mother is soon to be released from the hospital and her psychiatrist suggests they rent a house so she will feel more at home. Their father is also due out on parole before too long, but Rebecca says she can't live in the same house with him; she has not been able to visit him since the trial. They find a modest but comfortable house to rent and begin to fix it up. The day her mother is due home, Rebecca drives to the prison to see her father. As she walks into the visiting room she says, "I'm finally here."

Caught in a complex web of needs and emotions, four strikingly individual young people try to keep their equilibrium during a stressful, tragic time in their lives. Eric, Sarah, and Eliza are all shown reacting to the turmoil in various ways, but the book focuses on Rebecca: the family mainstay, the strong one, the surrogate mother. As long as she clings to her unrealistic beliefs about her father, she avoids reality. When reality comes, it crushes and disorients her. At the end, Rebecca's visit to the prison seems a step toward peace —with her father and with herself. No easy solutions are proposed. But it's clear that Rebecca and her family have come through some unusually difficult months with tattered bits of their family flag still flying. Strong characterizations make for an absorbing story.

Ages 12 and up

Also available in:
Paperbound—*The Masquerade*
Dell Publishing Company, Inc.

## 592
Shura, Mary Francis Craig

## The Barkley Street Six-pack
Black/white illustrations by Gene Sparkman.
Dodd, Mead & Company, Inc., 1979.
(159 pages)

FRIENDSHIP: Best Friend
PEER RELATIONSHIPS: Peer Pressures
    Animals: love for
    Change: new home
    Friendship: meaning of
    Honesty/Dishonesty
    Manipulation: peer
    Neighbors/Neighborhood

When Natalie Lowery moves in across the street from thirteen-year-old Jane Todd, the shy, lonely Jane doesn't like her at all. But she finds herself drawn to fascinating Natalie, who claims she knows how to use magic. Both girls are new to the neighborhood and soon are friends. But Natalie will allow Jane no other friends. New young families keep moving in and the children of each, it seems, discover some reason to distrust Natalie and, by extension, Jane. The Jarvis boys, for example: Natalie tangles her kite strings with those of Steve Jarvis's very special, much-admired kite, making his kite fall into a tree. Later, the younger Jarvis boy's roller skate disappears. When Tracy moves in, Natalie loses a special ring and allows suspicion to fall on Tracy and her little brother. Always Natalie denies guilt, always she accuses others of lying and picking on her, and always she seeks affirmations of Jane's trust. Soon nobody in the neighborhood will even speak to Jane. Then Natalie's father is transferred and her family moves to Germany. One night a lonely Jane sees a dark shape moving on the porch of Natalie's empty house. It is a dog, alone and starving. Jane names it Stilts because of its long legs, feeds it and loves it, but keeps it a secret because she knows her parents won't let her keep it. Winter nears and she worries about the dog's safety. When Mr. Garvic, divorced and with a young son who visits on weekends, moves into the Lowery house, Jane is frantic because Stilts sleeps beneath the house. Trying to sneak a visit, she meets the son, Duke Garvic, who knows Jane's reputation in the neighborhood as Natalie's friend and already dislikes her. Jane realizes that Duke is a bit afraid of her too because his father's lease forbids children in the house. Seeing a way to get rid of the Garvics and protect Stilts, Jane writes to Natalie, telling her of Duke so Natalie's parents will evict the Garvics. Natalie's response speaks only of a new friend: "I've taken her under my wing, just like I did you." Slowly, Jane begins to suspect that there was no magic, that Natalie did all the things she denied and blamed on others. Then one day Jane glances into the Garvics' house and sees Stilts, happy, healthy, and obviously loved. She worries about her letter to Natalie, now that she has begun to like the Garvics and especially when Duke tells her he will be living permanently with his father. Her fears about Natalie are confirmed when Natalie's ring, missing since the episode with Tracy, is found behind the lattice enclosure under Natalie's house. Then Natalie writes to Jane again, telling about her new best friend and adding that her father no longer owns the house; he has accepted Mr. Garvic's recent offer to buy it. Duke invites Jane to a skating party with the two Jarvis boys, Tracy, and her brother. The Barkley Street Six-pack, as Jane's father calls it, begins to be a real team.

Complex emotions and ambiguous situations force a young girl to admit some unpleasant truths about her manipulative friend and her own judgment in this first-person study of relationships. Jane's loneliness in a new neighborhood, her love for Stilts, her initial ambivalence about Natalie and later the control Natalie exerts over her are all realistically described, as is the resolution of her problem and her happy return to the neighborhood children. The book will amply reward discussion about friendship, manipulation, and peer pressures.

Ages 9-12

**Also available in:**
Paperbound—*The Barkley Street Six-pack*
Scholastic Book Services

## 593

**Shura, Mary Francis Craig**

## Chester

Black/white illustrations by Susan Swan.
Dodd, Mead & Company, Inc., 1980.
(92 pages)

---

*JEALOUSY: Peer*
  *Friendship: meaning of*
  *Neighbors/Neighborhood*

---

Five friends live in a neighborhood known for having its "own living, breathing *Guinness Book of World*

*Records.*" All five consider themselves record-breakers. With twenty-seven freckles on his face, Jamie is estimated to have more freckles than any other kid in the world. Amy is the oldest of seven children, undoubtedly the largest family in existence. George is the fastest runner, Edie's family has the baldest baby, and Zach has the greatest home zoo. The five are proud of their notoriety and of the distinction enjoyed by their neighborhood—a great place to live except for Wally Parsons, the neighborhood bully who has recently managed to get a driver's license. His reckless driving makes him a menace, but the police need to catch him in the act before they can do anything about him. Now a new boy, Chester, has moved into the neighborhood. When the five friends meet Chester, they get quite a shock. First, they discover that he has forty-three freckles. Jamie is crushed. As he explains, "When you are used to being the most of something and it gets taken away from you, something you didn't even know was loose falls with a thud in the bottom of your stomach and just lies there." They next discover that Chester has eight children in his family, one more than Amy's family has. Not only that, but neither of his twin baby brothers has a hair on his head. They don't even have eyebrows yet, which makes them balder than Edie's baby. Then Chester beats George in a foot race and describes a home zoo far more interesting than Zach's. Later, the five friends talk dejectedly about how special they had felt before, how they now feel like five nothings. Jamie says, "Everybody deep down inside wants to be the best of something, even if it isn't anything really important. Nobody wants to be second best. Nobody wants to be a loser." Then Chester's sister comes to report that their pet goat, Tui, is missing. Everyone spends the evening searching. The next day at school, Jamie spots the goat across the street. When they rush out to catch him, they see Wally Parsons speeding down the street right towards him. They watch as the car heads toward the goat and the goat decides to chase the car, so unnerving Wally that he crashes into a telephone pole. A policeman who observes the incident asks for Wally's license and calls a tow truck for the ruined car. A classmate of the five friends predicts that Chester will now be a hero. "My dad says that anyone who gets Wally Parsons off the street should get the keys to the city." When one of the other kids says that it must be great to be friends with someone like Chester, the five friends admit that it is.

Five friends struggle with their jealousy of a newcomer who shows them up at everything they had thought themselves best at. He even manages to do in the neighborhood bully. One of the friends, Jamie, narrates the story, expressing clearly the group's disappointment and envy. He does not explain why they finally decide to befriend Chester, but the story might lead to discussion about how it feels to be second-best. The plot moves swiftly and is supported by clever illustrations and by many witty and believable details.

Ages 8-10

**Also available in:**
No other form known

**594**

Shyer, Marlene Fanta

## My Brother, the Thief

Charles Scribner's Sons, 1980.
(138 pages)

---

*STEALING*
*Adoption: feelings about*
*Family: unity*
*Self-esteem*
*Sibling: relationships*

---

Carolyn Desmond, twelve, and her fifteen-year-old brother, Richard, spend most of their summer vacation in each other's company, since both parents work. Richard is really Carolyn's half-brother. His father walked out when he was two; when he was three his mother married Dr. Desmond. Richard is an angry, hostile boy, but Dr. Desmond, who has adopted him, thinks of him as his own son. He is a loving but demanding parent who makes sure both children have plenty of chores to keep them busy. Since he worked his way through high school, college, and dental school, he believes in the merits of hard work; as a dentist, he hates junk food and concerns himself greatly with his children's diets. When Carolyn begins to notice that Richard is hiding things in his room that do not belong to him, she feels she should tell her parents. She knows, however, that if she does, Richard will reveal to her friends her hated middle name of Frankfurter. So she decides to keep quiet. One day she overhears Richard's friend, nicknamed Flim Flam, asking him to hide some more stolen property in their house. When Richard refuses, Flim Flam threatens to tell a special girl named Cookie that Richard can't swim. Since he is very ashamed of this fact, Richard agrees to do what Flim Flam wants. Preoccupied with guilt and the fear of being caught, Richard becomes careless about his chores, angering Dr. Desmond. Their relationship worsens when Richard takes the key Carolyn is using to care for the neighbor's cat and lets himself into their house. Mrs. Desmond thinks it might help if Richard saw his father. She makes arrangements for them to meet, but when the time arrives, his father fails to show up. After this Richard begins to steal. When the neighbors return from their vacation, they find a silver cream pitcher, an antique silver whistle, and forty-five dollars in cash missing from their home. Dr. and Mrs. Desmond cannot believe that Richard has had anything to do with this, but Carolyn discovers that her brother has given both the missing silver items to Cookie. She also finds a trunk full of stolen goods in their attic. When she asks Richard why he has taken these things, he replies, "Because I'm no good. . . . Because I'm just like my father." He'll never be "great, super, excellent, wonderful" like Dr. Desmond, "Mr. Perfect." Carolyn decides she must try to return a penlight and five dollars stolen from a member of the family's swim club. When she squeezes these things under the door of the appropriate beach locker, she is caught in the act by the club manager. They discover her family's locker filled with stolen goods; Flim Flam apparently stowed them there. The manager assumes Carolyn is the thief, compelling Richard to confess and explain his recent behavior. Flim Flam is apprehended and sent

to jail. His eyes opened, Dr. Desmond lets Richard know that he is not "Mr. Perfect." In fact, he gives the boy specific examples of his imperfections. The judge dismisses Richard's case and, though they must give up their club membership and withstand some ostracism and harassment, the family comes through this painful time with a deeper understanding of and commitment to each other.

In this first-person narrative, it is clear that Carolyn hates what her brother is doing and even at times believes she hates him. But as she attempts to help him without betraying him, she knows deep down that she will "always love him." When her father realizes that his high standards have contributed to Richard's poor self-image, he tries to be gentler with his children. Richard begins to see that he does not have to win trophies or love chores to be a good person, that one mistake does not make him irresponsible like his birth father. Readers will sympathize with these very human characters as they live through a critical time in their family relationship.

Ages 10-13

**Also available in:**
Paperbound—*My Brother, the Thief*
Scholastic Book Services

**595**

Simon, Norma

## Elly the Elephant

Black/white illustrations by Stanley Bleifeld.
Albert Whitman & Company, 1982.
(37 pages counted)

---

*TRANSITIONAL OBJECTS: Toys*
*Loss: of possessions*

---

Wendy has a little elephant named Elly that she's loved for so long he's worn out in spots and looks gray. Whenever Elly tells Wendy it's his birthday, Mama bakes a cake and they sing "Happy Birthday" to him. One day when Wendy can't find Elly, she remembers that he's visiting his invisible cousins. Wendy finds him later in the bathtub where he and his cousins always meet. When Wendy goes to the dentist, she leaves Elly with Mary the doll, his baby-sitter. But when Wendy comes home, Elly is crying. He missed her and fussed the whole time she was gone. One day Elly gets lost at school. No matter how hard Wendy looks, she can't find him and has to go home without him. She also has to sleep without him and is lonely all night. After searching everywhere, she finds him in the middle of the pile of dolls. Everyone is delighted to have found Elly, but Wendy is happiest of all. She tells him they'll live happily ever after.

A little girl and her stuffed elephant are inseparable friends. In a first-person account, Wendy tells about some of their adventures together. These experiences—having a sitter, visiting the dentist, going to school—potentially anxious times for a young child, are reassuringly presented. Text and illustrations are interspersed with five Elly Songs, their lyrics and melodies simple enough for most adults and some children to follow. The story is told on alternating yellow and green pages accented by line drawings. In a note preceding the story, the author urges readers to tell, or to have adults write down, stories about their own special toy friends.

Ages 2-5

**Also available in:**
No other form known

## 596

**Simon, Norma**

### I'm Busy, Too

Color illustrations by Dora Leder.
Albert Whitman & Company, 1980.
(32 pages counted)

---

*FAMILY: Relationships*
  *Day-care center, going to*

---

Mikey, Sara, and Charlie are all members of active, working families. When Monday morning comes, these preschool children and others like them must wake up and get ready for their own busy day. There is "stretching, yawning, grumbling, tumbling, tossing covers off, all over town." Soon everyone is on the way to work or school. The teachers are ready for the children, and the children are ready for their school day. Parents also work hard. Mikey's mother helps a dentist clean and repair teeth. Sara's mother works in their house; her father works in their restaurant. Charlie's father fixes broken television sets. When the day is over, everyone goes home. Now is "a time to talk together." Mikey tells his mother about the Halloween pirate's mask he made. She promises to help him make his costume. Sara's family admires her paintings, and her sister hangs them in their room. Charlie tells his father about building a garage for Mikey's truck. His father promises to visit school soon so he can see everything. Then there are "sleepy people, tired people, washing up to go to bed.... Happy dreams, all over town."

Three children of working parents are themselves "working playing, playing working, all day long." But when adults and kids come home, everyone's adventures during the day are taken seriously and shared. Realistic illustrations complement the happy, positive tone as the notion is quietly conveyed that close family relationships are still the norm in today's day-care-dependent society. The use of rhythmic repetition makes the book especially pleasant for reading aloud.

Ages 3-5

**Also available in:**
Large Print—*I'm Busy, Too*
Albert Whitman & Company

## 597

**Simon, Norma**

### Nobody's Perfect, Not Even My Mother

Color illustrations by Dora Leder.
Albert Whitman & Company, 1981.
(32 pages counted)

---

*PERSEVERANCE*
  *Encouragement*
  *Self, attitude toward: confidence*

---

Various young narrators tell of things they can do well, such as putting together puzzles or doing somersaults, and things they can't manage, such as baking birthday cakes. One admits, "When I really try to do something right and it comes out all wrong, I feel awful. Just awful!" But each child notices that parents, grandparents, and teachers have shortcomings too. One boy's mother is good at repairing cars, but she can't seem to stop smoking. A father yells at his children and frightens them, but he acknowledges the situation and is trying to change. A grandfather doesn't play his guitar very well, but he practices every night. In sum, "You're good at some things—I'm good at some things. Everyone's good at some things. But nobody's perfect!"

A cast of ethnically and racially varied children and adults, many shown pursuing untraditional tasks and occupations, helps young readers understand that everyone is good at something and that even adults fall far short of perfection. Children made anxious both by their own shortcomings and by the limitations of the adults in their lives will find reassurance in the examples of grown-ups facing everyday failures and weaknesses, just as children do. Illustrations are exceptionally realistic and appealing.

Ages 4-8

**Also available in:**
Large Print—*Nobody's Perfect, Not Even My Mother*
Albert Whitman & Company

## 598

**Simon, Norma**

### We Remember Philip

Color illustrations by Ruth Sanderson.
Albert Whitman & Company, 1979.
(31 pages counted)

---

*DEATH: Attitude Toward*
*MOURNING, STAGES OF*
  *Empathy*
  *School: pupil-teacher relationships*

---

Young Sam arrives home from school and tells his mother that Philip, the son of his favorite teacher, Mr. Hall, has been killed in a mountain climbing accident. "Oh, Mom, what would you do if that happened to me?" Sam asks. Sam's mother says she cannot imagine anything more terrible, but reassures him that such accidents are rare and that most people live to be very old. Sam has never thought about dying before, but he remembers the sorrow he felt at the death of his old collie dog, Skye. This memory prompts him to

**S**

empathize further with Mr. Hall's pain. Sam's mother says, "Crying helps when you hurt inside. I hope Mr. Hall lets himself cry." Sam and his classmates write letters of sympathy to Mr. Hall, listen to the grief-stricken man talk about his son, and look at pictures he shows them of Philip. Seeing how the photographs fill Mr. Hall's face with sadness, the children search for a less painful way to keep Philip alive in his father's memory. They decide to plant an oak tree as a memorial, because Philip loved the outdoors and was tall and straight as a young tree. Together with their teacher, they plant the tree on the school grounds in memory of Philip.

In this sensitively written book, Sam and his classmates share their teacher's pain and loss at the death of his son. Highlighted is the capacity of children to accept and respond appropriately to death. Thoughtful examples are given of ways to comfort a bereaved person. Although this is a picture book in format, its content appears better suited to older children. It could prompt valuable discussion when read aloud to a group. Photograph-like illustrations enhance the text.

Ages 7-10

**Also available in:**
No other form known

## 599

Sirof, Harriet

### Save the Dam!

Black/white illustrations by Jan Albrecht.
Crestwood House, Inc., 1981.
(63 pages)

---

*IMAGINATION*
  *Honesty/Dishonesty*

---

Cathy can't figure out why her social studies teacher, Ms. Taylor, left town so suddenly. She wonders what it would be like if Ms. Taylor's father had died in Texas and left her an oil well. She tells her friends that's why Ms. Taylor left town. But a classmate, Marlene, scornfully disputes the story. The new social studies teacher announces plans for a field trip to Wolf River Dam, an important addition to the community that saves it from flooding. When Cathy mentions the time a flood carried her grandmother's house downstream with her grandmother on the roof, Marlene scoffs and calls Cathy a liar. Still puzzling over Ms. Taylor's disappearance, Cathy decides she must have been kidnapped. Her cat has dragged in a glove with a charm caught on it, and Cathy remembers Ms. Taylor wearing a charm bracelet once. She goes to the police and tells them her suspicions. The police bring her home, and her resigned mother advises Cathy to curb her imagination. On the field trip, Cathy sees a diver in a wet suit come out of the water and remove a red flag from a nearby tree. Nobody believes her, of course, but she persuades two girls to help her search the area. They find tracks and an empty oxygen tank. Then Cathy visits Ms. Taylor's former apartment where the owner's son, Stan, lets her in, ostensibly to retrieve a map. They find the map, but on the back are strange lines and numbers. Stan says the lines and numbers remind him of some work he did in

drafting class, but he can't remember the building he was drawing. Soon a radio announcement warns the town that members of F.R.E.E., a radical group, have threatened to blow up the dam unless one million dollars is paid within two days. Stan recognizes the voice on the F.R.E.E. tape as Ms. Taylor's brother. They go to the police with the map and information, but the station is crowded with people worrying about the dam, and Cathy, understandably, has no credibility with the police. When they are also unable to get to the dam because of police roadblocks, Cathy and Stan decide to approach the problem from the other end. They've got to find Ms. Taylor's brother. They finally locate his van, but he locates them about the same time, coming at them with a gun and leaving them tied up all night. Ms. Taylor is with him. She had originally tried to talk her brother out of his plan, but now is afraid to turn him in. Cathy reminds her of what she said in class once: nobody can make you do anything. Hours later the police surround the van. Ms. Taylor's brother's hand hovers over the buttons that will blow up the dam, but she convinces him that their father would not have wanted him to do this. He surrenders. Cathy decides that she'll tell her grandchildren stories about the time the dam was nearly blown up—and every detail will be true.

One of a series of high-interest, shorter-length books, Cathy's story is a variation on "the boy who cried wolf." Because of her fertile imagination, she often presents as facts things that are merely fancies. Her inability to obtain support from adults when she desperately needs it shows her the importance of sticking to the literal truth in most situations.

Ages 9-12

**Also available in:**
Paperbound—*Save the Dam!*
Crestwood House, Inc.

## 600

Skolsky, Mindy Warshaw

### Carnival and Kopeck and More About Hannah

Black/white illustrations by Karen Ann Weinhaus.
Harper & Row, Publishers, Inc., 1979.
(74 pages)

---

*ARGUING*
*SELF-DISCIPLINE*
  *Anger*
  *Consideration, meaning of*
  *Grandparent: love for*
  *Grandparent: respect for*
  *Patience/Impatience*
  *Promise, keeping*

---

In the early summer of 1932, Hannah, about eight, excitedly looks forward to spending lots of time with her grandmother. Her grandparents have recently moved from New York City to Hannah's small hometown. But Hannah is an extremely excitable child, and she often goes too far. When she plays school with her Polish-born grandmother, she embarrasses the woman by asking her to spell difficult words. When Grandpa brings home a special dessert, Hannah tells him it's only third best, not her favorite. A carnival is coming to town, and Hannah begs her grandmother to take her. But both Mother and Grandma remind Hannah that on her last outing she became far too excited and misbehaved because of it. Mother tells Hannah she may go to the carnival if she will try her hardest to behave. For her part, Grandma extracts three promises from Hannah: not to get too excited, not to beg for hot dogs, and not to drag Grandma around to meet all the neighbors. Hannah wants to keep her promises but her self-control dissolves when, on their arrival at the carnival, her friend Mr. Branagan offers Grandma a beer and Hannah a hot dog. The child becomes frenzied with excitement; Grandma picks her up and takes her home without a word. In the middle of the night at Grandma's, Hannah wakes up and again raises a fuss. Grandma takes her home then and there, angrily dumping her at her mother's front door. The next morning Hannah tells her mother she is angry with her grandmother. But after thinking it over, Hannah decides she misses Grandma and wants to be with her. She wonders whether Grandma will "still be her same grandma." But it turns out that Grandma too regrets their quarrel. She reminds Hannah that people who spend lots of time together will inevitably have arguments. The two agree that the next time they are angry, they will tell each other. They also decide to return to the carnival that night. This time Hannah will try harder to control herself, and Grandma will be more polite to friendly neighbors.

Children will easily empathize with little Hannah, who means well but whose great energy and thoughtlessness cause problems for her and the people around her. Grandma too is vividly portrayed, with her own firm values, eccentricities, and imperfections. Hannah learns that people who love each other may not always get along, but that she needs to temper her enthusiasm and zest. Grandma learns to adapt to the neighborly ways of the small community that is now her home. Cheerful illustrations enhance the period, setting, and mood of the story, a universal one well suited for reading aloud.

Ages 7-9

Also available in:
Disc—*Carnival and Kopeck and More About Hannah*
Library of Congress (NLSBPH)

## 601

Skurzynski, Gloria Joan

## Honest Andrew

Color illustrations by David Wiesner.
Harcourt Brace Jovanovich, Inc., 1980.
(29 pages counted)

*HONESTY/DISHONESTY*

Andrew Otter wants to tell his mother that he doesn't like the crayfish they are having for dinner, but he hates to hurt her feelings. So he collects the food in his cheeks and goes outdoors to spit it into the river. Papa Otter follows him and sees him get rid of the food. But when he questions his son, Andrew says that he has only come out to bait the fish traps. Papa marches Andrew back indoors and reads him the otter motto: "AN OTTER

OUGHT TO BE HONEST." Andrew promises that from now on he will always tell the truth. The next day he and Mama Otter set out for the store. When they meet Professor Newton Beaver, the distinguished scholar asks Andrew, "How are you, young man?" Andrew, wanting to be entirely truthful, responds with a lengthy account of his recent problems. After a while, the smile on the Professor's face fades and he hurries off down the path. Next they meet Aunt Prissy Porcupine who is "very fussy about manners." Aunt Prissy comments on how big Andrew has grown. "That's not the truth. I am not a big otter," insists Andrew. Next Mrs. Hazel Woodchuck comes into sight. She is pushing a baby buggy and wants to introduce her newest child. Mrs. Otter comments that the baby is "darling." Andrew, however, looks into the buggy and expresses a different opinion: "Darling? She's ugly. . . . Her face is all wrinkled. She looks like she slid facedown on a mud slide." Mama Otter makes Andrew spend the rest of the day sitting on a chair facing the wall. When Papa gets home he has a talk with his son. He explains that Andrew has carried his honesty too far. He has bored Professor Beaver, insulted Aunt Prissy, and hurt Mrs. Woodchuck. He must be polite as well as honest. That evening they have salamander stew for dinner. Andrew does not like this dish either but tries to be diplomatic about telling his mother. He says she is "the sweetest, nicest mama in the whole world. Your eyes are big and bright. Your fur is warm and soft. You wear pretty earrings, and I HATE SALAMANDER STEW!"

First, Andrew's concern for his mother's feelings keeps him from being truthful. Then his truthfulness keeps him from being tactful. Finally, he attempts to reconcile the virtues of honesty and tact. The incongruous result will bring a smile to the reader's or listener's face. Expressive illustrations of the animal characters add to the humor of this easy reader.

Ages 4-7

Also available in:
Paperbound—*Honest Andrew*
Harcourt Brace Jovanovich, Inc.

## 602

Skurzynski, Gloria Joan

## Martin By Himself

Color illustrations by Lynn Munsinger.
Houghton Mifflin Company, 1979.
(36 pages)

*LIFE STYLE: Change in*
*PARENT/PARENTS: Mother Working Outside Home*
   *Loneliness*
   *Parent/Parents: single*
   *Problem solving*

Martin, about six, splashes through the mud and puddles on his way home from school. Once home, he remembers that his mother has started work again and is not there to greet him. He unlocks the door and enters the kitchen, aware of how quiet the house is. A note from his mother saying she will be home at five tells Martin he has an hour to be alone. Dropping his wet clothes on the way, he goes to his room and changes. Then he makes a peanut-butter and banana sandwich

**S**

and can't resist making peanut-butter designs all over the refrigerator door. Martin knows his mother won't like that, but then she isn't home. Bored, he wanders around the house. Then he spots Gus, the dog next door. Gus is wet and muddy and so Martin, feeling sorry for him, brings the dog into the house. Gus promptly shakes his coat, splashing mud and water all over the kitchen. Then he knocks over a large plant and, while Martin is trying to scoop up the dirt, urinates on the living room carpet. Martin throws good towels on the floor to mop up the wet spot and then fills the bathtub with bubble bath to soak the towels. The tub overflows. Frustrated beyond endurance, Martin yells at Gus to leave. He finally succeeds in getting the dog out of the house by luring him with the meatloaf intended for dinner. He then looks around the messy house and feels awful. Just then his mother arrives home. Surveying the scene, she tells Martin she will have to get him a baby-sitter. Martin begs for another chance. They resolve the problem by deciding that tomorrow Martin will come home from school, have a snack, and then go outside and take Gus for a nice, long walk. Both Martin and his mother are satisfied with this solution.

Lonely and bored while his mother is at work, a little boy and his neighbor's dog create chaos in the house. When his mother arrives home, they find a solution to "having nothing to do"—although parents and astute readers may question the mother's decision to continue leaving such a young child to fend for himself. Still, the colorful illustrations and humorous events keep the book lighthearted and nonthreatening to other "latchkey children."

Ages 6-9

**Also available in:**
No other form known

## 603

Slepian, Jan

### The Alfred Summer

Macmillan Publishing Company, Inc., 1980.
(119 pages)

---

*DEPENDENCE/INDEPENDENCE*
*FRIENDSHIP: Meaning of*
*SELF, ATTITUDE TOWARD: Accepting*
  *Cerebral palsy*
  *Epilepsy*
  *Limbs, abnormal or missing*
  *Mental retardation*
  *Peer relationships*
  *Rejection: parental*
  *Stealing*

---

At fourteen, Lester Klopper, who has cerebral palsy, wants friends and a full life. He is stymied by an overprotective mother and an aloof, uninterested father. Then he meets Alfie and Myron and his summer takes on new dimensions. Alfie is retarded and has a deformed hand and foot; Myron, who has recently lost his father, feels dominated and interfered with by his family. The friendship among the three boys begins at the beach one Sunday when Lester sees Alfie caught in rocks and in danger from the waves and incoming tide.

Alfie never thinks to call for help, so Lester tries frantically to alert someone to the situation. But he is unable to speak when excited, and his gestures succeed only in drawing an uncomprehending crowd. Then Lester's father arrives and the boy calms down enough to explain the situation. His father and Myron rescue Alfie. Afterwards, the three boys go off together for ice cream. Lester has to concentrate on getting the spoonfuls of ice cream to his lips, but soon realizes that he is enjoying the normality of eating ice cream and talking with friends. Myron tells them a secret; he is building a rowboat in his basement. In it he plans to escape from all the people who dominate his life. Excitedly, Alfie and Lester convince Myron to let them help him find materials for the boat, and the three quickly warm to the project. They are joined by another outcast, Claire. Myron decides they must all go to a park to examine the construction of rowboats. Lester's anxious mother is at first very reluctant to let him go without her, but she consents when she understands that Myron and Claire will be going also. At the park, Myron studies the boats and is dismayed to find that he has made no provision for oarlocks. Claire urges him to steal some. He tries, but is seen by an attendant who tells the four to leave the park. Only Claire has the courage to ask strangers for directions out, and the others admire her confidence. Later she admits that talking to people she doesn't know unnerves her. After much planning, Lester and Alfie return to the park and succeed in stealing a pair of oarlocks. But this triumph is forgotten when, on their way home, they ride a commuter train together and Alfie has a seizure. Nobody on the train makes a move to help and so, gathering composure and strength he didn't know he had, Lester gets Alfie off the train, forgetting the oarlocks in the process. People finally help the two, taking Alfie to a hospital and Lester home. Once there, Lester locks himself in his room. He is devastated by the limitations of his handicap, angry at the lack of sympathy and understanding he encounters all the time. His mother tries to draw him out of his room, but he bitterly rejects his attachment to her: "The strings are gone," he tells her. She accuses his father of never being home long enough to get to know his son, and the father replies angrily that she has pushed him away by preferring Lester. Finally, Lester's father knocks on the boy's door and Lester admits him. Told what he has lived to hear, that rescuing Alfie was the act of a man, Lester is now too embittered to care. But his father is able to console him and together they go to dinner. News of the rescue has spread, they discover, and Lester is a hero. Everyone but Alfie, who is still in the hospital, comes to the launching of Myron's boat, which he has renamed "Alfred." As he rows from shore, the boat begins to sink. But he keeps rowing until the boat is completely submerged, at which he stands up and raises his hands in victory. The laughing crowd begins applauding, and Lester is filled with triumph, pride, affection for his friends—many emotions he has never known before.

In this special book about special people, four friends, two outcast because of their disabilities and two because of personality and circumstance, find strength and self-acceptance through their relationship. Lester, who tells the story, gives reality and urgency to the people, emotions, and events he describes. He injects humor too, often leavening the seriousness of the story. The sequel to this richly rewarding book is *Lester's Turn*.

Ages 11-13

**Also available in:**
Cassette—*The Alfred Summer*
Library of Congress (NLSBPH)

**604**

**Slepian, Jan**

**Lester's Turn**

Macmillan Publishing Company, Inc., 1981.
(139 pages)

*FRIENDSHIP: Best Friend*
 *Boy-girl relationships*
 *Cerebral palsy*
 *Death: of friend*
 *Determination*
 *Love, meaning of*
 *Mental retardation*
 *Self, attitude toward: accepting*

When sixteen-year-old Lester, who has cerebral palsy, visits his retarded friend Alfie in the hospital where he lives now that his mother has died, he's appalled at how fat and pasty Alfie looks. Although Alfie has always loved the outdoors, the hospital staff finds it easier to keep him indoors so that if he has an epileptic seizure he won't get hurt. Lester feels an urgent need to get Alfie out of the place. But when his attempt to smuggle his friend out is foiled, Mrs. Brenner, the hospital director, explains to him what caring for Alfie would mean, why people can't just remove patients from the hospital. She realizes she has not convinced him, however, and says she recognizes an obsession when she sees one. Lester visits his good friend Claire, who introduces him to her upstairs neighbors, Lena Lensky and her violinist son, Alex. Lester tells them about Alfie, but Lena thinks it would be a mistake to remove him from the hospital. She asks Lester if he really cares that much about Alfie and Lester reflects, "It was not the caring I knew so much about, but the needing." He remains determined to devote his life to Alfie, the only person, he believes, who really needs him. Later that day he walks down to the beach and meets Tillie-Rose, a hospital volunteer. She and some friends are having a cookout and she invites Lester to join them. At first he refuses, unable to visualize himself with normal kids, afraid to eat with them because he often makes a mess. But Tillie-Rose persists, and Lester enjoys himself. Later, the group pairs off under blankets and Tillie-Rose kisses Lester, his first kiss. This experience awakens him to a "secret treasure"—he likes Tillie-Rose, but he really loves Claire. The next day the principal tells Lester that he could get a college scholarship if he would just try a

little harder. But Lester thinks he knows what his future holds, and it doesn't include college. That afternoon he gets a part-time job making deliveries for a drugstore, but after several days, one of his uncontrollable movements brings down a stack of pill bottles and he loses the job. Tillie-Rose offers to let Alfie live in her basement, and Claire offers to keep him with her family. But Lester wants to care for Alfie himself. Still, he accepts Lena's offer of a benefit violin concert performed by Alex. He also gets permission from Mrs. Brenner for Alfie to spend the weekend of the concert with Claire's family. Claire, Tillie-Rose, and Lester take Alfie around the hospital grounds, and Lester is amazed at how popular Alfie is. Too bad that such a beautiful place isn't good for Alfie, who appears to have gotten more forgetful and fanciful during his stay. Tillie-Rose reassures Lester that Alfie will be his old self again once they get him out of there. The afternoon of the violin concert, Lester and Alfie explore Claire's neighborhood and remember old times. After several hours, however, Alfie asks to go home. He looks sick—bent over, gray lips, a yellowish cast to his eyes. Lester leaves him with Claire, as they've arranged, planning to return after dinner. Claire's family discovers that Alfie is running a high temperature. Although they rush him to the hospital and he has emergency surgery, his appendix bursts and he dies. In the middle of the night, Lester creeps into Tillie-Rose's basement. She finds him there, calls Claire, and the three grieve together. Lester is guilt-ridden at the thought that he had been using Alfie just as he accused everyone else of doing. He goes to see Mrs. Brenner. She tells him he can either use his guilt as an excuse for failure, or he can use the example of Alfie's life to make something of himself. On Lester's way out of the hospital, Alfie's friends tell how they miss him and how special he was. Noticing a man with cerebral palsy in a wheelchair, Lester realizes that, unlike this man, he himself has choices, choices he intends to make wisely.

A teenager with cerebral palsy is forced to examine his relationship with a retarded friend, and in so doing learns quite a bit about love and friendship. The sequel to *The Alfred Summer,* this first-person narrative set in 1939 is universal in its emotions and especially rich in settings and characters. Lester's mother is overprotective and his father all but invisible, so the boy fastens on Alfie as a reason for living. Gradually, he sorts out his obligations to his friends and to himself. The book is powerfully effective in conveying the richness and complexity of the lives of disabled people. Lester and Alfie are very real, human, and likeable. The story makes good dramatic use of the ways love can highlight the similarities among all people.

Ages 11-14

**Also available in:**
No other form known

**S**

## 605

Slote, Alfred

## Love and Tennis

Macmillan Publishing Company, Inc., 1979.
(163 pages) o.p.

---

COMMUNICATION: Parent-Child
MATURATION
TALENTS: Athletic
    Boy-girl relationships: dating
    Competition
    Divorce: of parents
    Expectations
    Parent/Parents: remarriage of
    Parental: control
    Sports/Sportsmanship
    Values/Valuing: moral/ethical

---

When fifteen-year-old Buddy Berger beats a nationally ranked player in a local tennis tournament, his divorced mother, who has coached him, decides it's time for him to begin developing his talent in earnest. To Buddy's dismay, she and the man she's been dating, Matt, arrange a meeting for Buddy with Hans Steger, who owns the famed Tennis World, training ground for many of the world's top players. Steger invites Buddy to Tennis World for a one-week tryout. Although honored to meet the renowned teacher, Buddy finds the man hard, unbending, unsympathetic—like his mother. He does not have any wish to become part of Steger's pressure cooker, and he tells his girlfriend, Chris, that he won't do it. In the next stage of the local tournament, Buddy's mother insists that he defeat his superior opponent by using moonball, a sneaky technique of hitting the ball high so the opponent gets tired and dazed by the sun. Buddy, not wanting to play "disgraceful tennis," does so nevertheless and wins the match. His mother tells him he now must go to Tennis World. Buddy suspects the real reason she wants him to go is to prepare him for a sure win over his father, against whom he is pitted in the finals. The father, a doctor and local tennis enthusiast, has recently married Chris's mother. At Tennis World, Buddy meets the current teenage champion, Rick DeVere. Several other boys warn Buddy that he is "new meat" and thus fair game for much unkind criticism. Buddy plays a friendly, easy opening game with Steger but later, at a videotaped review of the match, Steger tears Buddy apart in front of all the other students. They, in turn, ruthlessly dissect his game and accuse him of having no will to win. Upset and discouraged, Buddy returns to his room to sleep but finds a welcome party instead, complete with girls and beer. When Rick arrives, he is carrying a protesting, pajama-clad girl. Buddy tells him to let her go. Rick refuses. Buddy tries to escort the girl back, but Rick moves to block him. Angry, Buddy lets loose, beating Rick until he has "damn near killed him." Steger interrupts the fracas and tells Buddy he must meet Rick in a match. Buddy begins to realize what it takes to be a star: not only drive and commitment, but a lack of concern for anything or anyone else. During the match, Buddy is surprised to find that Rick, so crude and brazen off the court, is courteous and serious when he plays his game. Nonetheless, he reminds Buddy of his mother, "all graceless, relentless attack." Rick wins, partly because Buddy stops trying, but Buddy is satisfied that he has not played "junk" tennis. Determined to quit the sport completely, he returns home. "I had seen all the worms that lived at the bottom of the tennis can," he muses. When his mother meets him at the airport, she seems changed. She apologizes for being the cause of his bad week and the two come clean. Buddy says he wants no more to do with tennis, and his mother explains that Matt has helped her see how she's been using Buddy in her war against his father. She plans to marry Matt and wants to work on a better relationship with Buddy. Buddy, still jarred and deeply hurt from his experience, lashes out, telling his mother all the details of his wretched week, until the two cry and embrace. When Buddy goes to see Chris, to whom he neglected to write, he finds her busy playing tennis with a visiting Swedish player, her manner toward Buddy decidedly cool. Feeling more wounded and uncertain, Buddy declines his father's invitation to dinner. His father tells him that time will heal the pain of losing Chris, but Buddy decides that time only "makes hurts permanent." Playing his best game, Buddy still loses to his father in the tournament finals. He announces he's through with tennis, but his father insists he has tennis in his blood and predicts he'll be back: "not for a living, but for life."

In this first-person narrative a boy tries to decide if his athletic talent obligates him to be ruthlessly competitive. Torn by his parents' divorce and his dawning love for Chris, Buddy struggles to discover and hold on to his emerging values. In the end, he has found strength in himself: he is wiser and more resilient. The dilemma of trying to remain loyal to both divorced parents is treated realistically, as are the relationships and the sequence of events.

Ages 12-14

**Also available in:**
No other form known

## 606

Slote, Alfred

## Rabbit Ears

J. B. Lippincott Company, 1982.
(110 pages)

---

NAME-CALLING
SELF-DISCIPLINE
    Sibling: relationships
    Sports/Sportsmanship
    Talents: musical

---

Fifteen-year-old baseball pitcher Tip O'Hara has rabbit ears; that is, the taunts and jeers of the opposition are capable of changing him from a great pitcher into a poor one. Everyone tries to help Tip, but his problem persists. Part of him knows the chatter is meaningless, but another part hears and takes to heart every little word. He even falls for the oldest line of all and looks down to see if his shoelaces really are untied—and then is called by the umpire for balking. His coach tells him he's got the pitching arm, but not the tough head. His father says he's got the physical equipment to play baseball, but not the emotional equipment. After a game that he helped lose, Tip takes out some of his frustration on his younger brother, Roland, who is practicing with his friends Wings and Peggy for a Battle of the Bands. The whole O'Hara family is musical, but Roland spends the most time at it. He begs Tip to join their group and help them win the contest, but Tip rudely refuses, preoccupied with his own problems. His coach and team continue trying to help him, but the earplugs and practice harassment they offer go for naught when they play Belden Hardware and Tip falls to pieces in the first inning. They win, but through no effort of his. He tells his mother he's going to quit baseball, and she suggests he help Roland with his band. So Tip apologizes to his brother and joins the band. When he calls the coach to tell him his decision, the coach just says he'll talk to Tip about it after Monday's game. Roland, Tip, Peggy, and Wings win the Battle of the Bands, and Roland's original song is a huge hit. Roland believes his music can help Tip. He makes Tip promise to join his band permanently if music can solve his rabbit ears problem. When they get home from the Battle of the Bands, the whole team is waiting on the lawn. They explain that one of their remaining two pitchers is out for the season and they need Tip. He agrees to pitch for them. Then Roland comes up with an idea for overcoming the problem of Tip's sensitive ears. At the next game, Tip takes each word he hears yelled at him and turns it inside his head into nonsense songs. By making fun of the taunts, he stays relaxed and pitches a terrific game. Roland takes him up on his promise to join the band; he always said that Tip's ears are musician's ears.

A young baseball pitcher is unable to shut out the jeers of the opposition. His musician brother comes up with an ingenious solution that allows Tip to overcome his instinctive recoiling from the taunts. Written in the first person, this funny, lively book will appeal to sports-minded readers as it demonstrates the inherent meaninglessness of name-calling.

Ages 10-12

**Also available in:**
Paperbound—*Rabbit Ears*
Harper & Row, Publishers, Inc.

## 607

**Smith, Anne Warren**

### Blue Denim Blues

Atheneum Publishers, 1982.
(126 pages)

---

*JOB*
*SHYNESS*
  *Anxiety*
  *Baby-sitting*
  *Child abuse*
  *Self, attitude toward: confidence*
  *Talents: musical*

---

Janet Donovan considers herself a fifteen-year-old failure. Her only strength, she's convinced, is that she's good with children, so she applies for a summer job as assistant to Mrs. Bailey at Little Britches Preschool. Her best friend, Horse, expects the job to ruin their summer. Janet's father plays bluegrass music with two friends and with Darrell Danielson, the president of Janet's

class, and so when Janet has to give an oral report in English she decides to talk about bluegrass. But she's terribly shy and dreads any sort of public performance. In the midst of her stumbling report, given with hiccups, Darrell comes to her rescue when she can't open a banjo case. He helps her and then demonstrates how to play the banjo. Meanwhile, Arlene Tuttle, mother of the little boy, Clancy, whom Janet often baby-sits for, recommends Janet to Mrs. Bailey. One night when Janet's father and his group are having a jam session, he asks Janet to play the washtub. She does so, very well. On the basis of Arlene Tuttle's recommendation and because Janet has stressed her interest in music, Mrs. Bailey offers Janet the preschool job on a temporary basis until a more qualified person applies. Janet enjoys the work, although her shyness won't let her lead the children in songs in front of Mrs. Bailey. She does love the children, especially her dear Clancy. But he seems to be changing in some way. One day he pounds on a doll so violently he frightens the other children. Janet's father suggests their little bluegrass group perform in public, beginning with a brief concert at the preschool. During their program, Clancy asks Janet to play on the autoharp, as she has many times for him at home. But in front of the group, Janet freezes and is unable to play. Another child, Cynthia, who hates getting messy, taunts Janet; Janet replies that if Cynthia will paint a picture with those messy paints she hates, she will play a song. Cynthia carries out her end of the bargain and Janet manages hers—by pretending that she and Clancy are alone and she's playing just for him. Then, while baby-sitting for Clancy, Janet discovers that he has been beaten and suspects his mother's rough new boyfriend, Tom. When she tells his mother, however, Arlene brushes her off, saying Tom won't be coming back and that Clancy got those bruises on the slide. Mrs. Bailey tells Janet she has found a more experienced assistant so Janet's job will end that week. While the new woman is filling out an application form, Clancy and his mother come in and Arlene accuses Janet of abusing the boy. In the end Arlene breaks down, admits beating Clancy, and asks for help. After putting Arlene in touch with agencies who can help her, Mrs. Bailey tells Janet she's decided to keep her on at full pay for the remainder of the summer. The girl has learned a great deal and is an excellent assistant.

A girl who thinks she has only one good point, her skill in dealing with young children, finds that she is also courageous enough to overcome a long-standing fear of speaking or performing in public, that she can attract a popular, intelligent boy, and that she can even play in a bluegrass band. Janet also reinforces her own conviction that working with children can be uniquely challenging. This is a capably written story with characters who act and react believably—but, unfortunately, none is fully developed. Janet's delightful relationship with Horse is never explored, leaving the reader unsatisfied. The slight hint of a romance with Darrell is also left unpursued. Nevertheless, the story will hold the reader's interest with its realistic, satisfying portrayal of a teenage girl plagued by shyness and her successful efforts to overcome her fear.

Ages 12 and up

**Also available in:**
No other form known

**608**

Smith, Doris Buchanan

## Last Was Lloyd

The Viking Press, Inc., 1981.
(124 pages)

---

*SELF-ESTEEM*
  *Friendship: making friends*
  *Parental: overprotection*
  *School: truancy*
  *Talents: athletic*
  *Weight control: overweight*

---

Unhappy and overweight, twelve-year-old Lloyd is pampered, almost smothered, by his overprotective, divorced mother. She cooks whatever he wants, insists on driving him everywhere he goes, has allowed him to miss sixty-four days of school, and defends him from the truant officer, Mr. Duggan. Lloyd is a crackerjack baseball player, the star hitter on his mother's softball team. But no one at school knows of his prowess because his mother, fearing for his safety, insists that he play only under her watchful eye. Always the last chosen for the school team, he never tries to hit the ball and refuses to run when he accidentally does hit it. The kids make fun of him, but Lloyd thinks of himself as a turtle whom names and jeers cannot reach. Then Kirby, a classmate, sees Lloyd at one of his mother's practice sessions and discovers his hitting ability. Dismayed, and further embarrassed when Kirby learns that he is not allowed to ride a bike or walk to the ball park by himself, Lloyd still refuses to make any effort when Kirby chooses him for the school team. He does notice that Ancil, the spirited, "spaghetti-haired" new girl in class, is now the last to be chosen. Meanwhile, Mr. Duggan tries to learn why Lloyd is so often truant, what is bothering him. Lloyd confides in him and is surprised by the truant officer's sympathy and his concerned insistence that Lloyd attend school regularly. Touched by Mr. Duggan's interest and by Kirby's continuing attempts to befriend him, Lloyd begins to come out of his shell. Kirby refuses a birthday party invitation unless Lloyd is invited; Lloyd, in turn, refuses to go unless Ancil is invited. Then he convinces the friendless Ancil to attend. During the party baseball game, Ancil gets a hit. Rather than strand her at first base, Lloyd hits the ball and runs. Pleased by his classmates' approval, he even resolves to begin his diet—he will have only a small portion of cake and ice cream.

A lonely, overprotected boy responds quickly but credibly to the friendship and encouragement of several classmates and a truant officer. As his self-image improves, Lloyd can assert himself for the benefit of another outcast classmate and begin to loosen his dependence on his mother. Although sympathetically portrayed, Lloyd's complete metamorphosis may seem a bit too smooth and sudden.

Ages 8-11

**Also available in:**
Paperbound—*Last Was Lloyd*
Dell Publishing Company, Inc.

---

**609**

Smith, Doris Buchanan

## Salted Lemons

Four Winds Press, 1980.
(233 pages)

---

*PREJUDICE: Ethnic/Racial*
  *Change: new home*
  *Friendship: making friends*
  *Friendship: meaning of*
  *Peer relationships*

---

For ten-year-old Darby Bannister, moving from Washington, D.C., to Atlanta during World War II means starting all over again. In Washington she had "friends and cousins and familiar streets." Here the neighborhood children call her a "Yankee" and her teacher, Miss Hardy, scolds her constantly for forgetting to say "ma'am." School is very different too. The children have to sit at their desks all day, except for recess, lunch, and spelling bees. Darby is used to moving around and being away from her desk. The teachers and principal of this new school give spankings too, something Darby can hardly believe. Furthermore, the city limits line runs one-half block behind the Bannisters' house. So, although most children her age in the area go to the City school, she goes to the County. Darby's first new friend, Yoko Sasaki, lives across the street but attends the other school. Still, Darby delights in their relationship until someone calls her a "Jap lover." Suddenly she realizes why Yoko has been so reluctant to discuss her heritage, insisting that since she was born in Atlanta she is an American. For a while Darby is afraid Yoko may really be the enemy, but she soon sees that her friend is as much an American as she, a "Yankee." There is another person in the neighborhood who raises suspicion. Mr. Kaigler, who runs the grocery store, speaks with a heavy German accent and is called a "spy" by most of the children. Some of them even throw eggs at his store and soap his windows on Halloween. When his friend with the white Samoyed dog comes to talk with him, they follow the man. Mr. Kaigler understands Darby's loneliness and is kind to her. She thinks at first that he may really be a spy, but gradually realizes that this is just one more case of prejudice. The most narrow-minded child of all is a fifth grader named Gordon. He has had polio and "everyone thinks he's as important as President Roosevelt." His sister, Valerie, says that Gordon considers himself "general of the neighborhood." Gordon hates "Yankees" and makes sure that Darby doesn't get invited to attend the Saturday afternoon movies with the other neighborhood children. The first time he acknowledges her existence at all is when he challenges her to stand with him under the railroad trestle on Halloween night. There is supposed to be a ghost under the trestle, but Darby is determined not to let Gordon conquer her. When her father refuses to let her go, she loses the only chance she's had to prove herself to everyone. Later, when Gordon challenges her again, she sneaks out of the house at midnight and outlasts all the others under the trestle. The next day she is invited to the movies by "the general" himself. Now Darby, who has also made a special friend at school, begins to feel good about Atlanta. But then Yoko's family is forced to move; the government is sending everyone of Japanese descent to camps fenced in with barbed wire. Once again Darby is faced with the irrational behavior of people who are "afraid of anything or anyone different." When Mr. Kaigler defends the Sasaki family and is called a "Jap lover" by an angry customer, Darby fears that people will stop buying at his store. Then he disappears for several days, and she worries that he has been accused of spying and taken away. When he returns and tells her he has only been to see his new granddaughter, she is vastly relieved. Her delight increases when she learns that the Kaiglers have gotten a beautiful Samoyed puppy from their friend.

A young girl in Atlanta, ostracized for being a "Yankee," observes the prejudice against Japanese and German citizens during World War II, overcoming her own suspicions and developing special insight into people's irrational fears. Along the way she makes friends and learns to fit into her new neighborhood and school. Darby is bright and sensitive enough to catch and hold the reader's interest throughout each believable plot development in this compelling story.

Ages 9-12

**Also available in:**
No other form known

## 610

Smith, Janice Lee

### The Monster in the Third Dresser Drawer and Other Stories about Adam Joshua

Black/white illustrations by Dick Gackenbach.
Harper & Row, Publishers, Inc., 1981.
(86 pages)

---

*CHANGE: Resisting*
*Age: respect for*
*Baby-sitter*
*Fear: of darkness*
*Friendship: making friends*
*Moving*
*Sibling: new baby*
*Tooth, loss of*

---

Young Adam Joshua strongly objects to the move his family is planning. But the move takes place nevertheless, and he ends up in a new town, a new house, and a new room. While climbing a tree, he sees into a bedroom hung with Spiderman posters. He yells hello and gives his name, but the boy in the room slams down the window. Then he lifts it up a crack and says his name is Nelson. Later, Adam Joshua writes on his bedroom wall that moving is moving and there's not much he can do about it. Nobody asks Adam Joshua if he wants a baby in the family either. But Amanda Jane arrives all the same. Suddenly Adam Joshua is "too loud. And too babyish. And too in the way." While Amanda Jane's bedroom is readied she sleeps in her brother's room, waking him up repeatedly when she cries. Nelson, with whom he's become friends, has already warned him that babies get all the attention. One night, after Adam Joshua gets a little kiss and a little hug from his parents and Amanda Jane gets a big hug and a big kiss, he cuts up her teddy bear with a scissors. His parents respond

by hugging him and reading him a story. After they leave, Adam Joshua makes amends by tucking Amanda Jane in. When Adam Joshua gets a loose tooth, he and Nelson try to make it fall out with string, bubble gum, pounding on the back, and other ineffective measures. In due time, Adam Joshua swallows the tooth while eating cereal. The baby-sitter who comes one night does not understand about the monster hiding in Adam Joshua's third dresser drawer. As many times as he turns on the light, she turns it off. When Amanda Jane wakes up, the baby-sitter pats her back and takes her downstairs, but she tells Adam Joshua to get to sleep and keep the light off. When his parents return, he explains the monster to his mother. She tells the monster to scat, waves her arms around, and assures her son that it's gone. Adam Joshua is not happy when Great-Aunt Emily comes to visit. She is old, wears black, smells like lavender, and loves Amanda Jane. But this time she brings Adam Joshua a present—a very old picture of her family standing by their sod house in Kansas. The more she tells him about the old days, the more he likes her and the more she appreciates him. He is sorry to see her go. Adam Joshua's parents finally begin working in earnest on Amanda Jane's bedroom. He takes care of her while they carpet, paint, and wallpaper. When he complains about how much nicer her new room is compared with his, his father says he can choose between the two rooms. After sitting in both rooms Adam Joshua decides to remain in his own, and he paints stars and a moon on the ceiling and some flowers on the wall. The first night Amanda Jane sleeps in her new room, Adam Joshua worries she will be lonely. He brings her to his room and tucks her in bed with him, saying, "Now you don't have to worry, I'm right here."

In these anecdotal chapters, young Adam Joshua, helped by understanding parents, copes with a move, a new baby sister, and several less dramatic but very familiar events. Young readers will appreciate the humor of the little boy's escapades as he makes new friends and learns to love his baby sister. Delightful illustrations capture the lighthearted mood.

Ages 5-8

**Also available in:**
No other form known

## 611

Smith, Lucia B.

### My Mom Got a Job

Color illustrations by C. Christina Johanson.
Holt, Rinehart and Winston, Inc., 1979.
(32 pages counted)

---

*PARENT/PARENTS: Mother Working Outside Home*
*Change: accepting*
*Life style: change in*

---

Many things have changed for a young girl since her mother got a job. She misses the quiet after-school time they used to share, although she feels important about taking care of the baby at Mrs. Raynor's, where she now goes after school. Her mother can no longer help her teacher once a week, but now, on one special day, she comes to school to tell about her job. Her best friend's mother now takes both girls to their ballet lessons, and the narrator's mother no longer plays the piano for recitals. After their lessons, though, the three stop for ice cream. Helping her mother shop for groceries used to be a happy time, but shopping with Dad is turning out to be fun too—and since Dad knows little about how to select fruits and vegetables, his daughter is teaching him. She and her mother no longer go to the library on Fridays, and so the little girl looks forward instead to evenings by the fire, where her father reads *Treasure Island* to her. Even weekends are different: housecleaning is a joint effort, and Mom is less fussy about how her daughter's room looks. On Saturdays and Sundays the family spends time together biking or picnicking. One Sunday the girl's parents go out, leaving her with her grandparents. "My mom used to take care of Dad and me," says the girl. "Now we are all taking care of each other."

A young girl tells what she likes and what she doesn't like about her life when her mother gets a job. The child misses having her mother at home, but finds much that is special and satisfying about the family's new routine. Readers will respond—perhaps by sharing similar experiences—to the cheerful and resourceful manner in which the main character adapts to her changed home life. The illustrations warmly enhance the simple, lyrical text.

Ages 5-8

**Also available in:**
No other form known

## 612

**Smith, Nancy Covert**

## The Falling-Apart Winter

Walker and Company, 1982.
(112 pages)

---

*DEPRESSION*
*MENTAL ILLNESS: of Parent*
  *Change: new home*
  *Change: resisting*
  *Family: relationships*
  *Reality, escaping*
  *School: classmate relationships*

---

Twelve-year-old Addam Hanley misses his dog, his grandparents, and the friends he left in Ohio when his father's new job took him and his parents to an apartment (no pets allowed) in Virginia. He also misses the way his mother used to be. These days she's listless, apathetic, and cries a lot. She's too tired to do the housework or fix meals, and Addam's father won't take care of those chores either. Months after their move, boxes still sit unpacked. Addam's parents fight often, his mother crying that nobody understands, his father calling her crazy. A new friendship with a classmate named Bryan is hindered when Addam's mother makes a scene in front of Bryan. In response to all this, Addam's schoolwork suffers. Moose, the football team captain, compounds his misery by teasing him. One day Addam comes home to find that his mother has been hospitalized. Angry with his father for not averting the situation, partly relieved, anxious, guilty, he runs out of the house.

He tells friends that his mother works for the State Department and travels a lot, fantasizing about the wonderful gifts she brings when she returns home. When his father asks him to come along on the nightly visits to his mother, Addam refuses. He "didn't want to think about his real mother. His made-up mother was better." When Addam's mother finally returns home, she is somewhat better but still not herself. She will visit a mental health clinic daily as an outpatient. As part of her treatment, Addam and his father must also attend sessions with her therapist, Dr. Collier. Dr. Collier explains that his mother is suffering from depression. She asks Addam if he is willing to help his family be happy. He doesn't know. In subsequent visits, Dr. Collier helps Addam understand human psychology and family dynamics a bit better. Thanksgiving approaches, and Addam bemoans the TV turkey dinner he's expecting. However, his mother does fix the traditional dinner while Addam and his father watch the parade. While she does all the dishes, they watch the football game. Then an essay contest on freedom is announced at school, and Addam begins a paper about the freedom to be mentally healthy. Dr. Collier arranges a conference with all three Hanleys, during which Mrs. Hanley reports that on Thanksgiving she was once again taken for granted, doing all the cooking and cleaning up while her husband and son enjoyed their own pursuits. Addam watches as his parents assume their familiar postures: his father turning away from the problem, his mother crying. Mr. Hanley refuses to attend any more sessions with Dr. Collier and forbids Addam to also. Addam works hard on his essay and becomes one of six semi-finalists. All are to read their essays to the entire seventh grade, and the whole class will help choose the winner. Addam is horrified. He imagines the jeers when Moose and his other classmates learn his mother has been mentally ill. The night before the contest, Addam reads his essay to his parents, figuring his father will forbid him to read it in public. His father storms out of the apartment, and Addam isn't sure what his reaction is. His mother cries, this time with the relief of feeling that Addam actually understands some of what she's been going through. The next day, just before the essay reading, Addam tries to intercede when Moose bullies his friend Joanne. Furious with Moose, Addam, after reading his essay, lashes out extemporaneously at bullies who not only refuse to help others, but actually aggravate their problems. Addam's classmates choose his essay as the winner. Then Addam discovers that Moose's mother is an alcoholic; they may never be friends, but a truce is declared. Mr. Hanley finally admits to being wrongheaded, and the family resumes therapy sessions with Dr. Collier. When the question of returning to Ohio for Christmas comes up, all three agree that "home" is where they are. They know they can look forward now, not backward.

A young boy tries to make sense of his changed family situation while his mother suffers from acute depression. He must also cope with the loss of his dog, friends, and former home; a new school; a bully; and his father's tendency to offer less support, rather than more, in times of trouble. The book is never didactic, but does offer a number of suggestions to readers who live with mentally ill family members. Familiarizing themselves with mental illness in general and the person's condition in particular is a first step, and the book defuses anxiety about counseling, therapists, group sessions, and mental health clinics. Addam's negative feelings about his mother's illness—fear, shame, guilt, hostility, selfishness—are all shown to be natural, although he learns how to turn them around. This well-written story takes readers into the troubled Hanley home and leaves them with more empathy, understanding, and knowledge than they had before.

Ages 10-13

**Also available in:**
No other form known

## 613

**Smith, Pauline Coggeshall**

**Brush Fire!**

The Westminster Press, 1979.
(96 pages)

---

*MATURATION*
*RESPONSIBILITY: Accepting*
  *Courage, meaning of*
  *Gangs: being bothered by*
  *Identity, search for*
  *Resourcefulness*

---

Johnny, seventeen, is filled with excited plans to fix up the camper he's just bought and take to the road, leaving school, his job, and his Aunt Kate behind. She is appalled at the very sight of the camper and refuses to let him park it on her property. Then Mr. Miller, Johnny's shop and woodworking teacher, asks Johnny to house-sit and care for his animals for several weeks once school is out. Johnny, wondering why the Millers trust him, is delighted, determined that as soon as he finishes certain repairs on the camper, he will leave. School out, Johnny quits his job at the grocery store and goes to the Millers' house, out in the hills "at the end of nowhere." They give him detailed instructions and warn him about the warm Santa Ana winds and the danger of fires. For the first two weeks Johnny is absorbed in working on his camper. He establishes a compatible coexistence with the dog and cat, and the Millers' regular calls remind him to do the watering. Then one day, three motorcycles drive slowly up the long stretch of dusty road. Johnny recognizes Bo and Red, two boys from his high school, but he doesn't know the other, older man called Cam. Bo and Red taunt Johnny, threatening and then beginning to wreck his camper. Johnny calls for the dog, Macho, who leaps to stop the attack. In the ensuing fracas, Macho is badly cut and Johnny hurts his hand. The three leave without damaging the camper, and Johnny frantically tends to Macho's wounds. By nightfall he begins to fear the three will return and decides to call the police. But the phone wires have been cut. After a sleepless night he decides to set up the three overhead sprinkler systems, saturating the yard, garage, and house in the hope that the water will slow the three down if they return. They do, riding back and forth up the hill and down past the house. Suddenly they leave, and Johnny soon discovers why. A Santa Ana wind has started a fire. He resets the sprinklers, hoping to slow or ward off the fire. Next he

beats a repeated SOS on a washtub. Then he begins digging a firebreak. Soon fire trucks arrive, and Johnny helps them contain the fire. Hours later, the fire chief credits the boy's quick actions with saving the Millers' property. Investigators discover evidence that the fire was set, and Johnny tells of his encounter with the three motorcyclists. He's a hero, his story written up in the local newspaper. When the fire chief returns several days later to present Johnny with a fireman's helmet as a souvenir, he suggests that the boy finish school and take the civil service exam to join the fire department. He also mentions that Johnny could volunteer as a reserve firefighter in the mountains for the remainder of the summer. Johnny applies and is accepted. After the Millers' return, he takes back his job at the grocery store for the fall and heads for the mountains in his camper, dreaming new dreams of his future.

A restless and dissatisfied young man believes he wants only to restore his camper and drift around the country. Asked to house-sit, Johnny displays courage and quick thinking when he's faced with a motorcycle gang and a brush fire, and his experiences lead him to reassess his plans for the future. If the ending is a bit pat, this high-interest, low-vocabulary story is believable and exciting enough to appeal, especially to the reluctant reader.

Ages 11 and up

**Also available in:**
No other form known

S

## 614

**Smith, Robert Kimmel**

**Jelly Belly**

Black/white illustrations by Bob Jones.
Delacorte Press, 1981.
(155 pages)

---

*WEIGHT CONTROL: Overweight*
  *Camp experiences*
  *Determination*
  *Family: relationships*
  *Grandparent: living in child's home*
  *Self-discipline*

---

Eleven-year-old Ned Robbins is thirty pounds overweight. Ned used to be skinny until his grandmother came to live with his family five years ago. His grandmother loves to cook; Ned loves to eat. Now the kids call him names like Blimpie, Tubby, Piggy, Lard-Butt, and Jelly Belly. Ned's parents have put him on a diet but he has not lost any weight in four months—because he sneaks food and his grandmother helps him. One day in May, Ned's parents inform him he will be spending two months at Camp Lean-Too. Ned thinks the camp sounds "like a jail for fat kids." Jamie, his older brother, tells a depressed Ned that he must not want to lose the weight badly enough; if he did, he would try. By the first day of camp, Ned has gained seven pounds. Dr. Skinner, the camp dietician, tells him he should expect to lose twenty pounds in eight weeks. He encourages all the campers to think sports, not food. Ned meets his roommates: Richard, Max, Hog, Fred, and Brian. He immediately takes to Richard, the only one who managed to sneak food into camp. The regular camp food is so bad that

Ned, Richard, Max, and Hog raid the kitchen one night, stealing cheese and bread to make sandwiches. After three weeks Ned has only lost three pounds. Then Richard sneaks into town and buys large quantities of snack foods and candy. They stash the food and eat it each night after dinner. By the end of camp Ned is only fourteen pounds lighter. He feels guilty and regretful when an award is given to a boy who has lost forty-four pounds. Back home, Ned again begins to eat his grandmother's food heartily. His father makes a deal with him. If Ned can get down to seventy-five pounds by Easter, the family will go to Disney World. Ned is not sure he can do it. But while sitting in the school cafeteria, he comes to the realization that he indeed eats too much. He decides to lose weight. That afternoon he tells his grandmother to stop feeding him so much. He then tells Jamie of his determination, and Jamie encourages him to jog. By January Ned is down to seventy-nine pounds and cannot seem to lose any more. At his checkup, the doctor informs him that since he has grown one-and-a-half inches, his ideal weight is now seventy-nine pounds. Ned is elated; his father makes reservations at Disney World. Shortly thereafter, Ned receives a letter from Richard saying he will see him at Camp Lean-Too. Ned vows never to see Camp Lean-Too again.

Until Ned makes up his mind to lose weight, even sending him to a weight-loss camp doesn't solve his eating problem. When he becomes determined to win a coveted trip by losing weight, he succeeds. Ned's first-person narrative offers considerable insight into the struggle involved in losing weight, especially when one's grandmother plies the family with good food. Clever illustrations enhance the humor of the story.

Ages 10-12

**Also available in:**
Cassette—*Jelly Belly*
Library of Congress (NLSBPH)

Paperbound—*Jelly Belly*
Dell Publishing Company, Inc.

## 615

**Snyder, Zilpha Keatley**

## Come On, Patsy

Color illustrations by Margot Zemach.
Atheneum Publishers, 1982.
(32 pages)

---

*AGGRESSION*
*FRIENDSHIP: Lack of*
  *Autonomy*

---

"Come on, Patsy," says Patsy's friend. She knows a new way to get to the park. First they must jump over a low wire. The friend makes it, but Patsy trips. Next they must climb over a fence with a KEEP OUT sign on it. Patsy falls and hurts her knee. They tiptoe across a lawn with a KEEP OFF THE LAWN sign. When Patsy looks dubious about the big guard dog, her friend tells her not to worry and hurries off. The dog rips Patsy's dress. At the playground, the friend pushes Patsy too high on the swing and then wants to know why Patsy didn't tell her she doesn't like to go so high. Encouraged to jump over a mud hole, Patsy falls in and then is reproached by her friend for fussing about her dirty dress. When they pass an ice cream cart, the friend finds some money in Patsy's pocket and buys them an ice cream cone. She eats her "half" first, giving Patsy a nearly empty piece of cone. There is too some ice cream left, she insists. After a merry-go-round ride, the friend says she didn't realize the ride was making Patsy sick—as Patsy throws up. As they head back, Patsy's angry father comes for the bedraggled Patsy, dragging her off home with him. The next day when the friend comes by and says, "Come on, Patsy. Want to go play?" she can't understand why Patsy turns her back on her.

A little girl who is led willy-nilly by a domineering playmate seems unable to say no or to express her own opinions. However, after a day of getting into one fix after another, she does say no to any more "playing." Highly original and detailed illustrations, as well as a light-verse text, underscore a problem that sometimes has serious consequences: following a leader who is not too careful of life's rules and limits. Children might like to suggest what Patsy could have said each time her bossy, inconsiderate friend recommended an uncomfortable or disobedient course of action.

Ages 5-8

**Also available in:**
No other form known

## 616

**Sobol, Harriet Langsam**

## My Other-Mother, My Other-Father

Black/white photographs by Patricia Agre.
Macmillan Publishing Company, Inc., 1979.
(34 pages)

---

*FAMILY: Relationships*
  *Change: accepting*
  *Divorce: of parents*
  *Parent/Parents: remarriage of*
  *School: pupil-teacher relationships*
  *Stepparent: father*
  *Stepparent: mother*

---

Andrea Hayes, about twelve, has a favorite teacher: Ms. Burns, an English teacher who, until this year, taught Navaho children in Arizona. Only Ms. Burns seems to understand Andrea's complicated family situation without a lengthy explanation. The girl's parents divorced when she was eight. Her mother is now married to Larry Goodrich, her father to Sharon. Andrea and her younger brother live with their mother and Larry; Andrea calls her stepfather Larry because she already has a father. What is confusing is that her mother's last name is now different from her own. Andrea doesn't like the words "stepfather," "stepmother," and "stepchildren." She is sure there is a better word than "step." Ms. Burns suggests she call Sharon by the Navaho word "shema," meaning any woman old enough to be one's mother. Andrea wonders if the new word would help her any, since instead of explaining her relationship with Sharon she'd have to explain "shema." Still, she notes that there are both advantages and disadvantages to not having a regular family. She does have more family to love and more people to help celebrate birthdays and Christmas. But when she has fun with one parent, she feels guilty about not sharing her happiness with the other. Fortunately, her parents live near each other so she can spend time with both families. And they all get along quite well, so there is no fighting. Andrea sadly realizes that her parents will never get together again. But she decides she likes her stepparents so much she may call Sharon "my other-mother" and Larry "my other-father."

In this photographic essay, a child of divorce gives a candid account of her feelings about her parents' breakup and remarriages, and about her two families. Though she is not without sadness and confusion, Andrea seems to be making the best of her rather complicated family life. The photographs give immediacy to her story.

Ages 7-10

**Also available in:**
No other form known

## 617

Somerlott, Robert

**Blaze**

The Viking Press, Inc., 1981.
(221 pages)

---

ANIMALS: Love for
  Grandparent: living in home of
  Grandparent: love for
  Running away

---

Ten-year-old David has been living with his aunt and uncle in California since his parents died a year earlier. He is well cared for, but receives little affection. Now he is being sent to camp for a month so his guardians can take a vacation. A few hours before he is to leave, his grandfather, Cappy Holland, stops in for a brief visit. Cappy owns the Rancho San Pascual in the Rockies, where he has raised and trained German shepherd dogs for the past forty years. A few months earlier he had sent David a puppy, Blaze, but dogs aren't allowed in the apartment building and his uncle gave Blaze to a work associate who wanted a guard dog. The man, Cappy has learned, has mistreated and abused Blaze. So the dog "was familiar with abuse, but had no experience of kindness, and as his strength had grown, so had his anger." Cappy decides to visit Blaze; David, determined not to go to camp, stows away in the back of the truck. Very angry at Blaze's state and still retaining part ownership of the dog, Cappy puts Blaze into a cage in the back of the truck and sets off for his ranch. When he pulls up at a truck stop, he lets Blaze have the run of the truck, not knowing that David is hiding behind a flimsy curtain. Cappy tells the restaurant owner about the recent fire that killed all his dogs, saying he's too old to start over. Meanwhile, Blaze confronts David and shows every intention of attacking. David remembers that dogs like to be talked to and he tries to soothe Blaze.

Inside, Cappy hears Blaze's attack bark. He runs to the truck, tranquilizes and cages Blaze, and takes David into the restaurant. Cappy admires the boy's spirit, but doesn't know what to do with him. Finally he agrees to take David with him to the ranch. At San Pascual, David feeds Blaze and makes the first, tenuous attempts to befriend him. The dog begins to respond to the affectionate treatment. Cappy starts training him and is delighted to be once again doing the thing he loves best, working with an intelligent dog. For David, it's a magical new world with Blaze his constant, devoted companion. Cappy persuades David's uncle to let the boy spend the summer with him. One day they take Blaze for a walk and meet two little Indian girls and their flock of sheep. Blaze's dormant sheepherding instincts take over, and with great skill he carefully herds the sheep into the midst of a fancy cocktail party given by a local society woman, Mrs. Bradley. One night soon after, David sees Mrs. Bradley's car stop on the road without lights. The next day, Blaze eats a piece of meat he finds by the creek and nearly dies of strychnine poisoning. They have no proof, but David blames Mrs. Bradley. They train Blaze not to eat any food but what they give him. Intending that David and Blaze not be separated when the boy returns to California, Cappy invites David's uncle to come pick him up. He hopes the man will see how attached the boy and dog are to each other. But when Cappy and David's uncle return from the airport, David is missing. He has decided to lay low for a few days until Uncle Arthur gives up and goes home. Mrs. Bradley offers him a lift and her "shortcut" takes them into the treacherous wilderness area in the upper canyon. When her jeep can no longer penetrate the thick growth, they abandon it. Then starts a nightmare that includes a skirmish with a local wild man, a rattlesnake, and a fire. David learns that Mrs. Bradley's cats were poisoned by an employee she'd recently fired, a man who used to sponsor dog fights. He realizes that this was the man who'd poisoned Blaze. Meanwhile, Cappy sets out to find David, but injures his knee and must send Blaze on alone. After many adventures, the dog eventually finds David and Mrs. Bradley in a cave and leads them down the mountainside. Cappy promises himself that if David and Blaze return safely, he will insist that David remain with him. He knows now that he, David, and Blaze belong together.

A boy, his grandfather, and a dog, all starved for affection, help each other create a loving home together in this well-written story. Much information about the care and training of dogs is worked into the text, and the reader becomes sensitive to dogs in general—their fears, their capabilities and limitations, even their various barks. The "good training" that both Blaze and David receive from Cappy changes the lives of all three.

Ages 10-13

**Also available in:**
Paperbound—Blaze
Scholastic Book Services

**618**

Spence, Eleanor Rachel

## A Candle for Saint Antony

Oxford University Press, 1979.
(140 pages) o.p.

---

FRIENDSHIP: Best Friend
FRIENDSHIP: Meaning of
LOVE, MEANING OF
    Homosexuality: male
    Maturation
    Prejudice: social class
    Roman Catholic
    School: classmate relationships

---

Justin Vincent, fifteen, lives in a suburb of Sydney, Australia. Like his friends, Justin works only hard enough to get by at Bayside College, the preparatory school to which he'll be returning after summer vacation. His new classmate at Bayside, Rudolph (Rudi) Mayer, comes from an entirely different background. Born in Vienna, Austria, the son of a music teacher, Rudi emigrated to Australia with his family when he was seven. But his father died soon after the move, and Rudi's mother went to work. A devout Roman Catholic, Rudi is using the money he's saved to attend the non-Catholic Bayside College, a school he thinks well equipped to prepare him for medical school. Justin considers Rudi presumptuous for coming to Bayside. Egged on by his friends, he taunts Rudi and threatens him. But nothing Justin does seems to ruffle the solitary Rudi, and Justin finds himself inexplicably drawn to the boy. Eventually, the two develop a close friendship, usually excluding all other classmates. Justin's newfound friendship and his newly mature behavior puzzle his friends and his parents. With the announcement of an opportunity for the boys' German Conversation class to visit Austria, the two friends begin plotting ways to raise the money for the trip. Justin's father tells him he may go if he achieves a very high average in all his subjects. The two boys work to bring up certain of Justin's grades, with Rudi praying regularly for Justin and lighting candles to Saint Antony, the revered subject of a Brahms composition his father had loved. Justin manages the high grades, and Rudi is able to save enough money for his own expenses. A few nights before the class is to leave, Greg, once a close friend of Justin's, gives a party. Justin goes by himself, since Rudi has to work. At one point another old friend, Rick, makes a snide reference to the unusually close relationship between Justin and Rudi. In Vienna at last, Justin and Rudi go off on their own to tour the city, and Rudi shares points of interest from his childhood memories. Justin feels very close to Rudi and very happy. But the others now tease Justin often and treat the two as outsiders, implying that their relationship is homosexual. Then Justin and Rudi are invited to spend a few days with an Austrian family in their home in the Wienerwald—the Austrian woods. Exploring in the forest, they come upon the remains of an old church. Entranced with the beauty of the church and its idyllic surroundings, they decide to clean up the chapel and clear away its overgrown greenery. Back at the house, their hostess tells them the chapel was long ago dedicated to Saint Antony and that Brahms himself had

once seen it. Rudi is "positively radiant." On the last day of their stay, Rudi and Justin are stranded in the chapel during a violent thunderstorm. Huddled together under raincoats, they wait for the storm to subside. Rudi tells Justin he loves him and fears their intimacy will be lost or changed when they return to Sydney. He asks Justin to stay in Austria with him, where he believes they could "be together as much as we want without people noticing, or saying stupid things." Justin asks for time to decide what to do. Greg, who has followed them and overheard the conversation, later describes the episode to the whole group, hoping to humiliate the boys. In front of everyone, Rudi confirms that he said he loved Justin and he does. Justin unhappily tells Rudi that he can't stay in Austria, but Rudi says to their tormentors, "It was never the way you thought. It never would be." Justin says nothing, but in his heart is less sure about the nature of his feelings for Rudi. Rudi stays; Justin returns home. After months of struggling with a sense of having failed his friend, Justin finally acknowledges in letters to Rudi that the love they share is special and enduring. Rudi, for his part, comes to understand the pressures Justin was feeling and is able to forgive him for not showing more loyalty.

Two soulmates, whose relationship is neither romantic nor sexual, are the victims of a world that sets limits on the nature and variety of acceptable human relationships and self-expression. Rudi, more self-confident and mature, is able to understand his feelings for Justin; but Justin takes longer to sort things out, haunted by the knowledge that others are suspicious of the special bond they share. "You could say you love your parents . . . and your new jeans . . . and the surf when the wind was blowing. . . . But there should be another word to describe the feeling you had for a friend whose like you might never encounter again in a lifetime." This is a memorable, thought-provoking exploration of the meaning of love and friendship.

Ages 13 and up

**Also available in:**
No other form known

**619**

Springstubb, Tricia

**The Moon on a String**

Little, Brown and Company, 1982.
(201 pages)

---

AUTONOMY
MATURATION
    Boy-girl relationships
    Dependence/Independence
    Expectations
    Family: relationships
    Sibling: rivalry

---

Seventeen-year-old Deirdre Shea badly wants to leave the boring, predictable, uninspiring little town of Green River. Her mother says Deirdre has wanted the moon on a string ever since she was a baby. Her older sister, Angel, left home at Deirdre's age. But, as her mother points out, Angel had definite plans and is now living successfully in Boston, with a "big, important, not to mention lucrative" job and two years of college. Angel has been held up to Deirdre as a model of perfection for so long that the very name makes Deirdre bristle. Tim, Deirdre's long-time boyfriend, looks forward to remaining in Green River forever, with her as his wife. She can't imagine being apart from Tim, but when he suggests they become engaged, she pleads for more time. After graduation Deirdre moves to Boston, where Angel finds her a room at Mrs. Croghan's house. The only work Deirdre can find—and it's very hard work—is waitressing. A few days after she gets her job, she goes into a drugstore and finds Angel behind the cash register. Her embarrassed sister takes Deirdre to the apartment she shares with three other people, including Garth, her lover. She tells Deirdre she had a nervous breakdown in college because of the pressure to excel. Garth helped her see that she didn't have to live up to anybody else's expectations. Deirdre promises not to tell their parents about Angel's circumstances. The sisters attend the Fourth of July fireworks together, where Deirdre contracts poison ivy. Tad, a college freshman who also rooms at Mrs. Croghan's, takes care of her. When she returns to work, Deirdre decides that waitressing is boring and demeaning. Furthermore, Eddie, the fat cook, has been harassing her. She finally quits when his harassment becomes blatantly sexual. Home for a visit, she realizes that she left Boston that morning an independent woman but has become a child again at home. Back in Boston, Deirdre finds Angel grieving—Garth appears to be dating someone else. The sisters have words; Deirdre admits she has despised Angel by reputation for a long time. Through a social service agency, Deirdre volunteers to be a Big Sister to twelve-year-old Kenny. Inspired by this role, she finds a job as a file clerk in a children's home. When she sees the indifference of the counselors at the home, she feels sure she could do a better job and begins to think about attending college. While Deirdre is again home visiting, Angel calls and confesses to her mother that she has no money, no job, and is not attending college. When Deirdre returns to Boston, she and Angel make a new start with their relationship. A visit to Kenny's home makes Deirdre realize, "Even though his father beats him, Kenny can't stop wanting his love; even though I feel claustrophobic in Green River, I go on thinking of it as the one place I'll ever truly be safe." Tim comes unexpectedly to visit her, but finds her in Tad's room and leaves, shocked and hurt. Tad and Deirdre, however, see that their relationship is not working. They agree to separate and talk again in a month. Deirdre moves into Angel's apartment and takes Kenny home with her for Thanksgiving. She realizes she has never really left Green River. "Though she couldn't live here, this was her home."

A young woman's search for "home" leads to many discoveries about herself, her family, and other people; in the end she decides, "The place has to be inside you." Deirdre's main discovery is that she does not need to reject all the old values in order to consider herself independent. What she will eventually decide about

Tim and Tad is left open, since Deirdre is not finished growing and learning yet. This is an effective, believable study of a girl's gradual maturation. Especially well presented are her twin feelings of vulnerability and excitement at being on her own for the first time.

Ages 12 and up

**Also available in:**
Paperbound—*The Moon on a String*
Dell Publishing Company, Inc.

## 620
### Stanek, Muriel Novella
### Growl When You Say R
Color illustrations by Phil Smith.
Albert Whitman & Company, 1979.
(31 pages counted)

---

*SPEECH PROBLEMS*
  *Self, attitude toward: feeling different*
  *Success*
  *Teasing*

---

When young Robbie moves to a new school, his classmates laugh at him and tell him he talks funny. Robbie pronounces his name Wobbie, and he makes "Run, Harry, run!" into "Wun, Hawwy, wun!" After Robbie tries to get out of school by pretending he's sick, refuses to talk at all, and gets in a fight when he is teased, his teacher, Mrs. Rose, enrolls him in a speech class. There he learns to listen to sounds, to record his speech using a microphone, and to use mirrors to watch his mouth. He and the other students play games and work on pronouncing words that start with *R*, end with *R*, or have *R* in the middle. Although his speech is improving, Robbie is still hesitant about speaking in his regular classes, so he sometimes uses a puppet to speak for him. During a spring trip to the zoo, Robbie and two other children get separated from the class. At the Lost and Found, they're invited to use a microphone to contact their group. Steve, the boy who had teased Robbie most, says Robbie should make the announcement because he's had experience with microphones. Triumphantly and correctly, Robbie announces, "R-r-roberts School, Bus Number-r-r-r 9. Wait for-r-r us!" Mrs. Rose later tells Robbie she's proud of him. When he thanks her, they both smile—it's the first time he's said her name.

A young boy gains self-confidence and the admiration of his peers when he improves his speech with the help of a special class. Speech therapy techniques are accurately portrayed in the text and illustrations. An introductory note to teachers and parents includes an address where readers can write for more information. The book will be reassuring to those in need of speech therapy, informative for others.

Ages 4-8

**Also available in:**
No other form known

S

**621**

Stanek, Muriel Novella

## My Little Foster Sister

Color illustrations by Judith Cheng.
Albert Whitman & Company, 1981.
(32 pages counted)

---

*FOSTER HOME*
  *Friendship: meaning of*
  *Sharing/Not sharing*
  *Sibling: rivalry*

---

When Penny, a foster child, comes to live with a little girl's family, the girl, an only child, says, "But she doesn't belong here!" She crossly tells Penny not to sit in her chair and hangs a Keep Out sign on her bedroom door. She's unhappy when she has to push Penny in the grocery cart, share her toys, and watch Penny sit on her grandmother's lap. She objects when her mother gives Penny one of her outgrown sweaters and again when her mother asks her to take Penny to the playground. But when a bully pushes Penny off the slide ladder, the foster sister says, "She's my foster sister, and I'm here to see that she gets her turn." From then on, things get better between the two children. Sometimes when her big sister is due home from school, Penny hides behind the door and says, Boo! In turn, big sister reads to Penny, shows her how she practices her piano lessons, and lets her cuddle in her bed during a scary storm. The night after that, the older girl takes down the Keep Out sign and tells Penny she can play with her toys while she's at school. When Penny leaves to be adopted by an aunt and uncle in California, her foster sister cries and misses her. But "it was nice having a foster sister, even for a little while."

A little girl first resents and rejects a younger foster sister, then learns to love and enjoy her. A first-person narrative with delightful illustrations that focus on the changing feelings of the two girls, this simple story encourages understanding of what it means to be a foster child or have a foster sibling. The two girls' initial resentment grows naturally into a warm, caring relationship.

Ages 4-8

**Also available in:**
Large Print—*My Little Foster Sister*
Albert Whitman & Company

**622**

Stanek, Muriel Novella

## Starting School

Color illustrations by Betty and Tony DeLuna.
Albert Whitman & Company, 1981.
(32 pages counted)

---

*SCHOOL: Entering*

---

Mama tells her son that since next fall he'll start school, it's time to get ready. She shows him how to walk to school and they explore the school building. All summer long, the boy prepares for school: he counts to ten, says his address and telephone number, and practices writing his name. He gets a physical and has his teeth checked. He shops for new shoes and shows his father how he can tie them and zip his jacket. On the first day of school, his mother walks him to the classroom door. She cries, but he doesn't. The teacher greets him, as do his friends Mary and Timmy. One boy tries to return to his mother, but the teacher brings him back. Timmy's dog comes in, but is sent home. The teacher gives the children paper and crayons and shows them the science table and the hamster. Then she reads them a story and they all sing a song. When they line up to go to the water fountain, the narrator and Danny disagree about who's first. They are both told to go to the end of the line. When it's time to work, however, he and Danny work together. At dismissal time, his mother is waiting for him. He tells her the teacher must like him because she calls him "honey" just as his mother does. The next day he asks for permission to walk to school by himself. After he promises to be careful, his mother consents.

A little boy narrates in considerable detail his preparation for school and his first-day experiences. His attitude is positive and practical, the book useful for preparing preschoolers. Softly colored illustrations present a multi-ethnic class, a black doctor, a female dentist.

Ages 3-5

**Also available in:**
Braille—*Starting School*
Library of Congress (NLSBPH)

Disc—*Starting School*
Library of Congress (NLSBPH)

Large Print—*Starting School*
Library of Congress (NLSBPH)

**623**

Stanek, Muriel Novella

## Who's Afraid of the Dark?

Color illustrations by Helen Cogancherry.
Albert Whitman & Company, 1980.
(32 pages counted)

---

*FEAR: of Darkness*
  *Emotions: accepting*
  *School: classmate relationships*

---

Kenny is brave about most things, but he is very afraid of the dark. Kenny's grandfather says he'll get over it with time. One day there is a tornado warning at school, and the children have to go down into the basement. When the lights go out suddenly, Kenny begins to cry. Everyone hears him and Mark calls him a crybaby. When he tells his family about this experience, his father replies, "Everyone is afraid of something." To his surprise, Kenny learns that his father is afraid of flying in airplanes. His sister is afraid of roller coasters. His mother is afraid of starting her new job. His grandfather is afraid of something too, but he won't tell what it is. The next day at school, Mark makes fun of Kenny again. An angry Kenny resolves to get over his fear. That evening, he and his sister go upstairs together with all the lights off. She points out the light shining in at the window and coming in under the door. Kenny can see the numbers glowing on the face of his clock. When he thinks he sees a monster, they turn the lights on and he sees it is only the chair. Then one evening Grandpa tells Kenny what his fear is. He is afraid of falling, so he has gotten a cane to help him walk. He has gotten something to help Kenny too—a little flashlight that Kenny can carry with him wherever he goes. A few days later, the movie projector at school breaks down and the auditorium becomes dark. Kenny concentrates on finding light as he and his sister did. He sees the exit lights and the little yellow lights on the walls. He takes his flashlight from his pocket and turns it on. The new girl who is sitting next to him has started to cry, and Kenny comforts her. After the projector is fixed and the movie ends, Mark asks who was crying in the dark. Kenny replies that it wasn't him and asks, "Who's afraid of the dark anyway?" That night he tells his family about the incident and how he was only just a little scared. Everyone is proud of him. Grandpa says he knew all along that Kenny just needed "a little more time."

A little boy learns to cope with his fear of the dark, aided by his sympathetic, supportive family, all of whom admit to being afraid of something. Children who share Kenny's fear will find the story reassuring and may more easily accept and understand their own feelings. The illustrations emphasize light and darkness, effectively portraying Kenny's anxiety.

Ages 5-8

**Also available in:**
No other form known

## 624

**Stecher, Miriam B. and Alice S. Kandell**

**Daddy and Ben Together**

Black/white photographs by Alice S. Kandell.
Lothrop, Lee & Shepard Company, 1981.
(28 pages counted)

---

COMMUNICATION: Parent-Child
  Parent/Parents: mother working outside home

---

When Ben was younger, he used to dress up like his father. As he grew older, he and his father began to do things together. When his mother has to be away for a few days on business, Ben and Daddy say they can take care of each other. Mommy reminds them to laugh a lot, since laughter helps things work out. But they don't laugh when Ben drops eggshells in the omelette, when Daddy is late picking Ben up from school, or when Daddy has to fix Ben's hangnail. Daddy doesn't read to Ben long enough at bedtime, and he spends too much time with his newspaper on Saturday morning. When Ben wonders why he and Daddy are having such a hard time, he remembers what's missing. He makes funny faces so Daddy will laugh and then tells riddles. Daddy suggests a picnic in the park. There they play catch and then eat so much they both have stomachaches that night. But the next morning they are recovered enough to have a pillow fight, build a bike together, and make up nonsense songs. Just before Mommy is due home, they get all dressed up. Daddy doesn't think she'll know which is which because they look so much alike. "But, of course, she did!"

A little boy and his father strengthen and deepen their relationship when they are left to take care of each other without "Mommy" for a few days. This is a tender story of a loving family. Lively, realistic photographs show the minor trials and many happy times of Ben and his father.

Ages 4-6

**Also available in:**
No other form known

## 625

**Stein, Sara Bonnett**

**The Adopted One: An Open Family Book for Parents and Children Together**

Black/white photographs by Erika Stone.
Walker and Company, 1979.
(47 pages)

---

ADOPTION: Explaining
ADOPTION: Feelings About
ADOPTION: Identity Questions
  Family: relationships
  Identity, search for

---

Joshua, about four, is celebrating Thanksgiving with all his relatives. He realizes that everyone resembles everyone else and they all have dark hair—all except him. Blond Joshua is adopted. He does not know where he came from. When he asks his mother who his "real" mother is, she tries to reassure him, explaining that his birth mother loved him but could not care for him. She also mentions that she herself wanted to love a baby, but could not have one. Then she tells of the excitement of adopting Joshua and how all the relatives came to visit. The little boy has some trouble accepting the story. He thinks maybe his real mother would let him stick his fingers in the cranberry jelly. Maybe his real father would not make him eat asparagus. Maybe he wouldn't be in trouble for spilling milk. When his aunt and uncle both comment about Joshua's behavior at the dinner table, Joshua yells that his parents are not really his mother and father. His father yells back that Joshua is not their real child. But, his father says as he hugs Joshua, he is their special surprise gift.

Written and photographed with compassion and understanding, this book shows the confusion and doubt of an adopted child. Although reassured of his "real" mother's love and also of the love of his adoptive parents, Joshua still wonders if life would be better were he not adopted. At the close of the story Joshua once again is assured of his special value to his adoptive parents, but the emphasis here is on the child's unwillingness and inability to accept his adoption and his place in the adoptive family and to reconcile his feelings of rejection by his birth parents. This focus could be viewed as a negative, and therefore undesirable, point of view by some parents. This book is one of the Open Family Series, written to help parents prepare children for the "common hurts of childhood" and to facilitate communication between parents and children. A guide for parents, explaining how the contents may be used in relation to a child's feelings, is included on each page along with the text for the child.

**S**

Ages 4-8

**Also available in:**
Paperbound—*The Adopted One: An Open Family Book for Parents and Children Together*
Walker and Company

## 626

Stein, Sara Bonnett

### On Divorce: An Open Family Book for Parents and Children Together

Black/white photographs by Erika Stone.
Walker and Company, 1979.
(47 pages)

---

*DIVORCE: of Parents*
  *Communication: parent-child*

---

Becky, about four, loves to play house with her friends Heather and Tom. She is always the baby and they play the mother and father. One day during the game, Heather and Tom pretend to fight. Tom leaves and Heather says they will get a divorce. This upsets Becky and she tells the two to go home. At lunch that day Becky asks her mother where her father is. He's at work, her mother replies. After cartoons she asks again and is again told. At supper, she asks a third time. When her father is not home at Becky's bedtime, the little girl becomes frightened and, during the night, has a bad dream. She calls for her father, but he's still not home. Her mother comforts her, saying that her father is still at work but will return soon. Both parents are there as usual for breakfast, and Becky's mother tells her father that Heather and Tom's parents are divorcing. A frightened Becky cuddles up to her father and asks for a baby doll. Her parents argue when he agrees to buy her the doll, and Becky runs off and hides. When they find her, the alarmed child asks if they are getting a divorce. They explain to Becky that being angry does not mean hating, that people often quarrel with the ones they love. In the days that follow, Heather and Tom come over and the three again play house. Whether they pretend they are married or divorced, they still care for their baby as usual. Several days later, Becky's father brings her a doll and her mother a dress. While a sitter cares for Becky, her parents go out for the evening.

A little girl, hearing that her friends' parents are divorcing, fears her father will leave her. When her parents argue, Becky is sure they will divorce too. Reassured that even people who love each other can disagree, Becky's fear is alleviated. Photographs accompany and complement the text. This book is one of the Open Family Series, written to help parents prepare children for the "common hurts of childhood" and to facilitate communication between parents and children. A guide for parents, explaining how the contents may be used in relation to a child's feelings, is included on each page, along with the text for the child.

Ages 4-8

**Also available in:**
Paperbound—*On Divorce: An Open Family Book for Parents and Children Together*
Walker and Company

## 627

Steptoe, John Lewis

### Daddy Is a Monster . . . Sometimes

Color illustrations by the author.
J. B. Lippincott Company, 1980.
(30 pages counted)

---

*PARENTAL: Control*
  *Discipline, meaning of*
  *Family: relationships*

---

Javaka and Bweela think their daddy is nice most of the time. But sometimes he turns into a monster. For example, once he bought them each an ice-cream cone to eat while he did the grocery shopping. Later he decided to get one for himself but would not buy them a second cone because "one . . . is enough for one day." That's when it happened. Right in front of their eyes, "hair started comin' out of his face" and he began turning into a monster. Then a woman came into the store and saw the children pouting. She thought Daddy was treating himself to ice cream but making them go without. Their father tried to stop her, but before he could explain she bought two large strawberry cones for the delighted children. Their daddy was very angry and "his teeth started growing out like Dracula's." He even laughed when Bweela's cone dropped onto the sidewalk. Sometimes Daddy is a monster at bedtime when Javaka or Bweela ask for one more drink, make another trip to the bathroom, or have an argument that keeps them awake. Daddy also becomes a monster when he takes them to a restaurant. He warns them to stop playing with their food, and he turns into a scary creature right there at the table—"but only a little bit so nobody sees him doin' it." Sometimes he's a monster when they are messy, make noise, or have an accident. When the children ask him why he turns into a monster, Daddy replies, "Well, I'm probably a monster daddy when I got monster kids."

Most children find their parents to be monsters sometimes. These feelings find humorous and loving expression here as Javaka and Bweela discuss and recall several transformations of their usually quite human father. The idea that children can be monsters too will interest the young reader or listener, and the familiar, everyday occurrences and realistic relationships will appeal. Exceptional, surrealistic illustrations give the book special artistic value for children. Modified black dialect is used. Another story about Bweela and Javaka is *My Special Best Words*.

Ages 5-7

**Also available in:**
Paperbound—*Daddy Is a Monster . . . Sometimes*
Harper & Row, Publishers, Inc.

## 628

Stevens, Carla McBride

### Sara and the Pinch

Color illustrations by John Wallner.
Clarion Books, 1980.
(48 pages)

---

ATTENTION SEEKING
EGOCENTRISM
SCHOOL: Behavior
    Sharing/Not sharing

---

Seven-year-old Sara wants her own way. When her mother insists that she wear boots to school, Sara takes them off on the bus and leaves them there. Later that day it snows, and Sara must remain inside during recess because she has no boots. Then the kindly janitor, Mr. Zamatsky, lends her his own boots, which he fills with paper to fit her feet and ties at her ankles with string. When Sara gets home she tells her mother that she wore Mr. Zamatsky's boots because she preferred them to her own. Another day Sara's class plays school. When Sara is not allowed to be the teacher, she pinches a classmate. Then during story time she pinches another child and is made to sit apart from everyone else. Trying to get attention, she shuffles her feet and slides her chair noisily. At writing time no one wants to sit beside Sara because she pinches. Angry, she scribbles on two classmates' papers. Her teacher makes her sit in the hall, and Mr. Zamatsky finds her there. When he learns of her pinching he brings her a ball of clay and shows her how to model a face by pinching the clay. Her teacher sees the clay model when she comes to get Sara, and she asks the girl to show the class how to pinch a face in clay. The next day is Sara's birthday and she expects and gets her own way in everything. At her request the class sings "Happy Birthday." Then her mother appears with a tray of cupcakes. When Sara realizes there is no cupcake for Mr. Zamatsky and her mother won't allow her to overlook any classmate, Sara gives him her own. After all, she thinks, she's had her way all day and doesn't really need a cupcake "because I'm the birthday girl!"

Three stories show Sara demanding attention and her own way. In each, she is befriended and her aggression redirected by the perceptive and kind school janitor, whom she rewards at the end with her own birthday cupcake. This beginning reader presents for discussion several familiar situations and attitudes that children will recognize. Many of the simple illustrations show Sara's face filled with anger or determined to get attention by any means.

Ages 5-7

**Also available in:**
No other form known

## 629

Stevens, Margaret

### When Grandpa Died

Color photographs by Kenneth Uated.
Children's Press, Inc., 1979.
(31 pages)

---

DEATH: of Grandparent
    Death: attitude toward
    Death: funeral issues
    Grandparent: love for

---

A young girl, about eight, spends lots of time with her grandfather, who lives with the family. The two enjoy reading, storytelling, walking, and working in the garden. When they find a dead bird in the yard, the girl wonders aloud why it has died. Grandpa tells her there are many reasons things die: they become sick, they are hurt, or their bodies grow very old and weak. The two bury the bird in the garden. After its death, Grandpa says, the bird will continue to contribute to the earth's life cycle. The bird's body will change underground, and it will help the flowers grow. Soon afterwards, Grandpa becomes ill and goes to the hospital, where the girl's parents visit him every day. When they return from visiting one day, upset and crying, the girl feels frightened. Her father tells her Grandpa has died. At first she is angry with Grandpa, because she wants him to come back home and play with her. Soon, though, she goes to his bedroom, puts on his sweater, and cries and cries. Her father comforts her, telling her it is all right to cry, but she still regrets not having said goodbye to Grandpa. Her father explains that there will be a funeral and that funerals allow people to say goodbye to those they love. He takes her to see the dead man's closed casket, and the next day the girl and her parents attend the funeral. The girl says she now knows her grandfather will never return. She plans to tell her little sister all about Grandpa, as soon as the younger child is old enough to understand.

In this simple, first-person narrative, a young girl learns to see the death of her beloved grandfather as part of the continuing life cycle. Sensitive photographs help keep the story straightforward and realistic. The text conveys a sense of grief and the assurance that it is natural to experience and express sorrow. The photograph of the closed casket might be helpful in preparing a child for a visit to a funeral home.

Ages 4-8

**Also available in:**
Paperbound—When Grandpa Died
Children's Press, Inc.

S

**630**

Stolz, Mary Slattery

## Go and Catch a Flying Fish

Harper & Row, Publishers, Inc., 1979.
(213 pages)

---

*SEPARATION, MARITAL*
*Nature: appreciation of*
*Parental: unreliability*
*Sibling: relationships*

---

Each of the three Reddick children is becoming uneasy over the frequency and intensity of their parents' quarrels. The family lives in a spacious home on ten acres of prime land on the coast of Florida. Jem, a solitary ten-year-old, loves the undersea world and maintains a large saltwater aquarium stocked with fish he's caught. Taylor, thirteen, is a bird lover; she can identify most of the native birds of the Florida seacoast. Little B.J. is an energetic four-year-old. Tony, their father, is a chef and has taught Jem and Taylor to cook—well enough that they do most of the family's cooking. Junie, their mother, a free-spirited woman who believes that women have been slaves to their husbands for too long, has little regard for everyday household tasks. She is seldom home, preferring to spend her time attending estate sales, where she spends a great deal on ornamental items for the house. Her handling of the family finances is a major source of the quarrels with her husband. Junie wants to get a job so she can have her own money, but Tony wants her home with the children. When she overdraws the checking account to buy a picture of fish skeletons, the resulting fight ends with Junie packing a bag and leaving for her uncle's home in New York. Jem and Taylor are not surprised, though they are sad and somewhat confused. Jem blames his father for not letting Junie have money of her own. Taylor cannot figure out why Junie ever had children if she needs to be away from them so much. B.J. is distraught, disobedient to Jem and Taylor who must look after him, crying in the night. Because Tony is at work much of the first days after Junie's departure, he does not realize what their mother's leaving has done to the children. Then the family receives a letter from Junie. She will not be returning and soon will take a secretarial job. Tony tells Jem and Taylor that he will ask his mother, whom B.J. adores, to come and manage the house and look after B.J. temporarily. Although their feelings of emptiness persist, Jem and Taylor still hope that order will soon be restored to their lives.

A family breaks up because two parents are unable and unwilling to make compromises. Though Tony seems less self-centered than Junie, he insists that his wife play a traditional homemaker's role. Junie claims to love the children, but she has no sense of responsibility about caring for them or running the household. Their daughter, Taylor, mature and dependable, tries to be nonjudgmental as she contemplates the family's troubles. She and her brothers grow closer; Jem and Taylor pull together for little B.J.'s sake. The story provides a perceptive inside look at the feelings of each family

member. Beautiful descriptions of the plants and animals living on the Florida seacoast add interest and dimension. The Reddicks' story continues in the sequel, *What Time of Night Is It?*

Ages 10-13

**Also available in:**
Cassette—*Go and Catch a Flying Fish*
Library of Congress (NLSBPH)

Paperbound—*Go and Catch a Flying Fish*
Scholastic Book Services

---

**631**

Stolz, Mary Slattery

## What Time of Night Is It?

Harper & Row, Publishers, Inc., 1981.
(209 pages)

---

*FAMILY: Relationships*
*Friendship: best friend*
*Grandparent: living in child's home*
*Prejudice: sexual*
*Separation, marital*
*Sibling: oldest*

---

After her mother, Junie, leaves the family in Florida and goes to Connecticut, fourteen-year-old Taylor wonders how they can start over, how they can rebuild their broken home. Her father, Tony, is a chef who either works long hours or sails his sloop alone. When he is home, he's withdrawn. When Tony realizes that Taylor and ten-year-old Jem are unable to cope with little B.J. on their own, he sends for his mother, Grandmother Reddick, who lives in Boston. Although they need her, they are no happier than she is about the arrangement. The Florida heat bothers her, and so does nearly everything about the casual way her son and his children live. However, Jem feels his home situation is still better than that of his best friend, Dan. Dan's sister, Sandy, is Taylor's best friend. Their mother is an alcoholic and their father a domineering, cruelly insensitive man. A few weeks of Grandmother Reddick's presence weigh heavily on Taylor. B.J. is better behaved, but he's turned into what Taylor considers a zombie, clinging to Granny and watching television constantly. Jem is no help, since he hates confrontations and tries to keep peace at any price. Tony is hardly ever home. One morning he and Taylor talk, and she tries to tell him how bad things are. He says that if she will tolerate Grandmother Reddick, he'll spend more time at home. School starts, high school, and Taylor dreads the year in a new place. When she sleeps over at Sandy's house, Sandy confides her worry about her older sister, Amanda, who is perpetually depressed. Amanda and Dan both see a psychiatrist once a week, although their parents don't know that in nearly a year Dan has yet to say a word to the therapist. With a tyrant for a father, an alcoholic mother, and two disturbed siblings, Sandy needs the stable friendship she has with Taylor. That night, Amanda takes an overdose of Librium along with handfuls of aspirin, and the girls have to call the paramedics. Sandy accompanies her sister to the hospital while Taylor stays with Sandy's drunk mother. The next day Taylor picks up the phone to call Sandy and overhears her mother and father talking. Junie begs Tony to get himself and the children off the island before a hurricane, which has been threatening the area, strikes. She also asks him if he has spent the last few weeks feeling sorry for himself or if he has any idea why she left. He hangs up. Taylor finally finds the courage to read the letter her mother left her. In it, Junie expresses her love for Taylor and asks her to try and understand why she went away. One night, Grandmother Reddick tells Taylor that her mother has sent her another letter. She then proceeds to describe what's in it. Shocked and outraged at this invasion of privacy, Taylor locks herself in her room. Late that night Tony asks her to apologize to her grandmother. He wants peace in his house. Taylor wonders if her father's willingness to ask for completely unreasonable favors is part of why Junie left. Another hurricane threatens, but their coast is spared. Suddenly Junie arrives. As long as her family is going to be endangered by hurricanes, she will share the danger with them. Taylor notices that her mother has returned a grown woman, not the girl she has always been. Jem calls her "Mom" instead of Junie, and she seems more able to talk calmly with Tony in spite of several irritating, challenging remarks made by him and his mother. Junie is determined to give their marriage another try, and Tony agrees with some reservations. Taylor has no reason to think it will work out, but she is content to have a "moment of perfect joy."

Taylor and her two brothers adjust in different ways to their mother's leaving home: B.J. has behavior problems, Jem tries not to think about it, and Taylor struggles to understand why it has happened. Both she and her friend Sandy, whose family is even more troubled, must cope with their fathers' crippling sense of male superiority, which has helped drive Taylor's mother away and Sandy's to alcohol. Readers will suffer along with Taylor and Jem at the hands of insensitive, unjust Grandmother Reddick. They will find no solutions here to family conflicts, but they will find a compelling depiction of family relationships in this sequel to *Go and Catch a Flying Fish*. Taylor's interest in the natural beauty of Florida adds another dimension to an already well-rounded characterization.

Ages 11-14

**Also available in:**
Paperbound—*What Time of Night Is It?*
Scholastic Book Services

## 632

**Storr, Catherine Cole**

# Vicky

Faber and Faber Ltd., 1981.
(152 pages)

---

*ADOPTION: Identity Questions*
*IDENTITY, SEARCH FOR*
  *Family: relationships*
  *Friendship: meaning of*

---

When sixteen-year-old Vicky Stanford's adoptive mother dies, Vicky finds herself wondering with renewed intensity about her birth parents. Vicky and her adoptive sister, Chris, were born the same day to young women who shared a hospital room. Vicky's mother, registered as Jenny Morgan, died two days later. When a search revealed nothing about "Jenny Morgan," Chris's parents, told they could have no more children of their own, adopted Vicky. Now Mum is gone, and Vicky has always felt that her adoptive father cares less for her than for Chris. She decides she must know about her origins. The only clues she has are the name Jenny Morgan, which was probably not her mother's real name, some baby clothes, and a picture Jenny left of a young man. Stephen, a special friend who shares Vicky's gift of clairvoyance, tries to help her. Vicky tracks down a nurse who helped deliver her; the only clue she offers is that Vicky's mother had a Cornish accent. Next, Vicky visits Detective Chief Superintendent Price. He has Missing Persons check their records and finds two possible names. Stephen wants them to put their pieces of the Chinese Egg together through clairvoyance, but instead Vicky suggests that she, Chris, and their father vacation in Cornwall this year. While there, she sees a shawl knitted in the same pattern as her infant's shawl. She follows that trail to St. Riok, where she learns that "Jenny Morgan" died at the age of fourteen and couldn't possibly have been her mother. But there she runs into Superintendent Price; his trail has led to a former school headmistress, Mrs. Yelland, who had long ago reported a Helen Penrose missing. Helen, an orphan, had been cared for by Mrs. Yelland, and a picture of Helen as a schoolgirl convinces Price that she was Vicky's mother. He brings Vicky to see Mrs. Yelland. When Vicky shows the woman the picture of the man she thinks may be her father, Mrs. Yelland does not appear surprised. She is sure Vicky's mother did not tell the father she was pregnant, feeling it would disrupt his life. Just then Mrs. Yelland's son, Victor, and his family arrive for a visit. Victor is the man in the photograph. Vicky looks at her father but says nothing, allowing him to remain a stranger. Home again, she suspects her adoptive father really does love her. She's content now to be where she is. But "she felt as if she had spent most of her life up till now searching for a secret. . . . Now the secret was out, and she didn't feel any different, only flat and miserable." Later, when Stephen reminds her that the Chinese Egg is still incomplete, she regains her animation and suggests they try to put it together.

An adopted teenager successfully traces her birth parents, but finds that the knowledge in itself doesn't change her life. However, she has satisfied her deep need to know, which was her only motive. As Vicky learns more about her past, she comes to understand and appreciate her relationship with her adoptive family, particularly her father. The narrative's British flavor doesn't interfere with the meaning or suspense of this well-written account. Many of the characters appeared in *The Chinese Egg*, another engaging British story centered around a mystery. In the earlier book, Vicky's clairvoyance played a more important role than it does here.

Ages 12 and up

**Also available in:**
No other form known

**633**

**Strang, Celia**

## Foster Mary

McGraw-Hill Book Company, 1979.
(162 pages)

---

*FAMILY: Unity*
*RESPONSIBILITY: Accepting*
  *Abandonment*
  *Child abuse*
  *Education: value of*
  *Foster home*
  *Love, meaning of*
  *Migrant workers*
  *Work, attitude toward*

---

In the fall of 1959, fifteen-year-old Wallace (Bud) Meekin comes with his adoptive family to pick apples in Yakima, Washington. Bud, Bennie, and Ameilla were each abandoned by their parents and taken in by "Aunt" Foster Mary and "Uncle" Alonzo. Mary and Alonzo, migrant workers, have recently taken in another abandoned boy, Lonnie, about seven, who was beaten and left by his father, also a migrant worker. The brutalized Lonnie is at first violently hostile, even pointing a gun at Bennie and Bud. But once installed in Aunt Mary's care, Lonnie adapts easily to his new home. Mary has "a way of making a home out of any old place," but she clings to her dream of a permanent home where her children can attend school regularly. The picking over, the Meekin family stays on in Yakima so Alonzo can apply to Mr. Ransome, the orchard owner, for the job of caretaker. Bud is happy at the prospect of a settled life, but does not look forward to attending school regularly. Never having stayed in one school very long, he finds schoolwork difficult and is still in the eighth grade. He cannot imagine that he will ever go to college, although this is Mary's goal for all the children. Alonzo gets the job and he and Mary prepare to spend the winter, buying the necessary food, clothing, and supplies. A heavy snowfall necessitates an early opening of Christmas gifts—they need the warm clothing packed inside—and Alonzo and the children surprise Foster Mary with a sewing machine. Soon after, Alonzo goes to get a sled down for the kids and falls from the ladder, breaking his leg. Bud must go for help and, finding the snow too deep to accommodate car or truck, has to make his way to a neighbor's on foot. He gets through, and an ambulance comes and takes Alonzo to the hospital. It is soon learned that Alonzo's leg will require surgery, that it will be months before he will be able to walk or use his strength again. Together, Foster Mary and Bud must hang on to the caretaking job. Bud is daunted by the prospect, but Mary is confident they will find a way. Bud sees that keeping the job —and their settled life—is so important to Alonzo and Mary that he must help them succeed. He and Mary begin doing all the work they can by themselves, planning to have Alonzo supervise and teach them the rest after he comes home from the hospital. At the same time, Bud works on his schoolwork with a friend, Liz Holbrook. Liz, formerly a migrant worker with her mother, helps Bud see that education is the only way out of the migrant's hard life. Alonzo is released from the hospital in time to see all the children in their Christmas pageant at church. With a new confidence, Bud resolves that next summer Aunt Foster Mary will have the flower garden she has always wanted.

Bud narrates this story of a family's struggle to escape the hard life of migrant workers. His colloquial storytelling style and flair for using language inject humor into a rather slow, predictable account with more than a touch of unreality. The undiluted goodness of Mary and Alonzo's world may put some readers off; others may be encouraged and cheered. Characterizations are generally believable and complete, and the book offers some insight into a way of life that may be unfamiliar to many.

Ages 10-13

**Also available in:**
No other form known

**634**

**Strang, Celia**

## This Child Is Mine

Beaufort Books, Inc., 1981.
(156 pages)

---

*PROBLEM SOLVING*
*UNWED MOTHER: Child of*
  *Determination*
  *Family: relationships*
  *Love, meaning of*
  *Parent/Parents: single*
  *Poverty*
  *Responsibility: accepting*

---

It is early summer and fourteen-year-old Tally's unmarried sister, Leta, comes home from the hospital with her newborn son. The first thing Leta does is ask her mother to hem up a dress for her, and then she goes next door to make a phone call. She orders Tally to find her sandals for her since a boyfriend will soon arrive. When her mother protests, Leta retorts, "You made me have this kid. You got no kick coming." When Tally is slow to do her sister's bidding, Leta whacks her on the head. In the meantime, the baby has been crying steadily. Tally, shocked and angry at her sister's behavior, manages to change and feed him. Once he stops crying, he looks at her and something happens between them. "From that time on I belonged to him and he belonged to me." Beautiful Leta, in contrast, never looks at her baby, touches him, or refers to him. It is Tally who names him, feeds him, gets a neighbor to make him some diapers out of rags, and takes him to church. Nina, Tally's older, widowed sister, her two boys, and her teenage brother-in-law, Bernie, come by with vitamins. But Tally, virtually penniless, worries about how she can go on caring for baby Sean. Leta, meanwhile, keeps "borrowing" from their mother's slim grocery budget to buy clothes for herself. One day Tally sees Leta look closely at the baby, and she wonders what her plans are. Then when Tally and the baby are home alone, a richly dressed couple comes to inquire about Sean. Leta has shown them his picture and they badly want him. Tally knows Leta is not just looking out for Sean's welfare; there must be money in it for her. Stalling the couple, she takes Sean, some diapers, a little food, and the few dollars of grocery money and goes out the back door. She spends the entire Labor Day weekend hiding with Sean, first sleeping behind bushes in a park and then on the balcony of an apartment whose occupants, a mother and son she knows slightly, are gone for the long weekend. Tally becomes feverish and delirious and is found by the owners of the apartment and taken home. When she wakes up, she immediately fears that her mother will once again give in to Leta and allow her to sell Sean to the rich couple. But as she recovers she finds she has underestimated her mother. Leta is leaving for Denver with one of her boyfriends, leaving Sean at home. Nina and Tally's mother have found a perfect solution for their problems. Nina and the boys will move back home, Nina will work, and Tally's mother will care for the children. Tally's mother won't have to work, Nina won't have to pay a baby-sitter, and Tally and Sean will stay together. A relieved Tally wants Sean to be baptized. She makes a baptismal gown for him out of one of Leta's lacy slips and a shawl. Leta is too busy to attend the ceremony but the rest of the family, including the sympathetic Bernie, celebrate Sean's baptism.

A young teenager takes over the care of her unmarried sister's baby and forms a strong bond with him. Tally shows herself to be responsible and resourceful in trying to solve the problems that afflict this very poor family with one more mouth to feed. The first-person story grips the reader as it explores the opposing values of the two sisters—Leta, beautiful and entirely selfish, and Tally, loving and determined. This is a well-crafted novel.

Ages 11-14

**Also available in:**
No other form known

## 635

Strasser, Todd

**Angel Dust Blues**

Coward, McCann & Geoghegan, Inc., 1979.
(203 pages)

---

DRUGS: Abuse of
  Boy-girl relationships: dating
  Communication: lack of
  Crime/Criminals
  Drugs: dependence on
  Friendship: meaning of
  Parental: negligence
  Rebellion
  Sex: premarital
  Wealth/Wealthy

---

When wealthy, seventeen-year-old Alex Lazar, a good student and state tennis champ, becomes bored and rebellious, he turns to drug dealing for excitement. Alex's father, a retired businessman, and his mother, a former county executive, spend their time in Palm Beach, Florida, leaving Alex at home in suburban New York City with only Lucille, the housekeeper, for supervision. Alex's friend Michael, a dropout and a junkie, teaches him how to make big money in drugs. While picking up a kilo of marijuana in Brooklyn one morning,

Alex, nervous and hungry, mistakenly walks into G. Schapmann & Sons, the office of a commercial bakery, where he is impressed with the cool attractiveness of Schapmann's daughter, Ellen. He begins to cultivate a friendship with her. Becoming the number-one dealer in school gives Alex a certain satisfaction because he's reached this pinnacle through his own efforts—and because his parents would be shocked if they knew. When Michael informs Alex of a deal on angel dust (PCP—phencyclidine), a more potent drug than marijuana, the lucrative project appeals to him. Still, he can't help but notice Michael's deterioration as he grows more and more dependent on drugs. When Michael disappears, Alex, certain he has been arrested, is frightened into burying his share of the angel dust and marijuana. At this time his friendship with Ellen deepens. Her determination to attend the University of Southern California and become a film director makes him aware of how uncertain his own future is. All he knows is that he doesn't want to go to Columbia University and become a businessman like his father. When Alex learns that Michael has been at Hillcrest, a mental institution for drug abusers, he relaxes somewhat. But he discovers he no longer enjoys drug dealing and doesn't care for the feeling that people only like him for what they can get from him. He prefers getting high on his love for Ellen, and they become lovers. Michael finds a buyer for the angel dust buried in Alex's backyard, and Alex is only too glad to be rid of it. He is not aware that Michael has turned state's evidence and that the buyer is an undercover police officer. The next morning, a shocked, frightened Alex is arrested. His parents return from Palm Beach and Alex, arraigned and released on bail, confronts his mother angrily. "You managed to run a whole county filled with people, but you don't want to bother with me." But he knows he cannot change his parents and when they return to Palm Beach, planning to come back in two weeks to check up on him, he decides to take his lawyer's advice and get a summer job. He also applies to a small Maine college with a poor tennis team, where he is required to work for his acceptance rather than take an easy tennis scholarship. Then one day Alex finds Michael in his garage, stoned and very sick. He cares for him as best he can, but by the next afternoon Michael's condition worsens. Alex notifies the police. Soon after, he is summoned home from school to find that Michael has gotten into the house, ransacked it, found and taken prescription drugs, and collapsed. A blood test reveals angel dust in Michael's blood. He remains in a coma. The charges against Alex are reduced and he knows he has "crossed the line for good. Why he had made it and Michael hadn't he didn't know."

This is a taut, believable portrayal of teenage alienation and drug abuse. Character development and the portrayal of relationships, especially the one between Alex and Ellen, are well done, and readers will readily understand and sympathize with various characters as the story unfolds. The bitterness Alex feels toward his parents is vividly portrayed. Several brief, explicit sexual encounters between Alex and Ellen are included. This is strong, candid, informative, but not didactic, material.

**S**

Ages 14 and up

Also available in:
Braille—*Angel Dust Blues*
Library of Congress (NLSBPH)

Cassette—*Angel Dust Blues*
Library of Congress (NLSBPH)

Paperbound—*Angel Dust Blues*
Dell Publishing Company, Inc.

## 636

Strasser, Todd

**Friends till the End**

Delacorte Press, 1981.
(201 pages)

---

FRIENDSHIP: Meaning of
ILLNESSES: Terminal
    Boy-girl relationships: dating
    Careers: planning
    Death: attitude toward
    Leukemia

---

High school senior David Gilbert doesn't have much time in his life for a new friend. He is goalie for his school's soccer team and until last spring had planned to go to college on a soccer scholarship and eventually become a professional player. Recently, however, he has decided to enter pre-med and is studying hard. His remaining time is taken up by his independent and strong-willed girlfriend, Rena Steuben. David first meets Howie Jamison at a bus stop. Howie has just moved to Long Island from Florida and hasn't yet learned to dress and act like the typical Gold Coast teenager. But David finds him refreshing. Then, suddenly, after the first week of school, Howie is hospitalized for a form of leukemia called AML and his mother asks David to visit him. At the hospital he finds Mrs. Jamison upset over the move north and pessimistic about her son's illness. Howie, anxious to talk to someone more objective, tells David how sick the chemotherapy makes him. After leaving the hospital, David remembers hearing how smoking marijuana can help reduce the side effects of chemotherapy and decides to tell Howie about this. When he returns to the hospital a week later, David learns that Howie has contracted an infection. Howie's distraught mother talks about taking him back to Florida for Laetrile treatments. By now David is becoming quite preoccupied with Howie's problems and is upset that his classmates don't want to get involved. He tries to express his feelings to Rena, but finds her also uninterested—in him as well as in Howie. She's upset because he has given up his plans to become a pro soccer player. The following weekend David goes to Howie's house for dinner. Howie tells David he is in remission now. But his mother seems to believe that everything that goes wrong is part of a "big plot" against them. She still wants to return to Florida. David brings up the marijuana idea and both parents become very upset. He realizes he has probably lost their approval of his and Howie's friendship. The soccer team wins its ninth straight game, but instead of being elated, David worries about Rena's increasingly distant behavior. The next day he gets a note from her, breaking off their relationship. The team continues undefeated and is assured a place in the sectionals. When one of the team members gives a party to celebrate, David invites Howie to come along. Both boys lose track of the time, getting back late. Also, Howie has violated his doctor's instructions not to drink. His parents hold David responsible. Soon Howie returns to school. To David's surprise, Rena, who is in most of Howie's classes, offers to help him get caught up with his work. The next time he goes into the hospital, she organizes a blood drive. She admits to David that part of the reason she broke up with him was because of the pressure he was putting on her to "join the Howie Jamison bandwagon." Later, another friend tells him that he has resented David's "sister of mercy" attitude about Howie. David decides, however, that some things are "more important than being Mr. Cool Popular Nice Guy." David and Rena visit Howie in the hospital on the day before the soccer championship and learn from the doctor that he is getting worse. Later, Rena tells David that his involvement with Howie has made it impossible for her to think of him as just a fun, safe boyfriend whom she can drop at the end of high school. She knows she must take him seriously. For the first time in months, they make love. Two days later, after winning the championship, David returns home to find that the Jamisons are moving back south and that Howie has already been transferred to a hospital in Florida. Both David and Rena feel that something special has been taken away from them. Over the next couple of months David writes to his friend three times, but Howie never writes back.

It is a life-changing experience for David to realize that no one, regardless of age, is invulnerable to sickness and death. As his friendship with Howie grows, he is forced to ask the same searching questions his friend does: Why do these things happen to some people and not to others? Is there a God who punishes sin by letting people get sick? What happens to a human being after death? Since David does not believe in God or in life after death, the only persistent question for him is "Why?" He finally concludes that there is no answer: "Sometimes things just happen. The toughest part is learning to accept that." This is a convincing, substantive first-person narrative that skillfully integrates various issues—friendship, love, illness, career goals, attitudes toward life and death—within a compelling story line.

Ages 12 and up

Also available in:
No other form known

## 637

Strauss, Joyce

**How Does It Feel . . . ?**

Black/white illustrations by Sumishta Brahm.
Human Sciences Press, 1979.
(87 pages counted)

---

EMOTIONS: Identifying

---

The reader is asked, "How does it feel . . . when you smell a flower? when you are alone? when something dies? when you receive something new? when you are yelled at?'' There are forty such questions, encouraging children to stop and consider the feelings evoked by many everyday happenings.

Very simple line drawings illustrate each of the "how does it feel" questions, questions whose answers are probably best shared with an adult. The publisher suggests that the book can be instructive and valuable to parents, educators, and child psychologists, but it's unlikely that a child reading alone would actually reflect on the questions posed. The book asks children to consider feelings of rejection, approval, sadness, powerlessness, joy, wonder, loss, self-esteem, and others.

Ages 4-8

Also available in:
No other form known

## 638

Stren, Patti

### There's a Rainbow in My Closet

Color illustrations by the author.
Harper & Row, Publishers, Inc., 1979.
(136 pages)

---

AUTONOMY
SELF, ATTITUDE TOWARD: Feeling Different
TALENTS: Artistic
    Grandparent: living in child's home
    Grandparent: love for
    Parental: absence

---

Emma is nine and lives in Canada. Her favorite things are drawing, the feel of paint, the color purple, and her best friend, Edgar, who collects worms. When her busy mother, a publicity manager for a ballet company, tapes a ballet schedule over one of Emma's special drawings, Emma decides never to share her art again. Her teacher too seems unreceptive, but Emma believes her father, a clockmaker, loves clocks the way she loves to draw. Feelings of abandonment, hurt, and anger assail Emma when she learns her mother will be touring Europe for two months with the ballet company. When Emma's maternal grandmother is invited to visit from Florida, Emma decides to hate her. But to Emma's surprise, Gramma isn't at all what she expects. She keeps a hat with feathers and fruit on her dresser because it makes her laugh, and she hangs prints of famous paintings to make her feel at home. Emma has the sudden urge to show this strange Gramma her purple drawings. When she does, Gramma both appreciates and understands them. When Emma's teacher makes horrible red marks on her picture because Emma painted what was in her heart and not what the teacher asked for, Gramma admires the beautiful painting and ignores the red circles. Gramma and Emma have many memorable times together. They hold a special tea party just like the ones Gramma had in Russia and even go fishing with Edgar. Gramma teaches Emma about famous artists. She shares part of Van Gogh's diary, and Emma is amazed that he felt about his artwork as she does about hers. When Emma does poorly on a surprise test in school, Gramma gives her another surprise test with instructions to "Draw a rose," "Draw me a purple anything,"

and "Write me a song about a cat named Fred who drinks only chocolate milk." One day Gramma plans a wonderful surprise. With a mirror and her eyeglasses for a reflector she makes a rainbow in Emma's closet. When Emma's teacher assigns the class a speech, Emma is very apprehensive. But Gramma encourages her to just let her feelings flow. Emma's speech, illustrated with her drawings, impresses the entire class, including her teacher. That night Emma, her father, and Gramma stand on Emma's bed in the dark and gaze at the stars. Emma is happy that Gramma will stay with them until the weather gets cold and her arthritis forces her back to the warmth of Florida. She falls asleep in her grandmother's arms while Gramma sings a Russian lullaby.

Imaginative, artistic Emma finds it difficult to be different from other children. Her Russian-born grandmother, once a child just like Emma, provides her with the understanding and appreciation she craves—and that her busy mother doesn't offer. Some labored dialogue and a dash of sentimentality detract a bit, but this is essentially a worthwhile account of a very special relationship, one that includes Emma's father and her best friend, Edgar. Cartoon illustrations, touched with Emma's beloved purple, enhance the story's warmth and humor.

Ages 8-10

Also available in:
No other form known

## 639

Stretton, Barbara

### You Never Lose

Alfred A. Knopf, Inc., 1982.
(237 pages)

---

DEATH: Attitude Toward
ILLNESSES: Terminal
    Ambivalence, feelings of
    Anger
    Boy-girl relationships: dating
    Cancer
    Change: resisting
    Communication: parent-child
    Friendship: meaning of
    Guilt, feelings of
    Maturation
    Sports/Sportsmanship

---

Jim Halbert is not looking forward to the first day of his senior year. He's known for five weeks that his father, the popular football hero and coach, is dying of cancer. Soon everyone knows, and emotions run high throughout the school. Jim's English teacher, Dundee, begins a unit on "Death, the Final Taboo." Jim freezes up; the other students are shocked. One of Jim's problems in responding to people's sympathy is that he has ambivalent feelings about his father, who has always ridden him harder than anyone else. Most of his life, Jim has tried to stay out of his father's way. He remembers a game last year when he carried the ball ninety-five yards for a touchdown. Afterwards his father swore at him and benched him, calling him a Saturday hero. Jim's mood is lifted by a brash, noisy new girl from West Virginia, Gus (Agnes), but he's still looking forward to

S

seeing Mimi again. They dated last year, although they've been out of touch this summer. By noon, Mimi has begun organizing a campaign to make the school the best in the state as a tribute to Coach Halbert. She's proud to be Jim's girl, but mainly because everyone is talking about his father. At football practice, Coach Halbert (who insists on coaching the team this year although he doesn't need to) lashes into Jim as usual. He has never, in his eleven years of coaching, praised anyone. During practice, he falls as he's running across the field. He accepts the help of Jim's younger sister, Liz, but just yells at Jim. As always, Jim is puzzled and hurt by his father's rejection. At the next football practice, Coach Halbert harasses his son again. When he tells Jim to throw him the ball, Jim puts everything he has into it: "A lifetime of being told to be a man and somehow never quite making it, rode on the leather of that ball, in the power of that pass." The ball hits the coach in the stomach and knocks him out. He's taken to the hospital where he remains for several days. The first thing he says to Jim as soon as he can get the words out is that Jim's throw was a great pass. But Jim never again wants to feel the kind of anger that made him throw the ball that way. One afternoon Gus, who's become a good friend, skips school with Jim to visit the coach in the hospital. While Gus waits, Jim goes looking for his father. He finds him in a restroom, sobbing. Jim doesn't want his father to be discovered in his weakness, so he leaves. He and Gus make love, leaving Jim exhilarated at first but then depressed, wondering if he's just using her. Friends and family offer information and advice. Jim's mother talks about his father's defenses and how he can't ever admit to weakness. Then Dundee decides to shelve the death unit. He himself has unresolved feelings about his own father's suicide and, after being approached by a delegation of students about the way he's picked on Jim, admits he hasn't handled the situation well. But he tells Jim that anger is an important part of grief. At the first football game of the season, Mimi, a cheerleader, leads a cheer about Coach Halbert. Jim continues to believe she just wants to be part of all the attention and fame. After the game she's anxious to get to a favorite hangout, even though Jim wants to go to the hospital to tell his father about their victory. He's beginning to realize that he's probably the most important thing in his father's life, that his father loves him and that he loves his father. He promises the coach that he can die at home and not in a hospital, understanding at last what playing football means to his father, his need for the love that surges from the crowd in their cheers. Coach Halbert replies that his deepest wish has been that Jim would know that same feeling. Jim picks up Gus, who's been suspended for three days for skipping school to go to the hospital with him; he only received a reprimand. Jim knows Mimi isn't for him anymore and he lets Gus know they have a future together. He recalls his father's old saying after a lost game: "You didn't lose. The damned clock ran out, that's all."

When a young man learns that his football-coach father, whom he both loves and resents, is dying of cancer, he begins learning a lot about love, courage, and staying true to oneself. Relationships are more important than plot in this powerful book, which is not so much the story of a father's dying as of a son coming to understand some of the mystery that is his father. Another focus is change, inevitable whether it results from a death or from the growing human spirit. The reader is offered considerable insight into various attitudes toward impending death; also part of this narrative are profanity and some descriptive sexual passages, as Jim turns for comfort from the superficial Mimi to the down-to-earth Gus.

Ages 12 and up

**Also available in:**
Paperbound—*You Never Lose*
Scholastic Book Services

### 640

**Sullivan, Mary Beth and Alan J. Brightman and Joseph Blatt**

**Feeling Free**

Black/white illustrations by Marci Davis and Linda Bourke. Black/white photographs by Alan J. Brightman. Addison-Wesley Publishing Company, Inc., 1979. (192 pages)

---

*BLINDNESS*
*CEREBRAL PALSY*
*DEAFNESS*
*DEFORMITIES*
*DETERMINATION*
*DWARFISM*
*HANDICAPS*
*LEARNING DISABILITIES*
    *School: mainstreaming*
    *Self, attitude toward: accepting*
    *Wheelchair, dependence on*

---

Ginny, Gordon, Hollis, John, and Laurie are all considered handicapped, but all five consider themselves the same as everyone else. Ginny, thirteen, is a dwarf. She wants no special attention, only friends who understand. After joining the Little People of America organization, Ginny realizes she is not the only dwarf in the world. Gordon is deaf and communicates through sign language and finger spelling. The toughest thing for him is not hearing what others hear. He also wishes it were easier to get to know people and that everyone knew sign language. Hollis has cerebral palsy and wears braces on his legs. He likes friends who encourage him. John has learning disabilities. He used to be frustrated and angry, but since he entered a special class John has learned he is not stupid, only in need of extra help. School continues to be hard work, but John now believes he can succeed. Laurie, who used to be able to see, is now blind. But she can do almost anything she tries. Besides being a freshman in a regular high school, Laurie also attends a school for the blind where she is learning to use a cane and an abacus, and to read and write in Braille. All five of these special people object to being stared at or pitied. As Hollis says, "Me, I'm just happy with myself."

Written as a follow-up to the television series "Feeling Free," this book's theme could well be "handicapped children are the same as everyone else." Centering on five children, it also tells of others with handicaps and includes short plays, cartoons, mysteries, a test about Braille, games to understand handicaps and disabilities, and things to think about. The cartoons, illustrations, and especially the numerous photographs of the five main characters bring the book to life and personalize it. The writing is filled with understanding and compassion.

Ages 9 and up

**Also available in:**
Paperbound—*Feeling Free*
Addison-Wesley Publishing Company, Inc.

## 641

**Sussman, Susan**

## Hippo Thunder

Color illustrations by John C. Wallner.
Albert Whitman & Company, 1982.
(32 pages counted)

---

*FEAR: of Storms*

---

A little boy is afraid of the thunder. His sister tells him thunder is only the angels bowling. His brother says it's the stars snoring. Grandma says it's Mr. Boom-boom yelling for the flowers to wake up in time for spring. The boy goes into his parents' bedroom ("just to be sure they're all right"), and his father explains that the storm is far away. He can tell by counting hippopotamuses between the flash of the lightning and the clap of the thunder. He has counted five hippopotamuses, he tells his son, which means that the storm is about a mile away. The next time his father only gets to three hippopotamuses before they hear the thunder, meaning the storm is getting closer. "When it is right overhead," says his father, "lightning and thunder will come at the same time." The father asks his son to count with him the next time. They do and notice that the storm is moving away. They wait and listen for more thunder. Then the father tucks his little boy in bed with instructions to keep counting. After a while the thunder is so far away the boy can hardly hear it, but he keeps counting as he drifts off to sleep.

A little boy learns a simple and relatively accurate trick for overcoming his fear of thunder. Wonderful illustrations, most of cheerful hippopotamuses dressed as Norsemen, make this a charming and probably effective tool for talking to children who fear storms.

Ages 3-6

**Also available in:**
Large Print—*Hippo Thunder*
Albert Whitman & Company

## 642

**Swartley, David Warren**

## My Friend, My Brother

Black/white illustrations by James Converse.
Herald Press, 1980.
(102 pages)

---

*CHILD ABUSE*
*FAMILY: Unity*
  *Adoption: feelings about*
  *Communication: importance of*
  *Friendship: meaning of*
  *Mennonite*
  *Religion: faith*

---

When twelve-year-old Eric refuses the challenge of his classmate Jon Simon to enter the local pool hall on a hot Indiana summer day, Jon scornfully attributes Eric's refusal to his being a Mennonite. One day Jon tells Eric that his father gives him money all the time. Eric is therefore surprised to learn from his own father that Jon's parents were killed when Jon was an infant, that he lives with an aunt and uncle who are under investigation after complaints by neighbors about their poor treatment of the boy. A membership meeting for Boy Scouts during which Eric declines to join is another occasion for Jon to call attention to Eric's "strange" religion. Even so, Eric thinks about Jon often and hopes everything will work out well for him. One day as they're walking home from school together, Eric tells Jon that he knows about his tough time at home. Immediately defensive and angry, Jon shoves Eric into a snowbank. Eric forgets his own distress when he gets home and learns that his beloved grandfather has died. A few days before Christmas Jon gives Eric a present, with a card apologizing for his behavior and telling Eric he wants to be friends. During the vacation, the boys become better acquainted. One night Eric invites Jon to sleep over. As they prepare for bed, Eric asks Jon about the bruises on his back. After swearing Eric to secrecy, Jon tearfully tells him that his uncle beats him nearly every day and his aunt often puts the man up to it. Eric longs to help but doesn't know how. However, after he witnesses the uncle's dangerous and unreasonable anger directed at Jon, he feels he must tell his father about the beatings. Then, when Jon is absent from school for the next three days, Eric takes his father's advice and tells the teacher about the incident he saw. It is discovered that Jon has run away; the police find him unconscious and severely beaten in an abandoned railroad car. Jon spends several weeks in the hospital and then stays with Eric's family before he's moved to a foster home. Eric invites Jon to a weekend church retreat during which Jon reveals his unhappiness with his new school and foster family. Then Eric is distressed to learn that his grandmother plans to sell her home. His outlook brightens a bit when, told to choose a keepsake, he picks his grandfather's 1957 Oldsmobile, a car he had always treasured even though it hasn't run in years. Eric is delighted when his parents agree, at the request of a social worker, to have Jon come stay with them. At first the two boys feel awkward around one another. Then one day while they are polishing the Oldsmobile, Jon admits that he used to feel jealous of Eric's close family but that now he feels differently about Mennonites. That evening Eric's father announces that they have applied to adopt Jon, now a ward of the court, if the boy consents. Jon enthusiastically does. A newspaper article about his uncle's trial prompts Jon to tell Eric that he now feels sorry for his aunt and uncle. The last day of school, the family learns that Jon's adoption has been approved.

A friendship develops between a Mennonite boy and his hardened, abused detractor, who eventually is accepted into the loving Mennonite family. The most important aspect of this book is its emphasis on family togetherness and communication. Information about the Mennonite religion and way of life adds interest. The fast-moving plot is advanced mainly by narration, occasionally by stilted dialogue. Characterization lacks depth. Still, the book has a refreshingly wholesome tone, and the restricted vocabulary qualifies it as an easy reader for older children.

Ages 9-11

**Also available in:**
Paperbound—*My Friend, My Brother*
Herald Press

## 643

Tate, Eleanora E.

### Just an Overnight Guest

The Dial Press, Inc., 1980.
(182 pages)

---

FAMILY: Extended
  Afro-American
  Family: relationships
  Parental: control
  Parental: negligence
  Sibling: relationships

---

Nine-year-old Margie Carson likes softball, fishing, and the times when Daddy is home from his job as a furniture mover. She doesn't like Ethel Hardison, "that trashy little kid." But Margie's mother, Luvenia, realizes that Ethel's mother, Miz Mary, neglects wild, ill-mannered Ethel, and that if the Carsons don't take the child in during her mother's upcoming trip, she'll be sent to a Home. Nobody else in Nutbrush wants anything to do with the half-white, half-black Ethel. One night Margie's sister, Alberta, wakes Margie as their parents quarrel about taking Ethel into their home. Daddy objects strongly, but Momma says it's the right thing to do. The next morning, after Daddy goes on a job, Momma announces that Ethel is coming. Now Alberta and Margie object vigorously, but Momma is adamant. After Miz Mary drops Ethel off, the little girl breaks a plate, screams, tears around, and spits on the carpet. When they all go to a movie, Ethel runs down the aisle and it takes three ushers to catch her. The child behaves at the Nubia Missionary Baptist Church because Momma has promised her ice cream, but some members of the congregation tease the Carsons and offer unwanted advice about Ethel. Because Luvenia is a high school teacher and insists on good manners and proper behavior, some of the black community has always considered her a "white man's nigger." Taking Ethel in doesn't help matters. Miz Wilkins tells Margie about the time Miz Mary left Ethel with a family for ten whole days. But Margie insists that Ethel is just an overnight guest. However, when they next hear from Miz Mary she says she can't come for Ethel until a week from Monday. Margie's despair and sense of injustice grow. Ethel wets Margie's bed—again—and when Margie picks a fight with her, Momma spanks her. Then she discovers that her precious shell collection is now mostly broken pieces. "Something horrible had happened every day since Ethel came," Margie recalls. But when she and Alberta learn that Ethel has never had any toys, they both give her one of their shells— Margie's on loan only. After a softball game, Momma and Miz Good exchange words when Miz Good refers to Ethel as a "half-breed daughter of a white-trash whore." It's Ethel who stops the quarrel, reminding Momma that she herself said not to fight. Margie begins to wonder if Ethel is bad simply because nobody ever taught her to be good. When the little girl says she misses her own momma, Margie feels sorry for her. Miz Mary calls again to say she can't get home until Thursday. Margie is not quite so angry this time, especially since Ethel has told them that her mother wants to drop her down a well and be done with her. Then Daddy returns. He isn't pleased when he discovers that Ethel is still living with them, but Ethel takes to him immediately. When she's not cuddling up to him, Alberta is. Margie feels left out and angry. "Ethel already had Momma. And now she was after Daddy. If she took Daddy, then I wouldn't have anybody at all." Then Daddy announces that he has a new job, one that will not include any out-of-town work. Gradually, to Margie's dismay, Ethel is included in everything the family does. When Margie finally blows up and attacks Ethel, shouting at Daddy to make Ethel go away, he says they're going to have her for a long time. Ethel's father, he explains, is Margie's Uncle Jake, Momma's brother. Neither he nor Miz Mary seem to know how to care for a child, so the Carsons must keep her. Can Margie accept this situation? asks Daddy. Reassured of his love and support, Margie thinks she can.

Margie's vivid first-person narrative tells of her difficulty accepting mistreated, misbehaving little Ethel, and the reader shares her sense of betrayal and injustice. The other characters, especially Margie's loving father and strong, high-principled mother, are all well drawn, as are the attitudes and daily life of a small black community. Filled with wonderful details that are particular to that community, this story will nevertheless be understandable and appealing to a wide range of readers.

Ages 9-11

**Also available in:**
No other form known

**644**

Tate, Joan

## Luke's Garden and Gramp: Two Novels

Harper & Row, Publishers, Inc., 1981.
(138 pages)

---

*DIFFERENCES, HUMAN*
  *Age: aging*
  *Grandparent: living in child's home*
  *Love, meaning of*
  *Nature: appreciation of*
  *Resourcefulness*

---

Thirteen-year-old Luke, quiet and shy, lives in a shabby part of a big English city and has one of the only gardens around. People think he's strange. His mother wishes he'd play football "like the others do." After school Luke either works in his garden or delivers groceries for Mrs. Greenbaum. When Old Widow Lebber dies, her sister tells Luke that the widow wanted him to have her rosebush. In spite of being moved, the rosebush thrives. When it blooms, Luke takes the first rose to his mother. Then he takes some to his friend Big Bob, the blind newspaper seller. He also takes roses to various relatives and to his classmates and teachers. The more he cuts the roses, the more they seem to grow. Luke even takes some to Mrs. Greenbaum, who everyone thinks is a witch. She takes him to the room behind their store to meet her husband, who has never been the same since the Blitz. Luke notices how tenderly she cares for him and, as time goes on, he observes her little acts of kindness, such as slipping extra packets of tea into an old person's groceries. Meanwhile, one of Luke's teachers wants him to work harder so he can make something of himself. Luke asks what's wrong with growing up to be a good gardener. The art teacher rejects Luke's wild, colorful drawings of the way he sees flowers, substituting her own realistic drawings for him to color. One day Luke brings the last of the roses to school, placing one on each of his classmates' desks. One of the bullies from the Dodd gang makes fun of the flowers and of the students who like them. He picks a fight with another boy, and they are both taken to the principal's office to be punished. After school, the gang waylays Luke in his garden and beats him up. He doesn't want to go home looking so bad, so he crawls into a condemned cottage nearby. It collapses, killing Luke. He is found with the roses still in his hands, their thorns driven into his palms. That's Luke's story, which "ought to be told, so that others will know about him, and his garden, and his roses." In *Gramp*, ten-year-old Simon, his parents, and his grandfather are moved out of their row house, which is to be torn down, to an apartment on the twelfth floor of a new building. Gramp and Simon used to spend a lot of time in Gramp's shed behind their house, Gramp repairing and building things at his workbench, and Simon learning how to use tools. But there's no room in the new apartment for Gramp's workbench and tools. Although the rest of the family adjusts to their new home, Simon notices Gramp becoming listless and vague. His mother says Gramp is just getting old. Simon asks Gramp what's bothering him and Gramp says, "Nothing." But Simon knows the trouble is that Gramp has nothing to do. He begs his mother to help get Gramp a spot for his workbench, but she angrily says that's impossible and there's nothing wrong with Gramp. She shouts at Simon to find Gramp a place himself if he wants one so badly. So Simon approaches a workman at the building site across the street. Although sympathetic, the man says nobody but workmen are allowed on the site. He then asks the guards at a nearby factory about space for his grandfather to work, but they laugh at him. On his way home, he runs into the caretaker of their apartment building, who invites him to see the basement. In a corner, Simon sees an old, unused workbench, and he asks if his grandfather could use it. When the caretaker agrees, Simon brings Gramp down to look at it, and the three discuss details. Gramp installs his tools and begins repairing and building again. Every day he "seemed a little younger, a little quicker."

The first short novel in this book is the tragic tale of a gentle, flower-loving boy whose very existence appears to arouse deep hostility in a gang of bullies. The second tells the story of another person who doesn't fit the mold: an old man whose sense of usefulness depends on his workbench and tools. His loving grandson recognizes how important keeping busy is to his grandfather's health and happiness, and he finds a way around the problem of where to put a workbench in a small apartment. Both stories are vivid, gripping, and subtle. Readers are encouraged to look beyond stereotypes to the unique, creative, and productive people they hide.

Ages 10-13

**Also available in:**
No other form known

---

**645**

**Tax, Meredith**

## Families

Black/white illustrations by Marylin Hafner.
The Atlantic Monthly Press, 1981.
(32 pages counted)

---

*FAMILY: Extended*
*FAMILY: Relationships*
  *Adoption*
  *Differences, human*
  *Love, meaning of*
  *Stepbrother/Stepsister*
  *Stepparent*

---

Little Angie says, "Families are who you live with and who you love." Most of the time Angie lives with her mother in New York, but on vacations she lives with her father and stepmother in Boston. She likes to help care for their baby, Mickey, her half-brother but as good as a "whole." Angie's friend George lives with his father and mother and two brothers. Sometimes Angie and George play baseball with his older brother, but they never get to bat. Angie's friend Marisel lives with her mother, aunt, grandparents, brothers, and baby sister. Her father and another grandmother live in Puerto Rico. Angie's cousin Louis is adopted. "That means he didn't come from my Aunt Julie's belly, but they got him someplace else." He's theirs forever now. Angie learns about ant families from an ant farm in her classroom. Ants have lots of fathers and babies, she discovers, but only one mother—the queen. Chicken families, however, have many mothers and babies but only one father —the rooster. Another of Angie's friends stays with his grandmother during the week because his mother works at night. On the weekends he moves downstairs and stays with his mother. Angie's friend Willie lives with his father, and her friend Susie lives with her mother and godmother but has no father. When they hear that, George and another boy both volunteer to be Susie's father. So Angie and her friends play family and both boys are allowed to be father. Sometimes Angie wishes her parents lived together as George's do, but he wishes his parents were divorced so he could fly to Boston as she does. Families, it seems clear, come in different sizes and arrangements.

A little girl who divides her time between each divorced parent tells about the unique family arrangements of her friends. Only one can claim a traditional, nuclear family. Angie's matter-of-fact tone and the variety of family situations she presents, along with descriptions of her daily activities with her friends, should prove instructive and reassuring to young readers. As Angie says about families, "The main thing isn't where they live or how big they are—it's how much they love each other." Large, humorous illustrations reinforce the tone.

Ages 4-8

**Also available in:**
No other form known

### 646

Teibl, Margaret

**Davey Come Home**

Black/white illustrations by Jacqueline Bardner Smith.
Harper & Row, Publishers, Inc., 1979.
(60 pages)

LONELINESS
PARENT/PARENTS: Single
    Belonging
    Daydreaming
    Dependence/Independence

Third-grader Davey is a "latch-key child." His parents were divorced when Davey was four, and he lives with his caring, but busy, father. He and his father spend a lot of time together on weekends, but during the week, when he comes home from school, Davey must let himself into the apartment. There he is ignored by a teenage baby-sitter who has no interest in him. His mother lives in another city and calls now and then to talk with him, mainly on his birthday and at Christmas. Davey thinks his teacher is "okay," but he's sad that she disapproves of his daydreaming, a tendency he cannot seem to avoid. As imperfect as his life is, Davey would rather have it continue this way than be separated from his father and sent to live with his Aunt Betty—when the sitter suddenly quits, this becomes a real possibility. Then his father hires Mrs. Summers and she enters the boy's home and heart. More than a housekeeper, Mrs. Summers is the epitome of grandmotherly affection and concern. She invites Davey to call her Aunt Ruth, packs lunches, bakes pies, and zips jackets. But will she call him for supper as his friends' mothers do? To find out,

Davey deliberately stays outside at suppertime. Sure enough, she calls to him from the window: "Davey! Davey, come home now! Suppertime!"

This simple, perceptive book gives insight into the thoughts and feelings of a child forced to be independent before his time. Davey is not old enough to analyze his situation or his feelings. He just knows that, despite a warm relationship with his father, his life is different from that of his friends. Without realizing it, he longs for someone to replace his absent mother. The joy and contentment he feels when his need is met is quite touching. Sensitively drawn illustrations complement the text.

Ages 6-9

**Also available in:**
No other form known

### 647

Terris, Susan Dubinsky

**No Scarlet Ribbons**

Farrar, Straus & Giroux, Inc., 1981.
(154 pages)

FAMILY: Relationships
PARENT/PARENTS: Remarriage of
SECURITY/INSECURITY
    Death: of father
    Reality, escaping
    Self-esteem
    Stepbrother/Stepsister
    Stepparent: father

Before Rachel's father died of cancer some years ago, he said people must make things happen, that they shouldn't live passive lives. Now Rachel is thirteen and obsessed with following that advice. When her mother marries Norm, Rachel feels triumphantly responsible, since it was she who introduced them. Delighted with her new family, which includes Norm's son, Sandy, Rachel wants family closeness to blossom instantly and keeps engineering events to create those feelings. Even her mother, Ginger, who understands and often shares Rachel's enthusiasm, grows weary of her continual suggestions for family happenings: a Halloween sand-sculpture day at the beach, a roller-skate across the Golden Gate Bridge. At first Sandy is overwhelmed by Rachel. He dislikes her tireless attempts to befriend him, her needling, the embarrassing comments in front of his friends. Gradually, though, Sandy begins to warm to Rachel a bit. She tells him that the song she often sings and plays on her harp, "Scarlet Ribbons," reminds her of her father. He was the kind of man, she remembers, who would fill her bed with scarlet ribbons, as in the song. Sandy assures her that color-blind Norm never would. Norm himself is perplexed by his new stepdaughter. Once she asks him, "If something happens to Mom, Norm—if she dies, do I belong to you?" When he pauses to think of the proper answer to this and other questions, she changes the subject, refusing to be serious with him for long. One evening Ginger and Norm go out to dinner and leave an unhappy and jealous Rachel to fix dinner for herself and Sandy, who is confined to bed with a broken leg. She goes into Sandy's room to keep him company, and they begin an innocent conversation about sex. Hearing her mother and Norm return, Rachel suddenly jumps into bed with Sandy, telling her angry mother that they were talking about sex. Then Rachel flees to her grandmother's house nearby, where her mother and Norm decide she should spend a few days. Afraid that she is losing her mother and unsure of how Norm feels about her, Rachel does the forbidden and asks Sandy to come over and talk with her, meeting her that night in her grandmother's car. He reluctantly agrees when she says there will be a chaperone. The "chaperone" turns out to be an inflated plastic doll. When Norm discovers them, Rachel again says their conversation was about sex. The girl's behavior causes a tremendous strain between Norm and Ginger, Norm steadfastly trying to understand the cause of it and Ginger increasingly angry. When Rachel returns home the following day, she is sullen and belligerent. Christmastime arrives, a painful season for Rachel since it coincides with the day of her father's death and her own birthday. Everything comes to a head when Rachel refuses to join in her birthday outing to the movies but goes out alone after everyone leaves, returning to find they have all been frantic with worry about her. She hears Norm and Ginger argue bitterly and feels awful when she hears the front door slam. Assuming Norm has left and hearing loud, desperate sobs, she goes to comfort her mother. Instead she finds Norm crying—her mother has left the house. He speaks plainly and honestly to her about how she uses her dead father as an excuse, how he enjoys her enthusiasm but dislikes her pushiness, how he will always take care of her. Chastened, realizing that Norm, though angry, does love her, Rachel wants to make up and play her harp for him as he has so often asked her to. But Norm says she must first prove herself. The next morning Rachel apologizes to her mother. She begins making wild plans for atonement but checks herself, remembering her resolve to be less pushy and extravagant. Still, she tells her mother how marvelous it would be if Norm would fill her bed with red ribbons. That afternoon, Christmas Eve, after Rachel has surprised her family with a harp concert of Christmas carols at the Golden Gate Bridge, she returns home to find a small bundle of green ribbons on her bed. She knows the ribbons could only be from one person: her color-blind stepfather.

A young teenager still mourning the death of her father and anxious about her new stepfather hides behind a facade of unpredictability and extravagance. Only when she comes close to harming her mother's recent marriage does Rachel accept her stepfather's affection and her own need to make peace with her family and herself. Believable characterizations distinguish this realistic view of the challenges faced by two families merging into one. One caution: although this is probably a contemporary story, the jacket illustration looks old-fashioned and could mislead potential readers.

Ages 11-13

**Also available in:**
Paperbound—*No Scarlet Ribbons*
Avon Books

## 648

Tester, Sylvia Root

### Sandy's New Home

Color illustrations by Sher Sester.
The Child's World, Inc., 1979.
(32 pages)

*MOVING*
  *Change: resisting*
  *Empathy*
  *Grandparent: living in child's home*

Young Sandy is angry. She and her parents, brother and sister, and great-grandmother are moving far away to a new home. During the three-day moving trip, Sandy and her mother talk. Her mother assures her that the move is for the best; her father will have a better job and she will no longer have to share her bedroom with Great-Grandmother Pierce, whom the girl considers bossy. But Sandy angrily accuses her mother of not caring, of moving on purpose so she will lose her friends. When they stop to eat, Sandy locks herself in the car and refuses to get out. She writes a note she tucks in her shoe, promising to run away. After lunch, her father has Sandy ride in the truck with him. As they ride, he talks to her about her bad feelings toward her great-grandmother. Through the conversation, Sandy slowly becomes aware of how her own feelings about moving must be similar to the way her great-grandmother felt when she had to give up her own house and move in with the family. When they arrive at their new home, much larger than the other, they spend the rest of the day busily unloading the truck. Sandy is excited about her attic bedroom. Although she has to share it with her younger sister, Sandy gets to pick out the wallpaper. Wandering through the house later, she joins her mother in the three rooms that will be just for her great-grandmother, furnished with the old woman's things. When Sandy sees how happy her great-grandmother is with her own little rooms, she returns to her bedroom, tears up her note about running away, and goes to sleep dreaming of green wallpaper.

Upset and angry about moving, a little girl is grouchy and uncooperative, harboring unloving thoughts about the great-grandmother who has shared her bedroom. A conversation with her father helps Sandy connect her feelings of displacement with her great-grandmother's similar emotions about giving up her own house. Seeing the old woman's happiness with the little suite reserved for her in the new house, Sandy's anger and sadness disappear. This colorfully illustrated book is one in a series—Handling Difficult Times. Following the story is a guide suggesting discussion questions and offering additional information about the often-traumatic experience of moving.

Ages 5-8

**Also available in:**
No other form known

T

**649**

Tester, Sylvia Root

## Sometimes I'm Afraid

Color illustrations by Frances Hook.
Children's Press, Inc., 1979.
(30 pages)

---

*FEAR: of Animals*
*FEAR: of Darkness*
*FEAR: of Physical Harm*
  *Nightmares*
  *Separation anxiety*

---

A little girl is sometimes afraid. Once when she couldn't find her mother after searching through most of the house, she was frightened and cried. Her mother, it turned out, was in the basement. Now when she can't find her mother, she just calls and her mother answers. She used to be afraid of the neighbor's dog until she made friends with him. Once she was frightened by a huge shadow on the wall, but it was just her brother teasing her. After he hugged her, she wasn't afraid anymore. Sometimes she has nightmares, but when her father turns on the light and holds her close, everything is all right again. She used to be afraid of the slide because it's so high, but after seeing how much fun the little girl down the street was having, she tried it and now she's not afraid anymore. Once she chased a ball into the street and was almost hit by a car. She and her mother were both scared then. Her mother says there are things she ought to be afraid of; she must never again run in the street after a ball. The little girl remembers that she used to be much more afraid of things than she is now. Sometimes she's still afraid, but that's all right because "everyone is afraid sometimes."

A small child describes some of her fears and explains how she has become less fearful. Children will understand that fears are a normal and sometimes even necessary part of life. One of a series that deals with children's feelings, this straightforward text and full-page pastel illustrations capture everyday scenes and experiences.

Ages 3-5

**Also available in:**
No other form known

**650**

Tester, Sylvia Root

## We Laughed a Lot, My First Day of School

Color illustrations by Frances Hook.
Children's Press, Inc., 1979.
(31 pages)

---

*SCHOOL: Entering*
  *Fear: of school*
  *Mexican-American*
  *Separation anxiety*

---

Young Juan does not want to start school. He thinks of telling his father how he feels, but before he can begin his father tells him how very proud he is of Juan. He himself was unable to get much schooling in Mexico, but things will be different for his son in the United States. Juan considers telling his mother how reluctant he feels, but she too is proud of him, sure he will do well his first day at school. He doesn't tell his friend Jamie how he feels either—it's her first day too. After their teacher smiles at them, however, Juan decides school might not be so bad after all. Mr. Green lets Juan look for a surprise in his pocket, a green crayon to help the boy remember his teacher's name. But Juan knows he won't forget Mr. Green's name because "he is my first teacher. And he likes me." Juan colors with the crayon, plays with some trucks, sings, dances, and laughs with his classmates. After they play outside, Mr. Green reads to them and makes faces like the clown in the story. Before he knows it, Juan's first day of school is over. Jamie admits she was scared, but Juan says he wasn't; he's not scared of anything. Jamie doesn't quite believe that, and they both laugh all the way home.

A Mexican-American boy discovers that his fears about kindergarten are unfounded, and he enjoys a positive first-day experience just as his proud parents say he will. Part of a series that deals with children's feelings, this first-person account can help prepare and reassure children as they start school; it may have special appeal for minority-group children. Full-page pastel illustrations accompany a simple text.

Ages 3-6

**Also available in:**
No other form known

**651**

Thomas, Ianthe

## Hi, Mrs. Mallory!

Color illustrations by Ann Toulmin-Rothe.
Harper & Row, Publishers, Inc., 1979.
(48 pages)

---

*AGE: Respect for*
*DEATH: of Friend*
*FRIENDSHIP: Meaning of*
  *Helping*
  *Pets: love for*

---

Each day, after the school bus drops her off, a young black girl named Li'l Bits stops at the home of her elderly white neighbor and friend, Mrs. Mallory. She brings the woman's mail in and feeds her dogs cookies. Mrs. Mallory always has a snack waiting, and while they eat she tells Li'l Bits stories of the past and of her difficult life. The girl writes checks and letters for the old woman, whose hands have become stiff with age. She loves Mrs. Mallory's poor old house with the missing windows covered with cardboard and the floorboards so far apart that the ground can be seen through the spaces. In warm weather, little snakes sometimes poke their heads through the cracks and then are scared away by the dogs. One day Mrs. Mallory gets a letter from her son, a soldier stationed far away, and the happy woman dances on her porch. Li'l Bits agrees to return the next day to write an answer. But the next day after school Mrs. Mallory doesn't answer Li'l Bits's call. So the girl sits on the porch and waits. Her mother calls her, and when she gets home she is told that Mrs. Mallory died that day. Li'l Bits cries so hard she thinks "my heart is gone." Mrs. Mallory's son comes home, and he and Li'l Bits look for the dogs. The old one is gone but the other, who followed Li'l Bits home the day her friend died, becomes the girl's pet.

Li'l Bits tells this easy-to-read but unusually evocative story of a special friendship. Anecdotes of her relationship with Mrs. Mallory, expressive illustrations, and skillful use of the vernacular convey much about aging, poverty, caring, helping, and grief.

Ages 5-8

**Also available in:**
No other form known

## 652

**Thomas, Ianthe**

### Willie Blows a Mean Horn

Color illustrations by Ann Toulmin-Rothe.
Harper & Row, Publishers, Inc., 1981.
(22 pages)

---

*IDENTIFICATION WITH OTHERS: Adults*
*TALENTS: Musical*
 *Parent/Parents: respect for/lack of respect for*

---

Willie's young son describes how his father, "The Jazz King," plays his horn: "people start moving and swaying. Then I know Willie's brought the sunshine in." After Willie plays to thundering feet and nodding heads, sweat runs down his face. Sitting in the audience, his son knows when Willie has finished playing and it's time to head backstage. There he wipes the sweat off Willie's face with a clean white rag. When his father hands him his horn and invites him to play a little blues, the boy does, feeling "warm and dizzy inside." He admits, "My music isn't smooth and easy, but everybody stops and listens. And when I'm finished, Willie tells me that one day I'll play a lullaby to the wind." After they drive home together, Willie carries his sleepy son into the house, undresses him, and tucks him in bed. Half asleep, the boy wants to know what it means when people talk about blowing a mean horn. Willie says it means the musician is making beautiful music, just as the boy did when he played for Willie. The boy asks his mother if he can keep the white rag that he used to wipe Willie's face. His mother tucks it under his pillow and whispers goodnight. As he falls asleep the boy thinks, "Willie says someday I'll play a lullaby to the wind. And he should know, 'cause Willie blows a mean horn."

A young boy greatly admires his jazz-musician father and is encouraged by him to pursue his own music. This strong, lyrical, first-person narrative subtly conveys the boy's unsentimental attachment to his father. It also reflects the father's love and the many ways he helps build his son's self-esteem and confidence. The illustrations provide a sensitive counterpoint to the upbeat, spirited text.

Ages 5-8

**Also available in:**
No other form known

## 653

**Thomas, Jane Resh**

### The Comeback Dog

Black/white illustrations by Troy Howell.
Clarion Books, 1981.
(62 pages)

---

*ANIMALS: Love for*
 *Expectations*
*Responsibility: accepting*

---

Daniel, a nine-year-old farm boy, is still grieving over the recent death of his dog, Captain, when he finds a female English setter nearly dead in a culvert. Doc, the veterinarian, says the dog is close to starvation and predicts she won't last the night. He offers to put her away, but Daniel won't hear of it. His parents help him as he warms her with rags and feeds her broth. He takes time out to do his chores, but spends the night with the dog, calling her Lady. He imagines her herding cows as Captain used to do and playing Captain's old games. In the days that follow, Lady begins to regain her weight but reacts strangely to Daniel: she cringes or hides from him, even bares her teeth and snarls. Pa speculates that she's been beaten. Daniel tries to force her to accept his caresses and his company, but she generally ends up evading him. His mother reminds him he can't squeeze blood out of a turnip. Lady isn't a bit like Captain, and Daniel, grieving and angry, finds himself wishing she had died that first night. One day while checking fences, he puts Lady on a choke chain. His father suggests the choke chain can be cruel, and Daniel finally gets so exasperated with Lady's cringing ways that he removes the chain. Somewhat to his relief, she runs away. He watches for her every day, but it is nineteen days later when she returns, porcupine quills stuck all over her face. She snarls at Daniel's father when he tries to help her, but then approaches Daniel with imploring eyes. An angry Daniel kicks a bucket, hitting a cow in the shin and frightening all the cows in the barn. His father tells him to take a good look at himself, that it's now or never if he wants the dog. Tears running down his cheeks, Daniel hugs Lady and painstakingly removes the porcupine quills. With a swollen, infected face and sore paws, her ribs showing, Lady has nearly returned to the condition she was in when Daniel first saw her. But he plans to fatten her up again; maybe this time she'll stay.

In this warm story of Midwestern farm life, a boy grieving for his dead dog comes to love another animal with a very different temperament. Lady isn't at all what Daniel expected, but he can still accept responsibility for her once he's won her trust. Accompanied by illustrations that evoke the rural setting, this is a simple, well-told story that reflects traditional values: hard work, responsibility, satisfaction in a job well done.

Ages 7-9

**Also available in:**
Paperbound—*The Comeback Dog*
Bantam Books, Inc.

T

**654**

Thomas, Karen

**The Good Thing . . . The Bad Thing**

Color illustrations by Yaroslava.
Prentice-Hall, Inc., 1979.
(28 pages)

---

AMBIVALENCE, FEELINGS OF
   Cooperation
   Responsibility: accepting
   Sharing/Not Sharing

---

A young boy proclaims that "the good thing about pretending I'm sick is . . . I don't have to go to school!" But then he decides, "The bad thing about pretending I'm sick is . . . I have to pretend it all day," even when he sees other children playing in their yards. In similar fashion, he describes the good and the bad thing about jumping in a leaf pile (having to rake up the pile again), not sharing his raisins (others not sharing with him), sneaking his flashlight to bed (wearing out the batteries), not being a helper (not being helped), wandering off when Mom is shopping (losing Mom), leaving his bike outside (having it rust), and so on. In the last example, he gives the bad part first: "The bad thing about not doing the things I know I should is . . . I only feel good for a little while." The good part about doing the things he should is that he feels good "for a long, long time!"

A little boy contrasts the good and bad aspects of being naughty or thoughtless, perhaps encouraging young readers or listeners to make up their own "the good thing is," "the bad thing is" pairs. Not all will respond to the examples, especially those that convey a thinly hidden moral, but the book does show youngsters a new way of evaluating their experiences. Clever illustrations help the familiar situations come alive.

Ages 3-7

**Also available in:**
No other form known

---

**655**

Thomas, William E.

**The New Boy Is Blind**

Black/white photographs by the author.
Julian Messner, Inc., 1980.
(62 pages)

---

BLINDNESS
SCHOOL: Mainstreaming
   Parental: overprotection
   School: classmate relationships

---

When Ricky Conboy begins fourth grade, he must learn almost everything—and his classmates have a lot to learn too. Ricky is blind and has never before attended a regular school. He has to learn how to get called on in class, how to find his way around the building, how to locate his coat, how to use a Brailler, how to play on the gym set outside. The other fourth graders learn much about the needs of blind people and the opportunities available to them. They are eager, for example, to use the Brailler and even to try moving around the room with their eyes closed. Mr. Norman, a "trainer" from the Blind Institute, comes to school to help Ricky find his way around. He shows the class how to guide Ricky by letting him hold on to a classmate's right elbow. The children enjoy being "sighted guides." Soon Ricky is accepted as a regular member of the class. When older students tease him or hit him to test whether he is really blind, his classmates defend him. But Ricky's mother continues to shelter him, keeping him home when she thinks he might be upset, often taking him home for lunch instead of allowing him to eat at school, forbidding him field trips, and keeping him off the school bus. As time passes, however, Mrs. Conboy is able to relax more about her son. She realizes that "Ricky is not helpless, he's only blind." The next year Ricky rides the school bus and buys school lunches with his friends.

This is a simple, clear, easy-to-read account of what blind children and their sighted classmates can learn from each other. Also considered are the adjustments required of overprotective parents. Posed photographs help clarify and expand the text, which should lessen the awkwardness often felt by sighted people when they meet someone who is blind. Children preparing to receive a mainstreamed blind classmate will find the book especially valuable.

Ages 6-10

**Also available in:**
No other form known

---

**656**

Thompson, Jean, pseud.

**Don't Forget Michael**

Black/white illustrations by Margot Apple.
William Morrow & Company, Inc., 1979.
(64 pages)

---

FAMILY: Unity
SIBLING: Youngest
   Family: extended
   Privacy, need for

---

Seven-year-old Michael is the smallest and quietest of the McBrides, a very large family that includes his parents, five brothers and sisters, three grandparents, various aunts and uncles, twenty-five cousins, and a host of pets. Sometimes the boy feels lost and overlooked in the middle of this noisy, busy brood. One day, when the family goes on a picnic, Michael wanders off by himself for a while and returns to find he has been left behind. He is just about to cry when he realizes that he is hearing silence for the first time in his life. He enjoys nature's litle noises until suddenly, with horns and loud voices, the family returns for him. Everyone is so happy to see him that, although he enjoyed his time alone, he is glad to know he's been missed. Another day, several members of the family go to a farm to buy produce. Michael's older brother, Kevin, puts a bushel of very ripe tomatoes in the back seat with Michael. Then, while driving, he swerves to avoid another car and puts the front end of their car in the ditch. The tomatoes hit against Michael and split open, covering him with red pulp. Great-Aunt Olivia, thinking he is covered with blood, passes out. When she comes to, she hugs him and calls him her "own dear little Matthew." This is not the first time Michael has been called by his cousin's name, but now he doesn't mind because he knows Aunt Olivia loves him. Grandma Cameron cares about him too, he soon finds. One evening, when the rest of the family is out, she and her parrot, Captain Kid, come to stay with Michael and nine-year-old Connie. Grandma is tired because she stayed up late the night before reading a murder mystery called *The Empty Grave.* The scary title captures the children's imaginations, and later, when Grandma falls asleep and Captain Kid escapes into the night, they are at first afraid to go after him. But they do, and when they finally get him back into the house, Grandma wakes up and shows them how pleased she is with their "nice, quiet evening" together by giving them big scoops of ice cream. One day the McBride children decide to have a volleyball game. While getting the ball from the shed, Kevin drops the shed key through a crack in the porch. They all hurry around trying to devise ways to get the key back. They ignore Michael when he tells them he has a plan and are amazed when he retrieves the key all by himself, using a magnet attached to a yardstick. They call him a genius and promise to listen to him from now on. Reassured, the boy knows that no one will "ever really forget Michael again."

Life in a big family is realistically portrayed in four short episodes. Sometimes Michael feels that if he hears any more noise, he is "going to short out like a computer on TV, lights flashing wildly on and off, sparks flying out, and finally grind to a stop." The boy also frequently feels ignored. But once in a while he is reminded that he is a special part of the family, and then he feels very happy. The book should be appealing to the intended audience and can be read as a novel or as individual short stories. Clever illustrations help depict the hustle and bustle of the McBride household.

Ages 7-9

**Also available in:**
No other form known

## 657

**Thompson, Paul**

**The Hitchhikers**

Black/white photographs by Susan Kuklin.
Franklin Watts, Inc., 1980.
(83 pages)

---

*RUNNING AWAY*
 *Hitchhiking*
 *Rejection: parental*
 *Unwed mother*

---

Seventeen-year-old Shawn is hitchhiking when another hitchhiker, a girl in a red poncho, gets out of a car that stops near him. Soon a car with several men in it stops for the girl. When they try to pull her in, she resists and Shawn jumps to her defense. He gets a split lip for his trouble. The girl and Shawn are both headed for California, they discover, but after talking a bit they split up. Then Shawn loses the last of his money playing cards, to his great disgust: "It was just like everybody back home

said. He was stupid. He never did anything right." Hungry and broke, he gets some breakfast at a mission and is offered a bus ticket home. He refuses, determined to make his mother's life easier by leaving. He's on his way to see his father, who left his mother fourteen years ago. Later, he runs into the girl in the red poncho again, playing her harmonica in the park for the occasional donation. She's staying in a commune, she tells him, her name is Val, she's from Pittsburgh. Shawn works all day in the mission warehouse to earn a little money. That evening, he again finds Val in the park, looking sick. Shawn tells her about his home in New York and the two become friends. Two days later they hitchhike to New Mexico where a rancher picks them up. As they ride in the back of his truck, Shawn realizes why Val is sickly and doesn't eat much: she's pregnant. She's on her way to California to find the baby's father, Charlie. Her letters and calls have not been answered; she thinks his parents have intercepted them. Suddenly the truck plunges off a bridge into a rain-swollen river. Since the rancher is unconscious and Shawn can't swim, Val swims to the bank, towing a rope. She signals Shawn to get the rancher out. When he recovers, the rancher wants them to come home with him for a few days, but they refuse. So he buys them bus tickets to California and gives them each twenty-five dollars for food. In Los Angeles, Shawn leaves Val to catch a bus south, but gives her his father's address. He is shocked to find that this turns out to be a bar and that his father is an alcoholic who tells Shawn, "Why don't you go home. I ain't got nothing for you here." Before too long, Val comes to find Shawn. Neither Charlie's parents nor Charlie himself want her. She wants to go home, and so does Shawn. The next day they begin hitchhiking again.

Two lonely teenagers meet while hitchhiking to California in search of love, Shawn from his father and Val from the father of her unborn child. The very brief text has one sensitive, good-quality photograph for every two pages of text. Within the constraints of a high-interest, low-vocabulary format, this is an interesting story with credible characters. Running away and hitchhiking are romanticized a bit, but the rather desolate lives of these two young people are not. There is much here to promote discussion.

Ages 12 and up

**Also available in:**
No other form known

## 658

**Thrasher, Crystal Faye**

**Between Dark and Daylight**

Atheneum Publishers, 1979.
(251 pages)

---

*FAMILY: Unity*
*MOVING*
*POVERTY*
 *Change: new home*
 *Death: of friend*
 *Death: murder*
 *Friendship: making friends*
 *Violence*

---

The worst of the Depression is over, and twelve-year-old Seely Robinson and her family start their move to the site of her father's new job. When their borrowed, unreliable truck breaks a rear axle, they decide to camp for the night in the hills of southern Indiana. Sent for water, Seely meets the shy but helpful Meaders family, who offer the use of the abandoned Tyson home nearby. Seely's mother is unwilling to move to the house; she wants to move out of the county, not deeper into it. But a downpour forces them to leave their campsite, and with the help of young Johnny Meaders and his cousin, Byron Tyson, the Robinsons occupy the house. Seely's family learns that Byron and his father had moved out of their house and in with the Meaders when Byron's mother died. Johnny and Byron warn Seely that the "sneaky-mean" Fender twins are out to avenge themselves on Johnny's father, Jack, a door-to-door salesman who called them "bastards" when their unmarried mother could not pay her bill for his products. The seventeen-year-old twins, slow-witted, cruel, and destructive, spy on Seely's family and vandalize their truck. The girl begins to sense the menace in their hostility. Meanwhile, Mr. Robinson tries to find temporary work and the families become friends. The indispensable Johnny and Byron plow a garden for Seely's mother. Mrs. Meaders takes Mrs. Robinson and the children to a prayer meeting of the "Holy Rollers." Returning from the meeting, Seely, her brother, Byron, and Johnny are pelted with rocks by the Fender twins. Soon after, Seely begins working for Mrs. Meaders, caring for the ailing Grandma Stoner. The Fender boys follow Seely home through the woods, causing their mother, Nellie, to warn Seely about her sons, telling her that her own uncle "took me, and got me in the family way." One day Seely returns home to find the twins waiting for her. Nellie drives them off and from then on accompanies Seely home from the Meaders's house. Affections deepen, particularly between Seely and Johnny, but also between the mothers. Then the Meaders's home burns down. Grandma Stoner is killed, and the Meaders family moves into the Tyson house with the Robinsons. One Sunday, Seely's father takes his family to a baseball game. A violent storm halts the game and turns the roads to mud, forcing them to abandon their old car and walk back to the house. In the morning Johnny Meaders is found dead, tied to the Robinsons' abandoned car and dragged to death. The Fender twins are easily tracked through the mud, and they confess. The grieving parents try to shoulder the blame, Jack Meaders for insulting the twins, Nellie Fender for not having them institutionalized years earlier as she was advised. The Meaders family decides to move back to Kentucky, and Mrs. Robinson gives them the money she had saved for a sewing machine so they can buy a gravestone for Johnny. Byron and Seely realize they will have to help Nellie Fender, now alone. A part of her life, Seely thinks, is ended.

In an earlier novel, *The Dark Didn't Catch Me*, Seely learned about family discord and death when her parents argued sharply, her sister turned against them, and her beloved brother drowned. In this book, she is again forced to move, but is sustained by the concern and helpfulness of the Meaders family and by the special affection of Johnny. She deepens her sympathies by caring for the infirm Grandma Stoner, but is thrown into a relentless cycle of menace and violence, learning once again of death's finality as the grieving Meaders family drives away. In this memorable community of characters there is courage, humor, and endurance. The extraordinary manner of Johnny's death is strong material likely to provoke useful discussion. This engrossing book is followed by another, *End of a Dark Road*.

Ages 11-13

**Also available in:**
No other form known

## 659

**Tolan, Stephanie S.**

## The Last of Eden

Frederick Warne & Company, Inc., 1980.
(154 pages)

---

*FRIENDSHIP: Meaning of*
*HOMOSEXUALITY: Female*
*IDENTITY, SEARCH FOR*
*PEER RELATIONSHIPS*
*SCHOOLS, PRIVATE: Girls'*
  *Communication: rumor*
  *School: pupil-teacher relationships*
  *Talents: artistic*

---

Michelle ("Mike") Caine returns for her sophomore year to the girls' boarding school she thinks of as Eden. There she finds the family feeling she does not have at home. Mike's special friends are all back: Scovie, Bits, Jeannie, Tag, and Willie. Marty, Mike's best friend and her roommate this year, is also back. New on campus are houseparents Donald and Priscilla Kincaid. He is a history teacher, she a nationally known artist. Marty, a talented artist herself, is overjoyed at the chance to work with Priscilla. Mike's interest lies in poetry and her mentor is Miss Engles, an English teacher. Donald is extremely good-looking and most of the girls develop crushes on him, but Bits seems to go out of her way to attract his attention, sometimes succeeding. The family atmosphere at school begins to change: the Kincaids' door is kept shut and they are rarely seen together. Marty becomes obsessed with winning a contest to design a church stained-glass window. She is convinced she will win, both because of her artistic ability and her religious convictions. Marty does win the competition, and she and Priscilla are to travel to Detroit to meet with the architects. Bits, who has never liked Marty because Marty has money, becomes nasty and snide. The morning that Marty and Priscilla leave, Marty stops back at the Kincaids' apartment and finds Bits there alone with Donald. After that weekend, Bits is withdrawn and avoids Marty. When Bits faces expulsion for arriving late and dishevelled after the Spring Ball, she tells the headmistress that the trouble in the Kincaid marriage is not because of her and Donald, but because of Priscilla and Marty. The story spreads. As Marty's roommate, Mike finds herself also suspected of homosexuality. She stops associating with Miss Engles when she realizes that her frequent visits to discuss poetry could be misinterpreted. Rumors abound, notes and posters appear, and Marty and Mike are shunned. Adding to Marty's depression, the Kincaids are leaving to try to solve their marital problems elsewhere. Bits will not be returning either, as she has failed two subjects and lost her scholarship. After uneventful summers, the other girls return as juniors. Marty and Mike room together again, and Scovie has a new roommate, Sylva. Sylva asks Jeannie who the best friends in their class are; Jeannie says they're Marty and Mike. Sylva makes a remark that Jeannie doesn't understand about breaking up that friendship within a month. Soon Marty's behavior begins to change: she fails to meet commitments, skips her art lessons, joins the Altar Guild (which she has always scorned), and spends a lot of time with Sylva. Early one morning, Mike wakes up when Sylva comes in to get Marty for the early church service. Claiming to be freezing, Sylva asks to get under Marty's covers. Several days later, Scovie reports that Marty and Sylva have not spent the entire night in their own beds for the past three nights. The housemother tells Mike that Marty and Sylva have requested to become roommates. Then Mike receives a note from Marty in which Marty talks about her strengthened religious feelings and how she must put God first, ahead of her art or her friends. She adds that she now realizes her feelings for Priscilla were just what everyone said they were. Mike tears up the note, vomits repeatedly, and is placed in the infirmary for several days. Miss Engles comes to see her, and they talk about Mike's feelings of confusion and betrayal. Priscilla comes back to talk to Marty, trying to get the girl to continue with her art. Sylva takes an overdose of drugs, but she recovers and is taken out of school by her mother. Marty's wealthy father allows her to transfer to the arts-oriented school she wanted all along. Mike wonders what will become of Marty at another all-girls' school, what her future will be. Miss Engles tells Mike that "homosexuality is one area no one can be quite sure about. . . . A label is just too simple." Mike still grieves for the loss of the friendship, but she begins to write poetry again.

This is a story of relationships, of people who separate and then come together again as they grow and change. Mike, who narrates, is primarily the reactor to events and people around her, finding many of the changes in her world painful and unanticipated. In a sense, the story is also about loss of innocence, of Eden, as Mike discovers that Marty does in fact have sexually ambivalent feelings, that the rumors have some substance. Each relationship is explored in considerable depth, offering much to discuss in this well-written, thought-provoking book.

Ages 12 and up

**Also available in:**
Paperbound—*The Last of Eden*
Bantam Books, Inc.

**660**

**Townsend, Maryann and Ronnie Stern**

## Pop's Secret

Black/white photographs: a collection.
Addison-Wesley Publishing Company, Inc., 1980.
(26 pages)

---

AGE: Aging
DEATH: of Grandparent
GRANDPARENT: Love for
  Loss: feelings of

---

Young Mark remembers Pop, his grandfather. Pop seemed so old Mark thought he was never a baby. Yet Pop had a photograph of himself as an infant and other photographs showing how he grew. One picture showed Pop with his beloved sister; another showed him in a funny-looking bathing suit; one showed him with Mark's father, then a young boy. After Pop's wife died, he became too lonely living alone and moved in with Mark's family. He fit right in: Mark's friends even called him Pop. Mark loved him very much. One winter Pop became sick and, though no one told him, Mark knew Pop was not getting better. He died in the hospital, but Mark was only sure Pop was really gone when he saw the coffin at the funeral. Though friends try to console him, Mark remains angry and confused. He misses Pop and doesn't want to go into his room. He worries about small things: who will buy vitamins now that Pop is gone? Mom says she will. Mark worries about large things: what can he do now that Pop is dead? Mom has an idea. Why not assemble a book about Pop, put his photos in it, and write down memories of him? Mark and his family prepare the book and look at it often to refresh their memories of Pop.

This is a true story, enhanced and extended by family photographs, about a boy's love for his grandfather and his deep grief after the old man's death. Seemingly inconsolable, Mark responds favorably to his mother's suggestion of preparing a book about Pop so none of their memories will be lost—a useful idea that can be extended to other areas of children's lives. Here is a refreshingly positive look at aging and at the warm relationship among three generations of a family.

Ages 5-7

**Also available in:**
No other form known

T

**661**

**Truss, Jan**

**Bird at the Window**

Harper & Row, Publishers, Inc., 1980.
(215 pages)

---

*UNWED MOTHER*
*Abortion*
*Boy-girl relationships*
*Communication: lack of*
*Family: relationships*
*Identity, search for*
*Pregnancy*
*Visiting*

---

Eighteen-year-old Angela Moynahan tells her favorite teacher, Mr. Olson, that she is sure she is pregnant by Gordy Kopec, a "pale clod of a heavy boy-man who had slipped away from school to work around the farms, more than three years ago." Mr. Olson, appalled, suggests she tell her mother, get an abortion, at least see a doctor. But Angela rejects all three suggestions. She may even proceed with her plans to go to England in seven weeks when school ends. As she rides the bus home, Damion Good, with whom Angela has gradually been falling in love, sits beside her. How ironic that today of all days, Damion asks her out for the first time. Angela keeps hoping she's not really pregnant. She tries to miscarry by hauling heavy loads, leaping down stairs, taking purgatives, and pummeling her stomach. The day after her date with Damion, she drinks half a bottle of gin with grated nutmeg in it (a method she heard described in a rest room), gets on her horse, and rides as hard as she can. Nothing happens. Two months later, she leaves Canada to spend the year in England, at first with her maternal grandparents. She soon realizes they are not the strong, supportive grandparents of her fantasy. While with them, Angela finds some sketches that her mother drew years ago, before she went to Canada where she met and married Joe Moynahan. The eyes in the sketches are like Angela's. Angela visits a doctor and tells her she wants an abortion. The doctor ignores her request. Frustrated and angry, Angela gets a job at a bakeshop and wears girdles to disguise her pregnancy. Damion writes and tells her she won a coveted scholarship; her marks were the highest in the province. After an argument with her grandmother, who often makes disparaging remarks about Angela's mother, Angela rides off on her bike but has trouble with it in front of Clara Jonason's house. Clara (whose eyes remind Angela of her own) tells Angela about her son, Jeff, who was a great friend of Angela's mother, Dinah. Both won important scholarships, and Clara was always surprised that Dinah didn't return from her trip to Canada to pick hers up. Angela explains that on that trip her mother met and married Joe Moynahan. But now she understands that Jeff Jonason must be her father, not Joe. Bitterly, her grandmother tells her that Clara has never been married; the old woman hates and fears both mother and son, believing them somehow responsible for her daughter's departure. When Angela's two-month visit with her grandparents ends, she finds a flat and a job in London. The news from home is always that Gordy sends his love and that Joe Moynahan is

ailing. Two months early, Angela goes into labor and is delivered of a stillborn baby girl. Upon her return home from the hospital, Angela finds a letter from her mother. Joe is very sick and wants her to come home. She does and sits with Joe for a few minutes the day of his surgery. He dies that night. After the funeral her mother says she wants to sell the farm and move to a city. Angela mentions Jeff Jonason but her mother won't react or explain, except to say that Joe knew all along that Angela wasn't his child. Damion has gone north to work. At sea about her future, Angela tells Gordy she will marry him. She makes plans for a quick wedding, since her mother is going to England soon. However, after she opens all her gifts at a bridal shower, Angela calmly asks the women to take everything back. She won't marry Gordy after all—may not, in fact, ever marry anyone. Her mother invites Angela to accompany her to England, but Angela says she wants to continue writing her diaries and notebooks. She'll also await Damion's return.

An intelligent, perceptive, but confused young woman, pregnant by a boy she has no real feelings for, attempts to retain her independence and make wise choices about herself and her future. Angela's story is told in part through her notebooks; Mr. Olson had encouraged her to write down her thoughts. Curiously, despite all the events of the plot, Angela remains a two-dimensional character, perhaps because she habitually reacts rather than acts. Her decision at the end not to marry Gordy is the only real suggestion that she may now begin to take charge of her life. Through all the trials of her pregnancy and the stillborn birth, Angela remains strangely adrift, making no plans and expressing no real attitudes. The reader can't be sure she has learned anything from her experiences. Some may find this book slow and depressing; others, thought-provoking. Readers will note that the homespun abortion attempts Angela makes are neither effective nor safe.

Ages 13 and up

**Also available in:**
No other form known

**662**

**Udry, Janice May**

**Thump and Plunk**

Color illustrations by Ann Schweninger.
Harper & Row, Publishers, Inc., 1981.
(21 pages counted)

---

*AGGRESSION*
*Sibling: relationships*

---

Thump and Plunk, brother and sister mice, each have a doll: Thumpit and Plunkit. After the two sit quietly in their chairs for a while, Plunk plunks Thump's Thumpit and Thump returns the favor by thumping Plunk. They exchange a number of blows before their mother comes in and tries to determine who thumped or plunked the other first. She orders them to stop thumping and plunking each other and forbids them to thump or plunk each other or each other's dolls again. She then invites them into the kitchen for ice cream.

In a tongue-twisting exchange of thumps and plunks, two mice siblings go after each other and each other's dolls. The conflict is quickly begun and then authoritatively halted by their mother. Accompanied by soft, appealing illustrations, the slight, amusing text may encourage little children to talk about relationships with their own siblings. They will also enjoy the tongue twisters.

Ages 2-5

**Also available in:**
No other form known

## 663

**Van Leeuwen, Jean**

### Seems Like This Road Goes On Forever

The Dial Press, Inc., 1979.
(214 pages)

COMMUNICATION: Parent-Child
IDENTITY, SEARCH FOR
MENTAL ILLNESS: of Adolescent
    Accidents: automobile
    Deprivation, emotional
    Expectations
    Guilt, feelings of
    Parental: control
    Reality, escaping
    Religion: questioning
    Stealing: shoplifting

Seventeen-year-old Mary Alice Fletcher lies in a hospital bed feeling completely detached from what is going on around her. She doesn't speak, eat, or react to anyone or anything. Even the car accident that brought her to the hospital with a head injury and broken leg does not seem real. She cannot tell whether or not she is in pain. But her parents do not believe in "such things as emotional breakdowns and psychiatrists." Her father, a minister, believes Mary Alice is going through a spiritual crisis that can only be healed by prayer. Her mother thinks there is nothing wrong with her mind at all, except the shock of the accident. However, they do agree to let their daughter talk to Dr. Nyquist, a psychologist who works with young people. Even though Mary Alice feels she has "had no life" and therefore has nothing to discuss, Dr. Nyquist patiently helps her probe her feelings and memories to understand why she has found it necessary to retreat from the world. Most of Mary Alice's childhood memories center around her parents. She feels from all she has observed that her father is "a completely good person." She, by contrast, is very imperfect, and his penetrating eyes seem to look into her head and "see the bad thoughts there." She remembers that when he punished her, which was often, he never spanked her or even raised his voice. Instead, he would quote the Bible and make her think about how she had sinned against God. Since he always had all the answers, Mary Alice never talked back. She recalls how her older brother, Peter, used to make their father very angry by questioning him. But by

the time Peter was fifteen he had learned to keep his thoughts to himself. Mary Alice sees her father as "a silent reproachful shadow" looming over her hospital bed and her life. Her mother is also unapproachable, in a different way. She is not the warm and caring person she pretends to be, not even with her children. Since her father frowns on worldliness, Mary Alice has always worn homemade clothes of her mother's choice or clothes bought at rummage sales. Pretty accessories were not allowed. When Peter left for college, Mary Alice was panic-stricken at the thought of being without him. He advised her to remember that she would be leaving soon too, but that while still at home she must "buck the tide—they've got a strong tide going—but it's got to be done." About the time Peter left, their father was becoming more extreme in his religion. He had become a follower of Bob Parker, an evangelist who preached about the Power of Prayer and the Healing of the Holy Spirit. Mary Alice didn't understand any of this. Yet when it was time for her to think about college, her parents insisted that she apply only to Bob Parker University. She felt extremely uneasy when she "thought of turning herself over like a lump of clay to be molded—body, mind, and spirit—into a total Christian woman." In high school Mary Alice had felt invisible. At one point she had begun to think of herself as a good student. But when she wrote an exceptionally fine book report, her teacher accused her of plagiarism. After that, she didn't think good grades were worth the effort. Her job as a salesclerk gave her a sense of identity for a while, but this was ruined by her compulsion to take small, pretty items from the store. The breaking point came when a boy she thought was interested in her asked out her friend instead. Then Mary Alice started "spinning a cocoon" around herself. Shortly after this, she stole a sweater from the store and fled in her parents' car. She had an accident and was brought to the hospital. As Dr. Nyquist helps Mary Alice better understand herself and her family situation, she decides that with his and her brother's help, she may be able to take charge of her own future. She knows it won't be easy to "buck the tide," but she will try.

This book describes the inner life of a sensitive girl who is given no freedom to explore her own personality or ideas in a home dedicated totally to a stern, impersonal religion. Her brother is strong enough to survive his stifling home life, but Mary Alice, paralyzed by guilt and fear, does not have the willpower to resist her forceful parents. It is only after much painful self-analysis, helped by a skillful psychologist, that she begins to understand how her seemingly irrational behavior has been an expression of anger and despair. Not a fast-paced narrative, this study of a troubled girl is convincingly realistic but won't appeal to all readers.

Ages 12 and up

**Also available in:**
Cassette—Seems Like This Road Goes On Forever
Library of Congress (NLSBPH)

Paperbound—Seems Like This Road Goes On Forever
Dell Publishing Company, Inc.

V

**664**

Van Steenwyk, Elizabeth Ann

**Rivals on Ice**

Black/white illustrations by Rondi Anderson.
Albert Whitman & Company, 1979.
(63 pages)

---

COMPETITION
    Communication: parent-child
    Determination
    Parent/Parents: single
    Sports/Sportsmanship
    Talents: athletic

---

Tucker Cameron loves figure skating. In fact, at twelve she is the best Novice-level skater in the South Bay Skating Club and dreams of winning first place in the upcoming regional competition. She wonders if becoming number one would make her mother start to notice her again. Tucker's mother has been preoccupied since her divorce, and Tucker feels neglected. But the girl tries hard to push her personal life to the side and make skating "her one and only world." Then Sara Mars, the current Midwest Novice Champion, enters Tucker's life. Sara seems to have everything: "Talent, money, looks." Not only that, but Sara's mother is totally involved in her daughter's activities. When Tucker meets Sara, however, she notes that her eyes "don't look calm and confident like the rest of her face." There is "anger, with a touch of scared rabbit" in them. Tucker soon has her own reason to be disturbed when Mr. Billings, the rink manager, announces that fees are being raised. Tucker knows her mother will not be able to afford the additional expense. She thinks about trying for a scholarship, but can't get enough of her mother's time to discuss it with her. Finally, when they do talk, Mrs. Cameron just tells Tucker to quit. Instead, Tucker goes to Mr. Billings with a business arrangement he gladly accepts. She will baby-sit for the small children who run around the rink during Mothers' Hour in exchange for free early-morning skating time. Sara begins to practice then too and she asks her coach, Jack Barrett, to watch Tucker. Impressed, he offers to coach her without charge. A grateful Tucker is sorry she has ever been jealous of Sara. On the morning of the competition, the skaters meet in Mr. Billings's office so they can ride together to Polar Ice. Suddenly Sara bursts into the room; she has taken the bus to the club so she can ride in the van with the others. Mrs. Mars appears and tries to persuade Sara to drive over in her car. Sara resists, but her mother wins out; Sara seems almost afraid of her. When the others arrive at the rink, Sara is nowhere to be seen. Mrs. Mars reveals to Tucker that Sara gets sick when she rides in the back of buses or vans. Suddenly Tucker understands: Sara wanted to get sick so she would miss the competition. She isn't afraid of her mother, but of competing. Tucker finds Sara and convinces her that she doesn't want to become a champion by default. Both girls perform, finishing with very close scores. Though Sara remains the champion, the crowd gives Tucker a standing ovation for her nearly perfect routine, and the coach presents her with flowers

from her mother. Tucker, very happy, understands that her mother loves her and always has. And "maybe next year will be her turn to be first."

The pressures of competition are complicated for Tucker by her struggle to earn enough money to keep skating and by her desire to win back her mother's interest and affection. Sara, on the other hand, has every advantage, but she buckles under the pressure of trying to live up to her champion status. The two girls find in each other the friendship and support they need, learning that rivalry does not have to extend to the personal level, that even friends can compete. The few simple illustrations complement the plainly written text, which should appeal to the reluctant reader.

Ages 9-11

**Also available in:**
No other form known

**665**

Veglahn, Nancy Crary

**Fellowship of the Seven Stars**

Abingdon Press, 1981.
(175 pages)

---

CULTS
    Family: relationships
    Rebellion
    Religion: questioning
    Running away

---

Mazie Ffoulke, a plump high school senior who is "good" at home and at school, attends her first meeting of a religious organization, the Fellowship of the Seven Stars, after a particularly bad day. She has been replaced on the "A" debate team by Harrison Baker, and her older brother, Rich, who is continually in trouble, has stolen the family car. Nick Sorenson is the magnetic, good-looking leader of the Fellowship, and Mazie is drawn to him. At the first meeting she hears that members of the Fellowship never use each other selfishly, as other people do. Founded five years ago by a former Chicago businessman now known as Malakh, the Fellowship exists to spread the messages he receives from God. The next evening Mazie and Paul Clough, whom she's casually dated, attend another meeting. Everything the speakers say seems logical, and Mazie likes the feeling of unity and the kindness members show each other. The following morning, Mazie stays home from church—her father is a Methodist minister and, although she enjoys being in church, her religious feelings aren't deep—and hears Rich sneaking in. He's come to steal their grandfather's coin collection and warns Mazie not to say anything. Always full of get-rich-quick schemes, Rich is sure this stake will start him on the road to riches. After church Mazie's parents are so happy to see the returned car that she doesn't tell them about the coin collection. She knows they'll just make more excuses for Rich. All her life she's watched them argue about her brother and bail him out of trouble. Paul's distressed parents come by and report that Paul is joining the Fellowship. Mazie announces that she is joining too. Suddenly she wants to get away from everything, to be "free from all those answerless questions." She moves into the Fellowship house, a place of constant prayer and Bible reading. To her distress, she is told that every day she must try to sell forty dollars' worth of cheap ballpoint pens. But eventually she settles into her new routine. She promises her parents that she will finish high school and will call home once a week; in return, they are to leave her alone. One day Harrison sees her selling pens in a mall. He wonders how such an intelligent, analytical person could join a group like the Fellowship; Mazie replies that he simply doesn't understand. Then it's announced that the great Malakh is coming for a rally, and Mazie joins the publicity committee. When Harrison calls her at the Fellowship house to discuss debate, Nick tells Mazie that relationships outside the Fellowship are discouraged. Then Paul quits school to become an orderly in a nursing home so he can contribute more money to the Fellowship. His move shocks Mazie; Paul was in line for several top college scholarships. One of the girls, Ellen, who shares a bunk in Mazie's room suffers from severe headaches. After she faints one day, a healing service is held and Ellen says her headache is gone. But Mazie finds her very ill in the middle of the night and begs Nick to get a doctor for her. Nick insists that too little faith can make a person ill; Ellen will be all right if she has enough faith. But Ellen goes to a doctor who puts her in a hospital for tests. When Nick discovers where she is, he brings her back to the Fellowship house before all her tests are run. Malakh arrives in town, and Mazie accompanies him and his assistants to an interview she has set up with a local journalist. The reporter illustrates his story with photographs of a luxurious set of buildings in Chicago where only the elite of the Fellowship ever go, wondering how the Fellowship's huge income can come from teenagers working menial jobs and selling ballpoint pens. Harrison has kept in touch, and Mazie invites him to attend Malakh's upcoming rally. But when Mazie sees Paul wrapping up a scorpion to send to the skeptical journalist, something in her snaps. She leaves the Fellowship house and spends the night in her father's church. When she returns to pick up her things, Nick tells her she will leave the next morning for a rural retreat where troubled members can be helped. Mazie realizes it may not be easy to leave the Fellowship. During the rally, Mazie is kept close to Fellowship members. She sees her parents and Harrison in the audience, but is only able to break away and go to them when some bleachers collapse and cause a diversion. Back at home again, Mazie misses the sense of belonging. But when she learns that Ellen died of an operable brain tumor, her anger quells her desire to return to the Fellowship. She's dating Harrison and that helps. But she's "still bugged sometimes by having to think and decide—by not being sure of anything much."

In this first-person narrative, a teenager looks back at the time she spent with a religious cult, what drew her to join and then compelled her to leave. She also acknowledges the part of herself that is still vulnerable to the group's appeal. Readers will come away from the book knowing a little more about cults and how they operate. However, the story seems fuzzy because the one-dimensional characters exist only to further the plot. Readers will recognize the typical—perhaps stereotypical—cult tactics of poor food, little sleep, repetitive teachings, and no outside contacts. Many will also understand the implications of the Fellowship's finances.

Ages 12 and up

**Also available in:**
No other form known

### 666

**Vigna, Judith**

**Daddy's New Baby**

Color illustrations by the author.
Albert Whitman & Company, 1982.
(32 pages counted)

---

SIBLING: New Baby
    Parent/Parents: remarriage of
    Sibling: half brother/half sister
    Sibling: rivalry

---

A little girl's parents are divorced, her father is remarried, and he and his new wife have just had a baby. The girl doesn't understand why her father wanted a new baby when he has her to come visit on weekends. The baby is only a half-sister and doesn't even look like her; how will people know they are sisters? Before the baby came, she always had a room to herself when she visited her father. Now she shares the room—and her father's time—with the baby. One day her father plans to take her to a puppet show. But when his wife has a family emergency, the girl and her father take the baby to the park to feed the ducks instead. Big sister helps get the baby ready, chooses her clothes, helps prepare her bottle, and even pushes the stroller. As they go toward the pond, she inadvertently lets go of the stroller and it begins to roll toward the water. With just seconds to spare, she grabs it. Bystanders congratulate her for saving her little sister. When they get back home the baby is crying, so the older sister entertains her with a homemade puppet show. The baby seems to enjoy it, and her sister is glad they like the same games. She's also glad they have the same daddy.

A child who rescues her new little half-sister from danger (illustrations show the father's hand ready to grab the buggy himself) finds that her daddy's baby might be a plus in her life after all. Attractive pastel illustrations complement a text sparkling with short, rhythmic sentences. The feelings described are typical of many children with new siblings, regardless of their family situations.

Ages 4-7

**Also available in:**
Large Print—*Daddy's New Baby*
Albert Whitman & Company

V

**667**

Vigna, Judith

**The Hiding House**

Color illustrations by the author.
Albert Whitman & Company, 1979.
(32 pages counted)

---

*FRIENDSHIP: Best Friend*
  *Friendship: making friends*
  *Sharing/Not sharing*

---

Little Marybeth and Barbara are best friends, and they do everything together. They even share a house, an old shed in Marybeth's backyard that Barbara's father helped them fix up. The girls call it the "Hiding House," and they go there when they want to be by themselves. Sometimes they even sleep there. But Marybeth has a rule that no one else is allowed in the house, not even her own brother and sister. One night when the moon is full, the two girls go to the house and take an oath to be best friends forever. Then something unexpected happens. A new girl moves into the neighborhood and Barbara invites her to the Hiding House. Marybeth is so angry she locks herself in the house and won't let the other two come in. After several hours she opens a window and overhears Barbara talking to the new girl. Barbara says, "I must have done something terrible. Marybeth always said I was her BEST FRIEND!" Marybeth then realizes she need not be angry with Barbara; she opens the door. Soon Marybeth has two best friends and is pleased that Barbara isn't jealous at all.

Possessive Marybeth wants an exclusive relationship with Barbara, but Barbara is willing to let others into their small world. Eventually, Marybeth discovers how nice it is to have more than one playmate. Children who rely too much on one friend or are threatened by outsiders may gain insight from this story. The pictures enhance the text to make an appealing book.

Ages 4-7

**Also available in:**
Large Print—*The Hiding House*
Albert Whitman & Company

**668**

Vigna, Judith

**She's Not My Real Mother**

Color illustrations by the author.
Albert Whitman & Company, 1980.
(32 pages counted)

---

*PARENT/PARENTS: Remarriage of*
*STEPPARENT: Mother*
  *Change: resisting*

---

Miles, about five, lives with his divorced mother. He likes to visit Daddy in the city, but he doesn't like Daddy's new wife because "she's not my REAL mother." He's afraid that by befriending his stepmother, he may anger his mother. "Suppose Mommy found out and got mad and left me just the way Daddy did?" When Daddy's wife buys Miles a balloon at the zoo, Miles refuses to thank her. When she tells Miles she'd like to be his friend, he responds that he does not want to be hers. One Sunday afternoon, Miles and his stepmother go alone to the Ice Show. Though Miles enjoys the show he worries about being too nice to Daddy's wife, so he hides behind a column at the giant stadium just to scare her. But he quickly loses sight of his stepmother and grows frightened, fearing Daddy's wife has left him in the crowded arena and gone home. Actually, she has gone to the lost children department, and soon Miles hears his name over the loudspeaker. Reunited with his stepmother, Miles is now very happy to see her. When he realizes she is not going to tell his father "the bad thing" he did, he decides he can be friends with Daddy's wife after all without feeling disloyal to his mother.

A little boy tells in his own words how hurt and bewildered he is by his parents' divorce and his father's remarriage. His stepmother's kindness helps Miles realize he can be friends with her and still maintain his relationship with his mother. Although written in language that some children will be able to read on their own, this convincing and realistic story is also a good read-aloud selection and may stimulate discussion. The illustrations nicely complement the text.

Ages 4-8

**Also available in:**
Large Print—*She's Not My Real Mother*
Albert Whitman & Company

**669**

Vogel, Ilse-Margret

**Farewell, Aunt Isabell**

Black/white illustrations by the author.
Harper & Row, Publishers, Inc., 1979.
(54 pages)

---

*MENTAL ILLNESS*
  *Family: unity*
  *Relatives: living in child's home*

---

Twins Erika and Inge are curious to see their Aunt Isabell after her year-long absence. Mother, Grandmother, and Nurse Amelia have brought Isabell back from the hospital, that "terrible place," to live with the family in a cheerful room—cheerful despite recently installed bars on the window and a locked door. The family is determined to keep Isabell happy so she will get completely well. As Grandmother says, "Everything that makes her happy will also make her well faster." The girls greet Aunt Isabell, but are shocked when she insists upon talking about their "shit-yellow" shoes. Several days later they find her lying on her back in the brook with a flower circlet on her head and water streaming over her. At first they think she is dead, which delights Isabell. She explains that she was waiting for her bridegroom, but since he didn't come she lay in the brook and now she's married to him. She teaches the girls how to make wreaths of flowers, and all three sing and dance in the meadow. When they hear Mother and Nurse Amelia calling for Isabell, they don't answer. They know that the most important thing is to keep

380

Isabell happy, and she obviously does not want to be found. Later, when they walk to the railroad station, Isabell promises to show the girls the wonders of Greece and Paris someday. When their father gets off the commuter train, he calmly walks them all home. Later, when Inge tells the family what Isabell did that afternoon, she says, "She was so happy. . . . You will see she will be well very soon." The girls spend three days making Isabell a beautiful embroidered apron. Isabell says the correct way to wear it is back to front, and she turns the girls' aprons around too. Then she attempts to walk backwards down the stairs to show her sister the nice apron, falls, and hurts herself. The girls go outside to get away from Isabell's constant laughter and talk to their friend Magda, who lives next door. Magda wants to see their "crazy aunt," and they promise to arrange it. The next day Magda hides behind a bush in the meadow, but when Isabell, the girls, and Nurse Amelia arrive, she can't resist coming out of hiding. Isabell physically attacks her, accusing Magda of stealing her bridegroom. Magda later reproaches the girls for not warning her that their aunt was mean. They try to explain that she's not mean, just sick. Isabell disappears again and the girls find her at the railroad station watching the trains. She complains that she can only be happy with them, that the others want to keep her locked up. She again promises to take Inge and Erika to Paris with her—there, she tells them, people sometimes kill themselves by jumping off the Eiffel Tower. Isabell is now watched even more carefully, but she manages to escape again and is found in a narrow cistern. She refuses to come out until Inge reminds her of her promise to take them to Paris. Afterwards, the girls hear talk of an ambulance and a high fever. The next day an ambulance arrives, and Aunt Isabell is carried out on a stretcher. Inge cries because she's never told Isabell how much she loves her. Their mother calls them to come quickly; Isabell is awake and wants to say goodbye to them. Isabell says she knows they love her. She's very sick, she tells them, but someday she will get well. Then the three of them will go to Paris together.

In this affectionate and realistic first-person narrative, Inge describes her family's attempts to cope with the mental illness of Aunt Isabell. Mother and Grandmother seem to feel they can cure Isabell by making her happy, but it soon becomes obvious that there is more to the treatment of mental illness than providing a benign, loving environment. The portrayal of Aunt Isabell lets readers see her as a unique individual who can love and be loved. Yet, although the story is gently told, the barred windows and Isabell's attack on Magda are jarring notes. The author's own pen-and-ink drawings, suggesting a time earlier in the century, are very much in keeping with the lyrical and highly readable text. This is one of several books about Inge and her family and friends.

Ages 8-10

**Also available in:**
No other form known

---

**670**

Vogel, Ilse-Margret

**My Summer Brother**

Black/white illustrations by the author.
Harper & Row, Publishers, Inc., 1981.
(86 pages)

---

*FRIENDSHIP: Meaning of*
*LOVE, MEANING OF*
  *Death: of sibling*
  *Family: relationships*
  *Jealousy*
  *Mourning, stages of*

---

Six weeks after the death of Erika, her twin sister, nine-year-old Inge meets Dieter, an art student of twenty who is moving in next door, when he stops by her special backyard hiding place. When he offers to be her big brother, an important friendship begins. The two exchange notes and little gifts, leaving them in Inge's hiding place for the other to find. One day, Dieter leaves a large envelope containing a drawing he's made of Inge. When she goes to show it to her mother she finds her crying, not just about Erika's death but about Papa's preoccupation with his work. She tells Inge she is terribly lonely. A few days later, Dieter comes to sketch Inge again. He and Inge's mother begin a conversation so absorbing that Inge must interrupt impatiently. As Dieter sketches her, Inge's mother hovers nearby—not going off to prepare dinner, as Inge expects. That Sunday, when Dieter comes again to sketch Inge, he brings two baskets of raspberries, one for her and one for her mother. After he leaves, Inge finds at the bottom of her mother's basket a piece of paper with a poem written in a foreign language. All she can decipher is her mother's name, Margarete. Inge crumples up the poem, deciding to say nothing to her mother. Several days later, she wanders, bored, into her mother's room without knocking. Her mother is curling her hair and smiling a secret sort of smile Inge doesn't recognize. She is going to the village, she tells Inge, but doesn't want the girl to accompany her. Instead, Inge is to meet her at the station at six o'clock, the time of Papa's train. After she leaves, Inge amuses herself by trying on all her mother's jewelry. In the bottom of the jewelry box she finds a picture of her mother when she was younger. "The woman in the photo I did not know—and did not like." When Inge goes to meet Papa's train, her mother comes running up at the last minute, clutching a wilting red rose. That evening, Papa says he will not be able to accompany them on their vacation in the Zobten Mountains, so perhaps Dieter will go instead. Inge's mother objects, but Inge is "in seventh heaven." The evening they arrive at their hotel, Inge wants to take a walk in the moonlight. Her mother suggests they go to bed instead. At midnight Inge wakes to find both her mother and Dieter gone, taking the walk she wanted to take. But the week of vacation passes pleasantly enough. On Saturday night they attend a dance at the hotel. After Inge goes up to bed, she can't get her party dress unzipped and returns downstairs to ask her mother for help. She sees her mother and Dieter dancing very close together. She sits at their table, unthinkingly downing both their glasses of punch and trying to get their attention. When

V

they wander outside, Inge manages tipsily to get back upstairs. The last thing she remembers is lighting a candle and groggily watching the whole room light up. Four days later she awakes, hurting all over and with both arms bandaged. A bellhop had rescued her from her burning room. Her grandmother hands her letters from Dieter. When her mother comes into her hospital room, Inge accuses her of not really caring, of being too absorbed in Papa and Dieter. Her mother explains that all three are dear to her for different reasons. One of Dieter's letters tells Inge that he is accepting an exciting position in Berlin. Papa and Mother look happy when they welcome Inge home from the hospital. Dieter has left a last gift in Inge's secret place: a paperweight to hold down all the letters he will send her. She and her mother talk, her mother explaining that Dieter was a friend with whom she could share poems, books, and ideas when Papa was too busy with his work. The two are affectionately reconciled. That night when Inge closes her eyes, she walks "hand in hand with Dieter through dream-meadows, fields and woods."

A lonely young girl, grieving for her twin sister, becomes infatuated with a young man who is attracted to her mother. Dieter fulfills Inge's mother's need for sympathetic companionship but Inge, sensing a rival for Dieter's attentions, resents the relationship—an innocent but romantic one. Underlying the triangle is the story of a family trying to regain its balance after a death. Taking place in Germany and told by Inge, this is an introspective, skillfully written mixture of atmosphere, relationships, and feelings. Delicate drawings give a period flavor to the book, one of several about Inge and her family and friends.

Ages 8-10

**Also available in:**
No other form known

## 671

**Voigt, Cynthia**

**Dicey's Song**

Atheneum Publishers, 1982.
(196 pages)

---

FAMILY: Relationships
  Death: of mother
  Grandparent: living in home of
  Love, meaning of
  Parental: absence
  School: achievement/underachievement
  School: classmate relationships
  Sibling: relationships
  Talents: musical

---

Dicey Tillerman, thirteen, and her younger brothers and sister have been living with Gram since their mother abandoned them and later entered a mental institution. To help out, Dicey gets an after-school job. Gram plans to adopt the children and will register for welfare because she must, although she hates taking charity. Maybeth, eight, has always been considered retarded by everyone but the family. As usual, she's not doing well in school. Dicey believes Maybeth is only shy and slow, but even long, hard hours of studying don't improve her reading. However, Mr. Lingerle, the music teacher, considers Maybeth extremely talented, and he wants her to take piano lessons. So Dicey uses the income from her job to pay for the lessons. Later, Mr. Lingerle offers to give Maybeth an extra lesson each week at no charge. Dicey herself is prickly with everyone except her family. A classmate, Mina, picks Dicey for her science lab partner and tries in vain to make friends with her. After school Dicey often sees Jeff, a tenth grader, sitting on the steps playing his guitar and singing. But when he makes overtures to her, she always finds some excuse to leave. Dicey also chafes at having to take home ec. instead of the mechanical drawing she wanted. After school conferences, Gram decides that she and Dicey will go into the city, do some necessary winter shopping, and discuss the conferences. She buys Dicey a beautiful dress, definitely a luxury, and then reports what she learned at school. James, ten, is extremely intelligent, but he turned in an inferior paper to avoid his peers' teasing and seems to have trouble making friends. Seven-year-old Sammy's "problem" is that he is too well-behaved in school; he's not being himself, and Gram and Dicey worry about him. Maybeth is still not learning, and her teacher mentioned special tutors. Gram is a little concerned about Dicey too, but Dicey assures her that she knows what she needs to about sex and isn't interested in boys yet. At Dicey's request, James begins researching reading methods to find out why Maybeth can't read and if another teaching method would help her. He decides that she probably could learn if he taught her phonetically. He spends evenings tutoring her, and gradually Maybeth begins reading more easily and fluently. Sammy begins coming home looking as if he's been in a fight, but nobody can find out why he's fighting. Then Dicey gets an F in home ec., although she's done all the assignments. Her attitude seems to have hurt her. Even more of a shock is her C+ in English. She discovers that the English teacher believes she plagiarized an essay she wrote about Momma. Mina defends Dicey and the teacher eventually apologizes, giving her an A+ on the paper and an A on her report card. When Dicey tells Gram about the experience, Gram asks her not to stop reaching out to people just because she got her hand slapped this time. Sammy's fighting continues. Mina suggests that Sammy is defending Gram's name. Gram has something of a reputation as an eccentric and if Sammy's friends have been making fun of her, he may be fighting them over it. One day Gram shows up at the schoolyard with a bag of old marbles she found in the attic. She teaches Sammy and his friends how to really play, winning all their marbles from them. The troublemakers are impressed by Gram, and Sammy's fighting ends. That night at dinner Gram announces that the adoption papers have gone through and they are now officially her children. Mina and Dicey discuss the future; Dicey is impressed with Mina's determination to choose her future freely, not fall into something because she is black and female. Then they get word that Momma is dying. Gram and Dicey go to Boston to see her. They hold the sick woman's hand and talk to her, although Momma is unconscious. When she dies, they can't afford to have her body taken back home and so have her cremated. At home, they bury her ashes under the old mulberry tree. Dicey ponders Gram's reflection that, although Momma is gone, she's home at last.

Four children living with their grandmother learn the give-and-take of family life. The oldest, Dicey, learns what it means to let go, to reach out, and to hold on to those she loves. In this sequel to *Homecoming* (the story of the children's long, hard walk to Gram's house), all four children meet school and family problems with courage, humor, and perseverance. When Gram decides to adopt them with all the attendant worry, fear, and inconvenience, she does so determined to hold on to her grandchildren as she didn't her own three children. Readers familiar with the first book will be delighted to meet the Tillerman children again, and newcomers will be drawn into their world of strong values and family commitment. This is a richly rewarding story.

Ages 11 and up

**Also available in:**
Braille—*Dicey's Song*
Library of Congress (NLSBPH)

Cassette—*Dicey's Song*
Library of Congress (NLSBPH)

Film—*Dicey's Song*
Walt Disney Productions

Paperbound—*Dicey's Song*
Ballantine Books, Inc.

## 672

Voigt, Cynthia

**Homecoming**

Atheneum Publishers, 1981.
(312 pages)

---

*ABANDONMENT*
*DEPENDENCE/INDEPENDENCE*
   *Change: accepting*
   *Determination*
   *Family: unity*
   *Grandparent: living in home of*
   *Relatives: living in home of*
   *Sibling: relationships*

---

The last thing Momma says to the children before she abandons them in a shopping mall parking lot in Peewauket, Connecticut, is that they should mind Dicey. After waiting a night and a day for Momma to return, thirteen-year-old Dicey and her younger brothers and sister—James, Sammy, and Maybeth—begin walking to Bridgeport where their Great-Aunt Cilla lives. They have only a few dollars and a map that Dicey buys. James remembers that their father left them just before Sammy was born. He wonders if "we're the kind that people go off from." Through summer days of hot, hungry walking, their nights spent in parks, Dicey cares for her family. When all the money is gone, they earn more by carrying bags of groceries for shoppers. One rainy night a college student named Windy treats them to a meal and becomes interested in their story. His roommate, Stewart, offers to drive them the remaining distance to Bridgeport. But first the matter of James stealing twenty dollars from Stewart must be resolved. The boy has turned to stealing several times, despite Dicey's disapproval, and defiantly resists seeing it as wrong. Stewart says James owes it to himself, not to anyone else, to be honest. When they arrive in

Bridgeport they discover that Great-Aunt Cilla is dead. Her daughter, Cousin Eunice, doesn't know quite what to do with the children. She calls in her friend, Father Joseph, who makes plans for them. He will arrange to have someone check on their only other living relative, their maternal grandmother. He'll also contact the police so a missing-person report can be filed on their mother. In the meantime, James will go to a school camp and Maybeth and Sammy to a day camp. Although James is very bright and the school is pleased with him, the nuns find Maybeth slow and Sammy hostile. The priest tells Dicey she should think about adoption or foster homes for herself and the children. Cousin Eunice, who has been on the point of becoming a nun, says she will sacrifice her wishes and adopt the children herself. Dicey makes a little money from the sale of the car Momma abandoned along with the children. She also finds work washing windows. When the question of putting Maybeth in a special school and Sammy in a foster home becomes more immediate, Dicey decides she must go to their grandmother, apparently an acid-tongued recluse living in Crisfield, Maryland. The other children insist on going with her. With the money Dicey has saved, they set off on a bus. After various adventures, including traveling with a circus for a time, they finally arrive in Crisfield. Their grandmother is anything but welcoming, but Dicey is determined to stay and makes her plans. They begin immediately to work on their grandmother's badly neglected farm, pulling down overgrown honeysuckle bushes, repairing the screens and the back steps. Each night their grandmother acts as if it's their last, and each day the children find more work to do. Dicey refuses to let their grandmother mistreat the children: Sammy is not to be sent to bed without supper; Maybeth is not to be referred to as retarded. The grandmother seems to accept Dicey's stand, although she is not used to being crossed. Eventually, she explains to Dicey why she won't keep the children. She was married to an extremely domineering man for a long time and always obeyed him. Now she's gotten a taste of freedom and likes doing things her own way. She also feels she failed her own three children, and she doesn't want any more failure. However, she "temporarily" registers the children for school. Dicey is to start junior high, James is put in a program for gifted students, and Sammy will be in second grade. Maybeth has already repeated first grade, and her former school had strongly suggested she repeat second. But the Crisfield school counselor decides to test her in an effort to move her into third grade. While Maybeth is taking her tests, James suggests to his grandmother that she raise something to support them and pay the taxes on her farm: Christmas trees, chickens, pigs, or vegetables. Grandmother and Dicey go to the grocery store and Grandmother abruptly asks Millie, the widowed store owner, if she gets Social Security, something Grandmother has never applied for. Millie convinces Grandmother that there's nothing shameful about a widow's pension. On the way home, they all congratulate Maybeth for being promoted to third grade, and Dicey advises their grandmother to let them live with her. The old woman finally capitulates. She'll check into adoption procedures, Social Security pensions, and the possibilities of growing Christmas trees. The children are home at last.

V

Four children, led by the exceptionally resourceful Dicey, cope with the practical and emotional problems of being abandoned by their mother. Dicey loves her siblings, defends them, and finally wins them all a home with their sharp-tongued grandmother, whose life is changed through the children's determination to be accepted. Deft, strong characterizations and superbly developed relationships distinguish this story. Particularly noteworthy is the forcefully independent character of Dicey. This memorable odyssey is one of those rare books that can truly inspire readers. The story of Dicey and her family is continued in the sequel, *Dicey's Song*.

Ages 11 and up

**Also available in:**
Braille—*Homecoming*
Library of Congress (NLSBPH)

Cassette—*Homecoming*
Library of Congress (NLSBPH)

Film—*Homecoming*
Walt Disney Productions

Paperbound—*Homecoming*
Fawcett World Library

## 673

**Waber, Bernard**

**You're a Little Kid with a Big Heart**
Color illustrations by the author.
Houghton Mifflin Company, 1980.
(48 pages)

*MATURATION*
*WISHES*
   *Self, attitude toward: accepting*

Seven-year-old Octavia Blesswink finds a magic kite caught in a tree. It promises to grant her a wish if she frees it. She does so and wishes to be grown up, free to decide for herself what she wants and does not want to do. Suddenly she is thirty-nine, all grown up. For a while she is happy. But her mother and father are not, though both treat her as an adult. That night Octavia watches television until very late, eating until she is half sick. When she wakes the next morning, all the things she loves—stuffed animals, toys, games, rocking chair—are gone. Her mother put them away, thinking an adult wouldn't need or want them. Her friends think she's lucky, but then decide never to play with such an old person again. One friend doesn't even recognize her; he calls her "ma'am" and flees in terror when she threatens to twist his arm for calling her that. Soon Octavia is bored. She looks for work but has no skills, and she longs for her lost childhood. Several days later she sees the magic kite, again caught in a tree. Again she frees it and gets her wish: to be seven again. At home, her prized possessions are restored. She insists she will never again want to be an adult, but her parents tell her that in time she will be ready and happy to grow up. For now, though, they are all glad Octavia is a child.

A little girl is granted a familiar childhood wish, to be grown up, but finds that adulthood is not a state she

wants to live in—not yet, anyway. Lively illustrations and charming characters enhance this warm, wise book, presenting a view of the adult world bound to produce discussion.

Ages 5-7

**Also available in:**
No other form known

## 674

**Wade, Anne**

**A Promise Is for Keeping**
Color photographs by Jon Petersson.
Children's Press, Inc., 1979.
(30 pages)

*PROMISE, KEEPING*
   *Friendship: meaning of*
   *Trust/Distrust*

While collecting stones at the beach one day, Susan and Kathy, about nine, find a beautiful bracelet in the sand. They decide to share it, each of them wearing it for a week at a time. Susan thinks that maybe a week is too long; perhaps every other day would be better. But Kathy says a week isn't that long. She'll go first, she announces, and promises to let Susan have the bracelet the next week. Susan wants to know what will happen if Kathy forgets, but Kathy says she won't. They shake hands. Later, Kathy's father suggests they run an ad to find the bracelet's owner. They do, but no one responds. Kathy wears the bracelet, polishes it lovingly every night, and at the end of her week decides she doesn't want to give it up. After all, she saw it first and it's she who's been taking such good care of it. On Sunday she goes to the park to avoid Susan. Monday she goes to the playground. When she gets home she finds a note from Susan saying that since Kathy has broken her promise, they are no longer friends. Although Kathy is angry, she knows that Susan is right. But she decides she doesn't care about the friendship. Very soon, however, Kathy is lonely. She waits several days for Susan to come for the bracelet, but she doesn't. Kathy discovers that wearing the bracelet isn't as much fun as it used to be. Finally she takes the bracelet to Susan's house and apologizes. She offers to let Susan keep it for a month, or even two. Susan wants to know how she can believe what Kathy says. Kathy assures her that "a promise is a promise. And a promise is for keeping."

Two young girls discover the effects of a broken promise on their friendship. One of the most common effects is brought out clearly: the distrust created. Without being moralistic, the book allows children to see a broken promise in the context of a broken relationship. The full-page photographs seem somewhat posed, but they work fairly well. Although as a story this is meager, it would be suitable material to promote discussion.

Ages 4-7

**Also available in:**
Paperbound—*A Promise Is for Keeping*
Children's Press, Inc.

## 675

**Wallace, Bill**

## A Dog Called Kitty

Holiday House, Inc., 1980.
(153 pages)

---

*COURAGE, MEANING OF*
*FEAR: of Animals*
*PETS: Love for*
    *Death: of pet*
    *Fear: of physical harm*

---

Bitten and mauled by a rabid dog when he was small, Ricky, now in fifth grade, has been terrified by all dogs ever since. Though he has suppressed memories of the attack, he recalls vividly the pain of the rabies shots. Ricky's friend Brad admits he is afraid of spiders and invites Ricky to make friends with his own gentle dog. Ricky will not. When a puppy appears on Ricky's farm, a bedraggled, hungry stray, the boy reacts in panic to the little dog's friendliness. Later he finds the puppy in the barn, obviously starving. Though he decides to let it die, he cannot sleep. He takes the puppy table scraps and somehow makes himself touch it, moving the animal nearer the food. Soon he is feeding the dog by hand three times a day, never admitting he is going to keep it. His parents are aware of the situation, but keep silent. Soon the puppy chases the farm cats from their food, coming whenever anyone calls "Kitty." Ricky cannot admit his love for the dog, now named Kitty, but they are inseparable. He and his father build a pen to protect Kitty from the poisoned meat that area ranchers have left for the wild dogs preying on their livestock. But the puppy climbs out of the pen and, when they cover the top, digs beneath the walls. Ricky realizes Kitty will eat the poisoned meat if he is not taught to eat only from his dish. So he trains the puppy by scattering meat filled with hot peppers. Then Ricky's father is called away from the farm, and Ricky and his mother undertake the chores. One day Ricky finds a heifer and her newborn calf surrounded by wild dogs. Kitty challenges the pack but Ricky flees, the old panic overwhelming him. He trips and hears his dog in a fight for its life. Without thinking, he grabs a large stick and races to save Kitty. He breaks one dog's back and cripples another, but then is pulled down from behind. Kitty and Ricky manage to drive the dogs off, but Ricky is sure his savagely bitten dog is dead. Suddenly Kitty wags his tail and licks the boy's face. The two are bandaged and treated like returning heroes. Fortunately, the wild dogs were not rabid. Soon after, Ricky makes friends with oil drillers working nearby. One day, when they're unloading a pipe from a truck, Kitty runs underneath and the pipe falls and crushes him. Ricky feels a part of him has died too, but he hides his feelings. His parents give him a birthday party but he is uninterested, eager for it to end so he can be alone with his sorrow. Suddenly they hear dogs fighting in the barn and find a large dog mauling a puppy—another hungry, unwanted puppy. Ricky drives the big dog off. Later, he hears the cats attacking the puppy and sees it run for the barn. He laughs heartily, for the first time since Kitty's death, and takes food to the puppy.

A boy of good sense and good heart overcomes his fear of dogs when a stray wins his loyalty and affection. This first-person narrative is convincing: Ricky's changing emotions seem realistic, his concern for the new puppy touching and believable. Dog lovers especially will enjoy this exciting and affecting story.

Ages 9-11

**Also available in:**
No other form known

## 676

**Wallace-Brodeur, Ruth**

## The Kenton Year

Atheneum Publishers, 1980.
(93 pages)

---

*CHANGE: Accepting*
*DEATH: of Father*
    *Change: new home*
    *Friendship: making friends*
    *Mourning, stages of*

---

When her father is struck and killed by a truck, Mandy McPherson is overwhelmed by grief. The nine-year-old grows fearful and insecure, afraid to let her mother out of her sight, afraid to go to school. Her mother, Anne, hoping that a vacation in the small house where she herself grew up in Kenton, Vermont, will help Mandy, takes a summer leave of absence from her Boston newspaper job. In Kenton, Mandy and Anne make new friends: Carrie Marquand and her two brothers; Martin Wechsler, the editor of the local paper; and Shandee, the town eccentric, a gentle, independent recluse who takes a special interest in Mandy. One neighbor, Mr. Neele, is tight-fisted and condescending, always checking up on Shandee and making him look incompetent. To get back at him, Mandy and the Marquands, at Mandy's suggestion, take apart his heavy, slat-sided trailer and reassemble it on his garage roof. Mandy is nearly caught when she sneaks back to leave a dime and a note saying, "A dime to make you feel better," the very words Mr. Neele used to express his "sympathy" for the loss of her father. When the summer ends, to Mandy's delight her mother quits her job with the Boston newspaper, takes a job with Martin Wechsler, and makes arrangements to buy the house they are renting. Mandy enjoys her small country school with fourteen other children of varying ages. Ordinarily, celebrating her birthday without her father, who had always planned extravagant displays, would have been difficult for Mandy. But her mother and their friends surprise her with a lavish tenth-birthday picnic. As winter descends, Martin Wechsler buys skis for Mandy and her mother, allowing them mobility over the snowbound countryside. Christmas, a sorrowful time of remembering, is made special when good friends come together for tree trimming and sleigh rides. Mandy proves to have a natural ability on skis, and Martin convinces her to enter the Crawford County Winter Carnival competition. Training vigorously, she suddenly feels driven to be in the top ten. Her concerned mother and Martin decide this obsession is helping Mandy heal her hurt over her father's death. When she comes in sixth, she is exhausted but satisfied. Then a heckling student introduces Mandy to the idea of a romance between her mother and Martin. Although she isn't enthusiastic about the idea, she doesn't reject it entirely. In early spring Mandy brings home a chunk of wood from Shandee and spends days secretly carving it. On March 23, the anniversary of her father's death, she invites her mother to a special ceremony held at her favorite outdoor place. There she pounds her hand-carved sign into the soft ground, officially declaring the spot the William Clough McPherson Hill. She has made a special place in her new life for her father's memory.

This is a gently humorous, low-key story of how a young girl and her mother deal with the loss of a father and husband. Readers are eased with Mandy through the painful stages of grief as she begins, at first fearful and insecure, to develop new strengths and find happiness in her own way. Her decision to create a memorial for her father represents the final stage of healing.

Ages 9-11

**Also available in:**
No other form known

### 677

**Wallace-Brodeur, Ruth**

## One April Vacation

Atheneum Publishers, 1981.
(80 pages)

---

*DEATH: Attitude Toward*
*FEAR: of Death*
  *Maturation*
  *Superstition*

---

The loss of a nose hair on a quiet April Sunday sends nine-year-old Kate into a panic: smart Harlan Atwater announces that such a loss spells death in one week for the affected person. Although Kate knows this is silly, too silly to discuss with adults, she also fears it might be true. Troubled on this first day of her week-long spring break, Kate pays a visit to her vibrant, eighty-two-year-old Aunt Melindy. They discuss death; Aunt Melindy says that in her last days she would "be sure to do just the things that pleased me most." Kate decides to adopt this philosophy during her final week on earth. On the way home from her aunt's she rescues a cat from a group of boys tormenting it. Kate names the cat Arthur and takes it home, even though her mother has always refused a pet. To Kate's surprise and delight, her mother agrees to let Arthur stay. The next day, Kate decides that what she most wants is for her two best friends to come over, meet Arthur, and play with her in the attic. Their games culminate in the spooky speculation that a young girl was hanged in that very attic. But Kate says nothing to her parents because "parents could think up good explanations for anything." Watching her father repairing their family tent makes Kate think of past summer vacations and how much she will miss them when she's dead. The week goes by quickly and holds many adventures. One day Kate decides to bury some treasured mementos in a tin box, only to discover when she digs that another girl had the same idea in 1949. She puts the girl's old tin back in the ground along with her own and thinks, "It was good to get your affairs in order, no

matter what." On Friday she decides that just once she wants to beat her older sister, Allison, at something. Settling on badminton, Kate achieves her goal and Allison stalks off angrily, just as Kate usually does. Later, Kate shares a popsicle with her sister to soothe hard feelings, deciding that "things had changed." On Saturday, with only one day left, Kate feels grumpy and unable to focus on anything. She goes for a walk and spots the abandoned grange building. Suddenly she knows this is the day she will do what she has always been too frightened to do, what her friends consider a real mark of courage—she will jump off the grange roof. In bed later with a broken arm, Kate tells her mother she jumped because "I wanted to prove I could do it. It seemed the right thing." The next day Kate grows sullen and retreats to her room to watch the clock as the hour of her supposed death draws near. The time passes without mishap, to her great relief. Much later, when she tells her family about that week, she is pleased by their approval of her behavior. Aunt Melindy comments, "Death can get you anytime. You can be proud that you didn't just sit around waiting for it." Kate knows her aunt's advice helped her through a very trying week.

In this story of personal growth, a young girl decides to live her supposed last week to the fullest. In the process, Kate gains confidence in her own abilities and resourcefulness. Though Kate's fear of death is serious, the story's tone is light, in keeping with the comical origin of the death prophecy. Kate gets good advice from her spritely aunt, who has always been a source of inspiration and understanding. Because she uses her time so wisely and in one week accomplishes so many personal victories, the girl feels changed by the entire episode and views death differently than she had a week earlier. This aspect of the story might be helpful with children who are working through a fear of death.

Ages 9-11

**Also available in:**
No other form known

### 678

**Wartski, Maureen Crane**

## A Boat to Nowhere

Black/white illustrations by Dick Teicher.
The Westminster Press, 1980.
(191 pages)

---

*COURAGE, MEANING OF*
*LOVE, MEANING OF*
*REFUGEES*
*VIETNAM*
  *Age: respect for*
  *Belonging*
  *Maturation*

---

Mai, about twelve, and her younger brother, Loc, are Vietnamese war orphans. Years ago, the two fled their city with their grandfather, Van Chi, and came to live in a small village at the southern tip of Vietnam. Now fourteen-year-old Kien has arrived at the village, living "by his wits," traveling from town to town just a few steps ahead of the New Government officials. Van Chi, who has become the revered teacher and headman of the isolated village, listens uneasily while Kien tells of resettlement camps, economic zones, and dislocation. Bewildered by Kien's stories, Mai senses that her people's simple way of life is threatened. She resents the attention and credence her grandfather gives Kien; unlike her brother, who is Kien's friend immediately, Mai is suspicious. But gradually she comes to trust him, and the three young people become friends. One day, returning from a fishing trip, they find that officials of the New Government have arrived, bringing turmoil to the village. The officials accuse Van Chi of treason, set fire to the old man's books, and announce that he will be taken away to be "reeducated." With Kien's help, the grandfather, Mai, and Loc escape through the forest and set sail for Thailand in the village fishing boat, the *Sea Breeze.* Van Chi navigates the boat by the stars and sun, but they are beset by storms and thrown off course. Lost and without food, the four grow weak. Grandfather develops a serious cough and fever. Their joy at sighting Thailand is quickly squelched when Thai officials turn them away, refusing to accept more refugees. They must set sail for Malaysia, but their journey seems hopeless. As Van Chi's sickness worsens, Kien recognizes that he alone is responsible for the crew's fate. Overtaken by the worst storm yet and attacked by pirates, the four manage to survive and to reach land once more. But Outcast Island proves to be an evil place, controlled by Bác Thong, headman of a small band of Vietnamese refugees, who pretends kindness but actually covets their boat. The children narrowly escape with the dying old man. At sea again, the four are without food or medicine. Mai sickens. When Kien, weak and discouraged, spots a ship on the horizon, he swims toward the vessel but finds that the sailors on board intend to save only him. Unable to desert his helpless friends, Kien lets go of the lifeline and swims back to the *Sea Breeze.* Van Chi, dying, asks Kien to remain with Mai and Loc and see that they return someday to Vietnam. Kien declares that he owes allegiance to no one, but Van Chi insists that Mai and Loc are Kien's family now. "None of us choose to be born into a family," says the old man. "Nor do we choose those we come to love." Van Chi dies, and the three children bury him at sea. Mai is now delirious. Disheartened, Kien lets the *Sea Breeze* drift aimlessly. He prays that he, Mai, and Loc may die together, quickly and painlessly. But an American ship sights the craft and rescues them. After the ship's doctor reassures Kien that Mai will recover from her illness, the boy at last feels safe. He falls asleep between clean sheets, happy that he has not failed Grandfather Van Chi.

Victims of the dislocation of war, four people search for a haven in this engrossing, fast-paced account. Along the way, a solitary young man gains a family he can love and respect. Somewhat stilted dialogue and intrusive English translations of Vietnamese phrases (the glossary provides translation enough) mar the story's impact at times. But young people will learn much here about the plight of Vietnamese refugees. Evocative illustrations depict Vietnamese culture; especially valuable is a map of the characters' journey. The story of Kien, Mai, and Loc continues in the sequel, *A Long Way from Home.*

Ages 9-12

**Also available in:**
Cassette—*A Boat to Nowhere*
Library of Congress (NLSBPH)

Paperbound—*A Boat to Nowhere*
New American Library

### 679

**Wartski, Maureen Crane**

**The Lake Is On Fire**
The Westminster Press, 1981.
(130 pages)

ANIMALS: Love for
BLINDNESS
LOSS: Feelings of
   Change: resisting
   Courage, meaning of
   Fear: of the unknown
   Suicide: attempted

After an automobile accident that blinds him and kills his best friend, Leo, thirteen-year-old Ricky attempts suicide by slashing his wrists. His life is saved, but he remains deeply depressed. At the request of his parents, family friends Sol and Deidre take Ricky and their newest "orphan," King, a severely mistreated German shepherd named King, to their rented mountain cabin for a few weeks. The boy, apathetic and withdrawn, silently dwells on memories of past summers spent with Leo at this same cabin. He hates everything about it now, especially the snarling dog he fears. One evening, recognizing that Ricky may need to be alone, Sol and Deidre offer him the option of staying at the cabin while they go into town the next day. Then Sol tells Ricky about King's mistreatment, confident that King can learn to trust again. Ricky does not share his optimism. Choosing to stay alone the next day, Ricky listens as gathering thunder promises a much-needed rainstorm. Then a deafening crash sends Ricky outside only moments before the cabin is crushed by a falling pine. King's leash has snapped and he is free of his post. Ricky quickly grabs the leash, now forced to rely on the dog's eyes. A panicked King drags Ricky through trees and brush, and the boy begins to despair of finding any familiar landmarks. When he yells at King, the dog suddenly stops and will not move. So Ricky sets out on his own, soon falling into a large hole left by a fallen tree. King helps him out. Hot, tired, and thirsty, Ricky presses on with King, hoping to find water. Suddenly he hears a creek, and King hurries toward it. Thirst quenched, Ricky falls asleep. When he awakes and calls King, the dog is gone. "How right he had been not to trust that treacherous, mean, vicious canine!" thinks Ricky. But King returns and rescues Ricky from an attacking fisher, a weasel-like animal, getting himself wounded in the process. Painfully they make their way to a nearby lake, only minutes ahead of a raging forest fire. Several times, Ricky is ready to give up—the smoke and pain are too much—but King pulls him on. Even when they reach the lake King is restless, pushing Ricky out further into the water, where still smoke chokes them and smoldering bits of branch fly into their faces. At one point Ricky dives underwater with King to escape a falling tree.

**W**

Then he pushes the exhausted King onto a log, kicking until he has no more strength. At last a helicopter arrives. The rangers tell Ricky they can only come down once because of the dangerous wind currents and they cannot take the dog. Directed by the men, Ricky swims for the rescue line and wrestles to get the loop over his shoulder. He feels King at his side and suddenly grabs the dog. The men warn him that the dog will struggle and pull him down, but Ricky shouts, "I'm not going without him!" He hangs on, calmly steadying King with his voice, and they make it into the helicopter. Safe at last, headed for his family and friends, Ricky hears the rescuers marvel at his and King's survival. He "ached all over. His face was burned raw, his hair all singed off, and it hurt to breathe. He felt wonderful!"

A boy's numb despair over his own blindness and the death of his friend lifts when he embarks on a dangerous trek through a burning forest, forced to rely on the eyes of a dog he fears. During their treacherous journey to the lake, Ricky learns to trust again and recovers his will to live. This is an exciting, affecting, slightly sentimental story that animal lovers will especially enjoy. The development of a trusting relationship between Ricky and King is satisfying and believable. Ricky's feelings about the accident that has changed his life aren't explored in great depth, but what's there is realistically presented.

Ages 10-13

**Also available in:**
Paperbound—*The Lake Is On Fire*
New American Library

## 680

Wartski, Maureen Crane

**A Long Way from Home**

The Westminster Press, 1980.
(155 pages)

---

*REFUGEES*
*VIETNAM*
  *Belonging*
  *Bully: being bothered by*
  *Hostility*
  *Immigrants*
  *Prejudice: ethnic/racial*

---

Kien Ho, a fifteen-year-old Vietnamese refugee now living in the United States, struggles to adapt to American attitudes and habits. As a consequence of his promise to their dying grandfather during a sea crossing, Kien has become the adopted brother of Mai and Loc, two orphaned Vietnamese children. The three live with their sponsor family, the Olsons, in Bradley, California. Though Mai and Loc have readily adjusted to their new home and school, Kien cannot confide in the Olsons and is the target of the taunts and harassment of a racist bully at school. When he is physically attacked for the second time by the bully and two other boys, Kien, reverting to the fighting tactics that helped him survive when fleeing Vietnam, throws a rock at the bully, hitting his eye and injuring him seriously. Later, a witness verifies to the police and to the boy's furious—and equally racist—father that Kien had acted in self-

defense. Still, Kien is sure he has ruined his chances in Bradley and with the Olsons. Convinced that everyone will be better off without him, he decides to move to another, more congenial, place. An old newspaper account of a happy Vietnamese settlement in the California fishing town of Travor leads him there. Instead of the peaceful existence Kien expects, however, he and all the Vietnamese in Travor encounter intolerance and hatred from the local fishermen. Wealthy, influential Paul Orrin convinces the American fishermen in the town that they cannot make a living if the Vietnamese continue selling their catches at lower prices. Amid the resulting violence directed at the Vietnamese, Orrin sets fire to his own boat and then sees that a Vietnamese man is charged with arson. With a promise not to press charges, Orrin forces the Vietnamese fishermen to sell their boats to him. Only Kien knows of Orrin's blackmail and arson but feels powerless to prove it: he was out walking near the boats that night and heard a deep laugh just as the flames burst out. Later, when he heard Orrin laugh, he recognized him as the arsonist. On the night before the Vietnamese are to leave Travor, Kien rescues Orrin from a burning boat that had been struck by lightning, getting injured in the process. Hospitalized, Kien uses his new status as hero and his secret knowledge about Orrin to bring the leaders of the warring groups together in an attempt to work out their differences. After the turmoil ends, Kien finds himself thinking of Mai, Loc, and the Olsons. With life back to normal in Travor, he feels something is missing in his own life. As warm memories flood over him, he decides to return to Bradley, his home.

A young Vietnamese refugee, struggling to find a place for himself in an often-inhospitable America, comes to accept and draw strength from the love of his adopted family in this exciting, if at times melodramatic, sequel to *A Boat to Nowhere*. Occasionally stilted dialogue doesn't always ring true, but the characters are believable and the accounts of bigotry realistic. The story evokes sympathy and understanding for the plight of America's Vietnamese immigrants.

Ages 11-13

**Also available in:**
Paperbound—*A Long Way from Home*
New American Library

## 681

Wartski, Maureen Crane

**My Brother Is Special**

The Westminster Press, 1979.
(152 pages)

---

*FAMILY: Relationships*
*MENTAL RETARDATION*
  *Animals: love for*
  *Change: new home*
  *Honesty/Dishonesty*
  *Peer relationships*
  *School: transfer*
  *Sibling: love for*
  *Success*

---

Noni Harlow is an eighth-grade girl with a talent for running. She has recently joined the track team at Conan Junior High in Conan, Massachusetts. She and her family, originally from California, had first moved to another east-coast town, Lincoln. But both Noni and Kip, her nine-year-old retarded brother, had disliked their schools. Kip had even tried to run away. When their father was transferred to Conan, Noni hoped life would soon be good again. But then she met Denise Baxley—popular, pretty, smart, and the captain of the track team. Noni had sought Denise's friendship, but from their first meeting Denise made cutting remarks about Kip. Now it is the morning of the interscholastic meet with Franklin. Noni wakes up knowing she is going to beat Denise in the 100-yard dash. When she arrives at the track, Red Balkans, the girls' coach, is telling her team about the Special Olympics for handicapped and retarded children. Denise and her friends do not lose this opportunity to taunt Noni about her "special" brother. An angry Noni is very pleased when she does beat Denise in the race. When Kip sees her ribbon he insists on having it, and Noni realizes that Kip believes he'll never win anything. She decides that Kip must compete in the Special Olympics. The local meet will be held in a few weeks at the school for retarded children at Haymarket. Noni gets some pamphlets from her coach and waits for a chance to discuss the idea with her parents. They have had a growing conflict about Kip since his bad school experience in Lincoln. The father wants to push Kip out into the world and make him achieve. Mrs. Harlow wants to protect him and keep him from getting hurt again. On one issue, however, they agree: Kip should not compete in the Special Olympics. They don't want to subject him to such an experience. But Noni is determined to give Kip his moment of victory. She will train him herself. Kip's secret workouts start at the beach, where he finds a gull caught in an oil spill. He loves birds and insists on taking it home. With the help of Denise, whose mother heads the local ecology group, and Neill Oliver, Denise's sympathetic boyfriend, Noni and Kip clean the oil off the bird and devise a hammock in which to suspend it until its broken legs heal. Noni continues Kip's training, often in the garage so he can stay with Bird. Then a newspaper article about Mrs. Baxley, "A Lady with a Heart," reveals Noni's plan for Kip and compares Kip's efforts to those of the bird trying to get well; the Baxley children had told the reporter the story in their mother's absence. Noni's angry parents grow even more incensed when they discover she has forged both her father's and their doctor's signatures on the entry form. But when they realize how desperately Noni wants to do this for her brother and what a good runner he has become, they forgive and support her. This change, along with the increasing attentions of Neill Oliver, makes Noni very happy. Her pleasure is marred only by Denise's continuing harassment. Noni knows exactly whom to blame when, on the morning of the race, Kip discovers Bird's hammock torn to shreds and the gull flapping its wings on the floor. This so upsets Kip that he must be medicated to calm him down. The family takes

him to Haymarket, but does not plan to let him race. Kip, however, sneaks away and runs the course behind the others. His determination wins him everyone's admiration; he is a "real winner." Noni wins too when she comes to see Denise as a lonely girl who can only please her demanding parents by being best at everything. She even hopes that someday they'll be friends. Bird survives and the family makes plans to set him free.

A young teenage girl loves her retarded brother and cannot understand those who talk about handicapped and retarded people as though they are "creatures from another planet." Noni wants to prove to everyone, including Kip himself, that he can be a winner too. Along the way she comes to understand the reasons behind a classmate's hostility. Character development is slight here and the dialogue, situations, and conclusion are somewhat contrived. But the book has value in its emphasis on ways retarded people can succeed and in its examples of the varied responses retarded people can evoke from others. Sound information is given about the Special Olympics.

Ages 10-12

**Also available in:**
Cassette—*My Brother Is Special*
Library of Congress (NLSBPH)

Paperbound—*My Brother Is Special*
New American Library

**682**

**Watanabe, Shigeo**

**Get Set! Go!**

Color illustrations by Yasuo Ohtomo.
Philomel Books, 1981.
(28 pages)

*PERSEVERANCE*
*Success*

Bear starts the obstacle race by walking quickly along the beam. But, ouch, he falls off. When he swings on the bar, he lands on the mat with a thump. When he tries to jump over the horse, he lands on it instead. He heads into the tunnel but, oops! he exits from it backwards. Crawling under the net doesn't turn out very well either. But soon he's over the finish line. "Did I win?" he wants to know.

In this delightfully simple, cleverly illustrated read-aloud, Bear continues to follow an obstacle course in spite of mishaps along the way. Listeners may be encouraged to talk about times they have persevered. Setting the bear in a sports environment may be especially encouraging for children who shy away from sports because they don't feel "good enough."

Ages 3-5

**Also available in:**
Paperbound—*Get Set! Go!*
Philomel Books

W

**683**

Watanabe, Shigeo

## How Do I Put It On?

Color illustrations by Yasuo Ohtomo.
Philomel Books, 1979.
(28 pages)

---

*AUTONOMY*

---

A young bear says, "I can get dressed all by myself." He then holds up a shirt and asks, "Do I put it on like this?" He puts the shirt on his legs, answers "No!" and then demonstrates the correct way. He repeats his question and answer with pants, cap, and shoes, putting his arms in the pants, the cap on his foot, and the shoes on his ears. Finally, he gets dressed properly.

A bear illustrates the right and wrong way to put on shirt, pants, cap, and shoes in this first book of a series. Large, clear, softly colored illustrations will amuse and encourage children who are just learning to dress themselves. Many will enjoy "reading" the book independently.

Ages 2-5

**Also available in:**
Paperbound—*How Do I Put It On?*
Philomel Books

**684**

Watanabe, Shigeo

## I Can Ride It!

Color illustrations by Yasuo Ohtomo.
Translated from the Japanese.
Philomel Books, 1982.
(28 pages)

---

*GOALS*
*Perseverance*
*Success*

---

Little Bear can ride his tricycle by himself. He can also ride his two-wheeler with training wheels. Bear can even ride a skateboard—if he sits on it. He can roller skate just fine when he puts skates on his feet and on his hands. Bear can even drive a small toy car. Someday he hopes to drive a bus and maybe fly an airplane.

Bear tells and shows the read-aloud audience how he "masters" certain vehicles in this funny, colorful book, part of a series called "I Can Do It All By Myself." Each line of text faces a full-page illustration that shows Bear persisting in his attempts to keep from falling down. He never gives up and cheerfully continues to dream of further accomplishments.

Ages 2-5

**Also available in:**
Paperbound—*I Can Ride It!*
Philomel Books

**685**

Waterton, Betty Marie

## A Salmon for Simon

Color illustrations by Ann Blades.
Atheneum Publishers, 1980.
(28 pages counted)

---

*NATURE: Respect for*
*Animals: love for*
*Animals: responsibility for*
*Freedom, meaning of*
*Native American*
*Resourcefulness*

---

In September, near the west coast of Canada where young Simon lives, the salmon return from the sea to lay their eggs in the rivers and streams where they were born. Although Simon enjoys clam digging with his sisters, he wants more than anything to catch a salmon. All summer, every day, he tries and fails. So he decides to stop fishing, maybe forever. One day while walking along the beach digging clams, Simon looks up and sees a bald eagle with a salmon glistening in its talons. Excitedly, he flaps his arms and hops while screeching seagulls circle overhead. In all the excitement, the eagle drops the salmon and it lands with a splat in Simon's clam hole. Simon thinks Sukai, as he calls the salmon (from an Indian word meaning "king of the fish"), is the most beautiful thing he's ever seen. He watches with pity as Sukai tries to find his way out of the clam hole; he must find a way to save the salmon. So Simon decides to dig a channel to the sea. For hours he digs while his hands grow red and blistered and Sukai waits quietly. At last, when he can dig no more, he reaches the sea. He watches as Sukai feels the cold freshness and swims slowly down the channel. The salmon dives deep into the cool, green water and then gives one mighty leap as if to say thank-you to Simon. Exhausted, Simon returns to his home and supper. He decides he will go fishing tomorrow after all. "But not for a salmon."

This warm and simple story of a Canadian Indian boy who traps and then releases a salmon come to spawn speaks clearly of a child's sensitivity toward a living creature and the great satisfaction of having saved a life. The richly colored, full-page illustrations add much to the appealing tale.

Ages 4-7

**Also available in:**
No other form known

**686**

Weiman, Eiveen

**It Takes Brains**

Atheneum Publishers, 1982.
(261 pages)

---

BELONGING
  Education: special
  Friendship: making friends
  Loneliness
  Parental: absence
  School: achievement/underachievement
  School: classmate relationships

---

At eleven, Barbara Brainard feels lonely, unloved, depressed. Both her parents are doctors and seldom home. At school she's called Brains, but her report cards are always mediocre and teachers consider her lazy. Even attending an expensive private school doesn't make Barbara any more popular or successful. Then her parents move from California to Ohio, and one of her new teachers suspects Barbara may actually be very bright. She's put in Room 100, a group of fourth, fifth, and sixth graders who are considered gifted. In Room 100, students work on interesting projects of their own choosing, meet the terms of learning contracts they themselves write, and have special teachers for French, art, and music. Ned Ferris, one of Barbara's classmates and the nephew of the Brainards' housekeeper, talks Barbara into going sledding one Saturday and she's surprised at how much fun she has. Then Margery, another classmate, invites all the Room 100 girls to a slumber party where Barbara again has a good time. Barbara especially admires Ned, who studies hard in school and still holds down two part-time jobs. She helps him recover some shopping carts, for which he gets two dollars apiece, and then spends a delightful Saturday afternoon with his large family. The youngest, four-year-old Emily, has epilepsy and the others take special care of her. At the end of the year, Barbara herself has a very successful party. She decides to take French and computer classes during the summer, having discovered that she likes doing something more than just lazing around. She and Margery discuss Margery's older sisters, who both sought early marriages and have uninteresting jobs. Unlike them, Margery intends to be responsible for her own life. One day Margery, Barbara, and Ned discuss their families. Barbara feels her parents neglect her; she sees no sign of their love. Margery and Ned point out the different ways people express love and the drawbacks in their own families. The grass is always greener in someone else's family, they decide. While Barbara is baby-sitting for Emily, the little girl falls off a swing and is knocked unconscious. Barbara calls her father, who sends an ambulance. When a nonmalignant tumor is discovered, Barbara's father operates immediately and Emily begins her recovery. That same day is Barbara's twelfth birthday. Surrounded by good friends and parents who have lately been spending more time with her, Barbara awaits her next year in junior high with eagerness and confidence.

A bright but underachieving young girl finds a comfortable niche for herself at home and at school, largely due to her timely placement in a class for gifted children. Through the influence of her new friends, Barbara learns to compromise between what she wants from her busy parents and what they are able to give her. Not a particularly deep or thought-provoking book, this is nonetheless a realistic profile of an engaging, somewhat atypical eleven-year-old and touches on many feelings and situations that concern this age group: too-busy parents, loneliness, the need for peer acceptance, school difficulties, pets, moving, self-esteem.

Ages 10-12

**Also available in:**
No other form known

---

**687**

Weiss, Nicki

**Chuckie**

Color illustrations by the author.
Greenwillow Books, 1982.
(32 pages counted)

W

---

SIBLING: New Baby

---

Until Chuckie arrives, Lucy is a good little girl who makes her bed, puts away her toys, eats all her carrots, and helps her mother around the house. But in spite of her parents' obvious enchantment with Chuckie, Lucy thinks "he's just a dumb lump of baby." At first she thinks Chuckie will go away if she wishes hard enough, but he doesn't. Then she pretends he's not there. When he begins to grow hair, she tells her father that Chuckie seems to have a disease. Since Chuckie's arrival, Lucy hasn't made her bed, her toys are scattered all over her room, she leaves carrots on her plate, and she refuses to help around the house. Whenever she's naughty, she says Chuckie told her to do it. Her parents point out that Chuckie can't talk. She pulls the baby's hair, makes scary faces at him, and pushes him down in his crib. But Chuckie only laughs and giggles and wants to play some more. Her parents tell her that Chuckie likes her. Lucy wonders how they figured that out. Then Chuckie begins babbling, and Mama and Papa anxiously await his first word. Mama is sure it will be "Mama." Papa feels it certainly will be "Papa." But his first word is "Lucy"! From then on, things change. Lucy again makes her bed, puts away her toys, eats her carrots, and helps out. She also helps Chuckie make his bed and put away his toys. She even eats his carrots for him sometimes when no one is looking.

A little girl's resentment and hostility toward her baby brother are worn away by his persistent good humor and love for her. This funny and charmingly illustrated story will greatly appeal to the read-aloud audience. Despite the book's weaknesses—Lucy's parents' lack of awareness and concern about the child's feelings and behavior, the overly simple resolution—young children might be encouraged to discuss their own reactions to new siblings as they listen to Lucy's story.

Ages 3-6

**Also available in:**
Paperbound—*Chuckie*
Scholastic Book Services

## 688

### Weiss, Nicki

### Waiting

Color illustrations by the author.
Greenwillow Books, 1981.
(30 pages counted)

*PATIENCE/IMPATIENCE*
  *Nature: appreciation of*

Little Annalee walks with her mother, who's all dressed up, from the house to the gate. Before leaving, her mother closes the gate and tells Annalee to wait for her. Annalee watches until she can no longer see her mother. Soon she hears singing and is sure she's hearing her mother. But it is only a bird in a tree. With her eyes shut, Annalee sits in the grass and waits. Soon she smells something good and is sure she's smelling her mother. But it is the roses on the fence. When the grass rustles, Annalee is sure her mother is coming. It is only the wind blowing. As Annalee lies in the grass something tickles her. She is sure it is her mother. But it's only a ladybug on her leg. So Annalee begins to watch the clouds. She hears a noise by the gate, but ignores it. Then she hears a voice, her mother's, saying, "I bet you didn't even know I was gone."

A little girl waits outside for her mother to return. After mistaking the sounds, smells, and feelings she gets from the natural world for her returning mother, she becomes so absorbed in that world that her mother's actual return surprises her. Soft, colorful illustrations add to the quiet charm of this simple story. The read-aloud audience will sense the love between the lines.

Ages 3-5

**Also available in:**
No other form known

## 689

### Wells, Rosemary

### Timothy Goes to School

Color illustrations by the author.
The Dial Press, Inc., 1981.
(30 pages counted)

*SCHOOL: Entering*
  *Friendship: making friends*
  *Jealousy: peer*
  *School: classmate relationships*

On his first day of school Timothy excitedly hurries off in a new sunsuit with a new book and pencil. His teacher introduces him to a classmate, Claude. Claude promptly tells Timothy that nobody wears sunsuits on the first day of school. Upset, Timothy wishes Claude would fall in a puddle. At home Timothy tells his mother what Claude said. She makes him a new jacket for the second day of school, but Claude tells him he should not wear party clothes on the second day. Timothy goes home dejected. The next day Timothy wears his favorite shirt. But he is upstaged when Claude arrives wearing the same shirt. Timothy informs his mother that he won't be returning to school because he'll never measure up to Claude. Timothy does return to school, however, and there he meets Violet. Violet is mumbling, "I can't stand it anymore." When Timothy asks her what's wrong, she tells him she can't stand Grace, who can do anything. Timothy knows how she feels. During the day Timothy and Violet play together. Violet says, "I can't believe you've been here all along!" After school she invites Timothy home for a snack. On the way they laugh together about Claude and Grace.

Continually upstaged and second-guessed by a classmate, little Timothy is happy to make friends with Violet, who shares his feelings. Winning little animal characters in brightly colored illustrations add to the charm of this touching, funny story about some of the trials of entering school. Small children may find the book reassuring as they approach their own first days.

Ages 3-5

**Also available in:**
Paperbound—*Timothy Goes to School*
The Dial Press, Inc.

## 690

### Whelan, Gloria

### A Time to Keep Silent

G. P. Putnam's Sons, 1979.
(127 pages) o.p.

*FRIENDSHIP: Meaning of*
*LIFE STYLE: Change in*
*MUTENESS*
  *Change: resisting*
  *Child abuse*
  *Communication: parent-child*
  *Nature: living in harmony with*

After thirteen-year-old Clair Lothrop's mother dies, Claire stops talking "so my father would listen to me." Later that same evening, she suddenly finds she can't "utter a simple 'yes' or 'no' to save my life," and so it continues. Her distressed father, pastor of a large, affluent suburban church, resigns his post to start a mission in the isolated northern part of their state, hoping a change will help Clair. Also, such a mission effort has always been his dream. He promises Clair that they can return in six months if the move doesn't work out. During the first night in their little stone house, rustic and ill-equipped, Clair seeks the safety of their car to sleep. Soon, however, despite her silence, she strikes up a friendship with a girl her own age, Dorrie Norcher. Dorrie's mother is also dead and her father is a vicious bully, currently in jail for attempted arson. Her grandmother cares more for the welfare check Dorrie brings in than for the girl herself. So Dorrie has learned to survive on her own, escaping from her father's beatings by leaving their cellar house and going to her hideout in the woods. One day she takes Clair to this hideout, "a sort of teepee made of fir branches," cleverly concealed. Here she has blankets, water from the pond, and berry bushes nearby. Guinevere, her pet goat, comes also, but Dorrie keeps her on a rope, safe from poison plants and the many traps her father has set throughout the woods. While the girls spend days gathering lumber and building a room with a view of the pond on top of Dorrie's cellar house, Clair's father devotes himself to the old schoolhouse that's being turned into a church. When he learns that the girls are unsupervised, he promptly sends Clair on a weekend vacation with her aunt and uncle. When she returns, her father tells her he has made arrangements for a foster home for Dorrie. They go to say goodbye, but the "farewell" is sweet: Clair's father has volunteered himself as Dorrie's temporary foster parent. As the time approaches for Mr. Norcher's release, Clair's father supervises the girls closely. But Mr. Norcher gets his revenge for the foster home situation anyway. He sets fire to the new church on the Sunday it is to be initiated. Distraught and humiliated, Dorrie runs away. When Clair finds her in the woods that evening, Dorrie insists on going to the room they built. Mr. Norcher bursts in on them there, hitting Dorrie and kicking apart their room. The girls escape only footsteps ahead of Mr. Norcher. Clair regains her voice when she calls out Dorrie's name to locate her after she falls from a home-made raft into the water. After struggling to shore, they spend the night in the hideout. Next morning, Dorrie is sick and grows worse through the day; that evening, Clair goes to seek help. Mr. Norcher, however, is waiting for her when she returns to the pond, chasing her back through the woods until he is stopped by one of his own traps. At the hideout, Clair's father is waiting; after hours of fruitless searching, he remembered that Dorrie's goat knew the way. Clair tells him she has decided they can stay in their new home, which delights him nearly as much as the fact that she is now talking. On the ride home, Dorrie carefully avoids looking at her father in the passing sheriff's car. Later, Clair asks her father about this. He replies, "There must have been times . . . when you came close to hating me for taking you away. . . . Well, there must be times when, in spite of everything, Dorrie comes close to loving her father."

A drastic change in life style, immediately precipitated by Clair's mourning silence but more deeply motivated by her father's desire to start anew after his wife's death, fills Clair with anger and a renewed determination to keep silent. Her friendship with Dorrie, who has found her own sources of strength through years of parental neglect and abuse, helps Clair recover, enabling her to find joy and peace in nature and to come out of her self-imposed shell. Clair's stages of mourning for her mother are never explored in depth, but her minister father is shown to be compassionate, warm, and very likeable. The first-person narrative allows readers access to Clair's emotional progression from self-absorbed withdrawal to unselfishness and commitment. Unsentimental descriptions of the north woods setting enhance the quiet, healing resolution of this story, which is convincing if not especially profound.

Ages 11-14

**Also available in:**
No other form known

## 691

**Wilkinson, Brenda Scott**

## Ludell's New York Time

Harper & Row, Publishers, Inc., 1980.
(184 pages)

*AFRO-AMERICAN*
*CHANGE: Accepting*
*Life style: change in*
*Moving*
*Separation from loved ones*

Following the death of the beloved grandmother who raised her, Ludell is abruptly moved from her small hometown in Georgia to New York City, where her mother has lived and worked for many years. Young, black, and thoroughly unsophisticated, she leaves behind the only world she knows: her private room, the high school she is about to finish, her friends, and Willie, her sweetheart and fiancé. In New York, Ludell sleeps on a cot in her mother's living room, attends a large, impersonal high school, confronts sophisticated big-city teens, and misses Willie. She meets Regina, daughter of her mother's neighbor, who drinks, smokes, and sleeps with her boyfriend. Regina takes Ludell to parties and concerts, introduces her to boys, and encourages her to enjoy city pleasures. But Ludell, making her wedding plans, prefers the society of the neighborhood church members and the quiet company of the married Shirley, whom she befriended on the trip to New York. She finishes high school joylessly and can find only a low-paying typing job. While job hunting she meets Carolyn, newly awakened to her identity as a black woman, and is ashamed that she thinks only of herself and Willie. Her mother wants her to start college, to have more precise plans for the future. So Ludell seeks college admission, but indifferently. Christmas nears, and Willie, chief support of his father-less family in Georgia, tells Ludell he is finally free to join her in New York. They plan to marry in two weeks. Then Willie is drafted. Ludell leaves her job and the chance for college to marry and be with him in Georgia until he leaves for the service, planning to join him wherever he is finally stationed.

This third book about Ludell is a somber, clear-eyed look at growing up and at growing up black. Cut off from all she knows, surrounded by much she dislikes, Ludell finds the strength to survive in the values of the past, the courage to go on in her love for Willie. Readers will sympathize with her plight; her first-person narration is convincing, her innocence beguiling. This book is a sequel to *Ludell* and *Ludell and Willie*. Discussion is likely, since at various times characters confront discrimination, abortion, separation, premarital sex, moving, and nearly continuous frustration.

Ages 12 and up

**Also available in:**
No other form known

W

**692**

**Williams, Barbara Wright**

## So What If I'm a Sore Loser?

Black/white illustrations by Linda Strauss Edwards.
Harcourt Brace Jovanovich, Inc., 1981.
(38 pages counted)

---

*COMPETITION*
*SPORTS/SPORTSMANSHIP*
  *Boasting*
  *Success*

---

Blake, about seven, always seems to fall short of his cousin Maurice. Maurice lives across town in a large apartment building with a courteous doorman, five elevators, and an Olympic-sized swimming pool. Blake lives in a small building with a disgruntled super and four flights of stairs to climb. Maurice is a talented drummer, an excellent swimmer, and an avid boxer. Blake's talents are more sedate—working jigsaw puzzles and humming. Maurice eats broccoli and has a swimming teacher who predicts he will be a champion. Blake eats peanut brittle and has a dentist who predicts he will wear braces. One Sunday a month Blake and his mother visit Maurice and his mother. The women are delighted to see one another, but the boys eye each other warily. Athletic Maurice goads Blake into contests and always wins. Maurice is a better swimmer, a better boxer, even a better sauna-taker, and he always lets Blake know it. "Blake, you're a sore loser," he says. "Sore losers make me sick. I hate sore losers." Blake replies, "So what?" Then one Sunday when Maurice's apartment is being painted, he and his mother come to spend the day at Blake's apartment. After offering Maurice some peanut brittle and an opportunity to see what the pigeons might drop on his head, Blake challenges his cousin to a jigsaw puzzle contest. To make it fair, Blake offers Maurice a puzzle with only seventy-nine pieces. He himself works a completely new one with a hundred pieces. Blake still finishes first and rubs in his victory just as Maurice would. Maurice says, "You're a sore winner. I hate sore winners. If there's anything in this world that's worse than a sore loser, it's a sore winner." And Blake answers, "I thought you'd never notice."

A boy turns the tables on his conceited cousin, showing him what it's like to lose to a "sore winner." Readers will quickly sympathize with Blake's frustration and his defensive, "big-deal" attitude toward the irritating Maurice. Blake's wry, understated humor and the clever illustrations add to the fun.

Ages 5-8

**Also available in:**
No other form known

**693**

**Williams, Barbara Wright**

## Whatever Happened to Beverly Bigler's Birthday?

Color illustrations by Emily Arnold McCully.
Harcourt Brace Jovanovich, Inc., 1979.
(62 pages counted)

---

*ATTENTION SEEKING*
*EGOCENTRISM*
  *Communication: lack of*
  *Consideration, meaning of*

---

It is Beverly Bigler's seventh birthday but she seems to be the only one who cares, for it is also her sister's wedding day. Beverly's questions about her birthday cake are turned away as family members dress for the ceremony. She puts on her own special dress but, because she is angry, wears rolled-up blue jeans under it. Then she searches everywhere, the toolbox and doghouse included, but finds neither birthday cake nor presents. The wedding is delayed a little because Beverly, a flower girl, has torn and soiled her dress during her search. At the reception she thinks she should be dancing on her birthday. So she dances alone. Only her mother notices, and she tells Beverly to remove her sagging blue jeans. Seeing the wedding cake, Beverly decides she has found her birthday cake at last. It has no candles, so she takes seven from a sconce on the wall and puts them in the wedding cake. When they are removed by the bride, they leave large holes in the cake. Beverly sees the gift table and confirms what she expects: all the gifts are for the bride and groom. The reception ends, no one has even mentioned Beverly's birthday, and she decides to run away. Outside the hotel she meets her father. He takes her back inside where she finds her teacher, her classmates, and a band waiting for her. It is about time, she thinks, that they remembered her birthday.

A little girl who must share her birthday with her sister's wedding day manages to disrupt the wedding festivities considerably in her single-minded attempt to get everyone to realize their injustice to her. Though humorous, this easy reader should stimulate discussion about Beverly's self-centeredness and lack of consideration. Scribbly drawings convey her actions and reactions.

Ages 4-8

**Also available in:**
Paperbound—*Whatever Happened to Beverly Bigler's Birthday?*
Harcourt Brace Jovanovich, Inc.

**694**

**Willoughby, Elaine Macmann**

## Boris and the Monsters

Color illustrations by Lynn Munsinger.
Houghton Mifflin Company, 1980.
(32 pages)

---

*BEDTIME*
*FEAR: of Darkness*
  *Pets: love for*

---

Though little Boris is assured by his parents that there are no monsters, he cannot overcome his dread of bedtime. Every night he finds excuses to stay up later. He must feed his goldfish, work on his airplane, pump up his football. Despite his efforts, though, bedtime always comes and in the darkness he sees shapes that form and dance. Certain the shapes are monsters, Boris shuts his eyes tightly and whispers, "There are no monsters." It doesn't help, but luckily the monsters don't grab him. In the morning he searches his room, finding no sign of the strange nighttime shapes. One evening his father helps him look, but even together they find nothing. Boris decides he needs something ferocious to frighten the monsters away—like a tiger or at least a big, fierce dog. So he and his father bring Ivan the Terrible home from the pet shop. Although Ivan is only a small puppy, he will grow to be big and ferocious. Boris puts a soft rug beside his bed for Ivan, and then his mother turns off the light. Boris says firmly, "There are no monsters in this house." Suddenly loud, mournful sounds pierce the darkness. It is Ivan. Boris takes the puppy under his covers. "I shall just have to protect him until he isn't afraid of the dark anymore!" says Boris. "Like me."

A small boy masters his fear of the dark when he moves to protect something more helpless than he is, his frightened puppy. This amusing and reassuring story is enhanced by softly colored, cartoonlike illustrations. Young children will enjoy the funny resolution of Boris's and Ivan's fears.

Ages 4-7

**Also available in:**
Paperbound—*Boris and the Monsters*
Scholastic Book Services

## 695

Winthrop, Elizabeth

**I Think He Likes Me**

Color illustrations by Denise Saldutti.
Harper & Row, Publishers, Inc., 1980.
(32 pages)

---

*SIBLING: New Baby*
   *Determination*

---

Eliza, about five, is happy when her mother brings home her new baby brother, Andrew. "I think he likes me," she says after she has held him a while. She wants to share her toys with the baby. But, her parents tell her, her fire engine is too noisy, her doll too large, and her turtle "too slimy." Whenever Eliza wants to play with the baby, there are reasons she mustn't. Either her mother is busy rocking him to sleep or her father must bathe him. Andrew is always too heavy or too tired to be held. In frustration, Eliza whispers, "I think he wants to play with me." But no one hears her. One day Eliza's mother is in the garden and her father in the shower when Andrew begins to cry. Tiptoeing to his room, Eliza whispers his name and he stops. She climbs into his crib, builds him a tower of blocks, and plays "This Little Piggie" with his toes, which makes him giggle. When her mother comes in, Eliza says, "See, Mama, Andrew likes me." And her mother must agree.

A little girl determined to get to know her new baby brother convinces her parents that she should be included and can be trusted. This is a charming story of a small child's need to be involved with the new baby. Its quiet mood is captured by warm, homey illustrations.

Ages 3-7

**Also available in:**
No other form known

## 696

Winthrop, Elizabeth

**Marathon Miranda**

Holiday House, Inc., 1979.
(155 pages) o.p.

---

*ASTHMA*
*DETERMINATION*
*FRIENDSHIP: Meaning of*
   *Adoption: feelings about*
   *Fear: of failure*
   *Helping*
   *Running away*

---

Suffering her third asthma attack in a week, an embarrassed Miranda has to leave her ninth-grade gym class accompanied by her best friend, Katherine. The next day, when her neighbor and friend Margaret, an elderly widow, takes Miranda to the zoo, she sees Katherine with "nerdy old Viola" who has made unkind remarks about Miranda and her asthma. Feeling deserted, Miranda decides Margaret is now her best friend. But while walking her dog, Miranda meets and befriends an enthusiastic jogger, Phoebe. She also meets—and jealously resents—Margaret's friend Steven Delaney, a young television actor. Phoebe invites Miranda to dinner, during which Phoebe, an only child, gets the constant, undivided attention of her well-to-do, formal parents. At Phoebe's urging, Miranda reluctantly agrees to try jogging, thinking it may strengthen her lungs. She enjoys running more than she expected and becomes devoted to the routine. Soon Phoebe encourages her to train for an upcoming marathon. Miranda hesitates, whereupon Phoebe and Miranda's older brother hint that she uses her asthma to keep from having to risk failure. One day, while the girls are running, Miranda has a severe asthma attack. Phoebe calls the police, who rush Miranda to the hospital for adrenalin. She recovers swiftly and runs again the next day, but Phoebe now has doubts that this is wise. In the park Miranda sees Steven with a young woman. When Miranda visits Margaret, who is haggard and depressed, the woman shows her a picture of her adopted son, now dead, and admits that she hasn't seen Steven since he met the younger woman. Miranda's sympathetic family invites Margaret to join them on a visit to Miranda's grandfather's farm in Vermont. Before they leave, Miranda tries several times to see Phoebe but is told that her friend has a mysterious illness and is being kept isolated. When at last the girls meet, Phoebe tells Miranda she has suddenly, during a parental argument, learned a terrible truth about herself: she is adopted. She has been sick about the news, and her parents will not discuss it with her. The girls part, Miranda to the farm, Phoebe to Connecticut for a vacation. Then Phoebe's mother calls the farm to say that Phoebe has run away. Soon the girl appears at the farm and begs Miranda and her brother to hide her. They do, but she is discovered and runs away again. The family finds her and returns her to the farm, where Margaret, who has found much in common with Miranda's grandfather, befriends her. When Phoebe's parents come for her, they are persuaded to let Phoebe stay for a while with Margaret in a little cottage at the farm. Order is restored; the girls stay an extra week on the farm and then return to the city. Phoebe's parents agree to talk with her about her adoption, and she and Miranda successfully complete the marathon.

Miranda, a forthright and objective girl, narrates this warm story about friendship and relationships. She tells of refusing to allow her asthma to limit her unnecessarily, of confronting and overcoming her fear of failure. Miranda also makes a new friend, strengthens her ties with an old one, and unites both. Readers will find her a believable, caring protagonist. Miranda's story continues in the sequel, *Miranda in the Middle*.

Ages 9-11

**Also available in:**
Paperbound—*Marathon Miranda*
Bantam Books, Inc.

## 697

**Winthrop, Elizabeth**

**Miranda in the Middle**

Holiday House, Inc., 1980.
(128 pages)

---

*FRIENDSHIP: Meaning of*
*VALUES/VALUING: Moral/Ethical*
  *Asthma*
  *Friendship: best friend*
  *Honesty/Dishonesty*

---

When thirteen-year-old Miranda met her best friend, Phoebe, an avid jogger, she too took up jogging. Miranda runs with her dog, Frisbee, in hopes of curing her asthma. Recently Phoebe, who is angry with her parents for not telling her until now that she was adopted, has developed a rebellious attitude. When Phillip, a boy her parents wouldn't approve of because he smokes and drinks, asks her out, she begs Miranda to cover for her. Miranda does. One day, while she's jogging without Phoebe, Miranda meets ten-year-old Michael Oliver. Although she doesn't realize it, he is the unwitting guinea pig for a class experiment that Miranda's older brother, Alex, is conducting. Alex has observed Michael Oliver sitting on his fire escape day after day, apparently taking notes on the Methodist church below. When he informs Miranda of his suspicions that the church is being sold to a development corporation to be torn down for a high-rise, Miranda tells her father. Since a high-rise building will completely block their river view, Miranda's father forms a neighborhood committee to check into Michael Oliver's suspicions. When these suspicions are confirmed, the committee takes steps to prevent the destruction of the church. A member of this committee, an older friend of Miranda's family named Margaret, has recently

become romantically involved with Miranda's grandfather. Miranda is nervous about this romance, because she's afraid that if they marry she will lose her two favorite people. Meanwhile, Alex learns that his "subject" is Miranda's friend, and he connives to become Michael Oliver's extra-special friend so he can observe him better. The lonely, unsuspecting boy becomes very attached to Alex. Miranda, feeling guilty at her position in the middle, wishes Alex would drop the project and tells him so, but even though Alex too is conscience-stricken, it's too late for him to start another paper on another person. Michael Oliver is crushed the day he enters Miranda's apartment alone and discovers Alex's report. Neither Alex nor Miranda can console him. Now Miranda feels lost: Phoebe is dating and Michael Oliver is angry. When Phoebe wants Miranda to lie for her again, she refuses, telling Phoebe's mother the truth when she calls asking for Phoebe. Phoebe is furious; Miranda feels she's lost another friend. Then Alex and Miranda together ask Michael Oliver to be their friend again—Alex gives his report to Michael Oliver instead of handing it in. The boy forgives them. As a Christmas gift and peace offering, Miranda sends Phoebe the pedometer she's been wanting and their friendship resumes. Phoebe confides that Phillip hasn't called since their last fatal date and that she has been grounded for life. Miranda recommends building up her parents' trust by following all rules, and Phoebe agrees to try. It is finally decided that the church will be preserved as an architectural monument. And to cap Miranda's happiness, when her grandfather and Margaret announce their engagement and then marry, Miranda realizes she is not losing two friends—she is gaining a grandmother.

In this humorous first-person sequel to *Marathon Miranda*, Miranda must choose between her principles and her friendships. She finds to her relief and satisfaction that a true friend will appreciate her integrity. This story of friendship lost and restored will appeal to the intended audience.

Ages 9-13

**Also available in:**
Cassette—*Miranda in the Middle*
Library of Congress (NLSBPH)

Paperbound—*Miranda in the Middle*
Bantam Books, Inc.

## 698

**Winthrop, Elizabeth**

**Sloppy Kisses**

Color illustrations by Anne Burgess.
Macmillan Publishing Company, Inc., 1980.
(28 pages counted)

---

*PEER RELATIONSHIPS: Peer Pressures*
  *Communication: parent-child*
  *Embarrassment*

---

"Emmy Lou's family loved to kiss." This doesn't disturb little Emmy Lou until the day her friend Rosemary sees Emmy Lou's father kissing her goodbye at school. Rosemary informs Emmy Lou that kissing is for babies. The next time Emmy Lou's father wants to kiss her, she tells him what Rosemary said. From then on her parents kiss only her younger sister, Dolly, giving Emmy Lou pats on the shoulder. One night, Emmy Lou finds it hard to fall asleep. She tiptoes into her parents' room. They ask her if she wants some juice, another blanket, or a story, but each time she answers no. "I know what you need," says her father. He grabs her up and gives her a great big sloppy kiss. Then her mother kisses her softly. Tucked back into bed, Emmy Lou falls right to sleep. The next morning her father drops her off at school. Spying Rosemary, he pats Emmy Lou's shoulder and turns to leave. Emmy Lou begs him for her goodbye kiss as Rosemary watches, disgusted. Emmy Lou tells her, "Kissing is for everybody." And she gives the surprised Rosemary a quick little kiss on the cheek.

This appealing story gives a humorous account of the need children have for physical affection. The disarming Emmy Lou discovers this for herself and then teaches it to her doubting friend. The catchy title and small size of the book will delight young children, as will the bright pictures of the characters, a family of pigs.

Ages 4-7

**Also available in:**
Paperbound—*Sloppy Kisses*
Penguin Books, Inc.

## 699

**Wiseman, Bernard**

### The Lucky Runner
Color illustrations by the author.
Garrard Publishing Company, 1979.
(48 pages)

---

*SUPERSTITION*
  *Competition*
  *Talents: athletic*

---

Buddy, about ten, is a fast runner who trains hard, likes to win races, and usually does. However, he believes he wins because he wears his lucky socks with the red stripe. This disclosure amazes his friend Chub after he cheers Buddy to victory in a difficult race. Buddy's reliance on lucky socks also surprises his coach, who argues that talent and hard work, not luck or socks, account for Buddy's wins. Buddy will run the half-mile at the state championship meet, and the coach gives him new running shoes to increase his speed even more. Buddy trains hard, but still relies on his socks to pull him through. To his dismay, when he begins dressing for the meet he cannot find his lucky socks in his bag. His mother, it turns out, replaced the old, tattered socks with new ones, unaware that the old socks meant luck to Buddy. He calls home and asks his parents to bring his old socks when they come to watch the meet. The socks arrive just in time. Buddy quickly slips them on and runs a great race, coming from far back in the field to nip the leading runner at the tape. When he's congratulated, Buddy insists on attributing the victory to his lucky socks. Then he notices that his socks are not, in fact, the lucky socks. These have a black stripe instead of a red stripe. Not knowing that Buddy wanted a particular pair of old socks, his mother had simply grabbed any pair and sent them along.

A good runner insists on attributing his victories to a particular pair of socks. When he mistakenly believes he's wearing his lucky socks and runs a great race, Buddy learns that perseverance and hard work make a winner. The subject matter and the humor, enhanced by clever illustrations, will have great appeal in this easy reader.

Ages 6-9

**Also available in:**
No other form known

## 700

**Wittman, Sally Anne Christensen**

### The Wonderful Mrs. Trumbly
Color illustrations by Margot Apple.
Harper & Row, Publishers, Inc., 1982.
(40 pages)

---

*SCHOOL: Pupil-Teacher Relationships*
  *Friendship: meaning of*
  *Jealousy*

---

From the beginning, Martin likes his new teacher, Mrs. Trumbly. Because he defends her and seeks her out, his friends tease him. But even when the whole class likes Mrs. Trumbly, Martin feels he and she have a special relationship. He discovers that she has grown children but, to his relief, no grandchildren. Martin walks her to the bus stop every day, talks with her about his aquarium, and tells her all his knock-knock jokes. On rainy days they share her umbrella. Martin begins to feel they aren't just friends, but best friends. Then Mr. Klein, the music teacher, begins driving Mrs. Trumbly home from school. One day Martin sees them sharing a pot of tea in the faculty lunchroom, and he hears they've attended a concert together. Martin thinks about Mrs. Trumbly over Christmas vacation and wonders if she'd mind if he called her Cecilia, as he heard Mr. Klein doing. On Valentine's Day Mrs. Trumbly receives twenty-four small valentines and one big one. Martin knows the big one is from Mr. Klein. When Mr. Klein gives Mrs. Trumbly a canary, Martin decides he'll give her gifts too. He makes her a clay dinosaur and gives her an orchid from his mother's garden and a blue jawbreaker that he leaves on her desk with a note: "From your best friend." Mrs. Trumbly thanks him, and they seem to be good friends again. He wonders if she has forgotten about Mr. Klein. Then Martin sees her holding hands with the music teacher and dreams that he and Mr. Klein have a sword fight with violin bows. Then in May Mrs. Trumbly announces that she and Mr. Klein will be married the first day of summer vacation. The entire class is invited, but the news gives Martin a stomachache. The last day of school, Martin finds a note from Mrs. Trumbly tucked in his spelling book. She hopes they will be good friends, no matter what. Now Martin looks for a gift that will show Mrs. Trumbly he understands and that it's all right for her to marry Mr. Klein. At the wedding, Martin's gift, a bride-and-groom statue, decorates the top of the cake. This year Martin has a different teacher, but he takes violin lessons from Mr. Klein. At his first recital, Mrs. Trumbly—that is, Mrs. Klein—sits in the front row next to his parents.

A young boy with a crush on his teacher is upset when she begins keeping company with another teacher. When Martin learns that friendship does not exclude other relationships, he is able to accept and even enjoy his teacher's wedding. Martin's feelings about this special relationship are well portrayed. Any reader who has had a favorite teacher will sympathize, and others may see their teachers in a different light. The story is greatly enhanced by illustrations that manage to be simultaneously whimsical and realistic.

Ages 5-8

**Also available in:**
No other form known

## 701

Wolde, Gunilla

**Betsy and Peter Are Different**
Translated from the Swedish by Alison Winn.
Color illustrations by the author.
Random House, Inc., 1979.
(23 pages counted) o.p.

---

*DIFFERENCES, HUMAN*

---

Although little Betsy and Peter are the same age, they are different from each other. Peter lives in a small house; Betsy lives in a large apartment building. Betsy's mother and father take turns staying home with her; Peter has no father but does have his grandmother living with him and his mother. Betsy has a baby brother but no dog, and Peter has a dog but no baby brother. Betsy gets bored playing by herself, but when she plays with Peter they think up exciting games. Even when they dress up to look the same, they end up looking different. Betsy and Peter like being different from each other. They know it wouldn't be nearly as much fun if they were exactly alike.

Two preschoolers discover the advantages of human differences. Cheerful, attractive illustrations accompany the simple text and down-to-earth examples of the variety among human beings. This is one of a series of books about Betsy, her family and friends.

Ages 3-6

**Also available in:**
No other form known

## 702

Wolde, Gunilla

**Betsy and the Vacuum Cleaner**
Translated from the Swedish by Alison Winn.
Color illustrations by the author.
Random House, Inc., 1979.
(23 pages counted) o.p.

---

*CHORES*
  *Curiosity*
  *Fear: of vacuum cleaner*
  *Helping*

---

When Betsy's father vacuums, she likes to sit on the vacuum cleaner and pretend it's an animal making a whirring sound. She knows her father turns on a switch to make it go, and she also knows she's not to turn it on herself. Sometimes, though, he lets her help him. The vacuum sucks up all sorts of dust and sand and even a button, a Lego block, and a piece of paper. Betsy discovers that her teddy bear is too big to be vacuumed up. So is she, although some of her hair gets sucked into the tube of the vacuum. When she pretends to vacuum up her baby brother, he gets scared and yells for his father. So Betsy vacuums up his sock instead. In an attempt to retrieve the sock, Betsy takes the cover off the vacuum cleaner after her father has shut it off and unplugged it. She finds a bag full of dust and dirt, which she empties onto the floor. She also finds sand, the button, the Lego, the piece of paper, and the sock. Her brother is glad to have his sock back, but Betsy wonders how happy her father will be with the pile of dirt on the floor. She also wonders how the vacuum works. As she replaces the vacuum cleaner cover, she decides that some things shouldn't be vacuumed up. Next time she'll be more careful. She then cleans up the pile of dirt she made on the floor. Her little brother is afraid of the vacuum when it's on, but when it's turned off he sits on it, pretending he's riding an animal. However, he makes his own whirring sound.

A little girl's interest in an ordinary household chore leads her to help with the vacuuming and eventually to become curious about how the vacuum cleaner works. Betsy's father is apparently in charge of the vacuuming and at least some of the child care in this family; no mother is seen. Some safety guidelines about working with an electrical appliance are included in the story line. Included also is a diagram of a vacuum cleaner that will interest many preschoolers and may prove especially valuable in consoling youngsters who are afraid of vacuum cleaners. The illustrations are attractive and lighthearted, reflecting the touch of whimsy in the text. This is one of a series of books about Betsy, her family and friends.

Ages 3-6

**Also available in:**
No other form known

## 703

Wolkoff, Judie

**Happily Ever After . . . Almost**
Bradbury Press, Inc., 1982.
(215 pages)

---

*FAMILY: Extended*
*PARENT/PARENTS: Remarriage of*
  *Divorce: of parents*
  *Family: relationships*
  *Parental: custody*
  *Stepbrother/Stepsister*
  *Stepparent: father*
  *Stepparent: mother*

---

Kitty Birdsall, eleven, and her sister, Sarah, nine, are not surprised when they overhear Seth Krampner propose to their mother, Liz. They like Seth, a photographer who met their mother in her job of designing book-jacket layouts. On weekends the girls visit their father, a pediatrician, who lives with his new wife, Linda, in a New York suburb much like their own. Seth's eleven-year-old son, R.J., lives with his difficult mother, Kay, an heiress and a manipulator. Seth and Liz want their children to meet and get along, but R.J. and Kitty immediately dislike each other. Seth explains to Kitty that R.J. has been seeing a psychiatrist since his parents' divorce. He asks Kitty to be tolerant of the boy. For New Year's Eve, Seth, Liz, and the children, with numerous relatives, gather at Seth's parents' house. Kitty overhears R.J. on the phone in the bedroom, begging his mother not to give away the guinea pig he's just bought, and she begins to realize just what life must be like for him. Then her father and Linda announce they are expecting a baby. After Seth and Liz are married, they and the girls move into the loft of a huge old shoe factory and begin renovation. During the summer, R.J. attends camp and he and Kitty begin writing to each other. When he returns in time to celebrate his twelfth birthday, Kitty gives him an album of photographs she's taken. R.J., who was shaken by the sight of the bums on the Bowery, gives his generous birthday check from his wealthy maternal grandfather to the Bowery Home for the Homeless. While Kitty and Sarah are visiting their father and Linda one weekend, the girls' half-brother, Josh, is born. Kitty desperately wants a special vest for her birthday—a neighbor makes them for thirty dollars. However, she is so moved by reports of starving children in Zaire that she tells her mother she'd rather have the money to send to Africa. Her mother and Seth promptly double the amount; her father and Linda add to it. Then Kitty's mother, harassed by the renovation and worried about a lump in her breast, shows signs of depression and emotional strain. After surgery, which shows the lump to be benign, Seth and the girls take her from the hospital to a hotel for four days of rest and recreation. Seth accidentally discovers that R.J.'s mother has had his school records sent to a boys' prep school in London. A Christmas trip to London has been planned, and Seth and R.J. both fear that Kay means to remain in London—which is against the custody ruling. Seth immediately sets a custody battle in motion. The judge denies the trip to London, keeping R.J.'s passport so his mother can't take him anyway, and awards custody to Seth. Kay appeals. The resulting legal fees leave little money for Christmas, so they all start making gifts for each other. Sarah and R.J., with the neighbor's help, make the vest for Kitty. Christmas Day finds all the children together with Linda and the girls' father, joined by Linda's two children from her previous marriage and baby Josh. Kitty enjoys this gathering of all her brothers and sisters. Before the final custody hearing, R.J. tells Kitty that he now likes her; he wants her to know that in case they lose and he has to go to London. But the judge finds for Seth. Kay becomes abusive when she hears the verdict, and R.J. runs away in the middle of the night to the loft where he stays for good. Eventually, his mother begins working with a psychiatrist (just as R.J. stops seeing his), and their relationship improves slightly. Now Liz is pregnant and the children are delighted. Kitty thinks back to the most unhappy day of her life—when her father left them—and realizes that from it has come the happy beginning of a new life.

In this first-person view of the upbeat side of changing family configurations, Kitty records the confusing relationships she has with her sister, her stepbrother, her half-brother, extra grandparents, and various unrelated people who are still "family." Sharply drawn characters people this fast-moving, funny, vivid chronicle of family members jockeying for position. Although there are trials and troubles, the emphasis here is on the advantages and stimulation of family changes. Kitty would have counseled her unhappy younger self, "You'll live through today. And tomorrow. And the next. But you won't stay sad. Just wait! Around the corner is a happy beginning."

Ages 11-13

**Also available in:**
Braille—*Happily Ever After . . . Almost*
Library of Congress (NLSBPH)

Cassette—*Happily Ever After . . . Almost*
Library of Congress (NLSBPH)

Paperbound—*Happily Ever After . . . Almost*
Dell Publishing Company, Inc.

### 704

Wolkoff, Judie

## Where the Elf King Sings

Bradbury Press, Inc., 1980.
(178 pages)

*FAMILY: Relationships*
*VIETNAM*
  *Age: aging*
  *Alcoholism: of father*
  *Violence*

At twelve, Marcie Breckenridge watches her world fall apart. Her father, Billy, a Vietnam veteran haunted by flashbacks of his combat experiences, has lost his job and the family's car because of his violent, drunken behavior. At a slumber party, Marcie is taunted by some of the girls about her father's drinking. It is caused, they tell her, by the curse of a murdered servant girl who had worked for the store from which Marcie's father has just been fired. Determined to investigate this curse, Marcie goes to the old cemetery where the murdered girl is buried. There she meets the town eccentric, Mrs. King, who is wearing a bizarre outfit of hip boots and white gloves. At first Marcie finds the tales she's heard about the "town loon" confirmed. But soon she realizes that Mrs. King wears the boots and gloves to protect herself from the snakes and poison ivy in the graveyard. She goes there often to care for her brother's grave. Intrigued by the sharp-witted woman, Marcie accepts an invitation to tea. That night, unable to sleep, she recalls her family's happier times. In the middle of the night her father arrives, noisily drunk, having spent her mother's tip money from the diner where she works, not to redeem the car, but to buy liquor. Offended by the "racist" cast-iron black jockey on his neighbor's lawn, Billy drags it into the gutter. The next day Marcie takes her younger brother with her to have tea with Mrs. King. When they return home they find the house a shambles. Their grandmother, always willing to deny the truth, tries to blame the destruction on vandals, but the children know their father is responsible. Their mother had poured his liquor down the sink before she left for work. They spend that night at their grandmother's house. Next morning their father arrives, followed closely by their mother. She tells him, "You destroyed everything there ever was between us. You're not coming back. I won't let you." Billy promises to seek counseling at the V.A. hospital, but he's not allowed near the children. For a while the therapy seems to be working. Then Billy disappears and Marcie, her brother, and their grandmother search for him in vain. They go back home and find their mother with Curt, a member of Billy's therapy group. Curt, understanding what Billy could never tell his family, the horror of his Vietnam experiences, has found the tormented man at the grave of his best friend, killed in Vietnam while trying to save Billy, who had stepped on a mine. Mrs. King, aware that Billy goes to the cemetery on each anniversary of his friend's death, brings hot soup to comfort him. After this, Billy returns to the V.A. Alcoholic Unit and shows rapid improvement. The family looks forward to his return.

The unending agony of Vietnam, the terrible price still being paid by many veterans, and the impact of their traumas on their families are vividly conveyed in this powerful book. The story moves swiftly, the characters so well developed that each becomes an individual to whom the reader is closely drawn. This is a book rich in discussion possibilities.

Ages 12 and up

**Also available in:**
Braille—*Where the Elf King Sings*
Library of Congress (NLSBPH)

Cassette—*Where the Elf King Sings*
Library of Congress (NLSBPH)

Paperbound—*Where the Elf King Sings*
Scholastic Book Services

## 705

**Wood, Phyllis Anderson**

**Pass Me a Pine Cone**

Black/white photographs: a collection.
The Westminster Press, 1982.
(160 pages)

---

CHANGE: New Home
  Belonging
  Boy-girl relationships
  Family: unity
  Peer relationships
  Pets: love for
  School: pupil-teacher relationships
  School: transfer

---

When high school sophomore Sam Overton and his parents move from their oceanside community to a town in the California mountains, a neighbor asks them to deliver a box of pinecones to his niece, Sara Rudeen, who makes pinecone creatures to sell to gift shops. Sam worries mainly about how his cat, Monster, will adapt to new surroundings and about how he will face entering a new school as the new principal's son; delivering the pinecones seems only a nuisance until Sam meets Sara.

Monster does take to his new home, immediately establishing himself in a tall pine tree. Challenged by a squirrel, he falls out. Sam rushes him to Sara's house to inquire about a vet, since Sara has an equally eccentric pet, an Irish setter named Shashi. Sam likes school well enough except for Laney, an English teacher who hates administrators because he was once demoted from assistant principal. Laney (he insists on being called just that) makes trouble for Sam from the beginning and encourages a group of trouble-making boys to ridicule him. Sam, who secretly loves climbing trees, discovers that Sara also thinks Monster's pine tree is a natural for a tree house. They spend four weeks designing and building the structure, which has an alpine roof, windows, a snack cupboard, and a feather pillow for Monster—also enough space for the two of them. Then Laney, always playing to his "pet" group of boys, not only makes fun of Sam, but insults his father. Sam talks back; Laney requests that he be moved to another English class. Sam is delighted, but knows he's not seen the end of Laney's hostility. Sam spends a happy day with Sara visiting Cougar Valley up in the mountains. On the way home he offers to help her with her pinecone business, since she helped him build Monster's tree house. He wonders if they'll still be business partners if one of them decides to date other people, or even if they fall in love with each other. They decide their business relationship can handle either eventuality. Then some students from Cougar Valley tell Sam they've heard Laney has more or less inspired his band of bad boys to vandalize Monster's tree house on Halloween. When he hears that the rumor is true, Sam tells his father, who offers help. But Sam insists he has to lick the problem by himself. He and Sara work hard all week on their counterattack. On Halloween night when the vandals arrive, they are greeted with tape recordings of barking dogs, shrieks, police sirens, and whistles, and with a shower from the underground lawn-sprinkling system. An article in the newspaper that makes the would-be vandals look silly is the final touch. Sam has successfully solved his problem with his peers; his father will have to deal with Laney. Monster is made the school mascot, and Sam and Sara are honored for their part in handling the vandals.

"The principal's kid" manages to evade the easy labels people want to hang on him, making friends and winning the respect of his peers simply by being himself. "The Overton way," the way Sam has been raised, involves being your own best person without worrying what others think of you. Sam's relationship with his parents is almost ideal, and readers will enjoy seeing the downfall of the obnoxious Laney. The book's only real distinction is its glimpse of the running of a school from the principal's point of view and its perspective of a principal's child. But this is a satisfying, easy-to-read book that will appeal most to reluctant readers. Photographs of forest scenes and animals decorate the book almost randomly.

Ages 11 and up

**Also available in:**
No other form known

**706**

Wood, Phyllis Anderson

**This Time Count Me In**

The Westminster Press, 1980.
(119 pages)

---

BOY-GIRL RELATIONSHIPS: Dating
SCHOOL: Transfer
    Afro-American
    Fear: of physical harm
    Friendship: making friends
    School: classmate relationships
    Values/Valuing: moral/ethical

---

For her sophomore year Peggy Marklee transfers from her private girls' school to a public high school so she can make some nonwhite friends and have classes with boys in them. Shy and used to wearing uniforms, she worries about her clothes and whether the students will accept her. She is assigned to a Reading Lab and there meets Walter and Alfred, class troublemakers; Roxanne and Cheryl, stylish black girls she admires on sight; and Ron, who seems just the kind of boy she's hoped to meet. But trouble with Walter and Alfred begins almost immediately. They disrupt the class and pelt her with wadded paper. Alfred takes the folder and special gold pen from her desk, replacing the folder with a test answer key inside. His efforts backfire when Roxanne confronts him and demands that he return Peggy's pen. The teacher knows Peggy didn't steal the answer key—Alfred is already on probation. Although order is soon restored, Peggy feels unsettled and uneasy. All during her first week she has spent her lunch hour in the library because she was afraid to approach the busy, confusing cafeteria. When Ron, who has only been at the school for a short time himself, notices her plight, he walks her through the lunch line and soon they are eating together every day. One day they have lunch at a hamburger stand and overhear a conversation about two young men who have knocked a woman down and stolen her purse. From the descriptions, Peggy and Ron believe the thieves to be Walter and Alfred. Then in Reading Lab, Peggy sees Alfred steal the teacher's wallet. She knows that by reporting him she will make enemies, but she likes the teacher and feels compelled to speak up. Adding to her account of the theft at school, Ron tells the police about the episode at the hamburger stand. Later, two girls who are friends of Alfred's threaten Peggy with notes and phone calls, but Roxanne and Cheryl defend and protect her. In court several days later, Peggy testifies ably, despite her fears and self-consciousness. Later that day, in the school cafeteria, Alfred's two friends confront Peggy, call her a "snitch," and threaten to start a food fight with her as their target. Suddenly Peggy is surrounded protectively by twenty-five black girls, who face down her tormentors and the young tough who has come to help them. The crisis passes. Roxanne and Cheryl invite Peggy and Ron to a celebration dinner that evening at Cheryl's house. There they meet two more black friends. Returning to Peggy's house, they talk about the possibilities ahead when Ron gets his driver's license. He mentions that he wants to spend a day taking a friend up the coast. Shyly, Peggy realizes he means her.

An inexperienced girl hoping to make black friends and meet boys by attending a public high school for the first time overcomes her apprehensions and shyness, deals decisively with lawbreakers, and begins a first romance. Simply told with no complete characterizations other than Peggy's, this high-interest, low-vocabulary account rings true in its presentation of the trials of transferring schools and the joys of new friendships.

Ages 12 and up

**Also available in:**
Paperbound—*This Time Count Me In*
Pocket Books, Inc.

---

**707**

Wortis, Avi

**A Place Called Ugly**

Pantheon Books, 1981.
(141 pages)

---

CHANGE: Resisting
    Determination
    Maturation

---

Fourteen-year-old Owen Coughlin is determined to stop the destruction of the cottage on Grenlow's Island where he and his family have vacationed for the last ten years. His family has moved many times in those ten years, but this cottage has been a constant in a life of change. Many happy memories of the cottage tie Owen's life together. But the owner, Miss Devlin, has decided to build a hotel where the house now stands. On the day the family is to leave the cottage for the last time, Owen writes a note to his parents explaining that he plans to stay in the house. Then he hides from them. His parents decide to call his bluff and let him remain for a few days by himself. Owen's crusade is underway, yet he feels confused and uncertain about exactly what he can do to save his cottage. Terri Janick, whose parents own the general store in town, is sent to check on Owen, and their friendship develops quickly. She shows Owen how to cook clams and potatoes over an open fire and seems to understand what he's fighting for. The people who live on the island all year are very much in favor of the new hotel, which would bring more jobs, and they resent Owen's interference. One evening as Terri and Owen are talking, Terri's older brother, Bill, and two of his friends come to convince Owen to leave: a fight ensues. Owen goes to visit Miss Devlin, but fails to change her mind. However, she comes to the house to see for herself what is to be demolished. "I am sorry for you, Owen," she says, "but not about the house. I like you. But this . . . is ugly." To Owen the house is beautiful, and he is determined to have others see it as he does. With Terri's help in obtaining paint that was discarded by summer residents, he begins his renovation. The windows are all painted red, orange stars adorn the sides, and he proudly writes BEAUTIFUL in silver paint across the roof. The next morning as the bulldozer starts toward the house, Owen initiates his final plan. Remembering what he learned one summer from Mr. Hinks, the propane-gas man, Owen fills the house with gas and throws a jar containing burning paper through the window. As the house goes up in flames, Owen feels he has won. He's never lost control of the house's destiny.

This first-person narrative is laced with italicized flashbacks of happy boyhood summers. As the story unfolds, the reader is given subtle evidence of Owen's struggle to deal with numerous emotions: confusion, sadness, anger, mourning, determination. His sensitivity leads him to his final realization that memories gave the house beauty and they can never be destroyed. Once he sees this, he can destroy the place himself. Owen is a serious boy and this is a serious book. Readers will sympathize with the protagonist and his cause.

Ages 11-14

**Also available in:**
No other form known

## 708

Wortis, Avi

### Sometimes I Think I Hear My Name

Pantheon Books, 1982.
(144 pages)

---

*BOY-GIRL RELATIONSHIPS*
*MATURATION*
*REJECTION: Parental*
  *Deprivation, emotional*
  *Love, meaning of*
  *Relatives: living in home of*

---

Since his parent's divorce three years ago, thirteen-year-old Conrad Murray has lived in St. Louis with his Uncle Carl and Aunt Lu. They have told him that his parents wanted him to have a good home life with a stable family. Conrad loves his aunt and uncle but is increasingly concerned that his parents, both living in New York City, are forgetting him. Just before spring vacation, Conrad's aunt and uncle tell him they are sending him to England by himself to visit relatives. But Conrad tells them he would rather go see his parents. They don't consent. Asked to pick up his tickets at the travel agency, he meets Nancy Sterling, about his age, who is also buying a ticket. A boarding-school student in St. Louis, she is going to New York City to see her parents and is less than excited about it. The next day Conrad stops at Nancy's and offers to trade tickets. Nancy declines, but she does give him her New York telephone number. Conrad resigns himself to a trip to England. But in talking over the plans with his aunt and uncle, he discovers there will be a layover and change of planes in New York City. Accordingly, when he gets into the New York airport terminal, he slips past the stewardess who has been asked to look after him and calls Nancy. Nancy's sister gives Conrad their address. He takes a bus there and is surprised to see that Nancy and her sister live in one apartment, their parents in another. After some initial fabrications about his own situation, Conrad admits that his parents don't even know he's in town. He calls both but neither is home, so he spends that night at Nancy's apartment. The next day he and Nancy go to his mother's apartment and are let in by a neighbor. The phone rings and when the answer tape goes on automatically Conrad hears his Aunt Lu as

she leaves a message for his mother. Mortified, he realizes from her words that his mother did not want him to visit. When he goes to see his father, he notes the man's embarrassment. Suddenly he misses his aunt and uncle. The next morning he calls his mother and is invited over. After an uncomfortable visit, Conrad understands that his aunt and uncle were trying to protect him from his parents' indifference. That evening Conrad is invited to Nancy's parents' apartment for dinner. He sees the superficiality of their relationship with their daughters and understands why Nancy is so withdrawn and unemotional. Compelled to admit the truth to himself—his parents do not want him—Conrad flies back to St. Louis, glad to be home. Spring vacation ends and Nancy is still in New York, partly because her parents consider Conrad a bad influence on her. In a letter, she suggests that they "think each other's name. Hard." Maybe their "thoughts can connect." And each day at five o'clock, Conrad does just that. Sometimes he thinks he hears his name.

A young teenage boy abandons a trip to England to search for his divorced parents in New York City. With the help of a quiet, withdrawn girl who is similarly distanced from her parents, Conrad finds that the love and security he so desperately wants from his parents are already his from his aunt and uncle. Conrad tells this fast-paced story; readers will readily sympathize both with his hurt and longing and with Nancy's alienation and desire to separate completely from her own frustrating, unsatisfactory relationship with her parents. (The symbolism of the butterfly tattoo used to represent her feelings may elude some readers.) No reason is given for the emotional desert these young people face, but Conrad's loving aunt and uncle and his promising relationship with Nancy make the ending bittersweet.

Ages 10-13

**Also available in:**
No other form known

## 709

Wright, Betty Ren

### I Like Being Alone

Color illustrations by Krystyna Stasiak.
Raintree Publishers, Inc., 1981.
(31 pages)

---

*PRIVACY, NEED FOR*
  *Emotions: identifying*
  *Problem solving*
  *Relatives: living in child's home*

---

While showing her new friend Jason around her busy house, Brenda, about eight, feels vaguely out of sorts. Jason, an only child, admires the bunk bed she shares with her sister, her large and noisy family, the ready supply of constant companions. Brenda realizes that she feels just the opposite. "I'd like to be alone sometimes . . . I love my family, but they are always right there. Every minute." That night at dinner, surrounded by her family, not one of whom notices her sadness, the girl feels even more unhappy. Aunt Rose, a boarder and the only member of the household with a room of her own, finally does notice Brenda and invites her to her room.

As Brenda admires her aunt's homemade furnishings, she happens to glance at the single tree in their backyard and gets an idea. Using her aunt's leftover lumber, she builds a platform and puts it in the tree. When her father comes along, she tells him, "This is my very own place, Dad. I made it." He goes to get some rope to secure the platform in place. Then the whole family comes to see the tree house, including Aunt Rose who brings more lumber to build walls. Brenda happily spends that entire day in her tree house with only her books and the birds for company. When she wants to sleep there, Aunt Rose's encouragement overrides her parents' objections. Brenda stays awake for a long while, listening to the peaceful night sounds. In the middle of the night, however, she awakens to darkness and a strong wind. Hearing a noise beneath the tree, she summons all her courage, leans over, and shines the flashlight—onto Aunt Rose who has come to check on her. Relieved, Brenda settles back down and her aunt returns to the house. Tomorrow she will let her siblings and Jason take turns in her tree house. "But it will always be my place, when I want to be alone," she thinks before drifting back to sleep.

A need to escape from her large and ever-present family, to have a place of her own, is the impetus behind a girl's decision to build her own tree house. With the help and emotional support of an understanding aunt, Brenda creates her hideaway, a place she will share occasionally but will also reserve for herself when she wants it. There is good discussion material here on how people can balance their need for privacy with their need for social contact. Radiant, colorful illustrations emphasize the sense of emotional well-being Brenda achieves.

Ages 6-9

**Also available in:**
No other form known

## 710

Wright, Betty Ren

### My New Mom and Me

Color illustrations by Betsy Day.
Raintree Publishers, Inc., 1981.
(31 pages)

---

*CHANGE: Accepting*
*STEPPARENT: Mother*
*Loss: feelings of*
*Parent/Parents: remarriage of*
*Pets: substitute for human relationship*

---

A girl of about nine is comforted by the thought that Cat, once her mother's special pet and now hers, remembers the good times as well as the bad. The worst time for her was two summers ago when her mother suddenly became ill and died. The girl remembers feeling very angry at her mother for leaving; "If she knew how sad I was going to be, she would have found a way to stay alive." Cat seems lost also, searching the house for the absent woman and wary of the girl and her father. "He doesn't want to love us, because he's afraid we might die too," says the girl. But soon the cat begins to sleep

with her, and she tells him of her sadness and loneliness. Then the girl's father decides to remarry. Certain she will not like this new woman named Elena, the girl thinks, "We don't need her." She says nothing to her father, but demonstrates her unhappiness by refusing to let Elena hug her when she comes to live with them. Cat too keeps his distance, waiting for Elena to leave the room before approaching the food she has put in his bowl. Sometimes when Elena watches Cat and the girl her smile seems to fade, making the girl glad. Then one night her father must go out of town. After dinner the girl goes to her room and sprawls on her bed, regretting how different everything is now. Soon she hears Cat, meowing frantically. Although the sound seems to be coming from her closet, she cannot find him. Upset, she calls Elena, who comes into her room and searches the closet. They decide that somehow Cat is stuck inside the wall. The girl remembers a loose board at the back of her closet shelf, and Elena discovers a hole in the wall where Cat must have slipped through. Using a hammer the girl brings, Elena cracks open the wallboard and pulls the boards loose to the floor. Although the girl insists the cat will scratch, Elena softly and patiently calls to it and the frightened animal jumps right into her arms. For the first time, the girl really looks at Elena and thanks her for her help. Outside on the back steps Elena holds Cat, who buries his head under her arm. The girl tells Elena that he used to do that to her mother. Elena says, "Your mother taught Cat how to love. He'll never forget her, but maybe he's tired of keeping all that love locked inside." They sit quietly together. Elena puts her arm around the girl and she leans against her stepmother, surprised at how good the closeness feels.

In this first-person story of loss and change, a bereaved young girl withdraws from the affection her stepmother offers, clinging instead to the past as represented by her cat. Only when the cat needs rescuing and the stepmother acts quickly to provide it does the girl begin to accept the love of her new mother. This gentle story, appropriately illustrated, could serve as a starting point for a discussion of death and grief.

Ages 8-10

**Also available in:**
No other form known

## 711

Wright, Betty Ren

### My Sister Is Different

Color illustrations by Helen Cogancherry.
Raintree Publishers, Inc., 1981.
(31 pages)

---

*MENTAL RETARDATION*
*SIBLING: Younger*
*Sibling: love for*

---

Whenever Carlo goes out to play he must take his mentally retarded sister, Terry, with him. Terry, though older and taller than he is, is slow to learn, usually drops the ball or gets the rules wrong, and is laughed at by the other children. Sometimes Carlo dislikes her. He even made a birthday card for her that expressed just those sentiments, but he decided not to give it to her. His grandmother tells him to love Terry. "Is your heart so dried up and scrawny that it can't love?" she asks. At Christmastime, Carlo takes Terry shopping to get a present for their grandmother. Terry wants to buy her a powder puff doll; Carlo quickly agrees because he is embarrassed by Terry and wants to move on so the clerk will stop staring at them. When Terry has to go to the bathroom, Carlo gives her hasty directions rather than accompanying her. He sees her stumble as she walks away, excited to be on her own. Ten minutes pass. Then Carlo, first thinking how very slow Terry is, goes to find her, enlisting the aid of a helpful clerk. Finding the bathroom empty, the clerk reassures him that his older sister can certainly take care of herself. But Carlo knows better. Searching the store, he considers how his family will blame him, thinking he lost Terry on purpose. He then remembers the good things about Terry—the birthday card that said "To my dearest Brother"; the way she can always make the baby laugh; the times she wanted to take his turn doing the dishes. Remembering how people often laugh at her, Carlo begins to cry and starts to run—nearly tripping over Terry, who is sitting on the floor playing with a baby while the mother shops nearby. The woman compliments Terry on her help with the fussy child. Carlo resists the urge to yell at Terry and hugs her instead. Then they go home. After that, although he still feels annoyed at his sister sometimes, Carlo remembers the day she was lost and how he felt. On Terry's birthday he gives her a card, "To a wonderful sister," that she carries around for a week. His family is pleased, even his grandmother: "Your heart is in better shape than I thought it was."

A young boy's resentment toward his mentally retarded sister, who is often made his responsibility, changes when he loses track of her in a department store. Though it doesn't entirely eliminate his resentment, the episode does help him see his sister's special talents and qualities. Once Carlo perceives Terry as a person rather than a burden, he can acknowledge and express his love for her. Young readers may be helped to see that mentally retarded people are more similar to them than different. Illustrations clearly show the girl's warm, gentle, loving personality.

Ages 6-9

**Also available in:**
No other form known

## 712

Yep, Laurence Michael

### Kind Hearts and Gentle Monsters
Harper & Row, Publishers, Inc., 1982.
(175 pages)

---

MENTAL ILLNESS: of Parent
  Autonomy
  Boy-girl relationships: dating
  Differences, human
  Empathy
  Guilt, feelings of
  Self, attitude toward: confidence

---

High school sophomore Charley Sabini angrily confronts Chris Pomeroy with a Poison Chain Letter she wrote about how despicable he is. He soon discovers that eccentric Chris is more human than he'd expected, and Chris finds Charley isn't as stuffy as she'd thought. Chris has a knack for unsettling Charley and making him doubt things he's always accepted. Before Charley meets her mother, though, Chris remarks that her mother is the real monster of the family. Charley then discovers that Chris's mother has been in a mental institution, and he watches in horror as she saws at her wrist with a nail file until Chris stops her. He admires Chris's strength and courage in dealing with the explosive Mrs. Pomeroy every day. But Chris avoids Charley once he knows about her mother's condition. Finally, he goes to talk to her at the library where she works. Chris says her mother has chased away every friend she's ever had. They go to the zoo together, the place Chris and her father used to escape to when things were bad at home. Then nine-year-old Duane visits the library to look for books about Godzilla. He seems to need a "protector" and is very involved in his monster fantasies. Chris and Charley "adopt" him, but when Chris mentions the actor who plays Godzilla, Duane, who thinks Godzilla is real, turns on her in a rage. Upset by the boy's abuse, Chris remarks that Duane is as vicious and sick as her mother. Charley supports her, telling her not to believe her mother's and now Duane's criticisms and insults. Chris does try to lead her own life, as her mother's psychiatrist advised her to do. When she mentions spending Christmas Eve with Charley's family, her mother appears unhappy but refuses to go with her, even though Charley invites her. Chris demands that her mother pull herself together, accusing her of eating her husband alive (he died of a heart attack three years ago) and announcing that she'll not do the same thing to Chris. "I'm drowning, mother, and I've only got the strength to save myself." Chris gets into the Christmas spirit with a vengeance, intending to enjoy herself since her mother has made her last ten Christmases a misery. When Charley calls her Christmas morning, she says her mother's been hospitalized after a suicide attempt. They are in a hopeless cycle, Chris explains. Her mother always appears to get better, but then as soon as Chris tries to pull away she regresses. She has tried to kill herself once before. Chris says she can feel her mother reaching out to her, but she finds such emptiness inside herself. Charley comforts her. They visit the zoo; Chris talks about the daily appointment she and her mother will have with the psychiatrist and the line she'll have to walk between supporting her mother and living her own life. Charley promises to stay around long enough to convince Chris she's really a good person.

Chris's struggles to live with her emotionally fragile mother are narrated by her new friend, Charley, who learns from her to empathize with other people's pain and confusion. He helps encourage Chris, whose sense of worth has been damaged by her critical, obsessive mother. Chris's mother isn't a monster but a suffering human being, making the situation more confusing and painful for both Chris and Charley. This is a gripping, realistic story of growth and courage in the face of an insoluble, anguishing problem. The book may alert readers to the possibility that a cocky facade can hide a heartbreaking story, and it emphasizes the importance of understanding and empathy in human relationships.

Ages 12 and up

**Also available in:**
No other form known

## 713

Yep, Laurence Michael

**Sea Glass**

Harper & Row, Publishers, Inc., 1979.
(213 pages)

---

*CHINESE-AMERICAN
IDENTITY, SEARCH FOR*
  *Age: respect for
  Boy-girl relationships
  Communication: parent-child
  Friendship: meaning of
  Maturation
  Prejudice: ethnic/racial
  Pride/False pride*

---

Twelve-year-old Craig Chin respects his Chinese heritage, although he is taunted by classmates and encouraged by his father to be an all-American boy. Until recently, Craig and his parents lived in San Francisco's Chinatown, where Craig's total environment was Chinese. Now his family has moved to the town of Concepcion to manage a neighborhood grocery store. For Craig's father, the move is a dream realized: he is his own boss, his family lives in a private apartment, and the area behind the store provides perfect space for growing flowers and for a hoop to shoot baskets with Craig. Craig, however, is miserable. He misses his friends in Chinatown and, more than that, he misses the traditions of his Chinese culture. Craig's father, a champion basketball player in his youth, demands that Craig try to find acceptance with his American peers by becoming a sports hero. Craig, heavy-set and uncoordinated, prefers to study, although he tries hard at both football and basketball. His father insists that the two work out together daily and then loses his temper when Craig does poorly. Craig's upbringing does not permit him to challenge his father's position or even to express an opinion. One day while delivering groceries, Craig meets his father's elderly Chinese friend, fondly called Uncle Quail. Though a reclusive and stubborn man, Uncle takes a liking to Craig and seems to understand the boy's confusion. The two swim together in the ocean waters near Uncle's home, where the old man introduces Craig to the beautiful undersea life. One day a popular classmate, Kenyon, follows Craig to Uncle's. Secretly, she watches the two swim. When Craig discovers her presence he angrily confronts her, but later they become friends. Uncle Quail, however, remains angry, convinced that Craig has deceived him by telling a "white demon" of their secret cove. Kenyon, however, is uninterested in Uncle's prejudices and persists in wanting to join the two for a swim. In time Craig convinces Uncle to let her come, but when Kenyon herself backs out because of rain, Uncle convinces Craig that she's not worth bothering with. So Kenyon becomes angry with Craig. Then Craig, thinking Uncle has betrayed *him* over a promise to dive for abalone, turns against the old man. Meanwhile, at home, Craig's father continues to badger the boy about playing sports. Finally, Craig

defends himself, enraging his father by saying he does not choose to enter the white man's world in that way. Craig is overwhelmed by all the conflicts in his life, but his mother encourages him to be patient and wait for an opportunity to solve each dilemma. In time it is Uncle Quail who becomes the peacemaker. He misses Craig and comes to the boy's home to say that Kenyon may swim with them in the cove. Uncle speaks to Craig's father about permitting Craig to pursue his own dreams, and Mr. Chin reluctantly agrees. At last Uncle, Craig, and Kenyon swim together in the cove.

A Chinese boy, proud of his heritage, cannot understand why his peers, and especially his own father, want him to change his ways. An old Chinese man tells the boy to observe the world around him carefully and learn from it, to listen to his inner desires and act upon them. The result: a more mature young man who begins to know himself and how he wishes to live. The Chinese-American author captures the flavor of Chinese life as it is lived in the United States, particularly the respect of Chinese children for their elders. This authenticity enhances a warm story of family life and interpersonal relationships.

Ages 11-14

**Also available in:**
No other form known

## 714

York, Carol Beach

**Remember Me When I Am Dead**

Elsevier/Nelson Books, 1980.
(94 pages)

---

*JEALOUSY: Sibling
  Death: of mother
  Manipulation
  Stepparent: mother*

---

On the last day of school before Christmas vacation, nine-year-old Jenny Loring insists she has just seen old Mr. Hoffman, a family friend who has moved away. The mention of Mr. Hoffman brings back memories for Jenny's thirteen-year-old sister, Sara. It also leaves their stepmother of one month, Margaret, feeling the presence of their mother, killed the year before in a railway accident in Switzerland. Jenny had had nightmares for a long time afterwards, refusing to believe her mother was really dead. That night Margaret finds a verse penciled in the front of Jenny's geography book: "Roses are blue/Violets are red/Remember me/When I am dead/Momma." A tearful Jenny insists she didn't write it, that her mother did. Later, Mrs. Dow, the housekeeper, finds a letter addressed to Momma in Switzerland and gives it to Margaret. They assume it is in Jenny's handwriting. In the letter, Jenny asks her mother to come home for Christmas. When the girls propose to go Christmas shopping and Margaret tries to dissuade them because Jenny looks so pale and tired, Sara angrily remembers all the times Jenny has gotten her own way. Sara asks Mrs. Dow whether she thinks Jenny should go away to school, as the family had discussed when Jenny was having so much trouble adjusting to her mother's death. On Christmas day, after all the gifts have been opened, Margaret finds the last gift tucked behind the tree. It is addressed to "Jenny-wren from Momma." The next day finds Sara with a post-Christmas letdown. She has received a new pair of ice skates, as she does every Christmas, and remembers a day when Jenny was just three and recently recovered from a serious illness. Sara was ice skating, but Momma and Daddy weren't watching her; they were watching Jenny. So she decided to skate across the pond, ignoring their calls to come back in her delight at having their undivided attention. She fell through thin ice and had to be carried to Mr. Hoffman's cottage. Ever since then, Sara can't bear to ice skate, although her parents have never noticed and keep giving her new pairs of skates. Sara muses that Jenny looks like Momma, but she doesn't; that their mother called her younger daughter Jenny-wren, but had no special name for her older girl. Sara had hoped that things would change after her father married Margaret. But they hadn't; Jenny was still the favorite. So, after Jenny had said she saw Mr. Hoffman, Sara had hatched her plan. She knew that if Jenny got upset again about their mother's death, their father would send her away to school. Then she, Sara, would become the center of her father's and Margaret's lives and they would give her all their love. It was easy to imitate Jenny's handwriting in the poem and the letter. Now Sara writes a New Year's greeting to "Jenny-wren" and hides it in her schoolbook to use later. She goes downstairs to find her father, Margaret, and a tearful Jenny talking about boarding school. Sara has "no time to realize that everything was not exactly as she had planned." Jenny will indeed be sent away to school, but Sara will go with her to keep her company. Bursting with frustrated anger, Sara holds her tongue, because if she protests no one will love her. Jenny looks at Sara, not knowing that she is "the person in the world she should least trust," and says, "I'm glad you're going too, Sara. I don't want to go alone."

Deeply jealous of her younger sister, a girl hatches a plan to rid herself of the child, but it backfires. This suspenseful, almost brooding, story allows the reader to identify with Sara and her jealousy, which is revealed in her memories. The shocking ending offers no hope for a resolution of Sara's feelings, since her parents still don't know of her manipulations. The striving for atmospheric effect here deprives the characters of depth. Still, Sara's mental state and the unsettling conclusion may invite discussion.

Ages 9-11

**Also available in:**
Paperbound—*Remember Me When I Am Dead*
Lodestar Books

**715**

Young, Helen

**What Difference Does It Make, Danny?**
Black/white illustrations by Quentin Blake.
André Deutsch Ltd., 1980.
(93 pages)

---

*EPILEPSY*
*SELF, ATTITUDE TOWARD: Accepting*
  *School: classmate relationships*
  *School: pupil-teacher relationships*

---

Danny Blane, about nine, is a perfectly ordinary English schoolboy, except that he has epilepsy. His teachers and classmates know he has it and readily accept him. They also know he is on medication to control his seizures. Danny loves gym and all sports, especially swimming. At the school's sports day in the country, he comes in second in three running events. In a new event, swim races, he wins first place. One day in class Danny feels a seizure coming. He tells his teacher and then lies down. The children watch as Danny has a *grand mal* seizure. The teacher, who puts her folded jacket under his head, explains what is happening. Afterwards, the students ask Danny questions about his experience. Soon a new games master, Mr. Masterson, joins the school. Danny, because of his athletic ability, becomes one of Mr. Masterson's prized students—until he discovers that Danny has epilepsy. Then he refuses to let the boy participate in any sports. Any competitive stress, he fears, could cause Danny to have a seizure. Danny's teacher must tell him that his activities in gym will now be restricted to vaulting and mat routines. Hurt and bitter that Mr. Masterson didn't even bother to talk to him himself, Danny becomes extremely uncooperative in school. Soon he is "determined to behave as badly as he dared." His parents become increasingly distressed by his moods. Finally, his mother goes to talk with the principal. While the two converse, truant Danny is walking along a canal he's forbidden to go near. Suddenly he sees a small boy fall into the water. Danny dives in and, struggling to stay above water and reach shore, pulls the boy out. The boy's mother and neighbors rush both youngsters to the hospital, and soon Danny is a hero. Several days later he receives the Royal Humane Society Award at his school assembly. After the assembly Mr. Masterson apologizes to Danny. He also challenges the boy to prepare for the championship games.

A young epileptic boy proves his capabilities as an athlete in this well-written, informative book that emphasizes Danny's special needs rather than his limitations. Danny accepts and can freely discuss his condition, the information about which comes through clearly without didacticism. Lively pencil sketches add interest to this valuable book.

Ages 9-12

**Also available in:**
No other form known

**716**

Zalben, Jane Breskin

**Maybe It Will Rain Tomorrow**

Farrar, Straus & Giroux, Inc., 1982.
(181 pages)

---

REJECTION: Parental
  Belonging
  Change: accepting
  Parent/Parents: remarriage of
  Sex: premarital
  Stepparent: mother
  Suicide: of parent

---

When Beth Corey's mother commits suicide, sixteen-year-old Beth goes to live with her father, his wife, Linda, and their new baby. Beth's father left when she was ten, and Beth has never liked Linda. Starting at a new high school in April of her sophomore year, she meets Jonathan Schein, a good-looking, intelligent boy who has a scholarship at Juilliard for his Saturday morning flute lessons. One Saturday, when Beth takes the same train into New York City with him for a visit with her Aunt Ellen, they talk and make arrangements to meet. Beth wants to know from Ellen why her parents divorced and why her mother killed herself: "Wasn't I a good enough reason for Mom to stay around?" Her aunt sighs. "Of course you were, Beth." After her visit, Beth joins Jonathan and his friends as they play music for passersby, collecting money for it. Later in the week, Beth has dinner at Jonathan's house. She likes his family and plays one of her original songs for Jonathan. She also tells him about her mother's suicide and her own feelings of anger and guilt. One afternoon Beth and Jonathan skip school and go to the beach, where they make love, Beth for the first time. The next Saturday when Beth again joins Jonathan and his friends to play music on the New York sidewalks, they play one of her compositions. She and Jonathan decide to stay in town for a concert, and Beth declines to inform Linda; her father is out of town. They go to Jonathan's father's store and make love, falling asleep and not catching a train until very late. When Beth walks in, an angry Linda is waiting for her. Things are so uncomfortable between Linda and Beth all weekend that Beth packs a bag on Monday and arrives on her Aunt Ellen's doorstep. Beth tells Ellen about her involvement with Jonathan; Ellen matter-of-factly says she hopes they were careful and offers Beth her gynecologist's number. Beth confesses to her aunt her fears of being left alone again, as she was first by her father, then by her mother. What if Jonathan also abandons her? Ellen takes Beth home and talks to Linda, who resents being forced to deal with problems that her husband and his first wife should have dealt with. Beth accuses her father of keeping himself emotionally distant from everyone. She and Jonathan visit the country club, which isn't open for the season yet, and make love in one of the cabanas. Afterwards, Jonathan tells Beth he's going to spend the summer working in the Catskills. She feels betrayed; she'd never have made love with him if she'd known he wasn't going to be around. In the days before he leaves, Beth cannot bring herself to speak to him or respond to his notes. But they correspond during the summer, and Beth's life at home gets easier. When she visits Jonathan at the resort, she suspects he's seeing other girls. They make love and she knows, although she can't quite accept it, that it's the last time. By summer's end, Beth has made two new friends and is feeling more at home with her father and Linda. Then, in spite of several overtures from Jonathan, Beth decides not to resume any kind of relationship with him. "Alone no longer felt bad. It didn't mean loneliness; it meant I belonged to myself."

A teenage girl feels helpless in the face of relentless changes in her life: her mother's suicide, a new home with her father and his family, a new school, a first love affair. She learns that she must turn to herself for the sense of belonging and security she covets. This first-person account of a young woman struggling with feelings of rejection never provides a satisfying explanation for Beth's mother's suicide. But Beth's eventual response is to take charge of her own life and acknowledge that she has no control over other people's behavior. Beth's sexual relationship with Jonathan is presented as a fact, one of many things happening in Beth's life, of no great import or meaning; the book includes some rough language and sexual description. Beth's interaction with Linda, her stepmother, is something of a barometer of her increasing maturity. Toward the end, the reader knows there is hope for the relationship and for Beth as a competent, maturing person.

Ages 12 and up

**Also available in:**
No other form known

---

**Z**

**717**

Zalben, Jane Breskin

**Norton's Nighttime**

Color illustrations by the author.
William Collins Publishers, Inc., 1979.
(24 pages counted) o.p.

---

FEAR: of Darkness
LOST, BEING

---

A young raccoon named Norton wanders away from his pine tree and cannot find his way home before nightfall. He hears the sounds of the forest and wonders if something is coming to get him. He thinks of his friends Possum, Porcupine, and Rabbit and imagines what they would do in this situation. Finally, when he gets the courage to challenge the noises, he finds that he has only been hearing his friends—who have been as scared of him as he has been of them. As they walk home together, no one is afraid any longer. They all drift off to sleep, secure in the knowledge that if any one of them needs help, the others are close by.

Small children will understand Norton's feelings of fear and insecurity and will laugh with relief as the raccoon discovers his friends. This sweet, reassuring story with its charming, subdued illustrations would be especially appropriate for reading aloud at bedtime. The simple text makes it also suitable for the beginning reader.

Ages 2-6

Also available in:
No other form known

## 718

Zelonky, Joy

### I Can't Always Hear You

Color illustrations by Barbara Bejna and Shirlee Jensen.
Raintree Publishers, Inc., 1980.
(30 pages)

DEAFNESS
DIFFERENCES, HUMAN
  School: classmate relationships
  School: mainstreaming
  Self, attitude toward: feeling different

Kim, a hearing-impaired girl of about ten, is attending a regular school for the first time. On the first day, her teacher, Mr. Davis, speaks loudly to her until she tells him he doesn't need to shout. Although she cannot always hear, she usually can. During arithmetic, Kim's best subject, she answers a question with "Eight tickery three is five," whereupon the whole class laughs. Reassuring Kim that her answer was indeed correct, Mr. Davis repeats the problem and solution. Kim clearly hears the words "take away" and repeats them to herself. Then, removing his glasses, Mr. Davis points out to the class that many people need glasses to see better, just as Kim needs a hearing aid to hear better. During lunch, when Erik, a classmate, taunts Kim, she makes a sarcastic retort about his dental braces and runs out of the room. At home that night, she tells her mother that she is "the only one in the world with a hearing aid" and that people always treat her differently. Her mother responds that each person is unique in some way and that people just need to get used to one another. But the next day brings an intensely embarrassing mistake for Kim. She notices several students lining up and so joins them, unaware that the teacher has asked all the boys who need to use the lavatory to form a line. After school that afternoon, Kim tells Mr. Davis that she doesn't plan to come back anymore. She hates being made fun of, she explains. He suggests that it might have helped if she had laughed along with the others about the washroom incident, but Kim replies that she didn't find it funny. Taking the girl by the hand, Mr. Davis escorts her to the principal's office. Ms. Pinkowski reveals to Kim that she too wears a hearing aid and that she also had trouble being accepted in school. Being friendly and patient makes things easier. "Expect a lot from yourself," she tells the girl. "Soon others will too." The following day on the playground, Erik's ball lands at Kim's feet. Rather than make an accusing remark, she simply tosses the ball back to him with a courteous comment. He asks to see her hearing aid and she removes it to give him a look. After he examines it, Erik tells Kim that now he is pleased she is in his class. When Kim begins to explain how she is different from the others, Erik points out that her hearing aid is no stranger than his braces. Sasha, a very tall girl who has come up beside Erik and Kim, adds that her height makes her different. Others join in, confessing their own special differences: one is adopted, another has no television set at home, another is a twin, another learned to read at the age of four, another gets a rash from eating chocolate. When the bell rings, the children all run back into the school, laughing together.

Kim tells how she learned to adjust to a mainstreamed classroom and how her classmates learned to accept her. The girl has obviously managed to overcome her physical disability, but now must struggle with the way others treat her. An introductory note for parents and teachers points out that the book can not only help break down the walls between disabled and nondisabled people, but can also prompt readers to consider the special qualities of all people. Illustrations show children of various sizes, shapes, and ethnic backgrounds.

Ages 7-10

Also available in:
No other form known

## 719

Zelonky, Joy

### My Best Friend Moved Away

Color illustrations by Angela Adams.
Raintree Publishers, Inc., 1980.
(31 pages)

CHANGE: Accepting
FRIENDSHIP: Best Friend
  Moving

Young Brian does not like hearing that his best friend Nick's parents have bought a new house. As soon as his house is sold, Nick will be moving across town and will transfer schools. Hoping to obstruct the sale, Brian rips the For Sale sign in Nick's yard off its post and hurls it into the street. The next day Nick tells Brian that someone played a dirty trick and stole their For Sale sign, almost losing them some potential buyers. Brian realizes his gesture was wrong and futile. One morning Nick meets Brian on the way to school and announces that his house has been sold and they will move in a month. Miserably unhappy, Brian can't bring himself to say anything in the face of Nick's obvious happiness. On moving day, Brian presents Nick with a bag of his best marbles as a going-away present. Then he retreats to his room, feeling miserably lonely. His father comes in to comfort him, but Brian is sure he will never again have a friend like Nick. "No two people are alike," agrees his father. "That's why each friend is special." One day Nick calls and invites Brian to visit. While there, Brian suggests that the two of them play marbles or fly kites. But Nick pooh-poohs the ideas, declaring that none of the kids in this new neighborhood do such things. Instead, he takes Brian, who is sworn to secrecy, to a construction site. Scoffing at Brian's worry that this is a dangerous place to play, Nick proceeds to walk across a narrow board straddling a deep, muddy hole. Brian hesitates to follow, but Nick goads him. The board is unsteady and Brian marvels that Nick, who wears a leg brace, managed to cross it so easily. Brian, on the other hand, slips and falls into the mud. As she helps Brian clean up, Nick's mother reprimands her son for the escapade and grounds him for the next day. Nick blames Brian for his punishment and a distressed Brian runs outside, where he meets his father who has come to pick him up. On the way to the subway, Brian tells what happened and how different Nick seems. Brian's father points out that Nick has been through a lot of changes and that he is probably not as happy as he appears to be. Riding the subway, Brian thinks this over. He does not like the fact that people have to change. His father suggests that he remember all the good times he had with Nick. Brian decides that eventually he might change too, "but if I'm careful, maybe the good things about me will get better." When he suddenly remembers that he has promised to play marbles with some kids on his block, father and son disembark to buy replacement marbles for the ones Brian gave Nick.

In this first-person narrative, young Brian explains how time and his father's support help him accept his best friend's moving and changing. Brian's confusion and sense of loss come through clearly, enhanced by the bright, appealing illustrations. Especially noteworthy is the close father-son relationship. A note encourages parents and teachers to help children express and work through their feelings of personal loss.

Ages 6-9

**Also available in:**
No other form known

## 720

Zhitkov, Boris Stepanovich

### How I Hunted the Little Fellows

Translated from the Russian by Djemma Bider.
Black/white illustrations by Paul O. Zelinsky.
Dodd, Mead & Company, Inc., 1979.
(52 pages counted)

---

*IMAGINATION*
*PROMISE, KEEPING*
  *Guilt, feelings of*
  *Russia*
  *Self-discipline*

---

A young boy visiting his grandmother is captivated by the intricate model ship displayed on a special shelf on the wall. At his grandmother's urging he promises never to touch the treasured model, but soon his imagination has supplied the ship with a tiny crew the size of matches, who he believes come out at night. Convincing his grandmother to leave a lamp burning overnight, he tries to stay awake to glimpse the crew. When the bedsprings creak he is discouraged, thinking he has alerted them. Deciding to trick them, he puts a large piece of candy by the small cabin door. Perhaps, he thinks, they will chop the door down to get the candy inside. In the morning, however, the candy is untouched. That night he tries to stay awake, but falls asleep. Next morning the candy is gone. He leaves bread. Finding leftover crumbs, he decides the crew prefers candy. Frustrated at failing to see them, he finally decides to examine the ship. When his grandmother wants to take him visiting he feigns a headache. She leaves without him and he takes the ship down. He shakes it, but sees and hears nothing. He tries to pry the deck loose with a knife, but rope ladders hold it down. He cuts the ropes, pulls the

deck up, and slams his hand down to trap the crew. The inside of the ship is empty. He tries to reassemble the model, but it is ruined and he puts it back on the shelf. When his grandmother returns he is in bed, sobbing. She hurries to comfort him, and he realizes she has not yet seen the ruined ship.

The power of unchecked imagination leads a young boy to break his promise and destroy his grandmother's prized possession in this first-person account based on the author's experience in pre-revolutionary Russia. Detailed illustrations capture the time, place, and tone of the story, which has universal appeal and is open-ended to promote discussion. In an appended biographical note, the reader learns that the boy was so distraught over the destruction and his disobedience that he ran away and hid, and that his grandmother forgave him.

Ages 3-7

**Also available in:**
No other form known

## 721

Zindel, Bonnie and Paul Zindel

### A Star for the Latecomer

Harper & Row, Publishers, Inc., 1980.
(185 pages)

---

*CANCER*
*DEATH: of Mother*
*PARENTAL: Interference*
  *Autonomy*
  *Careers: dancer*
  *Illnesses: terminal*
  *Loss: feelings of*

---

Brooke Hillary loves to dance and attends a special high school for aspiring performers. But she goes to the school chiefly to please her mother, since Brooke suffers from stage fright and doesn't like to perform. Sometimes Brooke wishes she were a normal teenager attending a regular school, going to football games, but most of her attention now is consumed by her mother's worsening illness. The girl is convinced her mother has terminal cancer, and when her fears are confirmed Brooke vows to become a star before her mother dies. But her despair intensifies when it seems that all the people she loves are deserting her: Brandon, her boyfriend, in Alaska filming a movie, will be unable to return for Christmas. Determined to land a good part in a show, Brooke auditions frequently. After one successful tryout, however, she learns she will have to be "very friendly" to the agent and perhaps the director if she really wants the part. She refuses. Then Brooke and her mother are asked to represent Brooke's school on the "Tonight Show." Brooke's excitement is tempered by her mother's increasing sickness and then shattered by news that her best friend, a talented ice skater, will soon move away. Her mother gathers her remaining strength for the television show and it goes well. Brooke learns to give her mother injections of a pain-killing medicine. In a weak moment she writes a supplicating love letter to Brandon and then a letter from him crosses hers in the mail—a cool, shallow, egotistical letter. When Brooke graduates from high school, her mother gives her a pearl ring, a family symbol of freedom. Her mother now longs to die and, as death approaches, she apologizes to Brooke for pushing her so hard. Soon after, she dies. For a moment, Brooke hates her mother. Then she puts her dancing shoes into her mother's casket. She will choose her own path from now on. She speaks to her mother's body, forgiving her, affirming her love. Brooke is free.

Brooke's first-person narrative is a poignant record of insight gained through great emotional pain. Her mother's slow death brings home to her the fact that her own life has been shaped by her mother's wishes, that she must now set herself free. Brooke's feelings and thoughts about death and about her complicated relationship with her mother are revealing and instructive. The effects of terminal cancer on the victim and the family are portrayed with realism and restraint.

Ages 12 and up

**Also available in:**
Paperbound—*A Star for the Latecomer*
Bantam Books, Inc.

## 722

### Zolotow, Charlotte Shapiro

### If You Listen

Color illustrations by Marc Simont.
Harper & Row, Publishers, Inc., 1980.
(29 pages counted)

---

*PARENTAL: Absence*
*SEPARATION FROM LOVED ONES*
  *Communication: parent-child*
  *Imagination*

---

A little girl whose father has been away for a long time asks her mother how she can tell if someone far away loves her. Admitting she means her father, she wonders, "If I can't see him, or hear him, or feel his hugs, how can I know he loves me when he isn't here?" Her mother explains a special way of listening, like listening to the faraway church bells or feeling the night outside her dark bedroom, with the distant foghorn and the dog barking in the hills. This listening is like the flash of lightning on a still summer day when you hear the thunder coming behind it; like when a petal from the vase of roses in the living room falls onto the coffee table. Her mother advises the girl to listen hard inside herself so she can feel someone far away sending his love to her. The little girl isn't quite convinced. "I will listen hard, but I wish he'd come home."

A mother reassures her little daughter that her father loves her, even though he is far away. Young readers may need help understanding the rather fragmented and abstract text. No explanation is given for the father's absence, so this could fit a variety of family circumstances. Beautiful illustrations help convey the thoughtful, lyrical tone.

Ages 5-7

**Also available in:**
No other form known

## 723

### Zolotow, Charlotte Shapiro

### The New Friend

Color illustrations by Emily Arnold McCully.
Thomas Y. Crowell Company, Inc., 1981.
(31 pages counted)

---

*FRIENDSHIP: Best Friend*
  *Loss: feelings of*

---

A little girl has a close friend with long brown hair. The two girls play together often. They walk in the woods, pick wild flowers, and wade in the brook. They play in the attic when it rains and go barefoot in the grass when the rain stops. They share apples under the trees and talk together. One day the girl calls for her friend, but she is not home. The girl finds her in the woods with another friend. The girl watches as her friend shares the wild flowers and brook with this new friend. At home she sees them enjoying the activities she and her friend enjoyed, singing their songs and jumping rope. The girl goes home and cries herself to sleep. She dreams she finds a new friend and walks with her in the woods. The new friend shows her new paths and new flowers. When she wakes up she decides to look for this new friend. When she finds her she's sure to remember her other one with the long brown hair. "But maybe then I won't care!"

In this gentle first-person tale, a little girl feels hurt and disappointed when her friend forsakes her. Her dream shows her that new, different, perhaps even better friends await her. In time she will forget the hurt, but she will always remember the friend. Soft, pastel illustrations complement the spare, lyrical text.

Ages 3-7

**Also available in:**
No other form known

## 724

### Zolotow, Charlotte Shapiro

### One Step, Two . . .

Color illustrations by Cindy Wheeler.
Lothrop, Lee & Shepard Company, 1981.
(30 pages counted)

---

*COMMUNICATION: Parent-Child*
*SHARING/NOT SHARING*
  *Nature: appreciation of*

---

One spring morning a mother and her little daughter start out on a walk to the corner. The girl shows her mother a yellow crocus and a fat gray cat. Then the child sees a blue jay and stops to pick up a white stone that gleams like the moon. Walking on, she sees clothes dancing on a clothesline. Then she hears the garbage truck grinding up the garbage, and the church bells ringing. Going on, they pass a yellow school bus. When they reach the corner, the mother says it is time to go home for lunch. On the way the child stops to pick some daffodils, but her mother reminds her that the flowers do not belong to them. So she bends to smell the flowers instead and, when she stands up, discovers yellow powder on her nose. Mr. Peabody and his big dog approach, and the friendly dog licks the powder right off. Mother and child walk past a house with plants in the window, and the mother names them for the girl. Then they are home. The little girl stops at the bottom of the steps, holds up her arms, and is carried in by her mother. Fast asleep, she does not hear her mother thanking her for showing her so many lovely things on their walk.

For a young child and her mother, a spring walk becomes an occasion for sharing and appreciating many little discoveries and wonders. The charming, rhythmic text conveys the pleasures of a companionable stroll. Originally published in 1955, this is newly illustrated with warm, pastel pictures that emphasize mother and child.

Ages 2-5

**Also available in:**
No other form known

---

**725**

**Zolotow, Charlotte Shapiro**

## The White Marble

Black/white illustrations by Deborah Kogan Ray.
Thomas Y. Crowell Company, Inc., 1982.
(32 pages)

---

*FRIENDSHIP*
  *Nature: appreciation of*
  *Sharing/Not sharing*

---

One hot, still summer's night, John Henry and his parents walk to the park. John Henry picks up something from the grass. When his father asks him what he found, John Henry replies, "Nothing." Sitting between his parents on the bench, the only child in the park, John Henry feels lonely, even though he knows it is special to be allowed out late like this. Then he sees Pamela, a girl from school, arrive with her mother. He and she smile at each other and seem to understand that only children can know what a night like this really means. They run together, kicking off their shoes and enjoying the sweet, fresh-smelling air. Lying on the soft grass, John Henry shows Pamela the white marble he found. She thinks it's beautiful. "No grown-up would have known." They drink from the white, foamy fountain and let the icy water run down their necks. Their parents call them to the ice-cream man's cart and buy them pineapple sticks. When it's time to go, John Henry presses the white marble into Pamela's hand and tells her to keep it.

A young boy and girl share a special evening in the park, made magical by their sensuous appreciation of the soft breezes, fresh-smelling grass, icy fountain, and starry sky. Their friendship is a spontaneous one, formed from the simple bond of childhood. In this newly illustrated version of the story, soft, shaded pictures reinforce the lyrical mood established by the text.

Ages 4-8

**Also available in:**
No other form known

Z

# SUBJECT INDEX

To locate a book through the Subject Index, find the desired subject; titles of relevant books are listed under each subject. Numbers refer to annotation numbers.

# A

## Abandonment

**See also:** *Loss: feelings of; Rejection; Separation from loved ones*
Byars, Betsy Cromer. THE TWO-THOUSAND-POUND GOLDFISH.
Ages 9-12. 99
Culin, Charlotte. CAGES OF GLASS, FLOWERS OF TIME.
Ages 12 and up. 145
Dixon, Paige, pseud. SKIPPER.
Ages 12 and up. 165
Dunlop, Eileen Rhona. FOX FARM.
Ages 10-12. 175
Fairless, Caroline. HAMBONE.
Ages 8-11. 184
Hill, Margaret. TURN THE PAGE, WENDY.
Ages 10-14. 291
Hinton, Susan Eloise. TEX.
Ages 11-15. 292
Klass, Sheila Solomon. TO SEE MY MOTHER DANCE.
Ages 10-13. 344
Leach, Michael. DON'T CALL ME ORPHAN!
Ages 10-12. 360
Morgan, Alison Mary. ALL KINDS OF PRICKLES.
Ages 11-13. 450
Peterson, Jeanne Whitehouse. THAT IS THAT.
Ages 5-8. 497
Sargent, Sarah. SECRET LIES.
Ages 11 and up. 570
Strang, Celia. FOSTER MARY.
Ages 10-13. 633
Voigt, Cynthia. HOMECOMING.
Ages 11 and up. 672

## Abortion

**See also:** *Pregnancy*
Posner, Grace. IN MY SISTER'S EYES.
Ages 12 and up. 516
Prince, Alison. THE TURKEY'S NEST.
Ages 12 and up. 520
Rinaldi, Ann. PROMISES ARE FOR KEEPING.
Ages 12 and up. 534
Truss, Jan. BIRD AT THE WINDOW.
Ages 13 and up. 661

## Absent Parent

**See:** *Divorce: of parents; Parental: absence*

## Accidents

**See also:** *Guilt, feelings of; Hospital, going to*
Colman, Hila Crayder. ACCIDENT.
Ages 11 and up. 132
Marino, Barbara Pavis. ERIC NEEDS STITCHES.
Ages 4-10. 403
Richter, Elizabeth. THE TEENAGE HOSPITAL EXPERIENCE: YOU CAN HANDLE IT!
Ages 12 and up. 532

### Airplane
Milton, Hilary Herbert. MAYDAY! MAYDAY!
Ages 9-11. 427

### Automobile
Bates, Betty. PICKING UP THE PIECES.
Ages 10-13. 40
Butterworth, William Edmund. UNDER THE INFLUENCE.
Ages 12 and up. 94
McCaffrey, Mary. MY BROTHER ANGE.
Ages 8-11. 389
Mazer, Norma Fox. WHEN WE FIRST MET.
Ages 12 and up. 416

Van Leeuwen, Jean. SEEMS LIKE THIS ROAD GOES ON FOREVER.
Ages 12 and up. 663

### Fractures. *See: Fractures*

### Hit and run. *See also: Crime/Criminals*
Atkinson, Linda. HIT AND RUN.
Ages 11 and up. 31

## Achievement

**See:** *Competition; School: achievement/underachievement; Success*

## Addiction

**See:** *Alcoholism; Drugs; Marijuana; Peer relationships: peer pressures*

## Adolescence

**See:** *Maturation; Menstruation; Puberty*

## Adoption

**See also:** *Children's home, living in; Identity, search for; Orphan*
Tax, Meredith. FAMILIES.
Ages 4-8. 645

### Explaining
Drescher, Joan Elizabeth. YOUR FAMILY, MY FAMILY.
Ages 5-7. 173
Krementz, Jill. HOW IT FEELS TO BE ADOPTED.
Ages 9 and up. 351
Stein, Sara Bonnett. THE ADOPTED ONE: AN OPEN FAMILY BOOK FOR PARENTS AND CHILDREN TOGETHER.
Ages 4-8. 625

### Feelings about
Adler, Carole Schwerdtfeger. THE CAT THAT WAS LEFT BEHIND.
Ages 9-12. 3
Bates, Betty. IT MUST'VE BEEN THE FISH STICKS.
Ages 10-13. 37
First, Julia. I, REBEKAH, TAKE YOU, THE LAWRENCES.
Ages 11-13. 187
Gordon, Shirley. THE BOY WHO WANTED A FAMILY.
Ages 7-9. 222
Krementz, Jill. HOW IT FEELS TO BE ADOPTED.
Ages 9 and up. 351
Miner, Jane Claypool. MIRACLE OF TIME: ADOPTING A SISTER.
Ages 11 and up. 430
Myers, Walter Dean. WON'T KNOW TILL I GET THERE.
Ages 11-14. 460
Pfeffer, Susan Beth. ABOUT DAVID.
Ages 13 and up. 500
Pfeffer, Susan Beth. JUST BETWEEN US.
Ages 10-12. 502
Shyer, Marlene Fanta. MY BROTHER, THE THIEF.
Ages 10-13. 594
Stein, Sara Bonnett. THE ADOPTED ONE: AN OPEN FAMILY BOOK FOR PARENTS AND CHILDREN TOGETHER.
Ages 4-8. 625
Swartley, David Warren. MY FRIEND, MY BROTHER.
Ages 9-11. 642
Winthrop, Elizabeth. MARATHON MIRANDA.
Ages 9-11. 696

### Identity questions
Bates, Betty. IT MUST'VE BEEN THE FISH STICKS.
Ages 10-13. 37
Krementz, Jill. HOW IT FEELS TO BE ADOPTED.
Ages 9 and up. 351

## Alcoholism (cont.)

### Adolescent

Butterworth, William Edmund. UNDER THE
INFLUENCE.
Ages 12 and up. 94

Due, Linnea A. HIGH AND OUTSIDE.
Ages 13 and up. 174

Greene, Sheppard M. THE BOY WHO DRANK TOO
MUCH.
Ages 12 and up. 242

### Adult

Rinaldi, Ann. TERM PAPER.
Ages 12 and up. 535

### of Father

Greene, Sheppard M. THE BOY WHO DRANK TOO
MUCH.
Ages 12 and up. 242

Hassler, Jon Francis. JEMMY.
Ages 11 and up. 270

Miner, Jane Claypool. A DAY AT A TIME: DEALING
WITH AN ALCOHOLIC.
Ages 11 and up. 428

Wolkoff, Judie. WHERE THE ELF KING SINGS.
Ages 12 and up. 704

### of Mother

Adler, Carole Schwerdtfeger. IN OUR HOUSE
SCOTT IS MY BROTHER.
Ages 10-13. 5

Guy, Rosa Cuthbert. THE DISAPPEARANCE.
Ages 12 and up. 252

Harrah, Michael. FIRST OFFENDER.
Ages 11-13. 266

Holland, Isabelle. NOW IS NOT TOO LATE.
Ages 10-13. 301

Kenny, Kevin and Helen Krull. SOMETIMES MY
MOM DRINKS TOO MUCH.
Ages 5-8. 338

Rabinowich, Ellen. ROCK FEVER.
Ages 12 and up. 523

## Allergies

Allen, Marjorie N. ONE, TWO, THREE—AH-CHOO!
Ages 4-7. 13

## Alternatives

**See:** *Problem solving; Resourcefulness*

## Alzheimer's Disease

**See:** *Age: aging*

## Ambivalence, Feelings of

**See also:** *Problem solving*

Branscum, Robbie. FOR LOVE OF JODY.
Ages 9-12. 73

Dyer, Thomas A. THE WHIPMAN IS WATCHING.
Ages 10-14. 177

Guest, Elissa Haden. THE HANDSOME MAN.
Ages 12 and up. 251

Hughes, Dean. SWITCHING TRACKS.
Ages 10-14. 308

Iverson, Genie. I WANT TO BE BIG.
Ages 3-6. 327

Josephs, Rebecca. EARLY DISORDER.
Ages 13 and up. 335

Lorimar, Lawrence T. SECRETS.
Ages 12 and up. 382

Platt, Kin. BROGG'S BRAIN.
Ages 12 and up. 514

Rinaldi, Ann. PROMISES ARE FOR KEEPING.
Ages 12 and up. 534

Rodowsky, Colby F. A SUMMER'S WORTH OF
SHAME.
Ages 12-14. 548

Shreve, Susan Richards. THE MASQUERADE.
Ages 12 and up. 591

Stretton, Barbara. YOU NEVER LOSE.
Ages 12 and up. 639

Thomas, Karen. THE GOOD THING . . . THE BAD
THING.
Ages 3-7. 654

## Amputee

**See also:** *Hospital, going to; Limbs, abnormal or missing;
Surgery; Wheelchair, dependence on*

Sallis, Susan Diana. ONLY LOVE.
Ages 12 and up. 568

## Anger

**See also:** *Aggression; Depression; Hatred; Hostility*

Colman, Hila Crayder. ACCIDENT.
Ages 11 and up. 132

Grace, Fran. BRANIGAN'S DOG.
Ages 10 and up. 225

Greene, Constance Clarke. YOUR OLD PAL, AL.
Ages 9-13. 241

Hogan, Paula Z. SOMETIMES I GET SO MAD.
Ages 5-8. 298

Park, Barbara. DON'T MAKE ME SMILE.
Ages 8-11. 481

Platt, Kin. THE APE INSIDE ME.
Ages 12 and up. 513

Sharmat, Marjorie Weinman. ROLLO AND JULIET,
FOREVER!
Ages 4-8. 584

Sharmat, Mitchell. COME HOME, WILMA.
Ages 6-8. 588

Skolsky, Mindy Warshaw. CARNIVAL AND KOPECK
AND MORE ABOUT HANNAH.
Ages 7-9. 600

Stretton, Barbara. YOU NEVER LOSE.
Ages 12 and up. 639

## Animals

**See also:** *Pets; Transitional objects*

**Fear of.** *See: Fear: of animals*

### Love for

Adler, Carole Schwerdtfeger. THE CAT THAT WAS
LEFT BEHIND.
Ages 9-12. 3

Callen, Lawrence Willard. SORROW'S SONG.
Ages 9-12. 103

Crofford, Emily. STORIES FROM THE BLUE ROAD.
Ages 9-12. 143

Dolan, Sheila. THE WISHING BOTTLE.
Ages 7-9. 167

Dunne, Mary Collins. HOBY & STUB.
Ages 10-13. 176

Fairless, Caroline. HAMBONE.
Ages 8-11. 184

Graham, Ada and Frank Graham. JACOB AND OWL.
Ages 8-11. 228

Hall, Lynn. DANZA!
Ages 9-12. 254

Herzig, Alison Cragin and Jane Lawrence Mali. A
SEASON OF SECRETS.
Ages 11-13. 287

L'Engle, Madeleine Franklin. A RING OF ENDLESS
LIGHT.
Ages 11-14. 363

McPhail, David Michael. A WOLF STORY.
Ages 5-7. 399

Rounds, Glen Harold. BLIND OUTLAW.
Ages 9-11. 554

Shura, Mary Francis Craig. THE BARKLEY STREET
SIX-PACK.
Ages 9-12. 592

Somerlott, Robert. BLAZE.
Ages 10-13. 617

Thomas, Jane Resh. THE COMEBACK DOG.
Ages 7-9. 653

## Animals (cont.)

Wartski, Maureen Crane. THE LAKE IS ON FIRE.
Ages 10-13. 679
Wartski, Maureen Crane. MY BROTHER IS SPECIAL.
Ages 10-12. 681
Waterton, Betty Marie. A SALMON FOR SIMON.
Ages 4-7. 685

### Responsibility for

Billington, Elizabeth T. PART-TIME BOY.
Ages 8-10. 53
Carrick, Carol. A RABBIT FOR EASTER.
Ages 3-7. 105
Dolan, Sheila. THE WISHING BOTTLE.
Ages 7-9. 167
Gates, Doris. A MORGAN FOR MELINDA.
Ages 10-12. 203
Graeber, Charlotte Towner. GREY CLOUD.
Ages 9-11. 226
Waterton, Betty Marie. A SALMON FOR SIMON.
Ages 4-7. 685

## Anorexia Nervosa

See also: *Mental illness*
Hautzig, Deborah. SECOND STAR TO THE RIGHT.
Ages 12 and up. 272
Josephs, Rebecca. EARLY DISORDER.
Ages 13 and up. 335
Liu, Aimee. SOLITAIRE.
Ages 13 and up. 380
Richter, Elizabeth. THE TEENAGE HOSPITAL
EXPERIENCE: YOU CAN HANDLE IT!
Ages 12 and up. 532

## Anxiety

See also: *Fear; Separation anxiety*
Asher, Sandra Fenichel. JUST LIKE JENNY.
Ages 10-12. 27
Byars, Betsy Cromer. GOODBYE, CHICKEN LITTLE.
Ages 9-11. 97
Delton, Judy. MY MOTHER LOST HER JOB TODAY.
Ages 3-7. 156
Gordon, Shirley. THE BOY WHO WANTED A
FAMILY.
Ages 7-9. 222
Greenberg, Jan. A SEASON IN-BETWEEN.
Ages 11-13. 237
Helmering, Doris Wild. I HAVE TWO FAMILIES.
Ages 6-8. 279
Schuchman, Joan. TWO PLACES TO SLEEP.
Ages 5-7. 577
Smith, Anne Warren. BLUE DENIM BLUES.
Ages 12 and up. 607

## Apartheid

See also: *Prejudice: ethnic/racial*
Jones, Toeckey. GO WELL, STAY WELL.
Ages 12 and up. 334

## Apathy

See: *Depression*

## Appalachia

Bulla, Clyde Robert. DANIEL'S DUCK.
Ages 5-8. 85
Chaffin, Lillie Dorton. WE BE WARM TILL
SPRINGTIME COMES.
Ages 6-9. 110

## Appearance

See also: *Height; Weight control*

**Body concept.** *See: Self, attitude toward: body concept*

### Concern about

Belair, Richard L. DOUBLE TAKE.
Ages 13 and up. 44

Brown, Marc Tolan. ARTHUR'S EYES.
Ages 4-7. 80
Clifton, Lucille. SONORA BEAUTIFUL.
Ages 12-14. 123
First, Julia. LOOK WHO'S BEAUTIFUL!
Ages 10-12. 188
Guy, Rosa Cuthbert. THE DISAPPEARANCE.
Ages 12 and up. 252
Landis, James David. THE SISTERS IMPOSSIBLE.
Ages 9-11. 355
Okimoto, Jean Davies. IT'S JUST TOO MUCH.
Ages 10-12. 469
Robison, Nancy Louise. BALLET MAGIC.
Ages 9-11. 541
Rockwell, Anne F. and Harlow Rockwell. MY
BARBER.
Ages 3-6. 545
Sachs, Marilyn. BUS RIDE.
Ages 11-14. 563
Sachs, Marilyn. HELLO...WRONG NUMBER.
Ages 12-16. 565

**Deformities.** *See: Deformities*

**Glasses.** *See: Glasses, wearing of*

## Appendectomy

See: *Hospital, going to*

## Appetite

See: *Weight control*

## Apple Polishing

See: *Attention seeking*

## Approach-Avoidance Conflict

See: *Ambivalence, feelings of*

## Arguing

Byars, Betsy Cromer. THE ANIMAL, THE
VEGETABLE, AND JOHN D JONES.
Ages 10-12. 95
Delaney, Ned. BERT AND BARNEY.
Ages 3-7. 153
Oppenheimer, Joan Letson. GARDINE VS.
HANOVER.
Ages 11-14. 474
Ross, Pat. MEET M AND M.
Ages 6-8. 551
Skolsky, Mindy Warshaw. CARNIVAL AND KOPECK
AND MORE ABOUT HANNAH.
Ages 7-9. 600

## Arthritis, Juvenile rheumatoid

Jones, Rebecca Castaldi. ANGIE AND ME.
Ages 9-11. 333

## Asthma

Winthrop, Elizabeth. MARATHON MIRANDA.
Ages 9-11. 696
Winthrop, Elizabeth. MIRANDA IN THE MIDDLE.
Ages 9-13. 697

## Athletics

See: *Competition; Little League; Sports/Sportsmanship*

## Attention Seeking

See also: *Boasting*
Belair, Richard L. DOUBLE TAKE.
Ages 13 and up. 44
Blue, Rose. WISHFUL LYING.
Ages 6-9. 54
Dygard, Thomas J. SOCCER DUEL.
Ages 11-14. 179
Galbraith, Kathryn Osebold. KATIE DID!
Ages 3-7. 198

## Attention Seeking (cont.)

Giff, Patricia Reilly. FOURTH GRADE CELEBRITY.
Ages 8-10. 210
Lindgren, Astrid. I WANT A BROTHER OR SISTER.
Ages 3-7. 373
Stevens, Carla McBride. SARA AND THE PINCH.
Ages 5-7. 628
Williams, Barbara Wright. WHATEVER HAPPENED
TO BEVERLY BIGLER'S BIRTHDAY?
Ages 4-8. 693

## Attitude

See: Self, attitude toward; Work, attitude toward

## Aunt

See: Relatives

## Australia

Phipson, Joan Nash, pseud. FLY FREE.
Ages 11 and up. 508

## Autonomy

See also: Dependence/Independence
Ames, Mildred. NICKY AND THE JOYOUS NOISE.
Ages 9-12. 14
Billington, Elizabeth T. PART-TIME BOY.
Ages 8-10. 53
Colman, Hila Crayder. THE FAMILY TRAP.
Ages 12 and up. 134
Danziger, Paula. CAN YOU SUE YOUR PARENTS
FOR MALPRACTICE?
Ages 10-14. 149
Gilbert, Harriett. RUNNING AWAY.
Ages 11-14. 215
Greenberg, Jan. THE PIG-OUT BLUES.
Ages 12 and up. 236
Hansen, Joyce. THE GIFT-GIVER.
Ages 9-12. 263
Henkes, Kevin. ALL ALONE.
Ages 3-6. 280
Iverson, Genie. I WANT TO BE BIG.
Ages 3-6. 327
Johnston, Norma. MYSELF AND I.
Ages 11 and up. 330
Kerr, M. E., pseud. LITTLE LITTLE.
Ages 11 and up. 339
Korschunow, Irina. WHO KILLED CHRISTOPHER?
Ages 12 and up. 350
Levoy, Myron. A SHADOW LIKE A LEOPARD.
Ages 12 and up. 369
Mazer, Harry. THE ISLAND KEEPER.
Ages 10-14. 412
Mazer, Norma Fox. UP IN SETH'S ROOM.
Ages 13 and up. 415
Seuling, Barbara. THE TRIPLETS.
Ages 4-7. 581
Snyder, Zilpha Keatley. COME ON, PATSY.
Ages 5-8. 615
Springstubb, Tricia. THE MOON ON A STRING.
Ages 12 and up. 619
Stren, Patti. THERE'S A RAINBOW IN MY CLOSET.
Ages 8-10. 638
Watanabe, Shigeo. HOW DO I PUT IT ON?
Ages 2-5. 683
Yep, Laurence Michael. KIND HEARTS AND
GENTLE MONSTERS.
Ages 12 and up. 712
Zindel, Bonnie and Paul Zindel. A STAR FOR THE
LATECOMER.
Ages 12 and up. 721

## Avoidance

See: Peer relationships: avoiding others; Responsibility:
avoiding

## B

## Baby, New

See: Sibling: new baby

## Baby-Sitter

Delton, Judy and Elaine Knox-Wagner. THE BEST
MOM IN THE WORLD.
Ages 4-7. 159
Smith, Janice Lee. THE MONSTER IN THE THIRD
DRESSER DRAWER AND OTHER STORIES
ABOUT ADAM JOSHUA.
Ages 5-8. 610

## Baby-Sitting

See also: Job; Sibling: older; Sibling: oldest
Bates, Betty. LOVE IS LIKE PEANUTS.
Ages 10-14. 38
Byars, Betsy Cromer. THE NIGHT SWIMMERS.
Ages 10-12. 98
Farley, Carol J. TWILIGHT WAVES.
Ages 10-13. 186
Gerson, Corinne. TREAD SOFTLY.
Ages 9-12. 209
Gilson, Jamie. DO BANANAS CHEW GUM?
Ages 9-11. 216
Pascal, Francine. MY FIRST LOVE & OTHER
DISASTERS.
Ages 12 and up. 484
Ruby, Lois. WHAT DO YOU DO IN QUICKSAND?
Ages 12-14. 558
Smith, Anne Warren. BLUE DENIM BLUES.
Ages 12 and up. 607

## Involuntary

Girion, Barbara. MISTY AND ME.
Ages 10-12. 219
McCaffrey, Mary. MY BROTHER ANGE.
Ages 8-11. 389
McCord, Jean. TURKEYLEGS THOMPSON.
Ages 11-14. 390
Matthews, Ellen. THE TROUBLE WITH LESLIE.
Ages 8-11. 409

## Banned Books

See: Censorship, literary

## Barber, Going to

Rockwell, Anne F. and Harlow Rockwell. MY
BARBER.
Ages 3-6. 545

## Baths, Taking of

Cole, Brock. NO MORE BATHS.
Ages 3-6. 130

## Battered Child

See: Child abuse

## Beauty, Personal

See: Appearance

## Bed-Wetting

See: Enuresis

## Bedtime

Robison, Deborah. NO ELEPHANTS ALLOWED.
Ages 3-6. 540
Schubert, Ingrid and Dieter Schubert. THERE'S A
CROCODILE UNDER MY BED!
Ages 3-6. 576
Willoughby, Elaine Macmann. BORIS AND THE
MONSTERS.
Ages 4-7. 694

## Belonging

See also: *Clubs; Gangs: membership in; Loneliness; Peer relationships; Rejection*

Abercrombie, Barbara Mattes. CAT-MAN'S DAUGHTER.
Ages 11-13. 1

Adler, Carole Schwerdtfeger. THE CAT THAT WAS LEFT BEHIND.
Ages 9-12. 3

Adler, Carole Schwerdtfeger. SOME OTHER SUMMER.
Ages 10-13. 9

Angell, Judie. DEAR LOLA OR HOW TO BUILD YOUR OWN FAMILY.
Ages 10-13. 19

Ashley, Bernard. A KIND OF WILD JUSTICE.
Ages 12 and up. 30

Carrick, Malcolm. I'LL GET YOU.
Ages 11-13. 107

Drescher, Joan Elizabeth. YOUR FAMILY, MY FAMILY.
Ages 5-7. 173

Dunlop, Eileen Rhona. FOX FARM.
Ages 10-12. 175

Dunne, Mary Collins. HOBY & STUB.
Ages 10-13. 176

Ellis, Ella Thorp. SLEEPWALKER'S MOON.
Ages 12 and up. 181

Farley, Carol J. TWILIGHT WAVES.
Ages 10-13. 186

Galbraith, Kathryn Osebold. KATIE DID!
Ages 3-7. 198

Gauch, Patricia Lee. FRIDAYS.
Ages 11-13. 204

Hill, Margaret. TURN THE PAGE, WENDY.
Ages 10-14. 291

Kingman, Lee. THE REFINER'S FIRE.
Ages 12-14. 341

Lasker, Joe. THE DO-SOMETHING DAY.
Ages 3-7. 357

Leach, Michael. DON'T CALL ME ORPHAN!
Ages 10-12. 360

McKay, Robert W. THE RUNNING BACK.
Ages 12-14. 392

MacLachlan, Patricia. CASSIE BINEGAR.
Ages 9-12. 394

Mearian, Judy Frank. TWO WAYS ABOUT IT.
Ages 9-12. 418

Mendonca, Susan R. TOUGH CHOICES.
Ages 11 and up. 419

Morgan, Alison Mary. ALL KINDS OF PRICKLES.
Ages 11-13. 450

Morgan, Alison Mary. PAUL'S KITE.
Ages 10-13. 451

Prince, Alison. THE TURKEY'S NEST.
Ages 12 and up. 520

Reece, Colleen L. THE OUTSIDER.
Ages 12 and up. 527

Rodowsky, Colby F. H. MY NAME IS HENLEY.
Ages 10-13. 547

Ruby, Lois. TWO TRUTHS IN MY POCKET.
Ages 12 and up. 557

Sebestyen, Ouida. FAR FROM HOME.
Ages 12 and up. 579

Teibl, Margaret. DAVEY COME HOME.
Ages 6-9. 646

Wartski, Maureen Crane. A BOAT TO NOWHERE.
Ages 9-12. 678

Wartski, Maureen Crane. A LONG WAY FROM HOME.
Ages 11-13. 680

Weiman, Eiveen. IT TAKES BRAINS.
Ages 10-12. 686

Wood, Phyllis Anderson. PASS ME A PINE CONE.
Ages 11 and up. 705

Zalben, Jane Breskin. MAYBE IT WILL RAIN TOMORROW.
Ages 12 and up. 716

## Best Friend

See: *Friendship: best friend*

## Bias

See: *Prejudice*

## Birth Defects

See also: *Brain injury; Cerebral palsy; Cleft lip/palate; Learning disabilities; Limbs, abnormal or missing*

Richter, Elizabeth. THE TEENAGE HOSPITAL EXPERIENCE: YOU CAN HANDLE IT!
Ages 12 and up. 532

## Bizarre Thoughts/Behavior

See: *Mental illness*

## Black

See: *Afro-American*

## Blame

See also: *Guilt, feelings of; Justice/Injustice*

Carroll, Theodorus C. THE LOST CHRISTMAS STAR.
Ages 7-9. 109

Johnston, Norma. MYSELF AND I.
Ages 11 and up. 330

McKay, Robert W. THE RUNNING BACK.
Ages 12-14. 392

Mazer, Norma Fox. WHEN WE FIRST MET.
Ages 12 and up. 416

## Blindness

See also: *Education: special; Visual impairment*

Eyerly, Jeannette Hyde. THE SEEING SUMMER.
Ages 8-10. 183

Hall, Lynn. HALF THE BATTLE.
Ages 11 and up. 255

Kamien, Janet. WHAT IF YOU COULDN'T . . . ? A BOOK ABOUT SPECIAL NEEDS.
Ages 8-12. 336

MacLachlan, Patricia. THROUGH GRANDPA'S EYES.
Ages 5-8. 397

Montgomery, Elizabeth Rider. "SEEING" IN THE DARK.
Ages 5-7. 448

Reuter, Margaret. MY MOTHER IS BLIND.
Ages 5-8. 529

Rounds, Glen Harold. BLIND OUTLAW.
Ages 9-11. 554

Sullivan, Mary Beth and Alan J. Brightman and Joseph Blatt. FEELING FREE.
Ages 9 and up. 640

Thomas, William E. THE NEW BOY IS BLIND.
Ages 6-10. 655

Wartski, Maureen Crane. THE LAKE IS ON FIRE.
Ages 10-13. 679

## Boarding Schools

See: *Schools, private*

## Boasting

See also: *Attention seeking*

Blue, Rose. WISHFUL LYING.
Ages 6-9. 54

Greene, Bette. GET ON OUT OF HERE, PHILIP HALL.
Ages 9-12. 238

Williams, Barbara Wright. SO WHAT IF I'M A SORE LOSER?
Ages 5-8. 692

## Body Concept

**See:** *Name-calling; Self, attitude toward: body concept*

## Boy-Girl Relationships

**See also:** *Friendship; Peer relationships; Sex*

Adler, Carole Schwerdtfeger. SOME OTHER
SUMMER.
Ages 10-13. 9

Angell, Judie. SECRET SELVES.
Ages 11-13. 20

Asher, Sandra Fenichel. JUST LIKE JENNY.
Ages 10-12. 27

Bach, Alice Hendricks. WAITING FOR JOHNNY
MIRACLE.
Ages 12 and up. 32

Bates, Betty. LOVE IS LIKE PEANUTS.
Ages 10-14. 38

Bates, Betty. PICKING UP THE PIECES.
Ages 10-13. 40

Bates, Betty. THAT'S WHAT T.J. SAYS.
Ages 9-11. 41

Bulla, Clyde Robert. ALMOST A HERO.
Ages 11 and up. 84

Byars, Betsy Cromer. THE CYBIL WAR.
Ages 9-12. 96

Calhoun, Mary Huiskamp. KATIE JOHN AND
HEATHCLIFF.
Ages 9-11. 101

Cohen, Barbara Nash. FAT JACK.
Ages 11 and up. 125

Cohen, Barbara Nash. THE INNKEEPER'S
DAUGHTER.
Ages 11-14. 126

Colman, Hila Crayder. ACCIDENT.
Ages 11 and up. 132

Colman, Hila Crayder. CONFESSION OF A
STORYTELLER.
Ages 10-13. 133

Culin, Charlotte. CAGES OF GLASS, FLOWERS OF
TIME.
Ages 12 and up. 145

Danziger, Paula. THE DIVORCE EXPRESS.
Ages 11-14. 150

Danziger, Paula. THERE'S A BAT IN BUNK FIVE.
Ages 10-14. 151

Elfman, Blossom. THE BUTTERFLY GIRL.
Ages 13 and up. 180

Foley, June. IT'S NO CRUSH, I'M IN LOVE!
Ages 11-13. 192

Franco, Marjorie. SO WHO HASN'T GOT
PROBLEMS?
Ages 10-12. 194

Gerber, Merrill Joan. PLEASE DON'T KISS ME
NOW.
Ages 13 and up. 206

Greenberg, Jan. THE PIG-OUT BLUES.
Ages 12 and up. 236

Greene, Bette. GET ON OUT OF HERE, PHILIP
HALL.
Ages 9-12. 238

Greene, Sheppard M. THE BOY WHO DRANK TOO
MUCH.
Ages 12 and up. 242

Guest, Elissa Haden. THE HANDSOME MAN.
Ages 12 and up. 251

Hallman, Ruth. BREAKAWAY.
Ages 12 and up. 257

Hansen, Joyce. THE GIFT-GIVER.
Ages 9-12. 263

Harlan, Elizabeth. FOOTFALLS.
Ages 12-14. 265

Hest, Amy. MAYBE NEXT YEAR . . .
Ages 9-12. 288

Hinton, Susan Eloise. TEX.
Ages 11-15. 292

Hogan, Paula Z. I HATE BOYS  I HATE GIRLS.
Ages 5-8. 296

Hunter, Kristin Eggleston. LOU IN THE LIMELIGHT.
Ages 14 and up. 312

Irwin, Hadley, pseud. MOON AND ME.
Ages 11-14. 325

Kerr, M. E., pseud. LITTLE LITTLE.
Ages 11 and up. 339

Kropp, Paul Stephan. WILTED.
Ages 11-14. 354

L'Engle, Madeleine Franklin. A RING OF ENDLESS
LIGHT.
Ages 11-14. 363

Levinson, Nancy Smiler. WORLD OF HER OWN.
Ages 12 and up. 368

Marney, Dean. JUST GOOD FRIENDS.
Ages 11-13. 404

Mendonca, Susan R. TOUGH CHOICES.
Ages 11 and up. 419

Moeri, Louise. FIRST THE EGG.
Ages 12 and up. 438

Myers, Walter Dean. HOOPS.
Ages 12 and up. 459

Myers, Walter Dean. THE YOUNG LANDLORDS.
Ages 11-14. 461

Naylor, Phyllis Reynolds. A STRING OF CHANCES.
Ages 12 and up. 464

Newton, Suzanne. M.V. SEXTON SPEAKING.
Ages 11 and up. 466

Oppenheimer, Joan Letson. WORKING ON IT.
Ages 11-13. 475

Pascal, Francine. MY FIRST LOVE & OTHER
DISASTERS.
Ages 12 and up. 484

Pfeffer, Susan Beth. ABOUT DAVID.
Ages 13 and up. 500

Powers, Bill. A TEST OF LOVE.
Ages 12 and up. 519

Rabinowich, Ellen. ROCK FEVER.
Ages 12 and up. 523

Reader, Dennis J. COMING BACK ALIVE.
Ages 12 and up. 525

Rinaldi, Ann. PROMISES ARE FOR KEEPING.
Ages 12 and up. 534

Sachs, Marilyn. BEACH TOWELS.
Ages 12 and up. 562

Sachs, Marilyn. BUS RIDE.
Ages 11-14. 563

Sachs, Marilyn. HELLO . . . WRONG NUMBER.
Ages 12-16. 565

Sallis, Susan Diana. ONLY LOVE.
Ages 12 and up. 568

Slepian, Jan. LESTER'S TURN.
Ages 11-14. 604

Springstubb, Tricia. THE MOON ON A STRING.
Ages 12 and up. 619

Truss, Jan. BIRD AT THE WINDOW.
Ages 13 and up. 661

Wood, Phyllis Anderson. PASS ME A PINE CONE.
Ages 11 and up. 705

Wortis, Avi. SOMETIMES I THINK I HEAR MY
NAME.
Ages 10-13. 708

Yep, Laurence Michael. SEA GLASS.
Ages 11-14. 713

## Dating

Adler, Carole Schwerdtfeger. DOWN BY THE RIVER.
Ages 12 and up. 4

Angell, Judie. WHAT'S BEST FOR YOU.
Ages 11-14. 21

Banks, Lynne Reid. THE WRITING ON THE WALL.
Ages 12 and up. 33

Belair, Richard L. DOUBLE TAKE.
Ages 13 and up. 44

Bonham, Frank. GIMME AN H, GIMME AN E,
GIMME AN L, GIMME A P.
Ages 12 and up. 61

## Boy-Girl Relationships (cont.)

Bridgers, Sue Ellen. NOTES FOR ANOTHER LIFE.
Ages 12 and up. 75
Butterworth, William Edmund. UNDER THE
INFLUENCE.
Ages 12 and up. 94
Colman, Hila Crayder. THE FAMILY TRAP.
Ages 12 and up. 134
Dacquino, Vincent T. KISS THE CANDY DAYS
GOOD-BYE.
Ages 10-14. 148
Danziger, Paula. CAN YOU SUE YOUR PARENTS
FOR MALPRACTICE?
Ages 10-14. 149
Ellis, Ella Thorp. SLEEPWALKER'S MOON.
Ages 12 and up. 181
Geibel, James. THE BLOND BROTHER.
Ages 12 and up. 205
Girion, Barbara. A HANDFUL OF STARS.
Ages 12 and up. 217
Girion, Barbara. A TANGLE OF ROOTS.
Ages 12-16. 220
Graber, Richard Fredrick. BLACK COW SUMMER.
Ages 12 and up. 224
Hayes, Sheila. ME AND MY MONA LISA SMILE.
Ages 11-13. 274
Irwin, Hadley, pseud. WHAT ABOUT GRANDMA?
Ages 11 and up. 326
Johnston, Norma. MYSELF AND I.
Ages 11 and up. 330
Liu, Aimee. SOLITAIRE.
Ages 13 and up. 380
Luger, Harriett Mandelay. LAUREN.
Ages 12 and up. 387
McKay, Robert W. THE RUNNING BACK.
Ages 12-14. 392
Mazer, Norma Fox. UP IN SETH'S ROOM.
Ages 13 and up. 415
Mazer, Norma Fox. WHEN WE FIRST MET.
Ages 12 and up. 416
Miklowitz, Gloria D. DID YOU HEAR WHAT
HAPPENED TO ANDREA?
Ages 13 and up. 421
Peck, Richard. CLOSE ENOUGH TO TOUCH.
Ages 12 and up. 490
Pevsner, Stella. CUTE IS A FOUR-LETTER WORD.
Ages 10-12. 498
Pfeffer, Susan Beth. STARTING WITH MELODIE.
Ages 11-13. 504
Platt, Kin. BROGG'S BRAIN.
Ages 12 and up. 514
Posner, Grace. IN MY SISTER'S EYES.
Ages 12 and up. 516
Riley, Jocelyn. ONLY MY MOUTH IS SMILING.
Ages 12-14. 533
Robinson, Barbara Webb. TEMPORARY TIMES,
TEMPORARY PLACES.
Ages 11-13. 538
Ruby, Lois. TWO TRUTHS IN MY POCKET.
Ages 12 and up. 557
Savitz, Harriet May. RUN, DON'T WALK.
Ages 12 and up. 572
Slote, Alfred. LOVE AND TENNIS.
Ages 12-14. 605
Strasser, Todd. ANGEL DUST BLUES.
Ages 14 and up. 635
Strasser, Todd. FRIENDS TILL THE END.
Ages 12 and up. 636
Stretton, Barbara. YOU NEVER LOSE.
Ages 12 and up. 639
Wood, Phyllis Anderson. THIS TIME COUNT ME IN.
Ages 12 and up. 706
Yep, Laurence Michael. KIND HEARTS AND
GENTLE MONSTERS.
Ages 12 and up. 712

## Braces on Body/Limbs

See also: Limbs, abnormal or missing

Brooks, Jerome. THE BIG DIPPER MARATHON.
Ages 11-14. 77
Rabe, Berniece Louise. THE BALANCING GIRL.
Ages 5-7. 522

## Braces on Teeth

See: Orthodontia

## Bragging

See: Boasting

## Brain Injury

See also: Birth defects; Cerebral palsy; Epilepsy;
Learning disabilities; Mental retardation
Robinet, Harriette Gillem. RIDE THE RED CYCLE.
Ages 7-11. 537

## Bravery

See: Courage, meaning of

## Broken Bones

See: Fractures; Surgery

## Brother

See: Sibling

## Bully

See also: Harassment; Teasing
McCord, Jean. TURKEYLEGS THOMPSON.
Ages 11-14. 390

**Being bothered by**
Adler, Carole Schwerdtfeger. THE ONCE IN A
WHILE HERO.
Ages 10-13. 7
Alexander, Martha G. MOVE OVER, TWERP.
Ages 5-8. 11
Brooks, Jerome. MAKE ME A HERO.
Ages 9-12. 78
Chapman, Carol. HERBIE'S TROUBLES.
Ages 5-7. 113
Conford, Ellen. THE REVENGE OF THE
INCREDIBLE DR. RANCID AND HIS YOUTHFUL
ASSISTANT, JEFFREY.
Ages 10-12. 137
Cunningham, Julia Woolfolk. THE SILENT VOICE.
Ages 11-14. 146
Kropp, Paul Stephan. WILTED.
Ages 11-14. 354
Mauser, Pat Rhoads. A BUNDLE OF STICKS.
Ages 10-12. 410
Miner, Jane Claypool. NAVAJO VICTORY: BEING A
NATIVE AMERICAN.
Ages 11 and up. 432
Peck, Robert Newton. CLUNIE.
Ages 12 and up. 491
Robinson, Nancy Konheim. WENDY AND THE
BULLIES.
Ages 7-10. 539
Wartski, Maureen Crane. A LONG WAY FROM
HOME.
Ages 11-13. 680

**Fear of**
Robinson, Nancy Konheim. WENDY AND THE
BULLIES.
Ages 7-10. 539

# C

## Camp Experiences

See also: Separation anxiety
Brown, Marc Tolan. ARTHUR GOES TO CAMP.
Ages 5-8. 79

## Camp Experiences (cont.)

Danziger, Paula. THERE'S A BAT IN BUNK FIVE.
Ages 10-14. 151
Levy, Elizabeth. COME OUT SMILING.
Ages 12 and up. 370
O'Connor, Jane. YOURS TILL NIAGARA FALLS,
ABBY.
Ages 8-10. 467
Smith, Robert Kimmel. JELLY BELLY.
Ages 10-12. 614

## Cancer

**See also:** *Hodgkin's disease; Hospital, going to;
Leukemia; Surgery*
Bach, Alice Hendricks. WAITING FOR JOHNNY
MIRACLE.
Ages 12 and up. 32
Donnelly, Elfie. SO LONG, GRANDPA.
Ages 9-11. 168
Hermes, Patricia. YOU SHOULDN'T HAVE TO SAY
GOOD-BYE.
Ages 10-13. 286
Mearian, Judy Frank. TWO WAYS ABOUT IT.
Ages 9-12. 418
Richter, Elizabeth. THE TEENAGE HOSPITAL
EXPERIENCE: YOU CAN HANDLE IT!
Ages 12 and up. 532
Schotter, Roni. A MATTER OF TIME.
Ages 12 and up. 575
Stretton, Barbara. YOU NEVER LOSE.
Ages 12 and up. 639
Zindel, Bonnie and Paul Zindel. A STAR FOR THE
LATECOMER.
Ages 12 and up. 721

## Cardiac Conditions

Richter, Elizabeth. THE TEENAGE HOSPITAL
EXPERIENCE: YOU CAN HANDLE IT!
Ages 12 and up. 532

## Careers

### Dancer

Hest, Amy. MAYBE NEXT YEAR . . .
Ages 9-12. 288
Landis, James David. THE SISTERS IMPOSSIBLE.
Ages 9-11. 355
Zindel, Bonnie and Paul Zindel. A STAR FOR THE
LATECOMER.
Ages 12 and up. 721

**Planning.** *See also: Education; Work, attitude toward*
Bruna, Dick. WHEN I'M BIG.
Ages 2-4. 81
Strasser, Todd. FRIENDS TILL THE END.
Ages 12 and up. 636

## Catholic, Roman

**See:** *Roman Catholic*

## Censorship, Literary

Miles, Betty. MAUDIE AND ME AND THE DIRTY
BOOK.
Ages 10-12. 423

## Cerebral Palsy

**See also:** *Birth defects; Brain injury*
Adler, Carole Schwerdtfeger. DOWN BY THE RIVER.
Ages 12 and up. 4
Gould, Marilyn. GOLDEN DAFFODILS.
Ages 8-12. 223
Payne, Sherry Neuwirth. A CONTEST.
Ages 8-10. 486
Slepian, Jan. THE ALFRED SUMMER.
Ages 11-13. 603
Slepian, Jan. LESTER'S TURN.
Ages 11-14. 604

Sullivan, Mary Beth and Alan J. Brightman and Joseph
Blatt. FEELING FREE.
Ages 9 and up. 640

## Change

Hargreaves, Roger. MR. NOISY.
Ages 3-7. 264

### Accepting

Abercrombie, Barbara Mattes. CAT-MAN'S
DAUGHTER.
Ages 11-13. 1
Alda, Arlene. SONYA'S MOMMY WORKS.
Ages 4-7. 10
Ames, Mildred. NICKY AND THE JOYOUS NOISE.
Ages 9-12. 14
Angell, Judie. WHAT'S BEST FOR YOU.
Ages 11-14. 21
Bates, Betty. PICKING UP THE PIECES.
Ages 10-13. 40
Bawden, Nina Mary Kark. THE ROBBERS.
Ages 9-12. 43
Bennett, Jack. THE VOYAGE OF THE LUCKY
DRAGON.
Ages 11 and up. 45
Berman, Claire. WHAT AM I DOING IN A
STEP-FAMILY?
Ages 5-10. 51
Bernstein, Joanne Eckstein. DMITRY: A YOUNG
SOVIET IMMIGRANT.
Ages 11-13. 52
Bond, Nancy Barbara. THE VOYAGE BEGUN.
Ages 12 and up. 60
Bosse, Malcolm Joseph. GANESH.
Ages 11-14. 65
Brandenberg, Aliki Liacouras. WE ARE BEST
FRIENDS.
Ages 3-6. 72
Bunting, Anne Evelyn THE BIG RED BARN.
Ages 4-7. 88
Byars, Betsy Cromer. THE ANIMAL, THE
VEGETABLE, AND JOHN D JONES.
Ages 10-12. 95
Byars, Betsy Cromer. THE NIGHT SWIMMERS.
Ages 10-12. 98
Cheatham, Karyn Follis. THE BEST WAY OUT.
Ages 12 and up. 114
Cleary, Beverly Bunn. RAMONA AND HER
MOTHER.
Ages 7-10. 118
Coates, Belle. MAK.
Ages 12 and up. 124
Colman, Hila Crayder. ACCIDENT.
Ages 11 and up. 132
Dacquino, Vincent T. KISS THE CANDY DAYS
GOOD-BYE.
Ages 10-14. 148
Danziger, Paula. THE DIVORCE EXPRESS.
Ages 11-14. 150
Delton, Judy. THE NEW GIRL AT SCHOOL.
Ages 4-7. 157
Ellis, Ella Thorp. SLEEPWALKER'S MOON.
Ages 12 and up. 181
First, Julia. I, REBEKAH, TAKE YOU, THE
LAWRENCES.
Ages 11-13. 187
Freeman, Gaail. OUT FROM UNDER.
Ages 12 and up. 195
Gordon, Shirley. THE BOY WHO WANTED A
FAMILY.
Ages 7-9. 222
Green, Phyllis. GLOOMY LOUIE.
Ages 8-9. 234
Greenfield, Eloise. DARLENE.
Ages 5-7. 243
Greenfield, Eloise. GRANDMAMA'S JOY.
Ages 4-8. 244

## Change (cont.)

Grant, Cynthia D. JOSHUA FORTUNE.
Ages 10-13. 229
Gregory, Diana. THERE'S A CATERPILLAR IN MY LEMONADE.
Ages 10-12. 247
Harris, Mark Jonathan. WITH A WAVE OF THE WAND.
Ages 9-12. 267
Hogan, Paula Z. WILL DAD EVER MOVE BACK HOME?
Ages 7-10. 299
Jones, Penelope. I'M NOT MOVING!
Ages 3-6. 332
Josephs, Rebecca. EARLY DISORDER.
Ages 13 and up. 335
Klass, Sheila Solomon. TO SEE MY MOTHER DANCE.
Ages 10-13. 344
Levinson, Nancy Smiler. WORLD OF HER OWN.
Ages 12 and up. 368
Marangell, Virginia J. GIANNA MIA.
Ages 12-15. 402
Morgan, Alison Mary. ALL KINDS OF PRICKLES.
Ages 11-13. 450
Okimoto, Jean Davies. IT'S JUST TOO MUCH.
Ages 10-12. 469
Okimoto, Jean Davies. MY MOTHER IS NOT MARRIED TO MY FATHER.
Ages 9-11. 470
Oneal, Zibby. THE LANGUAGE OF GOLDFISH.
Ages 11-14. 473
Park, Barbara. DON'T MAKE ME SMILE.
Ages 8-11. 481
Pollock, Penny. KEEPING IT SECRET.
Ages 9-12. 515
Radley, Gail. NOTHING STAYS THE SAME FOREVER.
Ages 9-12. 524
Smith, Janice Lee. THE MONSTER IN THE THIRD DRESSER DRAWER AND OTHER STORIES ABOUT ADAM JOSHUA.
Ages 5-8. 610
Smith, Nancy Covert. THE FALLING-APART WINTER.
Ages 10-13. 612
Stretton, Barbara. YOU NEVER LOSE.
Ages 12 and up. 639
Tester, Sylvia Root. SANDY'S NEW HOME.
Ages 5-8. 648
Vigna, Judith. SHE'S NOT MY REAL MOTHER.
Ages 4-8. 668
Wartski, Maureen Crane. THE LAKE IS ON FIRE.
Ages 10-13. 679
Whelan, Gloria. A TIME TO KEEP SILENT.
Ages 11-14. 690
Wortis, Avi. A PLACE CALLED UGLY.
Ages 11-14. 707

## Chemical Dependency

**See:** *Alcoholism; Drugs; Marijuana; Reality, escaping*

## Child Abuse

**See also:** *Cruelty*
Adler, Carole Schwerdtfeger. DOWN BY THE RIVER.
Ages 12 and up. 4
Armstrong, Louise. SAVING THE BIG-DEAL BABY.
Ages 10 and up. 22
Ashley, Bernard. BREAK IN THE SUN.
Ages 11 and up. 29
Bulla, Clyde Robert. ALMOST A HERO.
Ages 11 and up. 84
Culin, Charlotte. CAGES OF GLASS, FLOWERS OF TIME.
Ages 12 and up. 145
Dodson, Susan. HAVE YOU SEEN THIS GIRL?
Ages 13 and up. 166

Greene, Sheppard M. THE BOY WHO DRANK TOO MUCH.
Ages 12 and up. 242
Hill, Margaret. TURN THE PAGE, WENDY.
Ages 10-14. 291
Kingman, Lee. THE REFINER'S FIRE.
Ages 12-14. 341
Levinson, Nancy Smiler. SILENT FEAR.
Ages 10-13. 367
Magorian, Michelle. GOOD NIGHT, MR. TOM.
Ages 11 and up. 401
Moeri, Louise. THE GIRL WHO LIVED ON THE FERRIS WHEEL.
Ages 13 and up. 439
Smith, Anne Warren. BLUE DENIM BLUES.
Ages 12 and up. 607
Strang, Celia. FOSTER MARY.
Ages 10-13. 633
Swartley, David Warren. MY FRIEND, MY BROTHER.
Ages 9-11. 642
Whelan, Gloria. A TIME TO KEEP SILENT.
Ages 11-14. 690

## Children's Home, Living in

**See also:** *Adoption; Foster home; Orphan*
Bulla, Clyde Robert. ALMOST A HERO.
Ages 11 and up. 84
First, Julia. I, REBEKAH, TAKE YOU, THE LAWRENCES.
Ages 11-13. 187
Hill, Margaret. TURN THE PAGE, WENDY.
Ages 10-14. 291
Leach, Michael. DON'T CALL ME ORPHAN!
Ages 10-12. 360

## Chinese-American

Bunting, Anne Evelyn. THE HAPPY FUNERAL.
Ages 5-9. 90
Yep, Laurence Michael. SEA GLASS.
Ages 11-14. 713

## Choice Making

**See:** *Decision making*

## Chores

**See also:** *Job; Responsibility*
Drescher, Joan Elizabeth. THE MARVELOUS MESS.
Ages 4-6. 172
Galbraith, Kathryn Osebold. COME SPRING.
Ages 9-13. 197
Reuter, Margaret. YOU CAN DEPEND ON ME.
Ages 6-9. 530
Wolde, Gunilla. BETSY AND THE VACUUM CLEANER.
Ages 3-6. 702

## Classmate Relationships

**See:** *School: classmate relationships*

## Claustrophobia

**See:** *Fear: of enclosed spaces*

## Cleanliness

**See:** *Baths, taking of*

## Cleft Lip/Palate

**See also:** *Birth defects; Speech problems; Surgery*
Richter, Elizabeth. THE TEENAGE HOSPITAL EXPERIENCE: YOU CAN HANDLE IT!
Ages 12 and up. 532

## Clowning

**See:** *Attention seeking*

## Clubs

**See also:** *Belonging; Gangs*
Bonsall, Crosby Newell. THE CASE OF THE DOUBLE CROSS.
Ages 6-8. 62
Gauch, Patricia Lee. FRIDAYS.
Ages 11-13. 204
Greene, Bette. GET ON OUT OF HERE, PHILIP HALL.
Ages 9-12. 238
Hogan, Paula Z. I HATE BOYS I HATE GIRLS.
Ages 5-8. 296

## Commune

**See also:** *Life style*
Elfman, Blossom. THE BUTTERFLY GIRL.
Ages 13 and up. 180
Kingman, Lee. THE REFINER'S FIRE.
Ages 12-14. 341

## Communicable Diseases

**See:** *Illnesses*

## Communication

**Importance of**
Dacquino, Vincent T. KISS THE CANDY DAYS GOOD-BYE.
Ages 10-14. 148
Hughes, Dean. HONESTLY, MYRON.
Ages 9-11. 307
Meyer, Carolyn. THE CENTER: FROM A TROUBLED PAST TO A NEW LIFE.
Ages 13 and up. 420
Miner, Jane Claypool. THIS DAY IS MINE: LIVING WITH LEUKEMIA.
Ages 10 and up. 436
Powers, Bill. A TEST OF LOVE.
Ages 12 and up. 519
Riskind, Mary L. APPLE IS MY SIGN.
Ages 10-14. 536
Rosen, Lillian D. JUST LIKE EVERYBODY ELSE.
Ages 11 and up. 549
Sachs, Marilyn. BEACH TOWELS.
Ages 12 and up. 562
Swartley, David Warren. MY FRIEND, MY BROTHER.
Ages 9-11. 642

**Lack of**
Arrick, Fran. TUNNEL VISION.
Ages 12 and up. 24
Bawden, Nina Mary Kark. THE ROBBERS.
Ages 9-12. 43
Grace, Fran. BRANIGAN'S DOG.
Ages 10 and up. 225
Hall, Lynn. THE LEAVING.
Ages 12 and up. 256
Herzig, Alison Cragin and Jane Lawrence Mali. A SEASON OF SECRETS.
Ages 11-13. 287
Miklowitz, Gloria D. THE LOVE BOMBERS.
Ages 12 and up. 422
Newton, Suzanne. M.V. SEXTON SPEAKING.
Ages 11 and up. 466
Osborne, Mary Pope. RUN, RUN, AS FAST AS YOU CAN.
Ages 9-12. 477
Pfeffer, Susan Beth. ABOUT DAVID.
Ages 13 and up. 500
Strasser, Todd. ANGEL DUST BLUES.
Ages 14 and up. 635
Truss, Jan. BIRD AT THE WINDOW.
Ages 13 and up. 661
Williams, Barbara Wright. WHATEVER HAPPENED TO BEVERLY BIGLER'S BIRTHDAY?
Ages 4-8. 693

**Misunderstandings**
Carroll, Theodorus C. THE LOST CHRISTMAS STAR.
Ages 7-9. 109
Hughes, Dean. HONESTLY, MYRON.
Ages 9-11. 307
Myers, Bernice. NOT AT HOME?
Ages 6-8. 458

**Parent-child.** *See also: Family: unity*
Adler, Carole Schwerdtfeger. THE SILVER COACH.
Ages 9-12. 8
Alda, Arlene. SONYA'S MOMMY WORKS.
Ages 4-7. 10
Alexander, Martha G. WHEN THE NEW BABY COMES, I'M MOVING OUT.
Ages 2-5. 12
Angell, Judie. WHAT'S BEST FOR YOU.
Ages 11-14. 21
Asher, Sandra Fenichel. DAUGHTERS OF THE LAW.
Ages 11-13. 26
Asher, Sandra Fenichel. SUMMER BEGINS.
Ages 10-13. 28
Bates, Betty. MY MOM, THE MONEY NUT.
Ages 10-12. 39
Blue, Rose. WISHFUL LYING.
Ages 6-9. 54
Blume, Judy Sussman. TIGER EYES.
Ages 11 and up. 57
Boutis, Victoria. KATY DID IT.
Ages 8-10. 69
Brooks, Jerome. THE BIG DIPPER MARATHON.
Ages 11-14. 77
Danziger, Paula. THE DIVORCE EXPRESS.
Ages 11-14. 150
Delton, Judy. MY MOTHER LOST HER JOB TODAY.
Ages 3-7. 156
Delton, Judy. A WALK ON A SNOWY NIGHT.
Ages 5-8. 158
Delton, Judy and Elaine Knox-Wagner. THE BEST MOM IN THE WORLD.
Ages 4-7. 159
Drescher, Joan Elizabeth. I'M IN CHARGE!
Ages 5-8. 171
Elfman, Blossom. THE BUTTERFLY GIRL.
Ages 13 and up. 180
First, Julia. LOOK WHO'S BEAUTIFUL!
Ages 10-12. 188
Galbraith, Kathryn Osebold. KATIE DID!
Ages 3-7. 198
Gerber, Merrill Joan. PLEASE DON'T KISS ME NOW.
Ages 13 and up. 206
Gerson, Corinne. HOW I PUT MY MOTHER THROUGH COLLEGE.
Ages 11 and up. 207
Graeber, Charlotte Towner. MUSTARD.
Ages 4-10. 227
Greenberg, Jan. THE PIG-OUT BLUES.
Ages 12 and up. 236
Hall, Lynn. THE LEAVING.
Ages 12 and up. 256
Hamilton, Morse and Emily Hamilton. MY NAME IS EMILY.
Ages 3-6. 259
Hanlon, Emily. THE SWING.
Ages 10-12. 261
Hentoff, Nat. DOES THIS SCHOOL HAVE CAPITAL PUNISHMENT?
Ages 11 and up. 282
Hogan, Paula Z. WILL DAD EVER MOVE BACK HOME?
Ages 7-10. 299
Hopkins, Lee Bennett. MAMA & HER BOYS.
Ages 8-11. 303
Hughes, Dean. HONESTLY, MYRON.
Ages 9-11. 307

## Communication (cont.)

Irwin, Hadley, pseud. WHAT ABOUT GRANDMA?
Ages 11 and up. 326

Kenny, Kevin and Helen Krull. SOMETIMES MY MOM DRINKS TOO MUCH.
Ages 5-8. 338

Levy, Elizabeth. COME OUT SMILING.
Ages 12 and up. 370

Lindsay, Jeanne Warren. DO I HAVE A DADDY? A STORY ABOUT A SINGLE-PARENT CHILD.
Ages 4-8. 376

Love, Sandra Weller. CROSSING OVER.
Ages 10-12. 383

Luger, Harriett Mandelay. LAUREN.
Ages 12 and up. 387

Lyle, Katie Letcher. DARK BUT FULL OF DIAMONDS.
Ages 12-14. 388

Mazer, Norma Fox. UP IN SETH'S ROOM.
Ages 13 and up. 415

Mills, Claudia. AT THE BACK OF THE WOODS.
Ages 9-11. 426

Morton, Jane. RUNNING SCARED.
Ages 10-14. 455

Okimoto, Jean Davies. NORMAN SCHNURMAN, AVERAGE PERSON.
Ages 10-12. 471

Park, Barbara. DON'T MAKE ME SMILE.
Ages 8-11. 481

Platt, Kin. BROGG'S BRAIN.
Ages 12 and up. 514

Robinson, Nancy Konheim. WENDY AND THE BULLIES.
Ages 7-10. 539

Sallis, Susan Diana. A TIME FOR EVERYTHING.
Ages 13 and up. 569

Schotter, Roni. A MATTER OF TIME.
Ages 12 and up. 575

Sebestyen, Ouida. FAR FROM HOME.
Ages 12 and up. 579

Sebestyen, Ouida. WORDS BY HEART.
Ages 10-13. 580

Slote, Alfred. LOVE AND TENNIS.
Ages 12-14. 605

Stecher, Miriam B. and Alice S. Kandell. DADDY AND BEN TOGETHER.
Ages 4-6. 624

Stein, Sara Bonnett. ON DIVORCE: AN OPEN FAMILY BOOK FOR PARENTS AND CHILDREN TOGETHER.
Ages 4-8. 626

Stretton, Barbara. YOU NEVER LOSE.
Ages 12 and up. 639

Van Leeuwen, Jean. SEEMS LIKE THIS ROAD GOES ON FOREVER.
Ages 12 and up. 663

Van Steenwyk, Elizabeth Ann. RIVALS ON ICE.
Ages 9-11. 664

Whelan, Gloria. A TIME TO KEEP SILENT.
Ages 11-14. 690

Winthrop, Elizabeth. SLOPPY KISSES.
Ages 4-7. 698

Yep, Laurence Michael. SEA GLASS.
Ages 11-14. 713

Zolotow, Charlotte Shapiro. IF YOU LISTEN.
Ages 5-7. 722

Zolotow, Charlotte Shapiro. ONE STEP, TWO...
Ages 2-5. 724

## Rumor

Hayes, Sheila. ME AND MY MONA LISA SMILE.
Ages 11-13. 274

Rinaldi, Ann. PROMISES ARE FOR KEEPING.
Ages 12 and up. 534

Tolan, Stephanie S. THE LAST OF EDEN.
Ages 12 and up. 659

## Competition

**See also:** *Little League; Sports/Sportsmanship*

Douglass, Barbara. SKATEBOARD SCRAMBLE.
Ages 9-11. 170

Hall, Lynn. HALF THE BATTLE.
Ages 11 and up. 255

Landis, James David. THE SISTERS IMPOSSIBLE.
Ages 9-11. 355

Levy, Elizabeth. COME OUT SMILING.
Ages 12 and up. 370

Marshall, Lydia. NOBODY LIKES TO LOSE.
Ages 7-9. 405

Platt, Kin. BROGG'S BRAIN.
Ages 12 and up. 514

Slote, Alfred. LOVE AND TENNIS.
Ages 12-14. 605

Van Steenwyk, Elizabeth Ann. RIVALS ON ICE.
Ages 9-11. 664

Williams, Barbara Wright. SO WHAT IF I'M A SORE LOSER?
Ages 5-8. 692

Wiseman, Bernard. THE LUCKY RUNNER.
Ages 6-9. 699

## Compromise

**See:** *Communication; Cooperation*

## Conflict

**See:** *Ambivalence, feelings of; Problem solving*

## Conscience

**See:** *Guilt, feelings of*

## Consideration, Meaning of

Hargreaves, Roger. MR. NOISY.
Ages 3-7. 264

Moncure, Jane Belk. CARING.
Ages 3-6. 441

Moncure, Jane Belk. KINDNESS.
Ages 3-6. 445

Moncure, Jane Belk. LOVE.
Ages 3-6. 446

Skolsky, Mindy Warshaw. CARNIVAL AND KOPECK AND MORE ABOUT HANNAH.
Ages 7-9. 600

Williams, Barbara Wright. WHATEVER HAPPENED TO BEVERLY BIGLER'S BIRTHDAY?
Ages 4-8. 693

## Cooperation

**See also:** *Helping; Neighbors/Neighborhood; Sharing/Not sharing*

Delaney, Ned. BERT AND BARNEY.
Ages 3-7. 153

Moncure, Jane Belk. KINDNESS.
Ages 3-6. 445

Thomas, Karen. THE GOOD THING...THE BAD THING.
Ages 3-7. 654

### In play

Pfeffer, Susan Beth. AWFUL EVELINA.
Ages 6-8. 501

### In work

Bond, Nancy Barbara. THE VOYAGE BEGUN.
Ages 12 and up. 60

Hoban, Lillian Aberman. ARTHUR'S FUNNY MONEY.
Ages 6-8. 294

Matthews, Ellen. THE TROUBLE WITH LESLIE.
Ages 8-11. 409

Myers, Walter Dean. THE YOUNG LANDLORDS.
Ages 11-14. 461

Naylor, Phyllis Reynolds. EDDIE, INCORPORATED.
Ages 9-11. 463

## Cruelty (cont.)

Fox, Paula. A PLACE APART.
Ages 12 and up. 193

## Cults

Miklowitz, Gloria D. THE LOVE BOMBERS.
Ages 12 and up. 422
Veglahn, Nancy Crary. FELLOWSHIP OF THE
SEVEN STARS.
Ages 12 and up. 665

## Cultural/Ethnic Groups

See: *Specific group (e.g. Afro-American; Puerto Rican-
American)*

## Curiosity

See also: *Creativity*
Fisher, Aileen Lucia. I STOOD UPON A
MOUNTAIN.
Ages 4-8. 189
Wolde, Gunilla. BETSY AND THE VACUUM
CLEANER.
Ages 3-6. 702

## Custody

See: *Parental: custody*

# D

## Danger

See: *Risk, taking of*

## Dating

See: *Boy-girl relationships: dating; Sex*

## Day-Care Center, Going to

Simon, Norma. I'M BUSY, TOO.
Ages 3-5. 596

## Daydreaming

See also: *Fantasy formation; Magical thinking;
Nightmares; Reality, escaping; Wishes*
Byars, Betsy Cromer. THE
TWO-THOUSAND-POUND GOLDFISH.
Ages 9-12. 99
Hayes, Sheila. ME AND MY MONA LISA SMILE.
Ages 11-13. 274
Shreve, Susan Richards. THE BAD DREAMS OF A
GOOD GIRL.
Ages 8-10. 589
Teibl, Margaret. DAVEY COME HOME.
Ages 6-9. 646

## Deafness

See also: *Education: special; Muteness*
Arthur, Catherine. MY SISTER'S SILENT WORLD.
Ages 5-9. 25
Bunting, Anne Evelyn. THE WAITING GAME.
Ages 10 and up. 91
Hallman, Ruth. BREAKAWAY.
Ages 12 and up. 257
Hanlon, Emily. THE SWING.
Ages 10-12. 261
Hlibok, Bruce. SILENT DANCER.
Ages 8-11. 293
Kamien, Janet. WHAT IF YOU COULDN'T . . . ? A
BOOK ABOUT SPECIAL NEEDS.
Ages 8-12. 336
Levinson, Nancy Smiler. WORLD OF HER OWN.
Ages 12 and up. 368
Litchfield, Ada Bassett. WORDS IN OUR HANDS.
Ages 7-9. 378
Morgenroth, Barbara. WILL THE REAL RENIE LAKE
PLEASE STAND UP?
Ages 12 and up. 453

Pollock, Penny. KEEPING IT SECRET.
Ages 9-12. 515
Riskind, Mary L. APPLE IS MY SIGN.
Ages 10-14. 536
Rosen, Lillian D. JUST LIKE EVERYBODY ELSE.
Ages 11 and up. 549
Sullivan, Mary Beth and Alan J. Brightman and Joseph
Blatt. FEELING FREE.
Ages 9 and up. 640
Zelonky, Joy. I CAN'T ALWAYS HEAR YOU.
Ages 7-10. 718

## Death

See also: *Guilt, feelings of; Loss: feelings of; Mourning,
stages of*
Maruki, Toshi. HIROSHIMA NO PIKA.
Ages 7 and up. 406
Naylor, Phyllis Reynolds. A STRING OF CHANCES.
Ages 12 and up. 464
Sallis, Susan Diana. A TIME FOR EVERYTHING.
Ages 13 and up. 569

## Attitude toward

Anderson, Leone Castell. IT'S O.K. TO CRY.
Ages 5-8. 16
Donnelly, Elfie. SO LONG, GRANDPA.
Ages 9-11. 168
Hermes, Patricia. YOU SHOULDN'T HAVE TO SAY
GOOD-BYE.
Ages 10-13. 286
Ipswitch, Elaine. SCOTT WAS HERE.
Ages 12 and up. 322
Jacobs, Dee. LAURA'S GIFT.
Ages 10-13. 328
Krementz, Jill. HOW IT FEELS WHEN A PARENT
DIES.
Ages 8 and up. 352
L'Engle, Madeleine Franklin. A RING OF ENDLESS
LIGHT.
Ages 11-14. 363
Peavy, Linda S. ALLISON'S GRANDFATHER.
Ages 6-9. 489
Sallis, Susan Diana. ONLY LOVE.
Ages 12 and up. 568
Simon, Norma. WE REMEMBER PHILIP.
Ages 7-10. 598
Stevens, Margaret. WHEN GRANDPA DIED.
Ages 4-8. 629
Strasser, Todd. FRIENDS TILL THE END.
Ages 12 and up. 636
Stretton, Barbara. YOU NEVER LOSE.
Ages 12 and up. 639
Wallace-Brodeur, Ruth. ONE APRIL VACATION.
Ages 9-11. 677

## of Father

Blume, Judy Sussman. TIGER EYES.
Ages 11 and up. 57
Bosse, Malcolm Joseph. GANESH.
Ages 11-14. 65
Foley, June. IT'S NO CRUSH, I'M IN LOVE!
Ages 11-13. 192
Fox, Paula. A PLACE APART.
Ages 12 and up. 193
Greenberg, Jan. A SEASON IN-BETWEEN.
Ages 11-13. 237
Harlan, Elizabeth. FOOTFALLS.
Ages 12-14. 265
Hopper, Nancy J. SECRETS.
Ages 11-14. 304
Krementz, Jill. HOW IT FEELS WHEN A PARENT
DIES.
Ages 8 and up. 352
Miner, Jane Claypool. A MAN'S PRIDE: LOSING A
FATHER.
Ages 11 and up. 429
Pierik, Robert. ROOKFLEAS IN THE CELLAR.
Ages 8-13. 512

## Dependence/Independence (cont.)

Slepian, Jan. THE ALFRED SUMMER.
Ages 11-13. 603
Springstubb, Tricia. THE MOON ON A STRING.
Ages 12 and up. 619
Teibl, Margaret. DAVEY COME HOME.
Ages 6-9. 646
Voigt, Cynthia. HOMECOMING.
Ages 11 and up. 672

## Depression

**See also:** *Anger; Guilt, feelings of; Loneliness; Loss: feelings of; Mental illness*
Arrick, Fran. TUNNEL VISION.
Ages 12 and up. 24
Bridgers, Sue Ellen. NOTES FOR ANOTHER LIFE.
Ages 12 and up. 75
Hughes, Dean. SWITCHING TRACKS.
Ages 10-14. 308
Oneal, Zibby. THE LANGUAGE OF GOLDFISH.
Ages 11-14. 473
Smith, Nancy Covert. THE FALLING-APART WINTER.
Ages 10-13. 612

## Deprivation, Emotional

**See also:** *Parental: negligence; Security/Insecurity*
Bonham, Frank. GIMME AN H, GIMME AN E, GIMME AN L, GIMME A P.
Ages 12 and up. 61
Greene, Sheppard M. THE BOY WHO DRANK TOO MUCH.
Ages 12 and up. 242
Magorian, Michelle. GOOD NIGHT, MR. TOM.
Ages 11 and up. 401
Van Leeuwen, Jean. SEEMS LIKE THIS ROAD GOES ON FOREVER.
Ages 12 and up. 663
Wortis, Avi. SOMETIMES I THINK I HEAR MY NAME.
Ages 10-13. 708

## Desegregation

**See:** *Integration; Prejudice*

## Desertion

**See:** *Abandonment*

## Detention Home, Living in

**See also:** *Crime/Criminals; Delinquency, juvenile; Imprisonment*
Grace, Fran. BRANIGAN'S DOG.
Ages 10 and up. 225
Harrah, Michael. FIRST OFFENDER.
Ages 11-13. 266
Meyer, Carolyn. THE CENTER: FROM A TROUBLED PAST TO A NEW LIFE.
Ages 13 and up. 420

## Determination

Bond, Nancy Barbara. THE VOYAGE BEGUN.
Ages 12 and up. 60
Bottner, Barbara. DUMB OLD CASEY IS A FAT TREE.
Ages 6-9. 66
Boutis, Victoria. KATY DID IT.
Ages 8-10. 69
Chaffin, Lillie Dorton. WE BE WARM TILL SPRINGTIME COMES.
Ages 6-9. 110
De Roo, Anne Louise. SCRUB FIRE.
Ages 9-12. 162
Dolan, Sheila. THE WISHING BOTTLE.
Ages 7-9. 167
Dunne, Mary Collins. HOBY & STUB.
Ages 10-13. 176

Elfman, Blossom. THE BUTTERFLY GIRL.
Ages 13 and up. 180
Farley, Carol J. TWILIGHT WAVES.
Ages 10-13. 186
Gardiner, John Reynolds. STONE FOX.
Ages 8-10. 202
Geibel, James. THE BLOND BROTHER.
Ages 12 and up. 205
Greenfield, Eloise and Alesia Revis. ALESIA.
Ages 10-14. 245
Knudson, R. Rozanne. RINEHART LIFTS.
Ages 10-12. 348
Lexau, Joan M. I HATE RED ROVER.
Ages 6-8. 371
Myers, Walter Dean. HOOPS.
Ages 12 and up. 459
Ruby, Lois. TWO TRUTHS IN MY POCKET.
Ages 12 and up. 557
Sachs, Marilyn. A SUMMER'S LEASE.
Ages 11-14. 566
Slepian, Jan. LESTER'S TURN.
Ages 11-14. 604
Smith, Robert Kimmel. JELLY BELLY.
Ages 10-12. 614
Strang, Celia. THIS CHILD IS MINE.
Ages 11-14. 634
Sullivan, Mary Beth and Alan J. Brightman and Joseph Blatt. FEELING FREE.
Ages 9 and up. 640
Van Steenwyk, Elizabeth Ann. RIVALS ON ICE.
Ages 9-11. 664
Voigt, Cynthia. HOMECOMING.
Ages 11 and up. 672
Winthrop, Elizabeth. I THINK HE LIKES ME.
Ages 3-7. 695
Winthrop, Elizabeth. MARATHON MIRANDA.
Ages 9-11. 696
Wortis, Avi. A PLACE CALLED UGLY.
Ages 11-14. 707

## Diabetes

Dacquino, Vincent T. KISS THE CANDY DAYS GOOD-BYE.
Ages 10-14. 148
Giff, Patricia Reilly. THE GIFT OF THE PIRATE QUEEN.
Ages 9-12. 211
Kipnis, Lynne and Susan Adler. YOU CAN'T CATCH DIABETES FROM A FRIEND.
Ages 7-12. 343
Richter, Elizabeth. THE TEENAGE HOSPITAL EXPERIENCE: YOU CAN HANDLE IT!
Ages 12 and up. 532

## Diet/Dieting

**See:** *Weight control: overweight*

## Differences, Human

**See also:** *Poverty; Prejudice; Self, attitude toward: feeling different; Values/Valuing; Wealth/Wealthy*
Billington, Elizabeth T. PART-TIME BOY.
Ages 8-10. 53
Brooks, Jerome. THE BIG DIPPER MARATHON.
Ages 11-14. 77
Burch, Robert Joseph. IDA EARLY COMES OVER THE MOUNTAIN.
Ages 8-10. 92
Cohen, Miriam. SO WHAT?
Ages 4-7. 129
Crofford, Emily. STORIES FROM THE BLUE ROAD.
Ages 9-12. 143
DeClements, Barthe. NOTHING'S FAIR IN FIFTH GRADE.
Ages 8-11. 152
Hanlon, Emily. THE WING AND THE FLAME.
Ages 13 and up. 262

## Differences, Human (cont.)

Hautzig, Deborah. THE HANDSOMEST FATHER.
Ages 4-7. 271

Kamien, Janet. WHAT IF YOU COULDN'T . . . ? A
BOOK ABOUT SPECIAL NEEDS.
Ages 8-12. 336

Lasker, Joe. NICK JOINS IN.
Ages 5-8. 358

MacLachlan, Patricia. ARTHUR, FOR THE VERY
FIRST TIME.
Ages 8-10. 393

MacLachlan, Patricia. CASSIE BINEGAR.
Ages 9-12. 394

Mazer, Norma Fox. MRS. FISH, APE, AND ME, THE
DUMP QUEEN.
Ages 10-12. 414

Oppenheimer, Joan Letson. GARDINE VS.
HANOVER.
Ages 11-14. 474

Payne, Sherry Neuwirth. A CONTEST.
Ages 8-10. 486

Ruby, Lois. TWO TRUTHS IN MY POCKET.
Ages 12 and up. 557

Tate, Joan. LUKE'S GARDEN AND GRAMP: TWO
NOVELS.
Ages 10-13. 644

Tax, Meredith. FAMILIES.
Ages 4-8. 645

Wolde, Gunilla. BETSY AND PETER ARE
DIFFERENT.
Ages 3-6. 701

Yep, Laurence Michael. KIND HEARTS AND
GENTLE MONSTERS.
Ages 12 and up. 712

Zelonky, Joy. I CAN'T ALWAYS HEAR YOU.
Ages 7-10. 718

## Disabilities

See: *Handicaps: multiple; Illnesses; Learning disabilities;
Mental retardation*

## Disagreements

See: *Aggression; Parent/Parents: fighting between; Peer
relationships; Problem solving; Sibling: rivalry*

## Discipline, Meaning of

See also: *Parental: control; Self-discipline*

Buerger, Jane. OBEDIENCE.
Ages 3-6. 83

Dyer, Thomas A. THE WHIPMAN IS WATCHING.
Ages 10-14. 177

Hazen, Barbara Shook. EVEN IF I DID SOMETHING
AWFUL.
Ages 3-6. 275

Love, Sandra Weller. CROSSING OVER.
Ages 10-12. 383

Morgenroth, Barbara. TRAMPS LIKE US.
Ages 12 and up. 452

Sharmat, Mitchell. COME HOME, WILMA.
Ages 6-8. 588

Steptoe, John Lewis. DADDY IS A
MONSTER . . . SOMETIMES.
Ages 5-7. 627

## Discouragement

See: *Encouragement*

## Discrimination

See: *Apartheid; Integration; Prejudice*

## Dishonesty

See: *Honesty/Dishonesty*

## Distrust

See: *Trust/Distrust*

## Divorce

See also: *Separation, marital*

Shreve, Susan Richards. FAMILY SECRETS: FIVE
VERY IMPORTANT STORIES.
Ages 9-11. 590

**of Parents.** *See also: Parental: custody*

Abercrombie, Barbara Mattes. CAT-MAN'S
DAUGHTER.
Ages 11-13. 1

Adler, Carole Schwerdtfeger. THE SILVER COACH.
Ages 9-12. 8

Anderson, Penny S. A PRETTY GOOD TEAM.
Ages 5-8. 18

Angell, Judie. WHAT'S BEST FOR YOU.
Ages 11-14. 21

Danziger, Paula. THE DIVORCE EXPRESS.
Ages 11-14. 150

Drescher, Joan Elizabeth. YOUR FAMILY, MY
FAMILY.
Ages 5-7. 173

Gaeddert, LouAnn Bigge. JUST LIKE SISTERS.
Ages 8-12. 196

Gerson, Corinne. HOW I PUT MY MOTHER
THROUGH COLLEGE.
Ages 11 and up. 207

Graham, Ada and Frank Graham. JACOB AND OWL.
Ages 8-11. 228

Grant, Cynthia D. JOSHUA FORTUNE.
Ages 10-13. 229

Helmering, Doris Wild. I HAVE TWO FAMILIES.
Ages 6-8. 279

Hogan, Paula Z. WILL DAD EVER MOVE BACK
HOME?
Ages 7-10. 299

Irwin, Hadley, pseud. BRING TO A BOIL AND
SEPARATE.
Ages 10-12. 323

Love, Sandra Weller. CROSSING OVER.
Ages 10-12. 383

Miles, Betty. THE TROUBLE WITH THIRTEEN.
Ages 9-13. 424

Miner, Jane Claypool. SPLIT DECISION: FACING
DIVORCE.
Ages 11 and up. 435

Okimoto, Jean Davies. MY MOTHER IS NOT
MARRIED TO MY FATHER.
Ages 9-11. 470

Paris, Lena. MOM IS SINGLE.
Ages 6-8. 480

Park, Barbara. DON'T MAKE ME SMILE.
Ages 8-11. 481

Pfeffer, Susan Beth. JUST BETWEEN US.
Ages 10-12. 502

Pfeffer, Susan Beth. STARRING PETER AND LEIGH.
Ages 12-14. 503

Pfeffer, Susan Beth. STARTING WITH MELODIE.
Ages 11-13. 504

Rabinowich, Ellen. ROCK FEVER.
Ages 12 and up. 523

Reader, Dennis J. COMING BACK ALIVE.
Ages 12 and up. 525

Schuchman, Joan. TWO PLACES TO SLEEP.
Ages 5-7. 577

Slote, Alfred. LOVE AND TENNIS.
Ages 12-14. 605

Sobol, Harriet Langsam. MY OTHER-MOTHER, MY
OTHER-FATHER.
Ages 7-10. 616

Stein, Sara Bonnett. ON DIVORCE: AN OPEN
FAMILY BOOK FOR PARENTS AND CHILDREN
TOGETHER.
Ages 4-8. 626

Wolkoff, Judie. HAPPILY EVER AFTER . . . ALMOST.
Ages 11-13. 703

## Doctor, Going to

**See also:** *Fractures; Hospital, going to; Illnesses; Surgery; Sutures*
Chalmers, Mary Eileen. COME TO THE DOCTOR, HARRY.
Ages 2-5. 112
Rockwell, Anne F. and Harlow Rockwell. SICK IN BED.
Ages 3-6. 546

## Doubt

**See:** *Inferiority, feelings of; Trust/Distrust*

## Dreams

**See:** *Daydreaming; Nightmares; Wishes*

## Drinking

**See:** *Alcoholism*

## Dropout, School

Hassler, Jon Francis. JEMMY.
Ages 11 and up. 270
Reader, Dennis J. COMING BACK ALIVE.
Ages 12 and up. 525

## Drugs

**See also:** *Alcoholism; Marijuana; Reality, escaping*
Banks, Lynne Reid. THE WRITING ON THE WALL.
Ages 12 and up. 33
Kinter, Judith. CROSS-COUNTRY CAPER.
Ages 11-14. 342

**Abuse of**
Dodson, Susan. HAVE YOU SEEN THIS GIRL?
Ages 13 and up. 166
Hunter, Kristin Eggleston. LOU IN THE LIMELIGHT.
Ages 14 and up. 312
Meyer, Carolyn. THE CENTER: FROM A TROUBLED PAST TO A NEW LIFE.
Ages 13 and up. 420
Rabinowich, Ellen. ROCK FEVER.
Ages 12 and up. 523
Strasser, Todd. ANGEL DUST BLUES.
Ages 14 and up. 635

**Dependence on**
Strasser, Todd. ANGEL DUST BLUES.
Ages 14 and up. 635

## Dwarfism

Kerr, M. E., pseud. LITTLE LITTLE.
Ages 11 and up. 339
Sullivan, Mary Beth and Alan J. Brightman and Joseph Blatt. FEELING FREE.
Ages 9 and up. 640

## Dyslexia

**See:** *Learning disabilities*

# E

## Eating Problems

**See:** *Anorexia nervosa; Weight control*

## Ecology

**See:** *Nature*

## Economic Adversity

**See:** *Parent/Parents: unemployed*

## Economic Status

**See:** *Poverty; Wealth/Wealthy*

## Education

**See also:** *Careers: planning; School*

**Special.** *See also: Blindness; Deafness; Handicaps; Learning disabilities; Mental retardation; Talents*
Cheatham, Karyn Follis. THE BEST WAY OUT.
Ages 12 and up. 114
Cohen, Miriam. FIRST GRADE TAKES A TEST.
Ages 5-7. 127
Gilson, Jamie. DO BANANAS CHEW GUM?
Ages 9-11. 216
Hlibok, Bruce. SILENT DANCER.
Ages 8-11. 293
Riskind, Mary L. APPLE IS MY SIGN.
Ages 10-14. 536
Weiman, Eiveen. IT TAKES BRAINS.
Ages 10-12. 686

**Value of**
Hutchins, Patricia. THE TALE OF THOMAS MEADE.
Ages 5-7. 320
Jones, Toeckey. GO WELL, STAY WELL.
Ages 12 and up. 334
Ross, Pat. M AND M AND THE BIG BAG.
Ages 6-8. 550
Strang, Celia. FOSTER MARY.
Ages 10-13. 633

## Ego Ideal

**See:** *Identification with others*

## Egocentrism

**See also:** *Empathy; Sharing/Not sharing*
Brochmann, Elizabeth. WHAT'S THE MATTER, GIRL?
Ages 12 and up. 76
Matthews, Ellen. PUTTING UP WITH SHERWOOD.
Ages 9-11. 408
Miner, Jane Claypool. SHE'S MY SISTER: HAVING A RETARDED SISTER.
Ages 11 and up. 434
Moeri, Louise. FIRST THE EGG.
Ages 12 and up. 438
Morgenroth, Barbara. TRAMPS LIKE US.
Ages 12 and up. 452
Perl, Lila. PIEFACE AND DAPHNE.
Ages 9-11. 494
Sachs, Marilyn. A SUMMER'S LEASE.
Ages 11-14. 566
Stevens, Carla McBride. SARA AND THE PINCH.
Ages 5-7. 628
Williams, Barbara Wright. WHATEVER HAPPENED TO BEVERLY BIGLER'S BIRTHDAY?
Ages 4-8. 693

## Emancipation of Minor

Colman, Hila Crayder. THE FAMILY TRAP.
Ages 12 and up. 134

## Embarrassment

**See also:** *Enuresis; Shame*
Winthrop, Elizabeth. SLOPPY KISSES.
Ages 4-7. 698

## Emigration

**See:** *Immigrants*

## Emotional Deprivation

**See:** *Deprivation, emotional*

## Emotions

**See also:** *Self, attitude toward; Specific feeling (e.g. Anger; Jealousy)*

## Emotions (cont.)

### Accepting

Berman, Claire. WHAT AM I DOING IN A STEP-FAMILY?
Ages 5-10. 51

Colman, Hila Crayder. CONFESSION OF A STORYTELLER.
Ages 10-13. 133

Hill, Margaret. TURN THE PAGE, WENDY.
Ages 10-14. 291

Hogan, Paula Z. SOMETIMES I GET SO MAD.
Ages 5-8. 298

Jenkins, Jordan. LEARNING ABOUT LOVE.
Ages 4-8. 329

Kamien, Janet. WHAT IF YOU COULDN'T . . . ? A BOOK ABOUT SPECIAL NEEDS.
Ages 8-12. 336

Oneal, Zibby. A FORMAL FEELING.
Ages 12 and up. 472

Peyton, K. M., pseud. MARION'S ANGELS.
Ages 11-14. 499

Stanek, Muriel Novella. WHO'S AFRAID OF THE DARK?
Ages 5-8. 623

### Identifying

Moncure, Jane Belk. JOY.
Ages 3-6. 444

Oneal, Zibby. A FORMAL FEELING.
Ages 12 and up. 472

Strauss, Joyce. HOW DOES IT FEEL . . . ?
Ages 4-8. 637

Wright, Betty Ren. I LIKE BEING ALONE.
Ages 6-9. 709

## Empathy

See also: Egocentrism; Identification with others

Greenfield, Eloise. GRANDMAMA'S JOY.
Ages 4-8. 244

Knox-Wagner, Elaine. MY GRANDPA RETIRED TODAY.
Ages 4-7. 346

Leggett, Linda Rodgers and Linda Gambee Andrews. THE ROSE-COLORED GLASSES: MELANIE ADJUSTS TO POOR VISION.
Ages 8-11. 362

Lexau, Joan M. I HATE RED ROVER.
Ages 6-8. 371

Robinson, Barbara Webb. TEMPORARY TIMES, TEMPORARY PLACES.
Ages 11-13. 538

Roy, Ronald. FRANKIE IS STAYING BACK.
Ages 8-10. 556

Simon, Norma. WE REMEMBER PHILIP.
Ages 7-10. 598

Tester, Sylvia Root. SANDY'S NEW HOME.
Ages 5-8. 648

Yep, Laurence Michael. KIND HEARTS AND GENTLE MONSTERS.
Ages 12 and up. 712

## Encouragement

See also: Courage, meaning of

Robison, Nancy Louise. BALLET MAGIC.
Ages 9-11. 541

Simon, Norma. NOBODY'S PERFECT, NOT EVEN MY MOTHER.
Ages 4-8. 597

## Enuresis

See also: Embarrassment; Shame

Ashley, Bernard. BREAK IN THE SUN.
Ages 11 and up. 29

McCord, Jean. TURKEYLEGS THOMPSON.
Ages 11-14. 390

## Epilepsy

See also: Brain injury

Corcoran, Barbara. CHILD OF THE MORNING.
Ages 10 and up. 139

Girion, Barbara. A HANDFUL OF STARS.
Ages 12 and up. 217

Gould, Marilyn. GOLDEN DAFFODILS.
Ages 8-12. 223

Hermes, Patricia. WHAT IF THEY KNEW?
Ages 9-11. 285

Herzig, Alison Cragin and Jane Lawrence Mali. A SEASON OF SECRETS.
Ages 11-13. 287

Slepian, Jan. THE ALFRED SUMMER.
Ages 11-13. 603

Young, Helen. WHAT DIFFERENCE DOES IT MAKE, DANNY?
Ages 9-12. 715

## Equal Rights

See: Integration; Prejudice

## Equality

See: Differences, human; Integration; Prejudice

## Escaping Reality

See: Reality, escaping

## Eskimo

Houston, James Archibald. LONG CLAWS: AN ARCTIC ADVENTURE.
Ages 9-11. 305

## Ethnic Differences

See: Prejudice: ethnic/racial

## Exceptional Children

See: Education: special; Learning disabilities; Mental retardation; Talents

## Exile

See: Ostracism

## Expectancy, Power of

See: Expectations

## Expectations

See also: Peer relationships: peer pressures

Adler, Carole Schwerdtfeger. SOME OTHER SUMMER.
Ages 10-13. 9

Arrick, Fran. TUNNEL VISION.
Ages 12 and up. 24

Dygard, Thomas J. SOCCER DUEL.
Ages 11-14. 179

Ellis, Ella Thorp. SLEEPWALKER'S MOON.
Ages 12 and up. 181

Greenberg, Jan. THE PIG-OUT BLUES.
Ages 12 and up. 236

Greene, Constance Clarke. YOUR OLD PAL, AL.
Ages 9-13. 241

Greenwald, Sheila. GIVE US A GREAT BIG SMILE, ROSY COLE.
Ages 8-10. 246

Miner, Jane Claypool. NAVAJO VICTORY: BEING A NATIVE AMERICAN.
Ages 11 and up. 432

Okimoto, Jean Davies. NORMAN SCHNURMAN, AVERAGE PERSON.
Ages 10-12. 471

Platt, Kin. BROGG'S BRAIN.
Ages 12 and up. 514

Slote, Alfred. LOVE AND TENNIS.
Ages 12-14. 605

### Expectations (cont.)

Springstubb, Tricia. THE MOON ON A STRING.
Ages 12 and up. 619

Thomas, Jane Resh. THE COMEBACK DOG.
Ages 7-9. 653

Van Leeuwen, Jean. SEEMS LIKE THIS ROAD GOES
ON FOREVER.
Ages 12 and up. 663

### Extended Family

**See:** *Family: extended*

## F

### Fairness

**See:** *Honesty/Dishonesty; Sharing/Not sharing*

### Family

**See also:** *Age; Grandparent; Parent/Parents; Relatives;
Sibling; Stepbrother/Stepsister; Stepparent*

**Extended**

Angell, Judie. DEAR LOLA OR HOW TO BUILD
YOUR OWN FAMILY.
Ages 10-13. 19

Dixon, Paige, pseud. SKIPPER.
Ages 12 and up. 165

Drescher, Joan Elizabeth. YOUR FAMILY, MY
FAMILY.
Ages 5-7. 173

Harrah, Michael. FIRST OFFENDER.
Ages 11-13. 266

Hest, Amy. MAYBE NEXT YEAR . . .
Ages 9-12. 288

MacLachlan, Patricia. CASSIE BINEGAR.
Ages 9-12. 394

Marangell, Virginia J. GIANNA MIA.
Ages 12-15. 402

Tate, Eleanora E. JUST AN OVERNIGHT GUEST.
Ages 9-11. 643

Tax, Meredith. FAMILIES.
Ages 4-8. 645

Thompson, Jean, pseud. DON'T FORGET MICHAEL.
Ages 7-9. 656

Wolkoff, Judie. HAPPILY EVER AFTER. . .ALMOST.
Ages 11-13. 703

**Relationships.** *See also: Sibling: relationships*

Adler, Carole Schwerdtfeger. THE ONCE IN A
WHILE HERO.
Ages 10-13. 7

Angell, Judie. WHAT'S BEST FOR YOU.
Ages 11-14. 21

Asher, Sandra Fenichel. JUST LIKE JENNY.
Ages 10-12. 27

Bach, Alice Hendricks. WAITING FOR JOHNNY
MIRACLE.
Ages 12 and up. 32

Banks, Lynne Reid. THE WRITING ON THE WALL.
Ages 12 and up. 33

Barrett, John M. DANIEL DISCOVERS DANIEL.
Ages 7-9. 35

Bates, Betty. MY MOM, THE MONEY NUT.
Ages 10-12. 39

Berman, Claire. WHAT AM I DOING IN A
STEP-FAMILY?
Ages 5-10. 51

Blue, Rose. WISHFUL LYING.
Ages 6-9. 54

Blume, Judy Sussman. SUPERFUDGE.
Ages 8-10. 56

Branscum, Robbie. FOR LOVE OF JODY.
Ages 9-12. 73

Brochmann, Elizabeth. WHAT'S THE MATTER,
GIRL?
Ages 12 and up. 76

Buchan, Stuart. A SPACE OF HIS OWN.
Ages 12 and up. 82

Burch, Robert Joseph. IDA EARLY COMES OVER
THE MOUNTAIN.
Ages 8-10. 92

Byars, Betsy Cromer. GOODBYE, CHICKEN LITTLE.
Ages 9-11. 97

Cameron, Ann. THE STORIES JULIAN TELLS.
Ages 7-9. 104

Carrick, Malcolm. I'LL GET YOU.
Ages 11-13. 107

Chaikin, Miriam. I SHOULD WORRY, I SHOULD
CARE.
Ages 8-11. 111

Cheatham, Karyn Follis. THE BEST WAY OUT.
Ages 12 and up. 114

Cleary, Beverly Bunn. RAMONA AND HER
MOTHER.
Ages 7-10. 118

Cleary, Beverly Bunn. RAMONA QUIMBY, AGE 8.
Ages 8-10. 119

Clifton, Lucille. SONORA BEAUTIFUL.
Ages 12-14. 123

Colman, Hila Crayder. WHAT'S THE MATTER WITH
THE DOBSONS?
Ages 10-13. 135

Crofford, Emily. STORIES FROM THE BLUE ROAD.
Ages 9-12. 143

Dacquino, Vincent T. KISS THE CANDY DAYS
GOOD-BYE.
Ages 10-14. 148

Danziger, Paula. CAN YOU SUE YOUR PARENTS
FOR MALPRACTICE?
Ages 10-14. 149

Dixon, Jeanne. LADY CAT LOST.
Ages 10-12. 164

Dixon, Paige, pseud. SKIPPER.
Ages 12 and up. 165

Dodson, Susan. HAVE YOU SEEN THIS GIRL?
Ages 13 and up. 166

Donnelly, Elfie. SO LONG, GRANDPA.
Ages 9-11. 168

Drescher, Joan Elizabeth. YOUR FAMILY, MY
FAMILY.
Ages 5-7. 173

Foley, June. IT'S NO CRUSH, I'M IN LOVE!
Ages 11-13. 192

Gaeddert, LouAnn Bigge. JUST LIKE SISTERS.
Ages 8-12. 196

Galbraith, Kathryn Osebold. COME SPRING.
Ages 9-13. 197

Gates, Doris. A MORGAN FOR MELINDA.
Ages 10-12. 203

Giff, Patricia Reilly. THE GIFT OF THE PIRATE
QUEEN.
Ages 9-12. 211

Giff, Patricia Reilly. THE WINTER WORM
BUSINESS.
Ages 8-10. 214

Girion, Barbara. A HANDFUL OF STARS.
Ages 12 and up. 217

Girion, Barbara. LIKE EVERYBODY ELSE.
Ages 10-13. 218

Grant, Cynthia D. JOSHUA FORTUNE.
Ages 10-13. 229

Green, Phyllis. GLOOMY LOUIE.
Ages 8-9. 234

Greenberg, Jan. THE ICEBERG AND ITS SHADOW.
Ages 10-12. 235

Greenwald, Sheila. GIVE US A GREAT BIG SMILE,
ROSY COLE.
Ages 8-10. 246

Guest, Elissa Haden. THE HANDSOME MAN.
Ages 12 and up. 251

Haas, Dorothy. POPPY AND THE OUTDOORS CAT.
Ages 7-10. 253

## Family (cont.)

Hall, Lynn. DANZA!
Ages 9-12. 254
Hall, Lynn. THE LEAVING.
Ages 12 and up. 256
Harlan, Elizabeth. FOOTFALLS.
Ages 12-14. 265
Hautzig, Deborah. SECOND STAR TO THE RIGHT.
Ages 12 and up. 272
Hautzig, Esther Rudomin. A GIFT FOR MAMA.
Ages 8-12. 273
Heck, Bessie Holland. CAVE-IN AT MASON'S MINE.
Ages 8-10. 278
Herman, Charlotte. WHAT HAPPENED TO
HEATHER HOPKOWITZ?
Ages 10-13. 283
Hunter, Kristin Eggleston. LOU IN THE LIMELIGHT.
Ages 14 and up. 312
Hurd, Edith Thacher. THE BLACK DOG WHO WENT
INTO THE WOODS.
Ages 5-7. 313
Hurwitz, Johanna. TOUGH-LUCK KAREN.
Ages 10-13. 319
Jacobs, Dee. LAURA'S GIFT.
Ages 10-13. 328
Josephs, Rebecca. EARLY DISORDER.
Ages 13 and up. 335
Kherdian, David. THE ROAD FROM HOME: THE
STORY OF AN ARMENIAN GIRL.
Ages 12 and up. 340
Kingman, Lee. THE REFINER'S FIRE.
Ages 12-14. 341
Lifton, Betty Jean. I'M STILL ME.
Ages 12 and up. 372
Liu, Aimee. SOLITAIRE.
Ages 13 and up. 380
McCaffrey, Mary. MY BROTHER ANGE.
Ages 8-11. 389
MacLachlan, Patricia. CASSIE BINEGAR.
Ages 9-12. 394
McLendon, Gloria Houston. MY BROTHER JOEY
DIED.
Ages 9-11. 398
Marzollo, Jean. AMY GOES FISHING.
Ages 4-7. 407
Mazer, Harry. THE ISLAND KEEPER.
Ages 10-14. 412
Mazer, Norma Fox. UP IN SETH'S ROOM.
Ages 13 and up. 415
Mendonca, Susan R. TOUGH CHOICES.
Ages 11 and up. 419
Miklowitz, Gloria D. DID YOU HEAR WHAT
HAPPENED TO ANDREA?
Ages 13 and up. 421
Miner, Jane Claypool. A DAY AT A TIME: DEALING
WITH AN ALCOHOLIC.
Ages 11 and up. 428
Miner, Jane Claypool. SPLIT DECISION: FACING
DIVORCE.
Ages 11 and up. 435
Moeri, Louise. FIRST THE EGG.
Ages 12 and up. 438
Morton, Jane. I AM RUBBER, YOU ARE GLUE.
Ages 9-11. 454
Naylor, Phyllis Reynolds. A STRING OF CHANCES.
Ages 12 and up. 464
Neigoff, Mike. IT WILL NEVER BE THE SAME
AGAIN.
Ages 12-14. 465
Okimoto, Jean Davies. IT'S JUST TOO MUCH.
Ages 10-12. 469
Oneal, Zibby. A FORMAL FEELING.
Ages 12 and up. 472
Oneal, Zibby. THE LANGUAGE OF GOLDFISH.
Ages 11-14. 473
Oppenheimer, Joan Letson. GARDINE VS.
HANOVER.
Ages 11-14. 474

Pearson, Susan. SATURDAY I RAN AWAY.
Ages 5-7. 488
Perl, Lila. DON'T ASK MIRANDA.
Ages 10-13. 492
Pfeffer, Susan Beth. WHAT DO YOU DO WHEN
YOUR MOUTH WON'T OPEN?
Ages 10-13. 505
Posner, Grace. IN MY SISTER'S EYES.
Ages 12 and up. 516
Potter, Marian. THE SHARED ROOM.
Ages 10-12. 517
Power, Barbara. I WISH LAURA'S MOMMY WAS
MY MOMMY.
Ages 4-7. 518
Richter, Alice and Laura Joffe Numeroff. YOU CAN'T
PUT BRACES ON SPACES.
Ages 5-9. 531
Riley, Jocelyn. ONLY MY MOUTH IS SMILING.
Ages 12-14. 533
Rinaldi, Ann. TERM PAPER.
Ages 12 and up. 535
Riskind, Mary L. APPLE IS MY SIGN.
Ages 10-14. 536
Robinson, Barbara Webb. TEMPORARY TIMES,
TEMPORARY PLACES.
Ages 11-13. 538
Rodowsky, Colby F. A SUMMER'S WORTH OF
SHAME.
Ages 12-14. 548
Ruby, Lois. TWO TRUTHS IN MY POCKET.
Ages 12 and up. 557
Shreve, Susan Richards. THE BAD DREAMS OF A
GOOD GIRL.
Ages 8-10. 589
Shreve, Susan Richards. FAMILY SECRETS: FIVE
VERY IMPORTANT STORIES.
Ages 9-11. 590
Shreve, Susan Richards. THE MASQUERADE.
Ages 12 and up. 591
Simon, Norma. I'M BUSY, TOO.
Ages 3-5. 596
Smith, Nancy Covert. THE FALLING-APART
WINTER.
Ages 10-13. 612
Smith, Robert Kimmel. JELLY BELLY.
Ages 10-12. 614
Sobol, Harriet Langsam. MY OTHER-MOTHER, MY
OTHER-FATHER.
Ages 7-10. 616
Springstubb, Tricia. THE MOON ON A STRING.
Ages 12 and up. 619
Stein, Sara Bonnett. THE ADOPTED ONE: AN OPEN
FAMILY BOOK FOR PARENTS AND CHILDREN
TOGETHER.
Ages 4-8. 625
Steptoe, John Lewis. DADDY IS A MONSTER . . .
SOMETIMES.
Ages 5-7. 627
Stolz, Mary Slattery. WHAT TIME OF NIGHT IS IT?
Ages 11-14. 631
Storr, Catherine Cole. VICKY.
Ages 12 and up. 632
Strang, Celia. THIS CHILD IS MINE.
Ages 11-14. 634
Tate, Eleanora E. JUST AN OVERNIGHT GUEST.
Ages 9-11. 643
Tax, Meredith. FAMILIES.
Ages 4-8. 645
Terris, Susan Dubinsky. NO SCARLET RIBBONS.
Ages 11-13. 647
Truss, Jan. BIRD AT THE WINDOW.
Ages 13 and up. 661
Veglahn, Nancy Crary. FELLOWSHIP OF THE
SEVEN STARS.
Ages 12 and up. 665
Vogel, Ilse-Margret. MY SUMMER BROTHER.
Ages 8-10. 670

## Family (cont.)

Voigt, Cynthia. DICEY'S SONG.
Ages 11 and up. 671
Wartski, Maureen Crane. MY BROTHER IS SPECIAL.
Ages 10-12. 681
Wolkoff, Judie. HAPPILY EVER AFTER . . . ALMOST.
Ages 11-13. 703
Wolkoff, Judie. WHERE THE ELF KING SINGS.
Ages 12 and up. 704

**Unity.** *See also: Communication: parent-child*
Bauer, Caroline Feller. MY MOM TRAVELS A LOT.
Ages 5-8. 42
Bennett, Jack. THE VOYAGE OF THE LUCKY DRAGON.
Ages 11 and up. 45
Bond, Felicia. POINSETTIA & HER FAMILY.
Ages 4-7. 59
Cohen, Barbara Nash. THE INNKEEPER'S DAUGHTER.
Ages 11-14. 126
Crofford, Emily. A MATTER OF PRIDE.
Ages 8-11. 142
Fairless, Caroline. HAMBONE.
Ages 8-11. 184
Girion, Barbara. A TANGLE OF ROOTS.
Ages 12-16. 220
Gray, Nigel. IT'LL ALL COME OUT IN THE WASH.
Ages 4-6. 233
Greenberg, Jan. A SEASON IN-BETWEEN.
Ages 11-13. 237
Hermes, Patricia. YOU SHOULDN'T HAVE TO SAY GOOD-BYE.
Ages 10-13. 286
Hurmence, Belinda. TOUGH TIFFANY.
Ages 10-13. 315
Ipswitch, Elaine. SCOTT WAS HERE.
Ages 12 and up. 322
Jones, Penelope. HOLDING TOGETHER.
Ages 9-11. 331
L'Engle, Madeleine Franklin. A RING OF ENDLESS LIGHT.
Ages 11-14. 363
Madler, Trudy. WHY DID GRANDMA DIE?
Ages 4-9. 400
Marangell, Virginia J. GIANNA MIA.
Ages 12-15. 402
Mearian, Judy Frank. TWO WAYS ABOUT IT.
Ages 9-12. 418
Mohr, Nicholasa. FELITA.
Ages 8-10. 440
Pierik, Robert. ROOKFLEAS IN THE CELLAR.
Ages 8-13. 512
Reuter, Margaret. MY MOTHER IS BLIND.
Ages 5-8. 529
Rosen, Lillian D. JUST LIKE EVERYBODY ELSE.
Ages 11 and up. 549
Shyer, Marlene Fanta. MY BROTHER, THE THIEF.
Ages 10-13. 594
Strang, Celia. FOSTER MARY.
Ages 10-13. 633
Swartley, David Warren. MY FRIEND, MY BROTHER.
Ages 9-11. 642
Thompson, Jean, pseud. DON'T FORGET MICHAEL.
Ages 7-9. 656
Thrasher, Crystal Faye. BETWEEN DARK AND DAYLIGHT.
Ages 11-13. 658
Vogel, Ilse-Margret. FAREWELL, AUNT ISABELL.
Ages 8-10. 669
Voigt, Cynthia. HOMECOMING.
Ages 11 and up. 672
Wood, Phyllis Anderson. PASS ME A PINE CONE.
Ages 11 and up. 705

## Fantasy Formation

**See also:** *Creativity; Daydreaming; Imagination; Magical thinking; Play; Wishes*
Klass, Sheila Solomon. TO SEE MY MOTHER DANCE.
Ages 10-13. 344
Lyle, Katie Letcher. DARK BUT FULL OF DIAMONDS.
Ages 12-14. 388
Sargent, Sarah. SECRET LIES.
Ages 11 and up. 570

## Fat

**See:** *Weight control: overweight*

## Father

**See:** *Communication: parent-child; Parent/Parents: single*

## Fear

**See also:** *Anxiety; Courage, meaning of; Nightmares; Security/Insecurity*
Childress, Alice. RAINBOW JORDAN.
Ages 12 and up. 115
Crofford, Emily. A MATTER OF PRIDE.
Ages 8-11. 142
De Roo, Anne Louise. SCRUB FIRE.
Ages 9-12. 162
Heck, Bessie Holland. CAVE-IN AT MASON'S MINE.
Ages 8-10. 278
Miner, Jane Claypool. MOUNTAIN FEAR: WHEN A BROTHER DIES.
Ages 10 and up. 431
Osborn, Lois. MY BROTHER IS AFRAID OF JUST ABOUT EVERYTHING.
Ages 4-7. 476
Pfeffer, Susan Beth. WHAT DO YOU DO WHEN YOUR MOUTH WON'T OPEN?
Ages 10-13. 505
Sachs, Elizabeth-Ann. JUST LIKE ALWAYS.
Ages 10-13. 561

**of Animals**
Gates, Doris. A MORGAN FOR MELINDA.
Ages 10-12. 203
Hickman, Janet. THE THUNDER-PUP.
Ages 9-11. 289
Tester, Sylvia Root. SOMETIMES I'M AFRAID.
Ages 3-5. 649
Wallace, Bill. A DOG CALLED KITTY.
Ages 9-11. 675

**of Being lost.** *See: Lost, being*

**of Darkness**
Bonsall, Crosby Newell. WHO'S AFRAID OF THE DARK?
Ages 3-7. 64
Robison, Deborah. NO ELEPHANTS ALLOWED.
Ages 3-6. 540
Schubert, Ingrid and Dieter Schubert. THERE'S A CROCODILE UNDER MY BED!
Ages 3-6. 576
Smith, Janice Lee. THE MONSTER IN THE THIRD DRESSER DRAWER.
Ages 5-8. 610
Stanek, Muriel Novella. WHO'S AFRAID OF THE DARK?
Ages 5-8. 623
Tester, Sylvia Root. SOMETIMES I'M AFRAID.
Ages 3-5. 649
Willoughby, Elaine Macmann. BORIS AND THE MONSTERS.
Ages 4-7. 694

## Foster Home (cont.)

Myers, Walter Dean. WON'T KNOW TILL I GET THERE.
Ages 11-14. 460

Piepgras, Ruth. MY NAME IS MIKE TRUMSKY.
Ages 5-8. 511

Stanek, Muriel Novella. MY LITTLE FOSTER SISTER.
Ages 4-8. 621

Strang, Celia. FOSTER MARY.
Ages 10-13. 633

## Fractures

See also: *Doctor, going to; Hospital, going to*
Richter, Elizabeth. THE TEENAGE HOSPITAL EXPERIENCE: YOU CAN HANDLE IT!
Ages 12 and up. 532

## Freedom, Meaning of

Bennett, Jack. THE VOYAGE OF THE LUCKY DRAGON.
Ages 11 and up. 45

Bulla, Clyde Robert. POOR BOY, RICH BOY.
Ages 5-8. 87

Callen, Lawrence Willard. SORROW'S SONG.
Ages 9-12. 103

Colman, Hila Crayder. THE FAMILY TRAP.
Ages 12 and up. 134

McPhail, David Michael. A WOLF STORY.
Ages 5-7. 399

Phipson, Joan Nash, pseud. FLY FREE.
Ages 11 and up. 508

Waterton, Betty Marie. A SALMON FOR SIMON.
Ages 4-7. 685

## Friendship

See also: *Boy-girl relationships; Gangs: membership in; Identification with others: peers*
Zolotow, Charlotte Shapiro. THE WHITE MARBLE.
Ages 4-8. 725

### Best friend

Angell, Judie. WHAT'S BEST FOR YOU.
Ages 11-14. 21

Asher, Sandra Fenichel. DAUGHTERS OF THE LAW.
Ages 11-13. 26

Asher, Sandra Fenichel. JUST LIKE JENNY.
Ages 10-12. 27

Bawden, Nina Mary Kark. THE ROBBERS.
Ages 9-12. 43

Bonsall, Crosby Newell. THE GOODBYE SUMMER.
Ages 9-11. 63

Brandenberg, Aliki Liacouras. WE ARE BEST FRIENDS.
Ages 3-6. 72

Butterworth, William Edmund. UNDER THE INFLUENCE.
Ages 12 and up. 94

Byars, Betsy Cromer. THE CYBIL WAR.
Ages 9-12. 96

Byars, Betsy Cromer. GOODBYE, CHICKEN LITTLE.
Ages 9-11. 97

Carrick, Carol. SOME FRIEND!
Ages 9-12. 106

Clifton, Lucille. MY FRIEND JACOB.
Ages 4-7. 122

Cuyler, Margery S. THE TROUBLE WITH SOAP.
Ages 10-13. 147

Danziger, Paula. THE DIVORCE EXPRESS.
Ages 11-14. 150

Delaney, Ned. BERT AND BARNEY.
Ages 3-7. 153

Delton, Judy. LEE HENRY'S BEST FRIEND.
Ages 4-8. 155

Douglass, Barbara. SKATEBOARD SCRAMBLE.
Ages 9-11. 170

Due, Linnea A. HIGH AND OUTSIDE.
Ages 13 and up. 174

Eyerly, Jeannette Hyde. THE SEEING SUMMER.
Ages 8-10. 183

Foley, June. IT'S NO CRUSH, I'M IN LOVE!
Ages 11-13. 192

Franco, Marjorie. SO WHO HASN'T GOT PROBLEMS?
Ages 10-12. 194

Freeman, Gaail. OUT FROM UNDER.
Ages 12 and up. 195

Giff, Patricia Reilly. FOURTH GRADE CELEBRITY.
Ages 8-10. 210

Gilbert, Harriett. RUNNING AWAY.
Ages 11-14. 215

Girion, Barbara. LIKE EVERYBODY ELSE.
Ages 10-13. 218

Girion, Barbara. A TANGLE OF ROOTS.
Ages 12-16. 220

Greenberg, Jan. THE ICEBERG AND ITS SHADOW.
Ages 10-12. 235

Greene, Constance Clarke. AL(EXANDRA) THE GREAT.
Ages 10-12. 239

Greene, Constance Clarke. YOUR OLD PAL, AL.
Ages 9-13. 241

Greene, Sheppard M. THE BOY WHO DRANK TOO MUCH.
Ages 12 and up. 242

Gregory, Diana. THERE'S A CATERPILLAR IN MY LEMONADE.
Ages 10-12. 247

Guest, Elissa Haden. THE HANDSOME MAN.
Ages 12 and up. 251

Haas, Dorothy. POPPY AND THE OUTDOORS CAT.
Ages 7-10. 253

Hautzig, Deborah. SECOND STAR TO THE RIGHT.
Ages 12 and up. 272

Hickman, Martha Whitmore. MY FRIEND WILLIAM MOVED AWAY.
Ages 4-7. 290

Hinton, Susan Eloise. TEX.
Ages 11-15. 292

Irwin, Hadley, pseud. BRING TO A BOIL AND SEPARATE.
Ages 10-12. 323

Knudson, R. Rozanne. RINEHART LIFTS.
Ages 10-12. 348

Korschunow, Irina. WHO KILLED CHRISTOPHER?
Ages 12 and up. 350

Marney, Dean. JUST GOOD FRIENDS.
Ages 11-13. 404

Miles, Betty. THE TROUBLE WITH THIRTEEN.
Ages 9-13. 424

Mohr, Nicholasa. FELITA.
Ages 8-10. 440

Myers, Bernice. NOT AT HOME?
Ages 6-8. 458

Oppenheimer, Joan Letson. WORKING ON IT.
Ages 11-13. 475

Perl, Lila. HEY, REMEMBER FAT GLENDA?
Ages 9-12. 493

Pfeffer, Susan Beth. ABOUT DAVID.
Ages 13 and up. 500

Pfeffer, Susan Beth. STARTING WITH MELODIE.
Ages 11-13. 504

Pfeffer, Susan Beth. WHAT DO YOU DO WHEN YOUR MOUTH WON'T OPEN?
Ages 10-13. 505

Phipson, Joan Nash, pseud. FLY FREE.
Ages 11 and up. 508

Ross, Pat. MEET M AND M.
Ages 6-8. 551

Roy, Ronald. FRANKIE IS STAYING BACK.
Ages 8-10. 556

Sachs, Marilyn. CLASS PICTURES.
Ages 10-13. 564

Schotter, Roni. A MATTER OF TIME.
Ages 12 and up. 575

## Friendship (cont.)

Sharmat, Marjorie Weinman. ROLLO AND JULIET,
FOREVER!
Ages 4-8. 584

Shreve, Susan Richards. FAMILY SECRETS: FIVE
VERY IMPORTANT STORIES.
Ages 9-11. 590

Shura, Mary Francis Craig. THE BARKLEY STREET
SIX-PACK.
Ages 9-12. 592

Slepian, Jan. LESTER'S TURN.
Ages 11-14. 604

Spence, Eleanor Rachel. A CANDLE FOR SAINT
ANTONY.
Ages 13 and up. 618

Stolz, Mary Slattery. WHAT TIME OF NIGHT IS IT?
Ages 11-14. 631

Vigna, Judith. THE HIDING HOUSE.
Ages 4-7. 667

Winthrop, Elizabeth. MIRANDA IN THE MIDDLE.
Ages 9-13. 697

Zelonky, Joy. MY BEST FRIEND MOVED AWAY.
Ages 6-9. 719

Zolotow, Charlotte Shapiro. THE NEW FRIEND.
Ages 3-7. 723

## Keeping friends

Panek, Dennis. MATILDA HIPPO HAS A BIG
MOUTH.
Ages 4-7. 478

Sharmat, Marjorie Weinman. LUCRETIA THE
UNBEARABLE.
Ages 4-7. 583

## Lack of

Conford, Ellen. ANYTHING FOR A FRIEND.
Ages 9-11. 136

Graham, Ada and Frank Graham. JACOB AND OWL.
Ages 8-11. 228

Matthews, Ellen. PUTTING UP WITH SHERWOOD.
Ages 9-11. 408

Sachs, Marilyn. A SUMMER'S LEASE.
Ages 11-14. 566

Snyder, Zilpha Keatley. COME ON, PATSY.
Ages 5-8. 615

## Making friends

Blume, Judy Sussman. SUPERFUDGE.
Ages 8-10. 56

Bograd, Larry. LOST IN THE STORE.
Ages 4-7. 58

Brandenberg, Aliki Liacouras. WE ARE BEST
FRIENDS.
Ages 3-6. 72

Cameron, Ann. THE STORIES JULIAN TELLS.
Ages 7-9. 104

Carrick, Malcolm. I'LL GET YOU.
Ages 11-13. 107

Chaikin, Miriam. I SHOULD WORRY, I SHOULD
CARE.
Ages 8-11. 111

Conford, Ellen. ANYTHING FOR A FRIEND.
Ages 9-11. 136

Corcoran, Barbara. CHILD OF THE MORNING.
Ages 10 and up. 139

Cuyler, Margery S. THE TROUBLE WITH SOAP.
Ages 10-13. 147

DeClements, Barthe. NOTHING'S FAIR IN FIFTH
GRADE.
Ages 8-11. 152

Delton, Judy. LEE HENRY'S BEST FRIEND.
Ages 4-8. 155

Dixon, Jeanne. LADY CAT LOST.
Ages 10-12. 164

Galbraith, Kathryn Osebold. COME SPRING.
Ages 9-13. 197

Gerson, Corinne. SON FOR A DAY.
Ages 10-12. 208

Giff, Patricia Reilly. THE WINTER WORM
BUSINESS.
Ages 8-10. 214

Hamilton-Merritt, Jane. MY FIRST DAY OF SCHOOL.
Ages 3-6. 260

Hickman, Martha Whitmore. MY FRIEND WILLIAM
MOVED AWAY.
Ages 4-7. 290

Hughes, Dean. SWITCHING TRACKS.
Ages 10-14. 308

Hurwitz, Johanna. ALDO APPLESAUCE.
Ages 7-9. 316

Hurwitz, Johanna. TOUGH-LUCK KAREN.
Ages 10-13. 319

Kropp, Paul Stephan. WILTED.
Ages 11-14. 354

Lipp, Frederick J. SOME LOSE THEIR WAY.
Ages 10-13. 377

Liu, Aimee. SOLITAIRE.
Ages 13 and up. 380

Lowry, Lois. ANASTASIA AGAIN!
Ages 9-12. 384

Lowry, Lois. ANASTASIA AT YOUR SERVICE.
Ages 9-12. 385

McCord, Jean. TURKEYLEGS THOMPSON.
Ages 11-14. 390

Magorian, Michelle. GOOD NIGHT, MR. TOM.
Ages 11 and up. 401

Miles, Betty. MAUDIE AND ME AND THE DIRTY
BOOK.
Ages 10-12. 423

Montgomery, Elizabeth Rider. "SEEING" IN THE
DARK.
Ages 5-7. 448

Newton, Suzanne. M.V. SEXTON SPEAKING.
Ages 11 and up. 466

O'Connor, Jane. YOURS TILL NIAGARA FALLS,
ABBY.
Ages 8-10. 467

Pascal, Francine. THE HAND-ME-DOWN KID.
Ages 10-13. 483

Pearson, Susan. MOLLY MOVES OUT.
Ages 5-8. 487

Perl, Lila. DON'T ASK MIRANDA.
Ages 10-13. 492

Pollock, Penny. KEEPING IT SECRET.
Ages 9-12. 515

Riskind, Mary L. APPLE IS MY SIGN.
Ages 10-14. 536

Robinson, Nancy Konheim. WENDY AND THE
BULLIES.
Ages 7-10. 539

Sachs, Marilyn. BEACH TOWELS.
Ages 12 and up. 562

Schultz, Gwendolyn. THE BLUE VALENTINE.
Ages 5-8. 578

Sharmat, Marjorie Weinman. SAY HELLO, VANESSA.
Ages 4-7. 585

Smith, Doris Buchanan. LAST WAS LLOYD.
Ages 8-11. 608

Smith, Doris Buchanan. SALTED LEMONS.
Ages 9-12. 609

Smith, Janice Lee. THE MONSTER IN THE THIRD
DRESSER DRAWER AND OTHER STORIES
ABOUT ADAM JOSHUA.
Ages 5-8. 610

Thrasher, Crystal Faye. BETWEEN DARK AND
DAYLIGHT.
Ages 11-13. 658

Vigna, Judith. THE HIDING HOUSE.
Ages 4-7. 667

Wallace-Brodeur, Ruth. THE KENTON YEAR.
Ages 9-11. 676

Weiman, Eiveen. IT TAKES BRAINS.
Ages 10-12. 686

Wells, Rosemary. TIMOTHY GOES TO SCHOOL.
Ages 3-5. 689

## Glasses, Wearing of

**See also:** *Visual impairment*

Brown, Marc Tolan. ARTHUR'S EYES.
   Ages 4-7. 80
Keller, Holly. CROMWELL'S GLASSES.
   Ages 3-6. 337
Kropp, Paul Stephan. WILTED.
   Ages 11-14. 354
Leggett, Linda Rodgers and Linda Gambee
   Andrews. THE ROSE-COLORED GLASSES:
   MELANIE ADJUSTS TO POOR VISION.
   Ages 8-11. 362

## Goals

Bunting, Anne Evelyn. THE WAITING GAME.
   Ages 10 and up. 91
Hoban, Lillian Aberman. ARTHUR'S FUNNY
   MONEY.
   Ages 6-8. 294
Watanabe, Shigeo. I CAN RIDE IT!
   Ages 2-5. 684

## God

**See:** *Religion*

## Going Away

**See:** *Abandonment; Camp experiences; Hospital, going
to; Moving; Schools, private; Separation anxiety;
Separation from loved ones*

## Going Steady

**See:** *Boy-girl relationships: dating*

## Grandparent

**See also:** *Age; Family; Retirement*

**Death of.** *See: Death: of grandparent*

**Illness of.** *See: Illnesses: of grandparent*

**Living in child's home**
Angell, Judie. SECRET SELVES.
   Ages 11-13. 20
Donnelly, Elfie. SO LONG, GRANDPA.
   Ages 9-11. 168
Langner, Nola. FREDDY MY GRANDFATHER.
   Ages 5-8. 356
Mearian, Judy Frank. SOMEONE SLIGHTLY
   DIFFERENT.
   Ages 10-12. 417
Paterson, Katherine Womeldorf. JACOB HAVE I
   LOVED.
   Ages 12 and up. 485
Sachs, Marilyn. CLASS PICTURES.
   Ages 10-13. 564
Shreve, Susan Richards. FAMILY SECRETS: FIVE
   VERY IMPORTANT STORIES.
   Ages 9-11. 590
Smith, Robert Kimmel. JELLY BELLY.
   Ages 10-12. 614
Stolz, Mary Slattery. WHAT TIME OF NIGHT IS IT?
   Ages 11-14. 631
Stren, Patti. THERE'S A RAINBOW IN MY CLOSET.
   Ages 8-10. 638
Tate, Joan. LUKE'S GARDEN AND GRAMP: TWO
   NOVELS.
   Ages 10-13. 644
Tester, Sylvia Root. SANDY'S NEW HOME.
   Ages 5-8. 648

**Living in home of**
Adler, Carole Schwerdtfeger. THE SILVER COACH.
   Ages 9-12. 8
Ames, Mildred. NICKY AND THE JOYOUS NOISE.
   Ages 9-12. 14
Bates, Betty. THAT'S WHAT T.J. SAYS.
   Ages 9-11. 41

Bridgers, Sue Ellen. ALL TOGETHER NOW.
   Ages 11 and up. 74
Bridgers, Sue Ellen. NOTES FOR ANOTHER LIFE.
   Ages 12 and up. 75
Butterworth, William Edmund. LEROY AND THE
   OLD MAN.
   Ages 12 and up. 93
Byars, Betsy Cromer. THE
   TWO-THOUSAND-POUND GOLDFISH.
   Ages 9-12. 99
Dyer, Thomas A. THE WHIPMAN IS WATCHING.
   Ages 10-14. 177
Farley, Carol J. TWILIGHT WAVES.
   Ages 10-13. 186
Gardiner, John Reynolds. STONE FOX.
   Ages 8-10. 202
Gerson, Corinne. TREAD SOFTLY.
   Ages 9-12. 209
Greenfield, Eloise. GRANDMAMA'S JOY.
   Ages 4-8. 244
Hermes, Patricia. WHAT IF THEY KNEW?
   Ages 9-11. 285
Hest, Amy. MAYBE NEXT YEAR . . .
   Ages 9-12. 288
Holland, Isabelle. NOW IS NOT TOO LATE.
   Ages 10-13. 301
Irwin, Hadley, pseud. MOON AND ME.
   Ages 11-14. 325
Irwin, Hadley, pseud. WHAT ABOUT GRANDMA?
   Ages 11 and up. 326
Phipson, Joan Nash, pseud. A TIDE FLOWING.
   Ages 12 and up. 509
Potter, Marian. THE SHARED ROOM.
   Ages 10-12. 517
Somerlott, Robert. BLAZE.
   Ages 10-13. 617
Voigt, Cynthia. DICEY'S SONG.
   Ages 11 and up. 671
Voigt, Cynthia. HOMECOMING.
   Ages 11 and up. 672

**Love for**
Abercrombie, Barbara Mattes. CAT-MAN'S
   DAUGHTER.
   Ages 11-13. 1
Bates, Betty. MY MOM, THE MONEY NUT.
   Ages 10-12. 39
Bawden, Nina Mary Kark. THE ROBBERS.
   Ages 9-12. 43
Brancato, Robin Fidler. SWEET BELLS JANGLED
   OUT OF TUNE.
   Ages 11-14. 70
Brandenberg, Aliki Liacouras. THE TWO OF THEM.
   Ages 3-7. 71
Bridgers, Sue Ellen. NOTES FOR ANOTHER LIFE.
   Ages 12 and up. 75
Caines, Jeannette Franklin. WINDOW WISHING.
   Ages 4-7. 100
Clifton, Lucille. THE LUCKY STONE.
   Ages 8-10. 121
De Paola, Thomas Anthony. NOW ONE FOOT, NOW
   THE OTHER.
   Ages 4-7. 160
Donnelly, Elfie. SO LONG, GRANDPA.
   Ages 9-11. 168
Farber, Norma. HOW DOES IT FEEL TO BE OLD?
   Ages 8 and up. 185
Gardiner, John Reynolds. STONE FOX.
   Ages 8-10. 202
Goldman, Susan. GRANDPA AND ME TOGETHER.
   Ages 2-6. 221
Greenfield, Eloise. GRANDMAMA'S JOY.
   Ages 4-8. 244
Harris, Robin. HELLO KITTY SLEEPS OVER.
   Ages 2-5. 269
Henriod, Lorraine. GRANDMA'S WHEELCHAIR.
   Ages 3-7. 281

## Guilt, Feelings of (cont.)

Yep, Laurence Michael. KIND HEARTS AND GENTLE MONSTERS.
Ages 12 and up. 712

Zhitkov, Boris Stepanovich. HOW I HUNTED THE LITTLE FELLOWS.
Ages 3-7. 720

# H

## Half Brother/Half Sister

**See:** *Sibling: half brother/half sister*

## Handicaps

**See also:** *Education: special*

**Amputee.** *See: Amputee*

**Asthma.** *See: Asthma*

**Birth defects.** *See: Birth defects*

**Blindness.** *See: Blindness*

**Braces on body/limbs.** *See: Braces on body/limbs*

**Brain injury.** *See: Brain injury*

**Cardiac conditions.** *See: Cardiac conditions*

**Cleft lip/palate.** *See: Cleft lip/palate*

**Deafness.** *See: Deafness*

**Deformities.** *See: Deformities*

**Hemophilia.** *See: Hemophilia*

**Limbs, abnormal or missing.** *See: Limbs, abnormal or missing*

**Multiple**

Greenfield, Eloise and Alesia Revis. ALESIA.
Ages 10-14. 245

Robinet, Harriette Gillem. RIDE THE RED CYCLE.
Ages 7-11. 537

**Muteness.** *See: Muteness*

**Paraplegia.** *See: Paraplegia*

**Prejudice.** *See: Prejudice: toward handicapped persons*

**Speech problems.** *See: Speech problems*

**Visual impairment.** *See: Visual impairment*

**Wheelchair.** *See: Wheelchair, dependence on*

## Harassment

**See also:** *Bully; Practical jokes/pranks*

Arrick, Fran. CHERNOWITZ!
Ages 12 and up. 23

Garden, Nancy. ANNIE ON MY MIND.
Ages 13 and up. 201

Graber, Richard Fredrick. BLACK COW SUMMER.
Ages 12 and up. 224

Mohr, Nicholasa. FELITA.
Ages 8-10. 440

## Hard of Hearing

**See:** *Deafness*

## Hatred

**See also:** *Aggression; Anger; Hostility; Prejudice*

Arrick, Fran. CHERNOWITZ!
Ages 12 and up. 23

## Hearing Aid

**See:** *Deafness*

## Heart Trouble

**See:** *Cardiac conditions*

## Heaven

**See:** *Religion*

## Height

**See also:** *Appearance*

**Short**

Barrett, Judith. I'M TOO SMALL. YOU'RE TOO BIG.
Ages 4-6. 36

**Tall**

Robison, Nancy Louise. BALLET MAGIC.
Ages 9-11. 541

## Hell

**See:** *Religion*

## Helping

**See also:** *Cooperation*

Bond, Nancy Barbara. THE VOYAGE BEGUN.
Ages 12 and up. 60

Delton, Judy and Elaine Knox-Wagner. THE BEST MOM IN THE WORLD.
Ages 4-7. 159

De Paola, Thomas Anthony. NOW ONE FOOT, NOW THE OTHER.
Ages 4-7. 160

Gray, Nigel. IT'LL ALL COME OUT IN THE WASH.
Ages 4-6. 233

Green, Phyllis. GLOOMY LOUIE.
Ages 8-9. 234

Henriod, Lorraine. GRANDMA'S WHEELCHAIR.
Ages 3-7. 281

Lasker, Joe. THE DO-SOMETHING DAY.
Ages 3-7. 357

Moncure, Jane Belk. LOVE.
Ages 3-6. 446

Morton, Jane. I AM RUBBER, YOU ARE GLUE.
Ages 9-11. 454

Reuter, Margaret. YOU CAN DEPEND ON ME.
Ages 6-9. 530

Rockwell, Anne F. and Harlow Rockwell. CAN I HELP?
Ages 3-6. 543

Ruffins, Reynold. MY BROTHER NEVER FEEDS THE CAT.
Ages 3-7. 559

Schick, Eleanor Grossman. JOEY ON HIS OWN.
Ages 5-8. 574

Sharmat, Marjorie Weinman. TAKING CARE OF MELVIN.
Ages 4-8. 587

Thomas, Ianthe. HI, MRS. MALLORY!
Ages 5-8. 651

Winthrop, Elizabeth. MARATHON MIRANDA.
Ages 9-11. 696

Wolde, Gunilla. BETSY AND THE VACUUM CLEANER.
Ages 3-6. 702

## Hemophilia

Pfeffer, Susan Beth. STARRING PETER AND LEIGH.
Ages 12-14. 503

## Hippie

**See:** *Commune; Life style; Running away*

## Hitchhiking

Dunne, Mary Collins. HOBY & STUB.
Ages 10-13. 176

Miklowitz, Gloria D. DID YOU HEAR WHAT HAPPENED TO ANDREA?
Ages 13 and up. 421

Thompson, Paul. THE HITCHHIKERS.
Ages 12 and up. 657

## Hodgkin's Disease

**See also:** *Cancer; Hospital, going to*

Ipswitch, Elaine. SCOTT WAS HERE.
Ages 12 and up. 322

## Illnesses (cont.)

De Paola, Thomas Anthony. NOW ONE FOOT, NOW
THE OTHER.
Ages 4-7. 160
Gardiner, John Reynolds. STONE FOX.
Ages 8-10. 202
L'Engle, Madeleine Franklin. A RING OF ENDLESS
LIGHT.
Ages 11-14. 363

**Hemophilia.** *See: Hemophilia*

**Hodgkin's disease.** *See: Hodgkin's disease*

**Leukemia.** *See: Leukemia*

### of Parent

Blue, Rose. WISHFUL LYING.
Ages 6-9. 54
Carris, Joan Davenport. WHEN THE BOYS RAN THE
HOUSE.
Ages 8-12. 108
Greene, Constance Clarke. AL(EXANDRA) THE
GREAT.
Ages 10-12. 239
Mearian, Judy Frank. TWO WAYS ABOUT IT.
Ages 9-12. 418

### of Sibling

Herzig, Alison Cragin and Jane Lawrence Mali. A
SEASON OF SECRETS.
Ages 11-13. 287

**Terminal.** *See also: Fear: of death*
Bach, Alice Hendricks. WAITING FOR JOHNNY
MIRACLE.
Ages 12 and up. 32
Donnelly, Elfie. SO LONG, GRANDPA.
Ages 9-11. 168
Greenberg, Jan. A SEASON IN-BETWEEN.
Ages 11-13. 237
Harlan, Elizabeth. FOOTFALLS.
Ages 12-14. 265
Hermes, Patricia. YOU SHOULDN'T HAVE TO SAY
GOOD-BYE.
Ages 10-13. 286
Ipswitch, Elaine. SCOTT WAS HERE.
Ages 12 and up. 322
Irwin, Hadley, pseud. WHAT ABOUT GRANDMA?
Ages 11 and up. 326
Jones, Penelope. HOLDING TOGETHER.
Ages 9-11. 331
Jones, Rebecca Castaldi. ANGIE AND ME.
Ages 9-11. 333
L'Engle, Madeleine Franklin. A RING OF ENDLESS
LIGHT.
Ages 11-14. 363
Miner, Jane Claypool. THIS DAY IS MINE: LIVING
WITH LEUKEMIA.
Ages 10 and up. 436
Peavy, Linda S. ALLISON'S GRANDFATHER.
Ages 6-9. 489
Schotter, Roni. A MATTER OF TIME.
Ages 12 and up. 575
Shreve, Susan Richards. FAMILY SECRETS: FIVE
VERY IMPORTANT STORIES.
Ages 9-11. 590
Strasser, Todd. FRIENDS TILL THE END.
Ages 12 and up. 636
Stretton, Barbara. YOU NEVER LOSE.
Ages 12 and up. 639
Zindel, Bonnie and Paul Zindel. A STAR FOR THE
LATECOMER.
Ages 12 and up. 721

## Imaginary Friend

*See: Fantasy formation; Imagination; Magical thinking;
Play*

## Imagination

**See also:** *Creativity; Fantasy formation; Magical
thinking; Play; Reality, escaping*
Adler, Carole Schwerdtfeger. THE MAGIC OF THE
GLITS.
Ages 9-12. 6
Adler, Carole Schwerdtfeger. THE SILVER COACH.
Ages 9-12. 8
Byars, Betsy Cromer. THE
TWO-THOUSAND-POUND GOLDFISH.
Ages 9-12. 99
Calhoun, Mary Huiskamp. THE NIGHT THE
MONSTER CAME.
Ages 8-10. 102
Cameron, Ann. THE STORIES JULIAN TELLS.
Ages 7-9. 104
Collins, David R. IF I COULD, I WOULD.
Ages 6-8. 131
Conford, Ellen. THE REVENGE OF THE
INCREDIBLE DR. RANCID AND HIS YOUTHFUL
ASSISTANT, JEFFREY.
Ages 10-12. 137
Delton, Judy. MY MOTHER LOST HER JOB TODAY.
Ages 3-7. 156
Gerson, Corinne. TREAD SOFTLY.
Ages 9-12. 209
Giff, Patricia Reilly. FOURTH GRADE CELEBRITY.
Ages 8-10. 210
Griffith, Helen V. MINE WILL, SAID JOHN.
Ages 4-6. 248
Gross, Alan. THE I DON'T WANT TO GO TO
SCHOOL BOOK.
Ages 5-9. 249
Peterson, Esther Allen. FREDERICK'S ALLIGATOR.
Ages 4-7. 496
Peyton, K. M., pseud. MARION'S ANGELS.
Ages 11-14. 499
Pfeffer, Susan Beth. AWFUL EVELINA.
Ages 6-8. 501
Robison, Deborah. NO ELEPHANTS ALLOWED.
Ages 3-6. 540
Sachs, Elizabeth-Ann. JUST LIKE ALWAYS.
Ages 10-13. 561
Schubert, Ingrid and Dieter Schubert. THERE'S A
CROCODILE UNDER MY BED!
Ages 3-6. 576
Sharmat, Marjorie Weinman. LUCRETIA THE
UNBEARABLE.
Ages 4-7. 583
Sharmat, Mitchell. COME HOME, WILMA.
Ages 6-8. 588
Sirof, Harriet. SAVE THE DAM!
Ages 9-12. 599
Zhitkov, Boris Stepanovich. HOW I HUNTED THE
LITTLE FELLOWS.
Ages 3-7. 720
Zolotow, Charlotte Shapiro. IF YOU LISTEN.
Ages 5-7. 722

## Immigrants

**See also:** *Prejudice: ethnic/racial; Refugees; Vietnam*
Bernstein, Joanne Eckstein. DMITRY: A YOUNG
SOVIET IMMIGRANT.
Ages 11-13. 52
Marangell, Virginia J. GIANNA MIA.
Ages 12-15. 402
Wartski, Maureen Crane. A LONG WAY FROM
HOME.
Ages 11-13. 680

## Impatience

*See: Patience/Impatience*

## Imprisonment

**See also:** *Crime/Criminals; Delinquency, juvenile; Detention home, living in; Internment*
Rodowsky, Colby F. A SUMMER'S WORTH OF SHAME.
Ages 12-14. 548
Shreve, Susan Richards. THE MASQUERADE.
Ages 12 and up. 591

## Independence

**See:** *Dependence/Independence*

## Independent Thinking

**See:** *Autonomy*

## Indian, American

**See:** *Native American*

## Individuality

**See:** *Autonomy*

## Individuation

**See:** *Autonomy; Dependence/Independence; Separation anxiety*

## Infant

**See:** *Sibling: new baby*

## Inferiority, Feelings of

**See also:** *Shyness*
Ashley, Bernard. A KIND OF WILD JUSTICE.
Ages 12 and up. 30
Barrett, John M. DANIEL DISCOVERS DANIEL.
Ages 7-9. 35
Bates, Betty. THAT'S WHAT T.J. SAYS.
Ages 9-11. 41
Brooks, Jerome. MAKE ME A HERO.
Ages 9-12. 78
Cohen, Barbara Nash. THE INNKEEPER'S DAUGHTER.
Ages 11-14. 126
Delton, Judy. I NEVER WIN!
Ages 4-7. 154
Giff, Patricia Reilly. FOURTH GRADE CELEBRITY.
Ages 8-10. 210
Giff, Patricia Reilly. THE GIRL WHO KNEW IT ALL.
Ages 8-10. 212
Giff, Patricia Reilly. TODAY WAS A TERRIBLE DAY.
Ages 6-7. 213
Gilson, Jamie. DO BANANAS CHEW GUM?
Ages 9-11. 216
Green, Phyllis. GLOOMY LOUIE.
Ages 8-9. 234
Kroll, Steven. FRIDAY THE 13TH.
Ages 4-7. 353
LeRoy, Gen. BILLY'S SHOES.
Ages 5-8. 364
Morton, Jane. RUNNING SCARED.
Ages 10-14. 455
Oppenheimer, Joan Letson. WORKING ON IT.
Ages 11-13. 475
St. George, Judith. CALL ME MARGO.
Ages 12-14. 567

## Inhibition

**See:** *Inferiority, feelings of; Shyness*

## Initiative, Taking

**See:** *Autonomy; Leader/Leadership; Work, attitude toward*

## Injuries

**See:** *Accidents; Doctor, going to; Fractures; Hospital, going to; Surgery; Sutures*

## Injustice

**See:** *Justice/Injustice*

## Insanity

**See:** *Mental illness*

## Insecurity

**See:** *Security/Insecurity*

## Institutions/Institutionalization

**See:** *Children's home, living in; Detention home, living in; Nursing home, living in; Schools, private*

## Integration

**See also:** *Prejudice; School*
Miner, Jane Claypool. THE TOUGH GUY: BLACK IN A WHITE WORLD.
Ages 11 and up. 437

**School busing**
Cheatham, Karyn Follis. THE BEST WAY OUT.
Ages 12 and up. 114

## Internment

**See also:** *Imprisonment; Prejudice: ethnic/racial*
Asher, Sandra Fenichel. DAUGHTERS OF THE LAW.
Ages 11-13. 26

## Intolerance

**See:** *Patience/Impatience; Prejudice*

## Isolation

**See:** *Loneliness; Ostracism; Peer relationships: avoiding others*

## Israel

**See also:** *Jewish*
Ofek, Uriel. SMOKE OVER GOLAN.
Ages 9-13. 468

## Italian-American

Marangell, Virginia J. GIANNA MIA.
Ages 12-15. 402

# J

## Jail

**See:** *Detention home, living in; Imprisonment*

## Japan

Maruki, Toshi. HIROSHIMA NO PIKA.
Ages 7 and up. 406

## Jealousy

Adler, Carole Schwerdtfeger. SOME OTHER SUMMER.
Ages 10-13. 9
Colman, Hila Crayder. CONFESSION OF A STORYTELLER.
Ages 10-13. 133
Freeman, Gaail. OUT FROM UNDER.
Ages 12 and up. 195
Vogel, Ilse-Margret. MY SUMMER BROTHER.
Ages 8-10. 670
Wittman, Sally Anne Christensen. THE WONDERFUL MRS. TRUMBLY.
Ages 5-8. 700

## Jealousy (cont.)

### Peer

Asher, Sandra Fenichel. JUST LIKE JENNY.
Ages 10-12. 27
Brooks, Jerome. MAKE ME A HERO.
Ages 9-12. 78
Greene, Constance Clarke. YOUR OLD PAL, AL.
Ages 9-13. 241
Mearian, Judy Frank. TWO WAYS ABOUT IT.
Ages 9-12. 418
Perl, Lila. PIEFACE AND DAPHNE.
Ages 9-11. 494
Pfeffer, Susan Beth. STARTING WITH MELODIE.
Ages 11-13. 504
Sachs, Marilyn. A SUMMER'S LEASE.
Ages 11-14. 566
Shura, Mary Francis Craig. CHESTER.
Ages 8-10. 593
Wells, Rosemary. TIMOTHY GOES TO SCHOOL.
Ages 3-5. 689

### Sibling

Barrett, John M. DANIEL DISCOVERS DANIEL.
Ages 7-9. 35
Branscum, Robbie. FOR LOVE OF JODY.
Ages 9-12. 73
Byars, Betsy Cromer. THE ANIMAL, THE
VEGETABLE, AND JOHN D JONES.
Ages 10-12. 95
Colman, Hila Crayder. WHAT'S THE MATTER WITH
THE DOBSONS?
Ages 10-13. 135
Drescher, Joan Elizabeth. THE MARVELOUS MESS.
Ages 4-6. 172
Ewing, Kathryn. THINGS WON'T BE THE SAME.
Ages 8-10. 182
Giff, Patricia Reilly. FOURTH GRADE CELEBRITY.
Ages 8-10. 210
Landis, James David. THE SISTERS IMPOSSIBLE.
Ages 9-11. 355
Leech, Jay and Zane Spencer. BRIGHT FAWN AND
ME.
Ages 4-8. 361
LeRoy, Gen. LUCKY STIFF!
Ages 4-7. 365
Paterson, Katherine Womeldorf. JACOB HAVE I
LOVED.
Ages 12 and up. 485
Pfeffer, Susan Beth. WHAT DO YOU DO WHEN
YOUR MOUTH WON'T OPEN?
Ages 10-13. 505
York, Carol Beach. REMEMBER ME WHEN I AM
DEAD.
Ages 9-11. 714

## Jewish

See also: Ghetto; Israel
Arrick, Fran. CHERNOWITZ!
Ages 12 and up. 23
Asher, Sandra Fenichel. DAUGHTERS OF THE LAW.
Ages 11-13. 26
Bernstein, Joanne Eckstein. DMITRY: A YOUNG
SOVIET IMMIGRANT.
Ages 11-13. 52
Brooks, Jerome. MAKE ME A HERO.
Ages 9-12. 78
Chaikin, Miriam. I SHOULD WORRY, I SHOULD
CARE.
Ages 8-11. 111
Girion, Barbara. LIKE EVERYBODY ELSE.
Ages 10-13. 218
Girion, Barbara. A TANGLE OF ROOTS.
Ages 12-16. 220
Herman, Charlotte. WHAT HAPPENED TO
HEATHER HOPKOWITZ?
Ages 10-13. 283
Hurwitz, Johanna. ONCE I WAS A PLUM TREE.
Ages 9-11. 317

Mazer, Harry. THE LAST MISSION.
Ages 12-14. 413
Ruby, Lois. TWO TRUTHS IN MY POCKET.
Ages 12 and up. 557

## Job

See also: Baby-sitting; Chores; Money: earning;
Responsibility; Work, attitude toward
Belair, Richard L. DOUBLE TAKE.
Ages 13 and up. 44
Lowry, Lois. ANASTASIA AT YOUR SERVICE.
Ages 9-12. 385
Miner, Jane Claypool. A MAN'S PRIDE: LOSING A
FATHER.
Ages 11 and up. 429
Naylor, Phyllis Reynolds. EDDIE, INCORPORATED.
Ages 9-11. 463
Newton, Suzanne. M.V. SEXTON SPEAKING.
Ages 11 and up. 466
Smith, Anne Warren. BLUE DENIM BLUES.
Ages 12 and up. 607

## Judgment, Effect of Emotions on

Carroll, Theodorus C. THE LOST CHRISTMAS
STAR.
Ages 7-9. 109

## Justice/Injustice

See also: Blame; Guilt, feelings of; Prejudice
Carrick, Malcolm. I'LL GET YOU.
Ages 11-13. 107
Garden, Nancy. ANNIE ON MY MIND.
Ages 13 and up. 201
Guy, Rosa Cuthbert. THE DISAPPEARANCE.
Ages 12 and up. 252
Harrah, Michael. FIRST OFFENDER.
Ages 11-13. 266
Hentoff, Nat. DOES THIS SCHOOL HAVE CAPITAL
PUNISHMENT?
Ages 11 and up. 282
Knox-Wagner, Elaine. THE OLDEST KID.
Ages 4-8. 347
Naylor, Phyllis Reynolds. ALL BECAUSE I'M OLDER.
Ages 7-9. 462
Sarnoff, Jane and Reynold Ruffins. THAT'S NOT
FAIR.
Ages 4-7. 571

## Juvenile Delinquency

See: Delinquency, juvenile

## Juvenile Detention

See: Detention home, living in

# K

## Kidnapping

See also: Crime/Criminals
Eyerly, Jeannette Hyde. THE SEEING SUMMER.
Ages 8-10. 183
Fitzhugh, Louise. SPORT.
Ages 9-12. 190
Hopper, Nancy J. SECRETS.
Ages 11-14. 304

## Killing

See: Death: murder; Violence; War

## Kissing

See: Boy-girl relationships; Sex

# L

## Language Problems

See: *Communication; Speech problems*

## Latchkey Child

See: *Parent/Parents: mother working outside home;
Parent/Parents: single*

## Laziness

See: *Chores; Daydreaming; Responsibility: avoiding;
School: achievement/underachievement; Work, attitude
toward*

## Leader/Leadership

See also: *Identification with others; Responsibility:
accepting*
Greene, Bette. GET ON OUT OF HERE, PHILIP
HALL.
Ages 9-12. 238

## Learning, Love of

See: *Education: value of*

## Learning Disabilities

See also: *Brain injury; Birth defects; Education: special;
Mental retardation*
Gilson, Jamie. DO BANANAS CHEW GUM?
Ages 9-11. 216
Kamien, Janet. WHAT IF YOU COULDN'T . . . ? A
BOOK ABOUT SPECIAL NEEDS.
Ages 8-12. 336
Matthews, Ellen. PUTTING UP WITH SHERWOOD.
Ages 9-11. 408
Morton, Jane. RUNNING SCARED.
Ages 10-14. 455
Sullivan, Mary Beth and Alan J. Brightman and Joseph
Blatt. FEELING FREE.
Ages 9 and up. 640

## Lesbianism

See: *Homosexuality: female*

## Leukemia

See also: *Cancer; Hospital, going to*
L'Engle, Madeleine Franklin. A RING OF ENDLESS
LIGHT.
Ages 11-14. 363
Miner, Jane Claypool. THIS DAY IS MINE: LIVING
WITH LEUKEMIA.
Ages 10 and up. 436
Strasser, Todd. FRIENDS TILL THE END.
Ages 12 and up. 636

## Life, Meaning of

See: *Identity, search for; Religion*

## Life Style

See also: *Commune*
Bauer, Caroline Feller. MY MOM TRAVELS A LOT.
Ages 5-8. 42
Clifton, Lucille. SONORA BEAUTIFUL.
Ages 12-14. 123
Cohen, Barbara Nash. THE INNKEEPER'S
DAUGHTER.
Ages 11-14. 126
Drescher, Joan Elizabeth. YOUR FAMILY, MY
FAMILY.
Ages 5-7. 173
Girion, Barbara. LIKE EVERYBODY ELSE.
Ages 10-13. 218

Mazer, Norma Fox. MRS. FISH, APE, AND ME, THE
DUMP QUEEN.
Ages 10-12. 414

**Change in.** See also: *Change: new home*
Bernstein, Joanne Eckstein. DMITRY: A YOUNG
SOVIET IMMIGRANT.
Ages 11-13. 52
Bosse, Malcolm Joseph. GANESH.
Ages 11-14. 65
Bulla, Clyde Robert. POOR BOY, RICH BOY.
Ages 5-8. 87
Butterworth, William Edmund. LEROY AND THE
OLD MAN.
Ages 12 and up. 93
Ellis, Ella Thorp. SLEEPWALKER'S MOON.
Ages 12 and up. 181
Ewing, Kathryn. THINGS WON'T BE THE SAME.
Ages 8-10. 182
Graeber, Charlotte Towner. GREY CLOUD.
Ages 9-11. 226
Grant, Cynthia D. JOSHUA FORTUNE.
Ages 10-13. 229
Kingman, Lee. THE REFINER'S FIRE.
Ages 12-14. 341
Knox-Wagner, Elaine. MY GRANDPA RETIRED
TODAY.
Ages 4-7. 346
Love, Sandra Weller. CROSSING OVER.
Ages 10-12. 383
Morgenroth, Barbara. WILL THE REAL RENIE LAKE
PLEASE STAND UP?
Ages 12 and up. 453
Park, Barbara. DON'T MAKE ME SMILE.
Ages 8-11. 481
Prince, Alison. THE TURKEY'S NEST.
Ages 12 and up. 520
Rodowsky, Colby F. A SUMMER'S WORTH OF
SHAME.
Ages 12-14. 548
Shreve, Susan Richards. THE MASQUERADE.
Ages 12 and up. 591
Skurzynski, Gloria Joan. MARTIN BY HIMSELF.
Ages 6-9. 602
Smith, Lucia B. MY MOM GOT A JOB.
Ages 5-8. 611
Whelan, Gloria. A TIME TO KEEP SILENT.
Ages 11-14. 690
Wilkinson, Brenda Scott. LUDELL'S NEW YORK
TIME.
Ages 12 and up. 691

## Limbs, Abnormal or Missing

See also: *Amputee; Birth defects; Braces on body/limbs;
Deformities*
Donovan, Pete. CAROL JOHNSTON: THE ONE-
ARMED GYMNAST.
Ages 8-12. 169
Kamien, Janet. WHAT IF YOU COULDN'T . . . ? A
BOOK ABOUT SPECIAL NEEDS.
Ages 8-12. 336
Richter, Elizabeth. THE TEENAGE HOSPITAL
EXPERIENCE: YOU CAN HANDLE IT!
Ages 12 and up. 532
Slepian, Jan. THE ALFRED SUMMER.
Ages 11-13. 603

## Little Brother/Sister

See: *Sibling: younger; Sibling: youngest*

## Little League

See also: *Competition; Sports/Sportsmanship*
Morton, Jane. I AM RUBBER, YOU ARE GLUE.
Ages 9-11. 454

## Love, Meaning of (cont.)

Garden, Nancy. ANNIE ON MY MIND.
Ages 13 and up. 201
Graber, Richard Fredrick. BLACK COW SUMMER.
Ages 12 and up. 224
Guest, Elissa Haden. THE HANDSOME MAN.
Ages 12 and up. 251
Hallman, Ruth. BREAKAWAY.
Ages 12 and up. 257
Hanlon, Emily. THE WING AND THE FLAME.
Ages 13 and up. 262
Hautzig, Esther Rudomin. A GIFT FOR MAMA.
Ages 8-12. 273
Hazen, Barbara Shook. EVEN IF I DID SOMETHING AWFUL.
Ages 3-6. 275
Holland, Isabelle. NOW IS NOT TOO LATE.
Ages 10-13. 301
Hopkins, Lee Bennett. MAMA & HER BOYS.
Ages 8-11. 303
Ipswitch, Elaine. SCOTT WAS HERE.
Ages 12 and up. 322
Irwin, Hadley, pseud. THE LILITH SUMMER.
Ages 9-13. 324
Jenkins, Jordan. LEARNING ABOUT LOVE.
Ages 4-8. 329
Johnston, Norma. MYSELF AND I.
Ages 11 and up. 330
Lyle, Katie Letcher. DARK BUT FULL OF DIAMONDS.
Ages 12-14. 388
MacLachlan, Patricia. THE SICK DAY.
Ages 4-7. 396
Magorian, Michelle. GOOD NIGHT, MR. TOM.
Ages 11 and up. 401
Marangell, Virginia J. GIANNA MIA.
Ages 12-15. 402
Mazer, Norma Fox. MRS. FISH, APE, AND ME, THE DUMP QUEEN.
Ages 10-12. 414
Mazer, Norma Fox. WHEN WE FIRST MET.
Ages 12 and up. 416
Moncure, Jane Belk. CARING.
Ages 3-6. 441
Moncure, Jane Belk. KINDNESS.
Ages 3-6. 445
Moncure, Jane Belk. LOVE.
Ages 3-6. 446
Peck, Richard. CLOSE ENOUGH TO TOUCH.
Ages 12 and up. 490
Power, Barbara. I WISH LAURA'S MOMMY WAS MY MOMMY.
Ages 4-7. 518
Prince, Alison. THE TURKEY'S NEST.
Ages 12 and up. 520
Rinaldi, Ann. PROMISES ARE FOR KEEPING.
Ages 12 and up. 534
Rinaldi, Ann. TERM PAPER.
Ages 12 and up. 535
Ruby, Lois. TWO TRUTHS IN MY POCKET.
Ages 12 and up. 557
Ruby, Lois. WHAT DO YOU DO IN QUICKSAND?
Ages 12-14. 558
Sallis, Susan Diana. ONLY LOVE.
Ages 12 and up. 568
Sallis, Susan Diana. A TIME FOR EVERYTHING.
Ages 13 and up. 569
Sebestyen, Ouida. FAR FROM HOME.
Ages 12 and up. 579
Sebestyen, Ouida. WORDS BY HEART.
Ages 10-13. 580
Slepian, Jan. LESTER'S TURN.
Ages 11-14. 604
Spence, Eleanor Rachel. A CANDLE FOR SAINT ANTONY.
Ages 13 and up. 618
Strang, Celia. FOSTER MARY.
Ages 10-13. 633

Strang, Celia. THIS CHILD IS MINE.
Ages 11-14. 634
Tate, Joan. LUKE'S GARDEN AND GRAMP: TWO NOVELS.
Ages 10-13. 644
Tax, Meredith. FAMILIES.
Ages 4-8. 645
Vogel, Ilse-Margret. MY SUMMER BROTHER.
Ages 8-10. 670
Voigt, Cynthia. DICEY'S SONG.
Ages 11 and up. 671
Wartski, Maureen Crane. A BOAT TO NOWHERE.
Ages 9-12. 678
Wortis, Avi. SOMETIMES I THINK I HEAR MY NAME.
Ages 10-13. 708

## Loyalty

See also: *Patriotism*
Brancato, Robin Fidler. SWEET BELLS JANGLED OUT OF TUNE.
Ages 11-14. 70
Carrick, Carol. SOME FRIEND!
Ages 9-12. 106
Little, Mary E. OLD CAT AND THE KITTEN.
Ages 8-12. 379
Sachs, Marilyn. CLASS PICTURES.
Ages 10-13. 564

## Lying

See: *Honesty/Dishonesty; Values/Valuing*

# M

## Magical Thinking

See also: *Daydreaming; Fantasy formation; Imagination; Wishes*
Dolan, Sheila. THE WISHING BOTTLE.
Ages 7-9. 167
Harris, Mark Jonathan. WITH A WAVE OF THE WAND.
Ages 9-12. 267

## Mainstreaming

See: *School: mainstreaming*

## Make-Believe

See: *Fantasy formation; Imagination; Play*

## Manipulation

York, Carol Beach. REMEMBER ME WHEN I AM DEAD.
Ages 9-11. 714

### Peer

Freeman, Gaail. OUT FROM UNDER.
Ages 12 and up. 195
Shura, Mary Francis Craig. THE BARKLEY STREET SIX-PACK.
Ages 9-12. 592

## Manliness

See: *Gender role identity: male*

## Marijuana

See also: *Drugs*
Hentoff, Nat. DOES THIS SCHOOL HAVE CAPITAL PUNISHMENT?
Ages 11 and up. 282

## Marriage

### Teenage

Armstrong, Louise. SAVING THE BIG-DEAL BABY.
Ages 10 and up. 22

## Masculinity

**See:** *Gender role identity: male*

## Maturation

**See also:** *Puberty*

Adler, Carole Schwerdtfeger. THE SILVER COACH.
Ages 9-12. 8

Adler, Carole Schwerdtfeger. SOME OTHER
SUMMER.
Ages 10-13. 9

Bargar, Gary W. WHAT HAPPENED TO MR.
FORSTER?
Ages 10-13. 34

Bates, Betty. LOVE IS LIKE PEANUTS.
Ages 10-14. 38

Bates, Betty. MY MOM, THE MONEY NUT.
Ages 10-12. 39

Bates, Betty. THAT'S WHAT T.J. SAYS.
Ages 9-11. 41

Blume, Judy Sussman. TIGER EYES.
Ages 11 and up. 57

Bond, Nancy Barbara. THE VOYAGE BEGUN.
Ages 12 and up. 60

Bonsall, Crosby Newell. THE GOODBYE SUMMER.
Ages 9-11. 63

Bridgers, Sue Ellen. ALL TOGETHER NOW.
Ages 11 and up. 74

Bruna, Dick. WHEN I'M BIG.
Ages 2-4. 81

Buchan, Stuart. A SPACE OF HIS OWN.
Ages 12 and up. 82

Byars, Betsy Cromer. THE ANIMAL, THE
VEGETABLE, AND JOHN D JONES.
Ages 10-12. 95

Byars, Betsy Cromer. THE
TWO-THOUSAND-POUND GOLDFISH.
Ages 9-12. 99

Calhoun, Mary Huiskamp. KATIE JOHN AND
HEATHCLIFF.
Ages 9-11. 101

Danziger, Paula. THERE'S A BAT IN BUNK FIVE.
Ages 10-14. 151

Dodson, Susan. HAVE YOU SEEN THIS GIRL?
Ages 13 and up. 166

Ellis, Ella Thorp. SLEEPWALKER'S MOON.
Ages 12 and up. 181

Freeman, Gaail. OUT FROM UNDER.
Ages 12 and up. 195

Gates, Doris. A MORGAN FOR MELINDA.
Ages 10-12. 203

Gilbert, Harriett. RUNNING AWAY.
Ages 11-14. 215

Girion, Barbara. A HANDFUL OF STARS.
Ages 12 and up. 217

Girion, Barbara. LIKE EVERYBODY ELSE.
Ages 10-13. 218

Girion, Barbara. A TANGLE OF ROOTS.
Ages 12-16. 220

Graham, Ada and Frank Graham. JACOB AND OWL.
Ages 8-11. 228

Greenberg, Jan. A SEASON IN-BETWEEN.
Ages 11-13. 237

Greene, Constance Clarke. AL(EXANDRA) THE
GREAT.
Ages 10-12. 239

Gregory, Diana. THERE'S A CATERPILLAR IN MY
LEMONADE.
Ages 10-12. 247

Hallman, Ruth. BREAKAWAY.
Ages 12 and up. 257

Hanlon, Emily. THE WING AND THE FLAME.
Ages 13 and up. 262

Hansen, Joyce. THE GIFT-GIVER.
Ages 9-12. 263

Harris, Robie H. I HATE KISSES.
Ages 2-5. 268

Hayes, Sheila. ME AND MY MONA LISA SMILE.
Ages 11-13. 274

Hest, Amy. MAYBE NEXT YEAR . . .
Ages 9-12. 288

Hinton, Susan Eloise. TEX.
Ages 11-15. 292

Holland, Isabelle. NOW IS NOT TOO LATE.
Ages 10-13. 301

Hull, Eleanor Means. ALICE WITH GOLDEN HAIR.
Ages 11 and up. 311

Irwin, Hadley, pseud. MOON AND ME.
Ages 11-14. 325

Iverson, Genie. I WANT TO BE BIG.
Ages 3-6. 327

Jacobs, Dee. LAURA'S GIFT.
Ages 10-13. 328

Jones, Rebecca Castaldi. ANGIE AND ME.
Ages 9-11. 333

Jones, Toeckey. GO WELL, STAY WELL.
Ages 12 and up. 334

Konigsburg, Elaine Lobl. THROWING SHADOWS.
Ages 10-12. 349

L'Engle, Madeleine Franklin. A RING OF ENDLESS
LIGHT.
Ages 11-14. 363

Levoy, Myron. A SHADOW LIKE A LEOPARD.
Ages 12 and up. 369

Liu, Aimee. SOLITAIRE.
Ages 13 and up. 380

Love, Sandra Weller. CROSSING OVER.
Ages 10-12. 383

Lowry, Lois. ANASTASIA KRUPNIK.
Ages 9-11. 386

McCord, Jean. TURKEYLEGS THOMPSON.
Ages 11-14. 390

Marangell, Virginia J. GIANNA MIA.
Ages 12-15. 402

Mazer, Norma Fox. UP IN SETH'S ROOM.
Ages 13 and up. 415

Miles, Betty. THE TROUBLE WITH THIRTEEN.
Ages 9-13. 424

Moeri, Louise. FIRST THE EGG.
Ages 12 and up. 438

Myers, Walter Dean. HOOPS.
Ages 12 and up. 459

Myers, Walter Dean. WON'T KNOW TILL I GET
THERE.
Ages 11-14. 460

Naylor, Phyllis Reynolds. A STRING OF CHANCES.
Ages 12 and up. 464

Neigoff, Mike. IT WILL NEVER BE THE SAME
AGAIN.
Ages 12-14. 465

Newton, Suzanne. M.V. SEXTON SPEAKING.
Ages 11 and up. 466

O'Connor, Jane. YOURS TILL NIAGARA FALLS,
ABBY.
Ages 8-10. 467

Okimoto, Jean Davies. IT'S JUST TOO MUCH.
Ages 10-12. 469

Oneal, Zibby. THE LANGUAGE OF GOLDFISH.
Ages 11-14. 473

Pascal, Francine. MY FIRST LOVE & OTHER
DISASTERS.
Ages 12 and up. 484

Paterson, Katherine Womeldorf. JACOB HAVE I
LOVED.
Ages 12 and up. 485

Petersen, P. J. WOULD YOU SETTLE FOR
IMPROBABLE?
Ages 11-13. 495

Platt, Kin. BROGG'S BRAIN.
Ages 12 and up. 514

Potter, Marian. THE SHARED ROOM.
Ages 10-12. 517

## Middle Child

**See:** *Sibling: middle*

## Migrant Workers

Strang, Celia. FOSTER MARY.
Ages 10-13. 633

## Minding

**See:** *Discipline, meaning of*

## Minor, Emancipation of

**See:** *Emancipation of minor*

## Minority Groups

**See:** *Differences, human; Prejudice; Specific group (e.g. Afro-American; Native American)*

## Misunderstandings

**See:** *Communication: misunderstandings*

## Money

**Earning.** *See also: Job*
Bates, Betty. LOVE IS LIKE PEANUTS.
Ages 10-14. 38
Dolan, Sheila. THE WISHING BOTTLE.
Ages 7-9. 167
First, Julia. LOOK WHO'S BEAUTIFUL!
Ages 10-12. 188
Hoban, Lillian Aberman. ARTHUR'S FUNNY MONEY.
Ages 6-8. 294
Hurwitz, Johanna. SUPERDUPER TEDDY.
Ages 4-7. 318
Lowry, Lois. ANASTASIA AT YOUR SERVICE.
Ages 9-12. 385
Naylor, Phyllis Reynolds. EDDIE, INCORPORATED.
Ages 9-11. 463
Neigoff, Mike. IT WILL NEVER BE THE SAME AGAIN.
Ages 12-14. 465
Ruthstrom, Dorotha. THE BIG KITE CONTEST.
Ages 6-8. 560

**Management**
Cleary, Beverly Bunn. RAMONA QUIMBY, AGE 8.
Ages 8-10. 119
Hurmence, Belinda. TOUGH TIFFANY.
Ages 10-13. 315

## Moral Values

**See:** *Values/Valuing: moral/ethical*

## Mother

**See:** *Communication: parent-child; Parent/Parents: mother working outside home; Parent/Parents: single*

## Mountain People

**See:** *Appalachia*

## Mourning, Stages of

**See also:** *Death; Guilt, feelings of; Loss: feelings of; Separation from loved ones*
Arrick, Fran. TUNNEL VISION.
Ages 12 and up. 24
Blume, Judy Sussman. TIGER EYES.
Ages 11 and up. 57
Byars, Betsy Cromer. GOODBYE, CHICKEN LITTLE.
Ages 9-11. 97
Dixon, Paige, pseud. SKIPPER.
Ages 12 and up. 165
Girion, Barbara. A TANGLE OF ROOTS.
Ages 12-16. 220

Krementz, Jill. HOW IT FEELS WHEN A PARENT DIES.
Ages 8 and up. 352
Lobel, Arnold. UNCLE ELEPHANT.
Ages 4-7. 381
McLendon, Gloria Houston. MY BROTHER JOEY DIED.
Ages 9-11. 398
Mazer, Norma Fox. WHEN WE FIRST MET.
Ages 12 and up. 416
Oneal, Zibby. A FORMAL FEELING.
Ages 12 and up. 472
Peck, Richard. CLOSE ENOUGH TO TOUCH.
Ages 12 and up. 490
Pfeffer, Susan Beth. ABOUT DAVID.
Ages 13 and up. 500
Pierik, Robert. ROOKFLEAS IN THE CELLAR.
Ages 8-13. 512
Reader, Dennis J. COMING BACK ALIVE.
Ages 12 and up. 525
Simon, Norma. WE REMEMBER PHILIP.
Ages 7-10. 598
Vogel, Ilse-Margret. MY SUMMER BROTHER.
Ages 8-10. 670
Wallace-Brodeur, Ruth. THE KENTON YEAR.
Ages 9-11. 676

## Moving

**See also:** *Change: new home; Separation from loved ones*
Brandenberg, Aliki Liacouras. WE ARE BEST FRIENDS.
Ages 3-6. 72
Conford, Ellen. ANYTHING FOR A FRIEND.
Ages 9-11. 136
Delton, Judy. LEE HENRY'S BEST FRIEND.
Ages 4-8. 155
Franco, Marjorie. SO WHO HASN'T GOT PROBLEMS?
Ages 10-12. 194
Galbraith, Kathryn Osebold. COME SPRING.
Ages 9-13. 197
Green, Phyllis. GLOOMY LOUIE.
Ages 8-9. 234
Greenfield, Eloise. GRANDMAMA'S JOY.
Ages 4-8. 244
Hickman, Janet. THE THUNDER-PUP.
Ages 9-11. 289
Hickman, Martha Whitmore. MY FRIEND WILLIAM MOVED AWAY.
Ages 4-7. 290
Hughes, Shirley. MOVING MOLLY.
Ages 3-5. 310
Hurwitz, Johanna. ALDO APPLESAUCE.
Ages 7-9. 316
Jones, Penelope. I'M NOT MOVING!
Ages 3-6. 332
Lowry, Lois. ANASTASIA AGAIN!
Ages 9-12. 384
Miles, Betty. THE TROUBLE WITH THIRTEEN.
Ages 9-13. 424
Mohr, Nicholasa. FELITA.
Ages 8-10. 440
Perl, Lila. DON'T ASK MIRANDA.
Ages 10-13. 492
Pollock, Penny. KEEPING IT SECRET.
Ages 9-12. 515
Smith, Janice Lee. THE MONSTER IN THE THIRD DRESSER DRAWER AND OTHER STORIES ABOUT ADAM JOSHUA.
Ages 5-8. 610
Tester, Sylvia Root. SANDY'S NEW HOME.
Ages 5-8. 648
Thrasher, Crystal Faye. BETWEEN DARK AND DAYLIGHT.
Ages 11-13. 658

## Moving (cont.)

Wilkinson, Brenda Scott. LUDELL'S NEW YORK
TIME.
Ages 12 and up. 691
Zelonky, Joy. MY BEST FRIEND MOVED AWAY.
Ages 6-9. 719

## Murder

**See:** *Death: murder*

## Muscular Dystrophy

**See also:** *Wheelchair, dependence on*
Jacobs, Dee. LAURA'S GIFT.
Ages 10-13. 328

## Muteness

**See also:** *Deafness*
Callen, Lawrence Willard. SORROW'S SONG.
Ages 9-12. 103
Cunningham, Julia Woolfolk. THE SILENT VOICE.
Ages 11-14. 146
Rounds, Glen Harold. BLIND OUTLAW.
Ages 9-11. 554
Whelan, Gloria. A TIME TO KEEP SILENT.
Ages 11-14. 690

# N

## Name, Dissatisfaction with

Clifton, Lucille. SONORA BEAUTIFUL.
Ages 12-14. 123
Conford, Ellen. ANYTHING FOR A FRIEND.
Ages 9-11. 136
Grant, Cynthia D. JOSHUA FORTUNE.
Ages 10-13. 229
Grant, Eva. I HATE MY NAME.
Ages 5-8. 230
Hurwitz, Johanna. ALDO APPLESAUCE.
Ages 7-9. 316

## Name-Calling

**See also:** *Aggression; Teasing*
Bottner, Barbara. MEAN MAXINE.
Ages 4-6. 67
Brown, Marc Tolan. ARTHUR'S EYES.
Ages 4-7. 80
De Paola, Thomas Anthony. OLIVER BUTTON IS A
SISSY.
Ages 4-7. 161
Mazer, Norma Fox. MRS. FISH, APE, AND ME, THE
DUMP QUEEN.
Ages 10-12. 414
Panek, Dennis. MATILDA HIPPO HAS A BIG
MOUTH.
Ages 4-7. 478
Philips, Barbara. DON'T CALL ME FATSO.
Ages 5-9. 507
Slote, Alfred. RABBIT EARS.
Ages 10-12. 606

## Narcotic Habit

**See:** *Drugs*

## Native American

Coates, Belle. MAK.
Ages 12 and up. 124
Dyer, Thomas A. THE WHIPMAN IS WATCHING.
Ages 10-14. 177
Hassler, Jon Francis. JEMMY.
Ages 11 and up. 270
Houston, James Archibald. RIVER RUNNERS: A
TALE OF HARDSHIP AND BRAVERY.
Ages 11 and up. 306
Leech, Jay and Zane Spencer. BRIGHT FAWN AND
ME.
Ages 4-8. 361

Miner, Jane Claypool. NAVAJO VICTORY: BEING A
NATIVE AMERICAN.
Ages 11 and up. 432
Waterton, Betty Marie. A SALMON FOR SIMON.
Ages 4-7. 685

## Nature

### Appreciation of

Boutis, Victoria. KATY DID IT.
Ages 8-10. 69
Delton, Judy. A WALK ON A SNOWY NIGHT.
Ages 5-8. 158
Fisher, Aileen Lucia. I STOOD UPON A
MOUNTAIN.
Ages 4-8. 189
Hoopes, Lyn Littlefield. NANA.
Ages 5-8. 302
Lasky, Kathryn. MY ISLAND GRANDMA.
Ages 4-7. 359
Lipp, Frederick J. SOME LOSE THEIR WAY.
Ages 10-13. 377
Phelan, Terry Wolfe. THE WEEK MOM
UNPLUGGED THE TVS.
Ages 8-10. 506
Phipson, Joan Nash, pseud. FLY FREE.
Ages 11 and up. 508
Stolz, Mary Slattery. GO AND CATCH A FLYING
FISH.
Ages 10-13. 630
Tate, Joan. LUKE'S GARDEN AND GRAMP: TWO
NOVELS.
Ages 10-13. 644
Weiss, Nicki. WAITING.
Ages 3-5. 688
Zolotow, Charlotte Shapiro. ONE STEP, TWO...
Ages 2-5. 724
Zolotow, Charlotte Shapiro. THE WHITE MARBLE.
Ages 4-8. 725

### Living in harmony with

Bond, Nancy Barbara. THE VOYAGE BEGUN.
Ages 12 and up. 60
Houston, James Archibald. RIVER RUNNERS: A
TALE OF HARDSHIP AND BRAVERY.
Ages 11 and up. 306
Mazer, Harry. THE ISLAND KEEPER.
Ages 10-14. 412
Reader, Dennis J. COMING BACK ALIVE.
Ages 12 and up. 525
Whelan, Gloria. A TIME TO KEEP SILENT.
Ages 11-14. 690

### Respect for

Callen, Lawrence Willard. SORROW'S SONG.
Ages 9-12. 103
Houston, James Archibald. LONG CLAWS: AN
ARCTIC ADVENTURE.
Ages 9-11. 305
Lipp, Frederick J. SOME LOSE THEIR WAY.
Ages 10-13. 377
McPhail, David Michael. A WOLF STORY.
Ages 5-7. 399
Waterton, Betty Marie. A SALMON FOR SIMON.
Ages 4-7. 685

## Naughty Child

**See:** *Discipline, meaning of*

## Negative Attitude

**See:** *Inferiority, feelings of; Shame*

## Neglect

**See:** *Chores; Job; Parental: negligence*

## Neglected Child

**See:** *Abandonment; Deprivation, emotional; Parental:
negligence*

**Negro**

See: *Afro-American*

**Neighbors/Neighborhood**

See also: *Cooperation*
Franco, Marjorie. SO WHO HASN'T GOT
PROBLEMS?
Ages 10-12. 194
Myers, Walter Dean. THE YOUNG LANDLORDS.
Ages 11-14. 461
Shura, Mary Francis Craig. THE BARKLEY STREET
SIX-PACK.
Ages 9-12. 592
Shura, Mary Francis Craig. CHESTER.
Ages 8-10. 593

**Nervous Breakdown**

See: *Mental illness*

**Neurosis**

See: *Mental illness*

**New Baby**

See: *Sibling: new baby*

**New Home**

See: *Change: new home; Moving*

**Nightmares**

See also: *Daydreaming; Fear*
Holland, Isabelle. NOW IS NOT TOO LATE.
Ages 10-13. 301
Tester, Sylvia Root. SOMETIMES I'M AFRAID.
Ages 3-5. 649

**Nursing Home, Living in**

Hull, Eleanor Means. ALICE WITH GOLDEN HAIR.
Ages 11 and up. 311
Sallis, Susan Diana. ONLY LOVE.
Ages 12 and up. 568

# O

**Obedience/Disobedience**

See: *Discipline, meaning of*

**Obesity**

See: *Weight control: overweight*

**Old Age**

See: *Age*

**One-Parent Home**

See: *Parent/Parents: single*

**Only Child**

Gaeddert, LouAnn Bigge. JUST LIKE SISTERS.
Ages 8-12. 196
Perl, Lila. PIEFACE AND DAPHNE.
Ages 9-11. 494

**Operation**

See: *Hospital, going to; Surgery*

**Orphan**

See also: *Adoption; Chiildren's home, living in; Foster
home*
Angell, Judie. DEAR LOLA OR HOW TO BUILD
YOUR OWN FAMILY.
Ages 10-13. 19
Bulla, Clyde Robert. ALMOST A HERO.
Ages 11 and up. 84

Bulla, Clyde Robert. POOR BOY, RICH BOY.
Ages 5-8. 87
Coates, Belle. MAK.
Ages 12 and up. 124
Cunningham, Julia Woolfolk. THE SILENT VOICE.
Ages 11-14. 146
Dunne, Mary Collins. HOBY & STUB.
Ages 10-13. 176
Farley, Carol J. TWILIGHT WAVES.
Ages 10-13. 186
First, Julia. I, REBEKAH, TAKE YOU, THE
LAWRENCES.
Ages 11-13. 187
Gerson, Corinne. TREAD SOFTLY.
Ages 9-12. 209
Kerr, M. E., pseud. LITTLE LITTLE.
Ages 11 and up. 339
Magorian, Michelle. GOOD NIGHT, MR. TOM.
Ages 11 and up. 401
Miner, Jane Claypool. MIRACLE OF TIME:
ADOPTING A SISTER.
Ages 11 and up. 430
Newton, Suzanne. M.V. SEXTON SPEAKING.
Ages 11 and up. 466

**Orphanage**

See: *Children's home, living in*

**Orthodontia**

Richter, Alice and Laura Joffe Numeroff. YOU CAN'T
PUT BRACES ON SPACES.
Ages 5-9. 531

**Ostracism**

See also: *Prejudice; Rejection*
Arrick, Fran. CHERNOWITZ!
Ages 12 and up. 23
Cohen, Barbara Nash. FAT JACK.
Ages 11 and up. 125
Gauch, Patricia Lee. FRIDAYS.
Ages 11-13. 204
Greenberg, Jan. THE ICEBERG AND ITS SHADOW.
Ages 10-12. 235
Mazer, Norma Fox. MRS. FISH, APE, AND ME, THE
DUMP QUEEN.
Ages 10-12. 414

**Overprotection**

See: *Autonomy; Dependence/Independence; Parental:
overprotection*

**Overweight**

See: *Weight control: overweight*

# P

**Pain**

See: *Accidents; Depression; Doctor, going to; Hospital,
going to; Illnesses; Surgery*

**Paralysis**

See: *Paraplegia; Wheelchair, dependence on*

**Paranoid Thoughts**

See: *Mental illness; Trust/Distrust*

**Paraplegia**

See also: *Wheelchair, dependence on*
Miner, Jane Claypool. NEW BEGINNING: AN
ATHLETE IS PARALYZED.
Ages 11 and up. 433
Phipson, Joan Nash, pseud. A TIDE FLOWING.
Ages 12 and up. 509

## Parent/Parents (cont.)

Bonsall, Crosby Newell. THE GOODBYE SUMMER.
Ages 9-11. 63
Butterworth, William Edmund. UNDER THE INFLUENCE.
Ages 12 and up. 94
Byars, Betsy Cromer. THE ANIMAL, THE VEGETABLE, AND JOHN D JONES.
Ages 10-12. 95
Byars, Betsy Cromer. THE NIGHT SWIMMERS.
Ages 10-12. 98
Chaffin, Lillie Dorton. WE BE WARM TILL SPRINGTIME COMES.
Ages 6-9. 110
Cohen, Barbara Nash. THE INNKEEPER'S DAUGHTER.
Ages 11-14. 126
Foley, June. IT'S NO CRUSH, I'M IN LOVE!
Ages 11-13. 192
Freeman, Gaail. OUT FROM UNDER.
Ages 12 and up. 195
Gerber, Merrill Joan. PLEASE DON'T KISS ME NOW.
Ages 13 and up. 206
Gerson, Corinne. SON FOR A DAY.
Ages 10-12. 208
Gordon, Shirley. THE BOY WHO WANTED A FAMILY.
Ages 7-9. 222
Greene, Constance Clarke. AL(EXANDRA) THE GREAT.
Ages 10-12. 239
Greene, Sheppard M. THE BOY WHO DRANK TOO MUCH.
Ages 12 and up. 242
Hopkins, Lee Bennett. MAMA & HER BOYS.
Ages 8-11. 303
Kingman, Lee. THE REFINER'S FIRE.
Ages 12-14. 341
Lindsay, Jeanne Warren. DO I HAVE A DADDY? A STORY ABOUT A SINGLE-PARENT CHILD.
Ages 4-8. 376
Lyle, Katie Letcher. DARK BUT FULL OF DIAMONDS.
Ages 12-14. 388
Mearian, Judy Frank. SOMEONE SLIGHTLY DIFFERENT.
Ages 10-12. 417
Peyton, K. M., pseud. MARION'S ANGELS.
Ages 11-14. 499
Rodowsky, Colby F. H. MY NAME IS HENLEY.
Ages 10-13. 547
Skurzynski, Gloria Joan. MARTIN BY HIMSELF.
Ages 6-9. 602
Strang, Celia. THIS CHILD IS MINE.
Ages 11-14. 634
Teibl, Margaret. DAVEY COME HOME.
Ages 6-9. 646
Van Steenwyk, Elizabeth Ann. RIVALS ON ICE.
Ages 9-11. 664

**Stepparent.** See: Parent/Parents: remarriage of; Stepparent

**Substitute.** See also: Foster home
Gerson, Corinne. SON FOR A DAY.
Ages 10-12. 208
MacLachlan, Patricia. MAMA ONE, MAMA TWO.
Ages 4-7. 395
Mazer, Norma Fox. MRS. FISH, APE, AND ME, THE DUMP QUEEN.
Ages 10-12. 414

**Suicide of.** See: Suicide: of parent

## Unemployed
Delton, Judy. MY MOTHER LOST HER JOB TODAY.
Ages 3-7. 156
Hansen, Joyce. THE GIFT-GIVER.
Ages 9-12. 263

Hazen, Barbara Shook. TIGHT TIMES.
Ages 5-7. 277
Neigoff, Mike. IT WILL NEVER BE THE SAME AGAIN.
Ages 12-14. 465

**Unwed father.** See: Unwed father

**Unwed mother.** See: Unwed mother

## Parental

**See also:** Parent/Parents

**Abandonment.** See: Abandonment

## Absence
Ames, Mildred. NICKY AND THE JOYOUS NOISE.
Ages 9-12. 14
Bates, Betty. THAT'S WHAT T.J. SAYS.
Ages 9-11. 41
Bonham, Frank. GIMME AN H, GIMME AN E, GIMME AN L, GIMME A P.
Ages 12 and up. 61
Bridgers, Sue Ellen. NOTES FOR ANOTHER LIFE.
Ages 12 and up. 75
Byars, Betsy Cromer. THE CYBIL WAR.
Ages 9-12. 96
Byars, Betsy Cromer. THE TWO-THOUSAND-POUND GOLDFISH.
Ages 9-12. 99
Carris, Joan Davenport. WHEN THE BOYS RAN THE HOUSE.
Ages 8-12. 108
Dixon, Jeanne. LADY CAT LOST.
Ages 10-12. 164
Gerson, Corinne. SON FOR A DAY.
Ages 10-12. 208
Irwin, Hadley, pseud. MOON AND ME.
Ages 11-14. 325
Levoy, Myron. A SHADOW LIKE A LEOPARD.
Ages 12 and up. 369
Lindsay, Jeanne Warren. DO I HAVE A DADDY? A STORY ABOUT A SINGLE-PARENT CHILD.
Ages 4-8. 376
Lobel, Arnold. UNCLE ELEPHANT.
Ages 4-7. 381
Matthews, Ellen. THE TROUBLE WITH LESLIE.
Ages 8-11. 409
Mearian, Judy Frank. SOMEONE SLIGHTLY DIFFERENT.
Ages 10-12. 417
Potter, Marian. THE SHARED ROOM.
Ages 10-12. 517
Rodowsky, Colby F. A SUMMER'S WORTH OF SHAME.
Ages 12-14. 548
Sargent, Sarah. SECRET LIES.
Ages 11 and up. 570
Stren, Patti. THERE'S A RAINBOW IN MY CLOSET.
Ages 8-10. 638
Voigt, Cynthia. DICEY'S SONG.
Ages 11 and up. 671
Weiman, Eiveen. IT TAKES BRAINS.
Ages 10-12. 686
Zolotow, Charlotte Shapiro. IF YOU LISTEN.
Ages 5-7. 722

**Abuse.** See: Child abuse

**Alcoholism.** See: Alcoholism: of father; Alcoholism: of mother

**Control.** See also: Discipline, meaning of
Greenberg, Jan. THE PIG-OUT BLUES.
Ages 12 and up. 236
Mazer, Norma Fox. UP IN SETH'S ROOM.
Ages 13 and up. 415
Morgenroth, Barbara. TRAMPS LIKE US.
Ages 12 and up. 452

## Parental (cont.)

Phelan, Terry Wolfe. THE WEEK MOM
UNPLUGGED THE TVS.
Ages 8-10. 506
Slote, Alfred. LOVE AND TENNIS.
Ages 12-14. 605
Steptoe, John Lewis. DADDY IS A MONSTER . . .
SOMETIMES.
Ages 5-7. 627
Tate, Eleanora E. JUST AN OVERNIGHT GUEST.
Ages 9-11. 643
Van Leeuwen, Jean. SEEMS LIKE THIS ROAD GOES
ON FOREVER.
Ages 12 and up. 663

**Custody.** See also: Divorce: of parents
Angell, Judie. WHAT'S BEST FOR YOU.
Ages 11-14. 21
Fitzhugh, Louise. SPORT.
Ages 9-12. 190
Mendonca, Susan R. TOUGH CHOICES.
Ages 11 and up. 419
Pfeffer, Susan Beth. STARTING WITH MELODIE.
Ages 11-13. 504
Wolkoff, Judie. HAPPILY EVER AFTER . . . ALMOST.
Ages 11-13. 703

**Interference**
Douglass, Barbara. SKATEBOARD SCRAMBLE.
Ages 9-11. 170
LeRoy, Gen. BILLY'S SHOES.
Ages 5-8. 364
Okimoto, Jean Davies. NORMAN SCHNURMAN,
AVERAGE PERSON.
Ages 10-12. 471
Zindel, Bonnie and Paul Zindel. A STAR FOR THE
LATECOMER.
Ages 12 and up. 721

**Negligence.** See also: Deprivation, emotional
Ashley, Bernard. A KIND OF WILD JUSTICE.
Ages 12 and up. 30
Childress, Alice. RAINBOW JORDAN.
Ages 12 and up. 115
DeClements, Barthe. NOTHING'S FAIR IN FIFTH
GRADE.
Ages 8-11. 152
Morgan, Alison Mary. PAUL'S KITE.
Ages 10-13. 451
Strasser, Todd. ANGEL DUST BLUES.
Ages 14 and up. 635
Tate, Eleanora E. JUST AN OVERNIGHT GUEST.
Ages 9-11. 643

**Overprotection**
Brooks, Jerome. THE BIG DIPPER MARATHON.
Ages 11-14. 77
Hallman, Ruth. BREAKAWAY.
Ages 12 and up. 257
Kerr, M. E., pseud. LITTLE LITTLE.
Ages 11 and up. 339
Smith, Doris Buchanan. LAST WAS LLOYD.
Ages 8-11. 608
Thomas, William E. THE NEW BOY IS BLIND.
Ages 6-10. 655

**Rejection.** See: Rejection: parental

**Unreliability**
Childress, Alice. RAINBOW JORDAN.
Ages 12 and up. 115
Gerson, Corinne. HOW I PUT MY MOTHER
THROUGH COLLEGE.
Ages 11 and up. 207
Mendonca, Susan R. TOUGH CHOICES.
Ages 11 and up. 419
Rodowsky, Colby F. H. MY NAME IS HENLEY.
Ages 10-13. 547
Stolz, Mary Slattery. GO AND CATCH A FLYING
FISH.
Ages 10-13. 630

**Weakness**
Lorimar, Lawrence T. SECRETS.
Ages 12 and up. 382
Shreve, Susan Richards. THE MASQUERADE.
Ages 12 and up. 591

## Parting

**See:** Separation from loved ones

## Patience/Impatience

Corey, Dorothy. EVERYBODY TAKES TURNS.
Ages 2-6. 140
Rounds, Glen Harold. BLIND OUTLAW.
Ages 9-11. 554
Skolsky, Mindy Warshaw. CARNIVAL AND KOPECK
AND MORE ABOUT HANNAH.
Ages 7-9. 600
Weiss, Nicki. WAITING.
Ages 3-5. 688

## Patriotism

**See also:** Loyalty
Ofek, Uriel. SMOKE OVER GOLAN.
Ages 9-13. 468

## Peer Relationships

**See also:** Belonging; Boy-girl relationships; Play
Banks, Lynne Reid. THE WRITING ON THE WALL.
Ages 12 and up. 33
Bonsall, Crosby Newell. THE CASE OF THE
DOUBLE CROSS.
Ages 6-8. 62
Bottner, Barbara. DUMB OLD CASEY IS A FAT
TREE.
Ages 6-9. 66
Bulla, Clyde Robert. LAST LOOK.
Ages 8-10. 86
Byars, Betsy Cromer. THE ANIMAL, THE
VEGETABLE, AND JOHN D JONES.
Ages 10-12. 95
Carroll, Theodorus C. THE LOST CHRISTMAS
STAR.
Ages 7-9. 109
Crofford, Emily. STORIES FROM THE BLUE ROAD.
Ages 9-12. 143
Franco, Marjorie. SO WHO HASN'T GOT
PROBLEMS?
Ages 10-12. 194
Greene, Bette. GET ON OUT OF HERE, PHILIP
HALL.
Ages 9-12. 238
Klass, Sheila Solomon. TO SEE MY MOTHER
DANCE.
Ages 10-13. 344
Klein, Monica. BACKYARD BASKETBALL
SUPERSTAR.
Ages 6-8. 345
Levy, Elizabeth. COME OUT SMILING.
Ages 12 and up. 370
McDonnell, Christine. DON'T BE MAD, IVY.
Ages 7-8. 391
Matthews, Ellen. PUTTING UP WITH SHERWOOD.
Ages 9-11. 408
Miner, Jane Claypool. SHE'S MY SISTER: HAVING A
RETARDED SISTER.
Ages 11 and up. 434
Myers, Walter Dean. HOOPS.
Ages 12 and up. 459
Osborne, Mary Pope. RUN, RUN, AS FAST AS YOU
CAN.
Ages 9-12. 477
Platt, Kin. THE APE INSIDE ME.
Ages 12 and up. 513
Slepian, Jan. THE ALFRED SUMMER.
Ages 11-13. 603

## Pets (cont.)

Savitz, Harriet May. RUN, DON'T WALK.
Ages 12 and up. 572
Thomas, Ianthe. HI, MRS. MALLORY!
Ages 5-8. 651
Wallace, Bill. A DOG CALLED KITTY.
Ages 9-11. 675
Willoughby, Elaine Macmann. BORIS AND THE
MONSTERS.
Ages 4-7. 694
Wood, Phyllis Anderson. PASS ME A PINE CONE.
Ages 11 and up. 705

### Responsibility for

Girion, Barbara. MISTY AND ME.
Ages 10-12. 219
Little, Mary E. OLD CAT AND THE KITTEN.
Ages 8-12. 379
Rockwell, Anne F. and Harlow Rockwell. I LOVE MY
PETS.
Ages 3-5. 544

### Substitute for human relationship

Graham, Ada and Frank Graham. JACOB AND OWL.
Ages 8-11. 228
Wright, Betty Ren. MY NEW MOM AND ME.
Ages 8-10. 710

## Phobia

See: *Fear*

## Physical Handicaps

See: *Handicaps*

## Planning

See: *Careers: planning; Problem solving; Responsibility*

## Play

See also: *Fantasy formation; Imagination; Peer
relationships; Reality, escaping; Sharing/Not sharing*
Lexau, Joan M. I HATE RED ROVER.
Ages 6-8. 371
Lindgren, Barbro. SAM'S CAR.
Ages 2-5. 374
McDonnell, Christine. DON'T BE MAD, IVY.
Ages 7-8. 391

## Popularity

See: *Boy-girl relationships; Friendship; Peer
relationships*

## Poverty

See also: *Differences, human; Ghetto; Prejudice: social
class*
Branscum, Robbie. FOR LOVE OF JODY.
Ages 9-12. 73
Chaffin, Lillie Dorton. WE BE WARM TILL
SPRINGTIME COMES.
Ages 6-9. 110
Crofford, Emily. A MATTER OF PRIDE.
Ages 8-11. 142
Crofford, Emily. STORIES FROM THE BLUE ROAD.
Ages 9-12. 143
Hurmence, Belinda. TOUGH TIFFANY.
Ages 10-13. 315
Letchworth, Beverly J. PAX AND THE MUTT.
Ages 8-11. 366
Strang, Celia. THIS CHILD IS MINE.
Ages 11-14. 634
Thrasher, Crystal Faye. BETWEEN DARK AND
DAYLIGHT.
Ages 11-13. 658

## Power Struggle

See: *Parent/Parents: power struggle with*

## Practical Jokes/Pranks

See also: *Harassment; Teasing*
Addy, Sharon. WE DIDN'T MEAN TO.
Ages 8-10. 2
Lowry, Lois. ANASTASIA AT YOUR SERVICE.
Ages 9-12. 385

## Pregnancy

See also: *Abortion; Sex; Unwed mother*
Elfman, Blossom. THE BUTTERFLY GIRL.
Ages 13 and up. 180
Posner, Grace. IN MY SISTER'S EYES.
Ages 12 and up. 516
Powers, Bill. A TEST OF LOVE.
Ages 12 and up. 519
Prince, Alison. THE TURKEY'S NEST.
Ages 12 and up. 520
Truss, Jan. BIRD AT THE WINDOW.
Ages 13 and up. 661

## Prejudice

See also: *Differences, human; Hatred; Hostility;
Integration; Justice/Injustice; Ostracism; Rejection*

### Ethnic/Racial. See also: *Apartheid; Immigrants;
Internment; Refugees*

Bernstein, Joanne Eckstein. DMITRY: A YOUNG
SOVIET IMMIGRANT.
Ages 11-13. 52
Cheatham, Karyn Follis. THE BEST WAY OUT.
Ages 12 and up. 114
Geibel, James. THE BLOND BROTHER.
Ages 12 and up. 205
Guy, Rosa Cuthbert. THE DISAPPEARANCE.
Ages 12 and up. 252
Hassler, Jon Francis. JEMMY.
Ages 11 and up. 270
Jones, Toeckey. GO WELL, STAY WELL.
Ages 12 and up. 334
Miner, Jane Claypool. NAVAJO VICTORY: BEING A
NATIVE AMERICAN.
Ages 11 and up. 432
Miner, Jane Claypool. THE TOUGH GUY: BLACK IN
A WHITE WORLD.
Ages 11 and up. 437
Mohr, Nicholasa. FELITA.
Ages 8-10. 440
Ruby, Lois. TWO TRUTHS IN MY POCKET.
Ages 12 and up. 557
Sebestyen, Ouida. WORDS BY HEART.
Ages 10-13. 580
Smith, Doris Buchanan. SALTED LEMONS.
Ages 9-12. 609
Wartski, Maureen Crane. A LONG WAY FROM
HOME.
Ages 11-13. 680
Yep, Laurence Michael. SEA GLASS.
Ages 11-14. 713

### toward Handicapped persons

Savitz, Harriet May. RUN, DON'T WALK.
Ages 12 and up. 572

### Religious. See also: *Refugees; Religion*

Arrick, Fran. CHERNOWITZ!
Ages 12 and up. 23
Asher, Sandra Fenichel. DAUGHTERS OF THE LAW.
Ages 11-13. 26
Hurwitz, Johanna. ONCE I WAS A PLUM TREE.
Ages 9-11. 317

### Sexual

Angell, Judie. SECRET SELVES.
Ages 11-13. 20
Bargar, Gary W. WHAT HAPPENED TO MR.
FORSTER?
Ages 10-13. 34

## Prejudice (cont.)

Bonsall, Crosby Newell. THE CASE OF THE
DOUBLE CROSS.
Ages 6-8. 62
Douglass, Barbara. SKATEBOARD SCRAMBLE.
Ages 9-11. 170
Klein, Monica. BACKYARD BASKETBALL
SUPERSTAR.
Ages 6-8. 345
Stolz, Mary Slattery. WHAT TIME OF NIGHT IS IT?
Ages 11-14. 631

**Social class.** *See also: Poverty*
Carrick, Malcolm. I'LL GET YOU.
Ages 11-13. 107
Graber, Richard Fredrick. BLACK COW SUMMER.
Ages 12 and up. 224
Lowry, Lois. ANASTASIA AT YOUR SERVICE.
Ages 9-12. 385
Sallis, Susan Diana. A TIME FOR EVERYTHING.
Ages 13 and up. 569
Spence, Eleanor Rachel. A CANDLE FOR SAINT
ANTONY.
Ages 13 and up. 618

## Premarital Sex

**See:** *Sex: premarital; Unwed father; Unwed mother*

## Presents

**See:** *Giving, meaning of*

## Pretending

**See:** *Daydreaming; Fantasy formation; Imagination;
Reality, escaping*

## Pride/False Pride

Bulla, Clyde Robert. DANIEL'S DUCK.
Ages 5-8. 85
Miner, Jane Claypool. A MAN'S PRIDE: LOSING A
FATHER.
Ages 11 and up. 429
Yep, Laurence Michael. SEA GLASS.
Ages 11-14. 713

## Priorities, Establishing

**See:** *Problem solving; Values/Valuing*

## Prison

**See:** *Crime/Criminals; Delinquency, juvenile; Detention
home, living in; Imprisonment*

## Privacy, Need for

Billington, Elizabeth T. PART-TIME BOY.
Ages 8-10. 53
Bond, Felicia. POINSETTIA & HER FAMILY.
Ages 4-7. 59
Henkes, Kevin. ALL ALONE.
Ages 3-6. 280
Hurmence, Belinda. TOUGH TIFFANY.
Ages 10-13. 315
MacLachlan, Patricia. CASSIE BINEGAR.
Ages 9-12. 394
Thompson, Jean, pseud. DON'T FORGET MICHAEL.
Ages 7-9. 656
Wright, Betty Ren. I LIKE BEING ALONE.
Ages 6-9. 709

## Private Schools

**See:** *Schools, private*

## Problem Solving

**See also:** *Ambivalence, feelings of; Creativity; Decision
making; Resourcefulness*
Alexander, Martha G. MOVE OVER, TWERP.
Ages 5-8. 11

Bonsall, Crosby Newell. THE CASE OF THE
DOUBLE CROSS.
Ages 6-8. 62
Bosse, Malcolm Joseph. GANESH.
Ages 11-14. 65
Bottner, Barbara. MEAN MAXINE.
Ages 4-6. 67
Carris, Joan Davenport. WHEN THE BOYS RAN THE
HOUSE.
Ages 8-12. 108
Chapman, Carol. HERBIE'S TROUBLES.
Ages 5-7. 113
Cooney, Nancy Evans. THE BLANKET THAT HAD
TO GO.
Ages 3-5. 138
Dickinson, Mary. ALEX'S BED.
Ages 3-6. 163
Flournoy, Valerie. THE TWINS STRIKE BACK.
Ages 6-8. 191
Greenwald, Sheila. GIVE US A GREAT BIG SMILE,
ROSY COLE.
Ages 8-10. 246
Haas, Dorothy. POPPY AND THE OUTDOORS CAT.
Ages 7-10. 253
Hogan, Paula Z. SOMETIMES I DON'T LIKE
SCHOOL.
Ages 6-9. 297
Hogan, Paula Z. SOMETIMES I GET SO MAD.
Ages 5-8. 298
Hopper, Nancy J. SECRETS.
Ages 11-14. 304
Hughes, Shirley. ALFIE GETS IN FIRST.
Ages 3-5. 309
Inkiow, Dimiter. ME AND CLARA AND CASIMER
THE CAT.
Ages 7-9. 321
Landis, James David. THE SISTERS IMPOSSIBLE.
Ages 9-11. 355
McDonnell, Christine. DON'T BE MAD, IVY.
Ages 7-8. 391
Mauser, Pat Rhoads. HOW I FOUND MYSELF AT
THE FAIR.
Ages 7-9. 411
Moskin, Marietta Dunston. ROSIE'S BIRTHDAY
PRESENT.
Ages 4-7. 456
Myers, Walter Dean. THE YOUNG LANDLORDS.
Ages 11-14. 461
Pascal, Francine. THE HAND-ME-DOWN KID.
Ages 10-13. 483
Pfeffer, Susan Beth. WHAT DO YOU DO WHEN
YOUR MOUTH WON'T OPEN?
Ages 10-13. 505
Ruthstrom, Dorotha. THE BIG KITE CONTEST.
Ages 6-8. 560
Seuling, Barbara. THE TRIPLETS.
Ages 4-7. 581
Skurzynski, Gloria Joan. MARTIN BY HIMSELF.
Ages 6-9. 602
Strang, Celia. THIS CHILD IS MINE.
Ages 11-14. 634
Wright, Betty Ren. I LIKE BEING ALONE.
Ages 6-9. 709

## Promise, Keeping

Skolsky, Mindy Warshaw. CARNIVAL AND KOPECK
AND MORE ABOUT HANNAH.
Ages 7-9. 600
Wade, Anne. A PROMISE IS FOR KEEPING.
Ages 4-7. 674
Zhitkov, Boris Stepanovich. HOW I HUNTED THE
LITTLE FELLOWS.
Ages 3-7. 720

## Psychosis

**See:** *Mental illness*

## Report Cards

**See:** *School: achievement/underachievement*

## Reputation

Guy, Rosa Cuthbert. THE DISAPPEARANCE.
Ages 12 and up. 252
McKay, Robert W. THE RUNNING BACK.
Ages 12-14. 392

## Resourcefulness

**See also:** *Creativity; Problem solving*
Alexander, Martha G. MOVE OVER, TWERP.
Ages 5-8. 11
Bennett, Jack. THE VOYAGE OF THE LUCKY
DRAGON.
Ages 11 and up. 45
Benson, Ellen. PHILIP'S LITTLE SISTER.
Ages 5-8. 46
Calhoun, Mary Huiskamp. THE NIGHT THE
MONSTER CAME.
Ages 8-10. 102
Chaffin, Lillie Dorton. WE BE WARM TILL
SPRINGTIME COMES.
Ages 6-9. 110
Crowley, Arthur. BONZO BEAVER.
Ages 3-6. 144
De Roo, Anne Louise. SCRUB FIRE.
Ages 9-12. 162
Drescher, Joan Elizabeth. I'M IN CHARGE!
Ages 5-8. 171
Gardiner, John Reynolds. STONE FOX.
Ages 8-10. 202
Gerson, Corinne. SON FOR A DAY.
Ages 10-12. 208
Giff, Patricia Reilly. FOURTH GRADE CELEBRITY.
Ages 8-10. 210
Gray, Nigel. IT'LL ALL COME OUT IN THE WASH.
Ages 4-6. 233
Greenwald, Sheila. GIVE US A GREAT BIG SMILE,
ROSY COLE.
Ages 8-10. 246
Hautzig, Esther Rudomin. A GIFT FOR MAMA.
Ages 8-12. 273
Hoban, Lillian Aberman. ARTHUR'S FUNNY
MONEY.
Ages 6-8. 294
Hughes, Shirley. ALFIE GETS IN FIRST.
Ages 3-5. 309
Inkiow, Dimiter. ME AND CLARA AND CASIMER
THE CAT.
Ages 7-9. 321
Irwin, Hadley, pseud. MOON AND ME.
Ages 11-14. 325
Letchworth, Beverly J. PAX AND THE MUTT.
Ages 8-11. 366
Naylor, Phyllis Reynolds. ALL BECAUSE I'M OLDER.
Ages 7-9. 462
Naylor, Phyllis Reynolds. EDDIE, INCORPORATED.
Ages 9-11. 463
Ofek, Uriel. SMOKE OVER GOLAN.
Ages 9-13. 468
Pearson, Susan. SATURDAY I RAN AWAY.
Ages 5-7. 488
Phelan, Terry Wolfe. THE WEEK MOM
UNPLUGGED THE TVS.
Ages 8-10. 506
Reader, Dennis J. COMING BACK ALIVE.
Ages 12 and up. 525
Roy, Ronald. AVALANCHE!
Ages 10 and up. 555
Ruthstrom, Dorotha. THE BIG KITE CONTEST.
Ages 6-8. 560
Smith, Pauline Coggeshall. BRUSH FIRE!
Ages 11 and up. 613

Tate, Joan. LUKE'S GARDEN AND GRAMP: TWO
NOVELS.
Ages 10-13. 644
Waterton, Betty Marie. A SALMON FOR SIMON.
Ages 4-7. 685

## Respect

**See:** *Age: respect for; Grandparent: respect for;
Parent/Parents: respect for/lack of respect for*

## Responsibility

**See also:** *Chores; Job; Work, attitude toward*

**Accepting.** *See also: Leader/Leadership*
Adler, Carole Schwerdtfeger. THE MAGIC OF THE
GLITS.
Ages 9-12. 6
Brancato, Robin Fidler. SWEET BELLS JANGLED
OUT OF TUNE.
Ages 11-14. 70
Branscum, Robbie. FOR LOVE OF JODY.
Ages 9-12. 73
Buchan, Stuart. A SPACE OF HIS OWN.
Ages 12 and up. 82
Butterworth, William Edmund. LEROY AND THE
OLD MAN.
Ages 12 and up. 93
Byars, Betsy Cromer. THE NIGHT SWIMMERS.
Ages 10-12. 98
Carris, Joan Davenport. WHEN THE BOYS RAN THE
HOUSE.
Ages 8-12. 108
Chaffin, Lillie Dorton. WE BE WARM TILL
SPRINGTIME COMES.
Ages 6-9. 110
Danziger, Paula. THERE'S A BAT IN BUNK FIVE.
Ages 10-14. 151
Drescher, Joan Elizabeth. I'M IN CHARGE!
Ages 5-8. 171
Graeber, Charlotte Towner. GREY CLOUD.
Ages 9-11. 226
Hall, Lynn. DANZA!
Ages 9-12. 254
Hansen, Joyce. THE GIFT-GIVER.
Ages 9-12. 263
Herman, Charlotte. WHAT HAPPENED TO
HEATHER HOPKOWITZ?
Ages 10-13. 283
Johnston, Norma. MYSELF AND I.
Ages 11 and up. 330
Konigsburg, Elaine Lobl. THROWING SHADOWS.
Ages 10-12. 349
Lowry, Lois. ANASTASIA AT YOUR SERVICE.
Ages 9-12. 385
Matthews, Ellen. THE TROUBLE WITH LESLIE.
Ages 8-11. 409
Miner, Jane Claypool. A MAN'S PRIDE: LOSING A
FATHER.
Ages 11 and up. 429
Moeri, Louise. FIRST THE EGG.
Ages 12 and up. 438
Moncure, Jane Belk. CARING.
Ages 3-6. 441
Myers, Walter Dean. THE YOUNG LANDLORDS.
Ages 11-14. 461
Neigoff, Mike. IT WILL NEVER BE THE SAME
AGAIN.
Ages 12-14. 465
Newton, Suzanne. M.V. SEXTON SPEAKING.
Ages 11 and up. 466
Pascal, Francine. MY FIRST LOVE & OTHER
DISASTERS.
Ages 12 and up. 484
Philips, Barbara. DON'T CALL ME FATSO.
Ages 5-9. 507
Pierik, Robert. ROOKFLEAS IN THE CELLAR.
Ages 8-13. 512

## Responsibility (cont.)

Reuter, Margaret. YOU CAN DEPEND ON ME.
Ages 6-9. 530
Ross, Pat. M AND M AND THE BIG BAG.
Ages 6-8. 550
Shreve, Susan Richards. THE MASQUERADE.
Ages 12 and up. 591
Smith, Pauline Coggeshall. BRUSH FIRE!
Ages 11 and up. 613
Strang, Celia. FOSTER MARY.
Ages 10-13. 633
Strang, Celia. THIS CHILD IS MINE.
Ages 11-14. 634
Thomas, Jane Resh. THE COMEBACK DOG.
Ages 7-9. 653
Thomas, Karen. THE GOOD THING . . . THE BAD
THING.
Ages 3-7. 654

### Avoiding

Atkinson, Linda. HIT AND RUN.
Ages 11 and up. 31
Delton, Judy and Elaine Knox-Wagner. THE BEST
MOM IN THE WORLD.
Ages 4-7. 159
Drescher, Joan Elizabeth. THE MARVELOUS MESS.
Ages 4-6. 172
Giff, Patricia Reilly. THE GIRL WHO KNEW IT ALL.
Ages 8-10. 212

## Retardation

See: *Mental retardation*

## Retirement

See also: *Age; Grandparent*
Knox-Wagner, Elaine. MY GRANDPA RETIRED
TODAY.
Ages 4-7. 346

## Revenge

See also: *Aggression*
Arrick, Fran. CHERNOWITZ!
Ages 12 and up. 23
Ashley, Bernard. A KIND OF WILD JUSTICE.
Ages 12 and up. 30
Bulla, Clyde Robert. ALMOST A HERO.
Ages 11 and up. 84
Bulla, Clyde Robert. LAST LOOK.
Ages 8-10. 86
Lowry, Lois. ANASTASIA AT YOUR SERVICE.
Ages 9-12. 385
Panek, Dennis. MATILDA HIPPO HAS A BIG
MOUTH.
Ages 4-7. 478

## Risk, Taking of

Greene, Constance Clarke. DOUBLE-DARE O'TOOLE.
Ages 9-11. 240
Houston, James Archibald. LONG CLAWS: AN
ARCTIC ADVENTURE.
Ages 9-11. 305

## Rivalry

See: *Competition; Jealousy; Parent/Parents: power
struggle with; Sibling: rivalry; Sports/Sportsmanship*

## Roman Catholic

Foley, June. IT'S NO CRUSH, I'M IN LOVE!
Ages 11-13. 192
Marangell, Virginia J. GIANNA MIA.
Ages 12-15. 402
Spence, Eleanor Rachel. A CANDLE FOR SAINT
ANTONY.
Ages 13 and up. 618

## Rumor

See: *Communication: rumor*

## Running Away

Angell, Judie. DEAR LOLA OR HOW TO BUILD
YOUR OWN FAMILY.
Ages 10-13. 19
Ashley, Bernard. BREAK IN THE SUN.
Ages 11 and up. 29
Brown, Marc Tolan. ARTHUR GOES TO CAMP.
Ages 5-8. 79
Cole, Brock. NO MORE BATHS.
Ages 3-6. 130
Dodson, Susan. HAVE YOU SEEN THIS GIRL?
Ages 13 and up. 166
Dunne, Mary Collins. HOBY & STUB.
Ages 10-13. 176
Elfman, Blossom. THE BUTTERFLY GIRL.
Ages 13 and up. 180
Hallman, Ruth. BREAKAWAY.
Ages 12 and up. 257
Hamilton, Morse and Emily Hamilton. MY NAME IS
EMILY.
Ages 3-6. 259
Hill, Margaret. TURN THE PAGE, WENDY.
Ages 10-14. 291
Hogan, Paula Z. WILL DAD EVER MOVE BACK
HOME?
Ages 7-10. 299
Lasker, Joe. THE DO-SOMETHING DAY.
Ages 3-7. 357
Mendonca, Susan R. TOUGH CHOICES.
Ages 11 and up. 419
Miles, Miska, pseud. JENNY'S CAT.
Ages 6-8. 425
Morgenroth, Barbara. TRAMPS LIKE US.
Ages 12 and up. 452
Pearson, Susan. SATURDAY I RAN AWAY.
Ages 5-7. 488
Somerlott, Robert. BLAZE.
Ages 10-13. 617
Thompson, Paul. THE HITCHHIKERS.
Ages 12 and up. 657
Veglahn, Nancy Crary. FELLOWSHIP OF THE
SEVEN STARS.
Ages 12 and up. 665
Winthrop, Elizabeth. MARATHON MIRANDA.
Ages 9-11. 696

## Russia

Bernstein, Joanne Eckstein. DMITRY: A YOUNG
SOVIET IMMIGRANT.
Ages 11-13. 52
Zhitkov, Boris Stepanovich. HOW I HUNTED THE
LITTLE FELLOWS.
Ages 3-7. 720

# S

## Sadness

See: *Depression*

## Schizophrenia

See: *Mental illness*

## School

See also: *Education; Integration*

### Achievement/Underachievement

Ashley, Bernard. A KIND OF WILD JUSTICE.
Ages 12 and up. 30
Giff, Patricia Reilly. THE GIRL WHO KNEW IT ALL.
Ages 8-10. 212
Giff, Patricia Reilly. TODAY WAS A TERRIBLE DAY.
Ages 6-7. 213
Gilson, Jamie. DO BANANAS CHEW GUM?
Ages 9-11. 216

## School (cont.)

Hobby, Janice Hale with Gabrielle Rubin and Daniel Rubin. STAYING BACK.
Ages 6-12. 295

Hogan, Paula Z. SOMETIMES I DON'T LIKE SCHOOL.
Ages 6-9. 297

Hurwitz, Johanna. TOUGH-LUCK KAREN.
Ages 10-13. 319

Morton, Jane. RUNNING SCARED.
Ages 10-14. 455

Roy, Ronald. FRANKIE IS STAYING BACK.
Ages 8-10. 556

Voigt, Cynthia. DICEY'S SONG.
Ages 11 and up. 671

Weiman, Eiveen. IT TAKES BRAINS.
Ages 10-12. 686

### Behavior

Cuyler, Margery S. THE TROUBLE WITH SOAP.
Ages 10-13. 147

Danziger, Paula. THE DIVORCE EXPRESS.
Ages 11-14. 150

Jacobs, Dee. LAURA'S GIFT.
Ages 10-13. 328

Morton, Jane. RUNNING SCARED.
Ages 10-14. 455

Stevens, Carla McBride. SARA AND THE PINCH.
Ages 5-7. 628

### Busing. See: Integration: school busing

### Classmate relationships

Adler, Carole Schwerdtfeger. THE ONCE IN A WHILE HERO.
Ages 10-13. 7

Asher, Sandra Fenichel. SUMMER BEGINS.
Ages 10-13. 28

Bargar, Gary W. WHAT HAPPENED TO MR. FORSTER?
Ages 10-13. 34

Bates, Betty. MY MOM, THE MONEY NUT.
Ages 10-12. 39

Bates, Betty. PICKING UP THE PIECES.
Ages 10-13. 40

Bates, Betty. THAT'S WHAT T.J. SAYS.
Ages 9-11. 41

Bonham, Frank. GIMME AN H, GIMME AN E, GIMME AN L, GIMME A P.
Ages 12 and up. 61

Calhoun, Mary Huiskamp. KATIE JOHN AND HEATHCLIFF.
Ages 9-11. 101

Chapman, Carol. HERBIE'S TROUBLES.
Ages 5-7. 113

Cleary, Beverly Bunn. RAMONA QUIMBY, AGE 8.
Ages 8-10. 119

Cohen, Barbara Nash. FAT JACK.
Ages 11 and up. 125

Cohen, Miriam. FIRST GRADE TAKES A TEST.
Ages 5-7. 127

Cohen, Miriam. NO GOOD IN ART.
Ages 5-7. 128

Cohen, Miriam. SO WHAT?
Ages 4-7. 129

Conford, Ellen. THE REVENGE OF THE INCREDIBLE DR. RANCID AND HIS YOUTHFUL ASSISTANT, JEFFREY.
Ages 10-12. 137

Dacquino, Vincent T. KISS THE CANDY DAYS GOOD-BYE.
Ages 10-14. 148

Danziger, Paula. CAN YOU SUE YOUR PARENTS FOR MALPRACTICE?
Ages 10-14. 149

Dygard, Thomas J. SOCCER DUEL.
Ages 11-14. 179

Fox, Paula. A PLACE APART.
Ages 12 and up. 193

Gauch, Patricia Lee. FRIDAYS.
Ages 11-13. 204

Geibel, James. THE BLOND BROTHER.
Ages 12 and up. 205

Gerber, Merrill Joan. PLEASE DON'T KISS ME NOW.
Ages 13 and up. 206

Giff, Patricia Reilly. FOURTH GRADE CELEBRITY.
Ages 8-10. 210

Giff, Patricia Reilly. THE GIFT OF THE PIRATE QUEEN.
Ages 9-12. 211

Gilson, Jamie. DO BANANAS CHEW GUM?
Ages 9-11. 216

Girion, Barbara. A HANDFUL OF STARS.
Ages 12 and up. 217

Girion, Barbara. LIKE EVERYBODY ELSE.
Ages 10-13. 218

Gould, Marilyn. GOLDEN DAFFODILS.
Ages 8-12. 223

Grace, Fran. BRANIGAN'S DOG.
Ages 10 and up. 225

Greenberg, Jan. THE ICEBERG AND ITS SHADOW.
Ages 10-12. 235

Greenberg, Jan. A SEASON IN-BETWEEN.
Ages 11-13. 237

Greene, Constance Clarke. DOUBLE-DARE O'TOOLE.
Ages 9-11. 240

Hautzig, Deborah. THE HANDSOMEST FATHER.
Ages 4-7. 271

Hentoff, Nat. DOES THIS SCHOOL HAVE CAPITAL PUNISHMENT?
Ages 11 and up. 282

Hughes, Dean. HONESTLY, MYRON.
Ages 9-11. 307

Hughes, Dean. SWITCHING TRACKS.
Ages 10-14. 308

Hurwitz, Johanna. ALDO APPLESAUCE.
Ages 7-9. 316

Knudson, R. Rozanne. RINEHART LIFTS.
Ages 10-12. 348

Leggett, Linda Rodgers and Linda Gambee Andrews. THE ROSE-COLORED GLASSES: MELANIE ADJUSTS TO POOR VISION.
Ages 8-11. 362

Lexau, Joan M. I HATE RED ROVER.
Ages 6-8. 371

McKay, Robert W. THE RUNNING BACK.
Ages 12-14. 392

Marney, Dean. JUST GOOD FRIENDS.
Ages 11-13. 404

Mauser, Pat Rhoads. A BUNDLE OF STICKS.
Ages 10-12. 410

Mazer, Norma Fox. MRS. FISH, APE, AND ME, THE DUMP QUEEN.
Ages 10-12. 414

Mearian, Judy Frank. SOMEONE SLIGHTLY DIFFERENT.
Ages 10-12. 417

Miles, Betty. MAUDIE AND ME AND THE DIRTY BOOK.
Ages 10-12. 423

Miner, Jane Claypool. NAVAJO VICTORY: BEING A NATIVE AMERICAN.
Ages 11 and up. 432

Miner, Jane Claypool. THE TOUGH GUY: BLACK IN A WHITE WORLD.
Ages 11 and up. 437

Moore, Emily. SOMETHING TO COUNT ON.
Ages 8-10. 449

Morgenroth, Barbara. WILL THE REAL RENIE LAKE PLEASE STAND UP?
Ages 12 and up. 453

Oppenheimer, Joan Letson. WORKING ON IT.
Ages 11-13. 475

Payne, Sherry Neuwirth. A CONTEST.
Ages 8-10. 486

## School (cont.)

## Self, Attitude Toward (cont.)

Colman, Hila Crayder. CONFESSION OF A STORYTELLER.
Ages 10-13. 133

Corcoran, Barbara. CHILD OF THE MORNING.
Ages 10 and up. 139

Delton, Judy. I NEVER WIN!
Ages 4-7. 154

Giff, Patricia Reilly. FOURTH GRADE CELEBRITY.
Ages 8-10. 210

Green, Phyllis. GLOOMY LOUIE.
Ages 8-9. 234

Greenberg, Jan. A SEASON IN-BETWEEN.
Ages 11-13. 237

Hallman, Ruth. BREAKAWAY.
Ages 12 and up. 257

Hobby, Janice Hale with Gabrielle Rubin and Daniel Rubin. STAYING BACK.
Ages 6-12. 295

Kropp, Paul Stephan. WILTED.
Ages 11-14. 354

Leggett, Linda Rodgers and Linda Gambee Andrews. THE ROSE-COLORED GLASSES: MELANIE ADJUSTS TO POOR VISION.
Ages 8-11. 362

Mauser, Pat Rhoads. A BUNDLE OF STICKS.
Ages 10-12. 410

Mendonca, Susan R. TOUGH CHOICES.
Ages 11 and up. 419

Miklowitz, Gloria D. THE LOVE BOMBERS.
Ages 12 and up. 422

Montgomery, Elizabeth Rider. "SEEING" IN THE DARK.
Ages 5-7. 448

Morgenroth, Barbara. TRAMPS LIKE US.
Ages 12 and up. 452

Oppenheimer, Joan Letson. WORKING ON IT.
Ages 11-13. 475

Pollock, Penny. KEEPING IT SECRET.
Ages 9-12. 515

Sachs, Marilyn. BUS RIDE.
Ages 11-14. 563

Sachs, Marilyn. HELLO . . . WRONG NUMBER.
Ages 12-16. 565

Savitz, Harriet May. RUN, DON'T WALK.
Ages 12 and up. 572

Slepian, Jan. THE ALFRED SUMMER.
Ages 11-13. 603

Slepian, Jan. LESTER'S TURN.
Ages 11-14. 604

Sullivan, Mary Beth and Alan J. Brightman and Joseph Blatt. FEELING FREE.
Ages 9 and up. 640

Waber, Bernard. YOU'RE A LITTLE KID WITH A BIG HEART.
Ages 5-7. 673

Young, Helen. WHAT DIFFERENCE DOES IT MAKE, DANNY?
Ages 9-12. 715

## Blame. See: Blame

## Body concept

First, Julia. LOOK WHO'S BEAUTIFUL!
Ages 10-12. 188

Hautzig, Deborah. SECOND STAR TO THE RIGHT.
Ages 12 and up. 272

Liu, Aimee. SOLITAIRE.
Ages 13 and up. 380

Perl, Lila. HEY, REMEMBER FAT GLENDA?
Ages 9-12. 493

Robison, Nancy Louise. BALLET MAGIC.
Ages 9-11. 541

## Confidence

Greene, Bette. GET ON OUT OF HERE, PHILIP HALL.
Ages 9-12. 238

Gross, Alan. WHAT IF THE TEACHER CALLS ON ME?
Ages 5-7. 250

Hurwitz, Johanna. SUPERDUPER TEDDY.
Ages 4-7. 318

Matthews, Ellen. THE TROUBLE WITH LESLIE.
Ages 8-11. 409

Simon, Norma. NOBODY'S PERFECT, NOT EVEN MY MOTHER.
Ages 4-8. 597

Smith, Anne Warren. BLUE DENIM BLUES.
Ages 12 and up. 607

Yep, Laurence Michael. KIND HEARTS AND GENTLE MONSTERS.
Ages 12 and up. 712

## Doubt. See: Identity, search for; Inferiority, feelings of

## Embarrassment. See: Embarrassment

## Feeling different. See also: Differences, human

Bargar, Gary W. WHAT HAPPENED TO MR. FORSTER?
Ages 10-13. 34

Barrett, John M. DANIEL DISCOVERS DANIEL.
Ages 7-9. 35

Belair, Richard L. DOUBLE TAKE.
Ages 13 and up. 44

Clifton, Lucille. SONORA BEAUTIFUL.
Ages 12-14. 123

Cohen, Barbara Nash. FAT JACK.
Ages 11 and up. 125

Cohen, Miriam. SO WHAT?
Ages 4-7. 129

Conford, Ellen. THE REVENGE OF THE INCREDIBLE DR. RANCID AND HIS YOUTHFUL ASSISTANT, JEFFREY.
Ages 10-12. 137

Dixon, Jeanne. LADY CAT LOST.
Ages 10-12. 164

Gilson, Jamie. DO BANANAS CHEW GUM?
Ages 9-11. 216

Greenberg, Jan. A SEASON IN-BETWEEN.
Ages 11-13. 237

Hermes, Patricia. WHAT IF THEY KNEW?
Ages 9-11. 285

Litchfield, Ada Bassett. WORDS IN OUR HANDS.
Ages 7-9. 378

McKay, Robert W. THE RUNNING BACK.
Ages 12-14. 392

Morgenroth, Barbara. TRAMPS LIKE US.
Ages 12 and up. 452

Paterson, Katherine Womeldorf. JACOB HAVE I LOVED.
Ages 12 and up. 485

Payne, Sherry Neuwirth. A CONTEST.
Ages 8-10. 486

Peyton, K. M., pseud. MARION'S ANGELS.
Ages 11-14. 499

Philips, Barbara. DON'T CALL ME FATSO.
Ages 5-9. 507

Pollock, Penny. KEEPING IT SECRET.
Ages 9-12. 515

Stanek, Muriel Novella. GROWL WHEN YOU SAY R.
Ages 4-8. 620

Stren, Patti. THERE'S A RAINBOW IN MY CLOSET.
Ages 8-10. 638

Zelonky, Joy. I CAN'T ALWAYS HEAR YOU.
Ages 7-10. 718

## Hatred. See: Hatred

## Pride/False pride. See: Pride/False pride

## Respect

Ames, Mildred. NICKY AND THE JOYOUS NOISE.
Ages 9-12. 14

Bunting, Anne Evelyn. THE WAITING GAME.
Ages 10 and up. 91

## Sex (cont.)

Gerber, Merrill Joan. PLEASE DON'T KISS ME NOW.
  Ages 13 and up. 206
Harlan, Elizabeth. FOOTFALLS.
  Ages 12-14. 265
Hunter, Kristin Eggleston. LOU IN THE LIMELIGHT.
  Ages 14 and up. 312
Mazer, Norma Fox. UP IN SETH'S ROOM.
  Ages 13 and up. 415
Okimoto, Jean Davies. NORMAN SCHNURMAN, AVERAGE PERSON.
  Ages 10-12. 471

### Extramarital

Lorimar, Lawrence T. SECRETS.
  Ages 12 and up. 382
Sallis, Susan Diana. A TIME FOR EVERYTHING.
  Ages 13 and up. 569

### Premarital. See also: Unwed father; Unwed mother

Adler, Carole Schwerdtfeger. DOWN BY THE RIVER.
  Ages 12 and up. 4
Banks, Lynne Reid. THE WRITING ON THE WALL.
  Ages 12 and up. 33
Elfman, Blossom. THE BUTTERFLY GIRL.
  Ages 13 and up. 180
Lifton, Betty Jean. I'M STILL ME.
  Ages 12 and up. 372
Lorimar, Lawrence T. SECRETS.
  Ages 12 and up. 382
Posner, Grace. IN MY SISTER'S EYES.
  Ages 12 and up. 516
Strasser, Todd. ANGEL DUST BLUES.
  Ages 14 and up. 635
Zalben, Jane Breskin. MAYBE IT WILL RAIN TOMORROW.
  Ages 12 and up. 716

## Sex Role

See: Gender role identity

## Sexism

See: Prejudice: sexual

## Sexual Assault

See also: Rape; Violence
Peck, Robert Newton. CLUNIE.
  Ages 12 and up. 491

## Sexuality

See: Gender role identity; Prejudice: sexual

## Shame

See also: Embarrassment; Enuresis; Guilt, feelings of
Rodowsky, Colby F. A SUMMER'S WORTH OF SHAME.
  Ages 12-14. 548

## Sharing/Not Sharing

See also: Cooperation; Egocentrism; Play
Benson, Ellen. PHILIP'S LITTLE SISTER.
  Ages 5-8. 46
Corey, Dorothy. EVERYBODY TAKES TURNS.
  Ages 2-6. 140
Corey, Dorothy. WE ALL SHARE.
  Ages 2-6. 141
Douglass, Barbara. SKATEBOARD SCRAMBLE.
  Ages 9-11. 170
Knox-Wagner, Elaine. THE OLDEST KID.
  Ages 4-8. 347
Lindgren, Barbro. SAM'S CAR.
  Ages 2-5. 374
Lindgren, Barbro. SAM'S COOKIE.
  Ages 2-5. 375
Lobel, Arnold. UNCLE ELEPHANT.
  Ages 4-7. 381

McDonnell, Christine. DON'T BE MAD, IVY.
  Ages 7-8. 391
Moncure, Jane Belk. KINDNESS.
  Ages 3-6. 445
Parsons, Elizabeth. THE UPSIDE-DOWN CAT.
  Ages 8-11. 482
Perl, Lila. PIEFACE AND DAPHNE.
  Ages 9-11. 494
Stanek, Muriel Novella. MY LITTLE FOSTER SISTER.
  Ages 4-8. 621
Stevens, Carla McBride. SARA AND THE PINCH.
  Ages 5-7. 628
Thomas, Karen. THE GOOD THING . . . THE BAD THING.
  Ages 3-7. 654
Vigna, Judith. THE HIDING HOUSE.
  Ages 4-7. 667
Zolotow, Charlotte Shapiro. ONE STEP, TWO . . .
  Ages 2-5. 724
Zolotow, Charlotte Shapiro. THE WHITE MARBLE.
  Ages 4-8. 725

## Shoplifting

See: Stealing: shoplifting

## Showing Off

See: Attention seeking; Boasting

## Shyness

See also: Inferiority, feelings of
Billington, Elizabeth T. PART-TIME BOY.
  Ages 8-10. 53
Carroll, Theodorus C. THE LOST CHRISTMAS STAR.
  Ages 7-9. 109
Hayes, Sheila. ME AND MY MONA LISA SMILE.
  Ages 11-13. 274
Hurwitz, Johanna. SUPERDUPER TEDDY.
  Ages 4-7. 318
Oppenheimer, Joan Letson. WORKING ON IT.
  Ages 11-13. 475
St. George, Judith. CALL ME MARGO.
  Ages 12-14. 567
Sharmat, Marjorie Weinman. SAY HELLO, VANESSA.
  Ages 4-7. 585
Smith, Anne Warren. BLUE DENIM BLUES.
  Ages 12 and up. 607

## Sibling

See also: Family

Death of. See: Death: of sibling

Half brother/Half sister
Vigna, Judith. DADDY'S NEW BABY.
  Ages 4-7. 666

Illness of. See: Illnesses: of sibling

Jealousy. See: Jealousy: sibling

Love for
Adler, Carole Schwerdtfeger. DOWN BY THE RIVER.
  Ages 12 and up. 4
Arthur, Catherine. MY SISTER'S SILENT WORLD.
  Ages 5-9. 25
Bates, Betty. THAT'S WHAT T.J. SAYS.
  Ages 9-11. 41
Grant, Eva. WILL I EVER BE OLDER?
  Ages 5-8. 231
Herzig, Alison Cragin and Jane Lawrence Mali. A SEASON OF SECRETS.
  Ages 11-13. 287
Hinton, Susan Eloise. TEX.
  Ages 11-15. 292
Leech, Jay and Zane Spencer. BRIGHT FAWN AND ME.
  Ages 4-8. 361

## Sibling (cont.)

LeRoy, Gen. BILLY'S SHOES.
Ages 5-8. 364
McCord, Jean. TURKEYLEGS THOMPSON.
Ages 11-14. 390
Posner, Grace. IN MY SISTER'S EYES.
Ages 12 and up. 516
Roy, Ronald. AVALANCHE!
Ages 10 and up. 555
Wartski, Maureen Crane. MY BROTHER IS SPECIAL.
Ages 10-12. 681
Wright, Betty Ren. MY SISTER IS DIFFERENT.
Ages 6-9. 711

### Middle

Blume, Judy Sussman. THE ONE IN THE MIDDLE IS THE GREEN KANGAROO.
Ages 7-9. 55

### New baby

Alexander, Martha G. WHEN THE NEW BABY COMES, I'M MOVING OUT.
Ages 2-5. 12
Blume, Judy Sussman. SUPERFUDGE.
Ages 8-10. 56
Galbraith, Kathryn Osebold. KATIE DID!
Ages 3-7. 198
Grant, Jan. OUR NEW BABY.
Ages 4-7. 232
Hamilton, Morse. BIG SISTERS ARE BAD WITCHES.
Ages 3-6. 258
Hamilton, Morse and Emily Hamilton. MY NAME IS EMILY.
Ages 3-6. 259
LeRoy, Gen. LUCKY STIFF!
Ages 4-7. 365
Lindgren, Astrid. I WANT A BROTHER OR SISTER.
Ages 3-7. 373
Lowry, Lois. ANASTASIA KRUPNIK.
Ages 9-11. 386
MacLachlan, Patricia. ARTHUR, FOR THE VERY FIRST TIME.
Ages 8-10. 393
Moncure, Jane Belk. MY BABY BROTHER NEEDS A FRIEND.
Ages 3-7. 447
Relf, Patricia. THAT NEW BABY!
Ages 4-7. 528
Ruffins, Reynold. MY BROTHER NEVER FEEDS THE CAT.
Ages 3-7. 559
Shane, Ruth and Harold Shane. THE NEW BABY.
Ages 2-6. 582
Smith, Janice Lee. THE MONSTER IN THE THIRD DRESSER DRAWER AND OTHER STORIES ABOUT ADAM JOSHUA.
Ages 5-8. 610
Vigna, Judith. DADDY'S NEW BABY.
Ages 4-7. 666
Weiss, Nicki. CHUCKIE.
Ages 3-6. 687
Winthrop, Elizabeth. I THINK HE LIKES ME.
Ages 3-7. 695

### Older. *See also: Baby-sitting*

Branscum, Robbie. FOR LOVE OF JODY.
Ages 9-12. 73
Girion, Barbara. MISTY AND ME.
Ages 10-12. 219
Hogan, Paula Z. SOMETIMES I GET SO MAD.
Ages 5-8. 298
Knox-Wagner, Elaine. THE OLDEST KID.
Ages 4-8. 347
McCaffrey, Mary. MY BROTHER ANGE.
Ages 8-11. 389
Matthews, Ellen. THE TROUBLE WITH LESLIE.
Ages 8-11. 409

Naylor, Phyllis Reynolds. ALL BECAUSE I'M OLDER.
Ages 7-9. 462

### Oldest. *See also: Baby-sitting*

Byars, Betsy Cromer. THE NIGHT SWIMMERS.
Ages 10-12. 98
Stolz, Mary Slattery. WHAT TIME OF NIGHT IS IT?
Ages 11-14. 631

**Rejection.** *See: Rejection: sibling*

**Relationships.** *See also: Family: relationships*
Arrick, Fran. TUNNEL VISION.
Ages 12 and up. 24
Blume, Judy Sussman. SUPERFUDGE.
Ages 8-10. 56
Bond, Felicia. POINSETTIA & HER FAMILY.
Ages 4-7. 59
Bridgers, Sue Ellen. NOTES FOR ANOTHER LIFE.
Ages 12 and up. 75
Bunting, Anne Evelyn. THE EMPTY WINDOW.
Ages 8-12. 89
Cameron, Ann. THE STORIES JULIAN TELLS.
Ages 7-9. 104
Carris, Joan Davenport. WHEN THE BOYS RAN THE HOUSE.
Ages 8-12. 108
Colman, Hila Crayder. THE FAMILY TRAP.
Ages 12 and up. 134
De Roo, Anne Louise. SCRUB FIRE.
Ages 9-12. 162
Greene, Constance Clarke. DOUBLE-DARE O'TOOLE.
Ages 9-11. 240
Harris, Mark Jonathan. WITH A WAVE OF THE WAND.
Ages 9-12. 267
Hassler, Jon Francis. JEMMY.
Ages 11 and up. 270
Hazen, Barbara Shook. IF IT WEREN'T FOR BENJAMIN (I'D ALWAYS GET TO LICK THE ICING SPOON).
Ages 3-7. 276
Hoban, Lillian Aberman. ARTHUR'S FUNNY MONEY.
Ages 6-8. 294
Hopkins, Lee Bennett. MAMA & HER BOYS.
Ages 8-11. 303
Houston, James Archibald. LONG CLAWS: AN ARCTIC ADVENTURE.
Ages 9-11. 305
Hurwitz, Johanna. SUPERDUPER TEDDY.
Ages 4-7. 318
Inkiow, Dimiter. ME AND CLARA AND CASIMER THE CAT.
Ages 7-9. 321
Jones, Penelope. HOLDING TOGETHER.
Ages 9-11. 331
Keller, Holly. CROMWELL'S GLASSES.
Ages 3-6. 337
Kroll, Steven. FRIDAY THE 13TH.
Ages 4-7. 353
Miklowitz, Gloria D. THE LOVE BOMBERS.
Ages 12 and up. 422
Miner, Jane Claypool. MIRACLE OF TIME: ADOPTING A SISTER.
Ages 11 and up. 430
Osborn, Lois. MY BROTHER IS AFRAID OF JUST ABOUT EVERYTHING.
Ages 4-7. 476
Pascal, Francine. THE HAND-ME-DOWN KID.
Ages 10-13. 483
Pearson, Susan. MOLLY MOVES OUT.
Ages 5-8. 487
Peterson, Jeanne Whitehouse. THAT IS THAT.
Ages 5-8. 497
Pierik, Robert. ROOKFLEAS IN THE CELLAR.
Ages 8-13. 512
Reece, Colleen L. THE OUTSIDER.
Ages 12 and up. 527

## Surgery (cont.)

Hogan, Paula Z. and Kirk Hogan. THE HOSPITAL SCARES ME.
Ages 3-8. 300
Richter, Elizabeth. THE TEENAGE HOSPITAL EXPERIENCE: YOU CAN HANDLE IT!
Ages 12 and up. 532

### Tonsillectomy

Anderson, Penny S. THE OPERATION.
Ages 3-8. 17

## Sutures

See also: *Doctor, going to; Surgery*
Marino, Barbara Pavis. ERIC NEEDS STITCHES.
Ages 4-10. 403

## Sympathy

See: *Empathy*

# T

## Talents

See also: *Education: special*
Asher, Sandra Fenichel. JUST LIKE JENNY.
Ages 10-12. 27
Corcoran, Barbara. CHILD OF THE MORNING.
Ages 10 and up. 139
Cunningham, Julia Woolfolk. THE SILENT VOICE.
Ages 11-14. 146
Hest, Amy. MAYBE NEXT YEAR . . .
Ages 9-12. 288
Hlibok, Bruce. SILENT DANCER.
Ages 8-11. 293
Landis, James David. THE SISTERS IMPOSSIBLE.
Ages 9-11. 355
Robison, Nancy Louise. BALLET MAGIC.
Ages 9-11. 541
Sachs, Marilyn. A SUMMER'S LEASE.
Ages 11-14. 566

### Artistic

Ames, Mildred. NICKY AND THE JOYOUS NOISE.
Ages 9-12. 14
Bulla, Clyde Robert. DANIEL'S DUCK.
Ages 5-8. 85
Cohen, Miriam. NO GOOD IN ART.
Ages 5-7. 128
Culin, Charlotte. CAGES OF GLASS, FLOWERS OF TIME.
Ages 12 and up. 145
Hassler, Jon Francis. JEMMY.
Ages 11 and up. 270
Love, Sandra Weller. CROSSING OVER.
Ages 10-12. 383
Magorian, Michelle. GOOD NIGHT, MR. TOM.
Ages 11 and up. 401
Stren, Patti. THERE'S A RAINBOW IN MY CLOSET.
Ages 8-10. 638
Tolan, Stephanie S. THE LAST OF EDEN.
Ages 12 and up. 659

### Athletic

Donovan, Pete. CAROL JOHNSTON: THE ONE-ARMED GYMNAST.
Ages 8-12. 169
Dygard, Thomas J. SOCCER DUEL.
Ages 11-14. 179
Geibel, James. THE BLOND BROTHER.
Ages 12 and up. 205
Hallman, Ruth. BREAKAWAY.
Ages 12 and up. 257
Klein, Monica. BACKYARD BASKETBALL SUPERSTAR.
Ages 6-8. 345
Morton, Jane. RUNNING SCARED.
Ages 10-14. 455

Myers, Walter Dean. HOOPS.
Ages 12 and up. 459
Platt, Kin. BROGG'S BRAIN.
Ages 12 and up. 514
Slote, Alfred. LOVE AND TENNIS.
Ages 12-14. 605
Smith, Doris Buchanan. LAST WAS LLOYD.
Ages 8-11. 608
Van Steenwyk, Elizabeth Ann. RIVALS ON ICE.
Ages 9-11. 664
Wiseman, Bernard. THE LUCKY RUNNER.
Ages 6-9. 699

### Musical

Ames, Mildred. NICKY AND THE JOYOUS NOISE.
Ages 9-12. 14
Bates, Betty. MY MOM, THE MONEY NUT.
Ages 10-12. 39
Bridgers, Sue Ellen. NOTES FOR ANOTHER LIFE.
Ages 12 and up. 75
Delton, Judy. I NEVER WIN!
Ages 4-7. 154
Greenwald, Sheila. GIVE US A GREAT BIG SMILE, ROSY COLE.
Ages 8-10. 246
Hunter, Kristin Eggleston. LOU IN THE LIMELIGHT.
Ages 14 and up. 312
Peyton, K. M., pseud. MARION'S ANGELS.
Ages 11-14. 499
Slote, Alfred. RABBIT EARS.
Ages 10-12. 606
Smith, Anne Warren. BLUE DENIM BLUES.
Ages 12 and up. 607
Thomas, Ianthe. WILLIE BLOWS A MEAN HORN.
Ages 5-8. 652
Voigt, Cynthia. DICEY'S SONG.
Ages 11 and up. 671

## Teachers

See: *School: pupil-teacher relationships*

## Teasing

See also: *Aggression; Bully; Name-calling; Practical jokes/pranks*
Bottner, Barbara. MEAN MAXINE.
Ages 4-6. 67
Cohen, Barbara Nash. FAT JACK.
Ages 11 and up. 125
De Paola, Thomas Anthony. OLIVER BUTTON IS A SISSY.
Ages 4-7. 161
Flournoy, Valerie. THE TWINS STRIKE BACK.
Ages 6-8. 191
Giff, Patricia Reilly. THE GIRL WHO KNEW IT ALL.
Ages 8-10. 212
Gould, Marilyn. GOLDEN DAFFODILS.
Ages 8-12. 223
Grant, Eva. I HATE MY NAME.
Ages 5-8. 230
Hogan, Paula Z. I HATE BOYS  I HATE GIRLS.
Ages 5-8. 296
Hurwitz, Johanna. ALDO APPLESAUCE.
Ages 7-9. 316
Keller, Holly. CROMWELL'S GLASSES.
Ages 3-6. 337
Lexau, Joan M. I HATE RED ROVER.
Ages 6-8. 371
Pascal, Francine. THE HAND-ME-DOWN KID.
Ages 10-13. 483
Peck, Robert Newton. CLUNIE.
Ages 12 and up. 491
Stanek, Muriel Novella. GROWL WHEN YOU SAY R.
Ages 4-8. 620

## Temper

See: *Aggression; Anger; Violence*

## Unwed Mother (cont.)

Lindsay, Jeanne Warren. DO I HAVE A DADDY? A
STORY ABOUT A SINGLE-PARENT CHILD.
Ages 4-8. 376
Sebestyen, Ouida. FAR FROM HOME.
Ages 12 and up. 579
Strang, Celia. THIS CHILD IS MINE.
Ages 11-14. 634

# V

## Vacuum Cleaner

See: *Fear: of vacuum cleaner*

## Values/Valuing

See also: *Differences, human; Identification with others*

### Aesthetic

Ames, Mildred. NICKY AND THE JOYOUS NOISE.
Ages 9-12. 14
Fisher, Aileen Lucia. I STOOD UPON A
MOUNTAIN.
Ages 4-8. 189

### Materialistic

Bates, Betty. MY MOM, THE MONEY NUT.
Ages 10-12. 39
Bulla, Clyde Robert. POOR BOY, RICH BOY.
Ages 5-8. 87

### Moral/Ethical

Adler, Carole Schwerdtfeger. IN OUR HOUSE
SCOTT IS MY BROTHER.
Ages 10-13. 5
Asher, Sandra Fenichel. SUMMER BEGINS.
Ages 10-13. 28
Bawden, Nina Mary Kark. THE ROBBERS.
Ages 9-12. 43
Butterworth, William Edmund. LEROY AND THE
OLD MAN.
Ages 12 and up. 93
Dygard, Thomas J. POINT SPREAD.
Ages 10 and up. 178
Hentoff, Nat. DOES THIS SCHOOL HAVE CAPITAL
PUNISHMENT?
Ages 11 and up. 282
Jones, Toeckey. GO WELL, STAY WELL.
Ages 12 and up. 334
Korschunow, Irina. WHO KILLED CHRISTOPHER?
Ages 12 and up. 350
Mazer, Norma Fox. UP IN SETH'S ROOM.
Ages 13 and up. 415
Meyer, Carolyn. THE CENTER: FROM A TROUBLED
PAST TO A NEW LIFE.
Ages 13 and up. 420
Moeri, Louise. FIRST THE EGG.
Ages 12 and up. 438
Morgenroth, Barbara. TRAMPS LIKE US.
Ages 12 and up. 452
Murphy, Jim. DEATH RUN.
Ages 11 and up. 457
Naylor, Phyllis Reynolds. A STRING OF CHANCES.
Ages 12 and up. 464
Pascal, Francine. MY FIRST LOVE & OTHER
DISASTERS.
Ages 12 and up. 484
Pevsner, Stella. CUTE IS A FOUR-LETTER WORD.
Ages 10-12. 498
Phipson, Joan Nash, pseud. FLY FREE.
Ages 11 and up. 508
Roth, David. THE HERMIT OF FOG HOLLOW
STATION.
Ages 9-12. 553
Sebestyen, Ouida. WORDS BY HEART.
Ages 10-13. 580
Slote, Alfred. LOVE AND TENNIS.
Ages 12-14. 605

Winthrop, Elizabeth. MIRANDA IN THE MIDDLE.
Ages 9-13. 697
Wood, Phyllis Anderson. THIS TIME COUNT ME IN.
Ages 12 and up. 706

## Vandalism

See also: *Crime/Criminals; Delinquency, juvenile*
Addy, Sharon. WE DIDN'T MEAN TO.
Ages 8-10. 2

## Vanity

See: *Pride/False pride*

## Vietnam

See also: *Immigrants; Refugees*
Bennett, Jack. THE VOYAGE OF THE LUCKY
DRAGON.
Ages 11 and up. 45
Wartski, Maureen Crane. A BOAT TO NOWHERE.
Ages 9-12. 678
Wartski, Maureen Crane. A LONG WAY FROM
HOME.
Ages 11-13. 680
Wolkoff, Judie. WHERE THE ELF KING SINGS.
Ages 12 and up. 704

## Violence

See also: *Aggression; Cruelty; Death: murder;
Delinquency, juvenile; Rape; Sexual assault; War*
Ashley, Bernard. A KIND OF WILD JUSTICE.
Ages 12 and up. 30
Clifford, Ethel Rosenberg. THE KILLER SWAN.
Ages 10-12. 120
Geibel, James. THE BLOND BROTHER.
Ages 12 and up. 205
Harrah, Michael. FIRST OFFENDER.
Ages 11-13. 266
Levoy, Myron. A SHADOW LIKE A LEOPARD.
Ages 12 and up. 369
Maruki, Toshi. HIROSHIMA NO PIKA.
Ages 7 and up. 406
Mauser, Pat Rhoads. A BUNDLE OF STICKS.
Ages 10-12. 410
Mazer, Harry. THE LAST MISSION.
Ages 12-14. 413
Murphy, Jim. DEATH RUN.
Ages 11 and up. 457
Myers, Walter Dean. HOOPS.
Ages 12 and up. 459
Riley, Jocelyn. ONLY MY MOUTH IS SMILING.
Ages 12-14. 533
Thrasher, Crystal Faye. BETWEEN DARK AND
DAYLIGHT.
Ages 11-13. 658
Wolkoff, Judie. WHERE THE ELF KING SINGS.
Ages 12 and up. 704

## Visiting

Brooks, Jerome. THE BIG DIPPER MARATHON.
Ages 11-14. 77
Caines, Jeannette Franklin. WINDOW WISHING.
Ages 4-7. 100
Greenfield, Eloise. DARLENE.
Ages 5-7. 243
Harris, Robin. HELLO KITTY SLEEPS OVER.
Ages 2-5. 269
Hickman, Janet. THE THUNDER-PUP.
Ages 9-11. 289
Hurd, Edith Thacher. I DANCE IN MY RED
PAJAMAS.
Ages 3-6. 314
Pfeffer, Susan Beth. AWFUL EVELINA.
Ages 6-8. 501
Truss, Jan. BIRD AT THE WINDOW.
Ages 13 and up. 661

## Visual Impairment

**See also:** *Blindness; Glasses, wearing of*
Leggett, Linda Rodgers and Linda Gambee
Andrews. THE ROSE-COLORED GLASSES:
MELANIE ADJUSTS TO POOR VISION.
Ages 8-11. 362

## W

## War

**See also:** *Violence*
Bennett, Jack. THE VOYAGE OF THE LUCKY
DRAGON.
Ages 11 and up. 45
Brochmann, Elizabeth. WHAT'S THE MATTER,
GIRL?
Ages 12 and up. 76
Ellis, Ella Thorp. SLEEPWALKER'S MOON.
Ages 12 and up. 181
Kherdian, David. THE ROAD FROM HOME: THE
STORY OF AN ARMENIAN GIRL.
Ages 12 and up. 340
Magorian, Michelle. GOOD NIGHT, MR. TOM.
Ages 11 and up. 401
Maruki, Toshi. HIROSHIMA NO PIKA.
Ages 7 and up. 406
Mazer, Harry. THE LAST MISSION.
Ages 12-14. 413
Ofek, Uriel. SMOKE OVER GOLAN.
Ages 9-13. 468
Sallis, Susan Diana. A TIME FOR EVERYTHING.
Ages 13 and up. 569

## War Orphan

**See:** *Orphan*

## Wealth/Wealthy

**See also:** *Differences, human*
Strasser, Todd. ANGEL DUST BLUES.
Ages 14 and up. 635

## Weight Control

**See also:** *Appearance*

**Overweight**
Bottner, Barbara. DUMB OLD CASEY IS A FAT
TREE.
Ages 6-9. 66
Cohen, Barbara Nash. FAT JACK.
Ages 11 and up. 125
Cohen, Barbara Nash. THE INNKEEPER'S
DAUGHTER.
Ages 11-14. 126
DeClements, Barthe. NOTHING'S FAIR IN FIFTH
GRADE.
Ages 8-11. 152
Greenberg, Jan. THE PIG-OUT BLUES.
Ages 12 and up. 236
Perl, Lila. HEY, REMEMBER FAT GLENDA?
Ages 9-12. 493
Philips, Barbara. DON'T CALL ME FATSO.
Ages 5-9. 507
Smith, Doris Buchanan. LAST WAS LLOYD.
Ages 8-11. 608
Smith, Robert Kimmel. JELLY BELLY.
Ages 10-12. 614

## Wetting

**See:** *Enuresis*

## Wheelchair, Dependence on

**See also:** *Amputee; Muscular dystrophy; Paraplegia*

Colman, Hila Crayder. ACCIDENT.
Ages 11 and up. 132
Greenfield, Eloise. DARLENE.
Ages 5-7. 243
Greenfield, Eloise and Alesia Revis. ALESIA.
Ages 10-14. 245
Henriod, Lorraine. GRANDMA'S WHEELCHAIR.
Ages 3-7. 281
Jacobs, Dee. LAURA'S GIFT.
Ages 10-13. 328
Lasker, Joe. NICK JOINS IN.
Ages 5-8. 358
Miner, Jane Claypool. NEW BEGINNING: AN
ATHLETE IS PARALYZED.
Ages 11 and up. 433
Payne, Sherry Neuwirth. A CONTEST.
Ages 8-10. 486
Pieper, Elizabeth. A SCHOOL FOR TOMMY.
Ages 5-8. 510
Rabe, Berniece Louise. THE BALANCING GIRL.
Ages 5-7. 522
Redpath, Ann. JIM BOEN: A MAN OF OPPOSITES.
Ages 9 and up. 526
Robinet, Harriette Gillem. RIDE THE RED CYCLE.
Ages 7-11. 537
Sallis, Susan Diana. ONLY LOVE.
Ages 12 and up. 568
Savitz, Harriet May. RUN, DON'T WALK.
Ages 12 and up. 572
Sullivan, Mary Beth and Alan J. Brightman and Joseph
Blatt. FEELING FREE.
Ages 9 and up. 640

## Wishes

**See also:** *Daydreaming; Fantasy formation; Magical
thinking*
Collins, David R. IF I COULD, I WOULD.
Ages 6-8. 131
Dolan, Sheila. THE WISHING BOTTLE.
Ages 7-9. 167
Waber, Bernard. YOU'RE A LITTLE KID WITH A
BIG HEART.
Ages 5-7. 673

## Withdrawal

**See:** *Reality, escaping*

## Womanliness

**See:** *Gender role identity: female*

## Work, Attitude Toward

**See also:** *Careers: planning; Job; Responsibility*
Naylor, Phyliss Reynolds. EDDIE, INCORPORATED.
Ages 9-11 463
Neigoff, Mike. IT WILL NEVER BE THE SAME
AGAIN.
Ages 12-14 465
Strang, Celia. FOSTER MARY.
Ages 10-13 633

## Working Mother

**See:** *Parent/Parents: mother working outside home*

## Worries

**See:** *Anxiety; Fear*

## Y

## Youngest Child

**See:** *Sibling: youngest*

# AUTHOR INDEX

To locate a book through the
Author Index, find the
author's name; titles are listed
alphabetically under each
author's name. Numbers refer
to annotation numbers.

# Q

**Quackenbush, Robert M.**
FIRST GRADE JITTERS. 521

# R

**Rabe, Berniece Louise**
BALANCING GIRL, THE. 522

**Rabinowich, Ellen**
ROCK FEVER. 523

**Radley, Gail**
NOTHING STAYS THE SAME FOREVER. 524

**Reader, Dennis J.**
COMING BACK ALIVE. 525

**Redpath, Ann**
JIM BOEN: A MAN OF OPPOSITES. 526

**Reece, Colleen L.**
OUTSIDER, THE. 527

**Relf, Patricia**
THAT NEW BABY! 528

**Reuter, Margaret**
MY MOTHER IS BLIND. 529
YOU CAN DEPEND ON ME. 530

**Revis, Alesia, joint author**
*See: Greenfield, Eloise*

**Richter, Alice and Laura Joffe Numeroff**
YOU CAN'T PUT BRACES ON SPACES. 531

**Richter, Elizabeth**
TEENAGE HOSPITAL EXPERIENCE, THE: YOU CAN
  HANDLE IT! 532

**Riley, Jocelyn**
ONLY MY MOUTH IS SMILING. 533

**Rinaldi, Ann**
PROMISES ARE FOR KEEPING. 534
TERM PAPER. 535

**Riskind, Mary L.**
APPLE IS MY SIGN. 536

**Robinet, Harriette Gillem**
RIDE THE RED CYCLE. 537

**Robinson, Barbara Webb**
TEMPORARY TIMES, TEMPORARY PLACES. 538

**Robinson, Nancy Konheim**
WENDY AND THE BULLIES. 539

**Robison, Deborah**
NO ELEPHANTS ALLOWED. 540

**Robison, Nancy Louise**
BALLET MAGIC. 541

**Roche, Patricia K.**
GOOD-BYE, ARNOLD. 542

**Rockwell, Anne F. and Harlow Rockwell**
CAN I HELP? 543
I LOVE MY PETS. 544
MY BARBER. 545
SICK IN BED. 546

**Rockwell, Harlow, joint author**
*See: Rockwell, Anne F.*

**Rodowsky, Colby F.**
H. MY NAME IS HENLEY. 547
SUMMER'S WORTH OF SHAME, A. 548

**Rosen, Lillian D.**
JUST LIKE EVERYBODY ELSE. 549

**Rosenberg, Ethel Clifford**
*See: Clifford, Ethel Rosenberg*

**Ross, Pat**
M AND M AND THE BIG BAG. 550
MEET M AND M. 551
MOLLY AND THE SLOW TEETH. 552

**Roth, David**
HERMIT OF FOG HOLLOW STATION, THE. 553

**Rounds, Glen Harold**
BLIND OUTLAW. 554

**Roy, Ron**
*See: Roy, Ronald*

**Roy, Ronald**
AVALANCHE! 555
FRANKIE IS STAYING BACK. 556

**Rubin, Daniel, joint author**
*See: Hobby, Janice Hale*

**Rubin, Gabrielle, joint author**
*See: Hobby, Janice Hale*

**Ruby, Lois**
TWO TRUTHS IN MY POCKET. 557
WHAT DO YOU DO IN QUICKSAND? 558

**Ruffins, Reynold**
MY BROTHER NEVER FEEDS THE CAT. 559

**Ruffins, Reynold, joint author**
*See: Sarnoff, Jane*

**Ruthstrom, Dorotha**
BIG KITE CONTEST, THE. 560

# S

**Sachs, Elizabeth-Ann**
JUST LIKE ALWAYS. 561

**Sachs, Marilyn**
BEACH TOWELS. 562
BUS RIDE. 563
CLASS PICTURES. 564
HELLO . . . WRONG NUMBER. 565
SUMMER'S LEASE, A. 566

**St. George, Judith**
CALL ME MARGO. 567

**Sallis, Susan Diana**
ONLY LOVE. 568
TIME FOR EVERYTHING, A. 569

**Sargent, Sarah**
SECRET LIES. 570

**Sarnoff, Jane and Reynold Ruffins**
THAT'S NOT FAIR. 571

**Savitz, Harriet May**
RUN, DON'T WALK. 572

**Schick, Eleanor Grossman**
HOME ALONE. 573
JOEY ON HIS OWN. 574

**Schotter, Roni**
MATTER OF TIME, A. 575

**Schubert, Dieter, joint author**
*See: Schubert, Ingrid*

**Schubert, Ingrid and Dieter Schubert**
THERE'S A CROCODILE UNDER MY BED! 576

**Schuchman, Joan**
TWO PLACES TO SLEEP. 577

**Schultz, Gwendolyn**
BLUE VALENTINE, THE. 578

**Sebestyen, Ouida**
FAR FROM HOME. 579
WORDS BY HEART. 580

Terris, Susan Dubinsky
NO SCARLET RIBBONS. 647

Tester, Sylvia Root
SANDY'S NEW HOME. 648
SOMETIMES I'M AFRAID. 649
WE LAUGHED A LOT, MY FIRST DAY OF SCHOOL. 650

Thomas, Ianthe
HI, MRS. MALLORY! 651
WILLIE BLOWS A MEAN HORN. 652

Thomas, Jane Resh
COMEBACK DOG, THE. 653

Thomas, Karen
GOOD THING, THE . . . THE BAD THING. 654

Thomas, William E.
NEW BOY IS BLIND, THE. 655

Thompson, Jean, pseud.
DON'T FORGET MICHAEL. 656

Thompson, Paul
HITCHHIKERS, THE. 657

Thrasher, Crystal Faye
BETWEEN DARK AND DAYLIGHT. 658

Tolan, Stephanie S.
LAST OF EDEN, THE. 659

Townsend, Maryann and Ronnie Stern
POP'S SECRET. 660

Truss, Jan
BIRD AT THE WINDOW. 661

# U

Udry, Janice May
THUMP AND PLUNK. 662

# V

Van Leeuwen, Jean
SEEMS LIKE THIS ROAD GOES ON FOREVER. 663

Van Steenwyk, Elizabeth Ann
RIVALS ON ICE. 664

Veglahn, Nancy Crary
FELLOWSHIP OF THE SEVEN STARS. 665

Vigna, Judith
DADDY'S NEW BABY. 666
HIDING HOUSE, THE. 667
SHE'S NOT MY REAL MOTHER. 668

Vogel, Ilse-Margret
FAREWELL, AUNT ISABELL. 669
MY SUMMER BROTHER. 670

Voigt, Cynthia
DICEY'S SONG. 671
HOMECOMING. 672

# W

Waber, Bernard
YOU'RE A LITTLE KID WITH A BIG HEART. 673

Wade, Anne
PROMISE IS FOR KEEPING, A. 674

Wallace, Bill
DOG CALLED KITTY, A. 675

Wallace-Brodeur, Ruth
KENTON YEAR, THE. 676
ONE APRIL VACATION. 677

Wartski, Maureen Crane
BOAT TO NOWHERE, A. 678
LAKE IS ON FIRE, THE. 679
LONG WAY FROM HOME, A. 680
MY BROTHER IS SPECIAL. 681

Watanabe, Shigeo
GET SET! GO! 682
HOW DO I PUT IT ON? 683
I CAN RIDE IT! 684

Waterton, Betty Marie
SALMON FOR SIMON, A. 685

Weiman, Eiveen
IT TAKES BRAINS. 686

Weiss, Nicki
CHUCKIE. 687
WAITING. 688

Wells, Rosemary
TIMOTHY GOES TO SCHOOL. 689

Whelan, Gloria
TIME TO KEEP SILENT, A. 690

Whitehouse, Jeanne
See: Peterson, Jeanne Whitehouse

Wilkinson, Brenda Scott
LUDELL'S NEW YORK TIME. 691

Williams, Barbara Wright
SO WHAT IF I'M A SORE LOSER? 692
WHATEVER HAPPENED TO BEVERLY BIGLER'S
BIRTHDAY? 693

Willoughby, Elaine Macmann
BORIS AND THE MONSTERS. 694

Winthrop, Elizabeth
I THINK HE LIKES ME. 695
MARATHON MIRANDA. 696
MIRANDA IN THE MIDDLE. 697
SLOPPY KISSES. 698

Wiseman, Bernard
LUCKY RUNNER, THE. 699

Wittman, Sally Anne Christensen
WONDERFUL MRS. TRUMBLY, THE. 700

Wolde, Gunilla
BETSY AND PETER ARE DIFFERENT. 701
BETSY AND THE VACUUM CLEANER. 702

Wolkoff, Judie
HAPPILY EVER AFTER . . . ALMOST. 703
WHERE THE ELF KING SINGS. 704

Wood, Phyllis Anderson
PASS ME A PINE CONE. 705
THIS TIME COUNT ME IN. 706

Wortis, Avi
PLACE CALLED UGLY, A. 707
SOMETIMES I THINK I HEAR MY NAME. 708

Wright, Betty Ren
I LIKE BEING ALONE. 709
MY NEW MOM AND ME. 710
MY SISTER IS DIFFERENT. 711

# Y

Yep, Laurence Michael
KIND HEARTS AND GENTLE MONSTERS. 712
SEA GLASS. 713

York, Carol Beach
REMEMBER ME WHEN I AM DEAD. 714

Young, Helen
WHAT DIFFERENCE DOES IT MAKE, DANNY? 715

## Z

# TITLE INDEX

To locate a book through the Title Index, find the title of the book; titles are listed alphabetically. Numbers refer to annotation numbers.

# A

ABOUT DAVID
Pfeffer, Susan Beth. 500

ACCIDENT
Colman, Hila Crayder. 132

ADOPTED ONE, THE: AN OPEN FAMILY BOOK FOR PARENTS AND CHILDREN TOGETHER
Stein, Sara Bonnett. 625

ALDO APPLESAUCE
Hurwitz, Johanna. 316

ALESIA
Greenfield, Eloise and Alesia Revis. 245

AL(EXANDRA) THE GREAT
Greene, Constance Clarke. 239

ALEX'S BED
Dickinson, Mary. 163

ALFIE GETS IN FIRST
Hughes, Shirley. 309

ALFRED SUMMER, THE
Slepian, Jan. 603

ALICE WITH GOLDEN HAIR
Hull, Eleanor Means. 311

ALL ALONE
Henkes, Kevin. 280

ALL BECAUSE I'M OLDER
Naylor, Phyllis Reynolds. 462

ALL KINDS OF PRICKLES
Morgan, Alison Mary. 450

ALL TOGETHER NOW
Bridgers, Sue Ellen. 74

ALLISON'S GRANDFATHER
Peavy, Linda S. 489

ALMOST A HERO
Bulla, Clyde Robert. 84

AMY GOES FISHING
Marzollo, Jean. 407

ANASTASIA AGAIN!
Lowry, Lois. 384

ANASTASIA AT YOUR SERVICE
Lowry, Lois. 385

ANASTASIA KRUPNIK
Lowry, Lois. 386

ANGEL DUST BLUES
Strasser, Todd. 635

ANGIE AND ME
Jones, Rebecca Castaldi. 333

ANIMAL, THE VEGETABLE, AND JOHN D JONES, THE
Byars, Betsy Cromer. 95

ANNIE ON MY MIND
Garden, Nancy. 201

ANYTHING FOR A FRIEND
Conford, Ellen. 136

APE INSIDE ME, THE
Platt, Kin. 513

APPLE IS MY SIGN
Riskind, Mary L. 536

ARTHUR, FOR THE VERY FIRST TIME
MacLachlan, Patricia. 393

ARTHUR GOES TO CAMP
Brown, Marc Tolan. 79

ARTHUR'S EYES
Brown, Marc Tolan. 80

ARTHUR'S FUNNY MONEY
Hoban, Lillian Aberman. 294

AT THE BACK OF THE WOODS
Mills, Claudia. 426

AVALANCHE!
Roy, Ronald. 555

AWFUL EVELINA
Pfeffer, Susan Beth. 501

# B

BACKYARD BASKETBALL SUPERSTAR
Klein, Monica. 345

BAD DREAMS OF A GOOD GIRL, THE
Shreve, Susan Richards. 589

BALANCING GIRL, THE
Rabe, Berniece Louise. 522

BALLET MAGIC
Robison, Nancy Louise. 541

BARKLEY STREET SIX-PACK, THE
Shura, Mary Francis Craig. 592

BEACH TOWELS
Sachs, Marilyn. 562

BERT AND BARNEY
Delaney, Ned. 153

BEST MOM IN THE WORLD, THE
Delton, Judy and Elaine Knox-Wagner. 159

BEST WAY OUT, THE
Cheatham, Karyn Follis. 114

BETSY AND PETER ARE DIFFERENT
Wolde, Gunilla. 701

BETSY AND THE VACUUM CLEANER
Wolde, Gunilla. 702

BETWEEN DARK AND DAYLIGHT
Thrasher, Crystal Faye. 658

BIG DIPPER MARATHON, THE
Brooks, Jerome. 77

BIG KITE CONTEST, THE
Ruthstrom, Dorotha. 560

# PUBLISHERS/PRODUCERS DIRECTORY

# A

**Abingdon Press**
201 Eighth Avenue South
P.O. 801
Nashville TN 37202

**Addison-Wesley Publishing Company, Inc.**
Jacob Way
Reading MA 01867

**Albert Whitman & Company**
*See: Whitman (Albert) & Company*

**Alfred A. Knopf, Inc.**
*See: Random House, Inc.*

**American Guidance Service, Inc.**
Publishers' Building
Circle Pines MN 55014-1796

**André Deutsch**
*See: Dutton (E. P.) & Company, Inc.*

**Atheneum Publishers**
597 Fifth Avenue
New York NY 10017

**Atlantic Monthly Press, The**
*See: Little, Brown and Company*

**Avon Books**
959 Eighth Avenue
New York NY 10019

# B

**BFA Educational Media**
468 Park Avenue South
New York NY 10016

**Ballantine Books, Inc.**
201 East 50 Street
New York NY 10022

**Bantam Books, Inc.**
666 Fifth Avenue
New York NY 10019

**Beaufort Books, Inc.**
9 East 40 Street
New York NY 10016

**Bradbury Press, Inc.**
An affiliate of Macmillan, Inc.
866 Third Avenue
New York NY 10022

# C

**Carolrhoda Books, Inc.**
241 First Avenue North
Minneapolis MN 55401

**Chas. Franklin Press, The**
*See: Franklin (Chas.) Press, The*

**Charles Scribner's Sons**
*See: Scribner Book Companies, Inc., The*

**Children's Press, Inc.**
1224 West Van Buren Street
Chicago IL 60607

**Child's World, Inc., The**
P.O. Box 681
Elgin IL 60120

**Clarion Books**
*See: Houghton Mifflin Company*

**Collins (William) Publishers, Inc.**
*See: Putnam Publishing Group, The*

**Coward, McCann & Geoghegan, Inc.**
*See: Putnam Publishing Group, The*

**Creative Education, Inc.**
123 South Broad Street
Mankato MN 56001

**Crestwood House, Inc.**
Box 3427 Highway 66 South
Mankato MN 56001

**Crowell (Thomas Y.) Company, Inc.**
10 East 53 Street
New York NY 10022

**Crown Publishers, Inc.**
One Park Avenue
New York NY 10016

# D

**Delacorte Press**
*See: Dell Publishing Company, Inc.*

**Dell Publishing Company, Inc.**
245 East 47 Street
New York NY 10017

**Deutsch (André)**
*See: Dutton (E. P.) & Company, Inc.*

**Dial Press, Inc., The**
245 East 47 Street
New York NY 10017

**Disney (Walt) Productions**
Educational Film Division
500 South Buena Vista Avenue
Burbank CA 91503

**Dodd, Mead & Company, Inc.**
79 Madison Avenue
New York NY 10016

**Doubleday & Company, Inc.**
245 Park Avenue
New York NY 10017

**Dutton (E. P.) & Company, Inc.**
Two Park Avenue
New York NY 10016

# E

**EMC Publishing**
300 York Avenue
St. Paul MN 55101

**E. P. Dutton & Company, Inc.**
*See: Dutton (E. P.) & Company, Inc.*

**Educational Enrichment Corporation**
357 Adams Street
Bedford Hills NY 10507

# F

**Faber & Faber Ltd.**
39 Thompson Street
Winchester MA 01890

**Farrar, Straus & Giroux, Inc.**
19 Union Square West
New York NY 10003

**Fawcett Book Group**
1515 Broadway
New York NY 10036

**Fawcett World Library**
*See: Fawcett Book Group*

**Feminist Press, The**
Box 334
Old Westbury NY 11568

**Follett Publishing Company**
1010 West Washington Boulevard
Chicago IL 60607

**Four Winds Press**
*See: Scholastic Book Services*

**Franklin (Chas.) Press, The**
18409-90 Avenue West
Edmonds WA 98020

**Franklin Watts, Inc.**
*See: Watts (Franklin), Inc.*

**Frederick Warne & Company, Inc.**
*See: Viking Penguin, Inc.*

# G

**G. P. Putnam's Sons**
*See: Putnam Publishing Group, The*

**Garrard Publishing Company**
107 Cherry Street
New Canaan CT 06840

**Ginn and Company**
191 Spring Street
Lexington MA 02173

**Golden Press**
*See: Western Publishing Company, Inc.*

**Greenwillow Books**
*See: Morrow (William) & Company, Inc.*

**Grosset & Dunlap, Inc.**
*See: Putnam Publishing Group, The*

# H

**Harcourt Brace Jovanovich, Inc.**
757 Third Avenue
New York NY 10017

**Harper & Row, Publishers, Inc.**
10 East 53 Street
New York NY 10022

**Harvey House, Inc.**
20 Waterside Plaza
New York NY 10010

**Hastings House Publishers, Inc.**
10 East 40 Street
New York NY 10016

**Herald Press**
616 Walnut Avenue
Scottdale PA 15683

**Holiday House, Inc.**
18 East 53 Street
New York NY 10022

**Holt, Rinehart and Winston, Inc.**
383 Madison Avenue
New York NY 10017

**Houghton Mifflin Company**
Two Park Street
Boston MA 02107

**Human Sciences Press**
72 Fifth Avenue
New York NY 10011

# J

**J. B. Lippincott Company**
*See: Lippincott (J. B.) Company*

**Julian Messner, Inc.**
*See: Messner (Julian), Inc.*

# K

**Knopf (Alfred A.), Inc.**
*See: Random House, Inc.*

# L

**Learning Corporation of America**
1350 Avenue of the Americas
New York NY 10019

**Library of Congress**
National Library Service for
the Blind and Physically Handicapped
Washington DC 20540

**Lippincott (J. B.) Company**
10 East 53 Street
New York NY 10022

**Little, Brown and Company**
34 Beacon Street
Boston MA 02106

**Live Oaks Media**
Box 116
Selmer NY 10589

**Lodestar Books**
Two Park Avenue
New York NY 10016

**Lothrop, Lee & Shepard Company**
*See: Morrow (William) & Company, Inc.*

**Lyle Stuart, Inc.**
*See: Stuart (Lyle), Inc.*

# M

**McGraw-Hill Book Company**
1221 Avenue of the Americas
New York NY 10020

**Macmillan Publishing Company, Inc.**
866 Third Avenue
New York NY 10022

**Merrimack Publishers' Circle**
99 Main Street
Salem NH 03079

**Messner (Julian), Inc.**
1230 Avenue of the Americas
New York NY 10020

**Methuen, Inc.**
733 Third Avenue
New York NY 10017

**Miller-Brody Productions**
*See: Random House, Inc., School Division*

**Morning Glory Press**
6595 San Haroldo Way
Buena Park CA 90620

**Morrow (William) & Company, Inc.**
6 Henderson Drive
West Caldwell NJ 07006

# N

**New American Library**
1301 Avenue of the Americas
New York NY 10019

# O

**Oriel Press**
P.O. Box 12373
Portland OR 97212

**Oxford University Press**
*See: Merrimack Publishers' Circle*

# P

**Pantheon Books**
*See: Random House, Inc.*

**Penguin Books, Inc.**
*See: Viking Penguin, Inc.*

**Phillips (S. G.), Inc.**
305 West 86 Street
New York NY 10024

**Philomel Books**
*See: Putnam Publishing Group, The*

**Pied Piper Productions**
P.O. Box 320
Verdugo City CA 91046

**Pocket Books, Inc.**
1230 Avenue of the Americas
New York NY 10020

**Prentice-Hall, Inc.**
Englewood Cliffs NJ 07632

**Putnam Publishing Group, The**
200 Madison Avenue
New York NY 10016

**Putnam's (G. P.) Sons**
*See: Putnam Publishing Group, The*

# R

**Raintree Publishers, Inc.**
205 West Highland Avenue
Milwaukee WI 53203

**Raintree Publishers Ltd.**
*See: Raintree Publishers, Inc.*

**Random House, Inc.**
201 East 50 Street
New York NY 10022

**Random House, Inc.**
School Division
400 Hahn Road
Westminster MD 21157

# S

**S. G. Phillips, Inc.**
*See: Phillips (S. G.), Inc.*

**St. Martin's Press, Inc.**
175 Fifth Avenue
New York NY 10010

**Scholastic Book Services**
50 West 44 Street
New York NY 10036

**Scribner Book Companies, Inc., The**
597 Fifth Avenue
New York NY 10017

**Scribner's (Charles) Sons**
*See: Scribner Book Companies, Inc., The*

**Seabury Press, Inc.**
*See: Houghton Mifflin Company*

**Stuart (Lyle), Inc.**
120 Enterprise Avenue
Secaucus NJ 07094

# T

**Thomas Y. Crowell Company, Inc.**
*See: Crowell (Thomas Y.) Company, Inc.*

**Triad Publishing Company, Inc.**
P.O. Box 13096
Gainesville FL 32604

**Tundra Books of Northern New York**
Box 1030, 51 Clinton Street
Plattsburgh NY 12901

# V

**Viking Penguin, Inc.**
40 West 23 Street
New York NY 10010

**Viking Press, Inc., The**
*See: Viking Penguin, Inc.*

# W

**Walker and Company**
720 Fifth Avenue
New York NY 10019

**Walt Disney Productions**
*See: Disney (Walt) Productions*

**Warne (Frederick) & Company, Inc.**
*See: Viking Penguin, Inc.*

**Watts (Franklin), Inc.**
387 Park Avenue South
New York NY 10016

**Western Publishing Company, Inc.**
1220 Mound Avenue
Racine WI 53404

**Westminster Press, The**
925 Chestnut Street
Philadelphia PA 19107

**Weston Wood Studios, Inc.**
Weston CT 06883

**Westport Communications**
155 Post Road East
Westport CT 06880

**Whitman (Albert) & Company**
5747 Howard Street
Niles IL 60648

**William Collins Publishers, Inc.**
*See: Putnam Publishing Group, The*

**Wisconsin Department of Public Instruction**
P.O. Box 7841
Madison WI 53707

# X

**Xerox Publishing Division**
1200 High Ridge Road
Stamford CT 06905

# CUMULATIVE SUBJECT INDEX

To locate a book through the Cumulative Subject Index, find the desired subject; titles of relevant books from all three volumes of the *Bookfinder* are listed under each subject. Numbers refer to annotation numbers.

# A

## Abandonment

**See also:** *Loss: feelings of; Rejection; Separation from loved ones*
Broderick, Dorothy M. HANK.
Ages 11 and up. 122, Vol. 1
Buck, Pearl Sydenstricker. MATTHEW, MARK, LUKE, AND JOHN.
Ages 8-12. 130, Vol. 1
Byars, Betsy Cromer. THE HOUSE OF WINGS.
Ages 9-12. 156, Vol. 1
Byars, Betsy Cromer. THE TWO-THOUSAND-POUND GOLDFISH.
Ages 9-12. 99, Vol. 3
Childress, Alice. A HERO AIN'T NOTHIN' BUT A SANDWICH.
Ages 12 and up. 183, Vol. 1
Clymer, Eleanor Lowenton. LUKE WAS THERE.
Ages 8-12. 211, Vol. 1
Coleman, William Laurence. ORPHAN JIM: A NOVEL.
Ages 13 and up. 158, Vol. 2
Culin, Charlotte. CAGES OF GLASS, FLOWERS OF TIME.
Ages 12 and up. 145, Vol. 3
Dixon, Paige, pseud. SKIPPER.
Ages 12 and up. 165, Vol. 3
Dunlop, Eileen Rhona. FOX FARM.
Ages 10-12. 175, Vol. 3
Engebrecht, P. A. UNDER THE HAYSTACK.
Ages 11 and up. 289, Vol. 1
Fairless, Caroline. HAMBONE.
Ages 8-11. 184, Vol. 3
Hill, Margaret. TURN THE PAGE, WENDY.
Ages 10-14. 291, Vol. 3
Hinton, Susan Eloise. TEX.
Ages 11-15. 292, Vol. 3
Jordan, June. HIS OWN WHERE.
Ages 12 and up. 474, Vol. 1
Kerr, M. E., pseud. IF I LOVE YOU, AM I TRAPPED FOREVER?
Ages 12 and up. 492, Vol. 1
Kerr, M. E., pseud. IS THAT YOU, MISS BLUE?
Ages 11-14. 379, Vol. 2
Klass, Sheila Solomon. TO SEE MY MOTHER DANCE.
Ages 10-13. 344, Vol. 3
Leach, Michael. DON'T CALL ME ORPHAN!
Ages 10-12. 360, Vol. 3
LeShan, Eda J. WHAT'S GOING TO HAPPEN TO ME? WHEN PARENTS SEPARATE OR DIVORCE.
Ages 8 and up. 402, Vol. 2
Morgan, Alison Mary. ALL KINDS OF PRICKLES.
Ages 11-13. 450, Vol. 3
O'Dell, Scott. ISLAND OF THE BLUE DOLPHINS.
Ages 10 and up. 681, Vol. 1
Peterson, Jeanne Whitehouse. THAT IS THAT.
Ages 5-8. 497, Vol. 3
Renvoize, Jean. A WILD THING.
Ages 13 and up. 727, Vol. 1
Rinkoff, Barbara Jean Rich. HEADED FOR TROUBLE.
Ages 12 and up. 736, Vol. 1
Sachs, Marilyn. THE BEARS' HOUSE.
Ages 9-12. 760, Vol. 1
Sargent, Sarah. SECRET LIES.
Ages 11 and up. 570, Vol. 3
Strang, Celia. FOSTER MARY.
Ages 10-13. 633, Vol. 3
Thiele, Colin Milton. FIRE IN THE STONE.
Ages 12 and up. 893, Vol. 1

Townsend, John Rowe. TROUBLE IN THE JUNGLE.
Ages 12 and up. 902, Vol. 1
Voigt, Cynthia. HOMECOMING.
Ages 11 and up. 672, Vol. 3
Weik, Mary Hays. THE JAZZ MAN.
Ages 9-11. 958, Vol. 1

## Abortion

**See also:** *Pregnancy*
Beckman, Gunnel. MIA ALONE.
Ages 12 and up. 46, Vol. 2
Eyerly, Jeannette Hyde. BONNIE JO, GO HOME.
Ages 12 and up. 295, Vol. 1
Head, Ann. MR. AND MRS. BO JO JONES.
Ages 13 and up. 408, Vol. 1
Klein, Norma. IT'S NOT WHAT YOU EXPECT.
Ages 12 and up. 504, Vol. 1
Madison, Winifred. GROWING UP IN A HURRY.
Ages 12 and up. 606, Vol. 1
Posner, Grace. IN MY SISTER'S EYES.
Ages 12 and up. 516, Vol. 1
Prince, Alison. THE TURKEY'S NEST.
Ages 12 and up. 520, Vol. 3
Rinaldi, Ann. PROMISES ARE FOR KEEPING.
Ages 12 and up. 534, Vol. 3
Sherburne, Zoa. TOO BAD ABOUT THE HAINES GIRL.
Ages 12 and up. 814, Vol. 1
Truss, Jan. BIRD AT THE WINDOW.
Ages 13 and up. 661, Vol. 3

## Absent Parent

**See:** *Divorce; Divorce: of parents; Parental: absence*

## Abuse

**See:** *Child abuse*

## Accidents

**See also:** *Guilt, feelings of; Hospital, going to*
Cate, Dick. FLYING FREE.
Ages 8-10. 124, Vol. 2
Colman, Hila Crayder. ACCIDENT.
Ages 11 and up. 132, Vol. 3
Haar, Jaap ter. THE WORLD OF BEN LIGHTHART.
Ages 10-13. 287, Vol. 2
Kay, Eleanor. THE EMERGENCY ROOM.
Ages 9-12. 481, Vol. 1
Marino, Barbara Pavis. ERIC NEEDS STITCHES.
Ages 4-10. 403, Vol. 3
Richter, Elizabeth. THE TEENAGE HOSPITAL EXPERIENCE: YOU CAN HANDLE IT!
Ages 12 and up. 532, Vol. 3
Wolde, Gunilla. BETSY AND THE DOCTOR.
Ages 3-7. 697, Vol. 2
Wolff, Angelika. MOM! I BROKE MY ARM!
Ages 5-8. 988, Vol. 1

## Airplane

Milton, Hilary Herbert. MAYDAY! MAYDAY!
Ages 9-11. 427, Vol. 2
Rivera, Geraldo. A SPECIAL KIND OF COURAGE: PROFILES OF YOUNG AMERICANS.
Ages 12 and up. 544, Vol. 2
Stapp, Arthur Donald. ORDEAL BY MOUNTAINS.
Ages 11 and up. 853, Vol. 1

## Automobile

Bates, Betty. PICKING UP THE PIECES.
Ages 10-13. 40, Vol. 3
Butterworth, William Edmund. UNDER THE INFLUENCE.
Ages 12 and up. 94, Vol. 3
Campanella, Roy. IT'S GOOD TO BE ALIVE.
Ages 13 and up. 160, Vol. 1

## Accidents (cont.)

Cook, Marjorie. TO WALK ON TWO FEET.
Ages 11-14. 177, Vol. 2

Friis-Baastad, Babbis Ellinor. KRISTY'S COURAGE.
Ages 8-10. 339, Vol. 1

Huntsberry, William Emery. THE BIG HANG-UP.
Ages 12 and up. 445, Vol. 1

Jordan, Hope Dahle. HAUNTED SUMMER.
Ages 11 and up. 472, Vol. 1

Kingman, Lee. HEAD OVER WHEELS.
Ages 12 and up. 383, Vol. 2

McCaffrey, Mary. MY BROTHER ANGE.
Ages 8-11. 389, Vol. 3

Mazer, Norma Fox. WHEN WE FIRST MET.
Ages 12 and up. 416, Vol. 3

Nicholson, William G. PETE GRAY: ONE-ARMED MAJOR LEAGUER.
Ages 9-12. 479, Vol. 2

Van Leeuwen, Jean. SEEMS LIKE THIS ROAD GOES ON FOREVER.
Ages 12 and up. 663, Vol. 3

### Bicycle

Byars, Betsy Cromer. AFTER THE GOAT MAN.
Ages 9-11. 153, Vol. 1

### Fractures. *See: Fractures*

### Hit and run. See also: Crime/Criminals

Atkinson, Linda. HIT AND RUN.
Ages 11 and up. 31, Vol. 3

Hinton, Nigel. COLLISION COURSE.
Ages 11 and up. 315, Vol. 2

## Achievement

**See:** *Competition; School: achievement/underachievement; Success*

## Acne

**See also:** *Puberty*

Van Leeuwen, Jean. I WAS A 98-POUND DUCKLING.
Ages 11 and up. 918, Vol. 1

## Addiction

**See:** *Alcoholism; Drugs; Marijuana; Peer relationships: peer pressures; Smoking*

## Adolescence

**See:** *Maturation; Menstruation; Puberty*

## Adoption

**See also:** *Children's home, living in; Identity, search for; Orphan*

Gates, Doris. SENSIBLE KATE.
Ages 9-11. 349, Vol. 1

Pursell, Margaret Sanford. A LOOK AT ADOPTION.
Ages 3-7. 523, Vol. 2

Rivera, Geraldo. A SPECIAL KIND OF COURAGE: PROFILES OF YOUNG AMERICANS.
Ages 12 and up. 544, Vol. 2

Tax, Meredith. FAMILIES.
Ages 4-8. 645, Vol. 3

### Explaining

Arthur, Ruth M. REQUIEM FOR A PRINCESS.
Ages 12 and up. 34, Vol. 1

Bradbury, Bianca. LAURIE.
Ages 11 and up. 109, Vol. 1

Bunin, Catherine and Sherry Bunin. IS THAT YOUR SISTER? A TRUE STORY OF ADOPTION.
Ages 4-8. 94, Vol. 2

Caines, Jeannette Franklin. ABBY.
Ages 3-7. 157, Vol. 1

Drescher, Joan Elizabeth. YOUR FAMILY, MY FAMILY.
Ages 5-7. 173, Vol. 3

Fitzgerald, John Dennis. ME AND MY LITTLE BRAIN.
Ages 9-12. 319, Vol. 1

Krementz, Jill. HOW IT FEELS TO BE ADOPTED.
Ages 9 and up. 351, Vol. 3

Stein, Sara Bonnett. THE ADOPTED ONE: AN OPEN FAMILY BOOK FOR PARENTS AND CHILDREN TOGETHER.
Ages 4-8. 625, Vol. 3

Wasson, Valentina Pavlovna. THE CHOSEN BABY.
Ages 3-9. 948, Vol. 1

Wasson, Valentina Pavlovna. THE CHOSEN BABY, 3D ED. REV.
Ages 3-9. 674, Vol. 2

### Feelings about

Adler, Carole Schwerdtfeger. THE CAT THAT WAS LEFT BEHIND.
Ages 9-12. 3, Vol. 3

Bates, Betty. BUGS IN YOUR EARS.
Ages 10-13. 40, Vol. 2

Bates, Betty. IT MUST'VE BEEN THE FISH STICKS.
Ages 10-13. 37, Vol. 3

Bradbury, Bianca. LAURIE.
Ages 11 and up. 109, Vol. 1

Budbill, David. BONES ON BLACK SPRUCE MOUNTAIN.
Ages 10-13. 91, Vol. 2

Daringer, Helen Fern. ADOPTED JANE.
Ages 9-12. 263, Vol. 1

Fall, Thomas, pseud. EDDIE NO-NAME.
Ages 8-10. 303, Vol. 1

First, Julia. I, REBEKAH, TAKE YOU, THE LAWRENCES.
Ages 11-13. 187, Vol. 3

Glass, Frankcina. MARVIN & TIGE.
Ages 12 and up. 250, Vol. 2

Gordon, Shirley. THE BOY WHO WANTED A FAMILY.
Ages 7-9. 222, Vol. 3

Krementz, Jill. HOW IT FEELS TO BE ADOPTED.
Ages 9 and up. 351, Vol. 3

Lapsley, Susan. I AM ADOPTED!
Ages 3-7. 529, Vol. 1

Lowry, Lois. FIND A STRANGER, SAY GOODBYE.
Ages 12 and up. 422, Vol. 2

Miles, Miska, pseud. AARON'S DOOR.
Ages 5-9. 458, Vol. 2

Miner, Jane Claypool. MIRACLE OF TIME: ADOPTING A SISTER.
Ages 11 and up. 430, Vol. 3

Myers, Walter Dean. WON'T KNOW TILL I GET THERE.
Ages 11-14. 460, Vol. 3

Parker, Richard. PAUL AND ETTA.
Ages 9-11. 689, Vol. 1

Parker, Richard. SECOND-HAND FAMILY.
Ages 9-12. 690, Vol. 1

Pfeffer, Susan Beth. ABOUT DAVID.
Ages 13 and up. 500, Vol. 3

Pfeffer, Susan Beth. JUST BETWEEN US.
Ages 10-12. 502, Vol. 3

Roth, Arthur J. THE SECRET LOVER OF ELMTREE.
Ages 12 and up. 563, Vol. 2

Shyer, Marlene Fanta. MY BROTHER, THE THIEF.
Ages 10-13. 594, Vol. 3

Silman, Roberta. SOMEBODY ELSE'S CHILD.
Ages 9-11. 599, Vol. 2

Stein, Sara Bonnett. THE ADOPTED ONE: AN OPEN FAMILY BOOK FOR PARENTS AND CHILDREN TOGETHER.
Ages 4-8. 625, Vol. 3

Swartley, David Warren. MY FRIEND, MY BROTHER.
Ages 9-11. 642, Vol. 3

## Afro-American (cont.)

Lexau, Joan M. ME DAY.
Ages 7-10. 558, Vol. 1

Lexau, Joan M. STRIPED ICE CREAM.
Ages 8-11. 559, Vol. 1

Lipsyte, Robert. THE CONTENDER.
Ages 12 and up. 569, Vol. 1

Mathis, Sharon Bell. THE HUNDRED PENNY BOX.
Ages 8-10. 445, Vol. 2

Mathis, Sharon Bell. LISTEN FOR THE FIG TREE.
Ages 12 and up. 617, Vol. 1

Mathis, Sharon Bell. SIDEWALK STORY.
Ages 8-10. 618, Vol. 1

Meriwether, Louise. DON'T RIDE THE BUS ON MONDAY: THE ROSA PARKS STORY.
Ages 9-11. 635, Vol. 1

Miner, Jane Claypool. THE TOUGH GUY: BLACK IN A WHITE WORLD.
Ages 11 and up. 437, Vol. 3

Murray, Michele. NELLIE CAMERON.
Ages 9-12. 655, Vol. 1

Myers, Walter Dean. FAST SAM, COOL CLYDE, AND STUFF.
Ages 11-14. 469, Vol. 2

Myers, Walter Dean. HOOPS.
Ages 12 and up. 459, Vol. 3

Myers, Walter Dean. IT AIN'T ALL FOR NOTHIN'.
Ages 11-13. 470, Vol. 3

Myers, Walter Dean. THE YOUNG LANDLORDS.
Ages 11-14. 461, Vol. 3

Nolan, Madeena Spray. MY DADDY DON'T GO TO WORK.
Ages 4-7. 480, Vol. 2

Norris, Gunilla Brodde. THE GOOD MORROW.
Ages 9-11. 674, Vol. 1

Robinson, John Roosevelt and Alfred Duckett. BREAKTHROUGH TO THE BIG LEAGUE: THE STORY OF JACKIE ROBINSON.
Ages 10 and up. 746, Vol. 1

Rowe, Jeanne A. AN ALBUM OF MARTIN LUTHER KING, JR.
Ages 10 and up. 755, Vol. 1

Sargent, Sarah. EDWARD TROY AND THE WITCH CAT.
Ages 9-11. 569, Vol. 2

Scoppettone, Sandra. TRYING HARD TO HEAR YOU.
Ages 13 and up. 799, Vol. 1

Screen, Robert Martin. WITH MY FACE TO THE RISING SUN.
Ages 11 and up. 580, Vol. 2

Sebestyen, Ouida. WORDS BY HEART.
Ages 10-13. 580, Vol. 3

Shearer, John. I WISH I HAD AN AFRO.
Ages 9-11. 809, Vol. 1

Steptoe, John Lewis. MARCIA.
Ages 12 and up. 621, Vol. 2

Tate, Eleanora E. JUST AN OVERNIGHT GUEST.
Ages 9-11. 643, Vol. 3

Taylor, Mildred D. ROLL OF THUNDER, HEAR MY CRY.
Ages 10 and up. 636, Vol. 2

Taylor, Mildred D. SONG OF THE TREES.
Ages 8-11. 637, Vol. 2

Tester, Sylvia Root. BILLY'S BASKETBALL.
Ages 5-7. 642, Vol. 2

Tobias, Tobi. ARTHUR MITCHELL.
Ages 7-10. 649, Vol. 2

Tobias, Tobi. MARIAN ANDERSON.
Ages 7-10. 898, Vol. 1

Vroman, Mary Elizabeth. HARLEM SUMMER.
Ages 12 and up. 936, Vol. 1

Wilkinson, Brenda Scott. LUDELL.
Ages 10-14. 680, Vol. 2

Wilkinson, Brenda Scott. LUDELL AND WILLIE.
Ages 12 and up. 681, Vol. 2

Wilkinson, Brenda Scott. LUDELL'S NEW YORK TIME.
Ages 12 and up. 691, Vol. 3

Wood, Phyllis Anderson. THIS TIME COUNT ME IN.
Ages 12 and up. 706, Vol. 3

## Age

**See also:** *Family; Grandparent; Great-grandparent; Retirement*

### Aging

Anders, Rebecca. A LOOK AT AGING.
Ages 3-7. 14, Vol. 2

Brancato, Robin Fidler. SWEET BELLS JANGLED OUT OF TUNE.
Ages 11-14. 70, Vol. 3

Burch, Robert Joseph. TWO THAT WERE TOUGH.
Ages 9-11. 99, Vol. 2

Campbell, R. Wright. WHERE PIGEONS GO TO DIE.
Ages 12 and up. 112, Vol. 2

Clifford, Ethel Rosenberg. THE ROCKING CHAIR REBELLION.
Ages 11-13. 142, Vol. 2

Farber, Norma. HOW DOES IT FEEL TO BE OLD?
Ages 8 and up. 185, Vol. 3

First, Julia. LOOK WHO'S BEAUTIFUL!
Ages 10-12. 188, Vol. 3

Girion, Barbara. MISTY AND ME.
Ages 10-12. 219, Vol. 3

Hentoff, Nat. DOES THIS SCHOOL HAVE CAPITAL PUNISHMENT?
Ages 11 and up. 282, Vol. 3

Herman, Charlotte. OUR SNOWMAN HAD OLIVE EYES.
Ages 9-11. 313, Vol. 2

Hughes, Dean. SWITCHING TRACKS.
Ages 10-14. 308, Vol. 3

Hull, Eleanor Means. ALICE WITH GOLDEN HAIR.
Ages 11 and up. 311, Vol. 3

Hurd, Edith Thacher. I DANCE IN MY RED PAJAMAS.
Ages 3-6. 314, Vol. 3

Irwin, Hadley, pseud. WHAT ABOUT GRANDMA?
Ages 11 and up. 326, Vol. 3

Lowry, Lois. ANASTASIA AGAIN!
Ages 9-12. 384, Vol. 3

Lowry, Lois. ANASTASIA KRUPNIK.
Ages 9-11. 386, Vol. 3

Myers, Walter Dean. WON'T KNOW TILL I GET THERE.
Ages 11-14. 460, Vol. 3

Paterson, Katherine Womeldorf. JACOB HAVE I LOVED.
Ages 12 and up. 485, Vol. 3

Perl, Lila. PIEFACE AND DAPHNE.
Ages 9-11. 494, Vol. 3

Pollowitz, Melinda. CINNAMON CANE.
Ages 10-12. 519, Vol. 3

Radley, Gail. NOTHING STAYS THE SAME FOREVER.
Ages 9-12. 524, Vol. 3

Ruby, Lois. TWO TRUTHS IN MY POCKET.
Ages 12 and up. 557, Vol. 3

Shanks, Ann Zane. OLD IS WHAT YOU GET: DIALOGUES ON AGING BY THE OLD AND THE YOUNG.
Ages 10 and up. 582, Vol. 2

Tate, Joan. LUKE'S GARDEN AND GRAMP: TWO NOVELS.
Ages 10-13. 644, Vol. 3

Thiele, Colin Milton. THE HAMMERHEAD LIGHT.
Ages 10-12. 645, Vol. 2

## Alcoholism (cont.)

Windsor, Patricia. DIVING FOR ROSES.
Ages 13 and up. 687, Vol. 2
Woody, Regina Llewellyn Jones. ONE DAY AT A
TIME.
Ages 11 and up. 992, Vol. 1

### of Parents

Colman, Hila Crayder. CAR-CRAZY GIRL.
Ages 12 and up. 227, Vol. 1

## Allergies

Allen, Marjorie N. ONE, TWO, THREE—AH-CHOO!
Ages 4-7. 13, Vol. 3
Greene, Bette. PHILIP HALL LIKES ME. I RECKON
MAYBE.
Ages 10-13. 374, Vol. 1
LeRoy, Gen. EMMA'S DILEMMA.
Ages 9-12. 400, Vol. 2

## Alternatives

**See:** *Problem solving; Resourcefulness*

## Alzheimer's Disease

**See:** *Age: aging*

## Ambivalence, Feelings of

**See also:** *Problem solving*
Adelson, Leone. ALL READY FOR SCHOOL.
Ages 4-6. 2, Vol. 1
Berger, Terry. BIG SISTER, LITTLE BROTHER.
Ages 3-7. 72, Vol. 1
Bradbury, Bianca. WHERE'S JIM NOW?
Ages 11-13. 67, Vol. 2
Branscum, Robbie. FOR LOVE OF JODY.
Ages 9-12. 73, Vol. 3
Carlson, Natalie Savage. THE HALF SISTERS.
Ages 10-12. 166, Vol. 1
Cleaver, Vera and Bill Cleaver. ELLEN GRAE.
Ages 9-12. 197, Vol. 1
Colman, Hila Crayder. DIARY OF A FRANTIC KID
SISTER.
Ages 10-13. 230, Vol. 1
Dodd, Wayne. A TIME OF HUNTING.
Ages 11-14. 204, Vol. 2
Duncan, Lois, pseud. SEASON OF THE TWO-
HEART.
Ages 12 and up. 278, Vol. 1
Dyer, Thomas A. THE WHIPMAN IS WATCHING.
Ages 10-14. 177, Vol. 3
Fife, Dale. NORTH OF DANGER.
Ages 10-12. 227, Vol. 2
First, Julia. MOVE OVER, BEETHOVEN.
Ages 10-13. 231, Vol. 2
Guest, Elissa Haden. THE HANDSOME MAN.
Ages 12 and up. 251, Vol. 3
Herman, Charlotte. THE DIFFERENCE OF ARI
STEIN.
Ages 9-12. 312, Vol. 2
Hughes, Dean. SWITCHING TRACKS.
Ages 10-14. 308, Vol. 3
Iverson, Genie. I WANT TO BE BIG.
Ages 3-6. 327, Vol. 3
Josephs, Rebecca. EARLY DISORDER.
Ages 13 and up. 335, Vol. 3
LeShan, Eda J. WHAT'S GOING TO HAPPEN TO
ME? WHEN PARENTS SEPARATE OR DIVORCE.
Ages 8 and up. 402, Vol. 2
Little, Jean. TAKE WING.
Ages 10 and up. 577, Vol. 1
Lorimar, Lawrence T. SECRETS.
Ages 12 and up. 382, Vol. 3
Neufeld, John. TOUCHING.
Ages 12 and up. 665, Vol. 1

Norris, Gunilla Brodde. LILLAN.
Ages 9-12. 677, Vol. 1
Platt, Kin. BROGG'S BRAIN.
Ages 12 and up. 514, Vol. 3
Reynolds, Pamela. A DIFFERENT KIND OF SISTER.
Ages 12 and up. 729, Vol. 1
Rinaldi, Ann. PROMISES ARE FOR KEEPING.
Ages 12 and up. 534, Vol. 3
Rodowsky, Colby F. A SUMMER'S WORTH OF
SHAME.
Ages 12-14. 548, Vol. 3
Rodowsky, Colby F. WHAT ABOUT ME?
Ages 11-13. 556, Vol. 2
Rosenblatt, Suzanne. EVERYONE IS GOING
SOMEWHERE.
Ages 4-6. 561, Vol. 2
Rosenberg, Sondra. ARE THERE ANY MORE AT
HOME LIKE YOU?.
Ages 11 and up. 753, Vol. 1
Schoen, Barbara. A PLACE AND A TIME.
Ages 12 and up. 784, Vol. 1
Shotwell, Louisa Rossiter. MAGDALENA.
Ages 10-12. 818, Vol. 1
Shreve, Susan Richards. THE MASQUERADE.
Ages 12 and up. 591, Vol. 3
Smith, Doris Buchanan. DREAMS & DRUMMERS.
Ages 10-12. 612, Vol. 2
Sobol, Harriet Langsam. MY BROTHER STEVEN IS
RETARDED.
Ages 7-10. 618, Vol. 2
Sommerfelt, Aimee. THE WHITE BUNGALOW.
Ages 10-13. 840, Vol. 1
Spence, Eleanor Rachel. THE DEVIL HOLE.
Ages 10-14. 619, Vol. 2
Stolz, Mary Slattery. A LOVE, OR A SEASON.
Ages 12 and up. 870, Vol. 1
Stretton, Barbara. YOU NEVER LOSE.
Ages 12 and up. 639, Vol. 3
Thomas, Karen. THE GOOD THING...THE BAD
THING.
Ages 3-7. 654, Vol. 3
Vigna, Judith. ANYHOW, I'M GLAD I TRIED.
Ages 3-6. 661, Vol. 2
Winthrop, Elizabeth. WALKING AWAY.
Ages 11 and up. 979, Vol. 1

## Amish

Jordan, Mildred. PROUD TO BE AMISH.
Ages 10-12. 475, Vol. 1
Sorenson, Virginia Eggertsen. PLAIN GIRL.
Ages 9-11. 844, Vol. 1

## Amputee

**See also:** *Hospital, going to; Limbs, abnormal or missing;
Prosthesis; Surgery; Wheelchair, dependence on*
Archibald, Joseph Stopford. THE FIFTH BASE.
Ages 12 and up. 28, Vol. 1
Cook, Marjorie. TO WALK ON TWO FEET.
Ages 11-14. 177, Vol. 2
Nicholson, William G. PETE GRAY: ONE-ARMED
MAJOR LEAGUER.
Ages 9-12. 479, Vol. 2
Rivera, Geraldo. A SPECIAL KIND OF COURAGE:
PROFILES OF YOUNG AMERICANS.
Ages 12 and up. 544, Vol. 2
Sallis, Susan Diana. ONLY LOVE.
Ages 12 and up. 568, Vol. 3
Viscardi, Henry. A LAUGHTER IN THE LONELY
NIGHT.
Ages 12 and up. 931, Vol. 1

## Amyotrophic Lateral Sclerosis

Dixon, Paige, pseud. MAY I CROSS YOUR GOLDEN RIVER?
  Ages 12 and up. 202, Vol. 2
Luce, Willard and Celia Luce. LOU GEHRIG: IRON MAN OF BASEBALL.
  Ages 8-10. 589, Vol. 1

## Anger

**See also:** *Aggression; Depression; Hatred; Hostility; Tantrums*

Adelman, Bob and Susan Hall. ON AND OFF THE STREET.
  Ages 8-10. 1, Vol. 1
Alexander, Anne. TO LIVE A LIE.
  Ages 9-12. 7, Vol. 2
Barkin, Carol and Elizabeth James. SOMETIMES I HATE SCHOOL.
  Ages 5-7. 34, Vol. 2
Colman, Hila Crayder. ACCIDENT.
  Ages 11 and up. 132, Vol. 3
Conaway, Judith. I'LL GET EVEN.
  Ages 4-7. 170, Vol. 2
Dobrin, Arnold. GILLY GILHOOLEY: A TALE OF IRELAND.
  Ages 5-8. 203, Vol. 2
Dunn, Judy. FEELINGS.
  Ages 3-8. 279, Vol. 1
Fitzhugh, Louise. THE LONG SECRET.
  Ages 9-12. 321, Vol. 1
Goff, Beth. WHERE IS DADDY? THE STORY OF A DIVORCE.
  Ages 4-8. 363, Vol. 1
Grace, Fran. BRANIGAN'S DOG.
  Ages 10 and up. 225, Vol. 3
Greene, Constance Clarke. YOUR OLD PAL, AL.
  Ages 9-13. 241, Vol. 3
Grohskopf, Bernice. SHADOW IN THE SUN.
  Ages 10 and up. 281, Vol. 2
Hall, Lynn. TROUBLEMAKER.
  Ages 11-14. 395, Vol. 1
Hapgood, Miranda. MARTHA'S MAD DAY.
  Ages 3-6. 293, Vol. 2
Hitte, Kathryn. BOY, WAS I MAD.
  Ages 5-8. 414, Vol. 1
Hogan, Paula Z. SOMETIMES I GET SO MAD.
  Ages 5-8. 298, Vol. 3
Houston, James Archibald. THE WHITE ARCHER: AN ESKIMO LEGEND.
  Ages 9-11. 436, Vol. 1
Kingman, Lee. HEAD OVER WHEELS.
  Ages 12 and up. 383, Vol. 2
Kroll, Steven. THAT MAKES ME MAD!
  Ages 4-7. 389, Vol. 2
Kugelmass, J. Alvin. LOUIS BRAILLE: WINDOWS FOR THE BLIND.
  Ages 11 and up. 523, Vol. 1
McGovern, Ann. SCRAM, KID!
  Ages 5-8. 596, Vol. 1
Park, Barbara. DON'T MAKE ME SMILE.
  Ages 8-11. 481, Vol. 3
Platt, Kin. THE APE INSIDE ME.
  Ages 12 and up. 513, Vol. 3
Riley, Susan. WHAT DOES IT MEAN? ANGRY.
  Ages 3-6. 539, Vol. 2
Sauer, Julia L. THE LIGHT AT TERN ROCK.
  Ages 9-11. 772, Vol. 1
Schlein, Miriam. I HATE IT.
  Ages 4-7. 575, Vol. 2
Sharmat, Marjorie Weinman. COME HOME, WILMA.
  Ages 6-8. 588, Vol. 3
Sharmat, Marjorie Weinman. I'M NOT OSCAR'S FRIEND ANYMORE.
  Ages 3-7. 586, Vol. 2

Sharmat, Marjorie Weinman. ROLLO AND JULIET.
  Ages 4-8. 584, Vol. 3
Simon, Norma. I WAS SO MAD.
  Ages 4-8. 823, Vol. 1
Skolsky, Mindy Warshaw. CARNIVAL AND KOPECK AND MORE ABOUT HANNAH.
  Ages 7-9. 600, Vol. 3
Stolz, Mary Slattery. MAXIMILIAN'S WORLD.
  Ages 7-10. 871, Vol. 1
Stretton, Barbara. YOU NEVER LOSE.
  Ages 12 and up. 639, Vol. 3
Terris, Susan Dubinsky. THE CHICKEN POX PAPERS.
  Ages 10-12. 640, Vol. 2
Tester, Sylvia Root. FEELING ANGRY.
  Ages 3-6. 643, Vol. 2
Udry, Janice May. LET'S BE ENEMIES.
  Ages 3-7. 911, Vol. 1
Viorst, Judith. ALEXANDER AND THE TERRIBLE, HORRIBLE, NO GOOD, VERY BAD DAY.
  Ages 3-8. 926, Vol. 1
Watson, Jane Werner, Robert E. Switzer, and J. Cotter Hirschberg. SOMETIMES I GET ANGRY.
  Ages 3-6. 952, Vol. 1
Williams, Barbara Wright. JEREMY ISN'T HUNGRY.
  Ages 4-7. 684, Vol. 2
Wittels, Harriet and Joan Greisman. THINGS I HATE.
  Ages 4-8. 982, Vol. 1
Wojciechowska, Maia Rodman. THE HOLLYWOOD KID.
  Ages 12 and up. 984, Vol. 1
Zolotow, Charlotte Shapiro. THE HATING BOOK.
  Ages 3-7. 1021, Vol. 1

## Animals

**See also:** *Pets; Transitional objects*

**Fear of.** *See: Fear: of animals*

**Love for**

Adler, Carole Schwerdtfeger. THE CAT THAT WAS LEFT BEHIND.
  Ages 9-12. 3, Vol. 3
Baylor, Byrd. HAWK, I'M YOUR BROTHER.
  Ages 5-8. 45, Vol. 2
Bradbury, Bianca. IN HER FATHER'S FOOTSTEPS.
  Ages 11 and up. 66, Vol. 2
Brown, Fern G. HARD LUCK HORSE.
  Ages 9-11. 85, Vol. 2
Brown, Fern G. JOCKEY — OR ELSE!
  Ages 9-12. 86, Vol. 2
Brown, Fern G. YOU'RE SOMEBODY SPECIAL ON A HORSE.
  Ages 10-13. 87, Vol. 2
Callen, Lawrence Willard. SORROW'S SONG.
  Ages 9-12. 103, Vol. 3
Crofford, Emily. STORIES FROM THE BLUE ROAD.
  Ages 9-12. 143, Vol. 3
Dolan, Sheila. THE WISHING BOTTLE.
  Ages 7-9. 167, Vol. 3
Dunne, Mary Collins. HOBY & STUB.
  Ages 10-13. 176, Vol. 3
Fairless, Caroline. HAMBONE.
  Ages 8-11. 184, Vol. 3
Francis, Dorothy Brenner. THE FLINT HILLS FOAL.
  Ages 8-11. 234, Vol. 2
Godden, Rumer. MR. MCFADDEN'S HALLOWE'EN.
  Ages 9-11. 252, Vol. 2
Graham, Ada and Frank Graham. JACOB AND OWL.
  Ages 8-11. 228, Vol. 3
Hall, Lynn. DANZA!
  Ages 9-12. 254, Vol. 3
Herzig, Alison Cragin and Jane Lawrence Mali. A SEASON OF SECRETS.
  Ages 11-13. 287, Vol. 3

## Animals (cont.)

La Farge, Phyllis. JOANNA RUNS AWAY.
   Ages 7-9. 524, Vol. 1
Lee, H. Alton. SEVEN FEET FOUR AND GROWING.
   Ages 9-12. 396, Vol. 2
L'Engle, Madeleine Franklin. A RING OF ENDLESS LIGHT.
   Ages 11-14. 363, Vol. 3
McPhail, David Michael. A WOLF STORY.
   Ages 5-7. 399, Vol. 3
Morey, Walter. YEAR OF THE BLACK PONY.
   Ages 10-13. 465, Vol. 2
Neville, Emily Cheney. GARDEN OF BROKEN GLASS.
   Ages 11-14. 477, Vol. 2
Rounds, Glen Harold. BLIND OUTLAW.
   Ages 9-11. 554, Vol. 3
Shura, Mary Francis Craig. THE BARKLEY STREET SIX-PACK.
   Ages 9-12. 592, Vol. 3
Skorpen, Liesel Moak. BIRD.
   Ages 6-8. 606, Vol. 2
Somerlott, Robert. BLAZE.
   Ages 10-13. 617, Vol. 3
Stoutenburg, Adrien. WHERE TO NOW, BLUE?
   Ages 10-12. 628, Vol. 2
Thiele, Colin Milton. THE HAMMERHEAD LIGHT.
   Ages 10-12. 645, Vol. 2
Thomas, Jane Resh. THE COMEBACK DOG.
   Ages 7-9. 653, Vol. 3
Wartski, Maureen Crane. THE LAKE IS ON FIRE.
   Ages 10-13. 679, Vol. 3
Wartski, Maureen Crane. MY BROTHER IS SPECIAL.
   Ages 10-12. 681, Vol. 3
Waterton, Betty Marie. A SALMON FOR SIMON.
   Ages 4-7. 685, Vol. 3

## Responsibility for

Aaron, Chester. SPILL.
   Ages 12-14. 1, Vol. 2
Billington, Elizabeth T. PART-TIME BOY.
   Ages 8-10. 53, Vol. 3
Bunting, Anne Evelyn. MAGIC AND THE NIGHT RIVER.
   Ages 5-9. 96, Vol. 2
Carrick, Carol. A RABBIT FOR EASTER.
   Ages 3-7. 105, Vol. 3
Cleaver, Vera and Bill Cleaver. DUST OF THE EARTH.
   Ages 12 and up. 139, Vol. 2
Dexter, Pat Egan. ARROW IN THE WIND.
   Ages 10-13. 200, Vol. 2
Dolan, Sheila. THE WISHING BOTTLE.
   Ages 7-9. 167, Vol. 3
Gates, Doris. A MORGAN FOR MELINDA.
   Ages 10-12. 203, Vol. 2
Graeber, Charlotte Towner. GREY CLOUD.
   Ages 9-11. 226, Vol. 3
Holmes, Efner Tudor. AMY'S GOOSE.
   Ages 8-11. 330, Vol. 2
Huston, Anne and Jane H. Yolan. TRUST A CITY KID.
   Ages 11 and up. 448, Vol. 1
Lenski, Lois. CORN-FARM BOY.
   Ages 9-12. 544, Vol. 1
Renner, Beverly Hollett. THE HIDEAWAY SUMMER.
   Ages 10-13. 531, Vol. 2
Skorpen, Liesel Moak. BIRD.
   Ages 6-8. 606, Vol. 2
Skorpen, Liesel Moak. MICHAEL.
   Ages 4-8. 609, Vol. 2
Waterton, Betty Marie. A SALMON FOR SIMON.
   Ages 4-7. 685, Vol. 3
Wier, Ester Alberti. THE LONG YEAR.
   Ages 10 and up. 971, Vol. 1

## Anorexia Nervosa

**See also:** *Mental illness*
Hautzig, Deborah. SECOND STAR TO THE RIGHT.
   Ages 12 and up. 272, Vol. 3
Josephs, Rebecca. EARLY DISORDER.
   Ages 13 and up. 335, Vol. 3
Liu, Aimee. SOLITAIRE.
   Ages 13 and up. 380, Vol. 3
Richter, Elizabeth. THE TEENAGE HOSPITAL EXPERIENCE: YOU CAN HANDLE IT!
   Ages 12 and up. 532, Vol. 3

## Anxiety

**See also:** *Fear; Separation anxiety*
Asher, Sandra Fenichel. JUST LIKE JENNY.
   Ages 10-12. 27, Vol. 3
Beckman, Gunnel. MIA ALONE.
   Ages 12 and up. 46, Vol. 2
Blume, Judy Sussman. IT'S NOT THE END OF THE WORLD.
   Ages 10-12. 91, Vol. 1
Blume, Judy Sussman. THEN AGAIN, MAYBE I WON'T.
   Ages 12 and up. 94, Vol. 1
Byars, Betsy Cromer. THE 18TH EMERGENCY.
   Ages 9-11. 154, Vol. 1
Byars, Betsy Cromer. GOODBYE, CHICKEN LITTLE.
   Ages 9-11. 97, Vol. 3
Corcoran, Barbara. THE FARAWAY ISLAND.
   Ages 10-13. 179, Vol. 2
Crayder, Dorothy. SHE, THE ADVENTURESS.
   Ages 10-13. 258, Vol. 1
Delton, Judy. MY MOTHER LOST HER JOB TODAY.
   Ages 3-7. 156, Vol. 3
Fassler, Joan. THE BOY WITH A PROBLEM.
   Ages 4-8. 304, Vol. 1
Fassler, Joan. DON'T WORRY DEAR.
   Ages 4-6. 305, Vol. 1
Gordon, Shirley. THE BOY WHO WANTED A FAMILY.
   Ages 7-9. 222, Vol. 3
Greenberg, Jan. A SEASON IN-BETWEEN.
   Ages 11-13. 237, Vol. 3
Hall, Lynn. STICKS AND STONES.
   Ages 14 and up. 393, Vol. 1
Hamilton, Virginia. M. C. HIGGINS, THE GREAT.
   Ages 12 and up. 396, Vol. 1
Harris, Dorothy Joan. THE SCHOOL MOUSE.
   Ages 6-8. 294, Vol. 2
Helmering, Doris Wild. I HAVE TWO FAMILIES.
   Ages 6-8. 279, Vol. 3
Jackson, Jacqueline. THE TASTE OF SPRUCE GUM.
   Ages 10-13. 454, Vol. 1
Klein, Norma. TAKING SIDES.
   Ages 10 and up. 506, Vol. 1
Marshall, James. GEORGE AND MARTHA — ONE FINE DAY.
   Ages 3-6. 442, Vol. 2
Orgel, Doris. THE MULBERRY MUSIC.
   Ages 10-12. 685, Vol. 1
Schuchman, Joan. TWO PLACES TO SLEEP.
   Ages 5-7. 577, Vol. 3
Smith, Anne Warren. BLUE DENIM BLUES.
   Ages 12 and up. 607, Vol. 3
Stanek, Muriel Novella. I WON'T GO WITHOUT A FATHER.
   Ages 8-10. 850, Vol. 1
Valencak, Hannelore. A TANGLED WEB.
   Ages 9-11. 659, Vol. 2

## Apartheid

**See also:** *Prejudice: ethnic/racial*

## Arguing (cont.)

Madison, Winifred. MARINKA, KATINKA AND ME (SUSIE).
Ages 7-10. 438, Vol. 1
Oppenheimer, Joan Letson. GARDINE VS. HANOVER.
Ages 11-14. 474, Vol. 3
Platt, Kin. CHLORIS AND THE WEIRDOS.
Ages 11 and up. 516, Vol. 2
Ross, Pat. MEET M AND M.
Ages 6-8. 551, Vol. 3
Skolsky, Mindy Warshaw. CARNIVAL AND KOPECK AND MORE ABOUT HANNAH.
Ages 7-9. 600, Vol. 3

## Arthritis, Juvenile Rheumatoid

Jones, Rebecca Castaldi. ANGIE AND ME.
Ages 9-11. 333, Vol. 3

## Artificial Limbs

See: Prosthesis

## Asthma

Danziger, Paula. THE PISTACHIO PRESCRIPTION: A NOVEL.
Ages 11-13. 190, Vol. 2
Wilkinson, Brenda Scott. LUDELL.
Ages 10-14. 680, Vol. 2
Winthrop, Elizabeth. MARATHON MIRANDA.
Ages 9-11. 696, Vol. 3
Winthrop, Elizabeth. MIRANDA IN THE MIDDLE.
Ages 9-13. 697, Vol. 3

## Athletics

See: Competition; Little League; Sports/Sportsmanship

## Attention Seeking

See also: Boasting
Beim, Jerrold. THE SMALLEST BOY IN THE CLASS.
Ages 5-8. 64, Vol. 1
Belair, Richard L. DOUBLE TAKE.
Ages 13 and up. 44, Vol. 3
Blue, Rose. WISHFUL LYING.
Ages 6-9. 54, Vol. 3
Brandenberg, Franz. I WISH I WAS SICK, TOO!
Ages 3-7. 73, Vol. 2
Calhoun, Mary Huiskamp. IT'S GETTING BEAUTIFUL NOW.
Ages 12 and up. 158, Vol. 1
Delaney, Ned. RUFUS THE DOOFUS.
Ages 4-6. 195, Vol. 2
Duvoisin, Roger Antoine. VERONICA.
Ages 4-7. 283, Vol. 1
Dygard, Thomas J. SOCCER DUEL.
Ages 11-14. 179, Vol. 3
Galbraith, Kathryn Osebold. KATIE DID!
Ages 3-7. 198, Vol. 3
Giff, Patricia Reilly. FOURTH GRADE CELEBRITY.
Ages 8-10. 210, Vol. 3
Lindgren, Astrid. I WANT A BROTHER OR SISTER.
Ages 3-7. 373, Vol. 3
Rodowsky, Colby F. P.S. WRITE SOON.
Ages 10-12. 555, Vol. 2
Rogers, Pamela. THE STONE ANGEL.
Ages 10-12. 558, Vol. 2
Stevens, Carla McBride. SARA AND THE PINCH.
Ages 5-7. 628, Vol. 3
Terris, Susan Dubinsky. AMANDA, THE PANDA, AND THE REDHEAD.
Ages 5-7. 639, Vol. 2
Tunis, John Roberts. HIGHPOCKETS.
Ages 10 and up. 905, Vol. 1
Wahl, Jan. WHO WILL BELIEVE TIM KITTEN?
Ages 5-8. 671, Vol. 2

Wallace, Art. TOBY.
Ages 9-11. 945, Vol. 1
Watson, Jane Werner, Robert E. Switzer, and J. Cotter Hirschberg. SOMETIMES I'M JEALOUS.
Ages 3-6. 954, Vol. 1
Wells, Rosemary. NOISY NORA.
Ages 4-7. 962, Vol. 1
Williams, Barbara Wright. WHATEVER HAPPENED TO BEVERLY BIGLER'S BIRTHDAY?
Ages 4-8. 693, Vol. 3

## Attitude

See: Self, attitude toward; Work, attitude toward

## Aunt

See: Relatives; Relatives: living in home of

## Australia

Norman, Lilith. CLIMB A LONELY HILL.
Ages 11-14. 671, Vol. 1
Ottley, Reginald. BOY ALONE.
Ages 10-13. 688, Vol. 1
Phipson, Joan Nash, pseud. FLY FREE.
Ages 11 and up. 508, Vol. 3
Phipson, Joan Nash, pseud. PETER AND BUTCH.
Ages 10 and up. 709, Vol. 1
Ruhen, Olaf. CORCORAN'S THE NAME.
Ages 12 and up. 758, Vol. 1
Southall, Ivan. LET THE BALLOON GO.
Ages 12 and up. 847, Vol. 1
Spence, Eleanor Rachel. THE DEVIL HOLE.
Ages 10-14. 619, Vol. 2
Thiele, Colin Milton. FIRE IN THE STONE.
Ages 12 and up. 893, Vol. 1

## Autism

See also: Mental illness: of child
D'Ambrosio, Richard. NO LANGUAGE BUT A CRY.
Ages 13 and up. 891, Vol. 1
Gold, Phyllis. PLEASE DON'T SAY HELLO.
Ages 7 and up. 253, Vol. 2
Spence, Eleanor Rachel. THE DEVIL HOLE.
Ages 10-14. 619, Vol. 2
Terris, Susan Dubinsky. THE DROWNING BOY.
Ages 10 and up. 891, Vol. 1

## Autonomy

See also: Dependence/Independence
Ames, Mildred. NICKY AND THE JOYOUS NOISE.
Ages 9-12. 14, Vol. 3
Arkin, Alan. THE LEMMING CONDITION.
Ages 10 and up. 23, Vol. 2
Bennett, Rainey. THE SECRET HIDING PLACE.
Ages 5-8. 69, Vol. 1
Billington, Elizabeth T. PART-TIME BOY.
Ages 8-10. 53, Vol. 3
Branscum, Robbie. THE THREE WARS OF BILLY JOE TREAT.
Ages 9-11. 79, Vol. 2
Burn, Doris. ANDREW HENRY'S MEADOW.
Ages 5-8. 146, Vol. 1
Charlip, Remy and Lilian Moore. HOORAY FOR ME!
Ages 3-6. 127, Vol. 2
Colman, Hila Crayder. THE FAMILY TRAP.
Ages 12 and up. 134, Vol. 3
Danziger, Paula. CAN YOU SUE YOUR PARENTS FOR MALPRACTICE?
Ages 10-14. 149, Vol. 3
De Regniers, Beatrice Schenk A LITTLE HOUSE OF YOUR OWN.
Ages 3-8. 273, Vol. 1
Ellis, Ella Thorp. CELEBRATE THE MORNING.
Ages 12 and up. 286, Vol. 1

## Autonomy (cont.)

George, Jean Craighead. GULL NUMBER 737.
Ages 12 and up. 352, Vol. 1

George, Jean Craighead. MY SIDE OF THE MOUNTAIN.
Ages 11-14. 354, Vol. 1

Gilbert, Harriett. RUNNING AWAY.
Ages 11-14. 215, Vol. 3

Greenberg, Jan. THE PIG-OUT BLUES.
Ages 12 and up. 236, Vol. 3

Greenwald, Sheila. THE SECRET IN MIRANDA'S CLOSET.
Ages 8-11. 274, Vol. 2

Hansen, Joyce. THE GIFT-GIVER.
Ages 9-12. 263, Vol. 3

Henkes, Kevin. ALL ALONE.
Ages 3-6. 280, Vol. 3

Holl, Adelaide Hinkle. SMALL BEAR BUILDS A PLAYHOUSE.
Ages 5-7 326, Vol. 2

Iverson, Genie. I WANT TO BE BIG.
Ages 3-6. 327, Vol. 3

Johnson, Annabel Jones and Edgar Raymond Johnson. WILDERNESS BRIDE.
Ages 12 and up. 465, Vol. 1

Johnston, Norma. MYSELF AND I.
Ages 11 and up. 330, Vol. 3

Kerr, M. E., pseud. LITTLE LITTLE.
Ages 11 and up. 339, Vol. 3

Kingman, Lee. THE PETER PAN BAG.
Ages 12 and up. 498, Vol. 1

Korschunow, Irina. WHO KILLED CHRISTOPHER?
Ages 12 and up. 350, Vol. 3

Levoy, Myron. A SHADOW LIKE A LEOPARD.
Ages 12 and up. 369, Vol. 3

McKay, Robert W. THE TROUBLEMAKER: A STORY ABOUT NOW, AND THEN, AND ALWAYS.
Ages 12 and up. 598, Vol. 1

Mazer, Harry. THE ISLAND KEEPER.
Ages 10-14 412, Vol. 3

Mazer, Norma Fox. UP IN SETH'S ROOM.
Ages 13 and up. 415, Vol. 3

Molarsky, Osmond. RIGHT THUMB, LEFT THUMB.
Ages 4-7. 640, Vol. 1

O'Dell, Scott. ZIA.
Ages 10 and up. 486, Vol. 2

Perrine, Mary. SALT BOY.
Ages 7-10. 703, Vol. 1

Platt, Kin. CHLORIS AND THE WEIRDOS.
Ages 11 and up. 516, Vol. 2

Rabe, Berniece Louise. NAOMI.
Ages 12 and up. 527, Vol. 2

Richardson, Grace. APPLES EVERY DAY.
Ages 12 and up. 733, Vol. 1

Seuling, Barbara. THE TRIPLETS.
Ages 4-7. 581, Vol. 3

Simon, Norma. WHY AM I DIFFERENT?
Ages 4-8. 603, Vol. 2

Snyder, Zilpha Keatley. COME ON, PATSY.
Ages 5-8. 615, Vol. 3

Springstubb, Tricia. THE MOON ON A STRING.
Ages 12 and up. 619, Vol. 3

Stren, Patti. THERE'S A RAINBOW IN MY CLOSET.
Ages 8-10. 638, Vol. 3

Watanabe, Shigeo. HOW DO I PUT IT ON?
Ages 2-5. 683, Vol. 3

Watson, Nancy Dingman. TOMMY'S MOMMY'S FISH.
Ages 5-8. 955, Vol. 1

Welber, Robert. THE TRAIN
Ages 7-9. 959, Vol. 1

Wells, Rosemary. THE FOG COMES ON LITTLE PIG FEET.
Ages 11 and up. 961, Vol. 1

Wolde, Gunilla. THIS IS BETSY.
Ages 2-5. 700, Vol. 2

Wrenn, C. Gilbert and Shirley Schwarzrock. SOME COMMON CRUTCHES.
Ages 11 and up. 1006, Vol. 1

Yep, Laurence Michael. KIND HEARTS AND GENTLE MONSTERS.
Ages 12 and up. 712, Vol. 3

Zindel, Bonnie and Paul Zindel. A STAR FOR THE LATECOMER.
Ages 12 and up. 721, Vol. 3

Zolotow, Charlotte Shapiro. BIG SISTER AND LITTLE SISTER.
Ages 3-7. 1018, Vol. 1

## Avoidance

See: *Peer relationships: avoiding others; Responsibility: avoiding*

# B

## Baby, New

See: *Sibling: new baby*

## Baby-Sitter

Chalmers, Mary Eileen. BE GOOD, HARRY.
Ages 3-5. 178, Vol. 1

Delton, Judy and Elaine Knox-Wagner. THE BEST MOM IN THE WORLD.
Ages 4-7. 159, Vol. 3

Duczman, Linda. THE BABY-SITTER.
Ages 4-7. 209, Vol. 2

Gripe, Maria Kristina. THE NIGHT DADDY.
Ages 8-11. 387, Vol. 1

Harris, Robie H. DON'T FORGET TO COME BACK.
Ages 3-7. 295, Vol. 2

Hughes, Shirley. GEORGE, THE BABYSITTER.
Ages 4-7. 336, Vol. 2

Klein, Norma. BLUE TREES, RED SKY.
Ages 7-10. 384, Vol. 2

Smith, Janice Lee. THE MONSTER IN THE THIRD DRESSER DRAWER AND OTHER STORIES ABOUT ADAM JOSHUA.
Ages 5-8. 610, Vol. 3

Vestley, Anne-Catharina. AURORA AND SOCRATES.
Ages 8-10. 660, Vol. 2

Watson, Jane Werner, Robert E. Switzer, and J. Cotter Hirschberg. MY FRIEND THE BABYSITTER.
Ages 2-5. 949, Vol. 1

Wells, Rosemary. STANLEY & RHODA.
Ages 4-7. 677, Vol. 2

## Baby-Sitting

See also: *Job; Sibling: older; Sibling: oldest*

Bates, Betty. LOVE IS LIKE PEANUTS.
Ages 10-14. 38, Vol. 3

Byars, Betsy Cromer. THE NIGHT SWIMMERS.
Ages 10-12. 98, Vol. 3

Farley, Carol J. TWILIGHT WAVES.
Ages 10-13. 186, Vol. 3

Gerson, Corinne. TREAD SOFTLY.
Ages 9-12. 209, Vol. 3

Gilson, Jamie. DO BANANAS CHEW GUM?
Ages 9-11. 216, Vol. 3

Greenberg, Barbara. THE BRAVEST BABYSITTER.
Ages 4-8. 265, Vol. 3

Pascal, Francine. MY FIRST LOVE & OTHER DISASTERS.
Ages 12 and up. 484, Vol. 3

Ruby, Lois. WHAT DO YOU DO IN QUICKSAND?
Ages 12-14. 558, Vol. 3

Smith, Anne Warren. BLUE DENIM BLUES.
Ages 12 and up. 607, Vol. 3

## Baby-Sitting (cont.)

### Involuntary

Bonsall, Crosby Newell. THE DAY I HAD TO PLAY WITH MY SISTER.
Ages 3-8. 100, Vol. 1

Carlson, Natalie Savage. MARIE LOUISE'S HEYDAY.
Ages 3-6. 116, Vol. 2

Clymer, Eleanor Lowenton. HOW I WENT SHOPPING AND WHAT I GOT.
Ages 8-10. 210, Vol. 1

Girion, Barbara. MISTY AND ME.
Ages 10-12. 219, Vol. 3

Greenfield, Eloise. GOOD NEWS.
Ages 5-6. 271, Vol. 2

Lexau, Joan M. EMILY AND THE KLUNKY BABY AND THE NEXT-DOOR DOG.
Ages 5-8. 555, Vol. 1

McCaffrey, Mary. MY BROTHER ANGE.
Ages 8-11. 389, Vol. 3

McCord, Jean. TURKEYLEGS THOMPSON.
Ages 11-14. 390, Vol. 3

Matthews, Ellen. THE TROUBLE WITH LESLIE.
Ages 8-11. 409, Vol. 3

Rosenberg, Sondra. ARE THERE ANY MORE AT HOME LIKE YOU?
Ages 11 and up. 753, Vol. 1

Steptoe, John Lewis. STEVIE.
Ages 6-8. 860, Vol. 1

Watson, Pauline. CURLEY CAT BABY-SITS.
Ages 5-8. 675, Vol. 2

Williams, Barbara Wright. JEREMY ISN'T HUNGRY.
Ages 4-7. 684, Vol. 2

### Voluntary

Byars, Betsy Cromer. GO AND HUSH THE BABY.
Ages 3-6. 155, Vol. 1

Lattimore, Eleanor Frances. THE BUS TRIP.
Ages 8-10. 532, Vol. 1

Robertson, Keith. HENRY REED'S BABY-SITTING SERVICE.
Ages 9-12. 742, Vol. 1

## Banned Books

See: Censorship, Literary

## Barber, Going to

See also: Hair style, importance of
Rockwell, Anne F. and Harlow Rockwell. MY BARBER.
Ages 3-6. 545, Vol. 3

## Baths, Taking of

Barrett, Judith. I HATE TO TAKE A BATH.
Ages 4-6. 37, Vol. 2

Cole, Brock. NO MORE BATHS.
Ages 3-6. 130, Vol. 3

Zion, Gene. HARRY THE DIRTY DOG.
Ages 3-8. 1016, Vol. 1

## Battered Child

See: Child abuse

## Beauty, Personal

See: Appearance

## Bed-Wetting

See: Enuresis

## Bedtime

Barrett, Judith. I HATE TO GO TO BED.
Ages 4-6. 36, Vol. 2

Cole, William. FRANCES FACE-MAKER.
Ages 3-6. 221, Vol. 1

Crowe, Robert L. CLYDE MONSTER.
Ages 3-6. 186, Vol. 2

Hoban, Russell Conwell. BEDTIME FOR FRANCES.
Ages 3-7. 418, Vol. 1

Low, Joseph. BENNY RABBIT AND THE OWL.
Ages 4-7. 419, Vol. 2

Marzollo, Jean. CLOSE YOUR EYES.
Ages 2-5. 444, Vol. 2

Robison, Deborah. NO ELEPHANTS ALLOWED.
Ages 3-6. 540, Vol. 3

Schubert, Ingrid and Dieter Schubert. THERE'S A CROCODILE UNDER MY BED!
Ages 3-6. 576, Vol. 3

Sharmat, Marjorie Weinman. GOODNIGHT, ANDREW; GOODNIGHT, CRAIG.
Ages 3-7. 806, Vol. 1

Tobias, Tobi. CHASING THE GOBLINS AWAY.
Ages 4-7. 650, Vol. 2

Willoughby, Elaine Macmann. BORIS AND THE MONSTERS.
Ages 4-7. 694, Vol. 3

## Belonging

See also: Cliques; Clubs; Gangs: membership in; Loneliness; Peer relationships; Rejection

Abercrombie, Barbara Mattes. CAT-MAN'S DAUGHTER.
Ages 11-13. 1, Vol. 3

Adler, Carole Schwerdtfeger. THE CAT THAT WAS LEFT BEHIND.
Ages 9-12. 3, Vol. 3

Adler, Carole Schwerdtfeger. SOME OTHER SUMMER.
Ages 10-13. 9, Vol. 3

Alcock, Gudrun. DUFFY.
Ages 11-13. 4, Vol. 1

Anderson, Clarence William. LONESOME LITTLE COLT.
Ages 4-7. 18, Vol. 1

Angell, Judie. DEAR LOLA OR HOW TO BUILD YOUR OWN FAMILY.
Ages 10-13. 19, Vol. 3

Ashley, Bernard. A KIND OF WILD JUSTICE.
Ages 12 and up. 30, Vol. 3

Bailey, Pearl. DUEY'S TALE.
Ages 12 and up. 29, Vol. 2

Ball, Zachary, pseud. BRISTLE FACE.
Ages 10 and up. 49, Vol. 1

Blue, Rose. A QUIET PLACE.
Ages 8-11. 86, Vol. 1

Burchardt, Nellie. A SURPRISE FOR CARLOTTA.
Ages 9-11. 144, Vol. 1

Burnett, Frances Hodgson. THE SECRET GARDEN.
Ages 10 and up. 147, Vol. 1

Cameron, Eleanor Butler. A SPELL IS CAST.
Ages 10-12. 159, Vol. 1

Carrick, Malcolm. I'LL GET YOU.
Ages 11-13. 107, Vol. 3

Chandler, Edna Walker. INDIAN PAINTBRUSH.
Ages 9-11. 126, Vol. 2

Coatsworth, Elizabeth Jane. MARRA'S WORLD.
Ages 8-11. 150, Vol. 2

Delaney, Ned. RUFUS THE DOOFUS.
Ages 4-6. 195, Vol. 2

Drescher, Joan Elizabeth. YOUR FAMILY, MY FAMILY.
Ages 5-7. 173, Vol. 3

Duncan, Lois, pseud. SEASON OF THE TWO-HEART.
Ages 12 and up. 278, Vol. 1

Dunlop, Eileen Rhona. FOX FARM.
Ages 10-12. 175, Vol. 3

Dunne, Mary Collins. HOBY & STUB.
Ages 10-13. 176, Vol. 3

Ellis, Ella Thorp. SLEEPWALKER'S MOON.
Ages 12 and up. 181, Vol. 3

## Blame (cont.)

Flory, Jane Trescott. ONE HUNDRED AND EIGHT
BELLS.
Ages 9-11. 324, Vol. 1
Hoban, Russell Conwell and Lillian Aberman
Hoban. THE SORELY TRYING DAY.
Ages 3-7. 421, Vol. 1
Johnston, Norma. MYSELF AND I.
Ages 11 and up. 330, Vol. 3
Low, Joseph. MY DOG, YOUR DOG.
Ages 4-6. 421, Vol. 2
McKay, Robert W. THE RUNNING BACK.
Ages 12-14. 392, Vol. 3
Mazer, Norma Fox. WHEN WE FIRST MET.
Ages 12 and up. 416, Vol. 3
Snyder, Zilpha Keatley. THE HEADLESS CUPID!
Ages 10-13. 837, Vol. 1

## Blindness

See also: Education: special; Pets: guide dog; Visual
impairment
Brown, Marion Marsh and Ruth Crone. THE SILENT
STORM.
Ages 10-13. 125, Vol. 1
Butler, Beverly Kathleen. GIFT OF GOLD.
Ages 11 and up. 151, Vol. 1
Butler, Beverly Kathleen. LIGHT A SINGLE
CANDLE.
Ages 10 and up. 152, Vol. 1
Canty, Mary. THE GREEN GATE.
Ages 9-11. 162, Vol. 1
Clewes, Dorothy. GUIDE DOG.
Ages 10 and up. 205, Vol. 1
DeGering, Etta Fowler. SEEING FINGERS: THE
STORY OF LOUIS BRAILLE.
Ages 10-12. 268, Vol. 1
Eyerly, Jeannette Hyde. THE SEEING SUMMER.
Ages 8-10. 183, Vol. 3
Garfield, James B. FOLLOW MY LEADER.
Ages 9-11. 346, Vol. 1
Gill, Derek Lewis Theodore. TOM SULLIVAN'S
ADVENTURES IN DARKNESS.
Ages 10-14. 247, Vol. 2
Haar, Jaap ter. THE WORLD OF BEN LIGHTHART.
Ages 10-13. 287, Vol. 2
Hall, Lynn. HALF THE BATTLE.
Ages 11 and up. 255, Vol. 3
Heide, Florence Parry. SOUND OF SUNSHINE,
SOUND OF RAIN.
Ages 8-10. 409, Vol. 1
Hocken, Sheila. EMMA AND I.
Ages 12 and up. 324, Vol. 2
Hunter, Edith Fisher. CHILD OF THE SILENT
NIGHT.
Ages 9-11. 440, Vol. 1
Kamien, Janet. WHAT IF YOU COULDN'T...? A
BOOK ABOUT SPECIAL NEEDS.
Ages 8-12. 336, Vol. 3
Keller, Helen Adams. THE STORY OF MY LIFE.
Ages 11 and up. 488, Vol. 1
Kent, Deborah. BELONGING: A NOVEL.
Ages 11-14. 375, Vol. 2
Kugelmass, J. Alvin. LOUIS BRAILLE: WINDOWS
FOR THE BLIND.
Ages 11 and up. 523, Vol. 1
Little, Jean. LISTEN FOR THE SINGING.
Ages 10-14. 413, Vol. 2
MacLachlan, Patricia. THROUGH GRANDPA'S EYES.
Ages 5-8. 397, Vol. 3
Mathis, Sharon Bell. LISTEN FOR THE FIG TREE.
Ages 12 and up. 617, Vol. 1
Montgomery, Elizabeth Rider. "SEEING" IN THE
DARK.
Ages 5-7. 448, Vol. 3

Nelson, Mary Carroll. MICHAEL NARANJO: THE
STORY OF AN AMERICAN INDIAN.
Ages 9-12. 476, Vol. 2
Peare, Catherine Owens. THE HELEN KELLER
STORY.
Ages 10 and up. 693, Vol. 1
Petersen, Palle. SALLY CAN'T SEE.
Ages 5-8. 506, Vol. 1
Putnam, Peter. "KEEP YOUR HEAD UP, MR.
PUTNAM!"
Ages 12 and up. 718, Vol. 1
Quigley, Lillian Fox. THE BLIND MEN AND THE
ELEPHANT: AN OLD TALE FROM THE LAND OF
INDIA.
Ages 6-9. 719, Vol. 1
Rappaport, Eva. "BANNER, FORWARD!" THE
PICTORIAL BIOGRAPHY OF A GUIDE DOG.
Ages 10 and up. 722, Vol. 1
Resnick, Rose. SUN AND SHADOW: THE
AUTOBIOGRAPHY OF A WOMAN WHO
CLEARED A PATHWAY TO THE SEEING WORLD
FOR THE BLIND.
Ages 12 and up. 532, Vol. 2
Reuter, Margaret. MY MOTHER IS BLIND.
Ages 5-8. 529, Vol. 3
Rounds, Glen Harold. THE BLIND COLT.
Ages 8-12. 754, Vol. 1
Rounds, Glen Harold. BLIND OUTLAW.
Ages 9-11. 554, Vol. 3
Saint-Marcoux, Jeanne. THE LIGHT.
Ages 12 and up. 766, Vol. 1
Sommerfelt, Aimee. THE ROAD TO AGRA.
Ages 10-13. 839, Vol. 1
Stinetorf, Louise Allender. A CHARM FOR PACO'S
MOTHER.
Ages 9 and up. 862, Vol. 1
Sullivan, Mary Beth and Alan J. Brightman and Joseph
Blatt. FEELING FREE.
Ages 9 and up. 640, Vol. 3
Thomas, William E. THE NEW BOY IS BLIND.
Ages 6-10. 655, Vol. 3
Vance, Marguerite Schlund. WINDOWS FOR
ROSEMARY.
Ages 8-10. 921, Vol. 1
Vinson, Kathryn. RUN WITH THE RING.
Ages 12 and up. 925, Vol. 1
Viscardi, Henry. A LAUGHTER IN THE LONELY
NIGHT.
Ages 12 and up. 931, Vol. 1
Waite, Helen Elmira. VALIANT COMPANIONS:
HELEN KELLER AND ANNE SULLIVAN MACY.
Ages 10 and up. 941, Vol. 1
Wartski, Maureen Crane. THE LAKE IS ON FIRE.
Ages 10-13. 679, Vol. 3
Wilder, Laura Ingalls. BY THE SHORES OF SILVER
LAKE.
Ages 8-11. 974, Vol. 1
Witheridge, Elizabeth P. DEAD END BLUFF.
Ages 10-12. 981, Vol. 1
Wolf, Bernard. CONNIE'S NEW EYES.
Ages 9 and up. 703, Vol. 2
Woody, Regina Llewellyn Jones. SECOND SIGHT FOR
TOMMY.
Ages 12 and up. 933, Vol. 1
Wosmek, Frances. A BOWL OF SUN.
Ages 7-9. 710, Vol. 2

## Boarding Schools

See: Schools, private

## Boasting

See also: Attention seeking
Blue, Rose. WISHFUL LYING.
Ages 6-9. 54, Vol. 3

## Boasting (cont.)

Blume, Judy Sussman. OTHERWISE KNOWN AS SHEILA THE GREAT.
Ages 9-11. 92, Vol. 1
Bonsall, Crosby Newell. MINE'S THE BEST.
Ages 3-8. 101, Vol. 1
Brenner, Barbara Johnes. MR. TALL AND MR. SMALL.
Ages 4-8. 116, Vol. 1
Duvoisin, Roger Antoine. PETUNIA'S TREASURE.
Ages 5-8. 212, Vol. 2
Greene, Bette. GET ON OUT OF HERE, PHILIP HALL.
Ages 9-12. 238, Vol. 3
Lopshire, Robert. I AM BETTER THAN YOU!
Ages 4-8. 579, Vol. 1
Rodowsky, Colby F. P.S. WRITE SOON.
Ages 10-12. 555, Vol. 2
Sharmat, Marjorie Weinman. I'M TERRIFIC.
Ages 4-7. 587, Vol. 1
Williams, Barbara Wright. SO WHAT IF I'M A SORE LOSER?
Ages 5-8. 692, Vol. 3

## Body Concept

**See:** *Name-calling; Self, attitude toward: body concept*

## Boy-Girl Relationships

**See also:** *Friendship; Peer relationships; Sex*
Adler, Carole Schwerdtfeger. SOME OTHER SUMMER.
Ages 10-13. 9, Vol. 3
Alexander, Anne. CONNIE.
Ages 10-13. 6, Vol. 2
Angell, Judie. RONNIE AND ROSEY.
Ages 11 and up. 20, Vol. 2
Angell, Judie. SECRET SELVES.
Ages 11-13. 20, Vol. 3
Annixter, Paul, pseud. SWIFTWATER.
Ages 13 and up. 26, Vol. 1
Asher, Sandra Fenichel. JUST LIKE JENNY.
Ages 10-12. 27, Vol. 3
Bach, Alice Hendricks. A FATHER EVERY FEW YEARS.
Ages 11-13. 27, Vol. 2
Bach, Alice Hendricks. MOLLIE MAKE-BELIEVE.
Ages 12 and up. 41, Vol. 1
Bach, Alice Hendricks. WAITING FOR JOHNNY MIRACLE.
Ages 12 and up. 32, Vol. 3
Bates, Betty. LOVE IS LIKE PEANUTS.
Ages 10-14. 38, Vol. 3
Bates, Betty. PICKING UP THE PIECES.
Ages 10-13. 40, Vol. 3
Bates, Betty. THAT'S WHAT T.J. SAYS.
Ages 9-11. 41, Vol. 3
Brancato, Robin Fidler. BLINDED BY THE LIGHT.
Ages 11-14. 70, Vol. 2
Brancato, Robin Fidler. WINNING.
Ages 12 and up. 72, Vol. 2
Branscum, Robbie. JOHNNY MAY.
Ages 9-12. 77, Vol. 2
Bridgers, Sue Ellen. HOME BEFORE DARK.
Ages 12 and up. 81, Vol. 2
Bulla, Clyde Robert. ALMOST A HERO.
Ages 11 and up. 84, Vol. 1
Burch, Robert Joseph. THE WHITMAN KICK.
Ages 12 and up. 100, Vol. 2
Butler, Beverly Kathleen. GIFT OF GOLD.
Ages 11 and up. 151, Vol. 1
Byars, Betsy Cromer. THE CYBIL WAR.
Ages 9-12. 96, Vol. 3
Calhoun, Mary Huiskamp. KATIE JOHN AND HEATHCLIFF.
Ages 9-11. 101, Vol. 3

Campbell, Hope, pseud. NO MORE TRAINS TO TOTTENVILLE.
Ages 12 and up. 161, Vol. 1
Carlson, Dale Bick. TRIPLE BOY.
Ages 13 and up. 115, Vol. 2
Cleaver, Vera and Bill Cleaver. TRIAL VALLEY.
Ages 12 and up. 141, Vol. 2
Cohen, Barbara Nash. BITTER HERBS AND HONEY.
Ages 11-13. 153, Vol. 2
Cohen, Barbara Nash. FAT JACK.
Ages 11 and up. 125, Vol. 3
Cohen, Barbara Nash. THE INNKEEPER'S DAUGHTER.
Ages 11-14. 126, Vol. 3
Colman, Hila Crayder. ACCIDENT.
Ages 11 and up. 132, Vol. 3
Colman, Hila Crayder. CONFESSION OF A STORYTELLER.
Ages 10-13. 133, Vol. 3
Colman, Hila Crayder. SOMETIMES I DON'T LOVE MY MOTHER.
Ages 12 and up. 166, Vol. 2
Corcoran, Barbara. AXE-TIME, SWORD-TIME.
Ages 11 and up. 178, Vol. 2
Culin, Charlotte. CAGES OF GLASS, FLOWERS OF TIME.
Ages 12 and up. 145, Vol. 3
Danziger, Paula. THE DIVORCE EXPRESS.
Ages 11-14. 150, Vol. 3
Danziger, Paula. THE PISTACHIO PRESCRIPTION: A NOVEL.
Ages 11-13. 190, Vol. 2
Danziger, Paula. THERE'S A BAT IN BUNK FIVE.
Ages 10-14. 151, Vol. 3
Dodd, Wayne. A TIME OF HUNTING.
Ages 11-14. 204, Vol. 2
Elfman, Blossom. THE BUTTERFLY GIRL.
Ages 13 and up. 180, Vol. 3
Feagles, Anita Macrae. THE YEAR THE DREAMS CAME BACK.
Ages 11-14. 225, Vol. 2
Ferry, Charles. UP IN SISTER BAY.
Ages 12 and up. 226, Vol. 2
Foley, June. IT'S NO CRUSH, I'M IN LOVE!
Ages 11-13. 192, Vol. 3
Forman, James. MY ENEMY, MY BROTHER.
Ages 12 and up. 326, Vol. 1
Franco, Marjorie. SO WHO HASN'T GOT PROBLEMS?
Ages 10-12. 194, Vol. 3
Frank, Anne. ANNE FRANK: THE DIARY OF A YOUNG GIRL.
Ages 11 and up. 330, Vol. 1
Garden, Nancy. THE LONERS.
Ages 12 and up. 343, Vol. 1
Gerber, Merrill Joan. PLEASE DON'T KISS ME NOW.
Ages 13 and up. 206, Vol. 3
Greenberg, Jan. THE PIG-OUT BLUES.
Ages 12 and up. 236, Vol. 3
Greene, Bette. GET ON OUT OF HERE, PHILIP HALL.
Ages 9-12. 238, Vol. 3
Greene, Sheppard M. THE BOY WHO DRANK TOO MUCH.
Ages 12 and up. 242, Vol. 3
Guest, Elissa Haden. THE HANDSOME MAN.
Ages 12 and up. 251, Vol. 3
Hallman, Ruth. BREAKAWAY.
Ages 12 and up. 257, Vol. 3
Hamilton, Virginia. M. C. HIGGINS, THE GREAT.
Ages 12 and up. 396, Vol. 1
Hanlon, Emily. IT'S TOO LATE FOR SORRY.
Ages 11-14. 292, Vol. 2

**Boy-Girl Relationships (cont.)**

Hansen, Joyce. THE GIFT-GIVER.
Ages 9-12. 263, Vol. 3

Harlan, Elizabeth. FOOTFALLS.
Ages 12-14. 265, Vol. 3

Hest, Amy. MAYBE NEXT YEAR...
Ages 9-12. 288, Vol. 3

Hinton, Susan Eloise. TEX.
Ages 11-15. 292, Vol. 3

Hoff, Sydney. IRVING AND ME.
Ages 12 and up. 424, Vol. 1

Hogan, Paula Z. I HATE BOYS  I HATE GIRLS.
Ages 5-8. 296, Vol. 3

Hopkins, Lee Bennett. I LOVED ROSE ANN.
Ages 6-9. 333, Vol. 2

Hunter, Kristin Eggleston. LOU IN THE LIMELIGHT.
Ages 14 and up. 312, Vol. 3

Irwin, Hadley, pseud. MOON AND ME.
Ages 11-14. 325, Vol. 3

Johnston, Norma. THE KEEPING DAYS.
Ages 11 and up. 468, Vol. 1

Johnston, Norma. A MUSTARD SEED OF MAGIC.
Ages 12 and up. 355, Vol. 2

Johnston, Norma. THE SANCTUARY TREE.
Ages 12 and up. 356, Vol. 2

Jordan, June. HIS OWN WHERE.
Ages 12 and up. 474, Vol. 1

Kerr, M. E., pseud. DINKY HOCKER SHOOTS SMACK.
Ages 12 and up. 491, Vol. 1

Kerr, M. E., pseud. I'LL LOVE YOU WHEN YOU'RE MORE LIKE ME.
Ages 12 and up. 378, Vol. 2

Kerr, M. E., pseud. LITTLE LITTLE.
Ages 11 and up. 339, Vol. 3

Kingman, Lee. BREAK A LEG, BETSY MAYBE!
Ages 12 and up. 382, Vol. 3

Kropp, Paul Stephan. WILTED.
Ages 11-14. 354, Vol. 3

Le Guin, Ursula Kroeber. VERY FAR AWAY FROM ANYWHERE ELSE.
Ages 12 and up. 397, Vol. 2

L'Engle, Madeleine Franklin. CAMILLA.
Ages 12 and up. 540, Vol. 1

L'Engle, Madeleine Franklin. A RING OF ENDLESS LIGHT.
Ages 11-14. 363, Vol. 3

Levinson, Nancy Smiler. WORLD OF HER OWN.
Ages 12 and up. 368, Vol. 3

McKillip, Patricia A. THE NIGHT GIFT.
Ages 11 and up. 430, Vol. 2

Madison, Winifred. GETTING OUT.
Ages 12 and up. 437, Vol. 2

Marney, Dean. JUST GOOD FRIENDS.
Ages 11-13. 404, Vol. 3

Mendonca, Susan R. TOUGH CHOICES.
Ages 11 and up. 419, Vol. 3

Moeri, Louise. FIRST THE EGG.
Ages 12 and up. 438, Vol. 3

Myers, Walter Dean. HOOPS.
Ages 12 and up. 459, Vol. 3

Myers, Walter Dean. THE YOUNG LANDLORDS.
Ages 11-14. 461, Vol. 3

Naylor, Phyllis Reynolds. A STRING OF CHANCES.
Ages 12 and up. 464, Vol. 3

Naylor, Phyllis Reynolds. WALKING THROUGH THE DARK.
Ages 12 and up. 473, Vol. 2

Newton, Suzanne. M.V. SEXTON SPEAKING.
Ages 11 and up. 466, Vol. 3

Oppenheimer, Joan Letson. WORKING ON IT.
Ages 11-13. 475, Vol. 3

Pascal, Francine. MY FIRST LOVE & OTHER DISASTERS.
Ages 12 and up. 484, Vol. 3

Pevsner, Stella. AND YOU GIVE ME A PAIN, ELAINE.
Ages 10-13. 508, Vol. 2

Pfeffer, Susan Beth. ABOUT DAVID.
Ages 13 and up. 500, Vol. 3

Pohlmann, Lillian Grenfell. SING LOOSE.
Ages 12 and up. 714, Vol. 1

Powers, Bill. A TEST OF LOVE.
Ages 12 and up. 519, Vol. 3

Rabinowich, Ellen. ROCK FEVER.
Ages 12 and up. 523, Vol. 3

Reader, Dennis J. COMING BACK ALIVE.
Ages 12 and up. 525, Vol. 3

Rees, David. RISKS.
Ages 11 and up. 529, Vol. 2

Rinaldi, Ann. PROMISES ARE FOR KEEPING.
Ages 12 and up. 534, Vol. 3

Riter, Dorris. THE EDGE OF VIOLENCE.
Ages 12 and up. 741, Vol. 1

Rock, Gail. ADDIE AND THE KING OF HEARTS.
Ages 9-12. 550, Vol. 2

Roth, Arthur J. THE SECRET LOVER OF ELMTREE.
Ages 12 and up. 563, Vol. 2

Sachs, Marilyn. BEACH TOWELS.
Ages 12 and up. 562, Vol. 3

Sachs, Marilyn. BUS RIDE.
Ages 11-14. 563, Vol. 3

Sachs, Marilyn. HELLO...WRONG NUMBER.
Ages 12-16. 565, Vol. 3

Sachs, Marilyn. PETER AND VERONICA.
Ages 10-12. 762, Vol. 1

Sachs, Marilyn. VERONICA GANZ.
Ages 10-12. 765, Vol. 1

Sallis, Susan Diana. ONLY LOVE.
Ages 12 and up. 568, Vol. 3

Sherburne, Zoa. ALMOST APRIL.
Ages 12 and up. 810, Vol. 1

Shura, Mary Frances Craig. THE SEASON OF SILENCE.
Ages 10-14. 597, Vol. 2

Singer, Marilyn. NO APPLAUSE, PLEASE.
Ages 10-12. 605, Vol. 2

Slepian, Jan. LESTER'S TURN.
Ages 11-14. 604, Vol. 3

Smith, Doris Buchanan. DREAMS & DRUMMERS.
Ages 10-12. 612, Vol. 2

Snyder, Anne. FIRST STEP.
Ages 11-13. 615, Vol. 2

Snyder, Anne. MY NAME IS DAVY — I'M AN ALCOHOLIC.
Ages 12 and up. 616, Vol. 2

Springstubb, Tricia. THE MOON ON A STRING.
Ages 12 and up. 619, Vol. 3

Stolz, Mary Slattery. BY THE HIGHWAY HOME.
Ages 12 and up. 864, Vol. 1

Truss, Jan. BIRD AT THE WINDOW.
Ages 13 and up. 661, Vol. 3

Van Iterson, Siny Rose. VILLAGE OF OUTCASTS.
Ages 12 and up. 917, Vol. 1

Wilkinson, Brenda Scott. LUDELL.
Ages 10-14. 680, Vol. 2

Wolitzer, Hilma. OUT OF LOVE.
Ages 10-13. 704, Vol. 2

Wood, Phyllis Anderson. GET A LITTLE LOST, TIA.
Ages 11-13. 708, Vol. 2

Wood, Phyllis Anderson. PASS ME A PINE CONE.
Ages 11 and up. 705, Vol. 2

Wood, Phyllis Anderson. WIN ME AND YOU LOSE.
Ages 10-13. 709, Vol. 2

Wortis, Avi. SOMETIMES I THINK I HEAR MY NAME.
Ages 10-13. 708, Vol. 3

Worth, Kathryn. THEY LOVED TO LAUGH.
Ages 12 and up. 996, Vol. 1

## Boy-Girl Relationships (cont.)

## Boy-Girl Relationships (cont.)

Schoen, Barbara. A PLACE AND A TIME.
Ages 12 and up. 784, Vol. 1
Scoppettone, Sandra. THE LATE GREAT ME.
Ages 12 and up. 579, Vol. 2
Sherburne, Zoa. STRANGER IN THE HOUSE.
Ages 11 and up. 813, Vol. 1
Slote, Alfred. LOVE AND TENNIS.
Ages 12-14. 605, Vol. 3
Smith, Doris Buchanan. KICK A STONE HOME.
Ages 11 and up. 830, Vol. 1
Steptoe, John Lewis. MARCIA.
Ages 12 and up. 621, Vol. 2
Stolz, Mary Slattery. A LOVE, OR A SEASON.
Ages 12 and up. 870, Vol. 1
Strasser, Todd. ANGEL DUST BLUES.
Ages 14 and up. 635, Vol. 3
Strasser, Todd. FRIENDS TILL THE END.
Ages 12 and up. 636, Vol. 3
Stretton, Barbara. YOU NEVER LOSE.
Ages 12 and up. 639, Vol. 3
Van Leeuwen, Jean. I WAS A 98-POUND DUCKLING.
Ages 11 and up. 918, Vol. 1
Wilkinson, Brenda Scott. LUDELL AND WILLIE.
Ages 12 and up. 681, Vol. 2
Wood, Phyllis Anderson. THIS TIME COUNT ME IN.
Ages 12 and up. 706, Vol. 3
Woodford, Peggy. PLEASE DON'T GO.
Ages 12 and up. 991, Vol. 1
Yep, Laurence Michael. KIND HEARTS AND
GENTLE MONSTERS.
Ages 12 and up. 712, Vol. 3

## Braces on Body/Limbs

See also: *Limbs, abnormal or missing; Poliomyelitis*
Blume, Judy Sussman. DEENIE.
Ages 10-12. 88, Vol. 1
Brooks, Jerome. THE BIG DIPPER MARATHON.
Ages 11-14. 77, Vol. 3
Rabe, Berniece Louise. THE BALANCING GIRL.
Ages 5-7. 522, Vol. 3
Rodowsky, Colby F. P.S. WRITE SOON.
Ages 10-12. 555, Vol. 2
Wolf, Bernard. DON'T FEEL SORRY FOR PAUL.
Ages 8 and up. 987, Vol. 1

## Braces on Teeth

See: *Orthodontia*

## Bragging

See: *Boasting*

## Brain Injury

See also: *Birth defects; Cerebral palsy; Epilepsy;
Learning disabilities; Mental retardation; Spastic*
Goldreich, Gloria. SEASON OF DISCOVERY.
Ages 11-13. 256, Vol. 2
Melton, David. A BOY CALLED HOPELESS.
Ages 10 and up. 451, Vol. 2
Robinet, Harriette Gillem. RIDE THE RED CYCLE.
Ages 7-11. 537, Vol. 3

## Bravery

See: *Courage, meaning of*

## Broken Bones

See: *Fractures; Surgery*

## Brother

See: *Sibling*

## Buddhist

Coutant, Helen. FIRST SNOW.
Ages 7-9. 255, Vol. 1

## Bully

See also: *Harassment; Teasing*
McCord, Jean. TURKEYLEGS THOMPSON.
Ages 11-14. 390, Vol. 3

### Being a

Sachs, Marilyn. VERONICA GANZ.
Ages 10-12. 765, Vol. 1
Stolz, Mary Slattery. THE BULLY OF BARKHAM
STREET.
Ages 8-11. 863, Vol. 1

### Being bothered by

Adler, Carole Schwerdtfeger. THE ONCE IN A
WHILE HERO.
Ages 10-13. 7, Vol. 3
Alexander, Martha G. MOVE OVER, TWERP.
Ages 5-8. 11, Vol. 3
Anderson, Mary Quirk. JUST THE TWO OF THEM.
Ages 12 and up. 19, Vol. 1
Brooks, Jerome. MAKE ME A HERO.
Ages 9-12. 78, Vol. 3
Chapman, Carol. HERBIE'S TROUBLES.
Ages 5-7. 113, Vol. 3
Conford, Ellen. THE REVENGE OF THE
INCREDIBLE DR. RANCID AND HIS YOUTHFUL
ASSISTANT, JEFFREY.
Ages 10-12. 137, Vol. 3
Cunningham, Julia Woolfolk. THE SILENT VOICE.
Ages 11-14. 146, Vol. 3
Degens, T. THE GAME ON THATCHER ISLAND.
Ages 11-14. 193, Vol. 2
Evans, Mari. JD.
Ages 9-12. 294, Vol. 1
Hoff, Sydney. IRVING AND ME.
Ages 12 and up. 424, Vol. 1
Keats, Ezra Jack. GOGGLES.
Ages 4-8. 484, Vol. 1
Kesselman, Wendy Ann. ANGELITA.
Ages 5-9. 494, Vol. 1
Kropp, Paul Stephan. WILTED.
Ages 11-14. 354, Vol. 3
Maddock, Reginald. DANNY ROWLEY.
Ages 11-13. 602, Vol. 1
Maddock, Reginald. THE DRAGON IN THE
GARDEN.
Ages 10-13. 603, Vol. 1
Mauser, Pat Rhodes. A BUNDLE OF STICKS.
Ages 10-12. 410, Vol. 3
Meddaugh, Susan. TOO SHORT FRED.
Ages 6-8. 450, Vol. 2
Miles, Miska, pseud. GERTRUDE'S POCKET.
Ages 7-9. 639, Vol. 1
Miner, Jane Claypool. NAVAJO VICTORY: BEING A
NATIVE AMERICAN.
Ages 11 and up. 432, Vol. 3
Peck, Robert Newton. CLUNIE.
Ages 12 and up. 491, Vol. 3
Rinaldo, C. L. DARK DREAMS.
Ages 11 and up. 734, Vol. 1
Rinkoff, Barbara Jean Rich. HEADED FOR
TROUBLE.
Ages 12 and up. 736, Vol. 1
Robinson, Charles. NEW KID IN TOWN.
Ages 4-7. 548, Vol. 2
Robinson, Nancy Konheim. WENDY AND THE
BULLIES.
Ages 7-10. 539, Vol. 3
Wartski, Maureen Crane. A LONG WAY FROM
HOME.
Ages 11-13. 680, Vol. 3

### Fear of

Cleary, Beverly Bunn. MITCH AND AMY.
Ages 9-11. 193, Vol. 1
Friis-Baastad, Babbis Ellinor. KRISTY'S COURAGE.
Ages 8-10. 339, Vol. 1

## Bully (cont.)

Leigh, Bill. THE FAR SIDE OF FEAR.
Ages 10-14. 398, Vol. 2
Norris, Gunilla Brodde. GREEN AND SOMETHING ELSE.
Ages 8-11. 675, Vol. 1
Rinaldo, C. L. DARK DREAMS.
Ages 11 and up. 734, Vol. 1
Robinson, Nancy Konheim. WENDY AND THE BULLIES.
Ages 7-10. 539, Vol. 3
Stolz, Mary Slattery. A DOG ON BARKHAM STREET.
Ages 8-11. 865, Vol. 1
Wells, Rosemary. BENJAMIN & TULIP.
Ages 3-7. 960, Vol. 1

# C

## Camp Experiences

**See also:** *Separation anxiety*
Angell, Judie. IN SUMMERTIME IT'S TUFFY.
Ages 11-13. 19, Vol. 2
Brown, Marc Tolan. ARTHUR GOES TO CAMP.
Ages 5-8. 79, Vol. 3
Cone, Molly Lamken. CALL ME MOOSE.
Ages 9-11. 174, Vol. 2
Danziger, Paula. THERE'S A BAT IN BUNK FIVE.
Ages 10-14. 151, Vol. 3
Hodges, Margaret Moore. THE HATCHING OF JOSHUA COBB.
Ages 8-12. 423, Vol. 1
Jones, Ron. THE ACORN PEOPLE.
Ages 10 and up. 360, Vol. 2
Levy, Elizabeth. COME OUT SMILING.
Ages 12 and up. 370, Vol. 3
Norris, Gunilla Brodde. THE GOOD MORROW.
Ages 9-11. 674, Vol. 1
O'Connor, Jane. YOURS TILL NIAGARA FALLS, ABBY.
Ages 8-10. 467, Vol. 3
Shaw, Richard. SHAPE UP, BURKE.
Ages 10-14. 593, Vol. 2
Smith, Robert Kimmel. JELLY BELLY.
Ages 10-12. 614, Vol. 3
Stolz, Mary Slattery. A WONDERFUL, TERRIBLE TIME.
Ages 9-11. 877, Vol. 1
Terris, Susan Dubinsky. WHIRLING RAINBOWS.
Ages 11 and up. 892, Vol. 1

## Canada

Little, Jean. LISTEN FOR THE SINGING.
Ages 10-14. 413, Vol. 2
Little, Jean. STAND IN THE WIND.
Ages 8-11. 414, Vol. 2
Madison, Winifred. CALL ME DANICA.
Ages 10-13. 435, Vol. 2

## Cancer

**See also:** *Hodgkin's disease; Hospital, going to; Surgery*
Bach, Alice Hendricks. WAITING FOR JOHNNY MIRACLE.
Ages 12 and up. 32, Vol. 3
Brady, Mari. PLEASE REMEMBER ME: A YOUNG WOMAN'S STORY OF HER FRIENDSHIP WITH AN UNFORGETTABLE FIFTEEN-YEAR-OLD BOY.
Ages 12 and up. 68, Vol. 2
Donnelly, Elfie. SO LONG, GRANDPA.
Ages 9-11. 168, Vol. 3
Hermes, Patricia. YOU SHOULDN'T HAVE TO SAY GOOD-BYE.
Ages 10-13. 286, Vol. 3

Mann, Peggy. THERE ARE TWO KINDS OF TERRIBLE.
Ages 9-12. 441, Vol. 2
Mearian, Judy Frank. TWO WAYS ABOUT IT.
Ages 9-12. 418, Vol. 3
Morris, Jeannie. BRIAN PICCOLO: A SHORT SEASON.
Ages 13 and up. 647, Vol. 1
Richter, Elizabeth. THE TEENAGE HOSPITAL EXPERIENCE: YOU CAN HANDLE IT!
Ages 12 and up. 532, Vol. 3
Rivera, Geraldo. A SPECIAL KIND OF COURAGE: PROFILES OF YOUNG AMERICANS.
Ages 12 and up. 544, Vol. 2
Schotter, Roni. A MATTER OF TIME.
Ages 12 and up. 575, Vol. 3
Stretton, Barbara. YOU NEVER LOSE.
Ages 12 and up. 639, Vol. 3
Zindel, Bonnie and Paul Zindel. A STAR FOR THE LATECOMER.
Ages 12 and up. 721, Vol. 3

### Brain tumor

Gunther, John. DEATH BE NOT PROUD: A MEMOIR.
Ages 12 and up. 389, Vol. 1

### Leukemia. *See also: Leukemia*

Lund, Doris Harold. ERIC.
Ages 12 and up. 590, Vol. 1
Slote, Alfred. HANG TOUGH, PAUL MATHER.
Ages 10 and up. 827, Vol. 1

## Cardiac Conditions

**See also:** *Rheumatic fever; Surgery: heart*
Beckman, Gunnel. THAT EARLY SPRING.
Ages 12 and up. 47, Vol. 2
Corbin, William, pseud. GOLDEN MARE.
Ages 9-12. 246, Vol. 1
Lenski, Lois. CORN-FARM BOY.
Ages 9-12. 544, Vol. 1
Richter, Elizabeth. THE TEENAGE HOSPITAL EXPERIENCE: YOU CAN HANDLE IT!
Ages 12 and up. 532, Vol. 3
Rinaldo, C. L. DARK DREAMS.
Ages 11 and up. 734, Vol. 1
Rogers, Dale Evans. ANGEL UNAWARE.
Ages 12 and up. 750, Vol. 1

## Careers

### Dancer

Hest, Amy. MAYBE NEXT YEAR...
Ages 9-12. 288, Vol. 3
Landis, James David. THE SISTERS IMPOSSIBLE.
Ages 9-11. 355, Vol. 3
Tobias, Tobi. ARTHUR MITCHELL.
Ages 7-10. 649, Vol. 2
Zindel, Bonnie and Paul Zindel. A STAR FOR THE LATECOMER.
Ages 12 and up. 721, Vol. 3

### Nurse

Greene, Carla. DOCTORS AND NURSES: WHAT DO THEY DO?
Ages 4-8. 376, Vol. 1
Grey, Elizabeth, pseud. FRIEND WITHIN THE GATES: THE STORY OF NURSE EDITH CAVELL.
Ages 12 and up. 384, Vol. 1

### Physician

Baker, Rachel Mininberg. THE FIRST WOMAN DOCTOR: THE STORY OF ELIZABETH BLACKWELL, M.D.
Ages 12 and up. 46, Vol. 1

## Careers (cont.)

Greene, Carla. DOCTORS AND NURSES: WHAT DO THEY DO?
Ages 4-8. 376, Vol. 1
Hardwick, Richard. CHARLES RICHARD DREW, PIONEER IN BLOOD RESEARCH.
Ages 12 and up. 399, Vol. 1

**Planning.** See also: Education; Work, attitude toward
Anckarsvärd, Karin. DOCTOR'S BOY.
Ages 9-11. 15, Vol. 1
Brown, Fern G. JOCKEY — OR ELSE!
Ages 9-12. 86, Vol. 2
Bruna, Dick. WHEN I'M BIG.
Ages 2-4. 81, Vol. 3
Butler, Beverly Kathleen. GIFT OF GOLD.
Ages 11 and up. 151, Vol. 1
Clewes, Dorothy. GUIDE DOG.
Ages 10 and up. 205, Vol. 1
Clifford, Ethel Rosenberg. THE ROCKING CHAIR REBELLION.
Ages 11-13. 142, Vol. 2
Cohen, Peter Zachary. THE MUSKIE HOOK.
Ages 12 and up. 218, Vol. 1
Felton, Harold William. JAMES WELDON JOHNSON.
Ages 9-12. 309, Vol. 1
Jacobs, Helen Hull. THE TENNIS MACHINE.
Ages 12 and up. 455, Vol. 1
Johnson, Annabel Jones and Edgar Raymond Johnson. COUNT ME GONE.
Ages 13 and up. 459, Vol. 1
Kerr, Judith. THE OTHER WAY ROUND.
Ages 12 and up. 376, Vol. 2
Lipsyte, Robert. THE CONTENDER.
Ages 12 and up. 569, Vol. 1
Pedersen, Elsa Kienitz. FISHERMAN'S CHOICE.
Ages 12 and up. 698, Vol. 1
Saint-Marcoux, Jeanne. THE LIGHT.
Ages 12 and up. 766, Vol. 1
Schwarzrock, Shirley and C. Gilbert Wrenn. CHANGING ROLES OF MEN AND WOMEN: WHAT IT MEANS TO YOUTH.
Ages 11 and up. 787, Vol. 1
Schwarzrock, Shirley and C. Gilbert Wrenn. MY LIFE —WHAT SHALL I DO WITH IT?
Ages 13 and up. 794, Vol. 1
Sommerfelt, Aimee. THE WHITE BUNGALOW.
Ages 10-13. 840, Vol. 1
Strasser, Todd. FRIENDS TILL THE END.
Ages 12 and up. 636, Vol. 3

## Singer

Taylor, Paula. JOHNNY CASH.
Ages 7-10. 638, Vol. 2
Tobias, Tobi. MARIAN ANDERSON.
Ages 7-10. 898, Vol. 1

## Sports

Jacobs, Helen Hull. THE TENNIS MACHINE.
Ages 12 and up. 455, Vol. 1
Robinson, John Roosevelt and Alfred Duckett. BREAKTHROUGH TO THE BIG LEAGUE: THE STORY OF JACKIE ROBINSON.
Ages 10 and up. 746, Vol. 1
Rudeen, Kenneth. JACKIE ROBINSON.
Ages 7-9. 757, Vol. 1

## Catholic, Roman

**See:** Roman Catholic

## Censorship, Literary

Miles, Betty. MAUDIE AND ME AND THE DIRTY BOOK.
Ages 10-12. 423, Vol. 3

## Cerebral Palsy

**See also:** Birth defects; Brain injury; Spastic
Adler, Carole Schwerdtfeger. DOWN BY THE RIVER.
Ages 12 and up. 4, Vol. 3

Fassler, Joan. HOWIE HELPS HIMSELF.
Ages 5-8. 224, Vol. 2
Gerson, Corinne. PASSING THROUGH.
Ages 12 and up. 245, Vol. 2
Gould, Marilyn. GOLDEN DAFFODILS.
Ages 8-12. 223, Vol. 3
Killilea, Marie Lyons. KAREN.
Ages 12 and up. 495, Vol. 1
Killilea, Marie Lyons. WITH LOVE FROM KAREN.
Ages 12 and up. 496, Vol. 1
Little, Jean. MINE FOR KEEPS.
Ages 10-13. 574, Vol. 1
Mack, Nancy. TRACY.
Ages 4-8. 428, Vol. 2
Neufeld, John. TOUCHING.
Ages 12 and up. 665, Vol. 1
Payne, Sherry Neuwirth. A CONTEST.
Ages 8-10. 486, Vol. 3
Rivera, Geraldo. A SPECIAL KIND OF COURAGE: PROFILES OF YOUNG AMERICANS.
Ages 12 and up. 544, Vol. 2
Robinet, Harriette Gillem. JAY AND THE MARIGOLD.
Ages 6-9. 547, Vol. 2
Slepian, Jan. THE ALFRED SUMMER.
Ages 11-13. 603, Vol. 3
Slepian, Jan. LESTER'S TURN.
Ages 11-14. 604, Vol. 3
Stein, Sara Bonnett. ABOUT HANDICAPS: AN OPEN FAMILY BOOK FOR PARENTS AND CHILDREN TOGETHER.
Ages 4-8. 856, Vol. 1
Sullivan, Mary Beth and Alan J. Brightman and Joseph Blatt. FEELING FREE.
Ages 9 and up. 640, Vol. 3
Viscardi, Henry. A LAUGHTER IN THE LONELY NIGHT.
Ages 12 and up. 931, Vol. 1

## Change

Hargreaves, Roger. MR. NOISY.
Ages 3-7. 264, Vol. 3

## Accepting

Abercrombie, Barbara Mattes. CAT-MAN'S DAUGHTER.
Ages 11-13. 1, Vol. 3
Agle, Nan Hayden. SUSAN'S MAGIC.
Ages 9-11. 3, Vol. 1
Alda, Arlene. SONYA'S MOMMY WORKS.
Ages 4-7. 10, Vol. 3
Ames, Mildred. NICKY AND THE JOYOUS NOISE.
Ages 9-12. 14, Vol. 3
Angell, Judie. WHAT'S BEST FOR YOU.
Ages 11-14. 21, Vol. 3
Bachmann, Evelyn Trent. TRESSA.
Ages 8-12. 42, Vol. 1
Bates, Betty. PICKING UP THE PIECES.
Ages 10-13. 40, Vol. 3
Bawden, Nina Mary Kark. THE ROBBERS.
Ages 9-12. 43, Vol. 3
Behrens, June York. SOO LING FINDS A WAY.
Ages 4-8. 62, Vol. 1
Bennett, Jack. THE VOYAGE OF THE LUCKY DRAGON.
Ages 11 and up. 45, Vol. 3
Berman, Claire. WHAT AM I DOING IN A STEP-FAMILY?
Ages 5-10. 51, Vol. 3
Bernstein, Joanne Eckstein. DMITRY: A YOUNG SOVIET IMMIGRANT.
Ages 11-13. 52, Vol. 3
Blaine, Margery Kay. THE TERRIBLE THING THAT HAPPENED AT OUR HOUSE.
Ages 3-7. 56, Vol. 2

## Change (cont.)

**Change (cont.)**

Sobol, Harriet Langsam. MY OTHER-MOTHER, MY OTHER-FATHER.
  Ages 7-10. 616, Vol. 3
Strete, Craig Kee. PAINT YOUR FACE ON A DROWNING IN THE RIVER.
  Ages 12 and up. 629, Vol. 2
Sugarman, Daniel A. and Rolaine A. Hochstein. SEVEN STORIES FOR GROWTH.
  Ages 6-12. 880, Vol. 1
Thiele, Colin Milton. THE HAMMERHEAD LIGHT.
  Ages 10-12. 645, Vol. 2
Voigt, Cynthia. HOMECOMING.
  Ages 11 and up. 672, Vol. 3
Walker, Mary Alexander. YEAR OF THE CAFETERIA.
  Ages 12 and up. 943, Vol. 1
Wallace-Brodeur, Ruth. THE KENTON YEAR.
  Ages 9-11. 676, Vol. 3
Watson, Pauline. DAYS WITH DADDY.
  Ages 5-8. 676, Vol. 2
Watson, Sally. OTHER SANDALS.
  Ages 12 and up. 956, Vol. 1
Wilkinson, Brenda Scott. LUDELL'S NEW YORK TIME.
  Ages 12 and up. 691, Vol. 3
Winthrop, Elizabeth. WALKING AWAY.
  Ages 11 and up. 979, Vol. 1
Wright, Betty Ren. MY NEW MOM AND ME.
  Ages 8-10. 710, Vol. 3
Zalben, Jane Breskin. MAYBE IT WILL RAIN TOMORROW.
  Ages 12 and up. 716, Vol. 3
Zelonky, Joy. MY BEST FRIEND MOVED AWAY.
  Ages 6-9. 719, Vol. 3

**New home.** *See also: Life style: change in; Moving*
Armer, Alberta. SCREWBALL.
  Ages 9-11. 29, Vol. 1
Bachmann, Evelyn Trent. TRESSA.
  Ages 8-12. 42, Vol. 1
Bernays, Anne. GROWING UP RICH.
  Ages 13 and up. 52, Vol. 2
Bethancourt, T. Ernesto, pseud. NEW YORK CITY TOO FAR FROM TAMPA BLUES.
  Ages 10-14. 55, Vol. 2
Blue, Rose. A MONTH OF SUNDAYS.
  Ages 9-11. 84, Vol. 1
Blume, Judy Sussman. SUPERFUDGE.
  Ages 8-10. 56, Vol. 3
Brandenberg, Franz. NICE NEW NEIGHBORS.
  Ages 6-8. 74, Vol. 2
Brink, Carol Ryrie. THE BAD TIMES OF IRMA BAUMLEIN.
  Ages 10-13. 119, Vol. 1
Bulla, Clyde Robert. OPEN THE DOOR AND SEE ALL THE PEOPLE.
  Ages 8-11. 136, Vol. 1
Carpelan, Bo Gustaf Bertelsson. DOLPHINS IN THE CITY.
  Ages 12-14. 118, Vol. 2
Chaikin, Miriam. I SHOULD WORRY, I SHOULD CARE.
  Ages 8-11. 111, Vol. 3
Chandler, Edna Walker. INDIAN PAINTBRUSH.
  Ages 9-11. 126, Vol. 2
Chetin, Helen. HOW FAR IS BERKELEY?
  Ages 11-13. 128, Vol. 2
Cleaver, Vera and Bill Cleaver. DUST OF THE EARTH.
  Ages 12 and up. 139, Vol. 2
Colman, Hila Crayder. MIXED MARRIAGE DAUGHTER.
  Ages 11 and up. 232, Vol. 1
Conford, Ellen. ANYTHING FOR A FRIEND.
  Ages 9-11. 136, Vol. 3

Corcoran, Barbara. MAKE NO SOUND.
  Ages 10-13. 181, Vol. 2
Danziger, Paula. THE DIVORCE EXPRESS.
  Ages 11-14. 150, Vol. 3
Dixon, Jeanne. LADY CAT LOST.
  Ages 10-12. 164, Vol. 3
Friedman, Frieda. CAROL FROM THE COUNTRY.
  Ages 9-12. 334, Vol. 1
Gage, Wilson, pseud. BIG BLUE ISLAND.
  Ages 9-11. 341, Vol. 1
Galbraith, Kathryn Osebold. COME SPRING.
  Ages 9-13. 197, Vol. 3
Garrigue, Sheila. BETWEEN FRIENDS.
  Ages 9-12. 243, Vol. 2
Giff, Patricia Reilly. THE WINTER WORM BUSINESS.
  Ages 8-10. 214, Vol. 3
Gordon, Shirley. THE BOY WHO WANTED A FAMILY.
  Ages 7-9. 222, Vol. 3
Graeber, Charlotte Towner. GREY CLOUD.
  Ages 9-11. 226, Vol. 3
Green, Phyllis. MILDRED MURPHY, HOW DOES YOUR GARDEN GROW?
  Ages 9-11. 263, Vol. 2
Guy, Rosa Cuthbert. THE FRIENDS.
  Ages 12 and up. 391, Vol. 1
Harris, Mark Jonathan. WITH A WAVE OF THE WAND.
  Ages 9-12. 267, Vol. 3
Hautzig, Esther Rudomin. THE ENDLESS STEPPE: A GROWING UP IN SIBERIA.
  Ages 11 and up. 406, Vol. 1
Hickman, Janet. THE THUNDER-PUP.
  Ages 9-11. 289, Vol. 3
Hoff, Sydney. IRVING AND ME.
  Ages 12 and up. 424, Vol. 1
Hughes, Shirley. MOVING MOLLY.
  Ages 3-5. 310, Vol. 3
Hurwitz, Johanna. ALDO APPLESAUCE.
  Ages 7-9. 316, Vol. 3
Hurwitz, Johanna. TOUGH-LUCK KAREN.
  Ages 10-13. 319, Vol. 3
Irion, Ruth Hershey. THE CHRISTMAS COOKIE TREE.
  Ages 8-10. 345, Vol. 2
Isadora, Rachel. THE POTTERS' KITCHEN.
  Ages 4-8. 347, Vol. 2
Jackson, Jacqueline. THE TASTE OF SPRUCE GUM.
  Ages 10-13. 454, Vol. 1
Jacobson, Jane. CITY, SING FOR ME: A COUNTRY CHILD MOVES TO THE CITY.
  Ages 6-10. 349, Vol. 2
Johnson, Annabel Jones and Edgar Raymond Johnson. THE RESCUED HEART.
  Ages 12 and up. 464, Vol. 1
Keats, Ezra Jack. THE TRIP.
  Ages 4-7. 368, Vol. 2
Kerr, Judith. WHEN HITLER STOLE PINK RABBIT.
  Ages 10-12. 490, Vol. 1
Kesselman, Wendy Ann. ANGELITA.
  Ages 5-9. 494, Vol. 1
Krumgold, Joseph E. HENRY 3.
  Ages 11 and up. 522, Vol. 1
Lewiton, Mina Simon. CANDITA'S CHOICE.
  Ages 8-11. 551, Vol. 1
Lewiton, Mina Simon. THAT BAD CARLOS.
  Ages 8-11. 552, Vol. 1
Lingard, Joan. A PROPER PLACE.
  Ages 12 and up. 407, Vol. 2
Litchfield, Ada Bassett. WORDS IN OUR HANDS.
  Ages 7-9. 378, Vol. 3
Little, Jean. FROM ANNA.
  Ages 9-11. 570, Vol. 1

## Classmate Relationships

**See:** *School: classmate relationships*

## Claustrophobia

**See:** *Fear: of enclosed spaces*

## Cleanliness

**See:** *Baths, taking of*

## Cleft Lip/Palate

**See also:** *Birth defects; Speech problems; Surgery*
Lowery, Bruce. SCARRED.
  Ages 12 and up. 588, Vol. 1
McKillip, Patricia A. THE NIGHT GIFT.
  Ages 11 and up. 430, Vol. 2
Richter, Elizabeth. THE TEENAGE HOSPITAL
  EXPERIENCE: YOU CAN HANDLE IT!
  Ages 12 and up. 532, Vol. 3

## Cliques

**See also:** *Belonging; Clubs; Gangs*
Wrenn, C. Gilbert and Shirley Schwarzrock. COPING
  WITH CLIQUES.
  Ages 11 and up. 998, Vol. 1

## Clowning

**See:** *Attention seeking*

## Clubs

**See also:** *Belonging; Cliques; Gangs*
Bonsall, Crosby Newell. THE CASE OF THE
  DOUBLE CROSS.
  Ages 6-8. 62, Vol. 3
Bunting, Anne Evelyn. SKATEBOARD FOUR.
  Ages 8-10. 98, Vol. 2
Fife, Dale. WHAT'S THE PRIZE, LINCOLN?
  Ages 8-10. 313, Vol. 1
Fife, Dale. WHO GOES THERE, LINCOLN?
  Ages 8-10. 228, Vol. 2
Gauch, Patricia Lee. FRIDAYS.
  Ages 11-13. 204, Vol. 3
Greene, Bette. GET ON OUT OF HERE, PHILIP
  HALL.
  Ages 9-12. 238, Vol. 3
Hodges, Margaret Moore. A CLUB AGAINST KEATS.
  Ages 8-10. 422, Vol. 1
Hogan, Paula Z. I HATE BOYS I HATE GIRLS.
  Ages 5-8. 296, Vol. 3
Huntsberry, William Emery. THE BIG WHEELS.
  Ages 12 and up. 446, Vol. 1
Myers, Walter Dean. FAST SAM, COOL CLYDE, AND
  STUFF.
  Ages 11-14. 469, Vol. 2
Perl, Lila. THE TELLTALE SUMMER OF TINA C.
  Ages 10-13. 503, Vol. 2
Phipson, Joan Nash, pseud. PETER AND BUTCH.
  Ages 10 and up. 709, Vol. 1
Robinson, Jean. THE SECRET LIFE OF T.K.
  DEARING.
  Ages 10 and up. 744, Vol. 1
Wrenn, C. Gilbert and Shirley Schwarzrock. IN
  FRONT OF THE TABLE AND BEHIND IT.
  Ages 11 and up. 1003, Vol. 1

## Commune

**See also:** *Life style*
Arundel, Honor. A FAMILY FAILING.
  Ages 12 and up. 36, Vol. 1
Corcoran, Barbara. DON'T SLAM THE DOOR WHEN
  YOU GO.
  Ages 12 and up. 249, Vol. 1

Elfman, Blossom. THE BUTTERFLY GIRL.
  Ages 13 and up. 180, Vol. 3
Forman, James. MY ENEMY, MY BROTHER.
  Ages 12 and up. 326, Vol. 1
Kingman, Lee. THE REFINER'S FIRE.
  Ages 12-14. 341, Vol. 3
Loree, Sharron. THE SUNSHINE FAMILY AND THE
  PONY.
  Ages 6-8. 585, Vol. 1
Rich, Louise Dickinson. SUMMER AT HIGH
  KINGDOM.
  Ages 12 and up. 536, Vol. 2
Shaw, Richard. THE HARD WAY HOME.
  Ages 11-13. 592, Vol. 2
Watson, Sally. OTHER SANDALS.
  Ages 12 and up. 956, Vol. 1

## Communicable Diseases

**See also:** *Illnesses*

### Chicken pox

Galbraith, Kathryn Osebold. SPOTS ARE SPECIAL!
  Ages 4-7. 241, Vol. 2
Lerner, Marguerite Rush. PETER GETS THE
  CHICKENPOX.
  Ages 3-7. 549, Vol. 1
Terris, Susan Dubinsky. THE CHICKEN POX
  PAPERS.
  Ages 10-12. 640, Vol. 2
Wolde, Gunilla. BETSY AND THE CHICKEN POX.
  Ages 3-7. 696, Vol. 2

### Measles

Lerner, Marguerite Rush. MICHAEL GETS THE
  MEASLES.
  Ages 3-7. 548, Vol. 1

### Mumps

Lerner, Marguerite Rush. DEAR LITTLE MUMPS
  CHILD.
  Ages 3-7. 546, Vol. 1

## Communication

Berger, Terry. A FRIEND CAN HELP.
  Ages 3-7. 73, Vol. 1
Conta, Marcia Maher and Maureen
  Reardon. FEELINGS BETWEEN KIDS AND
  GROWNUPS.
  Ages 3-6. 243, Vol. 1
Gripe, Maria Kristina. THE NIGHT DADDY.
  Ages 8-11. 387, Vol. 1
Schwarzrock, Shirley and C. Gilbert Wrenn. YOU
  ALWAYS COMMUNICATE SOMETHING.
  Ages 11 and up. 798, Vol. 1
Wrenn, C. Gilbert and Shirley Schwarzrock. CAN
  YOU TALK WITH SOMEONE ELSE?
  Ages 11 and up. 997, Vol. 1

### Importance of

Baldwin, Anne Norris. A LITTLE TIME.
  Ages 9-11. 30, Vol. 2
Barkin, Carol and Elizabeth James. SOMETIMES I
  HATE SCHOOL.
  Ages 5-7. 34, Vol. 2
Brooks, Jerome. THE TESTING OF CHARLIE
  HAMMELMAN.
  Ages 10-13. 84, Vol. 2
Castle, Sue. FACE TALK, HAND TALK, BODY TALK.
  Ages 4-7. 123, Vol. 2
Dacquino, Vincent T. KISS THE CANDY DAYS
  GOOD-BYE.
  Ages 10-14. 148, Vol. 3
Gerson, Corinne. PASSING THROUGH.
  Ages 12 and up. 245, Vol. 2
Grohskopf, Bernice. SHADOW IN THE SUN.
  Ages 10 and up. 281, Vol. 2

## Communication (cont.)

Peck, Richard. FATHER FIGURE: A NOVEL.
Ages 11 and up. 501, Vol. 2
Peck, Robert Newton. A DAY NO PIGS WOULD DIE.
Ages 12 and up. 697, Vol. 1
Perl, Lila. DUMB, LIKE ME, OLIVIA POTTS.
Ages 9-12. 502, Vol. 2
Perl, Lila. ME AND FAT GLENDA.
Ages 9-12. 700, Vol. 1
Perl, Lila. THAT CRAZY APRIL.
Ages 10-12. 701, Vol. 1
Platt, Kin. BROGG'S BRAIN.
Ages 12 and up. 514, Vol. 3
Platt, Kin. CHLORIS AND THE WEIRDOS.
Ages 11 and up. 516, Vol. 2
Potok, Chaim. THE CHOSEN.
Ages 13 and up. 715, Vol. 1
Rabe, Berniece Louise. RASS.
Ages 12 and up. 720, Vol. 1
Rinkoff, Barbara Jean Rich. NAME: JOHNNY
PIERCE.
Ages 10-12. 738, Vol. 1
Robinson, Nancy Konheim. WENDY AND THE
BULLIES.
Ages 7-10. 539, Vol. 3
Rodgers, Mary. FREAKY FRIDAY.
Ages 10-13. 749, Vol. 1
Rogers, Pamela. THE STONE ANGEL.
Ages 10-12. 558, Vol. 2
Roth, Arthur J. THE SECRET LOVER OF ELMTREE.
Ages 12 and up. 563, Vol. 2
Sachs, Marilyn. AMY AND LAURA.
Ages 9-12. 759, Vol. 1
Sachs, Marilyn. DORRIE'S BOOK.
Ages 9-12. 566, Vol. 2
Sallis, Susan Diana. A TIME FOR EVERYTHING.
Ages 13 and up. 569, Vol. 3
Sandberg, Inger and Lasse Sandberg. COME ON
OUT, DADDY.
Ages 4-7. 769, Vol. 1
Schotter, Roni. A MATTER OF TIME.
Ages 12 and up. 575, Vol. 3
Schwarzrock, Shirley and C. Gilbert
Wrenn. PARENTS CAN BE A PROBLEM.
Ages 11 and up. 795, Vol. 1
Sebestyen, Ouida. FAR FROM HOME.
Ages 12 and up. 579, Vol. 3
Sebestyen, Ouida. WORDS BY HEART.
Ages 10-13. 580, Vol. 3
Shaw, Richard. SHAPE UP, BURKE.
Ages 10-14. 593, Vol. 2
Sherburne, Zoa. STRANGER IN THE HOUSE.
Ages 11 and up. 813, Vol. 1
Skorpen, Liesel Moak. MICHAEL.
Ages 4-8. 609, Vol. 2
Slote, Alfred. LOVE AND TENNIS.
Ages 12-14. 605, Vol. 3
Stecher, Miriam B. and Alice S. Kandell. DADDY
AND BEN TOGETHER.
Ages 4-6. 624, Vol. 3
Stein, Sara Bonnett. ON DIVORCE: AN OPEN
FAMILY BOOK FOR PARENTS AND CHILDREN
TOGETHER.
Ages 4-8. 626, Vol. 3
Stolz, Mary Slattery. LEAP BEFORE YOU LOOK.
Ages 12 and up. 869, Vol. 1
Stolz, Mary Slattery. A LOVE, OR A SEASON.
Ages 12 and up. 870, Vol. 1
Stretton, Barbara. YOU NEVER LOSE.
Ages 12 and up. 639, Vol. 3
Talbot, Charlene Joy. THE GREAT RAT ISLAND
ADVENTURE.
Ages 10-13. 634, Vol. 2
Tobias, Tobi. THE QUITTING DEAL.
Ages 7-9. 654, Vol. 2

Towne, Mary. THE GLASS ROOM.
Ages 11 and up. 899, Vol. 1
Townsend, John Rowe. NOAH'S CASTLE.
Ages 11 and up. 656, Vol. 2
Udry, Janice May. THE SUNFLOWER GARDEN.
Ages 6-10. 913, Vol. 1
Valencak, Hannelore. A TANGLED WEB.
Ages 9-11. 659, Vol. 2
Van Leeuwen, Jean. SEEMS LIKE THIS ROAD GOES
ON FOREVER.
Ages 12 and up. 663, Vol. 3
Van Steenwyk, Elizabeth Ann. RIVALS ON ICE.
Ages 9-11. 664, Vol. 3
Watson, Pauline. DAYS WITH DADDY.
Ages 5-8. 676, Vol. 3
Whelan, Gloria. A TIME TO KEEP SILENT.
Ages 11-14. 690, Vol. 3
Winthrop, Elizabeth. SLOPPY KISSES.
Ages 4-7. 698, Vol. 3
Wood, Phyllis Anderson. WIN ME AND YOU LOSE.
Ages 10-13. 709, Vol. 2
Woody, Regina Llewellyn Jones. ONE DAY AT A
TIME.
Ages 11 and up. 992, Vol. 1
Yep, Laurence Michael. DRAGONWINGS.
Ages 12 and up. 712, Vol. 2
Yep, Laurence Michael. SEA GLASS.
Ages 11-14. 713, Vol. 3
Zolotow, Charlotte Shapiro. IF YOU LISTEN.
Ages 5-7. 722, Vol. 3
Zolotow, Charlotte Shapiro. ONE STEP, TWO...
Ages 2-5. 724, Vol. 3
Zolotow, Charlotte Shapiro. WHEN THE WIND
STOPS.
Ages 5-7. 722, Vol. 2

## Rumor

Hayes, Sheila. ME AND MY MONA LISA SMILE.
Ages 11-13. 274, Vol. 3
Rinaldi, Ann. PROMISES ARE FOR KEEPING.
Ages 12 and up. 534, Vol. 3
Rinkoff, Barbara Jean Rich. THE WATCHERS.
Ages 11-14. 740, Vol. 1
Terris, Susan Dubinsky. TWO P'S IN A POD.
Ages 9-12. 641, Vol. 2
Tolan, Stephanie S. THE LAST OF EDEN.
Ages 12 and up. 659, Vol. 3
Vigna, Judith. GREGORY'S STITCHES.
Ages 4-7. 924, Vol. 1

## Compensation

Arthur, Ruth M. MY DAUGHTER, NICOLA.
Ages 10-13. 33, Vol. 1
Beim, Jerrold. THE SMALLEST BOY IN THE CLASS.
Ages 5-8. 64, Vol. 1
Little, Jean. ONE TO GROW ON.
Ages 10-12. 575, Vol. 1
White, Elwyn Brooks. THE TRUMPET OF THE
SWAN.
Ages 9-13. 968, Vol. 1

## Competition

See also: Little League; Sports/Sportsmanship
Bach, Alice. THE MEAT IN THE SANDWICH.
Ages 10-13. 28, Vol. 2
Douglass, Barbara. SKATEBOARD SCRAMBLE.
Ages 9-11. 170, Vol. 3
Gilbert, Nan, pseud. CHAMPIONS DON'T CRY.
Ages 10-13. 358, Vol. 1
Hall, Lynn. HALF THE BATTLE.
Ages 11 and up. 255, Vol. 3
Katz, Bobbi. VOLLEYBALL JINX.
Ages 9-11. 364, Vol. 2
Knudson, R. Rozanne. ZANBANGER.
Ages 10-13. 387, Vol. 2

**Cooperation (cont.)**

**in Work**

Barkin, Carol and Elizabeth James. DOING THINGS
TOGETHER.
Ages 4-7. 32, Vol. 2

Beskow, Elsa Maartman. PELLE'S NEW SUIT.
Ages 4-7. 75, Vol. 1

Bishop, Claire Huchet. ALL ALONE.
Ages 7-10. 78, Vol. 1

Black, Irma Simonton. THE LITTLE OLD MAN WHO
COOKED AND CLEANED.
Ages 4-8. 79, Vol. 1

Blaine, Margery Kay. THE TERRIBLE THING THAT
HAPPENED AT OUR HOUSE.
Ages 3-7. 56, Vol. 2

Bond, Nancy Barbara. THE VOYAGE BEGUN.
Ages 12 and up. 60, Vol. 3

Bradbury, Bianca. "I'M VINNY, I'M ME".
Ages 12 and up. 65, Vol. 2

Buckley, Peter and Hortense Jones. WILLIAM, ANDY,
AND RAMON.
Ages 6-8. 133, Vol. 1

Cleaver, Vera and Bill Cleaver. DUST OF THE
EARTH.
Ages 12 and up. 139, Vol. 2

Dauer, Rosamond. BULLFROG BUILDS A HOUSE.
Ages 4-7. 191, Vol. 2

Delton, Judy. TWO GOOD FRIENDS.
Ages 5-7. 269, Vol. 1

Hoban, Lillian Aberman. ARTHUR'S FUNNY
MONEY.
Ages 6-8. 294, Vol. 3

Hunt, Irene. WILLIAM: A NOVEL.
Ages 12 and up. 338, Vol. 2

Jones, Adrienne. SAIL, CALYPSO!
Ages 10-13. 469, Vol. 1

Lionni, Leo. SWIMMY.
Ages 3-7. 567, Vol. 1

Mann, Peggy. THE STREET OF THE FLOWER
BOXES.
Ages 8-11. 610, Vol. 1

Matthews, Ellen. THE TROUBLE WITH LESLIE.
Ages 8-11. 409, Vol. 3

Melton, David. A BOY CALLED HOPELESS.
Ages 10 and up. 451, Vol. 2

Molarsky, Osmond. WHERE THE GOOD LUCK WAS.
Ages 8-10. 641, Vol. 1

Myers, Walter Dean. THE YOUNG LANDLORDS.
Ages 11-14. 461, Vol. 3

Naylor, Phyllis Reynolds. EDDIE, INCORPORATED.
Ages 9-11. 463, Vol. 3

Renner, Beverly Hollett. THE HIDEAWAY SUMMER.
Ages 10-13. 531, Vol. 2

Sachs, Marilyn. A SUMMER'S LEASE.
Ages 11-14. 566, Vol. 3

Wiesner, William. TURNABOUT: A NORWEGIAN
TALE.
Ages 4-8. 973, Vol. 1

**Coping**

**See:** *Problem solving; Resourcefulness*

**Copycat**

**See:** *Name-calling*

**Copying**

**See:** *Honesty/Dishonesty; Imitation*

**Courage, Meaning of**

**See also:** *Encouragement; Fear*

Adler, Carole Schwerdtfeger. THE ONCE IN A
WHILE HERO.
Ages 10-13. 7, Vol. 3

Annixter, Jane, pseud. and Paul Annixter,
pseud. WINDIGO.
Ages 10 and up. 25, Vol. 1

Arthur, Ruth M. MY DAUGHTER, NICOLA.
Ages 10-13. 33, Vol. 1

Asher, Sandra Fenichel. DAUGHTERS OF THE LAW.
Ages 11-13. 26, Vol. 3

Bach, Alice Hendricks. WAITING FOR JOHNNY
MIRACLE.
Ages 12 and up. 32, Vol. 3

Bailey, Carolyn Sherwin. FLICKERTAIL.
Ages 8-10. 43, Vol. 1

Balderson, Margaret. WHEN JAYS FLY TO BARBMO.
Ages 12 and up. 48, Vol. 1

Ball, Zachary, pseud. KEP.
Ages 10 and up. 50, Vol. 1

Beatty, Hetty Burlingame. LITTLE OWL INDIAN.
Ages 4-7. 59, Vol. 1

Bell, Frederic. JENNY'S CORNER.
Ages 8-11. 65, Vol. 1

Bennett, Jack. THE VOYAGE OF THE LUCKY
DRAGON.
Ages 11 and up. 45, Vol. 3

Bishop, Claire Huchet. ALL ALONE.
Ages 7-10. 78, Vol. 1

Bosworth, J. Allan. ALL THE DARK PLACES.
Ages 12 and up. 104, Vol. 1

Bosworth, J. Allan. WHITE WATER, STILL WATER.
Ages 11 and up. 105, Vol. 1

Brady, Mari. PLEASE REMEMBER ME: A YOUNG
WOMAN'S STORY OF HER FRIENDSHIP WITH
AN UNFORGETTABLE FIFTEEN-YEAR-OLD BOY.
Ages 12 and up. 68, Vol. 2

Brancato, Robin Fidler. WINNING.
Ages 12 and up. 72, Vol. 2

Breisky, William. I THINK I CAN.
Ages 12 and up. 115, Vol. 1

Brink, Carol Ryrie. CADDIE WOODLAWN: A
FRONTIER STORY.
Ages 9-12. 120, Vol. 1

Brooks, Jerome. MAKE ME A HERO.
Ages 9-12. 78, Vol. 3

Bunting, Anne Evelyn. HIGH TIDE FOR LABRADOR.
Ages 9-11. 95, Vol. 2

Calhoun, Mary Huiskamp. THE NIGHT THE
MONSTER CAME.
Ages 8-10. 102, Vol. 3

Campanella, Roy. IT'S GOOD TO BE ALIVE.
Ages 13 and up. 160, Vol. 1

Chaffin, Lillie Dorton. WE BE WARM TILL
SPRINGTIME COMES.
Ages 6-9. 110, Vol. 3

Christman, Elizabeth. A NICE ITALIAN GIRL.
Ages 12 and up. 132, Vol. 2

Church, Richard. FIVE BOYS IN A CAVE.
Ages 9-12. 185, Vol. 1

Clayton, Edward Taylor. MARTIN LUTHER KING:
THE PEACEFUL WARRIOR.
Ages 8-10. 189, Vol. 1

Clyne, Patricia Edwards. TUNNELS OF TERROR.
Ages 10-12. 149, Vol. 2

Coates, Belle. MAK.
Ages 12 and up. 124, Vol. 3

Coerr, Eleanor. SADAKO AND THE THOUSAND
PAPER CRANES.
Ages 11 and up. 151, Vol. 2

Cohen, Peter Zachary. BEE.
Ages 10-13. 157, Vol. 2

Conford, Ellen. THE REVENGE OF THE
INCREDIBLE DR. RANCID AND HIS YOUTHFUL
ASSISTANT, JEFFREY.
Ages 10-12. 137, Vol. 3

Corbin, William, pseud. GOLDEN MARE.
Ages 9-12. 246, Vol. 1

**Courage, Meaning of (cont.)**

Rogers, Helen Spelman. MORRIS AND HIS BRAVE LION.
Ages 4-7. 557, Vol. 2
Roy, Ronald. AVALANCHE!
Ages 10 and up. 555, Vol. 3
Rudeen, Kenneth. JACKIE ROBINSON.
Ages 7-9. 757, Vol. 1
Saint-Marcoux, Jeanne. THE LIGHT.
Ages 12 and up. 766, Vol. 1
Sandoz, Mari. THE HORSECATCHER.
Ages 12 and up. 771, Vol. 1
Savitz, Harriet May. ON THE MOVE.
Ages 10 and up. 775, Vol. 1
Schaefer, Jack Warner. OLD RAMON.
Ages 10 and up. 777, Vol. 1
Scoppettone, Sandra. HAPPY ENDINGS ARE ALL ALIKE.
Ages 12 and up. 578, Vol. 2
Sebestyen, Ouida. WORDS BY HEART.
Ages 10-13. 580, Vol. 3
Simon, Marcia L. A SPECIAL GIFT.
Ages 10-13. 601, Vol. 2
Slote, Alfred. HANG TOUGH, PAUL MATHER.
Ages 10 and up. 827, Vol. 1
Smith, Pauline Coggeshall. BRUSH FIRE!
Ages 11 and up. 613, Vol. 3
Sommerfelt, Aimee. THE ROAD TO AGRA.
Ages 10-13. 839, Vol. 1
Southall, Ivan. HILLS END.
Ages 11 and up. 846, Vol. 1
Sperry, Armstrong. CALL IT COURAGE.
Ages 9 and up. 849, Vol. 1
Stapp, Arthur Donald. ORDEAL BY MOUNTAINS.
Ages 11 and up. 853, Vol. 1
Steele, William Owen. FLAMING ARROWS.
Ages 10-12. 854, Vol. 1
Stolz, Mary Slattery. SIRI THE CONQUISTADOR.
Ages 8-11. 875, Vol. 1
Swarthout, Glendon Fred and Kathryn Swarthout. WHICHAWAY.
Ages 10 and up. 883, Vol. 1
Taylor, Mildred D. SONG OF THE TREES.
Ages 8-11. 637, Vol. 2
Tester, Sylvia Root. THAT BIG BRUNO.
Ages 3-7. 644, Vol. 2
Treffinger, Carolyn. LI LUN, LAD OF COURAGE.
Ages 8-11. 903, Vol. 1
Turkle, Brinton. THE FIDDLER OF HIGH LONESOME.
Ages 5-10. 907, Vol. 1
Uchida, Yoshiko. JOURNEY TO TOPAZ: A STORY OF THE JAPANESE-AMERICAN EVACUATION.
Ages 9-12. 910, Vol. 1
Ullman, James Ramsey. BANNER IN THE SKY.
Ages 12 and up. 915, Vol. 1
Viscardi, Henry. A MAN'S STATURE.
Ages 12 and up. 932, Vol. 1
Wallace, Bill. A DOG CALLED KITTY.
Ages 9-11. 675, Vol. 3
Wartski, Maureen Crane. A BOAT TO NOWHERE.
Ages 9-12. 678, Vol. 3
Wartski, Maureen Crane. THE LAKE IS ON FIRE.
Ages 10-13. 679, Vol. 3
Wier, Ester Alberti. THE BARREL.
Ages 10-13. 970, Vol. 1
Wojciechowska, Maia Rodman. SHADOW OF A BULL.
Ages 11 and up. 985, Vol. 1

**Courtesy**

See: *Etiquette*

**Cousin**

See: *Relatives; Relatives: living in home of*

**Crackers**

Lenski, Lois. STRAWBERRY GIRL.
Ages 9-11. 545, Vol. 1

**Crazy**

See: *Mental illness*

**Creativity**

See also: *Curiosity; Fantasy formation; Imagination; Problem solving; Resourcefulness*
Bulla, Clyde Robert. DANIEL'S DUCK.
Ages 5-8. 85, Vol. 3
Byars, Betsy Cromer. THE CARTOONIST.
Ages 8-12. 107, Vol. 2
Byars, Betsy Cromer. GO AND HUSH THE BABY.
Ages 3-6. 155, Vol. 1
Coatsworth, Elizabeth Jane. LONELY MARIA.
Ages 4-8. 214, Vol. 1
Fife, Dale. WHO'LL VOTE FOR LINCOLN?
Ages 8-10. 229, Vol. 2
Garlan, Patricia Wallace and Maryjane Dunstan. THE BOY WHO PLAYED TIGER.
Ages 9-11. 347, Vol. 1
Gauch, Patricia Lee. CHRISTINA KATERINA & THE BOX.
Ages 4-7. 350, Vol. 1
Greenwald, Sheila. THE SECRET IN MIRANDA'S CLOSET.
Ages 8-11. 274, Vol. 2
Hodges, Margaret Moore. A CLUB AGAINST KEATS.
Ages 8-10. 422, Vol. 1
Holl, Adelaide Hinkle. SMALL BEAR BUILDS A PLAYHOUSE.
Ages 5-7. 326, Vol. 2
Lionni, Leo. FREDERICK.
Ages 5-8. 566, Vol. 1
Phelan, Terry Wolfe. THE WEEK MOM UNPLUGGED THE TVS.
Ages 8-10. 506, Vol. 3
Robinson, Jean. THE STRANGE BUT WONDERFUL COSMIC AWARENESS OF DUFFY MOON.
Ages 9-12. 745, Vol. 1
Sachs, Marilyn. MARV.
Ages 10-12. 761, Vol. 1
Wosmek, Frances. A BOWL OF SUN.
Ages 7-9. 710, Vol. 2
Yep, Laurence Michael. DRAGONWINGS.
Ages 12 and up. 712, Vol. 2

**Crime/Criminals**

See also: *Accidents: hit and run; Death: murder; Delinquency, juvenile; Detention home, living in; Guilt, feelings of; Imprisonment; Kidnapping; Parole; Probation; Prostitution; Rape; Stealing; Vandalism*
Alter, Judy. AFTER PA WAS SHOT.
Ages 10-13. 11, Vol. 2
Banks, Lynne Reid. THE WRITING ON THE WALL.
Ages 12 and up. 33, Vol. 3
Bawden, Nina Mary Kark. THE ROBBERS.
Ages 9-12. 43, Vol. 3
Bonham, Frank. DURANGO STREET.
Ages 11 and up. 97, Vol. 1
Bradbury, Bianca. THOSE TRAVER KIDS.
Ages 12 and up. 111, Vol. 1
Bradbury, Bianca. WHERE'S JIM NOW?
Ages 11-13. 67, Vol. 2
Butterworth, William Edmund. LEROY AND THE OLD MAN.
Ages 12 and up. 93, Vol. 3
Dunnahoo, Terry. WHO CARES ABOUT ESPIE SANCHEZ?
Ages 10-12. 210, Vol. 2

## Daydreaming (cont.)

O'Hara, Mary, pseud. MY FRIEND FLICKA.
Ages 11 and up. 683, Vol. 1
Sachs, Marilyn. MARV.
Ages 10-12. 761, Vol. 1
Shreve, Susan Richards. THE BAD DREAMS OF A
GOOD GIRL.
Ages 8-10. 589, Vol. 3
Teibl, Margaret. DAVEY COME HOME.
Ages 6-9. 646, Vol. 3
Viorst, Judith. I'LL FIX ANTHONY.
Ages 3-6. 927, Vol. 1
Willard, Mildred Wilds. THE LUCK OF HARRY
WEAVER.
Ages 8-10. 977, Vol. 1
Williams, Barbara Wright. SOMEDAY, SAID
MITCHELL.
Ages 3-6. 686, Vol. 2
Zolotow, Charlotte Shapiro. IF IT WEREN'T FOR
YOU.
Ages 3-6. 1022, Vol. 1

## Deafness

**See also:** *Education: special; Muteness*
Arthur, Catherine. MY SISTER'S SILENT WORLD.
Ages 5-9. 25, Vol. 3
Brown, Marion Marsh and Ruth Crone. THE SILENT
STORM.
Ages 10-13. 125, Vol. 1
Bunting, Anne Evelyn. THE WAITING GAME.
Ages 10 and up. 91, Vol. 3
Coolidge, Olivia Ensor. COME BY HERE.
Ages 11 and up. 245, Vol. 1
Hallman, Ruth. BREAKAWAY.
Ages 12 and up. 257, Vol. 3
Hanlon, Emily. THE SWING.
Ages 10-12. 261, Vol. 3
Hlibok, Bruce. SILENT DANCER.
Ages 8-11. 293, Vol. 3
Hunter, Edith Fisher. CHILD OF THE SILENT
NIGHT.
Ages 9-11. 440, Vol. 1
Kamien, Janet. WHAT IF YOU COULDN'T...? A
BOOK ABOUT SPECIAL NEEDS.
Ages 8-12. 336, Vol. 3
Keller, Helen Adams. THE STORY OF MY LIFE.
Ages 11 and up. 488, Vol. 1
Levine, Edna S. LISA AND HER SOUNDLESS
WORLD.
Ages 5-9. 550, Vol. 1
Levinson, Nancy Smiler. WORLD OF HER OWN.
Ages 12 and up. 368, Vol. 3
Litchfield, Ada Bassett. A BUTTON IN HER EAR.
Ages 5-8. 411, Vol. 2
Litchfield, Ada Bassett. WORDS IN OUR HANDS.
Ages 7-9. 378, Vol. 3
Montgomery, Elizabeth Rider. THE MYSTERY OF
THE BOY NEXT DOOR.
Ages 5-8. 464, Vol. 2
Morgenroth, Barbara. WILL THE REAL RENIE LAKE
PLEASE STAND UP?
Ages 12 and up. 453, Vol. 3
Peare, Catherine Owens. THE HELEN KELLER
STORY.
Ages 10 and up. 693, Vol. 1
Peter, Diana. CLAIRE AND EMMA.
Ages 5-8. 505, Vol. 2
Peterson, Jeanne Whitehouse. I HAVE A SISTER —
MY SISTER IS DEAF.
Ages 4-7. 507, Vol. 1
Pollock, Penny. KEEPING IT SECRET.
Ages 9-12. 515, Vol. 3
Riskind, Mary L. APPLE IS MY SIGN.
Ages 10-14. 536, Vol. 3

Robinson, Veronica. DAVID IN SILENCE.
Ages 12 and up. 747, Vol. 1
Rosen, Lillian D. JUST LIKE EVERYBODY ELSE.
Ages 11 and up. 549, Vol. 3
Sullivan, Mary Beth and Alan J. Brightman and Joseph
Blatt. FEELING FREE.
Ages 9 and up. 640, Vol. 3
Wahl, Jan. JAMIE'S TIGER.
Ages 4-8. 670, Vol. 2
Waite, Helen Elmira. VALIANT COMPANIONS:
HELEN KELLER AND ANNE SULLIVAN MACY.
Ages 10 and up. 941, Vol. 1
Wolf, Bernard. ANNA'S SILENT WORLD.
Ages 5-9. 702, Vol. 2
Zelonky, Joy. I CAN'T ALWAYS HEAR YOU.
Ages 7-10. 718, Vol. 3

## Death

**See also:** *Guilt, feelings of; Loss: feelings of; Mourning,
stages of*
Maruki, Toshi. HIROSHIMA NO PIKA.
Ages 7 and up. 406, Vol. 3
Naylor, Phyllis Reynolds. A STRING OF CHANCES.
Ages 12 and up. 464, Vol. 3
Sallis, Susan Diana. A TIME FOR EVERYTHING.
Ages 13 and up. 569, Vol. 3

### Accidental

Annixter, Paul, pseud. SWIFTWATER.
Ages 13 and up. 26, Vol. 1
Burch, Robert Joseph. SIMON AND THE GAME OF
CHANCE.
Ages 10-12. 142, Vol. 1
Norman, Lilith. CLIMB A LONELY HILL.
Ages 11-14. 671, Vol. 1
Peck, Richard. DREAMLAND LAKE.
Ages 12 and up. 695, Vol. 1

### Attitude toward

Anckarsvard, Karin. SPRINGTIME FOR EVA.
Ages 12 and up. 16, Vol. 1
Anders, Rebecca. A LOOK AT DEATH.
Ages 3-7. 15, Vol. 2
Anderson, Leone Castell. IT'S O.K. TO CRY.
Ages 5-8. 16, Vol. 3
Arnothy, Christine. I AM FIFTEEN AND I DON'T
WANT TO DIE.
Ages 12 and up. 31, Vol. 1
Beckman, Gunnel. THAT EARLY SPRING.
Ages 12 and up. 47, Vol. 2
Bernstein, Joanne Eckstein. and Stephen V.
Gullo. WHEN PEOPLE DIE.
Ages 5-9. 53, Vol. 2
Buck, Pearl Sydenstricker. THE BIG WAVE.
Ages 9-11. 129, Vol. 1
Campbell, R. Wright. WHERE PIGEONS GO TO DIE.
Ages 12 and up. 112, Vol. 2
Coerr, Eleanor. SADAKO AND THE THOUSAND
PAPER CRANES.
Ages 11 and up. 151, Vol. 2
Coutant, Helen. FIRST SNOW.
Ages 7-9. 255, Vol. 1
Dixon, Paige, pseud. MAY I CROSS YOUR GOLDEN
RIVER?
Ages 12 and up. 202, Vol. 2
Dobrin, Arnold. SCAT.
Ages 6-9. 276, Vol. 1
Donnelly, Elfie. SO LONG, GRANDPA.
Ages 9-11. 168, Vol. 3
Farley, Carol J. THE GARDEN IS DOING FINE.
Ages 11 and up. 223, Vol. 2
Gelman, Rita Golden and Warner Friedman. UNCLE
HUGH: A FISHING STORY.
Ages 5-8. 244, Vol. 2

**Death (cont.)**

Lutters, Valerie. THE HAUNTING OF JULIE UNGER.
Ages 10-13. 425, Vol. 2
Madison, Winifred. CALL ME DANICA.
Ages 10-13. 435, Vol. 2
Miner, Jane Claypool. A MAN'S PRIDE: LOSING A
FATHER.
Ages 11 and up. 429, Vol. 3
Molloy, Anne Stearns. THE GIRL FROM TWO
MILES HIGH.
Ages 10-12. 642, Vol. 1
Peck, Robert Newton. A DAY NO PIGS WOULD DIE.
Ages 12 and up. 697, Vol. 1
Pierik, Robert. ROOKFLEAS IN THE CELLAR.
Ages 8-13. 512, Vol. 3
Rabin, Gil. CHANGES.
Ages 12 and up. 721, Vol. 1
Reader, Dennis J. COMING BACK ALIVE.
Ages 12 and up. 525, Vol. 3
Rinaldi, Ann. TERM PAPER.
Ages 12 and up. 535, Vol. 3
Sebestyen, Ouida. WORDS BY HEART.
Ages 10-13. 580, Vol. 3
Sherburne, Zoa. GIRL IN THE MIRROR.
Ages 11 and up. 811, Vol. 1
Terris, Susan Dubinsky. NO SCARLET RIBBONS.
Ages 11-13. 647, Vol. 3
Viscardi, Henry. A MAN'S STATURE.
Ages 12 and up. 932, Vol. 1
Wallace-Brodeur, Ruth. THE KENTON YEAR.
Ages 9-11. 676, Vol. 3
Wersba, Barbara. RUN SOFTLY, GO FAST.
Ages 13 and up. 965, Vol. 1
Wolff, Ruth. A CRACK IN THE SIDEWALK.
Ages 12 and up. 990, Vol. 1

**of Fiancé/Fiancée**

Bro, Margueritte Harmon. SARAH.
Ages 12 and up. 121, Vol. 1
O'Dell, Scott. KATHLEEN, PLEASE COME HOME.
Ages 12 and up. 485, Vol. 2

**of Friend**

Aaron, Chester. SPILL.
Ages 12-14. 1, Vol. 2
Anckarsvärd, Karin. SPRINGTIME FOR EVA.
Ages 12 and up. 16, Vol. 1
Armstrong, Richard. THE ALBATROSS.
Ages 12 and up. 30, Vol. 1
Brooks, Jerome. MAKE ME A HERO.
Ages 9-12. 78, Vol. 3
Bunting, Anne Evelyn. THE EMPTY WINDOW.
Ages 8-12. 89, Vol. 3
Cohen, Barbara Nash. THANK YOU, JACKIE
ROBINSON.
Ages 10-13. 215, Vol. 1
Colman, Hila Crayder. CAR-CRAZY GIRL.
Ages 12 and up. 227, Vol. 1
Distad, Audree. THE DREAM RUNNER.
Ages 10-13. 201, Vol. 2
Gerber, Merrill Joan. PLEASE DON'T KISS ME
NOW.
Ages 13 and up. 206, Vol. 3
Goldreich, Gloria. SEASON OF DISCOVERY.
Ages 11-13. 256, Vol. 2
Greene, Constance Clarke. DOUBLE-DARE O'TOOLE.
Ages 9-11. 240, Vol. 3
Greene, Constance Clarke. A GIRL CALLED AL.
Ages 11 and up. 378, Vol. 1
Hinton, Susan Eloise. THE OUTSIDERS.
Ages 12 and up. 412, Vol. 1
Hunt, Irene. THE LOTTERY ROSE.
Ages 11 and up. 337, Vol. 2
Huntsberry, William Emery. THE BIG HANG-UP.
Ages 12 and up. 445, Vol. 1

Ish-Kishor, Sulamith. OUR EDDIE.
Ages 12 and up. 450, Vol. 1
Jones, Rebecca Castaldi. ANGIE AND ME.
Ages 9-11. 333, Vol. 3
Korschunow, Irina. WHO KILLED CHRISTOPHER?
Ages 12 and up. 350, Vol. 3
Lee, Mildred Scudder. FOG.
Ages 12 and up. 534, Vol. 1
Magorian, Michelle. GOOD NIGHT, MR. TOM.
Ages 11 and up. 401, Vol. 3
Mazer, Harry. THE LAST MISSION.
Ages 12-14. 413, Vol. 3
Moe, Barbara. PICKLES AND PRUNES.
Ages 10-13. 461, Vol. 2
Paterson, Katherine Womeldorf. BRIDGE TO
TERABITHIA.
Ages 9-12. 493, Vol. 2
Paulsen, Gary. THE FOXMAN.
Ages 11-14. 495, Vol. 2
Peck, Richard. CLOSE ENOUGH TO TOUCH.
Ages 12 and up. 490, Vol. 3
Pfeffer, Susan Beth. ABOUT DAVID.
Ages 13 and up. 500, Vol. 3
Phipson, Joan Nash, pseud. A TIDE FLOWING.
Ages 12 and up. 509, Vol. 3
Rees, David. RISKS.
Ages 11 and up. 529, Vol. 2
Slepian, Jan. LESTER'S TURN.
Ages 11-14. 604, Vol. 3
Smith, Doris Buchanan. A TASTE OF
BLACKBERRIES.
Ages 8-11. 831, Vol. 1
Stevens, Carla McBride. STORIES FROM A SNOWY
MEADOW.
Ages 3-7. 623, Vol. 2
Thomas, Ianthe. HI, MRS. MALLORY!
Ages 5-8. 651, Vol. 3
Thrasher, Crystal Faye. BETWEEN DARK AND
DAYLIGHT.
Ages 11-13. 658, Vol. 3
Wersba, Barbara. THE DREAM WATCHER.
Ages 12 and up. 964, Vol. 1
White, Elwyn Brooks. CHARLOTTE'S WEB.
Ages 8-12. 967, Vol. 1
Woodford, Peggy. PLEASE DON'T GO.
Ages 12 and up. 991, Vol. 1
Zindel, Paul. THE PIGMAN.
Ages 12 and up. 1015, Vol. 1

**Funeral issues**

Bernstein, Joanne Eckstein. and Stephen V.
Gullo. WHEN PEOPLE DIE.
Ages 5-9. 53, Vol. 2
Brown, Margaret Wise. THE DEAD BIRD.
Ages 4-7. 124, Vol. 1
Bunting, Anne Evelyn. THE HAPPY FUNERAL.
Ages 5-9. 90, Vol. 3
Madler, Trudy. WHY DID GRANDMA DIE?
Ages 4-9. 400, Vol. 3
Orgel, Doris. THE MULBERRY MUSIC.
Ages 10-12. 685, Vol. 3
Stevens, Margaret. WHEN GRANDPA DIED.
Ages 4-8. 629, Vol. 3

**of Grandparent**

Barnwell, D. Robinson. SHADOW ON THE WATER.
Ages 12 and up. 52, Vol. 1
Bartoli, Jennifer. NONNA.
Ages 4-9. 38, Vol. 2
Blue, Rose. THE THIRTEENTH YEAR: A BAR
MITZVAH STORY.
Ages 10-12. 60, Vol. 2
Brandenberg, Aliki Liacouras. THE TWO OF THEM.
Ages 3-7. 71, Vol. 3

## Death (cont.)

Bunting, Anne Evelyn. THE HAPPY FUNERAL.
Ages 5-9. 90, Vol. 3

Byars, Betsy Cromer. THE TWO-THOUSAND-POUND GOLDFISH.
Ages 9-12. 99, Vol. 3

Coutant, Helen. FIRST SNOW.
Ages 7-9. 255, Vol. 1

Crawford, Deborah. SOMEBODY WILL MISS ME.
Ages 12 and up. 257, Vol. 1

De Paola, Thomas Anthony. NANA UPSTAIRS AND NANA DOWNSTAIRS.
Ages 3-8. 272, Vol. 1

Donnelly, Elfie. SO LONG, GRANDPA.
Ages 9-11. 168, Vol. 3

Fassler, Joan. MY GRANDPA DIED TODAY.
Ages 4-8. 306, Vol. 1

Fenton, Edward. DUFFY'S ROCKS.
Ages 12 and up. 311, Vol. 1

Fitzhugh, Louise. SPORT.
Ages 9-12. 190, Vol. 3

Garden, Nancy. THE LONERS.
Ages 12 and up. 343, Vol. 1

Hoopes, Lyn Littlefield. NANA.
Ages 5-8. 302, Vol. 3

Irwin, Hadley, pseud. WHAT ABOUT GRANDMA?
Ages 11 and up. 326, Vol. 3

Johnston, Norma. GLORY IN THE FLOWER.
Ages 11 and up. 467, Vol. 1

Johnston, Norma. IF YOU LOVE ME, LET ME GO.
Ages 12 and up. 354, Vol. 2

Madler, Trudy. WHY DID GRANDMA DIE?
Ages 4-9. 400, Vol. 3

Mazer, Norma Fox. A FIGURE OF SPEECH.
Ages 12 and up. 628, Vol. 1

Mearian, Judy Frank. SOMEONE SLIGHTLY DIFFERENT.
Ages 10-12. 417, Vol. 3

Mohr, Nicholasa. FELITA.
Ages 8-10. 440, Vol. 3

Morgan, Alison Mary. ALL KINDS OF PRICKLES.
Ages 11-13. 450, Vol. 3

Naylor, Phyllis Reynolds. TO WALK THE SKY PATH.
Ages 10-13. 658, Vol. 1

Orgel, Doris. THE MULBERRY MUSIC.
Ages 10-12. 685, Vol. 1

Peavy, Linda S. ALLISON'S GRANDFATHER.
Ages 6-9. 489, Vol. 3

Pollowitz, Melinda. CINNAMON CANE.
Ages 10-12. 519, Vol. 2

Rabin, Gil. CHANGES.
Ages 12 and up. 721, Vol. 1

Ruby, Lois. TWO TRUTHS IN MY POCKET.
Ages 12 and up. 557, Vol. 3

Schoen, Barbara. A PLACE AND A TIME.
Ages 12 and up. 784, Vol. 1

Shura, Mary Frances Craig. THE SEASON OF SILENCE.
Ages 10-14. 597, Vol. 2

Stein, Sara Bonnett. ABOUT DYING: AN OPEN FAMILY BOOK FOR PARENTS AND CHILDREN TOGETHER.
Ages 3-8. 855, Vol. 1

Stevens, Margaret. WHEN GRANDPA DIED.
Ages 4-8. 629, Vol. 3

Talbot, Toby. DEAR GRETA GARBO.
Ages 11-13. 635, Vol. 2

Townsend, Maryann and Ronnie Stern. POP'S SECRET.
Ages 5-7. 660, Vol. 3

Walker, Mary Alexander. YEAR OF THE CAFETERIA.
Ages 12 and up. 943, Vol. 1

Wilkinson, Brenda Scott. LUDELL AND WILLIE.
Ages 12 and up. 681, Vol. 2

Wilkinson, Sylvia. A KILLING FROST.
Ages 13 and up. 975, Vol. 1

Winthrop, Elizabeth. WALKING AWAY.
Ages 11 and up. 979, Vol. 1

Zolotow, Charlotte Shapiro. MY GRANDSON LEW.
Ages 3-7. 1025, Vol. 1

### of Great-grandparent

De Paola, Thomas Anthony. NANA UPSTAIRS AND NANA DOWNSTAIRS.
Ages 3-8. 272, Vol. 1

### of Infant

Head, Ann. MR. AND MRS. BO JO JONES.
Ages 13 and up. 408, Vol. 1

Klein, Norma. CONFESSIONS OF AN ONLY CHILD.
Ages 9-11. 502, Vol. 1

### of Mother

Arundel, Honor. THE BLANKET WORD.
Ages 13 and up. 35, Vol. 1

Bernays, Anne. GROWING UP RICH.
Ages 13 and up. 52, Vol. 2

Bridgers, Sue Ellen. HOME BEFORE DARK.
Ages 12 and up. 81, Vol. 2

Giff, Patricia Reilly. THE GIFT OF THE PIRATE QUEEN.
Ages 9-12. 211, Vol. 3

Girion, Barbara. A TANGLE OF ROOTS.
Ages 12-16. 220, Vol. 3

Guy, Rosa Cuthbert. THE FRIENDS.
Ages 12 and up. 391, Vol. 1

Harnden, Ruth Peabody. THE HIGH PASTURE.
Ages 11-14. 401, Vol. 1

Hermes, Patricia. YOU SHOULDN'T HAVE TO SAY GOOD-BYE.
Ages 10-13. 286, Vol. 3

Holland, Isabelle. OF LOVE AND DEATH AND OTHER JOURNEYS.
Ages 11 and up. 329, Vol. 2

Hunt, Irene. WILLIAM: A NOVEL.
Ages 12 and up. 338, Vol. 2

Jones, Penelope. HOLDING TOGETHER.
Ages 9-11. 331, Vol. 3

Kaplan, Bess. THE EMPTY CHAIR.
Ages 10-14. 363, Vol. 2

Krementz, Jill. HOW IT FEELS WHEN A PARENT DIES.
Ages 8 and up. 352, Vol. 3

Lee, Mildred Scudder. THE ROCK AND THE WILLOW.
Ages 12 and up. 535, Vol. 1

LeShan, Eda J. LEARNING TO SAY GOOD-BY: WHEN A PARENT DIES.
Ages 12 and up. 401, Vol. 2

Lyle, Katie Letcher. DARK BUT FULL OF DIAMONDS.
Ages 12-14. 388, Vol. 3

Mann, Peggy. THERE ARE TWO KINDS OF TERRIBLE.
Ages 9-12. 441, Vol. 2

Ogilvie, Elizabeth. THAT PIGEON PAIR.
Ages 12 and up. 682, Vol. 1

Oneal, Zibby. A FORMAL FEELING.
Ages 12 and up. 472, Vol. 3

Peck, Richard. FATHER FIGURE: A NOVEL.
Ages 11 and up. 501, Vol. 2

Phipson, Joan Nash, pseud. A TIDE FLOWING.
Ages 12 and up. 509, Vol. 3

Radley, Gail. NOTHING STAYS THE SAME FOREVER.
Ages 9-12. 524, Vol. 3

Reader, Dennis J. COMING BACK ALIVE.
Ages 12 and up. 525, Vol. 3

Sachs, Marilyn. BEACH TOWELS.
Ages 12 and up. 562, Vol. 3

**Death (cont.)**

Schotter, Roni. A MATTER OF TIME.
Ages 12 and up. 575, Vol. 3

Stolz, Mary Slattery. THE EDGE OF NEXT YEAR.
Ages 12 and up. 866, Vol. 1

Stolz, Mary Slattery. A LOVE, OR A SEASON.
Ages 12 and up. 870, Vol. 1

Voigt, Cynthia. DICEY'S SONG.
Ages 11 and up. 671, Vol. 3

Whitehead, Ruth. THE MOTHER TREE.
Ages 10-13. 969, Vol. 1

York, Carol Beach. REMEMBER ME WHEN I AM
DEAD.
Ages 9-11. 714, Vol. 3

Zindel, Bonnie and Paul Zindel. A STAR FOR THE
LATECOMER.
Ages 12 and up. 721, Vol. 3

**Murder.** *See also: Crime/Criminals; Violence*

Armstrong, Richard. THE ALBATROSS.
Ages 12 and up. 30, Vol. 1

Clifford, Ethel Rosenberg. THE YEAR OF THE
THREE-LEGGED DEER.
Ages 12 and up. 207, Vol. 1

Ellis, Melvin Richard. NO MAN FOR MURDER.
Ages 12 and up. 287, Vol. 1

Guy, Rosa Cuthbert. THE DISAPPEARANCE.
Ages 12 and up. 252, Vol. 3

Hinton, Susan Eloise. THE OUTSIDERS.
Ages 12 and up. 412, Vol. 1

Houston, James Archibald. THE WHITE ARCHER:
AN ESKIMO LEGEND.
Ages 9-11. 436, Vol. 1

Pfeffer, Susan Beth. ABOUT DAVID.
Ages 13 and up. 500, Vol. 3

Rees, David. RISKS.
Ages 11 and up. 529, Vol. 2

Roberts, Willo Davis. THE VIEW FROM THE
CHERRY TREE.
Ages 9-12. 546, Vol. 2

Ruby, Lois. ARRIVING AT A PLACE YOU'VE
NEVER LEFT.
Ages 12 and up. 564, Vol. 2

Sebestyen, Ouida. WORDS BY HEART.
Ages 10-13. 580, Vol. 3

Thrasher, Crystal Faye. BETWEEN DARK AND
DAYLIGHT.
Ages 11-13. 658, Vol. 3

**of Parents.** *See also: Orphan*

Ball, Zachary, pseud. KEP.
Ages 10 and up. 50, Vol. 1

Buck, Pearl Sydenstricker. THE BIG WAVE.
Ages 9-11. 129, Vol. 1

Coolidge, Olivia Ensor. COME BY HERE.
Ages 11 and up. 245, Vol. 1

Eyerly, Jeannette Hyde. THE GIRL INSIDE.
Ages 12 and up. 298, Vol. 1

Fitzgerald, John Dennis. ME AND MY LITTLE
BRAIN.
Ages 9-12. 319, Vol. 1

Gordon, Ethel Edison. SO FAR FROM HOME.
Ages 11 and up. 369, Vol. 1

Pfeffer, Susan Beth. JUST MORGAN.
Ages 12 and up. 707, Vol. 1

Shotwell, Louisa Rossiter. ADAM BOOKOUT.
Ages 11-13. 817, Vol. 1

Wier, Ester Alberti. THE RUMPTYDOOLERS.
Ages 11-13. 972, Vol. 1

**of Pet**

Ball, Zachary, pseud. BRISTLE FACE.
Ages 10 and up. 49, Vol. 1

Borack, Barbara. SOMEONE SMALL.
Ages 4-7. 103, Vol. 1

Carrick, Carol. THE ACCIDENT.
Ages 4-8. 119, Vol. 2

Cate, Dick. NEVER IS A LONG, LONG TIME.
Ages 9-11. 125, Vol. 2

Corbin, William, pseud. GOLDEN MARE.
Ages 9-12. 246, Vol. 1

Crofford, Emily. STORIES FROM THE BLUE ROAD.
Ages 9-12. 143, Vol. 3

Fairless, Caroline. HAMBONE.
Ages 8-11. 184, Vol. 3

Graeber, Charlotte Towner. MUSTARD.
Ages 4-10. 227, Vol. 3

Hall, Lynn. FLOWERS OF ANGER.
Ages 10-12. 288, Vol. 2

Hegwood, Mamie. MY FRIEND FISH.
Ages 4-8. 304, Vol. 2

Hurd, Edith Thacher. THE BLACK DOG WHO WENT
INTO THE WOODS.
Ages 5-7. 313, Vol. 3

Little, Mary E. OLD CAT AND THE KITTEN.
Ages 8-12. 379, Vol. 3

Miles, Betty. THE TROUBLE WITH THIRTEEN.
Ages 9-13. 424, Vol. 3

Morgan, Alison Mary. ALL KINDS OF PRICKLES.
Ages 11-13. 450, Vol. 3

Norris, Gunilla Brodde. THE FRIENDSHIP HEDGE.
Ages 8-11. 673, Vol. 1

Ottley, Reginald. BOY ALONE.
Ages 10-13. 688, Vol. 1

Peck, Robert Newton. A DAY NO PIGS WOULD DIE.
Ages 12 and up. 697, Vol. 1

Rawlings, Marjorie Kinnan. THE YEARLING.
Ages 12 and up. 725, Vol. 1

Shreve, Susan Richards. FAMILY SECRETS: FIVE
VERY IMPORTANT STORIES.
Ages 9-11. 590, Vol. 3

Smith, Doris Buchanan. KICK A STONE HOME.
Ages 11 and up. 830, Vol. 1

Thiele, Colin Milton. STORM BOY.
Ages 8-11. 646, Vol. 2

Tobias, Tobi. PETEY.
Ages 6-9. 653, Vol. 2

Viorst, Judith. THE TENTH GOOD THING ABOUT
BARNEY.
Ages 4-8. 930, Vol. 1

Wagner, Jane. J.T.
Ages 8-10. 939, Vol. 1

Wallace, Bill. A DOG CALLED KITTY.
Ages 9-11. 675, Vol. 3

Warburg, Sandol Stoddard. GROWING TIME.
Ages 7-9. 947, Vol. 1

Winthrop, Elizabeth. A LITTLE DEMONSTRATION
OF AFFECTION.
Ages 12-16. 689, Vol. 2

**of Relative**

Anderson, Leone Castell. IT'S O.K. TO CRY.
Ages 5-8. 16, Vol. 3

Balderson, Margaret. WHEN JAYS FLY TO BÁRBMO.
Ages 12 and up. 48, Vol. 1

Byars, Betsy Cromer. GOODBYE, CHICKEN LITTLE.
Ages 9-11. 97, Vol. 3

Godden, Rumer. THE DIDDAKOI.
Ages 10-12. 362, Vol. 1

Raskin, Ellen. FIGGS & PHANTOMS.
Ages 12 and up. 723, Vol. 1

**of Sibling**

Bawden, Nina Mary Kark. SQUIB.
Ages 10-13. 58, Vol. 1

Blue, Rose. NIKKI 108.
Ages 10-12. 85, Vol. 1

Brooks, Jerome. UNCLE MIKE'S BOY.
Ages 11 and up. 123, Vol. 1

Carlson, Natalie Savage. THE HALF SISTERS.
Ages 10-12. 166, Vol. 1

## Death (cont.)

### of Stepparent

**Suicide.** *See: Suicide*

## Decision Making

**See also:** *Problem solving*

## Decision Making (cont.)

Snyder, Anne. MY NAME IS DAVY — I'M AN ALCOHOLIC.
Ages 12 and up. 616, Vol. 2

Sugarman, Daniel A. and Rolaine A. Hochstein. SEVEN STORIES FOR GROWTH.
Ages 6-12. 880, Vol. 1

Townsend, John Rowe. NOAH'S CASTLE.
Ages 11 and up. 656, Vol. 2

Waber, Bernard. IRA SLEEPS OVER.
Ages 6-8. 937, Vol. 1

Young, Miriam Burt. MISS SUZY'S BIRTHDAY.
Ages 3-7. 1012, Vol. 1

## Deformities

See also: Limbs, abnormal or missing

Forbes, Esther. JOHNNY TREMAIN.
Ages 10 and up. 325, Vol. 1

Gallico, Paul. THE SNOW GOOSE.
Ages 12 and up. 342, Vol. 1

Guy, Anne Welsh. STEINMETZ: WIZARD OF LIGHT.
Ages 9-12. 390, Vol. 1

Hassler, Jon Francis. JEMMY.
Ages 11 and up. 270, Vol. 3

Sullivan, Mary Beth and Alan J. Brightman and Joseph Blatt. FEELING FREE.
Ages 9 and up. 640, Vol. 3

Sutcliff, Rosemary. THE WITCH'S BRAT.
Ages 11-13. 882, Vol. 1

Viscardi, Henry. THE PHOENIX CHILD: A STORY OF LOVE.
Ages 13 and up. 665, Vol. 2

## Delinquency, Juvenile

See also: Crime/Criminals; Detention home, living in; Gangs; Imprisonment; Probation; Rebellion; Stealing; Vandalism; Violence

Alcock, Gudrun. RUN, WESTY, RUN.
Ages 10-12. 5, Vol. 1

Ashley, Bernard. TERRY ON THE FENCE.
Ages 12 and up. 25, Vol. 2

Bonham, Frank. DURANGO STREET.
Ages 11 and up. 97, Vol. 1

Bonham, Frank. VIVA CHICANO.
Ages 12 and up. 99, Vol. 1

Bova, Benjamin William. ESCAPE.
Ages 10 and up. 107, Vol. 1

Broderick, Dorothy M. HANK.
Ages 11 and up. 122, Vol. 1

Burch, Robert Joseph. QUEENIE PEAVY.
Ages 11-13. 140, Vol. 1

Clark, Mavis Thorpe. THE MIN-MIN.
Ages 12 and up. 188, Vol. 1

Clifford, Ethel Rosenberg. THE WILD ONE.
Ages 11 and up. 206, Vol. 1

Dunne, Mary Collins. HOBY & STUB.
Ages 10-13. 176, Vol. 3

Fleischman, H. Samuel. GANG GIRL.
Ages 11 and up. 322, Vol. 1

Hall, Lynn. TROUBLEMAKER.
Ages 11-14. 395, Vol. 1

Harrah, Michael. FIRST OFFENDER.
Ages 11-13. 266, Vol. 3

Hinton, Susan Eloise. THE OUTSIDERS.
Ages 12 and up. 412, Vol. 1

Hinton, Susan Eloise. THAT WAS THEN, THIS IS NOW.
Ages 12 and up. 413, Vol. 1

Levoy, Myron. A SHADOW LIKE A LEOPARD.
Ages 12 and up. 369, Vol. 3

Luger, Harriett Mandelay. THE ELEPHANT TREE.
Ages 12 and up. 424, Vol. 2

McKay, Robert W. THE RUNNING BACK.
Ages 12-14. 392, Vol. 3

Maddock, Reginald. THIN ICE.
Ages 12 and up. 605, Vol. 1

Meyer, Carolyn. THE CENTER: FROM A TROUBLED PAST TO A NEW LIFE.
Ages 13 and up. 420, Vol. 3

Morgenroth, Barbara. WILL THE REAL RENIE LAKE PLEASE STAND UP?
Ages 12 and up. 453, Vol. 3

Morton, Jane. RUNNING SCARED.
Ages 10-14. 455, Vol. 3

Murphy, Barbara Beasley. NO PLACE TO RUN.
Ages 12 and up. 467, Vol. 2

Murphy, Jim. DEATH RUN.
Ages 11 and up. 457, Vol. 3

Myers, Walter Dean. WON'T KNOW TILL I GET THERE.
Ages 11-14. 460, Vol. 3

Pascal, Francine. THE HAND-ME-DOWN KID.
Ages 10-13. 483, Vol. 3

Petersen, P. J. WOULD YOU SETTLE FOR IMPROBABLE?
Ages 11-13. 495, Vol. 3

Peyton, K.M., pseud. PENNINGTON'S LAST TERM.
Ages 12 and up. 706, Vol. 1

Platt, Kin. HEADMAN.
Ages 13-19. 517, Vol. 2

Schwarzrock, Shirley and C. Gilbert Wrenn. UNDERSTANDING THE LAW OF OUR LAND.
Ages 11 and up. 797, Vol. 1

## Denial

Crane, Caroline. A GIRL LIKE TRACY.
Ages 12 and up. 256, Vol. 1

Eyerly, Jeannette Hyde. THE WORLD OF ELLEN MARCH.
Ages 12 and up. 301, Vol. 1

Platt, Kin. CHLORIS AND THE CREEPS.
Ages 10-14. 713, Vol. 1

## Dentist, Going to

See also: Orthodontia

Barnett, Naomi. I KNOW A DENTIST.
Ages 6-8. 35, Vol. 2

Rockwell, Harlow. MY DENTIST.
Ages 4-7. 552, Vol. 2

Schalebin-Lewis, Joy. THE DENTIST AND ME.
Ages 4-7. 572, Vol. 2

Watson, Jane Werner, Robert E. Switzer, and J. Cotter Hirschberg. MY FRIEND THE DENTIST.
Ages 3-6. 950, Vol. 1

Ziegler, Sandra. AT THE DENTIST: WHAT DID CHRISTOPHER SEE?
Ages 4-7. 715, Vol. 2

## Dependability

See: Responsibility: accepting

## Dependence/Independence

See also: Autonomy

Adler, Carole Schwerdtfeger. THE CAT THAT WAS LEFT BEHIND.
Ages 9-12. 3, Vol. 3

Alter, Judy. AFTER PA WAS SHOT.
Ages 10-13. 11, Vol. 2

Angell, Judie. RONNIE AND ROSEY.
Ages 11 and up. 20, Vol. 2

Arrick, Fran. STEFFIE CAN'T COME OUT TO PLAY.
Ages 12 and up. 24, Vol. 2

Bloch, Marie Halun. DISPLACED PERSON.
Ages 10-13. 57, Vol. 2

Bradbury, Bianca. BOY ON THE RUN.
Ages 11-13. 64, Vol. 2

## Deprivation, Emotional

**See also:** *Parental: negligence; Security/Insecurity*
Bonham, Frank. GIMME AN H, GIMME AN E,
GIMME AN L, GIMME A P.
Ages 12 and up. 61, Vol. 3
Byars, Betsy Cromer. THE CARTOONIST.
Ages 8-12. 107, Vol. 2
Corcoran, Barbara. MAKE NO SOUND.
Ages 10-13. 181, Vol. 2
Greene, Sheppard M. THE BOY WHO DRANK TOO
MUCH.
Ages 12 and up. 242, Vol. 3
Hinton, Susan Eloise. RUMBLE FISH.
Ages 12 and up. 316, Vol. 2
Holman, Felice. SLAKE'S LIMBO.
Ages 12 and up. 430, Vol. 1
Hunt, Irene. THE LOTTERY ROSE.
Ages 11 and up. 337, Vol. 2
Magorian, Michelle. GOOD NIGHT, MR. TOM.
Ages 11 and up. 401, Vol. 3
Myers, Walter Dean. IT AIN'T ALL FOR NOTHIN'.
Ages 11-13. 470, Vol. 2
Paterson, Katherine Womeldorf. THE GREAT GILLY
HOPKINS.
Ages 10-13. 494, Vol. 2
Platt, Kin. THE BOY WHO COULD MAKE HIMSELF
DISAPPEAR.
Ages 12 and up. 712, Vol. 1
Reynolds, Pamela. WILL THE REAL MONDAY
PLEASE STAND UP.
Ages 11-14. 533, Vol. 2
Sachs, Marilyn. A DECEMBER TALE.
Ages 9-12. 565, Vol. 2
Smith, Doris Buchanan. TOUGH CHAUNCEY.
Ages 12 and up. 832, Vol. 1
Van Leeuwen, Jean. SEEMS LIKE THIS ROAD GOES
ON FOREVER.
Ages 12 and up. 663, Vol. 3
Windsor, Patricia. MAD MARTIN.
Ages 10-14. 688, Vol. 2
Wortis, Avi. SOMETIMES I THINK I HEAR MY
NAME.
Ages 10-13. 708, Vol. 3

## Desegregation

**See:** *Integration; Prejudice*

## Desertion

**See:** *Abandonment*

## Detention Home, Living in

**See also:** *Crime/Criminals; Delinquency, juvenile;
Imprisonment; Probation*
Alcock, Gudrun. RUN, WESTY, RUN.
Ages 10-12. 5, Vol. 1
Bova, Benjamin William. ESCAPE.
Ages 10 and up. 107, Vol. 1
Fleischman, H. Samuel. GANG GIRL.
Ages 11 and up. 322, Vol. 1
Grace, Fran. BRANIGAN'S DOG.
Ages 10 and up. 225, Vol. 3
Harrah, Michael. FIRST OFFENDER.
Ages 11-13. 266, Vol. 3
Meyer, Carolyn. THE CENTER: FROM A TROUBLED
PAST TO A NEW LIFE.
Ages 13 and up. 420, Vol. 3
Platt, Kin. HEADMAN.
Ages 13-19. 517, Vol. 2

## Determination

Allen, Alex B., pseud. THE TENNIS MENACE.
Ages 8-10. 10, Vol. 2

Annixter, Jane, pseud. and Paul Annixter,
pseud. WINDIGO.
Ages 10 and up. 25, Vol. 1
Bond, Nancy Barbara. THE VOYAGE BEGUN.
Ages 12 and up. 60, Vol. 3
Bonham, Frank. CHIEF.
Ages 11 and up. 95, Vol. 1
Bottner, Barbara. DUMB OLD CASEY IS A FAT
TREE.
Ages 6-9. 66, Vol. 3
Boutis, Victoria. KATY DID IT.
Ages 8-10. 69, Vol. 3
Brancato, Robin Fidler. WINNING.
Ages 12 and up. 72, Vol. 2
Breinburg, Petronella. SHAWN'S RED BIKE.
Ages 3-6. 80, Vol. 2
Breisky, William. I THINK I CAN.
Ages 12 and up. 115, Vol. 1
Brooks, Jerome. THE TESTING OF CHARLIE
HAMMELMAN.
Ages 10-13. 84, Vol. 2
Brown, Fern G. HARD LUCK HORSE.
Ages 9-11. 85, Vol. 2
Brown, Fern G. JOCKEY — OR ELSE!
Ages 9-12. 86, Vol. 2
Carlson, Natalie Savage. MARCHERS FOR THE
DREAM.
Ages 9-11. 168, Vol. 1
Carruth, Ella Kaiser. SHE WANTED TO READ: THE
STORY OF MARY MCLEOD BETHUNE.
Ages 9-12. 173, Vol. 1
Chaffin, Lillie Dorton. WE BE WARM TILL
SPRINGTIME COMES.
Ages 6-9. 110, Vol. 3
Chorao, Kay. MOLLY'S MOE.
Ages 4-7. 131, Vol. 2
Chukovsky, Kornei Ivanovich. THE SILVER CREST:
MY RUSSIAN BOYHOOD.
Ages 12 and up. 135, Vol. 2
De Roo, Ann Louise. SCRUB FIRE.
Ages 9-12. 162, Vol. 3
Dolan, Sheila. THE WISHING BOTTLE.
Ages 7-9. 167, Vol. 3
Dunne, Mary Collins. HOBY & STUB.
Ages 10-13. 176, Vol. 3
Elfman, Blossom. THE BUTTERFLY GIRL.
Ages 13 and up. 180, Vol. 3
Farley, Carol J. TWILIGHT WAVES.
Ages 10-13. 186, Vol. 3
Gardiner, John Reynolds. STONE FOX.
Ages 8-10. 202, Vol. 3
Geibel, James. THE BLOND BROTHER.
Ages 12 and up. 205, Vol. 3
Gibson, Althea. I ALWAYS WANTED TO BE
SOMEBODY.
Ages 12 and up. 357, Vol. 1
Gill, Derek Lewis Theodore. TOM SULLIVAN'S
ADVENTURES IN DARKNESS.
Ages 10-14. 247, Vol. 2
Gorsline, Douglas Warren. FARM BOY.
Ages 10-12. 370, Vol. 1
Greenfield, Eloise. FIRST PINK LIGHT.
Ages 3-6. 270, Vol. 2
Greenfield, Eloise and Alesia Revis. ALESIA.
Ages 10-14. 245, Vol. 3
Gripe, Maria Kristina. THE GREEN COAT.
Ages 13 and up. 279, Vol. 2
Houston, James Archibald. AKAVAK: AN ESKIMO
JOURNEY.
Ages 9-12. 435, Vol. 1
Howard, Moses L. THE OSTRICH CHASE.
Ages 10-13. 437, Vol. 1
Hunt, Irene. WILLIAM: A NOVEL.
Ages 12 and up. 338, Vol. 2

## Determination (cont.)

Killilea, Marie Lyons. KAREN.
Ages 12 and up. 495, Vol. 1

Knudson, R. Rozanne. RINEHART LIFTS.
Ages 10-12. 348, Vol. 3

Knudson, R. Rozanne. ZANBOOMER.
Ages 10-13. 388, Vol. 2

Lexau, Joan M. I HATE RED ROVER.
Ages 6-8. 371, Vol. 3

Lipsyte, Robert. ONE FAT SUMMER.
Ages 12-14. 409, Vol. 2

Long, Judy. VOLUNTEER SPRING.
Ages 11-14. 416, Vol. 2

Majerus, Janet. GRANDPA AND FRANK.
Ages 12 and up. 440, Vol. 2

Myers, Walter Dean. HOOPS.
Ages 12 and up. 459, Vol. 3

Nicholson, William G. PETE GRAY: ONE-ARMED
MAJOR LEAGUER.
Ages 9-12. 479, Vol. 2

Noble, Iris Davis. FIRST WOMAN AMBULANCE
SURGEON, EMILY BARRINGER.
Ages 12 and up. 669, Vol. 1

O'Dell, Scott. ZIA.
Ages 10 and up. 486, Vol. 2

Piper, Watty. THE LITTLE ENGINE THAT COULD.
Ages 3-7. 711, Vol. 1

Piper, Watty. THE LITTLE ENGINE THAT COULD.
Ages 3-7. 514, Vol. 2

Platt, Kin. RUN FOR YOUR LIFE.
Ages 9-12. 518, Vol. 2

Robertson, Keith. IN SEARCH OF A SANDHILL
CRANE.
Ages 11 and up. 743, Vol. 1

Robinet, Harriette Gillem. JAY AND THE
MARIGOLD.
Ages 6-9. 547, Vol. 2

Ruby, Lois. TWO TRUTHS IN MY POCKET.
Ages 12 and up. 557, Vol. 3

Sachs, Marilyn. A SUMMER'S LEASE.
Ages 11-14. 566, Vol. 3

Sandoz, Mari. THE HORSECATCHER.
Ages 12 and up. 771, Vol. 1

Sawyer, Ruth. MAGGIE ROSE: HER BIRTHDAY
CHRISTMAS.
Ages 8-10. 776, Vol. 1

Slepian, Jan. LESTER'S TURN.
Ages 11-14. 604, Vol. 3

Smith, Robert Kimmel. JELLY BELLY.
Ages 10-12. 614, Vol. 3

Strang, Celia. THIS CHILD IS MINE.
Ages 11-14. 634, Vol. 3

Sullivan, Mary Beth and Alan J. Brightman and Joseph
Blatt. FEELING FREE.
Ages 9 and up. 640, Vol. 3

Treffinger, Carolyn. LI LUN, LAD OF COURAGE.
Ages 8-11. 903, Vol. 1

Ullman, James Ramsey. BANNER IN THE SKY.
Ages 12 and up. 915, Vol. 1

Van Steenwyk, Elizabeth Ann. RIVALS ON ICE.
Ages 9-11. 664, Vol. 3

Voigt, Cynthia. HOMECOMING.
Ages 11 and up. 672, Vol. 3

Winthrop, Elizabeth. I THINK HE LIKES ME.
Ages 3-7. 695, Vol. 3

Winthrop, Elizabeth. MARATHON MIRANDA.
Ages 9-11. 696, Vol. 3

Wojciechowska, Maia Rodman. SHADOW OF A
BULL.
Ages 11 and up. 985, Vol. 1

Wortis, Avi. A PLACE CALLED UGLY.
Ages 11-14. 707, Vol. 3

## Diabetes

Branfield, John. WHY ME?
Ages 11 and up. 114, Vol. 1

Dacquino, Vincent T. KISS THE CANDY DAYS
GOOD-BYE.
Ages 10-14. 148, Vol. 3

Dolan, Edward Francis and Richard B. Lyttle. BOBBY
CLARKE.
Ages 10-12. 205, Vol. 2

Giff, Patricia Reilly. THE GIFT OF THE PIRATE
QUEEN.
Ages 9-12. 211, Vol. 3

Kipnis, Lynne and Susan Adler. YOU CAN'T CATCH
DIABETES FROM A FRIEND.
Ages 7-12. 343, Vol. 3

Richter, Elizabeth. THE TEENAGE HOSPITAL
EXPERIENCE: YOU CAN HANDLE IT!
Ages 12 and up. 532, Vol. 3

## Diet/Dieting

**See:** *Weight control: overweight; Weight control:
underweight*

## Differences, Human

**See also:** *Poverty; Prejudice; Self, attitude toward:
feeling different; Values/Valuing; Wealth/Wealthy*

Anders, Rebecca. A LOOK AT MENTAL
RETARDATION.
Ages 3-7. 16, Vol. 2

Anders, Rebecca. A LOOK AT PREJUDICE AND
UNDERSTANDING.
Ages 3-7. 17, Vol. 2

Billington, Elizabeth T. PART-TIME BOY.
Ages 8-10. 53, Vol. 3

Brightman, Alan. LIKE ME.
Ages 3-8. 82, Vol. 2

Brooks, Jerome. THE BIG DIPPER MARATHON.
Ages 11-14. 77, Vol. 3

Burch, Robert Joseph. IDA EARLY COMES OVER
THE MOUNTAIN.
Ages 8-10. 92, Vol. 3

Cohen, Miriam. SO WHAT?
Ages 4-7. 129, Vol. 3

Crofford, Emily. STORIES FROM THE BLUE ROAD.
Ages 9-12. 143, Vol. 3

DeClements, Barthe. NOTHING'S FAIR IN FIFTH
GRADE.
Ages 8-11. 152, Vol. 3

Friskey, Margaret Richards. RACKETY, THAT VERY
SPECIAL RABBIT.
Ages 3-5. 237, Vol. 2

Hanlon, Emily. THE WING AND THE FLAME.
Ages 13 and up. 262, Vol. 3

Hautzig, Deborah. THE HANDSOMEST FATHER.
Ages 4-7. 271, Vol. 3

Herman, Charlotte. THE DIFFERENCE OF ARI
STEIN.
Ages 9-12. 312, Vol. 2

Hurwitz, Johanna. THE LAW OF GRAVITY.
Ages 10-13. 341, Vol. 2

Huston, Anne and Jane H. Yolen. TRUST A CITY
KID.
Ages 11 and up. 448, Vol. 1

Kamien, Janet. WHAT IF YOU COULDN'T . . . ? A
BOOK ABOUT SPECIAL NEEDS.
Ages 8-12. 336, Vol. 3

Klein, Gerda Weissmann. THE BLUE ROSE.
Ages 8 and up. 500, Vol. 1

Lasker, Joe. NICK JOINS IN.
Ages 5-8. 358, Vol. 3

Leigh, Frances THE LOST BOY.
Ages 10-13. 399, Vol. 2

Lionni, Leo. TICO AND THE GOLDEN WINGS.
Ages 4-8. 568, Vol. 1

## Differences, Human (cont.)

MacLachlan, Patricia. ARTHUR, FOR THE VERY
FIRST TIME.
   Ages 8-10. 393, Vol. 3
MacLachlan, Patricia. CASSIE BINEGAR.
   Ages 9-12. 394, Vol. 3
Mazer, Norma Fox. MRS. FISH, APE, AND ME, THE
DUMP QUEEN.
   Ages 10-12. 414, Vol. 3
Merriam, Eve. BOYS & GIRLS, GIRLS & BOYS.
   Ages 5-8. 636, Vol. 1
Oppenheimer, Joan Letson. GARDINE VS.
HANOVER.
   Ages 11-14. 474, Vol. 3
Payne, Sherry Neuwirth. A CONTEST.
   Ages 8-10. 486, Vol. 3
Ruby, Lois. TWO TRUTHS IN MY POCKET.
   Ages 12 and up. 557, Vol. 3
Scoppettone, Sandra. HAPPY ENDINGS ARE ALL
ALIKE.
   Ages 12 and up. 578, Vol. 2
Simon, Norma. WHY AM I DIFFERENT?
   Ages 4-8. 603, Vol. 2
Swarthout, Glendon Fred and Kathryn
Swarthout. WHALES TO SEE THE.
   Ages 10-12. 632, Vol. 2
Tate, Joan. LUKE'S GARDEN AND GRAMP: TWO
NOVELS.
   Ages 10-13. 644, Vol. 3
Tax, Meredith. FAMILIES.
   Ages 4-8. 645, Vol. 3
Wolde, Gunilla. BETSY AND PETER ARE
DIFFERENT.
   Ages 3-6. 701, Vol. 3
Yep, Laurence Michael. KIND HEARTS AND
GENTLE MONSTERS.
   Ages 12 and up. 712, Vol. 3
Zelonky, Joy. I CAN'T ALWAYS HEAR YOU.
   Ages 7-10. 718, Vol. 3

## Disabilities

See: *Handicaps: multiple; Illnesses; Learning disabilities;
Mental retardation*

## Disagreements

See: *Aggression; Parent/Parents: fighting between;
Parent/Parents: fighting with; Peer relationships;
Problem solving; Sibling: rivalry*

## Discipline, Meaning of

See also: *Parental: control; Self-discipline*
Buerger, Jane. OBEDIENCE.
   Ages 3-6. 83, Vol. 3
Charnley, Nathaniel and Betty Jo Charnley. MARTHA
ANN AND THE MOTHER STORE.
   Ages 5-9. 180, Vol. 1
Cohen, Barbara Nash. WHERE'S FLORRIE?
   Ages 6-8. 154, Vol. 2
Dyer, Thomas A. THE WHIPMAN IS WATCHING.
   Ages 10-14. 177, Vol. 3
Gordon, Shirley. CRYSTAL IS THE NEW GIRL.
   Ages 4-7. 259, Vol. 2
Hazen, Barbara Shook. EVEN IF I DID SOMETHING
AWFUL.
   Ages 3-6. 275, Vol. 3
Hentoff, Nat. THIS SCHOOL IS DRIVING ME
CRAZY.
   Ages 11-15. 311, Vol. 2
Love, Sandra Weller. CROSSING OVER.
   Ages 10-12. 383, Vol. 3
Morgenroth, Barbara. TRAMPS LIKE US.
   Ages 12 and up. 452, Vol. 3
Potter, Beatrix. THE TALE OF PETER RABBIT.
   Ages 3-7. 716, Vol. 1

Sharmat, Mitchell. COME HOME, WILMA.
   Ages 6-8. 588, Vol. 3
Steptoe, John Lewis. DADDY IS A
MONSTER...SOMETIMES
   Ages 5-7. 627, Vol. 3

## Discouragement

See: *Encouragement*

## Discrimination

See: *Apartheid; Integration; Prejudice*

## Dishonesty

See: *Conscience; Honesty/Dishonesty*

## Displacement of Aggression

See: *Aggression, displacement of*

## Distrust

See: *Trust/Distrust*

## Divorce

See also: *Separation, marital*
Bawden, Nina Mary Kark. THE RUNAWAY
SUMMER.
   Ages 9-12. 57, Vol. 1
Berger, Terry. A FRIEND CAN HELP.
   Ages 3-7. 73, Vol. 1
Bradbury, Bianca. THE BLUE YEAR.
   Ages 12 and up. 108, Vol. 1
Brooks, Jerome. UNCLE MIKE'S BOY.
   Ages 11 and up. 123, Vol. 1
Cleaver, Vera and Bill Cleaver. ELLEN GRAE.
   Ages 9-12. 197, Vol. 1
Cleaver, Vera and Bill Cleaver. LADY ELLEN GRAE.
   Ages 9-12. 199, Vol. 1
Corcoran, Barbara. THIS IS A RECORDING.
   Ages 12 and up. 252, Vol. 1
Eyerly, Jeannette Hyde. THE WORLD OF ELLEN
MARCH.
   Ages 12 and up. 301, Vol. 1
Gardner, Richard A. THE BOYS AND GIRLS BOOK
ABOUT DIVORCE.
   Ages 7-14. 344, Vol. 1
Goff, Beth. WHERE IS DADDY? THE STORY OF A
DIVORCE.
   Ages 4-8. 363, Vol. 1
Greene, Constance Clarke. A GIRL CALLED AL.
   Ages 11 and up. 378, Vol. 1
Gunther, John. DEATH BE NOT PROUD: A
MEMOIR.
   Ages 12 and up. 389, Vol. 1
Holland, Isabelle. THE MAN WITHOUT A FACE.
   Ages 13 and up. 427, Vol. 1
Klein, Norma. TAKING SIDES.
   Ages 10 and up. 506, Vol. 1
Konigsburg, Elaine Lobl. (GEORGE)
   Ages 11-14. 511, Vol. 1
Lexau, Joan M. EMILY AND THE KLUNKY BABY
AND THE NEXT-DOOR DOG.
   Ages 5-8. 555, Vol. 1
Lexau, Joan M. ME DAY.
   Ages 7-10. 558, Vol. 1
Norris, Gunilla Brodde. LILLAN.
   Ages 9-12. 677, Vol. 1
Platt, Kin. THE BOY WHO COULD MAKE HIMSELF
DISAPPEAR.
   Ages 12 and up. 712, Vol. 1
Platt, Kin. CHLORIS AND THE CREEPS.
   Ages 10-14. 713, Vol. 1
Pursell, Margaret Sanford. A LOOK AT DIVORCE.
   Ages 3-7. 524, Vol. 2

## Divorce (cont.)

Shreve, Susan Richards. FAMILY SECRETS: FIVE VERY IMPORTANT STORIES.
Ages 9-11. 590, Vol. 3
Smith, Doris Buchanan. KICK A STONE HOME.
Ages 11 and up. 830, Vol. 1
Stolz, Mary Slattery. LEAP BEFORE YOU LOOK.
Ages 12 and up. 869, Vol. 1

**of Parents.** *See also: Parental: custody*

Abercrombie, Barbara Mattes. CAT-MAN'S DAUGHTER.
Ages 11-13. 1, Vol. 3
Adler, Carole Schwerdtfeger. THE SILVER COACH.
Ages 9-12. 8, Vol. 3
Alexander, Anne. TO LIVE A LIE.
Ages 9-12. 7, Vol. 2
Ames, Mildred. WHAT ARE FRIENDS FOR?
Ages 9-11. 12, Vol. 2
Anderson, Penny S. A PRETTY GOOD TEAM.
Ages 5-8. 18, Vol. 3
Angell, Judie. WHAT'S BEST FOR YOU.
Ages 11-14. 21, Vol. 3
Berger, Terry. HOW DOES IT FEEL WHEN YOUR PARENTS GET DIVORCED?
Ages 6-11. 50, Vol. 2
Bradbury, Bianca. BOY ON THE RUN.
Ages 11-13. 64, Vol. 2
Butler, Beverly Kathleen. A GIRL CALLED WENDY.
Ages 12 and up. 106, Vol. 2
Caines, Jeannette Franklin. DADDY.
Ages 4-8. 110, Vol. 2
Christopher, Matthew F. THE FOX STEALS HOME.
Ages 8-10. 133, Vol. 2
Corcoran, Barbara. HEY, THAT'S MY SOUL YOU'RE STOMPING ON.
Ages 11-14. 180, Vol. 2
Danziger, Paula. THE DIVORCE EXPRESS.
Ages 11-14. 150, Vol. 3
Dexter, Pat Egan. ARROW IN THE WIND.
Ages 10-13. 200, Vol. 2
Drescher, Joan Elizabeth. YOUR FAMILY, MY FAMILY.
Ages 5-7. 173, Vol. 3
Gaeddert, LouAnn Bigge. JUST LIKE SISTERS.
Ages 8-12. 196, Vol. 3
Gerson, Corinne. HOW I PUT MY MOTHER THROUGH COLLEGE.
Ages 11 and up. 207, Vol. 3
Graham, Ada and Frank Graham. JACOB AND OWL.
Ages 8-11. 228, Vol. 3
Grant, Cynthia D. JOSHUA FORTUNE.
Ages 10-13. 229, Vol. 3
Grollman, Earl A. TALKING ABOUT DIVORCE: A DIALOGUE BETWEEN PARENT AND CHILD.
Ages 7-10. 283, Vol. 2
Hazen, Barbara Shook. TWO HOMES TO LIVE IN: A CHILD'S-EYE VIEW OF DIVORCE.
Ages 5-8. 302, Vol. 2
Helmering, Doris Wild. I HAVE TWO FAMILIES.
Ages 6-8. 279, Vol. 3
Hogan, Paula Z. WILL DAD EVER MOVE BACK HOME?
Ages 7-10. 299, Vol. 3
Hunter, Evan. ME AND MR. STENNER.
Ages 10-13. 339, Vol. 2
Irwin, Hadley, pseud. BRING TO A BOIL AND SEPARATE.
Ages 10-12. 323, Vol. 3
LeShan, Eda J. WHAT'S GOING TO HAPPEN TO ME? WHEN PARENTS SEPARATE OR DIVORCE.
Ages 8 and up. 402, Vol. 2
Lisker, Sonia Olson and Leigh Dean. TWO SPECIAL CARDS.
Ages 6-9. 410, Vol. 2

Love, Sandra Weller. CROSSING OVER.
Ages 10-12. 383, Vol. 3
Madison, Winifred. THE GENESSEE QUEEN.
Ages 11 and up. 436, Vol. 2
Meyer, Carolyn. C. C. POINDEXTER.
Ages 12 and up. 453, Vol. 2
Miles, Betty. THE TROUBLE WITH THIRTEEN.
Ages 9-13. 424, Vol. 3
Miner, Jane Claypool. SPLIT DECISION: FACING DIVORCE.
Ages 11 and up. 435, Vol. 3
Newfield, Marcia. A BOOK FOR JODAN.
Ages 8-12. 478, Vol. 2
Okimoto, Jean Davies. MY MOTHER IS NOT MARRIED TO MY FATHER.
Ages 9-11. 470, Vol. 3
Paris, Lena. MOM IS SINGLE.
Ages 6-8. 480, Vol. 3
Park, Barbara. DON'T MAKE ME SMILE.
Ages 8-11. 481, Vol. 3
Perry, Patricia and Marietta Lynch. MOMMY AND DADDY ARE DIVORCED.
Ages 3-6. 504, Vol. 2
Pevsner, Stella. A SMART KID LIKE YOU.
Ages 10-13. 510, Vol. 2
Pfeffer, Susan Beth. JUST BETWEEN US.
Ages 10-12. 502, Vol. 3
Pfeffer, Susan Beth. STARRING PETER AND LEIGH.
Ages 12-14. 503, Vol. 3
Pfeffer, Susan Beth. STARTING WITH MELODIE.
Ages 11-13. 504, Vol. 3
Platt, Kin. CHLORIS AND THE FREAKS.
Ages 11 and up. 515, Vol. 2
Rabinowich, Ellen. ROCK FEVER.
Ages 12 and up. 523, Vol. 3
Reader, Dennis J. COMING BACK ALIVE.
Ages 12 and up. 525, Vol. 3
Rogers, Helen Spelman. MORRIS AND HIS BRAVE LION.
Ages 4-7. 557, Vol. 2
Schuchman, Joan. TWO PLACES TO SLEEP.
Ages 5-7. 577, Vol. 3
Sheffield, Janet N. NOT JUST SUGAR AND SPICE.
Ages 9-12. 594, Vol. 2
Slote, Alfred. LOVE AND TENNIS.
Ages 12-14. 605, Vol. 3
Sobol, Harriet Langsam. MY OTHER-MOTHER, MY OTHER-FATHER.
Ages 7-10. 616, Vol. 3
Stein, Sara Bonnett. ON DIVORCE: AN OPEN FAMILY BOOK FOR PARENTS AND CHILDREN TOGETHER.
Ages 4-8. 626, Vol. 3
Thomas, Ianthe. ELIZA'S DADDY.
Ages 4-7. 647, Vol. 2
Wolitzer, Hilma. OUT OF LOVE.
Ages 10-13. 704, Vol. 2
Wolkoff, Judie. HAPPILY EVER AFTER...ALMOST.
Ages 11-13. 703, Vol. 3
Wood, Phyllis Anderson. WIN ME AND YOU LOSE.
Ages 10-13. 709, Vol. 2

## Doctor, Going to

**See also:** *Fractures; Hospital, going to; Illnesses; Surgery; Sutures*

Berger, Knute. A VISIT TO THE DOCTOR.
Ages 4-7. 70, Vol. 1
Blume, Judy Sussman. DEENIE.
Ages 10-12. 88, Vol. 1
Chalmers, Mary Eileen. COME TO THE DOCTOR, HARRY.
Ages 2-5. 112, Vol. 3

## Emotions (cont.)

Colman, Hila Crayder. CONFESSION OF A STORYTELLER.
Ages 10-13. 133, Vol. 3

Conta, Marcia Maher and Maureen Reardon. FEELINGS BETWEEN BROTHERS AND SISTERS.
Ages 3-7. 241, Vol. 1

Conta, Marcia Maher and Maureen Reardon. FEELINGS BETWEEN FRIENDS.
Ages 3-7. 242, Vol. 1

Dobrin, Arnold. SCAT!
Ages 6-9. 276, Vol. 1

Dunn, Judy. FEELINGS.
Ages 3-8. 279, Vol. 1

Hill, Margaret. TURN THE PAGE, WENDY.
Ages 10-14. 291, Vol. 3

Hogan, Paula Z. SOMETIMES I GET SO MAD.
Ages 5-8. 298, Vol. 3

Jenkins, Jordan. LEARNING ABOUT LOVE.
Ages 4-8. 329, Vol. 3

Kamien, Janet. WHAT IF YOU COULDN'T...? A BOOK ABOUT SPECIAL NEEDS.
Ages 8-12. 336, Vol. 3

Kroll, Steven. THAT MAKES ME MAD!
Ages 4-7. 389, Vol. 2

LeRoy, Gen. EMMA'S DILEMMA.
Ages 9-12. 400, Vol. 2

LeShan, Eda J. WHAT'S GOING TO HAPPEN TO ME? WHEN PARENTS SEPARATE OR DIVORCE.
Ages 8 and up. 402, Vol. 2

Oneal, Zibby. A FORMAL FEELING.
Ages 12 and up. 472, Vol. 3

Peyton, K. M., pseud. MARION'S ANGELS.
Ages 11-14. 499, Vol. 3

Riley, Susan. WHAT DOES IT MEAN? AFRAID.
Ages 3-6. 538, Vol. 2

Riley, Susan. WHAT DOES IT MEAN? ANGRY.
Ages 3-6. 539, Vol. 2

Schlein, Miriam. I HATE IT.
Ages 4-7. 575, Vol. 2

Sharmat, Marjorie Weinman. I DON'T CARE.
Ages 3-6. 585, Vol. 2

Simon, Norma. HOW DO I FEEL?
Ages 4-8. 822, Vol. 1

Sobol, Harriet Langsam. MY BROTHER STEVEN IS RETARDED.
Ages 7-10. 618, Vol. 2

Stanek, Muriel Novella. WHO'S AFRAID OF THE DARK?
Ages 5-8. 623, Vol. 3

Stanton, Elizabeth and Henry Stanton. SOMETIMES I LIKE TO CRY.
Ages 4-7. 620, Vol. 2

Sugarman, Daniel A. and Rolaine A. Hochstein. SEVEN STORIES FOR GROWTH.
Ages 6-12. 880, Vol. 1

Windsor, Patricia. MAD MARTIN.
Ages 10-14. 688, Vol. 2

Winthrop, Elizabeth. A LITTLE DEMONSTRATION OF AFFECTION.
Ages 12-16. 689, Vol. 2

Winthrop, Elizabeth. POTBELLIED POSSUMS.
Ages 4-6. 690, Vol. 2

Wolitzer, Hilma. TOBY LIVED HERE.
Ages 10-12. 705, Vol. 2

## Identifying

Behrens, June York. HOW I FEEL.
Ages 3-8. 61, Vol. 1

Conta, Marcia Maher and Maureen Reardon. FEELINGS BETWEEN KIDS AND GROWNUPS.
Ages 3-6. 243, Vol. 1

Conta, Marcia Maher and Maureen Reardon. FEELINGS BETWEEN KIDS AND PARENTS.
Ages 4-8. 244, Vol. 1

Grimes, Nikki. SOMETHING ON MY MIND.
Ages 5-9. 278, Vol. 2

Johnston, Norma. THE SWALLOW'S SONG.
Ages 12 and up. 357, Vol. 2

Moncure, Jane Belk. JOY.
Ages 3-6. 444, Vol. 3

Oneal, Zibby. A FORMAL FEELING.
Ages 12 and up. 472, Vol. 3

Riley, Susan. WHAT DOES IT MEAN? AFRAID.
Ages 3-6. 538, Vol. 2

Riley, Susan. WHAT DOES IT MEAN? I'M SORRY.
Ages 3-6. 541, Vol. 2

Strauss, Joyce. HOW DOES IT FEEL...?
Ages 4-8. 637, Vol. 3

Vogel, Ilse-Margret. DODO EVERY DAY.
Ages 7-9. 666, Vol. 2

Wallace, Barbara Brooks. THE SECRET SUMMER OF L.E.B.
Ages 11 and up. 946, Vol. 1

Windsor, Patricia. MAD MARTIN.
Ages 10-14. 688, Vol. 2

Wright, Betty Ren. I LIKE BEING ALONE.
Ages 6-9. 709, Vol. 3

## Empathy

**See also:** *Egocentrism; Identification with others*

Cohen, Barbara Nash. BENNY.
Ages 9-11. 152, Vol. 2

Conaway, Judith. WAS MY FACE RED!
Ages 4-7. 172, Vol. 2

Greenfield, Eloise. GRANDMAMA'S JOY.
Ages 4-8. 244, Vol. 3

Klein, Leonore. ONLY ONE ANT.
Ages 4-7. 501, Vol. 1

Knox-Wagner, Elaine. MY GRANDPA RETIRED TODAY.
Ages 4-7. 346, Vol. 3

Leggett, Linda Rogers and Linda Gambee Andrews. THE ROSE-COLORED GLASSES: MELANIE ADJUSTS TO POOR VISION.
Ages 8-11. 362, Vol. 3

Lexau, Joan M. I HATE RED ROVER.
Ages 6-8. 371, Vol. 3

Myers, Walter Dean. FAST SAM, COOL CLYDE, AND STUFF.
Ages 11-14. 469, Vol. 2

Naylor, Phyllis Reynolds. WALKING THROUGH THE DARK.
Ages 12 and up. 473, Vol. 2

Robinson, Barbara Webb. TEMPORARY TIMES, TEMPORARY PLACES.
Ages 11-13. 538, Vol. 3

Rodgers, Mary. FREAKY FRIDAY.
Ages 10-13. 749, Vol. 1

Roy, Ronald. FRANKIE IS STAYING BACK.
Ages 8-10. 556, Vol. 3

Simon, Norma. WE REMEMBER PHILIP.
Ages 7-10. 598, Vol. 3

Tester, Sylvia Root. SANDY'S NEW HOME.
Ages 5-8. 648, Vol. 3

Tolan, Stephanie S. GRANDPA — AND ME.
Ages 10-13. 655, Vol. 2

Yep, Laurence Michael. KIND HEARTS AND GENTLE MONSTERS.
Ages 12 and up. 712, Vol. 3

## Encouragement

**See also:** *Courage, meaning of*

Blue, Rose. I AM HERE. YO ESTOY AQUÍ.
Ages 5-8. 83, Vol. 1

**Family (cont.)**

Bond, Felicia. POINSETTIA & HER FAMILY.
Ages 4-7. 59, Vol. 3

Bradbury, Bianca. "I'M VINNY, I'M ME".
Ages 12 and up. 65, Vol. 2

Breisky, William. I THINK I CAN.
Ages 12 and up. 115, Vol. 1

Bridgers, Sue Ellen. HOME BEFORE DARK.
Ages 12 and up. 81, Vol. 2

Brink, Carol Ryrie. CADDIE WOODLAWN: A
FRONTIER STORY.
Ages 9-12. 120, Vol. 1

Burch, Robert Joseph. SIMON AND THE GAME OF
CHANCE.
Ages 10-12. 142, Vol. 1

Burchardt, Nellie. A SURPRISE FOR CARLOTTA.
Ages 9-11. 144, Vol. 1

Carlson, Natalie Savage. THE EMPTY
SCHOOLHOUSE.
Ages 8-12. 165, Vol. 1

Carlson, Natalie Savage. THE HALF SISTERS.
Ages 10-12. 166, Vol. 1

Cate, Dick. NEVER IS A LONG, LONG TIME.
Ages 9-11. 125, Vol. 2

Child Study Association of America. FAMILIES ARE
LIKE THAT! STORIES TO READ TO YOURSELF.
Ages 6-9. 129, Vol. 2

Clark, Ann Nolan. LITTLE NAVAJO BLUEBIRD.
Ages 9-12. 186, Vol. 1

Cleaver, Vera and Bill Cleaver. DUST OF THE
EARTH.
Ages 12 and up. 139, Vol. 2

Cleaver, Vera and Bill Cleaver. THE MIMOSA TREE.
Ages 10-13. 201, Vol. 1

Cleaver, Vera and Bill Cleaver. TRIAL VALLEY.
Ages 12 and up. 141, Vol. 2

Cleaver, Vera and Bill Cleaver. WHERE THE LILIES
BLOOM.
Ages 11 and up. 203, Vol. 1

Clifton, Lucille. EVERETT ANDERSON'S NINE
MONTH LONG.
Ages 4-7. 145, Vol. 2

Cohen, Barbara Nash. BENNY.
Ages 9-11. 152, Vol. 2

Cohen, Barbara Nash. THE INNKEEPER'S
DAUGHTER.
Ages 11-14. 126, Vol. 3

Cone, Molly Lamken. A PROMISE IS A PROMISE.
Ages 11-13. 234, Vol. 1

Crofford, Emily. A MATTER OF PRIDE.
Ages 8-11. 142, Vol. 3

Dexter, Pat Egan. ARROW IN THE WIND.
Ages 10-13. 200, Vol. 2

Dixon, Paige, pseud. MAY I CROSS YOUR GOLDEN
RIVER?
Ages 12 and up. 202, Vol. 2

Fairless, Caroline. HAMBONE.
Ages 8-11. 184, Vol. 3

George, John Lothar and Jean Craighead
George. VULPES, THE RED FOX.
Ages 10 and up. 355, Vol. 1

Girion, Barbara. A TANGLE OF ROOTS.
Ages 12-16. 220, Vol. 3

Gray, Nigel. IT'LL ALL COME OUT IN THE WASH.
Ages 4-6. 233, Vol. 3

Greenberg, Jan. A SEASON IN-BETWEEN.
Ages 11-13. 237, Vol. 3

Haar, Jaap ter. THE WORLD OF BEN LIGHTHART.
Ages 10-13. 287, Vol. 2

Hamilton, Gail, pseud. TITANIA'S LODESTONE.
Ages 11-13. 290, Vol. 1

Hautzig, Esther Rudomin. THE ENDLESS STEPPE: A
GROWING UP IN SIBERIA.
Ages 11 and up. 406, Vol. 1

Hermes, Patricia. YOU SHOULDN'T HAVE TO SAY
GOOD-BYE.
Ages 10-13. 286, Vol. 3

Hoban, Russell Conwell and Lillian Aberman
Hoban. THE SORELY TRYING DAY.
Ages 3-7. 421, Vol. 1

Holland, Isabelle. DINAH AND THE GREEN FAT
KINGDOM.
Ages 10-13. 328, Vol. 2

Hunt, Irene. WILLIAM: A NOVEL.
Ages 12 and up. 338, Vol. 2

Hurmence, Belinda. TOUGH TIFFANY.
Ages 10-13. 315, Vol. 3

Hutchins, Patricia. THE BEST TRAIN SET EVER.
Ages 5-8. 342, Vol. 2

Ipswitch, Elaine. SCOTT WAS HERE.
Ages 12 and up. 322, Vol. 3

Isadora, Rachel. THE POTTERS' KITCHEN.
Ages 4-8. 347, Vol. 2

Johnston, Norma. GLORY IN THE FLOWER.
Ages 11 and up. 467, Vol. 1

Johnston, Norma. THE KEEPING DAYS.
Ages 11 and up. 468, Vol. 1

Jones, Penelope. HOLDING TOGETHER.
Ages 9-11. 331, Vol. 3

Kerr, Judith. THE OTHER WAY ROUND.
Ages 12 and up. 376, Vol. 2

Killilea, Marie Lyons. KAREN.
Ages 12 and up. 495, Vol. 1

Killilea, Marie Lyons. WITH LOVE FROM KAREN.
Ages 12 and up. 496, Vol. 1

Kingman, Lee. HEAD OVER WHEELS.
Ages 12 and up. 383, Vol. 2

Lapsley, Susan. I AM ADOPTED.
Ages 3-7. 529, Vol. 1

Lee, Harper. TO KILL A MOCKINGBIRD
Ages 12 and up. 533, Vol. 1

Lee, Virginia. THE MAGIC MOTH.
Ages 8-11. 539, Vol. 1

L'Engle, Madeleine Franklin. MEET THE AUSTINS.
Ages 11-13. 541, Vol. 1

L'Engle, Madeleine Franklin. A RING OF ENDLESS
LIGHT.
Ages 11-14. 363, Vol. 3

Lenski, Lois. STRAWBERRY GIRL.
Ages 9-11. 545, Vol. 1

Lexau, Joan M. EVERY DAY A DRAGON.
Ages 3-8. 556, Vol. 1

Lexau, Joan M. STRIPED ICE CREAM.
Ages 8-11. 559, Vol. 1

Little, Jean. LISTEN FOR THE SINGING.
Ages 10-14. 413, Vol. 2

Little, Jean. SPRING BEGINS IN MARCH.
Ages 10-12. 576, Vol. 1

Lowry, Lois. A SUMMER TO DIE.
Ages 10-14. 423, Vol. 2

Madison, Winifred. BECKY'S HORSE
Ages 10-12. 434, Vol. 2

Madler, Trudy. WHY DID GRANDMA DIE?
Ages 4-9. 400, Vol. 3

Marangell, Virginia J. GIANNA MIA.
Ages 12-15. 402, Vol. 3

May, Julian. HOW WE ARE BORN.
Ages 8-12. 621, Vol. 1

May, Julian. LIVING THINGS AND THEIR YOUNG.
Ages 8-12. 622, Vol. 1

May, Julian. MEN AND WOMEN.
Ages 9-12. 623, Vol. 1

Mearian, Judy Frank. TWO WAYS ABOUT IT.
Ages 9-12. 418, Vol. 3

Meeks, Esther K. and Elizabeth Bagwell. FAMILIES
LIVE TOGETHER.
Ages 4-8. 631, Vol. 1

## Family (cont.)

Meeks, Esther K. and Elizabeth Bagwell. THE WORLD OF LIVING THINGS.
Ages 4-8. 633, Vol. 1

Melton, David. A BOY CALLED HOPELESS.
Ages 10 and up. 451, Vol. 2

Mohr, Nicholasa. FELITA.
Ages 8-10. 440, Vol. 3

Neville, Emily Cheney. GARDEN OF BROKEN GLASS.
Ages 11-14. 477, Vol. 2

Nolan, Madeena Spray. MY DADDY DON'T GO TO WORK.
Ages 4-7. 480, Vol. 2

Norris, Gunilla Brodde. A FEAST OF LIGHT.
Ages 9-12. 672, Vol. 1

O'Hara, Mary, pseud. MY FRIEND FLICKA
Ages 11 and up. 683, Vol. 1

Patterson, Katheryn. NO TIME FOR TEARS.
Ages 12 and up. 692, Vol. 1

Phipson, Joan Nash, pseud. THE FAMILY CONSPIRACY.
Ages 10-13. 708, Vol. 1

Pierik, Robert. ROOKFLEAS IN THE CELLAR.
Ages 8-13. 512, Vol. 3

Rawlings, Marjorie Kinnan. THE YEARLING.
Ages 12 and up. 725, Vol. 1

Reuter, Margaret. MY MOTHER IS BLIND.
Ages 5-8. 529, Vol. 3

Rosen, Lillian D. JUST LIKE EVERYBODY ELSE.
Ages 11 and up. 549, Vol. 3

Shyer, Marlene Fanta. MY BROTHER, THE THIEF.
Ages 10-13. 594, Vol. 3

Simon, Norma. ALL KINDS OF FAMILIES.
Ages 5-8. 602, Vol. 2

Sommerfelt, Aimee. THE WHITE BUNGALOW.
Ages 10-13. 840, Vol. 1

Sonneborn, Ruth A. FRIDAY NIGHT IS PAPA NIGHT.
Ages 5-8. 841, Vol. 1

Stolz, Mary Slattery. BY THE HIGHWAY HOME.
Ages 12 and up. 864, Vol. 1

Strang, Celia. FOSTER MARY.
Ages 10-13. 633, Vol. 3

Swartley, David Warren. MY FRIEND, MY BROTHER.
Ages 9-11. 642, Vol. 3

Taylor, Mildred D. ROLL OF THUNDER, HEAR MY CRY.
Ages 10 and up. 636, Vol. 2

Thompson, Jean, pseud. DON'T FORGET MICHAEL.
Ages 7-9. 656, Vol. 3

Thrasher, Crystal Faye. BETWEEN DARK AND DAYLIGHT.
Ages 11-13. 658, Vol. 3

Tobias, Tobi. JANE, WISHING.
Ages 6-9. 651, Vol. 2

Uchida, Yoshiko. JOURNEY HOME.
Ages 12-14. 657, Vol. 2

Vestley, Anne-Catharina. HELLO, AURORA.
Ages 8-11. 922, Vol. 1

Viscardi, Henry. A MAN'S STATURE.
Ages 12 and up. 932, Vol. 1

Vogel, Ilse-Margret. FAREWELL, AUNT ISABELL.
Ages 8-10. 669, Vol. 3

Voigt, Cynthia. HOMECOMING.
Ages 11 and up. 672, Vol. 3

Wallace, Barbara Brooks. JULIA AND THE THIRD BAD THING.
Ages 8-10. 673, Vol. 2

Wilder, Laura Ingalls. BY THE SHORES OF SILVER LAKE.
Ages 8-11. 974, Vol. 1

Wolff, Ruth. A CRACK IN THE SIDEWALK.
Ages 12 and up. 990, Vol. 1

Wood, Phyllis Anderson. PASS ME A PINE CONE.
Ages 11 and up. 705, Vol. 3

Worth, Kathryn. THEY LOVED TO LAUGH.
Ages 12 and up. 996, Vol. 1

## Fantasy Formation

**See also:** *Creativity; Daydreaming; Imaginary friend; Imagination; Magical thinking; Play; Wishes*

Agle, Nan Hayden. SUSAN'S MAGIC.
Ages 9-11. 3, Vol. 1

Barrett, Anne. MIDWAY.
Ages 11-13. 53, Vol. 1

Bawden, Nina Mary Kark. SQUIB.
Ages 10-13. 58, Vol. 1

Bonham, Frank. THE NITTY GRITTY.
Ages 12 and up. 98, Vol. 1

Colman, Hila Crayder. THE SECRET LIFE OF HAROLD THE BIRD WATCHER.
Ages 8-10. 165, Vol. 2

Conford, Ellen. DREAMS OF VICTORY.
Ages 9-12. 238, Vol. 1

Estes, Eleanor. THE HUNDRED DRESSES.
Ages 8-10. 291, Vol. 1

Klass, Sheila Solomon. TO SEE MY MOTHER DANCE.
Ages 10-13. 344, Vol. 3

Lutters, Valerie. THE HAUNTING OF JULIE UNGER.
Ages 10-13. 425, Vol. 2

Lyle, Katie Letcher. DARK BUT FULL OF DIAMONDS.
Ages 12-14. 388, Vol. 3

Madison, Winifred. THE GENESSEE QUEEN.
Ages 11 and up. 436, Vol. 2

Pinkwater, Manus. WINGMAN.
Ages 9-12. 513, Vol. 2

Rolerson, Darrell A. A BOY CALLED PLUM.
Ages 10-12. 752, Vol. 1

Sargent, Sarah. SECRET LIES.
Ages 11 and up. 570, Vol. 3

Schick, Eleanor Grossman. NEIGHBORHOOD KNIGHT.
Ages 5-7. 573, Vol. 2

Screen, Robert Martin. WITH MY FACE TO THE RISING SUN.
Ages 11 and up. 580, Vol. 2

Stolz, Mary Slattery. JUAN.
Ages 8-11. 868, Vol. 1

Valencak, Hannelore. A TANGLED WEB.
Ages 9-11. 659, Vol. 2

Zolotow, Charlotte Shapiro. A FATHER LIKE THAT.
Ages 4-6. 1020, Vol. 1

## Fat

**See:** *Weight control: overweight*

## Father

**See:** *Communication: parent-child; Parent/Parents: single*

## Fatso

**See:** *Name-calling; Weight control: overweight*

## Fear

**See also:** *Anxiety; Courage, meaning of; Nightmares; Security/Insecurity*

Bachmann, Evelyn Trent. TRESSA.
Ages 8-12. 42, Vol. 1

Berkey, Barry R. and Velma A. Berkey. ROBBERS, BONES & MEAN DOGS.
Ages 5-9. 51, Vol. 2

Bloch, Marie Halun. DISPLACED PERSON.
Ages 10-13. 57, Vol. 2

## Fear (cont.)

Blume, Judy Sussman. OTHERWISE KNOWN AS
SHEILA THE GREAT.
Ages 9-11. 92, Vol. 1

Bosworth, J. Allan. WHITE WATER, STILL WATER.
Ages 11 and up. 105, Vol. 1

Childress, Alice. RAINBOW JORDAN.
Ages 12 and up. 115, Vol. 3

Church, Richard. FIVE BOYS IN A CAVE.
Ages 9-12. 185, Vol. 1

Clifton, Lucille. AMIFIKA.
Ages 4-7. 143, Vol. 2

Conaway, Judith. SOMETIMES IT SCARES ME.
Ages 3-7. 171, Vol. 2

Crofford, Emily. A MATTER OF PRIDE.
Ages 8-11. 142, Vol. 3

Dalgliesh, Alice. THE COURAGE OF SARAH
NOBLE.
Ages 8-10. 210, Vol. 1

De Roo, Anne Louise. SCRUB FIRE.
Ages 9-12. 162, Vol. 3

Dragonwagon, Crescent. WILL IT BE OKAY?
Ages 3-7. 207, Vol. 2

Dunn, Judy. FEELINGS.
Ages 3-8. 279, Vol. 1

Fisher, Dorothy Canfield. UNDERSTOOD BETSY.
Ages 9-12. 317, Vol. 1

Fox, Paula. THE STONE-FACED BOY.
Ages 10-12. 329, Vol. 1

Griese, Arnold Alfred. THE WAY OF OUR PEOPLE.
Ages 9-12. 275, Vol. 2

Heck, Bessie Holland. CAVE-IN AT MASON'S MINE.
Ages 8-10. 278, Vol. 3

Heide, Florence Parry. GROWING ANYWAY UP.
Ages 12-14. 305, Vol. 2

Holman, Felice. SLAKE'S LIMBO.
Ages 12 and up. 430, Vol. 1

Leigh, Bill. THE FAR SIDE OF FEAR.
Ages 10-14. 398, Vol. 2

Marshall, James Vance, pseud. WALKABOUT.
Ages 12 and up. 614, Vol. 1

Mason, Mariam Evangeline. THE MIDDLE SISTER.
Ages 8-10. 615, Vol. 1

Miles, Miska, pseud. AARON'S DOOR.
Ages 5-9. 458, Vol. 2

Miner, Jane Claypool. MOUNTAIN FEAR: WHEN A
BROTHER DIES.
Ages 10 and up. 431, Vol. 3

Norris, Gunilla Brodde. GREEN AND SOMETHING
ELSE.
Ages 8-11. 675, Vol. 1

Osborn, Lois. MY BROTHER IS AFRAID OF JUST
ABOUT EVERYTHING.
Ages 4-7. 476, Vol. 3

Pfeffer, Susan Beth. WHAT DO YOU DO WHEN
YOUR MOUTH WON'T OPEN?
Ages 10-13. 505, Vol. 3

Riley, Susan. WHAT DOES IT MEAN? AFRAID.
Ages 3-6. 538, Vol. 2

Sachs, Elizabeth-Ann. JUST LIKE ALWAYS.
Ages 10-13. 561, Vol. 3

Shanks, Ann Zane. OLD IS WHAT YOU GET:
DIALOGUES ON AGING BY THE OLD AND THE
YOUNG.
Ages 10 and up. 582, Vol. 2

Shaw, Richard. SHAPE UP, BURKE.
Ages 10-14. 593, Vol. 2

Showers, Paul. A BOOK OF SCARY THINGS.
Ages 3-6. 596, Vol. 2

Sperry, Armstrong. CALL IT COURAGE.
Ages 9 and up. 849, Vol. 1

Watson, Jane Werner, Robert E. Switzer, and J. Cotter
Hirschberg. SOMETIMES I'M AFRAID.
Ages 2-5. 953, Vol. 1

Wittels, Harriet and Joan Greisman. THINGS I HATE.
Ages 4-8. 982, Vol. 1

### of Animals

Gates, Doris. A MORGAN FOR MELINDA.
Ages 10-12. 203, Vol. 3

Hickman, Janet. THE THUNDER-PUP.
Ages 9-11. 289, Vol. 3

Little, Lessie Jones and Eloise Greenfield. I CAN DO
IT BY MYSELF.
Ages 5-7. 415, Vol. 2

Low, Joseph. BOO TO A GOOSE.
Ages 5-8. 420, Vol. 2

Tester, Sylvia Root. SOMETIMES I'M AFRAID.
Ages 3-5. 649, Vol. 3

Tester, Sylvia Root. THAT BIG BRUNO.
Ages 3-7. 644, Vol. 2

Wallace, Bill. A DOG CALLED KITTY.
Ages 9-11. 675, Vol. 3

### of Being lost. See also: Lost, being

Eckert, Allan W. INCIDENT AT HAWK'S HILL.
Ages 11 and up. 284, Vol. 1

Vogel, Ilse-Margaret. HELLO, HENRY.
Ages 4-7. 933, Vol. 1

### of Darkness

Babbitt, Natalie. THE SOMETHING.
Ages 4-7. 40, Vol. 1

Bonsall, Crosby Newell. WHO'S AFRAID OF THE
DARK?
Ages 3-7. 64, Vol. 3

Cleary, Beverly Bunn. RAMONA THE BRAVE.
Ages 7-10. 138, Vol. 2

Conford, Ellen. EUGENE THE BRAVE.
Ages 5-7. 175, Vol. 2

Corbin, William, pseud. SMOKE.
Ages 11 and up. 247, Vol. 1

Crowe, Robert L. CLYDE MONSTER.
Ages 3-6. 186, Vol. 2

Hoban, Russell Conwell. BEDTIME FOR FRANCES.
Ages 3-7. 418, Vol. 1

Holman, Felice. PROFESSOR DIGGINS' DRAGONS.
Ages 9-11. 429, Vol. 1

Johnston, Tony. NIGHT NOISES: AND OTHER
MOLE AND TROLL STORIES.
Ages 4-7. 358, Vol. 2

Low, Joseph. BENNY RABBIT AND THE OWL.
Ages 4-7. 419, Vol. 2

Marzollo, Jean. CLOSE YOUR EYES.
Ages 2-5. 444, Vol. 2

Mayer, Mercer. THERE'S A NIGHTMARE IN MY
CLOSET.
Ages 3-7. 624, Vol. 1

Mayer, Mercer. YOU'RE THE SCAREDY-CAT.
Ages 4-8. 625, Vol. 1

Memling, Carl. WHAT'S IN THE DARK?
Ages 4-7. 634, Vol. 1

Robison, Deborah. NO ELEPHANTS ALLOWED.
Ages 3-6. 540, Vol. 3

Schubert, Ingrid and Dieter Schubert. THERE'S A
CROCODILE UNDER MY BED!
Ages 3-6. 576, Vol. 3

Smith, Janice Lee. THE MONSTER IN THE THIRD
DRESSER DRAWER.
Ages 5-8. 610, Vol. 3

Stanek, Muriel Novella. WHO'S AFRAID OF THE
DARK?
Ages 5-8. 623, Vol. 3

Tester, Sylvia Root. SOMETIMES I'M AFRAID.
Ages 3-5. 649, Vol. 3

Tobias, Tobi. CHASING THE GOBLINS AWAY.
Ages 4-7. 650, Vol. 2

## Freedom, Meaning of (cont.)

Waterton, Betty Marie. A SALMON FOR SIMON.
Ages 4-7. 685, Vol. 3
Yashima, Taró, pseud. and Hatoju Moku. THE
GOLDEN FOOTPRINTS.
Ages 8-10. 1009, Vol. 1

## Friendship

**See also:** *Boy-girl relationships; Gangs: membership in;
Identification with others: peers*
Anker, Charlotte. LAST NIGHT I SAW
ANDROMEDA.
Ages 9-11. 22, Vol. 2
Bailey, Pearl. DUEY'S TALE.
Ages 12 and up. 29, Vol. 2
Behrens, June York. TOGETHER.
Ages 4-7. 49, Vol. 2
Godden, Rumer. MR. MCFADDEN'S HALLOWE'EN.
Ages 9-11. 252, Vol. 2
Ichikawa, Satomi. FRIENDS.
Ages 3-7. 344, Vol. 2
Kelley, Sally. TROUBLE WITH EXPLOSIVES.
Ages 10-13. 373, Vol. 2
Mohr, Nicholasa. IN NUEVA YORK.
Ages 13 and up. 462, Vol. 2
Shanks, Ann Zane. OLD IS WHAT YOU GET:
DIALOGUES ON AGING BY THE OLD AND THE
YOUNG.
Ages 10 and up. 582, Vol. 2
Zolotow, Charlotte Shapiro. THE WHITE MARBLE.
Ages 4-8. 725, Vol. 3

**Best friend**
Adelman, Bob and Susan Hall. ON AND OFF THE
STREET.
Ages 8-10. 1, Vol. 1
Ames, Mildred. WHAT ARE FRIENDS FOR?
Ages 9-11. 12, Vol. 2
Angell, Judie. WHAT'S BEST FOR YOU.
Ages 11-14. 21, Vol. 3
Asher, Sandra Fenichel. DAUGHTERS OF THE LAW.
Ages 11-13. 26, Vol. 3
Asher, Sandra Fenichel. JUST LIKE JENNY.
Ages 10-12. 27, Vol. 3
Barkin, Carol and Elizabeth James. ARE WE STILL
BEST FRIENDS?
Ages 4-7. 31, Vol. 2
Bawden, Nina Mary Kark. THE ROBBERS.
Ages 9-12. 43, Vol. 3
Berger, Terry. A FRIEND CAN HELP.
Ages 3-7. 73, Vol. 1
Bethancourt, T. Ernesto, pseud. NEW YORK CITY
TOO FAR FROM TAMPA BLUES.
Ages 10-14. 55, Vol. 2
Bonsall, Crosby Newell. THE GOODBYE SUMMER.
Ages 9-11. 63, Vol. 3
Brancato, Robin Fidler. SOMETHING LEFT TO
LOSE.
Ages 12-14. 71, Vol. 2
Brandenberg, Aliki Liacouras. WE ARE BEST
FRIENDS.
Ages 3-6. 72, Vol. 3
Brown, Myra Berry. BEST FRIENDS.
Ages 3-7. 127, Vol. 1
Burningham, John Mackintosh. THE FRIEND.
Ages 2-5. 104, Vol. 2
Butterworth, William Edmund. UNDER THE
INFLUENCE.
Ages 12 and up. 94, Vol. 3
Byars, Betsy Cromer. THE CYBIL WAR.
Ages 9-12. 96, Vol. 3
Byars, Betsy Cromer. GOODBYE, CHICKEN LITTLE.
Ages 9-11. 97, Vol. 3
Carlson, Natalie Savage. ANN AURELIA AND
DOROTHY.
Ages 8-10. 164, Vol. 1

Carrick, Carol. SOME FRIEND!
Ages 9-12. 106, Vol. 3
Clifton, Lucille. MY FRIEND JACOB.
Ages 4-7. 122, Vol. 3
Coatsworth, Elizabeth Jane. MARRA'S WORLD.
Ages 8-11. 150, Vol. 2
Cohen, Miriam. BEST FRIENDS.
Ages 5-7. 216, Vol. 1
Cone, Molly Lamken. CALL ME MOOSE.
Ages 9-11. 174, Vol. 2
Cuyler, Margery S. THE TROUBLE WITH SOAP.
Ages 10-13. 147, Vol. 3
Danziger, Paula. THE DIVORCE EXPRESS.
Ages 11-14. 150, Vol. 3
Delaney, Ned. BERT AND BARNEY.
Ages 3-7. 153, Vol. 3
Delton, Judy. LEE HENRY'S BEST FRIEND.
Ages 4-8. 155, Vol. 3
Delton, Judy. TWO IS COMPANY.
Ages 4-7. 199, Vol. 2
Desbarats, Peter. GABRIELLE AND SELENA.
Ages 8-10. 274, Vol. 1
Douglass, Barbara. SKATEBOARD SCRAMBLE.
Ages 9-11. 170, Vol. 3
Due, Linnea A. HIGH AND OUTSIDE.
Ages 13 and up. 174, Vol. 3
Eyerly, Jeannette Hyde. THE SEEING SUMMER.
Ages 8-10. 183, Vol. 3
Fletcher, David. THE KING'S GOBLET.
Ages 12 and up. 323, Vol. 1
Foley, June. IT'S NO CRUSH, I'M IN LOVE!
Ages 11-13. 192, Vol. 3
Franco, Marjorie. SO WHO HASN'T GOT
PROBLEMS?
Ages 10-12. 194, Vol. 3
Freeman, Gaail. OUT FROM UNDER.
Ages 12 and up. 195, Vol. 3
Gackenbach, Dick. HOUND AND BEAR.
Ages 4-6. 240, Vol. 2
Gantos, Jack. FAIR-WEATHER FRIENDS.
Ages 4-7. 242, Vol. 2
Giff, Patricia Reilly. FOURTH GRADE CELEBRITY.
Ages 8-10. 210, Vol. 3
Gilbert, Harriett. RUNNING AWAY.
Ages 11-14. 215, Vol. 3
Gilbert, Nan, pseud. THE UNCHOSEN.
Ages 11 and up. 359, Vol. 1
Girion, Barbara. LIKE EVERYBODY ELSE.
Ages 10-13. 218, Vol. 3
Girion, Barbara. A TANGLE OF ROOTS.
Ages 12-16. 220, Vol. 3
Glovach, Linda. LET'S MAKE A DEAL.
Ages 8-11. 251, Vol. 3
Gordon, Shirley. CRYSTAL IS MY FRIEND.
Ages 6-9. 258, Vol. 2
Gordon, Shirley. CRYSTAL IS THE NEW GIRL.
Ages 4-7. 259, Vol. 2
Greenberg, Jan. THE ICEBERG AND ITS SHADOW.
Ages 10-12. 235, Vol. 3
Greene, Constance Clarke. AL(EXANDRA) THE
GREAT.
Ages 10-12. 239, Vol. 3
Greene, Constance Clarke. I KNOW YOU, AL.
Ages 11 and up. 268, Vol. 2
Greene, Constance Clarke. YOUR OLD PAL, AL.
Ages 9-13. 241, Vol. 3
Greene, Sheppard M. THE BOY WHO DRANK TOO
MUCH.
Ages 12 and up. 242, Vol. 3
Gregory, Diana. THERE'S A CATERPILLAR IN MY
LEMONADE.
Ages 10-12. 247, Vol. 3
Grimes, Nikki. GROWIN'.
Ages 9-11. 277, Vol. 2

## Friendship (cont.)

**Imaginary friend.** *See: Imaginary friend*

## Keeping friends

## Lack of

## Making friends

## Friendship (cont.)

Carlson, Natalie Savage. LUVVY AND THE GIRLS.
Ages 10-13. 167, Vol. 1

Carrick, Malcolm. I'LL GET YOU.
Ages 11-13. 107, Vol. 3

Carrick, Malcolm. TRAMP.
Ages 7-9. 122, Vol. 2

Chaikin, Miriam. I SHOULD WORRY, I SHOULD CARE.
Ages 8-11. 111, Vol. 3

Chetin, Helen. HOW FAR IS BERKELEY?
Ages 11-13. 128, Vol. 2

Christopher, Matthew F. JOHNNY LONG LEGS.
Ages 9-11. 184, Vol. 1

Cleary, Beverly Bunn. HENRY AND THE PAPER ROUTE.
Ages 7-10. 192, Vol. 1

Cohen, Miriam. WILL I HAVE A FRIEND?
Ages 4-6. 217, Vol. 1

Cole, Sheila R. MEANING WELL.
Ages 9-12. 220, Vol. 1

Colman, Hila Crayder. THE SECRET LIFE OF HAROLD THE BIRD WATCHER.
Ages 8-10. 165, Vol. 2

Conford, Ellen. ANYTHING FOR A FRIEND.
Ages 9-11. 136, Vol. 3

Conford, Ellen. FELICIA THE CRITIC.
Ages 9-11. 239, Vol. 1

Corcoran, Barbara. CHILD OF THE MORNING.
Ages 10 and up. 139, Vol. 3

Corcoran, Barbara. SAM.
Ages 12 and up. 251, Vol. 1

Crawford, Deborah. SOMEBODY WILL MISS ME.
Ages 12 and up. 257, Vol. 1

Cuyler, Margery S. THE TROUBLE WITH SOAP.
Ages 10-13. 147, Vol. 3

DeClements, Barthe. NOTHING'S FAIR IN FIFTH GRADE.
Ages 8-11. 152, Vol. 3

Delton, Judy. LEE HENRY'S BEST FRIEND.
Ages 4-8. 155, Vol. 3

Dixon, Jeanne. LADY CAT LOST.
Ages 10-12. 164, Vol. 3

Dunnahoo, Terry. WHO CARES ABOUT ESPIE SANCHEZ?
Ages 10-12. 210, Vol. 2

Duvoisin, Roger Antoine. PERIWINKLE.
Ages 4-7. 211, Vol. 2

Fall, Thomas, pseud. DANDY'S MOUNTAIN.
Ages 12 and up. 302, Vol. 1

Fox, Paula. PORTRAIT OF IVAN.
Ages 11 and up. 328, Vol. 1

Friedman, Frieda. THE JANITOR'S GIRL.
Ages 10-12. 336, Vol. 1

Galbraith, Kathryn Osebold. COME SPRING.
Ages 9-13. 197, Vol. 3

Gerson, Corinne. SON FOR A DAY.
Ages 10-12. 208, Vol. 3

Giff, Patricia Reilly. THE WINTER WORM BUSINESS.
Ages 8-10. 214, Vol. 3

Glass, Frankcina. MARVIN & TIGE.
Ages 12 and up. 250, Vol. 2

Gordon, Ethel Edison. SO FAR FROM HOME.
Ages 11 and up. 369, Vol. 1

Gordon, Shirley. CRYSTAL IS THE NEW GIRL.
Ages 4-7. 259, Vol. 2

Green, Phyllis. MILDRED MURPHY, HOW DOES YOUR GARDEN GROW?
Ages 9-11. 263, Vol. 2

Hamilton-Merritt, Jane. MY FIRST DAY OF SCHOOL.
Ages 3-6. 260, Vol. 3

Harris, Dorothy Joan. THE SCHOOL MOUSE.
Ages 6-8. 294, Vol. 2

Haugaard, Kay. MYEKO'S GIFT.
Ages 9-12. 405, Vol. 1

Hayes, Sheila. THE CAROUSEL HORSE.
Ages 10-12. 300, Vol. 2

Hickman, Martha Whitmore. MY FRIEND WILLIAM MOVED AWAY.
Ages 4-7. 290, Vol. 3

Hodges, Margaret Moore. A CLUB AGAINST KEATS.
Ages 8-10. 422, Vol. 1

Hodges, Margaret Moore. THE HATCHING OF JOSHUA COBB.
Ages 8-12. 423, Vol. 1

Hooker, Ruth. GERTRUDE KLOPPENBERG (PRIVATE)
Ages 8-12. 432, Vol. 1

Horvath, Betty. BE NICE TO JOSEPHINE.
Ages 5-8. 433, Vol. 1

Hughes, Dean. SWITCHING TRACKS.
Ages 10-14. 308, Vol. 3

Hurwitz, Johanna. ALDO APPLESAUCE.
Ages 7-9. 316, Vol. 3

Hurwitz, Johanna. THE LAW OF GRAVITY.
Ages 10-13. 341, Vol. 2

Hurwitz, Johanna. TOUGH-LUCK KAREN.
Ages 10-13. 319, Vol. 3

Huston, Anne. OLLIE'S GO-KART.
Ages 9-11. 447, Vol. 1

Irion, Ruth Hershey. THE CHRISTMAS COOKIE TREE.
Ages 8-10. 345, Vol. 2

Iwasaki, Chihiro. WILL YOU BE MY FRIEND?
Ages 3-5. 453, Vol. 1

Jacobson, Jane. CITY, SING FOR ME: A COUNTRY CHILD MOVES TO THE CITY.
Ages 6-10. 349, Vol. 2

Jewell, Nancy. BUS RIDE.
Ages 4-8. 352, Vol. 2

Jones, Adrienne. SAIL, CALYPSO!
Ages 10-13. 469, Vol. 1

Jones, Cordelia. A CAT CALLED CAMOUFLAGE.
Ages 11-14. 470, Vol. 1

Keith, Harold Verne. THE RUNT OF ROGERS SCHOOL.
Ages 9-12. 487, Vol. 1

Keller, Beverly Lou. FIONA'S BEE.
Ages 5-8. 371, Vol. 2

Kent, Deborah. BELONGING: A NOVEL.
Ages 11-14. 375, Vol. 2

Konigsburg, Elaine Lobl. ABOUT THE B'NAI BAGELS.
Ages 10-13. 508, Vol. 1

Konigsburg, Elaine Lobl. JENNIFER, HECATE, MACBETH, WILLIAM MCKINLEY AND ME, ELIZABETH.
Ages 9-11. 512, Vol. 1

Krasilovsky, Phyllis. THE POPULAR GIRLS CLUB.
Ages 10-13. 514, Vol. 1

Krasilovsky, Phyllis. THE SHY LITTLE GIRL.
Ages 4-8. 515, Vol. 1

Krasilovsky, Phyllis. SUSAN SOMETIMES.
Ages 3-5. 516, Vol. 1

Kropp, Paul Stephan. WILTED.
Ages 11-14. 354, Vol. 3

Krumgold, Joseph E. HENRY 3.
Ages 11 and up. 522, Vol. 1

Lampman, Evelyn Sibley. THE YEAR OF SMALL SHADOW.
Ages 10-12. 528, Vol. 1

Lee, Mildred Scudder. SYCAMORE YEAR.
Ages 12 and up. 537, Vol. 1

Lingard, Joan. THE TWELFTH DAY OF JULY: A NOVEL OF MODERN IRELAND.
Ages 12 and up. 564, Vol. 1

## Friendship (cont.)

Lionni, Leo. A COLOR OF HIS OWN.
  Ages 3-5. 408, Vol. 2
Lipp, Frederick J. SOME LOSE THEIR WAY.
  Ages 10-13. 377, Vol. 3
Little, Jean. LISTEN FOR THE SINGING.
  Ages 10-14. 413, Vol. 2
Little, Jean. LOOK THROUGH MY WINDOW.
  Ages 10-14. 573, Vol. 1
Little, Jean. STAND IN THE WIND.
  Ages 8-11. 414, Vol. 2
Little, Jean. TAKE WING.
  Ages 10 and up. 577, Vol. 1
Liu, Aimee. SOLITAIRE.
  Ages 13 and up. 380, Vol. 3
Lovelace, Maud Hart. THE VALENTINE BOX.
  Ages 8-11. 587, Vol. 1
Lowry, Lois. ANASTASIA AGAIN!
  Ages 9-12. 384, Vol. 3
Lowry, Lois. ANASTASIA AT YOUR SERVICE.
  Ages 9-12. 385, Vol. 3
Lystad, Mary. THAT NEW BOY.
  Ages 6-7. 593, Vol. 1
McCord, Jean. TURKEYLEGS THOMPSON.
  Ages 11-14. 390, Vol. 3
McGovern, Ann. SCRAM, KID!
  Ages 5-8. 596, Vol. 1
Madison, Winifred. MARIA LUISA.
  Ages 9-12. 607, Vol. 1
Magorian, Michelle. GOOD NIGHT, MR. TOM.
  Ages 11 and up. 401, Vol. 3
Mann, Peggy. HOW JUAN GOT HOME.
  Ages 8-10. 608, Vol. 1
Miles, Betty. ALL IT TAKES IS PRACTICE.
  Ages 9-12. 454, Vol. 2
Miles, Betty. HAVING A FRIEND.
  Ages 3-6. 637, Vol. 1
Miles, Betty. MAUDIE AND ME AND THE DIRTY
  BOOK.
  Ages 10-12. 423, Vol. 3
Miller, Ruth White. THE CITY ROSE.
  Ages 11-13. 460, Vol. 2
Molloy, Anne Stearns. THE GIRL FROM TWO
  MILES HIGH.
  Ages 10-12. 642, Vol. 1
Moncure, Jane Belk. A NEW BOY IN
  KINDERGARTEN.
  Ages 4-7. 463, Vol. 2
Montgomery, Elizabeth Rider. THE MYSTERY OF
  THE BOY NEXT DOOR.
  Ages 5-8. 464, Vol. 2
Montgomery, Elizabeth Rider. "SEEING" IN THE
  DARK.
  Ages 5-7. 448, Vol. 3
Neville, Emily Cheney. GARDEN OF BROKEN
  GLASS.
  Ages 11-14. 477, Vol. 2
Neville, Emily Cheney. THE SEVENTEENTH-
  STREET GANG.
  Ages 10-13. 668, Vol. 1
Newton, Suzanne. M.V. SEXTON SPEAKING.
  Ages 11 and up. 466, Vol. 3
Norris, Gunilla Brodde. A FEAST OF LIGHT.
  Ages 9-12. 672, Vol. 1
Norris, Gunilla Brodde. THE GOOD MORROW.
  Ages 9-11. 674, Vol. 1
O'Connor, Jane. YOURS TILL NIAGARA FALLS,
  ABBY.
  Ages 8-10. 467, Vol. 3
Pascal, Francine. THE HAND-ME-DOWN KID.
  Ages 10-13. 483, Vol. 3
Pearson, Susan. MOLLY MOVES OUT.
  Ages 5-8. 487, Vol. 3
Peck, Richard. REPRESENTING SUPER DOLL.
  Ages 12 and up. 696, Vol. 1

Perl, Lila. DON'T ASK MIRANDA.
  Ages 10-13. 492, Vol. 3
Perrine, Mary. NANNABAH'S FRIEND.
  Ages 7-10. 702, Vol. 1
Phipson, Joan Nash, pseud. PETER AND BUTCH.
  Ages 10 and up. 709, Vol. 1
Pollock, Penny. KEEPING IT SECRET.
  Ages 9-12. 515, Vol. 3
Prather, Ray. NEW NEIGHBORS.
  Ages 4-7. 522, Vol. 2
Pundt, Helen Marie. SPRING COMES FIRST TO
  THE WILLOWS.
  Ages 11 and up. 717, Vol. 1
Rinkoff, Barbara Jean Rich. A GUY CAN BE
  WRONG.
  Ages 10-12. 735, Vol. 1
Rinkoff, Barbara Jean Rich. HEADED FOR
  TROUBLE.
  Ages 12 and up. 736, Vol. 1
Rinkoff, Barbara Jean Rich. RUTHERFORD T. FINDS
  21B.
  Ages 5-7. 739, Vol. 1
Rinkoff, Barbara Jean Rich. THE WATCHERS.
  Ages 11-14. 740, Vol. 1
Riskind, Mary L. APPLE IS MY SIGN.
  Ages 10-14. 536, Vol. 3
Robinet, Harriette Gillem. JAY AND THE
  MARIGOLD.
  Ages 6-9. 547, Vol. 2
Robinson, Charles. NEW KID IN TOWN.
  Ages 4-7. 548, Vol. 2
Robinson, Nancy Konheim. WENDY AND THE
  BULLIES.
  Ages 7-10. 539, Vol. 3
Rockwell, Thomas. THE THIEF.
  Ages 8-10. 554, Vol. 2
Sachs, Marilyn. BEACH TOWELS.
  Ages 12 and up. 562, Vol. 3
Sachs, Marilyn. A SECRET FRIEND.
  Ages 10-12. 567, Vol. 2
Schick, Eleanor Grossman. 5A AND 7B.
  Ages 3-5. 779, Vol. 1.
Schulman, Janet. THE BIG HELLO.
  Ages 3-7. 576, Vol. 2
Schultz, Gwendolyn. THE BLUE VALENTINE.
  Ages 5-8. 785, Vol. 1
Schultz, Gwendolyn. THE BLUE VALENTINE.
  Ages 5-8. 578, Vol. 3
Schwarzrock, Shirley and C. Gilbert Wrenn. EASING
  THE SCENE.
  Ages 11 and up. 790, Vol. 1
Schwarzrock, Shirley and C. Gilbert Wrenn. TO LIKE
  AND BE LIKED.
  Ages 11 and up. 796, Vol. 1
Sharmat, Marjorie Weinman. SAY HELLO, VANESSA.
  Ages 4-7. 585, Vol. 3
Sherburne, Zoa. JENNIFER.
  Ages 12 and up. 812, Vol. 1
Shotwell, Louisa Rossiter. MAGDALENA.
  Ages 10-12. 818, Vol. 1
Shura, Mary Francis Craig. RUN AWAY HOME.
  Ages 9-11. 820, Vol. 1
Singer, Marilyn. IT CAN'T HURT FOREVER.
  Ages 9-12. 604, Vol. 2
Smith, Doris Buchanan. LAST WAS LLOYD.
  Ages 8-11. 608, Vol. 2
Smith, Doris Buchanan. SALTED LEMONS.
  Ages 9-12. 609, Vol. 3
Smith, Janice Lee. THE MONSTER IN THE THIRD
  DRESSER DRAWER AND OTHER STORIES
  ABOUT ADAM JOSHUA.
  Ages 5-8. 610, Vol. 3
Snyder, Zilpha Keatley. THE EGYPT GAME.
  Ages 10-13. 836, Vol. 1

## Friendship (cont.)

Speevack, Yetta. THE SPIDER PLANT.
Ages 9-11. 848, Vol. 1

Stolz, Mary Slattery. CIDER DAYS.
Ages 8-11. 626, Vol. 2

Stolz, Mary Slattery. FERRIS WHEEL.
Ages 8-11. 627, Vol. 2

Stolz, Mary Slattery. WAIT FOR ME, MICHAEL.
Ages 12 and up. 876, Vol. 1

Talbot, Charlene Joy. THE GREAT RAT ISLAND
ADVENTURE.
Ages 10-13. 634, Vol. 2

Thrasher, Crystal Faye. BETWEEN DARK AND
DAYLIGHT.
Ages 11-13. 658, Vol. 3

Towne, Mary. THE GLASS ROOM.
Ages 11 and up. 899, Vol. 1

Townsend, John Rowe. HELL'S EDGE.
Ages 12 and up. 901, Vol. 1

Van Leeuwen, Jean. TIMOTHY'S FLOWER.
Ages 6-8. 919, Vol. 1

Vigna, Judith. THE HIDING HOUSE.
Ages 4-7. 667, Vol. 3

Vogel, Ilse-Margaret. HELLO, HENRY.
Ages 4-7. 933, Vol. 1

Von Gebhardt, Hertha Antonie Mathilde Triepel. THE
GIRL FROM NOWHERE.
Ages 9-12. 934, Vol. 1

Vroman, Mary Elizabeth. HARLEM SUMMER.
Ages 12 and up. 936, Vol. 1

Walker, Mary Alexander. YEAR OF THE
CAFETERIA.
Ages 12 and up. 943, Vol. 1

Wallace, Art. TOBY.
Ages 9-11. 945, Vol. 1

Wallace-Brodeur, Ruth. THE KENTON YEAR.
Ages 9-11. 676, Vol. 3

Weiman, Eiveen. IT TAKES BRAINS.
Ages 10-12. 686, Vol. 3

Wells, Rosemary. TIMOTHY GOES TO SCHOOL.
Ages 3-5. 689, Vol. 3

Willard, Mildred Wilds. THE LUCK OF HARRY
WEAVER.
Ages 8-10. 977, Vol. 1

Wood, Phyllis Anderson. THIS TIME COUNT ME IN.
Ages 12 and up. 706, Vol. 3

Wrenn, C. Gilbert and Shirley Schwarzrock. LIVING
WITH LONELINESS.
Ages 11 and up. 1004, Vol. 1

Zolotow, Charlotte Shapiro. A TIGER NAMED
THOMAS.
Ages 4-7. 1029, Vol. 1

### Meaning of

Adler, Carole Schwerdtfeger. THE MAGIC OF THE
GLITS.
Ages 9-12. 6, Vol. 3

Ames, Mildred. WHAT ARE FRIENDS FOR?
Ages 9-11. 12, Vol. 2

Anckarsvärd, Karin. SPRINGTIME FOR EVA.
Ages 12 and up. 16, Vol. 1

Anderson, Mary Quirk. JUST THE TWO OF THEM.
Ages 12 and up. 19, Vol. 1

Angell, Judie. IN SUMMERTIME IT'S TUFFY.
Ages 11-13. 19, Vol. 2

Anglund, Joan Walsh. A FRIEND IS SOMEONE WHO
LIKES YOU.
Ages 4-9. 21, Vol. 1

Annett, Cora. WHEN THE PORCUPINE MOVED IN.
Ages 6-9. 22, Vol. 1

Asher, Sandra Fenichel. SUMMER BEGINS.
Ages 10-13. 28, Vol. 3

Ball, Zachary, pseud. KEP.
Ages 10 and up. 50, Vol. 1

Bates, Betty. LOVE IS LIKE PEANUTS.
Ages 10-14. 38, Vol. 3

Bates, Betty. PICKING UP THE PIECES.
Ages 10-13. 40, Vol. 3

Baudouy, Michel-Aime. MORE THAN COURAGE.
Ages 12 and up. 56, Vol. 1

Bawden, Nina Mark Kark. THE RUNAWAY
SUMMER.
Ages 9-12. 57, Vol. 1

Bell, Frederic. JENNY'S CORNER.
Ages 8-11. 65, Vol. 1

Berger, Terry. BEING ALONE, BEING TOGETHER.
Ages 3-7. 71, Vol. 1

Berger, Terry. FRIENDS.
Ages 7-11. 48, Vol. 3

Berger, Terry. SPECIAL FRIENDS.
Ages 8-11. 49, Vol. 3

Bethancourt, T. Ernesto, pseud. THE DOG DAYS OF
ARTHUR CANE.
Ages 11 and up. 54, Vol. 2

Billington, Elizabeth T. PART-TIME BOY.
Ages 8-10. 53, Vol. 3

Blume, Judy Sussman. TIGER EYES.
Ages 11 and up. 57, Vol. 3

Bond, Nancy Barbara. THE VOYAGE BEGUN.
Ages 12 and up. 60, Vol. 3

Bonham, Frank. COOL CAT.
Ages 12 and up. 96, Vol. 1

Bonsall, Crosby Newell. THE GOODBYE SUMMER.
Ages 9-11. 63, Vol. 3

Brancato, Robin Fidler. SOMETHING LEFT TO
LOSE.
Ages 12-14. 71, Vol. 2

Bridgers, Sue Ellen. ALL TOGETHER NOW.
Ages 11 and up. 74, Vol. 3

Brooks, Jerome. MAKE ME A HERO.
Ages 9-12. 78, Vol. 3

Brown, Myra Berry. BEST FRIENDS.
Ages 3-7. 127, Vol. 1

Buck, Pearl Sydenstricker. THE BIG WAVE.
Ages 9-11. 129, Vol. 1

Buckley, Peter and Hortense Jones. WILLIAM, ANDY,
AND RAMÓN.
Ages 6-8. 133, Vol. 1

Bulla, Clyde Robert. DEXTER.
Ages 9-11. 135, Vol. 1

Bulla, Clyde Robert. SHOESHINE GIRL.
Ages 8-10. 93, Vol. 2

Bunting, Anne Evelyn. THE EMPTY WINDOW.
Ages 8-12. 89, Vol. 3

Bunting, Anne Evelyn. THE WAITING GAME.
Ages 10 and up. 91, Vol. 3

Burch, Robert Joseph. THE WHITMAN KICK.
Ages 12 and up. 100, Vol. 2

Burnett, Frances Hodgson. THE SECRET GARDEN.
Ages 10 and up. 147, Vol. 1

Burton, Virginia Lee. MIKE MULLIGAN AND HIS
STEAM SHOVEL.
Ages 4-8. 149, Vol. 1

Byars, Betsy Cromer. AFTER THE GOAT MAN.
Ages 9-11. 153, Vol. 1

Byars, Betsy Cromer. THE CYBIL WAR.
Ages 9-12. 96, Vol. 3

Byars, Betsy Cromer. THE PINBALLS.
Ages 10-13. 108, Vol. 2

Callen, Lawrence Willard. SORROW'S SONG.
Ages 9-12. 103, Vol. 3

Carlson, Dale Bick. TRIPLE BOY.
Ages 13 and up. 115, Vol. 2

Carlson, Natalie Savage. THE EMPTY
SCHOOLHOUSE.
Ages 8-12. 165, Vol. 1

Carpelan, Bo Gustaf Bertelsson. BOW ISLAND: THE
STORY OF A SUMMER THAT WAS DIFFERENT.
Ages 11-14. 171, Vol. 1

## Friendship (cont.)

Whelan, Gloria. A TIME TO KEEP SILENT.
Ages 11-14. 690, Vol. 3
White, Elwyn Brooks. CHARLOTTE'S WEB.
Ages 8-12. 967, Vol. 1
Winthrop, Elizabeth. MARATHON MIRANDA.
Ages 9-11. 696, Vol. 3
Winthrop, Elizabeth. MIRANDA IN THE MIDDLE.
Ages 9-13. 697, Vol. 3
Wittman, Sally Anne Christensen. A SPECIAL
TRADE.
Ages 2-5. 693, Vol. 2
Wittman, Sally Anne Christensen. THE WONDERFUL
MRS. TRUMBLY.
Ages 5-8. 700, Vol. 3
Wrightson, Patricia. A RACECOURSE FOR ANDY.
Ages 9-12. 1007, Vol. 1
Yep, Laurence Michael. SEA GLASS.
Ages 11-14. 713, Vol. 3
York, Carol Beach. NOTHING EVER HAPPENS
HERE.
Ages 12 and up. 1011, Vol. 1
Zalben, Jane Breskin. LYLE AND HUMUS.
Ages 3-6. 1014, Vol. 1
Zolotow, Charlotte Shapiro. JANEY.
Ages 4-7. 1023, Vol. 1
Zolotow, Charlotte Shapiro. MY FRIEND JOHN.
Ages 4-6. 1024, Vol. 1
Zolotow, Charlotte Shapiro. THE UNFRIENDLY
BOOK.
Ages 4-8. 721, Vol. 2

## Funerals

See: Death: funeral issues

## Future

See: Careers: planning; Education; Ego ideal; Goals

# G

## Gambling

Dygard, Thomas J. POINT SPREAD.
Ages 10 and up. 178, Vol. 3
Rinkoff, Barbara Jean Rich. THE WATCHERS.
Ages 11-14. 740, Vol. 1
Yep, Laurence Michael. CHILD OF THE OWL.
Ages 11 and up. 711, Vol. 2

## Ganging Up On

See: Aggression

## Gangs

See also: Cliques; Clubs; Delinquency, juvenile

**Being bothered by**
Alexander, Anne. TROUBLE ON TREAT STREET.
Ages 10-12. 7, Vol. 1
Ashley, Bernard. TERRY ON THE FENCE.
Ages 12 and up. 25, Vol. 2
Bond, Nancy Barbara. THE VOYAGE BEGUN.
Ages 12 and up. 60, Vol. 3
Bova, Benjamin William. CITY OF DARKNESS: A
NOVEL.
Ages 12 and up. 63, Vol. 2
Butterworth, William Edmund. LEROY AND THE
OLD MAN.
Ages 12 and up. 93, Vol. 3
Mazer, Harry. THE WAR ON VILLA STREET: A
NOVEL.
Ages 11-13. 448, Vol. 2
Platt, Kin. HEADMAN.
Ages 13-19. 517, Vol. 2
Smith, Pauline Coggeshall. BRUSH FIRE!
Ages 11 and up. 613, Vol. 3

**Conflict between**
Bonham, Frank. COOL CAT.
Ages 12 and up. 96, Vol. 1
Bonham, Frank. DURANGO STREET.
Ages 11 and up. 97, Vol. 1
Bonham, Frank. VIVA CHICANO.
Ages 12 and up. 99, Vol. 1
Hinton, Susan Eloise. THE OUTSIDERS.
Ages 12 and up. 412, Vol. 1

**Membership in.** See also: Belonging; Friendship
Bonham, Frank. DURANGO STREET.
Ages 11 and up. 97, Vol. 1
Bova, Benjamin William. CITY OF DARKNESS: A
NOVEL.
Ages 12 and up. 63, Vol. 2
Fleischman, H. Samuel. GANG GIRL.
Ages 11 and up. 322, Vol. 1
Hinton, Susan Eloise. RUMBLE FISH.
Ages 12 and up. 316, Vol. 2
Levoy, Myron. A SHADOW LIKE A LEOPARD.
Ages 12 and up. 369, Vol. 3
Maddock, Reginald. THIN ICE.
Ages 12 and up. 605, Vol. 1
Mann, Peggy. WHEN CARLOS CLOSED THE
STREET.
Ages 8-11. 612, Vol. 1
Neville, Emily Cheney. THE SEVENTEENTH-
STREET GANG.
Ages 10-13. 668, Vol. 1
Platt, Kin. HEADMAN.
Ages 13-19. 517, Vol. 2
Rinkoff, Barbara Jean Rich. MEMBER OF THE
GANG.
Ages 10-12. 737, Vol. 1
Rinkoff, Barbara Jean Rich. NAME: JOHNNY
PIERCE.
Ages 10-12. 738, Vol. 1
Wrenn, C. Gilbert and Shirley Schwarzrock. COPING
WITH CLIQUES.
Ages 11 and up. 998, Vol. 1

## Gender Role Identity

Pearson, Susan. EVERYBODY KNOWS THAT!
Ages 4-7. 496, Vol. 2

**Female.** See also: Women's rights
Arthur, Ruth M. MY DAUGHTER, NICOLA.
Ages 10-13. 33, Vol. 1
Baker, Rachel Mininberg. THE FIRST WOMAN
DOCTOR: THE STORY OF ELIZABETH
BLACKWELL, M.D.
Ages 12 and up. 46, Vol. 1
Brink, Carol Ryrie. CADDIE WOODLAWN: A
FRONTIER STORY.
Ages 9-12. 120, Vol. 1
Carlson, Dale Bick. GIRLS ARE EQUAL TOO: THE
WOMEN'S MOVEMENT FOR TEENAGERS.
Ages 12 and up. 163, Vol. 1
Cleaver, Vera and Bill Cleaver. LADY ELLEN GRAE.
Ages 9-12. 199, Vol. 1
Clifton, Lucille. EVERETT ANDERSON'S FRIEND.
Ages 4-7. 144, Vol. 2
Colman, Hila Crayder. DAUGHTER OF
DISCONTENT.
Ages 12 and up. 229, Vol. 1
Flory, Jane Trescott. ONE HUNDRED AND EIGHT
BELLS.
Ages 9-11. 324, Vol. 1
Gibson, Althea. I ALWAYS WANTED TO BE
SOMEBODY.
Ages 12 and up. 357, Vol. 1
Greene, Bette. PHILIP HALL LIKES ME. I RECKON
MAYBE.
Ages 10-13. 374, Vol. 1

## Gender Role Identity (cont.)

Greenwald, Sheila. THE SECRET IN MIRANDA'S CLOSET.
Ages 8-11. 274, Vol. 2

Ho, Minfong. SING TO THE DAWN.
Ages 10-13. 320, Vol. 2

Howard, Moses L. THE OSTRICH CHASE.
Ages 10-13. 437, Vol. 1

Klein, Norma. GIRLS CAN BE ANYTHING.
Ages 4-7. 503, Vol. 1

Knudson, R. Rozanne. ZANBANGER.
Ages 10-13. 387, Vol. 2

Lasker, Joe. MOTHERS CAN DO ANYTHING.
Ages 3-6. 531, Vol. 1

Lexau, Joan M. THE TROUBLE WITH TERRY.
Ages 8-11. 560, Vol. 1

Madden, Betsy. THE ALL-AMERICAN COEDS.
Ages 12 and up. 601, Vol. 1

Marney, Dean. JUST GOOD FRIENDS.
Ages 11-13. 404, Vol. 3

Merriam, Eve. BOYS & GIRLS, GIRLS & BOYS.
Ages 5-8. 636, Vol. 1

Noble, Iris Davis. FIRST WOMAN AMBULANCE SURGEON, EMILY BARRINGER.
Ages 12 and up. 669, Vol. 1

O'Dell, Scott. ISLAND OF THE BLUE DOLPHINS.
Ages 10 and up. 681, Vol. 1

Peck, Richard. REPRESENTING SUPER DOLL.
Ages 12 and up. 696, Vol. 1

Perl, Lila. THAT CRAZY APRIL.
Ages 10-12. 701, Vol. 1

Schlein, Miriam. THE GIRL WHO WOULD RATHER CLIMB TREES.
Ages 4-8. 574, Vol. 2

Schwarzrock, Shirley and C. Gilbert Wrenn. CHANGING ROLES OF MEN AND WOMEN: WHAT IT MEANS TO YOUTH.
Ages 11 and up. 787, Vol. 1

Skorpen, Liesel Moak. MANDY'S GRANDMOTHER.
Ages 4-7. 608, Vol. 2

Udry, Janice May. THE SUNFLOWER GARDEN.
Ages 6-10. 913, Vol. 1

Vestley, Anne-Catharina. HELLO, AURORA.
Ages 8-11. 922, Vol. 1

Walden, Amelia Elizabeth. BASKETBALL GIRL OF THE YEAR.
Ages 12 and up. 942, Vol. 1

Zolotow, Charlotte Shapiro. WHEN I HAVE A LITTLE GIRL.
Ages 4-6. 1030, Vol. 1

### Male

Adler, Carole Schwerdtfeger. THE ONCE IN A WHILE HERO.
Ages 10-13. 7, Vol. 3

Black, Irma Simonton. THE LITTLE OLD MAN WHO COOKED AND CLEANED.
Ages 4-8. 79, Vol. 1

Carol, Bill J., pseud. SINGLE TO CENTER.
Ages 9-11. 170, Vol. 1

Colman, Hila Crayder. THAT'S THE WAY IT IS, AMIGO.
Ages 11-13. 168, Vol. 2

De Paola, Thomas Anthony. OLIVER BUTTON IS A SISSY.
Ages 4-7. 161, Vol. 3

Hooks, William Harris. DOUG MEETS THE NUTCRACKER.
Ages 8-11. 332, Vol. 2

Isadora, Rachel. MAX.
Ages 4-7. 346, Vol. 2

Levoy, Myron. A SHADOW LIKE A LEOPARD.
Ages 12 and up. 369, Vol. 3

Marney, Dean. JUST GOOD FRIENDS.
Ages 11-13. 404, Vol. 3

Merriam, Eve. BOYS & GIRLS, GIRLS & BOYS.
Ages 5-8. 636, Vol. 1

Okimoto, Jean Davies. NORMAN SCHNURMAN, AVERAGE PERSON.
Ages 10-12. 471, Vol. 3

Peck, Richard. FATHER FIGURE: A NOVEL.
Ages 11 and up. 501, Vol. 2

Phipson, Joan Nash, pseud. PETER AND BUTCH.
Ages 10 and up. 709, Vol. 1

Schwarzrock, Shirley and C. Gilbert Wrenn. CHANGING ROLES OF MEN AND WOMEN: WHAT IT MEANS TO YOUTH.
Ages 11 and up. 787, Vol. 1

Simon, Marcia L. A SPECIAL GIFT.
Ages 10-13. 601, Vol. 2

Stewart, Robert. THE DADDY BOOK.
Ages 3-5. 861, Vol. 1

Vestley, Anne-Catharina. AURORA AND SOCRATES.
Ages 8-10. 660, Vol. 1

Vestley, Anne-Catharina. HELLO, AURORA.
Ages 8-11. 922, Vol. 1

Wiesner, William. TURNABOUT: A NORWEGIAN TALE.
Ages 4-8. 973, Vol. 1

Zolotow, Charlotte Shapiro. WILLIAM'S DOLL.
Ages 4-7. 1031, Vol. 1

## Generation Gap

See: *Communication: lack of; Communication: parent-child*

## Generosity

See: *Sharing/Not sharing*

## German-American

Irion, Ruth Hershey. THE CHRISTMAS COOKIE TREE.
Ages 8-10. 345, Vol. 2

Pundt, Helen Marie. SPRING COMES FIRST TO THE WILLOWS.
Ages 11 and up. 717, Vol. 1

## Getting Along With Others

See: *Communication: parent-child; Cooperation: in play; Cooperation: in work*

## Ghetto

See also: *Afro-American; Jew/Jewish; Poverty*

Blue, Rose. NIKKI 108.
Ages 10-12. 85, Vol. 1

Bonham, Frank. COOL CAT.
Ages 12 and up. 96, Vol. 1

Coles, Robert. DEAD END SCHOOL.
Ages 9-11. 222, Vol. 1

Colman, Hila Crayder. THE GIRL FROM PUERTO RICO.
Ages 11 and up. 231, Vol. 1

Hinton, Susan Eloise. THAT WAS THEN, THIS IS NOW.
Ages 12 and up. 413, Vol. 1

Hunter, Kristin Eggleston. SOUL BROTHERS AND SISTER LOU.
Ages 12 and up. 443, Vol. 1

Hunter, Kristin Eggleston. THE SURVIVORS.
Ages 12 and up. 340, Vol. 2

Keats, Ezra Jack. LOUIE.
Ages 3-7. 367, Vol. 2

Myers, Walter Dean. THE YOUNG LANDLORDS.
Ages 11-14. 461, Vol. 3

Neville, Emily Cheney. GARDEN OF BROKEN GLASS.
Ages 11-14. 477, Vol. 2

## Ghetto (cont.)

Rinkoff, Barbara Jean Rich. MEMBER OF THE GANG.
Ages 10-12. 737, Vol. 1
Rivera, Geraldo. A SPECIAL KIND OF COURAGE: PROFILES OF YOUNG AMERICANS.
Ages 12 and up. 544, Vol. 2
Walden, Amelia Elizabeth. BASKETBALL GIRL OF THE YEAR.
Ages 12 and up. 942, Vol. 1
Weik, Mary Hays. THE JAZZ MAN.
Ages 9-11. 958, Vol. 1

## Giftedness

See: *Talents*

## Giving, Meaning of

Agle, Nan Hayden. SUSAN'S MAGIC.
Ages 9-11. 3, Vol. 1
Brandenberg, Franz. A SECRET FOR GRANDMOTHER'S BIRTHDAY.
Ages 3-7. 75, Vol. 2
Burch, Robert Joseph. RENFROE'S CHRISTMAS.
Ages 8-11. 141, Vol. 1
Caudill, Rebecca. A CERTAIN SMALL SHEPHERD.
Ages 8 and up. 174, Vol. 1
Charlip, Remy and Burton Supree. HARLEQUIN AND THE GIFT OF MANY COLORS.
Ages 4-8. 179, Vol. 1
Collins, David R. IF I COULD, I WOULD.
Ages 6-8. 131, Vol. 3
Gerson, Mary-Joan. OMOTEJI'S BABY BROTHER.
Ages 6-8. 356, Vol. 1
Goffstein, Marilyn Brooke. GOLDIE, THE DOLLMAKER.
Ages 7-9. 364, Vol. 1
Hautzig, Esther Rudomin. A GIFT FOR MAMA.
Ages 8-12. 273, Vol. 3
Hughes, Shirley. DAVID AND DOG.
Ages 4-7. 335, Vol. 2
Hunt, Irene. THE LOTTERY ROSE.
Ages 11 and up. 337, Vol. 2
Hutchins, Patricia. THE BEST TRAIN SET EVER.
Ages 5-8. 342, Vol. 2
Kaye, Geraldine. TIM AND THE RED INDIAN HEADDRESS.
Ages 5-7. 365, Vol. 2
Lionni, Leo. TICO AND THE GOLDEN WINGS.
Ages 4-8. 568, Vol. 1
Moskin, Marietta Dunston. ROSIE'S BIRTHDAY PRESENT.
Ages 4-7. 456, Vol. 3
Ness, Evaline Michelow. EXACTLY ALIKE.
Ages 5-8. 660, Vol. 1
Ness, Evaline Michelow. JOSEFINA FEBRUARY.
Ages 4-8. 661, Vol. 1
Riley, Susan. WHAT DOES IT MEAN? HELP.
Ages 3-6. 540, Vol. 2
Sharmat, Marjorie Weinman. TAKING CARE OF MELVIN.
Ages 4-8. 587, Vol. 3
Shippen, Katherine Binney. ANDREW CARNEGIE AND THE AGE OF STEEL.
Ages 9-11. 816, Vol. 1
Silverstein, Shel. THE GIVING TREE.
Ages 4 and up. 821, Vol. 1
Stuart, Jesse. THE BEATINEST BOY.
Ages 10-12. 879, Vol. 1
Taylor, Mark. A TIME FOR FLOWERS.
Ages 4-7. 888, Vol. 1
Taylor, Paula. JOHNNY CASH.
Ages 7-10. 638, Vol. 1
Van Stockum, Hilda. MOGO'S FLUTE.
Ages 10-12. 920, Vol. 1

Watson, Nancy Dingman. TOMMY'S MOMMY'S FISH.
Ages 5-8. 955, Vol. 1
Williams, Barbara Wright. SOMEDAY, SAID MITCHELL.
Ages 3-6. 686, Vol. 2
Young, Miriam Burt. MISS SUZY'S BIRTHDAY.
Ages 3-7. 1012, Vol. 1

## Glasses, Wearing of

See also: *Visual impairment*
Brown, Marc Tolan. ARTHUR'S EYES.
Ages 4-7. 80, Vol. 3
Delaney, Ned. TWO STRIKES, FOUR EYES.
Ages 5-8. 196, Vol. 2
Goodsell, Jane. KATIE'S MAGIC GLASSES.
Ages 5-8. 368, Vol. 1
Keller, Holly. CROMWELL'S GLASSES.
Ages 3-6. 337, Vol. 3
Kropp, Paul Stephan. WILTED.
Ages 11-14. 354, Vol. 3
Leggett, Linda Rogers and Linda Gambee Andrews. THE ROSE-COLORED GLASSES: MELANIE ADJUSTS TO POOR VISION.
Ages 8-11. 362, Vol. 3
Little, Jean. FROM ANNA.
Ages 9-11. 570, Vol. 1
Lord, Beman. GUARDS FOR MATT.
Ages 8-10. 581, Vol. 1
Neigoff, Mike. SOCCER HERO.
Ages 9-11. 475, Vol. 2
Raskin, Ellen. SPECTACLES.
Ages 4-9. 724, Vol. 1
Wise, William. THE COWBOY SURPRISE.
Ages 5-8. 980, Vol. 1
Wolff, Angelika. MOM! I NEED GLASSES!
Ages 5-9. 989, Vol. 1

## Goals

Bunting, Anne Evelyn. THE WAITING GAME.
Ages 10 and up. 91, Vol. 3
Cohen, Miriam. WHEN WILL I READ?
Ages 4-6. 156, Vol. 2
Distad, Audree. THE DREAM RUNNER.
Ages 10-13. 201, Vol. 2
Hoban, Lillian Aberman. ARTHUR'S FUNNY MONEY.
Ages 6-8. 294, Vol. 3
Lipsyte, Robert. THE CONTENDER.
Ages 12 and up. 569, Vol. 1
Love, Sandra Weller. MELISSA'S MEDLEY.
Ages 10-13. 418, Vol. 2
Sargent, Sarah. EDWARD TROY AND THE WITCH CAT.
Ages 9-11. 569, Vol. 2
Ullman, James Ramsey. BANNER IN THE SKY.
Ages 12 and up. 915, Vol. 1
Watanabe, Shigeo. I CAN RIDE IT!
Ages 2-5. 684, Vol. 3

## God

See: *Religion*

## Going Away

See: *Abandonment; Camp experiences; Hospital, going to; Moving; Schools, private; Separation anxiety; Separation from loved ones*

## Going Steady

See: *Boy-girl relationships: dating*

## Grandparent

See also: *Age; Family; Great-grandparent; Retirement*

## Grandparent (cont.)

Shanks, Ann Zane. OLD IS WHAT YOU GET: DIALOGUES ON AGING BY THE OLD AND THE YOUNG.
  Ages 10 and up. 582, Vol. 2

**Death of.** *See: Death: of grandparent*

**Illness of.** *See: Illnesses: of grandparent*

**Interfering**

Barnwell, D. Robinson. SHADOW ON THE WATER.
  Ages 12 and up. 52, Vol. 1

**Living in child's home**

Angell, Judie. SECRET SELVES.
  Ages 11-13. 20, Vol. 3
Beckman, Gunnel. THAT EARLY SPRING.
  Ages 12 and up. 47, Vol. 2
Blue, Rose. GRANDMA DIDN'T WAVE BACK.
  Ages 8-11. 82, Vol. 1
Coatsworth, Elizabeth Jane. MARRA'S WORLD.
  Ages 8-11. 150, Vol. 2
Dobrin, Arnold. SCAT!
  Ages 6-9. 276, Vol. 1
Donnelly, Elfie. SO LONG, GRANDPA.
  Ages 9-11. 168, Vol. 3
Herman, Charlotte. OUR SNOWMAN HAD OLIVE EYES.
  Ages 9-11. 313, Vol. 2
Johnston, Norma. IF YOU LOVE ME, LET ME GO.
  Ages 12 and up. 354, Vol. 2
Kleberger, Ilse. GRANDMOTHER OMA.
  Ages 8-11. 499, Vol. 1
Langner, Nola. FREDDY MY GRANDFATHER.
  Ages 5-8. 356, Vol. 3
LeRoy, Gen. EMMA'S DILEMMA.
  Ages 9-12. 400, Vol. 2
Levy, Elizabeth. LIZZIE LIES A LOT.
  Ages 9-11. 405, Vol. 2
Little, Jean. SPRING BEGINS IN MARCH.
  Ages 10-12. 576, Vol. 1
Lorenzo, Carol Lee. MAMA'S GHOSTS.
  Ages 10-12. 586, Vol. 1
Mazer, Norma Fox. A FIGURE OF SPEECH.
  Ages 12 and up. 628, Vol. 1
Mearian, Judy Frank. SOMEONE SLIGHTLY DIFFERENT.
  Ages 10-12. 417, Vol. 3
Miles, Miska, pseud. ANNIE AND THE OLD ONE.
  Ages 6-9. 638, Vol. 1
Palay, Steven. I LOVE MY GRANDMA.
  Ages 4-7. 491, Vol. 2
Paterson, Katherine Womeldorf. JACOB HAVE I LOVED.
  Ages 12 and up. 485, Vol. 3
Pollowitz, Melinda. CINNAMON CANE.
  Ages 10-12. 519, Vol. 2
Rabin, Gil. CHANGES.
  Ages 12 and up. 721, Vol. 1
Robinson, Jean. THE SECRET LIFE OF T.K. DEARING.
  Ages 10 and up. 744, Vol. 1
Sachs, Marilyn. CLASS PICTURES.
  Ages 10-13. 564, Vol. 3
Shreve, Susan Richards. FAMILY SECRETS: FIVE VERY IMPORTANT STORIES.
  Ages 9-11. 590, Vol. 3
Simon, Shirley. BEST FRIEND.
  Ages 9-12. 824, Vol. 1
Smith, Robert Kimmel. JELLY BELLY.
  Ages 10-12. 614, Vol. 3
Sonneborn, Ruth A. I LOVE GRAM.
  Ages 4-7. 842, Vol. 1
Stolz, Mary Slattery. WHAT TIME OF NIGHT IS IT?
  Ages 11-14. 631, Vol. 3
Stren, Patti. THERE'S A RAINBOW IN MY CLOSET.
  Ages 8-10. 638, Vol. 3

Talbot, Toby. DEAR GRETA GARBO.
  Ages 11-13. 635, Vol. 2
Tate, Joan. LUKE'S GARDEN AND GRAMP: TWO NOVELS.
  Ages 10-13. 644, Vol. 3
Taylor, Mark. A TIME FOR FLOWERS.
  Ages 4-7. 888, Vol. 1
Tester, Sylvia Root. SANDY'S NEW HOME.
  Ages 5-8. 648, Vol. 3
Tolan, Stephanie S. GRANDPA — AND ME.
  Ages 10-13. 655, Vol. 2

**Living in home of**

Adler, Carole Schwerdtfeger. THE SILVER COACH.
  Ages 9-12. 8, Vol. 3
Ames, Mildred. NICKY AND THE JOYOUS NOISE.
  Ages 9-12. 14, Vol. 3
Arthur, Ruth M. MY DAUGHTER, NICOLA.
  Ages 10-13. 33, Vol. 1
Bates, Betty. THAT'S WHAT T.J. SAYS.
  Ages 9-11. 41, Vol. 3
Bloch, Marie Halun. THE TWO WORLDS OF DAMYAN.
  Ages 9-12. 81, Vol. 1
Brenner, Barbara Johnes. A YEAR IN THE LIFE OF ROSIE BERNARD.
  Ages 9-11. 118, Vol. 1
Bridgers, Sue Ellen. ALL TOGETHER NOW.
  Ages 11 and up. 74, Vol. 3
Bridgers, Sue Ellen. NOTES FOR ANOTHER LIFE.
  Ages 12 and up. 75, Vol. 3
Butterworth, William Edmund. LEROY AND THE OLD MAN.
  Ages 12 and up. 93, Vol. 3
Byars, Betsy Cromer. AFTER THE GOAT MAN.
  Ages 9-11. 153, Vol. 1
Byars, Betsy Cromer. THE HOUSE OF WINGS.
  Ages 9-12. 156, Vol. 1
Byars, Betsy Cromer. THE TWO-THOUSAND-POUND GOLDFISH.
  Ages 9-12. 99, Vol. 3
Cameron, Eleanor Butler. A SPELL IS CAST.
  Ages 10-12. 159, Vol. 1
Cleaver, Vera and Bill Cleaver. QUEEN OF HEARTS.
  Ages 10-13. 140, Vol. 2
Cleaver, Vera and Bill Cleaver. THE WHYS AND WHEREFORES OF LITTABELLE LEE.
  Ages 12 and up. 204, Vol. 1
Clymer, Eleanor Lowenton. MY BROTHER STEVIE.
  Ages 8-11. 213, Vol. 1
Colman, Hila Crayder. THE AMAZING MISS LAURA.
  Ages 11-14. 161, Vol. 2
Corcoran, Barbara. THE FARAWAY ISLAND.
  Ages 10-13. 179, Vol. 2
Corcoran, Barbara. HEY, THAT'S MY SOUL YOU'RE STOMPING ON.
  Ages 11-14. 180, Vol. 2
Corcoran, Barbara. THIS IS A RECORDING.
  Ages 12 and up. 252, Vol. 1
Crawford, Deborah. SOMEBODY WILL MISS ME.
  Ages 12 and up. 257, Vol. 1
Daringer, Helen Fern. STEPSISTER SALLY.
  Ages 9-12. 264, Vol. 1
Dyer, Thomas A. THE WHIPMAN IS WATCHING.
  Ages 10-14. 177, Vol. 3
Farley, Carol J. TWILIGHT WAVES.
  Ages 10-13. 186, Vol. 3
Fenton, Edward. DUFFY'S ROCKS.
  Ages 12 and up. 311, Vol. 1
Fitzhugh, Louise. THE LONG SECRET.
  Ages 9-12. 321, Vol. 1
Gardiner, John Reynolds. STONE FOX.
  Ages 8-10. 202, Vol. 3

## Grandparent (cont.)

Garlan, Patricia Wallace and Maryjane Dunstan. THE BOY WHO PLAYED TIGER.
Ages 9-11. 347, Vol. 1

Gauch, Patricia Lee. GRANDPA AND ME.
Ages 5-8. 351, Vol. 1

Gerson, Corinne. TREAD SOFTLY.
Ages 9-12. 209, Vol. 3

Goffstein, Marilyn Brooke. TWO PIANO TUNERS.
Ages 8-10. 365, Vol. 1

Greene, Constance Clarke. THE UNMAKING OF RABBIT.
Ages 10-13. 380, Vol. 1

Greenfield, Eloise. GRANDMAMA'S JOY.
Ages 4-8. 244, Vol. 3

Härtling, Peter. OMA.
Ages 8-11. 296, Vol. 2

Hermes, Patricia. WHAT IF THEY KNEW?
Ages 9-11. 285, Vol. 3

Hest, Amy. MAYBE NEXT YEAR...
Ages 9-12. 288, Vol. 3

Holland, Isabelle. NOW IS NOT TOO LATE.
Ages 10-13. 301, Vol. 3

Irwin, Hadley, pseud. MOON AND ME.
Ages 11-14. 325, Vol. 3

Irwin, Hadley, pseud. WHAT ABOUT GRANDMA?
Ages 11 and up. 326, Vol. 3

Johnston, Norma. THE SWALLOW'S SONG.
Ages 12 and up. 357, Vol. 2

Kerr, M. E., pseud. THE SON OF SOMEONE FAMOUS.
Ages 11 and up. 493, Vol. 1

Lexau, Joan M. BENJIE ON HIS OWN.
Ages 6-9. 554, Vol. 1

Lingard, Joan. THE CLEARANCE.
Ages 12 and up. 562, Vol. 1

Lutters, Valerie. THE HAUNTING OF JULIE UNGER.
Ages 10-13. 425, Vol. 2

Maher, Ramona. ALICE YAZZIE'S YEAR.
Ages 9-12. 439, Vol. 2

Majerus, Janet. GRANDPA AND FRANK.
Ages 12 and up. 440, Vol. 2

Molloy, Anne Stearns. THE GIRL FROM TWO MILES HIGH.
Ages 10-12. 642, Vol. 1

Moskin, Marietta Dunston. A PAPER DRAGON.
Ages 11 and up. 651, Vol. 1

Ness, Evaline Michelow. JOSEFINA FEBRUARY.
Ages 4-8. 661, Vol. 1

Perl, Lila. THE TELLTALE SUMMER OF TINA C.
Ages 10-13. 503, Vol. 2

Phipson, Joan Nash, pseud. A TIDE FLOWING.
Ages 12 and up. 509, Vol. 3

Potter, Marian. THE SHARED ROOM.
Ages 10-12. 517, Vol. 3

Rinaldo, C. L. DARK DREAMS.
Ages 11 and up. 734, Vol. 1

Rolerson, Darrell A. A BOY CALLED PLUM.
Ages 10-12. 752, Vol. 1

Screen, Robert Martin. WITH MY FACE TO THE RISING SUN.
Ages 11 and up. 580, Vol. 2

Simon, Norma. HOW DO I FEEL?
Ages 4-8. 822, Vol. 1

Smith, Doris Buchanan. TOUGH CHAUNCEY.
Ages 12 and up. 832, Vol. 1

Snyder, Zilpha Keatley. THE EGYPT GAME.
Ages 10-13. 836, Vol. 1

Somerlott, Robert. BLAZE.
Ages 10-13. 617, Vol. 3

Sorenson, Virginia Eggertsen. LOTTE'S LOCKET.
Ages 10-12. 843, Vol. 1

Stolz, Mary Slattery. THE MYSTERY OF THE WOODS.
Ages 7-10. 872, Vol. 1

Stuart, Jesse. THE BEATINEST BOY.
Ages 10-12. 879, Vol. 1

Uchida, Yoshiko. HISAKO'S MYSTERIES.
Ages 9-11. 909, Vol. 1

Voigt, Cynthia. DICEY'S SONG.
Ages 11 and up. 671, Vol. 3

Voigt, Cynthia. HOMECOMING.
Ages 11 and up. 672, Vol. 3

Wier, Ester Alberti. THE BARREL.
Ages 10-13. 970, Vol. 1

Wilkinson, Brenda Scott. LUDELL.
Ages 10-14. 680, Vol. 2

Wilkinson, Brenda Scott. LUDELL AND WILLIE.
Ages 12 and up. 681, Vol. 2

Winthrop, Elizabeth. WALKING AWAY.
Ages 11 and up. 979, Vol. 1

Yep, Laurence Michael. CHILD OF THE OWL.
Ages 11 and up. 711, Vol. 2

### Love for

Abercrombie, Barbara Mattes. CAT-MAN'S DAUGHTER.
Ages 11-13. 1, Vol. 3

Adler, David A. A LITTLE AT A TIME.
Ages 4-6. 2, Vol. 2

Bartoli, Jennifer. NONNA.
Ages 4-9. 38, Vol. 2

Bates, Betty. MY MOM, THE MONEY NUT.
Ages 10-12. 39, Vol. 3

Bawden, Nina Mary Kark. THE ROBBERS.
Ages 9-12. 43, Vol. 3

Beckman, Gunnel. THAT EARLY SPRING.
Ages 12 and up. 47, Vol. 2

Behrens, June York. SOO LING FINDS A WAY.
Ages 4-8. 62, Vol. 1

Blue, Rose. THE THIRTEENTH YEAR: A BAR MITZVAH STORY.
Ages 10-12. 60, Vol. 2

Borack, Barbara. GRANDPA.
Ages 3-6. 102, Vol. 1

Brancato, Robin Fidler. SWEET BELLS JANGLED OUT OF TUNE.
Ages 11-14. 70, Vol. 3

Brandenberg, Aliki Liacouras. THE TWO OF THEM.
Ages 3-7. 71, Vol. 3

Brandenberg, Franz. A SECRET FOR GRANDMOTHER'S BIRTHDAY.
Ages 3-7. 75, Vol. 2

Bridgers, Sue Ellen. NOTES FOR ANOTHER LIFE.
Ages 12 and up. 75, Vol. 3

Buckley, Helen Elizabeth. THE WONDERFUL LITTLE BOY.
Ages 3-7. 132, Vol. 1

Bunting, Anne Evelyn. MAGIC AND THE NIGHT RIVER.
Ages 5-9. 96, Vol. 2

Caines, Jeannette Franklin. WINDOW WISHING.
Ages 4-7. 100, Vol. 3

Campbell, R. Wright. WHERE PIGEONS GO TO DIE.
Ages 12 and up. 112, Vol. 2

Cate, Dick. NEVER IS A LONG, LONG TIME.
Ages 9-11. 125, Vol. 2

Clifton, Lucille. THE LUCKY STONE.
Ages 8-10. 121, Vol. 3

Corcoran, Barbara. ALL THE SUMMER VOICES.
Ages 11-14. 248, Vol. 1

Coutant, Helen. FIRST SNOW.
Ages 7-9. 255, Vol. 1

De Paola, Thomas Anthony. NANA UPSTAIRS AND NANA DOWNSTAIRS.
Ages 3-8. 272, Vol. 1

De Paola, Thomas Anthony. NOW ONE FOOT, NOW THE OTHER.
Ages 4-7. 160, Vol. 3

## Grandparent (cont.)

### Respect for

## Grandparent (cont.)

Hall, Lynn. DANZA!
Ages 9-12. 254, Vol. 3
Houston, James Archibald. AKAVAK: AN ESKIMO
JOURNEY.
Ages 9-12. 435, Vol. 1
Hurmence, Belinda. TOUGH TIFFANY.
Ages 10-13. 315, Vol. 3
Kerr, M. E., pseud. GENTLEHANDS.
Ages 11-14. 377, Vol. 2
Lingard, Joan. THE CLEARANCE.
Ages 12 and up. 562, Vol. 1
Mazer, Norma Fox. A FIGURE OF SPEECH.
Ages 12 and up. 628, Vol. 1
Naylor, Phyllis Reynolds. TO WALK THE SKY PATH.
Ages 10-13. 658, Vol. 1
Rabin, Gil. CHANGES.
Ages 12 and up. 721, Vol. 1
Robinson, Jean. THE SECRET LIFE OF T.K.
DEARING.
Ages 10 and up. 744, Vol. 1
Shotwell, Louisa Rossiter. MAGDALENA.
Ages 10-12. 818, Vol. 1
Skolsky, Mindy Warshaw. CARNIVAL AND KOPECK
AND MORE ABOUT HANNAH.
Ages 7-9. 600, Vol. 3
Walker, Mary Alexander. YEAR OF THE
CAFETERIA.
Ages 12 and up. 943, Vol. 1

## Gratitude

Brenner, Barbara Johnes. MR. TALL AND MR.
SMALL.
Ages 4-8. 116, Vol. 1
Duvoisin, Roger Antoine. PETUNIA, I LOVE YOU.
Ages 3-7. 282, Vol. 1

## Great-Grandparent

**See also:** *Age; Family; Grandparent*
Bulla, Clyde Robert. THE SUGAR PEAR TREE.
Ages 8-10. 137, Vol. 1
Carlson, Natalie Savage. MARCHERS FOR THE
DREAM.
Ages 9-11. 168, Vol. 1
De Paola, Thomas Anthony. NANA UPSTAIRS AND
NANA DOWNSTAIRS.
Ages 3-8. 272, Vol. 1
Knotts, Howard. GREAT-GRANDFATHER, THE
BABY AND ME.
Ages 5-8. 385, Vol. 2
Pevsner, Stella. KEEP STOMPIN' TILL THE MUSIC
STOPS.
Ages 9-12. 509, Vol. 2
Sneve, Virginia Driving Hawk. JIMMY YELLOW
HAWK.
Ages 8-10. 834, Vol. 1

**Death of.** *See: Death: of great-grandparent*

## Greed

Armstrong, Richard. THE ALBATROSS.
Ages 12 and up. 30, Vol. 1
Duvoisin, Roger Antoine. PETUNIA, I LOVE YOU.
Ages 3-7. 282, Vol. 1
Duvoisin, Roger Antoine. PETUNIA'S TREASURE.
Ages 5-8. 212, Vol. 2
Fitzhugh, Louise. SPORT.
Ages 9-12. 190, Vol. 3
Ginsburg, Mirra. TWO GREEDY BEARS.
Ages 3-8. 248, Vol. 2
Jones, Penelope. I DIDN'T WANT TO BE NICE.
Ages 4-7. 359, Vol. 1
Kimishima, Hisako. LUM FU AND THE GOLDEN
MOUNTAIN.
Ages 6-8. 497, Vol. 1

## Grief

**See:** *Death; Depression; Loss: feelings of; Mourning,
stages of; Separation from loved ones*

## Growing Up

**See:** *Maturation*

## Growth

**See:** *Height: short; Height: tall; Maturation*

## Guide Dog

**See:** *Blindness; Pets: guide dog*

## Guilt, Feelings of

**See also:** *Accidents; Blame; Conscience;
Crime/Criminals; Death; Depression; Justice/Injustice;
Mourning, stages of; Self-esteem; Shame*
Arrick, Fran. CHERNOWITZ!
Ages 12 and up. 23, Vol. 3
Arrick, Fran. TUNNEL VISION.
Ages 12 and up. 24, Vol. 3
Asher, Sandra Fenichel. DAUGHTERS OF THE LAW.
Ages 11-13. 26, Vol. 3
Atkinson, Linda. HIT AND RUN.
Ages 11 and up. 31, Vol. 3
Bach, Alice Hendricks. A FATHER EVERY FEW
YEARS.
Ages 11-13. 27, Vol. 2
Bawden, Nina Mary Kark. SQUIB.
Ages 10-13. 58, Vol. 1
Blume, Judy Sussman. TIGER EYES.
Ages 11 and up. 57, Vol. 3
Bradbury, Bianca. THE BLUE YEAR.
Ages 12 and up. 108, Vol. 1
Brooks, Jerome. UNCLE MIKE'S BOY.
Ages 11 and up. 123, Vol. 1
Burch, Robert Joseph. D. J.'S WORST ENEMY.
Ages 9-12. 139, Vol. 1
Burch, Robert Joseph. SIMON AND THE GAME OF
CHANCE.
Ages 10-12. 142, Vol. 1
Byars, Betsy Cromer. GOODBYE, CHICKEN LITTLE.
Ages 9-11. 97, Vol. 3
Carlson, Dale Bick. TRIPLE BOY.
Ages 13 and up. 115, Vol. 2
Christman, Elizabeth. A NICE ITALIAN GIRL.
Ages 12 and up. 132, Vol. 2
Clifford, Ethel Rosenberg. THE KILLER SWAN.
Ages 10-12. 120, Vol. 3
Clifford, Ethel Rosenberg. THE YEAR OF THE
THREE-LEGGED DEER.
Ages 12 and up. 207, Vol. 1
Clymer, Eleanor Lowenton. HOW I WENT
SHOPPING AND WHAT I GOT.
Ages 8-10. 210, Vol. 1
Colman, Hila Crayder. ACCIDENT.
Ages 11 and up. 132, Vol. 3
Colman, Hila Crayder. CAR-CRAZY GIRL.
Ages 12 and up. 227, Vol. 1
Colman, Hila Crayder. CONFESSION OF A
STORYTELLER.
Ages 10-13. 133, Vol. 3
Crawford, Charles P. LETTER PERFECT.
Ages 12 and up. 184, Vol. 2
Dunn, Judy. FEELINGS.
Ages 3-8. 279, Vol. 1
Estes, Eleanor. THE HUNDRED DRESSES.
Ages 8-10. 291, Vol. 1
Eyerly, Jeannette Hyde. THE GIRL INSIDE.
Ages 12 and up. 298, Vol. 1
Eyerly, Jeannette Hyde. THE WORLD OF ELLEN
MARCH.
Ages 12 and up. 301, Vol. 1

# H

## Habits

## Hair Style, Importance of

## Hair Style, Importance of (cont.)

Van Leeuwen, Jean. I WAS A 98-POUND DUCKLING.
Ages 11 and up. 918, Vol. 1

## Half Brother/Half Sister

See: *Sibling: half brother/half sister*

## Handicaps

See also: *Education: special*
Brown, Fern G. YOU'RE SOMEBODY SPECIAL ON A HORSE.
Ages 10-13. 87, Vol. 2
Fanshawe, Elizabeth. RACHEL.
Ages 4-6. 222, Vol. 2
Jones, Ron. THE ACORN PEOPLE.
Ages 10 and up. 360, Vol. 2
Mack, Nancy. TRACY.
Ages 4-8. 428, Vol. 2
Pursell, Margaret Sanford. A LOOK AT PHYSICAL HANDICAPS.
Ages 3-7. 525, Vol. 2
Stein, Sara Bonnett. ABOUT HANDICAPS: AN OPEN FAMILY BOOK FOR PARENTS AND CHILDREN TOGETHER.
Ages 4-8. 856, Vol. 1
Viscardi, Henry. A LAUGHTER IN THE LONELY NIGHT.
Ages 12 and up. 931, Vol. 1

Amputee. *See: Amputee*

Asthma. *See: Asthma*

Birth defects. *See: Birth defects*

Blindness. *See: Blindness*

Braces on body/limbs. *See: Braces on body/limbs*

Brain injury. *See: Brain injury; Cerebral palsy; Epilepsy; Learning disabilities; Mental retardation; Spastic*

Cardiac conditions. *See: Cardiac conditions*

Cleft lip/palate. *See: Cleft lip/palate*

Deafness. *See: Deafness*

Deformities. *See: Deformities*

Down's syndrome. *See: Down's syndrome*

Hemophilia. *See: Hemophilia*

Hydrocephalus. *See: Hydrocephalus*

Lameness. *See: Lameness*

Limbs, abnormal or missing. *See: Limbs, abnormal or missing*

### Multiple

Brown, Marion Marsh and Ruth Crone. THE SILENT STORM.
Ages 10-13. 125, Vol. 1
Greenfield, Eloise and Alesia Revis. ALESIA.
Ages 10-14. 245, Vol. 3
Robinet, Harriette Gillem. RIDE THE RED CYCLE.
Ages 7-11. 537, Vol. 3
Viscardi, Henry. THE PHOENIX CHILD: A STORY OF LOVE.
Ages 13 and up. 665, Vol. 2

Muteness. *See: Muteness*

Paralysis. *See: Paralysis*

Paraplegia. *See: Paraplegia*

Prejudice. *See: Prejudice: toward handicapped persons*

Prosthesis. *See: Prosthesis*

Quadriplegia. *See: Quadriplegia*

Rheumatic fever. *See: Rheumatic fever*

Spastic. *See: Spastic*

Speech problems. *See: Speech problems*

Visual impairment. *See: Visual impairment*

Wheelchair. *See: Wheelchair, dependence on*

## Harassment

See also: *Bully; Practical jokes/pranks*
Arrick, Fran. CHERNOWITZ!
Ages 12 and up. 23, Vol. 3
Garden, Nancy. ANNIE ON MY MIND.
Ages 13 and up. 201, Vol. 3
Graber, Richard Fredrick. BLACK COW SUMMER.
Ages 12 and up. 224, Vol. 3
Hickman, Janet. THE STONES.
Ages 9-12. 314, Vol. 2
Holland, Isabelle. DINAH AND THE GREEN FAT KINGDOM.
Ages 10-13. 328, Vol. 2
Mohr, Nicholasa. FELITA.
Ages 8-10. 440, Vol. 3

## Hard of Hearing

See: *Deafness*

## Hatred

See also: *Aggression; Anger; Hostility; Prejudice*
Arrick, Fran. CHERNOWITZ!
Ages 12 and up. 23, Vol. 3
Coolidge, Olivia Ensor. COME BY HERE.
Ages 11 and up. 245, Vol. 1
Engebrecht, P. A. UNDER THE HAYSTACK.
Ages 11 and up. 289, Vol. 1
Holland, Isabelle. AMANDA'S CHOICE.
Ages 10-13. 425, Vol. 1
Houston, James Archibald. THE WHITE ARCHER: AN ESKIMO LEGEND.
Ages 9-11. 436, Vol. 1
Hunt, Irene. THE LOTTERY ROSE.
Ages 11 and up. 337, Vol. 2

## Hearing Aid

See: *Deafness*

## Heart Trouble

See: *Cardiac conditions; Surgery: heart*

## Heaven

See: *Religion*

## Height

See also: *Appearance*

### Short

Barrett, Judith. I'M TOO SMALL. YOU'RE TOO BIG.
Ages 4-6. 36, Vol. 3
Beim, Jerrold. THE SMALLEST BOY IN THE CLASS.
Ages 5-8. 64, Vol. 1
Burchardt, Nellie. A SURPRISE FOR CARLOTTA.
Ages 9-11. 144, Vol. 1
Hoff, Sydney. THE LITTLEST LEAGUER.
Ages 5-8. 325, Vol. 2
Hutchins, Patricia. HAPPY BIRTHDAY, SAM.
Ages 5-7. 343, Vol. 2
Keith, Harold Verne. THE RUNT OF ROGERS SCHOOL.
Ages 9-12. 487, Vol. 1
Krasilovsky, Phyllis. THE VERY LITTLE BOY.
Ages 3-7. 517, Vol. 1
Krasilovsky, Phyllis. THE VERY LITTLE GIRL.
Ages 3-7. 518, Vol. 1
Lee, Robert C. IT'S A MILE FROM HERE TO GLORY.
Ages 10 and up. 538, Vol. 1
Lord, Beman. SHRIMP'S SOCCER GOAL.
Ages 8-11. 584, Vol. 1

## Homesickness (cont.)

Beckman, Gunnel. A ROOM OF HIS OWN.
Ages 12 and up. 60, Vol. 1

Brown, Marc Tolan. ARTHUR GOES TO CAMP.
Ages 5-8. 79, Vol. 3

Carlson, Natalie Savage. LUVVY AND THE GIRLS.
Ages 10-13. 167, Vol. 1

Cleaver, Vera and Bill Cleaver. LADY ELLEN GRAE.
Ages 9-12. 199, Vol. 1

Hoban, Lillian Aberman. I MET A TRAVELLER.
Ages 10-12. 322, Vol. 2

Kesselman, Wendy Ann. ANGELITA.
Ages 5-9. 494, Vol. 1

Lewiton, Mina Simon. CANDITA'S CHOICE.
Ages 8-11. 551, Vol. 1

Mann, Peggy. HOW JUAN GOT HOME.
Ages 8-10. 608, Vol. 1

Nordstrom, Ursula. THE SECRET LANGUAGE.
Ages 8-10. 670, Vol. 1

Norris, Gunilla Brodde. THE GOOD MORROW.
Ages 9-11. 674, Vol. 1

Robertson, Keith. IN SEARCH OF A SANDHILL CRANE.
Ages 11 and up. 743, Vol. 1

Stolz, Mary Slattery. A WONDERFUL, TERRIBLE TIME.
Ages 9-11. 877, Vol. 1

Sugarman, Daniel A. and Rolaine A. Hochstein. SEVEN STORIES FOR GROWTH.
Ages 6-12. 880, Vol. 1

Uchida, Yoshiko. HISAKO'S MYSTERIES.
Ages 9-11. 909, Vol. 1

## Homosexuality

**See also:** *Sex*

### Female

Garden, Nancy. ANNIE ON MY MIND.
Ages 13 and up. 201, Vol. 3

Hautzig, Deborah. HEY, DOLLFACE.
Ages 12 and up. 298, Vol. 2

Levy, Elizabeth. COME OUT SMILING.
Ages 12 and up. 370, Vol. 3

Mohr, Nicholasa. IN NUEVA YORK.
Ages 13 and up. 462, Vol. 2

St. George, Judith. CALL ME MARGO.
Ages 12-14. 567, Vol. 3

Samuels, Gertrude. RUN, SHELLEY, RUN.
Ages 12 and up. 768, Vol. 1

Scoppettone, Sandra. HAPPY ENDINGS ARE ALL ALIKE.
Ages 12 and up. 578, Vol. 2

Tolan, Stephanie S. THE LAST OF EDEN.
Ages 12 and up. 659, Vol. 3

### Male

Bargar, Gary W. WHAT HAPPENED TO MR. FORSTER?
Ages 10-13. 34, Vol. 3

Gerson, Corinne. PASSING THROUGH.
Ages 12 and up. 245, Vol. 2

Hall, Lynn. STICKS AND STONES.
Ages 14 and up. 393, Vol. 1

Hanlon, Emily. THE WING AND THE FLAME.
Ages 13 and up. 262, Vol. 3

Holland, Isabelle. THE MAN WITHOUT A FACE.
Ages 13 and up. 427, Vol. 1

Meyer, Carolyn. THE CENTER: FROM A TROUBLED PAST TO A NEW LIFE.
Ages 13 and up. 420, Vol. 3

Mohr, Nicholasa. IN NUEVA YORK.
Ages 13 and up. 462, Vol. 2

Scoppettone, Sandra. TRYING HARD TO HEAR YOU.
Ages 13 and up. 799, Vol. 1

Spence, Eleanor Rachel. A CANDLE FOR SAINT ANTONY.
Ages 13 and up. 618, Vol. 3

## Honesty/Dishonesty

**See also:** *Conscience*

Alexander, Anne. TO LIVE A LIE.
Ages 9-12. 7, Vol. 2

Allen, Elizabeth. THE LOSER.
Ages 12 and up. 12, Vol. 1

Angell, Judie. RONNIE AND ROSEY.
Ages 11 and up. 20, Vol. 2

Atkinson, Linda. HIT AND RUN.
Ages 11 and up. 31, Vol. 3

Bawden, Nina Mark Kark. THE RUNAWAY SUMMER.
Ages 9-12. 57, Vol. 1

Blue, Rose. WISHFUL LYING.
Ages 6-9. 54, Vol. 3

Blume, Judy Sussman. OTHERWISE KNOWN AS SHEILA THE GREAT.
Ages 9-11. 92, Vol. 1

Brink, Carol Ryrie. THE BAD TIMES OF IRMA BAUMLEIN.
Ages 10-13. 119, Vol. 1

Childress, Alice. RAINBOW JORDAN.
Ages 12 and up. 115, Vol. 3

Chorao, Kay. MOLLY'S LIES.
Ages 4-7. 116, Vol. 3

Cleaver, Vera and Bill Cleaver. ELLEN GRAE.
Ages 9-12. 197, Vol. 1

Colman, Hila Crayder. CONFESSION OF A STORYTELLER.
Ages 10-13. 133, Vol. 3

Colman, Hila Crayder. TELL ME NO LIES.
Ages 10-12. 167, Vol. 2

Crofford, Emily. STORIES FROM THE BLUE ROAD.
Ages 9-12. 143, Vol. 3

Cusack, Isabel Langis. IVAN THE GREAT.
Ages 7-10. 188, Vol. 3

Degens, T. THE GAME ON THATCHER ISLAND.
Ages 11-14. 193, Vol. 2

Duvoisin, Roger Antoine. PETUNIA, I LOVE YOU.
Ages 3-7. 282, Vol. 1

Fife, Dale. WHO'LL VOTE FOR LINCOLN?
Ages 8-10. 229, Vol. 1

Fife, Dale. WHO'S IN CHARGE OF LINCOLN?
Ages 8-10. 314, Vol. 1

Fitzgerald, John Dennis. THE GREAT BRAIN REFORMS.
Ages 10-13. 318, Vol. 1

Gerson, Corinne. TREAD SOFTLY.
Ages 9-12. 209, Vol. 3

Gessner, Lynne. MALCOLM YUCCA SEED.
Ages 8-10. 246, Vol. 2

Girion, Barbara. MISTY AND ME.
Ages 10-12. 219, Vol. 3

Grey, Elizabeth, pseud. FRIEND WITHIN THE GATES: THE STORY OF NURSE EDITH CAVELL.
Ages 12 and up. 384, Vol. 1

Hall, Lynn. THE SIEGE OF SILENT HENRY.
Ages 12 and up. 392, Vol. 1

Hanlon, Emily. THE SWING.
Ages 10-12. 261, Vol. 3

Helena, Ann. THE LIE.
Ages 5-8. 309, Vol. 2

Hinton, Nigel. COLLISION COURSE.
Ages 11 and up. 315, Vol. 2

Hughes, Dean. HONESTLY, MYRON.
Ages 9-11. 307, Vol. 3

Johnson, Annabel Jones and Edgar Raymond Johnson. PICKPOCKET RUN.
Ages 12 and up. 463, Vol. 1

## Honesty/Dishonesty (cont.)

Karp, Naomi J. NOTHING RHYMES WITH APRIL.
Ages 9-11. 479, Vol. 1

Lagercrantz, Rose. TULLA'S SUMMER.
Ages 8-11. 390, Vol. 2

Levy, Elizabeth. LIZZIE LIES A LOT.
Ages 9-11. 405, Vol. 2

Lewiton, Mina Simon. THAT BAD CARLOS.
Ages 8-11. 552, Vol. 1

Lexau, Joan M. I'LL TELL ON YOU.
Ages 5-8. 406, Vol. 2

Little, Jean. ONE TO GROW ON.
Ages 10-12. 575, Vol. 1

Lorimar, Lawrence T. SECRETS.
Ages 12 and up. 382, Vol. 3

Lowery, Bruce. SCARRED.
Ages 12 and up. 588, Vol. 1

McLenighan, Valjean. I KNOW YOU CHEATED.
Ages 6-8. 431, Vol. 2

Maddock, Reginald. THE PIT.
Ages 12 and up. 604, Vol. 1

Matsuno, Masako. A PAIR OF RED CLOGS.
Ages 4-7. 620, Vol. 1

Meyer, Carolyn. THE CENTER: FROM A TROUBLED
PAST TO A NEW LIFE.
Ages 13 and up. 420, Vol. 3

Molarsky, Osmond. WHERE THE GOOD LUCK WAS.
Ages 8-10. 641, Vol. 1

Moncure, Jane Belk. HONESTY.
Ages 3-6. 443, Vol. 3

Morgan, Alison Mary. A BOY CALLED FISH.
Ages 10-12. 645, Vol. 1

Myers, Walter Dean. IT AIN'T ALL FOR NOTHIN'.
Ages 11-13. 470, Vol. 2

Ness, Evaline Michelow. SAM, BANGS, AND
MOONSHINE.
Ages 4-8. 662, Vol. 1

Nöstlinger, Christine. GIRL MISSING: A NOVEL.
Ages 11 and up. 482, Vol. 2

Pascal, Francine. THE HAND-ME-DOWN KID.
Ages 10-13. 483, Vol. 3

Perl, Lila. DON'T ASK MIRANDA.
Ages 10-13. 492, Vol. 3

Peterson, Esther Allen. FREDERICK'S ALLIGATOR.
Ages 4-7. 496, Vol. 3

Reece, Colleen L. THE OUTSIDER.
Ages 12 and up. 527, Vol. 3

Rodowsky, Colby F. P.S. WRITE SOON.
Ages 10-12. 555, Vol. 3

Sharmat, Marjorie Weinman. A BIG FAT
ENORMOUS LIE.
Ages 3-7. 583, Vol. 2

Shreve, Susan Richards. FAMILY SECRETS: FIVE
VERY IMPORTANT STORIES.
Ages 9-11. 590, Vol. 3

Shura, Mary Francis Craig. THE BARKLEY STREET
SIX-PACK.
Ages 9-12. 592, Vol. 3

Sirof, Harriet. SAVE THE DAM!
Ages 9-12. 599, Vol. 3

Skurzynski, Gloria Joan. HONEST ANDREW.
Ages 4-7. 601, Vol. 3

Southall, Ivan. HILLS END.
Ages 11 and up. 846, Vol. 1

Taylor, Theodore. THE MALDONADO MIRACLE.
Ages 11-13. 889, Vol. 1

Turkle, Brinton. THE ADVENTURES OF OBADIAH.
Ages 4-8. 906, Vol. 1

Wahl, Jan. WHO WILL BELIEVE TIM KITTEN?
Ages 5-8. 671, Vol. 2

Wartski, Maureen Crane. MY BROTHER IS SPECIAL.
Ages 10-12. 681, Vol. 3

Wells, Rosemary. THE FOG COMES ON LITTLE PIG
FEET.
Ages 11 and up. 961, Vol. 1

White, Elwyn Brooks. THE TRUMPET OF THE
SWAN.
Ages 9-13. 968, Vol. 1

Willard, Nancy. STRANGERS' BREAD.
Ages 3-8. 682, Vol. 2

Winthrop, Elizabeth. MIRANDA IN THE MIDDLE.
Ages 9-13. 697, Vol. 3

Young, Miriam Burt. TRUTH AND
CONSEQUENCES.
Ages 9-12. 714, Vol. 2

## Hope

**See also:** *Ego ideal; Expectations*

Blue, Rose. NIKKI 108.
Ages 10-12. 85, Vol. 1

Blume, Judy Sussman. IT'S NOT THE END OF THE
WORLD.
Ages 10-12. 91, Vol. 1

Breisky, William. I THINK I CAN.
Ages 12 and up. 115, Vol. 1

Gates, Doris. BLUE WILLOW.
Ages 9-11. 348, Vol. 1

Hamilton, Virginia. M. C. HIGGINS, THE GREAT.
Ages 12 and up. 396, Vol. 1

## Hospital, Going to

**See also:** *Accidents; Amputee; Cancer; Doctor, going to;
Fractures; Hodgkin's disease; Illnesses; Leukemia;
Mental hospital, living in; Separation anxiety;
Separation from loved ones; Surgery*

Anderson, Penny S. THE OPERATION.
Ages 3-8. 17, Vol. 3

Arundel, Honor. THE GIRL IN THE OPPOSITE BED.
Ages 12 and up. 37, Vol. 1

Bach, Alice Hendricks. WAITING FOR JOHNNY
MIRACLE.
Ages 12 and up. 32, Vol. 3

Bemelmans, Ludwig. MADELINE.
Ages 3-8. 67, Vol. 1

Bruna, Dick. MIFFY IN THE HOSPITAL.
Ages 2-5. 90, Vol. 2

Chase, Francine. A VISIT TO THE HOSPITAL.
Ages 4-8. 181, Vol. 1

Ciliotta, Claire and Carole Livingston. WHY AM I
GOING TO THE HOSPITAL?
Ages 5-10. 117, Vol. 3

Collier, James Lincoln. DANNY GOES TO THE
HOSPITAL.
Ages 5-8. 225, Vol. 1

Cosgrove, Margaret Leota. YOUR HOSPITAL, A
MODERN MIRACLE.
Ages 10 and up. 254, Vol. 1

Dacquino, Vincent T. KISS THE CANDY DAYS
GOOD-BYE.
Ages 10-14. 148, Vol. 3

Deegan, Paul and Bruce Larson. A HOSPITAL: LIFE
IN A MEDICAL CENTER.
Ages 10-12. 267, Vol. 1

Hautzig, Deborah. SECOND STAR TO THE RIGHT.
Ages 12 and up. 272, Vol. 3

Hogan, Paula Z. and Kirk Hogan. THE HOSPITAL
SCARES ME.
Ages 3-8. 300, Vol. 3

Ipswitch, Elaine. SCOTT WAS HERE.
Ages 12 and up. 322, Vol. 3

Jones, Rebecca Castaldi. ANGIE AND ME.
Ages 9-11. 333, Vol. 3

Kay, Eleanor. THE EMERGENCY ROOM.
Ages 9-12. 481, Vol. 1

Kay, Eleanor. LET'S FIND OUT ABOUT THE
HOSPITAL.
Ages 4-7. 482, Vol. 1

Kay, Eleanor. THE OPERATING ROOM.
Ages 9-12. 483, Vol. 1

# CUMULATIVE SUBJECT INDEX

## Hospital, Going to (cont.)

Marino, Barbara Pavis. ERIC NEEDS STITCHES.
Ages 4-10. 403, Vol. 3

Miner, Jane Claypool. THIS DAY IS MINE: LIVING WITH LEUKEMIA.
Ages 10 and up. 436, Vol. 3

Rey, Margret Elisabeth Waldstein and Hans Augusto Rey. CURIOUS GEORGE GOES TO THE HOSPITAL.
Ages 4-9. 728, Vol. 1

Richter, Elizabeth. THE TEENAGE HOSPITAL EXPERIENCE: YOU CAN HANDLE IT!
Ages 12 and up. 532, Vol. 3

Rowland, Florence Wightman. LET'S GO TO A HOSPITAL.
Ages 7-10. 756, Vol. 1

Sachs, Elizabeth-Ann. JUST LIKE ALWAYS.
Ages 10-13. 561, Vol. 3

Sharmat, Marjorie Weinman. I WANT MAMA.
Ages 4-8. 807, Vol. 1

Shay, Arthur. WHAT HAPPENS WHEN YOU GO TO THE HOSPITAL.
Ages 4-7. 808, Vol. 1

Singer, Marilyn. IT CAN'T HURT FOREVER.
Ages 9-12. 604, Vol. 2

Sobol, Harriet Langsam. JEFF'S HOSPITAL BOOK.
Ages 2-7. 617, Vol. 2

Stein, Sara Bonnett. A HOSPITAL STORY: AN OPEN FAMILY BOOK FOR PARENTS AND CHILDREN TOGETHER.
Ages 3-8. 857, Vol. 1

Tamburine, Jean. I THINK I WILL GO TO THE HOSPITAL.
Ages 4-8. 885, Vol. 1

Thomas, Dawn C. PABLITO'S NEW FEET.
Ages 8-10. 894, Vol. 1

Weber, Alfons. ELIZABETH GETS WELL.
Ages 6-8. 957, Vol. 1

Wolde, Gunilla. BETSY AND THE DOCTOR.
Ages 3-7. 697, Vol. 2

Ziegler, Sandra. AT THE HOSPITAL: A SURPRISE FOR KRISSY.
Ages 3-6. 716, Vol. 2

## Hostility

See also: Aggression; Anger; Hatred; Prejudice; Trust/Distrust

Arrick, Fran. CHERNOWITZ!
Ages 12 and up. 23, Vol. 3

Gaeddert, LouAnn Bigge. JUST LIKE SISTERS.
Ages 8-12. 196, Vol. 3

Gerson, Corinne. PASSING THROUGH.
Ages 12 and up. 245, Vol. 2

McCord, Jean. TURKEYLEGS THOMPSON.
Ages 11-14. 390, Vol. 3

Paterson, Katherine Womeldorf. THE GREAT GILLY HOPKINS.
Ages 10-13. 494, Vol. 2

Rinkoff, Barbara Jean Rich. A GUY CAN BE WRONG.
Ages 10-12. 735, Vol. 1

Robison, Nancy Louise. ON THE BALANCE BEAM.
Ages 8-10. 549, Vol. 2

Stevenson, James. THE WORST PERSON IN THE WORLD.
Ages 4-8. 625, Vol. 2

Strete, Craig Kee. PAINT YOUR FACE ON A DROWNING IN THE RIVER.
Ages 12 and up. 629, Vol. 2

Wartski, Maureen Crane. A LONG WAY FROM HOME.
Ages 11-13. 680, Vol. 3

Zolotow, Charlotte Shapiro. THE QUARRELING BOOK.
Ages 4-7. 1026, Vol. 1

## Human Differences

See: Differences, human

## Hydrocephalus

Patterson, Katheryn. NO TIME FOR TEARS.
Ages 12 and up. 692, Vol. 1

## Hyperactivity

Green, Phyllis. WALKIE-TALKIE.
Ages 10-13. 264, Vol. 2

# I

## Ideals

See: Ego ideal; Identification with others; Values/Valuing

## Identification With Others

See also: Ego ideal; Empathy; Imitation; Leader/Leadership; Values/Valuing

### Adults

Colman, Hila Crayder. CONFESSION OF A STORYTELLER.
Ages 10-13. 133, Vol. 3

Gripe, Maria Kristina. THE GREEN COAT.
Ages 13 and up. 279, Vol. 2

Hall, Lynn. DANZA!
Ages 9-12. 254, Vol. 3

Miles, Betty. LOOKING ON.
Ages 11-14. 457, Vol. 2

Schaefer, Jack Warner. OLD RAMON.
Ages 10 and up. 777, Vol. 1

Thomas, Ianthe. WILLIE BLOWS A MEAN HORN.
Ages 5-8. 652, Vol. 3

### Parents

Wersba, Barbara. RUN SOFTLY, GO FAST.
Ages 13 and up. 965, Vol. 1

### Peers. See also: Friendship

Blume, Judy Sussman. FRECKLE JUICE.
Ages 8-11. 89, Vol. 1

Clymer, Eleanor Lowenton. HOW I WENT SHOPPING AND WHAT I GOT.
Ages 8-10. 210, Vol. 1

Degens, T. THE GAME ON THATCHER ISLAND.
Ages 11-14. 193, Vol. 2

Eyerly, Jeannette Hyde. ESCAPE FROM NOWHERE.
Ages 12 and up. 297, Vol. 1

Hinton, Susan Eloise. THE OUTSIDERS.
Ages 12 and up. 412, Vol. 1

Horvath, Betty. WILL THE REAL TOMMY WILSON PLEASE STAND UP?
Ages 5-8. 434, Vol. 1

Korschunow, Irina. WHO KILLED CHRISTOPHER?
Ages 12 and up. 350, Vol. 3

Maddock, Reginald. THIN ICE.
Ages 12 and up. 605, Vol. 1

Mills, Claudia. AT THE BACK OF THE WOODS.
Ages 9-11. 426, Vol. 3

Pfeffer, Susan Beth. STARRING PETER AND LEIGH.
Ages 12-14. 503, Vol. 3

Quackenbush, Robert M. FIRST GRADE JITTERS.
Ages 5-7. 521, Vol. 3

Wallace, Barbara Brooks. THE SECRET SUMMER OF L.E.B.
Ages 11 and up. 946, Vol. 1

### Story characters

Cone, Molly Lamken. CALL ME MOOSE.
Ages 9-11. 174, Vol. 2

Foley, June. IT'S NO CRUSH, I'M IN LOVE!
Ages 11-13. 192, Vol. 3

## Identification With Others (cont.)

Vreeken, Elizabeth. THE BOY WHO WOULD NOT
SAY HIS NAME.
Ages 5-8. 935, Vol. 1

## Identity, Search for

**See also:** *Adoption; Ego ideal*

Adler, Carole Schwerdtfeger. SOME OTHER
SUMMER.
Ages 10-13. 9, Vol. 3

Alcock, Gudrun. DUFFY.
Ages 11-13. 4, Vol. 1

Allen, Elizabeth. THE LOSER.
Ages 12 and up. 12, Vol. 1

Ames, Mildred. WITHOUT HATS, WHO CAN TELL
THE GOOD GUYS?
Ages 9-12. 13, Vol. 2

Angell, Judie. SECRET SELVES.
Ages 11-13. 20, Vol. 3

Angier, Bradford and Barbara Corcoran. ASK FOR
LOVE AND THEY GIVE YOU RICE PUDDING.
Ages 12-14. 21, Vol. 2

Arkin, Alan. THE LEMMING CONDITION.
Ages 10 and up. 23, Vol. 2

Armer, Alberta. SCREWBALL.
Ages 9-11. 29, Vol. 1

Asher, Sandra Fenichel. DAUGHTERS OF THE LAW.
Ages 11-13. 26, Vol. 3

Asher, Sandra Fenichel. JUST LIKE JENNY.
Ages 10-12. 27, Vol. 3

Asher, Sandra Fenichel. SUMMER BEGINS.
Ages 10-13. 28, Vol. 3

Bach, Alice Hendricks. THE MEAT IN THE
SANDWICH.
Ages 10-13. 28, Vol. 2

Bach, Alice Hendricks. MOLLIE MAKE-BELIEVE.
Ages 12 and up. 41, Vol. 1

Bailey, Pearl. DUEY'S TALE.
Ages 12 and up. 29, Vol. 2

Balderson, Margaret. WHEN JAYS FLY TO BARBMO.
Ages 12 and up. 48, Vol. 1

Banks, Lynne Reid. THE WRITING ON THE WALL.
Ages 12 and up. 33, Vol. 3

Barrett, Anne. MIDWAY.
Ages 11-13. 53, Vol. 1

Barrett, John M. DANIEL DISCOVERS DANIEL.
Ages 7-9. 35, Vol. 3

Bernays, Anne. GROWING UP RICH.
Ages 13 and up. 52, Vol. 2

Blue, Rose. NIKKI 108.
Ages 10-12. 85, Vol. 1

Blume, Judy Sussman. THE ONE IN THE MIDDLE IS
THE GREEN KANGAROO.
Ages 7-9. 55, Vol. 3

Bosse, Malcolm Joseph. GANESH.
Ages 11-14. 65, Vol. 3

Bradbury, Bianca. BOY ON THE RUN.
Ages 11-13. 64, Vol. 2

Bradbury, Bianca. LAURIE.
Ages 11 and up. 109, Vol. 1

Bragdon, Elspeth. THERE IS A TIDE.
Ages 12 and up. 113, Vol. 1

Branscum, Robbie. THE SAVING OF P.S.
Ages 9-12. 78, Vol. 2

Bridgers, Sue Ellen. HOME BEFORE DARK.
Ages 12 and up. 81, Vol. 2

Broderick, Dorothy M. HANK.
Ages 11 and up. 122, Vol. 1

Brown, Fern G. JOCKEY — OR ELSE!
Ages 9-12. 86, Vol. 2

Bruna, Dick. WHEN I'M BIG.
Ages 2-4. 81, Vol. 3

Buchan, Stuart. A SPACE OF HIS OWN.
Ages 12 and up. 82, Vol. 3

Budbill, David. BONES ON BLACK SPRUCE
MOUNTAIN.
Ages 10-13. 91, Vol. 2

Bunting, Anne Evelyn. ONE MORE FLIGHT.
Ages 10-13. 97, Vol. 2

Butler, Beverly Kathleen. A GIRL CALLED WENDY.
Ages 12 and up. 106, Vol. 2

Calhoun, Mary Huiskamp. IT'S GETTING
BEAUTIFUL NOW.
Ages 12 and up. 158, Vol. 1

Carrick, Malcolm. I'LL GET YOU.
Ages 11-13. 107, Vol. 3

Cavanna, Betty. ALMOST LIKE SISTERS.
Ages 11 and up. 176, Vol. 1

Charlip, Remy and Lilian Moore. HOORAY FOR ME!
Ages 3-6. 127, Vol. 2

Cheatham, Karyn Follis. THE BEST WAY OUT.
Ages 12 and up. 114, Vol. 3

Clark, Mavis Thorpe. IRON MOUNTAIN.
Ages 12 and up. 187, Vol. 1

Cleary, Beverly Bunn. RAMONA THE PEST.
Ages 8-10. 195, Vol. 1

Cleaver, Vera and Bill Cleaver. THE MOCK REVOLT.
Ages 10-14. 202, Vol. 1

Clifton, Lucille. ALL US COME CROSS THE WATER.
Ages 6-9. 208, Vol. 1

Cohen, Barbara Nash. BITTER HERBS AND HONEY.
Ages 11-13. 153, Vol. 2

Colman, Hila Crayder. BRIDE AT EIGHTEEN.
Ages 12 and up. 226, Vol. 1

Colman, Hila Crayder. CLAUDIA, WHERE ARE
YOU?
Ages 12 and up. 228, Vol. 1

Colman, Hila Crayder. DAUGHTER OF
DISCONTENT.
Ages 12 and up. 229, Vol. 1

Colman, Hila Crayder. TELL ME NO LIES.
Ages 10-12. 167, Vol. 2

Cone, Molly Lamken. THE TROUBLE WITH TOBY.
Ages 11-13. 236, Vol. 1

Cunningham, Julia Woolfolk. COME TO THE EDGE.
Ages 9-13. 187, Vol. 2

DeLage, Ida. AM I A BUNNY?
Ages 3-6. 194, Vol. 2

Delton, Judy. I NEVER WIN!
Ages 4-7. 154, Vol. 3

Distad, Audree. THE DREAM RUNNER.
Ages 10-13. 201, Vol. 2

Dixon, Paige, pseud. SKIPPER.
Ages 12 and up. 165, Vol. 3

Dunnahoo, Terry. WHO CARES ABOUT ESPIE
SANCHEZ?
Ages 10-12. 210, Vol. 2

Dyer, Thomas A. THE WHIPMAN IS WATCHING.
Ages 10-14. 177, Vol. 3

Embry, Margaret Jacob. MY NAME IS LION.
Ages 9-11. 288, Vol. 1

Etter, Les. GET THOSE REBOUNDS!
Ages 10-13. 220, Vol. 2

Farley, Carol J. TWILIGHT WAVES.
Ages 10-13. 186, Vol. 3

Fitzgerald, John Dennis. ME AND MY LITTLE
BRAIN.
Ages 9-12. 319, Vol. 1

Foley, June. IT'S NO CRUSH, I'M IN LOVE!
Ages 11-13. 192, Vol. 3

Forbes, Esther. JOHNNY TREMAIN.
Ages 10 and up. 325, Vol. 1

Forman, James. MY ENEMY, MY BROTHER.
Ages 12 and up. 326, Vol. 1

Fox, Paula. PORTRAIT OF IVAN.
Ages 11 and up. 328, Vol. 1

Friedman, Frieda. ELLEN AND THE GANG.
Ages 9-12. 335, Vol. 1

## Identity, Search for (cont.)

Screen, Robert Martin. WITH MY FACE TO THE RISING SUN.
Ages 11 and up. 580, Vol. 2

Sebestyen, Ouida. FAR FROM HOME.
Ages 12 and up. 579, Vol. 3

Sharmat, Marjorie Weinman. I'M TERRIFIC.
Ages 4-7. 587, Vol. 2

Smith, Doris Buchanan. KICK A STONE HOME.
Ages 11 and up. 830, Vol. 1

Smith, Pauline Coggeshall. BRUSH FIRE!
Ages 11 and up. 613, Vol. 3

Sneve, Virginia Driving Hawk. JIMMY YELLOW HAWK.
Ages 8-10. 834, Vol. 1

Sorenson, Virginia Eggertsen. PLAIN GIRL.
Ages 9-11. 844, Vol. 1

Stein, Sara Bonnett. THE ADOPTED ONE: AN OPEN FAMILY BOOK FOR PARENTS AND CHILDREN TOGETHER.
Ages 4-8. 625, Vol. 3

Stolz, Mary Slattery. WAIT FOR ME, MICHAEL.
Ages 12 and up. 876, Vol. 1

Storr, Catherine Cole. VICKY.
Ages 12 and up. 632, Vol. 3

Strete, Craig Kee. PAINT YOUR FACE ON A DROWNING IN THE RIVER.
Ages 12 and up. 629, Vol. 2

Terris, Susan Dubinsky. WHIRLING RAINBOWS.
Ages 11 and up. 892, Vol. 1

Tolan, Stephanie S. THE LAST OF EDEN.
Ages 12 and up. 659, Vol. 3

Truss, Jan. BIRD AT THE WINDOW.
Ages 13 and up. 661, Vol. 3

Van Leeuwen, Jean. SEEMS LIKE THIS ROAD GOES ON FOREVER.
Ages 12 and up. 663, Vol. 3

Viereck, Phillip. THE SUMMER I WAS LOST.
Ages 11 and up. 923, Vol. 1

Vroman, Mary Elizabeth. HARLEM SUMMER.
Ages 12 and up. 936, Vol. 1

Wells, Rosemary. NONE OF THE ABOVE.
Ages 12 and up. 963, Vol. 1

Wersba, Barbara. THE DREAM WATCHER.
Ages 12 and up. 964, Vol. 1

Windsor, Patricia. DIVING FOR ROSES.
Ages 13 and up. 687, Vol. 2

Wolff, Ruth. A CRACK IN THE SIDEWALK.
Ages 12 and up. 990, Vol. 1

Yep, Laurence Michael. SEA GLASS.
Ages 11-14. 713, Vol. 3

## Illegitimate Child

See also: Unwed father; Unwed mother: child of

Klein, Norma. MOM, THE WOLF MAN AND ME.
Ages 11 and up. 505, Vol. 1

Mazer, Harry. THE DOLLAR MAN.
Ages 12 and up. 626, Vol. 1

Rolerson, Darrell A. A BOY CALLED PLUM.
Ages 10-12. 752, Vol. 1

Wilkinson, Sylvia. A KILLING FROST.
Ages 13 and up. 975, Vol. 1

## Illnesses

See also: Communicable diseases; Doctor, going to; Hospital, going to; Mental illness; Surgery

Hunter, Kristin Eggleston. THE SURVIVORS.
Ages 12 and up. 340, Vol. 2

**Amyotrophic Lateral Sclerosis.** See: Amyotrophic Lateral Sclerosis

**Anorexia nervosa.** See: Anorexia nervosa

**Arthritis, juvenile rheumatoid.** See: Arthritis, juvenile rheumatoid

**Asthma.** See: Asthma

**Being ill**

Brandenberg, Franz. I WISH I WAS SICK, TOO!
Ages 3-7. 73, Vol. 2

Hirsch, Linda. THE SICK STORY.
Ages 6-9. 319, Vol. 2

MacLachlan, Patricia. THE SICK DAY.
Ages 4-7. 396, Vol. 3

Miner, Jane Claypool. THIS DAY IS MINE: LIVING WITH LEUKEMIA.
Ages 10 and up. 436, Vol. 3

Numeroff, Laura Joffe. PHOEBE DEXTER HAS HARRIET PETERSON'S SNIFFLES.
Ages 4-7. 484, Vol. 2

Richter, Elizabeth. THE TEENAGE HOSPITAL EXPERIENCE: YOU CAN HANDLE IT!
Ages 12 and up. 532, Vol. 3

Rockwell, Anne F. and Harlow Rockwell. SICK IN BED.
Ages 3-6. 546, Vol. 3

**Cancer.** See: Cancer

**Cardiac conditions.** See: Cardiac conditions

**Cerebral palsy.** See: Cerebral palsy

**Chronic**

Judson, Clara Ingram. CITY NEIGHBOR: THE STORY OF JANE ADDAMS.
Ages 9-12. 476, Vol. 1

Parker, Richard. SECOND-HAND FAMILY.
Ages 9-12. 690, Vol. 1

Van Stockum, Hilda. MOGO'S FLUTE.
Ages 10-12. 920, Vol. 1

**Diabetes.** See: Diabetes

**Epilepsy.** See: Epilepsy

**of Grandparent**

Bach, Alice Hendricks. MOLLIE MAKE-BELIEVE.
Ages 12 and up. 41, Vol. 1

Brancato, Robin Fidler. SWEET BELLS JANGLED OUT OF TUNE.
Ages 11-14. 70, Vol. 3

Campbell, R. Wright. WHERE PIGEONS GO TO DIE.
Ages 12 and up. 112, Vol. 2

Cate, Dick. NEVER IS A LONG, LONG TIME.
Ages 9-11. 125, Vol. 2

De Paola, Thomas Anthony. NOW ONE FOOT, NOW THE OTHER.
Ages 4-7. 160, Vol. 3

Gardiner, John Reynolds. STONE FOX.
Ages 8-10. 202, Vol. 3

L'Engle, Madeleine Franklin. A RING OF ENDLESS LIGHT.
Ages 11-14. 363, Vol. 3

Orgel, Doris. THE MULBERRY MUSIC.
Ages 10-12. 685, Vol. 1

Pollowitz, Melinda. CINNAMON CANE.
Ages 10-12. 519, Vol. 2

Sonneborn, Ruth A. I LOVE GRAM.
Ages 4-7. 842, Vol. 1

**Hemophilia.** See: Hemophilia

**Hodgkin's disease.** See: Hodgkin's disease

**Hyperactivity.** See: Hyperactivity

**Leprosy.** See: Leprosy

**Leukemia.** See: Leukemia

**of Parent**

Bates, Betty. THE UPS AND DOWNS OF JORIE JENKINS.
Ages 9-12. 41, Vol. 2

Blue, Rose. WISHFUL LYING.
Ages 6-9. 54, Vol. 3

## Illnesses (cont.)

Carris, Joan Davenport. WHEN THE BOYS RAN THE
HOUSE.
Ages 8-12. 108, Vol. 3
Cleaver, Vera and Bill Cleaver. GROVER.
Ages 9-12. 198, Vol. 1
Delton, Judy. IT HAPPENED ON THURSDAY.
Ages 5-8. 197, Vol. 2
Farley, Carol J. THE GARDEN IS DOING FINE.
Ages 11 and up. 223, Vol. 2
Greene, Constance Clarke. AL(EXANDRA) THE
GREAT.
Ages 10-12. 239, Vol. 3
Holland, Isabelle. OF LOVE AND DEATH AND
OTHER JOURNEYS.
Ages 11 and up. 329, Vol. 2
Honig, Donald. HURRY HOME.
Ages 7-9. 331, Vol. 2
Johnston, Norma. THE SANCTUARY TREE.
Ages 12 and up. 356, Vol. 2
Jordan, June. HIS OWN WHERE.
Ages 12 and up. 474, Vol. 1
Mearian, Judy Frank. TWO WAYS ABOUT IT.
Ages 9-12. 418, Vol. 3
Sachs, Marilyn. AMY AND LAURA.
Ages 9-12. 759, Vol. 1

**Rheumatic fever.** *See: Rheumatic fever*

## of Sibling

Burch, Robert Joseph. D. J.'S WORST ENEMY.
Ages 9-12. 139, Vol. 1
Butler, Beverly Kathleen. A GIRL CALLED WENDY.
Ages 12 and up. 106, Vol. 2
Friis-Baastad, Babbis Ellinor. DON'T TAKE TEDDY.
Ages 11 and up. 338, Vol. 1
Graber, Richard Fredrick. A LITTLE BREATHING
ROOM.
Ages 10-14. 260, Vol. 2
Herzig, Alison Cragin and Jane Lawrence Mali. A
SEASON OF SECRETS.
Ages 11-13. 287, Vol. 3
Johnston, Norma. THE KEEPING DAYS.
Ages 11 and up. 468, Vol. 1
Wolde, Gunilla. BETSY AND THE CHICKEN POX.
Ages 3-7. 696, Vol. 2

**Terminal.** *See also: Fear: of death*
Bach, Alice Hendricks. WAITING FOR JOHNNY
MIRACLE.
Ages 12 and up. 32, Vol. 3
Blue, Rose. THE THIRTEENTH YEAR: A BAR
MITZVAH STORY.
Ages 10-12. 60, Vol. 2
Brady, Mari. PLEASE REMEMBER ME: A YOUNG
WOMAN'S STORY OF HER FRIENDSHIP WITH
AN UNFORGETTABLE FIFTEEN-YEAR-OLD BOY.
Ages 12 and up. 68, Vol. 2
Coerr, Eleanor. SADAKO AND THE THOUSAND
PAPER CRANES.
Ages 11 and up. 151, Vol. 2
Donnelly, Elfie. SO LONG, GRANDPA.
Ages 9-11. 168, Vol. 3
Farley, Carol J. THE GARDEN IS DOING FINE.
Ages 11 and up. 223, Vol. 2
Greenberg, Jan. A SEASON IN-BETWEEN.
Ages 11-13. 237, Vol. 3
Harlan, Elizabeth. FOOTFALLS.
Ages 12-14. 265, Vol. 3
Hermes, Patricia. YOU SHOULDN'T HAVE TO SAY
GOOD-BYE.
Ages 10-13. 286, Vol. 3
Ipswitch, Elaine. SCOTT WAS HERE.
Ages 12 and up. 322, Vol. 3
Irwin, Hadley, pseud. WHAT ABOUT GRANDMA?
Ages 11 and up. 326, Vol. 3

Jones, Penelope. HOLDING TOGETHER.
Ages 9-11. 331, Vol. 3
Jones, Rebecca Castaldi. ANGIE AND ME.
Ages 9-11. 333, Vol. 3
L'Engle, Madeleine Franklin. A RING OF ENDLESS
LIGHT.
Ages 11-14. 363, Vol. 3
Lowry, Lois. A SUMMER TO DIE.
Ages 10-14. 423, Vol. 2
Mann, Peggy. THERE ARE TWO KINDS OF
TERRIBLE.
Ages 9-12. 441, Vol. 2
Mazer, Norma Fox. DEAR BILL, REMEMBER ME?
AND OTHER STORIES.
Ages 12 and up. 449, Vol. 2
Miner, Jane Claypool. THIS DAY IS MINE: LIVING
WITH LEUKEMIA.
Ages 10 and up. 436, Vol. 3
Moe, Barbara. PICKLES AND PRUNES.
Ages 10-13. 461, Vol. 2
Peavy, Linda S. ALLISON'S GRANDFATHER.
Ages 6-9. 489, Vol. 3
Ruby, Lois. ARRIVING AT A PLACE YOU'VE
NEVER LEFT.
Ages 12 and up. 564, Vol. 2
Schotter, Roni. A MATTER OF TIME.
Ages 12 and up. 575, Vol. 3
Shreve, Susan Richards. FAMILY SECRETS: FIVE
VERY IMPORTANT STORIES.
Ages 9-11. 590, Vol. 3
Strasser, Todd. FRIENDS TILL THE END.
Ages 12 and up. 636, Vol. 3
Stretton, Barbara. YOU NEVER LOSE.
Ages 12 and up. 639, Vol. 3
Zindel, Bonnie and Paul Zindel. A STAR FOR THE
LATECOMER.
Ages 12 and up. 721, Vol. 3

## Imaginary Friend

**See also:** *Fantasy formation; Imagination; Magical
thinking; Play*
Choate, Judith Newkirk. AWFUL ALEXANDER.
Ages 4-7. 130, Vol. 2
Dauer, Rosamond. MY FRIEND, JASPER JONES.
Ages 3-6. 192, Vol. 2
Greenfield, Eloise. ME AND NEESIE.
Ages 4-7. 272, Vol. 2
Hazen, Barbara Shook. GORILLA WANTS TO BE
THE BABY.
Ages 3-5 301, Vol. 2
King, Cynthia. THE YEAR OF MR. NOBODY.
Ages 6-8. 381, Vol. 2
Krasilovsky, Phyllis. SUSAN SOMETIMES.
Ages 3-5. 516, Vol. 1
Sachs, Marilyn. A DECEMBER TALE.
Ages 9-12. 565, Vol. 2
Sharmat, Marjorie Weinman. GOODNIGHT,
ANDREW; GOODNIGHT, CRAIG.
Ages 3-7. 806, Vol. 1
Young, Michael. THE IMAGINARY FRIEND.
Ages 4-7. 713, Vol. 1
Zolotow, Charlotte Shapiro. THE THREE FUNNY
FRIENDS.
Ages 4-6. 1028, Vol. 1

## Imagination

**See also:** *Creativity; Fantasy formation; Imaginary
friend; Magical thinking; Play; Reality, escaping*
Adler, Carole Schwerdtfeger. THE MAGIC OF THE
GLITS.
Ages 9-12. 6, Vol. 3
Adler, Carole Schwerdtfeger. THE SILVER COACH.
Ages 9-12. 8, Vol. 3

## Imagination (cont.)

Alexander, Martha G. AND MY MEAN OLD MOTHER WILL BE SORRY, BLACKBOARD BEAR.
Ages 3-8. 8, Vol. 1

Babbitt, Natalie. THE EYES OF THE AMARYLLIS.
Ages 11-14. 26, Vol. 2

Barrett, Anne. MIDWAY.
Ages 11-13. 53, Vol. 1

Baylor, Byrd. HAWK, I'M YOUR BROTHER.
Ages 5-8. 45, Vol. 2

Binzen, Bill. MIGUEL'S MOUNTAIN.
Ages 5-9. 77, Vol. 1

Burningham, John Mackintosh. COME AWAY FROM THE WATER, SHIRLEY.
Ages 4-7. 103, Vol. 2

Byars, Betsy Cromer. THE TV KID.
Ages 9-12. 109, Vol. 2

Byars, Betsy Cromer. THE TWO-THOUSAND-POUND GOLDFISH.
Ages 9-12. 99, Vol. 3

Calhoun, Mary Huiskamp. THE NIGHT THE MONSTER CAME.
Ages 8-10. 102, Vol. 3

Cameron, Ann. THE STORIES JULIAN TELLS.
Ages 7-9. 104, Vol. 3

Cleary, Beverly Bunn. THE REAL HOLE.
Ages 3-6. 196, Vol. 1

Coatsworth, Elizabeth Jane. LONELY MARIA.
Ages 4-8. 214, Vol. 1

Collins, David R. IF I COULD, I WOULD.
Ages 6-8. 131, Vol. 3

Conford, Ellen. THE REVENGE OF THE INCREDIBLE DR. RANCID AND HIS YOUTHFUL ASSISTANT, JEFFREY.
Ages 10-12. 137, Vol. 3

Delton, Judy. MY MOTHER LOST HER JOB TODAY.
Ages 3-7. 156, Vol. 3

Ewing, Kathryn. A PRIVATE MATTER.
Ages 8-10. 221, Vol. 2

Galbraith, Kathryn Osebold. SPOTS ARE SPECIAL!
Ages 4-7. 241, Vol. 2

Gerson, Corinne. TREAD SOFTLY.
Ages 9-12. 209, Vol. 3

Giff, Patricia Reilly. FOURTH GRADE CELEBRITY.
Ages 8-10. 210, Vol. 3

Griffith, Helen V. MINE WILL, SAID JOHN.
Ages 4-6. 248, Vol. 3

Gross, Alan. THE I DON'T WANT TO GO TO SCHOOL BOOK.
Ages 5-9. 249, Vol. 3

Hoban, Russell Conwell. BEDTIME FOR FRANCES.
Ages 3-7. 418, Vol. 1

Holland, Isabelle. DINAH AND THE GREEN FAT KINGDOM.
Ages 10-13. 328, Vol. 2

Johnston, Johanna. SUPPOSINGS.
Ages 3-6. 466, Vol. 1

Keats, Ezra Jack. THE TRIP.
Ages 4-7. 368, Vol. 2

Keith, Eros. A SMALL LOT.
Ages 4-7. 486, Vol. 1

Konigsburg, Elaine Lobl. JENNIFER, HECATE, MACBETH, WILLIAM MCKINLEY, AND ME, ELIZABETH.
Ages 9-11. 512, Vol. 1

Lexau, Joan M. EVERY DAY A DRAGON.
Ages 3-8. 556, Vol. 1

Lionni, Leo. FISH IS FISH.
Ages 4-8. 565, Vol. 1

Low, Joseph. BENNY RABBIT AND THE OWL.
Ages 4-7. 419, Vol. 2

Lund, Doris Herold. YOU OUGHT TO SEE HERBERT'S HOUSE.
Ages 4-7. 591, Vol. 1

Marzollo, Jean. CLOSE YOUR EYES.
Ages 2-5. 444, Vol. 2

Mayer, Mercer. YOU'RE THE SCAREDY-CAT.
Ages 4-8. 625, Vol. 2

Ness, Evaline Michelow. SAM, BANGS, AND MOONSHINE.
Ages 4-8. 662, Vol. 1

Numeroff, Laura Joffe. PHOEBE DEXTER HAS HARRIET PETERSON'S SNIFFLES.
Ages 4-7. 484, Vol. 3

Paterson, Katherine Womeldorf. BRIDGE TO TERABITHIA.
Ages 9-12. 493, Vol. 2

Peterson, Esther Allen. FREDERICK'S ALLIGATOR.
Ages 4-7. 496, Vol. 3

Peyton, K. M., pseud. MARION'S ANGELS.
Ages 11-14. 499, Vol. 3

Pfeffer, Susan Beth. AWFUL EVELINA.
Ages 6-8. 501, Vol. 3

Pinkwater, Manus. FAT ELLIOT & THE GORILLA.
Ages 8-10. 710, Vol. 1

Pomerantz, Charlotte. THE MANGO TOOTH.
Ages 4-7. 521, Vol. 2

Robison, Deborah. NO ELEPHANTS ALLOWED.
Ages 3-6. 540, Vol. 3

Sachs, Elizabeth-Ann. JUST LIKE ALWAYS.
Ages 10-13. 561, Vol. 3

Schick, Eleanor Grossman. NEIGHBORHOOD KNIGHT.
Ages 5-7. 573, Vol. 2

Schubert, Ingrid and Dieter Schubert. THERE'S A CROCODILE UNDER MY BED!
Ages 3-6. 576, Vol. 3

Sharmat, Marjorie Weinman. LUCRETIA THE UNBEARABLE.
Ages 4-7. 583, Vol. 3

Sharmat, Mitchell. COME HOME, WILMA.
Ages 6-8. 588, Vol. 3

Shimin, Symeon. I WISH THERE WERE TWO OF ME.
Ages 4-7. 595, Vol. 2

Sirof, Harriet. SAVE THE DAM!
Ages 9-12. 599, Vol. 3

Snyder, Zilpha Keatley. THE CHANGELING.
Ages 11-14. 835, Vol. 1

Snyder, Zilpha Keatley. THE EGYPT GAME.
Ages 10-13. 836, Vol. 1

Turkle, Brinton. THE ADVENTURES OF OBADIAH.
Ages 4-8. 906, Vol. 1

Viorst, Judith. MY MAMA SAYS THERE AREN'T ANY ZOMBIES, GHOSTS, VAMPIRES.
Ages 4-7. 928, Vol. 1

Vogel, Ilse-Margaret. HELLO, HENRY.
Ages 4-7. 933, Vol. 1

Von Gebhardt, Hertha Antonie Mathilde Triepel. THE GIRL FROM NOWHERE.
Ages 9-12. 934, Vol. 1

Wahl, Jan. A WOLF OF MY OWN.
Ages 3-7. 940, Vol. 1

Wojciechowska, Maia Rodman. THE HOLLYWOOD KID.
Ages 12 and up. 984, Vol. 1

Wrightson, Patricia. A RACECOURSE FOR ANDY.
Ages 9-12. 1007, Vol. 1

Zhitkov, Boris Stepanovich. HOW I HUNTED THE LITTLE FELLOWS.
Ages 3-7. 720, Vol. 3

Zolotow, Charlotte Shapiro. IF YOU LISTEN.
Ages 5-7. 722, Vol. 1

Zolotow, Charlotte Shapiro. WHEN I HAVE A LITTLE GIRL.
Ages 4-6. 1030, Vol. 1

## Imitation

**See also:** *Identification with others*
Blume, Judy Sussman. FRECKLE JUICE.
  Ages 8-11. 89, Vol. 1
Fitzgerald, John Dennis. ME AND MY LITTLE
  BRAIN.
  Ages 9-12. 319, Vol. 1
Freeman, Don. DANDELION.
  Ages 3-8. 333, Vol. 1
Hinton, Susan Eloise. RUMBLE FISH.
  Ages 12 and up. 316, Vol. 2
Horvath, Betty. WILL THE REAL TOMMY WILSON
  PLEASE STAND UP?
  Ages 5-8. 434, Vol. 1
Sachs, Marilyn. THE TRUTH ABOUT MARY ROSE.
  Ages 10-13. 764, Vol. 1

## Immigrants

**See also:** *Emigration; Prejudice: ethnic/racial; Refugees;
Vietnam*
Bernstein, Joanne Eckstein. DMITRY: A YOUNG
  SOVIET IMMIGRANT.
  Ages 11-13. 52, Vol. 3
Ets, Marie Hall. BAD BOY, GOOD BOY.
  Ages 6-10. 292, Vol. 1
Little, Jean. FROM ANNA.
  Ages 9-11. 570, Vol. 1
Madison, Winifred. CALL ME DANICA.
  Ages 10-13. 435, Vol. 2
Marangell, Virginia J. GIANNA MIA.
  Ages 12-15. 402, Vol. 3
Nathan, Dorothy. THE SHY ONE.
  Ages 9-12. 656, Vol. 1
Norris, Gunilla Brodde. A FEAST OF LIGHT.
  Ages 9-12. 672, Vol. 1
Wartski, Maureen Crane. A LONG WAY FROM
  HOME.
  Ages 11-13. 680, Vol. 3
Yep, Laurence Michael. DRAGONWINGS.
  Ages 12 and up. 712, Vol. 2

## Impatience

**See:** *Patience/Impatience*

## Imprisonment

**See also:** *Crime/Criminals; Delinquency, juvenile;
Detention home, living in; Internment*
Burch, Robert Joseph. QUEENIE PEAVY.
  Ages 11-13. 140, Vol. 1
Hautzig, Esther Rudomin. THE ENDLESS STEPPE: A
  GROWING UP IN SIBERIA.
  Ages 11 and up. 406, Vol. 1
Lampman, Evelyn Sibley. THE YEAR OF SMALL
  SHADOW.
  Ages 10-12. 528, Vol. 1
McKay, Robert W. CANARY RED.
  Ages 12 and up. 597, Vol. 1
Pohlmann, Lillian Grenfell. SING LOOSE.
  Ages 12 and up. 714, Vol. 1
Rodowsky, Colby F. A SUMMER'S WORTH OF
  SHAME.
  Ages 12-14. 548, Vol. 3
Samuels, Gertrude. RUN, SHELLEY, RUN.
  Ages 12 and up. 768, Vol. 1
Shreve, Susan Richards. THE MASQUERADE.
  Ages 12 and up. 591, Vol. 3
Trivers, James. I CAN STOP ANY TIME I WANT.
  Ages 12 and up. 904, Vol. 1

## Inconsistency

**See:** *Parental: inconsistency*

## Independence

**See:** *Dependence/Independence*

## Independent Thinking

**See:** *Autonomy*

## Indian, American

**See:** *Native American*

## Individuality

**See:** *Autonomy*

## Individuation

**See:** *Autonomy; Dependence/Independence; Separation
anxiety*

## Infant

**See:** *Death: of infant; Sibling: new baby*

## Inferiority, Feelings of

**See also:** *Shyness*
Andersen, Hans Christian. THE UGLY DUCKLING.
  Ages 4-8. 17, Vol. 1
Armer, Alberta. SCREWBALL.
  Ages 9-11. 29, Vol. 1
Ashley, Bernard. A KIND OF WILD JUSTICE.
  Ages 12 and up. 30, Vol. 3
Bach, Alice Hendricks. MOLLIE MAKE-BELIEVE.
  Ages 12 and up. 41, Vol. 1
Barrett, Anne. MIDWAY.
  Ages 11-13. 53, Vol. 1
Barrett, John M. DANIEL DISCOVERS DANIEL.
  Ages 7-9. 35, Vol. 3
Bates, Betty. THAT'S WHAT T.J. SAYS.
  Ages 9-11. 41, Vol. 3
Bradbury, Bianca. THE LONER.
  Ages 12 and up. 110, Vol. 1
Brooks, Jerome. MAKE ME A HERO.
  Ages 9-12. 78, Vol. 3
Byars, Betsy Cromer. THE CARTOONIST.
  Ages 8-12. 107, Vol. 2
Carol, Bill J., pseud. SINGLE TO CENTER.
  Ages 9-11. 170, Vol. 1
Cohen, Barbara Nash. BENNY.
  Ages 9-11. 152, Vol. 2
Cohen, Barbara Nash. THE INNKEEPER'S
  DAUGHTER.
  Ages 11-14. 126, Vol. 3
Conaway, Judith. WILL I EVER BE GOOD ENOUGH?
  Ages 6-9. 173, Vol. 2
Cone, Molly Lamken. THE TROUBLE WITH TOBY.
  Ages 11-13. 236, Vol. 1
Conford, Ellen. DREAMS OF VICTORY.
  Ages 9-12. 238, Vol. 1
Danziger, Paula. THE CAT ATE MY GYMSUIT.
  Ages 11 and up. 262, Vol. 1
Danziger, Paula. THE PISTACHIO PRESCRIPTION:
  A NOVEL.
  Ages 11-13. 190, Vol. 2
Delton, Judy. I NEVER WIN!
  Ages 4-7. 154, Vol. 3
Fall, Thomas, pseud. EDDIE NO-NAME.
  Ages 8-10. 303, Vol. 1
Fitzhugh, Louise. THE LONG SECRET.
  Ages 9-12. 321, Vol. 1
Fox, Paula. THE STONE-FACED BOY.
  Ages 10-12. 329, Vol. 1
Friedman, Frieda. ELLEN AND THE GANG.
  Ages 9-12. 335, Vol. 1
Giff, Patricia Reilly. FOURTH GRADE CELEBRITY.
  Ages 8-10. 210, Vol. 3

## Inferiority, Feelings of (cont.)

Giff, Patricia Reilly. THE GIRL WHO KNEW IT ALL.
Ages 8-10. 212, Vol. 3
Giff, Patricia Reilly. TODAY WAS A TERRIBLE DAY.
Ages 6-7. 213, Vol. 3
Gilson, Jamie. DO BANANAS CHEW GUM?
Ages 9-11. 216, Vol. 3
Glass, Frankcina. MARVIN & TIGE.
Ages 12 and up. 250, Vol. 2
Green, Phyllis. GLOOMY LOUIE.
Ages 8-9. 234, Vol. 3
Greene, Bette. THE SUMMER OF MY GERMAN
SOLDIER.
Ages 12 and up. 375, Vol. 1
Grohskopf, Bernice. CHILDREN IN THE WIND.
Ages 11-13. 280, Vol. 2
Haugaard, Kay. MYEKO'S GIFT.
Ages 9-12. 405, Vol. 1
Hodges, Margaret Moore. THE HATCHING OF
JOSHUA COBB.
Ages 8-12. 423, Vol. 1
Horvath, Betty. WILL THE REAL TOMMY WILSON
PLEASE STAND UP?
Ages 5-8. 434, Vol. 1
Huston, Anne and Jane H. Yolan. TRUST A CITY
KID.
Ages 11 and up. 448, Vol. 1
Katz, Bobbi. VOLLEYBALL JINX.
Ages 9-11. 364, Vol. 2
Keats, Ezra Jack. LOUIE.
Ages 3-7. 367, Vol. 2
Keller, Beverly Lou. THE BEETLE BUSH.
Ages 5-8. 369, Vol. 2
Kroll, Steven. FRIDAY THE 13TH.
Ages 4-7. 353, Vol. 3
Lee, Mildred Scudder. THE SKATING RINK.
Ages 10-13. 536, Vol. 1
LeRoy, Gen. BILLY'S SHOES.
Ages 5-8. 364, Vol. 3
Lipsyte, Robert. ONE FAT SUMMER.
Ages 12-14. 409, Vol. 2
Little, Jean. ONE TO GROW ON.
Ages 10-12. 575, Vol. 1
Madison, Winfred. GROWING UP IN A HURRY.
Ages 12 and up. 606, Vol. 1
Mazer, Harry. THE WAR ON VILLA STRET: A
NOVEL.
Ages 11-13. 448, Vol. 2
Mazer, Norma Fox. DEAR BILL, REMEMBER ME?
AND OTHER STORIES.
Ages 12 and up. 449, Vol. 2
Miles, Betty. JUST THE BEGINNING.
Ages 10-12. 456, Vol. 2
Morton, Jane. RUNNING SCARED.
Ages 10-14. 455, Vol. 3
Moskin, Marietta Dunston. A PAPER DRAGON.
Ages 11 and up. 651, Vol. 1
Nathan, Dorothy. THE SHY ONE.
Ages 9-12. 656, Vol. 1
Neigoff, Mike. RUNNER-UP.
Ages 9-11. 474, Vol. 2
Norris, Gunilla Brodde. TAKE MY WAKING SLOW.
Ages 10-13. 678, Vol. 1
Olds, Helen Diehl. JIM CAN SWIM.
Ages 6-8. 684, Vol. 1
Oppenheimer, Joan Letson. WORKING ON IT.
Ages 11-13. 475, Vol. 3
Perl, Lila. DUMB, LIKE ME, OLIVIA POTTS.
Ages 9-12. 502, Vol. 2
Perl, Lila. THE TELLTALE SUMMER OF TINA C.
Ages 10-13. 503, Vol. 2
Rinkoff, Barbara Jean Rich. A GUY CAN BE
WRONG.
Ages 10-12. 735, Vol. 1

Rodowsky, Colby F. P.S. WRITE SOON.
Ages 10-12. 555, Vol. 2
Sachs, Marilyn. PETER AND VERONICA.
Ages 10-12. 762, Vol. 1
St. George, Judith. CALL ME MARGO.
Ages 12-14. 567, Vol. 3
Snyder, Zilpha Keatley. THE CHANGELING.
Ages 11-14. 835, Vol. 1
Swetnam, Evelyn. YES, MY DARLING DAUGHTER.
Ages 9-12. 633, Vol. 2
Udry, Janice May. HOW I FADED AWAY.
Ages 5-8. 658, Vol. 2
Viereck, Phillip. THE SUMMER I WAS LOST.
Ages 11 and up. 923, Vol. 1
Walker, Pamela. TWYLA.
Ages 12 and up. 944, Vol. 1
Wersba, Barbara. THE DREAM WATCHER.
Ages 12 and up. 964, Vol. 1
Wier, Ester Alberti. THE BARREL.
Ages 10-13. 970, Vol. 1
Willard, Mildred Wilds. THE LUCK OF HARRY
WEAVER.
Ages 8-10. 977, Vol. 1
Wojciechowska, Maia Rodman. THE HOLLYWOOD
KID.
Ages 12 and up. 984, Vol. 1
Woolley, Catherine. GINNIE JOINS IN.
Ages 9-12. 995, Vol. 1

## Inhibition

**See:** *Inferiority, feelings of; Shyness*

## Initiative, Taking

**See:** *Autonomy; Leader/Leadership; Work, attitude
toward*

## Injuries

**See:** *Accidents; Doctor, going to; Fractures; Hospital,
going to; Surgery; Sutures*

## Injustice

**See:** *Justice/Injustice*

## Insanity

**See:** *Mental illness*

## Insecurity

**See:** *Security/Insecurity*

## Institutions/Institutionalization

**See:** *Children's home, living in; Detention home, living
in; Mental hospital, living in; Nursing home, living in;
Schools, private*

## Integration

**See also:** *Prejudice; School*
Carlson, Natalie Savage. THE EMPTY
SCHOOLHOUSE.
Ages 8-12. 165, Vol. 1
Coles, Robert. DEAD END SCHOOL.
Ages 9-11. 222, Vol. 1
Miner, Jane Claypool. THE TOUGH GUY: BLACK IN
A WHITE WORLD.
Ages 11 and up. 437, Vol. 3
Rowe, Jeanne A. AN ALBUM OF MARTIN LUTHER
KING, JR.
Ages 10 and up. 755, Vol. 1
Rudeen, Kenneth. JACKIE ROBINSON.
Ages 7-9. 757, Vol. 1
Waldron, Ann Wood. THE INTEGRATION OF
MARY-LARKIN THORNHILL.
Ages 10-13. 672, Vol. 2

## Integration (cont.)
### School busing
Blue, Rose. THE PREACHER'S KID.
Ages 9-12. 58, Vol. 2
Cheatham, Karyn Follis. THE BEST WAY OUT.
Ages 12 and up. 114, Vol. 3
Ormsby, Virginia H. TWENTY-ONE CHILDREN PLUS TEN.
Ages 5-8. 687, Vol. 1

## Internment
**See also:** *Imprisonment; Prejudice: ethnic/racial*
Asher, Sandra Fenichel. DAUGHTERS OF THE LAW.
Ages 11-13. 26, Vol. 3
Kerr, Judith. THE OTHER WAY ROUND.
Ages 12 and up. 376, Vol. 2
Uchida, Yoshiko. JOURNEY HOME.
Ages 12-14. 657, Vol. 2
Uchida, Yoshiko. JOURNEY TO TOPAZ: A STORY OF THE JAPANESE-AMERICAN EVACUATION.
Ages 9-12. 910, Vol. 1

## Interracial Marriage
**See:** *Marriage: interracial*

## Intolerance
**See:** *Patience/Impatience; Prejudice*

## Ireland
Lingard, Joan. ACROSS THE BARRICADES.
Ages 12 and up. 561, Vol. 1
Lingard, Joan. INTO EXILE.
Ages 12 and up. 563, Vol. 1
Lingard, Joan. A PROPER PLACE.
Ages 12 and up. 407, Vol. 2
Lingard, Joan. THE TWELFTH DAY OF JULY: A NOVEL OF MODERN IRELAND.
Ages 12 and up. 564, Vol. 1

## Irish-American
Fenton, Edward. DUFFY'S ROCKS.
Ages 12 and up. 311, Vol. 1

## Isolation
**See:** *Loneliness; Ostracism; Peer relationships: avoiding others*

## Israel
**See also:** *Jew/Jewish*
Forman, James. MY ENEMY, MY BROTHER.
Ages 12 and up. 326, Vol. 1
Hoban, Lillian Aberman. I MET A TRAVELLER.
Ages 10-12. 322, Vol. 2
Ofek, Uriel. SMOKE OVER GOLAN.
Ages 9-13. 468, Vol. 3
Watson, Sally. OTHER SANDALS.
Ages 12 and up. 956, Vol. 1

## Italian-American
Marangell, Virginia J. GIANNA MIA.
Ages 12-15. 402, Vol. 3

# J

## Jail
**See:** *Detention home, living in; Imprisonment*

## Japan
Buck, Pearl Sydenstricker. THE BIG WAVE.
Ages 9-11. 129, Vol. 1
Bunting, Anne Evelyn. MAGIC AND THE NIGHT RIVER.
Ages 5-9. 96, Vol. 2
Coerr, Eleanor. SADAKO AND THE THOUSAND PAPER CRANES.
Ages 11 and up. 151, Vol. 2
Flory, Jane Trescott. ONE HUNDRED AND EIGHT BELLS.
Ages 9-11. 324, Vol. 1
Maruki, Toshi. HIROSHIMA NO PIKA.
Ages 7 and up. 406, Vol. 3
Yashima, Taro, pseud. CROW BOY.
Ages 3-7. 1008, Vol. 1

## Japanese-American
Haugaard, Kay. MYEKO'S GIFT.
Ages 9-12. 405, Vol. 1
Taylor, Mark. A TIME FOR FLOWERS.
Ages 4-7. 888, Vol. 1
Uchida, Yoshiko. JOURNEY HOME.
Ages 12-14. 657, Vol. 2
Uchida, Yoshiko. JOURNEY TO TOPAZ: A STORY OF THE JAPANESE-AMERICAN EVACUATION.
Ages 9-12. 910, Vol. 1

## Jealousy
Adler, Carole Schwerdtfeger. SOME OTHER SUMMER.
Ages 10-13. 9, Vol. 3
Colman, Hila Crayder. CONFESSION OF A STORYTELLER.
Ages 10-13. 133, Vol. 3
Dunn, Judy. FEELINGS.
Ages 3-8. 279, Vol. 1
Freeman, Gaail. OUT FROM UNDER.
Ages 12 and up. 195, Vol. 3
Greene, Constance Clarke. I AND SPROGGY.
Ages 9-11. 267, Vol. 2
Grohskopf, Bernice. SHADOW IN THE SUN.
Ages 10 and up. 281, Vol. 2
Hunt, Irene. UP A ROAD SLOWLY.
Ages 12 and up. 438, Vol. 1
Marshall, James Vance, pseud. WALKABOUT.
Ages 12 and up. 614, Vol. 1
Moskin, Marietta Dunston. WITH AN OPEN HAND.
Ages 10-12. 653, Vol. 1
Norris, Gunilla Brodde. THE FRIENDSHIP HEDGE.
Ages 8-11. 673, Vol. 1
Norris, Gunilla Brodde. THE GOOD MORROW.
Ages 9-11. 674, Vol. 1
Pedersen, Elsa Kienitz. FISHERMAN'S CHOICE.
Ages 12 and up. 698, Vol. 1
Rich, Louise Dickinson. THREE OF A KIND.
Ages 10-12. 731, Vol. 1
Sherburne, Zoa. GIRL IN THE MIRROR.
Ages 11 and up. 811, Vol. 1
Skorpen, Liesel Moak. HIS MOTHER'S DOG.
Ages 5-8. 607, Vol. 2
Stolz, Mary Slattery. MAXIMILIAN'S WORLD.
Ages 7-10. 871, Vol. 1
Taylor, Theodore. TEETONCEY.
Ages 10 and up. 890, Vol. 1
Thorvall, Kerstin. AND LEFFE WAS INSTEAD OF A DAD.
Ages 10 and up. 897, Vol. 1
Vogel, Ilse-Margret. MY SUMMER BROTHER.
Ages 8-10. 670, Vol. 3
Wittman, Sally Anne Christensen. THE WONDERFUL MRS. TRUMBLY.
Ages 5-8. 700, Vol. 3

## Peer
Alexander, Anne. CONNIE.
Ages 10-13. 6, Vol. 2
Asher, Sandra Fenichel. JUST LIKE JENNY.
Ages 10-12. 27, Vol. 3
Branscum, Robbie. JOHNNY MAY.
Ages 9-12. 77, Vol. 2

## Jealousy (cont.)

Brooks, Jerome. MAKE ME A HERO.
Ages 9-12. 78, Vol. 3
Bunting, Anne Evelyn. SKATEBOARD FOUR.
Ages 8-10. 98, Vol. 2
Delton, Judy. TWO IS COMPANY.
Ages 4-7. 199, Vol. 2
Greene, Constance Clarke. YOUR OLD PAL, AL.
Ages 9-13. 241, Vol. 3
Jones, Penelope. I DIDN'T WANT TO BE NICE.
Ages 4-7. 359, Vol. 2
Mearian, Judy Frank. TWO WAYS ABOUT IT.
Ages 9-12. 418, Vol. 3
Perl, Lila. PIEFACE AND DAPHNE.
Ages 9-11. 494, Vol. 3
Pfeffer, Susan Beth. STARTING WITH MELODIE.
Ages 11-13. 504, Vol. 3
Sachs, Marilyn. A SUMMER'S LEASE.
Ages 11-14. 566, Vol. 3
Shura, Mary Francis Craig. CHESTER.
Ages 8-10. 593, Vol. 3
Wells, Rosemary. TIMOTHY GOES TO SCHOOL.
Ages 3-5. 689, Vol. 3
Zolotow, Charlotte Shapiro. IT'S NOT FAIR.
Ages 5-7. 718, Vol. 2

**Sibling.** *See also: Sibling: jealousy*

Barrett, John M. DANIEL DISCOVERS DANIEL.
Ages 7-9. 35, Vol. 3
Blue, Rose. SEVEN YEARS FROM HOME.
Ages 8-12. 59, Vol. 2
Brandenberg, Franz. I WISH I WAS SICK, TOO!
Ages 3-7. 73, Vol. 2
Branscum, Robbie. FOR LOVE OF JODY.
Ages 9-12. 73, Vol. 3
Byars, Betsy Cromer. THE ANIMAL, THE VEGETABLE, AND JOHN D JONES.
Ages 10-12. 95, Vol. 3
Byars, Betsy Cromer. THE CARTOONIST.
Ages 8-12. 107, Vol. 2
Colman, Hila Crayder. WHAT'S THE MATTER WITH THE DOBSONS?
Ages 10-13. 135, Vol. 3
Drescher, Joan Elizabeth. THE MARVELOUS MESS.
Ages 4-6. 172, Vol. 3
Ewing, Kathryn. THINGS WON'T BE THE SAME.
Ages 8-10. 182, Vol. 3
Giff, Patricia Reilly. FOURTH GRADE CELEBRITY.
Ages 8-10. 210, Vol. 3
Hamilton, Virginia. ARILLA SUN DOWN.
Ages 12 and up. 291, Vol. 2
Hazen, Barbara Shook. GORILLA WANTS TO BE THE BABY.
Ages 3-5. 301, Vol. 2
Ho, Minfong. SING TO THE DAWN.
Ages 10-13. 320, Vol. 2
Kerr, M. E., pseud. LOVE IS A MISSING PERSON.
Ages 12 and up. 380, Vol. 2
Landis, James David. THE SISTERS IMPOSSIBLE.
Ages 9-11. 355, Vol. 3
Leech, Jay and Jane Spencer. BRIGHT FAWN AND ME.
Ages 4-8. 361, Vol. 3
LeRoy, Gen. LUCKY STIFF!
Ages 4-7. 365, Vol. 3
Paterson, Katherine Womeldorf. JACOB HAVE I LOVED.
Ages 12 and up. 485, Vol. 3
Pfeffer, Susan Beth. WHAT DO YOU DO WHEN YOUR MOUTH WON'T OPEN?
Ages 10-13. 505, Vol. 3
Rodowsky, Colby F. WHAT ABOUT ME?
Ages 11-13. 556, Vol. 2
Rogers, Pamela. THE STONE ANGEL.
Ages 10-12. 558, Vol. 2

Terris, Susan Dubinsky. AMANDA, THE PANDA, AND THE REDHEAD.
Ages 5-7. 639, Vol. 2
Tester, Sylvia Root. FEELING ANGRY.
Ages 3-6. 643, Vol. 2
Winthrop, Elizabeth. A LITTLE DEMONSTRATION OF AFFECTION.
Ages 12-16. 689, Vol. 2
Wolde, Gunilla. BETSY AND THE CHICKEN POX.
Ages 3-7. 696, Vol. 2
York, Carol Beach. REMEMBER ME WHEN I AM DEAD.
Ages 9-11. 714, Vol. 3

## Jew/Jewish

**See also:** *Ghetto; Israel*

Arrick, Fran. CHERNOWITZ!
Ages 12 and up. 23, Vol. 3
Asher, Sandra Fenichel. DAUGHTERS OF THE LAW.
Ages 11-13. 26, Vol. 3
Bernays, Anne. GROWING UP RICH.
Ages 13 and up. 52, Vol. 2
Bernstein, Joanne Eckstein. DMITRY: A YOUNG SOVIET IMMIGRANT.
Ages 11-13. 52, Vol. 3
Blue, Rose. THE THIRTEENTH YEAR: A BAR MITZVAH STORY.
Ages 10-12. 60, Vol. 2
Brooks, Jerome. MAKE ME A HERO.
Ages 9-12. 78, Vol. 3
Chaikin, Miriam. I SHOULD WORRY, I SHOULD CARE.
Ages 8-11. 111, Vol. 3
Cohen, Barbara Nash. BENNY.
Ages 9-11. 152, Vol. 2
Cohen, Barbara Nash. BITTER HERBS AND HONEY.
Ages 11-13. 153, Vol. 2
Colman, Hila Crayder. MIXED MARRIAGE DAUGHTER.
Ages 11 and up. 232, Vol. 1
Cone, Molly Lamken. A PROMISE IS A PROMISE.
Ages 11-13. 234, Vol. 1
Eisenberg, Phyllis Rose. A MITZVAH IS SOMETHING SPECIAL.
Ages 5-8. 214, Vol. 2
Frank, Anne. ANNE FRANK: THE DIARY OF A YOUNG GIRL.
Ages 11 and up. 330, Vol. 1
Girion, Barbara. LIKE EVERYBODY ELSE.
Ages 10-13. 218, Vol. 3
Girion, Barbara. A TANGLE OF ROOTS.
Ages 12-16. 220, Vol. 3
Goldreich, Gloria. SEASON OF DISCOVERY.
Ages 11-13. 256, Vol. 2
Green, Hannah, pseud. I NEVER PROMISED YOU A ROSE GARDEN.
Ages 13 and up. 373, Vol. 1
Herman, Charlotte. THE DIFFERENCE OF ARI STEIN.
Ages 9-12. 312, Vol. 2
Herman, Charlotte. WHAT HAPPENED TO HEATHER HOPKOWITZ?
Ages 10-13. 283, Vol. 3
Hoban, Lillian Aberman. I MET A TRAVELLER.
Ages 10-12. 322, Vol. 2
Hurwitz, Johanna. ONCE I WAS A PLUM TREE.
Ages 9-11. 317, Vol. 3
Kaplan, Bess. THE EMPTY CHAIR.
Ages 10-14. 363, Vol. 2
Kerr, Judith. THE OTHER WAY ROUND.
Ages 12 and up. 376, Vol. 2
Kerr, Judith. WHEN HITLER STOLE PINK RABBIT.
Ages 10-12. 490, Vol. 1

## Jew/Jewish (cont.)

Konigsburg, Elaine Lobl. ABOUT THE B'NAI
BAGELS.
Ages 10-13. 508, Vol. 1
Levoy, Myron. ALAN AND NAOMI.
Ages 11-14. 404, Vol. 2
Little, Jean. KATE.
Ages 10-14. 572, Vol. 1
Little, Jean. LOOK THROUGH MY WINDOW.
Ages 10-14. 573, Vol. 1
Madison, Winifred. BECKY'S HORSE.
Ages 10-12. 434, Vol. 2
Mazer, Harry. THE LAST MISSION.
Ages 12-14. 413, Vol. 3
Morris, Terry. SHALOM, GOLDA.
Ages 12 and up. 648, Vol. 1
Neville, Emily Cheney. BERRIES GOODMAN.
Ages 11 and up. 666, Vol. 1
Potok, Chaim. THE CHOSEN.
Ages 13 and up. 715, Vol. 1
Reiss, Johanna. THE JOURNEY BACK.
Ages 10-14. 530, Vol. 2
Rose, Anne K. REFUGEE.
Ages 10-14. 559, Vol. 2
Ruby, Lois. TWO TRUTHS IN MY POCKET.
Ages 12 and up. 557, Vol. 3
Sachs, Marilyn. PETER AND VERONICA.
Ages 10-12. 762, Vol. 1
Sachs, Marilyn. A POCKET FULL OF SEEDS.
Ages 10-12. 763, Vol. 1
Terris, Susan Dubinsky. WHIRLING RAINBOWS.
Ages 11 and up. 892, Vol. 1

## Job

**See also:** *Baby-sitting; Chores; Money: earning;*
*Responsibility; Retirement; Work, attitude toward*
Belair, Richard L. DOUBLE TAKE.
Ages 13 and up. 44, Vol. 3
Bethancourt, T. Ernesto, pseud. NEW YORK CITY
TOO FAR FROM TAMPA BLUES.
Ages 10-14. 55, Vol. 2
Bulla, Clyde Robert. SHOESHINE GIRL.
Ages 8-10. 93, Vol. 2
Cleary, Beverly Bunn. HENRY AND THE PAPER
ROUTE.
Ages 7-10. 192, Vol. 1
Collier, James Lincoln. GIVE DAD MY BEST.
Ages 10-14. 159, Vol. 2
Lipsyte, Robert. ONE FAT SUMMER.
Ages 12-14. 409, Vol. 2
Lowry, Lois. ANASTASIA AT YOUR SERVICE.
Ages 9-12. 385, Vol. 3
Madison, Winifred. CALL ME DANICA.
Ages 10-13. 435, Vol. 2
Miner, Jane Claypool. A MAN'S PRIDE: LOSING A
FATHER.
Ages 11 and up. 429, Vol. 3
Naylor, Phyllis Reynolds. EDDIE, INCORPORATED.
Ages 9-11. 463, Vol. 3
Newton, Suzanne. M.V. SEXTON SPEAKING.
Ages 11 and up. 466, Vol. 3
Pfeffer, Susan Beth. KID POWER.
Ages 9-12. 511, Vol. 2
Shaw, Richard. THE HARD WAY HOME.
Ages 11-13. 592, Vol. 2
Smith, Anne Warren. BLUE DENIM BLUES.
Ages 12 and up. 607, Vol. 3

## Judgment, Effect of Emotions on

Bernays, Anne. GROWING UP RICH.
Ages 13 and up. 52, Vol. 2
Bunting, Anne Evelyn. HIGH TIDE FOR LABRADOR.
Ages 9-11. 95, Vol. 2

Carroll, Theodorus C. THE LOST CHRISTMAS
STAR.
Ages 7-9. 109, Vol. 3
Christman, Elizabeth. A NICE ITALIAN GIRL.
Ages 12 and up. 132, Vol. 2
Cone, Molly Lamken. THE REAL DREAM.
Ages 12 and up. 235, Vol. 1
Degens, T. THE GAME ON THATCHER ISLAND.
Ages 11-14. 193, Vol. 2
Hinton, Nigel. COLLISION COURSE.
Ages 11 and up. 315, Vol. 2
Leigh, Frances. THE LOST BOY.
Ages 10-13. 399, Vol. 2
O'Dell, Scott. KATHLEEN, PLEASE COME HOME.
Ages 12 and up. 485, Vol. 2
Platt, Kin. CHLORIS AND THE WEIRDOS.
Ages 11 and up. 516, Vol. 2
Stolz, Mary Slattery. SIRI THE CONQUISTADOR.
Ages 8-11. 875, Vol. 1

## Justice/Injustice

**See also:** *Blame; Guilt, feelings of; Prejudice*
Carrick, Malcolm. I'LL GET YOU.
Ages 11-13. 107, Vol. 3
Christman, Elizabeth. A NICE ITALIAN GIRL.
Ages 12 and up. 132, Vol. 2
Cleaver, Vera and Bill Cleaver. THE WHYS AND
WHEREFORES OF LITTABELLE LEE.
Ages 12 and up. 204, Vol. 1
Colman, Hila Crayder. THE CASE OF THE STOLEN
BAGELS.
Ages 7-10. 162, Vol. 2
Ellis, Melvin Richard. NO MAN FOR MURDER.
Ages 12 and up. 287, Vol. 1
Fitzgerald, John Dennis. THE GREAT BRAIN
REFORMS.
Ages 10-13. 318, Vol. 1
Garden, Nancy. ANNIE ON MY MIND.
Ages 13 and up. 201, Vol. 3
Guy, Rosa Cuthbert. THE DISAPPEARANCE.
Ages 12 and up. 252, Vol. 3
Harrah, Michael. FIRST OFFENDER.
Ages 11-13. 266, Vol. 3
Hentoff, Nat. DOES THIS SCHOOL HAVE CAPITAL
PUNISHMENT?
Ages 11 and up. 282, Vol. 3
Karp, Naomi J. NOTHING RHYMES WITH APRIL.
Ages 9-11. 364, Vol. 1
Knox-Wagner, Elaine. THE OLDEST KID.
Ages 4-8. 347, Vol. 3
Knudson, R. Rozanne. ZANBANGER.
Ages 10-13. 387, Vol. 2
Lee, Harper. TO KILL A MOCKINGBIRD.
Ages 12 and up. 533, Vol. 1
Naylor, Phyllis Reynolds. ALL BECAUSE I'M OLDER.
Ages 7-9. 462, Vol. 3
Samuels, Gertrude. ADAM'S DAUGHTER.
Ages 13 and up. 568, Vol. 2
Samuels, Gertrude. RUN, SHELLEY, RUN.
Ages 12 and up. 768, Vol. 1
Sarnoff, Jane and Reynold Ruffins. THAT'S NOT
FAIR.
Ages 4-7. 571, Vol. 3
Taylor, Mildred D. ROLL OF THUNDER, HEAR MY
CRY.
Ages 10 and up. 636, Vol. 2
Wier, Ester Alberti. THE LONG YEAR.
Ages 10 and up. 971, Vol. 1

## Juvenile Delinquency

**See:** *Delinquency, juvenile*

## Juvenile Detention

**See:** *Detention home, living in*

# K

## Kidnapping

**See also:** *Crime/Criminals*
Eyerly, Jeannette Hyde. THE SEEING SUMMER.
  Ages 8-10. 183, Vol. 3
Fitzhugh, Louise. SPORT.
  Ages 9-12. 190, Vol. 3
Hopper, Nancy J. SECRETS.
  Ages 11-14. 304, Vol. 3

## Killing

**See:** *Death: murder; Violence; War*

## Kissing

**See:** *Boy-girl relationships; Sex*

# L

## Lameness

**See also:** *Birth defects; Limbs, abnormal or missing; Poliomyelitis*
Annixter, Jane, pseud. and Paul Annixter, pseud. THE RUNNER.
  Ages 11-13. 24, Vol. 1
Armer, Alberta. SCREWBALL.
  Ages 9-11. 29, Vol. 1
Fletcher, David. THE KING'S GOBLET.
  Ages 12 and up. 323, Vol. 1
Watson, Sally. OTHER SANDALS.
  Ages 12 and up. 956, Vol. 1
Weik, Mary Hays. THE JAZZ MAN.
  Ages 9-11. 958, Vol. 1

## Language Problems

**See:** *Communication; Speech problems*

## Latchkey Child

**See:** *Parent/Parents: mother working outside home; Parent/Parents: single*

## Latter-day Saints

**See:** *Church of Jesus Christ of Latter-day Saints (Mormon)*

## Laziness

**See:** *Chores; Daydreaming; Responsibility: avoiding; School: achievement/underachievement; Work, attitude toward*

## Leader/Leadership

**See also:** *Identification with others; Responsibility: accepting*
Balch, Glenn. BRAVE RIDERS.
  Ages 10-13. 47, Vol. 1
Bunting, Anne Evelyn. SKATEBOARD FOUR.
  Ages 8-10. 98, Vol. 2
Church, Richard. FIVE BOYS IN A CAVE.
  Ages 9-12. 185, Vol. 1
Clayton, Edward Taylor. MARTIN LUTHER KING: THE PEACEFUL WARRIOR.
  Ages 8-10. 189, Vol. 1
Clyne, Patricia Edwards. TUNNELS OF TERROR.
  Ages 10-12. 149, Vol. 2
Dolan, Edward Francis and Richard B. Lyttle. BOBBY CLARKE.
  Ages 10-12. 205, Vol. 2
Dygard, Thomas J. WINNING KICKER.
  Ages 11-14. 213, Vol. 2
Fife, Dale. WHO'LL VOTE FOR LINCOLN?
  Ages 8-10. 229, Vol. 2

Greene, Bette. GET ON OUT OF HERE, PHILIP HALL.
  Ages 9-12. 238, Vol. 3
Huntsberry, William Emery. THE BIG WHEELS.
  Ages 12 and up. 446, Vol. 1
Jeffries, Roderic. TRAPPED.
  Ages 11-13. 457, Vol. 1
Leigh, Bill. THE FAR SIDE OF FEAR.
  Ages 10-14. 398, Vol. 2
Neigoff, Mike. SOCCER HERO.
  Ages 9-11. 475, Vol. 2
Rowe, Jeanne A. AN ALBUM OF MARTIN LUTHER KING, JR.
  Ages 10 and up. 755, Vol. 1
Sharmat, Marjorie Weinman. MAGGIE MARMELSTEIN FOR PRESIDENT.
  Ages 9-12. 588, Vol. 2
Terris, Susan Dubinsky. TWO P'S IN A POD.
  Ages 9-12. 641, Vol. 2
Wrenn, C. Gilbert and Shirley Schwarzrock. IN FRONT OF THE TABLE AND BEHIND IT.
  Ages 11 and up. 1003, Vol. 1

## Learning, Love of

**See:** *Education: Value of*

## Learning Disabilities

**See also:** *Birth defects; Brain injury; Education: special; Mental retardation*
Albert, Louise. BUT I'M READY TO GO.
  Ages 11-14. 5, Vol. 2
Breisky, William. I THINK I CAN.
  Ages 12 and up. 115, Vol. 1
Corcoran, Barbara. AXE-TIME, SWORD-TIME.
  Ages 11 and up. 178, Vol. 2
Gardner, Richard A. MBD: THE FAMILY BOOK ABOUT MINIMAL BRAIN DYSFUNCTION.
  Ages 9-12. 345, Vol. 1
Gilson, Jamie. DO BANANAS CHEW GUM?
  Ages 9-11. 216, Vol. 3
Kamien, Janet. WHAT IF YOU COULDN'T...? A BOOK ABOUT SPECIAL NEEDS.
  Ages 8-12. 336, Vol. 3
Konigsburg, Elaine Lobl. ALTOGETHER, ONE AT A TIME.
  Ages 9-11. 509, Vol. 1
Lasker, Joe. HE'S MY BROTHER.
  Ages 4-9. 530, Vol. 1
Matthews, Ellen. PUTTING UP WITH SHERWOOD.
  Ages 9-11. 408, Vol. 3
Morton, Jane. RUNNING SCARED.
  Ages 10-14. 455, Vol. 3
Pevsner, Stella. KEEP STOMPIN' TILL THE MUSIC STOPS.
  Ages 9-12. 509, Vol. 2
Rinkoff, Barbara Jean Rich. THE WATCHERS.
  Ages 11-14. 740, Vol. 1
Smith, Doris Buchanan. KELLY'S CREEK.
  Ages 8-13. 613, Vol. 2
Sullivan, Mary Beth and Alan J. Brightman and Joseph Blatt. FEELING FREE.
  Ages 9 and up. 640, Vol. 3
Swarthout, Glendon Fred and Kathryn Swarthout. WHALES TO SEE THE.
  Ages 10-12. 632, Vol. 2

## Left-Handedness

Lerner, Marguerite Rush. LEFTY: THE STORY OF LEFT-HANDEDNESS.
  Ages 9-11. 547, Vol. 1

## Leprosy

Van Iterson, Siny Rose. VILLAGE OF OUTCASTS.
  Ages 12 and up. 917, Vol. 1

## Lesbianism

**See:** *Homosexuality: female*

## Leukemia

**See also:** *Cancer: leukemia; Hospital, going to*
Coerr, Eleanor. SADAKO AND THE THOUSAND PAPER CRANES.
Ages 11 and up. 151, Vol. 2
L'Engle, Madeleine Franklin. A RING OF ENDLESS LIGHT.
Ages 11-14. 363, Vol. 3
Lowry, Lois. A SUMMER TO DIE.
Ages 10-14. 423, Vol. 2
Miner, Jane Claypool. THIS DAY IS MINE: LIVING WITH LEUKEMIA.
Ages 10 and up. 436, Vol. 3
Strasser, Todd. FRIENDS TILL THE END.
Ages 12 and up. 636, Vol. 3

## Life, Meaning of

**See:** *Identity, search for; Religion*

## Life Style

**See also:** *Commune*
Bauer, Caroline Feller. MY MOM TRAVELS A LOT.
Ages 5-8. 42, Vol. 3
Clifton, Lucille. SONORA BEAUTIFUL.
Ages 12-14. 123, Vol. 3
Cohen, Barbara Nash. THE INNKEEPER'S DAUGHTER.
Ages 11-14. 126, Vol. 3
Colman, Hila Crayder. AFTER THE WEDDING.
Ages 12 and up. 160, Vol. 2
Cone, Molly Lamken. ANNIE ANNIE.
Ages 10-13. 233, Vol. 1
Corcoran, Barbara. SAM.
Ages 12 and up. 251, Vol. 1
Drescher, Joan Elizabeth. YOUR FAMILY, MY FAMILY.
Ages 5-7. 173, Vol. 3
Girion, Barbara. LIKE EVERYBODY ELSE.
Ages 10-13. 218, Vol. 3
Hamilton, Gail, pseud. TITANIA'S LODESTONE.
Ages 11-13. 290, Vol. 2
Lampman, Evelyn Sibley. GO UP THE ROAD.
Ages 9-12. 526, Vol. 1
Mazer, Norma Fox. MRS. FISH, APE, AND ME, THE DUMP QUEEN.
Ages 10-12. 414, Vol. 3
Naylor, Phyllis Reynolds. TO WALK THE SKY PATH.
Ages 10-13. 658, Vol. 1
Perl, Lila. ME AND FAT GLENDA.
Ages 9-12. 700, Vol. 1
Richard, Adrienne. INTO THE ROAD.
Ages 12 and up. 537, Vol. 2
Rogers, Pamela. THE RARE ONE.
Ages 10-12. 751, Vol. 1
Ruhen, Olaf. CORCORAN'S THE NAME.
Ages 12 and up. 758, Vol. 1
Shanks, Ann Zane. OLD IS WHAT YOU GET: DIALOGUES ON AGING BY THE OLD AND THE YOUNG.
Ages 10 and up. 582, Vol. 2
Simon, Norma. ALL KINDS OF FAMILIES.
Ages 5-8. 602, Vol. 2
Vestley, Anne-Catharina. HELLO, AURORA.
Ages 8-11. 922, Vol. 1
Zolotow, Charlotte Shapiro. IT'S NOT FAIR.
Ages 5-7. 718, Vol. 2

**Change in.** *See also: Change: new home*
Bernays, Anne. GROWING UP RICH.
Ages 13 and up. 52, Vol. 2

Bernstein, Joanne Eckstein. DMITRY: A YOUNG SOVIET IMMIGRANT.
Ages 11-13. 52, Vol. 3
Blaine, Margery Kay. THE TERRIBLE THING THAT HAPPENED AT OUR HOUSE.
Ages 3-7. 56, Vol. 2
Blume, Judy Sussman. THEN AGAIN, MAYBE I WON'T.
Ages 12 and up. 94, Vol. 1
Bosse, Malcolm Joseph. GANESH.
Ages 11-14. 65, Vol. 3
Bridgers, Sue Ellen. HOME BEFORE DARK.
Ages 12 and up. 81, Vol. 2
Bulla, Clyde Robert. OPEN THE DOOR AND SEE ALL THE PEOPLE.
Ages 8-11. 136, Vol. 1
Bulla, Clyde Robert. POOR BOY, RICH BOY.
Ages 5-8. 87, Vol. 3
Butler, Beverly Kathleen. A GIRL CALLED WENDY.
Ages 12 and up. 106, Vol. 2
Butterworth, William Edmund. LEROY AND THE OLD MAN.
Ages 12 and up. 93, Vol. 3
Chandler, Edna Walker. INDIAN PAINTBRUSH.
Ages 9-11. 126, Vol. 2
Chetin, Helen. HOW FAR IS BERKELEY?
Ages 11-13. 128, Vol. 2
Colman, Hila Crayder. THE GIRL FROM PUERTO RICO.
Ages 11 and up. 231, Vol. 1
Dunnahoo, Terry. WHO CARES ABOUT ESPIE SANCHEZ?
Ages 10-12. 210, Vol. 2
Ellis, Ella Thorp. SLEEPWALKER'S MOON.
Ages 12 and up. 181, Vol. 3
Ewing, Kathryn. THINGS WON'T BE THE SAME.
Ages 8-10. 182, Vol. 3
Flory, Jane Trescott. THE UNEXPECTED GRANDCHILDREN.
Ages 4-7. 232, Vol. 2
Godden, Rumer. THE DIDDAKOI.
Ages 10-12. 362, Vol. 1
Graeber, Charlotte Towner. GREY CLOUD.
Ages 9-11. 226, Vol. 3
Grant, Cynthia D. JOSHUA FORTUNE.
Ages 10-13. 229, Vol. 3
Holland, Isabelle. OF LOVE AND DEATH AND OTHER JOURNEYS.
Ages 11 and up. 329, Vol. 2
Kingman, Lee. THE PETER PAN BAG.
Ages 12 and up. 498, Vol. 1
Kingman, Lee. THE REFINER'S FIRE.
Ages 12-14. 341, Vol. 3
Knox-Wagner, Elaine. MY GRANDPA RETIRED TODAY.
Ages 4-7. 346, Vol. 3
Love, Sandra Weller. CROSSING OVER.
Ages 10-12. 383, Vol. 3
Means, Florence Crannell. OUR CUP IS BROKEN.
Ages 12 and up. 629, Vol. 1
Molloy, Anne Stearns. THE GIRL FROM TWO MILES HIGH.
Ages 10-12. 642, Vol. 1
Morgenroth, Barbara. WILL THE REAL RENIE LAKE PLEASE STAND UP?
Ages 12 and up. 453, Vol. 3
Park, Barbara. DON'T MAKE ME SMILE.
Ages 8-11. 481, Vol. 3
Pfeffer, Susan Beth. JUST MORGAN.
Ages 12 and up. 707, Vol. 1
Prince, Alison. THE TURKEY'S NEST.
Ages 12 and up. 520, Vol. 3
Rabin, Gil. CHANGES.
Ages 12 and up. 721, Vol. 1

## Life Style (cont.)

Raymond, Charles. JUD.
Ages 9-12. 726, Vol. 1
Rodowsky, Colby F. A SUMMER'S WORTH OF
SHAME.
Ages 12-14. 548, Vol. 3
Seredy, Kate. THE SINGING TREE.
Ages 10-14. 803, Vol. 1
Shreve, Susan Richards. THE MASQUERADE.
Ages 12 and up. 591, Vol. 3
Skurzynski, Gloria Joan. MARTIN BY HIMSELF.
Ages 6-9. 602, Vol. 3
Smith, Lucia B. MY MOM GOT A JOB.
Ages 5-8. 611, Vol. 3
Stevenson, James. THE WORST PERSON IN THE
WORLD.
Ages 4-8. 625, Vol. 2
Stolz, Mary Slattery. BY THE HIGHWAY HOME.
Ages 12 and up. 864, Vol. 1
Taylor, Theodore. THE MALDONADO MIRACLE.
Ages 11-13. 889, Vol. 1
Uchida, Yoshiko. JOURNEY TO TOPAZ: A STORY OF
THE JAPANESE-AMERICAN EVACUATION.
Ages 9-12. 910, Vol. 1
Vestley, Anne-Catharina. AURORA AND SOCRATES.
Ages 8-10. 660, Vol. 2
Whelan, Gloria. A TIME TO KEEP SILENT.
Ages 11-14. 690, Vol. 3
Wier, Ester Alberti. THE BARREL.
Ages 10-13. 970, Vol. 1
Wilkinson, Brenda Scott. LUDELL'S NEW YORK
TIME.
Ages 12 and up. 691, Vol. 3
Yep, Laurence Michael. CHILD OF THE OWL.
Ages 11 and up. 711, Vol. 2

## Limbs, Abnormal or Missing

**See also:** *Amputee; Birth defects; Braces on body/limbs;
Deformities; Lameness; Prosthesis*
Cook, Marjorie. TO WALK ON TWO FEET.
Ages 11-14. 177, Vol. 2
Donovan, Pete. CAROL JOHNSTON: THE ONE-
ARMED GYMNAST.
Ages 8-12. 169, Vol. 3
Griese, Arnold Alfred. AT THE MOUTH OF THE
LUCKIEST RIVER.
Ages 8-11. 385, Vol. 1
Kamien, Janet. WHAT IF YOU COULDN'T . . . ? A
BOOK ABOUT SPECIAL NEEDS.
Ages 8-12. 336, Vol. 3
Richter, Elizabeth. THE TEENAGE HOSPITAL
EXPERIENCE: YOU CAN HANDLE IT!
Ages 12 and up. 532, Vol. 3
Slepian, Jan. THE ALFRED SUMMER.
Ages 11-13. 603, Vol. 3
Stein, Sara Bonnett. ABOUT HANDICAPS: AN OPEN
FAMILY BOOK FOR PARENTS AND CHILDREN
TOGETHER.
Ages 4-8. 856, Vol. 1
Viscardi, Henry. A LAUGHTER IN THE LONELY
NIGHT.
Ages 12 and up. 931, Vol. 1
Viscardi, Henry. A MAN'S STATURE.
Ages 12 and up. 932, Vol. 1
Wolf, Bernard. DON'T FEEL SORRY FOR PAUL.
Ages 8 and up. 987, Vol. 1

## Little Brother/Sister

**See:** *Sibling: younger; Sibling: youngest*

## Little League

**See also:** *Competition; Sports/Sportsmanship*
Carol, Bill J., pseud. SINGLE TO CENTER.
Ages 9-11. 170, Vol. 1

Harmon, A. W. BASE HIT.
Ages 9-12. 400, Vol. 1
Hoff, Sydney. THE LITTLEST LEAGUER.
Ages 5-8. 325, Vol. 2
Konigsburg, Elaine Lobl. ABOUT THE B'NAI
BAGELS.
Ages 10-13. 508, Vol. 1
Lexau, Joan M. I'LL TELL ON YOU.
Ages 5-8. 406, Vol. 2
Morton, Jane. I AM RUBBER, YOU ARE GLUE.
Ages 9-11. 454, Vol. 3
Rivera, Geraldo. A SPECIAL KIND OF COURAGE:
PROFILES OF YOUNG AMERICANS.
Ages 12 and up. 544, Vol. 2
Slote, Alfred. MATT GARGAN'S BOY.
Ages 9-11. 611, Vol. 2
Slote, Alfred. MY FATHER, THE COACH.
Ages 11-13. 828, Vol. 1

## Loneliness

**See also:** *Belonging; Depression; Separation anxiety;
Separation from loved ones*
Anderson, Clarence William. LONESOME LITTLE
COLT.
Ages 4-7. 18, Vol. 1
Anderson, Mary Quirk. JUST THE TWO OF THEM.
Ages 12 and up. 19, Vol. 1
Angier, Bradford and Barbara Corcoran. ASK FOR
LOVE AND THEY GIVE YOU RICE PUDDING.
Ages 12-14. 21, Vol. 2
Balderson, Margaret. WHEN JAYS FLY TO BARBMO.
Ages 12 and up. 48, Vol. 1
Ball, Zachary, pseud. KEP.
Ages 10 and up. 50, Vol. 1
Bates, Betty. THE UPS AND DOWNS OF JORIE
JENKINS.
Ages 9-12. 41, Vol. 2
Bawden, Nina Mary Kark. SQUIB.
Ages 10-13. 58, Vol. 1
Beckwith, Lillian. THE SPUDDY: A NOVEL.
Ages 11 and up. 48, Vol. 2
Bishop, Claire Huchet. ALL ALONE.
Ages 7-10. 78, Vol. 1
Bloch, Marie Halun. DISPLACED PERSON.
Ages 10-13. 57, Vol. 2
Bosworth, J. Allan. WHITE WATER, STILL WATER.
Ages 11 and up. 105, Vol. 1
Bradbury, Bianca. THE LONER.
Ages 12 and up. 110, Vol. 1
Brink, Carol Ryrie. THE BAD TIMES OF IRMA
BAUMLEIN.
Ages 10-13. 119, Vol. 1
Budbill, David. BONES ON BLACK SPRUCE
MOUNTAIN.
Ages 10-13. 91, Vol. 2
Bulla, Clyde Robert. WHITE BIRD.
Ages 9 and up. 138, Vol. 1
Byars, Betsy Cromer. THE CARTOONIST.
Ages 8-12. 107, Vol. 2
Byars, Betsy Cromer. THE NIGHT SWIMMERS.
Ages 10-12. 98, Vol. 3
Carrick, Malcolm. I'LL GET YOU.
Ages 11-13. 107, Vol. 3
Carrick, Malcolm. TRAMP.
Ages 7-9. 122, Vol. 2
Clymer, Eleanor Lowenton. LUKE WAS THERE.
Ages 8-12. 211, Vol. 1
Coatsworth, Elizabeth Jane. LONELY MARIA.
Ages 4-8. 214, Vol. 1
Cole, Sheila R. MEANING WELL.
Ages 9-12. 220, Vol. 1
Colman, Hila Crayder. CONFESSION OF A
STORYTELLER.
Ages 10-13. 133, Vol. 3

## Love, Meaning of (cont.)

Schlein, Miriam. THE WAY MOTHERS ARE.
Ages 3-6. 783, Vol. 1

Sebestyen, Ouida. FAR FROM HOME.
Ages 12 and up. 579, Vol. 3

Sebestyen, Ouida. WORDS BY HEART.
Ages 10-13. 580, Vol. 3

Silman, Roberta. SOMEBODY ELSE'S CHILD.
Ages 9-11. 599, Vol. 2

Slepian, Jan. LESTER'S TURN.
Ages 11-14. 604, Vol. 3

Spence, Eleanor Rachel. A CANDLE FOR SAINT
ANTONY.
Ages 13 and up. 618, Vol. 3

Stinetorf, Louise Allender. A CHARM FOR PACO'S
MOTHER.
Ages 9 and up. 862, Vol. 1

Stolz, Mary Slattery. WAIT FOR ME, MICHAEL.
Ages 12 and up. 876, Vol. 1

Strang, Celia. FOSTER MARY.
Ages 10-13. 633, Vol. 3

Strang, Celia. THIS CHILD IS MINE.
Ages 11-14. 634, Vol. 3

Street, James Howell. GOOD-BYE, MY LADY.
Ages 11 and up. 878, Vol. 1

Swetnam, Evelyn. YES, MY DARLING DAUGHTER.
Ages 9-12. 633, Vol. 2

Talbot, Toby. DEAR GRETA GARBO.
Ages 11-13. 635, Vol. 2

Tate, Joan. LUKE'S GARDEN AND GRAMP: TWO
NOVELS.
Ages 10-13. 644, Vol. 3

Tax, Meredith. FAMILIES.
Ages 4-8. 645, Vol. 3

Viscardi, Henry. THE PHOENIX CHILD: A STORY
OF LOVE.
Ages 13 and up. 665, Vol. 2

Vogel, Ilse-Margret. MY SUMMER BROTHER.
Ages 8-10. 670, Vol. 3

Voigt, Cynthia. DICEY'S SONG.
Ages 11 and up. 671, Vol. 3

Wahl, Jan. DOCTOR RABBIT'S FOUNDLING.
Ages 4-7. 669, Vol. 2

Wartski, Maureen Crane. A BOAT TO NOWHERE.
Ages 9-12. 678, Vol. 3

Wersba, Barbara. THE DREAM WATCHER.
Ages 12 and up. 964, Vol. 1

Wersba, Barbara. RUN SOFTLY, GO FAST.
Ages 13 and up. 965, Vol. 1

Williams, Margery Bianco. THE VELVETEEN
RABBIT; OR, HOW TOYS BECOME REAL.
Ages 5-10. 978, Vol. 1

Wolitzer, Hilma. OUT OF LOVE.
Ages 10-13. 704, Vol. 2

Wortis, Avi. SOMETIMES I THINK I HEAR MY
NAME.
Ages 10-13. 708, Vol. 3

Wosmek, Frances. A BOWL OF SUN.
Ages 7-9. 710, Vol. 2

Yashima, Taró, pseud. and Hatoju Muku. THE
GOLDEN FOOTPRINTS.
Ages 8-10. 1009, Vol. 1

Zindel, Paul. I LOVE MY MOTHER.
Ages 3-7. 717, Vol. 2

Zindel, Paul. THE PIGMAN.
Ages 12 and up. 1015, Vol. 1

Zolotow, Charlotte Shapiro. MAY I VISIT?
Ages 4-7. 719, Vol. 2

## Loyalty

**See also:** *Patriotism; Sibling: loyalty*
Angell, Judie. IN SUMMERTIME IT'S TUFFY.
Ages 11-13. 19, Vol. 2

Brancato, Robin Fidler. SOMETHING LEFT TO
LOSE.
Ages 12-14. 71, Vol. 2

Brancato, Robin Fidler. SWEET BELLS JANGLED
OUT OF TUNE.
Ages 11-14. 70, Vol. 3

Burton, Virginia Lee. MIKE MULLIGAN AND HIS
STEAM SHOVEL.
Ages 4-8. 149, Vol. 1

Byars, Betsy Cromer. AFTER THE GOAT MAN.
Ages 9-11. 153, Vol. 1

Carrick, Carol. SOME FRIEND!
Ages 9-12. 106, Vol. 3

Conklin, Paul. CHOCTAW BOY.
Ages 9-12. 176, Vol. 2

Fall, Thomas, pseud. DANDY'S MOUNTAIN.
Ages 12 and up. 302, Vol. 1

Hassler, Jon Francis. FOUR MILES TO PINECONE.
Ages 10-14. 297, Vol. 2

Horvath, Betty. BE NICE TO JOSEPHINE.
Ages 5-8. 433, Vol. 1

Huntsberry, William Emery. THE BIG WHEELS.
Ages 12 and up. 446, Vol. 1

Knudson, R. Rozanne. ZANBOOMER.
Ages 10-13. 388, Vol. 2

Little, Mary E. OLD CAT AND THE KITTEN.
Ages 8-12. 379, Vol. 3

Mazer, Norma Fox. A FIGURE OF SPEECH.
Ages 12 and up. 628, Vol. 1

Nöstlinger, Christine. GIRL MISSING: A NOVEL.
Ages 11 and up. 482, Vol. 2

Sachs, Marilyn. CLASS PICTURES.
Ages 10-13. 564, Vol. 3

Schaefer, Jack Warner. OLD RAMON.
Ages 10 and up. 777, Vol. 1

Scoppettone, Sandra. HAPPY ENDINGS ARE ALL
ALIKE.
Ages 12 and up. 578, Vol. 2

Singer, Marilyn. NO APPLAUSE, PLEASE.
Ages 10-12. 605, Vol. 2

Uchida, Yoshiko. JOURNEY TO TOPAZ: A STORY OF
THE JAPANESE-AMERICAN EVACUATION.
Ages 9-12. 910, Vol. 1

Viorst, Judith. ROSIE AND MICHAEL.
Ages 4-7. 929, Vol. 1

White, Dori. SARAH AND KATIE.
Ages 9-11. 966, Vol. 1

White, Elwyn Brooks. CHARLOTTE'S WEB.
Ages 8-12. 967, Vol. 1

Winthrop, Elizabeth. WALKING AWAY.
Ages 11 and up. 979, Vol. 1

## Lying

**See:** *Honesty/Dishonesty; Values/Valuing*

# M

## Magical Thinking

**See also:** *Daydreaming; Fantasy formation; Imaginary
friend; Imagination; Reality testing; Wishes*
Corcoran, Barbara. MAKE NO SOUND.
Ages 10-13. 181, Vol. 2

Dolan, Sheila. THE WISHING BOTTLE.
Ages 7-9. 167, Vol. 3

Goff, Beth. WHERE IS DADDY? THE STORY OF A
DIVORCE.
Ages 4-8. 363, Vol. 1

Harris, Mark Jonathan. WITH A WAVE OF THE
WAND.
Ages 9-12. 267, Vol. 3

Lorenzo, Carol Lee. MAMA'S GHOSTS.
Ages 10-12. 586, Vol. 1

## Maturation (cont.)

## Maturation (cont.)

Love, Sandra Weller. MELISSA'S MEDLEY.
Ages 10-13. 418, Vol. 2

Lowry, Lois. ANASTASIA KRUPNIK.
Ages 9-11. 386, Vol. 3

Luger, Harriett Mandelay. THE ELEPHANT TREE.
Ages 12 and up. 424, Vol. 2

McCloskey, Robert. ONE MORNING IN MAINE.
Ages 5-8. 595, Vol. 1

McCord, Jean. TURKEYLEGS THOMPSON.
Ages 11-14. 390, Vol. 3

McKillip, Patricia A. THE NIGHT GIFT.
Ages 11 and up. 430, Vol. 2

MacPherson, Margaret McLean. THE ROUGH ROAD.
Ages 12 and up. 600, Vol. 1

Madison, Winifred. GETTING OUT.
Ages 12 and up. 437, Vol. 2

Marangell, Virginia J. GIANNA MIA.
Ages 12-15. 402, Vol. 3

Mason, Miriam Evangeline. STEVIE AND HIS
SEVEN ORPHANS.
Ages 8-10. 616, Vol. 1

Matthews, Ellen. GETTING RID OF ROGER.
Ages 8-10. 466, Vol. 2

May, Julian. MAN AND WOMAN.
Ages 9-12. 623, Vol. 1

Mazer, Norma Fox. UP IN SETH'S ROOM.
Ages 13 and up. 415, Vol. 3

Means, Florence Crannell. US MALTBYS.
Ages 12 and up. 630, Vol. 1

Meyer, Carolyn. C. C. POINDEXTER.
Ages 12 and up. 453, Vol. 2

Miles, Betty. JUST THE BEGINNING.
Ages 10-12. 456, Vol. 2

Miles, Betty. LOOKING ON.
Ages 11-14. 457, Vol. 2

Miles, Betty. THE TROUBLE WITH THIRTEEN.
Ages 9-13. 424, Vol. 3

Moeri, Louise. FIRST THE EGG.
Ages 12 and up. 438, Vol. 3

Morgan, Alison. PETE.
Ages 11-13. 646, Vol. 1

Myers, Walter Dean. FAST SAM, COOL CLYDE, AND
STUFF.
Ages 11-14. 469, Vol. 2

Myers, Walter Dean. HOOPS.
Ages 12 and up. 459, Vol. 3

Myers, Walter Dean. WON'T KNOW TILL I GET
THERE.
Ages 11-14. 460, Vol. 3

Naylor, Phyllis Reynolds. A STRING OF CHANCES.
Ages 12 and up. 464, Vol. 3

Naylor, Phyllis Reynolds. WALKING THROUGH THE
DARK.
Ages 12 and up. 473, Vol. 2

Neigoff, Mike. IT WILL NEVER BE THE SAME
AGAIN.
Ages 12-14. 465, Vol. 3

Newton, Suzanne. M.V. SEXTON SPEAKING.
Ages 11 and up. 466, Vol. 3

Nöstlinger, Christine. FLY AWAY HOME.
Ages 10-13. 481, Vol. 2

Nöstlinger, Christine. GIRL MISSING: A NOVEL.
Ages 11 and up. 482, Vol. 3

O'Connor, Jane. YOURS TILL NIAGARA FALLS,
ABBY.
Ages 8-10. 467, Vol. 3

O'Hara, Mary, pseud. MY FRIEND FLICKA.
Ages 11 and up. 683, Vol. 1

Okimoto, Jean Davies. IT'S JUST TOO MUCH.
Ages 10-12. 469, Vol. 3

Oneal, Zibby. THE LANGUAGE OF GOLDFISH.
Ages 11-14. 473, Vol. 3

Pascal, Francine. MY FIRST LOVE & OTHER
DISASTERS.
Ages 12 and up. 484, Vol. 3

Paterson, Katherine Womeldorf. JACOB HAVE I
LOVED.
Ages 12 and up. 485, Vol. 3

Paulsen, Gary. THE FOXMAN.
Ages 11-14. 495, Vol. 2

Peck, Richard. FATHER FIGURE: A NOVEL.
Ages 11 and up. 501, Vol. 2

Peck, Robert Newton. A DAY NO PIGS WOULD DIE.
Ages 12 and up. 697, Vol. 1

Pedersen, Elsa Kienitz. FISHERMAN'S CHOICE.
Ages 12 and up. 698, Vol. 1

Petersen, P. J. WOULD YOU SETTLE FOR
IMPROBABLE?
Ages 11-13. 495, Vol. 3

Pevsner, Stella. AND YOU GIVE ME A PAIN,
ELAINE.
Ages 10-13. 508, Vol. 2

Pevsner, Stella. A SMART KID LIKE YOU.
Ages 10-13. 510, Vol. 2

Peyton, K.M., pseud. PENNINGTON'S HEIR.
Ages 12 and up. 705, Vol. 1

Pfeffer, Susan Beth. MARLY THE KID.
Ages 11-13. 512, Vol. 2

Platt, Kin. BROGG'S BRAIN.
Ages 12 and up. 514, Vol. 3

Pollowitz, Melinda. CINNAMON CANE.
Ages 10-12. 519, Vol. 2

Potok, Chaim. THE CHOSEN.
Ages 13 and up. 715, Vol. 1

Potter, Marian. THE SHARED ROOM.
Ages 10-12. 517, Vol. 3

Rabe, Berniece Louise. NAOMI.
Ages 12 and up. 527, Vol. 2

Radley, Gail. NOTHING STAYS THE SAME
FOREVER.
Ages 9-12. 524, Vol. 3

Rees, David. RISKS.
Ages 11 and up. 529, Vol. 2

Reiss, Johanna. THE JOURNEY BACK.
Ages 10-14. 530, Vol. 2

Richard, Adrienne. INTO THE ROAD.
Ages 12 and up. 537, Vol. 2

Richard, Adrienne. PISTOL.
Ages 12 and up. 732, Vol. 1

Richardson, Grace. APPLES EVERY DAY.
Ages 12 and up. 733, Vol. 1

Rock, Gail. ADDIE AND THE KING OF HEARTS.
Ages 9-12. 550, Vol. 2

Rogers, Pamela. THE STONE ANGEL.
Ages 10-12. 558, Vol. 2

Ruhen, Olaf. CORCORAN'S THE NAME.
Ages 12 and up. 758, Vol. 1

Sachs, Marilyn. CLASS PICTURES.
Ages 10-13. 564, Vol. 3

Sachs, Marilyn. A SUMMER'S LEASE.
Ages 11-14. 566, Vol. 3

Sallis, Susan Diana. A TIME FOR EVERYTHING.
Ages 13 and up. 569, Vol. 3

Samson, Joan. WATCHING THE NEW BABY.
Ages 9-11. 767, Vol. 1

Sargent, Sarah. EDWARD TROY AND THE WITCH
CAT.
Ages 9-11. 569, Vol. 2

Sargent, Sarah. SECRET LIES.
Ages 11 and up. 570, Vol. 3

Schoen, Barbara. A PLACE AND A TIME.
Ages 12 and up. 784, Vol. 1

Sebestyen, Ouida. FAR FROM HOME.
Ages 12 and up. 579, Vol. 3

Seredy, Kate. THE GOOD MASTER.
Ages 9-12. 802, Vol. 1

## Mental Illness (cont.)

### of Child. See also: Autism

### of Parent

## Mental Retardation

## Mental Retardation (cont.)

Mazer, Harry. THE WAR ON VILLA STREET: A NOVEL.
Ages 11-13. 448, Vol. 2

Miner, Jane Claypool. SHE'S MY SISTER: HAVING A RETARDED SISTER.
Ages 11 and up. 434, Vol. 3

Peck, Robert Newton. CLUNIE.
Ages 12 and up. 491, Vol. 3

Posner, Grace. IN MY SISTER'S EYES.
Ages 12 and up. 516, Vol. 3

Reynolds, Pamela. A DIFFERENT KIND OF SISTER.
Ages 12 and up. 729, Vol. 1

Rinaldo, C. L. DARK DREAMS.
Ages 11 and up. 734, Vol. 1

Rogers, Dale Evans. ANGEL UNAWARE.
Ages 12 and up. 750, Vol. 1

Ruby, Lois. TWO TRUTHS IN MY POCKET.
Ages 12 and up. 557, Vol. 3

Sallis, Susan Diana. A TIME FOR EVERYTHING.
Ages 13 and up. 569, Vol. 3

Shyer, Marlene Fanta. WELCOME HOME, JELLYBEAN.
Ages 10-13. 598, Vol. 2

Slepian, Jan. THE ALFRED SUMMER.
Ages 11-13. 603, Vol. 3

Slepian, Jan. LESTER'S TURN.
Ages 11-14. 604, Vol. 3

Smith, Gene. THE HAYBURNERS.
Ages 9-12. 833, Vol. 1

Sobol, Harriet Langsam. MY BROTHER STEVEN IS RETARDED.
Ages 7-10. 618, Vol. 2

Wartski, Maureen Crane. MY BROTHER IS SPECIAL.
Ages 10-12. 681, Vol. 3

Wright, Betty Ren. MY SISTER IS DIFFERENT.
Ages 6-9. 711, Vol. 3

Wrightson, Patricia. A RACECOURSE FOR ANDY.
Ages 9-12. 1007, Vol. 1

**Down's syndrome.** *See: Down's syndrome*

## Messiness

Bottner, Barbara. MESSY.
Ages 4-7. 68, Vol. 3

Dickinson, Mary. ALEX'S BED.
Ages 3-6. 163, Vol. 3

Drescher, Joan Elizabeth. THE MARVELOUS MESS.
Ages 4-6. 172, Vol. 3

## Mexican-American

Alexander, Anne. TROUBLE ON TREAT STREET.
Ages 10-12. 7, Vol. 1

Bonham, Frank. VIVA CHICANO.
Ages 12 and up. 99, Vol. 1

Ets, Marie Hall. BAD BOY, GOOD BOY.
Ages 6-10. 292, Vol. 1

Lampman, Evelyn Sibley. GO UP THE ROAD.
Ages 9-12. 526, Vol. 1

Madison, Winifred. MARIA LUISA.
Ages 9-12. 607, Vol. 1

O'Dell, Scott. ZIA.
Ages 10 and up. 486, Vol. 2

Smith, Nancy Covert. JOSIE'S HANDFUL OF QUIETNESS.
Ages 9-11. 614, Vol. 2

Stolz, Mary Slattery. CIDER DAYS.
Ages 8-11. 626, Vol. 2

Tester, Sylvia Root. WE LAUGHED A LOT, MY FIRST DAY OF SCHOOL.
Ages 3-6. 650, Vol. 3

## Middle Child

**See:** *Sibling: middle*

## Migrant Workers

Bridgers, Sue Ellen. HOME BEFORE DARK.
Ages 12 and up. 81, Vol. 2

Cleaver, Vera and Bill Cleaver. THE MOCK REVOLT.
Ages 10-14. 202, Vol. 1

Gates, Doris. BLUE WILLOW.
Ages 9-11. 348, Vol. 1

Lampman, Evelyn Sibley. GO UP THE ROAD.
Ages 9-12. 526, Vol. 1

Smith, Nancy Covert. JOSIE'S HANDFUL OF QUIETNESS.
Ages 9-11. 614, Vol. 2

Strang, Celia. FOSTER MARY.
Ages 10-13. 633, Vol. 3

Taylor, Theodore. THE MALDONADO MIRACLE.
Ages 11-13. 889, Vol. 1

## Minding

**See:** *Discipline, meaning of*

## Minor, Emancipation of

**See:** *Emancipation of minor*

## Minority Groups

**See:** *Differences, human; Prejudice; Specific group (e.g. Afro-American; Native American)*

## Mistakes, Making

Lexau, Joan M. I SHOULD HAVE STAYED IN BED!
Ages 6-8. 557, Vol. 1

## Misunderstandings

**See:** *Communication: misunderstandings*

## Mixed Marriage

**See:** *Marriage: interracial; Marriage: interreligious*

## Money

Shanks, Ann Zane. OLD IS WHAT YOU GET: DIALOGUES ON AGING BY THE OLD AND THE YOUNG.
Ages 10 and up. 582, Vol. 2

**Earning.** *See also: Job*

Bates, Betty. LOVE IS LIKE PEANUTS.
Ages 10-14. 38, Vol. 3

Bonham, Frank. COOL CAT.
Ages 12 and up. 96, Vol. 1

Bonham, Frank. THE NITTY GRITTY.
Ages 12 and up. 98, Vol. 1

Dolan, Sheila. THE WISHING BOTTLE.
Ages 7-9. 167, Vol. 3

First, Julia. LOOK WHO'S BEAUTIFUL!
Ages 10-12. 188, Vol. 3

Hall, Lynn. THE SIEGE OF SILENT HENRY.
Ages 12 and up. 392, Vol. 1

Hoban, Lillian Aberman. ARTHUR'S FUNNY MONEY.
Ages 6-8. 294, Vol. 3

Hurwitz, Johanna. SUPERDUPER TEDDY.
Ages 4-7. 318, Vol. 3

Lowry, Lois. ANASTASIA AT YOUR SERVICE.
Ages 9-12. 385, Vol. 3

Molarsky, Osmond. WHERE THE GOOD LUCK WAS.
Ages 8-10. 641, Vol. 1

Naylor, Phyllis Reynolds. EDDIE, INCORPORATED.
Ages 9-11. 463, Vol. 3

Neigoff, Mike. IT WILL NEVER BE THE SAME AGAIN.
Ages 12-14. 465, Vol. 3

Phipson, Joan Nash, pseud. THE FAMILY CONSPIRACY.
Ages 10-13. 708, Vol. 1

## Muteness (cont.)

Whelan, Gloria. A TIME TO KEEP SILENT.
Ages 11-14. 690, Vol. 3
White, Elwyn Brooks. THE TRUMPET OF THE SWAN.
Ages 9-13. 968, Vol. 1

# N

## Name, Dissatisfaction with

Alexander, Martha G. SABRINA.
Ages 3-7. 10, Vol. 1
Clifton, Lucille. SONORA BEAUTIFUL.
Ages 12-14. 123, Vol. 3
Conford, Ellen. ANYTHING FOR A FRIEND.
Ages 9-11. 136, Vol. 3
Gessner, Lynne. MALCOLM YUCCA SEED.
Ages 8-10. 246, Vol. 2
Grant, Cynthia D. JOSHUA FORTUNE.
Ages 10-13. 229, Vol. 3
Grant, Eva. I HATE MY NAME.
Ages 5-8. 230, Vol. 3
Hunt, Mabel Leigh. LITTLE GIRL WITH SEVEN NAMES.
Ages 7-10. 439, Vol. 1
Hurwitz, Johanna. ALDO APPLESAUCE.
Ages 7-9. 316, Vol. 3
Mosel, Arlene. TIKKI TIKKI TEMBO.
Ages 4-9. 650, Vol. 1
Rice, Eve. EBBIE.
Ages 3-7. 534, Vol. 2
Waber, Bernard. BUT NAMES WILL NEVER HURT ME.
Ages 4-8. 668, Vol. 2

## Name-Calling

**See also:** *Aggression; Nicknames; Teasing*

Bottner, Barbara. MEAN MAXINE.
Ages 4-6. 67, Vol. 3
Brown, Marc Tolan. ARTHUR'S EYES.
Ages 4-7. 80, Vol. 3
Christopher, Matthew F. JOHNNY LONG LEGS.
Ages 9-11. 184, Vol. 1
Crayder, Dorothy. ISHKABIBBLE!
Ages 9-12. 185, Vol. 2
De Paola, Thomas Anthony. OLIVER BUTTON IS A SISSY.
Ages 4-7. 161, Vol. 3
Greene, Constance Clarke. THE EARS OF LOUIS.
Ages 8-11. 377, Vol. 1
Hoban, Russell Conwell. HARVEY'S HIDEOUT.
Ages 5-8. 420, Vol. 1
Lee, Mildred Scudder. THE SKATING RINK.
Ages 10-13. 536, Vol. 1
Mazer, Norma Fox. MRS. FISH, APE, AND ME, THE DUMP QUEEN.
Ages 10-12. 414, Vol. 3
Panek, Dennis. MATILDA HIPPO HAS A BIG MOUTH.
Ages 4-7. 478, Vol. 3
Philips, Barbara. DON'T CALL ME FATSO.
Ages 5-9. 507, Vol. 1
Slote, Alfred. RABBIT EARS.
Ages 10-12. 606, Vol. 3
Sneve, Virginia Driving Hawk. JIMMY YELLOW HAWK.
Ages 8-10. 834, Vol. 1
Stolz, Mary Slattery. THE BULLY OF BARKHAM STREET.
Ages 8-11. 863, Vol. 1

## Narcotic Habit

**See:** *Drugs*

## Native American

Balch, Glenn. BRAVE RIDERS.
Ages 10-13. 47, Vol. 1
Bannon, Laura May. WHEN THE MOON IS NEW: A SEMINOLE INDIAN STORY.
Ages 5-9. 51, Vol. 1
Baylor, Byrd. HAWK, I'M YOUR BROTHER.
Ages 5-8. 45, Vol. 2
Beatty, Hetty Burlingame. LITTLE OWL INDIAN.
Ages 4-7. 59, Vol. 1
Bonham, Frank. CHIEF.
Ages 11 and up. 95, Vol. 1
Butler, Beverly Kathleen. A GIRL CALLED WENDY.
Ages 12 and up. 106, Vol. 2
Chandler, Edna Walker. INDIAN PAINTBRUSH.
Ages 9-11. 126, Vol. 2
Clark, Ann Nolan. LITTLE NAVAJO BLUEBIRD.
Ages 9-12. 186, Vol. 1
Coates, Belle. MAK.
Ages 12 and up. 124, Vol. 3
Conklin, Paul. CHOCTAW BOY.
Ages 9-12. 176, Vol. 2
Distad, Audree. DAKOTA SONS.
Ages 9-11. 275, Vol. 1
Duncan, Lois, pseud. SEASON OF THE TWO-HEART.
Ages 12 and up. 278, Vol. 1
Dyer, Thomas A. THE WHIPMAN IS WATCHING.
Ages 10-14. 177, Vol. 3
Embry, Margaret Jacob. MY NAME IS LION.
Ages 9-11. 288, Vol. 1
Fife, Dale. RIDE THE CROOKED WIND.
Ages 10-12. 312, Vol. 1
Fowler, Carol. DAISY HOOEE NAMPEYO.
Ages 11 and up. 233, Vol. 2
Fredericksen, Hazel. HE-WHO-RUNS-FAR.
Ages 10-13. 331, Vol. 1
Gessner, Lynne. MALCOLM YUCCA SEED.
Ages 8-10. 246, Vol. 2
Griese, Arnold Alfred. AT THE MOUTH OF THE LUCKIEST RIVER.
Ages 8-11. 385, Vol. 1
Griese, Arnold Alfred. THE WAY OF OUR PEOPLE.
Ages 9-12. 275, Vol. 2
Hamilton, Virginia. ARILLA SUN DOWN.
Ages 12 and up. 291, Vol. 2
Hassler, Jon Francis. JEMMY.
Ages 11 and up. 270, Vol. 3
Hood, Flora Mae. SOMETHING FOR THE MEDICINE MAN.
Ages 7-10. 431, Vol. 1
Houston, James Archibald. RIVER RUNNERS: A TALE OF HARDSHIP AND BRAVERY.
Ages 11 and up. 306, Vol. 3
Jones, Weyman B. EDGE OF TWO WORLDS.
Ages 10 and up. 471, Vol. 1
Knudson, R. Rozanne. FOX RUNNING: A NOVEL.
Ages 11 and up. 386, Vol. 2
Laing, Frederick. THE BRIDE WORE BRAIDS.
Ages 12 and up. 525, Vol. 1
Lampman, Evelyn Sibley. HALF-BREED.
Ages 10-12. 527, Vol. 1
Lampman, Evelyn Sibley. THE YEAR OF SMALL SHADOW.
Ages 10-12. 528, Vol. 1
Leech, Jay and Zane Spencer. BRIGHT FAWN AND ME.
Ages 4-8. 361, Vol. 3
Lockett, Sharon. NO MOCCASINS TODAY.
Ages 11-13. 578, Vol. 1
Maher, Ramona. ALICE YAZZIE'S YEAR.
Ages 9-12. 439, Vol. 2
Means, Florence Crannell. OUR CUP IS BROKEN.
Ages 12 and up. 629, Vol. 1

## Native American (cont.)

Miles, Miska, pseud. ANNIE AND THE OLD ONE.
Ages 6-9. 638, Vol. 1

Miner, Jane Claypool. NAVAJO VICTORY: BEING A NATIVE AMERICAN.
Ages 11 and up. 432, Vol. 3

Naylor, Phyllis Reynolds. TO WALK THE SKY PATH.
Ages 10-13. 658, Vol. 1

Nelson, Mary Carroll. MICHAEL NARANJO: THE STORY OF AN AMERICAN INDIAN.
Ages 9-12. 476, Vol. 2

O'Dell, Scott. ISLAND OF THE BLUE DOLPHINS.
Ages 10 and up. 681, Vol. 1

Perrine, Mary. NANNABAH'S FRIEND.
Ages 7-10. 702, Vol. 1

Perrine, Mary. SALT BOY.
Ages 7-10. 703, Vol. 1

Sandoz, Mari. THE HORSECATCHER.
Ages 12 and up. 771, Vol. 1

Sneve, Virginia Driving Hawk. JIMMY YELLOW HAWK.
Ages 8-10. 834, Vol. 1

Strete, Craig Kee. PAINT YOUR FACE ON A DROWNING IN THE RIVER.
Ages 12 and up. 629, Vol. 2

Udry, Janice May. THE SUNFLOWER GARDEN.
Ages 6-10. 913, Vol. 1

Waterton, Betty Marie. A SALMON FOR SIMON.
Ages 4-7. 685, Vol. 3

## Nature

### Appreciation of

Aaron, Chester. SPILL.
Ages 12-14. 1, Vol. 2

Annixter, Jane, pseud. and Paul Annixter, pseud. HORNS OF PLENTY.
Ages 11 and up. 23, Vol. 1

Beatty, Hetty Burlingame. LITTLE OWL INDIAN.
Ages 4-7. 59, Vol. 1

Bell, Frederic. JENNY'S CORNER.
Ages 8-11. 65, Vol. 1

Bourne, Miriam Anne. RACCOONS ARE FOR LOVING.
Ages 6-9. 106, Vol. 1

Boutis, Victoria. KATY DID IT.
Ages 8-10. 69, Vol. 3

Caudill, Rebecca. A POCKETFUL OF CRICKET.
Ages 4-7. 175, Vol. 1

Dahl, Roald. DANNY: THE CHAMPION OF THE WORLD.
Ages 10 and up. 189, Vol. 2

Delton, Judy. A WALK ON A SNOWY NIGHT.
Ages 5-8. 158, Vol. 3

Dragonwagon, Crescent. WHEN LIGHT TURNS INTO NIGHT.
Ages 4-7. 206, Vol. 2

Ernst, Kathryn. MR. TAMARIN'S TREES.
Ages 5-8. 218, Vol. 2

Ets, Marie Hall. PLAY WITH ME.
Ages 3-7. 293, Vol. 1

Ferry, Charles. UP IN SISTER BAY.
Ages 12 and up. 226, Vol. 2

Fisher, Aileen Lucia. BEST LITTLE HOUSE.
Ages 5-8. 315, Vol. 1

Fisher, Aileen Lucia. I STOOD UPON A MOUNTAIN.
Ages 4-8. 189, Vol. 3

Fisher, Aileen Lucia. MY MOTHER AND I.
Ages 5-8. 316, Vol. 1

Gallico, Paul. THE SNOW GOOSE.
Ages 12 and up. 342, Vol. 1

Gauch, Patricia Lee. GRANDPA AND ME.
Ages 5-8. 351, Vol. 1

Gelman, Rita Golden and Warner Friedman. UNCLE HUGH: A FISHING STORY.
Ages 5-8. 244, Vol. 2

George, Jean Craighead. MY SIDE OF THE MOUNTAIN.
Ages 11-14. 354, Vol. 1

Hood, Flora Mae. SOMETHING FOR THE MEDICINE MAN.
Ages 7-10. 431, Vol. 1

Hoopes, Lyn Littlefield. NANA.
Ages 5-8. 302, Vol. 3

Kesselman, Wendy Ann. ANGELITA.
Ages 5-9. 494, Vol. 1

Lapp, Eleanor J. IN THE MORNING MIST.
Ages 4-8. 392, Vol. 2

Lasky, Kathryn. MY ISLAND GRANDMA.
Ages 4-7. 359, Vol. 3

Lipp, Frederick J. SOME LOSE THEIR WAY.
Ages 10-13. 377, Vol. 2

McNulty, Faith. MOUSE AND TIM.
Ages 5-7. 433, Vol. 2

Meeks, Esther K. and Elizabeth Bagwell. HOW NEW LIFE BEGINS.
Ages 4-8. 632, Vol. 1

North, Sterling. RASCAL: A MEMOIR OF A BETTER ERA.
Ages 11 and up. 680, Vol. 1

Phelan, Terry Wolfe. THE WEEK MOM UNPLUGGED THE TVS.
Ages 8-10. 506, Vol. 3

Phipson, Joan Nash, pseud. FLY FREE.
Ages 11 and up. 508, Vol. 3

Rawlings, Marjorie Kinnan. THE YEARLING.
Ages 12 and up. 725, Vol. 1

Robertson, Keith. IN SEARCH OF A SANDHILL CRANE.
Ages 11 and up. 743, Vol. 1

Ruhen, Olaf. CORCORAN'S THE NAME.
Ages 12 and up. 758, Vol. 1

Shura, Mary Frances Craig. THE SEASON OF SILENCE.
Ages 10-14. 597, Vol. 2

Stolz, Mary Slattery. GO AND CATCH A FLYING FISH.
Ages 10-13. 630, Vol. 3

Tate, Joan. LUKE'S GARDEN AND GRAMP: TWO NOVELS.
Ages 10-13. 644, Vol. 3

Taylor, Mildred D. SONG OF THE TREES.
Ages 8-11. 637, Vol. 2

Weiss, Nicki. WAITING.
Ages 3-5. 688, Vol. 3

Wood, Joyce. GRANDMOTHER LUCY IN HER GARDEN.
Ages 4-8. 707, Vol. 2

Zolotow, Charlotte Shapiro. ONE STEP, TWO...
Ages 2-5. 724, Vol. 3

Zolotow, Charlotte Shapiro. WHEN THE WIND STOPS.
Ages 5-7. 722, Vol. 2

Zolotow, Charlotte Shapiro. THE WHITE MARBLE.
Ages 4-8. 725, Vol. 3

Zweifel, Frances William. BONY.
Ages 6-7. 723, Vol. 2

### Living in harmony with

Annixter, Paul, pseud. SWIFTWATER.
Ages 13 and up. 26, Vol. 1

Baylor, Byrd. HAWK, I'M YOUR BROTHER.
Ages 5-8. 45, Vol. 2

Bond, Nancy Barbara. THE VOYAGE BEGUN.
Ages 12 and up. 60, Vol. 3

George, Jean Craighead. MY SIDE OF THE MOUNTAIN.
Ages 11-14. 354, Vol. 1

## Nature (cont.)

Houston, James Archibald. RIVER RUNNERS: A
TALE OF HARDSHIP AND BRAVERY.
Ages 11 and up. 306, Vol. 3
Mazer, Harry. THE ISLAND KEEPER.
Ages 10-14. 412, Vol. 3
Morey, Walter. HOME IS THE NORTH.
Ages 12 and up. 644, Vol. 1
Reader, Dennis J. COMING BACK ALIVE.
Ages 12 and up. 525, Vol. 3
Thiele, Colin Milton. STORM BOY.
Ages 8-11. 646, Vol. 2
Whelan, Gloria. A TIME TO KEEP SILENT.
Ages 11-14. 690, Vol. 3

### Respect for

Annixter, Paul, pseud. SWIFTWATER.
Ages 13 and up. 26, Vol. 1
Byars, Betsy Cromer. THE HOUSE OF WINGS.
Ages 9-12. 156, Vol. 1
Callen, Lawrence Willard. SORROW'S SONG.
Ages 9-12. 103, Vol. 3
Dodd, Wayne. A TIME OF HUNTING.
Ages 11-14. 204, Vol. 2
Ernst, Kathryn. MR. TAMARIN'S TREES.
Ages 5-8. 218, Vol. 2
Gackenbach, Dick. DO YOU LOVE ME?
Ages 5-8. 238, Vol. 2
Holmes, Efner Tudor. AMY'S GOOSE.
Ages 8-11. 330, Vol. 2
Houston, James Archibald. LONG CLAWS: AN
ARCTIC ADVENTURE.
Ages 9-11. 305, Vol. 3
Lipp, Frederick J. SOME LOSE THEIR WAY.
Ages 10-13. 377, Vol. 3
McPhail, David Michael. A WOLF STORY.
Ages 5-7. 399, Vol. 3
Paulsen, Gary. THE FOXMAN.
Ages 11-14. 495, Vol. 2
Raymond, Charles. JUD.
Ages 9-12. 726, Vol. 1
Robertson, Keith. IN SEARCH OF A SANDHILL
CRANE.
Ages 11 and up. 743, Vol. 1
Thiele, Colin Milton. STORM BOY.
Ages 8-11. 646, Vol. 2
Waterton, Betty Marie. A SALMON FOR SIMON.
Ages 4-7. 685, Vol. 3

## Naughty Child

See: *Discipline, meaning of*

## Negative Attitude

See: *Inferiority, feelings of; Shame*

## Neglect

See: *Chores; Job; Parental: negligence; Responsibility: neglecting*

## Neglected Child

See: *Abandonment; Deprivation, emotional; Parental: negligence*

## Negro

See: *Afro-American*

## Neighbors/Neighborhood

See also: *Cooperation*
Conta, Marcia Maher and Maureen
Reardon. FEELINGS BETWEEN KIDS AND
GROWNUPS.
Ages 3-6. 243, Vol. 1
Franco, Marjorie. SO WHO HASN'T GOT
PROBLEMS?
Ages 10-12. 194, Vol. 3

Green, Phyllis. MILDRED MURPHY, HOW DOES
YOUR GARDEN GROW?
Ages 9-11. 263, Vol. 2
Lenski, Lois. STRAWBERRY GIRL.
Ages 9-11. 545, Vol. 1
McNeill, Janet. GOODBYE, DOVE SQUARE.
Ages 10-13. 599, Vol. 1
Mann, Peggy. THE STREET OF THE FLOWER
BOXES.
Ages 8-11. 610, Vol. 1
Mohr, Nicholasa. IN NUEVA YORK.
Ages 13 and up. 462, Vol. 2
Myers, Walter Dean. THE YOUNG LANDLORDS.
Ages 11-14. 461, Vol. 3
Seredy, Kate. A TREE FOR PETER.
Ages 9-12. 804, Vol. 1
Shura, Mary Francis Craig. THE BARKLEY STREET
SIX-PACK.
Ages 9-12. 592, Vol. 3
Shura, Mary Francis Craig. CHESTER.
Ages 8-10. 593, Vol. 3

## Nervous Breakdown

See: *Mental illness*

## Neurosis

See: *Mental illness*

## New Baby

See: *Sibling: new baby*

## New Home

See: *Change: new home; Moving*

## Nicknames

See also: *Name-calling*
Beim, Jerrold. THE SMALLEST BOY IN THE CLASS.
Ages 5-8. 64, Vol. 1

## Nightmares

See also: *Daydreaming; Dreams; Fear*
Anderson, Mary Quirk. STEP ON A CRACK.
Ages 12 and up. 18, Vol. 2
Holland, Isabelle. NOW IS NOT TOO LATE.
Ages 10-13. 301, Vol. 3
Hunter, Mollie, pseud. A SOUND OF CHARIOTS.
Ages 12 and up. 444, Vol. 1
Kingman, Lee. HEAD OVER WHEELS.
Ages 12 and up. 383, Vol. 2
Mayer, Mercer. THERE'S A NIGHTMARE IN MY
CLOSET.
Ages 3-7. 624, Vol. 1
Nardine, Elisabeth. DAYDREAMS AND NIGHT.
Ages 4-7. 472, Vol. 2
Tester, Sylvia Root. SOMETIMES I'M AFRAID.
Ages 3-5. 649, Vol. 3

## Nursery School

See also: *Day-care center, going to*
Rockwell, Harlow. MY NURSERY SCHOOL.
Ages 3-5. 553, Vol. 2
Wolde, Gunilla. BETSY'S FIRST DAY AT NURSERY
SCHOOL.
Ages 2-5. 699, Vol. 2

## Nursing Home, Living in

Blue, Rose. GRANDMA DIDN'T WAVE BACK.
Ages 8-11. 82, Vol. 1
Clifford, Ethel Rosenberg. THE ROCKING CHAIR
REBELLION.
Ages 11-13. 142, Vol. 2
Hull, Eleanor Means. ALICE WITH GOLDEN HAIR.
Ages 11 and up. 311, Vol. 3

# O

## Obedience/Disobedience

**See:** *Discipline, meaning of*

## Obesity

**See:** *Weight control: overweight*

## Old Age

**See:** *Age*

## Oldest Child

**See:** *Sibling: oldest*

## One-Parent Home

**See:** *Parent/Parents: single*

## Only Child

## Operation

**See:** *Hospital, going to; Surgery*

## Orphan

## Parent/Parents (cont.)

## Respect for/Lack of respect for

Separation of. *See: Separation, marital*

## Single

**Parent/Parents (cont.)**

Bates, Betty. THAT'S WHAT T.J. SAYS.
  Ages 9-11. 41, Vol. 3
Berman, Claire. WHAT AM I DOING IN A STEP-FAMILY?
  Ages 5-10. 51, Vol. 3
Bonham, Frank. DURANGO STREET.
  Ages 11 and up. 97, Vol. 1
Bonsall, Crosby Newell. THE GOODBYE SUMMER.
  Ages 9-11. 63, Vol. 3
Bradbury, Bianca. IN HER FATHER'S FOOTSTEPS.
  Ages 11 and up. 66, Vol. 2
Bradbury, Bianca. WHERE'S JIM NOW?
  Ages 11-13. 67, Vol. 2
Bragdon, Elspeth. THERE IS A TIDE.
  Ages 12 and up. 113, Vol. 1
Broderick, Dorothy M. HANK.
  Ages 11 and up. 122, Vol. 1
Buckley, Peter and Hortense Jones. WILLIAM, ANDY, AND RAMON.
  Ages 6-8. 133, Vol. 1
Bulla, Clyde Robert. THE SUGAR PEAR TREE.
  Ages 8-10. 137, Vol. 1
Bunting, Anne Evelyn. HIGH TIDE FOR LABRADOR.
  Ages 9-11. 95, Vol. 2
Butler, Beverly Kathleen. CAPTIVE THUNDER.
  Ages 11 and up. 150, Vol. 1
Butterworth, William Edmund. UNDER THE INFLUENCE.
  Ages 12 and up. 94, Vol. 3
Byars, Betsy Cromer. THE ANIMAL, THE VEGETABLE, AND JOHN D JONES.
  Ages 10-12. 95, Vol. 3
Byars, Betsy Cromer. THE NIGHT SWIMMERS.
  Ages 10-12. 98, Vol. 3
Byars, Betsy Cromer. THE TV KID.
  Ages 9-12. 109, Vol. 2
Chaffin, Lillie Dorton. WE BE WARM TILL SPRINGTIME COMES.
  Ages 6-9. 110, Vol. 3
Chetin, Helen. HOW FAR IS BERKELEY?
  Ages 11-13. 128, Vol. 2
Cohen, Barbara Nash. THE INNKEEPER'S DAUGHTER.
  Ages 11-14. 126, Vol. 3
Coles, Robert. DEAD END SCHOOL.
  Ages 9-11. 222, Vol. 1
Colman, Hila Crayder. DAUGHTER OF DISCONTENT.
  Ages 12 and up. 229, Vol. 1
Corcoran, Barbara. A ROW OF TIGERS.
  Ages 10-12. 250, Vol. 1
Dahl, Roald. DANNY: THE CHAMPION OF THE WORLD.
  Ages 10 and up. 189, Vol. 2
Dexter, Pat Egan. ARROW IN THE WIND.
  Ages 10-13. 200, Vol. 2
Ellis, Ella Thorp. CELEBRATE THE MORNING.
  Ages 12 and up. 286, Vol. 1
Ewing, Kathryn. A PRIVATE MATTER.
  Ages 8-10. 221, Vol. 2
Foley, June. IT'S NO CRUSH, I'M IN LOVE!
  Ages 11-13. 192, Vol. 3
Freeman, Gaail. OUT FROM UNDER.
  Ages 12 and up. 195, Vol. 3
Friermood, Elisabeth Hamilton. FOCUS THE BRIGHT LAND.
  Ages 11 and up. 337, Vol. 1
Gerber, Merrill Joan. PLEASE DON'T KISS ME NOW.
  Ages 13 and up. 206, Vol. 3
Gerson, Corinne. SON FOR A DAY.
  Ages 10-12. 208, Vol. 3

Gordon, Shirley. THE BOY WHO WANTED A FAMILY.
  Ages 7-9. 222, Vol. 3
Greene, Constance Clarke. AL(EXANDRA) THE GREAT.
  Ages 10-12. 239, Vol. 3
Greene, Constance Clarke. I KNOW YOU, AL.
  Ages 11 and up. 268, Vol. 2
Greene, Sheppard M. THE BOY WHO DRANK TOO MUCH.
  Ages 12 and up. 242, Vol. 3
Harmon, A. W. BASE HIT.
  Ages 9-12. 400, Vol. 1
Hoban, Lillian Aberman. I MET A TRAVELLER.
  Ages 10-12. 322, Vol. 2
Hopkins, Lee Bennett. MAMA & HER BOYS.
  Ages 8-11. 303, Vol. 3
Houston, James Archibald. FROZEN FIRE: A TALE OF COURAGE.
  Ages 10-13. 334, Vol. 2
Jacobs, Helen Hull. THE TENNIS MACHINE.
  Ages 12 and up. 455, Vol. 1
Johnson, Annabel Jones and Edgar Raymond Johnson. A GOLDEN TOUCH.
  Ages 11-14. 460, Vol. 1
Johnson, Annabel Jones and Edgar Raymond Johnson. WILDERNESS BRIDE.
  Ages 12 and up. 465, Vol. 1
Keith, Harold Verne. THE RUNT OF ROGERS SCHOOL.
  Ages 9-12. 487, Vol. 1
Kerr, M. E., pseud. IF I LOVE YOU, AM I TRAPPED FOREVER?
  Ages 12 and up. 492, Vol. 1
Kerr, M. E., pseud. THE SON OF SOMEONE FAMOUS.
  Ages 11 and up. 493, Vol. 1
Kingman, Lee. THE REFINER'S FIRE.
  Ages 12-14. 341, Vol. 3
Klein, Norma. BLUE TREES, RED SKY.
  Ages 7-10. 384, Vol. 2
Klein, Norma. MOM, THE WOLF MAN AND ME.
  Ages 11 and up. 505, Vol. 1
Klein, Norma. TAKING SIDES.
  Ages 10 and up. 506, Vol. 1
La Farge, Phyllis. JOANNA RUNS AWAY.
  Ages 7-9. 524, Vol. 1
LeShan, Eda J. WHAT'S GOING TO HAPPEN TO ME? WHEN PARENTS SEPARATE OR DIVORCE.
  Ages 8 and up. 402, Vol. 2
Lexau, Joan M. THE TROUBLE WITH TERRY.
  Ages 8-11. 560, Vol. 1
Lindsay, Jeanne Warren. DO I HAVE A DADDY? A STORY ABOUT A SINGLE-PARENT CHILD.
  Ages 4-8. 376, Vol. 3
Lyle, Katie Letcher. DARK BUT FULL OF DIAMONDS.
  Ages 12-14. 388, Vol. 3
Matthews, Ellen. GETTING RID OF ROGER.
  Ages 8-10. 446, Vol. 2
Mazer, Harry. THE DOLLAR MAN.
  Ages 12 and up. 626, Vol. 1
Mearian, Judy Frank. SOMEONE SLIGHTLY DIFFERENT.
  Ages 10-12. 417, Vol. 3
Moe, Barbara. PICKLES AND PRUNES.
  Ages 10-13. 461, Vol. 2
Murphy, Shirley Rousseau. POOR JENNY, BRIGHT AS A PENNY.
  Ages 10-13. 654, Vol. 1
North, Sterling. RASCAL: A MEMOIR OF A BETTER ERA.
  Ages 11 and up. 680, Vol. 1

## Parent/Parents (cont.)

Peck, Richard. DON'T LOOK AND IT WON'T HURT.
Ages 12 and up. 694, Vol. 1
Pegis, Jessie Corrigan. BEST FRIENDS: A CANADIAN STORY.
Ages 9-11. 699, Vol. 1
Peyton, K. M., pseud. MARION'S ANGELS.
Ages 11-14. 499, Vol. 3
Platt, Kin. CHLORIS AND THE WEIRDOS.
Ages 11 and up. 516, Vol. 2
Rodowsky, Colby F. H. MY NAME IS HENLEY.
Ages 10-13. 547, Vol. 3
Sargent, Sarah. EDWARD TROY AND THE WITCH CAT.
Ages 9-11. 569, Vol. 2
Schick, Eleanor Grossman. NEIGHBORHOOD KNIGHT.
Ages 5-7. 573, Vol. 2
Simon, Shirley. BEST FRIEND.
Ages 9-12. 824, Vol. 1
Skurzynski, Gloria Joan. MARTIN BY HIMSELF.
Ages 6-9. 602, Vol. 3
Slote, Alfred. MATT GARGAN'S BOY.
Ages 9-11. 611, Vol. 2
Smith, Doris Buchanan. KICK A STONE HOME.
Ages 11 and up. 830, Vol. 1
Smith, Doris Buchanan. TOUGH CHAUNCEY.
Ages 12 and up. 832, Vol. 1
Stanek, Muriel Novella. I WON'T GO WITHOUT A FATHER.
Ages 8-10. 850, Vol. 1
Strang, Celia. THIS CHILD IS MINE.
Ages 11-14. 634, Vol. 3
Taylor, Theodore. THE MALDONADO MIRACLE.
Ages 11-13. 889, Vol. 1
Taylor, Theodore. TEETONCEY.
Ages 10 and up. 890, Vol. 1
Teibl, Margaret. DAVEY COME HOME.
Ages 6-9. 646, Vol. 3
Thorvall, Kerstin. AND LEFFE WAS INSTEAD OF A DAD.
Ages 10 and up. 897, Vol. 1
Townsend, John Rowe. HELL'S EDGE.
Ages 12 and up. 901, Vol. 1
Ullman, James Ramsey. BANNER IN THE SKY.
Ages 12 and up. 915, Vol. 1
Van Steenwyk, Elizabeth Ann. RIVALS ON ICE.
Ages 9-11. 664, Vol. 3
Wagner, Jane. J.T.
Ages 8-10. 939, Vol. 1
Wojciechowska, Maia Rodman. "HEY, WHAT'S WRONG WITH THIS ONE?"
Ages 8-10. 983, Vol. 1
Zindel, Paul. I LOVE MY MOTHER.
Ages 3-7. 717, Vol. 2
Zolotow, Charlotte Shapiro. A FATHER LIKE THAT.
Ages 4-6. 1020, Vol. 1

**Stepparent.** *See: Parent/Parents: remarriage of; Stepparent*

**Substitute.** *See also: Foster home*
Ball, Zachary, pseud. BRISTLE FACE.
Ages 10 and up. 49, Vol. 1
Bulla, Clyde Robert. WHITE BIRD.
Ages 9 and up. 138, Vol. 1
Clark, Mavis Thorpe. IF THE EARTH FALLS IN.
Ages 11-14. 136, Vol. 2
Cohen, Barbara Nash THANK YOU, JACKIE ROBINSON.
Ages 10-13. 215, Vol. 1
Fisher, Dorothy Canfield. UNDERSTOOD BETSY.
Ages 9-12. 317, Vol. 1
Gerson, Corinne. SON FOR A DAY.
Ages 10-12. 208, Vol. 3

Greene, Bette. THE SUMMER OF MY GERMAN SOLDIER.
Ages 12 and up. 375, Vol. 1
Härtling, Peter. OMA.
Ages 8-11. 296, Vol. 2
Hunt, Irene. UP A ROAD SLOWLY.
Ages 12 and up. 438, Vol. 1
MacLachlan, Patricia. MAMA ONE, MAMA TWO.
Ages 4-7. 395, Vol. 3
Mazer, Norma Fox. MRS. FISH, APE, AND ME, THE DUMP QUEEN.
Ages 10-12. 414, Vol. 3
Seredy, Kate. THE GOOD MASTER.
Ages 9-12. 802, Vol. 1
Sherburne, Zoa. STRANGER IN THE HOUSE.
Ages 11 and up. 813, Vol. 1
Stolz, Mary Slattery. JUAN.
Ages 8-11. 868, Vol. 1
Terris, Susan Dubinsky. THE DROWNING BOY.
Ages 10 and up. 891, Vol. 1
Thorvall, Kerstin. AND LEFFE WAS INSTEAD OF A DAD.
Ages 10 and up. 897, Vol. 1
Wilkinson, Brenda Scott. LUDELL.
Ages 10-14. 680, Vol. 2
Wilkinson, Brenda Scott. LUDELL AND WILLIE.
Ages 12 and up. 681, Vol. 2

**Suicide of.** *See: Suicide: of parent*

**Unemployed**
Delton, Judy. MY MOTHER LOST HER JOB TODAY.
Ages 3-7. 156, Vol. 3
Hansen, Joyce. THE GIFT-GIVER.
Ages 9-12. 263, Vol. 3
Hazen, Barbara Shook. TIGHT TIMES.
Ages 5-7. 277, Vol. 3
Neigoff, Mike. IT WILL NEVER BE THE SAME AGAIN.
Ages 12-14. 465, Vol. 3
Nolan, Madeena Spray. MY DADDY DON'T GO TO WORK.
Ages 4-7. 480, Vol. 2

**Unwed father.** *See: Unwed father*

**Unwed mother.** *See: Unwed mother*

## Parental

**See also:** *Parent/Parents*

**Abandonment.** *See: Abandonment*

**Absence**
Alcock, Gudrun. DUFFY.
Ages 11-13. 4, Vol. 1
Ames, Mildred. NICKY AND THE JOYOUS NOISE.
Ages 9-12. 14, Vol. 3
Anckarsvärd, Karin. AUNT VINNIE'S VICTORIOUS SIX.
Ages 10-12. 14, Vol. 1
Arthur, Ruth M. MY DAUGHTER, NICOLA.
Ages 10-13. 33, Vol. 1
Bates, Betty. THAT'S WHAT T.J. SAYS.
Ages 9-11. 41, Vol. 3
Bawden, Nina Mary Kark. THE PEPPERMINT PIG.
Ages 9-14. 44, Vol. 2
Bonham, Frank. GIMME AN H, GIMME AN E, GIMME AN L, GIMME A P.
Ages 12 and up. 61, Vol. 3
Bridgers, Sue Ellen. NOTES FOR ANOTHER LIFE.
Ages 12 and up. 75, Vol. 3
Byars, Betsy Cromer. THE CYBIL WAR.
Ages 9-12. 96, Vol. 3
Byars, Betsy Cromer. THE TWO-THOUSAND-POUND GOLDFISH.
Ages 9-12. 99, Vol. 3

## Parental (cont.)

Campbell, Hope, pseud. NO MORE TRAINS TO
TOTTENVILLE.
Ages 12 and up. 161, Vol. 1

Carris, Joan Davenport. WHEN THE BOYS RAN THE
HOUSE.
Ages 8-12. 108, Vol. 3

Clifton, Lucille. AMIFIKA.
Ages 4-7. 143, Vol. 2

Clymer, Eleanor Lowenton. MY BROTHER STEVIE.
Ages 8-11. 213, Vol. 1

Dixon, Jeanne. LADY CAT LOST.
Ages 10-12. 164, Vol. 3

Elfman, Blossom. A HOUSE FOR JONNIE O.
Ages 12 and up. 215, Vol. 2

Fenton, Edward. DUFFY'S ROCKS.
Ages 12 and up. 311, Vol. 1

Fitzhugh, Louise. THE LONG SECRET.
Ages 9-12. 321, Vol. 1

Fox, Paula. PORTRAIT OF IVAN.
Ages 11 and up. 328, Vol. 1

Gerson, Corinne. SON FOR A DAY.
Ages 10-12. 208, Vol. 3

Greene, Constance Clarke. I KNOW YOU, AL.
Ages 11 and up. 268, Vol. 2

Greene, Constance Clarke. THE UNMAKING OF
RABBIT.
Ages 10-13. 380, Vol. 1

Hickman, Janet. THE STONES.
Ages 9-12. 314, Vol. 2

Irwin, Hadley, pseud. MOON AND ME.
Ages 11-14. 325, Vol. 3

Iwasaki, Chihiro. STAYING HOME ALONE ON A
RAINY DAY.
Ages 5-8. 452, Vol. 1

Lampman, Evelyn Sibley. HALF-BREED.
Ages 10-12. 527, Vol. 1

Levoy, Myron. A SHADOW LIKE A LEOPARD.
Ages 12 and up. 369, Vol. 1

Lindsay, Jeanne Warren. DO I HAVE A DADDY? A
STORY ABOUT A SINGLE-PARENT CHILD.
Ages 4-8. 376, Vol. 3

Lobel, Arnold. UNCLE ELEPHANT.
Ages 4-7. 381, Vol. 3

Matthews, Ellen. THE TROUBLE WITH LESLIE.
Ages 8-11. 409, Vol. 3

Mearian, Judy Frank. SOMEONE SLIGHTLY
DIFFERENT.
Ages 10-12. 417, Vol. 3

Morgan, Alison. PETE.
Ages 11-13. 646, Vol. 1

Parker, Richard. PAUL AND ETTA.
Ages 9-11. 689, Vol. 1

Peck, Richard. FATHER FIGURE: A NOVEL.
Ages 11 and up. 501, Vol. 2

Pedersen, Elsa Kienitz. FISHERMAN'S CHOICE.
Ages 12 and up. 698, Vol. 1

Potter, Marian. THE SHARED ROOM.
Ages 10-12. 517, Vol. 3

Rinaldo, C. L. DARK DREAMS.
Ages 11 and up. 734, Vol. 1

Rodowsky, Colby F. A SUMMER'S WORTH OF
SHAME.
Ages 12-14. 548, Vol. 3

Ruhen, Olaf. CORCORAN'S THE NAME.
Ages 12 and up. 758, Vol. 1

Sargent, Sarah. SECRET LIES.
Ages 11 and up. 570, Vol. 3

Shiefman, Vicky. MINDY.
Ages 8-10. 815, Vol. 1

Sonneborn, Ruth A. FRIDAY NIGHT IS PAPA
NIGHT.
Ages 5-8. 841, Vol. 1

Stren, Patti. THERE'S A RAINBOW IN MY CLOSET.
Ages 8-10. 638, Vol. 3

Uchida, Yoshiko. HISAKO'S MYSTERIES.
Ages 9-11. 909, Vol. 1

Uchida, Yoshiko. JOURNEY TO TOPAZ: A STORY OF
THE JAPANESE-AMERICAN EVACUATION.
Ages 9-12. 910, Vol. 1

Voigt, Cynthia. DICEY'S SONG.
Ages 11 and up. 671, Vol. 3

Weiman, Eiveen. IT TAKES BRAINS.
Ages 10-12. 686, Vol. 3

Zolotow, Charlotte Shapiro. IF YOU LISTEN.
Ages 5-7. 722, Vol. 3

**Abuse.** *See: Child abuse*

**Alcoholism.** *See: Alcoholism: of father; Alcoholism: of
mother; Alcoholism: of parents*

**Control.** *See also: Discipline, meaning of*

Burch, Robert Joseph. SIMON AND THE GAME OF
CHANCE.
Ages 10-12. 142, Vol. 1

Colman, Hila Crayder. DAUGHTER OF
DISCONTENT.
Ages 12 and up. 229, Vol. 1

Eyerly, Jeannette Hyde. DROP-OUT.
Ages 11 and up. 296, Vol. 1

First, Julia. MOVE OVER, BEETHOVEN.
Ages 10-13. 231, Vol. 2

Greenberg, Jan. THE PIG-OUT BLUES.
Ages 12 and up. 236, Vol. 3

Harmon, A. W. BASE HIT.
Ages 9-12. 400, Vol. 1

Jacobs, Helen Hull. THE TENNIS MACHINE.
Ages 12 and up. 455, Vol. 1

Maddock, Reginald. THIN ICE.
Ages 12 and up. 605, Vol. 1

Mazer, Norma Fox. UP IN SETH'S ROOM.
Ages 13 and up. 415, Vol. 3

Morgenroth, Barbara. TRAMPS LIKE US.
Ages 12 and up. 452, Vol. 3

Peck, Richard. REPRESENTING SUPER DOLL.
Ages 12 and up. 696, Vol. 1

Phelan, Terry Wolfe. THE WEEK MOM
UNPLUGGED THE TVS.
Ages 8-10. 506, Vol. 3

Raymond, Charles. JUD.
Ages 9-12. 726, Vol. 1

Slote, Alfred. LOVE AND TENNIS.
Ages 12-14. 605, Vol. 3

Steptoe, John Lewis. DADDY IS A
MONSTER...SOMETIMES.
Ages 5-7. 627, Vol. 3

Tate, Eleanora E. JUST AN OVERNIGHT GUEST.
Ages 9-11. 643, Vol. 3

Terris, Susan Dubinsky. THE DROWNING BOY.
Ages 10 and up. 891, Vol. 1

Van Leeuwen, Jean. SEEMS LIKE THIS ROAD GOES
ON FOREVER.
Ages 12 and up. 663, Vol. 3

Wolff, Ruth. A CRACK IN THE SIDEWALK.
Ages 12 and up. 990, Vol. 1

**Custody.** *See also: Divorce: of parents*

Angell, Judie. WHAT'S BEST FOR YOU.
Ages 11-14. 21, Vol. 3

Fitzhugh, Louise. SPORT.
Ages 9-12. 190, Vol. 3

Mendonca, Susan R. TOUGH CHOICES.
Ages 11 and up. 419, Vol. 3

Pfeffer, Susan Beth. STARTING WITH MELODIE.
Ages 11-13. 504, Vol. 3

Wolkoff, Judie. HAPPILY EVER AFTER...ALMOST.
Ages 11-13. 703, Vol. 3

**Drug abuse.** *See: Drugs: abuse of*

## Parental (cont.)
Fitzhugh, Louise. THE LONG SECRET.
Ages 9-12. 321, Vol. 1
Greene, Bette. THE SUMMER OF MY GERMAN
SOLDIER.
Ages 12 and up. 375, Vol. 1
Greene, Constance Clarke. A GIRL CALLED AL.
Ages 11 and up. 378, Vol. 1
Greene, Constance Clarke. THE UNMAKING OF
RABBIT.
Ages 10-13. 380, Vol. 1
Holland, Isabelle. AMANDA'S CHOICE.
Ages 10-13. 425, Vol. 1
Ish-Kishor, Sulamith. OUR EDDIE.
Ages 12 and up. 450, Vol. 1
Mazer, Norma Fox. A FIGURE OF SPEECH.
Ages 12 and up. 628, Vol. 1
Morgan, Alison. A BOY CALLED FISH.
Ages 10-12. 645, Vol. 1
Platt, Kin. THE BOY WHO COULD MAKE HIMSELF
DISAPPEAR.
Ages 12 and up. 712, Vol. 1
Snyder, Zilpha Keatley. THE EGYPT GAME.
Ages 10-13. 836, Vol. 1
Swarthout, Glendon Fred and Kathryn
Swarthout. WHICHAWAY.
Ages 10 and up. 883, Vol. 1
Wier, Ester Alberti. THE BARREL.
Ages 10-13. 970, Vol. 1

## Unreliability
Campbell, Hope, pseud. NO MORE TRAINS TO
TOTTENVILLE.
Ages 12 and up. 161, Vol. 1
Childress, Alice. RAINBOW JORDAN.
Ages 12 and up. 115, Vol. 3
Collier, James Lincoln. GIVE DAD MY BEST.
Ages 10-14. 159, Vol. 2
Corcoran, Barbara. MAKE NO SOUND.
Ages 10-13. 181, Vol. 2
Fenton, Edward. DUFFY'S ROCKS.
Ages 12 and up. 311, Vol. 1
Gerson, Corinne. HOW I PUT MY MOTHER
THROUGH COLLEGE.
Ages 11 and up. 207, Vol. 3
Madison, Winifred. THE GENESSEE QUEEN.
Ages 11 and up. 436, Vol. 2
Mathis, Sharon Bell. LISTEN FOR THE FIG TREE.
Ages 12 and up. 617, Vol. 1
Mendonca, Susan R. TOUGH CHOICES.
Ages 11 and up. 419, Vol. 3
Myers, Walter Dean. IT AIN'T ALL FOR NOTHIN'.
Ages 11-13. 470, Vol. 2
Ogilvie, Elisabeth. THE PIGEON PAIR.
Ages 12 and up. 682, Vol. 1
Rodowsky, Colby F. H. MY NAME IS HENLEY.
Ages 10-13. 547, Vol. 3
Sawyer, Ruth. MAGGIE ROSE: HER BIRTHDAY
CHRISTMAS.
Ages 8-10. 776, Vol. 1
Stolz, Mary Slattery. GO AND CATCH A FLYING
FISH.
Ages 10-13. 630, Vol. 3
Stolz, Mary Slattery. THE NOONDAY FRIENDS.
Ages 9-11. 873, Vol. 1

## Weakness
Lorimar, Lawrence T. SECRETS.
Ages 12 and up. 382, Vol. 3
Shreve, Susan Richards. THE MASQUERADE.
Ages 12 and up. 591, Vol. 3
Slote, Alfred. MY FATHER, THE COACH.
Ages 11-13. 828, Vol. 1
Stoutenburg, Adrien. WHERE TO NOW, BLUE?
Ages 10-12. 628, Vol. 2

## Parole
See also: Crime/Criminals; Probation
Samuels, Gertrude. ADAM'S DAUGHTER.
Ages 13 and up. 568, Vol. 2

## Parting
See: Separation from loved ones

## Patience/Impatience
Corey, Dorothy. EVERYBODY TAKES TURNS.
Ages 2-6. 140, Vol. 3
Delton, Judy. MY MOM HATES ME IN JANUARY.
Ages 3-6. 198, Vol. 2
Ets, Marie Hall. PLAY WITH ME.
Ages 3-7. 293, Vol. 1
Merriam, Eve. UNHURRY HARRY.
Ages 5-8. 452, Vol. 2
Rounds, Glen Harold. THE BLIND COLT.
Ages 8-12. 754, Vol. 1
Rounds, Glen Harold. BLIND OUTLAW.
Ages 9-11. 554, Vol. 3
Skolsky, Mindy Warshaw. CARNIVAL AND KOPECK
AND MORE ABOUT HANNAH.
Ages 7-9. 600, Vol. 3
Steptoe, John Lewis. STEVIE.
Ages 6-8. 860, Vol. 1
Weiss, Nicki. WAITING.
Ages 3-5. 688, Vol. 3

## Patriotism
See also: Loyalty
Hickman, Janet. THE STONES.
Ages 9-12. 314, Vol. 2
Ofek, Uriel. SMOKE OVER GOLAN.
Ages 9-13. 468, Vol. 3
Sorenson, Virginia Eggertsen. LOTTE'S LOCKET.
Ages 10-12. 843, Vol. 1

## Peer Relationships
See also: Belonging; Boy-girl relationships; Play
Bach, Alice Hendricks. THE MEAT IN THE
SANDWICH.
Ages 10-13. 28, Vol. 2
Banks, Lynne Reid. THE WRITING ON THE WALL.
Ages 12 and up. 33, Vol. 3
Blume, Judy Sussman. DEENIE.
Ages 10-12. 88, Vol. 1
Bonsall, Crosby Newell. THE CASE OF THE
DOUBLE CROSS.
Ages 6-8. 62, Vol. 3
Bottner, Barbara. DUMB OLD CASEY IS A FAT
TREE.
Ages 6-9. 66, Vol. 3
Bulla, Clyde Robert. LAST LOOK.
Ages 8-10. 86, Vol. 3
Butler, Beverly Kathleen. LIGHT A SINGLE
CANDLE.
Ages 10 and up. 152, Vol. 1
Byars, Betsy Cromer. THE ANIMAL, THE
VEGETABLE, AND JOHN D JONES.
Ages 10-12. 95, Vol. 3
Carroll, Theodorus C. THE LOST CHRISTMAS
STAR.
Ages 7-9. 109, Vol. 3
Cleary, Beverly Bunn. HENRY AND THE PAPER
ROUTE.
Ages 7-10. 192, Vol. 1
Conaway, Judith. WAS MY FACE RED!
Ages 4-7. 172, Vol. 2
Crofford, Emily. STORIES FROM THE BLUE ROAD.
Ages 9-12. 143, Vol. 3

## Peer Relationships (cont.)

Franco, Marjorie. SO WHO HASN'T GOT PROBLEMS?
Ages 10-12. 194, Vol. 3

Greene, Bette. GET ON OUT OF HERE, PHILIP HALL.
Ages 9-12. 238, Vol. 3

Hanlon, Emily. IT'S TOO LATE FOR SORRY.
Ages 11-14. 292, Vol. 2

Hassler, Jon Francis. FOUR MILES TO PINECONE.
Ages 10-14. 297, Vol. 2

Kingman, Lee. BREAK A LEG, BETSY MAYBE!
Ages 12 and up. 382, Vol. 2

Klass, Sheila Solomon. TO SEE MY MOTHER DANCE.
Ages 10-13. 344, Vol. 3

Klein, Monica. BACKYARD BASKETBALL SUPERSTAR.
Ages 6-8. 345, Vol. 3

Lee, H. Alton. SEVEN FEET FOUR AND GROWING.
Ages 9-12. 396, Vol. 2

Levy, Elizabeth. COME OUT SMILING.
Ages 12 and up. 370, Vol. 3

Lewiton, Mina Simon. THAT BAD CARLOS.
Ages 8-11. 552, Vol. 1

Luger, Harriett Mandelay. THE ELEPHANT TREE.
Ages 12 and up. 424, Vol. 2

McDonnell, Christine. DON'T BE MAD, IVY.
Ages 7-8. 391, Vol. 3

Matthews, Ellen. PUTTING UP WITH SHERWOOD.
Ages 9-11. 408, Vol. 3

Miner, Jane Claypool. SHE'S MY SISTER: HAVING A RETARDED SISTER.
Ages 11 and up. 434, Vol. 3

Myers, Walter Dean. HOOPS.
Ages 12 and up. 459, Vol. 3

Osborne, Mary Pope. RUN, RUN, AS FAST AS YOU CAN.
Ages 9-12. 477, Vol. 3

Perl, Lila. ME AND FAT GLENDA.
Ages 9-12. 700, Vol. 1

Platt, Kin. THE APE INSIDE ME.
Ages 12 and up. 513, Vol. 3

Schwarzrock, Shirley and C. Gilbert Wrenn. TO LIKE AND BE LIKED.
Ages 11 and up. 796, Vol. 1

Shaw, Richard. SHAPE UP, BURKE.
Ages 10-14. 593, Vol. 2

Slepian, Jan. THE ALFRED SUMMER.
Ages 11-13. 603, Vol. 3

Smith, Doris Buchanan. SALTED LEMONS.
Ages 9-12. 609, Vol. 3

Tolan, Stephanie S. THE LAST OF EDEN.
Ages 12 and up. 659, Vol. 3

Wartski, Maureen Crane. MY BROTHER IS SPECIAL.
Ages 10-12. 681, Vol. 3

Watson, Sally. OTHER SANDALS.
Ages 12 and up. 956, Vol. 1

Wood, Phyllis Anderson. PASS ME A PINE CONE.
Ages 11 and up. 705, Vol. 3

### Avoiding others

Albert, Louise. BUT I'M READY TO GO.
Ages 11-14. 5, Vol. 2

Colman, Hila Crayder. THE SECRET LIFE OF HAROLD THE BIRD WATCHER.
Ages 8-10. 165, Vol. 2

Fitzhugh, Louise. HARRIET THE SPY.
Ages 10-12. 320, Vol. 1

Gilbert, Harriett. RUNNING AWAY.
Ages 11-14. 215, Vol. 3

Guy, Rosa Cuthbert. THE FRIENDS.
Ages 12 and up. 391, Vol. 1

Robinson, Nancy Konheim. WENDY AND THE BULLIES.
Ages 7-10. 539, Vol. 3

Wosmek, Frances. A BOWL OF SUN.
Ages 7-9. 710, Vol. 2

**Cliques.** *See: Cliques*

**Clubs.** *See: Clubs*

**Gangs.** *See: Gangs*

**Identification with peers.** *See: Friendship; Identification with others: peers; Leader/Leadership*

**Isolation.** *See: Peer relationships: avoiding others*

**Jealousy.** *See: Jealousy: peer*

**Manipulation.** *See: Manipulation: peer*

**Ostracism.** *See: Ostracism*

### Peer pressures. *See also: Expectations*

Bates, Betty. PICKING UP THE PIECES.
Ages 10-13. 40, Vol. 3

Brancato, Robin Fidler. SOMETHING LEFT TO LOSE.
Ages 12-14. 71, Vol. 2

Brown, Marc Tolan. ARTHUR'S EYES.
Ages 4-7. 80, Vol. 3

Burch, Robert Joseph. IDA EARLY COMES OVER THE MOUNTAIN.
Ages 8-10. 92, Vol. 3

Cole, Sheila R. MEANING WELL.
Ages 9-12. 220, Vol. 1

Coles, Robert. THE GRASS PIPE.
Ages 11 and up. 223, Vol. 1

Conaway, Judith. I DARE YOU!
Ages 5-7. 169, Vol. 2

Crawford, Charles P. LETTER PERFECT.
Ages 12 and up. 184, Vol. 2

Cuyler, Margery S. THE TROUBLE WITH SOAP.
Ages 10-13. 147, Vol. 3

Danziger, Paula. CAN YOU SUE YOUR PARENTS FOR MALPRACTICE?
Ages 10-14. 149, Vol. 3

Delaney, Ned. TWO STRIKES, FOUR EYES.
Ages 5-8. 196, Vol. 3

Gauch, Patricia Lee. FRIDAYS.
Ages 11-13. 204, Vol. 3

Gold, Sharlya. AMELIA QUACKENBUSH.
Ages 10-13. 366, Vol. 1

Greenberg, Jan. THE ICEBERG AND ITS SHADOW.
Ages 10-12. 235, Vol. 3

Herman, Charlotte. THE DIFFERENCE OF ARI STEIN.
Ages 9-12. 312, Vol. 2

Hickman, Janet. THE STONES.
Ages 9-12. 314, Vol. 2

Hogan, Paula Z. I HATE BOYS  I HATE GIRLS.
Ages 5-8. 296, Vol. 3

Jeffries, Roderic. TRAPPED.
Ages 11-13. 457, Vol. 1

Johnson, Annabel Jones and Edgar Raymond Johnson. PICKPOCKET RUN.
Ages 12 and up. 463, Vol. 1

Kerr, M. E., pseud. GENTLEHANDS.
Ages 11-14. 377, Vol. 2

Levoy, Myron. ALAN AND NAOMI.
Ages 11-14. 404, Vol. 2

McClinton, Leon. CROSS-COUNTRY RUNNER.
Ages 12 and up. 594, Vol. 1

Murphy, Jim. DEATH RUN.
Ages 11 and up. 457, Vol. 3

Neigoff, Mike. IT WILL NEVER BE THE SAME AGAIN.
Ages 12-14. 465, Vol. 3

Neufeld, John. EDGAR ALLAN.
Ages 10 and up. 663, Vol. 1

O'Dell, Scott. KATHLEEN, PLEASE COME HOME.
Ages 12 and up. 485, Vol. 2

## Perseverance (cont.)

Watanabe, Shigeo. GET SET! GO!
  Ages 3-5. 682, Vol. 3
Watanabe, Shigeo. I CAN RIDE IT!
  Ages 2-5. 684, Vol. 3
Watson, Nancy Dingman. TOMMY'S MOMMY'S FISH.
  Ages 5-8. 955, Vol. 1

## Persistence

**See:** *Perseverance*

## Personal Appearance

**See:** *Appearance*

## Pets

**See also:** *Animals*
Allen, Marjorie N. ONE, TWO, THREE — AH-CHOO!
  Ages 4-7. 13, Vol. 3
Ernst, Kathryn. CHARLIE'S PETS.
  Ages 5-8. 217, Vol. 2
Gantos, Jack. THE PERFECT PAL.
  Ages 4-7. 200, Vol. 3
Griffith, Helen V. MINE WILL, SAID JOHN.
  Ages 4-6. 248, Vol. 3
Hurwitz, Johanna. SUPERDUPER TEDDY.
  Ages 4-7. 318, Vol. 3
Lindgren, Barbro. SAM'S COOKIE.
  Ages 2-5. 375, Vol. 3
Skorpen, Liesel Moak. HIS MOTHER'S DOG.
  Ages 5-8. 607, Vol. 2

### Adjustment to

Hunter, Kristin Eggleston. BOSS CAT.
  Ages 8-10. 442, Vol. 1
Loree, Sharron. THE SUNSHINE FAMILY AND THE PONY.
  Ages 6-8. 585, Vol. 1

### Death of. *See: Death: of pet*

### Guide dog. *See also: Blindness*

Butler, Beverly Kathleen. GIFT OF GOLD.
  Ages 11 and up. 151, Vol. 1
Butler, Beverly Kathleen. LIGHT A SINGLE CANDLE.
  Ages 10 and up. 152, Vol. 1
Clewes, Dorothy. GUIDE DOG.
  Ages 10 and up. 205, Vol. 1
Garfield, James B. FOLLOW MY LEADER.
  Ages 9-11. 346, Vol. 1
Gill, Derek Lewis Theodore. TOM SULLIVAN'S ADVENTURES IN DARKNESS.
  Ages 10-14. 247, Vol. 2
Hocken, Sheila. EMMA AND I.
  Ages 12 and up. 324, Vol. 2
Putnam, Peter. "KEEP YOUR HEAD UP, MR. PUTNAM!"
  Ages 12 and up. 718, Vol. 1
Rappaport, Eva. "BANNER, FORWARD!" THE PICTORIAL BIOGRAPHY OF A GUIDE DOG.
  Ages 10 and up. 722, Vol. 1
Resnick, Rose. SUN AND SHADOW: THE AUTOBIOGRAPHY OF A WOMAN WHO CLEARED A PATHWAY TO THE SEEING WORLD FOR THE BLIND.
  Ages 12 and up. 532, Vol. 2
Wolf, Bernard. CONNIE'S NEW EYES.
  Ages 9 and up. 703, Vol. 2

### Love for

Bawden, Nina Mary Kark. THE PEPPERMINT PIG.
  Ages 9-14. 44, Vol. 2
Beckwith, Lillian. THE SPUDDY: A NOVEL.
  Ages 11 and up. 48, Vol. 2

Belpre, Pura. SANTIAGO.
  Ages 4-8. 66, Vol. 1
Borack, Barbara. SOMEONE SMALL.
  Ages 4-7. 103, Vol. 1
Bosworth, J. Allan. WHITE WATER, STILL WATER.
  Ages 11 and up. 105, Vol. 1
Bradbury, Bianca. THE LONER.
  Ages 12 and up. 110, Vol. 1
Branfield, John. WHY ME?
  Ages 11 and up. 114, Vol. 1
Burchardt, Nellie. A SURPRISE FOR CARLOTTA.
  Ages 9-11. 144, Vol. 1
Carrick, Carol. THE FOUNDLING.
  Ages 5-8. 120, Vol. 2
Clifford, Ethel Rosenberg. THE KILLER SWAN.
  Ages 10-12. 120, Vol. 1
Corbin, William, pseud. GOLDEN MARE.
  Ages 9-12. 246, Vol. 1
Dixon, Jeanne. LADY CAT LOST.
  Ages 10-12. 164, Vol. 3
Dunlop, Eileen Rhona. FOX FARM.
  Ages 10-12. 175, Vol. 3
Eckert, Allan W. INCIDENT AT HAWK'S HILL.
  Ages 11 and up. 284, Vol. 1
Gackenbach, Dick. DO YOU LOVE ME?
  Ages 5-8. 238, Vol. 2
Galbraith, Kathryn Osebold. COME SPRING.
  Ages 9-13. 197, Vol. 3
Gardiner, John Reynolds. STONE FOX.
  Ages 8-10. 202, Vol. 3
Glovach, Linda. LET'S MAKE A DEAL.
  Ages 8-11. 251, Vol. 2
Grace, Fran. BRANIGAN'S DOG.
  Ages 10 and up. 225, Vol. 3
Green, Phyllis. ICE RIVER.
  Ages 8-10. 262, Vol. 3
Haas, Dorothy. POPPY AND THE OUTDOORS CAT.
  Ages 7-10. 253, Vol. 3
Harnden, Ruth Peabody. THE HIGH PASTURE.
  Ages 11-14. 401, Vol. 1
Hickman, Janet. THE THUNDER-PUP.
  Ages 9-11. 289, Vol. 3
Holland, Isabelle. ALAN AND THE ANIMAL KINGDOM.
  Ages 10-13. 327, Vol. 2
Iwasaki, Chihiro. WHAT'S FUN WITHOUT A FRIEND?
  Ages 4-7. 348, Vol. 2
LeRoy, Gen. EMMA'S DILEMMA.
  Ages 9-12. 400, Vol. 2
Letchworth, Beverly J. PAX AND THE MUTT.
  Ages 8-11. 366, Vol. 3
Lexau, Joan M. I'LL TELL ON YOU.
  Ages 5-8. 406, Vol. 2
Little, Mary E. OLD CAT AND THE KITTEN.
  Ages 8-12. 379, Vol. 3
Low, Joseph. MY DOG, YOUR DOG.
  Ages 4-6. 421, Vol. 2
Miles, Miska, pseud. JENNY'S CAT.
  Ages 6-8. 425, Vol. 1
Morey, Walter. HOME IS THE NORTH.
  Ages 12 and up. 644, Vol. 1
North, Sterling. RASCAL: A MEMOIR OF A BETTER ERA.
  Ages 11 and up. 680, Vol. 1
O'Hara, Mary, pseud. MY FRIEND FLICKA.
  Ages 11 and up. 683, Vol. 1
Parsons, Elizabeth. THE UPSIDE-DOWN CAT.
  Ages 8-11. 482, Vol. 3
Peck, Robert Newton. A DAY NO PIGS WOULD DIE.
  Ages 12 and up. 697, Vol. 1
Rockwell, Anne F. and Harlow Rockwell. I LOVE MY PETS.
  Ages 3-5. 544, Vol. 3

## Pets (cont.)

Ross, G. Maxim. WHEN LUCY WENT AWAY.
Ages 3-7. 562, Vol. 2
Savitz, Harriet May. RUN, DON'T WALK.
Ages 12 and up. 572, Vol. 3
Simmons, Anthony. THE OPTIMISTS OF NINE ELMS.
Ages 8-11. 600, Vol. 2
Stolz, Mary Slattery. THE BULLY OF BARKHAM STREET.
Ages 8-11. 863, Vol. 1
Stolz, Mary Slattery. A DOG ON BARKHAM STREET.
Ages 8-11. 865, Vol. 1
Street, James Howell. GOOD-BYE, MY LADY.
Ages 11 and up. 878, Vol. 1
Thiele, Colin Milton. STORM BOY.
Ages 8-11. 646, Vol. 2
Thomas, Ianthe. HI, MRS. MALLORY!
Ages 5-8. 651, Vol. 3
Wallace, Bill. A DOG CALLED KITTY.
Ages 9-11. 675, Vol. 3
Willoughby, Elaine Macmann. BORIS AND THE MONSTERS.
Ages 4-7. 694, Vol. 3
Wood, Phyllis Anderson. PASS ME A PINE CONE.
Ages 11 and up. 705, Vol. 3

## Responsibility for

Baker, Charlotte. COCKLEBURR QUARTERS.
Ages 9-12. 44, Vol. 1
Barton, Byron. WHERE'S AL?
Ages 3-7. 54, Vol. 1
Blegvad, Lenore Hochman and Erik Blegvad. THE GREAT HAMSTER HUNT.
Ages 8-10. 80, Vol. 1
Bulla, Clyde Robert. DEXTER.
Ages 9-11. 135, Vol. 1
Campbell, R. Wright. WHERE PIGEONS GO TO DIE.
Ages 12 and up. 112, Vol. 2
Carroll, Ruth Robinson and Latrobe Carroll. TOUGH ENOUGH.
Ages 8-10. 172, Vol. 1
Caudill, Rebecca. A POCKETFUL OF CRICKET.
Ages 4-7. 175, Vol. 1
Ernst, Kathryn. CHARLIE'S PETS.
Ages 5-8. 217, Vol. 2
Girion, Barbara. MISTY AND ME.
Ages 10-12. 219, Vol. 3
Lexau, Joan M. I'LL TELL ON YOU.
Ages 5-8. 406, Vol. 2
Little, Jean. MINE FOR KEEPS.
Ages 10-13. 574, Vol. 1
Little, Jean. SPRING BEGINS IN MARCH.
Ages 10-12. 576, Vol. 1
Little, Mary E. OLD CAT AND THE KITTEN.
Ages 8-12. 379, Vol. 3
Low, Joseph. MY DOG, YOUR DOG.
Ages 4-6. 421, Vol. 2
McNulty, Faith. MOUSE AND TIM.
Ages 5-7. 433, Vol. 2
Mason, Miriam Evangeline. STEVIE AND HIS SEVEN ORPHANS.
Ages 8-10. 616, Vol. 1
Norris, Gunilla Brodde. GREEN AND SOMETHING ELSE.
Ages 8-11. 675, Vol. 1
North, Sterling. RASCAL: A MEMOIR OF A BETTER ERA.
Ages 11 and up. 680, Vol. 1
Rockwell, Anne F. and Harlow Rockwell. I LOVE MY PETS.
Ages 3-5. 544, Vol. 3
Wagner, Jane. J.T.
Ages 8-10. 939, Vol. 1

Witheridge, Elizabeth P. DEAD END BLUFF.
Ages 10-12. 981, Vol. 1
Zweifel, Frances William. BONY.
Ages 6-7. 723, Vol. 2

## Substitute for human relationship

Asch, Frank. REBECKA.
Ages 3-6. 39, Vol. 1
Graham, Ada and Frank Graham. JACOB AND OWL.
Ages 8-11. 228, Vol. 3
Hall, Lynn. STRAY.
Ages 8-11. 394, Vol. 1
Hall, Lynn. TROUBLEMAKER.
Ages 11-14. 395, Vol. 1
Holland, Isabelle. ALAN AND THE ANIMAL KINGDOM.
Ages 10-13. 327, Vol. 2
Holland, Isabelle. DINAH AND THE GREEN FAT KINGDOM.
Ages 10-13. 328, Vol. 2
Iwasaki, Chihiro. WHAT'S FUN WITHOUT A FRIEND?
Ages 4-7. 348, Vol. 2
Morgan, Alison. A BOY CALLED FISH.
Ages 10-12. 645, Vol. 1
Neville, Emily Cheney. IT'S LIKE THIS, CAT.
Ages 11 and up. 667, Vol. 1
North, Sterling. RASCAL: A MEMOIR OF A BETTER ERA.
Ages 11 and up. 680, Vol. 1
Ottley, Reginald. BOY ALONE.
Ages 10-13. 688, Vol. 1
Wagner, Jane. J.T.
Ages 8-10. 939, Vol. 1
Woolley, Catherine. CATHY'S LITTLE SISTER.
Ages 9-12. 994, Vol. 1
Wright, Betty Ren. MY NEW MOM AND ME.
Ages 8-10. 710, Vol. 3
Yates, Elizabeth. SKEEZER: DOG WITH A MISSION.
Ages 11 and up. 1010, Vol. 1

## Phobia

See: Fear

## Physical Handicaps

See: Handicaps

## Pimples

See: Acne

## Planning

See: Careers: planning; Problem solving; Responsibility

## Play

See also: Fantasy formation; Imaginary friend; Imagination; Peer relationships; Reality, escaping; Sharing/Not sharing
Burningham, John Mackintosh. COME AWAY FROM THE WATER, SHIRLEY.
Ages 4-7. 103, Vol. 2
Gauch, Patricia Lee. CHRISTINA KATERINA & THE BOX.
Ages 4-7. 350, Vol. 1
Holl, Adelaide Hinkle. SMALL BEAR BUILDS A PLAYHOUSE.
Ages 5-7. 326, Vol. 2
Isadora, Rachel. MAX.
Ages 4-7. 346, Vol. 2
Keith, Eros. A SMALL LOT.
Ages 4-7. 486, Vol. 1
Krasilovsky, Phyllis. SUSAN SOMETIMES.
Ages 3-5. 516, Vol. 1
Lexau, Joan M. EVERY DAY A DRAGON.
Ages 3-8. 556, Vol. 1

## Practical Jokes/Pranks (cont.)

Gackenbach, Dick. HOUND AND BEAR.
Ages 4-6. 240, Vol. 2
Lowry, Lois. ANASTASIA AT YOUR SERVICE.
Ages 9-12. 385, Vol. 3
Walker, Pamela. TWYLA.
Ages 12 and up. 944, Vol. 1

## Pregnancy

**See also:** *Abortion; Childbirth; Sex; Unwed mother*
Christman, Elizabeth. A NICE ITALIAN GIRL.
Ages 12 and up. 132, Vol. 2
Elfman, Blossom. THE BUTTERFLY GIRL.
Ages 13 and up. 180, Vol. 3
Elfman, Blossom. A HOUSE FOR JONNIE O.
Ages 12 and up. 215, Vol. 2
Head, Ann. MR. AND MRS. BO JO JONES.
Ages 13 and up. 408, Vol. 1
Laing, Frederick. THE BRIDE WORE BRAIDS.
Ages 12 and up. 525, Vol. 1
Madison, Winifred. GROWING UP IN A HURRY.
Ages 12 and up. 606, Vol. 1
O'Dell, Scott. KATHLEEN, PLEASE COME HOME.
Ages 12 and up. 485, Vol. 2
Peyton, K.M., pseud. PENNINGTON'S HEIR.
Ages 12 and up. 705, Vol. 1
Posner, Grace. IN MY SISTER'S EYES.
Ages 12 and up. 516, Vol. 3
Powers, Bill. A TEST OF LOVE.
Ages 12 and up. 519, Vol. 3
Prince, Alison. THE TURKEY'S NEST.
Ages 12 and up. 520, Vol. 3
Sherburne, Zoa. TOO BAD ABOUT THE HAINES
GIRL.
Ages 12 and up. 814, Vol. 1
Thompson, Jean, pseud. THE HOUSE OF
TOMORROW.
Ages 12 and up. 895, Vol. 1
Truss, Jan. BIRD AT THE WINDOW.
Ages 13 and up. 661, Vol. 3

## Prejudice

**See also:** *Differences, human; Hatred; Hostility;*
*Integration; Justice/Injustice; Ostracism; Rejection*
Anders, Rebecca. A LOOK AT PREJUDICE AND
UNDERSTANDING.
Ages 3-7. 17, Vol. 2.
Corcoran, Barbara. DON'T SLAM THE DOOR WHEN
YOU GO.
Ages 12 and up. 249, Vol. 1
Schwarzrock, Shirley and C. Gilbert Wrenn. LIVING
WITH DIFFERENCES.
Ages 11 and up. 793, Vol. 1

**Ethnic/Racial.** *See also: Apartheid; Immigrants;*
*Internment; Marriage: interracial; Refugees*
Adelman, Bob and Susan Hall. ON AND OFF THE
STREET.
Ages 8-10. 1, Vol. 1
Alexander, Anne. TROUBLE ON TREAT STREET.
Ages 10-12. 7, Vol. 1
Archibald, Joseph Stopford. THE FIFTH BASE.
Ages 12 and up. 28, Vol. 1
Bartusis, Constance. SHADES OF DIFFERENCE.
Ages 12 and up. 55, Vol. 1
Bennett, Jay. MASKS: A LOVE STORY.
Ages 13 and up. 68, Vol. 1
Bernstein, Joanne Eckstein. DMITRY: A YOUNG
SOVIET IMMIGRANT.
Ages 11-13. 52, Vol. 3
Blue, Rose. THE PREACHER'S KID.
Ages 9-12. 58, Vol. 2
Blume, Judy Sussman. IGGIE'S HOUSE.
Ages 10 and up. 90, Vol. 1
Butler, Beverly Kathleen. A GIRL CALLED WENDY.
Ages 12 and up. 106, Vol. 2

Carlson, Natalie Savage. THE EMPTY
SCHOOLHOUSE.
Ages 8-12. 165, Vol. 1
Carlson, Natalie Savage. MARCHERS FOR THE
DREAM.
Ages 9-11. 168, Vol. 1
Cavanna, Betty. JENNY KIMURA.
Ages 11 and up. 177, Vol. 1
Cheatham, Karyn Follis. THE BEST WAY OUT.
Ages 12 and up. 114, Vol. 3
Clayton, Edward Taylor. MARTIN LUTHER KING:
THE PEACEFUL WARRIOR.
Ages 8-10. 189, Vol. 1
Clifford, Ethel Rosenberg. THE YEAR OF THE
THREE-LEGGED DEER.
Ages 12 and up. 207, Vol. 1
Cohen, Barbara Nash. BITTER HERBS AND HONEY.
Ages 11-13. 153, Vol. 2
Coleman, William Laurence. ORPHAN JIM: A
NOVEL.
Ages 13 and up. 158, Vol. 2
Colman, Hila Crayder. THE GIRL FROM PUERTO
RICO.
Ages 11 and up. 231, Vol. 1
Colman, Hila Crayder. MIXED-MARRIAGE
DAUGHTER.
Ages 11 and up. 232, Vol. 1
Corcoran, Barbara. THIS IS A RECORDING.
Ages 12 and up. 252, Vol. 1
De Angeli, Marguerite Loefft. BRIGHT APRIL.
Ages 8-10. 266, Vol. 1
Distad, Audree. DAKOTA SONS.
Ages 9-11. 275, Vol. 1
Duncan, Lois, pseud. SEASON OF THE TWO-
HEART.
Ages 12 and up. 278, Vol. 1
Estes, Eleanor. THE HUNDRED DRESSES.
Ages 8-10. 291, Vol. 1
Felton, Harold William. JAMES WELDON JOHNSON.
Ages 9-12. 309, Vol. 1
Ferry, Charles. UP IN SISTER BAY.
Ages 12 and up. 226, Vol. 2
First, Julia. AMY.
Ages 8-11. 230, Vol. 2
Friedman, Frieda. THE JANITOR'S GIRL.
Ages 10-12. 336, Vol. 1
Geibel, James. THE BLOND BROTHER.
Ages 12 and up. 205, Vol. 3
Gerson, Corinne. PASSING THROUGH.
Ages 12 and up. 245, Vol. 2
Godden, Rumer. THE DIDDAKOI.
Ages 10-12. 362, Vol. 1
Goldreich, Gloria. SEASON OF DISCOVERY.
Ages 11-13. 256, Vol. 2
Green, Hannah, pseud. I NEVER PROMISED YOU A
ROSE GARDEN.
Ages 13 and up. 373, Vol. 1
Griffin, John Howard. BLACK LIKE ME.
Ages 12 and up. 386, Vol. 1
Guy, Rosa Cuthbert. THE DISAPPEARANCE.
Ages 12 and up. 252, Vol. 1
Hardwick, Richard. CHARLES RICHARD DREW,
PIONEER IN BLOOD RESEARCH.
Ages 12 and up. 399, Vol. 1
Harris, Marilyn. THE PEPPERSALT LAND.
Ages 12 and up. 403, Vol. 1
Hassler, Jon Francis. JEMMY.
Ages 11 and up. 270, Vol. 3
Heide, Florence Parry. SOUND OF SUNSHINE,
SOUND OF RAIN.
Ages 8-10. 409, Vol. 1
Hickman, Janet. THE STONES.
Ages 9-12. 314, Vol. 2

## Prejudice (cont.)

Hunter, Kristin Eggleston. SOUL BROTHERS AND SISTER LOU.
Ages 12 and up. 443, Vol. 1

Jones, Toeckey. GO WELL, STAY WELL.
Ages 12 and up. 334, Vol. 3

Jones, Weyman B. EDGE OF TWO WORLDS.
Ages 10 and up. 471, Vol. 1

Jordan, June. FANNIE LOU HAMER.
Ages 8-10. 473, Vol. 1

Kaufman, Mervyn D. JESSE OWENS.
Ages 7-10. 480, Vol. 1

Kerr, Judith. THE OTHER WAY ROUND.
Ages 12 and up. 376, Vol. 2

Kerr, M. E., pseud. LOVE IS A MISSING PERSON.
Ages 12 and up. 380, Vol. 2

Konigsburg, Elaine Lobl. ABOUT THE B'NAI BAGELS.
Ages 10-13. 508, Vol. 1

Konigsburg, Elaine Lobl. ALTOGETHER, ONE AT A TIME.
Ages 9-11. 509, Vol. 1

Lampman, Evelyn Sibley. GO UP THE ROAD.
Ages 9-12. 526, Vol. 1

Lampman, Evelyn Sibley. HALF-BREED.
Ages 10-12. 527, Vol. 1

Lampman, Evelyn Sibley. THE YEAR OF SMALL SHADOW.
Ages 10-12. 528, Vol. 1

Lee, Harper. TO KILL A MOCKINGBIRD.
Ages 12 and up. 533, Vol. 1

Levoy, Myron. ALAN AND NAOMI.
Ages 11-14. 404, Vol. 2

Maddock, Reginald. DANNY ROWLEY.
Ages 11-13. 602, Vol. 1

Madison, Winifred. MARIA LUISA.
Ages 9-12. 607, Vol. 1

Mann, Peggy. WHEN CARLOS CLOSED THE STREET.
Ages 8-11. 612, Vol. 1

Marshall, James Vance, pseud. WALKABOUT.
Ages 12 and up. 614, Vol. 1

Means, Florence Crannell. US MALTBYS.
Ages 12 and up. 630, Vol. 1

Meriwether, Louise. DON'T RIDE THE BUS ON MONDAY: THE ROSA PARKS STORY.
Ages 9-11. 635, Vol. 1

Miles, Betty. ALL IT TAKES IS PRACTICE.
Ages 9-12. 454, Vol. 2

Miller, Ruth White. THE CITY ROSE.
Ages 11-13. 460, Vol. 2

Miner, Jane Claypool. NAVAJO VICTORY: BEING A NATIVE AMERICAN.
Ages 11 and up. 432, Vol. 3

Miner, Jane Claypool. THE TOUGH GUY: BLACK IN A WHITE WORLD.
Ages 11 and up. 437, Vol. 3

Mohr, Nicholasa. FELITA.
Ages 8-10. 440, Vol. 3

Neufeld, John. EDGAR ALLAN.
Ages 10 and up. 663, Vol. 1

Neville, Emily Cheney. BERRIES GOODMAN.
Ages 11 and up. 666, Vol. 1

Pinkwater, Manus. WINGMAN.
Ages 9-12. 513, Vol. 2

Rinkoff, Barbara Jean Rich. HEADED FOR TROUBLE.
Ages 12 and up. 736, Vol. 1

Rivera, Geraldo. A SPECIAL KIND OF COURAGE: PROFILES OF YOUNG AMERICANS.
Ages 12 and up. 544, Vol. 2

Robinson, John Roosevelt and Alfred Duckett. BREAKTHROUGH TO THE BIG LEAGUE: THE STORY OF JACKIE ROBINSON.
Ages 10 and up. 746, Vol. 1

Rowe, Jeanne A. AN ALBUM OF MARTIN LUTHER KING, JR.
Ages 10 and up. 755, Vol. 1

Ruby, Lois. ARRIVING AT A PLACE YOU'VE NEVER LEFT.
Ages 12 and up. 564, Vol. 2

Ruby, Lois. TWO TRUTHS IN MY POCKET.
Ages 12 and up. 557, Vol. 3

Rudeen, Kenneth. JACKIE ROBINSON.
Ages 7-9. 757, Vol. 1

Sachs, Marilyn. A POCKET FULL OF SEEDS.
Ages 10-12. 763, Vol. 1

Scoppettone, Sandra. TRYING HARD TO HEAR YOU.
Ages 13 and up. 799, Vol. 1

Screen, Robert Martin. WITH MY FACE TO THE RISING SUN.
Ages 11 and up. 580, Vol. 2

Seredy, Kate. THE SINGING TREE.
Ages 10-14. 803, Vol. 1

Sebestyen, Ouida. WORDS BY HEART.
Ages 10-13. 580, Vol. 3

Smith, Doris Buchanan. SALTED LEMONS.
Ages 9-12. 609, Vol. 3

Taylor, Mildred D. ROLL OF THUNDER, HEAR MY CRY.
Ages 10 and up. 636, Vol. 2

Tobias, Tobi. ARTHUR MITCHELL.
Ages 7-10. 649, Vol. 2

Tobias, Tobi. MARIAN ANDERSON.
Ages 7-10. 898, Vol. 1

Uchida, Yoshiko. JOURNEY HOME.
Ages 12-14. 657, Vol. 2

Waldron, Ann Wood. THE INTEGRATION OF MARY-LARKIN THORNHILL.
Ages 10-13. 672, Vol. 2

Wartski, Maureen Crane. A LONG WAY FROM HOME.
Ages 11-13. 680, Vol. 3

Watson, Sally. OTHER SANDALS.
Ages 12 and up. 956, Vol. 1

Yep, Laurence Michael. DRAGONWINGS.
Ages 12 and up. 712, Vol. 2

Yep, Laurence Michael. SEA GLASS.
Ages 11-14. 713, Vol. 3

### toward Handicapped persons

Ferry, Charles. UP IN SISTER BAY.
Ages 12 and up. 226, Vol. 2

Garrigue, Sheila. BETWEEN FRIENDS.
Ages 9-12. 243, Vol. 2

Gerson, Corinne. PASSING THROUGH.
Ages 12 and up. 245, Vol. 2

Hanlon, Emily. IT'S TOO LATE FOR SORRY.
Ages 11-14. 292, Vol. 2

Hocken, Sheila. EMMA AND I.
Ages 12 and up. 324, Vol. 2

Robinson, Veronica. DAVID IN SILENCE.
Ages 12 and up. 747, Vol. 1

Savitz, Harriet May. RUN, DON'T WALK.
Ages 12 and up. 572, Vol. 3

Smith, Gene. THE HAYBURNERS.
Ages 9-12. 833, Vol. 1

Viscardi, Henry. A MAN'S STATURE.
Ages 12 and up. 932, Vol. 1

### Religious. See also: Marriage: interreligious; Refugees; Religion

Arrick, Fran. CHERNOWITZ!
Ages 12 and up. 23, Vol. 3

Asher, Sandra Fenichel. DAUGHTERS OF THE LAW.
Ages 11-13. 26, Vol. 3

Bloch, Marie Halun. THE TWO WORLDS OF DAMYAN.
Ages 9-12. 81, Vol. 1

## Pride/False Pride (cont.)

Bunting, Anne Evelyn. MAGIC AND THE NIGHT RIVER.
Ages 5-9. 96, Vol. 2

Carlson, Natalie Savage. SCHOOL BELL IN THE VALLEY.
Ages 8-11. 169, Vol. 1

Cavanna, Betty. JENNY KIMURA.
Ages 11 and up. 177, Vol. 1

Distad, Audree. DAKOTA SONS.
Ages 9-11. 275, Vol. 1

Duvoisin, Roger Antoine. PETUNIA.
Ages 4-8. 281, Vol. 1

Fowler, Carol. DAISY HOOEE NAMPEYO.
Ages 11 and up. 233, Vol. 2

Friskey, Margaret Richards. RACKETY, THAT VERY SPECIAL RABBIT.
Ages 3-5. 237, Vol. 2

Greenfield, Eloise. GOOD NEWS.
Ages 5-6. 271, Vol. 2

Guy, Rosa Cuthbert THE FRIENDS.
Ages 12 and up. 391, Vol. 1

Hamilton, Virginia. ARILLA SUN DOWN.
Ages 12 and up. 291, Vol. 2

Karp, Naomi J. NOTHING RHYMES WITH APRIL.
Ages 9-11. 479, Vol. 1

Lampman, Evelyn Sibley. THE POTLATCH FAMILY.
Ages 11-13. 391, Vol. 2

Lexau, Joan M. STRIPED ICE CREAM.
Ages 8-11. 559, Vol. 1

Little, Lessie Jones and Eloise Greenfield. I CAN DO IT BY MYSELF.
Ages 5-7. 415, Vol. 2

Lopshire, Robert. I AM BETTER THAN YOU.
Ages 4-8. 579, Vol. 1

Mann, Peggy. THE STREET OF THE FLOWER BOXES.
Ages 8-11. 610, Vol. 1

Meddaugh, Susan. TOO SHORT FRED.
Ages 6-8. 450, Vol. 2

Miles, Betty. JUST THE BEGINNING.
Ages 10-12. 456, Vol. 2

Miner, Jane Claypool. A MAN'S PRIDE: LOSING A FATHER.
Ages 11 and up. 429, Vol. 3

Naylor, Phyllis Reynolds. WALKING THROUGH THE DARK.
Ages 12 and up. 473, Vol. 2

Riley, Susan. WHAT DOES IT MEAN? SUCCESS.
Ages 3-6. 543, Vol. 2

Rosenblatt, Suzanne. EVERYONE IS GOING SOMEWHERE.
Ages 4-6. 561, Vol. 2

Seredy, Kate. A TREE FOR PETER.
Ages 9-12. 804, Vol. 1

Sharmat, Marjorie Weinman. I'M TERRIFIC.
Ages 4-7. 587, Vol. 2

Strete, Craig Kee. PAINT YOUR FACE ON A DROWNING IN THE RIVER.
Ages 12 and up. 629, Vol. 2

Tobias, Tobi. ARTHUR MITCHELL.
Ages 7-10. 649, Vol. 2

Vroman, Mary Elizabeth. HARLEM SUMMER.
Ages 12 and up. 936, Vol. 1

Wolf, Bernard. ADAM SMITH GOES TO SCHOOL.
Ages 4-7. 701, Vol. 2

Yep, Laurence Michael. SEA GLASS.
Ages 11-14. 713, Vol. 3

## Priorities, Establishing

**See:** *Problem solving; Values/Valuing*

## Prison

**See:** *Crime/Criminals; Delinquency, juvenile; Detention home, living in; Imprisonment*

## Privacy, Need for

Bennett, Rainey. THE SECRET HIDING PLACE.
Ages 5-8. 69, Vol. 1

Berger, Terry. BEING ALONE, BEING TOGETHER.
Ages 3-7. 71, Vol. 1

Billington, Elizabeth T. PART-TIME BOY.
Ages 8-10. 53, Vol. 3

Blue, Rose. A QUIET PLACE.
Ages 8-11. 86, Vol. 1

Bond, Felicia. POINSETTIA & HER FAMILY.
Ages 4-7. 59, Vol. 3

Byars, Betsy Cromer. THE CARTOONIST.
Ages 8-12. 107, Vol. 2

Child Study Association of America. BROTHERS AND SISTERS ARE LIKE THAT! STORIES TO READ TO YOURSELF.
Ages 7-9. 182, Vol. 1

De Regniers, Beatrice Schenk. A LITTLE HOUSE OF YOUR OWN.
Ages 3-8. 273, Vol. 1

Dragonwagon, Crescent. WHEN LIGHT TURNS INTO NIGHT.
Ages 4-7. 206, Vol. 2

Hayes, Geoffrey. BEAR BY HIMSELF.
Ages 4-6. 299, Vol. 2

Henkes, Kevin. ALL ALONE.
Ages 3-6. 280, Vol. 3

Hill, Elizabeth Starr. EVAN'S CORNER.
Ages 6-9. 411, Vol. 1

Hunter, Kristin Eggleston. SOUL BROTHERS AND SISTER LOU.
Ages 12 and up. 443, Vol. 1

Hurmence, Belinda. TOUGH TIFFANY.
Ages 10-13. 315, Vol. 3

MacLachlan, Patricia. CASSIE BINEGAR.
Ages 9-12. 394, Vol. 3

Marshall, James. GEORGE AND MARTHA — ONE FINE DAY.
Ages 3-6. 442, Vol. 2

Thompson, Jean, pseud. DON'T FORGET MICHAEL.
Ages 7-9. 656, Vol. 3

Wells, Rosemary. THE FOG COMES ON LITTLE PIG FEET.
Ages 11 and up. 961, Vol. 1

Wright, Betty Ren. I LIKE BEING ALONE.
Ages 6-9. 709, Vol. 3

## Private Schools, Living at

**See:** *Schools, private*

## Probation

**See also:** *Crime/Criminals; Delinquency, juvenile; Detention home, living in; Parole*

Peyton, K.M., pseud. THE BEETHOVEN MEDAL.
Ages 12 and up. 704, Vol. 1

Riter, Dorris. THE EDGE OF VIOLENCE.
Ages 12 and up. 741, Vol. 1

Trivers, James. I CAN STOP ANY TIME I WANT.
Ages 12 and up. 904, Vol. 1

## Problem Solving

**See also:** *Ambivalence, feelings of; Creativity; Decision making; Resourcefulness*

Alexander, Martha G. MOVE OVER, TWERP.
Ages 5-8. 11, Vol. 3

Alexander, Martha G. SABRINA.
Ages 3-7. 10, Vol. 1

Anderson, Mary Quirk. STEP ON A CRACK.
Ages 12 and up. 18, Vol. 2

Baldwin, Anne Norris. A LITTLE TIME.
Ages 9-11. 30, Vol. 2

Barton, Byron. WHERE'S AL?
Ages 3-7. 54, Vol. 1

## Problem Solving (cont.)

Behrens, June York. SOO LING FINDS A WAY.
Ages 4-8. 62, Vol. 1

Binzen, Bill. MIGUEL'S MOUNTAIN.
Ages 5-9. 77, Vol. 1

Blegvad, Lenore Hochman and Erik Blegvad. THE GREAT HAMSTER HUNT.
Ages 8-10. 80, Vol. 1

Bonsall, Crosby Newell. THE CASE OF THE DOUBLE CROSS.
Ages 6-8. 62, Vol. 3

Bosse, Malcolm Joseph. GANESH.
Ages 11-14. 65, Vol. 3

Bottner, Barbara. MEAN MAXINE.
Ages 4-6. 67, Vol. 3

Bronin, Andrew. GUS AND BUSTER WORK THINGS OUT.
Ages 4-7. 83, Vol. 2

Brown, Fern G. JOCKEY — OR ELSE!
Ages 9-12. 86, Vol. 2

Carris, Joan Davenport. WHEN THE BOYS RAN THE HOUSE.
Ages 8-12. 108, Vol. 3

Chapman, Carol. HERBIE'S TROUBLES.
Ages 5-7. 113, Vol. 3

Cleary, Beverly Bunn. HENRY AND THE CLUBHOUSE.
Ages 8-10. 191, Vol. 1

Cleary, Beverly Bunn. HENRY AND THE PAPER ROUTE.
Ages 7-10. 192, Vol. 1

Clifford, Ethel Rosenberg. THE ROCKING CHAIR REBELLION.
Ages 11-13. 142, Vol. 2

Colman, Hila Crayder. THE CASE OF THE STOLEN BAGELS.
Ages 7-10. 162, Vol. 2

Cooney, Nancy Evans. THE BLANKET THAT HAD TO GO.
Ages 3-5. 138, Vol. 3

Crayder, Dorothy. ISHKABIBBLE!
Ages 9-12. 185, Vol. 2

Dahl, Roald. DANNY: THE CHAMPION OF THE WORLD.
Ages 10 and up. 189, Vol. 2

Dickinson, Mary. ALEX'S BED.
Ages 3-6. 163, Vol. 3

Dobrin, Arnold. GILLY GILHOOLEY: A TALE OF IRELAND.
Ages 5-8. 203, Vol. 2

Erskine, Jim. THE SNOWMAN.
Ages 3-6. 219, Vol. 2

Fassler, Joan. THE BOY WITH A PROBLEM.
Ages 4-8. 304, Vol. 1

Fife, Dale. WHO GOES THERE, LINCOLN?
Ages 8-10. 228, Vol. 2

Fife, Dale. WHO'S IN CHARGE OF LINCOLN?
Ages 8-10. 314, Vol. 1

First, Julia. MOVE OVER, BEETHOVEN.
Ages 10-13. 231, Vol. 2

Fitzgerald, John Dennis. ME AND MY LITTLE BRAIN.
Ages 9-12. 319, Vol. 1

Flournoy, Valerie. THE TWINS STRIKE BACK.
Ages 6-8. 191, Vol. 3

Gantos, Jack. FAIR-WEATHER FRIENDS.
Ages 4-7. 242, Vol. 2

Glovach, Linda. LET'S MAKE A DEAL.
Ages 8-11. 251, Vol. 2

Golding, William. LORD OF THE FLIES.
Ages 13 and up. 367, Vol. 1

Greenwald, Sheila. GIVE US A GREAT BIG SMILE, ROSY COLE.
Ages 8-10. 246, Vol. 3

Gunther, Louise. A TOOTH FOR THE TOOTH FAIRY.
Ages 5-8. 286, Vol. 2

Haas, Dorothy. POPPY AND THE OUTDOORS CAT.
Ages 7-10. 253, Vol. 3

Hoban, Russell Conwell. A BARGAIN FOR FRANCES.
Ages 5-7. 417, Vol. 1

Hogan, Paula Z. SOMETIMES I DON'T LIKE SCHOOL.
Ages 6-9. 297, Vol. 3

Hogan, Paula Z. SOMETIMES I GET SO MAD.
Ages 5-8. 298, Vol. 3

Holland, Isabelle. ALAN AND THE ANIMAL KINGDOM.
Ages 10-13. 327, Vol. 2

Holman, Felice. PROFESSOR DIGGINS' DRAGONS.
Ages 9-11. 429, Vol. 1

Hopper, Nancy J. SECRETS.
Ages 11-14. 304, Vol. 3

Hughes, Shirley. ALFIE GETS IN FIRST.
Ages 3-5. 309, Vol. 3

Inkiow, Dimiter. ME AND CLARA AND CASIMER THE CAT.
Ages 7-9. 321, Vol. 3

Jensen, Virginia Allen. SARA AND THE DOOR.
Ages 2-5. 350, Vol. 2

Jordan, June. NEW LIFE: NEW ROOM.
Ages 4-8. 361, Vol. 2

Keats, Ezra Jack. GOGGLES!
Ages 4-8. 484, Vol. 1

Keith, Eros. A SMALL LOT.
Ages 4-7. 486, Vol. 1

Kleberger, Ilse. GRANDMOTHER OMA.
Ages 8-11. 499, Vol. 1

Klein, Leonore. ONLY ONE ANT.
Ages 4-7. 501, Vol. 1

Knudson, R. Rozanne. ZANBANGER.
Ages 10-13. 387, Vol. 2

Landis, James David. THE SISTERS IMPOSSIBLE.
Ages 9-11. 355, Vol. 3

Lesikin, Joan. DOWN THE ROAD.
Ages 4-6. 403, Vol. 2

Lexau, Joan M. BENJIE ON HIS OWN.
Ages 6-9. 554, Vol. 1

Lionni, Leo. SWIMMY.
Ages 3-7. 567, Vol. 1

Lord, Beman. GUARDS FOR MATT.
Ages 8-10. 581, Vol. 1

Lord, Beman. SHRIMP'S SOCCER GOAL.
Ages 8-11. 584, Vol. 1

Low, Joseph. BOO TO A GOOSE.
Ages 5-8. 420, Vol. 2

Lystad, Mary. JAMES, THE JAGUAR.
Ages 3-7. 592, Vol. 1

McDonnell, Christine. DON'T BE MAD, IVY.
Ages 7-8. 391, Vol. 3

Mann, Peggy. WHEN CARLOS CLOSED THE STREET.
Ages 8-11. 612, Vol. 1

Mathis, Sharon Bell. SIDEWALK STORY.
Ages 8-10. 618, Vol. 1

Mauser, Pat Rhoads. HOW I FOUND MYSELF AT THE FAIR.
Ages 7-9. 411, Vol. 3

Moskin, Marietta Dunston. ROSIE'S BIRTHDAY PRESENT.
Ages 4-7. 456, Vol. 3

Myers, Walter Dean. THE YOUNG LANDLORDS.
Ages 11-14. 461, Vol. 3

Pascal, Francine. THE HAND-ME-DOWN KID.
Ages 10-13. 483, Vol. 3

## Problem Solving (cont.)

Pfeffer, Susan Beth. WHAT DO YOU DO WHEN YOUR MOUTH WON'T OPEN?
Ages 10-13. 505, Vol. 3

Piper, Watty. THE LITTLE ENGINE THAT COULD.
Ages 3-7. 711, Vol. 1

Piper, Watty. THE LITTLE ENGINE THAT COULD.
Ages 3-7. 514, Vol. 2

Roberts, Willo Davis. THE VIEW FROM THE CHERRY TREE.
Ages 9-12. 546, Vol. 2

Robertson, Keith. HENRY REED'S BABY-SITTING SERVICE.
Ages 9-12. 742, Vol. 1

Robinson, Charles. NEW KID IN TOWN.
Ages 4-7. 548, Vol. 2

Ruthstrom, Dorotha. THE BIG KITE CONTEST.
Ages 6-8. 560, Vol. 3

Schwarzrock, Shirley and C. Gilbert Wrenn. I'D RATHER DO IT MYSELF, IF YOU DON'T MIND.
Ages 11 and up. 792, Vol. 1

Schwarzrock, Shirley and C. Gilbert Wrenn. UNDERSTANDING THE LAW OF OUR LAND.
Ages 11 and up. 797, Vol. 1

Seuling, Barbara. THE TRIPLETS.
Ages 4-7. 581, Vol. 3

Skurzynski, Gloria Joan. MARTIN BY HIMSELF.
Ages 6-9. 602, Vol. 3

Southall, Ivan. HILLS END.
Ages 11 and up. 846, Vol. 1

Stanek, Muriel Novella. LEFT, RIGHT, LEFT, RIGHT.
Ages 5-8. 851, Vol. 1

Strang, Celia. THIS CHILD IS MINE.
Ages 11-14. 634, Vol. 3

Sugarman, Daniel A. and Rolaine A. Hochstein. SEVEN STORIES FOR GROWTH.
Ages 6-12. 880, Vol. 1

Watson, Pauline. CURLEY CAT BABY-SITS.
Ages 5-8. 675, Vol. 2

Willard, Barbara. STORM FROM THE WEST.
Ages 10-13. 976, Vol. 1

Witheridge, Elizabeth P. DEAD END BLUFF.
Ages 10-12. 981, Vol. 1

Wold, Jo Anne. TELL THEM MY NAME IS AMANDA.
Ages 5-8. 694, Vol. 2

Wright, Betty Ren. I LIKE BEING ALONE.
Ages 6-9. 709, Vol. 3

Zolotow, Charlotte Shapiro. THE HATING BOOK.
Ages 3-7. 1021, Vol. 1

## Promise, Keeping

See also: Forgetting

Cleaver, Vera and Bill Cleaver. WHERE THE LILIES BLOOM.
Ages 11 and up. 203, Vol. 1

Clifton, Lucille. DON'T YOU REMEMBER?
Ages 4-7. 209, Vol. 1

Cone, Molly Lamken. A PROMISE IS A PROMISE.
Ages 11-13. 234, Vol. 1

Hentoff, Nat. THIS SCHOOL IS DRIVING ME CRAZY.
Ages 11-15. 311, Vol. 2

Hoban, Russell Conwell. A BARGAIN FOR FRANCES.
Ages 5-7. 417, Vol. 1

Perrine, Mary. SALT BOY.
Ages 7-10. 703, Vol. 1

Skolsky, Mindy Warshaw. CARNIVAL AND KOPECK AND MORE ABOUT HANNAH.
Ages 7-9. 600, Vol. 3

Wade, Anne. A PROMISE IS FOR KEEPING.
Ages 4-7. 674, Vol. 3

Zhitkov, Boris Stepanovich. HOW I HUNTED THE LITTLE FELLOWS.
Ages 3-7. 720, Vol. 3

## Prosthesis

See also: Amputee; Limbs, abnormal or missing; Wheelchair, dependence on

Cook, Marjorie. TO WALK ON TWO FEET.
Ages 11-14. 177, Vol. 2

Wolf, Bernard. DON'T FEEL SORRY FOR PAUL.
Ages 8 and up. 987, Vol. 1

## Prostitution

See also: Crime/Criminals; Sex: extramarital; Sex: premarital

Arrick, Fran. STEFFIE CAN'T COME OUT TO PLAY.
Ages 12 and up. 24, Vol. 2

## Psychosis

See: Mental illness

## Puberty

See also: Acne; Maturation; Menstruation

Blume, Judy Sussman. THEN AGAIN, MAYBE I WON'T.
Ages 12 and up. 94, Vol. 1

Branscum, Robbie. JOHNNY MAY.
Ages 9-12. 77, Vol. 2

Engebrecht, P. A. UNDER THE HAYSTACK.
Ages 11 and up. 289, Vol. 1

Greene, Constance Clarke. I KNOW YOU, AL.
Ages 11 and up. 268, Vol. 2

Josephs, Rebecca. EARLY DISORDER.
Ages 13 and up. 335, Vol. 3

Lee, Mildred Scudder. SYCAMORE YEAR.
Ages 12 and up. 537, Vol. 1

Marney, Dean. JUST GOOD FRIENDS.
Ages 11-13. 404, Vol. 3

Okimoto, Jean Davies. IT'S JUST TOO MUCH.
Ages 10-12. 469, Vol. 3

Rabe, Berniece Louise. NAOMI.
Ages 12 and up. 527, Vol. 2

Stolz, Mary Slattery. LEAP BEFORE YOU LOOK.
Ages 12 and up. 869, Vol. 1

## Puerto Rican-American

Belpré, Pura. SANTIAGO.
Ages 4-8. 66, Vol. 1

Blue, Rose. I AM HERE. YO ESTOY AQUÍ.
Ages 5-8. 83, Vol. 1

Burchardt, Nellie. A SURPRISE FOR CARLOTTA.
Ages 9-11. 144, Vol. 1

Colman, Hila Crayder. THE GIRL FROM PUERTO RICO.
Ages 11 and up. 231, Vol. 1

Fleischman, H. Samuel. GANG GIRL.
Ages 11 and up. 322, Vol. 1

Gonzalez, Gloria. GAUCHO.
Ages 10-13. 257, Vol. 2

Kesselman, Wendy Ann. ANGELITA.
Ages 5-9. 494, Vol. 1

Levoy, Myron. A SHADOW LIKE A LEOPARD.
Ages 12 and up. 369, Vol. 3

Lewiton, Mina Simon. CANDITA'S CHOICE.
Ages 8-11. 551, Vol. 1

Lewiton, Mina Simon. THAT BAD CARLOS.
Ages 8-11. 552, Vol. 1

Mann, Peggy. HOW JUAN GOT HOME.
Ages 8-10. 608, Vol. 1

Mohr, Nicholasa. FELITA.
Ages 8-10. 440, Vol. 3

Mohr, Nicholasa. IN NUEVA YORK.
Ages 13 and up. 462, Vol. 2

## Puerto Rican-American (cont.)

Shotwell, Louisa Rossiter. MAGDALENA.
Ages 10-12. 818, Vol. 1
Speevack, Yetta. THE SPIDER PLANT.
Ages 9-11. 848, Vol. 1
Thomas, Dawn C. PABLITO'S NEW FEET.
Ages 8-10. 894, Vol. 1

## Punishment

**See:** *Detention home, living in; Discipline, meaning of;*
*Imprisonment; Parent/Parents: punitive*

## Pupil-Teacher Relationships

**See:** *School: pupil-teacher relationships*

## Purse Snatching

**See:** *Stealing: purse snatching*

# Q

## Quadriplegia

**See also:** *Paralysis; Paraplegia; Wheelchair, dependence*
*on*
Brancato, Robin Fidler. WINNING.
Ages 12 and up. 72, Vol. 2
Campanella, Roy. IT'S GOOD TO BE ALIVE.
Ages 13 and up. 160, Vol. 1
Kingman, Lee. HEAD OVER WHEELS.
Ages 12 and up. 383, Vol. 2

## Quaker

**See:** *Society of Friends (Quaker)*

# R

## Rage

**See:** *Aggression; Anger; Tantrums*

## Rape

**See also:** *Crime/Criminals; Sexual assault; Violence*
Miklowitz, Gloria D. DID YOU HEAR WHAT
HAPPENED TO ANDREA?
Ages 13 and up. 421, Vol. 3
Peck, Richard. ARE YOU IN THE HOUSE ALONE?
Ages 12 and up. 500, Vol. 2
Scoppettone, Sandra. HAPPY ENDINGS ARE ALL
ALIKE.
Ages 12 and up. 578, Vol. 2

## Reality, Escaping

**See also:** *Daydreaming; Drugs; Imagination; Mental*
*illness; Play*
Arrick, Fran. TUNNEL VISION.
Ages 12 and up. 24, Vol. 3
Byars, Betsy Cromer. THE TV KID.
Ages 9-12. 109, Vol. 2
Conford, Ellen. THE REVENGE OF THE
INCREDIBLE DR. RANCID AND HIS YOUTHFUL
ASSISTANT, JEFFREY.
Ages 10-12. 137, Vol. 3
Corcoran, Barbara. A ROW OF TIGERS.
Ages 10-12. 250, Vol. 1
Dixon, Jeanne. LADY CAT LOST.
Ages 10-12. 164, Vol. 3
Eyerly, Jeannette Hyde. THE GIRL INSIDE.
Ages 12 and up. 298, Vol. 1
Fox, Paula. BLOWFISH LIVE IN THE SEA.
Ages 11 and up. 327, Vol. 1
Grace, Fran. BRANIGAN'S DOG.
Ages 10 and up. 225, Vol. 3

Green, Hannah, pseud. I NEVER PROMISED YOU A
ROSE GARDEN.
Ages 13 and up. 373, Vol. 1
Heide, Florence Parry. GROWING ANYWAY UP.
Ages 12-14. 305, Vol. 2
Hermes, Patricia. NOBODY'S FAULT.
Ages 10-12. 284, Vol. 3
Holman, Felice. SLAKE'S LIMBO.
Ages 12 and up. 430, Vol. 1
Hopper, Nancy J. SECRETS.
Ages 11-14. 304, Vol. 3
Klass, Sheila Solomon. TO SEE MY MOTHER
DANCE.
Ages 10-13. 344, Vol. 3
Levoy, Myron. ALAN AND NAOMI.
Ages 11-14. 404, Vol. 2
Lipp, Frederick J. SOME LOSE THEIR WAY.
Ages 10-13. 377, Vol. 3
Lutters, Valerie. THE HAUNTING OF JULIE UNGER.
Ages 10-13. 425, Vol. 2
McCord, Jean. TURKEYLEGS THOMPSON.
Ages 11-14. 390, Vol. 3
MacLachlan, Patricia. ARTHUR, FOR THE VERY
FIRST TIME.
Ages 8-10. 393, Vol. 3
Morgan, Alison Mary. ALL KINDS OF PRICKLES.
Ages 11-13. 450, Vol. 3
Ness, Evaline Michelow. SAM, BANGS, AND
MOONSHINE.
Ages 4-8. 662, Vol. 1
Pinkwater, Manus. WINGMAN.
Ages 9-12. 513, Vol. 2
Rabinowich, Ellen. ROCK FEVER.
Ages 12 and up. 523, Vol. 3
Reader, Dennis J. COMING BACK ALIVE.
Ages 12 and up. 525, Vol. 3
Rodowsky, Colby F. P.S. WRITE SOON.
Ages 10-12. 555, Vol. 2
Ruby, Lois. WHAT DO YOU DO IN QUICKSAND?
Ages 12-14. 558, Vol. 3
Sachs, Marilyn. THE BEARS' HOUSE.
Ages 9-12. 760, Vol. 1
Sallis, Susan Diana. ONLY LOVE.
Ages 12 and up. 568, Vol. 3
Smith, Nancy Covert. THE FALLING-APART
WINTER.
Ages 10-13. 612, Vol. 3
Terris, Susan Dubinsky. NO SCARLET RIBBONS.
Ages 11-13. 647, Vol. 3
Trivers, James. I CAN STOP ANY TIME I WANT.
Ages 12 and up. 904, Vol. 1
Van Leeuwen, Jean. SEEMS LIKE THIS ROAD GOES
ON FOREVER.
Ages 12 and up. 663, Vol. 3
Wojciechowska, Maia Rodman. TUNED OUT.
Ages 12 and up. 986, Vol. 1

## Reality Testing

**See also:** *Magical thinking*
Clymer, Eleanor Lowenton. ME AND THE EGGMAN.
Ages 10-13. 212, Vol. 1

## Rebellion

**See also:** *Delinquency, juvenile*
Banks, Lynne Reid. THE WRITING ON THE WALL.
Ages 12 and up. 33, Vol. 3
Bova, Benjamin William. CITY OF DARKNESS: A
NOVEL.
Ages 12 and up. 63, Vol. 2
Campbell, Hope, pseud. NO MORE TRAINS TO
TOTTENVILLE.
Ages 12 and up. 161, Vol. 1
Colman, Hila Crayder. CAR-CRAZY GIRL.
Ages 12 and up. 227, Vol. 1

## Rebellion (cont.)

## Reconciliation, Parental

## Refugees

## Regionalism

## Rejection

## Parental. See also: *Parental: rejection*

**Rejection (cont.)**

Ruby, Lois. ARRIVING AT A PLACE YOU'VE
NEVER LEFT.
Ages 12 and up. 564, Vol. 2

Sachs, Marilyn. A DECEMBER TALE.
Ages 9-12. 565, Vol. 2

Sebestyen, Ouida. FAR FROM HOME.
Ages 12 and up. 579, Vol. 3

Slepian, Jan. THE ALFRED SUMMER.
Ages 11-13. 603, Vol. 3

Thompson, Paul. THE HITCHHIKERS.
Ages 12 and up. 657, Vol. 3

Wortis, Avi. SOMETIMES I THINK I HEAR MY
NAME.
Ages 10-13. 708, Vol. 3

Zalben, Jane Breskin. MAYBE IT WILL RAIN
TOMORROW.
Ages 12 and up. 716, Vol. 3

**Peer.** *See also: Peer relationships: rejection*

Albert, Louise. BUT I'M READY TO GO.
Ages 11-14. 5, Vol. 2

Blue, Rose. THE PREACHER'S KID.
Ages 9-12. 58, Vol. 2

Bulla, Clyde Robert. LAST LOOK.
Ages 8-10. 86, Vol. 3

Carrick, Malcolm. TRAMP.
Ages 7-9. 122, Vol. 2

De Clements, Barthe. NOTHING'S FAIR IN FIFTH
GRADE.
Ages 8-11. 152, Vol. 3

Giff, Patricia Reilly. THE WINTER WORM
BUSINESS.
Ages 8-10. 214, Vol. 3

Roth, David. THE HERMIT OF FOG HOLLOW
STATION.
Ages 9-12. 553, Vol. 3

Sachs, Marilyn. A SECRET FRIEND.
Ages 10-12. 567, Vol. 2

Sawyer, Paul. NEW NEIGHBORS.
Ages 5-8. 571, Vol. 2

Udry, Janice May. HOW I FADED AWAY.
Ages 5-8. 658, Vol. 2

Vigna, Judith. ANYHOW, I'M GLAD I TRIED.
Ages 3-6. 661, Vol. 2

**Sibling**

Conaway, Judith. I'LL GET EVEN.
Ages 4-7. 170, Vol. 2

Crowley, Arthur. BONZO BEAVER.
Ages 3-6. 144, Vol. 3

Kroll, Steven. FRIDAY THE 13TH.
Ages 4-7. 353, Vol. 3

McCaffrey, Mary. MY BROTHER ANGE.
Ages 8-11. 389, Vol. 3

McCord, Jean. TURKEYLEGS THOMPSON.
Ages 11-14. 390, Vol. 3

Miner, Jane Claypool. SHE'S MY SISTER: HAVING A
RETARDED SISTER.
Ages 11 and up. 434, Vol. 3

**Relatives**

**See also:** *Family*

Goldman, Susan. COUSINS ARE SPECIAL.
Ages 3-5. 254, Vol. 2

Orgel, Doris. A CERTAIN MAGIC.
Ages 11-13. 490, Vol. 2

**Grandparent.** *See: Grandparent*

**Great-grandparent.** *See: Great-grandparent*

**Living in child's home**

Gaeddert, LouAnn Bigge. JUST LIKE SISTERS.
Ages 8-12. 196, Vol. 3

Giff, Patricia Reilly. THE GIFT OF THE PIRATE
QUEEN.
Ages 9-12. 211, Vol. 3

Little, Jean. LOOK THROUGH MY WINDOW.
Ages 10-14. 573, Vol. 1

Mathis, Sharon Bell. THE HUNDRED PENNY BOX.
Ages 8-10. 445, Vol. 2

Mearian, Judy Frank. TWO WAYS ABOUT IT.
Ages 9-12. 418, Vol. 3

Nathan, Dorothy. THE SHY ONE.
Ages 9-12. 656, Vol. 1

Perl, Lila. PIEFACE AND DAPHNE.
Ages 9-11. 494, Vol. 3

Robinson, Barbara Webb. TEMPORARY TIMES,
TEMPORARY PLACES.
Ages 11-13. 538, Vol. 3

Shiefman, Vicky. MINDY.
Ages 8-10. 815, Vol. 1

Vogel, Ilse-Margret. FAREWELL, AUNT ISABELL.
Ages 8-10. 669, Vol. 3

Wright, Betty Ren. I LIKE BEING ALONE.
Ages 6-9. 709, Vol. 3

**Living in home of**

Adler, Carole Schwerdtfeger. SOME OTHER
SUMMER.
Ages 10-13. 9, Vol. 3

Anckarsvärd, Karin. AUNT VINNIE'S VICTORIOUS
SIX.
Ages 10-12. 14, Vol. 1

Annixter, Jane, pseud. and Paul Annixter, pseud. THE
RUNNER.
Ages 11-13. 24, Vol. 1

Arundel, Honor. THE HIGH HOUSE.
Ages 11 and up. 38, Vol. 1

Bawden, Nina Mary Kark. THE RUNAWAY
SUMMER.
Ages 9-12. 57, Vol. 1

Beckwith, Lillian. THE SPUDDY: A NOVEL.
Ages 11 and up. 48, Vol. 2

Blume, Judy Sussman. TIGER EYES.
Ages 11 and up. 57, Vol. 3

Bosse, Malcolm Joseph. GANESH.
Ages 11-14. 65, Vol. 3

Bulla, Clyde Robert. BENITO.
Ages 8-10. 134, Vol. 1

Bulla, Clyde Robert. POOR BOY, RICH BOY.
Ages 5-8. 87, Vol. 3

Bulla, Clyde Robert. SHOESHINE GIRL.
Ages 8-10. 93, Vol. 2

Butler, Beverly Kathleen. A GIRL CALLED WENDY.
Ages 12 and up. 106, Vol. 2

Carlson, Natalie Savage. SCHOOL BELL IN THE
VALLEY.
Ages 8-11. 169, Vol. 1

Coleman, William Laurence. ORPHAN JIM: A
NOVEL.
Ages 13 and up. 158, Vol. 2

Coolidge, Olivia Ensor. COME BY HERE.
Ages 11 and up. 245, Vol. 1

Fisher, Dorothy Canfield. UNDERSTOOD BETSY.
Ages 9-12. 317, Vol. 1

Gage, Wilson, pseud. BIG BLUE ISLAND.
Ages 9-11. 341, Vol. 1

Hunt, Irene. UP A ROAD SLOWLY.
Ages 12 and up. 438, Vol. 1

Lobel, Arnold. UNCLE ELEPHANT.
Ages 4-7. 381, Vol. 3

McKay, Robert W. CANARY RED.
Ages 12 and up. 597, Vol. 1

MacLachlan, Patricia. ARTHUR, FOR THE VERY
FIRST TIME.
Ages 8-10. 393, Vol. 3

Madison, Winifred. MARIA LUISA.
Ages 9-12. 607, Vol. 1

Mazer, Norma Fox. MRS. FISH, APE, AND ME, THE
DUMP QUEEN.
Ages 10-12. 414, Vol. 3

## Relatives (cont.)

Miller, Ruth White. THE CITY ROSE.
Ages 11-13. 460, Vol. 2

Morgan, Alison Mary. ALL KINDS OF PRICKLES.
Ages 11-13. 450, Vol. 3

Morgan, Alison Mary. PAUL'S KITE.
Ages 10-13. 451, Vol. 3

Naylor, Phyllis Reynolds. A STRING OF CHANCES.
Ages 12 and up. 464, Vol. 3

Newton, Suzanne. M.V. SEXTON SPEAKING.
Ages 11 and up. 466, Vol. 3

Paulsen, Gary. THE FOXMAN.
Ages 11-14. 495, Vol. 2

Pfeffer, Susan Beth. JUST MORGAN.
Ages 12 and up. 707, Vol. 1

Prince, Alison. THE TURKEY'S NEST.
Ages 12 and up. 520, Vol. 3

Rinaldi, Ann. PROMISES ARE FOR KEEPING.
Ages 12 and up. 534, Vol. 3

Sargent, Sarah. SECRET LIES.
Ages 11 and up. 570, Vol. 3

Seredy, Kate. THE GOOD MASTER.
Ages 9-12. 802, Vol. 1

Shotwell, Louisa Rossiter. ADAM BOOKOUT.
Ages 11-13. 817, Vol. 1

Street, James Howell. GOOD-BYE, MY LADY.
Ages 11 and up. 878, Vol. 1

Townsend, John Rowe. GOOD-BYE TO THE JUNGLE.
Ages 11-13. 900, Vol. 1

Townsend, John Rowe. TROUBLE IN THE JUNGLE.
Ages 12 and up. 902, Vol. 1

Voigt, Cynthia. HOMECOMING.
Ages 11 and up. 672, Vol. 3

Wier, Ester Alberti. THE RUMPTYDOOLERS.
Ages 11-13. 972, Vol. 1

Wortis, Avi. SOMETIMES I THINK I HEAR MY NAME.
Ages 10-13. 708, Vol. 3

**Parents.** *See: Parent/Parents; Parental*

**Sibling.** *See: Sibling*

## Religion

**See also:** *Prejudice: religious*

### Faith

Herman, Charlotte. WHAT HAPPENED TO HEATHER HOPKOWITZ?
Ages 10-13. 283, Vol. 3

Ipswitch, Elaine. SCOTT WAS HERE.
Ages 12 and up. 322, Vol. 3

Killilea, Marie Lyons. KAREN.
Ages 12 and up. 495, Vol. 1

Killilea, Marie Lyons. WITH LOVE FROM KAREN.
Ages 12 and up. 496, Vol. 1

L'Engle, Madeleine Franklin. A RING OF ENDLESS LIGHT.
Ages 11-14. 363, Vol. 1

Marangell, Virginia J. GIANNA MIA.
Ages 12-15. 402, Vol. 1

Rogers, Dale Evans. ANGEL UNAWARE.
Ages 12 and up. 750, Vol. 1

Sebestyen, Ouida. WORDS BY HEART.
Ages 10-13. 580, Vol. 3

Swartley, David Warren. MY FRIEND, MY BROTHER.
Ages 9-11. 642, Vol. 3

### Questioning

Branscum, Robbie. THE SAVING OF P.S.
Ages 9-12. 78, Vol. 2

Fisher, Aileen Lucia. I STOOD UPON A MOUNTAIN.
Ages 4-8. 189, Vol. 3

Hurwitz, Johanna. ONCE I WAS A PLUM TREE.
Ages 9-11. 317, Vol. 3

Johnston, Norma. THE KEEPING DAYS.
Ages 11 and up. 468, Vol. 1

Naylor, Phyllis Reynolds. A STRING OF CHANCES.
Ages 12 and up. 464, Vol. 3

Van Leeuwen, Jean. SEEMS LIKE THIS ROAD GOES ON FOREVER.
Ages 12 and up. 663, Vol. 3

Veglahn, Nancy Crary. FELLOWSHIP OF THE SEVEN STARS.
Ages 12 and up. 665, Vol. 3

## Religions

**Amish.** *See: Amish*

**Buddhist.** *See: Buddhist*

**Choice of**
Blume, Judy Sussman. ARE YOU THERE GOD? IT'S ME, MARGARET.
Ages 10-13. 87, Vol. 1

**Jewish.** *See: Jew/Jewish*

**Mennonite.** *See: Mennonite*

**Mormon.** *See: Church of Jesus Christ of Latter-day Saints (Mormon)*

**Quaker.** *See: Society of Friends (Quaker)*

**Roman Catholic.** *See: Roman Catholic*

## Remarriage

**See:** *Parent/Parents: remarriage of; Stepparent*

## Remorse

**See:** *Conscience; Guilt, feelings of; Values/Valuing*

## Report Cards

**See:** *School: achievement/underachievement*

## Reputation

Bonham, Frank. VIVA CHICANO.
Ages 12 and up. 99, Vol. 1

Colman, Hila Crayder. THE CASE OF THE STOLEN BAGELS.
Ages 7-10. 162, Vol. 2

Conford, Ellen. FELICIA THE CRITIC.
Ages 9-11. 239, Vol. 1

Etter, Les. GET THOSE REBOUNDS!
Ages 10-13. 220, Vol. 2

Fife, Dale. WHO'S IN CHARGE OF LINCOLN?
Ages 8-10. 314, Vol. 1

Guy, Rosa Cuthbert. THE DISAPPEARANCE.
Ages 12 and up. 252, Vol. 3

Hall, Lynn. TROUBLEMAKER.
Ages 11-14. 395, Vol. 1

McKay, Robert W. THE RUNNING BACK.
Ages 12-14. 392, Vol. 3

Peyton, K.M., pseud. THE BEETHOVEN MEDAL.
Ages 12 and up. 704, Vol. 1

Stolz, Mary Slattery. THE BULLY OF BARKHAM STREET.
Ages 8-11. 863, Vol. 1

Turkle, Brinton. THE ADVENTURES OF OBADIAH.
Ages 4-8. 906, Vol. 1

## Resourcefulness

**See also:** *Creativity; Problem solving*

Alexander, Martha G. MOVE OVER, TWERP.
Ages 5-8. 11, Vol. 3

Alexander, Martha G. WE NEVER GET TO DO ANYTHING.
Ages 3-6. 11, Vol. 1

Baker, Charlotte. COCKLEBURR QUARTERS.
Ages 9-12. 44, Vol. 1

Baker, Margaret Joyce. HOME FROM THE HILL.
Ages 11-13. 45, Vol. 1

## Resourcefulness (cont.)

Balderson, Margaret. WHEN JAYS FLY TO BARBMO.
Ages 12 and up. 48, Vol. 1

Bennett, Jack. THE VOYAGE OF THE LUCKY DRAGON.
Ages 11 and up. 45, Vol. 3

Benson, Ellen. PHILIP'S LITTLE SISTER.
Ages 5-8. 46, Vol. 3

Beskow, Elsa Maartman. PELLE'S NEW SUIT.
Ages 4-7. 75, Vol. 1

Bethancourt, T. Ernesto, pseud. NEW YORK CITY TOO FAR FROM TAMPA BLUES.
Ages 10-14. 55, Vol. 2

Binzen, Bill. MIGUEL'S MOUNTAIN.
Ages 5-9. 77, Vol. 1

Bosworth, J. Allan. ALL THE DARK PLACES.
Ages 12 and up. 104, Vol. 1

Bradbury, Bianca. "I'M VINNY, I'M ME".
Ages 12 and up. 65, Vol. 2

Bulla, Clyde Robert. KEEP RUNNING, ALLEN!
Ages 4-6. 92, Vol. 2

Calhoun, Mary Huiskamp. THE NIGHT THE MONSTER CAME.
Ages 8-10. 102, Vol. 3

Carruth, Ella Kaiser. SHE WANTED TO READ: THE STORY OF MARY MCLEOD BETHUNE.
Ages 9-12. 173, Vol. 1

Chaffin, Lillie Dorton. WE BE WARM TILL SPRINGTIME COMES.
Ages 6-9. 110, Vol. 3

Church, Richard. FIVE BOYS IN A CAVE.
Ages 9-12. 185, Vol. 1

Cleaver, Vera and Bill Cleaver. WHERE THE LILIES BLOOM.
Ages 11 and up. 203, Vol. 1

Clyne, Patricia Edwards. TUNNELS OF TERROR.
Ages 10-12. 149, Vol. 2

Corcoran, Barbara. DON'T SLAM THE DOOR WHEN YOU GO.
Ages 12 and up. 249, Vol. 1

Crowley, Arthur. BONZO BEAVER.
Ages 3-6. 144, Vol. 3

De Roo, Anne Louise. SCRUB FIRE.
Ages 9-12. 162, Vol. 3

Drescher, Joan Elizabeth. I'M IN CHARGE!
Ages 5-8. 171, Vol. 3

Fife, Dale. WHAT'S THE PRIZE, LINCOLN?
Ages 8-10. 313, Vol. 1

Fife, Dale. WHO'S IN CHARGE OF LINCOLN?
Ages 8-10. 314, Vol. 1

Gardiner, John Reynolds. STONE FOX.
Ages 8-10. 202, Vol. 3

George, Jean Craighead. JULIE OF THE WOLVES.
Ages 10 and up. 353, Vol. 1

George, Jean Craighead. MY SIDE OF THE MOUNTAIN.
Ages 11-14. 354, Vol. 1

Gerson, Corinne. SON FOR A DAY.
Ages 10-12. 208, Vol. 3

Giff, Patricia Reilly. FOURTH GRADE CELEBRITY.
Ages 8-10. 210, Vol. 3

Gray, Nigel. IT'LL ALL COME OUT IN THE WASH.
Ages 4-6. 233, Vol. 3

Greenwald, Sheila. GIVE US A GREAT BIG SMILE, ROSY COLE.
Ages 8-10. 246, Vol. 3

Griese, Arnold Alfred. THE WIND IS NOT A RIVER.
Ages 9-12. 276, Vol. 2

Hamre, Leif. OPERATION ARCTIC.
Ages 11 and up. 398, Vol. 1

Hautzig, Esther Rudomin. A GIFT FOR MAMA.
Ages 8-12. 273, Vol. 3

Hill, Elizabeth Starr. EVAN'S CORNER.
Ages 6-9. 411, Vol. 1

Hoban, Lillian Aberman. ARTHUR'S FUNNY MONEY.
Ages 6-8. 294, Vol. 3

Hoban, Lillian Aberman. ARTHUR'S HONEY BEAR.
Ages 4-8. 415, Vol. 1

Hocken, Sheila. EMMA AND I.
Ages 12 and up. 324, Vol. 2

Holman, Felice. SLAKE'S LIMBO.
Ages 12 and up. 430, Vol. 1

Houston, James Archibald. FROZEN FIRE: A TALE OF COURAGE.
Ages 10-13. 334, Vol. 2

Hughes, Shirley. ALFIE GETS IN FIRST.
Ages 3-5. 309, Vol. 3

Hutchins, Patricia. HAPPY BIRTHDAY, SAM.
Ages 5-7. 343, Vol. 2

Inkiow, Dimiter. ME AND CLARA AND CASIMER THE CAT.
Ages 7-9. 321, Vol. 3

Irwin, Hadley, pseud. MOON AND ME.
Ages 11-14. 325, Vol. 3

Jewell, Nancy. CHEER UP, PIG!
Ages 4-8. 353, Vol. 2

Keller, Beverly Lou. THE BEETLE BUSH.
Ages 5-8. 369, Vol. 2

Kellogg, Steven. MUCH BIGGER THAN MARTIN.
Ages 4-7. 374, Vol. 2

Klein, Norma. IT'S NOT WHAT YOU EXPECT.
Ages 12 and up. 504, Vol. 1

Lattimore, Eleanor Frances. ADAM'S KEY.
Ages 7-9. 395, Vol. 2

Letchworth, Beverly J. PAX AND THE MUTT.
Ages 8-11. 366, Vol. 3

Lingard, Joan. A PROPER PLACE.
Ages 12 and up. 407, Vol. 2

Mann, Peggy. WHEN CARLOS CLOSED THE STREET.
Ages 8-11. 612, Vol. 1

Mathis, Sharon Bell. SIDEWALK STORY.
Ages 8-10. 618, Vol. 1

Meddaugh, Susan. TOO SHORT FRED.
Ages 6-8. 450, Vol. 2

Naylor, Phyllis Reynolds. ALL BECAUSE I'M OLDER.
Ages 7-9. 462, Vol. 3

Naylor, Phyllis Reynolds. EDDIE, INCORPORATED.
Ages 9-11. 463, Vol. 3

Neigoff, Mike. SOCCER HERO.
Ages 9-11. 475, Vol. 2

Norman, Lilith. CLIMB A LONELY HILL.
Ages 11-14. 671, Vol. 1

O'Dell, Scott. ISLAND OF THE BLUE DOLPHINS.
Ages 10 and up. 681, Vol. 1

Ofek, Uriel. SMOKE OVER GOLAN.
Ages 9-13. 468, Vol. 3

Pape, Donna Lugg. SNOWMAN FOR SALE.
Ages 5-7. 492, Vol. 2

Pearson, Susan. SATURDAY I RAN AWAY.
Ages 5-7. 488, Vol. 3

Perrine, Mary. NANNABAH'S FRIEND.
Ages 7-10. 702, Vol. 1

Pfeffer, Susan Beth. KID POWER.
Ages 9-12. 511, Vol. 2

Phelan, Terry Wolfe. THE WEEK MOM UNPLUGGED THE TVS.
Ages 8-10. 506, Vol. 3

Reader, Dennis J. COMING BACK ALIVE.
Ages 12 and up. 525, Vol. 3

Resnick, Rose. SUN AND SHADOW: THE AUTOBIOGRAPHY OF A WOMAN WHO CLEARED A PATHWAY TO THE SEEING WORLD FOR THE BLIND.
Ages 12 and up. 532, Vol. 2

## Resourcefulness (cont.)

Robertson, Keith. HENRY REED'S BABY-SITTING SERVICE.
Ages 9-12. 742, Vol. 1

Robinson, Jean. THE STRANGE BUT WONDERFUL COSMIC AWARENESS OF DUFFY MOON.
Ages 9-12. 745, Vol. 1

Rounds, Glen Harold. THE BLIND COLT.
Ages 8-12. 754, Vol. 1

Roy, Ronald. AVALANCHE!
Ages 10 and up. 555, Vol. 3

Ruthstrom, Dorotha. THE BIG KITE CONTEST.
Ages 6-8. 560, Vol. 3

Sargent, Sarah. EDWARD TROY AND THE WITCH CAT.
Ages 9-11. 569, Vol. 2

Sawyer, Ruth. MAGGIE ROSE: HER BIRTHDAY CHRISTMAS.
Ages 8-10. 776, Vol. 1

Schlein, Miriam. THE GIRL WHO WOULD RATHER CLIMB TREES.
Ages 4-8. 574, Vol. 2

Smith, Pauline Coggeshall. BRUSH FIRE!
Ages 11 and up. 613, Vol. 3

Southall, Ivan. HILLS END.
Ages 11 and up. 846, Vol. 1

Sperry, Armstrong. CALL IT COURAGE.
Ages 9 and up. 849, Vol. 1

Stapp, Arthur Donald. THE FABULOUS EARTHWORM DEAL.
Ages 10-13. 852, Vol. 1

Tate, Joan. LUKE'S GARDEN AND GRAMP: TWO NOVELS.
Ages 10-13. 644, Vol. 3

Udry, Janice May. MARY JO'S GRANDMOTHER.
Ages 6-8. 912, Vol. 1

Udry, Janice May. THE SUNFLOWER GARDEN.
Ages 6-10. 913, Vol. 1

Viereck, Phillip. THE SUMMER I WAS LOST.
Ages 11 and up. 923, Vol. 1

Waterton, Betty Marie. A SALMON FOR SIMON.
Ages 4-7. 685, Vol. 3

## Respect

**See:** *Age: respect for; Grandparent: respect for; Parent/Parents: respect for/lack of respect for; Sibling: respect for*

## Responsibility

**See also:** *Chores; Job; Work, attitude toward*

*Accepting.* See also: *Leader/Leadership*
Adler, Carole Schwerdtfeger. THE MAGIC OF THE GLITS.
Ages 9-12. 6, Vol. 3

Alter, Judy. AFTER PA WAS SHOT.
Ages 10-13. 11, Vol. 2

Annixter, Jane, pseud. and Paul Annixter, pseud. HORNS OF PLENTY.
Ages 11 and up. 23, Vol. 1

Annixter, Jane, pseud. and Paul Annixter, pseud. THE RUNNER.
Ages 11-13. 24, Vol. 1

Annixter, Jane, pseud. and Paul Annixter, pseud. WINDIGO.
Ages 10 and up. 25, Vol. 1

Annixter, Paul, pseud. SWIFTWATER.
Ages 13 and up. 26, Vol. 1

Bach, Alice Hendricks. A FATHER EVERY FEW YEARS.
Ages 11-13. 27, Vol. 2

Beatty, Hetty Burlingame. LITTLE OWL INDIAN.
Ages 4-7. 59, Vol. 1

Bishop, Claire Huchet. ALL ALONE.
Ages 7-10. 78, Vol. 1

Blegvad, Lenore Hochman and Erik Blegvad. THE GREAT HAMSTER HUNT.
Ages 8-10. 80, Vol. 1

Bloch, Marie Halun. DISPLACED PERSON.
Ages 10-13. 57, Vol. 2

Blue, Rose. THE THIRTEENTH YEAR: A BAR MITZVAH STORY.
Ages 10-12. 60, Vol. 2

Bova, Benjamin William. CITY OF DARKNESS: A NOVEL.
Ages 12 and up. 63, Vol. 2

Bradbury, Bianca. "I'M VINNY, I'M ME".
Ages 12 and up. 65, Vol. 2

Bradbury, Bianca. THOSE TRAVER KIDS.
Ages 12 and up. 111, Vol. 1

Bradford, Richard. RED SKY AT MORNING.
Ages 13 and up. 112, Vol. 1

Brancato, Robin Fidler. SWEET BELLS JANGLED OUT OF TUNE.
Ages 11-14. 70, Vol. 3

Branfield, John. WHY ME?
Ages 11 and up. 114, Vol. 1

Branscum, Robbie. FOR LOVE OF JODY.
Ages 9-12. 73, Vol. 3

Buchan, Stuart. A SPACE OF HIS OWN.
Ages 12 and up. 82, Vol. 3

Buck, Pearl Sydenstricker. MATTHEW, MARK, LUKE, AND JOHN.
Ages 8-12. 130, Vol. 1

Bulla, Clyde Robert. DEXTER.
Ages 9-11. 135, Vol. 1

Bulla, Clyde Robert. OPEN THE DOOR AND SEE ALL THE PEOPLE.
Ages 8-11. 136, Vol. 1

Bulla, Clyde Robert. SHOESHINE GIRL.
Ages 8-10. 93, Vol. 2

Bunting, Anne Evelyn. SKATEBOARD FOUR.
Ages 8-10. 98, Vol. 2

Burleson, Elizabeth. A MAN OF THE FAMILY.
Ages 11 and up. 145, Vol. 1

Burton, Virginia Lee. KATY AND THE BIG SNOW.
Ages 3-6. 148, Vol. 1

Butterworth, William Edmund. LEROY AND THE OLD MAN.
Ages 12 and up. 93, Vol. 3

Byars, Betsy Cromer. THE NIGHT SWIMMERS.
Ages 10-12. 98, Vol. 3

Carris, Joan Davenport. WHEN THE BOYS RAN THE HOUSE.
Ages 8-12. 108, Vol. 3

Chaffin, Lillie Dorton. WE BE WARM TILL SPRINGTIME COMES.
Ages 6-9. 110, Vol. 3

Choate, Judith Newkirk. AWFUL ALEXANDER.
Ages 4-7. 130, Vol. 2

Clark, Mavis Thorpe. IRON MOUNTAIN.
Ages 12 and up. 187, Vol. 1

Clark, Mavis Thorpe. THE MIN-MIN.
Ages 12 and up. 188, Vol. 1

Cleary, Beverly Bunn. HENRY AND THE CLUBHOUSE.
Ages 8-10. 191, Vol. 1

Cleary, Beverly Bunn. HENRY AND THE PAPER ROUTE.
Ages 7-10. 192, Vol. 1

Cleaver, Vera and Bill Cleaver. THE MOCK REVOLT.
Ages 10-14. 202, Vol. 1

Cleaver, Vera and Bill Cleaver. QUEEN OF HEARTS.
Ages 10-13. 140, Vol. 2

Cleaver, Vera and Bill Cleaver. TRIAL VALLEY.
Ages 12 and up. 141, Vol. 2

Cleaver, Vera and Bill Cleaver. WHERE THE LILIES BLOOM.
Ages 11 and up. 203, Vol. 1

## Responsibility (cont.)

Pfeffer, Susan Beth. KID POWER.
Ages 9-12. 511, Vol. 2

Philips, Barbara. DON'T CALL ME FATSO.
Ages 5-9. 507, Vol. 3

Pierik, Robert. ROOKFLEAS IN THE CELLAR.
Ages 8-13. 512, Vol. 3

Raymond, Charles. JUD.
Ages 9-12. 726, Vol. 1

Reuter, Margaret. YOU CAN DEPEND ON ME.
Ages 6-9. 530, Vol. 3

Richard, Adrienne. PISTOL.
Ages 12 and up. 732, Vol. 1

Rivera, Geraldo. A SPECIAL KIND OF COURAGE:
PROFILES OF YOUNG AMERICANS.
Ages 12 and up. 544, Vol. 2

Robertson, Keith. HENRY REED'S BABY-SITTING
SERVICE.
Ages 9-12. 742, Vol. 1

Robinson, John Roosevelt and Alfred
Duckett. BREAKTHROUGH TO THE BIG LEAGUE:
THE STORY OF JACKIE ROBINSON.
Ages 10 and up. 746, Vol. 1

Rodgers, Mary. FREAKY FRIDAY.
Ages 10-13. 749, Vol. 1

Ross, Pat. M AND M AND THE BIG BAG.
Ages 6-8. 550, Vol. 3

Ruby, Lois. ARRIVING AT A PLACE YOU'VE
NEVER LEFT.
Ages 12 and up. 564, Vol. 2

Ruhen, Olaf. CORCORAN'S THE NAME.
Ages 12 and up. 758, Vol. 1

Sachs, Marilyn. THE BEARS' HOUSE.
Ages 9-12. 760, Vol. 1

Schaefer, Jack Warner. OLD RAMON.
Ages 10 and up. 777, Vol. 1

Schwarzrock, Shirley and C. Gilbert Wrenn. I'D
RATHER DO IT MYSELF, IF YOU DON'T MIND.
Ages 11 and up. 792, Vol. 1

Schwarzrock, Shirley and C. Gilbert
Wrenn. UNDERSTANDING THE LAW OF OUR
LAND.
Ages 11 and up. 797, Vol. 1

Shreve, Susan Richards. THE MASQUERADE.
Ages 12 and up. 591, Vol. 3

Smith, Nancy Covert. JOSIE'S HANDFUL OF
QUIETNESS.
Ages 9-11. 614, Vol. 2

Smith, Pauline Coggeshall. BRUSH FIRE!
Ages 11 and up. 613, Vol. 3

Snyder, Anne. MY NAME IS DAVY — I'M AN
ALCOHOLIC.
Ages 12 and up. 616, Vol. 2

Sommerfelt, Aimee. THE ROAD TO AGRA.
Ages 10-13. 839, Vol. 1

Sommerfelt, Aimee. THE WHITE BUNGALOW.
Ages 10-13. 840, Vol. 1

Southall, Ivan. BENSON BOY.
Ages 9-11. 845, Vol. 1

Spence, Eleanor Rachel. THE DEVIL HOLE.
Ages 10-14. 619, Vol. 2

Stapp, Arthur Donald. THE FABULOUS
EARTHWORM DEAL.
Ages 10-13. 852, Vol. 1

Stapp, Arthur Donald. ORDEAL BY MOUNTAINS.
Ages 11 and up. 853, Vol. 1

Stinetorf, Louise Allender. A CHARM FOR PACO'S
MOTHER.
Ages 9 and up. 862, Vol. 1

Stolz, Mary Slattery. A DOG ON BARKHAM
STREET.
Ages 8-11. 865, Vol. 1

Stolz, Mary Slattery. THE EDGE OF NEXT YEAR.
Ages 12 and up. 866, Vol. 1

Strang, Celia. FOSTER MARY.
Ages 10-13. 633, Vol. 3

Strang, Celia. THIS CHILD IS MINE.
Ages 11-14. 634, Vol. 3

Sutcliff, Rosemary. THE WITCH'S BRAT!
Ages 11-13. 882, Vol. 1

Thomas, Jane Resh. THE COMEBACK DOG.
Ages 7-9. 653, Vol. 3

Thomas, Karen. THE GOOD THING...THE BAD
THING.
Ages 3-7. 654, Vol. 3

Tobias, Tobi. ARTHUR MITCHELL.
Ages 7-10. 649, Vol. 2

Townsend, John Rowe. GOOD-BYE TO THE JUNGLE.
Ages 11-13. 900, Vol. 1

Townsend, John Rowe. TROUBLE IN THE JUNGLE.
Ages 12 and up. 902, Vol. 1

Udry, Janice May. THE SUNFLOWER GARDEN.
Ages 6-10. 913, Vol. 1

Viscardi, Henry. A MAN'S STATURE.
Ages 12 and up. 932, Vol. 1

White, Elwyn Brooks. THE TRUMPET OF THE
SWAN.
Ages 9-13. 968, Vol. 1

Whitehead, Ruth. THE MOTHER TREE.
Ages 10-13. 969, Vol. 1

Wilkinson, Brenda Scott. LUDELL AND WILLIE.
Ages 12 and up. 681, Vol. 2

Wood, Phyllis Anderson. GET A LITTLE LOST, TIA.
Ages 11-13. 708, Vol. 2

Woody, Regina Llewellyn Jones. SECOND SIGHT FOR
TOMMY.
Ages 12 and up. 993, Vol. 1

Zion, Gene. THE PLANT SITTER.
Ages 4-7. 1017, Vol. 1

## Avoiding

Atkinson, Linda. HIT AND RUN.
Ages 11 and up. 31, Vol. 3

Dauer, Rosamond. MY FRIEND, JASPER JONES.
Ages 3-6. 192, Vol. 2

Delton, Judy and Elaine Knox-Wagner. THE BEST
MOM IN THE WORLD.
Ages 4-7. 159, Vol. 3

Drescher, Joan Elizabeth. THE MARVELOUS MESS.
Ages 4-6. 172, Vol. 3

Giff, Patricia Reilly. THE GIRL WHO KNEW IT ALL.
Ages 8-10. 212, Vol. 3

Hinton, Nigel. COLLISION COURSE.
Ages 11 and up. 315, Vol. 2

Holman, Felice. PROFESSOR DIGGINS' DRAGONS.
Ages 9-11. 429, Vol. 1

Jordan, Hope Dahle. HAUNTED SUMMER.
Ages 11 and up. 472, Vol. 1

Lexau, Joan M. I'LL TELL ON YOU.
Ages 5-8. 406, Vol. 2

Polushkin, Maria. BUBBA AND BABBA.
Ages 3-8. 520, Vol. 2

Snyder, Anne. MY NAME IS DAVY — I'M AN
ALCOHOLIC.
Ages 12 and up. 616, Vol. 2

## Neglecting. See also: Forgetting

Branfield, John. WHY ME?
Ages 11 and up. 114, Vol. 1

Clymer, Eleanor Lowenton. HOW I WENT
SHOPPING AND WHAT I GOT.
Ages 8-10. 210, Vol. 1

Fletcher, David. THE KING'S GOBLET.
Ages 12 and up. 323, Vol. 1

Ness, Evaline Michelow. DO YOU HAVE THE TIME,
LYDIA?
Ages 5-8. 659, Vol. 1

Shaw, Richard. THE HARD WAY HOME.
Ages 11-13. 592, Vol. 2

## Retardation

**See:** *Mental retardation*

## Retirement

**See also:** *Age; Grandparent; Job*
Knox-Wagner, Elaine. MY GRANDPA RETIRED
TODAY.
Ages 4-7. 346, Vol. 3

## Revenge

**See also:** *Aggression*
Alexander, Martha G. AND MY MEAN OLD
MOTHER WILL BE SORRY, BLACKBOARD BEAR.
Ages 3-8. 8, Vol. 1
Arrick, Fran. CHERNOWITZ!
Ages 12 and up. 23, Vol. 3
Ashley, Bernard. A KIND OF WILD JUSTICE.
Ages 12 and up. 30, Vol. 3
Bulla, Clyde Robert. ALMOST A HERO.
Ages 11 and up. 84, Vol. 3
Bulla, Clyde Robert. LAST LOOK.
Ages 8-10. 86, Vol. 3
Hall, Lynn. FLOWERS OF ANGER.
Ages 10-12. 288, Vol. 2
Houston, James Archibald. THE WHITE ARCHER:
AN ESKIMO LEGEND.
Ages 9-11. 436, Vol. 1
Lowry, Lois. ANASTASIA AT YOUR SERVICE.
Ages 9-12. 385, Vol. 3
Panek, Dennis. MATILDA HIPPO HAS A BIG
MOUTH.
Ages 4-7. 478, Vol. 3
Sharmat, Marjorie Weinman. MAGGIE
MARMELSTEIN FOR PRESIDENT.
Ages 9-12. 588, Vol. 2
Wallace, Art. TOBY.
Ages 9-11. 945, Vol. 1

## Rheumatic Fever

**See also:** *Cardiac conditions*
Lenski, Lois. CORN-FARM BOY.
Ages 9-12. 544, Vol. 1

## Rights

**See:** *Prejudice; Women's rights*

## Risk, Taking of

Bosworth, J. Allan. ALL THE DARK PLACES.
Ages 12 and up. 104, Vol. 1
Clyne, Patricia Edwards. TUNNELS OF TERROR.
Ages 10-12. 149, Vol. 2
Conaway, Judith. I DARE YOU!
Ages 5-7. 169, Vol. 2
Fife, Dale. NORTH OF DANGER.
Ages 10-12. 227, Vol. 2
Greene, Constance Clarke. DOUBLE-DARE O'TOOLE.
Ages 9-11. 240, Vol. 3
Houston, James Archibald. AKAVAK: AN ESKIMO
JOURNEY.
Ages 9-12. 435, Vol. 1
Houston, James Archibald. LONG CLAWS: AN
ARCTIC ADVENTURE.
Ages 9-11. 305, Vol. 3
Jeffries, Roderic. TRAPPED.
Ages 11-13. 457, Vol. 1
Potter, Beatrix. THE TALE OF PETER RABBIT.
Ages 3-7. 716, Vol. 1
Rees, David. RISKS.
Ages 11 and up. 529, Vol. 2
Stoutenburg, Adrien. WHERE TO NOW, BLUE?
Ages 10-12. 628, Vol. 2

## Rivalry

**See:** *Competition; Jealousy; Parent/Parents: power
struggle with; Sibling: rivalry; Sports/Sportsmanship*

## Roman Catholic

Christman, Elizabeth. A NICE ITALIAN GIRL.
Ages 12 and up. 132, Vol. 2
Foley, June. IT'S NO CRUSH, I'M IN LOVE!
Ages 11-13. 192, Vol. 3
Killilea, Marie Lyons. WITH LOVE FROM KAREN.
Ages 12 and up. 496, Vol. 1
Marangell, Virginia J. GIANNA MIA.
Ages 12-15. 402, Vol. 3
Spence, Eleanor Rachel. A CANDLE FOR SAINT
ANTONY.
Ages 13 and up. 618, Vol. 3

## Rumor

**See:** *Communication: rumor*

## Running Away

Alcock, Gudrun. RUN, WESTY, RUN.
Ages 10-12. 5, Vol. 1
Alexander, Martha G. AND MY MEAN OLD
MOTHER WILL BE SORRY, BLACKBOARD BEAR.
Ages 3-8. 8, Vol. 1
Angell, Judie. DEAR LOLA OR HOW TO BUILD
YOUR OWN FAMILY.
Ages 10-13. 19, Vol. 3
Anonymous. GO ASK ALICE.
Ages 13 and up. 27, Vol. 1
Arrick, Fran. STEFFIE CAN'T COME OUT TO PLAY.
Ages 12 and up. 24, Vol. 2
Ashley, Bernard. BREAK IN THE SUN.
Ages 11 and up. 29, Vol. 3
Baker, Margaret Joyce. HOME FROM THE HILL.
Ages 11-13. 45, Vol. 1
Ball, Zachary, pseud. BRISTLE FACE.
Ages 10 and up. 49, Vol. 1
Bauer, Marion Dane. SHELTER FROM THE WIND.
Ages 10-13. 43, Vol. 2
Beckman, Gunnel. A ROOM OF HIS OWN.
Ages 12 and up. 60, Vol. 1
Blume, Judy Sussman. IT'S NOT THE END OF THE
WORLD.
Ages 10-12. 91, Vol. 1
Bonham, Frank. VIVA CHICANO.
Ages 12 and up. 99, Vol. 1
Bova, Benjamin William. CITY OF DARKNESS: A
NOVEL.
Ages 12 and up. 63, Vol. 2
Bradbury, Bianca. BOY ON THE RUN.
Ages 11-13. 64, Vol. 2
Branscum, Robbie. THE SAVING OF P.S.
Ages 9-12. 78, Vol. 2
Brown, Marc Tolan. ARTHUR GOES TO CAMP.
Ages 5-8. 79, Vol. 3
Bunting, Anne Evelyn. ONE MORE FLIGHT.
Ages 10-13. 97, Vol. 2
Burn, Doris. ANDREW HENRY'S MEADOW.
Ages 5-8. 146, Vol. 1
Butler, Beverly Kathleen. CAPTIVE THUNDER.
Ages 11 and up. 150, Vol. 1
Butler, Beverly Kathleen. A GIRL CALLED WENDY.
Ages 12 and up. 106, Vol. 2
Campbell, Hope, pseud. NO MORE TRAINS TO
TOTTENVILLE.
Ages 12 and up. 161, Vol. 1
Carlson, Natalie Savage. RUNAWAY MARIE LOUISE.
Ages 3-6. 117, Vol. 2
Clark, Mavis Thorpe. IRON MOUNTAIN.
Ages 12 and up. 187, Vol. 1
Clark, Mavis Thorpe. THE MIN-MIN.
Ages 12 and up. 188, Vol. 1
Clifton, Lucille. MY BROTHER FINE WITH ME.
Ages 5-8. 147, Vol. 2

## Running Away (cont.)

Clymer, Eleanor Lowenton. ME AND THE EGGMAN.
Ages 10-13. 212, Vol. 1

Cohen, Barbara Nash. WHERE'S FLORRIE?
Ages 6-8. 154, Vol. 2

Cole, Brock. NO MORE BATHS.
Ages 3-6. 130, Vol. 3

Coleman, William Laurence. ORPHAN JIM: A NOVEL.
Ages 13 and up. 158, Vol. 2

Coles, Robert. RIDING FREE.
Ages 11 and up. 224, Vol. 1

Colman, Hila Crayder. CLAUDIA, WHERE ARE YOU?
Ages 12 and up. 228, Vol. 1

Colman, Hila Crayder. THAT'S THE WAY IT IS, AMIGO.
Ages 11-13. 168, Vol. 2

Cone, Molly Lamken. YOU CAN'T MAKE ME IF I DON'T WANT TO.
Ages 12 and up. 237, Vol. 1

Corcoran, Barbara. DON'T SLAM THE DOOR WHEN YOU GO.
Ages 12 and up. 249, Vol. 1

Corcoran, Barbara. A ROW OF TIGERS.
Ages 10-12. 250, Vol. 1

Cunningham, Julia Woolfolk. COME TO THE EDGE.
Ages 9-13. 187, Vol. 2

Dodson, Susan. HAVE YOU SEEN THIS GIRL?
Ages 13 and up. 166, Vol. 3

Dunnahoo, Terry. WHO CARES ABOUT ESPIE SANCHEZ?
Ages 10-12. 210, Vol. 2

Dunne, Mary Collins. HOBY & STUB.
Ages 10-13. 176, Vol. 3

Elfman, Blossom. THE BUTTERFLY GIRL.
Ages 13 and up. 180, Vol. 3

Eyerly, Jeannette Hyde. DROP-OUT.
Ages 11 and up. 296, Vol. 1

Eyerly, Jeannette Hyde. THE WORLD OF ELLEN MARCH.
Ages 12 and up. 301, Vol. 1

Fenisong, Ruth. BOY WANTED.
Ages 8-11. 310, Vol. 1

Fenton, Edward. DUFFY'S ROCKS.
Ages 12 and up. 311, Vol. 1

Friis-Baastad, Babbis Ellinor. DON'T TAKE TEDDY.
Ages 11 and up. 338, Vol. 1

George, Jean Craighead. JULIE OF THE WOLVES.
Ages 10 and up. 353, Vol. 1

George, Jean Craighead. MY SIDE OF THE MOUNTAIN.
Ages 11-14. 354, Vol. 1

Hall, Lynn. STRAY.
Ages 8-11. 394, Vol. 1

Hallman, Ruth. BREAKAWAY.
Ages 12 and up. 257, Vol. 3

Hallman, Ruth. I GOTTA BE FREE.
Ages 10-13. 289, Vol. 2

Hamilton, Morse and Emily Hamilton. MY NAME IS EMILY.
Ages 3-6. 259, Vol. 3

Hamre, Leif. OPERATION ARCTIC.
Ages 11 and up. 398, Vol. 1

Harris, Marilyn. THE RUNAWAY'S DIARY.
Ages 11 and up. 404, Vol. 1

Helena, Ann. I'M RUNNING AWAY.
Ages 5-8. 308, Vol. 2

Hill, Margaret. TURN THE PAGE, WENDY.
Ages 10-14. 291, Vol. 3

Hitte, Kathryn. BOY, WAS I MAD!
Ages 5-8. 414, Vol. 1

Hoban, Russell Conwell. A BABY SISTER FOR FRANCES.
Ages 3-7. 416, Vol. 1

Hogan, Paula Z. WILL DAD EVER MOVE BACK HOME?
Ages 7-10. 299, Vol. 3

Holland, Isabelle. AMANDA'S CHOICE.
Ages 10-13. 425, Vol. 1

Holman, Felice. SLAKE'S LIMBO.
Ages 12 and up. 430, Vol. 1

Karp, Naomi J. NOTHING RHYMES WITH APRIL.
Ages 9-11. 479, Vol. 1

Keats, Ezra Jack. PETER'S CHAIR.
Ages 3-7. 485, Vol. 1

Kingman, Lee. THE PETER PAN BAG.
Ages 12 and up. 498, Vol. 1

Konigsburg, Elaine Lobl. FROM THE MIXED-UP FILES OF MRS. BASIL E. FRANKWEILER.
Ages 9-12. 510, Vol. 1

LaFarge, Phyllis. JOANNA RUNS AWAY.
Ages 7-9. 524, Vol. 1

Lasker, Joe. THE DO-SOMETHING DAY.
Ages 3-7. 357, Vol. 3

Lexau, Joan M. EMILY AND THE KLUNKY BABY AND THE NEXT-DOOR DOG.
Ages 5-8. 555, Vol. 1

MacPherson, Margaret McLean. THE ROUGH ROAD.
Ages 12 and up. 961, Vol. 1

Mendonca, Susan R. TOUGH CHOICES.
Ages 11 and up. 419, Vol. 3

Miles, Miska, pseud. JENNY'S CAT.
Ages 6-8. 425, Vol. 3

Morgan, Alison. A BOY CALLED FISH.
Ages 10-12. 645, Vol. 1

Morgan, Alison. PETE.
Ages 11-13. 646, Vol. 1

Morgenroth, Barbara. TRAMPS LIKE US.
Ages 12 and up. 452, Vol. 3

Naylor, Phyllis Reynolds. MAKING IT HAPPEN.
Ages 11-14. 657, Vol. 1

Norris, Gunilla Brodde. IF YOU LISTEN.
Ages 10 and up. 676, Vol. 1

Nöstlinger, Christine. GIRL MISSING: A NOVEL.
Ages 11 and up. 482, Vol. 2

O'Dell, Scott. KATHLEEN, PLEASE COME HOME.
Ages 12 and up. 485, Vol. 2

Pearson, Susan. SATURDAY I RAN AWAY.
Ages 5-7. 488, Vol. 3

Pevsner, Stella. AND YOU GIVE ME A PAIN, ELAINE.
Ages 10-13. 508, Vol. 2

Renvoize, Jean. A WILD THING.
Ages 13 and up. 727, Vol. 1

Rich, Louise Dickinson. STAR ISLAND BOY.
Ages 10-12. 730, Vol. 1

Riley, Susan. WHAT DOES IT MEAN? ANGRY.
Ages 3-6. 539, Vol. 2

Samuels, Gertrude. RUN, SHELLEY, RUN.
Ages 12 and up. 768, Vol. 1

Shaw, Richard. THE HARD WAY HOME.
Ages 11-13. 592, Vol. 2

Shotwell, Louisa Rossiter. ADAM BOOKOUT.
Ages 11-13. 817, Vol. 1

Somerlott, Robert. BLAZE.
Ages 10-13. 617, Vol. 3

Stoutenburg, Adrien. WHERE TO NOW, BLUE?
Ages 10-12. 628, Vol. 2

Talbot, Charlene Joy. THE GREAT RAT ISLAND ADVENTURE.
Ages 10-13. 634, Vol. 2

Thompson, Jean, pseud. I'M GOING TO RUN AWAY!
Ages 4-8. 648, Vol. 2

Thompson, Paul. THE HITCHHIKERS.
Ages 12 and up. 657, Vol. 3

Veglahn, Nancy Crary. FELLOWSHIP OF THE SEVEN STARS.
Ages 12 and up. 665, Vol. 3

## Running Away (cont.)

Wells, Rosemary. THE FOG COMES ON LITTLE PIG FEET.
Ages 11 and up. 961, Vol. 1
Wier, Ester Alberti. THE LONG YEAR.
Ages 10 and up. 971, Vol. 1
Winthrop, Elizabeth. MARATHON MIRANDA.
Ages 9-11. 696, Vol. 3
Zion, Gene. HARRY THE DIRTY DOG.
Ages 3-8. 1016, Vol. 1

## Russia

Bernstein, Joanne Eckstein. DMITRY: A YOUNG SOVIET IMMIGRANT.
Ages 11-13. 52, Vol. 3
Chukovsky, Kornei Ivanovich. THE SILVER CREST: MY RUSSIAN BOYHOOD.
Ages 12 and up. 135, Vol. 2
Wallace, Barbara Brooks. JULIA AND THE THIRD BAD THING.
Ages 8-10. 673, Vol. 2
Zhitkov, Boris Stepanovich. HOW I HUNTED THE LITTLE FELLOWS.
Ages 3-7. 720, Vol. 3

# S

## Sadness

**See:** *Depression*

## Scapegoat

**See:** *Aggression, displacement of*

## Scars

Friis-Baastad, Babbis Ellinor. KRISTY'S COURAGE.
Ages 8-10. 339, Vol. 1
Lowery, Bruce. SCARRED.
Ages 12 and up. 588, Vol. 1

## Schizophrenia

**See:** *Mental illness*

## School

**See also:** *Education; Integration*

### Achievement/Underachievement

Ashley, Bernard. A KIND OF WILD JUSTICE.
Ages 12 and up. 30, Vol. 3
Baudouy, Michel-Aime. MORE THAN COURAGE.
Ages 12 and up. 56, Vol. 1
Byars, Betsy Cromer. THE TV KID.
Ages 9-12. 109, Vol. 2
Cleary, Beverly Bunn. MITCH AND AMY.
Ages 9-11. 193, Vol. 1
Colman, Hila Crayder. ETHAN'S FAVORITE TEACHER.
Ages 7-9. 163, Vol. 2
First, Julia. AMY.
Ages 8-11. 230, Vol. 2
Giff, Patricia Reilly. THE GIRL WHO KNEW IT ALL.
Ages 8-10. 212, Vol. 3
Giff, Patricia Reilly. TODAY WAS A TERRIBLE DAY.
Ages 6-7. 213, Vol. 3
Gilson, Jamie. DO BANANAS CHEW GUM?
Ages 9-11. 216, Vol. 3
Hobby, Janice Hale with Gabrielle Rubin and Daniel Rubin. STAYING BACK.
Ages 6-12. 295, Vol. 3
Hogan, Paula Z. SOMETIMES I DON'T LIKE SCHOOL.
Ages 6-9. 297, Vol. 3
Hunter, Edith Fisher. SUE ELLEN.
Ages 10-12. 441, Vol. 1

Hurwitz, Johanna. TOUGH-LUCK KAREN.
Ages 10-13. 319, Vol. 3
Krumgold, Joseph E. HENRY 3.
Ages 11 and up. 522, Vol. 1
Little, Jean. SPRING BEGINS IN MARCH.
Ages 10-12. 576, Vol. 1
McKillip, Patricia A. THE NIGHT GIFT.
Ages 11 and up. 430, Vol. 2
Morrison, Bill. LOUIS JAMES HATES SCHOOL.
Ages 5-7. 466, Vol. 2
Morton, Jane. RUNNING SCARED.
Ages 10-14. 455, Vol. 3
Perl, Lila. DUMB, LIKE ME, OLIVIA POTTS.
Ages 9-12. 502, Vol. 2
Roy, Ronald. FRANKIE IS STAYING BACK.
Ages 8-10. 556, Vol. 3
Smith, Doris Buchanan. DREAMS & DRUMMERS.
Ages 10-12. 612, Vol. 2
Voigt, Cynthia. DICEY'S SONG.
Ages 11 and up. 671, Vol. 3
Walker, Pamela. TWYLA.
Ages 12 and up. 944, Vol. 1
Weiman, Eiveen. IT TAKES BRAINS.
Ages 10-12. 686, Vol. 3
Wrenn, C. Gilbert and Shirley Schwarzrock. GRADES, WHAT'S SO IMPORTANT ABOUT THEM ANYWAY?
Ages 13 and up. 1002, Vol. 1

### Behavior

Allard, Harry. MISS NELSON IS MISSING!
Ages 5-8. 9, Vol. 2
Cleary, Beverly Bunn. OTIS SPOFFORD.
Ages 8-10. 194, Vol. 1
Colman, Hila Crayder. THE CASE OF THE STOLEN BAGELS.
Ages 7-10. 162, Vol. 2
Cuyler, Margery S. THE TROUBLE WITH SOAP.
Ages 10-13. 147, Vol. 3
Danziger, Paula. THE DIVORCE EXPRESS.
Ages 11-14. 150, Vol. 3
Glasser, Barbara. LEROY OOPS.
Ages 6-10. 361, Vol. 1
Jacobs, Dee. LAURA'S GIFT.
Ages 10-13. 328, Vol. 3
Morton, Jane. RUNNING SCARED.
Ages 10-14. 455, Vol. 3
Stevens, Carla McBride. SARA AND THE PINCH.
Ages 5-7. 628, Vol. 3

**Busing.** *See: Integration: school busing*

### Classmate relationships

Adler, Carole Schwerdtfeger. THE ONCE IN A WHILE HERO.
Ages 10-13. 7, Vol. 3
Ames, Mildred. WHAT ARE FRIENDS FOR?
Ages 9-11. 12, Vol. 2
Asher, Sandra Fenichel. SUMMER BEGINS.
Ages 10-13. 28, Vol. 3
Bargar, Gary W. WHAT HAPPENED TO MR. FORSTER?
Ages 10-13. 34, Vol. 3
Barkin, Carol and Elizabeth James. DOING THINGS TOGETHER.
Ages 4-7. 32, Vol. 2
Barkin, Carol and Elizabeth James. I'D RATHER STAY HOME.
Ages 4-6. 33, Vol. 2
Bates, Betty. MY MOM, THE MONEY NUT.
Ages 10-12. 39, Vol. 3
Bates, Betty. PICKING UP THE PIECES.
Ages 10-13. 40, Vol. 3
Bates, Betty. THAT'S WHAT T.J. SAYS.
Ages 9-11. 41, Vol. 3

## School (cont.)

Belpre, Pura. SANTIAGO.
Ages 4-8. 66, Vol. 1

Blue, Rose. THE PREACHER'S KID.
Ages 9-12. 58, Vol. 2

Bonham, Frank. GIMME AN H, GIMME AN E, GIMME AN L, GIMME A P.
Ages 12 and up. 61, Vol. 3

Branscum, Robbie. THE THREE WARS OF BILLY JOE TREAT.
Ages 9-11. 79, Vol. 2

Byars, Betsy Cromer. THE 18TH EMERGENCY.
Ages 9-11. 154, Vol. 1

Calhoun, Mary Huiskamp. KATIE JOHN AND HEATHCLIFF.
Ages 9-11. 101, Vol. 3

Chapman, Carol. HERBIE'S TROUBLES.
Ages 5-7. 113, Vol. 3

Cleary, Beverly Bunn. RAMONA QUIMBY, AGE 8.
Ages 8-10. 119, Vol. 3

Cleary, Beverly Bunn. RAMONA THE PEST.
Ages 8-10. 195, Vol. 1

Cohen, Barbara Nash. FAT JACK.
Ages 11 and up. 125, Vol. 3

Cohen, Miriam. "BEE MY VALENTINE!"
Ages 5-7. 155, Vol. 3

Cohen, Miriam. BEST FRIENDS.
Ages 5-7. 216, Vol. 1

Cohen, Miriam. FIRST GRADE TAKES A TEST.
Ages 5-7. 127, Vol. 3

Cohen, Miriam. NO GOOD IN ART.
Ages 5-7. 128, Vol. 3

Cohen, Miriam. SO WHAT?
Ages 4-7. 129, Vol. 3

Cohen, Miriam. WHEN WILL I READ?
Ages 4-6. 156, Vol. 2

Cole, Joanna. THE SECRET BOX.
Ages 6-8. 219, Vol. 1

Colman, Hila Crayder. ETHAN'S FAVORITE TEACHER.
Ages 7-9. 163, Vol. 2

Conford, Ellen. THE REVENGE OF THE INCREDIBLE DR. RANCID AND HIS YOUTHFUL ASSISTANT, JEFFREY.
Ages 10-12. 137, Vol. 3

Crayder, Dorothy. ISHKABIBBLE!
Ages 9-12. 185, Vol. 2

Dacquino, Vincent T. KISS THE CANDY DAYS GOOD-BYE.
Ages 10-14. 148, Vol. 3

Danziger, Paula. CAN YOU SUE YOUR PARENTS FOR MALPRACTICE?
Ages 10-14. 149, Vol. 3

Delaney, Ned. RUFUS THE DOOFUS.
Ages 4-6. 195, Vol. 2

Dygard, Thomas J. SOCCER DUEL.
Ages 11-14. 179, Vol. 3

Fife, Dale. RIDE THE CROOKED WIND.
Ages 10-12. 312, Vol. 1

Fife, Dale. WHO'LL VOTE FOR LINCOLN?
Ages 8-10. 229, Vol. 2

First, Julia. AMY.
Ages 8-11. 230, Vol. 2

First, Julia. MOVE OVER, BEETHOVEN.
Ages 10-13. 231, Vol. 2

Fox, Paula. A PLACE APART.
Ages 12 and up. 193, Vol. 3

Friis-Baastad, Babbis Ellinor. KRISTY'S COURAGE.
Ages 8-10. 339, Vol. 1

Gauch, Patricia Lee. FRIDAYS.
Ages 11-13. 204, Vol. 3

Geibel, James. THE BLOND BROTHER.
Ages 12 and up. 205, Vol. 3

Gerber, Merrill Joan. PLEASE DON'T KISS ME NOW.
Ages 13 and up. 206, Vol. 3

Giff, Patricia Reilly. FOURTH GRADE CELEBRITY.
Ages 8-10. 210, Vol. 3

Giff, Patricia Reilly. THE GIFT OF THE PIRATE QUEEN.
Ages 9-12. 211, Vol. 3

Gilson, Jamie. DO BANANAS CHEW GUM?
Ages 9-11. 216, Vol. 3

Girion, Barbara. A HANDFUL OF STARS.
Ages 12 and up. 217, Vol. 3

Girion, Barbara. LIKE EVERYBODY ELSE.
Ages 10-13. 218, Vol. 3

Gould, Marilyn. GOLDEN DAFFODILS.
Ages 8-12. 223, Vol. 3

Grace, Fran. BRANIGAN'S DOG.
Ages 10 and up. 225, Vol. 3

Greenberg, Jan. THE ICEBERG AND ITS SHADOW.
Ages 10-12. 235, Vol. 3

Greenberg, Jan. A SEASON IN-BETWEEN.
Ages 11-13. 237, Vol. 3

Greene, Constance Clarke. DOUBLE-DARE O'TOOLE.
Ages 9-11. 240, Vol. 3

Grohskopf, Bernice. CHILDREN IN THE WIND.
Ages 11-13. 280, Vol. 2

Hautzig, Deborah. THE HANDSOMEST FATHER.
Ages 4-7. 271, Vol. 3

Hentoff, Nat. DOES THIS SCHOOL HAVE CAPITAL PUNISHMENT?
Ages 11 and up. 282, Vol. 3

Hughes, Dean. HONESTLY, MYRON.
Ages 9-11. 307, Vol. 3

Hughes, Dean. SWITCHING TRACKS.
Ages 10-14. 308, Vol. 3

Huntsberry, William Emery. THE BIG WHEELS.
Ages 12 and up. 446, Vol. 1

Hurwitz, Johanna. ALDO APPLESAUCE.
Ages 7-9. 316, Vol. 3

Johnston, Norma. A MUSTARD SEED OF MAGIC.
Ages 12 and up. 355, Vol. 2

Keller, Beverly Lou. THE GENUINE, INGENIOUS, THRIFT SHOP GENIE, CLARISSA MAE BEAN & ME.
Ages 10 and up. 372, Vol. 2

Kerr, M. E., pseud. IS THAT YOU, MISS BLUE?
Ages 11-14. 379, Vol. 2

Knudson, R. Rozanne. RINEHART LIFTS.
Ages 10-12. 348, Vol. 3

Koob, Theodora Johanna Foth. THE DEEP SEARCH.
Ages 12 and up. 513, Vol. 1

Leggett, Linda Rodgers and Linda Gambee Andrews. THE ROSE-COLORED GLASSES: MELANIE ADJUSTS TO POOR VISION.
Ages 8-11. 362, Vol. 3

Lexau, Joan M. I HATE RED ROVER.
Ages 6-8. 371, Vol. 3

McKay, Robert W. THE RUNNING BACK.
Ages 12-14. 392, Vol. 3

McLenighan, Valjean. I KNOW YOU CHEATED.
Ages 6-8. 431, Vol. 2

Maddock, Reginald. THE DRAGON IN THE GARDEN.
Ages 10-13. 603, Vol. 1

Maddock, Reginald. THE PIT.
Ages 12 and up. 604, Vol. 1

Marney, Dean. JUST GOOD FRIENDS.
Ages 11-13. 404, Vol. 3

Mauser, Pat Rhoads. A BUNDLE OF STICKS.
Ages 10-12. 410, Vol. 3

Mazer, Norma Fox. MRS. FISH, APE, AND ME, THE DUMP QUEEN.
Ages 10-12. 414, Vol. 3

**School (cont.)**

Mearian, Judy Frank. SOMEONE SLIGHTLY DIFFERENT.
Ages 10-12. 417, Vol. 3

Miles, Betty. MAUDIE AND ME AND THE DIRTY BOOK.
Ages 10-12. 423, Vol. 3

Miner, Jane Claypool. NAVAJO VICTORY: BEING A NATIVE AMERICAN.
Ages 11 and up. 432, Vol. 3

Miner, Jane Claypool. THE TOUGH GUY: BLACK IN A WHITE WORLD.
Ages 11 and up. 437, Vol. 3

Moore, Emily. SOMETHING TO COUNT ON.
Ages 8-10. 449, Vol. 3

Morgan, Alison Mary. A BOY CALLED FISH.
Ages 10-12. 645, Vol. 1

Morgenroth, Barbara. WILL THE REAL RENIE LAKE PLEASE STAND UP?
Ages 12 and up. 453, Vol. 3

Nordstrom, Ursula. THE SECRET LANGUAGE.
Ages 8-10. 670, Vol. 1

Oppenheimer, Joan Letson. WORKING ON IT.
Ages 11-13. 475, Vol. 3

Ormsby, Virginia H. TWENTY-ONE CHILDREN PLUS TEN.
Ages 5-8. 687, Vol. 1

Payne, Sherry Neuwirth. A CONTEST.
Ages 8-10. 486, Vol. 3

Perl, Lila. DON'T ASK MIRANDA.
Ages 10-13. 492, Vol. 3

Perl, Lila. HEY, REMEMBER FAT GLENDA?
Ages 9-12. 493, Vol. 3

Petersen, P. J. WOULD YOU SETTLE FOR IMPROBABLE?
Ages 11-13. 495, Vol. 3

Peyton, K.M., pseud. PENNINGTON'S LAST TERM.
Ages 12 and up. 706, Vol. 1

Pfeffer, Susan Beth. ABOUT DAVID.
Ages 13 and up. 500, Vol. 3

Pinkwater, Manus. WINGMAN.
Ages 9-12. 513, Vol. 2

Potter, Marian. THE SHARED ROOM.
Ages 10-12. 517, Vol. 3

Pundt, Helen Marie. SPRING COMES FIRST TO THE WILLOWS.
Ages 11 and up. 717, Vol. 1

Rabe, Berniece Louise. THE BALANCING GIRL.
Ages 5-7. 522, Vol. 3

Riley, Jocelyn. ONLY MY MOUTH IS SMILING.
Ages 12-14. 533, Vol. 3

Ross, Pat. MOLLY AND THE SLOW TEETH.
Ages 6-8. 552, Vol. 3

Sachs, Marilyn. A SECRET FRIEND.
Ages 10-12. 567, Vol. 2

Sachs, Marilyn. A SUMMER'S LEASE.
Ages 11-14. 566, Vol. 3

Sharmat, Marjorie Weinman. MAGGIE MARMELSTEIN FOR PRESIDENT.
Ages 9-12. 588, Vol. 2

Shreve, Susan Richards. THE BAD DREAMS OF A GOOD GIRL.
Ages 8-10. 589, Vol. 3

Shura, Mary Francis Craig. RUN AWAY HOME.
Ages 9-11. 820, Vol. 1

Smith, Nancy Covert. THE FALLING-APART WINTER.
Ages 10-13. 612, Vol. 3

Snyder, Anne. FIRST STEP.
Ages 11-13. 615, Vol. 2

Spence, Eleanor Rachel. A CANDLE FOR SAINT ANTONY.
Ages 13 and up. 618, Vol. 3

Stanek, Muriel Novella. WHO'S AFRAID OF THE DARK?
Ages 5-8. 623, Vol. 3

Terris, Susan Dubinsky. TWO P'S IN A POD.
Ages 9-12. 641, Vol. 2

Thomas, William E. THE NEW BOY IS BLIND.
Ages 6-10. 655, Vol. 3

Voigt, Cynthia. DICEY'S SONG.
Ages 11 and up. 671, Vol. 3

Waldron, Ann Wood. THE INTEGRATION OF MARY-LARKIN THORNHILL.
Ages 10-13. 67, Vol. 2

Walker, Pamela. TWYLA.
Ages 12 and up. 944, Vol. 1

Weiman, Eiveen. IT TAKES BRAINS.
Ages 10-12. 686, Vol. 3

Wells, Rosemary. TIMOTHY GOES TO SCHOOL.
Ages 3-5. 689, Vol. 3

White, Dori. SARAH AND KATIE.
Ages 9-11. 966, Vol. 1

Willard, Mildred Wilds. THE LUCK OF HARRY WEAVER.
Ages 8-10. 977, Vol. 1

Wise, William. THE COWBOY SURPRISE.
Ages 5-8. 980, Vol. 1

Wood, Phyllis Anderson. THIS TIME COUNT ME IN.
Ages 12 and up. 706, Vol. 3

Young, Helen. WHAT DIFFERENCE DOES IT MAKE, DANNY?
Ages 9-12. 715, Vol. 3

Zelonky, Joy. I CAN'T ALWAYS HEAR YOU.
Ages 7-10. 718, Vol. 3

**Dropout.** *See: Dropout, school*

**Entering.** *See also: Separation anxiety*

Adelson, Leone. ALL READY FOR SCHOOL.
Ages 4-6. 2, Vol. 1

Binzen, Bill. FIRST DAY IN SCHOOL.
Ages 4-6. 76, Vol. 1

Blue, Rose. I AM HERE. YO ESTOY AQUI.
Ages 5-8. 83, Vol. 1

Bram, Elizabeth. I DON'T WANT TO GO TO SCHOOL.
Ages 3-5. 69, Vol. 2

Brandenberg, Franz. SIX NEW STUDENTS.
Ages 5-7. 76, Vol. 2

Burningham, John Mackintosh. THE SCHOOL.
Ages 3-5. 105, Vol. 2

Caudill, Rebecca. A POCKETFUL OF CRICKET.
Ages 4-7. 175, Vol. 1

Chorao, Kay. MOLLY'S LIES.
Ages 4-7. 116, Vol. 3

Cleary, Beverly Bunn. RAMONA THE PEST.
Ages 8-10. 195, Vol. 1

Cohen, Miriam. WILL I HAVE A FRIEND?
Ages 4-6. 217, Vol. 1

Cooney, Nancy Evans. THE BLANKET THAT HAD TO GO.
Ages 3-5. 138, Vol. 3

Greenfield, Eloise. ME AND NEESIE.
Ages 4-7. 272, Vol. 2

Hamilton-Merritt, Jane. MY FIRST DAY OF SCHOOL.
Ages 3-6. 260, Vol. 3

Kantrowitz, Mildred. WILLY BEAR.
Ages 4-6. 362, Vol. 1

Pearson, Susan. EVERYBODY KNOWS THAT!
Ages 4-7. 496, Vol. 2

Rinkoff, Barbara Jean Rich. RUTHERFORD T. FINDS 21B.
Ages 5-7. 739, Vol. 1

Schick, Eleanor Grossman. THE LITTLE SCHOOL AT COTTONWOOD CORNERS.
Ages 3-6. 780, Vol. 1

## School Phobia

**See:** *Fear: of school; Separation anxiety*

## Schools, Private

**See also:** *Separation anxiety*
Love, Sandra Weller. CROSSING OVER.
Ages 10-12. 383, Vol. 3
Richardson, Grace. APPLES EVERY DAY.
Ages 12 and up. 733, Vol. 1
Riskind, Mary L. APPLE IS MY SIGN.
Ages 10-14. 536, Vol. 3
Vinson, Kathryn. RUN WITH THE RING.
Ages 12 and up. 925, Vol. 1

### Boys'
Hentoff, Nat. DOES THIS SCHOOL HAVE CAPITAL
PUNISHMENT?
Ages 11 and up. 282, Vol. 3
Hentoff, Nat. THIS SCHOOL IS DRIVING ME
CRAZY.
Ages 11-15. 311, Vol. 2

### Girls'
Carlson, Natalie Savage. LUVVY AND THE GIRLS.
Ages 10-13. 167, Vol. 1
Cuyler, Margery S. THE TROUBLE WITH SOAP.
Ages 10-13. 147, Vol. 3
Gilbert, Harriett. RUNNING AWAY.
Ages 11-14. 215, Vol. 3
Gordon, Ethel Edison. SO FAR FROM HOME.
Ages 11 and up. 369, Vol. 1
Kerr, M. E., pseud. IS THAT YOU, MISS BLUE?
Ages 11-14. 379, Vol. 2
Nordstrom, Ursula. THE SECRET LANGUAGE.
Ages 8-10. 670, Vol. 1
St. George, Judith. CALL ME MARGO.
Ages 12-14. 567, Vol. 3
Tolan, Stephanie S. THE LAST OF EDEN.
Ages 12 and up. 659, Vol. 3
Wells, Rosemary. THE FOG COMES ON LITTLE PIG
FEET.
Ages 11 and up. 961, Vol. 1

## Scoliosis
Richter, Elizabeth. THE TEENAGE HOSPITAL
EXPERIENCE: YOU CAN HANDLE IT!
Ages 12 and up. 532, Vol. 3
Sachs, Elizabeth-Ann. JUST LIKE ALWAYS.
Ages 10-13. 561, Vol. 3

## Secret, Keeping
Brandenberg, Franz. A SECRET FOR
GRANDMOTHER'S BIRTHDAY.
Ages 3-7. 75, Vol. 2
Bulla, Clyde Robert. DEXTER.
Ages 9-11. 135, Vol. 1
Cleaver, Vera and Bill Cleaver. ELLEN GRAE.
Ages 9-12. 197, Vol. 1
Fife, Dale. NORTH OF DANGER.
Ages 10-12. 227, Vol. 2
Girion, Barbara. MISTY AND ME.
Ages 10-12. 219, Vol. 3
Herman, Charlotte. WHAT HAPPENED TO
HEATHER HOPKOWITZ?
Ages 10-13. 283, Vol. 3
Hermes, Patricia. WHAT IF THEY KNEW?
Ages 9-11. 285, Vol. 3
Herzig, Alison Cragin and Jane Lawrence Mali. A
SEASON OF SECRETS.
Ages 11-13. 287, Vol. 3
Pfeffer, Susan Beth. JUST BETWEEN US.
Ages 10-12. 502, Vol. 3
Pohlmann, Lillian Grenfell. SING LOOSE.
Ages 12 and up. 714, Vol. 1
Townsend, John Rowe. NOAH'S CASTLE.
Ages 11 and up. 656, Vol. 2
Van Iterson, Siny Rose. VILLAGE OF OUTCASTS.
Ages 12 and up. 917, Vol. 1

Young, Miriam Burt. MISS SUZY'S BIRTHDAY.
Ages 3-7. 1012, Vol. 1

## Security Blanket
**See:** *Transitional objects: security blanket*

## Security/Insecurity
**See also:** *Deprivation, emotional; Fear; Trust/Distrust*
Ames, Mildred. NICKY AND THE JOYOUS NOISE.
Ages 9-12. 14, Vol. 3
Anker, Charlotte. LAST NIGHT I SAW
ANDROMEDA.
Ages 9-11. 22, Vol. 2
Ashley, Bernard. A KIND OF WILD JUSTICE.
Ages 12 and up. 30, Vol. 3
Bachmann, Evelyn Trent. TRESSA.
Ages 8-12. 42, Vol. 1
Bulla, Clyde Robert. WHITE BIRD.
Ages 9 and up. 138, Vol. 1
Bunting, Anne Evelyn. THE BIG RED BARN.
Ages 4-7. 88, Vol. 3
Byars, Betsy Cromer. THE PINBALLS.
Ages 10-13. 108, Vol. 2
Corcoran, Barbara. THE FARAWAY ISLAND.
Ages 10-13. 179, Vol. 2
Corcoran, Barbara. MAKE NO SOUND.
Ages 10-13. 181, Vol. 2
Delton, Judy. MY MOTHER LOST HER JOB TODAY.
Ages 3-7. 156, Vol. 3
Dragonwagon, Crescent. WILL IT BE OKAY?
Ages 3-7. 207, Vol. 2
Dunn, Judy. FEELINGS.
Ages 3-8. 279, Vol. 1
Hall, Lynn. HALF THE BATTLE.
Ages 11 and up. 255, Vol. 3
Hoban, Lillian Aberman. I MET A TRAVELLER.
Ages 10-12. 322, Vol. 2
Holland, Isabelle. DINAH AND THE GREEN FAT
KINGDOM.
Ages 10-13. 328, Vol. 2
Kerr, M. E., pseud. THE SON OF SOMEONE
FAMOUS.
Ages 11 and up. 493, Vol. 1
Lee, Robert C. IT'S A MILE FROM HERE TO
GLORY.
Ages 10 and up. 538, Vol. 1
Mearian, Judy Frank. TWO WAYS ABOUT IT.
Ages 9-12. 418, Vol. 3
Rodowsky, Colby F. H. MY NAME IS HENLEY.
Ages 10-13. 547, Vol. 3
Swetnam, Evelyn. YES, MY DARLING DAUGHTER.
Ages 9-12. 633, Vol. 2
Terris, Susan Dubinsky. NO SCARLET RIBBONS.
Ages 11-13. 647, Vol. 3
Uchida, Yoshiko. JOURNEY HOME.
Ages 12-14. 657, Vol. 2
Valencak, Hannelore. A TANGLED WEB.
Ages 9-11. 659, Vol. 2
Wrenn, C. Gilbert and Shirley Schwarzrock. SOME
COMMON CRUTCHES.
Ages 11 and up. 1006, Vol. 1

## Seeing Eye Dog
**See:** *Blindness; Pets: guide dog*

## Segregation
**See:** *Integration; Prejudice; School*

## Seizures
**See:** *Cerebral palsy; Epilepsy; Spastic*

## Self, Attitude Toward
**See also:** *Emotions; Self-esteem*

## Self, Attitude Toward (cont.)

Schwarzrock, Shirley and C. Gilbert Wrenn. DO I KNOW THE "ME" OTHERS SEE?
Ages 11 and up. 789, Vol. 1

## Accepting

Adler, Carole Schwerdtfeger. THE SILVER COACH.
Ages 9-12. 8, Vol. 3

Bailey, Pearl. DUEY'S TALE.
Ages 12 and up. 29, Vol. 2

Banks, Lynne Reid. THE WRITING ON THE WALL.
Ages 12 and up. 33, Vol. 3

Behrens, June York. WHO AM I?
Ages 3-6. 63, Vol. 1

Billington, Elizabeth T. PART-TIME BOY.
Ages 8-10. 53, Vol. 3

Bonham, Frank. CHIEF.
Ages 11 and up. 95, Vol. 1

Bornstein, Ruth. LITTLE GORILLA.
Ages 2-5. 61, Vol. 2

Brooks, Jerome. THE BIG DIPPER MARATHON.
Ages 11-14. 77, Vol. 3

Brown, Marc Tolan. ARTHUR'S NOSE.
Ages 3-7. 88, Vol. 2

Carle, Eric. THE MIXED-UP CHAMELEON.
Ages 4-8. 114, Vol. 2

Childress, Alice. RAINBOW JORDAN.
Ages 12 and up. 115, Vol. 3

Colman, Hila Crayder. CONFESSION OF A STORYTELLER.
Ages 10-13. 133, Vol. 3

Conford, Ellen. JUST THE THING FOR GERALDINE.
Ages 5-8. 240, Vol. 1

Corcoran, Barbara. CHILD OF THE MORNING.
Ages 10 and up. 139, Vol. 3

D'Ambrosio, Richard. NO LANGUAGE BUT A CRY.
Ages 13 and up. 261, Vol. 1

Delton, Judy. I NEVER WIN!
Ages 4-7. 154, Vol. 3

Desbarats, Peter. GABRIELLE AND SELENA.
Ages 8-10. 274, Vol. 1

Dunn, Judy. FEELINGS.
Ages 3-8. 279, Vol. 1

Duvoisin, Roger Antoine. VERONICA.
Ages 4-7. 283, Vol. 1

Flory, Jane Trescott. ONE HUNDRED AND EIGHT BELLS.
Ages 9-11. 324, Vol. 1

Freeman, Don. DANDELION.
Ages 3-8. 333, Vol. 1

Gardner, Richard A. MBD: THE FAMILY BOOK ABOUT MINIMAL BRAIN DYSFUNCTION.
Ages 9-12. 345, Vol. 1

Giff, Patricia Reilly. FOURTH GRADE CELEBRITY.
Ages 8-10. 210, Vol. 3

Green, Phyllis. GLOOMY LOUIE.
Ages 8-9. 234, Vol. 3

Greenberg, Jan. A SEASON IN-BETWEEN.
Ages 11-13. 237, Vol. 3

Greene, Constance Clarke. THE UNMAKING OF RABBIT.
Ages 10-13. 380, Vol. 1

Greenwald, Sheila. THE SECRET IN MIRANDA'S CLOSET.
Ages 8-11. 274, Vol. 2

Hallman, Ruth. BREAKAWAY.
Ages 12 and up. 257, Vol. 3

Hamilton, Virginia. ZEELY.
Ages 10-12. 397, Vol. 1

Herman, Charlotte. THE DIFFERENCE OF ARI STEIN.
Ages 9-12. 312, Vol. 2

Hobby, Janice Hale with Gabrielle Rubin and Daniel Rubin. STAYING BACK.
Ages 6-12. 295, Vol. 3

Hunter, Edith Fisher. SUE ELLEN.
Ages 10-12. 441, Vol. 1

Jeschke, Susan. SIDNEY.
Ages 4-7. 351, Vol. 2

Johnson, Annabel Jones and Edgar Raymond Johnson. THE RESCUED HEART.
Ages 12 and up. 464, Vol. 1

Johnston, Johanna. SUPPOSINGS.
Ages 3-6. 466, Vol. 1

Kent, Jack. THE WIZARD OF WALLABY WALLOW.
Ages 4-7. 489, Vol. 1

Kropp, Paul Stephan. WILTED.
Ages 11-14. 354, Vol. 3

Lampman, Evelyn Sibley. THE POTLATCH FAMILY.
Ages 11-13. 391, Vol. 2

Lee, H. Alton. SEVEN FEET FOUR AND GROWING.
Ages 9-12. 396, Vol. 2

Leggett, Linda Rodgers and Linda Gambee Andrews. THE ROSE-COLORED GLASSES: MELANIE ADJUSTS TO POOR VISION.
Ages 8-11. 362, Vol. 3

Little, Jean. STAND IN THE WIND.
Ages 8-11. 414, Vol. 2

Mauser, Pat Rhoads. A BUNDLE OF STICKS.
Ages 10-12. 410, Vol. 3

Meddaugh, Susan. TOO SHORT FRED.
Ages 6-8. 450, Vol. 2

Mendonca, Susan R. TOUGH CHOICES.
Ages 11 and up. 419, Vol. 3

Miklowitz, Gloria D. THE LOVE BOMBERS.
Ages 12 and up. 422, Vol. 3

Montgomery, Elizabeth Rider. "SEEING" IN THE DARK.
Ages 5-7. 448, Vol. 3

Morgenroth, Barbara. TRAMPS LIKE US.
Ages 12 and up. 452, Vol. 3

Oppenheimer, Joan Letson. WORKING ON IT.
Ages 11-13. 475, Vol. 3

Pfeffer, Susan Beth. MARLY THE KID.
Ages 11-13. 512, Vol. 2

Pollock, Penny. KEEPING IT SECRET.
Ages 9-12. 515, Vol. 3

Sachs, Marilyn. BUS RIDE.
Ages 11-14. 563, Vol. 3

Sachs, Marilyn. HELLO...WRONG NUMBER.
Ages 12-16. 565, Vol. 3

Sachs, Marilyn. MARV.
Ages 10-12. 761, Vol. 1

Savitz, Harriet May. FLY, WHEELS, FLY.
Ages 10 and up. 774, Vol. 1

Savitz, Harriet May. RUN, DON'T WALK.
Ages 12 and up. 572, Vol. 3

Schlein, Miriam. BILLY, THE LITTLEST ONE.
Ages 3-5. 782, Vol. 1

Schulman, Janet. JENNY AND THE TENNIS NUT.
Ages 7-9. 577, Vol. 2

Schwarzrock, Shirley and C. Gilbert Wrenn. EASING THE SCENE.
Ages 11 and up. 790, Vol. 1

Scoppettone, Sandra. HAPPY ENDINGS ARE ALL ALIKE.
Ages 12 and up. 578, Vol. 2

Screen, Robert Martin. WITH MY FACE TO THE RISING SUN.
Ages 11 and up. 580, Vol. 2

Sharmat, Marjorie Weinman. WALTER THE WOLF.
Ages 4-7. 591, Vol. 2

Shearer, John. I WISH I HAD AN AFRO.
Ages 9-11. 809, Vol. 1

Slepian, Jan. THE ALFRED SUMMER.
Ages 11-13. 603, Vol. 3

Slepian, Jan. LESTER'S TURN.
Ages 11-14. 604, Vol. 3

## Self, Attitude Toward (cont.)

Slobodkin, Louis. MAGIC MICHAEL.
Ages 4-8. 826, Vol. 1

Slote, Alfred. LOVE AND TENNIS.
Ages 12-14. 605, Vol. 3

Sugarman, Daniel A. and Rolaine A.
Hochstein. SEVEN STORIES FOR GROWTH.
Ages 6-12. 880, Vol. 1

Sullivan, Mary Beth and Alan J. Brightman and Joseph
Blatt. FEELING FREE.
Ages 9 and up. 640, Vol. 3

Swarthout, Glendon Fred and Kathryn
Swarthout. WHICHAWAY.
Ages 10 and up. 883, Vol. 1

Taylor, Paula. JOHNNY CASH.
Ages 7-10. 638, Vol. 2

Vigna, Judith. EVERYONE GOES AS A PUMPKIN.
Ages 3-6. 663, Vol. 2

Waber, Bernard. YOU'RE A LITTLE KID WITH A
BIG HEART.
Ages 5-7. 673, Vol. 3

Wittman, Sally. PELLY AND PEAK.
Ages 4-8. 692, Vol. 2

Woodford, Peggy. PLEASE DON'T GO.
Ages 12 and up. 991, Vol. 1

Yep, Laurence Michael. CHILD OF THE OWL.
Ages 11 and up. 711, Vol. 2

Young, Helen. WHAT DIFFERENCE DOES IT MAKE,
DANNY?
Ages 9-12. 715, Vol. 3

**Blame.** *See: Blame*

## Body concept

Brenner, Barbara Johnes. MR. TALL AND MR.
SMALL.
Ages 4-8. 116, Vol. 1

Brooks, Jerome. THE TESTING OF CHARLIE
HAMMELMAN.
Ages 10-13. 84, Vol. 2

Brown, Marc Tolan. ARTHUR'S NOSE.
Ages 3-7. 88, Vol. 2

Danziger, Paula. THE CAT ATE MY GYMSUIT.
Ages 11 and up. 262, Vol. 1

First, Julia. LOOK WHO'S BEAUTIFUL!
Ages 10-12. 188, Vol. 3

Hautzig, Deborah. SECOND STAR TO THE RIGHT.
Ages 12 and up. 272, Vol. 3

Lionni, Leo. FISH IS FISH.
Ages 4-8. 565, Vol. 1

Liu, Aimee. SOLITAIRE.
Ages 13 and up. 380, Vol. 3

Perl, Lila. HEY, REMEMBER FAT GLENDA?
Ages 9-12. 493, Vol. 3

Pinkwater, Manus. FAT ELLIOT & THE GORILLA.
Ages 8-10. 710, Vol. 1

Robison, Nancy Louise. BALLET MAGIC.
Ages 9-11. 541, Vol. 3

Viereck, Phillip. THE SUMMER I WAS LOST.
Ages 11 and up. 923, Vol. 1

Waber, Bernard. YOU LOOK RIDICULOUS, SAID
THE RHINOCEROS TO THE HIPPOPOTAMUS.
Ages 5-8. 938, Vol. 1

## Confidence

Blue, Rose. A QUIET PLACE.
Ages 8-11. 86, Vol. 1

Burleson, Elizabeth. A MAN OF THE FAMILY.
Ages 11 and up. 145, Vol. 1

Burton, Virginia Lee. KATY AND THE BIG SNOW.
Ages 3-6. 148, Vol. 1

Carol, Bill J., pseud. SINGLE TO CENTER.
Ages 9-11. 170, Vol. 1

Conaway, Judith. WILL I EVER BE GOOD ENOUGH?
Ages 6-9. 173, Vol. 2

De Paola, Thomas Anthony. ANDY (THAT'S MY
NAME).
Ages 3-5. 271, Vol. 1

Eckert, Allan W. INCIDENT AT HAWK'S HILL.
Ages 11 and up. 284, Vol. 1

Etter, Les. GET THOSE REBOUNDS!
Ages 10-13. 220, Vol. 2

Gackenbach, Dick. HARRY AND THE TERRIBLE
WHATZIT.
Ages 4-7. 239, Vol. 2

Greene, Bette. GET ON OUT OF HERE, PHILIP
HALL.
Ages 9-12. 238, Vol. 3

Greene, Bette. PHILIP HALL LIKES ME. I RECKON
MAYBE.
Ages 10-13. 374, Vol. 1

Gross, Alan. WHAT IF THE TEACHER CALLS ON
ME?
Ages 5-7. 250, Vol. 3

Hurwitz, Johanna. SUPERDUPER TEDDY.
Ages 4-7. 318, Vol. 3

Johnston, Norma. IF YOU LOVE ME, LET ME GO.
Ages 12 and up. 354, Vol. 2

Lattimore, Eleanor Frances. ADAM'S KEY.
Ages 7-9. 395, Vol. 3

Matthews, Ellen. THE TROUBLE WITH LESLIE.
Ages 8-11. 409, Vol. 3

Mazer, Norma Fox. DEAR BILL, REMEMBER ME?
AND OTHER STORIES.
Ages 12 and up. 449, Vol. 2

Peck, Richard. REPRESENTING SUPER DOLL.
Ages 12 and up. 696, Vol. 1

Richard, Adrienne. INTO THE ROAD.
Ages 12 and up. 537, Vol. 2

Simon, Norma. NOBODY'S PERFECT, NOT EVEN
MY MOTHER.
Ages 4-8. 597, Vol. 3

Smith, Anne Warren. BLUE DENIM BLUES.
Ages 12 and up. 607, Vol. 3

Stapp, Arthur Donald. ORDEAL BY MOUNTAINS.
Ages 11 and up. 853, Vol. 1

Yep, Laurence Michael. KIND HEARTS AND
GENTLE MONSTERS.
Ages 12 and up. 712, Vol. 3

**Doubt.** *See: Identity, search for; Inferiority, feelings of*

**Embarrassment.** *See: Embarrassment*

**Feeling different.** *See also: Differences, human*

Albert, Louise. BUT I'M READY TO GO.
Ages 11-14. 5, Vol. 2

Bargar, Gary W. WHAT HAPPENED TO MR.
FORSTER?
Ages 10-13. 34, Vol. 3

Barrett, John M. DANIEL DISCOVERS DANIEL.
Ages 7-9. 35, Vol. 3

Belair, Richard L. DOUBLE TAKE.
Ages 13 and up. 44, Vol. 3

Chandler, Edna Walker. INDIAN PAINTBRUSH.
Ages 9-11. 126, Vol. 2

Clifton, Lucille. SONORA BEAUTIFUL.
Ages 12-14. 123, Vol. 3

Cohen, Barbara Nash. FAT JACK.
Ages 11 and up. 125, Vol. 3

Cohen, Miriam. SO WHAT?
Ages 4-7. 129, Vol. 3

Colman, Hila Crayder. THE SECRET LIFE OF
HAROLD THE BIRD WATCHER.
Ages 8-10. 165, Vol. 2

Conford, Ellen. THE REVENGE OF THE
INCREDIBLE DR. RANCID AND HIS YOUTHFUL
ASSISTANT, JEFFREY.
Ages 10-12. 137, Vol. 3

Cook, Marjorie. TO WALK ON TWO FEET.
Ages 11-14. 177, Vol. 2

## Self, Attitude Toward (cont.)

Danziger, Paula. THE CAT ATE MY GYMSUIT.
Ages 11 and up. 262, Vol. 1
Dixon, Jeanne. LADY CAT LOST.
Ages 10-12. 164, Vol. 3
Gilson, Jamie. DO BANANAS CHEW GUM?
Ages 9-11. 216, Vol. 3
Greenberg, Jan. A SEASON IN-BETWEEN.
Ages 11-13. 237, Vol. 3
Guy, Rosa Cuthbert THE FRIENDS.
Ages 12 and up. 391, Vol. 1
Hamilton, Gail, pseud. TITANIA'S LODESTONE.
Ages 11-13. 290, Vol. 2
Haugaard, Kay. MYEKO'S GIFT.
Ages 9-12. 405, Vol. 1
Herman, Charlotte. THE DIFFERENCE OF ARI
STEIN.
Ages 9-12. 312, Vol. 2
Hermes, Patricia. WHAT IF THEY KNEW?
Ages 9-11. 285, Vol. 3
Hooks, William Harris. DOUG MEETS THE
NUTCRACKER.
Ages 8-11. 332, Vol. 2
Hunt, Mabel Leigh. LITTLE GIRL WITH SEVEN
NAMES.
Ages 7-10. 439, Vol. 1
Hunter, Edith Fisher. SUE ELLEN.
Ages 10-12. 441, Vol. 1
Keller, Beverly Lou. THE GENUINE, INGENIOUS,
THRIFT SHOP GENIE, CLARISSA MAE BEAN &
ME.
Ages 10 and up. 372, Vol. 2
Kerr, M. E., pseud. THE SON OF SOMEONE
FAMOUS.
Ages 11 and up. 493, Vol. 1
Kingman, Lee. HEAD OVER WHEELS.
Ages 12 and up. 383, Vol. 1
Le Guin, Ursula Kroeber. VERY FAR AWAY FROM
ANYWHERE ELSE.
Ages 12 and up. 397, Vol. 2
Lionni, Leo. A COLOR OF HIS OWN.
Ages 3-5. 408, Vol. 2
Litchfield, Ada Bassett. WORDS IN OUR HANDS.
Ages 7-9. 378, Vol. 3
McKay, Robert W. THE RUNNING BACK.
Ages 12-14. 392, Vol. 3
Morgenroth, Barbara. TRAMPS LIKE US.
Ages 12 and up. 452, Vol. 3
Paterson, Katherine Womeldorf. JACOB HAVE I
LOVED.
Ages 12 and up. 485, Vol. 3
Payne, Sherry Neuwirth. A CONTEST.
Ages 8-10. 486, Vol. 3
Peyton, K. M., pseud. MARION'S ANGELS.
Ages 11-14. 499, Vol. 3
Philips, Barbara. DON'T CALL ME FATSO.
Ages 5-9. 507, Vol. 3
Pollock, Penny. KEEPING IT SECRET.
Ages 9-12. 515, Vol. 3
Rosen, Winifred. HENRIETTA, THE WILD WOMAN
OF BORNEO.
Ages 4-7. 560, Vol. 2
Southall, Ivan. LET THE BALLOON GO.
Ages 12 and up. 847, Vol. 1
Stanek, Muriel Novella. GROWL WHEN YOU SAY R.
Ages 4-8. 620, Vol. 3
Stanek, Muriel Novella. I WON'T GO WITHOUT A
FATHER.
Ages 8-10. 850, Vol. 1
Stren, Patti. THERE'S A RAINBOW IN MY CLOSET.
Ages 8-10. 638, Vol. 3
Zelonky, Joy. I CAN'T ALWAYS HEAR YOU.
Ages 7-10. 718, Vol. 3

**Hatred.** *See: Hatred*

### Pity

Arundel, Honor. THE GIRL IN THE OPPOSITE BED.
Ages 12 and up. 37, Vol. 1
Cook, Marjorie. TO WALK ON TWO FEET.
Ages 11-14. 177, Vol. 2
Little, Jean. MINE FOR KEEPS.
Ages 10-13. 574, Vol. 1
Patterson, Katheryn. NO TIME FOR TEARS.
Ages 12 and up. 692, Vol. 1
Shaw, Richard. THE HARD WAY HOME.
Ages 11-13. 592, Vol. 2
Stanek, Muriel Novella. I WON'T GO WITHOUT A
FATHER.
Ages 8-10. 850, Vol. 1

**Pride/False pride.** *See: Pride/False pride*

### Respect

Adoff, Arnold. BIG SISTER TELLS ME THAT I'M
BLACK.
Ages 4-8. 3, Vol. 2
Ames, Mildred. NICKY AND THE JOYOUS NOISE.
Ages 9-12. 14, Vol. 3
Bradbury, Bianca. "I'M VINNY, I'M ME".
Ages 12 and up. 65, Vol. 2
Bunting, Anne Evelyn. THE WAITING GAME.
Ages 10 and up. 91, Vol. 3
Carrick, Carol. SOME FRIEND!
Ages 9-12. 106, Vol. 3
De Angeli, Marguerite Loefft. BRIGHT APRIL.
Ages 8-10. 266, Vol. 1
De Paola, Thomas Anthony. ANDY (THAT'S MY
NAME).
Ages 3-5. 271, Vol. 1
Dunnahoo, Terry. WHO CARES ABOUT ESPIE
SANCHEZ?
Ages 10-12. 210, Vol. 2
Hayes, Sheila. THE CAROUSEL HORSE.
Ages 10-12. 300, Vol. 2
Lipsyte, Robert. THE CONTENDER.
Ages 12 and up. 569, Vol. 1
Taylor, Mildred D. SONG OF THE TREES.
Ages 8-11. 637, Vol. 2
Wilkinson, Brenda Scott. LUDELL.
Ages 10-14. 680, Vol. 2

**Shame.** *See: Shame*

**Success.** *See: Success*

## Self-Concept

**See:** *Self, attitude toward; Values/Valuing*

## Self-Control

**See:** *Self-discipline*

## Self-Discipline

**See also:** *Discipline, meaning of*
Chukovsky, Kornei Ivanovich. THE SILVER CREST:
MY RUSSIAN BOYHOOD.
Ages 12 and up. 135, Vol. 2
Clifford, Ethel Rosenberg. THE WILD ONE.
Ages 11 and up. 206, Vol. 1
De Angeli, Marguerite Loefft. BRIGHT APRIL.
Ages 8-10. 266, Vol. 1
Gaeddert, LouAnn Bigge. NOISY NANCY NORRIS.
Ages 6-8. 340, Vol. 1
Gambill, Henrietta. SELF-CONTROL.
Ages 3-6. 199, Vol. 3
Giff, Patricia Reilly. THE GIRL WHO KNEW IT ALL.
Ages 8-10. 212, Vol. 3
Gilbert, Nan, pseud. CHAMPIONS DON'T CRY.
Ages 10-13. 358, Vol. 1
Hargreaves, Roger. MR. NOISY.
Ages 3-7. 264, Vol. 3

## Self-Discipline (cont.)

Hogan, Paula Z. SOMETIMES I GET SO MAD.
Ages 5-8. 298, Vol. 3

Huston, Anne and Jane H. Yolen. TRUST A CITY
KID.
Ages 11 and up. 448, Vol. 1

Meyer, Carolyn. THE CENTER: FROM A TROUBLED
PAST TO A NEW LIFE.
Ages 13 and up. 420, Vol. 3

Peyton, K. M., pseud. MARION'S ANGELS.
Ages 11-14. 499, Vol. 3

Platt, Kin. THE APE INSIDE ME.
Ages 12 and up. 513, Vol. 3

Robison, Nancy Louise. ON THE BALANCE BEAM.
Ages 8-10. 549, Vol. 2

Skolsky, Mindy Warshaw. CARNIVAL AND KOPECK
AND MORE ABOUT HANNAH.
Ages 7-9. 600, Vol. 3

Slote, Alfred. RABBIT EARS.
Ages 10-12. 606, Vol. 3

Smith, Robert Kimmel. JELLY BELLY.
Ages 10-12. 614, Vol. 3

Zhitkov, Boris Stepanovich. HOW I HUNTED THE
LITTLE FELLOWS.
Ages 3-7. 720, Vol. 3

## Self-Esteem

**See also:** *Guilt, feelings of; Self, attitude toward*

Christopher, Matthew F. GLUE FINGERS.
Ages 7-9. 134, Vol. 2

Ets, Marie Hall. BAD BOY, GOOD BOY.
Ages 6-10. 292, Vol. 1

Friskey, Margaret Richards. RACKETY, THAT VERY
SPECIAL RABBIT.
Ages 3-5. 237, Vol. 2

Greenberg, Jan. THE PIG-OUT BLUES.
Ages 12 and up. 236, Vol. 3

Hall, Lynn. TROUBLEMAKER.
Ages 11-14. 395, Vol. 1

Leach, Michael. DON'T CALL ME ORPHAN!
Ages 10-12. 360, Vol. 3

Mack, Nancy. WHY ME?
Ages 5-8. 429, Vol. 2

Moore, Emily. SOMETHING TO COUNT ON.
Ages 8-10. 449, Vol. 3

Neigoff, Mike. RUNNER-UP.
Ages 9-11. 474, Vol. 2

Pevsner, Stella. KEEP STOMPIN' TILL THE MUSIC
STOPS.
Ages 9-12. 509, Vol. 2

Reece, Colleen L. THE OUTSIDER.
Ages 12 and up. 527, Vol. 3

Schick, Eleanor Grossman. JOEY ON HIS OWN.
Ages 5-8. 574, Vol. 3

Shaw, Richard. SHAPE UP, BURKE.
Ages 10-14. 593, Vol. 2

Shyer, Marlene Fanta. MY BROTHER, THE THIEF.
Ages 10-13. 594, Vol. 3

Smith, Doris Buchanan. KELLY'S CREEK.
Ages 8-13. 613, Vol. 2

Smith, Doris Buchanan. LAST WAS LLOYD.
Ages 8-11. 608, Vol. 3

Smith, Doris Buchanan. TOUGH CHAUNCEY.
Ages 12 and up. 832, Vol. 1

Stevens, Carla McBride. PIG AND THE BLUE FLAG.
Ages 6-8. 622, Vol. 2

Terris, Susan Dubinsky. NO SCARLET RIBBONS.
Ages 11-13. 647, Vol. 3

Udry, Janice May. HOW I FADED AWAY.
Ages 5-8. 658, Vol. 2

Van Iterson, Siny Rose. PULGA.
Ages 12 and up. 916, Vol. 1

Williams, Barbara Wright. SOMEDAY, SAID
MITCHELL.
Ages 3-6. 686, Vol. 2

## Self-Identity

**See:** *Ego ideal; Identity, search for*

## Self-Image

**See:** *Self, attitude toward*

## Self-Improvement

Bonham, Frank. COOL CAT.
Ages 12 and up. 96, Vol. 1

Forbes, Esther. JOHNNY TREMAIN.
Ages 10 and up. 325, Vol. 1

Greene, Constance Clarke. A GIRL CALLED AL.
Ages 11 and up. 378, Vol. 1

Holland, Isabelle. DINAH AND THE GREEN FAT.
KINGDOM.
Ages 10-13. 328, Vol. 2

Hurwitz, Johanna. TOUGH-LUCK KAREN.
Ages 10-13. 319, Vol. 3

Kaufman, Mervyn D. JESSE OWENS.
Ages 7-10. 480, Vol. 1

Lee, Mildred Scudder. THE ROCK AND THE
WILLOW.
Ages 12 and up. 535, Vol. 1

Lipsyte, Robert. THE CONTENDER.
Ages 12 and up. 569, Vol. 1

Meyer, Carolyn. THE CENTER: FROM A TROUBLED
PAST TO A NEW LIFE.
Ages 13 and up. 420, Vol. 3

Shippen, Katherine Binney. ANDREW CARNEGIE
AND THE AGE OF STEEL.
Ages 9-11. 816, Vol. 1

Van Iterson, Siny Rose. PULGA.
Ages 12 and up. 916, Vol. 1

## Self-Reliance

**See:** *Dependence/Independence*

## Self-Respect

**See:** *Self, attitude toward: respect*

## Selfishness/Unselfishness

**See:** *Egocentrism; Giving, meaning of; Sharing/Not
sharing*

## Senility

**See:** *Age: aging; Age: senility*

## Separation, Marital

**See also:** *Divorce*

Arundel, Honor. A FAMILY FAILING.
Ages 12 and up. 36, Vol. 1

Bach, Alice Hendricks. A FATHER EVERY FEW
YEARS.
Ages 11-13. 27, Vol. 2

Barnwell, D. Robinson. SHADOW ON THE WATER.
Ages 12 and up. 52, Vol. 1

Beckman, Gunnel. MIA ALONE.
Ages 12 and up. 46, Vol. 2

Beckman, Gunnel. THAT EARLY SPRING.
Ages 12 and up. 47, Vol. 2

Blue, Rose. A MONTH OF SUNDAYS.
Ages 9-11. 84, Vol. 1

Blume, Judy Sussman. IT'S NOT THE END OF THE
WORLD.
Ages 10-12. 91, Vol. 1

Cameron, Eleanor Butler. TO THE GREEN
MOUNTAINS.
Ages 11 and up. 111, Vol. 2

Cleaver, Vera and Bill Cleaver. ME TOO.
Ages 9-11. 200, Vol. 1

Colman, Hila Crayder. NOBODY HAS TO BE A KID
FOREVER.
Ages 10-13. 164, Vol. 2

## Shame (cont.)

## Sharing/Not Sharing

## Shoplifting

## Showing Off

## Shyness

## Shyness (cont.)

Hurwitz, Johanna. SUPERDUPER TEDDY.
  Ages 4-7. 318, Vol. 3
Keller, Beverly Lou. FIONA'S BEE.
  Ages 5-8. 371, Vol. 2
Konigsburg, Elaine Lobl. JENNIFER, HECATE,
  MACBETH, WILLIAM MCKINLEY, AND ME,
  ELIZABETH.
  Ages 9-11. 512, Vol. 1
Krasilovsky, Phyllis. THE SHY LITTLE GIRL.
  Ages 4-8. 515, Vol. 1
Lee, H. Alton. SEVEN FEET FOUR AND GROWING.
  Ages 9-12. 396, Vol. 2
Lexau, Joan M. BENJIE.
  Ages 6-8. 553, Vol. 1
Miles, Betty. ALL IT TAKES IS PRACTICE.
  Ages 9-12. 454, Vol. 2
Miller, Ruth White. THE CITY ROSE.
  Ages 11-13. 460, Vol. 2
Nathan, Dorothy. THE SHY ONE.
  Ages 9-12. 656, Vol. 1
Oppenheimer, Joan Letson. WORKING ON IT.
  Ages 11-13. 475, Vol. 3
St. George, Judith. CALL ME MARGO.
  Ages 12-14. 567, Vol. 3
Sharmat, Marjorie Weinman. SAY HELLO, VANESSA.
  Ages 4-7. 585, Vol. 3
Skorpen, Liesel Moak. PLENTY FOR THREE.
  Ages 4-8. 825, Vol. 1
Smith, Anne Warren. BLUE DENIM BLUES.
  Ages 12 and up. 607, Vol. 3
Snyder, Zilpha Keatley. THE CHANGELING.
  Ages 11-14. 835, Vol. 1
Stolz, Mary Slattery. CIDER DAYS.
  Ages 8-11. 626, Vol. 2
Udry, Janice May. WHAT MARY JO SHARED.
  Ages 5-8. 914, Vol. 1
Wold, Jo Anne. TELL THEM MY NAME IS
  AMANDA.
  Ages 5-8. 694, Vol. 2
Yashima, Taro, pseud. CROW BOY.
  Ages 3-7. 1008, Vol. 1
Zolotow, Charlotte Shapiro. A TIGER CALLED
  THOMAS.
  Ages 4-7. 1029, Vol. 1

## Sibling

**See also:** *Family*

**Death of.** *See: Death: of sibling*

**Half brother/Half sister**
Bernays, Anne. GROWING UP RICH.
  Ages 13 and up. 52, Vol. 2
Bradbury, Bianca. WHERE'S JIM NOW?
  Ages 11-13. 67, Vol. 2
Carlson, Natalie Savage. THE HALF SISTERS.
  Ages 10-12. 166, Vol. 1
Corcoran, Barbara. MAKE NO SOUND.
  Ages 10-13. 181, Vol. 2
Fox, Paula. BLOWFISH LIVE IN THE SEA.
  Ages 11 and up. 327, Vol. 1
Vigna, Judith. DADDY'S NEW BABY.
  Ages 4-7. 666, Vol. 3

**Illness of.** *See: Illnesses: of sibling*

**Jealousy.** *See also: Jealousy: sibling*
Alexander, Martha G. NOBODY ASKED ME IF I
  WANTED A BABY SISTER.
  Ages 3-6. 9, Vol. 1
Arnstein, Helene S. BILLY AND OUR NEW BABY.
  Ages 3-6. 32, Vol. 1
Bradbury, Bianca. LAURIE.
  Ages 11 and up. 109, Vol. 1
Branfield, John. WHY ME?
  Ages 11 and up. 114, Vol. 1

Brenner, Barbara Johnes. NICKY'S SISTER.
  Ages 4-7. 117, Vol. 1
Burchardt, Nellie. A SURPRISE FOR CARLOTTA.
  Ages 9-11. 144, Vol. 1
Carol, Bill J. pseud. SINGLE TO CENTER.
  Ages 9-11. 170, Vol. 1
Child Study Association of America. BROTHERS AND
  SISTERS ARE LIKE THAT! STORIES TO READ TO
  YOURSELF.
  Ages 7-9. 182, Vol. 1
Colman, Hila Crayder. DIARY OF A FRANTIC KID
  SISTER.
  Ages 10-13. 230, Vol. 1
Crane, Caroline. A GIRL LIKE TRACY.
  Ages 12 and up. 256, Vol. 1
Friedman, Frieda. ELLEN AND THE GANG.
  Ages 9-12. 335, Vol. 1
Gerson, Mary-Joan. OMOTEJI'S BABY BROTHER.
  Ages 6-8. 356, Vol. 1
Gill, Joan. HUSH, JON!
  Ages 5-8. 360, Vol. 1
Greenfield, Eloise. SHE COME BRINGING ME
  THAT LITTLE BABY GIRL.
  Ages 3-7. 382, Vol. 1
Hoban, Russell Conwell. A BABY SISTER FOR
  FRANCES.
  Ages 3-7. 416, Vol. 1
Keats, Ezra Jack. PETER'S CHAIR.
  Ages 3-7. 485, Vol. 1
Schick, Eleanor Grossman. PEGGY'S NEW
  BROTHER.
  Ages 4-7. 781, Vol. 1
Scott, Ann Herbert. ON MOTHER'S LAP.
  Ages 3-7. 800, Vol. 1
Watson, Jane Werner, Robert E. Switzer, and J. Cotter
  Hirschberg. SOMETIMES I'M JEALOUS.
  Ages 3-6. 954, Vol. 1
Zolotow, Charlotte Shapiro. IF IT WEREN'T FOR
  YOU.
  Ages 3-6. 1022, Vol. 1

**Love for**
Adler, Carole Schwerdtfeger. DOWN BY THE RIVER.
  Ages 12 and up. 4, Vol. 3
Arthur, Catherine. MY SISTER'S SILENT WORLD.
  Ages 5-9. 25, Vol. 3
Bates, Betty. THAT'S WHAT T.J. SAYS.
  Ages 9-11. 41, Vol. 3
Bradbury, Bianca. "I'M VINNY, I'M ME".
  Ages 12 and up. 65, Vol. 2
Bradbury, Bianca. THOSE TRAVER KIDS.
  Ages 12 and up. 111, Vol. 1
Brancato, Robin Fidler. BLINDED BY THE LIGHT.
  Ages 11-14. 70, Vol. 2
Butler, Beverly Kathleen. A GIRL CALLED WENDY.
  Ages 12 and up. 106, Vol. 2
Child Study Association of America. BROTHERS AND
  SISTERS ARE LIKE THAT! STORIES TO READ TO
  YOURSELF.
  Ages 7-9. 182, Vol. 1
Clifton, Lucille. MY BROTHER FINE WITH ME.
  Ages 5-8. 147, Vol. 2
Freeman, Lucy. THE ELEVEN STEPS.
  Ages 8-10. 235, Vol. 2
Friis-Baastad, Babbis Ellinor. DON'T TAKE TEDDY.
  Ages 11 and up. 338, Vol. 1
Gordon, Ethel Edison. SO FAR FROM HOME.
  Ages 11 and up. 369, Vol. 1
Graber, Richard Fredrick. A LITTLE BREATHING
  ROOM.
  Ages 10-14. 260, Vol. 2
Grant, Eva. WILL I EVER BE OLDER?
  Ages 5-8. 231, Vol. 3

**Sibling (cont.)**

Greene, Constance Clarke. BEAT THE TURTLE
DRUM.
Ages 10-13. 266, Vol. 2
Herzig, Alison Cragin and Jane Lawrence Mali. A
SEASON OF SECRETS.
Ages 11-13. 287, Vol. 3
Hinton, Susan Eloise. THE OUTSIDERS.
Ages 12 and up. 412, Vol. 1
Hinton, Susan Eloise. TEX.
Ages 11-15. 292, Vol. 3
Ho, Minfong. SING TO THE DAWN.
Ages 10-13. 320, Vol. 2
Hughes, Shirley. DAVID AND DOG.
Ages 4-7. 335, Vol. 2
Leech, Jay and Zane Spencer. BRIGHT FAWN AND
ME.
Ages 4-8. 361, Vol. 3
LeRoy, Gen. BILLY'S SHOES.
Ages 5-8. 364, Vol. 3
Lexau, Joan M. STRIPED ICE CREAM.
Ages 8-11. 559, Vol. 1
Little, Jean. LISTEN FOR THE SINGING.
Ages 10-14. 413, Vol. 2
Lowery, Bruce. SCARRED.
Ages 12 and up. 588, Vol. 1
McCord, Jean. TURKEYLEGS THOMPSON.
Ages 11-14. 390, Vol. 3
Norman, Lilith. CLIMB A LONELY HILL.
Ages 11-14. 671, Vol. 1
Nöstlinger, Christine. GIRL MISSING: A NOVEL.
Ages 11 and up. 482, Vol. 2
Posner, Grace. IN MY SISTER'S EYES.
Ages 12 and up. 516, Vol. 3
Roy, Ronald. AVALANCHE!
Ages 10 and up. 555, Vol. 3
Shyer, Marlene Fanta. WELCOME HOME,
JELLYBEAN.
Ages 10-13. 598, Vol. 2
Stapp, Arthur Donald. THE FABULOUS
EARTHWORM DEAL.
Ages 10-13. 852, Vol. 1
Wartski, Maureen Crane. MY BROTHER IS SPECIAL.
Ages 10-12. 681, Vol. 3
Winthrop, Elizabeth. A LITTLE DEMONSTRATION
OF AFFECTION.
Ages 12-16. 689, Vol. 2
Wojciechowska, Maia Rodman. TUNED OUT.
Ages 12 and up. 986, Vol. 1
Wright, Betty Ren. MY SISTER IS DIFFERENT.
Ages 6-9. 711, Vol. 3
Zolotow, Charlotte Shapiro. BIG SISTER AND LITTLE
SISTER.
Ages 3-7. 1018, Vol. 1
Zolotow, Charlotte Shapiro. DO YOU KNOW WHAT
I'LL DO?
Ages 3-7. 1019, Vol. 1

**Loyalty.** See also: Loyalty
Berger, Terry. BIG SISTER, LITTLE BROTHER.
Ages 3-7. 72, Vol. 1
Carol, Bill J., pseud. SINGLE TO CENTER.
Ages 9-11. 170, Vol. 1
Crane, Caroline. A GIRL LIKE TRACY.
Ages 12 and up. 256, Vol. 1
Engebrecht, P.A. UNDER THE HAYSTACK.
Ages 11 and up. 289, Vol. 1
Friis-Baastad, Babbis Ellinor. DON'T TAKE TEDDY.
Ages 11 and up. 338, Vol. 1
Gordon, Ethel Edison. SO FAR FROM HOME.
Ages 11 and up. 369, Vol. 1
Hamre, Leif. OPERATION ARCTIC.
Ages 11 and up. 398, Vol. 1
Johnston, Norma. THE KEEPING DAYS.
Ages 11 and up. 468, Vol. 1

Konigsburg, Elaine Lobl. FROM THE MIXED-UP
FILES OF MRS. BASIL E. FRANKWEILER.
Ages 9-12. 510, Vol. 1
Lasker, Joe. HE'S MY BROTHER.
Ages 4-9. 530, Vol. 1
Mathis, Sharon Bell. TEACUP FULL OF ROSES.
Ages 12 and up. 619, Vol. 1
Murphy, Shirley Rousseau. POOR JENNY, BRIGHT
AS A PENNY.
Ages 10-13. 654, Vol. 1
Noble, Iris Davis. FIRST WOMAN AMBULANCE
SURGEON, EMILY BARRINGER.
Ages 12 and up. 669, Vol. 1
Norman, Lilith. CLIMB A LONELY HILL.
Ages 11-14. 671, Vol. 1
Platt, Kin. CHLORIS AND THE CREEPS.
Ages 10-14. 713, Vol. 1
Stapp, Arthur Donald. THE FABULOUS
EARTHWORM DEAL.
Ages 10-13. 852, Vol. 1
Zolotow, Charlotte Shapiro. IF IT WEREN'T FOR
YOU.
Ages 3-6. 1022, Vol. 1

**Middle**
Amoss, Berthe. TOM IN THE MIDDLE.
Ages 3-7. 13, Vol. 1
Barrett, Anne. MIDWAY.
Ages 11-13. 53, Vol. 1
Blume, Judy Sussman. THE ONE IN THE MIDDLE IS
THE GREEN KANGAROO.
Ages 7-9. 55, Vol. 3
Burch, Robert Joseph. D. J.'S WORST ENEMY.
Ages 9-12. 139, Vol. 1
Burn, Doris. ANDREW HENRY'S MEADOW.
Ages 5-8. 146, Vol. 1
Byars, Betsy Cromer. GO AND HUSH THE BABY.
Ages 3-6. 155, Vol. 1
Carlson, Natalie Savage. THE HALF SISTERS.
Ages 10-12. 166, Vol. 1
Child Study Association of America. BROTHERS AND
SISTERS ARE LIKE THAT! STORIES TO READ TO
YOURSELF.
Ages 7-9. 182, Vol. 1
Fox, Paula. THE STONE-FACED BOY.
Ages 10-12. 329, Vol. 1
Friedman, Frieda. ELLEN AND THE GANG.
Ages 9-12. 335, Vol. 1
King, Cynthia. THE YEAR OF MR. NOBODY.
Ages 6-8. 381, Vol. 2
Mason, Miriam Evangeline. THE MIDDLE SISTER.
Ages 8-10. 615, Vol. 1
Murray, Michele. NELLIE CAMERON.
Ages 9-12. 655, Vol. 1
Peck, Richard. DON'T LOOK AND IT WON'T HURT.
Ages 12 and up. 694, Vol. 1
Wells, Rosemary. NOISY NORA.
Ages 4-7. 962, Vol. 1
Woolley, Catherine. CATHY'S LITTLE SISTER.
Ages 8-10. 994, Vol. 1

**New baby.** See also: Childbirth
Alexander, Martha G. NOBODY ASKED ME IF I
WANTED A BABY SISTER.
Ages 3-6. 9, Vol. 1
Alexander, Martha G. WHEN THE NEW BABY
COMES, I'M MOVING OUT.
Ages 2-5. 12, Vol. 3
Andry, Andrew C. and Suzanne C. Kratka. HI, NEW
BABY: A BOOK TO HELP YOUR CHILD LEARN
ABOUT THE NEW BABY.
Ages 5-9. 20, Vol. 1
Arnstein, Helene S. BILLY AND OUR NEW BABY.
Ages 3-6. 32, Vol. 1

## Sibling (cont.)

Knox-Wagner, Elaine. THE OLDEST KID.
Ages 4-8. 347, Vol. 3

McCaffrey, Mary. MY BROTHER ANGE.
Ages 8-11. 389, Vol. 3

Matthews, Ellen. GETTING RID OF ROGER.
Ages 8-10. 446, Vol. 2

Matthews, Ellen. THE TROUBLE WITH LESLIE.
Ages 8-11. 409, Vol. 3

Morrow, Suzanne Stark. INATUK'S FRIEND.
Ages 5-8. 649, Vol. 1

Naylor, Phyllis Reynolds. ALL BECAUSE I'M OLDER.
Ages 7-9. 462, Vol. 2

Peck, Richard. FATHER FIGURE: A NOVEL.
Ages 11 and up. 501, Vol. 2

Peterson, Jeanne Whitehouse. I HAVE A SISTER —
MY SISTER IS DEAF.
Ages 4-7. 507, Vol. 2

Supraner, Robyn. IT'S NOT FAIR!
Ages 3-7. 631, Vol. 2

Williams, Barbara Wright. JEREMY ISN'T HUNGRY.
Ages 4-7. 684, Vol. 2

**Oldest.** See also: Baby-sitting

Blume, Judy Sussman. TALES OF A FOURTH
GRADE NOTHING.
Ages 8-11. 93, Vol. 1

Byars, Betsy Cromer. THE NIGHT SWIMMERS.
Ages 10-12. 98, Vol. 3

Engebrecht, P. A. UNDER THE HAYSTACK.
Ages 11 and up. 289, Vol. 1

Rinkoff, Barbara Jean Rich. NAME: JOHNNY
PIERCE.
Ages 10-12. 738, Vol. 1

Sommerfelt, Aimée. THE ROAD TO AGRA.
Ages 10-13. 839, Vol. 1

Stolz, Mary Slattery. WHAT TIME OF NIGHT IS IT?
Ages 11-14. 631, Vol. 3

Zolotow, Charlotte Shapiro. IF IT WEREN'T FOR
YOU.
Ages 3-6. 1022, Vol. 1

**Rejection.** See: Rejection: sibling

**Relationships.** See also: Family: relationships

Alexander, Martha G. I'LL BE THE HORSE IF
YOU'LL PLAY WITH ME.
Ages 3-6. 8, Vol. 2

Anckarsvärd, Karin. AUNT VINNIE'S VICTORIOUS
SIX.
Ages 10-12. 14, Vol. 1

Arrick, Fran. TUNNEL VISION.
Ages 12 and up. 24, Vol. 3

Bawden, Nina Mary Kark. THE PEPPERMINT PIG.
Ages 9-14. 44, Vol. 2

Blume, Judy Sussman. SUPERFUDGE.
Ages 8-10. 56, Vol. 3

Bond, Felicia. POINSETTIA & HER FAMILY.
Ages 4-7. 59, Vol. 3

Bottner, Barbara. JUNGLE DAY OR, HOW I
LEARNED TO LOVE MY NOSEY LITTLE
BROTHER.
Ages 4-7. 62, Vol. 2

Bridgers, Sue Ellen. NOTES FOR ANOTHER LIFE.
Ages 12 and up. 75, Vol. 3

Bunting, Anne Evelyn. THE EMPTY WINDOW.
Ages 8-12. 89, Vol. 3

Cameron, Ann. THE STORIES JULIAN TELLS.
Ages 7-9. 104, Vol. 3

Carris, Joan Davenport. WHEN THE BOYS RAN THE
HOUSE.
Ages 8-12. 108, Vol. 3

Child Study Association of America. BROTHERS AND
SISTERS ARE LIKE THAT! STORIES TO READ TO
YOURSELF.
Ages 7-9. 182, Vol. 1

Cleary, Beverly Bunn. RAMONA THE BRAVE.
Ages 7-10. 138, Vol. 2

Coleman, William Laurence. ORPHAN JIM: A
NOVEL.
Ages 13 and up. 158, Vol. 2

Colman, Hila Crayder. THE FAMILY TRAP.
Ages 12 and up. 134, Vol. 3

Conaway, Judith. I'LL GET EVEN.
Ages 4-7. 170, Vol. 2

Conford, Ellen. EUGENE THE BRAVE.
Ages 5-7. 175, Vol. 2

Conta, Marcia Maher and Maureen
Reardon. FEELINGS BETWEEN BROTHERS AND
SISTERS.
Ages 3-7. 241, Vol. 1

De Roo, Anne Louise. SCRUB FIRE.
Ages 9-12. 162, Vol. 3

Dixon, Paige, pseud. MAY I CROSS YOUR GOLDEN
RIVER?
Ages 12 and up. 202, Vol. 2

Erickson, Russell E. WARTON AND MORTON.
Ages 4-7. 216, Vol. 2

Fitzgerald, John Dennis. THE GREAT BRAIN
REFORMS.
Ages 10-13. 318, Vol. 1

Friermood, Elisabeth Hamilton. FOCUS THE BRIGHT
LAND.
Ages 11 and up. 337, Vol. 1

Galbraith, Kathryn Osebold. SPOTS ARE SPECIAL!
Ages 4-7. 241, Vol. 2

Goldreich, Gloria. SEASON OF DISCOVERY.
Ages 11-13. 256, Vol. 2

Greene, Constance Clarke. DOUBLE-DARE O'TOOLE.
Ages 9-11. 240, Vol. 3

Greenfield, Eloise. SISTER.
Ages 10-12. 383, Vol. 1

Greenfield, Eloise. TALK ABOUT A FAMILY.
Ages 8-10. 273, Vol. 2

Grollman, Sharon Hya. MORE TIME TO GROW.
EXPLAINING MENTAL RETARDATION TO
CHILDREN: A STORY.
Ages 6-10. 284, Vol. 2

Hamre, Leif. OPERATION ARCTIC.
Ages 11 and up. 398, Vol. 1

Harris, Mark Jonathan. WITH A WAVE OF THE
WAND.
Ages 9-12. 267, Vol. 3

Hassler, Jon Francis. JEMMY.
Ages 11 and up. 270, Vol. 3

Hazen, Barbara Shook. IF IT WEREN'T FOR
BENJAMIN (I'D ALWAYS GET TO LICK THE
ICING SPOON).
Ages 3-7. 276, Vol. 3

Hazen, Barbara Shook. WHY COULDN'T I BE AN
ONLY KID LIKE YOU, WIGGER.
Ages 4-7. 303, Vol. 2

Hoban, Lillian Aberman. ARTHUR'S FUNNY
MONEY.
Ages 6-8. 294, Vol. 3

Hoban, Russell Conwell. BEST FRIENDS FOR
FRANCES.
Ages 4-7. 419, Vol. 1

Hoban, Russell Conwell. HARVEY'S HIDEOUT.
Ages 5-8. 420, Vol. 1

Hopkins, Lee Bennett. MAMA & HER BOYS.
Ages 8-11. 303, Vol. 3

Houston, James Archibald. LONG CLAWS: AN
ARCTIC ADVENTURE.
Ages 9-11. 305, Vol. 3

Hurwitz, Johanna. SUPERDUPER TEDDY.
Ages 4-7. 318, Vol. 3

Inkiow, Dimiter. ME AND CLARA AND CASIMER
THE CAT.
Ages 7-9. 321, Vol. 3

## Sibling (cont.)

Johnston, Norma. THE KEEPING DAYS.
Ages 11 and up. 468, Vol. 1

Jones, Penelope. HOLDING TOGETHER.
Ages 9-11. 331, Vol. 3

Jordan, June. NEW LIFE: NEW ROOM.
Ages 4-8. 361, Vol. 2

Keller, Holly. CROMWELL'S GLASSES.
Ages 3-6. 337, Vol. 3

Kroll, Steven. FRIDAY THE 13TH.
Ages 4-7. 353, Vol. 3

Lattimore, Eleanor Frances. ADAM'S KEY.
Ages 7-9. 395, Vol. 2

Lattimore, Eleanor Frances. THE BUS TRIP.
Ages 8-10. 532, Vol. 1

Lee, Mildred Scudder. THE SKATING RINK.
Ages 10-13. 536, Vol. 1

Leigh, Frances. THE LOST BOY.
Ages 10-13. 399, Vol. 2

LeShan, Eda J. WHAT'S GOING TO HAPPEN TO
ME? WHEN PARENTS SEPARATE OR DIVORCE.
Ages 8 and up. 402, Vol. 2

Little, Jean. STAND IN THE WIND.
Ages 8-11. 414, Vol. 2

Lowry, Lois. A SUMMER TO DIE.
Ages 10-14. 423, Vol. 2

Marshall, James Vance, pseud. WALKABOUT.
Ages 12 and up. 614, Vol. 1

Miklowitz, Gloria D. THE LOVE BOMBERS.
Ages 12 and up. 422, Vol. 3

Miner, Jane Claypool. MIRACLE OF TIME:
ADOPTING A SISTER.
Ages 11 and up. 430, Vol. 3

Moskin, Marietta Dunston. A PAPER DRAGON.
Ages 11 and up. 651, Vol. 1

Neville, Emily Cheney. GARDEN OF BROKEN
GLASS.
Ages 11-14. 477, Vol. 2

Osborn, Lois. MY BROTHER IS AFRAID OF JUST
ABOUT EVERYTHING.
Ages 4-7. 476, Vol. 3

Pascal, Francine. THE HAND-ME-DOWN KID.
Ages 10-13. 483, Vol. 3

Paterson, Katherine Womeldorf. BRIDGE TO
TERABITHIA.
Ages 9-12. 493, Vol. 2

Pearson, Susan. MOLLY MOVES OUT.
Ages 5-8. 487, Vol. 3

Perl, Lila. DUMB, LIKE ME, OLIVIA POTTS.
Ages 9-12. 502, Vol. 2

Peterson, Jeanne Whitehouse. THAT IS THAT.
Ages 5-8. 497, Vol. 3

Pevsner, Stella. AND YOU GIVE ME A PAIN,
ELAINE.
Ages 10-13. 508, Vol. 2

Phipson, Joan Nash, pseud. THE FAMILY
CONSPIRACY.
Ages 10-13. 708, Vol. 1

Pierik, Robert. ROOKFLEAS IN THE CELLAR.
Ages 8-13. 512, Vol. 3

Platt, Kin. CHLORIS AND THE CREEPS.
Ages 10-14. 713, Vol. 1

Platt, Kin. CHLORIS AND THE FREAKS.
Ages 11 and up. 515, Vol. 2

Platt, Kin. CHLORIS AND THE WEIRDOS.
Ages 11 and up. 516, Vol. 2

Rabe, Berniece Louise. THE GIRL WHO HAD NO
NAME.
Ages 12 and up. 526, Vol. 2

Reece, Colleen L. THE OUTSIDER.
Ages 12 and up. 527, Vol. 3

Renner, Beverly Hollett. THE HIDEAWAY SUMMER.
Ages 10-13. 531, Vol. 2

Reynolds, Pamela. WILL THE REAL MONDAY
PLEASE STAND UP.
Ages 11-14. 533, Vol. 2

Richard, Adrienne. INTO THE ROAD.
Ages 12 and up. 537, Vol. 2

Rinaldi, Ann. PROMISES ARE FOR KEEPING.
Ages 12 and up. 534, Vol. 3

Rinaldi, Ann. TERM PAPER.
Ages 12 and up. 535, Vol. 3

Robinet, Harriette Gillem. RIDE THE RED CYCLE.
Ages 7-11. 537, Vol. 3

Rockwell, Thomas. THE THIEF.
Ages 8-10. 554, Vol. 2

Ruthstrom, Dorotha. THE BIG KITE CONTEST.
Ages 6-8. 560, Vol. 3

Sachs, Marilyn. AMY AND LAURA.
Ages 9-12. 759, Vol. 1

Sachs, Marilyn. A DECEMBER TALE.
Ages 9-12. 565, Vol. 2

Sachs, Marilyn. MARV.
Ages 10-12. 761, Vol. 1

Sarnoff, Jane and Reynold Ruffins. THAT'S NOT
FAIR.
Ages 4-7. 571, Vol. 3

Shyer, Marlene Fanta. MY BROTHER, THE THIEF.
Ages 10-13. 594, Vol. 3

Simmons, Anthony. THE OPTIMISTS OF NINE
ELMS.
Ages 8-11. 600, Vol. 2

Slote, Alfred. RABBIT EARS.
Ages 10-12. 606, Vol. 3

Sobol, Harriet Langsam. MY BROTHER STEVEN IS
RETARDED.
Ages 7-10. 618, Vol. 2

Spence, Eleanor Rachel. THE DEVIL HOLE.
Ages 10-14. 619, Vol. 2

Stolz, Mary Slattery. GO AND CATCH A FLYING
FISH.
Ages 10-13. 630, Vol. 3

Tate, Eleanora E. JUST AN OVERNIGHT GUEST.
Ages 9-11. 643, Vol. 3

Tester, Sylvia Root. BILLY'S BASKETBALL.
Ages 5-7. 642, Vol. 3

Udry, Janice May. THUMP AND PLUNK.
Ages 2-5. 662, Vol. 3

Vestley, Anne-Catharina. AURORA AND SOCRATES.
Ages 8-10. 660, Vol. 3

Viorst, Judith. ALEXANDER, WHO USED TO BE
RICH LAST SUNDAY.
Ages 5-9. 664, Vol. 2

Voigt, Cynthia. DICEY'S SONG.
Ages 11 and up. 671, Vol. 3

Voigt, Cynthia. HOMECOMING.
Ages 11 and up. 664, Vol. 2

Wallace, Barbara Brooks. JULIA AND THE THIRD
BAD THING.
Ages 8-10. 673, Vol. 2

Wells, Rosemary. STANLEY & RHODA.
Ages 4-7. 678, Vol. 2

Wier, Ester Alberti. THE BARREL.
Ages 10-13. 970, Vol. 1

Winthrop, Elizabeth. POTBELLIED POSSUMS.
Ages 4-6. 690, Vol. 2

Wojciechowska, Maia Rodman. "HEY, WHAT'S
WRONG WITH THIS ONE?"
Ages 8-10. 983, Vol. 1

Wood, Phyllis Anderson. GET A LITTLE LOST, TIA.
Ages 11-13. 708, Vol. 2

Zolotow, Charlotte Shapiro. BIG SISTER AND LITTLE
SISTER.
Ages 3-7. 1018, Vol. 1

## Respect for

Burch, Robert Joseph. D. J.'S WORST ENEMY.
Ages 9-12. 139, Vol. 1

**Sibling (cont.)**

Johnson, Annabel Jones and Edgar Raymond Johnson. THE LAST KNIFE.
Ages 12 and up. 462, Vol. 1

Konigsburg, Elaine Lobl. FROM THE MIXED-UP FILES OF MRS. BASIL E. FRANKWEILER.
Ages 9-12. 510, Vol. 1

Lystad, Mary. JAMES, THE JAGUAR.
Ages 3-7. 592, Vol. 1

Ness, Evaline Michelow. DO YOU HAVE THE TIME, LYDIA?
Ages 5-8. 659, Vol. 1

**Rivalry**

Alexander, Anne. CONNIE.
Ages 10-13. 6, Vol. 2

Blume, Judy Sussman. TALES OF A FOURTH GRADE NOTHING.
Ages 8-11. 93, Vol. 1

Bradbury, Bianca. LAURIE.
Ages 11 and up. 109, Vol. 1

Bradbury, Bianca. THE LONER.
Ages 12 and up. 110, Vol. 1

Bronin, Andrew. GUS AND BUSTER WORK THINGS OUT.
Ages 4-7. 83, Vol. 2

Burch, Robert Joseph. D. J.'S WORST ENEMY.
Ages 9-12. 139, Vol. 1

Cleary, Beverly Bunn. RAMONA AND HER MOTHER.
Ages 7-10. 118, Vol. 3

Cohen, Barbara Nash. BENNY.
Ages 9-11. 152, Vol. 2

Colman, Hila Crayder. DIARY OF A FRANTIC KID SISTER.
Ages 10-13. 230, Vol. 1

Danziger, Paula. THE PISTACHIO PRESCRIPTION: A NOVEL.
Ages 11-13. 190, Vol. 2

Etter, Les. GET THOSE REBOUNDS!
Ages 10-13. 220, Vol. 2

Grant, Eva. WILL I EVER BE OLDER?
Ages 5-8. 231, Vol. 3

Hall, Lynn. HALF THE BATTLE.
Ages 11 and up. 255, Vol. 3

Hazen, Barbara Shook. IF IT WEREN'T FOR BENJAMIN (I'D ALWAYS GET TO LICK THE ICING SPOON).
Ages 3-7. 276, Vol. 3

Ho, Minfong. SING TO THE DAWN.
Ages 10-13. 320, Vol. 2

Johnson, Annabel Jones and Edgar Raymond Johnson. COUNT ME GONE.
Ages 13 and up. 459, Vol. 1

Klein, Monica. BACKYARD BASKETBALL SUPERSTAR.
Ages 6-8. 345, Vol. 3

Little, Jean. FROM ANNA.
Ages 9-11. 570, Vol. 1

Miles, Betty. JUST THE BEGINNING.
Ages 10-12. 456, Vol. 2

Myers, Walter Dean. WON'T KNOW TILL I GET THERE.
Ages 11-14. 460, Vol. 3

Pearson, Susan. MONNIE HATES LYDIA.
Ages 7-10. 498, Vol. 2

Richard, Adrienne. PISTOL.
Ages 12 and up. 732, Vol. 1

Roche, Patricia K. GOOD-BYE, ARNOLD.
Ages 3-7. 542, Vol. 3

Rosen, Winifred. HENRIETTA, THE WILD WOMAN OF BORNEO.
Ages 4-7. 560, Vol. 2

Shreve, Susan Richards. THE BAD DREAMS OF A GOOD GIRL.
Ages 8-10. 589, Vol. 3

Springstubb, Tricia. THE MOON ON A STRING.
Ages 12 and up. 619, Vol. 3

Stanek, Muriel Novella. MY LITTLE FOSTER SISTER.
Ages 4-8. 621, Vol. 3

Stolz, Mary Slattery. BY THE HIGHWAY HOME.
Ages 12 and up. 864, Vol. 1

Stolz, Mary Slattery. CIDER DAYS.
Ages 8-11. 626, Vol. 2

Stolz, Mary Slattery. FERRIS WHEEL.
Ages 8-11. 627, Vol. 2

Vigna, Judith. DADDY'S NEW BABY.
Ages 4-7. 666, Vol. 3

Viorst, Judith. I'LL FIX ANTHONY.
Ages 3-6. 927, Vol. 1

Vogel, Ilse-Margret. MY TWIN SISTER ERIKA.
Ages 6-10. 667, Vol. 2

Wells, Rosemary. NONE OF THE ABOVE.
Ages 12 and up. 963, Vol. 1

Zalben, Jane Breskin. CECILIA'S OLDER BROTHER.
Ages 4-6. 1013, Vol. 1

**Stepbrother/Stepsister.** *See: Parent/Parents: remarriage of; Stepbrother/Stepsister*

**Suicide of.** *See: Suicide: of sibling*

**Triplets.** *See: Triplets*

**Twins.** *See: Twins*

**Younger**

Alexander, Martha G. I'LL BE THE HORSE IF YOU'LL PLAY WITH ME.
Ages 3-6. 8, Vol. 2

Benson, Ellen. PHILIP'S LITTLE SISTER.
Ages 5-8. 46, Vol. 3

Bonsall, Crosby Newell. THE DAY I HAD TO PLAY WITH MY SISTER.
Ages 3-8. 100, Vol. 1

Caines, Jeannette Franklin. ABBY.
Ages 3-7. 157, Vol. 1

Cleary, Beverly Bunn. BEEZUS AND RAMONA.
Ages 8-10. 190, Vol. 1

Cleary, Beverly Bunn. RAMONA AND HER MOTHER.
Ages 7-10. 118, Vol. 3

Crowley, Arthur. BONZO BEAVER.
Ages 3-6. 144, Vol. 3

Grant, Eva. WILL I EVER BE OLDER?
Ages 5-8. 231, Vol. 3

Hamilton, Morse and Emily Hamilton. BIG SISTERS ARE BAD WITCHES.
Ages 3-6. 258, Vol. 3

Hamilton, Virginia. ARILLA SUN DOWN.
Ages 12 and up. 291, Vol. 3

Hinton, Susan Eloise. RUMBLE FISH.
Ages 12 and up. 316, Vol. 2

Hoban, Lillian Aberman. ARTHUR'S HONEY BEAR.
Ages 4-8. 415, Vol. 1

Landis, James David. THE SISTERS IMPOSSIBLE.
Ages 9-11. 355, Vol. 3

LeRoy, Gen. BILLY'S SHOES.
Ages 5-8. 364, Vol. 3

Mosel, Arlene. TIKKI TIKKI TEMBO.
Ages 4-9. 650, Vol. 1

Ness, Evaline Michelow. EXACTLY ALIKE.
Ages 5-8. 660, Vol. 1

Pearson, Susan. MONNIE HATES LYDIA.
Ages 7-10. 498, Vol. 2

Reuter, Margaret. YOU CAN DEPEND ON ME.
Ages 6-9. 530, Vol. 3

Roche, Patricia K. GOOD-BYE, ARNOLD.
Ages 3-7. 542, Vol. 3

Rosenberg, Sondra. ARE THERE ANY MORE AT HOME LIKE YOU?
Ages 11 and up. 753, Vol. 1

## Sibling (cont.)

Wright, Betty Ren. MY SISTER IS DIFFERENT.
Ages 6-9. 711, Vol. 3
Zolotow, Charlotte Shapiro. MAY I VISIT?
Ages 4-7. 719, Vol. 2

### Youngest

Buckley, Helen Elizabeth. THE WONDERFUL
LITTLE BOY.
Ages 3-7. 132, Vol. 1
Bulla, Clyde Robert. KEEP RUNNING, ALLEN!
Ages 4-6. 92, Vol. 2
Clifton, Lucille. DON'T YOU REMEMBER?
Ages 4-7. 209, Vol. 1
Corey, Dorothy. TOMORROW YOU CAN.
Ages 2-5. 182, Vol. 2
Felt, Sue. ROSA-TOO-LITTLE.
Ages 4-7. 308, Vol. 1
Kellogg, Steven. MUCH BIGGER THAN MARTIN.
Ages 4-7. 374, Vol. 2
Kraus, Robert. BIG BROTHER.
Ages 3-6. 520, Vol. 1
Lattimore, Eleanor Frances. ADAM'S KEY.
Ages 7-9. 395, Vol. 2
Lexau, Joan M. STRIPED ICE CREAM.
Ages 8-11. 559, Vol. 1
Little, Jean. SPRING BEGINS IN MARCH.
Ages 10-12. 576, Vol. 1
Lystad, Mary. JAMES, THE JAGUAR.
Ages 3-7. 592, Vol. 1
Pape, Donna Lugg. SNOWMAN FOR SALE.
Ages 5-7. 492, Vol. 2
Pascal, Francine. THE HAND-ME-DOWN KID.
Ages 10-13. 483, Vol. 3
Pearson, Susan. SATURDAY I RAN AWAY.
Ages 5-7. 488, Vol. 3
Rodowsky, Colby F. P.S. WRITE SOON.
Ages 10-12. 555, Vol. 2
Scott, Ann Herbert. SAM.
Ages 3-7. 801, Vol. 1
Thompson, Jean, pseud. DON'T FORGET MICHAEL.
Ages 7-9. 656, Vol. 3
Viorst, Judith. I'LL FIX ANTHONY.
Ages 3-6. 927, Vol. 1

## Sickness

See: Illnesses; Mental illness

## Silliness

See: Attention seeking

## Sissy

See: Name-calling

## Sister

See: Sibling

## Size

See: Height; Weight control

## Skipping School

See: School: truancy

## Sleep

See: Bedtime; Dreams; Nightmares

## Slum

See: Ghetto; Poverty

## Slumber Party

See: Visiting

## Smart Aleck

See: Name-calling

## Smoking

See also: Drugs; Marijuana
Cleary, Beverly Bunn. RAMONA AND HER FATHER.
Ages 7-10. 137, Vol. 2
Sandberg, Inger and Lasse Sandberg. WHERE DOES
ALL THAT SMOKE COME FROM?
Ages 3-8. 770, Vol. 1
Tobias, Tobi. THE QUITTING DEAL.
Ages 7-9. 654, Vol. 2
Wrenn, C. Gilbert and Shirley Schwarzrock. FACTS
AND FANTASIES ABOUT SMOKING.
Ages 11 and up. 1001, Vol. 1

## Social Class

See: Poverty; Prejudice: social class; Wealth/Wealthy

## Society of Friends (Quaker)

Huston, Anne and Jane H. Yolen. TRUST A CITY
KID.
Ages 11 and up. 448, Vol. 1
Turkle, Brinton. THE ADVENTURES OF OBADIAH.
Ages 4-8. 906, Vol. 1
Turkle, Brinton. THY FRIEND, OBADIAH.
Ages 4-8. 908, Vol. 1
Worth, Kathryn. THEY LOVED TO LAUGH.
Ages 12 and up. 996, Vol. 1

## Sorrow

See: Death; Mourning, stages of; Separation from loved
ones

## Soviet Union

See: Russia

## Spastic

See also: Brain injury; Cerebral palsy
Southall, Ivan. LET THE BALLOON GO.
Ages 12 and up. 847, Vol. 1
Viscardi, Henry. A LAUGHTER IN THE LONELY
NIGHT.
Ages 12 and up. 931, Vol. 1

## Speech Problems

See also: Cleft lip/palate
Friis-Baastad, Babbis Ellinor. KRISTY'S COURAGE.
Ages 8-10. 339, Vol. 1
Platt, Kin. THE BOY WHO COULD MAKE HIMSELF
DISAPPEAR.
Ages 12 and up. 712, Vol. 1
Stanek, Muriel Novella. GROWL WHEN YOU SAY R.
Ages 4-8. 620, Vol. 3

### Stuttering

Christopher, Matthew F. GLUE FINGERS.
Ages 7-9. 134, Vol. 2
Fassler, Joan. DON'T WORRY DEAR.
Ages 4-6. 305, Vol. 1
Holland, Isabelle. ALAN AND THE ANIMAL
KINGDOM.
Ages 10-13. 327, Vol. 2
Kelley, Sally. TROUBLE WITH EXPLOSIVES.
Ages 10-13. 373, Vol. 2
Lee, Mildred Scudder. THE SKATING RINK.
Ages 10-13. 536, Vol. 1
Madison, Winifred. GROWING UP IN A HURRY.
Ages 12 and up. 606, Vol. 1
Watson, Sally. OTHER SANDALS.
Ages 12 and up. 956, Vol. 1

## Spine, Curvature of

See: Scoliosis

## Spoiled Child

**See:** *Parental: overpermissiveness*

## Sports/Sportsmanship

**See also:** *Competition; Little League*

Addy, Sharon. WE DIDN'T MEAN TO.
   Ages 8-10. 2, Vol. 3
Allen, Alex B., pseud. THE TENNIS MENACE.
   Ages 8-10. 10, Vol. 2
Archibald, Joseph Stopford. THE FIFTH BASE.
   Ages 12 and up. 28, Vol. 1
Bach, Alice Hendricks. THE MEAT IN THE
   SANDWICH.
   Ages 10-13. 28, Vol. 2
Block, Marie Halun. THE TWO WORLDS OF
   DAMYAN.
   Ages 9-12. 81, Vol. 1
Brown, Fern G. YOU'RE SOMEBODY SPECIAL ON
   A HORSE.
   Ages 10-13. 87, Vol. 2
Campanella, Roy. IT'S GOOD TO BE ALIVE.
   Ages 13 and up. 160, Vol. 1
Carol, Bill J., pseud. SINGLE TO CENTER.
   Ages 9-11. 170, Vol. 1
Christopher, Matthew F. THE FOX STEALS HOME.
   Ages 8-10. 133, Vol. 2
Christopher, Matthew F. GLUE FINGERS.
   Ages 7-9. 134, Vol. 2
Christopher, Matthew F. JOHNNY LONG LEGS.
   Ages 9-11. 184, Vol. 1
Cohen, Barbara Nash. BENNY.
   Ages 9-11. 152, Vol. 2
Cohen, Barbara Nash. THANK YOU, JACKIE
   ROBINSON.
   Ages 10-13. 215, Vol. 1
Dolan, Edward Francis and Richard B. Lyttle. BOBBY
   CLARKE.
   Ages 10-12. 205, Vol. 2
Donovan, Pete. CAROL JOHNSTON: THE ONE-
   ARMED GYMNAST.
   Ages 8-12. 169, Vol. 3
Douglass, Barbara. SKATEBOARD SCRAMBLE.
   Ages 9-11. 170, Vol. 3
Dygard, Thomas J. POINT SPREAD.
   Ages 10 and up. 178, Vol. 3
Dygard, Thomas J. SOCCER DUEL.
   Ages 11-14. 179, Vol. 3
Dygard, Thomas J. WINNING KICKER.
   Ages 11-14. 213, Vol. 2
Etter, Les. GET THOSE REBOUNDS!
   Ages 10-13. 220, Vol. 2
Geibel, James. THE BLOND BROTHER.
   Ages 12 and up. 205, Vol. 3
Gibson, Althea. I ALWAYS WANTED TO BE
   SOMEBODY.
   Ages 12 and up. 357, Vol. 1
Gilbert, Nan, pseud. CHAMPIONS DON'T CRY.
   Ages 10-13. 358, Vol. 1
Greene, Sheppard M. THE BOY WHO DRANK TOO
   MUCH.
   Ages 12 and up. 242, Vol. 3
Gregory, Diana. THERE'S A CATERPILLAR IN MY
   LEMONADE.
   Ages 10-12. 247, Vol. 3
Harlan, Elizabeth. FOOTFALLS.
   Ages 12-14. 265, Vol. 3
Harmon, A. W. BASE HIT.
   Ages 9-12. 400, Vol. 1
Jacobs, Helen Hull. THE TENNIS MACHINE.
   Ages 12 and up. 455, Vol. 1
Katz, Bobbi. VOLLEYBALL JINX.
   Ages 9-11. 364, Vol. 2
Kaufman, Mervyn D. JESSE OWENS.
   Ages 7-10. 480, Vol. 1

Kinter, Judith. CROSS-COUNTRY CAPER.
   Ages 11-14. 342, Vol. 3
Knudson, R. Rozanne. FOX RUNNING: A NOVEL.
   Ages 11 and up. 386, Vol. 2
Knudson, R. Rozanne. RINEHART LIFTS.
   Ages 10-12. 348, Vol. 3
Knudson, R. Rozanne. ZANBANGER.
   Ages 10-13. 387, Vol. 2
Knudson, R. Rozanne. ZANBOOMER.
   Ages 10-13. 388, Vol. 2
Lee, H. Alton. SEVEN FEET FOUR AND GROWING.
   Ages 9-12. 396, Vol. 2
Lee, Robert C. IT'S A MILE FROM HERE TO
   GLORY.
   Ages 10 and up. 538, Vol. 1
Lexau, Joan M. I HATE RED ROVER.
   Ages 6-8. 371, Vol. 3
Lexau, Joan M. I'LL TELL ON YOU.
   Ages 5-8. 406, Vol. 2
Lord, Beman. BATS AND BALLS.
   Ages 8-11. 580, Vol. 1
Lord, Beman. GUARDS FOR MATT.
   Ages 8-10. 581, Vol. 1
Lord, Beman. QUARTERBACK'S AIM.
   Ages 8-10. 582, Vol. 1
Lord, Beman. ROUGH ICE.
   Ages 8-11. 583, Vol. 1
Lord, Beman. SHRIMP'S SOCCER GOAL.
   Ages 8-11. 584, Vol. 1
Love, Sandra Weller. MELISSA'S MEDLEY.
   Ages 10-13. 418, Vol. 2
Luce, Willard and Celia Luce. LOU GEHRIG: IRON
   MAN OF BASEBALL.
   Ages 8-10. 589, Vol. 1
McClinton, Leon. CROSS-COUNTRY RUNNER.
   Ages 12 and up. 594, Vol. 1
McKay, Robert W. THE RUNNING BACK.
   Ages 12-14. 392, Vol. 3
Madden, Betsy. THE ALL-AMERICAN COEDS.
   Ages 12 and up. 601, Vol. 1
Marney, Dean. JUST GOOD FRIENDS.
   Ages 11-13. 404, Vol. 3
Marshall, Lydia. NOBODY LIKES TO LOSE.
   Ages 7-9. 405, Vol. 3
Mazer, Harry. THE WAR ON VILLA STREET: A
   NOVEL.
   Ages 11-13. 448, Vol. 2
Miner, Jane Claypool. NEW BEGINNING: AN
   ATHLETE IS PARALYZED.
   Ages 11 and up. 433, Vol. 3
Myers, Walter Dean. HOOPS.
   Ages 12 and up. 459, Vol. 3
Neigoff, Mike. RUNNER-UP.
   Ages 9-11. 474, Vol. 2
Neigoff, Mike. SOCCER HERO.
   Ages 9-11. 475, Vol. 2
Nicholson, William G. PETE GRAY: ONE-ARMED
   MAJOR LEAGUER.
   Ages 9-12. 479, Vol. 2
Platt, Kin. BROGG'S BRAIN.
   Ages 12 and up. 514, Vol. 3
Platt, Kin. RUN FOR YOUR LIFE.
   Ages 9-12. 518, Vol. 2
Robinson, John Roosevelt and Alfred
   Duckett. BREAKTHROUGH TO THE BIG LEAGUE:
   THE STORY OF JACKIE ROBINSON.
   Ages 10 and up. 746, Vol. 1
Robison, Nancy Louise. ON THE BALANCE BEAM.
   Ages 8-10. 549, Vol. 2
Rudeen, Kenneth. JACKIE ROBINSON.
   Ages 7-9. 757, Vol. 1
Slote, Alfred. THE HOTSHOT.
   Ages 8-11. 610, Vol. 2

## Stepbrother/Stepsister (cont.)

Okimoto, Jean Davies. IT'S JUST TOO MUCH.
Ages 10-12. 469, Vol. 3
Oppenheimer, Joan Letson. GARDINE VS.
HANOVER.
Ages 11-14. 474, Vol. 3
Pfeffer, Susan Beth. STARRING PETER AND LEIGH.
Ages 12-14. 503, Vol. 3
Roberts, Willo Davis. DON'T HURT LAURIE!
Ages 10-14. 545, Vol. 2
Tax, Meredith. FAMILIES.
Ages 4-8. 645, Vol. 3
Terris, Susan Dubinsky. NO SCARLET RIBBONS.
Ages 11-13. 647, Vol. 3
Thomas, Ianthe. ELIZA'S DADDY.
Ages 4-7. 647, Vol. 2
Wells, Rosemary. NONE OF THE ABOVE.
Ages 12 and up. 963, Vol. 1
Willard, Barbara. STORM FROM THE WEST.
Ages 10-13. 976, Vol. 1
Wolkoff, Judie. HAPPILY EVER AFTER...ALMOST.
Ages 11-13. 703, Vol. 3

## Stepparent

**See also:** *Family; Parent/Parents: remarriage of*
Berman, Claire. WHAT AM I DOING IN A STEP-
FAMILY?
Ages 5-10. 51, Vol. 3
Tax, Meredith. FAMILIES.
Ages 4-8. 645, Vol. 3

### Father

Ashley, Bernard. BREAK IN THE SUN.
Ages 11 and up. 29, Vol. 3
Bates, Betty. BUGS IN YOUR EARS.
Ages 10-13. 40, Vol. 2
Berger, Terry. STEPCHILD.
Ages 7-11. 50, Vol. 3
Bradbury, Bianca. THOSE TRAVER KIDS.
Ages 12 and up. 111, Vol. 1
Childress, Alice. A HERO AIN'T NOTHIN' BUT A
SANDWICH.
Ages 12 and up. 183, Vol. 1
Clifford, Ethel Rosenberg. THE KILLER SWAN.
Ages 10-12. 120, Vol. 3
Clifton, Lucille. EVERETT ANDERSON'S NINE
MONTH LONG.
Ages 4-7. 145, Vol. 2
Clifton, Lucille. EVERETT ANDERSON'S 1-2-3.
Ages 4-6. 146, Vol. 2
Corbin, William, pseud. SMOKE.
Ages 11 and up. 247, Vol. 1
Ewing, Kathryn. THINGS WON'T BE THE SAME.
Ages 8-10. 182, Vol. 3
Green, Phyllis. ICE RIVER.
Ages 8-10. 262, Vol. 2
Gregory, Diana. THERE'S A CATERPILLAR IN MY
LEMONADE.
Ages 10-12. 247, Vol. 3
Hanlon, Emily. THE SWING.
Ages 10-12. 261, Vol. 3
Hunter, Evan. ME AND MR. STENNER.
Ages 10-13. 339, Vol. 2
Huston, Anne. OLLIE'S GO-KART.
Ages 9-11. 447, Vol. 1
Jackson, Jacqueline. THE TASTE OF SPRUCE GUM.
Ages 10-13. 454, Vol. 1
LeShan, Eda J. WHAT'S GOING TO HAPPEN TO
ME? WHEN PARENTS SEPARATE OR DIVORCE.
Ages 8 and up. 402, Vol. 2
Maddock, Reginald. DANNY ROWLEY.
Ages 11-13. 602, Vol. 1
Mazer, Harry. GUY LENNY.
Ages 12 and up. 627, Vol. 1
Morey, Walter. YEAR OF THE BLACK PONY.
Ages 10-13. 465, Vol. 2

Nöstlinger, Christine. GIRL MISSING: A NOVEL.
Ages 11 and up. 482, Vol. 2
O'Hanlon, Jacklyn. FAIR GAME.
Ages 11-13. 487, Vol. 2
Okimoto, Jean Davies. IT'S JUST TOO MUCH.
Ages 10-12. 469, Vol. 3
Okimoto, Jean Davies. MY MOTHER IS NOT
MARRIED TO MY FATHER.
Ages 9-11. 470, Vol. 3
Platt, Kin. CHLORIS AND THE CREEPS.
Ages 10-14. 713, Vol. 1
Platt, Kin. CHLORIS AND THE FREAKS.
Ages 11 and up. 515, Vol. 2
Richardson, Grace. APPLES EVERY DAY.
Ages 12 and up. 733, Vol. 1
Roberts, Willo Davis. DON'T HURT LAURIE!
Ages 10-14. 545, Vol. 2
Samuels, Gertrude. RUN, SHELLEY, RUN.
Ages 12 and up. 768, Vol. 1
Snyder, Zilpha Keatley. THE HEADLESS CUPID.
Ages 10-13. 837, Vol. 1
Sobol, Harriet Langsam. MY OTHER-MOTHER, MY
OTHER-FATHER.
Ages 7-10. 616, Vol. 3
Sorenson, Virginia Eggertsen. LOTTE'S LOCKET.
Ages 10-12. 843, Vol. 1
Terris, Susan Dubinsky. NO SCARLET RIBBONS.
Ages 11-13. 647, Vol. 3
Willard, Barbara. STORM FROM THE WEST.
Ages 10-13. 976, Vol. 1
Wolkoff, Judie. HAPPILY EVER AFTER...ALMOST.
Ages 11-13. 703, Vol. 3

### Mother

Adler, Carole Schwerdtfeger. IN OUR HOUSE
SCOTT IS MY BROTHER.
Ages 10-13. 5, Vol. 3
Alcock, Gudrun. DUFFY.
Ages 11-13. 4, Vol. 1
Anckarsvärd, Karin. SPRINGTIME FOR EVA.
Ages 12 and up. 16, Vol. 1
Bates, Betty. BUGS IN YOUR EARS.
Ages 10-13. 40, Vol. 2
Bonham, Frank. GIMME AN H, GIMME AN E,
GIMME AN L, GIMME A P.
Ages 12 and up. 61, Vol. 3
Brenner, Barbara Johnes. A YEAR IN THE LIFE OF
ROSIE BERNARD.
Ages 9-11. 118, Vol. 1
Bunting, Anne Evelyn. THE BIG RED BARN.
Ages 4-7. 88, Vol. 3
Daringer, Helen Fern. STEPSISTER SALLY.
Ages 9-12. 264, Vol. 1
Ewing, Kathryn. THINGS WON'T BE THE SAME.
Ages 8-10. 182, Vol. 3
Eyerly, Jeannette Hyde. DROP-OUT.
Ages 11 and up. 296, Vol. 1
Francis, Dorothy Brenner. THE FLINT HILLS FOAL.
Ages 8-11. 234, Vol. 2
Gates, Doris. BLUE WILLOW.
Ages 9-11. 348, Vol. 1
Hunt, Irene. UP A ROAD SLOWLY.
Ages 12 and up. 438, Vol. 1
Kaplan, Bess. THE EMPTY CHAIR.
Ages 10-14. 363, Vol. 2
Klass, Sheila Solomon. TO SEE MY MOTHER
DANCE.
Ages 10-13. 344, Vol. 3
Lee, Mildred Scudder. THE SKATING RINK.
Ages 10-13. 536, Vol. 1
LeShan, Eda J. WHAT'S GOING TO HAPPEN TO
ME? WHEN PARENTS SEPARATE OR DIVORCE.
Ages 8 and up. 402, Vol. 2
Maddock, Reginald. DANNY ROWLEY.
Ages 11-13. 602, Vol. 1

## Stepparent (cont.)

Mazer, Harry. GUY LENNY.
Ages 12 and up. 627, Vol. 1

Mendonca, Susan R. TOUGH CHOICES.
Ages 11 and up. 419, Vol. 3

Neufeld, John. TOUCHING.
Ages 12 and up. 665, Vol. 1

Pevsner, Stella. A SMART KID LIKE YOU.
Ages 10-13. 510, Vol. 2

Pfeffer, Susan Beth. MARLY THE KID.
Ages 11-13. 512, Vol. 2

Reiss, Johanna. THE JOURNEY BACK.
Ages 10-14. 530, Vol. 2

Rogers, Pamela. THE RARE ONE.
Ages 10-12. 751, Vol. 1

Sherburne, Zoa. ALMOST APRIL.
Ages 12 and up. 810, Vol. 1

Sherburne, Zoa. GIRL IN THE MIRROR.
Ages 11 and up. 811, Vol. 1

Snyder, Zilpha Keatley. THE HEADLESS CUPID.
Ages 10-13. 837, Vol. 1

Sobol, Harriet Langsam. MY OTHER-MOTHER, MY
OTHER-FATHER.
Ages 7-10. 616, Vol. 3

Vigna, Judith. SHE'S NOT MY REAL MOTHER.
Ages 4-8. 668, Vol. 3

Wells, Rosemary. NONE OF THE ABOVE.
Ages 12 and up. 963, Vol. 1

Willard, Barbara. STORM FROM THE WEST.
Ages 10-13. 976, Vol. 1

Wolitzer, Hilma. OUT OF LOVE.
Ages 10-13. 704, Vol. 2

Wolkoff, Judie. HAPPILY EVER AFTER...ALMOST.
Ages 11-13. 703, Vol. 3

Wright, Betty Ren. MY NEW MOM AND ME.
Ages 8-10. 710, Vol. 3

York, Carol Beach. REMEMBER ME WHEN I AM
DEAD.
Ages 9-11. 714, Vol. 3

Zalben, Jane Breskin. MAYBE IT WILL RAIN
TOMORROW.
Ages 12 and up. 716, Vol. 3

## Stereotype

See: *Prejudice*

## Stitches

See: *Doctor, going to; Sutures*

## Stuttering

See: *Speech problems: stuttering*

## Substitute Parent

See: *Foster home; Parent/Parents: substitute*

## Success

Andersen, Karen Born. WHAT'S THE MATTER,
SYLVIE, CAN'T YOU RIDE?
Ages 4-7. 15, Vol. 3

Blume, Judy Sussman. THE ONE IN THE MIDDLE IS
THE GREEN KANGAROO.
Ages 7-9. 55, Vol. 3

Bottner, Barbara. DUMB OLD CASEY IS A FAT
TREE.
Ages 6-9. 66, Vol. 3

Boutis, Victoria. KATY DID IT.
Ages 8-10. 69, Vol. 3

Brown, Marc Tolan. ARTHUR GOES TO CAMP.
Ages 5-8. 79, Vol. 3

Cunningham, Julia Woolfolk. THE SILENT VOICE.
Ages 11-14. 146, Vol. 3

Delton, Judy. I NEVER WIN!
Ages 4-7. 154, Vol. 3

De Paola, Thomas Anthony. OLIVER BUTTON IS A
SISSY.
Ages 4-7. 154, Vol. 3

Giff, Patricia Reilly. TODAY WAS A TERRIBLE DAY.
Ages 6-7. 213, Vol. 3

Gorsline, Douglas Warren. FARM BOY.
Ages 10-12. 370, Vol. 1

Greene, Bette. GET ON OUT OF HERE, PHILIP
HALL.
Ages 9-12. 238, Vol. 3

Guy, Anne Welsh. STEINMETZ: WIZARD OF LIGHT.
Ages 9-12. 390, Vol. 1

Hallman, Ruth. BREAKAWAY.
Ages 12 and up. 257, Vol. 3

Hardwick, Richard. CHARLES RICHARD DREW,
PIONEER IN BLOOD RESEARCH.
Ages 12 and up. 399, Vol. 1

Hobby, Janice Hale with Gabrielle Rubin and Daniel
Rubin. STAYING BACK.
Ages 6-12. 295, Vol. 3

Hogan, Paula Z. SOMETIMES I DON'T LIKE
SCHOOL.
Ages 6-9. 297, Vol. 3

Hughes, Shirley. ALFIE GETS IN FIRST.
Ages 3-5. 309, Vol. 3

Hurwitz, Johanna. TOUGH-LUCK KAREN.
Ages 10-13. 319, Vol. 3

Jordan, June. FANNIE LOU HAMER.
Ages 8-10. 473, Vol. 1

Kroll, Steven. FRIDAY THE 13TH.
Ages 4-7. 353, Vol. 3

Lexau, Joan M. I HATE RED ROVER.
Ages 6-8. 371, Vol. 3

Marzollo, Jean. AMY GOES FISHING.
Ages 4-7. 407, Vol. 3

Melton, David. A BOY CALLED HOPELESS.
Ages 10 and up. 451, Vol. 2

Naylor, Phyllis Reynolds. EDDIE, INCORPORATED.
Ages 9-11. 463, Vol. 3

Pfeffer, Susan Beth. WHAT DO YOU DO WHEN
YOUR MOUTH WON'T OPEN?
Ages 10-13. 505, Vol. 3

Riley, Susan. WHAT DOES IT MEAN? SUCCESS.
Ages 3-6. 543, Vol. 2

Robinet, Harriette Gillem. RIDE THE RED CYCLE.
Ages 7-11. 537, Vol. 3

Robison, Nancy Louise. BALLET MAGIC.
Ages 9-11. 541, Vol. 3

Ross, Pat. M AND M AND THE BIG BAG.
Ages 6-8. 550, Vol. 3

Schick, Eleanor Grossman. JOEY ON HIS OWN.
Ages 5-8. 574, Vol. 3

Stanek, Muriel Novella. GROWL WHEN YOU SAY R.
Ages 4-8. 620, Vol. 3

Taylor, Paula. JOHNNY CASH.
Ages 7-10. 638, Vol. 2

Tobias, Tobi. ARTHUR MITCHELL.
Ages 7-10. 649, Vol. 2

Wartski, Maureen Crane. MY BROTHER IS SPECIAL.
Ages 10-12. 681, Vol. 3

Watanabe, Shigeo. GET SET! GO!
Ages 3-5. 682, Vol. 3

Watanabe, Shigeo. I CAN RIDE IT!
Ages 2-5. 684, Vol. 3

Williams, Barbara Wright. SO WHAT IF I'M A SORE
LOSER?
Ages 5-8. 692, Vol. 3

## Suicide

Arrick, Fran. TUNNEL VISION.
Ages 12 and up. 24, Vol. 3

Josephs, Rebecca. EARLY DISORDER.
Ages 13 and up. 335, Vol. 3

## Suicide (cont.)

Korschunow, Irina. WHO KILLED CHRISTOPHER?
Ages 12 and up. 350, Vol. 3
Peck, Robert Newton. CLUNIE.
Ages 12 and up. 491, Vol. 3
Pfeffer, Susan Beth. ABOUT DAVID.
Ages 13 and up. 500, Vol. 3
Shreve, Susan Richards. FAMILY SECRETS: FIVE
VERY IMPORTANT STORIES.
Ages 9-11. 590, Vol. 3
Tolan, Stephanie S. GRANDPA — AND ME.
Ages 10-13. 655, Vol. 2

### Attempted

Alexander, Anne. CONNIE.
Ages 10-13. 6, Vol. 2
Bonham, Frank. GIMME AN H, GIMME AN E,
GIMME AN L, GIMME A P.
Ages 12 and up. 61, Vol. 3
Bridgers, Sue Ellen. NOTES FOR ANOTHER LIFE.
Ages 12 and up. 75, Vol. 3
Carlson, Dale Bick. TRIPLE BOY.
Ages 13 and up. 115, Vol. 2
Due, Linnea A. HIGH AND OUTSIDE.
Ages 13 and up. 174, Vol. 3
Eyerly, Jeannette Hyde. THE GIRL INSIDE.
Ages 12 and up. 298, Vol. 1
Freeman, Gaail. OUT FROM UNDER.
Ages 12 and up. 195, Vol. 3
Johnson, A. E., pseud. A BLUES I CAN WHISTLE.
Ages 13 and up. 458, Vol. 1
L'Engle, Madeleine Franklin. CAMILLA.
Ages 12 and up. 540, Vol. 1
L'Engle, Madeleine Franklin. A RING OF ENDLESS
LIGHT.
Ages 11-14. 363, Vol. 3
Oneal, Zibby. THE LANGUAGE OF GOLDFISH.
Ages 11-14. 473, Vol. 3
Roth, Arthur J. THE SECRET LOVER OF ELMTREE.
Ages 12 and up. 563, Vol. 2
Terris, Susan Dubinsky. THE DROWNING BOY.
Ages 10 and up. 891, Vol. 1
Viscardi, Henry. A LAUGHTER IN THE LONELY
NIGHT.
Ages 12 and up. 931, Vol. 1
Wartski, Maureen Crane. THE LAKE IS ON FIRE.
Ages 10-13. 679, Vol. 3

### Consideration of

Brancato, Robin Fidler. WINNING.
Ages 12 and up. 72, Vol. 2
Elfman, Blossom. A HOUSE FOR JONNIE O.
Ages 12 and up. 215, Vol. 2
Freeman, Gaail. OUT FROM UNDER.
Ages 12 and up. 195, Vol. 3
Wersba, Barbara. THE DREAM WATCHER.
Ages 12 and up. 964, Vol. 1

### of Parent

Cleaver, Vera and Bill Cleaver. GROVER.
Ages 9-12. 198, Vol. 1
Clifford, Ethel Rosenberg. THE KILLER SWAN.
Ages 10-12. 120, Vol. 3
Feagles, Anita Macrae. THE YEAR THE DREAMS
CAME BACK.
Ages 11-14. 225, Vol. 2
Hughes, Dean. SWITCHING TRACKS.
Ages 10-14. 308, Vol. 3
Krementz, Jill. HOW IT FEELS WHEN A PARENT
DIES.
Ages 8 and up. 352, Vol. 3
Lorimar, Lawrence T. SECRETS.
Ages 12 and up. 382, Vol. 3
Peck, Richard. FATHER FIGURE: A NOVEL.
Ages 11 and up. 501, Vol. 2
Platt, Kin. CHLORIS AND THE FREAKS.
Ages 11 and up. 515, Vol. 2

Zalben, Jane Breskin. MAYBE IT WILL RAIN
TOMORROW.
Ages 12 and up. 716, Vol. 3

### of Sibling

Gerson, Corinne. PASSING THROUGH.
Ages 12 and up. 245, Vol. 2

## Superego

**See:** *Conscience; Identification with others;
Values/Valuing*

## Superstition

Babbitt, Natalie. THE EYES OF THE AMARYLLIS.
Ages 11-14. 26, Vol. 2
Delton, Judy. IT HAPPENED ON THURSDAY.
Ages 5-8. 197, Vol. 2
Katz, Bobbi. VOLLEYBALL JINX.
Ages 9-11. 364, Vol. 2
Mills, Claudia. AT THE BACK OF THE WOODS.
Ages 9-11. 426, Vol. 3
Wallace, Barbara Brooks. JULIA AND THE THIRD
BAD THING.
Ages 8-10. 673, Vol. 2
Wallace-Brodeur, Ruth. ONE APRIL VACATION.
Ages 9-11. 677, Vol. 3
Wiseman, Bernard. THE LUCKY RUNNER.
Ages 6-9. 699, Vol. 3

## Surgery

**See also:** *Amputee; Cancer; Cleft lip/palate; Doctor,
going to; Fear: of death; Hospital, going to; Illnesses;
Sutures*
Bach, Alice Hendricks. WAITING FOR JOHNNY
MIRACLE.
Ages 12 and up. 32, Vol. 3
Ciliotta, Claire and Carole Livingston. WHY AM I
GOING TO THE HOSPITAL?
Ages 5-10. 117, Vol. 3
Collier, James Lincoln. DANNY GOES TO THE
HOSPITAL.
Ages 5-8. 225, Vol. 1
Hogan, Paula Z. and Kirk Hogan. THE HOSPITAL
SCARES ME.
Ages 3-8. 300, Vol. 3
Kay, Eleanor. THE OPERATING ROOM.
Ages 9-12. 483, Vol. 1
Morris, Jeannie. BRIAN PICCOLO: A SHORT
SEASON.
Ages 13 and up. 647, Vol. 1
Rey, Margret Elisabeth Waldstein and Hans Augusto
Rey. CURIOUS GEORGE GOES TO THE
HOSPITAL.
Ages 4-9. 728, Vol. 1
Richter, Elizabeth. THE TEENAGE HOSPITAL
EXPERIENCE: YOU CAN HANDLE IT!
Ages 12 and up. 532, Vol. 3
Sobol, Harriet Langsam. JEFF'S HOSPITAL BOOK.
Ages 2-7. 617, Vol. 2
Viscardi, Henry. THE PHOENIX CHILD: A STORY
OF LOVE.
Ages 13 and up. 665, Vol. 2

### Appendectomy

Arundel, Honor. THE GIRL IN THE OPPOSITE BED.
Ages 12 and up. 37, Vol. 1
Bemelmans, Ludwig. MADELINE.
Ages 3-8. 67, Vol. 1
Weber, Alfons. ELIZABETH GETS WELL.
Ages 6-8. 957, Vol. 1

### Heart. See also: Cardiac conditions

Singer, Marilyn. IT CAN'T HURT FOREVER.
Ages 9-12. 604, Vol. 2

## Surgery (cont.)

### Tonsillectomy

Anderson, Penny S. THE OPERATION.
Ages 3-8. 17, Vol. 3

Bruna, Dick. MIFFY IN THE HOSPITAL.
Ages 2-5. 90, Vol. 2

Chase, Francine. A VISIT TO THE HOSPITAL.
Ages 4-8. 181, Vol. 1

Rowland, Florence Wightman. LET'S GO TO A
HOSPITAL.
Ages 7-10. 756, Vol. 1

Shay, Arthur. WHAT HAPPENS WHEN YOU GO TO
THE HOSPITAL.
Ages 4-7. 808, Vol. 1

Stein, Sara Bonnett. A HOSPITAL STORY: AN OPEN
FAMILY BOOK FOR PARENTS AND CHILDREN
TOGETHER.
Ages 3-8. 857, Vol. 1

Tamburine, Jean. I THINK I WILL GO TO THE
HOSPITAL.
Ages 4-8. 885, Vol. 1

Ziegler, Sandra. AT THE HOSPITAL: A SURPRISE
FOR KRISSY.
Ages 3-6. 716, Vol. 2

## Sutures

See also: *Doctor, going to; Surgery*

Marino, Barbara Pavis. ERIC NEEDS STITCHES.
Ages 4-10. 403, Vol. 3

Vigna, Judith. GREGORY'S STITCHES.
Ages 4-7. 924, Vol. 1

Wolde, Gunilla. BETSY AND THE DOCTOR.
Ages 3-7. 697, Vol. 2

## Sweden

Anckarsvärd, Karin. AUNT VINNIE'S VICTORIOUS
SIX.
Ages 10-12. 14, Vol. 1

Anckarsvärd, Karin. DOCTOR'S BOY.
Ages 9-11. 15, Vol. 1

## Sympathy

See: *Empathy*

# T

## Talents

See also: *Education: special*

Asher, Sandra Fenichel. JUST LIKE JENNY.
Ages 10-12. 27, Vol. 3

Conford, Ellen. JUST THE THING FOR
GERALDINE.
Ages 5-8. 240, Vol. 1

Corcoran, Barbara. CHILD OF THE MORNING.
Ages 10 and up. 139, Vol. 3

Cunningham, Julia Woolfolk. THE SILENT VOICE.
Ages 11-14. 146, Vol. 3

Grimes, Nikki. GROWIN'.
Ages 9-11. 277, Vol. 2

Hest, Amy. MAYBE NEXT YEAR...
Ages 9-12. 288, Vol. 3

Hlibok, Bruce. SILENT DANCER.
Ages 8-11. 293, Vol. 3

Landis, James David. THE SISTERS IMPOSSIBLE.
Ages 9-11. 355, Vol. 3

Robison, Nancy Louise. BALLET MAGIC.
Ages 9-11. 541, Vol. 3

Sachs, Marilyn. A SUMMER'S LEASE.
Ages 11-14. 566, Vol. 3

Sutcliff, Rosemary. THE WITCH'S BRAT.
Ages 11-13. 882, Vol. 1

## Artistic

Ames, Mildred. NICKY AND THE JOYOUS NOISE.
Ages 9-12. 14, Vol. 3

Bulla, Clyde Robert. BENITO.
Ages 8-10. 134, Vol. 1

Bulla, Clyde Robert. DANIEL'S DUCK.
Ages 5-8. 85, Vol. 3

Cohen, Miriam. NO GOOD IN ART.
Ages 5-7. 128, Vol. 3

Colman, Hila Crayder. THE AMAZING MISS
LAURA.
Ages 11-14. 161, Vol. 2

Cretan, Gladys Yessayan. ALL EXCEPT SAMMY.
Ages 6-9. 259, Vol. 1

Culin, Charlotte. CAGES OF GLASS, FLOWERS OF
TIME.
Ages 12 and up. 145, Vol. 3

Flory, Jane Trescott. ONE HUNDRED AND EIGHT
BELLS.
Ages 9-11. 324, Vol. 1

Fowler, Carol. DAISY HOOEE NAMPEYO.
Ages 11 and up. 233, Vol. 2

Hassler, Jon Francis. JEMMY.
Ages 11 and up. 270, Vol. 3

Kingman, Lee. BREAK A LEG, BETSY MAYBE!
Ages 12 and up. 382, Vol. 2

Love, Sandra Weller. CROSSING OVER.
Ages 10-12. 383, Vol. 3

Madison, Winifred. GETTING OUT.
Ages 12 and up. 437, Vol. 2

Magorian, Michelle. GOOD NIGHT, MR. TOM.
Ages 11 and up. 401, Vol. 3

Nelson, Mary Carroll. MICHAEL NARANJO: THE
STORY OF AN AMERICAN INDIAN.
Ages 9-12. 476, Vol. 2

Pinkwater, Manus. WINGMAN.
Ages 9-12. 513, Vol. 2

Riter, Dorris. THE EDGE OF VIOLENCE.
Ages 12 and up. 741, Vol. 1

Rock, Gail. A DREAM FOR ADDIE.
Ages 9-12. 551, Vol. 2

Rodowsky, Colby F. WHAT ABOUT ME?
Ages 11-13. 556, Vol. 2

Stren, Patti. THERE'S A RAINBOW IN MY CLOSET.
Ages 8-10. 638, Vol. 3

Tolan, Stephanie S. THE LAST OF EDEN.
Ages 12 and up. 659, Vol. 3

## Athletic

Cretan, Gladys Yessayan. ALL EXCEPT SAMMY.
Ages 6-9. 259, Vol. 1

Donovan, Pete. CAROL JOHNSTON: THE ONE-
ARMED GYMNAST.
Ages 8-12. 169, Vol. 3

Dygard, Thomas J. SOCCER DUEL.
Ages 11-14. 179, Vol. 3

Geibel, James. THE BLOND BROTHER.
Ages 12 and up. 205, Vol. 3

Hallman, Ruth. BREAKAWAY.
Ages 12 and up. 257, Vol. 3

Harmon, A. W. BASE HIT.
Ages 9-12. 400, Vol. 1

Klein, Monica. BACKYARD BASKETBALL
SUPERSTAR.
Ages 6-8. 345, Vol. 3

Knudson, R. Rozanne. FOX RUNNING: A NOVEL.
Ages 11 and up. 386, Vol. 2

Luce, Willard and Celia Luce. LOU GEHRIG: IRON
MAN OF BASEBALL.
Ages 8-10. 589, Vol. 1

Morton, Jane. RUNNING SCARED.
Ages 10-14. 455, Vol. 3

Myers, Walter Dean. HOOPS.
Ages 12 and up. 459, Vol. 3

## Teasing (cont.)

Gould, Marilyn. GOLDEN DAFFODILS.
Ages 8-12. 223, Vol. 3

Grant, Eva. I HATE MY NAME.
Ages 5-8. 230, Vol. 3

Hogan, Paula Z. I HATE BOYS I HATE GIRLS.
Ages 5-8. 296, Vol. 3

Hurwitz, Johanna. ALDO APPLESAUCE.
Ages 7-9. 316, Vol. 3

Keith, Harold Verne. THE RUNT OF ROGERS
SCHOOL.
Ages 9-12. 487, Vol. 1

Keller, Holly. CROMWELL'S GLASSES.
Ages 3-6. 337, Vol. 3

Lee, H. Alton. SEVEN FEET FOUR AND GROWING.
Ages 9-12. 396, Vol. 2

Lexau, Joan M. I HATE RED ROVER.
Ages 6-8. 371, Vol. 3

Miles, Miska, pseud. GERTRUDE'S POCKET.
Ages 7-9. 639, Vol. 1

Nicholson, William G. PETE GRAY: ONE-ARMED
MAJOR LEAGUER.
Ages 9-12. 479, Vol. 2

Pascal, Francine. THE HAND-ME-DOWN KID.
Ages 10-13. 483, Vol. 3

Peck, Robert Newton. CLUNIE.
Ages 12 and up. 491, Vol. 3

Stanek, Muriel Novella. GROWL WHEN YOU SAY R.
Ages 4-8. 620, Vol. 3

Turkle, Brinton. THY FRIEND, OBADIAH.
Ages 4-8. 908, Vol. 1

Walker, Pamela. TWYLA.
Ages 12 and up. 944, Vol. 1

Whitehead, Ruth. THE MOTHER TREE.
Ages 10-13. 969, Vol. 1

Wise, William. THE COWBOY SURPRISE.
Ages 5-8. 980, Vol. 1

Worth, Kathryn. THEY LOVED TO LAUGH.
Ages 12 and up. 996, Vol. 1

## Temper

See: Aggression; Anger; Tantrums; Violence

## Temptation

See: Conscience; Values/Valuing

## Theft

See: Stealing

## Thinking Ahead

See: Careers: planning; Responsibility: accepting

## Thrift

See: Money: management

## Thumb Sucking

Chorao, Kay. MOLLY'S LIES.
Ages 4-7. 116, Vol. 3

Ernst, Kathryn. DANNY AND HIS THUMB.
Ages 3-7. 290, Vol. 1

Fassler, Joan. DON'T WORRY DEAR.
Ages 4-6. 305, Vol. 1

Keith, Harold Verne. THE RUNT OF ROGERS
SCHOOL.
Ages 9-12. 487, Vol. 1

Klimowicz, Barbara. THE STRAWBERRY THUMB.
Ages 3-6. 507, Vol. 1

Sachs, Marilyn. THE BEARS' HOUSE.
Ages 9-12. 760, Vol. 1

Tobias, Tobi. THE QUITTING DEAL.
Ages 7-9. 654, Vol. 2

## Toilet Training

See: Enuresis

## Tolerance

See: Patience/Impatience; Prejudice

## Tomboy

See: Gender role identity: female; Name-calling

## Tonsillectomy

See: Hospital, going to; Surgery: tonsillectomy

## Tooth, Loss of

Bate, Lucy. LITTLE RABBIT'S LOOSE TOOTH.
Ages 4-6. 39, Vol. 2

Cameron, Ann. THE STORIES JULIAN TELLS.
Ages 7-9. 104, Vol. 3

Gunther, Louise. A TOOTH FOR THE TOOTH
FAIRY.
Ages 5-8. 286, Vol. 2

Johnston, Tony. NIGHT NOISES: AND OTHER
MOLE AND TROLL STORIES.
Ages 4-7. 358, Vol. 2

McCloskey, Robert. ONE MORNING IN MAINE.
Ages 5-8. 595, Vol. 1

Pomerantz, Charlotte. THE MANGO TOOTH.
Ages 4-7. 521, Vol. 2

Rice, Eve. EBBIE.
Ages 3-7. 534, Vol. 2

Ross, Pat. MOLLY AND THE SLOW TEETH.
Ages 6-8. 552, Vol. 3

Smith, Janice Lee. THE MONSTER IN THE THIRD
DRESSER DRAWER AND OTHER STORIES
ABOUT ADAM JOSHUA.
Ages 5-8. 610, Vol. 3

## Toys

See: Transitional objects: toys

## Transitional Objects

See also: Animals

### Security blanket

Brown, Myra Berry. BENJY'S BLANKET.
Ages 3-6. 126, Vol. 1

Burningham, John Mackintosh. THE BLANKET.
Ages 2-5. 102, Vol. 2

Cooney, Nancy Evans. THE BLANKET THAT HAD
TO GO.
Ages 3-5. 138, Vol. 3

Harris, Robie H. DON'T FORGET TO COME BACK.
Ages 3-7. 295, Vol. 2

### Toys

Arundel, Honor. THE GIRL IN THE OPPOSITE BED.
Ages 12 and up. 37, Vol. 1

Brown, Myra Berry. FIRST NIGHT AWAY FROM
HOME.
Ages 5-7. 128, Vol. 1

Hamilton-Merritt, Jane. MY FIRST DAY OF SCHOOL.
Ages 3-6. 260, Vol. 3

Harris, Robie H. I HATE KISSES.
Ages 2-5. 268, Vol. 3

Hoban, Lillian Aberman. ARTHUR'S HONEY BEAR.
Ages 4-8. 415, Vol. 1

Hughes, Shirley. DAVID AND DOG.
Ages 4-7. 335, Vol. 2

Kantrowitz, Mildred. WILLY BEAR.
Ages 4-6. 362, Vol. 2

Nakatani, Chiyoko. MY TEDDY BEAR.
Ages 2-5. 471, Vol. 2

Norris, Gunilla Brodde. IF YOU LISTEN.
Ages 10 and up. 676, Vol. 1

Pearson, Susan. IZZIE.
Ages 2-7. 497, Vol. 2

Schulman, Janet. THE BIG HELLO.
Ages 3-7. 576, Vol. 2

## Transitional Objects (cont.)

Simon, Norma. ELLY THE ELEPHANT.
Ages 2-5. 595, Vol. 3
Thompson, Vivian Laubach. SAD DAY, GLAD DAY.
Ages 5-8. 896, Vol. 1
Tobias, Tobi. MOVING DAY.
Ages 3-6. 652, Vol. 2
Waber, Bernard. IRA SLEEPS OVER.
Ages 6-8. 937, Vol. 1

## Triplets

Seuling, Barbara. THE TRIPLETS.
Ages 4-7. 581, Vol. 3

## Truancy

**See:** *Delinquency, juvenile; School: truancy*

## Trust/Distrust

**See also:** *Hostility; Security/Insecurity*
Alter, Judy. AFTER PA WAS SHOT.
Ages 10-13. 11, Vol. 2
Ashley, Bernard. A KIND OF WILD JUSTICE.
Ages 12 and up. 30, Vol. 3
Burch, Robert Joseph. SKINNY.
Ages 9-12. 143, Vol. 1
Carroll, Theodorus C. THE LOST CHRISTMAS STAR.
Ages 7-9. 109, Vol. 3
Culin, Charlotte. CAGES OF GLASS, FLOWERS OF TIME.
Ages 12 and up. 145, Vol. 3
Cusack, Isabel Langis. IVAN THE GREAT.
Ages 7-10. 188, Vol. 2
Fife, Dale. NORTH OF DANGER.
Ages 10-12. 227, Vol. 2
Guy, Rosa Cuthbert. THE DISAPPEARANCE.
Ages 12 and up. 252, Vol. 3
Holland, Isabelle. ALAN AND THE ANIMAL KINGDOM.
Ages 10-13. 327, Vol. 2
Hunt, Irene. THE LOTTERY ROSE.
Ages 11 and up. 337, Vol. 2
Hunter, Kristen Eggleston. THE SURVIVORS.
Ages 12 and up. 340, Vol. 2
Levoy, Myron. ALAN AND NAOMI.
Ages 11-14. 404, Vol. 2
Moncure, Jane Belk. HONESTY.
Ages 3-6. 443, Vol. 3
Pfeffer, Susan Beth. JUST BETWEEN US.
Ages 10-12. 502, Vol. 3
Rounds, Glen Harold. BLIND OUTLAW.
Ages 9-11. 554, Vol. 3
Shura, Mary Frances Craig. THE SEASON OF SILENCE.
Ages 10-14. 597, Vol. 2
Swetnam, Evelyn. YES, MY DARLING DAUGHTER.
Ages 9-12. 633, Vol. 2
Viorst, Judith. MY MAMA SAYS THERE AREN'T ANY ZOMBIES, GHOSTS, VAMPIRES, CREATURES, DEMONS, MONSTERS, FIENDS, GOBLINS, OR THINGS.
Ages 4-7. 928, Vol. 1
Wade, Anne. A PROMISE IS FOR KEEPING.
Ages 4-7. 674, Vol. 3
Walker, Pamela. TWYLA.
Ages 12 and up. 944, Vol. 1

## Trustworthiness

**See:** *Honesty/Dishonesty*

## Truth

**See:** *Honesty/Dishonesty*

## Twins

Armer, Alberta. SCREWBALL.
Ages 9-11. 29, Vol. 1

### Fraternal

Cleary, Beverly Bunn. MITCH AND AMY.
Ages 9-11. 193, Vol. 1
Cleary, Beverly Bunn. THE REAL HOLE.
Ages 3-6. 196, Vol. 1
Cleaver, Vera and Bill Cleaver. ME TOO.
Ages 9-11. 200, Vol. 1
Goldreich, Gloria. SEASON OF DISCOVERY.
Ages 11-13. 256, Vol. 2
Klein, Norma. IT'S NOT WHAT YOU EXPECT.
Ages 12 and up. 504, Vol. 1
Ogilvie, Elisabeth. THE PIGEON PAIR.
Ages 12 and up. 682, Vol. 1
Paterson, Katherine Womeldorf. JACOB HAVE I LOVED.
Ages 12 and up. 485, Vol. 3
Reece, Colleen L. THE OUTSIDER.
Ages 12 and up. 527, Vol. 3
Schatz, Letta. TAIWO AND HER TWIN.
Ages 8-10. 778, Vol. 1
Stolz, Mary Slattery. THE NOONDAY FRIENDS.
Ages 9-11. 873, Vol. 1

### Identical

Bach, Alice Hendricks. WAITING FOR JOHNNY MIRACLE.
Ages 12 and up. 32, Vol. 3
Flournoy, Valerie. THE TWINS STRIKE BACK.
Ages 6-8. 191, Vol. 3
Ipswitch, Elaine. SCOTT WAS HERE.
Ages 12 and up. 322, Vol. 3
Jacobs, Dee. LAURA'S GIFT.
Ages 10-13. 328, Vol. 3
Kingman, Lee. HEAD OVER WHEELS.
Ages 12 and up. 383, Vol. 2
Simon, Norma. HOW DO I FEEL?
Ages 4-8. 822, Vol. 1
Vogel, Ilse-Margret. MY TWIN SISTER ERIKA.
Ages 6-10. 667, Vol. 2

# U

## Uncle

**See:** *Relatives; Relatives: living in home of*

## Underweight

**See:** *Anorexia nervosa; Weight control: underweight*

## Unemployment

**See:** *Parent/Parents: unemployed*

## Unfairness

**See:** *Justice/Injustice*

## Untruthfulness

**See:** *Honesty/Dishonesty; Values/Valuing*

## Unwanted Child

**See:** *Abandonment; Rejection: parental*

## Unwed Father

**See also:** *Illegitimate child; Sex: premarital*
Ruby, Lois. WHAT DO YOU DO IN QUICKSAND?
Ages 12-14. 558, Vol. 3

## Unwed Mother

**See also:** *Pregnancy; Sex: premarital*
Beckman, Gunnel. MIA ALONE.
Ages 12 and up. 46, Vol. 2

## Unwed Mother (cont.)

Christman, Elizabeth. A NICE ITALIAN GIRL.
Ages 12 and up. 132, Vol. 2
Elfman, Blossom. THE BUTTERFLY GIRL.
Ages 13 and up. 180, Vol. 3
Elfman, Blossom. A HOUSE FOR JONNIE O.
Ages 12 and up. 215, Vol. 2
Eyerly, Jeannette Hyde. A GIRL LIKE ME.
Ages 12 and up. 299, Vol. 1
Gold, Sharlya. AMELIA QUACKENBUSH.
Ages 10-13. 366, Vol. 1
Hurmence, Belinda. TOUGH TIFFANY.
Ages 10-13. 315, Vol. 3
Johnston, Norma. A MUSTARD SEED OF MAGIC.
Ages 12 and up. 355, Vol. 2
Lee, Mildred Scudder. SYCAMORE YEAR.
Ages 12 and up. 537, Vol. 2
Luger, Harriett Mandelay. LAUREN.
Ages 12 and up. 387, Vol. 3
Means, Florence Crannell. OUR CUP IS BROKEN.
Ages 12 and up. 629, Vol. 1
Peck, Richard. DON'T LOOK AND IT WON'T HURT.
Ages 12 and up. 694, Vol. 1
Prince, Alison. THE TURKEY'S NEST.
Ages 12 and up. 520, Vol. 3
Ruby, Lois. ARRIVING AT A PLACE YOU'VE NEVER LEFT.
Ages 12 and up. 564, Vol. 2
Thompson, Jean, pseud. THE HOUSE OF TOMORROW.
Ages 12 and up. 895, Vol. 1
Thompson, Paul. THE HITCHHIKERS.
Ages 12 and up. 657, Vol. 3
Truss, Jan. BIRD AT THE WINDOW.
Ages 13 and up. 661, Vol. 3
Windsor, Patricia. DIVING FOR ROSES.
Ages 13 and up. 687, Vol. 2

### Child of. *See also: Illegitimate child*
Colman, Hila Crayder. TELL ME NO LIES.
Ages 10-12. 167, Vol. 2
Glass, Frankcina. MARVIN & TIGE.
Ages 12 and up. 250, Vol. 2
Johnston, Norma. MYSELF AND I.
Ages 11 and up. 330, Vol. 3
Lindsay, Jeanne Warren. DO I HAVE A DADDY? A STORY ABOUT A SINGLE-PARENT CHILD.
Ages 4-8. 376, Vol. 3
Sebestyen, Ouida. FAR FROM HOME.
Ages 12 and up. 579, Vol. 3
Strang, Celia. THIS CHILD IS MINE.
Ages 11-14. 634, Vol. 3

# V

## Vacuum Cleaner

**See:** *Fear: of vacuum cleaner*

## Values/Valuing

**See also:** *Conscience; Differences, human; Ego ideal; Identification with others*
Bethancourt, T. Ernesto, pseud. THE DOG DAYS OF ARTHUR CANE.
Ages 11 and up. 54, Vol. 2
Kerr, M. E., pseud. IS THAT YOU, MISS BLUE?
Ages 11-14. 379, Vol. 2
Schwarzrock, Shirley and C. Gilbert Wrenn. MY LIFE — WHAT SHALL I DO WITH IT?
Ages 13 and up. 794, Vol. 1

### Aesthetic
Ames, Mildred. NICKY AND THE JOYOUS NOISE.
Ages 9-12. 14, Vol. 3

Fisher, Aileen Lucia. I STOOD UPON A MOUNTAIN.
Ages 4-8. 189, Vol. 3
Hooks, William Harris. DOUG MEETS THE NUTCRACKER.
Ages 8-11. 332, Vol. 2
Lionni, Leo. FREDERICK.
Ages 5-8. 566, Vol. 1
Phipson, Joan Nash, pseud. PETER AND BUTCH.
Ages 10 and up. 709, Vol. 1
Towne, Mary. THE GLASS ROOM.
Ages 11 and up. 899, Vol. 1

### Materialistic
Bates, Betty. MY MOM, THE MONEY NUT.
Ages 10-12. 39, Vol. 3
Baudouy, Michel-Aime. MORE THAN COURAGE.
Ages 12 and up. 56, Vol. 1
Bloch, Marie Halun. THE TWO WORLDS OF DAMYAN.
Ages 9-12. 81, Vol. 1
Bulla, Clyde Robert. POOR BOY, RICH BOY.
Ages 5-8. 87, Vol. 3
Bulla, Clyde Robert. SHOESHINE GIRL.
Ages 8-10. 93, Vol. 2
Colman, Hila Crayder. AFTER THE WEDDING.
Ages 12 and up. 160, Vol. 2
Friedman, Frieda. CAROL FROM THE COUNTRY.
Ages 9-12. 334, Vol. 1
Gerson, Corinne. PASSING THROUGH.
Ages 12 and up. 245, Vol. 2
Hayes, Sheila. THE CAROUSEL HORSE.
Ages 10-12. 300, Vol. 2
Heide, Florence Parry. WHEN THE SAD ONE COMES TO STAY.
Ages 8-11. 307, Vol. 2
Kerr, M. E., pseud. LOVE IS A MISSING PERSON.
Ages 12 and up. 380, Vol. 2
Lenski, Lois. BOOM TOWN BOY.
Ages 9-11. 543, Vol. 1
Naylor, Phyllis Reynolds. WALKING THROUGH THE DARK.
Ages 12 and up. 473, Vol. 2
Ogilvie, Elisabeth. THE PIGEON PAIR.
Ages 12 and up. 682, Vol. 1
Pfeffer, Susan Beth. KID POWER.
Ages 9-12. 511, Vol. 2
Stolz, Mary Slattery. THE NOONDAY FRIENDS.
Ages 9-11. 873, Vol. 1
Wier, Ester Alberti. THE RUMPTYDOOLERS.
Ages 11-13. 972, Vol. 1

### Moral/Ethical
Adler, Carole Schwerdtfeger. IN OUR HOUSE SCOTT IS MY BROTHER.
Ages 10-13. 5, Vol. 3
Alexander, Anne. CONNIE.
Ages 10-13. 6, Vol. 2
Allen, Elizabeth. THE LOSER.
Ages 12 and up. 12, Vol. 1
Anckarsvärd, Karin. DOCTOR'S BOY.
Ages 9-11. 15, Vol. 1
Armstrong, Richard. THE ALBATROSS.
Ages 12 and up. 30, Vol. 1
Asher, Sandra Fenichel. SUMMER BEGINS.
Ages 10-13. 28, Vol. 3
Ashley, Bernard. TERRY ON THE FENCE.
Ages 12 and up. 25, Vol. 2
Bach, Alice Hendricks. THE MEAT IN THE SANDWICH.
Ages 10-13. 28, Vol. 2
Balch, Glenn. BRAVE RIDERS.
Ages 10-13. 47, Vol. 1
Bartusis, Constance. SHADES OF DIFFERENCE.
Ages 12 and up. 55, Vol. 1

## Values/Valuing (cont.)

Naylor, Phyllis Reynolds. A STRING OF CHANCES.
Ages 12 and up. 464, Vol. 3

Naylor, Phyllis Reynolds. TO WALK THE SKY PATH.
Ages 10-13. 658, Vol. 1

Neville, Emily Cheney. BERRIES GOODMAN.
Ages 11 and up. 666, Vol. 1

O'Dell, Scott. KATHLEEN, PLEASE COME HOME.
Ages 12 and up. 485, Vol. 2

Ogilvie, Elisabeth. THE PIGEON PAIR.
Ages 12 and up. 682, Vol. 1

Pascal, Francine. MY FIRST LOVE & OTHER DISASTERS.
Ages 12 and up. 484, Vol. 3

Pevsner, Stella. CUTE IS A FOUR-LETTER WORD.
Ages 10-12. 498, Vol. 3

Phipson, Joan Nash, pseud. FLY FREE.
Ages 11 and up. 508, Vol. 3

Phipson, Joan Nash, pseud. PETER AND BUTCH.
Ages 10 and up. 709, Vol. 1

Pundt, Helen Marie. SPRING COMES FIRST TO THE WILLOWS.
Ages 11 and up. 717, Vol. 1

Roth, David. THE HERMIT OF FOG HOLLOW STATION.
Ages 9-12. 553, Vol. 3

Samuels, Gertrude. ADAM'S DAUGHTER.
Ages 13 and up. 568, Vol. 2

Sandoz, Mari. THE HORSECATCHER.
Ages 12 and up. 771, Vol. 1

Sauer, Julia L. THE LIGHT AT TERN ROCK.
Ages 9-11. 772, Vol. 1

Scoppettone, Sandra. TRYING HARD TO HEAR YOU.
Ages 13 and up. 799, Vol. 1

Sebestyen, Ouida. WORDS BY HEART.
Ages 10-13. 580, Vol. 3

Shearer, John. I WISH I HAD AN AFRO.
Ages 9-11. 809, Vol. 1

Slote, Alfred. LOVE AND TENNIS.
Ages 12-14. 605, Vol. 3

Sommerfelt, Aimee. THE ROAD TO AGRA.
Ages 10-13. 839, Vol. 1

Steele, William Owen. FLAMING ARROWS.
Ages 10-12. 854, Vol. 1

Stevenson, James. WILFRED THE RAT.
Ages 4-7. 624, Vol. 2

Street, James Howell. GOOD-BYE, MY LADY.
Ages 11 and up. 878, Vol. 1

Townsend, John Rowe. GOOD-BYE TO THE JUNGLE.
Ages 11-13. 900, Vol. 1

Townsend, John Rowe. NOAH'S CASTLE.
Ages 11 and up. 656, Vol. 2

Turkle, Brinton. THE FIDDLER OF HIGH LONESOME.
Ages 5-10. 907, Vol. 1

Wallace, Barbara Brooks. THE SECRET SUMMER OF L.E.B.
Ages 11 and up. 946, Vol. 1

Winthrop, Elizabeth. MIRANDA IN THE MIDDLE.
Ages 9-13. 697, Vol. 3

Wood, Phyllis Anderson. THIS TIME COUNT ME IN.
Ages 12 and up. 706, Vol. 3

## Vandalism

See also: Crime/Criminals; Delinquency, juvenile

Addy, Sharon. WE DIDN'T MEAN TO.
Ages 8-10. 2, Vol. 3

Mann, Peggy. THE SECRET OF THE FLOWER BOXES.
Ages 8-11. 610, Vol. 1

Rockwell, Thomas. THE THIEF.
Ages 8-10. 554, Vol. 2

## Vanity

See: Pride/False pride

## Vietnam

See also: Immigrants; Refugees

Bennett, Jack. THE VOYAGE OF THE LUCKY DRAGON.
Ages 11 and up. 45, Vol. 3

Wartski, Maureen Crane. A BOAT TO NOWHERE.
Ages 9-12. 678, Vol. 3

Wartski, Maureen Crane. A LONG WAY FROM HOME.
Ages 11-13. 680, Vol. 3

Wolkoff, Judie. WHERE THE ELF KING SINGS.
Ages 12 and up. 704, Vol. 3

## Violence

See also: Aggression; Cruelty; Death: murder; Delinquency, juvenile; Rape; Sexual assault; War

Ashley, Bernard. A KIND OF WILD JUSTICE.
Ages 12 and up. 30, Vol. 3

Clifford, Ethel Rosenberg. THE KILLER SWAN.
Ages 10-12. 120, Vol. 3

Degens, T. THE GAME ON THATCHER ISLAND.
Ages 11-14. 193, Vol. 2

Geibel, James. THE BLOND BROTHER.
Ages 12 and up. 205, Vol. 3

Graham, Gail B. CROSS-FIRE: A VIETNAM NOVEL.
Ages 12 and up. 371, Vol. 1

Harrah, Michael. FIRST OFFENDER.
Ages 11-13. 266, Vol. 3

Levoy, Myron. A SHADOW LIKE A LEOPARD.
Ages 12 and up. 369, Vol. 3

Lingard, Joan. ACROSS THE BARRICADES.
Ages 12 and up. 561, Vol. 1

Maruki, Toshi. HIROSHIMA NO PIKA.
Ages 7 and up. 406, Vol. 3

Mauser, Pat Rhoads. A BUNDLE OF STICKS.
Ages 10-12. 410, Vol. 3

Mazer, Harry. THE LAST MISSION.
Ages 12-14. 413, Vol. 3

Murphy, Jim. DEATH RUN.
Ages 11 and up. 457, Vol. 3

Myers, Walter Dean. HOOPS.
Ages 12 and up. 459, Vol. 3

Riley, Jocelyn. ONLY MY MOUTH IS SMILING.
Ages 12-14. 533, Vol. 3

Thrasher, Crystal Faye. BETWEEN DARK AND DAYLIGHT.
Ages 11-13. 658, Vol. 3

Wolkoff, Judie. WHERE THE ELF KING SINGS.
Ages 12 and up. 704, Vol. 3

## Visiting

Brooks, Jerome. THE BIG DIPPER MARATHON.
Ages 11-14. 77, Vol. 3

Brown, Myra Berry. FIRST NIGHT AWAY FROM HOME.
Ages 5-7. 128, Vol. 1

Caines, Jeannette Franklin. WINDOW WISHING.
Ages 4-7. 100, Vol. 3

Daringer, Helen Fern. ADOPTED JANE.
Ages 9-12. 263, Vol. 1

Degens, T. THE GAME ON THATCHER ISLAND.
Ages 11-14. 193, Vol. 2

Goldman, Susan. GRANDMA IS SOMEBODY SPECIAL.
Ages 4-7. 255, Vol. 2

Greenfield, Eloise. DARLENE.
Ages 5-7. 243, Vol. 3

Harris, Robin. HELLO KITTY SLEEPS OVER.
Ages 2-5. 269, Vol. 3

## Visiting (cont.)

Hickman, Janet. THE THUNDER-PUP.
   Ages 9-11. 289, Vol. 3
Hurd, Edith Thacher. I DANCE IN MY RED
   PAJAMAS.
   Ages 3-6. 314, Vol. 3
Pfeffer, Susan Beth. AWFUL EVELINA.
   Ages 6-8. 501, Vol. 3
Robertson, Keith. IN SEARCH OF A SANDHILL
   CRANE.
   Ages 11 and up. 743, Vol. 1
Truss, Jan. BIRD AT THE WINDOW.
   Ages 13 and up. 661, Vol. 3
Waber, Bernard. IRA SLEEPS OVER.
   Ages 6-8. 937, Vol. 1
Wolkstein, Diane. THE VISIT.
   Ages 3-5. 706, Vol. 2

## Visual Impairment

**See also:** *Blindness; Glasses, wearing of*
Leggett, Linda Rodgers and Linda Gambee
   Andrews. THE ROSE-COLORED GLASSES:
   MELANIE ADJUSTS TO POOR VISION.
   Ages 8-11. 362, Vol. 3
Litchfield, Ada Bassett. A CANE IN HER HAND.
   Ages 6-9. 412, Vol. 2
Little, Jean. LISTEN FOR THE SINGING.
   Ages 10-14. 413, Vol. 2

# W

## War

**See also:** *Violence*
Arnothy, Christine. I AM FIFTEEN AND I DON'T
   WANT TO DIE.
   Ages 12 and up. 31, Vol. 1
Bennett, Jack. THE VOYAGE OF THE LUCKY
   DRAGON.
   Ages 11 and up. 45, Vol. 3
Bloch, Marie Halun. DISPLACED PERSON.
   Ages 10-13. 57, Vol. 2
Brochmann, Elizabeth. WHAT'S THE MATTER,
   GIRL?
   Ages 12 and up. 76, Vol. 3
Corcoran, Barbara. AXE-TIME, SWORD-TIME.
   Ages 11 and up. 178, Vol. 2
Ellis, Ella Thorp. SLEEPWALKER'S MOON.
   Ages 12 and up. 181, Vol. 3
Forman, James. MY ENEMY, MY BROTHER.
   Ages 12 and up. 326, Vol. 1
Frank, Anne. ANNE FRANK: THE DIARY OF A
   YOUNG GIRL.
   Ages 11 and up. 330, Vol. 1
Graham, Gail B. CROSS-FIRE: A VIETNAM NOVEL.
   Ages 12 and up. 371, Vol. 1
Griese, Arnold Alfred. THE WIND IS NOT A RIVER.
   Ages 9-12. 276, Vol. 2
Kerr, Judith. THE OTHER WAY ROUND.
   Ages 12 and up. 376, Vol. 2
Kherdian, David. THE ROAD FROM HOME: THE
   STORY OF AN ARMENIAN GIRL.
   Ages 12 and up. 340, Vol. 3
Little, Jean. LISTEN FOR THE SINGING.
   Ages 10-14. 413, Vol. 2
Magorian, Michelle. GOOD NIGHT, MR. TOM.
   Ages 11 and up. 401, Vol. 3
Maruki, Toshi. HIROSHIMA NO PIKA.
   Ages 7 and up. 406, Vol. 3
Mazer, Harry. THE LAST MISSION.
   Ages 12-14. 413, Vol. 3
Nöstlinger, Christine. FLY AWAY HOME.
   Ages 10-13. 481, Vol. 2
Ofek, Uriel. SMOKE OVER GOLAN.
   Ages 9-13. 468, Vol. 3

Reiss, Johanna. THE JOURNEY BACK.
   Ages 10-14. 530, Vol. 2
Rose, Anne K. REFUGEE.
   Ages 10-14. 559, Vol. 2
Sallis, Susan Diana. A TIME FOR EVERYTHING.
   Ages 13 and up. 569, Vol. 3
Seredy, Kate. THE SINGING TREE.
   Ages 10-14. 803, Vol. 1
Uchida, Yoshiko. JOURNEY HOME.
   Ages 12-14. 657, Vol. 2

## War Orphan

**See:** *Orphan*

## Water Head

**See:** *Hydrocephalus*

## Wealth/Wealthy

**See also:** *Differences, human*
Angier, Bradford and Barbara Corcoran. ASK FOR
   LOVE AND THEY GIVE YOU RICE PUDDING.
   Ages 12-14. 21, Vol. 2
Bernays, Anne. GROWING UP RICH.
   Ages 13 and up. 52, Vol. 2
Blume, Judy Sussman. THEN AGAIN, MAYBE I
   WON'T.
   Ages 12 and up. 94, Vol. 1
Kerr, M. E., pseud. GENTLEHANDS.
   Ages 11-14. 377, Vol. 2
Lenski, Lois. BOOM TOWN BOY.
   Ages 9-11. 543, Vol. 1
Shippen, Katherine Binney. ANDREW CARNEGIE
   AND THE AGE OF STEEL.
   Ages 9-11. 816, Vol. 1
Strasser, Todd. ANGEL DUST BLUES.
   Ages 14 and up. 635, Vol. 3

## Weight Control

**See also:** *Appearance*

### Overweight

Bottner, Barbara. DUMB OLD CASEY IS A FAT
   TREE.
   Ages 6-9. 66, Vol. 3
Brooks, Jerome. THE TESTING OF CHARLIE
   HAMMELMAN.
   Ages 10-13. 84, Vol. 2
Byars, Betsy Cromer. AFTER THE GOAT MAN.
   Ages 9-11. 153, Vol. 1
Cohen, Barbara Nash. FAT JACK.
   Ages 11 and up. 125, Vol. 3
Cohen, Barbara Nash. THE INNKEEPER'S
   DAUGHTER.
   Ages 11-14. 126, Vol. 3
Danziger, Paula. THE CAT ATE MY GYMSUIT.
   Ages 11 and up. 262, Vol. 1
DeClements, Barthe. NOTHING'S FAIR IN FIFTH
   GRADE.
   Ages 8-11. 152, Vol. 3
Du Bois, William Pène. PORKO VON POPBUTTON.
   Ages 9-12. 277, Vol. 1
Gilbert, Nan, pseud. THE UNCHOSEN.
   Ages 11 and up. 359, Vol. 1
Greenberg, Jan. THE PIG-OUT BLUES.
   Ages 12 and up. 236, Vol. 3
Greene, Constance Clarke. A GIRL CALLED AL.
   Ages 11 and up. 378, Vol. 1
Holland, Isabelle. DINAH AND THE GREEN FAT
   KINGDOM.
   Ages 10-13. 328, Vol. 2
Holland, Isabelle. HEADS YOU WIN, TAILS I LOSE.
   Ages 12 and up. 426, Vol. 1
Hurwitz, Johanna. THE LAW OF GRAVITY.
   Ages 10-13. 341, Vol. 2

## Weight Control (cont.)

Kerr, M. E., pseud. DINKY HOCKER SHOOTS
SMACK.
Ages 12 and up. 491, Vol. 1
Konigsburg, Elaine Lobl. ALTOGETHER, ONE AT A
TIME.
Ages 9-11. 509, Vol. 1
Lipsyte, Robert. ONE FAT SUMMER.
Ages 12-14. 409, Vol. 2
Mazer, Harry. THE DOLLAR MAN.
Ages 12 and up. 626, Vol. 1
Miles, Betty. LOOKING ON.
Ages 11-14. 457, Vol. 2
Neville, Emily Cheney. GARDEN OF BROKEN
GLASS.
Ages 11-14. 477, Vol. 2
Orgel, Doris. NEXT DOOR TO XANADU.
Ages 9-11. 686, Vol. 1
Perl, Lila. HEY, REMEMBER FAT GLENDA?
Ages 9-12. 493, Vol. 3
Perl, Lila. ME AND FAT GLENDA.
Ages 9-12. 700, Vol. 1
Perl, Lila. THAT CRAZY APRIL.
Ages 10-12. 701, Vol. 1
Philips, Barbara. DON'T CALL ME FATSO.
Ages 5-9. 507, Vol. 3
Pinkwater, Manus. FAT ELLIOT & THE GORILLA.
Ages 8-10. 710, Vol. 1
Schwarzrock, Shirley and C. Gilbert Wrenn. FOOD AS
A CRUTCH.
Ages 11 and up. 791, Vol. 1
Sherburne, Zoa. GIRL IN THE MIRROR.
Ages 11 and up. 811, Vol. 1
Smith, Doris Buchanan. LAST WAS LLOYD.
Ages 8-11. 608, Vol. 3
Smith, Robert Kimmel. JELLY BELLY.
Ages 10-12. 614, Vol. 3
Solot, Mary Lynn. 100 HAMBURGERS: THE
GETTING THIN BOOK.
Ages 7-10. 838, Vol. 1.
Stevens, Carla McBride. PIG AND THE BLUE FLAG.
Ages 6-8. 622, Vol. 2
Stolz, Mary Slattery. THE BULLY OF BARKHAM
STREET.
Ages 8-11. 863, Vol. 1
Talbot, Charlene Joy. THE GREAT RAT ISLAND
ADVENTURE.
Ages 10-13. 634, Vol. 2
Van Leeuwen, Jean. I WAS A 98-POUND DUCKLING.
Ages 11 and up. 918, Vol. 1
Winthrop, Elizabeth. POTBELLIED POSSUMS.
Ages 4-6. 690, Vol. 2
Woodford, Peggy. PLEASE DON'T GO.
Ages 12 and up. 991, Vol. 1
Woody, Regina Llewellyn Jones. ONE DAY AT A
TIME.
Ages 11 and up. 992, Vol. 1

### Underweight

Lord, Beman. QUARTERBACK'S AIM.
Ages 8-10. 582, Vol. 1
Van Leeuwen, Jean. I WAS A 98-POUND DUCKLING.
Ages 11 and up. 918, Vol. 1

## West Indian-American

Guy, Rosa Cuthbert. THE FRIENDS.
Ages 12 and up. 391, Vol. 1

## Wetting

See: Enuresis

## Wheelchair, Dependence on

See also: Amputee; Multiple sclerosis; Muscular
dystrophy; Paralysis; Paraplegia; Poliomyelitis;
Prosthesis; Quadriplegia

Burnett, Frances Hodgson. THE SECRET GARDEN.
Ages 10 and up. 147, Vol. 1
Colman, Hila Crayder. ACCIDENT.
Ages 11 and up. 132, Vol. 3
Cook, Marjorie. TO WALK ON TWO FEET.
Ages 11-14. 177, Vol. 2
Fanshawe, Elizabeth. RACHEL.
Ages 4-6. 222, Vol. 2
Fassler, Joan. HOWIE HELPS HIMSELF.
Ages 5-8. 224, Vol. 2
Green, Phyllis. WALKIE-TALKIE.
Ages 10-13. 264, Vol. 2
Greenfield, Eloise. DARLENE.
Ages 5-7. 243, Vol. 3
Greenfield, Eloise and Alesia Revis. ALESIA.
Ages 10-14. 245, Vol. 3
Grohskopf, Bernice. SHADOW IN THE SUN.
Ages 10 and up. 281, Vol. 2
Henriod, Lorraine. GRANDMA'S WHEELCHAIR.
Ages 3-7. 281, Vol. 3
Jacobs, Dee. LAURA'S GIFT.
Ages 10-13. 328, Vol. 3
Kingman, Lee. HEAD OVER WHEELS.
Ages 12 and up. 383, Vol. 2
Lasker, Joe. NICK JOINS IN.
Ages 5-8. 358, Vol. 3
Mack, Nancy. TRACY.
Ages 4-8. 428, Vol. 2
Miner, Jane Claypool. NEW BEGINNING: AN
ATHLETE IS PARALYZED.
Ages 11 and up. 433, Vol. 3
Payne, Sherry Neuwirth. A CONTEST.
Ages 8-10. 486, Vol. 3
Pieper, Elizabeth. A SCHOOL FOR TOMMY.
Ages 5-8. 510, Vol. 3
Rabe, Berniece Louise. THE BALANCING GIRL.
Ages 5-7. 522, Vol. 3
Redpath, Ann. JIM BOEN: A MAN OF OPPOSITES.
Ages 9 and up. 526, Vol. 3
Robinet, Harriette Gillem. RIDE THE RED CYCLE.
Ages 7-11. 537, Vol. 3
Sallis, Susan Diana. ONLY LOVE.
Ages 12 and up. 568, Vol. 3
Savitz, Harriet May. FLY, WHEELS, FLY.
Ages 10 and up. 774, Vol. 1
Schick, Eleanor Grossman. RUN, DON'T WALK.
Ages 12 and up. 573, Vol. 3
Sullivan, Mary Beth and Alan J. Brightman and Joseph
Blatt. FEELING FREE.
Ages 9 and up. 640, Vol. 3
Tate, Joan. BEN AND ANNIE.
Ages 9-12. 886, Vol. 1
Thomas, Dawn C. PABLITO'S NEW FEET.
Ages 8-10. 894, Vol. 1
White, Paul. JANET AT SCHOOL.
Ages 5-8. 679, Vol. 2

## Wishes

See also: Daydreaming; Dreams; Fantasy formation;
Magical thinking
Clifton, Lucille. THREE WISHES.
Ages 6-8. 148, Vol. 2
Collins, David R. IF I COULD, I WOULD.
Ages 6-8. 131, Vol. 3
Dolan, Sheila. THE WISHING BOTTLE.
Ages 7-9. 167, Vol. 3
Evans, Mari. JD.
Ages 9-12. 294, Vol. 1
Johnston, Tony. NIGHT NOISES: AND OTHER
MOLE AND TROLL STORIES.
Ages 4-7. 358, Vol. 2
Tobias, Tobi. JANE, WISHING.
Ages 6-9. 651, Vol. 2

## Wishes (cont.)

Waber, Bernard. YOU'RE A LITTLE KID WITH A BIG HEART.
Ages 5-7. 673, Vol. 3

## Withdrawal

**See:** *Reality, escaping*

## Womanliness

**See:** *Gender role identity: female*

## Women's Rights

**See also:** *Gender role identity: female; Prejudice: sexual*
Carlson, Dale Bick. GIRLS ARE EQUAL TOO: THE WOMEN'S MOVEMENT FOR TEENAGERS.
Ages 12 and up. 163, Vol. 1
Colman, Hila Crayder. NOBODY HAS TO BE A KID FOREVER.
Ages 10-13. 164, Vol. 2
Dygard, Thomas J. WINNING KICKER.
Ages 11-14. 213, Vol. 2
Friermood, Elisabeth Hamilton. FOCUS THE BRIGHT LAND.
Ages 11 and up. 337, Vol. 1
Gripe, Maria Kristina. THE GREEN COAT.
Ages 13 and up. 279, Vol. 2
Ho, Minfong. SING TO THE DAWN.
Ages 10-13. 320, Vol. 2
Klein, Norma. GIRLS CAN BE ANYTHING.
Ages 4-7. 503, Vol. 1
Lasker, Joe. MOTHERS CAN DO ANYTHING.
Ages 3-6. 531, Vol. 1
Morris, Terry. SHALOM, GOLDA.
Ages 12 and up. 648, Vol. 1

## Work, Attitude Toward

**See also:** *Careers: planning; Job; Responsibility*

Burton, Virginia Lee. KATY AND THE BIG SNOW.
Ages 3-6. 148, Vol. 1
Klein, Norma. BLUE TREES, RED SKY.
Ages 7-10. 384, Vol. 2
Naylor, Phyllis Reynolds. EDDIE, INCORPORATED.
Ages 9-11. 463, Vol. 3
Neigoff, Mike. IT WILL NEVER BE THE SAME AGAIN.
Ages 12-14. 465, Vol. 3
Ruhen, Olaf. CORCORAN'S THE NAME.
Ages 12 and up. 758, Vol. 1
Shaw, Richard. THE HARD WAY HOME.
Ages 11-13. 592, Vol. 2
Sonneborn, Ruth A. FRIDAY NIGHT IS PAPA NIGHT.
Ages 5-8. 841, Vol. 1
Strang, Celia. FOSTER MARY.
Ages 10-13. 633, Vol. 3
Treffinger, Carolyn. LI LUN, LAD OF COURAGE.
Ages 8-11. 903, Vol. 1

## Working Mother

**See:** *Parent/Parents: mother working outside home*

## Worries

**See:** *Anxiety; Fear*

# Y

## Youngest Child

**See:** *Sibling: youngest*